THE VICTORIA HISTORY
OF THE
COUNTIES OF ENGLAND

—

A HISTORY OF
MIDDLESEX

VOLUME VII

THE VICTORIA HISTORY
OF THE
COUNTIES OF ENGLAND

EDITED BY C. R. ELRINGTON

THE UNIVERSITY OF LONDON
INSTITUTE OF
HISTORICAL RESEARCH

Oxford University Press, Walton Street, Oxford OX2 6DP

London   Glasgow   New York   Toronto
Delhi   Bombay   Calcutta   Madras   Karachi
Kuala Lumpur   Singapore   Hong Kong   Tokyo
Nairobi   Dar es Salaam   Cape Town
Melbourne   Auckland
and associates in
Beirut   Berlin   Ibadan   Mexico City   Nicosia

Published in the United States by
Oxford University Press, New York

Printed in Great Britain
at the University Press, Oxford
by Eric Buckley
Printer to the University

East Acton: Manor House in the 18th century

INSCRIBED TO THE
MEMORY OF HER LATE MAJESTY
QUEEN VICTORIA
WHO GRACIOUSLY GAVE THE TITLE TO
AND ACCEPTED THE DEDICATION
OF THIS HISTORY

A HISTORY OF
MIDDLESEX

EDITED BY T. F. T. BAKER

VOLUME VII

ACTON, CHISWICK, EALING
AND WILLESDEN PARISHES

PUBLISHED FOR

THE INSTITUTE OF HISTORICAL RESEARCH

BY

OXFORD UNIVERSITY PRESS

1982

Distributed by Oxford University Press until 1 January 1985
thereafter by Dawsons of Pall Mall

CONTENTS OF VOLUME SEVEN

LIST OF ILLUSTRATIONS

For permission to reproduce material in their possession thanks are rendered to: the Greater London Council Photographic Library; London Borough of Brent, Grange Museum of Local History; London Borough of Ealing, Central Reference Library; London Borough of Hounslow, Chiswick Reference Library; the Museum of London; the National Monuments Record (N.M.R.) of the Royal Commission on Historical Monuments (England). Photographs dated 1980 were taken by A. P. Baggs. The coats of arms were drawn by H. Ellis Tomlinson and Patricia A. Tattersfield.

LIST OF ILLUSTRATIONS

LIST OF MAPS

All the maps except those showing the evolution of settlement were drawn by K. J. Wass of the Department of Geography, University College London, from drafts prepared by Diane K. Bolton, Patricia E. C. Croot, and T. F. T. Baker. The maps showing the evolution of settlement are taken from Ordnance Survey Maps 1″.

EDITORIAL NOTE

THE revival of the *Victoria History of Middlesex* in 1955 is described in the Editorial Note to Volume III, and later modifications of the arrangements are mentioned in that to Volume I. The structure and aims of the *Victoria History* series as a whole are outlined in the *General Introduction* to the History. The publication of the present volume completes the coverage of the administrative county as it existed up to 1965, and thus marks the fulfilment of the task which was assumed by the Middlesex *Victoria County History* Council. Further topographical volumes, on parishes which lay within the area of the former London County Council, are being prepared under a committee for the *Victoria County History* of (Inner) Middlesex.

That the compilation of the history of the former administrative county of Middlesex was initiated, has continued, and has been brought to a successful conclusion, in times of financial difficulty and of wide-ranging administrative changes in the contributing Local Authorities, results from the energetic, ingenious, and tenacious efforts of the successive chairmen (the late Sir Archer Hoare, C.B.E., 1955–63, Mr. R. M. Robbins, C.B.E., 1963–76, and Mr. I. W. Davies since 1976), members, and officers of the Middlesex *V.C.H.* Council. The University of London records its sincere appreciation of their work and of the generous contributions which originally were made by the Local Authorities of Middlesex and which have been continued by their successors, with the exception of Spelthorne. The membership of the council in 1981 is set out below. Miss Joan Coburn was succeeded as honorary secretary in 1979 by Miss Valerie Bott. The editorial staff has remained unchanged since the publication of the previous volume in 1980.

Many people have helped in the compilation of the present volume by providing information or by reading and commenting on parts of the text. Those who have read the drafts of individual parish articles are named in the footnotes. The co-operation of the librarians and other officers of the various Local Authorities is gratefully acknowledged. Special thanks are due to Mr. H. V. Borley, for help with the information on railways, to the Librarian of All Souls College, Oxford, to Mr. M. A. Jahn, to Miss Valerie Bott and the staff of the Grange Museum of Local History, and to the staff of the Greater London Record Office.

MIDDLESEX
VICTORIA COUNTY HISTORY
COUNCIL

As at 1 October 1981

Chairman
I. W. DAVIES, ESQ.†

Representatives of the following Local Authorities
The Greater London Council

London Boroughs
Barnet	Enfield	Hillingdon
Brent	Haringey	Hounslow
Ealing	Harrow	Richmond-upon-Thames

District

Hertsmere
(The District Council of Spelthorne, formerly represented on the Council,
has declined to make any contribution since 1975)

Representatives of

The London and Middlesex Archaeological Society
The Institute of Historical Research

Co-opted Members

MISS F. M. GREEN†

R. M. ROBBINS, ESQ., C.B.E.†

Hon. Secretary: MISS V. BOTT†

Hon. Treasurer: G. M. NOBLE, ESQ.†

General Editor: C. R. ELRINGTON, ESQ.†

Executive Committee

MISS A. CAMERON	DR. F. H. W. SHEPPARD
J. F. HEYWOOD, ESQ.	K. A. BAILEY, ESQ.
A. H. HALL, ESQ.	D. CLARK, ESQ.

together with the persons marked with a dagger

LIST OF CLASSES OF DOCUMENTS
IN THE PUBLIC RECORD OFFICE
USED IN THIS VOLUME
WITH THEIR CLASS NUMBERS

Chancery
                    Proceedings
C 1   Early
C 2   Series I
C 3   Series II
C 5   Six Clerks Series, Bridges
C 6   Collins
C 7   Hamilton
C 8   Mitford
C 10   Whittington
C 54   Close Rolls
C 66   Patent Rolls
C 78   Decree Rolls
C 88   Records upon Outlawries
C 90   Confirmations and Executions of
                    Decrees
C 93   Proceedings of Commissioners of
                    Charitable Uses, Inquisitions,
                    and Decrees
C 108   Masters' Exhibits, Farrar
                    Inquisitions post mortem
C 133   Series I, Edw. I
C 136   Ric. II
C 142   Series II
C 143   Inquisitions ad quod damnum
C 260   Chancery Files (Tower and Rolls
                    Chapel), Recorda

Court of Common Pleas
CP 25(1)   Feet of Fines, Series I
CP 25(2)   Feet of Fines, Series II
CP 40   Plea Rolls
CP 43   Recovery Rolls

Exchequer, Treasury of Receipt
E 36   Books
E 40   Ancient Deeds, Series A
E 42   Ancient Deeds, Series AS

Exchequer, King's Remembrancer
E 126   Decrees and Orders, Series IV
E 134   Depositions taken by Commis-
                    sion
E 154   Inventories of Goods and
                    Chattels
E 159   Memoranda Rolls
E 163   Minute Books, Miscellanea
E 178   Special Commissions of Inquiry
E 179   Subsidy Rolls, etc.

Exchequer, Augmentation Office
E 301   Certificates of Colleges and
                    Chantries
E 303   Conventual Leases
E 305   Deeds of Purchase and Exchange
E 308   Particulars of Sale of Fee-Farm
                    Rents

E 315   Miscellaneous Books
E 318   Particulars for Grants of Crown
                    Lands

Exchequer, Lord Treasurer's Remembrancer's
and Pipe Offices
E 367   Particulars and Warrants for
                    Leases
E 372   Pipe Rolls

Ministry of Education
ED 7   Public Elementary Schools, Pre-
                    liminary Statements
ED 16   Supply Files

Registry of Friendly Societies
FS 1   Rules and Amendments, Series I

Home Office
HO 107   Population Returns
HO 129   Ecclesiastical Returns

Board of Inland Revenue
IR 29   Tithe Apportionments
IR 30   Tithe Maps

Justices Itinerant, Assize and Gaol Delivery
Justices, etc.
JUST 1   Eyre Rolls, Assize Rolls, etc.

Court of King's Bench, Crown Side
KB 29   Controlment Rolls

Lord Steward's Department
LS 10   Gardens books

Ministry of Agriculture, Fisheries, and Food
MAF 9   Deeds and Awards of Enfran-
                    chisement
MAF 20   Manor Files
MAF 68   Agricultural Returns: Parish
                    Summaries

Maps and Plans
MPA 7   Map of Drayton in Ealing
                    (formerly C 113/259/4)

Prerogative Court of Canterbury
PROB 11   Registered Copies of Wills
                    proved in P.C.C.

Office of the Registrar General
RG 4   Authenticated Registers
RG 31   Registers of Places of Worship

Court of Requests
REQ 2   Proceedings

LIST OF CLASSES OF DOCUMENTS

Special Collections
SC 2   Court Rolls
SC 5   Hundred Rolls
SC 6   Ministers' and Receivers' Accounts

State Paper Office
SP 14   State Papers Domestic, Jas. I

Court of Star Chamber
STAC 8   Proceedings, Jas. I

Court of Wards and Liveries
WARD 2   Deeds and Evidences
WARD 5   Feodaries' Surveys

SELECT LIST OF
CLASSES OF DOCUMENTS IN THE
GREATER LONDON RECORD OFFICE
USED IN THIS VOLUME
WITH THEIR CLASS NUMBERS

Deposited Records

Acc. 262	Stowe Collection
Acc. 531	Records from Messrs. Prideaux (solicitors)
Acc. 638	Records of North Thames Gas Board
Acc. 890	Records concerning Brentford
Acc. 891	Records of Messrs. Fuller, Smith & Turner
Cal. Mdx. Rec.	Calendar of Sessions Records, 1607–12
Cal. Mdx. Sess. Bks.	Calendar of Sessions Books, 1638–1752
D.R.O. 37	Diocesan Records, Ealing Parish Records
F	Facsimile
EA	Enclosure Awards
MJ/SR	Sessions Rolls
MR/LV	Licensed Victuallers' Lists
MR/TH	Hearth Tax Assessments
PR	Prints
TA	Tithe Awards

NOTE ON ABBREVIATIONS

Among the abbreviations and short titles used the following may require elucidation, in addition to those noted in the V.C.H. *Handbook* (1970):

B.L.	British Library (used in references to documents transferred from the British Museum)
Bacon, *Atlas of Lond.* (1886)	*Ordnance Atlas of London and Suburbs*, ed. G. W. Bacon (1886)
Brewer, *Beauties of Eng. & Wales*, x (5)	J. N. Brewer, vol. x (1816) of *The Beauties of England and Wales* (1810–16), ed. E. W. Brayley and J. Britton. The part of the work cited is alternatively known either as the fifth part, or as the second part of vol. iv, of *London and Middlesex*, which is itself vol. x of *The Beauties*
Calamy Revised	A. G. Matthews, *Calamy Revised* (1934)
Ft. of F. Lond. & Mdx.	*Calendar to the Feet of Fines for London and Middlesex*, ed. W. J. Hardy and W. Page (2 vols. 1892–3)
Foot, *Agric. of Mdx.*	P. Foot, *General View of the Agriculture of the County of Middlesex* (1794)
Freshfield, *Communion Plate*	E. Freshfield, *The Communion Plate of the Parish Churches in the County of Middlesex* (1897)
Grange Mus.	London Borough of Brent, Grange Museum of Local History, Neasden
Guildhall MSS.	City of London, Guildhall Library. The collection includes bishops' registers (MS. 9531), diocesan administrative records (MSS. 9532–60), and records of bishops' estates (MSS. 10234–51)
Hennessy, *Novum Rep.*	G. Hennessy, *Novum Repertorium Ecclesiasticum Parochiale Londinense* (1898)
Hist. Lond. Transport	T. C. Barker and M. Robbins, *A History of London Transport* (2 vols. 1975 edn.)
Hist. Mon. Com. *Mdx.*	Royal Commission on Historical Monuments, *An Inventory of the Historical Monuments in Middlesex* (H.M.S.O. 1937)
Kelly's Dir. Mdx.	The Post Office *Directories*. The directories for Middlesex between 1845 and 1863 were published as part of the *Home Counties Directory*
Lond. Dioc. Bk.	*Yearbook* of the diocese of London (1940 to date)
Lysons, *Environs*	D. Lysons, *The Environs of London* (1792–6), vols. ii and iii (1795), Supplement (1811)
M.L.R.	Middlesex Land Registry. The enrolments, indexes, and volumes are at the Greater London Record Office
M.R.O.	Middlesex Record Office. On the incorporation of Middlesex within Greater London on 1 April 1965 the office became known as the Greater London Record Office (Middlesex Records)
Mdx. Cnty. Rec.	*Middlesex County Records* [1550–1688], ed. J. C. Jeaffreson (4 vols. 1886–92)
Mdx. Cnty. Rec. Sess. Bks. 1689–1709	*Middlesex County Records, Calendar of the Sessions Books 1689 to 1709*, ed. W. J. Hardy (1905)
Mdx. Sess. Rec.	*Calendar to the Sessions Records* [1612–18], ed. W. le Hardy (4 vols. 1935–41)
Middleton, *View*	J. Middleton, *View of the Agriculture of Middlesex* (1798)
Mudie-Smith, *Rel. Life*	R. Mudie-Smith, *The Religious Life of London* (1904)

NOTE ON ABBREVIATIONS

New Brentford MSS.

Records of St. Laurence's, New Brentford, at Brentford Library

Newcourt, *Rep.*

R. Newcourt, *Repertorium Ecclesiasticum Parochiale Londinense* (2 vols. 1708–10)

Norden, *Spec. Brit.*

J. Norden, *Speculum Britanniae* (Middlesex) (facsimile edn. 1971)

P.N. Mdx. (E.P.N.S.)

The Place-Names of Middlesex (English Place-Name Society, vol. xviii, 1942)

Pevsner, *Mdx.*

N. Pevsner, *The Buildings of England, Middlesex* (1951)

Rep. on Bridges in Mdx.

Report of the Committee of Magistrates Appointed to make Enquiry respecting the Public Bridges in the County of Middlesex (1826) in M.R.O.

Rep. Com. Eccl. Revenues

Report of the Commissioners Appointed to Inquire into the Ecclesiastical Revenues of England and Wales [67], H.C. (1835), xxii

Rep. Cttee. on Returns by Overseers, 1776

Report of the Select Committee on Returns by Overseers of the Poor 1776, H.C., 1st ser. ix

Robbins, *Mdx.*

M. Robbins, *Middlesex* (1953)

Rocque, *Map of Lond.* (1746)

J. Rocque, *An exact survey of the cities of London, Westminster, and the borough of Southwark, and the country near ten miles around* (1746, facsimile edn. 1971)

Thorne, *Environs*

J. Thorne, *Handbook to the Environs of London* [alphabetically arranged in two parts] (1876)

T.L.M.A.S.

Transactions of the London and Middlesex Archaeological Society (1856 to date). Consecutive numbers are used for the whole series, although vols. vii–xvii (1905–54) appeared as N.S. i–xi

W.A.M.

Westminster Abbey Muniments

Walker Revised

A. G. Matthews, *Walker Revised* (1948)

OSSULSTONE HUNDRED

(continued)

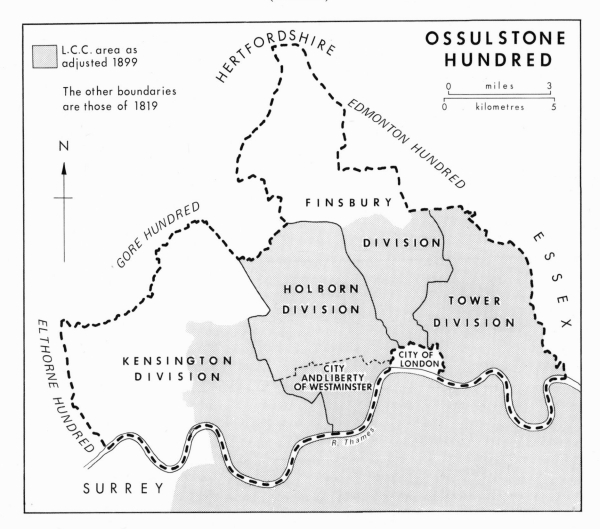

L.C.C. area as
adjusted 1899

The other boundaries
are those of 1819

N

OSSULSTONE HUNDRED

0   miles   3
0   kilometres   5

HERTFORDSHIRE

EDMONTON HUNDRED

GORE HUNDRED

FINSBURY

DIVISION

ESSEX

ELTHORNE HUNDRED

HOLBORN DIVISION

TOWER DIVISION

KENSINGTON DIVISION

CITY OF LONDON

CITY AND LIBERTY OF WESTMINSTER

R. Thames

SURREY

KENSINGTON DIVISION (OUTER PART)

ACTON

ACTON,[1] parish lies *c.* 8 km. west of Hyde Park Corner,[2] bounded on the north by Willesden and West Twyford, on the east by Hammersmith, on the south by Chiswick, and on the west by Ealing and Brentford. It is roughly rectangular in shape, measuring *c.* 2·4 km. from east to west by *c.* 4·8 km.,[3] although until 1894 a small peninsula jutted south-westward towards Brentford. The parish contained 2,305 a. in 1871 and had the same acreage after exchanges with Brentford, which received the south-western peninsula, in 1894 and Willesden in 1895. The civil parish was conterminous with Acton U.D., later M.B., which was enlarged to 2,319 a. by minor adjustments in the 1930s.[4] From 1965 Acton has formed the eastern part of Ealing L.B.

Most of the boundary with Hammersmith was formed by the eastern branch of Stamford brook, and the south-western boundary, from Fordhook south-eastward to Acton Green, by Bollo brook.

[1] The article was written in 1979. Any references to later events are dated.
[2] Following 4 paras. based on O.S. Maps 6″, Mdx. XVI.

NW., SW. (1874 and later edns.).
[3] M. S. Briggs, *Mdx. Old and New* (1934), 168.
[4] *Census,* 1871–1951; below, Chiswick, growth.

I

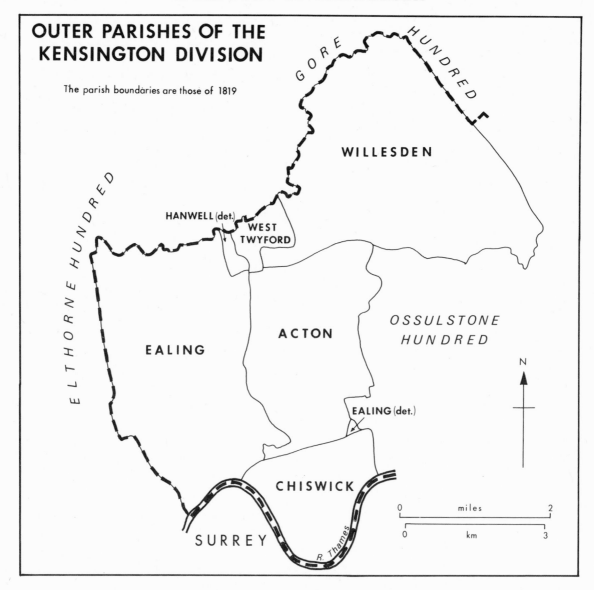

OUTER PARISHES OF THE
KENSINGTON DIVISION

The parish boundaries are those of 1819

GORE HUNDRED

WILLESDEN

ELTHORNE HUNDRED

HANWELL (det.)

WEST
TWYFORD

EALING

ACTON

OSSULSTONE
HUNDRED

N

EALING (det.)

CHISWICK

SURREY

R. Thames

| 0 | miles | 2 |
| 0 | km | 3 |

The southern boundary lay along the line of a Roman road, part of which remains as Chiswick High Road, but was adjusted in 1894 to follow the District and Piccadilly railway lines. The northern boundary and the remainder of the western were marked in 1842 by lanes,[5] which had probably existed much earlier.

London Clay covers the northern part of the parish as far south as Masons green, Acacia Avenue, East Acton village and the site of Manor House, and Acton park. Brickearth covers the rest of East Acton and the parish south of Uxbridge Road, except around Mill Hill and Heathfield, where Taplow Gravel lies along the south-western and western sides.[6]

The land slopes from 50 m. in the north-west corner of the parish to 6 m. in the south-east, drained by two main streams.[7] Bollo brook rises near Fordhook and flows south-eastward to Acton Green, passing into Chiswick. Stamford brook's western branch, apparently rising near

Acton Farm west of Horn Lane, flows south to meet another tributary, from Springfield near the Ealing boundary, at a point north of the Steyne and continues down the west side of the Steyne to cross the Oxford road at the foot of Acton hill. Thence it flows south-eastward south of Berrymead and across South field into Hammersmith, where it joins the eastern branch of Stamford brook from Old Oak common.

COMMUNICATIONS. Acton town lay on the high road from London to Oxford, which was not superseded until Western Avenue was built in the 1920s. Pavage was granted in 1358 and 1363 to men from Acton and Uxbridge to repair the highway in their parishes and as far as the City of London,[8] and a Londoner left money towards its repair in 1504.[9] Acton inhabitants often failed to repair the road in the 17th and 18th centuries, when landholders were ordered to cut back

[5] P.R.O., IR 30/21/1.
[6] Geol. Surv. Maps 1", drift, sheets 256 (1951 edn.) and 270 (1921 edn.).

[7] Para. based also on T. Milne, *Land Use Map of Lond.* (1800).   [8] *Cal. Pat.* 1358–61, 25; 1361–4, 382.
[9] P.R.O., PROB 11/14 (P.C.C. 12 Holgrave).

hedges to prevent robberies.[10] In 1737 it was proposed to use the spring east of Acton town to keep the road clear.[11] The worst stretch was Acton hill, which rose steeply from the water splash west of the church and towards which money was left for repairs in 1438.[12] The water splash was *c.* 4 m. lower than the modern road and waggoners were warned at the top of the hill, which as late as 1899 was a major obstacle: the R.S.P.C.A. and others provided a trace horse to help loads free of charge, and 22 horses laboured for 4 hours to haul a giant boiler over the hill.[13] The highway was turnpiked by the Uxbridge turnpike trust in the early 18th century,[14] with a tollgate at the 4-mile post, where Bromyard Avenue later joined Uxbridge Road by the former King's Arms.

A highway leading south from the top of Acton hill to Gunnersbury and Brentford was known as Bollo Bridge Lane in 1746,[15] Brentford Lane in 1769[16] and 1866,[17] and also as Gunnersbury Lane in the 1860s. The last name, once applied to a more westerly road in Ealing along the line of the modern Gunnersbury Avenue, was usual by 1889.[18] It was also occasionally known as Bollo Lane,[19] although that name normally referred to the way from Bollo bridge, where Gunnersbury Lane crossed the boundary, which followed Bollo brook to Acton common and existed by 1394.[20] The main route northward from Acton town, starting by the church, was called Horn Lane by 1746[21] and may have been the high road towards Harrow called Stone Lane in 1377.[22] It ran past Friars Place Farm before branching slightly north-westward along the modern Park Royal Road, known as Willesden Lane in 1842, to join Norwood or Green Lane at the boundary and lead thence to the Harrow road.

Minor roads included one which branched off Horn Lane to Friars Place and thence north-eastward to Harlesden green, skirting the west side of Old Oak common. Known as Holsden Green Lane in 1746 and Wales Farm Road in 1891, it probably became busier in the 18th century as the chief approach to Acton wells, then a fashionable resort. The parish was indicted in 1776 for the upkeep of the stretch from Harlesden green to Old Oak common,[23] but no path over the common was marked in 1842. Another lane led southward from Friars Place to the west end of East Acton and was called Worton Green Lane in 1639[24] and Batteridges Lane, after a local inhabitant, in 1746. East Acton was connected with Uxbridge Road by a lane from the west end of the green. The lane also ran across the green to the Hammersmith boundary and thence northward to Old Oak common as Old

Oak Lane in 1720[25] and Old Oak Common Lane in 1866. Also from East Acton a footpath led to the parish church along the modern Churchfield Road, being joined by another from the end of the green in the middle of Church field. As it left Church field the path formed a lane, apparently called Lyvyngeslane in 1380,[26] and continued across Horn Lane past the north side of the church. Acton Green was connected to the town by a cartway along the western edge of South field to Uxbridge Road and by a path which ran from the common to High Street just south of the church and partly survived in 1980. Farther west a lane ran north from Acton ponds to Masons green and thence as a path to West Twyford, marking part of the boundary. The portion as far as Masons green was called Mill Lane in 1746 and Green Lane in 1866. It was moved slightly westward by Samuel Wegg in 1758[27] and was also known as Wegg Avenue and then as Twyford Avenue.

The principal roads survived the spread of suburban housing and the fencing of most of the paths across Old Oak common by 1891. The vestry and its successors strove throughout the 19th century to keep open the path from Masons green to West Twyford. James Richard Wood tried to block it in 1813, together with the way south of Friars Place farm from Horn Lane past the moated site to Masons green, which probably had been important in the 15th century and earlier.[28] Harlesden Green Lane was also blocked by landowners, and committees were set up in 1868 and 1888 to protect rights of way.[29] A new road continued Old Oak Common Lane southward to Uxbridge Road by 1891. The road pattern was disrupted only in the late 1920s, when the arterial road called Western Avenue cut across the parish from just north of East Acton green to the north-west corner, near Twyford.

Two bridges carried Uxbridge Road in 1826.[30] Fordhook bridge at the western boundary, where Bollo brook passed under the road, was built by the Uxbridge turnpike trustees in 1776. A bridge at Acton Bottom, west of the church where Stamford brook met the high road, existed in 1742 and was rebuilt by the trustees in 1769. It may have been one of the four bridges between Notting Hill and Acton that the bishop of London or his tenant at Wormholt farm, Hammersmith, was liable to maintain,[31] but more probably they were responsible for a bridge at the east end of the parish, where Stamford brook's eastern branch crossed the road, which apparently was known as Mile End bridge in 1651.[32] In 1420 John Fyghter of Acton left money towards the new bridge between London and Acton, which may have been in the parish.[33]

[10] Hist. MSS. Com. 39, *15th Rep. II*, p. 260.
[11] R. Phillips, *Dissertation concerning High Roads* (1737), 28.
[12] Guildhall MS. 9171/3, f. 505v.
[13] Acton libr., notes on Acton hill by W. T. Poore.
[14] Robbins, *Mdx.* 71.
[15] J. Rocque, *Map of Lond., Westm. and Environs* (1746), sheet 14.
[16] Guildhall MS. 10465/84.
[17] O.S. Map 6″, Mdx. XVI. SW. (1874 edn.).
[18] R. N. G. Rowland, *Street Names of Acton* (1977), 20.
[19] P.R.O., IR 30/21/1. Perhaps also Bellow Lane, 1588: P.R.O., SC 2/189/24.
[20] *Public Works in Med. Law,* ii (Selden Soc. xi), p. 29.

[21] Rocque, *Map of Lond.* (1746). Following 2 paras. based on ibid.; P.R.O., IR 30/21/1; O.S. Maps 6″, Mdx. XVI. NW., SW. (1874 edn.).   [22] *Cal. Close,* 1374-7, 551.
[23] Acton par. church, vestry min. bk. (1776-1801).
[24] P.R.O., SC 2/190/10.
[25] Ibid. SC 2/190/16.   [26] *Cal. Close,* 1377-81, 468.
[27] M.R.O., Acc. 617/56.
[28] Ealing town hall, vestry min. bks. (1801-22), 8 Sept. 1813; (1822-57), 24 Aug. 1826.
[29] Ibid. highways cttee. min. bk. (1868); various cttees. bk. i, 31 Jan. 1888.
[30] Para. based on *Rep. on Bridges in Mdx.* 192-3.
[31] P.R.O., SP 14/203, no. 26.   [32] Ibid. SC 2/190/15.
[33] Guildhall MS. 9171/3, f. 85v.

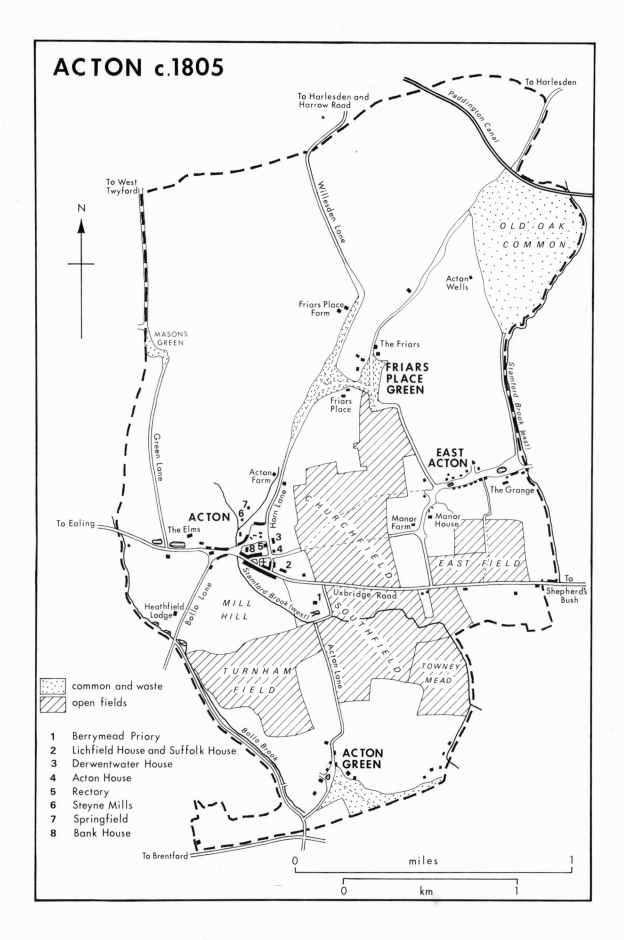

ACTON c.1805

N

To West Twyford

To Harlesden and Harrow Road

Paddington Canal

To Harlesden

OLD OAK COMMON

MASONS GREEN

Willesden Lane

Friars Place Farm

Acton Wells

The Friars

FRIARS PLACE GREEN

Friars Place

Stamford Brook (east)

Green Lane

Acton Farm

EAST ACTON

The Grange

ACTON

Horn Lane

7
6

CHURCHFIELD

Manor Farm

Manor House

EAST FIELD

To Ealing

The Elms

3
4

8 5

2

1

Uxbridge Road

To Shepherd's Bush

Heathfield Lodge

Bollo Lane

MILL HILL

Stamford Brook (west)

SOUTHFIELD

Acton Lane

TURNHAM FIELD

TOWNEY MEAD

Bollo Brook

ACTON GREEN

common and waste

open fields

1 Berrymead Priory
2 Lichfield House and Suffolk House
3 Derwentwater House
4 Acton House
5 Rectory
6 Steyne Mills
7 Springfield
8 Bank House

To Brentford

0   miles   1

0   km   1

The bishop in 1663 also repaired Bollo bridge,[34] in existence by 1239,[35] where the road from Acton hill to Gunnersbury crossed Bollo brook. It was decayed in 1554, when the bishop, as lord, was liable for its upkeep.[36] There were bridges on the road later called Acton Lane where it crossed Stamford brook east of Berrymead and at the north-west corner of Acton common where a stream called Mill Hill brook met the lane.

In the extreme north part of the parish the Paddington branch of the Grand Junction canal from Bull's Bridge junction, near Southall, to Paddington, was opened in 1801.[37] A bridge carrying Harlesden Green Lane across the canal was maintained by the Grand Junction Canal Co.,[38] but the canal itself made little local impact, since the area did not become industrial until the coming of the railways.

In 1764 the Acton Machine ran on Saturdays from the George at Acton to Oxford Street, returning two hours later, with a similar journey from London to Acton, returning an hour later, and every Saturday a coach went to Acton at 9 a.m.[39] In 1825 a short-stage coach from Acton to the City made four return journeys a day, [40] and in 1845 the London to Oxford coaches still passed, supplemented by an omnibus four times a day and by daily carriers.[41] In 1856 the London General Omnibus Co. took over the Bayswater horse bus fleet, which plied between the Victoria in Acton Bottom and London Bridge.[42]

Acton's first tram service, between the Princess Victoria in Askew Crescent, Acton Vale, and Uxbridge Road (Shepherd's Bush) station, was opened by the Southall, Ealing & Shepherd's Bush Tram-Railway Co. in 1874.[43] It soon closed but reopened and was said to carry 1,000 passengers daily, an extension to Acton Lane being opened in 1878. The line was taken over in 1881 by the West Metropolitan Tramways Co. but was in a bad state when sold in 1894. It was bought by the new London United Tramways Co., which extended it westward to the White Hart, Acton hill, in 1895 and replaced the Shepherd's Bush depot by one on the south side of Uxbridge Road west of the Red Lion, with 7 tracks and housing 50 cars. The line between Acton and Shepherd's Bush was doubled throughout and workmen's cars ran every morning from Acton to catch the early trains at Uxbridge Road station, with through tickets for tram and train. Birch Grove, near the Ealing boundary, was the limit for a 1d. journey from London.[44] An all-night service of horse cars ran by 1899.

London's first electric street tramway was started by the L.U.T. in 1901 between Acton and Shepherd's Bush, with extensions later in that year through Ealing to Southall.[45] A service from Hammersmith to Southall and Uxbridge by way of Acton started in 1904. A proposed line to Harlesden along Horn Lane and Old Oak Lane was dropped because of the county council's plans, although the route was opened finally, by the Metropolitan Electric Tramways Co., in 1909. A service from Acton to Putney (Surr.) began in 1928, run jointly by the L.U.T. and the L.C.C. In 1933 the tramways passed to the London Passenger Transport Board and in 1936 the Hammersmith and Acton section was converted for trolleybuses.[46]

Electric trams prompted the L.G.O.C. to improve its horse buses, provide a new service from Acton to Charing Cross, and cut fares,[47] but horses soon gave way to motor buses. By 1910 a motor bus ran daily from Ealing and Acton along Uxbridge Road through the City to East Ham (Essex), and by 1914 new services connected Acton with central London and Barking (Essex). By 1932 motor buses along Western Avenue connected East Acton with Putney bridge,[48] and in the 1920s independent companies ran a successful service from Finchley to Wandsworth (Surr.) through Willesden and Acton.[49]

Although its main line ran through the parish as early as 1838, the G.W.R. did not open Acton, later Acton main line, station until 1868.[50] Interested at first chiefly in long-distance traffic, the G.W.R. made little effort to develop suburban passenger services and neither did the two other main-line companies whose lines ran through Acton: the London & North Western in the extreme northern tip and the London & South Western in the extreme south.[51] Local passenger transport was left mostly to subsidiary companies and in 1891 the local board still pressed for fuller and cheaper train services.[52]

Acton's first station was opened in 1853 as Acton, renamed Acton Central in 1925. It was on the North & South Western Junction's line which ran southward through the middle of the parish, linking the L.N.W.R. line near Kensal Green with Old Kew junction on the L.S.W.R.'s Windsor loop.[53] The L.S.W.R. worked the first freight traffic, while passengers were left to the North London Railway, a subsidiary of the L.N.W.R. Passenger traffic was light at first but in 1858 trains were extended to Richmond (Surr.) and Twickenham and in 1863 to Kingston-upon-Thames (Surr.). When in 1865 the N.L.R. and L.N.W.R. jointly opened a station at Broad Street, Acton had a direct rail link with the City, which could be reached by a few fast trains in 30 minutes. From 1869 a line

[34] Guildhall MS. 10124A.
[35] *P. N. Mdx.* (E.P.N.S.), 82.
[36] P.R.O., SC 2/189/24.
[37] E. A. Course, *Lond. Rlys.* (1962), 171.
[38] *Rep. on Bridges in Mdx.* 158.
[39] Acton libr., cutting from *Acton Gaz.* 1911.
[40] Barker and Robbins, *Hist. Lond. Transport*, i. 391.
[41] *P.O. Dir. Mdx.* (1845).
[42] L.T.E. *Lond. General: Story of Lond. Bus, 1856–1956*, 70.
[43] Following 2 paras. based on G. Wilson, *Lond. Utd. Tramways* (1971).
[44] A. E. Davies and E. E. Gower, *Tramway Trips and Rambles* (1907), 10.

[45] Barker and Robbins, *Hist. Lond. Transport*, ii. 33.
[46] O. J. Morris, *Fares Please* (1953), 173.
[47] Wilson, *Lond. Utd. Tramways*, 67.
[48] A. A. Jackson, *Semi-detached Lond.* (1973), 333–4, 338.
[49] Barker and Robbins, *Hist. Lond. Transport*, ii. 227.
[50] T. B. Peacock, *Gt. Western Suburban Svces.* (1948), 99.
[51] J. R. Kellett, *Impact of Rlys. on Victorian Cities* (1969), 63; H. P. White, *Regional Hist. Rlys. of G.B.* iii (1963), 111, 118.
[52] Ealing town hall, Acton local bd., various cttees. bk. 1, 8 Dec. 1891.
[53] Para. based on M. Robbins, *N. Lond. Rly.* (1953), 3–5, 14, 16, 18.

from South Acton junction to Richmond provided a more direct route, and trains ran alternately to Richmond and Kew Bridge.[54] South Acton station, just north of South Acton junction, was opened in 1880; from 1909 almost all trains from Broad Street ran straight to Richmond, while Kew Bridge was served by a branch from Acton.

Later railways developed separately either in the north or in the south part of the parish. In the north the Midland & South Western Junction opened the Dudding Hill loop between the Midland's line at the Welsh Harp and the N.S.W.J.'s at Acton Wells junction, south of Willesden junction, in 1868.[55] Intermittent passenger services started in 1875 from Cricklewood to Acton, with trains at first running through to Richmond, later to Earl's Court on the District line, and finally from 1894 between Child's Hill and Gunnersbury only. Although the passenger service ceased in 1902, the line continued to be worked for freight by both the Midland and the L.S.W.R. and their successors. The Midland ran goods trains from Acton to its Kensington depot until 1878.[56]

The G.W.R. opened a spur in 1877 connecting its main line with the N.S.W.J. at Acton Wells junction, which was used chiefly for goods but also carried passengers from Southall to Willesden from 1888 until 1912.[57] In 1904 the company began another suburban service between Westbourne Park and Greenford on the first section of its new Birmingham line, using steam-powered motor cars.[58] The one regular station, at Park Royal, was first used in 1903 for the Royal Agricultural Society's show, but continental-style halts were provided at North Acton, opened in 1904, and Old Oak Lane, opened in 1906.[59] Services lasted until 1947 but remained infrequent, despite the speed of nearby building.

The Ealing and Shepherd's Bush railway was authorized in 1905, to link the G.W.R. with the Central London line, the first used by the G.W.R. for freight traffic to the West London line in 1917. Passenger services began only in 1920 when the Central London, which linked with the new line at Wood Lane (White City) station, began to run electric trains from the City and west end of London to Ealing Broadway, using electricity from the G.W.R.'s power station at Park Royal.[60] At first the only station within reach of Acton was East Acton, beyond the boundary in Hammersmith, opened in 1920 to serve the L.C.C.'s Old Oak housing estate. In 1923 West Acton and North Acton stations were added: the second, not far from the halt of 1904, allowed interchange between the Central London and the G.W.R.'s steam service. The G.W.R. itself provided workmen's trains between Greenford and Kensington over the line

from 1922 to 1938, extending them to Clapham junction from 1933.[61] Under the New Works Programme of 1935 the G.W.R. was to build extra tracks along its Birmingham line from North Acton to Ruislip, for the Central line to carry suburban traffic,[62] a project finally carried out in the late 1940s in collaboration with the L.P.T.B. Thereafter the G.W.R. closed its platforms at North Acton and confined its suburban activities to freight, running its steam trains on separate tracks.

In the south part of the parish the Hammersmith branch line ran from the N.S.W.J.'s line at a point slightly north of Acton Lane, called Acton Gatehouse junction.[63] From 1858 it carried passengers to its Hammersmith terminus north of Chiswick High Road, renamed Hammersmith and Chiswick in 1880. A rail motor car worked the line from 1909, when halts were built at Rugby Road, Woodstock Road, and Bath Road in an effort to revive traffic. Closed to passengers in 1916, the line continued to carry goods, mainly coal, until 1965.[64]

Passenger services to the City from the south part of the parish began with the opening in 1877 of the Hammersmith Junction line, a joint enterprise whereby the Metropolitan District Railway ran trains from the City to Richmond over the L.S.W.R.'s tracks and used its station at Turnham Green.[65] That station alone served the extreme south part of Acton until 1879, when the District built a line from Turnham Green to Ealing Broadway, with stations at Acton Green, renamed Chiswick Park and Acton Green in 1887 and Chiswick Park in 1910, and at Mill Hill Park, renamed Acton Town in 1910,[66] which was just outside the boundary. The District opened a new line from Mill Hill Park to Hounslow in 1883 and to Hounslow barracks in 1884. Its first electric service ran in 1903, from Mill Hill Park to Park Royal and South Harrow, and in 1905 the South Acton to Hounslow line was converted to electricity, followed by the service to Ealing.

A link between Acton Town on the District line and South Acton junction on the N.S.W.J., called the Acton loop line, was built in 1899, when it was used to carry materials to build the District's Ealing and South Harrow extension.[67] The loop followed the main District line from Acton Town before curving to cross Bollo Lane and join the N.S.W.J. line near South Acton station, where the District built an adjoining platform in 1905. Electric trains were run by the District from South Acton to Hounslow from 1905 and a 15-minute service from South Acton to South Harrow was started in 1922, with a few trains to Uxbridge or Hounslow barracks. Both the L.N.W.R. and the Midland used the Acton loop to send freight to Ealing Common. In 1913 additional sidings were laid for them near Acton

[54] White, *Rlys. of G.B.* iii. 129–30; inf. from Mr. H. V. Borley.

[55] Para. based on White, *Rlys. of G.B.* iii. 130; Barker and Robbins, *Hist. Lond. Transport*, i. 131.

[56] C. E. Lee, *Metropolitan Dist. Rly.* (1956), 8.

[57] Robbins, *N. Lond. Rly.* 14, 18.

[58] Rest of para. based on White, *Rlys. of G.B.* iii. 114–15; *Rly. Mag.* xiv (1904), 487–93.

[59] Barker and Robbins, *Hist. Lond. Transport*, ii. 158; Rowland, *Street Names*, 41.

[60] Para. based on White, *Rlys. of G.B.* iii. 116; Barker and Robbins, *Hist. Lond. Transport*, ii. 243.

[61] Peacock, *Gt. Western Suburban Svces.* 18.

[62] Course, *Lond. Rlys.* 225.

[63] Para. based on Robbins, *N. Lond. Rly.* 14; White, *Rlys. of G.B.* iii. 131.   [64] Rowland, *Street Names*, 41.

[65] Para. based on Lee, *Metropolitan Dist. Rly.*

[66] A. E. Bennett and H. V. Borley, *Lond. Transport Rlys.* 13, 20, 25, 27.

[67] Para. based on *Rly. Mag.* civ (1958), 817–19.

Town, but the route soon fell out of use and the connexion with the N.S.W.J. line was removed in 1930. The passenger service remained unchanged until 1932, when plans to use the District line for Piccadilly line trains to South Harrow led to the loop's reduction to a single track, with a shuttle service between South Acton and Acton Town. The line and the District's platform at South Acton were finally closed in 1959.[68]

In 1932 the Piccadilly line was extended from Hammersmith to South Harrow and later to Northfields, Uxbridge, and Hounslow. Piccadilly and District trains ran on parallel tracks, the Piccadilly non-stop from Hammersmith to Acton Town and the District calling at intervening stations,[69] and Chiswick Park was reconstructed for the District line alone. By 1963 the Piccadilly had taken over all the services to South Harrow, Hounslow, and Uxbridge, except for a few peak-hour trains; it extended the service to Hatton Cross in 1975 and to Heathrow in 1977.[70]

GROWTH. Prehistoric settlement is attested by finds of palaeolithic and neolithic Bronze-Age burials at Mill Hill Park, and Iron-Age coins near Bollo Lane.[71]

Although the name Acton, meaning 'oak town', is Anglo-Saxon, it was first recorded as that of a witness, Viel of Acton, in 1181.[72] In the Middle Ages the northern half of the parish was heavily wooded. Oaks and elms still stood along roads and hedgerows and in private grounds in the early 20th century,[73] but most of the woodland had been cleared by the 17th century, even on the extensive Old Oak common.[74]

Some landholders were resident by 1222[75] and houses were recorded from the late 13th century. The main settlement, Church Acton or Acton town, lay slightly west of the centre of the parish along the highway to Oxford, at the 5-mile post out of London.[76] By 1380 some of the tenements, such as the Tabard and the Cock, along the south side of the road, were inns.[77] The hamlet of East Acton, mentioned in 1294, consisted of farmhouses and cottages north and south of common land known as East Acton green by 1474.[78]

Medieval settlement was mainly around the two hamlets. At Church Acton most of the farmhouses lay along the Oxford road or Horn Lane, with only a few outlying farms. Friars Place Farm at the north end of Horn Lane and the moated site to the west, occupied until the 15th century, were early farms.[79] East of Friars

Place farm were commons, called Worton or Watton green and Rush green in the 16th and 17th centuries, and Friars Place in the 18th century, where there was some settlement by 1664. To the north-west were Acton or Old Oak wells, which were known by 1613.[80] In the extreme south part of the parish a few farmhouses on the northern side of Acton common or Acton Green were mentioned as in Turnham Green until the 19th century and were linked more closely with that village than with Acton. Gregories, mentioned in 1551 as a copyhold tenement with 30 a. near Bollo Lane and the Brentford high road, probably lay there.[81]

Londoners were increasingly involved in land sales from the early 14th century but apparently did not live in Acton until the late 15th. The manor, part of Fulham, had no demesne, and apart from a brief period before c. 1735, when the Somerset family lived in Acton in a house which was not part of the estate, there were no large resident landowners. Many of the tenements without land, including most of the inns, frequently changed hands, with the result that few local families can be traced over more than a hundred years.

By the 17th century Acton's proximity to London had made it a summer retreat for courtiers and lawyers. Sir Richard Sutton bought the seat at East Acton known later as Manor House in 1610 and Sir Henry Garraway probably rebuilt Acton House in 1638. Sir John Trevor bought several properties in the mid 17th century, including Berrymead where he probably lived, improving it with a lake and stream. Berrymead, home of the marquesses of Halifax in the late 17th century and afterwards of the duke of Kingston, was noted for its grounds.[82] The dowager countess of Leicester spent the summers c. 1700 in a house near the church.[83]

The parish had 158 communicants in 1548.[84] It had 72 chargeable households and 59 exempt, with 6 empty houses, in 1664. Fifty of the chargeable were in Acton town, 3 at Turnham Green, and 6 at Friars Place. Six houses had 10 or more hearths, 16 had from 5 to 9, 33 had 3 or 4, 23 had 2, and 53 had only 1.[85] There were c. 160 families in the mid 18th century.[86]

Acton was held to be blessed with very sweet air in 1706[87] and the rector accordingly urged a friend, in verse, to move there.[88] The fashion for medicinal waters brought a brief period of fame, with the exploitation of the wells at Old Oak common, when East Acton and Friars Place were said to be thronged with summer visitors, who had brought about improvement in the houses

[68] Bennett and Borley, *Lond. Transport Rlys.* 28.
[69] Para. based on White, *Rlys. of G.B.* iii. 134; Lee, *Metropolitan Dist. Rly.* 27.
[70] Inf. from Mr. Borley.
[71] C. H. Keene, *Field Monuments of Ealing* (Ealing L.B. Technical Svces. Group, 1975), 10–11 and map, 13–15; *V.C.H. Mdx.* i. 18–19, 35, 43, 45, 64; P. Jolliffe, *Acton and its Hist.* (1910), 3.
[72] *Domesday of St. Paul's* (Camd. Soc. [1st ser.], lxix), 128. A grant of land at Acton in 716 probably refers to a place in the west Midlands: *Cart. Sax.* ed. Birch, i, p. 198.
[73] e.g. illus. in W. K. Baker, *Acton* (1912); E. J. Tongue, *50 Yrs. in a Lond. Suburb* (jubilee souvenir of Acton Bapt. ch. 1915), 58.
[74] P.R.O., SC 2/190/5.

[75] *Bracton's Note Bk.* iii. 447–8.
[76] Tongue, *Lond. Suburb*, 57; below.
[77] *Cal. Close*, 1377–81, 468; below, social.
[78] *P.N. Mdx.* (E.P.N.S.), 82.
[79] Below, manors and other est.
[80] R. Morden, *Map. of Mdx.* (1694, 1701–8 edns.).
[81] P.R.O., SC 2/189/24; ibid. MAF 20/2/22 Turley.
[82] Below, manors and other est.
[83] J. Bowack, *Antiquities of Mdx.* (1705–6), 59.
[84] P.R.O., E 301/34, no. 161.
[85] M.R.O., MR/TH/3.
[86] Guildhall MS. 9550.
[87] Bowack, *Antiquities*, 59. Acton was still thought very salubrious in 1831: Lewis, *Topog. Dict. Eng.* (1831 edn.), 8.
[88] Jolliffe, *Acton*, 48.

there.[89] Although high society had left Acton by the mid 18th century, many professional and military men bought houses there, sometimes including a small park, until well into the 19th century. The break-up of the 800-a. Fetherstonhaugh estate, which had had no resident owner, produced four or five small estates whose owners, professional men such as Samuel Wegg, John Winter, and Richard White,[90] were active in parish affairs. Residences at East Acton, Friars Place, and Acton Green were altered and new ones were built: Heathfield Lodge, West Lodge, and East Lodge by Winter c. 1800, Mill Hill House by White, and Woodlands at Acton hill soon afterwards. Acton Green also became increasingly popular, being near Chiswick High Road or the Great West Road. Fairlawn, in its own grounds on the west side of the green, was the home of the botanist John Lindley (1797–1865)[91] and was substantial, as were the house to the north and Bedford House, another home of Lindley, and Melbourne House farther east.[92] A short row of houses had been built on the south side of the green by 1800.[93]

There were 241 inhabited houses in 1801 and 426 by 1831.[94] Growth took place mainly in the existing villages of Acton town and East Acton, but Acton Green also had acquired a cluster of cottages and houses at the bottom of Acton Lane by 1842.[95] Acton was, however, still a rural village, with agriculture providing the main employment in both 1801 and 1831.[96] The few mansions contrasted sharply with most of the houses, which were described as 'beneath mediocrity of character'.[97] Despite an overall rise in the number of houses, poor rates had to be increased in the 1820s because of a growing number of empty dwellings.[98]

More widespread building was planned in the 1850s. Mill Hill Terrace had been built by 1859 south of High Street,[99] the common fields were inclosed in 1859,[1] and the desire for improvements to attract new residents revealed belief in a potential demand.[2] From 1859 ratepayers were listed under the chief roads of the parish, their addresses in greater detail being given from 1862.[3]

The main village, known as CHURCH ACTON or ACTON TOWN to distinguish it from East Acton, grew up around the parish church and on either side of the main highway immediately south, later High Street, where there were inhabitants by 1222.[4] The ground rose steeply on each side of Stamford brook, where buildings near the church stood well above the road by the 18th century, as the name Bank House implied. By the 19th century a row of old cottages in High Street, close to the church, had a narrow raised footpath in front.[5]

Several tenements were inns, of which the Frowyk family held at least five c. 1500: the Tabard, the Cock on the Hoop, the White Lion, the Star, and the Hartshorn. Other tenements at that time were Scoriers and Patermanhall, and Butlers half way along Horn Lane.[6] A croft or close called the Steyne existed in 1520[7] and contained 4 a. c. 1533.[8] It gave its name to the area north of the church and nearby houses, such as Bank House, and included some waste land, which sloped from Horn Lane westward to Stamford brook, where gravel was dug in 1622.[9] Small inclosures were made from the waste from the 17th century and possibly earlier, to supplement the grounds of houses such as Bank House or for new buildings.[10] New cottages were increasingly recorded throughout the village from the mid 17th century.

In 1664 the town's 50 chargeable houses included all those in the parish with 8 or more hearths, apart from East Acton Manor House.[11] The high road formed the single street in 1706, when there were a few houses behind the church and in the Steyne. There were several inns, and some houses had been rebuilt in brick, although most were still of timber and plaster. The population remained agricultural, with only a few tradesmen in addition to farmers and gentry.[12] Among the improved houses, some of them large and with prominent residents, were Acton House or Skippon's house on the east side of Horn Lane, Fighters near the church, Bank House, and the house at Berrymead. An imposing Rectory was built on the west side of Horn Lane in 1725 and the Elms, near the western boundary, at about that date. The later Acton Farm, on the west side of Horn Lane, and Springfield House, on the east, were standing by 1746.[13] In 1766 Church Acton had 133 houses.[14]

In the late 18th century building covered very little new ground.[15] By 1800 dense rows of dwellings stretched from the north side of Acton hill around into the west side of the Steyne, forming a block in the middle of the Steyne, and similarly stretched on the south side of Acton hill from Gunnersbury Lane along the south side of High Street to a point opposite the junction with Horn Lane. The Elms and Hill House, on the north side of Uxbridge Road, and Woodlands, on the south side of Acton hill, stood in their own grounds. Then or soon afterwards a few middle-class houses were built away from the main settlement: Heathfield Lodge in Gunnersbury Lane, West Lodge and East Lodge in Uxbridge

[89] Below, social.
[90] Below, manors and other est.
[91] D.N.B.
[92] For their inclusion in Bedford Pk., see below, Chiswick, growth.
[93] Milne, Land Use Map of Lond. (1800).
[94] Census, 1801–31.
[95] P.R.O., IR 30/21/1.
[96] Census, 1801–31.
[97] Brewer, Beauties of Eng. & Wales, x (5), 329.
[98] Rep. Sel. Cttee. on Police of Metropolis, H.C. 533, p. 218 (1828), vi.
[99] Acton libr., vestry accts. rate bk. (1841–67).
[1] Below, econ.
[2] Below, local govt.
[3] Rate Bk. (1841–67).
[4] Bracton's Note Bk. iii. 447–8.
[5] Tongue, Lond. Suburb, 57.
[6] Below, social.
[7] P.R.O., C 142/79/231.
[8] Ibid. C 1/757/12.
[9] Guildhall MS. 10833.
[10] Ct. rolls, e.g. Guildhall MS. 10833 (1622); P.R.O., SC 2/190/5 (1650).
[11] M.R.O., MR/TH/3.
[12] Bowack, Antiquities, 59.
[13] Rocque, Map of Lond. (1746), sheet 14.
[14] Guildhall MS. 9558, f. 417.
[15] Para. based on Milne, Land Use Map of Lond. (1800).

Road, and Mill Hill or Acton Hill House amidst farmland south of the town. Apart from those isolated houses, building consisted mainly of infilling, especially in the Steyne where there were 50 or more tiny cottages by 1842,[16] or in closes behind High Street, such as Cock and Crown Yard. By 1860 housing along the south side of High Street had reached the wall of Berrymead Priory, with the building of the infants' school in 1837, Oldham's Terrace, and the National school.

The larger houses in the town began to outlive their purpose, although several such as Bank House, Orger House, and Hill House served as private schools. Bank House was demolished in the early 1870s and its grounds were covered with cottages, including Nelson Place, and the new local board offices at the junction of High Street and Steyne Road.[17] Orger House, set back from the road at the southern end of Horn Lane, was burned down c. 1855, and its site was used for an open market and fair in the 1860s. The land was sold in 1877 and shops were built along the Horn Lane frontage, which was probably then renamed Market Place.[18] Richards Cottages ran south from Churchfield Road behind the Market Place shops and were built between 1866 and 1871.[19]

Despite some infilling, there was still much open space in the old town in the early 1890s. On the north side of High Street, Lichfield House, Suffolk House, and Grove House retained their grounds, as did the houses on the east side of Horn Lane from Churchfield Road as far north as the Lodge and around the Rectory on the west side. Land north and west of the Steyne around Steyne mills was not yet built over, nor, on the south side of Acton hill, were the large grounds of Woodlands and adjoining land behind the High Street shops.[20]

In the 1890s the council began improving the roads, having already bought land on either side of High Street near Suffolk House to permit widening.[21] All the old cottages, with narrow frontages, north of the church between High Street and King Street were demolished in 1893, whereupon the road was widened by the west front of the church at the junction of the two streets, the rest of the land being left open as a small garden. The King's Head at the opposite corner of King Street and the forge and shop next to it in King Street were also bought, in order that the inn could be moved back from the main road, and other property to the west was soon bought for similar improvements, which continued during the next decade. Old houses in High Street opposite the church and Steyne Road were replaced by shops set farther back. Some 21 houses and 8 business premises, including those in Cock and Crown Yard, were

demolished in 1909 to make way for Crown Street. The Pineapple, at the west corner of Gunnersbury Lane and Acton hill, was demolished, the Red Lion was moved farther back, and more property was bought to widen King Street.

Before the First World War Acton House and Derwentwater House made way for a cinema and shops in Horn Lane, with housing behind, while Woodlands was replaced by a row of shops on Acton hill, with a public garden and the county school behind.[22] Further changes took place after the war. Suffolk House and Lichfield House were fronted with a row of shops in 1921, known as the Broadway, with a cinema beside them.[23] Grove House, at the eastern end of the town, made way in the 1920s for Acton technical college. The Steyne was considered the worst area of housing in the borough:[24] cottages in East Row and nearby property were pulled down in 1935, many of them having been condemned as early as 1903,[25] and the council built a four-storeyed block of flats called Steyne House in 1938.[26]

The main shopping streets in the early 1930s were High Street, Market Place, Horn Lane, Churchfield Road, and Church Road, the last having an open market that had been moved from Crown Street. By 1956 Churchfield Road and High Street were still a busy shopping area, but premises were in bad repair and used for other purposes at either end of High Street, where trade was declining. An area of 180 a., including Crown Street, was to be rebuilt over 25 years, leaving only the town hall and some churches and with 66 a. being included in plans by the county council for a ten-year scheme. One sixth of the 180 a. was for industry and commerce and 6 a. were for four open spaces.[27] In the early 1960s Lichfield House and Suffolk House, with the nearby cinema north of High Street, were replaced by a shopping precinct.[28] South of High Street almost all the sites behind the shops and on the south of Mill Hill Terrace as far as Avenue Road, from Langley Drive to Oldham's Terrace, were cleared, and by the late 1970s a community centre and new housing were nearly completed. In the Steyne old housing was demolished in Back Street and Steyne Road, besides Steyne mills and, in 1972, the Jubilee almshouses. Most of the area between Steyne and Lexden roads was left open, apart from the 22-storeyed blocks of flats, Rufford Tower and Moreton Tower, built in 1967 and 1968 respectively.[29] Further phases of the plan for the town centre were carried out in the 1970s. The bakery site next to Berrymead Priory was acquired for housing, which had been nearly finished by 1980, and the burial ground in Churchfield Road was converted into a garden and connected with the High Street shopping precinct to the south in 1980.[30]

Because it was on the Oxford road the town

[16] P.R.O., IR 30/21/1.
[17] Rowland, *Street Names*, 3.
[18] Jolliffe, *Acton*, 74; Rowland, *Street Names*, 25.
[19] O.S. Map 6″, Mdx. XVI. SW. (1874 edn.); Rowland, *Street Names*, 31.
[20] O.S. Maps 6″, Mdx. XVI. NW., SW. (1894–6 edn.).
[21] Para. based on Ealing libr., Acc. 19/1; *The Times*, 14 Jan. 1909.
[22] Rowland, *Street Names*, 1, 14, 40.   [23] Ibid. 8.
[24] *New Survey of Lond. Life and Labour* (1934), vi. 451.

[25] Rowland, *Street Names*, 35; Acton U.D.C. *Rep. of M.O.H.* (1903), 29.
[26] Acton U.D.C. *Rep. of M.O.H.* (1938), 35.
[27] J. Beasley, 'Architectural Survey of Central Acton' (Borough Rd. Coll., Isleworth, dissertation, 1956, TS. in Acton libr.), 28–9, 32, 34.
[28] Rowland, *Street Names*, 24.
[29] Ibid. 35.
[30] Acton libr., Acton town centre scheme progress rep. 1976.

was involved in the Civil War. In 1642 when the train bands of London were marching against the king to Turnham Green, a troop under John Hampden that swept around the royalist flank was probably the group that took part in a skirmish near Acton.[31] The citizens of London, in a procession of 300 coaches, met Oliver Cromwell at Acton on his return from his victory at Worcester in 1652.[32]

Eminent residents[33] not otherwise mentioned below included William Lloyd (1637–1710), non-juring bishop of Norwich, who lived for a time at Mitre House, High Street,[34] John Adams-Acton (1830–1910), sculptor, who was born at Acton hill,[35] and Samuel Newth (1821–98), principal of New College, London, who died at no. 23 Woodhurst Road.[36] Perhaps also resident in the town were William Ryley (d. 1667), herald and archivist, who moved to Acton in 1650, the actress Elizabeth Barry (1658–1713), who retired there c. 1709 and was buried in the church, and the engraver James Heath (1757–1834), who was also buried there.[37] The miniature-painter Alfred Tidey (1802–92) died at Glenelg, Pierrepoint Road, Springfield Park. North of the town the cricketer W. G. Grace (1848–1915) lived briefly at no. 1 Leamington Park and the aviator Sir John Alcock (1892–1919) in Allison Road.[38]

The hamlet of EAST ACTON consisted of farmhouses north and south of East Acton green. The name first occurred in 1294[39] and the settlement had free and copyhold tenements by 1394.[40] They included the freehold Bishops and Parkers in 1482,[41] Taygroves in 1489, also called Parkes in 1532, and, by 1532, Fowlers, Curles or Curlewyns, Dowyscroft, and the copyhold Fosters or Hill House.[42] A copyhold house with 30 a. was known by 1688 as the Farm House but also called Elm farm or the Elms by the late 18th century.[43]

In the early 17th century Sir Richard Sutton bought much of the surrounding land, including Fosters, where he moved East Acton Lane away from the house and laid out grounds.[44] In 1664 the house, later called Manor House, had 20 hearths and was the largest in the parish, while the other 14 chargeable houses in East Acton had 5 hearths or fewer.[45]

By 1800 the south side of the green was lined by houses, from a group of cottages at the eastern end as far as the later East Acton House and from the other side of Crown Lane as far as a house later called the Beeches. The north side had three detached houses and a row of cottages from the junction with Friars Place Lane to a point opposite Crown Lane. At the west end stood the Elms, in its own grounds, and Manor House.[46] Several of the former farmhouses were improved or rebuilt. The Grange, at the east end on the southern side of the green, was probably early 18th-century, having replaced a timber-framed building, and was afterwards extended. East Acton House was also 18th-century, with later alterations.[47] The Goldsmiths' Company of London built its almshouses facing towards Uxbridge Road in 1812 and other improvements around the green were reported in 1818, the ditch in front of the houses having been bricked over and railed enclosures made in front of the houses. In 1816 James Heath had been leased two cottages by the Goldsmiths' Company, on condition that he replaced them with a new house, as he had done by 1818,[48] probably with the Beeches. In 1829 the Goldsmiths' Arms was built at the corner of Friars Place Lane and East Acton Lane.

In 1842 the village consisted mainly of detached buildings.[49] The Elms, the Horse and Groom, and a forge stood at the west end of the green. On the north side were the Goldsmith's Arms, with some cottages next to it, then Hindley House, the White House, Glendun House, the Stud Farm, and a small house at the east end. On the south side from east to west stood the Bull's Head, some cottages and outbuildings, the Grange, East Acton House, the Chestnuts, the Lodge, Shakespeare House, Ivy Lodge, and the Beeches. East Acton Lane contained Manor House, Manor Farm, and the almshouses.

Few further additions were made until after the First World War, apart from the building of a National school in 1870.[50] The pond on the green near East Acton House had been filled by 1894.[51] Hindley House was demolished in 1902 and later replaced by a parish hall. The dilapidated Manor House was pulled down in 1911 and its site used for playing fields. Land around the village was rapidly built up in the late 1920s, when changes were made to the houses along the green. The White House was bought by the Goldsmiths' Company in 1935 and had made way for a block of flats called East Acton Court by 1937. Glendun House was used by Acton golf club until 1919 and demolished in the 1920s, Glendun Road being laid across the site, and the Stud Farm was probably pulled down at the same time. The Chestnuts, the Lodge, and Shakespeare House had all been replaced by semi-detached houses by 1938, the ground behind being taken for allotments, and a Baptist church was built in the grounds of Ivy Lodge. East Acton House became a private school but was damaged during the Second World War and demolished before 1955 to make way for Bromyard secondary

[31] V.C.H. Mdx. ii. 40.
[32] Baker, Acton, 46.
[33] Para. based on D.N.B.
[34] Rowland, Street Names, 27.
[35] Gunnersbury Pk. Mus., notes.
[36] Kelly's Dir. Mdx. (1890).
[37] B.L. Add. MS. 41794.
[38] Rowland, Street Names, p. iv.
[39] P.N. Mdx. (E.P.N.S.), 82.
[40] Goldsmiths' Hall, Acton Estate MS. B.III.1, no. 1.
[41] Guildhall MS. 9171/6, f. 347.
[42] Goldsmiths' Hall, Acton Estate MS. B.III.1, nos. 1–2.

[43] Guildhall MS. 10465/4; A. Harper Smith, 'East Acton: Mdx. Hamlet 1600–1866' (Univ. Extension Diploma essay, 1967, TS. in Acton libr.), 59.
[44] Below, manors and other est.
[45] M.R.O., MR/TH/3.
[46] Milne, Land Use Map of Lond. (1800).
[47] Hist. Mon. Com. Mdx. 2; Pevsner, Mdx. 25; Min. of Town and Country Planning, List of Bldgs. (1949).
[48] Goldsmiths' Hall, Acton Estate MS. B.III.13, no. 1.
[49] Based on P.R.O., IR 30/21/1; plans at Goldsmiths' Hall.
[50] Para. based on Goldsmiths' Hall, Acton Estate MSS.
[51] O.S. Map 6″, Mdx. XVI. SW. (1894–6 edn.).

school.[52] In 1956 the site of Manor Farm was built over with flats around a garden[53] and in 1977 a row of cottages next to the site of Hindley House was replaced by town houses.[54] In 1980 only the Beeches and Ivy Lodge remained of the older houses, while the green had been severely reduced by road widening.

Thomas Park (1759–1834), antiquary, and Nicholas Pearce (1779–1820), traveller, both spent their early years in East Acton. Thomas Davies (1837–91), mineralogist, died there.[55]

The inclosure of the four open fields in 1859 attracted speculative builders.[56] Before the award was confirmed, the British Land Co. had bought the 85 a. Mill Hill estate, where it immediately resold the house with 22 a., and it made several

may explain why much building was in the style of 30 years earlier.[57] Three-storeyed houses for the middle classes were built in Alfred Road by 1866 and Birkbeck Road c. 1870 near the N.L.R. line. Avenue Road and parts of Mill Hill Road also had several detached and semi-detached three-storeyed houses, as did Leamington Park and York Road, just north of the G.W.R. line, and Essex Road, to the south, where a few were built c. 1870 soon after the opening of the main-line station. Middle-class housing proved difficult to let, however, and supply constantly outstripped demand in the 19th century: in 1871 one in six of Acton's houses was unoccupied. Poor rail services may have been partly responsible, since links with the City, by the N.L.R. from 1865, were barely adequate and the west end of

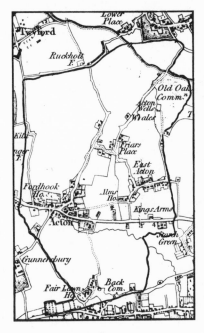

1822   1876–7   1914

ACTON: EVOLUTION OF SETTLEMENT, 1822–1914 (1 inch to 1 mile)

other purchases between 1860 and 1868: land in Church field adjoining Uxbridge Road and the N.L.R. line, a small site between Mill Hill and High Street where Church Road was laid out, two sites in Turnham field, and two at Acton Green, in all totalling 89 a. The Goldsmiths' Company bought 15 a. in 1862 east of the N.L.R. line for building, and at the same time 7 a. on the opposite side of the line were sold.

Building began in the 1860s. In Mill Hill and Church roads and Gunnersbury Lane, all near the town, and Shakespeare and Grove roads, near both town and railway, plots were sold quite quickly, mainly in small numbers. The new houses in general were two-storeyed terraces or semi-detached villas, with fairly low rentals, for those who worked locally. Such piecemeal sales

London was hard to reach. Building activity soon petered out and the Goldsmiths' Company's plan of 1868 for low-density housing on the 14-a. Churchfield estate produced very few houses.

Demand for cheaper housing continued steadily. While the larger plots on the Mill Hill estate farther from the town were slow to fill, plots in South Acton sold by the British Land Co. with some frontages only half the width of those north of Mill Hill House were soon covered with small houses, mostly for workers in laundries or such occupations as brickmaking. Building began in Enfield, Hanbury, Osborne, and Bollo Bridge roads in the mid 1860s, spreading south-eastward to the N.L.R. line after 1867. Beyond the railway Rothschild and Antrobus roads and Cunnington Street were built up c. 1870, as were

[52] Min. of Town and Country Planning, List of Bldgs. (1949); *Kelly's Dir. Acton* (1955).
[53] Mem. plaque.
[54] Mem. stone.   [55] *D.N.B.*
[56] Account of growth until 1900 based on M. A. Jahn, 'Rlys. and Suburban Development: Outer West Lond.

1850–1900' (Lond. Univ. M.Phil. thesis, 1971); O.S. Maps 6″, Mdx. XVI. NW., SW. (1874 and 1894–6 edns.); Bacon, *Atlas of Lond.* (1886). For a revised version of Jahn, 'Rlys. and Suburban Development', see *Rise of Suburbia*, ed. F. M. L. Thompson.
[57] e.g. surviving hos. in Mill Hill and Grove rds.

Berrymede and Priory roads east of Acton Lane, where the British Land Co. had bought land in 1868. Such building by land companies tended to be free from restrictions on use, with the result that South Acton quickly became a mixed industrial and residential district. Laundries were run in private houses,[58] several occupiers kept pigs, and businesses included bone-crushing plants and slaughterhouses. As early as 1869 the local board held an inquiry into conditions there, and officials constantly tried to remove pigs and noxious trades.[59] A characteristic mixture of use nonetheless survived in 1980, wherever the original houses still stood.

In the late 1870s building for the middle classes resumed north of the town. A few more large houses were built in Essex Road and along Horn Lane and in 1877 the 77-a. Springfield estate was divided into plots of $\frac{1}{5}$ a. About half of the plots had detached houses with 5 or 6 bedrooms by 1885, mainly in Rosemont, Pierrepoint, and Creswick roads, with a few farther north in Lynton Road. East of Horn Lane the Birkbeck Land Society laid out Allison and Brougham roads and Birkbeck Avenue on 9 a. purchased c. 1868, where most of the c. 70 terraced and small semi-detached villas planned had been built by 1885, although several sites remained vacant.

South of the town Mill Hill House and its land, which had been offered for building in 1869 and 1873, were finally sold in 1877. A private estate was laid out, with gates at its Avenue Road entrances and its three roads, Heathfield Road, Avenue Crescent, and Avenue Gardens, forming a cul-de-sac that made a barrier between the middle-class area to the north and working-class South Acton. By 1885 several large houses had been built, mainly at the Avenue Road end. Meanwhile a distinctive suburb was being built up at Bedford Park close to Acton Green, partly in Acton and partly in Chiswick.[60]

The Goldsmiths' Company began further attempts to build in 1879, granting leases incorporating brickmaking agreements for c. 40 a., mainly to George Wright for low-density housing, but again with only mixed success. Work began on $1\frac{1}{2}$ a. near the N.L.R. line on the north side of Churchfield Road East, with 12 houses, and spread to 14 a. to the north. By 1885 c. 50 houses, half the agreed number, had been built in Churchfield, Perryn, and Shaa roads. Another 25 were built between 1886 and 1892 but activity tailed off thereafter. A local builder, Frederick Bray, leased 9 a. in 1879 and had built 22 middle-class houses in Cumberland Park by 1882.

Although more workmen's trains were said to be needed in the 1880s to encourage residence in Acton, the demand for cheap housing persisted. Middle-class housing became still harder to let, not only because of poor train services but increasingly because the social status of Acton, with its many laundries, was declining. Between 1885 and 1895 no middle-class estates were started and very little building took place on the

existing ones. Grafton Road and Baldwin Gardens were laid out in the late 1880s but few plots were sold and only a handful of detached three-storeyed villas was built. The Goldsmiths' Company finally abandoned its earliest Churchfield scheme, selling the site to the local board in 1888 for Acton park.[61] On its other sites only 25 out of 190 planned houses were built between 1888 and 1892 and those were difficult to let, even at two thirds of the rent for similar houses in Ealing or Hampstead.

An injunction for the Metropolitan Board of Works, against connecting sewers to its system, also hampered building[62] until the local board provided comprehensive drainage. Inadequate drainage caused the board to refuse permission for more building in Leamington Park and seems also to have hindered work on the Berrymead, Beaumont Park, and Cowper-Essex estates. On the Elms estate, west of the town, building did not start, although roads across it linking Springfield Park with houses in Ealing were laid out in 1879.

Building leases were granted on the 130-a. Cowper-Essex estate in the Vale between 1878 and 1882 but only a few houses along Uxbridge Road were ready by 1885. In South Acton, 32 a. on either side of the N.L.R. line were sold by the Royal Society and offered for building as the South Acton station estate, where the first plots were bought quickly in 1882 but 50 remained unsold in 1889. The area around Brouncker Road was mostly built up by 1890, with narrow frontages as elsewhere in South Acton, while in Petersfield Road two-storeyed terraces formed maisonette flats, with double entrance doors and bow fronts, which became typical of much working-class housing of the period. Part of the estate remained open, as South Acton playing fields.[63]

The adjacent Beaumont Park estate was sold in 1882, to the National Liberal Land Co., and built up in a similar way. There, too, the lack of restriction on use, apart from noxious trades, produced small businesses among the dwellings. Although some plots were soon sold, the estate had been only partly completed by 1894. West of Acton Green and adjacent to the District line station, Fairlawn Park was planned in 1880 but approval for building was given only in 1888. On the Berrymead Priory estate, sold in 1882 to the Reading Land Co., later Berkshire Estates Co., plots were not sold until 1889, and by 1894 only half of Berrymead Gardens and part of the west side of Winchester Street had been built up, with two-storeyed terraces. Most of the rest of Winchester and Salisbury streets was sold to the U.D.C. for municipal buildings. The house itself remained, while the area south of it fronting Acton Lane became the site of a large bakery.

The last two major sites in South Acton were sold for building in 1895. One lay next to Bollo Lane north-west of the N.L.R. line and formed the South Acton estate. At first plots were advertised for medium-sized houses but the demand for cheaper property, as in the rest of the

[58] Below, trade and industry.
[59] Acton U.D.C. *Reps. of M.O.H. passim*; *Acton Gaz.* 19 July 1901.   [60] Below, Chiswick, growth.
[61] Ealing libr., Acc. 19/1.
[62] Acton U.D.C. *Rep. of M.O.H.* (1904), 16.
[63] Ealing libr., Acc. 19/1.

district, prevailed and cottages and laundries were proposed by 1896. In Stirling and Colville roads 178 cottages were approved, and most apparently had been built by the early 1900s. The other site was north of Acton Green and west of Bedford Park, where roads were laid out in 1898 but building started only after 1900. Building in the Southfield Park estate, off Southfield Road, and in Carlton Road, to the north, also began in 1900.[64]

By 1908 the houses south of Uxbridge Road, excluding Bedford Park, were described either as six-roomed houses of c. 1880, very often subdivided, or more recent two-storeyed terraces. North of Uxbridge Road the demand for the large villas of the 1860s had declined and many of those, too, had been subdivided.

Acton's population rose unusually rapidly, by half between 1901 and 1911, largely because of the spread of industry.[65] House building therefore greatly increased between 1901 and 1905, although it slackened before the First World War,[66] while electrification of the trams caused property values near by to rise sharply.[67] Building on the c. 100-a. Elms estate, on the north side of the tram route, at last started in 1904, although part of the earlier road system was abandoned and extensive sports grounds belonging to the Gas Light & Coke Co., later North Thames Gas, cut off most of the estate from Springfield Park. Land east and west of Twyford Avenue was quickly covered with three-storeyed semi-detached houses. Part of the Heathfield Lodge estate south of Uxbridge Road was also built up.

At the eastern end of Uxbridge Road, the Goldsmiths' Company still insisted on expensive housing whose attractions were diminished by industry on the south side of the Vale. The Town and General Estates Co. leased 111 a. bounded by East Acton Lane, Uxbridge Road, and Old Oak Road, and in 1903 advertised the Acton Park estate, where building was to begin on the eastern side. A grid of roads was laid out between Old Oak Road and Bromyard Avenue, and a road from the Vale to Crown Lane replaced the footpath across East field. Some building took place in Old Oak Road and in First, Second, and Third avenues c. 1905, but only about half of the plots had been filled by 1914.[68]

South of the Vale, in contrast, the land bounded by the main road and the Hammersmith branch line was rapidly being covered between 1900 and 1910 with large factory sites,[69] interspersed with a few short terraces of houses, giving Acton the industrial character that has since typified it.

Some building also took place in the northern part of the parish between 1900 and 1910. A few rows of cottages had been built in 1889 by the L.N.W.R. for its employees in Old Oak Lane near Willesden junction. Known as Railway

Cottages and later as Stephenson and Goodhall streets, with a railway institute and a mission church and school added soon afterwards, they had little connexion with the rest of Acton. Victoria Road was laid down in 1901 and some terraces were soon built in and around Victoria Road and Midland Terrace. Chandos, School, Bethune, and St. Leonard's roads were laid out at that time and a large school was built there in 1909. Terraced houses were also built on a triangular site, formerly Wells House farm, c. 1906, but they remained cut off on the south and west by railway lines.[70]

The First World War accelerated the growth of industry, by benefiting local engineering firms. In the north part of Acton it also led to the building of munitions factories, which were sold after the war to private companies. By 1919 almost all the area south of Uxbridge Road had been built over and the northern part was rapidly following. The density of South-East and South-West wards was 63 and 82 people an acre respectively, compared with only 15 and 17 in the two northern wards. Although housing in South-West ward was described as poor, the streets were wide, there were no back-to-back houses or courts, and every dwelling had its own garden and yard. Cheaper houses never met the demand, and rarely remained unlet. South-West ward had 157 overcrowded dwellings, out of 243 in the whole parish, and 1,700 new houses were needed.[71]

The council became the main builder after the First World War, buying two sites for working-class housing: 59 a. north of the Goldsmiths' land at East Acton between Old Oak Common Lane and the N.L.R. line, to which 15½ a. were later added, for 600 houses, and 18 a. west of Friars Place farm for 175 houses. At East Acton, also known briefly as Acton Wells estate, 268 houses were built under contract, and another 22 by direct labour. Thirty were built by the housing board of the Ministry of Health in order to demonstrate types of construction, including the 'Selfridge' concrete houses, and were opened in 1920. The cut in housing subsidies in 1921, however, forced the council to lease or sell the remaining land to private builders.[72]

The site near Friars Place farm, around North Acton playing fields which were opened in 1908,[73] was planned as a garden suburb in 1909,[74] but building apparently was not carried out until after the war, when the council sold or leased the land. The Victory Construction Co. built 70 bungalows for Gordon Selfridge in Lowfield and Westfield roads in 1919 and 1920, Acton residents receiving the first option to buy them.[75] The G.W.R. formed the Great Western (London) Garden Village Society in the 1920s, a co-operative which built an estate of 115 houses and shops between 1924 and 1931 on land just

[64] Acton U.D.C. Rep. of M.O.H. (1900), 21.
[65] Jackson, Semi-detached Lond. 36.
[66] Acton U.D.C. Rep. of M.O.H. (1919), 43.
[67] Barker and Robbins, Hist. Lond. Transport, ii. 34.
[68] Goldsmiths' Hall, Acton Estate MSS., old files nos. 178-88; Ealing libr., prospectus of Acton Pk. estate 1903.
[69] Below, trade and industry (Acton Vale).
[70] Rowland, Street Names; Acton U.D.C. Rep. of M.O.H. (1901), 28; (1904), 78; Procs. of Council (1906-7), 152.

[71] Acton U.D.C. Rep. of M.O.H. (1919), 5, 40, 44, 46, 48-9.
[72] Acton Boro. Rep. of M.O.H. (1933), 10; Ealing libr., Acc. 19/2; The Times, 9 Feb., 22 Nov. 1920.
[73] The Times, 4 Aug. 1908.
[74] Ibid. 28 Oct. 1909.
[75] Acton U.D.C. Rep. of M.O.H. (1919), 49; The Times, 18 Jan. 1921.

east of West Acton station. The houses were let to railwaymen, who held shares in the co-operative,[76] and were similar to council houses. West of the station, on land formerly part of Acton airfield, the private Hanger Hill Garden Estate was laid out between 1925 and 1933, with 325 houses on five-year leases and set in land-scaped gardens which contained a sports ground and club house managed by the tenants.[77] Most of the spaces on estates which had been started in the 1870s were filled in the period between the World Wars, with private housing for the middle classes.[78] After Western Avenue had been built, there was no new housing to the north except on the Friars estate and in Harold Road and Wesley Avenue, laid out for its employees by Harold Wesley Ltd. The area was almost entirely built up with factories by the mid 1930s, together with a part of Acton aerodrome south of Western Avenue.[79]

South of Western Avenue the Goldsmiths' Company built on the land between the road and East Acton village after 1928, with Bowes, Gibbon, and Foster roads, and the earlier gaps were filled in.[80] South of the village the company let a site in Bromyard Avenue for the huge Ministry of Pensions office in 1920 and built Perryn House with 36 flats to the north, but the rest of its land around Manor House was used mainly for sports grounds and allotments.[81] By 1932 the whole of East Acton south of Western Avenue, except the sports grounds, had been built up.

The council resumed building in 1930, with 4 blocks of 4 flats each in Perryn Road and 3 at the corner of Brassie Road and Old Oak Common Lane[82] and another 8 flats each in Enfield and Brouncker roads, South Acton, in 1931 and 1932. It also built 64 flats in blocks of 4 and a few semi-detached houses on the Friars estate in Conway Grove and Acorn Gardens, off Wales Farm Road, in 1932, and 52 flats and 2 houses in Canada Crescent near Friars Place farm in 1934.[83] After a survey in 1935 had found that 2.5 per cent of working-class dwellings were over-crowded,[84] the council built flats in the Steyne and the Vale: Steyne House was finished by 1939 and 32 flats were occupied by tenants transferred from the East Acton estate.[85]

After the Second World War the council began to build on 9½ a. on the north side of the Vale.[86] There were 318 flats by 1948, in 6 four-storeyed blocks along Beech Avenue, with a recreation ground on the north side.[87] By the end of 1951 the council had built 606 dwellings, mainly flats, since the war; another 132 were under construc-tion and 51 were planned, while 274 bombed dwellings had been rebuilt, mostly under private

licence.[88] By the end of 1961 post-war dwellings numbered 1,793.[89] Municipal building was mainly in South Acton, between Bollo Lane, Avenue Road, Strafford Road, and the N.L.R. line, where nearly all the older buildings except the Mill Hill Park estate were demolished. The area south of Bollo Bridge Road became the South Acton industrial estate. North of Bollo Bridge Road the houses were replaced by flats and maisonettes, with a few shops in Hanbury Road. Two tower blocks of 22 storeys and three of 13 dominated the open ground,[90] with several blocks of 6 storeys or less near by and some smaller blocks of maisonettes to the west. As elsewhere, however, the tower blocks were thought to breed crime, to the extent that an inquiry was held by the local M.P., Sir George Young, in 1977.[91] Later large building schemes, south of High Street and at Acton Green between Beaconsfield Road and Acton Lane, avoided the stark appearance of tower blocks and consisted of red-brick flats and maisonettes on varying levels.

The population of the parish was 1,425 in 1801, 1,929 in 1821, and 2,665 in 1841. It was only 2,582 in 1851 but rose to 3,151 in 1861 and 8,306 by 1871. Thereafter it increased rapidly to 17,126 in 1881, 24,206 in 1891, 37,744 in 1901, and 57,497 in 1911. Numbers reached 61,299 in 1921 and 70,510 in 1931, before falling to 64,471 in 1951 and 65,586 in 1961.[92]

SOCIAL AND CULTURAL ACTIVITIES. There were inns from an early date, due to Acton's position on the Oxford road. The Tabard on the Hope was mentioned in 1377 and 1505, the Cock on the Hoop from 1485, the Star and Hartshorn in 1505, and the White Lion in 1520.[93] The George existed by 1539.[94] The Cock and the Bell were listed among taverns around London by John Taylor, the 'water poet', in 1636[95] and the vestry met at the King's Head in 1674.[96] Thirteen alehouse keepers were licensed in 1716. The number had increased to 21 by 1751, probably because of trade generated by Acton wells, when inns included the Bull's Head and the Horse and Groom in East Acton and the King's Arms by the turnpike gate near East field. By 1801 the number had dropped to 9[97] but it rose again with the spread of housing and in 1873 there were 19, in addition to 24 beer retailers.[98] Almost all the older inns were rebuilt during the 19th century, the exception being the George and Dragon hotel in High Street: three-storeyed and with a projecting upper storey, partly timber-framed and partly refronted in brick, it was probably built early in the 17th century as two houses.[99]

[76] Jackson, *Semi-detached Lond.* 349.
[77] *The Times*, 5 Sept. 1933.
[78] Acton Boro. *Rep. of M.O.H.* (1933), 12.
[79] Ibid. (1931), 7; below, trade and industry (Park Royal).
[80] Goldsmiths' Hall, Acton Estate MS. B.III.14, no. 8.
[81] Ibid. 13, no. 26.
[82] Acton Boro. *Rep. of M.O.H.* (1931), 10.
[83] Ibid. (1938), 29–30.   [84] Ibid. (1936), 32.
[85] Ibid. (1938), 35.   [86] Ealing libr., Acc. 19/2.
[87] *The Times*, 19 May 1948.
[88] Acton Boro. *Rep. of M.O.H.* (1951), 25–6.
[89] Ibid. (1961), 23.

[90] Below, plate facing p. 17.
[91] Acton libr., Rep. on S. Acton estate, 1977 (TS.).
[92] *Census*, 1801–1961.
[93] *Cal. Close*, 1374–7, 551; *Cal. Inq. p.m. Hen. VII*, iii, p. 282; P.R.O., PROB 11/7 (P.C.C. 18 Logge); ibid. C 142/79, no. 231.
[94] P.R.O., C 1/1298/9.
[95] *Mdx. & Herts. N. & Q.* iv. 78.
[96] Acton par. church, chwdns. acct. bk. (1674–99).
[97] M.R.O., MR/LV3/4, 7/4, 10/98.
[98] *Green's Dir. Notting Hill and Acton* (1873–4).
[99] Hist. Mon. Com. *Mdx.* 2.

There was a 'bowling place' in 1622 next to the highway from London to Brentford, probably at Acton Green,[1] and a Bowling Alley field on the south side of Manor House at East Acton by the late 17th century.[2]

Acton wells, known as Old Oak wells in 1695,[3] a group of three wells on the western edge of Old Oak common, were mentioned in 1612 and widely known by 1699. The water, reputed to be one of the strongest purgatives around London, was whitish and sweet rather than salty, with a little of the bitterness of Epsom. By 1746 it was sold in large quantities in London, besides being drunk at the springs, especially in May and June. Public breakfasts were held c. 1775 and assemblies during the season. An assembly room was built, with a race course in the grounds, but by the end of the 18th century the wells were no longer in fashion and the assembly room became successively a school, a private dwelling, and a farmhouse, being pulled down in 1908.[4]

A short-lived successor to the wells was opened near by on the northern part of Old Oak common in 1870. Known as Willesden Gardens or the People's Garden, it was run by the German Club of Foley Street, London, c. 1876 as a summer *biergarten*, with a large dancing platform. It disappeared soon after 1885, the site becoming part of the extensive G.W.R. sidings and sheds.[5]

Friendly societies existed from 1800, meeting at public houses. The Ancient or Independent Britons met at the Blue Anchor in the Steyne from 1800 and the Young Britons also met there from 1817. The Acton friendly society met at the George and the Acton United friendly society at the King's Head, both from 1841. A court of the Ancient Order of Foresters met at the Duke of Sussex, Acton Green, from 1862 and a lodge of the Independent Order of Oddfellows of Manchester met at the Prince of Wales in Church Road from 1863.[6] The lodge built its own hall in Acton Lane in 1930.[7]

South Acton Working Men's Club, started in 1872, provided an important meeting place for the working class, despite some censure when one member died after a drinking bout.[8] When South Acton was rebuilt after the Second World War, the club was housed in a new building in Strafford Road.

The churches organized many social activities in the late 19th century: Baptists, for example,

founded Acton Baptist cricket club and a literary society.[9] Different denominations also joined together to promote temperance. In 1878 the rector, the Congregational minister, and five residents formed the Acton Coffee Public-House Co., to serve non-intoxicating drinks in a public house atmosphere.[10] In 1899 the various temperance societies were loosely united with the founding of Acton Temperance Federation, to which they and the churches sent delegates.[11] The non-sectarian Acton Adult Schools, started c. 1894, also worked for temperance and against Sunday business, providing bible study and a savings bank. A women's adult school was started in 1900 and the institution was soon said to be influential.[12]

Acton Literary Institution met regularly between 1868 and 1889,[13] and Acton Scientific Society and Field Club from 1901.[14] Acton Scientific and Literary Society in the 1920s[15] may have been an amalgam of those two societies and still met in 1963, at the public library.[16] A photographic society was formed in 1904 and met until 1924,[17] an art society met at the library between 1955 and 1963,[18] and Acton Piscatorial Society held its 20th annual dinner in 1901.[19] A chess club, which met at Beauchamp's, no. 160 High Street, was founded in 1881.[20]

Acton lecture hall, built in Church Road in 1866,[21] was used by many religious and secular bodies. A lecture association, which existed in 1901, met there ten times during the winter of 1908–9.[22] In winter the larger swimming pool in the public baths was boarded over and, as the Grand Hall, used for political and social functions and dances.[23]

A cinema in Horn Lane was licensed in 1910,[24] followed by the Crown cinema c. 1913 in Mill Hill Terrace.[25] In 1921 a third cinema, the Globe at no. 128 High Street, was opened by Vesta Tilley and was said to be the largest in Britain, accommodating 3,000.[26] By 1939 the Dominion in Uxbridge Road, the Odeon in King Street, and the Savoy in West Way, East Acton, had also been opened. The Dominion was bought by Granada in 1946 and renamed,[27] becoming a bingo club by 1977. The Globe was renamed the Gaumont and in the early 1960s made way for the shopping precinct.[28] The Crown and the Kinema, Horn Lane, had both been converted to other uses by 1964[29] and the Odeon was a shop in 1979.

The Y.W.C.A. opened the first part of its

[1] Guildhall MS. 10833.
[2] Goldsmiths' Hall, Acton Estate MS. B.III.1, no. 8, survey (probably 1682).
[3] Morden, *Map of Mdx.* (1695 edn.).
[4] *Gent. Mag.* lxxxiii (2), 556; B. Allen, *Nat. Hist. of Chalybeate Waters of Eng.* (1699), 126–8; S. Simpson, *Agreeable Historian*, ii. 620; Jolliffe, *Acton*, 65–7.
[5] Thorne, *Environs*, 4–5; Jolliffe, *Acton*, 8–9; Bacon, *Ordnance Atlas* (1886).
[6] P.R.O., FS 1/418/565; FS 1/422/950; FS 1/459/2176; FS 1/460/2183; FS 1/490/4169; FS 1/491/4198.
[7] Datestone.
[8] *Acton Gaz.* 8 Feb. 1901.
[9] Tongue, *Lond. Suburb*, 50, 52.
[10] Acton libr., articles of association (1878).
[11] *Acton Gaz.* 17 May 1901.
[12] Ibid. 1 Feb., 8 Mar. 1901.
[13] Acton libr., programmes of mtgs.
[14] *Acton Gaz.* 15 Mar. 1901.
[15] Acton libr., Acton Scientific and Lit. Soc. min. bk.
[16] Acton, *Official Guide* (1963), 14.
[17] Acton libr., min. bk.
[18] Acton, *Official Guide* (1955, 1963).
[19] *Acton Gaz.* 17 May 1901.
[20] Acton libr., photocopy of membership card.
[21] *Green's Dir. Notting Hill and Acton* (1873–4).
[22] Acton libr., programme.
[23] *The Times*, 8 July 1919, 7 Dec. 1926; Acton, *Official Guide* (1928), 26.
[24] *Mdx. Local Hist. Council Bull.* xviii. 21.
[25] M.R.O., MR/LMD, lic. application.
[26] *The Times*, 28 Mar. 1921; Acton libr., sale cat. Globe Kinemas Ltd. shares.
[27] *Mdx. Local Hist. Council Bull.* xviii. 8, 11.
[28] Rowland, *Street Names*, 8.
[29] *Mdx. Local Hist. Council Bull.* xviii. 12.

centre in East Acton Lane in 1931, intended to serve Acton, Hammersmith, and Chiswick.[30]

Flying displays were given at the London Aviation Co.'s airfield in North Acton c. 1910, and the Ruffy-Baumann flying school moved to Acton from Hendon in 1917 and operated there for two years.[31]

Acton golf club was formed in 1896, with an 18-hole course on land owned by the King Church family. The club house was Glendun House, on the north side of East Acton green, and a separate club and club house were formed for ladies.[32] The club ceased when the course was bought by the council in 1919 for a housing estate.

Much of the Goldsmiths' Company's charity estate at East Acton was used for sports grounds, leased to private clubs. Many came from elsewhere around London, such as Shepherd's Bush cricket club and West Kensington athletic club. Some local companies had sports grounds, including CAV, Eastman's, S.T.D., and Lowe & Bydone. The Gas Light & Coke Co. had a large ground on the former Elms estate and other private sports grounds were in East Acton Lane, Gunnersbury Lane, Friars Place Lane, and Willesden Lane. In 1924 there were some 17 athletic clubs and grounds, 4 cricket clubs, and 15 lawn tennis clubs. Acton bowling club met in Acton park and the council ran a badminton club.[33]

The *Acton Press* was founded in 1869, when it won notoriety for publishing criticism of the local board,[34] and may not have continued after 1871. A new series began c. 1898 but after 1900 was incorporated into the *County of Middlesex Independent*. The *Acton Gazette and General District Advertiser* was founded in 1871, published weekly, and continued as the *Acton, Chiswick and Turnham Green Gazette* from 1880 and the *Acton and Chiswick Gazette* from 1892. From 1900 it was known chiefly as the *Acton Gazette*. In 1918 it became the *Acton Gazette and Express*, incorporating the *Acton and Chiswick Express* which had been founded in 1900 as the *Acton Express*. Known from 1939 as the *Acton Gazette and West London Post*, it still appeared weekly in 1980. The *District Post* was founded in 1911 and renamed the *Acton and Chiswick District Post* and then the *Acton District Post* in the same year. In 1921 it was renamed the *Acton Borough Post* but in 1925 it was incorporated in the *Acton Gazette and Express*.[35]

MANORS AND OTHER ESTATES. The manor of *ACTON* was a division of the bishop of London's manor of Fulham, which he acquired between 704 and 709.[36] Acton was not described in Domesday and did not have a separate court until the 16th century, although views of frankpledge were taken separately for it and other members of Fulham from 1383.[37] The bishop held the manor until the 19th century except during the Interregnum, when Francis Allen held courts from 1651 to 1653.[38]

The bishop had no demesne in Acton, or so little that it was accounted for under Fulham or Ealing,[39] but held the wastes and commons, with liberty of fishing and hunting. In 1735 all the fishponds on the wastes of Ealing and Acton, with fishing and hunting, were leased to Thomas Langthorne of St. James's, Westminster, for 21 years,[40] and in 1738 he was appointed keeper of the game.[41] The premises consisted chiefly of Acton ponds, near the western boundary of the parish north of Uxbridge Road. They were leased to Samuel Wegg in 1777 and again in 1798.[42] By 1821 the lessee was his daughter Elizabeth and in 1842 her chief legatee Charles Gray Round,[43] in whose family they remained. In 1884 the homage of Acton confirmed the sale, made in 1877, of the freehold of the ponds to the trustees of James Round, receiving payments from his executors and the Ecclesiastical Commissioners in compensation for copyholders' rights.[44] In 1903 the Round family sold the site of the ponds to the council, which laid out Twyford Crescent and gardens on it.[45]

Some parcels of waste had been granted to individual tenants for front gardens in the 18th and 19th centuries. In 1881 the Ecclesiastical Commissioners, as successors to the bishop, conveyed their rights in the wastes of Friars Place green, the Steyne, East Acton Lane, and Acton Green common to Acton local board.[46] Enfranchisement of individual holdings began in 1846 and mostly took place after inclosure in 1859.[47]

The five-hide tenement held by Fulchered of the manor of Fulham, by knight service, in 1086 was probably the tenement in Acton later listed as $\frac{1}{2}$ knight's fee.[48] It was held in the mid 12th century by Alulf, whose son William recovered 1 hide between 1154 and 1189 from Simon Halvedieval, husband of Alulf's daughter Sabelina. In 1189–90 William pledged his estate to the king, and later it was described as $4\frac{1}{2}$ hides and rent, held from Ellis of Chicheworth. By 1211 William's widow and son Peter held the land.[49] Peter granted 50 a. in la Pulle to the bishop of London in fee c. 1222, on condition that the bishop paid his debts, and in 1230 granted to Osbert of Northbrook 150 a. held from him by rent and foreign services. Three houses were held by tenants, while Peter was left with $2\frac{1}{2}$ hides and 13 a. in demesne. About 1230 Peter granted to Geoffrey de Lucy, dean of St. Paul's, his mansion

[30] *The Times*, 30 Mar. 1931.
[31] *Acton Aerodrome* (Ealing L.B. libr. svce. 1978), 1–8.
[32] *V.C.H. Mdx.* ii. 281–2.
[33] Acton, *Official Guide* (1924), 44–6.
[34] Ealing town hall, Acton and Southall misc. file no. 5.
[35] B.L. Newspaper Cat.
[36] P. J. Taylor, 'Estates of Bishopric of Lond. from 7th to 16th cent.' (Lond. Univ. Ph.D. thesis, 1976), 430.
[37] P.R.O., SC 2/188/66.   [38] Ibid. SC 2/190/15.
[39] Taylor, 'Estates of Bishopric of Lond.' 274, 335 and n. 165.

[40] Guildhall MS. 10234/2, p. 247.
[41] Ibid. MS. 12348, deed 24 July 1738.
[42] Ibid. MS. 10242, p. 72.
[43] Ibid. MS. 10249, f. 105; cf. below (the Elms).
[44] Guildhall MS. 12697, deed 1 Dec. 1884.
[45] Ealing libr., Acc. 19/1.
[46] Guildhall MS. 12697, deed 4 May 1882.
[47] P.R.O., MAF 20/2/22.
[48] Account of estate based on *T.L.M.A.S.* xxviii. 316–22, which uses most of the sources cited below.
[49] *Cur. Reg. R.* vi. 161.

High Street and Belle Vue *c.* 1840

Berrymead Priory *c.* 1840

ACTON

High Street looking east *c.* 1904, with the Council Offices on the left

High-rise flats in South Acton

ACTON

house in Acton and 128 a., and later also granted land near Bollo bridge meadow and 20 a. of woodland. In 1239 the dean transferred the estate to the chapter of *ST. PAUL'S*, to be used for successive deans at a rent of £5 to support a chantry, and the estate was thereupon leased back to him for life.[50] It was augmented by the bishop's 50 a. and three houses on the north side of Uxbridge Road, given by Geoffrey Fitz-Walter, who held them from Peter FitzAlulf. In 1314 the chapter was granted exemption from purveyance[51] and in 1316 it was granted free warren in all its demesne lands of Acton.[52] The estate was occasionally called a manor.

Peter still held the rest of the tenement, and owed ½ knight's service to the bishop in 1242–3.[53] In 1256 William son of Peter granted a carucate in Acton to Thomas Tayland and his wife Edith, who were to pay William 5 marks a year for life.[54] In 1285 they granted a house and 2 carucates in Acton to William the seneschal of Evesham for rent.[55] Thomas Tayland still owed the ½ knight's service at Acton c. 1307 and presumably held the bulk of Alulf's tenement, which William the seneschal inherited with other property of Edith.

In 1312 William the seneschal granted to Adam de Herewinton a house, 1½ carucate of arable, 40 a. of meadow, 15 a. of wood, and a rent of pepper, held by Robert of Prestbury for life.[56] In 1316 Roger, son of William de Brok, heir of Philip of Cowley, transferred to Adam his rights in a carucate in Acton and Fulham to Adam,[57] which possibly derived from William son of Peter's grant of 1256. In 1318 Adam was the bishop's tenant by knight service for Tayland's tenement. He had also acquired houses and land in Acton in 1309 from John de Paris and Agnes his wife,[58] who had received a house and land from John, son of Isabel of Chicheworth, in 1304.[59]

Adam granted to the prior of *ST. BARTHOLOMEW'S*, Smithfield, in 1327 a house, land, and rents in Acton, held of the bishop of London as ¼ knight's fee, to support a chantry.[60] The estate presumably included most of the lands held by William the seneschal and Thomas Tayland. From 1353 the prior and convent owed the ½ knight's service in Acton.[61] St. Bartholomew's acquired much more land in Acton with a grant in 1349 by Edmund of Grimsby[62] and another in 1373 by John Chisnall, clerk, and others.[63]

The Crown secured St. Bartholomew's lands

at the Dissolution, when the Acton estate was described as a manor of itself, the bishop's interest being overlooked.[64] In 1544 the Crown also acquired the chapter's estate, as part of a forced exchange.[65] The two parts of the five-hide tenement were then reunited when John, Lord Russell (d. 1555), later earl of Bedford, was granted both in fee.[66] His son Francis, earl of Bedford (d. 1585), vested Acton manor in feoffees in 1574, when a description of it as containing 6,900 a., besides rents in Acton and Willesden, apparently referred to the whole of the bishop's manor rather than to the Russells' estate.[67] It passed to Anne Russell (d. 1639), daughter of Francis's second son and wife of Henry Somerset, later earl of Worcester (d. 1646). The Acton estate in 1645 consisted of 798 a., settled on the earl's second son Sir John Somerset,[68] but it was sequestrated and in 1646 was given to Richard Hill and William Pennoyer, merchants of London.[69] In 1653 Pennoyer and his wife Martha sold the 'manor' and 2 houses, 284 a. of arable, 50 a. of meadow, and 78 a. of pasture in Acton, to his brother Samuel and others,[70] who divided it.[71] By will proved 1654 Samuel Pennoyer left his share to his wife Rose and then to the Drapers' Company of London for family uses,[72] but the whole estate was restored to Worcester's heirs in 1660.[73]

The Acton estate formed part of the jointure for Anne, wife of Henry Somerset, Sir John's eldest son, in 1663.[74] Their only son having died childless,[75] the 'manor' in 1712 provided a jointure for Frances, wife of Charles Somerset, the eldest son of Henry's youngest brother.[76] By 1724 it had passed to Henry Somerset (d. 1727), probably the son of Charles and Frances, who settled it on his brother John (d. c. 1730),[77] whose widow Dorothy in 1732 relinquished her dower in return for an annuity.[78]

Under a Chancery decree of 1735 the estate was sold on behalf of John Somerset's sisters in 1736 to Christopher Lethieullier of Belmont (Hants). Consisting of 802 a. in Acton and Willesden,[79] it passed to his widow Sarah and son Benjamin by 1738.[80] Benjamin Lethieullier's Acton estate passed in 1797 to Sir Henry Fetherstonhaugh, Bt. (d. 1846), the son of his sister Sarah.[81] Although various sales had been made by Letheuillier, the estate c. 1799 still totalled 750 a. and covered nearly all the parish north and west of the footpath to Harlesden, Horn Lane, and Stamford brook's western

[50] *Early Charters of St. Paul's* (Camd. 3rd ser. lviii), 241, 264–7, 270.
[51] *Cal. Pat.* 1313–17, 190.
[52] *Cal. Chart. R.* 1300–26, 305.
[53] *Bk. of Fees*, ii. 897.
[54] P.R.O., CP 25(2)/149/19, no. 373.
[55] Ibid. CP 25(1)/148/30, no. 138.
[56] Ibid. CP 25(1)/149/42, no. 90.
[57] *Abbrev. Plac.* (Rec. Com.), 327.
[58] P.R.O., CP 25(1)/149/40, nos. 34, 42.
[59] Ibid. CP 25(1)/148/37, no. 303.
[60] *Cal. Pat.* 1327–30, 184; P.R.O., C 143/195, no. 11.
[61] *Feud. Aids*, iii. 376; vi. 487.
[62] P.R.O., C 143/294, no. 5.
[63] Ibid. C 143/380, no. 14; *Cal. Pat.* 1370–4, 380.
[64] P.R.O., E 318/Box 19/953, 16 June 35 Hen. VIII, section 3.
[65] Ibid. E 305/6/D7.

[66] *L. & P. Hen. VIII*, xviii (2), p. 140; xix (1), p. 496.
[67] P.R.O., C 66/1112, mm. 14–15.
[68] Wrongly called Sir Thomas: B.L. Add. MS. 5501, f. 70 and v.
[69] Ibid. f. 263.
[70] P.R.O., CP 25(2)/574/1653 Trin.
[71] Bodl. MS. Rawl. D. 715, f. 1.
[72] P.R.O., PROB 11/240 (P.C.C. 388 Alchin).
[73] W. Archer-Thomson, *Hist. Drapers' Co.'s Properties and Trusts* (1940), ii. 86; *L.J.* xi. 70.
[74] M.R.O., E.M.C. 53, no. 30.
[75] Brydges, *Collins's Peerage*, i. 232–3.
[76] M.R.O., E.M.C. 53, no. 87.
[77] Ibid. Acc. 617/40.
[78] Ibid. 44.
[79] Ibid. 45.
[80] Ibid. 49.
[81] Ibid. 64; G.E.C. *Baronetage*, v. 94.

branch, as far as Turnham field.[82] In 1800 Fetherstonhaugh began the piecemeal sale of the estate.[83]

The 'manor place' of St. Bartholomew's recorded in 1528[84] may, as has been suggested, have been on the moated site of Friars Place Farm, discussed below. The mansion granted by Peter FitzAlulf to the dean is less likely to have been Berrymead Priory, as local tradition has it, than either Acton Farm (later Springfield Farm) in Horn Lane or a house on the moated site west of Friars Place Farm, abandoned in or after the 15th century.[85]

Benjamin Lethieullier in 1795 sold 36 a. between Bollo brook and Gunnersbury Lane to John Winter,[86] who in 1802 owned the recently built *HEATHFIELD LODGE*, near Bollo bridge, and East Lodge[87] and West Lodge.[88] Heathfield Lodge was sold in 1843 on Winter's death to Baron Lionel de Rothschild,[89] and the land around it, with East Lodge, was also added to the Rothschilds' Gunnersbury Park estate.[90] West Lodge, owned in 1844 by George Aveling, the occupier in 1851,[91] survived in 1980, a two-storeyed brick building of c. 1800 with a slate roof, as the headquarters of the Acton Housing Association.

The Willan family bought Acton or *SPRING-FIELD* farm, with 145 a. north of Uxbridge Road, c. 1801.[92] After Thomas Willan's death the house and most of the land were sold in 1828[93] to the rector William Antrobus and his sons William Thomas and Edmund, who in 1842 jointly owned c. 90 a. with the farm and another house called Springfield, near Steyne mills.[94] After W. T. Antrobus's death c. 1877 the estate was sold for building. The farmhouse, at the corner of Horn Lane and Creswick Road, was in 1799 a two-storeyed brick house recently added to an older one.[95] Springfield faced the new Rosemont Road in 1908[96] but by the late 1930s had made way for flats called Rosemont Court.[97]

Richard White in 1809 bought 52 a. of the Lethieullier estate, in the middle of which he built *MILL HILL* or Acton Hill House. His widow Mary had succeeded by 1851 and in 1859 sold the estate to Walter Elliott Whittingham and the British Land Co.;[98] most of the land was sold for building, the house with its grounds being sold in 1860. It remained a private residence until Walter Willett, the London builder and originator of daylight saving, laid out a private housing

estate there in or before 1885.[99] Most of the house was pulled down, but the east wing, refronted, remained in 1980 as no. 11 Avenue Crescent.

FRIARS PLACE farm, with 227 a., was acquired by the Wood family of Ealing by 1811.[1] James Wood owned it between 1818 and 1827[2] and Edward Wood in 1842, when his holdings in the parish totalled 373½ a.[3] The land was gradually sold off from the early 20th century: in 1911 the U.D.C. bought 22½ a. from Col. Charles Boileau Wood, including the moated site west of Friars Place Farm, for a recreation ground, and in 1920 it bought 18 a. to the south for housing.[4] The moated farmhouse at no. 367 Horn Lane, thought to have belonged to St. Bartholomew's, was known as Friars Place Farm from 1664[5] and later also as Hamilton House, Narroway's Farm, or Snell's Farm. The last house, built or improved in 1818, was of two storeys in yellow brick, with a fluted door surround and an elaborate cast-iron balcony. At the rear two older cottages faced a paved courtyard. Joseph Narroway ran a home of rest there for 200 horses in 1901 and was succeeded by Francis Cave Snell. In the 1920s the land was laid out for 100 grass and hard tennis courts. In 1929 Col. Wood sold the house as a vicarage for St. Gabriel's church. The moat was filled and the house later became a private dwelling, but in 1975 it was badly damaged by fire and by 1980 it had been demolished.[6]

What was called *FOSTERS* manor in the 16th century may have comprised lands north of East Acton village known as Fosters in 1683. It was evidently distinct from the copyhold tenement called Fosters.[7] In 1517 Richard Copcot and his wife Grace sold c. 200 a. in Willesden, Harlesden, and Acton to Thomas Roberts and William Wass,[8] possibly including Fosters manor in Acton which Michael Roberts (d. 1544) devised to his brother John.[9] In 1632 Francis Roberts died holding Fosters of the bishop's manor of Fulham by fealty and rent.[10] His grandson Sir William Roberts, Bt. (d. 1662), owned 100 a. in Acton by 1646,[11] and in 1663 his widow Eleanor sold a comparable estate to John Attlee.[12] A Mr. Attlee owned land and leases in Acton in 1693,[13] but by 1713 Fosters had passed from John Marsh to his son Thomas and comprised 75 a. west of Old Oak common and Old Oak Lane.[14] By 1842 it belonged to the King Church family,[15] from which it was compulsorily purchased for council

[82] Guildhall libr., Pr. V/ACT (plan); Guildhall MS. 12697 (survey bk. and key).

[83] M.R.O., Acc. 617/60.

[84] P.R.O., E 303/9 Lond./289.

[85] Rowland, *Street Names*, 26. Berrymead is not known to have been part of the dean's estate. The lands of the two ecclesiastical bodies lay intermingled over the north and west parts of the parish; dean's field in 1811 lay not far from the moated site.

[86] M.L.R. 1795/2/161.   [87] Guildhall MS. 10465/117.

[88] P.R.O., MAF 20/2/22.

[89] Ealing libr., inventory of Heathfield Lodge.

[90] P.R.O., MAF 20/2/22.

[91] Guildhall MS. 12698; P.R.O., HO 107/1699.

[92] M.R.O., MR/PLT/1801.

[93] Acton libr., sale cert.

[94] P.R.O., IR 29/21/1.

[95] Guildhall MS. 12697.

[96] Acton libr., plan of fête at Springfield, 1908.

[97] Rowland, *Street Names*, 34.

[98] M.R.O., Acc. 487/1; P.R.O., HO 107/1699.

[99] Bacon, *Atlas of Lond.* (1886).

[1] M.R.O., MR/PLT/4579.

[2] Acton libr., Friars Place farm, list of owners.

[3] P.R.O., IR 29/21/1; Guildhall MS. 12697.

[4] Ealing libr., Acc. 19/1.

[5] M.R.O., MR/TH/3.

[6] Acton libr., notes on Friars Place farm and cutting from *Evening News*, 7 June 1927; *Ealing Local Historian* (1966), no. 1; *V.C.H. Mdx.* ii. 4; *Acton Gaz.* 4 Jan. 1901; Min. of Town and Country Planning, List of Bldgs. (1947).

[7] Below (Goldsmiths').

[8] P.R.O., CP 25(2)/27/179.

[9] Ibid. PROB 11/30 (P.C.C. 14 Pynnyng).

[10] Ibid. C 142/482, no. 65.

[11] Bodl. MS. Rawl. D. 715, f. 5.

[12] P.R.O., CP 25(2)/689/15 Chas. II Trin.

[13] M.R.O., F 34/1-10.

[14] M.L.R. 1713/5/136-7; 1714/1/186-8.

[15] P.R.O., IR 29/21/1.

housing in 1919, having been used as a golf course.[16]

The *FROWYKS'* large holding is traceable to 1303, when John de la Wodetone of Acton settled on Richard de la Wodetone a house, 74 a. of land, 4 a. of meadow, 40 a. of pasture, and rent in Acton and Chiswick.[17] In 1357 Bartholomew of Wodetone seems to have been in possession[18] and between 1374 and 1380 his son William made several conveyances of land in Acton to John Holmes. In 1382 William made over his remaining lands in Acton, Ealing, and Harlesden to John Knolte, fishmonger of London, and Thomas Wodetone his brother and heir.[19] By 1462 all or part of Holmes's lands had passed to the Frowyk family. Henry Frowyk, alderman of London (d. *c.* 1460)[20] and his son Thomas bought various estates in 1446 and 1458 in Acton, Ealing, and Willesden.[21] Land once of John Scorier and formerly of John Holmes may have formed part of them.[22]

Thomas Frowyk, knighted in 1478,[23] bought more property in Acton in 1484.[24] At his death in 1485 he held 6 houses, 70 a. of land, 10 a. of meadow, 20 a. of pasture, and 6 a. of wood in Acton and Willesden, all of the bishop of London.[25] His elder son Henry, knighted in 1501,[26] died in 1505 leaving sons Thomas and Henry (d. 1520), childless, and daughters Elizabeth wife of Sir John Spelman and Margaret wife of Sir Michael Fisher.[27] Sir Thomas's younger son, Sir Thomas (d. 1506), Chief Justice of Common Pleas,[28] held some of the property[29] and was succeeded by his daughter Frideswide, first wife of Sir Thomas Cheyney, K.G. (d. 1559).[30] Frideswide's grandson Thomas Parrott,[31] the Spelmans' sons Henry and Erasmus,[32] and the Fishers' granddaughter Agnes, wife of Oliver St. John, Lord St. John, each held portions.[33] Most of the Frowyks' land seems to have passed to two families, the Vincents of Harlesden and the Garraways or Garways.

Humphrey Vincent of Willesden (d. *c.* 1555) bought lands in Acton and left two sons William and Robert.[34] William was one of the principal free tenants in Acton in 1574[35] and left

his free land to his son William by will dated 1579.[36]

William's son and heir Gervase was one of three Vincents holding land freely in Acton in 1618,[37] and he later sold some of it.[38] Another William Vincent had land in 1618, and at his death in 1632 held Kingswood farm, 151 a. formerly Sir Thomas Frowyk's.[39] A third William Vincent had 150 a. in Acton in 1649.[40] In 1666 John Vincent of Harlesden green and others sold 139 a. in Acton and land in Willesden to William Rolleston (d. 1672). Notwithstanding an intention to use the lands to endow a charity at Rolleston (Staffs.), William's nieces Mary Mower and Elizabeth Jacob were in possession in 1708,[41] and in 1757 their heirs sold 128 a. to Robert Tubbs of St. James's, Westminster, horse dealer.[42] Tubbs bought Friars Place in 1765[43] and died in 1782, having conveyed the estate to his son Robert, who lived at Friars Place until his death in 1810.[44] A third Robert Tubbs owned 141 a. in 1842, but Friars Place then belonged to Thomas Street.[45] In 1850 the house was described as a beautiful villa with a balustraded terrace looking south over pleasure grounds.[46] Building began around it in 1886, and it had decayed before its demolition in 1902.[47] A sausage factory was built on the site in 1919.[48]

John Garraway or Garway, gentleman, who bought 176 a. in Acton in 1569,[49] was probably John Garraway of Buckhurst (Suss.), lessee of the parsonage and tithes.[50] He already held land in Acton through his wife Sibyl, widow of John Lane (d. *c.* 1550),[51] and carried out ditching in 1552 and 1554.[52] In 1616 his son Paul leased to John Collins of Acton his freehold farm called Scoriers, formerly Frowyk's, which included at least 60 a., and a cottage in the Steyne, and another 9 a.[53] Paul's eldest son Philip, who had freeholds in Acton and Ealing in 1624,[54] died seised of Scoriers *c.* 1625.[55] It passed to his brother John, who was apparently in possession in 1631.[56] A Capt. Garraway held 90 a. in 1646 and land valued at £95 in 1653.[57] In 1655 John Garraway sold a house, later called Bank House, and land near the Steyne to the Speaker Francis Rous (1579–1659).[58]

---

[16] Ealing libr., Acc. 19/2.
[17] P.R.O., CP 25(1)/148/36, no. 296.
[18] Ibid. CP 25(1)/150/67, no. 353.
[19] *Cal. Close*, 1374–7, 109, 551; 1377–81, 467–8; 1399–1402, 479.
[20] *Cal. of Wills in Ct. of Husting*, ii (2), 541–2, 579.
[21] P.R.O., CP 25(1)/152/93, nos. 131, 136; CP 25(1)/152/95, no. 188.
[22] *Cal. Close*, 1461–8, 136.
[23] Shaw, *Knights*, i. 138.
[24] P.R.O., CP 25(1)/152/99, no. 6.
[25] *Cal. Inq. p.m. Hen. VII*, i, p. 74.
[26] P.R.O., PROB 11/7 (P.C.C. 18 Logge); Shaw, *Knights*, i. 147.
[27] *Cal. Inq. p.m. Hen. VII*, iii, p. 282; P.R.O., C 142/79, no. 231; ibid. PROB 11/20 (P.C.C. 5 Maynwaryng).
[28] *D.N.B.*
[29] *Cal. Inq. p.m. Hen. VII*, iii, p. 111.
[30] P.R.O., PROB 11/15 (P.C.C. 15 Adeane).
[31] Ibid. C 142/119, no. 114.
[32] Ibid. PROB 11/20 (P.C.C. 5 Maynwaryng); PROB 11/39 (P.C.C. 5 Wrastley).
[33] Goldsmiths' Hall, Acton Estate MS. B.III.1, no. 4.
[34] Ibid.; P.R.O., CP 25(2)/27/181.
[35] B.L. Harl. MS. 1711, f. 1d.
[36] Goldsmiths' Hall, Acton Estate MS. B.III.1, no. 4.

[37] P.R.O., SC 2/190/5.
[38] Guildhall MS. 10833; P.R.O., C 2/Jas. I/T14/19; ibid. C 142/482, no. 65.
[39] P.R.O., C 142/715, no. 19.
[40] Bodl. MS. Rawl. D. 715, f. 3.
[41] Notts. R.O., Acc. 252, Rolleston of Watnall MSS. (N.R.A. Rep.) DDR. 19/2; 28/3; 130/5 and 7.
[42] M.L.R. 1757/2/480–2.
[43] M.L.R. 1765/6/457–60.
[44] Baker, *Acton*, 156.
[45] P.R.O., IR 29/21/1.
[46] Keane, *Beauties of Mdx.* 18–19.
[47] G. H. Monson, *Hist. Acton* (1934–5), 10; Rowland, *Street Names*, 15, 25.
[48] Below, trade and industry.
[49] P.R.O., CP 25(2)/171/11 Eliz. I East.
[50] Ibid. REQ 2/211/3.
[51] Ibid. C 1/1298/9–10; Hist. MSS. Com. 39, *15th Rep. II*, p. 259.
[52] P.R.O., SC 2/189/24.
[53] Ibid. C 3/343/17.
[54] Goldsmiths' Hall, Acton Estate MS. B.III.1, no. 8.
[55] P.R.O., PROB 11/145 (P.C.C. 38 Clarke).
[56] Goldsmiths' Hall, Acton Estate MS. B.III.1, no. 6.
[57] Bodl. MS. Rawl. D. 715, ff. 5, 3, 1.
[58] M.R.O., Acc. 156/1; *D.N.B.*

Most of the Garraways' estate was alienated in fragments,[59] Scoriers passing before 1800 to Nathan Carrington or his heir,[60] and the Garraways recorded as holding land in 1693 and 1780[61] may have inherited it from another branch of the family.[62]

BANK HOUSE was apparently acquired in 1663 by Richard Ogden from Francis Rous, son and heir of the Speaker's son and heir John,[63] and conveyed by Ogden in 1708 to Jane Thynne.[64] The property passed to Richard Allington Pye, son of Jane's daughter, Barbara Pershouse; in 1769 Pye sold the house to Sarah Ladds of Acton,[65] who rebuilt it further back from the road and was succeeded in 1771 by her niece Elizabeth Lehook (d. 1799), wife of Samuel Wegg. The house passed to Elizabeth's daughters, who ultimately inherited the estates bought by their father, but was sold in 1837;[66] it was later used as a school.

Thomas Thorney, barber-surgeon of London, bought the Bell on the north side of the highway and other property which in 1612 he left to his nephew Peter, also a barber-surgeon.[67] Peter bought land, including the tenement called Butlers, from Gervase Vincent[68] and died in 1628,[69] leaving a son Thomas, a minor, who had died by 1633, and a daughter Elizabeth, wife of John Glassington.[70] By 1646 only a house and 15 a. remained with Glassington,[71] and the property descended in separate parcels.

The farm called *BUTLERS* was owned by Henry Frowyk (d. 1520),[72] William Vincent in 1610,[73] and Peter Thorney in 1628.[74] It passed apparently to the Stevenson family, and may have been disposed of by the will of Henry Stevenson, proved in 1776. In 1775 the property was described as a new brick house and a wash house with 1½ a. In 1797 it belonged to Mrs. Elizabeth Hervey, passing between 1811 and 1821 to William Hervey, and in 1842 it consisted of the house, then called the Lodge or Acton Lodge, standing where Highlands Avenue later met Horn Lane, and 10 a. Hervey sold it in 1853–4 to Henry Scott Turner, whose son, Maj. Henry Scott Turner, lived at the Lodge from c. 1855 to 1871. in 1902 the house stood empty[75] before making way for the Highlands estate.[76]

The *BELL*, also held by Peter Thorney in 1628,[77] was known in 1637[78] but not listed as an inn in the early 18th century.[79] In 1729 Francis Ware sold it to Thomas Mandevil of Acton, apothecary,[80] who had replaced it with two adjoining brick houses by 1752, when he sold them to Nathan Carrington. Carrington's grandson Nathan Garrick, nephew of David Garrick the actor, had succeeded by 1780. The two houses were called Lichfield House and Suffolk House.[81]

A copyhold house with 4 a. acquired in 1611 by Thomas Thorney[82] was known as *ORGER HOUSE* in the 19th century and said to have been a fine Jacobean house.[83] In 1659 it was acquired by Sir John Trevor (1596–1673), gentleman of the Privy Chamber,[84] probably through his wife Anne, and after her death in 1663 it was conveyed to their son Richard (d. 1676).[85] Richard surrendered it in 1671 and 1674 to Thomas Coppin,[86] who left it in 1689 to his daughter Mary (d. c. 1699), wife of William Dickens,[87] and by 1702 it was held by Francis Dickens of Gray's Inn.[88] Thomas Eames was admitted in 1705 and succeeded by his youngest son William in 1711.[89] By 1797 the owners were the Revd. William Hall of Acton and his wife Frances Estcourt,[90] who in 1804 conveyed the house and adjoining land to the Clergy Orphans' school. The school occupied the house until 1812.[91] In 1834 John Bird was the owner, as in 1858 when the house had 'recently' been burned down.[92]

FIGHTERS perhaps had been the tenement which William Woodstone granted to Thomas Vighter, who had been succeeded by John Vighter by 1382.[93] Shortly before 1640 Anthony Bouchier sold it to Sir John Trevor, who lived there then.[94] In 1728 Dr. Thomas Pearson sold it to John Somerset,[95] whose widow Dorothy retained it when she surrendered other property in 1732.[96]

Sir John Trevor also acquired by 1661 the house later known as *BERRYMEAD PRIORY*.[97] In 1666 he had a great house with 16 hearths, another with 15, and an empty one with four.[98] His son John died before him and Berrymead apparently passed to a grandson Edward Trevor. By 1688 George Savile, marquess of Halifax (d. 1695), who settled at

[59] M.L.R. 1723/4/20; 1769/2/166–7.
[60] Guildhall Libr., Pr. V/ACT (plan of Fetherstonhaugh's est.). Plan perhaps copied from earlier one, as it gives Carrington's name rather than his nephew's.
[61] M.R.O., F 34/1–10; ibid. MR/PLT/4550.
[62] Below (Acton Ho.).
[63] Guildhall MS. 10312/100.
[64] Ibid. MS. 10465/24.
[65] M.L.R. 1769/2/451.
[66] Baker, *Acton*, 183.
[67] P.R.O., PROB 11/123 (P.C.C. 58 Lawe); ibid. SC 2/189/34.
[68] Ibid. C 2/Jas. I/T 14/19; Guildhall MS. 10833.
[69] P.R.O., C 142/491, no. 40.
[70] Ibid. SC 2/190/8.
[71] Bodl. MS. Rawl. D. 715, f. 5.
[72] P.R.O., C 142/79, no. 231.
[73] Goldsmiths' Hall, Acton Estate MS. B.III.1, no. 4.
[74] P.R.O., C 142/491, no. 40.
[75] B.R.A. 1180 (W. Suff. R.O., deeds of Wm. Hervey); Guildhall MSS. 10465/116–17; P.R.O., IR 29/21/1; ibid. MAF 20/2; M.R.O., Acc. 1385/9 and intro. in cal.
[76] Ealing libr., Acc. 19/2.
[77] P.R.O., C 142/491, no. 40.
[78] *Mdx. & Herts. N. & Q.* iv. 78.
[79] M.R.O., MR/LV.
[80] M.L.R. 1729/5/5–6.
[81] Monson, *Acton*, 29; M.R.O., MR/PLT/4550.
[82] P.R.O., SC 2/189/34.
[83] Jolliffe, *Acton*, 74.
[84] *D.N.B.*, amended in *B.I.H.R.* xviii. 136; *Glynde Place Archives*, facing p. xxvi.
[85] Guildhall MS. 10312/100.
[86] Ibid. 107, 109.
[87] P.R.O., PROB 11/398 (P.C.C. 3 Dyke).
[88] Guildhall MS. 10465/16.
[89] Ibid. 27.
[90] Ibid. 118.
[91] P.R.O., PROB. 11/285 (P.C.C. 714 Wootton); ibid. C 54/7842, no. 6; below, educ.
[92] Guildhall MS. 12698; P.R.O., MAF 20/2/22.
[93] *Cal. Close, 1381–5*, 221.
[94] Glynde Place MS. 691 (*Glynde Place Archives*, 65).
[95] M.L.R. 1728/5/143, 1723/3/274–5.
[96] M.R.O., Acc. 617/44.
[97] Guildhall MS. 10312/98.
[98] P.R.O., E 179/252/32.

Acton after the Revolution,[99] was in possession.[1] His son William, marquess of Halifax, died there in 1700[2] and was succeeded by four daughters.[3] Evelyn Pierrepont, earl and later duke of Kingston-upon-Hull (d. 1726) bought the property in 1708.[4] He used the house as a spring and summer residence, together with his daughters Mary, before her marriage to Edward Wortley Montagu in 1712, and Frances, who married the Jacobite John Erskine, earl of Mar (d. 1732), at Acton in 1714. It was left to his second wife Isabel (d. 1728) and then to her daughter Caroline Pierrepont.[5] In 1740 the house and 9 a. were sold to Miss Dorothy Fellowes,[6] whose brother William succeeded her in 1749 and immediately conveyed the estate to Henry Ord.[7] Ord's widow Anne in 1758 sold it to Thomas Fisher (d. 1769),[8] whose trustees sold it in 1787 to Thomas Whitmore.[9] Whitmore conveyed it in 1790 to Gen. Staats Long Morris (d. 1800),[10] whose wife Jane was succeeded by her brother James Edward Urquhart in 1802.[11] Urquhart surrendered it in 1803 to Thomas Clutton,[12] whose trustees sold it in 1807 to Edmund Fleming Akers (d. 1821).[13] By 1822 a Col. Peacocke (d. 1830) owned it, being succeeded by his widow (d. 1834).[14] Stephen Peacocke, owner 1834-7, was followed by Messrs. Nicholson and Westcar in 1838 and Mr. Croft by 1844.[15] Tenants included the novelist Edward Bulwer, Lord Lytton (1803-73), who took the house for his wife in the 1830s and lived there himself in 1835-6,[16] and nuns of the Sacred Heart from 1842 to 1850.[17] In 1842 the grounds totalled 11½ a.[18] Between 1849 and 1851 the house was owned by Lt. George Trafford Heald, who married Lola Montez but left England to escape bigamy charges, and c. 1856 it was bought by John Dawson.[19] In 1882 it was sold to the Berkshire Estates Co. but the house itself, with a small part of the garden, was bought by the Conservative party in 1885 and opened in 1886 as the Priory Constitutional Club. The club left after the Second World War, whereupon the house was used by the neighbouring Nevill's Bakery before passing c. 1977 to Ealing L.B.[20]

The house was described in 1705 as handsome, low, and regular, with fine gardens.[21] In 1802 it was known as Berrymead Lodge, and during the next five years Thomas Clutton, who probably gave it the name Berrymead Priory, remodelled it in a Gothic style.[22] Between 1882, when it had a galleried hall, 6 reception rooms, and 14 bedrooms on 3 floors,[23] and 1919 there was extensive rebuilding, but some Gothic detail survived inside.[24] Restoration was planned in 1980.

Sir Matthew Hale (1609-76), chief justice of King's Bench,[25] lived at Acton from c. 1666 until just before his death. His estate included *BAXTER'S* great house near the church where Richard Baxter had lived, describing it as small[26] although it had at least 10 hearths,[27] and *DAYCROFT* near East Acton Lane.[28] Daycroft may have belonged in 1461 to William Eston, fishmonger of London,[29] by purchase in 1458,[30] and was devised in 1658 by Thomas Child to his children.[31] Hale left all his property in Acton to his wife Anne (d. 1694) and then to his son Robert's son Gabriel.[32] In 1712 Gabriel settled it on his sister Frances and her husband Archibald Grosvenor;[33] they conveyed it to James Green, clothworker of London,[34] who in 1719 conveyed parts of it, including a house near the western boundary and Daycroft, to the chapter and to the almoner of St. Paul's.[35] The chapter c. 1758 exchanged its land with Samuel Wegg.[36] The almoner's land was later transferred to the Ecclesiastical Commissioners, including 8 a. south of Uxbridge Road awarded at inclosure in 1859[37] and built over c. 1900.[38] Daycroft was sold to the local board in 1889 and formed part of Acton park.[39]

The rest of Hale's estate, including Baxter's great house, was sold to Edward Gilbert in 1723.[40] The house may in fact already have been demolished, for it was not mentioned in subsequent conveyances and in 1705 Hale's house near the Rectory had been pulled down.[41] Gilbert at once conveyed the estate to James Joye, who had acquired *ACTON HOUSE*. That house had probably belonged in 1624 to Sir William Garraway, brother of John (fl. 1569).[42] Sir William's widow Elizabeth died in 1636 seised of a freehold house, occupied by Sir Henry Jernegan, which passed to her son Sir Henry (d. 1646), lord mayor of London.[43] 'The house and 40 a. had passed by 1649 to Matthew Herbert, by 1653 to Maj.-Gen. Philip Skippon

[99] *D.N.B.*
[1] Guildhall MS. 10465/4.
[2] Ibid. 15.
[3] Ibid. 16.
[4] Guildhall MS. 10465/56.
[5] *Complete Letters of Lady Mary Wortley Montagu*, ed. R. Halsband, i. 156 and *passim*; iii. 42 and n.; J. E. Lush, *Berrymead Priory* (1923), 13-14; *D.N.B.*
[6] M.L.R. 1740/3/75-7.
[7] Guildhall MS. 10465/65; M.L.R. 1749/1/372-3.
[8] Guildhall MS. 10465/84.
[9] M.L.R. 1787/5/382.
[10] Ibid. 1790/8/365-6.
[11] Guildhall MS. 10465/117.
[12] Ibid. 118.
[13] Ibid. 138.
[14] Lush, *Berrymead*, 19.
[15] Guildhall MS. 12698.
[16] Lush, *Berrymead*, 19-21.
[17] Below, Rom. Cathm.
[18] P.R.O., IR 29/21/1.
[19] Lush, *Berrymead*, 23, 25.
[20] Rowland, *Street Names*, 6.
[21] Bowack, *Antiquities*, 59.

[22] Lush, *Berrymead*, 17.
[23] Ibid. 25; Acton libr., Berrymead Priory, sale cats. 1882, 1889.
[24] Lush, *Berrymead*, 27-8.
[25] *D.N.B.*
[26] *Reliquiae Baxterianae*, ed. M. Sylvester (1696), pt. iii. 176, 181.
[27] P.R.O., E 179/252/32.
[28] M.L.R. 1719/5/106-7.
[29] P.R.O., SC 2/188/81.
[30] Ibid. CP 25(1)/152/95, no. 188.
[31] Ibid. PROB 11/285 (P.C.C. 714 Wootton).
[32] Ibid. PROB 11/353 (P.C.C. 19 Hale).
[33] Guildhall MS. 10465/27.
[34] M.L.R. 1719/5/106-7.
[35] Ibid. 1720/5/282-6.
[36] M.R.O., Acc. 617/38.
[37] Ibid. MR/DE/ACT.
[38] Below, econ. (Acton Vale).
[39] Ealing libr., Acc. 19/1.
[40] M.L.R. 1723/4/287-8; Guildhall MS. 10465/39.
[41] Bowack, *Antiquities*, 5.
[42] Goldsmiths' Hall, Acton Estate MS. B.III.1, no. 8.
[43] P.R.O., C 142/545, no. 79; *D.N.B.*

(d. 1660),[44] who left all his property in Acton to his wife Catherine,[45] and by 1686 to Skippon's son Sir Philip, traveller and writer,[46] who sold them to Sir Hele Hooke, Bt.[47] Sir Hele sold the house in 1696 to Daniel Sheldon,[48] whose trustees sold it in 1700 to Sir John Baber (d. 1704).[49] Francis Baber, brother and heir of Sir John's son John, sold it in 1721 to James Joye.[50]

On Joye's death c. 1742 his estate was sold to John Burton,[51] and in 1770 Capt. Charles Burton sold it to James Templar.[52] In 1786 Templar sold all his property in Acton to James Stratton, whose executors sold it in 1803 to Nicholas Selby.[53] The Selby family retained Acton House in 1845, but it was sold to Mary Robertson in 1860.[54] Probably rebuilt by Sir Henry Garraway in 1638,[55] it had 16 hearths in 1664[56] and was demolished c. 1904.[57]

There has been confusion between Acton House and another residence, called after the last countess of Derwentwater. The countess stayed during her husband's trial at Acton House, in whose grounds Selby built *DERWENT-WATER HOUSE*, possibly in 1804.[58] Selby sold it c. 1820 to George Kelly,[59] who owned it in 1842, but in 1859 it was sold to J. B. Nichols.[60] It remained a private house until it became Acton Liberal and Radical Club after 1890. The frontage was reduced for road widening, and the house itself was demolished in 1909.[61]

The *GOLDSMITHS'* estate grew from lands in East Acton left to the company by John Perryn, alderman of London, in 1656. The estate was first formed by Sir Richard Sutton (d. 1634), its nucleus being the copyhold capital messuage called Fosters or Hill House and later Manor House, which is recorded from 1532.[62] At his death Sutton held the capital messuage, 4 other houses, and c. 160 a. of copyhold and 50 a. of freehold.[63] His only child Elizabeth, wife of Sir John Ashfield, Bt., added to the estate, which by 1653 she had handed over to her son Sir Richard.[64] In 1654 the Ashfields sold it to John Perryn (d. 1657),[65] whose widow Alice married Sir Thomas Vyner, lord mayor of London (d. 1665), and after his death lived at the seat in Acton. On her death in 1682 the estate passed to the Goldsmiths' Company of London under Perryn's will.[66] It consisted of a large house, 2 farmhouses, and 3 cottages, with c. 166 a. of inclosed land and c. 60 a. in the fields in 1739, and was much enlarged in the 19th century and the early 20th. By the 1930s the company owned or had owned the whole area between the eastern parish boundary, Uxbridge Road, the green, and East Acton Lane, together with a wide band of land west of East Acton Lane, north of the green,

and on both sides of Friars Place Lane as far as the G.W.R. line, with the Friars beyond it. Until 1920 the only sales were to railway companies, besides those of 13 a. to the local board in 1886 for Acton park and of two leasehold houses and the Friars to the U.D.C. in 1902 for an isolation hospital. Building leases were granted over the western part of the estate and brickmaking leases for land south of the manor house, and sites were given for St. Dunstan's and other churches. After 1920 sales increased, including those of a large stretch of land to the U.D.C. for Western Avenue in 1921, the sites of several big houses for building, and parts of the charity estate for council housing and schools in the 1930s. Only the site of Manor House and some land around it had not been built on by 1945 and was still leased to private sports clubs in 1980.

Manor House became hard to let in the late 19th century and was demolished in 1911. The house was probably rebuilt by Henry Lambe, goldsmith, lessee from 1686.[67] In 1980 some wainscotting and a carved wooden overmantel were at Goldsmiths' Hall, London.[68] Of the Goldsmiths' other older houses only the Friars survives, as the administration block of Leamington Park hospital. It is an 18th-century house of three storeys and attics, with five bays, a central pediment, and cornices, which probably once had pilasters. A stuccoed porch was added in the 19th century.

The *ELMS* estate centred on a house called the Paddocks in 1817, Acton House in 1827, and the Elms by 1845. The precursor of the house was sold as a freehold cottage with a windmill and 2 a. in 1641. From 1722 the estate belonged to Charles Morren and his wife Elizabeth, and Elizabeth's son Henry Lloyd sold it in 1737 to Sir Joseph Ayloffe, Bt., and his wife Margaret. They sold it in 1750 to Samuel Wegg (d. 1802), who acquired much other property in Acton, including the lease of Acton ponds. His son George Samuel died in 1817, his heirs being his sisters Sarah, wife of the Revd. Richard Prosser, and Elizabeth. Elizabeth held most of the property and made additions to it, including Hill House; when she died in 1842, her sister having predeceased her without issue, she owned 169 a., which passed to Charles Gray Round, of Birch Hall (Essex), a distant relative. Parts were sold in 1895 and, to the Kensington Freehold Land Trust, in 1897, and the remainder was built on early in the 20th century.[69] The Elms was built probably in the 1720s in yellow brick with red-brick dressings, having three storeys with attics and a front of five bays with pilasters and a cornice. Single-storey wings with basements

[44] Bodl. MS. Rawl. D. 715, ff. 1, 3; *D.N.B.*; below, plate facing p. 32.
[45] P.R.O., PROB 11/300 (P.C.C. 193 Nabbs).
[46] *D.N.B.*   [47] Guildhall MS. 10465/2.
[48] Ibid. 11.   [49] Ibid. 15.
[50] M.L.R. 1721/5/281.
[51] Guildhall MS. 10465/58.
[52] Ibid. 85.   [53] Ibid. 118.
[54] P.R.O., IR 29/21/1; ibid. MAF 20/2/22.
[55] Lysons, *Environs*, ii. 15.
[56] M.R.O., MR/TH/3; P.R.O., E 179/252/32.
[57] Rowland, *Street Names*, 1.
[58] Jolliffe, *Acton*, 61; Lysons, *Environs*, ii. 15.
[59] Guildhall MS. 10465/118.
[60] P.R.O., IR 29/21/1; ibid. MAF 20/2/22.
[61] Jolliffe, *Acton*, 62.
[62] Goldsmiths' Hall, Acton Estate MSS. B.III.1-14.
[63] P.R.O., C 142/514, no. 45; ibid. SC 2/190/8.
[64] Bodl. MS. Rawl. D. 715, ff. 5, 3, 1.
[65] B.L. Add. MS. 38476, ff. 112-14.
[66] P.R.O., PROB 11/263 (P.C.C. 107 Ruthen).
[67] M.L.R. 1720/5/301; illus. in P. Norman, *E. Acton Manor Ho.* (L.C.C. *Survey*, monograph vii, 1921); above, frontispiece.
[68] Inf. from the librarian, Goldsmiths' Co.
[69] M.R.O., Acc. 617 and 1247; P.R.O., IR 29/21/1.

were added in the late 18th century. The house, let to private tenants in the 19th century, housed secondary schools from 1954, including Twyford high school in 1980.[70]

ECONOMIC HISTORY. AGRARIAN HISTORY. The field system of the five-hide holding that became the Somerset estate was distinct from that of Acton manor elsewhere in the parish. The estate, covering over a third of the parish, was granted out before 1086[71] and perhaps before the common fields were formed, since it had no holdings in those fields. The holding developed from inclosures and assarts in the northern clay belt and by 1229 was composed of several crofts of arable and pasture, with some remaining woodland, and at least two farms situated away from the main settlements.[72] One farm, leased by the chapter of St. Paul's to successive deans, c. 1230 had 4 oxen, 4 horses, and 100 sheep.[73] The arable was valued at 2d. an acre in 1327, 1349, and 1373, the value in 1349 being low because the land was poor and rarely cultivated; meadow was valued at 1s. an acre in 1327, 1s. 6d. in 1373, pasture at 3d. in 1327, and woodland at 6d. at both dates, being of slight growth in 1373.[74]

In 1460 the dean leased the fields called Goderhill, Dean's Bush field, and le Pylle, crofts called Dean's Reding and Dean's five acres, and a rod of meadow in Willesden for 99 years, at an annual rent of 8 marks and 4 bu. of wheatmeal and 4 of oatmeal. The lessee covenanted to clear the land and plough and sow it within 20 years. The dean also leased 24 a. of underwood called the dean's great wood. In 1545 no great trees, only underwood, grew on the dean's lands.[75] St. Bartholomew's leased its land to a London mercer in 1453 for 60 years[76] and in 1529 leased the fields called Parkstones for 7 years. The woods and underwoods were also leased.[77] In 1543 there were some 60 oaks and elms on the estate, partly mature timber and partly cropped for use in repairs.[78] The Frowyk estate included valuable woodland, probably in the north and east parts of the parish, in 1505 and 1518.[79] By the late 16th century, however, no woodland was recorded on the Frowyk estates and most, like the dean's woods, had probably been cleared, although a Garraway tenant was able to cut 700 faggots in 1600.[80]

The Somerset estate was let in several parcels in the 16th century to tenants who are likely to have sublet.[81] In 1636 more than 700 a. of the estate of nearly 800 a. was let to William Attlee of Fulham,[82] who sublet parcels of 5 a. and less for terms of six months.[83] By 1693 the estate had six tenants holding large portions and eight holding small ones.[84] In 1736 four tenants each held houses and large portions, from 113 a. to 260 a.; one tenement was let with 2 a. and six other tenants held from 3 a. to 72 a.[85] In 1799 Fetherstonhaugh had two tenants with farmhouses and c. 232 a. and c. 227 a. respectively, and three others with between 53 a. and 124 a., some of the estate having been sold off.[86]

The Goldsmiths' Company leased its estate for 61 years in 1686 and the whole, except the house, 10 a., and an orchard, was sublet to six tenants. In 1739 there were said to be c. 166 a. of inclosed land and c. 60 a. of arable in the common fields. The estate seems to have been leased out as a whole until the early 19th century, when the company began dealing directly with the sub-tenants.[87]

Apart from the Somerset estate, practically all the land was held of Acton manor in free socage or by copy of court roll, forming nucleated settlements at Church Acton and East Acton, with 4 or 5 open arable fields and inclosed meadow and pasture. In 1859 about two-thirds of the open arable was freehold,[88] as were most of the individual tenements without land, such as inns, while small inclosures of waste, many of them in front of houses, were copyhold. By the 17th century several houses and grounds were therefore held by mixed tenure. Copyholds descended by Borough English to the youngest surviving son or, failing sons, to the daughters as coheirs. Entry fines were fixed at one year's quitrent and a widow's dower was settled by the homage, if her husband had not made other arrangements. The eight houses liable to find the reeve had to pay a heriot, fixed at 3s. 4d. by 1697. Tenants could let their land for three-year periods without licence.[89]

In 1552 pasture was stinted at 3 sheep, 2 cows, and a horse for each acre of meadow and pasture held, 2 sheep for each acre of arable, a cow for every 4 a. of arable, and a horse for every 6 a. of stubble.[90] Such orders were often repeated in the early 17th century. In 1611 landholders living within the manor and parish could graze 3 sheep for every 2 a., while cottagers and inhabitants without land but possessing common rights could keep 4 sheep and 2 cows or a cow and a horse only. Occupants of cottages built within the last 20 years had no sheep commons but could keep a cow.[91] In 1612 landholders could again graze 2 sheep for every acre and 12 for each house or cottage, but bachelors could not keep any.[92] In 1637 tenants had to wait 20 days after the corn was cleared before turning sheep into the stubble, and in 1651 the order was repeated, with a 14-day wait, for Church field and South field only.[93]

[70] Below, educ.
[71] T.L.M.A.S. xxviii. 316.
[72] Early Charters of St. Paul's, 264–7.
[73] Ibid. 238–9.
[74] P.R.O., C 143/195, no. 11; C 143/294, no. 5; C 143/380, no. 14.
[75] Ibid. E 318/Bx 19/956.
[76] Ibid. PROB 11/4 (P.C.C. 4 Stokton).
[77] Ibid. E 303/9 Lond./271, 289.
[78] Ibid. E 318/Box 19/953.
[79] Ibid. PROB 11/15 (P.C.C. 15 Adeane); PROB 11/20 (P.C.C. 5 Maynwaryng).
[80] P.R.O., PROB 11/95 (P.C.C. 36 Wallopp, will of Hen. Fearne).
[81] Hist. MSS. Com. 39, 15th Rep. II, p. 259.
[82] B.L. Add. MS. 5501, ff. 70 and v.
[83] M.R.O., Cal. Mdx. Sess. Bks. i(A), p. 33.
[84] Ibid. F 34/1–10.   [85] Ibid. Acc. 617/46.
[86] Guildhall MS. 12697.
[87] Goldsmiths' Hall, Acton Estate MS. B.III.1, no. 8.
[88] M.R.O., MR/DE/ACT.
[89] Ibid. Acc. 538(i)/42/2.
[90] P.R.O., SC 2/189/24.   [91] Ibid. SC 2/189/34.
[92] Ibid. SC 2/190/2.   [93] Ibid. SC 2/190/10, 15.

Some 25 years before parliamentary inclosure in 1859 tenants had agreed not to turn animals into the fields.[94] Orders concerning the fields had ceased by 1670. Four open arable fields survived in 1859: Church field, South field, Turnham field, and East field, together with a small common meadow called Townham or Towney mead in the south-east corner of South field. They contained c. 360 a. in 1859, but some piecemeal inclosures had already been made.[95] An open field called North field had existed east of Friars Place green and north of East Acton in 1588;[96] 40 a. there were already inclosed by 1556 and held by one tenant. That tenant was one of four presented for converting areas of 30–120 a. to pasture.[97] In the late 17th century three fields called North fields, totalling 19 a. and belonging to the Goldsmiths' Company, were 'now inclosed' but to be common after the crops had been taken. Inclosures were also being made in East field, where a new 10-a. close south of the manor house existed at the same date,[98] and in Turnham field 5 a. had been recently inclosed by 1695.[99] Customary holdings in the open fields apparently had no standard size by the 16th century, and the land held by each tenant showed little sign of having been equally divided between the fields.[1] None of the orders indicates the existence of a common rotation, nor that one field remained fallow each year, but in 1637 tenants were not to inclose Lammas grounds, which were grazed in common from August to March,[2] and in 1641 all landholders in the common fields were to observe ancient custom and not crop their land out of rotation, with a heavy fine for every acre so ploughed.[3]

Commons listed in 1618 were Old Oak common of 60 a., which had been cleared of trees by the chapter of St. Paul's as part of Sutton Court manor in Chiswick, and Rushie green, 5 a. leading towards Willesden,[4] which apparently lay just east of Worton green.[5] The two greens together covered the area known later as Friars Place green. Householders and inhabitants of the manor were allowed to use the commons,[6] where grazing was stinted for certain categories. In 1611 cottagers could keep no more than 12 sheep on the common and bachelors could keep none.[7] In 1616 no cottage built on the waste during the previous 60 years was to have common for more than 6 sheep and a cow,[8] and in 1619 no cottager could keep more than 6 sheep, a cow, a heifer, and a colt on the common.[9]

Old Oak common was said to contain 200 a. in 1590, when it was called Old Holt wood, by then consisting mainly of oak scrub and thorn bushes.[10] Acton wells, with two houses including

the White House, stood there in 1758, and by 1821 some 3 a. around the wells and houses had been inclosed. In 1800 the chapter of St. Paul's sold its rights in the common to the duke of Devonshire, who in turn sold them in 1821 to Thomas Church. Since the parishioners had enjoyed pasture rights for all kinds of cattle throughout the year, they received compensation in 1805 for land taken for the Paddington canal and in 1837 for the G.W.R. Inclosure of the common, estimated at c. 120 a. of open grass and furze, was proposed in 1813 by the chief land-owners, and the vestry upheld the parish's claims by obtaining the key of a house built on the common for the Quarter-Master General, who had a lease from the chapter. In 1842 c. 104 a. were still supervised by the parish overseers,[11] but in 1862 Henry John King Church fenced most of the common and successfully sued eight leading landowners who pulled down his fences: usage by the commoners was adjudged to have originated through a 'blunder'. A small area in the south remained open, being used as an emergency landing ground for aircraft in the 1930s,[12] and later became part of the adjoining Wormwood Scrubs common in Hammersmith.

In 1842 there were 185 a. of common land outside the open fields. Apart from Old Oak common, the only large area was Acton Green common of c. 17 a.,[13] which had not been listed in 1618, probably because it was considered part of Turnham Green common.

Fragmentary evidence suggests that in the early modern period farming was mixed, with references to wheat, horses, fat cattle,[14] sheep,[15] and pigs.[16] An innholder claimed in 1668 that she had never heard of barren or dry cattle being pastured in the parish, although for many years she had grazed travelling and saddle horses for a single night.[17] In 1706 Acton was said to be sown every year with all sorts of grain, for which its soil was very suitable; crops were good, especially peas, and intermixed arable and meadow produced a chequered landscape.[18] By 1800 the land was mostly meadow and pasture. A little market garden ground existed around Acton Green, although only 10 a. had been recorded in the 1790s, and about a third of the rest of the parish was arable, mainly in the southern part in the four open fields.[19]

Of 740 a. of Fetherstonhaugh's estate leased in 1799, grassland amounted to 425 a. and arable to 315 a.; 70 a. of the arable were laid down to grass between 1800 and 1805. Most of the arable was on the two large farms each of over 200 a., whose tenants agreed to keep a total of 200 a. as meadow for the last seven years of their leases. On those

94 Harper Smith, 'East Acton', 27.
95 M.R.O., MR/DE/ACT.
96 Goldsmiths' Hall, Acton Estate MS. B. III. 1, no. 4.
97 Hist. MSS. Com. 39, 15th Rep. II, p. 259.
98 Goldsmiths' Hall, Acton Estate MS. B.III.1, no. 8.
99 Guildhall MS. 10465/11.
1 Based on ct. rolls and conveyances.
2 P.R.O., SC 2/190/10.
3 Ibid. SC 2/190/11.   4 Ibid. SC 2/190/5.
5 M.L.R. 1729/5/63-4.
6 M.R.O., Acc. 538(i)/42/2.
7 P.R.O., SC 2/189/34.   8 Ibid. SC 2/190/2.
9 Guildhall MS. 10833.

10 Para. based on M.R.O., Acc. 531/add./56-70.
11 P.R.O., IR 29/21/1.
12 Briggs, Mdx. Old and New, 168.
13 P.R.O., IR 29/21/1.
14 P.R.O., PROB 11/95 (P.C.C. 36 Wallopp, will of Hen. Fearne).
15 Guildhall MS. 9171/8, f. 105; P.R.O., PROB 11/30 (P.C.C. 1 Pynnyng, will of Rob. Evelyn).
16 Year Bk. 12 Edw. III (Selden Soc. lxxxi), 77; ct. rolls.
17 P.R.O., E 134/20-1 Chas. II/Hil. 9.
18 Bowack, Antiquities, 49, 59.
19 Milne, Land Use Map of Mdx. (1800); Lysons, Environs, ii. 1.

two farms the main arable crops between 1800 and 1805 were wheat, beans, and oats, with smaller acreages of tares and, in 1805, of peas, potatoes, and clover.[20] In 1870 in the parish as a whole 345 a. of crops were fairly equally distributed between corn and field vegetables, with another 916 a. returned as under grass.[21] There were 408 cattle, including 253 milk cows, 177 sheep, and 558 pigs. The number of milk cows had declined to c. 100 by 1890 but reached 166 in 1900; in 1888 there were 19 registered dairies or milkshops and in 1901 there were 8 cowkeepers and 68 dairies or shops. In 1914 there were 2 keepers with c. 110 cows and in 1919 there was only one, who stopped keeping cows during the year, although in 1920 there were still 21 milk cows in the parish.[22] From 1900 other cattle were generally young animals. Sheep were usually less numerous than cows but in 1917, possibly because of the war, there were c. 20 ewes and lambs and 773 sheep of one year or more. Pigs were recorded at 558 in 1870 and 322 in 1900, when returns probably underestimated the number of small keepers in South Acton. Farms in Old Oak Lane were well known for their piggeries in the late 19th century[23] and probably used Old Oak common for grazing. Discouragement by the medical officer of health had some success: 13 piggeries in 1901, 10 of them in Old Oak Lane, had been reduced to 3 in 1904, partly through persuading landlords to put pressure on their tenants,[24] but there were still at least 183 pigs in 1920.

The amount of arable declined from 412 a. in 1880 to 137 a. in 1890, 52 a. in 1910, and 7 a. in 1920; the proportion devoted to corn dropped to less than a quarter in 1890, while potatoes and field crops increased. Most of the farmland that survived the spread of building was converted to permanent grass, whose acreage in the returns rose to 1,211 a. in 1890. Thereafter it fell as the farmland shrank, although 423 a. remained in 1914 and 94 a. in 1920.

Market gardening was less widespread than in neighbouring Chiswick and developed later, as many surviving patches of open land were not large enough to be worth cultivating commercially. In 1873 four market gardens existed in the southern part of the parish, mostly near Acton Green.[25] In 1880 there were 92 a. of market garden, besides 12½ a. of orchard, and in 1890 79 a. of market garden, besides 50½ a. of orchard.

MILLS. Acton manor apparently had four mills in the 16th century,[26] although only two have been located with certainty. A windmill stood at the eastern end of Church field, south of the footpath to East Acton, on part of the modern Acton park,[27] where the waste in front of the mill was mentioned in 1622.[28] The occupier was William Harding, miller and corn dealer, in 1851[29] but the mill was pulled down probably before 1877, when the Goldsmiths' Company planned building near by. Another windmill stood on the site of the Elms or its grounds, in West Acton. It was sold in 1641, leased to a miller in the mid 17th century, and depicted c. 1677, but probably made way for the Elms in the early 18th century.[30] A third mill may have stood near Mill Hill Park, which was known as Windmill hill c. 1810.[31] Steyne mills included a mill house in 1728, when it was used as a tanyard, and may originally have been a water mill.[32]

TRADE AND INDUSTRY. First and Second brickfields, near Mason's green and so named in 1799, indicated early exploitation of Acton's extensive brickearth.[33] When suburban housing began to spread, several brickmaking agreements were drawn up, generally with building leases. The Goldsmiths' Company made agreements between 1868 and 1901 over the former Church field and East field, the latter passing to East Acton Brickworks & Estates in 1888.[34] Springfield Park brickworks on the north side of the G.W.R. line existed by 1894, as did brickworks in South field and the Atlas brick and tile works by the Grand Union canal;[35] the Willesden & Acton Brick Co. operated from Leamington Park by 1905.[36]

Gravel was dug from the banks of Stamford brook's western branch at the Steyne, where free tenants were ordered to stop taking gravel in 1622.[37] Gravel pit field bordered the stream just north of Acton Farm in 1828[38] and another field, just west of Church field along the London road, had a gravel pit in 1723.[39]

In 1232 the bishop of London was granted the right to hold a market at his manor of Acton every Monday,[40] but the market was not recorded later. Early occupations included those of a cordwainer in 1388,[41] a brewer in 1477,[42] a female tailor and a horse gelder in 1610,[43] a silkweaver in 1611,[44] a collar maker in 1641,[45] a draper in 1697,[46] a glazier in 1718,[47] a soapboiler in 1780,[48] and a peruke maker and a watchmaker in 1785.[49]

[20] Para. based on Guildhall MS. 12697 (survey bk.).
[21] Following 3 paras. based on P.R.O., MAF 68/250 (1870); MAF 68/706 (1880); MAF 68/1276 (1890); MAF 68/1846 (1900); MAF 68/2416 (1910); MAF 68/2815 (1917); MAF 2980 (1920).
[22] For dairies and cowkeepers: Acton U.D.C. Rep. of M.O.H. (1888), 16; (1901), 27; (1914), 71; (1919), 18.
[23] Baker, Acton, 147.
[24] Acton U.D.C. Rep. of M.O.H. (1901), 28; (1904), 78.
[25] Green's Dir. Notting Hill, Acton (1873–4).
[26] P.R.O., C 66/1112, mm. 14–15. The fig. is not reliable.
[27] P.R.O., IR 29/21/1.
[28] Guildhall MS. 10833.
[29] P.R.O., HO 107/1699.
[30] Above, manors and other est.; Ogilby, Map of Mdx. (c. 1677).
[31] Guildhall libr., Pr. V/ACT (plan of Fetherstonhaugh's est.).

[32] M.R.O., Acc. 276/27.   [33] Guildhall MS. 12697.
[34] Goldsmiths' Hall, Acton Estate MSS. old nos. 174–7, 238.
[35] O.S. Map 6", Mdx. XXI. NW. (1891–4 edn.).
[36] Suburban Dir., Trade (1905).
[37] Guildhall MS. 10833.
[38] Acton libr., Acton farm sale cat.
[39] M.L.R. 1725/1/529–30.
[40] P.R.O., C 54/43, m. 16.
[41] Ibid. CP 25(1)/151/78, no. 99.
[42] Guildhall MS. 9171/6, f. 225v.
[43] M.R.O., Cal. Mdx. Sess. Rec. iii. 165.
[44] Ibid. vii. 87.
[45] P.R.O., SC 2/190/11.
[46] Ibid. PROB 11/440 (P.C.C. 190 Pyne, will of Ezra Roome).
[47] M.L.R. 1718/3/143.
[48] Ibid. 1780/4/439.   [49] Ibid. 1785/2/292.

William Finch, a tanner in Acton in 1633, settled two tanyards and equipment in 1670 on his son William, who left them to his wife and son Thomas in 1701.[50] By 1728 the tanyard included a mill house[51] and was afterwards known as Steyne mills. It was later owned by Samuel Williams and William Wingfield, fellmongers, and then by William Gee, fellmonger. Gee bought the adjoining Finches field, which had warehouses and tanpits, with a piece of land in Diana's Spring field, in order to secure the water supply.[52] The property remained in the Gee family and was known as Steyne mills by 1832, when John Charles Gee & Co. made Lapland rugs and footwear, besides scouring blankets and counterpanes.[53] By 1873 it was the steam laundry of Rush & Co.,[54] later renamed the Empire Steam Laundry and owned by F. A. Baldwin. It was a jam and pickle factory of the Co-operative Wholesale Society from 1916 to 1962 and was afterwards demolished.[55]

In 1801, out of a population of 1,425, 141 people worked chiefly in trade, crafts, or manufacture, and 215 in agriculture. In 1831 128 families were engaged in trade or manufacture and 182 in agriculture.[56] Only services for the immediate neighbourhood were provided then and for most of the 19th century,[57] except by Steyne mills and later by the laundries.

Cheap housing in South Acton after 1860 seems to have attracted laundries from Notting Hill and Kensington, which were becoming too densely built up. Nearby brickworks, where laundresses' husbands could work, and the presence of soft water were also thought to explain the rapid growth of laundries. By 1873 there were c. 60, nearly all hand laundries on the Mill Hill estate and including a dye works in Enfield Road, and by 1890 there were over 170, still mainly small hand laundries in South Acton. In 1901 Acton's residents included 2,448 women and 568 men who worked in the laundry service, which was the largest employer of women. During the First World War many laundries closed and others installed power, although most firms remained small. In the 1930s Acton was still a centre of the trade and in 1956, when the borough had only 50 laundries, none of them hand laundries, it was still claimed to be the largest laundry town in Britain.[58]

In 1901 transport was the leading employer of men and was followed closely by building, the two together accounting for nearly a third of the male workforce, while laundries and domestic service accounted for about two-thirds of the female.[59] By 1921, after the arrival of large manufacturers, men were employed chiefly in metal work, including engineering and fitting,

followed by transport, commerce, and clerical work, which together accounted for half the male workers. Three-quarters of the employed women were still in personal service, laundries, and clerical work. Acton's 20th-century industrial growth, while attracting many non-resident workers, did not provide occupations for all its residents. In 1957, when nearly three times as many employees lived outside the borough as in it, the population increased by 20,000 during each working day. In 1979, out of c. 60,000 employed in Acton, only a quarter lived in the borough, while 25,000 residents worked elsewhere.[60]

Several large firms took sites in Acton Vale and South Acton between 1900 and 1908.[61] In the late 1920s and 1930s North Acton, linked with Park Royal, was built over with large and small factories.[62] After the Second World War redevelopment schemes permitted the separation of industrial from residential premises in part of South Acton and led to the creation of an industrial estate between Bollo Lane, Stanley Road, Bollo Bridge Road, and the North London railway, where there were several small light industries. In 1957 the borough had 719 factories, workshops, and other industrial premises, most of them in North Acton and Acton Vale,[63] and was said to have one of the two largest concentrations of industry south of Birmingham.[64] A small chamber of commerce was founded in 1909[65] and survived in 1980.[66]

Acton Vale. Large firms, mainly electrical and mechanical engineers seeking space near London, began moving into the district in 1900 and concentrated on the south side of Acton Vale, with a few major exceptions elsewhere in South Acton. By 1905 several small firms, including E. Bristow, makers of 'Roundwood' cycles, a plating works, and parquet flooring makers, were in the Parade, Acton Vale.[67] By 1932 the motor industry employed 5,400 or nearly four-fifths of the workers in the district and the chemical industry 1,300. Makers of musical instruments employed 250, of foodstuffs 200, of swords and razors and lithographic products 320, and of electrical heating equipment 50. Apart from one motor assembling factory, the seven largest firms, employing 6,000 between them, had all been founded between 1900 and 1908.[68] In 1952 there were some 29 firms with 7,430 workers.[69] Since the Second World War the closure of a few big factories, such as the Napier works whose site became Acton Park industrial estate, has made room for smaller concerns. Many newcomers, including clothing retailers and a brewery, acquired warehouse and distribution centres for London and the south of England.

[50] M.R.O., Acc. 276/22–4.
[51] Ibid. Acc. 276/27.
[52] M.L.R. 1789/1/269.
[53] Pigot, *Com. Dir.* (1832–4).
[54] *Ealing, Acton Dir.* (1873–4).
[55] Rowland, *Street Names*, 35.
[56] *Census*, 1801, 1831.
[57] Pigot, *Com. Dir.* (1832–4); *P.O. Dir. Mdx.* (1845); *Ealing, Acton Dir.* (1873–4).
[58] *The Times*, 31 Mar. 1956; *New Survey of Lond. Life and Labour*, v (1933), Lond. ind. II. 345–6; *Ealing, Acton Dir.* (1873–4); *Kelly's Dir. Mdx.* (1890); *Census*, 1901.

[59] *Census*, 1901, 1921.
[60] Acton libr., cutting from *Evening News*, 1957; Acton Chamber of Commerce, *Year Bk.* (1979–80), 14.
[61] Below (Acton Vale).
[62] Below (Park Royal).
[63] Acton libr., cutting from *Evening News*, 1957.
[64] *The Times*, 19 Apr. 1956.
[65] Ibid. 26 Nov. 1909.
[66] Acton Chamber of Commerce, *Year Bk.* (1979/80).
[67] *Suburban Dir., Trade* (1905).
[68] D. H. Smith, *Ind. of Gtr. Lond.* (1933), 96–7.
[69] P. G. Hall, *Ind. of Lond. since 1861* (1962), 126.

Eastman & Son built a new cleaning and dyeing works in 1901 on a 6-a. site east of Vale Grove, 1½ a. near St. Barnabas's church being used for housing and the rest for departments which included the silk dyeing formerly done in iron buildings in the Steyne.[70] The company was renamed Associated Dyers & Cleaners c. 1936.[71]

Wilkinson Sword Co. occupied a large site in Southfield Road, containing a former brickfield, by 1905. In addition to swords and razors, before the First World War the company made the Wilkinson Sword motor cycle and the Deemster motor car, which was made by the Ogston Motor Co. of Acton from 1914 until the 1920s. The firm sold part of its site to the U.D.C. in 1908 for Southfield Road recreation ground and by 1972 had moved to Brunel Road, near Old Oak common, where c. 40 craftsmen made up to 8,000 swords a year.[72]

D. Napier & Sons, engineers, in 1902 bought 3¾ a. in Stanley Gardens, a site easily accessible for customers. Another 2¾ a. were added in 1904, when c. 500 men were employed, and quickly built over. The most important work at the factory was on the first commercially successful six-cylinder engine, designed by S. F. Edge in 1903, Napier's major contribution to the development of the motor car. The works employed 1,000 by 1906, when over 200 cars a year were made, besides motor boat engines. Aero engines were built under government contract from 1914, followed by airframes, requiring a new workshop on land facing Uxbridge Road, east of the existing offices, and making a total factory area of 8½ a. In 1916 c. 1,700 were employed. The company concentrated on aero engines after the war, reaching a peak of 50 a month in 1927. In 1939 it took a building in Park Royal to test engines, but business declined after 1945. The Acton factories were closed c. 1960 and the site later became Acton Park industrial estate.[73]

Evershed & Vignoles, makers of electrical equipment, were founded in 1895 and moved to Acton Lane, near Acton Green, from Westbourne Park in 1903. They made steering and target equipment for the Royal Navy during the First World War and afterwards extended their site, employing c. 500 during the late 1920s. Numbers rose to over 1,000 in the Second World War, when aircraft instruments were also made, and to over 1,500 by the early 1960s. The company became part of Thorn Electronics in 1971 and concentrated the making of defence electronic equipment at Acton Lane, where c. 450 were employed in 1980.[74]

Charles A. Vandervell moved his company later known as CAV, which made accumulators, electric carriage lamps, and switchboards, from Willesden to Warple Way in 1904. Between 1904 and 1908 the firm pioneered the dynamo-charged battery principle and in 1911 it produced the world's first public service vehicle lighting system, used on a double-decker bus. Vehicle electrics and aircraft magnetos were made by 600 employees in 1916 and 1,000 by 1918. Wireless components were also made from 1923. In 1926 CAV was bought by Joseph Lucas Ltd. and in partnership with Robert Bosch Ltd. it began making fuel injection pumps for the new diesel industry and, in the Second World War, fuel systems for aircraft. From 1978 the company's name was Lucas CAV. The group's headquarters remained at Warple Way, where in 1980 c. 3,000 employees made heavy duty electric equipment for commercial vehicles.[75]

Other motor car manufacturers who arrived before the First World War included Panhard & Levasseur in Warple Way by 1909, where the site was later occupied by Sunbeam Talbot.[76] Darracq-Clement-Talbot and W. & G. du Cros had motor works in the Vale by 1924[77] and Smith Motor Accessories took part of the Bronnley factory in 1918.[78] The New Engine (Motor) Co. made N.E.C. aero engines at its Acton hill works in 1911.[79]

H. Bronnley & Co., which made soap and other toilet preparations, was founded in 1883 in Holborn by James Heilbron and built a factory in Warple Way in 1904, where it remained in 1958.[80]

H. W. Nevill Ltd. had built a factory on the Berrymead Priory estate by 1905, at no. 364 Acton Lane, to make patent bread.[81] It later took over the Priory as an administrative and welfare block and was still there in 1947, but by 1977 it had left and the bakery had been demolished.[82]

Although by 1923 hardly any of the meat sold locally was slaughtered in Acton, a few slaughterhouses were still operated by wholesale meat and food processing firms, the chief of which was T. Wall & Son. In 1926 an Aldgate firm bought a slaughterhouse in Hanbury Road, for producing kosher meat on a considerable scale, and was operating in 1938.[83] Walls bought the 6-a. site of Friars Place house and grounds in 1919 and built a factory there to make sausages, pies, and brawn, with a slaughterhouse in Warple Way to which pigs were driven from the G.W.R. line. In 1936 the company built a bacon factory for slaughtering and processing at Atlas Road, near Old Oak common; one of the largest of its kind, it employed 350 people, 200 of them in production, in 1949. From 1956 the Friary factory concentrated on ice cream, all the meat business moving to Atlas Road, and in 1958 the two factories together employed over 3,000, with 514 at Atlas Road in 1964. The Atlas Road factory was closed c. 1978 and the Friary factory employed 800 in 1980.[84]

[70] *Acton Gaz.* 1 Feb. 1901.
[71] Acton, *Official Guide* (1936), 27.
[72] Acton libr., cutting from *Soldier*, Sept. 1972; ibid. photocopy of D. Culshaw and P. Horobin, *Complete Cat. of Brit. Cars*; Rowland, *Street Names*, 33.
[73] C. H. Wilson and W. J. Reader, *Men and Machines* (1958), 79–81, 87, 102, 111, 134, 152; *Railway Mag.* xxxix. 91–7; Acton, *Official Guide* (1960, 1963).
[74] Inf. from the technical dir.
[75] Inf. from the pub. relations officer; below.

[76] Acton libr., copy of artesian wells map from Water Resources Bd.   [77] Acton, *Official Guide* (1924), 38.
[78] M.R.O., Acc. 1047/27.
[79] *Aviation World Dir.* (1911), 131, 273.
[80] Acton, *Official Guide* (1958), 59.
[81] *Suburban Dir., Trade* (1905).
[82] Rowland, *Street Names*, 6.
[83] Acton Boro. *Rep. of M.O.H.* (1926), 22; (1938), 38.
[84] Inf. from consumer research manager; Grange Mus., 1 A 2 (*Willesden Cit.* 12 Aug. 1949, 21 July 1964); Acton,

North Acton. A few factories appeared in the late 19th century near the Grand Junction canal and Willesden junction. Naphtha works were established in Old Oak Common Lane, beside the canal, by 1866[85] but closed between 1885 and 1894, when the site was occupied by saw mills.[86] Willesden Paper & Canvas Works, Old Oak Common Lane, south of the canal, formed a company in 1868 to pioneer waterproof paper and in 1873 opened an experimental factory, which was expanded in 1888. During the First World War the company made tents by applying its waterproofing process to textiles. In 1924 it was reorganized as Willesden Dux Oriental, still at the canal bank works, but by 1932 the site had been sold.[87]

In the north-west corner of the parish land south of the London Midland railway was used as an aerodrome by the London Aviation Co. in 1910, and Ruffy, Arnell & Baumann began developing an aeroplane there in 1917. They were taken over by the Alliance Aeroplane Co., formed by Waring & Gillow the furniture makers, and a huge factory and hangar were built on the airfield, a little south of the line later taken by Western Avenue. De Havilland triplanes and biplanes were made there at the end of the First World War but by 1919 Alliance had developed its own Seabird long-distance aeroplane, with a Napier 'Lion' engine, which won the Acton to Madrid air race in 1919. A projected flight to Australia was abandoned when a later model crashed and in 1920 the company closed. The factory was then used by several manufacturers, including Renault, which built another factory beside it, and was later leased to the Ministry of Aviation. During the Second World War parts of airframes were made there, until in 1945 W. H. Smith & Son bought the factory and used part for making stationery. Smith's sold it in 1973 and it then served various firms for storage.[88]

Park Royal. Industry in North Acton after the First World War was linked with the growth of Park Royal, whose centre lay in Willesden and which extended over West Twyford to form the leading industrial area in west Middlesex. There were good rail services with the G.W.R.'s Birmingham line, sidings built for the Royal Agricultural Society's show ground, and passenger transport from Willesden, the main source of labour. The opening of Western Avenue provided a quick route into the west end of London and further encouraged firms to move there.[89]

As in neighbouring North Acton, Park Royal had a few factories before 1914, the chief of which are noticed individually below. By 1919 Cumberland Avenue had several large factories, mainly engineering, employing over 1,200 workers; Acton Lane, Harlesden, had three, including the Metropolitan Electric Supply Co.'s generating station employing 320; Waxlow Road had two, employing 1,190, mostly at McVitie & Price, and Barratts Green Road had a laundry, employing 70.[90]

During the First World War, Park Royal was used as a large horse compound for the Royal Army Service Corps.[91] Munitions factories, employing mainly Willesden residents, were built in Willesden Lane and Victoria Road, Acton, and closed towards the end of 1918,[92] becoming derelict. In 1928 the government sold 5 a. with their buildings to Allnatt Ltd., for scrap metal sorting, and offers received for the premises revealed a growing demand for small ready-built factories.[93] Allnatts acquired more land and from 1929 built cheap all-purpose factories on what became the Chase estate, producing just over one a fortnight. Small plants thus predominated in the area and in two years most of the estate was covered.[94] In the 1930s bigger factories also were built, for particular firms, especially on the Western Avenue estate. In 1932 Park Royal consisted of Victoria Road with 28 factories, the Chase estate with 34, the Great Western estate with 5, Western Avenue with 6, and Cumberland Avenue with 10, together employing 13,400. The largest work-forces made foodstuffs, electrical equipment, motors, paper products, and non-electrical machinery.[95]

In 1952 industry in Park Royal covered 335 a. but only five firms had more than 1,000 employees. Engineering plants had an average of 73 workers, while electrical engineering firms were the largest with an average of 230 and food and drink firms had 202. In the northern part were a few very large factories, with an average workforce of 387, compared with 105 for the whole of Park Royal: Heinz, with 1,500, was the largest in 1952.[96]

By 1971 industry covered 1,290 a. between the Bakerloo line in the north-east and Western Avenue in the south, besides the former airfield south of the road, and 39,000 people were employed in *c.* 500 firms. The largest landowner, Allnatt (London) Ltd., was still building on several sites in the 1970s, including a large area in Park Royal Road, and another company was building on the former Walls site in Atlas Road, while major rebuilding in Cumberland Avenue involved new warehousing.[97] During a general industrial decline in north-west London, however, *c.* 70 firms left the Park Royal and Wembley estates in the six years to 1977, with the loss of nearly 6,000 jobs. In 1977 the G.L.C. decided to spend £1 million on Park Royal, in order to bring back skilled workers who were moving to new towns, but the plans were opposed by established firms who were already short of skilled labour.[98] The range of products made or stored in Park Royal is enormous. As in Acton Vale, the area is

Official Guide (1958), 39; Brent and Ealing L.B.s *Park Royal*; Goldsmiths' Hall, Acton Estate MS. B.III.13, no. 31.

[85] O.S. Map 6″, Mdx. XVI. NW., SW. (1874 edn.).

[86] Bacon, *Atlas of Lond.* (1886); O.S. Map 6″, Mdx. XVI. NW. (1894–6 edn.).

[87] Grange Mus. *Romance of Willesden Dux Oriental; Estates Exchange Yr. Bk.* (1932).

[88] *Acton Aerodrome* (Ealing L.B. libr. svce. 1978).

[89] Smith, *Ind. of Gtr. Lond.* 85.

[90] Grange Mus., Willesden educ. cttee. *Draft Rep.* (1919).

[91] *Acton Aerodrome*, addenda, June 1979.

[92] Acton U.D.C. *Rep. of M.O.H.* (1919), 42.

[93] Hall, *Ind. of Lond.* 128; *Geog. of Gtr. Lond.* ed. R. Clayton (1964), 138.   [94] Smith, *Ind. of Gtr. Lond.* 80.

[95] Ibid. 93–6.   [96] Hall, *Ind. of Lond.* 126–8.

[97] Brent and Ealing L.B.s *Park Royal*.

[98] Grange Mus., gen. files, Pk. Royal (*Willesden and Brent Chron.* 15, 22 Apr. 1977).

particularly useful as a warehousing and distribution centre for goods made elsewhere, and for service and spares depots for vehicles and household appliances. A few of the leading employers or manufacturers are noticed below.

McVitie & Price in 1902 built a biscuit-making factory in Waxlow Road, Harlesden, which employed 1,150 in 1919. By the Second World War 2,000 workers made 300 varieties of biscuit. In 1948 the company joined McFarlane Lang to become United Biscuits. A packing hall and warehouse were built between 1967 and 1969. In 1978 the factory, the largest biscuit factory in the western world, employed 1,600, with another 1,000 in the offices.[99]

Lancashire Dynamo & Crypto, Acton Lane, Harlesden, originated as Crypto Electrical Co., formed in 1899 in Bermondsey. It moved to Acton Lane in 1913 and employed 175 in 1919. In 1932 it merged with Lancashire Dynamo of Trafford Park (Manchester) and began making food-preparing machinery, employing 600 at Acton Lane in 1949 but reducing its staff in 1966.[1]

Park Royal Vehicles in Abbey Road, a division of British Leyland, originated as Hall, Lewis & Co., which began making railway waggons at Park Royal in 1919. In the 1920s it turned to motor car bodies and by 1925 it was also building motor buses. The firm was taken over in 1930 by Park Royal Coachworks and in 1946 became a public company as Park Royal Vehicles, chiefly making public vehicles. It became part of Leyland Motors in 1962 and employed c. 600 in 1978, mainly in building the new Titan double-decker motor buses, but in 1979 closure was announced for 1980.[2]

Rank Hovis McDougall Foods moved to Victoria Road from Tower Hill, London, in 1923, and made additions to its factory in 1936, 1956, and 1964. In 1978 the site was used for offices, garages, and warehousing, employing c. 420.[3]

Chesebrough-Pond also moved to Victoria Road in 1923, as the Chesebrough Manufacturing Co., which had formerly been in Holborn. The company took over Pond's Extract Co. of Perivale in 1956 and in 1964 Pond's, with three other companies which had become part of the group, moved to Park Royal. In 1978 the factory made Vaseline and Q-tips products, employing c. 350.[4]

H. J. Heinz & Co. opened a factory in Waxlow Road in 1925 for making bottled goods. By 1928 capacity had doubled and the introduction of can-making for baked beans led to steady expansion. The original site of 1¼ a. had increased to 48 a. by 1949 and 55 a. by 1964, while the staff of 2,000 in 1949 rose to c. 2,500 by 1953 and c. 3,500

in 1964. Administrative and research staff were moved to Hayes Park, in Hayes, in 1964, allowing a costly expansion programme on the factory site, where c. 2,500 were employed in 1978.[5]

Harold Wesley began making envelopes in the 1900s in Finsbury and moved to an 11-a. site in Acton Lane on the Willesden boundary in 1925. Part of the land was used for company housing, built by a subsidiary company called Wesley Estates. The factory made stationery and plastic articles, employing 1,000 at its peak but later only c. 150.[6]

Vandervell Products originated as the O. & S. Oilless Bearing Co. in Victoria Road and was bought in 1927 by Charles A. Vandervell, whose son G. A. Vandervell was made director. Known as Vandervell Products from 1933, the company produced the revolutionary thin-wall engine bearings from 1935, and a new factory, designed by Sir Aston Webb, was built in Western Avenue, where the staff was increased to 200. During the Second World War the company began making bearings for the Napier 'Sabre' aero engine, and after the war a special plant was built, producing 350 sets a week. From 1949 it made bearings for racing cars and from 1954 it raced its own car, the Vanwall Special. In 1958 Vanwalls won six of the ten championship races and dominated European Formula One racing, bringing British cars to the forefront and causing Acton to be compared with Modena, the Italian home of Ferrari. Racing ceased in 1959 on the retirement of G. A. (Tony) Vandervell and in 1967 the company was bought by G.K.N. Production of bearings was concentrated at Maidenhead (Berks.) and the Acton works were closed in 1970.[7]

Landis & Gyr, incorporated in 1912, built premises in Victoria Road in 1927, bringing together its offices from Stonebridge Park and its factory from Hampton Hill. The premises were later extended and a new office block was opened in 1961. Originally used for making electricity meters, from 1972 the factory also made heating and ventilating controls, and in 1979 most of the company's 1,000 employees worked in Acton.[8]

The British Can Co. was established by the American Can Co. in 1929 and fitted out a factory at Acton. In 1931 Metal Box took over British Can and continued to use the factory for making open-top cans for food processors, remaining a leading employer in the 1970s.[9]

Arthur Guinness, Son & Co. (Park Royal) bought c. 130 a. in Park Royal in 1933 and built what was the largest brewery in the country by 1949, when it had 1,100 workers. By 1976 the brewery employed between 750 and 1,000.[10]

Waterlow & Sons, printers, moved to a new factory in Twyford Abbey Road in 1936 from

[99] Inf. from communications officer; Grange Mus., 1 A 2 (*Willesden Cit.* 12 Aug. 1949).

[1] Grange Mus., 1 A 2 (*Willesden Cit.* 25 Mar. 1949); ibid. gen. files, ind. (*Willesden Mercury*, 16 Sept. 1966).

[2] Grange Mus., 1 A 2 (*Willesden Cit.* 17 Mar. 1950); inf. from the asst. commercial manager; *Evening Standard*, 4 Sept. 1979.

[3] Inf. from the pub. relations manager.

[4] Ibid.

[5] Inf. from the pub. relations asst.; Grange Mus., 1 A 2 (*Willesden Cit.* 15 July 1949, 10 Apr. 1964, 22 Jan. 1965).

[6] Grange Mus., 1 A 2 (*Willesden Cit.* 10 Mar. 1950); ibid. gen. files, ind.; Acton, *Official Guide* (1958), 45.

[7] D. Jenkinson and C. Posthumus, *Vanwall* (1975), 12, 22, 50, 143, 150, 153.

[8] Inf. from company sec.; Acton, *Official Guide* (1958), 35; (1963), 41.

[9] W. J. Reader, *Metal Box* (1976), 52, 68, 153; Brent and Ealing L.B.s *Park Royal*.

[10] Grange Mus., 1 A 2 (*Willesden Cit.* 30 Sept. 1949); ibid. gen. files, race relations (*Profile of Brent*, 1976).

premises in central London. In 1977 it had 700 employees.[11]

Elizabeth Arden moved its London factory from Coach and Horses Yard (Westm.) to a new factory at no. 140 Wales Farm Road in 1939. The company became part of Eli Lilly Pharmaceutical Co., U.S.A., in 1971. The Acton factory continued to make and distribute cosmetic products in the U.K., employing 311 in 1979.[12]

LOCAL GOVERNMENT. MANORIAL GOVERNMENT.

In 1294 the bishop of London successfully claimed view of frankpledge, infangthief, outfangthief, the assize of bread and of ale, fugitives, goods, and amercements of tenants in Acton, as part of his manor of Fulham.[13]

Views of frankpledge were held for the vill of Acton by 1383[14] and were taken at Fulham on the Sunday after Hocktide or another day generally in April. In 1750, and occasionally thereafter, the views for Ealing and Acton were taken together. The main business, apart from paying the common fine and appointing officers, concerned ditches and highways and the assize of bread and of ale. From the 16th century courts were increasingly concerned with grazing rights.[15]

The reeve collected quitrents for both Acton and Ealing. In 1697 it was stated that there were eight tenements in Acton from which the reeve was chosen every third year, Ealing tenants being chosen for the other years. The reeve received money, clothing, and food, and the reevable tenements were the only ones for which a heriot was paid.[16] Other manorial officers served Acton alone. Eight headboroughs were listed in the 14th and 15th centuries but only two by 1553. Two aletasters were recorded in 1393 and only one by 1486 and thereafter, until two were appointed in the early 19th century. A constable occurred in 1461 and there were two by 1528. Thereafter the two constables, with headboroughs and aletasters, were chosen annually until the views for Acton ceased c. 1815. In 1816 not enough tenants attended to form a jury, when the steward recommended that the vestry appoint manorial officers and resist encroachments by Chiswick inhabitants.[17] By that date business had been limited to elections and court baron transactions.

Land transfers took place at the court baron for Fulham until the 16th century, when some were recorded at the view of frankpledge. A court baron for Acton was held in 1607 and thereafter one for Ealing with Acton met regularly in the autumn for land transactions. By 1750 there were separate courts baron for Ealing and Acton. The view and the court baron were the only courts held every year and from the 17th century they were often adjourned over succeeding months. All the courts for Acton apparently were held in Fulham or Hammersmith. Court baron business continued to be recorded until 1951, by then mainly for extinguishment of quitrents, with a few conveyances and successions to property.[18] Enfranchisements began in 1846, most of the larger properties being enfranchised during the next 30 years.[19]

PARISH GOVERNMENT TO 1836.

Two churchwardens were recorded in 1554,[20] two overseers in 1583,[21] and two sidesmen from 1586 until the 17th century.[22] A parish clerk occurred in 1456[23] and two surveyors from 1627.[24] From 1777 the vestry clerk received a salary to carry out the business of the parish officers[25] and from the early 19th century he was also paid annually as an assistant overseer. The parish clerk and vestry clerk were different men in 1810.[26] Two inspectors of weights and balances were elected in 1798, and a beadle was appointed in 1800 to keep order in church, remove paupers, and report on new residents likely to become chargeable, for which he received a salary and uniform.[27] Churchwardens' accounts exist from 1674 to 1819, with a summary from the late 16th century,[28] overseers' accounts and poor rate books from 1772,[29] a highway surveyors' rate book from 1775 to 1811,[30] and vestry minutes from 1775.[31]

A vestry was held in 1586 with 14 present, but meetings were recorded only occasionally before 1775. The church rate, which included provision for the poor, was 3d. in the £ in 1675, when it raised £25 7s. 4d., and 4½d., in 1703, when it raised £51 10s. 9d. Eighteenth-century rates were generally annual and between 3d. and 4d. Vestries met in the church but were usually adjourned to the Cock, the King's Head, or another inn, until a new vestry room was built in 1781. Apart from elections, business mainly concerned apprenticeships and payments to the poor. Although the vestry met monthly, only the meetings which elected officers or made orders were minuted: eight meetings were recorded in 1776, six in 1780, and five in 1785. In 1800 the agenda was to be announced in advance and the monthly vestries on Sundays were to be confined to settling the overseers' accounts. The rector, William Antrobus, and his curates attended regularly from 1798. A select vestry was approved in 1821[32] but a meeting of 43 inhabitants reversed the decision, whereupon the open vestry continued to handle poor relief.[33]

[11] Grange Mus., gen. files, printers (*Kilburn Times*, 23 Sept. 1977).
[12] Inf. from the personnel officer.
[13] *Plac. de Quo Warr.* (Rec. Com.), 475.
[14] Following 3 paras. based on ct. rolls and bks. for Fulham manor including Acton or for Acton separately: Guildhall MSS. 10312/42–117 (1383–1682); 10832/1–138 (1682–1819); 10465/1–228 (1685–1951); P.R.O., SC 2/188/65–81 (1384–1462); SC 2/189/1–34 (1469–1612); SC 2/190/2–16 (1613–1722).
[15] P.R.O., SC 2/189/34.
[16] M.R.O., Acc. 538(1)/42/2.
[17] Vestry min. bk. (1801–22).
[18] Guildhall MS. 10465/228. Rolls for cts. leet and baron end in 1819.

[19] P.R.O., MAF 20/2/22.
[20] Guildhall MS. 9537/1.
[21] Ibid. 5.
[22] Chwdns. acct. bk. (1674–99), with notes from earlier records.
[23] Guildhall MS. 9171/5, f. 179.
[24] Chwdns. acct. bk.
[25] Vestry min. bk. (1775–1801).
[26] Ibid. (1801–22).
[27] Ibid. (1775–1801, 1801–22).
[28] At par. church.
[29] At par. church; one 19th-cent. rate bk. at Acton libr.
[30] At Ealing town hall.
[31] Vestry min. bk. (1775–1801) at par. church; later min. bks. (1801–68) at Ealing town hall.
[32] Chwdns. acct. bks. and vestry min. bks.
[33] Vestry min. bk. (1801–22), 9 Jan. 1822.

A separate poor rate apparently began in 1772.[34] The rate was 5*d.* in 1772, 7*d.* in 1790, and 20*d.* in 1801, and usually exceeded 1*s.* in the early 19th century, with two or more rates a year. In 1776 *c.* £220 was spent on the poor and in the early 1780s *c.* £290 a year.[35] From 1818 *c.* £1,000 was collected annually[36] and in 1836, the last year of parish poor relief, £1,174 was raised and £786 16*s.* was spent on the poor.[37] The parish was rated as a whole rather than by districts.[38]

Objections to the poor rate grew from 1785, when there were refusals to pay[39] and the vestry rejected a move to assess parishioners on improvements to their property.[40] Protests[41] eventually led to a revaluation by John Trumper and Richard Davis,[42] which thereafter formed the basis of rating. There were further disagreements in 1807 and 1821 and in 1823 Sir Richard Birnie, a resident, refused to sign the poor rate as a magistrate, whereupon some assessments were reduced.[43]

In 1629 William Ball of Willesden sold his house in Acton to the parish officers, who paid a rent for it as the parish house until 1681. There was no workhouse, but almshouses were built in 1725 on the site of a house in the Steyne which the churchwardens had bought from Charles Fox in 1681 for the use of the poor.[44] Pensioners were to be badged in 1706 but only one regular pension was paid, out of Ramsay's charity, in 1708.[45] Paupers were forbidden to keep dogs in 1792, when there were 14 receiving regular relief. Increasing poverty was met in 1799 by providing cheap meat, bread, and coals, paid for by voluntary subscriptions. In 1800 weekly allowances of 2*s.* 6*d.* to 12*s.* were arranged for 17 paupers and clothing was distributed yearly and half yearly to the aged.[46] A scheme of 1832 for part of Acton Green common to be cultivated by the poor was dropped when the bishop of London, after pressure from some residents and outsiders, withdrew his consent.[47] Acton was thought not to be a poor parish in 1828, when only three able bodied men were unemployed.[48]

By the late 18th century the vestry was assuming several functions of the manorial court. In 1792 it ordered that pigs should be controlled and from 1785 it dealt with encroachments on the wastes and lanes. In 1792 six inhabitants were allowed to inclose waste in front of their houses on making payments into the parish funds,[49] and compensation was also paid by the Grand Junction Canal Co., the G.W.R., and others for removal of common rights.[50] The vestry in 1810 sued a Hammersmith builder, who had erected six small houses on his strip in Church field, and won confirmation of common rights,[51] and it viewed an inclosure on Old Oak common in 1826 to protect the commoners there.[52] It also began to press for the general inclosure of wastes such as Acton Green common in 1794[53] and of all commons in 1805 and again in 1813, although without success. In 1816 gatehouses were planned at the entrances to the common fields and a gate was to be put up at the north end of Acton Lane, to protect South field.[54]

A temporary board of health, similar to one in Ealing, was formed in 1831 to counter the threat of cholera, with the rector as president and eleven other members.[55]

LOCAL GOVERNMENT AFTER 1836. Acton joined Brentford poor law union in 1836.[56] The vestry in 1848 appointed a short-lived committee to help the medical officers and guardians carry out the Nuisances Removal Act.[57] From the late 1850s there was disagreement between those who wished for improvements to attract new residents and those who wanted to do nothing until an increased population made improvements necessary. A meeting was called in 1859 to consider improving the footpaths and lighting the streets. Vestry meetings were moved from mid afternoon to 7 p.m. despite opposition, and those concerned with improvement drew such large numbers that they were adjourned to the George every time. In 1861 it was resolved to meet again before 3 p.m. and in 1862 it was finally agreed to adopt street lighting.[58]

In 1865 the Local Government Act, 1858,[59] was adopted to deal with sewerage,[60] and a local board of 12 members met twice monthly from 1866. A small house in High Street was rented for offices and a salaried clerk was appointed. The board also took over responsibility for the highways and for street lighting. A salaried surveyor and inspector of nuisances was appointed and committees for works and for finance were formed in 1866. Other committees were formed later, often of a temporary nature, such as a drainage committee in 1883 and a fire brigade committee in 1899. The local board exercised strict control over building, which led to criticism in 1869 and accusations of partiality. Examples of discrimination, supplied by 'Lucifer Doubtful' and published in the *Acton Press*, prompted the board to print a detailed refutation. Bylaws operated against the small builder, who could not afford to observe the regulations, and it was alleged that many sewers were being put

---

[34] Rest of subsection based on overseers' acct. bks.
[35] *Abstract of Returns by Overseers, 1787*, H.C. 1st ser. ix. 628.
[36] *Poor Rate Returns*, suppl. H.C. 556, p. 100 (1822), v.
[37] *Poor Law Com. 2nd Rep.* H.C. 595-II, pp. 214–15 (1836), xxix(2).
[38] *Rep. Com. Poor Laws*, H.C. 44, p. 81*f* (1834), xxxv.
[39] Vestry min. bk. (1775–1801), 2 Nov. 1785, 31 Oct. 1786.
[40] Ibid. 30 Nov. 1785.
[41] Vestry min. bk. (1801–22).
[42] Ibid. 2 Feb. 1805.
[43] Vestry min. bks. (1801–22, 1822–57).
[44] Ealing libr., Acton notes dep. by B. J. Taylor, 98, 89, 28.
[45] Chwdns. acct. bk. (1701–67).
[46] Vestry min. bk. (1775–1801).
[47] Ibid. (1822–57), 8 Mar. 1832, 18 Apr., 7 July 1833.

[48] *Rep. Sel. Cttee. on Police of Metropolis*, H.C. 533, p. 218 (1828), vi.
[49] Vestry min. bk. (1775–1801).
[50] Ibid. (1801–22), 4 Feb. 1805; M.R.O., Acc. 531/59, 65.
[51] Vestry min. bk. (1801–22).
[52] Ibid. (1822–57).
[53] Ibid. (1775–1801).
[54] Ibid. (1801–22).
[55] Ibid. (1822–57).
[56] G. A. Simonon, 'Treatment of Poor in Acton, 1601–1834' (Thos. Huxley Coll. of Educ. thesis, 1971), 47.
[57] Vestry min. bk. (1822–57), 21 Dec. 1848, 7 June 1849; below, pub. svces.
[58] Vestry min. bk. (1857–68).
[59] 21 & 22 Vic. c. 98.
[60] Vestry min. bk. (1857–68).

down in Horn Lane to accommodate gentlemen, while the badly flooded parts of Acton Green and around Bollo bridge had very few.[61]

Acton became a U.D. under the Local Government Act, 1894, and was divided into North, East, and West wards, returning 7, 4, and 4 members respectively. Four different wards, North-East, North-West, South-East, and South-West, each with 4 councillors, were created in 1906.[62] The incorporation of Acton as a borough, discussed as early as 1900,[63] was achieved with the grant of a charter in 1921.[64] The borough council consisted of a mayor, 6 aldermen, and 24 councillors, representing the 4 wards of the former U.D.[65] Conservatives controlled the council in the 1930s and the Labour party after the Second World War.[66] Acton remained a separate M.B. until 1965, when it was included in Ealing L.B.

BOROUGH OF ACTON. *Gules, an oak tree issuing from the base proper; on a chief or charged with a pale gules the arms of the Middlesex County Council, between on the dexter an open book and on the sinister a cog wheel, both proper*　　[Granted 1921]

An office was built by the local board in High Street, at the foot of Acton hill, in 1870.[67] In an Italianate Gothic style, it was used after 1910 by private firms until its demolition *c.* 1930.[68] New municipal offices on the Priory estate, next to the swimming baths, were opened in 1910,[69] accommodating both the council and departments which previously had been dispersed. A three-storeyed building, with its main entrance in Winchester Street, it was of red brick with stone facings in a free Renaissance style. The adjacent High Street site was opened as the King George V garden, but eventually was used for the new town hall, opened in 1939, which contained an assembly room.[70] After the formation of Ealing L.B., Acton town hall housed an information bureau, cash office, and the registrar of births, deaths, and marriages.[71]

Acton formed part of the parliamentary constituency of Middlesex until its inclusion in 1885 in the new Ealing division, which also contained Chiswick and returned a Conservative member. In 1918 Acton became a separate division of

Middlesex, returning a Conservative, as it did thereafter except between 1929 and 1931 and between 1945 and 1959, when there was a Labour member. As Ealing–Acton, the constituency was enlarged to include part of east Ealing and Twyford, with effect from 1974.[72]

PUBLIC SERVICES. A public conduit was constructed in High Street in the grounds of the Bell, later Suffolk House, by Thomas Thorney, who in 1612 left a rent charge on the adjacent Conduit close for its upkeep.[73] In 1755 a Chancery order confirmed the public use of the conduit and continuation of the rent charge.[74] In 1819 the rector paid for a new pump, as the conduit was in disrepair, and sunk a tank to exploit the spring.[75] The conduit later fell into disuse, allegedly because of the opening of the burial ground near by in 1863.[76] The pump, commemorated by a plaque in High Street, was eventually placed in Gunnersbury Park museum.

In addition to the medicinal springs at Acton wells,[77] several houses had their own wells. Butlers in Horn Lane had one in 1633[78] and access was granted in 1670 to a pump there;[79] Friars Place Farm had a pump behind the house;[80] two deep wells were found under Derwentwater House on its demolition.[81] Edward Tuffin dug a well in front of his house in 1666, and there was also a pump at the upper end of Acton town, by the main highway.[82] A parish well in 1832 was rendered unusable by a nearby privy,[83] perhaps the well dug in a watercourse by a Mr. Trafford, who put a tub there for the use of the inhabitants. Probably just west of the Steyne, it was known in 1802 as Trafford's well.[84]

In 1831 Acton was said to be plentifully supplied[85] but in 1848 the vestry's sanitary committee reported a general want of pure water. In 1855 a vestry was called to consider the serious shortage in East Acton, where the poor apparently had to rely on ponds.[86] In 1861 the Grand Junction Waterworks Co.'s area was allowed to include Acton[87] and in 1879 the company laid pipes to supply Acton Green.[88] By 1893 Acton obtained most of its water from the company as a continuous supply, although some railway cottages at Willesden junction were supplied by the L. & N.W.R. from a deep well in the chalk near Watford.[89] From 1903 Acton was supplied by the Metropolitan Water Board, which took over the Grand Junction and West Middlesex districts.[90] In 1908 the U.D.C. was

[61] Ealing town hall, local bd. and cttee. min. bks.; ibid. Acton and Southall misc. files, no. 5.
[62] M.R.O., *Rep. Local Inqs.* 1889–1912 (Acton U.D. 1909); *Kelly's Dir. Mdx.* (1908).
[63] *Acton Gaz.* 4 Jan. 1901.
[64] *The Times,* 26 Nov. 1917, 13 Oct. 1921.
[65] Ibid. 7, 17 Nov. 1921.
[66] Ibid. 3 Nov. 1936, 2 Nov. 1938, 14 May 1949, 10 May 1952.
[67] Ibid. 5 Apr. 1909.　　[68] Rowland, *Street Names,* 35.
[69] Baker, *Acton,* 281.
[70] Acton libr., brochure for opening of town hall, 1939; datestone.
[71] Ealing L.B. *Official Guide* [1966], 77.
[72] C. Hankinson, *Political Hist. of Ealing, 1832–1970* (Ealing L.B. [1971]); election results in *The Times.*
[73] Guildhall MS. 10371/1 (booklet, 'Chars. of Acton').

[74] Baker, *Acton,* 40; papers in par. church.
[75] *14th Rep. Com. Char.* H.C. 382, p. 171 (1826), xii.
[76] Baker, *Acton,* 40.
[77] Above, social.　　[78] M.R.O., Acc. 276/22.
[79] Ibid. 23.
[80] Ealing Local Hist. Soc. *Local Historian* (1966), i. 10.
[81] Baker, *Acton,* 109.
[82] Guildhall MS. 10312/102 (ct. baron 18 Apr. 1666).
[83] Vestry min. bk. (1822–57).
[84] Ibid. (1801–22).
[85] Lewis, *Topog. Dict. Eng.* (1831), i. 8.
[86] Vestry min. bk. (1822–57).
[87] 24 & 25 Vic. c. 151.
[88] Guildhall MS. 12697 (deed 30 Oct. 1879).
[89] Acton local bd. *Rep. of M.O.H.* (1893), 15–16.
[90] L. J. Flowerdew and G. C. Berry, *Lond.'s Water Supply* (1953), facing p. 44.

St. Mary's Church in 1795

Acton House *c.* 1800

ACTON

CHISWICK: HEATHFIELD HOUSE c. 1800

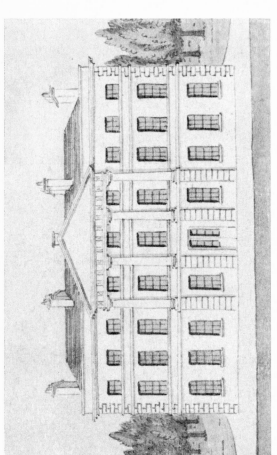

EALING GROVE c. 1800

CHISWICK: SUTTON COURT IN 1844

CHISWICK: MR. STEVENSON'S HOUSE c. 1800

permitted to seek funds to sink an artesian well, which thereafter supplied the public baths,[91] and in 1909 a well was sunk for Messrs. Panhard & Levasseur in Warple Way. A few other factories south of Acton Vale also used deep artesian wells by 1931.[92]

Bad sanitation and drainage were reported by the vestry's board of health in 1832, when householders were ordered to remove nuisances and it was recommended that the pond at the bottom of East Acton be filled in. The surveyors were to clear out the cesspool at the back of the churchyard and the culvert at the bottom of East Acton. In 1834 a rate was voted to make a proper sewer to improve Horn Lane. The sanitary committee which was formed in 1848 inspected nearly 400 premises and ascribed much disease to poor drainage and sanitation. The committee was disbanded in 1849, as its work was said to be finished.[93]

A nuisance removal committee was appointed under the Metropolis Local Management Act, 1855,[94] and accordingly a sewer rate was made in 1857. The Metropolitan Board of Works in 1857 levied money in Acton, probably because drainage passed into the board's area to the east. In 1858 the parish refused to pay a second levy or to make the poor-rate assessment available to the board. The board brought an action in 1861, after demanding three years' rates, which had not been paid when Acton local board was formed. Meanwhile the parish had appointed a salaried nuisance inspector in 1859 and a lower paid clerk and inspector in 1863.[95] When the local board came into being in 1866 its first action was to order a report on drainage.[96] The resulting plan, for drainage from Bollo bridge to Acton Green and for the main sewer there, was carried out at once, while private drainage was strictly supervised.[97]

In 1882 the Metropolitan Board of Works obtained an injunction to prevent the connexion of any more houses in Acton to sewers that discharged into London's sewers, so ending Acton's use of Stamford brook. In 1884, after the rapid spread of housing, the local board's drainage committee chose the alum, blood, and clay method of sewage treatment, whereupon works were built at the southern end of Warple Way.[98] Outlets were made into the Thames at Chiswick Eyot[99] and the new drainage system[1] was completed in 1888.[2] Septic tanks and filters were completed in 1902 in Warple Way.[3] By 1904

the sewage of nearly half the residents drained into the London system,[4] and in 1905 the U.D.C. secured an Act to allow all sewage to pass into the L.C.C.'s sewers, with only storm water draining into the Thames.[5] A scheme for the southern part of the district was finished in 1908 and one for the northern part was adopted,[6] although the northern relief sewer had not been laid in 1911.[7] In 1956 an agreement was made for Acton's sewage to be discharged into the West Middlesex drainage system.[8]

In 1866 the local board sought tenders for the removal of house refuse[9] and in 1893 scavenging was still done by contractors.[10] In 1902 the U.D.C. bought a site in Southfield Road for a dust destructor and electricity plant, but it was only after rubbish piled near the cemetery had become offensive that a destructor was built, on $3\frac{1}{2}$ a. near the Friars in Wales Farm Road, and opened in 1909.[11] By 1928 all rubbish was burnt in Wales Farm Road.[12] In 1955 house refuse was disposed of outside the borough.[13]

Gas lighting, under the Lighting and Watching Act, 1833, was adopted in 1862, when seven inspectors were appointed.[14] The area lit, known as the Town district, covered the high road from Berrymead Priory to Twyford Avenue, including the few existing side streets, the Steyne, and the lower end of Horn Lane.[15] In 1866 the new local board trebled the number of lamps to 79.[16] The Brentford Gas Co. was the supplier until 1926,[17] when it became part of the Gas Light and Coke Co. After nationalization in 1949 the supplier was the North Thames Gas Board.[18]

Under a provisional order of 1903 and after pressure from the Board of Trade[19] the U.D.C. arranged for the Metropolitan Electric Supply Co. to provide current to the council's transformer at the Friars, Wales Farm Road,[20] which was built in 1904. Service began in 1905 and in the first year cables were laid in c. 36 streets. Heavy costs led to the transfer of the municipal undertaking to the company in 1911, after much local dissension.[21] The company thereafter supplied electricity, buying the Wales Farm Road works in 1913. A station in Southfield Road, on land bought by the council in 1902,[22] supplied much of the borough in 1922[23] but by 1940 only two new substations, in Lynton Road and Leamington Park, were in use.[24] After nationalization the supplier was the Southern Electricity Board.[25]

A cage or round house beside the church was

[91] The Times, 2 Nov. 1908.
[92] Acton libr., artesian wells, copy of sketch map from Water Resources Bd. [1971]; Acton M.B. Rep. of M.O.H. (1931), 9.   [93] Vestry min. bk. (1822–57).
[94] Ibid. 3 Apr. 1856.   [95] Ibid. (1857–68).
[96] Local bd. min. bk. i. 16, 18.   [97] Ibid. 37 and passim.
[98] Acton drainage cttee. mins. (1883–8) in Ealing town hall.   [99] Ealing libr., Acc. 19/1, sewer easement 1886.
[1] Kelly's Dir. Mdx. (1890).
[2] Acton local bd. Rep. of M.O.H. (1888), 3, 5.
[3] Acton Gaz. 4 Jan. 1901; Acton U.D.C. Rep. of M.O.H. (1900), 3; ibid. (1903), 25.
[4] Acton U.D.C. Rep. of M.O.H. (1904), 46.
[5] 5 Edw. VII, c. 203 (Local).
[6] The Times, 10 Sept. 1908.   [7] Baker, Acton, 298.
[8] Ealing town hall, Acton Acts etc.
[9] Local bd. min. bk. i. 30.
[10] Acton local bd. Rep. of M.O.H. (1893), 17.

[11] Acton Gaz. 22 Feb. 1901; Ealing libr., Acc. 19/1; Baker, Acton, 298.
[12] Acton, Official Guide (1928), 37.
[13] Ibid. (1955), 12.
[14] Vestry min. bk. (1857–68).
[15] Ealing town hall, lighting inspectors' min. bk. 4 Dec. 1863 (recte 1862) to 19 Mar. 1866.
[16] Local bd. min. bk. i. 29.
[17] Kelly's Dir. Mdx. (1890).
[18] S. Everard, Gas Light and Coke Co. (1949), 327, 382.
[19] Baker, Acton, 290–2.
[20] Ealing town hall, Acton var. cttees. min. bk. ii (1900–5), elect. subcttee. passim.
[21] Baker, Acton, 290–2; The Times, 16 Nov. 1910, 1 Mar. 1911.   [22] Ealing libr., Acc. 19/1.
[23] The Times, 18 Apr. 1922.
[24] Kelly's Dir. Acton (1940).
[25] Acton, Official Guide [c. 1952], 14.

rebuilt in 1815 to incorporate the new school-room. Burglaries induced residents to subscribe in 1818 to a watch: three watchmen were employed for the town and one for East Acton, supervised nightly by the parish constable and others.[26] Only two watchmen patrolled the town in 1828, after a fall in subscriptions, but it was claimed that crime had been greatly reduced.[27] In 1819 two paupers were clothed and appointed to remove vagrants.[28]

Acton was included in the new Metropolitan Police Area in 1829.[29] Police broke up a riot at the King's Arms in 1837.[30] There was a station in 1845[31] and thereafter one remained at or near the site, no. 250 High Street,[32] with 2 inspectors, 2 sergeants, and 37 constables in 1890.[33] A magistrates' court was built in 1907 by the county council[34] in Winchester Street on the Priory estate.

A fire at Steyne mills in 1866, attended by engines from Chiswick and Hammersmith, prompted a call for local appliances.[35] In 1868 a fire brigade was formed and a manual engine was bought by the local board, being kept first in a shed by the churchyard and from the 1870s behind the local board offices. A fire station with a watch tower, and a mortuary at the rear, was built in 1899 on the north side of High Street at the bottom of Acton hill. A steam fire engine was bought and an engineer employed, helped by local volunteers. In 1936 the council purchased the sites of 15 houses on the east side of Gunnersbury Lane for a new fire station,[36] which was used from 1938. The former station was a welfare centre and kitchen for old people in 1979. Services were later provided by the Middlesex fire brigade.[37] By 1955 an ambulance and fire station had been built on the south side of Western Avenue.[38]

The vestry retained two residents in 1796 to attend the poor in pharmacy, surgery, and midwifery, at a salary which was doubled in 1813.[39] Acton cottage hospital, the gift of J. Passmore Edwards, was built on land in Gunnersbury Lane given by Lord Rothschild and opened in 1898 with 12 beds.[40] It was financed by voluntary subscriptions and gifts, which also paid for later extensions. Accommodation was nearly doubled in 1904[41] and raised to 30 beds in 1909, when a children's ward, operating theatre, and out-

patients' department were also added.[42] Patients paid according to their means from 1920,[43] when there were 35 beds.[44] In 1923 a further extension of 17 beds was built as part of the town's war memorial and praised by Neville Chamberlain, as Minister of Health.[45] Extensions in 1928, which included a nurses' hostel, gave a total of 62 beds. There were 72 in 1934 and 1935[46] and, after upgrading during the Second World War, 84 by 1958.[47] After nationalization the hospital was in the North-West Metropolitan region and in 1979 it was in the Ealing, Hammersmith, and Hounslow area of the North-West Thames region. It had 84 beds, for acute cases, at the end of 1977.[48]

Infectious cases were being sent to Willesden in 1899.[49] In 1902 the U.D.C. bought the Friars estate of 12¼ a. in Wales Farm Road for an isolation hospital and other purposes,[50] and the hospital, which was to take no smallpox cases,[51] opened in 1905 with 33 beds in three separate pavilions, while the Friars formed the administration block.[52] In 1909 a new pavilion of 30 beds was built[53] and there were 88 beds by 1931.[54] In 1939 the hospital was managed by the Acton and Wembley joint hospital committee,[55] but after 1946 it became an annexe to the Central Middlesex hospital in Acton Lane, Willesden.[56] From 1953 it was linked with Acton hospital for administration and nursing and by 1963 it was called Leamington Park hospital, with 96 beds for geriatric cases.[57] In 1979 it was in the Brent and Harrow area of the North-West Thames region.[58]

A collection was made for Acton general dispensary in 1877[59] and a public dispensary was operated in Mill Hill Grove in 1890.[60] In 1901 the Acton provident dispensary was opened at no. 1 Mill Hill Grove and directed by the staff of the cottage hospital.[61] In 1979 Acton health centre was held at nos. 35–61 Church Road and the community health services were directed from Avenue House, nos. 43–7 Avenue Road.[62]

There were privately owned baths at no. 91 Shakespeare Road in 1886.[63] The council in 1904 opened public swimming and spray baths on the Berrymead Priory site. Water came from an artesian well beneath the building, and by 1924 it had its own electricity, which also supplied the public library and municipal offices.[64] Another

[26] Vestry min. bk. (1801–22).
[27] Rep. Sel. Cttee. on Police of Metropolis, H.C. 533, pp. 216–20 (1828), vi.
[28] Vestry min. bk. (1801–22).   [29] 10 Geo. IV, c. 44.
[30] The Times, 3 May 1837.
[31] P.O. Dir. Six Home Counties (1845).
[32] Kelly's Dir. Mdx. (1890); Acton, Official Guide (1928), 22; (1934), 6.
[33] Kelly's Dir. Mdx. (1890).
[34] Datestone.
[35] Para. based on Baker, Acton, 283–5; Ealing town hall, Acton fire brigade mins. 30 May 1899 to 4 Apr. 1901, pp. 1, 3, 33.
[36] Ealing libr., Acc. 19/2.
[37] Acton, Official Guide [c. 1952], 14.
[38] Ibid. (1955), map.
[39] Vestry min. bks. (1775–1801, 1801–22).
[40] Acton U.D.C. Rep. of M.O.H. (1897), 4; Boro. of Acton (brochure, 1922).
[41] The Times, 6 Oct. 1904.
[42] Ibid. 13 May 1909; Boro. of Acton (brochure, 1922).
[43] The Times, 30 July 1920.

[44] Acton U.D.C. Rep. of M.O.H. (1920), 4.
[45] The Times, 13 July 1923.
[46] Acton, Official Guide (1932), 38; (1936), 13.
[47] Ibid. [c. 1952], 15; (1958), 12.
[48] Hospitals Year Bk. (1979), 134.
[49] Acton U.D.C. Rep. of M.O.H. (1899), 14.
[50] Ealing libr., Acc. 19/1; Acton Gaz. 11 Jan. 1901.
[51] Acton Gaz. 10 May 1901.
[52] Acton U.D.C. Rep. of M.O.H. (1904), 41; The Times, 19 Jan. 1905.
[53] The Times, 25 Dec. 1909.
[54] Acton M.B. Rep. of M.O.H. (1929), 6; (1931), 8.
[55] Acton, Official Guide [1939], 21.
[56] Ibid. [c. 1952], 15.   [57] Ibid. [1963], 13.
[58] Hospitals Year Bk. (1979), 130.
[59] Acton libr., churches, All Saints' 'Occasional Paper', June 1877.
[60] Kelly's Dir. Mdx. (1890).
[61] Acton Gaz. 4 Jan., 29 Mar. 1901.
[62] Hospitals Year Bk. (1979), 134.
[63] Ealing, Acton Dir. (1886).
[64] Acton Gaz. 4 Jan. 1901; Acton, Official Guide (1924), 26.

room for social functions, the King's room, was built c. 1928.[65]

There was a private lending library at no. 2 Churchfield Villas, at the corner of Myrtle Road, in 1886[66] and a subscription library near the U.D.C.'s offices in High Street before 1901.[67] The free public library at the corner of High Street and Winchester Street was opened in 1900, as a Tudor Gothic building of red brick with stone dressings, named after Passmore Edwards, who paid most of the building costs.[68] Branch libraries were built at the corner of Acton Lane and Beaconsfield Road, and at West Acton, near the Underground station, by 1952, but both had been replaced by mobile libraries by 1957. In 1966 there remained the central library and a branch at Acton Green.[69]

The churchyard was the only burial ground until 1863, when the vestry bought 1 a. on the south side of Church Lane, later Churchfield Road West.[70] In 1893 the U.D.C. bought 13 a. of Lower Place farm, at the junction of Horn Lane and Willesden Lane, where it built two chapels and opened 6½ a. as a cemetery in 1895.[71] Further portions were consecrated in 1915 and 1926.[72] In 1979 Churchfield Road cemetery was being cleared to make way for a public garden as part of a plan for the town centre. The mortuary behind the fire station had been replaced by one in Petersfield Road by 1940.[73]

In 1881 the local board acquired from the Ecclesiastical Commissioners the wastes and commons, and part of the largest, Acton Green common, thereupon became a recreation ground.[74] In 1888 the local board bought 21 a. from the Goldsmiths' Company and 4 a. from the Ecclesiastical Commissioners and laid out Acton park, between Churchfield Road East and Uxbridge Road,[75] with sports facilities.[76] Land in Bollo Bridge Road was bought in 1889 and 1890 to form South Acton recreation ground of 4 a.; the site of Acton ponds was bought from the Round estate in 1903 and laid out as Twyford gardens; Woodlands, with c. 6 a., was purchased in 1903 for the county school and a public park; North Acton playing fields of c. 22 a. were opened in 1908[77] and included a moated site, formerly part of Friars Place Farm; Southfield Road playing fields were formed from 12½ a. bought

from the Wilkinson Sword Co. in 1908; and Springfield park, Horn Lane, was formed from 5½ a. bought in 1920. By 1924 the district had 84 a. of parks and open spaces,[78] increased to 95 a. by 1934[79] and to 112 a. by 1952,[80] excluding private sports grounds.[81]

CHURCHES. A church dedicated to St. Mary existed by 1231, when Walter, rector of Acton, held a house from Peter FitzAlulf.[82] The church served the whole parish until 1872.[83] The benefice was a rectory in the gift of the bishop of London.[84]

The church was valued at £13 6s. 8d. in 1291,[85] and again in 1428.[86] In 1536 and 1549 it was valued at £14,[87] but c. 1570 the rectory and tithes were farmed to John Garraway for £50 a year.[88] The living consisted in 1650 of the parsonage house with outbuildings and 1 a. of pasture, valued at £10 a year, and the tithes valued at £190 a year;[89] the total was reduced to £160 for taxes in 1646 and 1653.[90] In the 18th century the total value was £300 to £350.[91] The tithes were valued at £759 in 1806,[92] £1,018 c. 1830, and £1,037 in 1851,[93] the sum at which the tithe rent charge was fixed. In 1889 the incumbent also received c. £165 a year in fees.[94]

The parsonage house, near the Steyne and Horn Lane, was rebuilt c. 1725 by William Hall, rector 1719-26, who died before moving in.[95] In 1889 it had 4 reception rooms and 14 bedrooms, with outbuildings and c. 1 a.[96] A new Rectory, on almost the same site, was built in 1925[97] and the old one was demolished.

No chantries were recorded in 1548,[98] although in Elizabeth I's reign a small piece of land, valued at 1d., was said to be for the maintenance of obits and lamps.[99] A fraternity of St. Mary had existed in 1464, 1477, and 1479.[1] Mrs Sarah Crayle left 40s. a year in 1730 for an annual sermon, as did Mrs. Ann Crayle in 1759 and John Cordy in 1799.[2]

Richard de Pertenhale, rector 1361-?1381, was certified as a pluralist in 1366, when he was appointed to a minor canonry in London.[3] John Holborn, rector 1405-26, held benefices in London,[4] Dr. Daniel Featley, rector 1628-43, also held Lambeth,[5] and Dr. Bruno Ryves, rector

[65] Acton, *Official Guide* (1928), 26.
[66] *Ealing, Acton Dir.* (1886).
[67] *Acton Gaz.* 18 Jan. 1901.
[68] Acton, *Official Guide* (1924), 28; Baker, *Acton*, 286.
[69] Acton, *Official Guide* (1930, 1932, 1939, c. 1952, 1957); Ealing L.B. *Guide* (1966), 59.
[70] Vestry min. bk. (1857-68).
[71] Ealing libr., Acc. 19/1; Acton local bd. *Rep. of M.O.H.* (1893), 17; Baker, *Acton*, 304.
[72] Acton libr., programme for consecration svce. 27 Jan. 1915; *The Times*, 2 Nov. 1926.
[73] Above; *Kelly's Dir. Acton* (1940).
[74] Guildhall MSS. 12697 (ind. May 1882); 12353 (ind. Aug. 1888).
[75] Rest of para. based on Ealing libr., Acc. 19/1-2.
[76] Baker, *Acton*, 299-300.
[77] *The Times*, 4 Aug. 1908.
[78] Acton, *Official Guide* (1924), 48.
[79] Briggs, *Mdx. Old and New*, 174.
[80] Acton, *Official Guide* [c. 1952].
[81] Above, social.
[82] *Early Charters of St. Paul's*, 264-7.
[83] Below, All Saints'.

[84] Newcourt, *Rep.* i. 569.
[85] *Tax. Eccl.* (Rec. Com.), 176.
[86] *Feud. Aids*, iii. 378.
[87] *Valor Eccl.* (Rec. Com.), i. 433; P.R.O., E 301/34, no. 161.
[88] P.R.O., REQ 2/211/3.
[89] *Home Counties Mag.* i. 224.
[90] Bodl. MS. Rawl. D. 715, ff. 1, 5.
[91] Guildhall MSS. 9550; 9556, p. 27; 9557, f. 20.
[92] Vestry min. bk. (1822-57), 16 Jan. 1822.
[93] P.R.O., HO 129/134/5/1/1; *Rep. Com. Eccl. Revenues*, 634.
[94] Guildhall MS. 10731/1.
[95] Baker, *Acton*, 164.
[96] Guildhall MS. 10731/1.
[97] Rowland, *Street Names*, 31.
[98] P.R.O., E 301/34, no. 161.
[99] Ibid. E 178/1503.
[1] Guildhall MSS. 9171/5, f. 353; 6, ff. 225v., 277.
[2] Ibid. MS. 10731/1.
[3] *Reg. Sudbury* (Cant. & York Soc.), ii. 159.
[4] Hennessy, *Novum Rep.* 71, 107, 436.
[5] Ibid. 71 and n.

1661–77, was dean of Windsor and Wolverhampton. A former chaplain to Charles I, Ryves was the author of *Mercurius Rusticus* and instrumental in prosecuting Richard Baxter.[6] Anthony Saunders, rector 1677–1719, was chancellor of St. Paul's from 1672;[7] Dr. Edward Cobden, rector 1726–64, held the prebend of Caddington Minor from 1726, a London benefice from 1730, and the archdeaconry of London from 1742;[8] William Antrobus, rector 1797–1852, also held a London benefice from 1794.[9]

A chaplain served the cure in 1377,[10] 1456, and 1458.[11] In 1549 Hugh Turnbull, rector 1542–63, was paying a priest out of his income to serve the cure,[12] as he still did in 1554.[13] Roger Cox served as assistant curate for most of Featley's incumbency,[14] Ryves had an assistant curate in 1664 and 1673,[15] and Cobden had as many as three curates, one a schoolmaster.[16] The assistant curate received £10 a year in 1768, £90 a year *c.* 1800, and £150 *c.* 1835.[17] There was at least one from the 18th century.

In 1637 a new communion table had been railed in and the church repaired, but the young were not properly catechized or instructed, because of failure to send children and servants to church.[18] Daniel Featley was known to be an exact observer of ceremonial, which caused a company of Metropolis Volunteers, lodging in Acton, to break into the church in August 1642, damaging the fittings.[19] Another report placed the incident later in that year, after the battle of Brentford, when soldiers also pulled down the font, smashed the windows, and set fire to the rector's outbuildings.[20] Featley's livings were sequestrated in 1643 and he complained that all his personal goods, rents, and a copyhold house were also seized.[21] He was succeeded by Philip Nye, minister 1643–54, described as an able preacher in 1650, assisted by John Nye,[22] and then by Thomas Elford, who was ejected in 1661.[23]

In 1685 Acton, with other parishes, was to keep the registers with more care and record the names of stranger preachers.[24] During the 18th century services were held twice every Sunday with two sermons, communion was taken once a month by between 20 and 40, and children were catechized in Lent. In 1766 evening prayers were held every Saturday and morning prayers on Wednesdays and Saturdays.[25] A piece of waste was added to the churchyard, which was nearly full, in 1792.[26] By 1810 the number of communicants had risen to 50 and St. Mary's could seat only 400 out of a population of 1,400.[27] In 1851, when attendance in the morning averaged 550, with 90 Sunday school children, there were 700 free sittings and 50 others,[28] but in 1865 the church was said to seat only 500 adults.[29] Attendance in 1903 was 729 in the morning and 476 in the evening.[30] The church ran St. Mary's mission house at no. 12 Priory Terrace, High Street, from the early 1880s, and a room and working men's club in the Steyne, possibly in the mission room and parish club house built at the back of the old Rectory stables and leased to the parish in 1879.[31]

The church of *ST. MARY* was rebuilt at least once on its existing site at the corner of High Street and Market Place. The building in the early 18th century was thought from its style to be of the 12th or 13th centuries, of flint and a soft stone. It was small with low walls and narrow windows,[32] and had a chancel, nave, and two aisles *c.* 1795, by which date the walls had been rebuilt in brick.[33] An altar table of black marble from Ashford-in-the-Water (Derb.), thought to be of the 12th or 13th century and probably from the medieval church, was repaired and placed in the existing church *c.* 1960.[34] In 1504 Richard Pontesbury, mercer of London, left stone towards paving the chancel and money to make a chapel on its north side, dedicated to the Virgin Mary, St. Anne, and St. Margaret and similarly paved.[35] There was a chapel of St. Catherine on the south side of the church by 1534.[36] The chancel was much decayed by the late 17th century and was repaired and whitewashed. The west tower was described as lofty and handsome in 1705 and was thought to be early 16th-century. It was square, of brick with stone dressings, and had a peal of six bells;[37] in 1766 it was cased with brick[38] and later had an octagonal turret at one corner.[39] The cupola needed repair in 1800 and again in 1821, when the surveyor recommended that it be replaced by a roof of lead or copper.[40]

The churchwardens in 1768 were to replace the vestry room with an octagonal one against the south side of the tower.[41] In 1780 repairs included making a coved ceiling over the body of the church, painting the gallery columns and wainscot, and building a new vestry room.[42] A north gallery was suggested in 1794, and changes to the gallery and pews were planned in 1802[43]

[6] *D.N.B.*; below, prot. nonconf.
[7] Hennessy, *Novum Rep.* 13, 71.
[8] Ibid. 7, 19, 71, 99.
[9] Ibid. 71, 93.
[10] Guildhall MS. 9171/1, f. 50v.
[11] Ibid. 5, f. 179; *Cal. Close,* 1454–61, 351.
[12] P.R.O., E 301/34, no. 161.
[13] Guildhall MS. 9537/1.
[14] Ibid. 13; 14, f. 31; 15, f. 49.
[15] Ibid. 16, f. 44; 20, p. 49.
[16] Ibid. MS. 9550.
[17] Ibid. MS. 9557, f. 20; *Rep. Com. Eccl. Revenues,* 634.
[18] Guildhall MS. 9583/1.
[19] *Cal. S.P. Dom.* 1641–3, 372.
[20] *D.N.B.* s.v. Featley.
[21] *Cal. S.P. Dom.* 1641–3, 489.
[22] *Home Counties Mag.* i. 224.
[23] Below, prot. nonconf.
[24] Guildhall MS. 9537/20, p. 118.
[25] Ibid. MS. 9557, f. 20.

[26] Vestry min. bk. (1775–1801); Jolliffe, *Acton,* 68.
[27] Guildhall MS. 9558, facing f. 417.
[28] P.R.O., HO 129/134/5/1/1.
[29] Acton libr., 'Churches' file, subscriptions for rebldg. [1865].
[30] Mudie-Smith, *Rel. Life,* 427.
[31] *Acton, Ealing Dir.* (1887–8); Guildhall MS. 10731/1.
[32] Bowack, *Antiquities,* 49.
[33] Lysons, *Environs,* ii. 5.
[34] Acton libr., 'Churches' file, TS. leaflet on altar slab [*c.* 1962].
[35] P.R.O., PROB 11/14 (P.C.C. 12 Holgrave).
[36] Guildhall MS. 9171/10, f. 230v.
[37] Bowack, *Antiquities,* 49.
[38] Plate facing p. 32; Lysons, *Environs,* ii. 5.
[39] Brewer, *Beauties of Eng. & Wales,* iv. 332.
[40] Vestry min. bks. (1775–1801, 1801–22).
[41] Guildhall MS. 9532/7, f. 237.
[42] Vestry min. bk. (1775–1801).
[43] Ibid. (1775–1801, 1801–22).

but perhaps not carried out. After plans for more seating in 1825 and 1830,[44] it was decided in 1836 partially to rebuild the church, whereupon services were held for a time in a schoolroom.[45] Part of the cost was met from the sale of Masons green and other waste and from compensation from the G.W.R.[46] The result was described by the bishop of London as the ugliest church in his diocese.[47]

The whole church, except the tower, was demolished in 1865, because it could seat only 500 and was considered unworthy in style.[48] Its successor, consisting of a chancel, nave with aisles, and south-east chapel, was built of red brick with stone dressings to the design of H. Francis in a Decorated style.[49] The tower in turn was rebuilt in 1876 and the vestry was extended over part of the churchyard in 1906, giving an additional, south-east, exit.[50] Planned to seat 1,050,[51] the church seated 950 in 1906 and 750 by 1979.[52]

A font from the previous church, possibly the medieval one described by Lysons,[53] was later used in St. Andrew's mission church,[54] but many other fittings were incorporated in the new building. They include a brass of Humphrey Cavell (d. 1558),[55] and several monuments and mural tablets, the earliest being to Anne, wife of Sir Thomas Southwell, 1636, Catherine, Viscountess Conway, 1639, Mary, wife of Maj.-Gen. Philip Skippon, 1655, John Perryn, 1656, and Philippa, wife of Francis Rous, 1657.[56]

The plate in 1552 consisted of a pyx, two crosses, two paxes, and two chalices of silver with patens.[57] In 1639 Alice, Lady Dudley, created Duchess Dudley in 1644, gave a set containing a flagon, possibly the largest in the diocese, a chalice, a paten on a foot, and a ciborium with cover by T. Bird, all silver-gilt with elaborate repoussé ornament.[58] A silver bowl had been added by 1685,[59] and an offertory plate by 1810.[60] In 1889 the plate consisted of Lady Dudley's gift, with another chalice and paten, and a spoon and cruet, all silver-gilt.[61]

A pair of organs lacked some pipes in 1552.[62] An organist was appointed in 1826 and a new organ placed in the west gallery, where the old one had stood, in 1859.[63] The tower held four bells and a sanctus bell in 1552.[64] The peal of

bells was increased to eight after recasting in 1877[65] and in 1937 included (vi) by James Bagley, 1712, and (vii) by Ellis Knight, 1637.[66] The registers begin in 1538.[67]

The rapid increase in population after 1860 brought not only the rebuilding of St. Mary's but the creation of separate parishes for South Acton in 1873, East Acton in 1880, and Acton Green in 1888, followed by districts for West Acton in 1907, Acton Vale in 1915, and North Acton in 1930. All Saints', South Acton, and St. Dunstan's, East Acton, were founded from the old parish church; thereafter most mission churches were run from All Saints'.[68]

ALL SAINTS, Bollo Bridge Rd., S. Acton. Dist. formed 1873.[69] Patron bp. of London.[70] Two asst. curates 1881, three by 1892, two in 1926, one in 1947, none by 1955. Attendance 1903: 479 a.m.; 393 p.m. Red brick bldg. with stone dressings in early Decorated style 1872 by J. Kelly: apsidal chancel, aisled nave, SW. tower; SE. chapel 1895 by E. Monson. Severe war damage to spire, since removed. Andrew Hunter Dunn, V. 1871–92, became bp. of Quebec 1892. James Macarthur, 1892–7, became bp. of Bombay, then of Southampton. Parish covered densely populated and poor area, where church ran several missions and other facilities, inc. Dolphin coffee tavern, Osborne Rd., a nursery and an institute and kitchen for the sick, Strafford Rd.[71] Missions:[72] mission ho., Osborne Rd., and Acton Green sch. 1877;[73] Stanley Rd. iron mission church by 1886 until 1902;[74] Fletcher Rd. by 1903, closed by 1926;[75] All Saints' parish hall, attendance 1903: 314 a.m.; 86 p.m.; Good Shepherd mission, Stirling Rd., by 1903 until 1934,[76] attendance 1903: 25 p.m.

ST. AIDAN'S mission church, Acton Lane. Bldg. just S. of N.L.R. line by 1894, served from All Saints' (q.v.) 1903.[77] Attendance 1903: 57 p.m. Closed by 1908.[78]

ST. ALBAN THE MARTYR, South Parade, Acton Green. Dist. formed 1888.[79] Patron bp. of London.[80] Two asst. curates 1892, one in 1905, none in 1926. Attendance 1903: 477 a.m.; 321 p.m. Originated in mission run by All Saints' (q.v.) in 1882 at temp. mission church and Sunday sch. in two bldgs. in Acton Lane near Beaumont

[44] Vestry min. bk. (1822–57).
[45] Ibid. 21 Dec. 1837.
[46] Ibid. 12 May 1836.
[47] Jolliffe, *Acton*, 72.
[48] Acton libr., 'Churches' file, subscriptions for rebldg.
[49] *T.L.M.A.S.* xviii (2), no. 1; *Ealing Churches* (Ealing Museum, Art and Hist. Soc. 1977), no. 15.
[50] *The Times*, 31 Mar. 1906.
[51] Acton libr., 'Churches' file, subscriptions for rebldg.
[52] Inf. from the rector.
[53] Lysons, *Environs*, ii. 5.
[54] Below.
[55] *T.L.M.A.S.* xvi. 267–9.
[56] Hist. Mon. Com. *Mdx.* i.
[57] *T.L.M.A.S.* xxv. 300–1.
[58] Freshfield, *Communion Plate*, i.
[59] Guildhall MS. 9537/20, p. 118.
[60] Vestry min. bk. (1801–22).
[61] Guildhall MS. 10731/1.
[62] *T.L.M.A.S.* xxv. 300–1.
[63] Vestry min. bks. (1822–57, 1857–68).
[64] *T.L.M.A.S.* xxv. 300–1.
[65] Baker, *Acton*, 190.
[66] Hist. Mon. Com. *Mdx.* i.

[67] Marriages 1566–1812 are in W. P. W. Phillimore, *Mdx. Par. Regs.* i (1). In 1979 the regs. were at the church.
[68] For the 19th- and 20th-century churches below, inf. about asst. curates is from *Clergy List* (1881 and later edns.); *Crockford* (1926 and later edns.); architectural descriptions based on *T.L.M.A.S.* xviii (2); *Ealing Churches*; attendance figs. 1903 from Mudie-Smith, *Rel. Life*, 427. The following abbreviations are used: asst., assistant; bldg., building; bp., bishop; demol., demolished; dist., district; ho., house; min., minister; sch., school; temp., temporary; V., vicar.
[69] *Lond. Gaz.* 27 June 1873, p. 3047.
[70] *Clergy List* (1881).
[71] Guildhall MS. 10731/1, terrier 1889–90; Acton ref. libr., 'Churches', All Saints' 'Occasional Paper', June 1877.
[72] See also St. Aidan and St. Cuthbert.
[73] *All Saints' 'Occasional Paper'*.
[74] *Ealing and Acton Dir.* (1886); *Kelly's Dir. N. Suburbs.* (1903).
[75] *Kelly's Dir. N. Suburbs* (1903); *Mdx.* (1926).
[76] *Kelly's Dir. Acton* (1934, 1935).
[77] *Kelly's Dir. N. Suburbs* (1894, 1903).
[78] *Kelly's Dir. Mdx.* (1908).
[79] Ibid. (1890).
[80] *Clergy List* (1892).

Rd.; later held at parish hall, a sch. bldg. on Acton Green common.[81] Red brick bldg. with stone dressings in neo-Gothic style 1887 by E. Monson, seating c. 750:[82] unusual roof steeply pitched in nave, low and circular in chancel, ending in modified apse. Chapel added 1908. Mission services continued in temp. church, sold c. 1938,[83] attendance 1903: 73 p.m.

ST. ANDREW'S mission church, Salisbury Street. Begun in shop premises. Church by 1894, contained font from old parish church, with which mission was connected.[84] Attendance 1903: 209 a.m.; 111 p.m. Curate-in-charge 1915.[85] Closed after Second World War, when bldg. demol.

ST. BARNABAS'S (temp.) church, Stanley Terrace, Acton Vale. Mission held by St. Dunstan's (q.v.) at no. 20 the Parade, Acton Vale, by 1884, called St. Barnabas's mission church by 1890.[86] Iron church in Stanley Terrace by 1894[87] and mission room closed by 1898.[88] Attendance 1903: 130 a.m.; 118 p.m. Replaced by St. Thomas's (q.v.) 1915, and bldg. and site sold 1919.[89]

ST. CUTHBERT'S mission church, Osborne Rd. Founded from All Saints' (q.v.) by 1880, called St. Cuthbert's by c. 1900, but still served from All Saints' in 1926.[90] Attendance 1903: 83 a.m.; 59 p.m. Closed c. 1934.[91]

ST. DUNSTAN, Friars Place Lane, E. Acton. Dist. formed 1880.[92] Mission services by curate from St. Mary's held in barn of Cotchings farm, E. Acton, and later in E. Acton infants' sch.[93] Goldsmiths' Co. of London gave land and bldg. and endowed living out of Perryn trust.[94] Patron Goldsmiths' Co.[95] Two asst. curates 1892, one in 1896, none in 1955. Attendance 1903: 201 a.m.; 136 p.m. Red brick bldg. with stone dressings in Early English style 1879 by R. Hesketh, seating c. 750: chancel, nave of five bays, N. and S. choir aisles, SE. chapel, SW. tower and spire. Mission at Acton Vale became St. Barnabas's mission church (q.v.).

ST. GABRIEL, Noel Rd., N. Acton. London Diocesan Home Missioner appointed for N. Acton in 1923, and services held in marquee[96] and in private ho. in Horn Lane.[97] Iron hut built in Noel Rd., afterwards used as parish hall until 1960s. Parish formed 1930.[98] Patron bp. of London.[99] Two asst. curates 1935, none in 1947. Brown brick bldg. with stone dressings in Decorated style 1931 by E. C. Shearman, seating c. 200: red brick interior with Gothic arches,

chancel unfinished, sanctuary in nave, NE. chapel; terracotta plaques given by George V and Queen Mary from Queen Alexandra's private chapel at Sandringham, said to be from old Danish church. Church was first of Bp. Winnington-Ingram's 'forty' commissioned for growing outskirts of London.[1]

ST. LUKE'S mission church, Old Oak Lane, Willesden Junction. Founded between 1894 and 1898.[2] Attendance 1903: 105 a.m.; 78 p.m. Formed part of parish of All Souls, Harlesden.[3]

ST. MARTIN, Hale Gardens, W. Acton. Parish formed 1907 from St. Mary's, with some parts of Christ Church and St. Mary's, Ealing.[4] Patron bp. of London.[5] One asst. curate 1915, none in 1965. Iron bldg. dedicated 1903,[6] later used as parish hall. Red brick bldg. with stone dressings 1906 by E. Monson, seating 750:[7] nave, N. and S. aisles, N. and S. transepts, SW. chapel; not oriented. New hall built c. 1960 replaced temp. chancel and used for worship in winter.

ST. PETER, Southfield Rd., Acton Green. Patron bp. of London.[8] Curate-in-charge and two assts. 1915, one asst. curate 1935 and 1973. Services held in tent on recreation ground 1906, and in a council sch.[9] Temp. church 1907, seating 300,[10] later used as parish hall. Buff brick bldg. with red brick facings and stone dressing to W. door, in basilican style, based on St. Paul's Outside the Walls, Rome, 1915 by William A. Pite, seating 750:[11] nave with apse, N. chapel. Chancel screen from Quebec Chapel, Marble Arch. Organ 1858 from St. Alphage, London Wall.

ST. SAVIOUR'S church for the Deaf, Old Oak Rd. Non-parochial. Built by Royal Assoc. in Aid of Deaf and Dumb 1924, on site given by Goldsmiths' Co. of London, with funds from sale of St. Saviour's church for the deaf in Oxford Street, from which statues and foundation stone were taken. Dark brown brick bldg. with stone dressings by Sir Edward Maufe, seating up to 110: on two levels, the upper being the church, the lower a recreation centre; church floor raked to make priest clearly visible;[12] nave, chancel, gallery, and side chapel.

ST. THOMAS, Bromyard Ave., Acton Vale. Parish formed 1915. Patron bp. of London.[13] Replaced St. Barnabas's (q.v.). Site, in proposed garden city, given by Goldsmiths' Co. of London. Bldg. funds from sale of site of St. Thomas Charterhouse, Goswell Rd. Brown

[81] *St. Alban the Martyr, Acton Green, 1888–1938* (brochure in Acton libr.); *Kelly's Dir. N. Suburbs* (1888).
[82] *The Times,* 9 Apr. 1908.
[83] *St. Alban the Martyr, 1888–1938.*
[84] Baker, *Acton,* 203–4; *Kelly's Dir. N. Suburbs* (1894).
[85] *Clergy List* (1915).
[86] *Kelly's Dir. N. Suburbs* (1884); *Mdx.* (1890).
[87] Possibly by 1891, as regs. held by St. Thomas's begin then.
[88] *Kelly's Dir. N. Suburbs* (1898).
[89] *The Times,* 5 Aug. 1919.
[90] *Kelly's Dir. N. Suburbs* (1880, 1900, 1926).
[91] *Kelly's Dir. Acton* (1934).
[92] *Lond. Gaz.* 2 Apr. 1880, p. 2355.
[93] *St. Dunstan Jubilee Souvenir*; Baker, *Acton,* 200; inf. from Mr. R. N. G. Rowland.
[94] For Perryn trust, see below, charities.
[95] *Clergy List* (1892).

[96] Photograph in *The Times,* 16 Apr. 1923.
[97] Inf. from the vicar; *Crockford* (1926).
[98] *Kelly's Dir. Acton* (1940).
[99] *Crockford* (1965–6).
[1] Inf. from the vicar.
[2] *Kelly's Dir. N. Suburbs* (1894, 1898).
[3] *Clergy List* (1915).
[4] *Kelly's Dir. Acton* (1940).
[5] *Clergy List* (1915).
[6] Baker, *Acton,* 205.
[7] Ealing central ref. libr., MS. of B. J. Taylor, notes from *Acton Par. Mag.* 1924; see also *The Times,* 14 Dec. 1912.
[8] *Crockford* (1955–6).
[9] Inf. from the vicar.
[10] *The Times,* 12 Apr. 1912.
[11] Inf. from the vicar.
[12] Inf. from the chaplain.
[13] *Crockford* (1965–6).

brick bldg. with red brick dressings in early Decorated style on cruciform plan 1915 by Sir A. Blomfield: apsidal chancel, vestries, and two bays of nave 1915; extended at W. end in Perpendicular style 1927. Parish centre added to N. side 1973: nave with unfinished aisles, NE. and SE. chapels. Two windows, early Victorian altar plate, and wardens' staves from St. Thomas Charterhouse.[14]

ROMAN CATHOLICISM. There was one absentee from church in 1626.[15] In 1640 the parish officials could find no recusants[16] and in 1706 the wife of Mr. John Keys, of Acton wells, and Catherine Acton, widow, who was living at the Old King's Head, were the only papists.[17] Catherine Acton was reported again in 1708, at the Crown alehouse, with George Hill, gentleman, and John Hyndham.[18] In 1767 a summary of papists in the diocese of London gave only one for Acton,[19] while none was found in 1790.[20]

Nicholas Selby housed 'Nuns of the Visitation' from more than one French convent in 1805,[21] probably represented by the nunnery from Rouen reported as in Acton in 1810, together with two families of papists.[22] The families were those of Selby, who had built Derwentwater House, and Peter Kelly, to whom Selby leased the new house, himself moving to Acton House next door. They were said to have maintained a priest between them and fitted out a chapel in the basement of Acton House. When Acton House was let in the summer, services took place in a wooden building in King Street, next to which lived the chaplain. Besides the two families and their servants, the congregation consisted of Irish workers from the market gardens at Turnham Green.[23]

In 1835 the Revd. Thomas Heptonstall, Selby's chaplain, was still holding services at a chapel in Acton, whose location is unknown. They continued in 1851, from which date Acton chapel was served from Turnham Green, but had apparently ceased by 1856.[24] It was not until 1880 that services were held again in Acton, preceding the opening of the church of Our Lady of Lourdes. That church and other Roman Catholic places of worship are described below.

St. Aidan's church founded 1922, using breeze-block hall in Old Oak Common Lane, E. Acton. New building 1961 by John Newton, seating 500:[25] brick and concrete, with open bell tower; nine bells by Whitechapel foundry; statue of St. Aidan by Kathleen Parbury on front of tower; altarpiece by Graham Sutherland; triptychs by

Roy de Maistre; stained glass windows by Pierre Fourmaintraux; stations of the cross in concrete by Arthur Fleischmann; ceramic wall to baptistery with design by Adam Kossowski.[26]

Church of the Holy Family, Hanger Vale Lane, built 1967, to serve W. side of Acton.[27]

Our Lady of Lourdes, High St., originated in services from 1880 at no. 2 Gloucester Villas, Shakespeare Rd. Replaced by temp. church of Our Lady, Strafford Rd., S. Acton, 1882.[28] Closed 1902 when permanent church of Our Lady of Lourdes opened on land bought 1892.[29] Attendance 1903: 427 a.m. and p.m.[30] Yellow brick building with pale red tiled roof in Romanesque style by Goldie of Kensington, seating 400.[31]

Sisters of Charity under Protection of St. Vincent de Paul had convent by 1902 at nos. 45 and 47 Avenue Rd., where they ran day school.[32] Moved to no. 9 Rosemont Rd. 1930. Chapel at no. 1 Pierrepoint Rd., adjoining convent, registered 1959, and chapel at no. 14 Rosemont Rd. 1964.[33] Also ran old people's home 1979 at Magnolia Court, no. 4 Pierrepoint Rd.

Sisters of Society of Sacred Heart from France formed first convent in England 1842 at Berrymead Priory, where they ran boarding and day schools. Moved to Roehampton (Surr.) 1850.[34]

Chapel and sacristy in Acacia House, Central Ave., registered 1960, cancelled 1964.[35]

Apostolic Exarchate for Ukrainians in Gt. Britain had chapel 1979 in St. Olga's House, no. 14 Newburgh Rd., residence of Titular Bishop and Apostolic Exarch.[36]

PROTESTANT NONCONFORMITY. Richard Baxter (1615-91), the puritan divine ejected from Kidderminster (Worcs.) in 1662, moved to Acton in 1663 and lived near the parish church.[37] He observed that the Independent ministries of Philip Nye, 1643-56, and Thomas Elford, 1656-61, had resulted in loss of support for 'the Independent separating vigour', because they had admitted to communion only two out of the entire parish. When the Act against Conventicles expired, many came from neighbouring parishes to hear Baxter preach, but since he also took his followers to services in the parish church, a separate church was not established and nonconformist meetings do not appear to have survived Baxter's departure in 1670, when he was prosecuted after complaints by the rector, Bruno Ryves, for holding a conventicle.[38] In 1690-2 Acton was considered to have nonconformist assemblies, but no minister was recorded.[39] Between 1703 and 1716 children were

[14] *The Times*, 6 Jan. 1926.
[15] *Mdx. County Rec.* iii. 5.
[16] B.L. Add. MS. 38856.
[17] Guildhall MS. 9800.
[18] M.R.O., MR/RR 11/4.
[19] Guildhall MS. 9557.
[20] Ibid. f. 20; 9558, f. 417.
[21] Lysons, *Environs* (Suppl.), 99.
[22] Guildhall MS. 9558, f. 417.
[23] H. Mitchell, quoted in Baker, *Acton*, 109-10.
[24] *Cath. Dir.* (1835 and later edns.).
[25] Inf. from the par. priest; G.R.O. Worship Reg. nos. 48618, 68323.
[26] *St. Aidan's E. Acton, Church and Its Art* (1964).
[27] Site is in former par. of Ealing: see Ealing, Rom. Cathm.
[28] *Cath. Dir.* (1880), 99; (1882), 101.

[29] G.R.O. Worship Reg. no. 39195; inf. from the par. priest.
[30] Mudie-Smith, *Rel. Life*, 428.
[31] Information from the par. priest; *Ealing Churches*, no. 9.
[32] *Kelly's Dir. N. Suburbs* (1902); below, private schs.
[33] *Kelly's Dir. Acton* (1930); G.R.O. Worship Reg. nos. 52495, 67329, 69871.
[34] P. F. Anson, *Rel. Orders and Congs. of Gt. Britain and Irel.* (1949), 390, 392.
[35] G.R.O. Worship Reg. no. 67611.
[36] *Cath. Dir.* (1969), 465.
[37] *Calamy Revised*, ed. Matthews, 182.
[38] *Reliquiae Baxterianae* (1696), pt. II, p. 46; pt. III, p. 48.
[39] Gordon, *Freedon after Ejection*, 73.

born to two dissenting families in the parish,[40] and in 1766 only one dissenting family was noted. By 1790, however, there were several Methodists, who were said to have a meeting house.[41]

In the early 19th century both Independents and Wesleyans were active. In 1804 Protestant dissenters registered for worship a house in the possession of William Gee,[42] and in 1810 Calvinists registered another house for worship and a Sunday school in the western end of the parish.[43] In 1817 Calvinists registered their newly built chapel on Acton hill, besides a shed adjoining the house of John Charles Gee,[44] and the chapel was also used by Baptists and Wesleyans until they built their own churches. Dissenters from East Acton and Hammersmith registered the ground floor of a house in East Acton belonging to Mrs. Ann Carter in 1820, the minister being Thomas Crabb of Belmont House academy, Turnham Green.[45] They registered another building in East Acton in 1831 and a house in the middle of the village in 1836.[46]

In 1851 only the Congregationalists and the Wesleyans had recognized congregations, with attendances of 80 and 176 respectively.[47] Nonconformist activity remained sporadic until the rise in population in the late 19th century. Wesleyans built a new chapel in 1857, Baptists in 1865, and Congregationalists in 1871, and all three sects had started missions in the south part of the parish by the 1880s.[48] By 1890 they had been joined by Primitive Methodists, United Methodists, Strict Baptists, and Plymouth Brethren,[49] and soon afterwards by the Salvation Army, Society of Friends, and Unitarians. On one Sunday in 1903 Baptists had the most attendances with 1,130, the Methodist sects had 874, and Congregationalists 845. The next largest groups were the Brethren with 305 and the Salvation Army with 235. Altogether nonconformist worshippers totalled 3,826, compared with 4,718 Anglicans and 427 Roman Catholics.[50]

New activity in the 20th century was mainly confined to missions, mostly short lived, by undesignated Christian sects. Buildings were erected by the established denominations between the World Wars at Acton Green and, with the spread of housing, in East Acton. After the Second World War declining attendances led to the amalgamation of two Baptist churches, and in 1976 the Congregationalists and Wesleyans agreed to share premises at Acton hill.[51]

CONGREGATIONALISTS. Calvinists reg. new chapel 1817, built by S. Smith of Davies St., Westminster, N. side of Acton hill, just W. of Red Lion.[52] Two-storeyed brick bldg.,[53] seating 200.[54] Membership rose from c. 12 to c. 40 1846.[55] Attendance 1851: 40 a.m.; 40 p.m.[56] Church re-formed 1855 but by 1864 most members worshipped elsewhere and chapel used by Bapts. Chapel reopened and new church formed with 16 members 1866. Moved to Acton hall, Church Rd., until new church built.[57]

Acton Cong. church, Churchfield Rd., built 1871, seating c. 900,[58] by J. Tarring & Son.[59] Seated 800 in 1894.[60] Attendance 1903: 405 a.m.; 282 p.m.[61] Renamed Acton United Reformed church 1972. Joined Acton Hill Meth. church 1976 to form Acton Hill church (Meth., later United Reformed), using Meths.' bldgs. Churchfield Rd. premises sold and demol.[62]

Mission work began in S. Acton c. 1882, with open-air services in Junction Terrace.[63] Laundry used for winter services and Sunday sch. added. Mission adopted by Acton Cong. church 1884, and iron hall built between nos. 11 and 13 Palmerston Rd. 1885, enlarged 1887, and reg. 1889 as S. Acton mission hall.[64] Seated 180 in 1894.[65] Attendance 1903: 37 a.m.; 121 p.m. Adjoining property bought and hall with kitchen and classroom built 1908. Mission closed after 1955.[66]

METHODISTS. Wes. Meths. acquired large ho. in Steyne near junction with High St. 1817,[67] reg. rooms for worship in Brentford (later Gunnersbury) Lane 1840, and opposite George inn 1843.[68] Chapel in Steyne built 1845, seating 140. Attendance 1851: 69 a.m.; 107 p.m.[69] New chapel with Sunday and day schs. and separate teacher's ho., built 1857 E. side Gunnersbury Lane, near High St.,[70] of Kentish ragstone in Gothic style. Chapel enlarged 1864 for over 100 additional seats.[71] Became mother church of new Ealing and Acton circuit 1867.[72] Attendance 1903: 198 a.m.; 177 p.m. Replaced 1907 by church built on site of the Oaks, whose grounds bounded existing chapel, and latter became church hall.[73] Acton Hill Meth. church, by

[40] Acton par. ch., front leaf bapt. reg. 1695–1726.
[41] Guildhall MS. 9558, f. 417.
[42] Ibid. MS. 9580/2, p. 124.   [43] Ibid. 3.
[44] Ibid. 4.   [45] Ibid. 5.
[46] Ibid. 7, ff. 50, 244.
[47] P.R.O., HO 129/134/5/1/6.
[48] Below.
[49] Kelly's Dir. Mdx. (1890).
[50] Mudie-Smith, Rel. Life, 427–8.
[51] The following abbreviations are used in the accounts of protestant nonconformist churches: Bapt., Baptist; bldg., building; Cong., Congregationalist; demol., demolished; ho., house; Meth., Methodist; min., minister; mtg., meeting; Presb., Presbyterian; reg., registered; sch., school; Wes., Wesleyan.
[52] Guildhall MS. 9580/4; Ealing Churches, no. 4; W. Bolton, Acton Cong. Ch. (1917), 16.
[53] Bolton, Acton Cong. Ch. photo. facing p. 16 shows former chapel but probably with altered front.
[54] P.R.O., HO 129/134/5/1/6.
[55] Bolton, Acton Cong. Ch. 26, 30.

[56] P.R.O., HO 129/134/5/1/6.
[57] Bolton, Acton Cong. Ch. 32–4, 36–7, 41.
[58] Inf. from the former min.; G.R.O. Worship Reg. no. 22299.
[59] Ealing Churches, no. 4.   [60] Cong. Yr. Bk. (1894).
[61] All attendances for 1903 are from Mudie-Smith, Rel. Life, 427–8.
[62] Inf. from the former min.
[63] Para. based on Bolton, Acton Cong. Ch. 61–5.
[64] G.R.O. Worship Reg. no. 31834.
[65] Cong. Yr. Bk. (1894).
[66] Kelly's Dir. Acton (1955).
[67] C. Hocking, Brief Hist. of Meth. Ch. in Acton (1957), 2.
[68] Guildhall MS. 9580/8, ff. 69, 181.
[69] P.R.O., HO 129/134/5/1/5.
[70] Hocking, op. cit. 3; inf. from Mr. Bamber and min.; P.R.O., C 54/15357, no. 3.
[71] Hocking, op. cit. 4; inf. from Mr. Bamber.
[72] Baker, Acton, 204.
[73] G.R.O. Worship Reg. no. 42367; Hocking, op. cit. 6; inf. from Mr. Bamber.

Gordon & Gordon, built of Kentish ragstone and dressings of Bath stone, with tower and Gothic detail.[74] Seated 780 on ground floor, 181 in gallery, 39 in choir.[75] W. transept converted to war memorial chapel 1921, reducing seats to 800. Agreement with Acton United Reformed church 1976, for joint use of Acton hill church. Extensive remodelling of interior 1978, reducing seating to c. 650.[76] Gunnersbury Lane chapel housed community relations centre 1979.

Acton Green Wes. church originated in mtgs. in ho. in Antrobus Rd. before 1885.[77] Wes. Meth. sch. chapel, Steele Rd., Acton Green, reg. 1885.[78] Attendance 1903: 173 a.m.; 100 p.m. New church built 1930 on site of chapel and sch., and reg. as Acton Green Wes. hall.[79] Rectangular, flat-roofed bldg. in red brick with stone dressings, by Smee & Houchin in style of Methodist Central Halls (Westminster). Large hall seating 350–400; small hall seating c. 100; classrooms, vestry, and others rooms; on two levels. All services in small hall 1978.[80]

Old Oak Wes. mtg. formed 1922, using disused day sch. at corner of Fitzquest St. and Old Oak Common Lane, E. Acton.[81] Old Oak Meth. church built in the Fairway, E. Acton, and reg. 1926.[82] Single-storeyed bldg. of red brick with steeply pitched tiled roof and small tower, seating c. 150. After fire 1977 members worshipped in other churches.

Primitive Meths. built Ebenezer chapel, Park Rd. North, 1867.[83] Seventh London circuit 1880, Ealing circuit 1898.[84] Attendance 1903: 56 a.m.; 60 p.m. Served from Ealing by 1911.[85] Closed c. 1934.[86]

United Meth. Free church, between nos. 41 and 43, Bollo Bridge Road, by 1880. Sixth London circuit 1880,[87] London (Willesden) circuit by 1926.[88] Attendance 1903: 54 a.m.; 56 p.m. Services in iron bldg. until church built adjoining.[89] Reg. 1903, renamed United Meth. church 1907.[90] Two-storeyed brick bldg. with stone dressings.[91] Demol. after 1955.

BAPTISTS. Acton Bapt. church originated in services held in Independent chapel, Acton hill, from c. 1856. Organized 1865.[92] Brick church with rendered front in Church Rd. 1864 by W. Mumford, seating 450.[93] Galleries added between 1875 and 1885 bringing seating to 650. Sunday sch. room added at rear of church, and halls on two floors 1899.[94] Church membership

46 c. 1866, reached peak of c. 275 on roll 1908. Attendance 1903: 277 a.m.; 204 p.m. Mission work in Bollo Bridge, E. Acton, and Acton Green, 1875–85, included cottage services and open-air mtgs.[95]

South Acton Bapt. church formed after split at Church Rd., when some members wanted visiting missioner to remain at Acton. Worshipped in Acton hall, Church Rd., 1894. Chapel built at corner of Newton Ave. and Avenue Rd. 1895:[96] yellow brick, by F. W. Stocking.[97] Reg. as Evangelistic Church 1897.[98] Attendance 1903: 236 a.m.; 308 p.m. Designation altered as pastors changed: Newton Ave. Bapt. church 1900–1; Evangelistic Free church 1902–8; Church of Christ 1909–11. Reverted to Bapt. church between 1912 and 1915. Withdrew from London Bapt. Assoc. and Bapt. Union between 1924 and 1926.[99] Reg. as Bapt. Free church 1944, and renamed S. Acton Bapt. church 1960.[1] Joined Church Rd. Bapts. 1977. Newton Ave. bldg. sold, and used by Ukrainian Autocephalic Orthodox church from 1977.[2]

Strict Bapts. began mission at no. 5 Richmond Terrace, Shakespeare Rd., 1881.[3] Church formed 1882. Worshipped in Churchfield hall 1885. Iron Beulah tabernacle in Acton Lane, at Leythe Rd., 1888. Attendance 1903: 35 a.m.; 34 p.m. Closed after 1955.[4]

Hope Bapt. church, Cromartie Rooms, Park Rd. North, formed 1901 by group from S. Acton church.[5] Attendance 1903: 14 a.m.; 22 p.m. Church re-formed 1904 and moved to Horn Lane, where Bapt. church at corner of Horn Lane and Faraday Rd. reg. 1905.[6] Closed 1934; bldg. renamed Faraday hall and used by Acton Liberal Assoc.[7]

East Acton Bapt. church, John Bradford Memorial, E. Acton Lane. Church of red brick with gabled roof of dark red tiles, by W. Hayne, built 1931.[8] Reg. by Bapts. 1937.[9]

Acton Green Bapt. mission rooms, no. 56 Antrobus Rd., opened c. 1887, but housed unsectarian mission by 1894.[10]

BRETHREN. Mtgs. held in Acton hall, Church Rd., by 1888, until c. 1900, and at Berrymead mission room, no. 38 Avenue Rd., by 1894.[11] Attendance 1903: 68 a.m.; 75 p.m. Renamed Berrymead gospel hall by 1940.[12] In 1903 mtgs. also held at no. 25 the Parade, Acton Vale; attendance: 70 a.m.; 66 p.m.; and at private ho.,

[74] Pevsner, Mdx. 23; Ealing Churches, no. 3.
[75] Hocking, op. cit. 8.
[76] Inf. from Mr. Bamber.
[77] Inf. from the min. and property steward.
[78] G.R.O. Worship Reg. no. 29021.
[79] Inf. from the property steward; G.R.O. Worship Reg. no. 52791.
[80] Ealing Churches, no. 2; inf. from the property steward.
[81] Para. based on inf. from the min.; Ealing Churches, no. 8.
[82] G.R.O. Worship Reg. no. 50381.
[83] Baker, Acton, 203; P.R.O., C 54/16842, no. 13.
[84] Kelly's Dir. N. Suburbs (1880, 1898).
[85] Baker, Acton, 203.
[86] Kelly's Dir. Acton (1934).
[87] Kelly's Dir. N. Suburbs. (1880).
[88] Kelly's Dir. Mdx. (1926).   [89] Baker, Acton, 202.
[90] G.R.O. Worship Reg. no. 39882.
[91] Acton libr., 'Churches', U.M.F.C. Souvenir [n.d.], photo.
[92] Tongue, Lond. Suburb, 12, 18.

[93] Ealing Churches, no. 1; G.R.O. Worship Reg. no. 17212.
[94] Inf. from Judge Granville Slack.
[95] Tongue, Lond. Suburb, 24, 48, 90–2.
[96] Ibid. 68–9; Whitley, Bapts. of Lond. 243.
[97] Ealing Churches, no. 19.
[98] G.R.O. Worship Reg. no. 36294.
[99] Whitley, op. cit. 243.
[1] G.R.O. Worship Reg. no. 60888.
[2] Inf. from Judge Granville Slack.
[3] Para. based on Whitley, op. cit. 227.
[4] Kelly's Dir. Acton (1955).
[5] Para. based on Whitley, op. cit. 252.
[6] G.R.O. Worship Reg. no. 41008.
[7] Kelly's Dir. Acton (1934, 1935).
[8] Ealing Churches, no. 6.
[9] G.R.O. Worship Reg. no. 57554.
[10] Ealing and Acton Dir. (1886–8); Kelly's Dir. N. Suburbs (1894).
[11] Kelly's Dir. N. Suburbs (1888, 1894, 1898, 1900).
[12] Kelly's Dir. Acton (1940).

no. 3 Birkbeck Rd.; attendance: 17 a.m.; 9 p.m. Mtgs. held 1958 at Larden Rd. hall and no. 50 Churchfield Rd.[13]

SOCIETY OF FRIENDS. Though George Fox held mtg. in fields near Acton 1654, and public mtg. took place 1802,[14] regular mtgs. not held until 1894, when Friends' mtg. and adult sch. started in private ho.[15] In 1896 mtg. ho. at no. 5 Avenue Rd. was reg.,[16] replaced 1901 with larger premises at no. 1 (later renumbered as no. 43) Avenue Rd. Iron hall seating c. 340 built 1902 in grounds to replace tent used for larger mtgs. Became particular mtg. 1903. Attendance 1903: 32 a.m.; 65 p.m. Joined Ealing mtg. 1940.[17]

SALVATION ARMY. No. 3 Grove Place, Grove Rd., reg. by 1893. Attendance 1903: 82 a.m.; 153 p.m. Replaced by hall in Church Rd. 1912. In 1922 replaced by citadel, Acton Lane, but moved to Crown Street 1926.[18] In use 1979.

OTHER DENOMINATIONS AND UNSPECIFIED MISSIONS. Acton Green Railway Mission, Cunnington St., opened 1900.[19] Attendance 1903: 82 a.m.; 92 p.m. Reg. 1924 as Railway Mission hall, by undesignated Christians, and renamed Acton Memorial Free church by 1958.[20] Services held in 1979 in iron bldg.

Unitarians met in Market Place 1903, when attendance was 32 p.m. Iron church in Creffield Rd., opposite Haberdashers' sch., reg. 1906. Still in use 1940 but closed by 1954.[21]

Presbs. held services in Willesden Junction Railway Institute, Railway Cottages, Old Oak Lane, 1903, when attendance was 54 a.m.; 80 p.m.

Acton Spiritual Mission held in two rooms at the Cottage, Woodhurst Rd., from 1929. Renamed Acton Spiritualist church 1960, where mtgs. were held 1979.[22]

Church of England Evangelical Protestants reg. St. Mark's Church Ho., on ground floor of no. 15 Newburgh Rd., 1946.[23]

Jehovah's Witnesses reg. Kingdom hall, nos. 318–20 Acton Lane, 1974.[24]

Ukrainian Autocephalic Orthodox Church took over former S. Acton Bapt. church, Newton Ave., 1977.[25]

Acton lecture hall, Church Rd., built c. 1866, reg. for unsectarian Christian mtgs. 1884, and used by several denominations. Closed c. 1900.[26]

Liberty Hall Evangelistic Mission, no. 2 Berrymead Gardens, reg. by undesignated Christians 1908. Still in use 1914 but United Services Club by 1933.[27] Christians' mtg. room at rear of no. 223 High St., reg. 1912, cancelled 1954.[28] Pentecostal Evangelistic Mission, no. 226 Acton Lane, reg. 1941. Still in use 1958 but cancelled 1964. Pentecostal free church held mtgs. in L.C.S. hall 1958.[29] York Rd. mtg. room, no. 83 York Rd., reg. 1972 by undesignated Christians.[30]

EDUCATION. Acton had two schoolmasters in 1628.[31] In 1637 Viscountess Conway bequeathed a rent charge for teaching six poor children at 1s. a week, which was paid out regularly by the churchwardens until 1816 and thereafter into the National school funds.[32] The rector, William Antrobus, in 1805 offered to assist the foundation of a school for the poor;[33] nothing further was mentioned, although a school for girls was said to have been established in 1808 under the auspices of the rector and supported by subscriptions.[34] In 1815 a special vestry meeting considered building a National school for 50 boys and 50 girls, supported by subscriptions and supervised by a committee of 14;[35] the round house and coal house by the north-west corner of the church were to be rebuilt, next to a new schoolroom.[36] In 1816 the school was formally united with the National Society[37] and by 1819 it had c. 110 pupils, taught by a salaried mistress with a house and supported entirely by subscriptions. The poor were said to possess sufficient means of educating their children in 1819, when there were also two boarding schools for tradesmen's children and two or three other small schools.[38]

In 1833 there were c. 100 pupils at the National school and c. 90, all fee paying, at four other day schools. There were also three boarding schools, one for 80 boys and the other two containing 50 girls, also supported by fees.[39] A separate infants' school was built by the parish in 1837,[40] and in 1843, in addition to the National school with 108 pupils and the infants' with 84, there was a common day school for 20 boys, besides three dame schools containing 35 pupils, two of them run by dissenters, for which 4d. to 6d. a week was charged.[41] One was probably a forerunner of the Wesleyan girls' school opened in the Steyne in 1846.[42] Poor children, regardless of religion,

---

[13] Acton libr., 'Churches', list of clergy in Acton.
[14] *Jnl. of Geo. Fox*, ed. N. Penney, i. 170; Friends' Ho. libr., Six Wks. Mtg. min. bk., vol. 18 (1801–21), p. 38.
[15] Para. based on *The Friend*, vol. 41, N.S., 2 Aug. 1901, pp. 505–6; *Friends' Mtg.-Ho. and Adult Sch., Acton* (leaflet 1906); Westminster and Longford M.M. min. bk., vol. 25, pp. 82, 139, 149, 171.
[16] G.R.O. Worship Reg. no. 35568.
[17] *Yearly Mtg. Procs. 1941*, 154; below, Ealing.
[18] G.R.O. Worship Reg. nos. 33799, 45213, 48392, 51872.
[19] *Kelly's Dir. N. Suburbs* (1900); *Acton Gaz.* 18 Jan. 1901.
[20] G.R.O. Worship Reg. no. 49360; Acton libr., 'Churches', list of clergy.
[21] Baker, *Acton*, 203; G.R.O. Worship Reg. no. 42166; *Kelly's Dir. Acton* (1940).
[22] G.R.O. Worship Reg. no. 55011; *Kelly's Dir. Acton* (1929).
[23] G.R.O. Worship Reg. no. 61558.
[24] Ibid. 73861.
[25] Above.

[26] G.R.O. Worship Reg. no. 28161; *Kelly's Dir. N. Suburbs* (1880, 1898, 1900).
[27] G.R.O. Worship Reg. no. 43292; *Kelly's Dir. Acton* (1914, 1933).
[28] G.R.O. Worship Reg. no. 45424.
[29] Ibid. 59937; Acton libr., 'Churches', list of clergy.
[30] G.R.O. Worship Reg. no. 73065.
[31] Guildhall MS. 9537/13.
[32] *V.C.H. Mdx.* i. 217; *Digest of Schs. and Chars. for Educ.* H.C. 435, pp. 66–7 (1843), xviii.
[33] Vestry min. bk. (1801–22).
[34] Lysons, *Environs* (Suppl.), 100.
[35] Vestry min. bk. (1801–22), 2 Aug. 1815.
[36] Ibid. 16 Oct. 1815.
[37] *Nat. Soc. 5th Ann. Rep.* (1816), 46.
[38] *Educ. of Poor Digest*, 533.
[39] *Educ. Enquiry Abs.* 554.
[40] P.R.O., C 54/11631, no. 8.
[41] *Jnl. Stat. Soc. of Lond.* vi. 128–9.
[42] Below.

were also taught by the nuns of the Sacred Heart at Berrymead Priory between 1842 and 1850.[43]

Anglican education increased with the new building of the National school in 1853 and 1862, and the opening of National schools at East Acton in 1862, Acton Green in 1863, and South Acton, All Saints', in 1868, while Turnham Green's Roman Catholic school moved to Acton Lane in 1864.[44] By 1870 there were eight elementary schools: four connected with the Church of England, the infants' forming part of Acton National school, two Wesleyan, one Roman Catholic, and one of no stated denomination. Five were public schools, secured by deeds and attended by 398 boys and 303 girls, and two were 'adventure' schools, of which one had 46 boys and 15 girls.[45] The four National schools, Turnham Green Roman Catholic, and the Wesleyan day school were all recognized as efficient in 1871, and it was considered that the total of 1,381 places sufficed.[46] Two evening schools were started in 1874, run as public elementary schools for boys, in Acton and South Acton.[47]

In 1875 a school board was requested by the managers of the National schools, whose threatened closure, on grounds of expense, would have lost 1,400 out of 1,800 places.[48] The board, with seven members, took over at the end of 1875,[49] but met much opposition, because it rented church schools for a nominal sum and allowed the school managers to control the premises until 9.45 a.m., in order that religious instruction could be given to pupils arriving early. Many nonconformists claimed that schools maintained from rates ought to be unsectarian, and the inspector in 1877 thought the practice likely to provoke conflicts of interest over financing between school managers and the board, who were often the same personnel.[50] Nevertheless the arrangement continued as long as the buildings were required.

The first board school was opened in 1880, with a second in 1882 and a third not until 1891. The board also took over the Wesleyan school in 1895 and opened a new temporary school in 1898. A persistent shortage of places was relieved by using nonconformist churches and mission rooms. Under the Education Act, 1902, Acton became a Part III authority and the U.D.C.'s education committee replaced the school board.[51] Four permanent schools and one temporary one had been opened by 1909, with another permanent school replacing the temporary one in 1912. In 1909 the council stopped negotiations for another new school on complaints of extravagance in building.[52]

An intermediate evening school was held at Priory school, with 119 students in 1902,[53] and from 1905 a central school provided higher elementary education, for which children had had to go outside the parish.[54] In 1906 the county grammar school for boys was opened, in which Acton boys made up a third.[55] A scheme was drawn up under the Act of 1918 to improve secondary and technical instruction, besides reducing elementary classes to 45 and abolishing temporary and older accommodation. In 1919 it was estimated that more than 3,000 additional places in elementary and central schools were needed for the next three years. Secondary provision was poor and many older pupils had to go outside the parish or to private schools. More than half of the secondary places in Acton were filled by children from outside.[56] Although the plans for new central schools were not carried out immediately, the sites chosen were eventually used in 1939 and 1955.

From 1924 the central school took seniors only, a new school being opened for the juniors. By 1930 reorganization into senior and junior schools was in progress, in accordance with the Hadow Report. Five schools were opened, including one completely new junior school, and three old ones closed. Montessori methods were adopted for the infants' classes and practice was afforded for Montessori students.[57] By 1936 the borough had seven senior schools formed from the central and elementary schools, although no new buildings were provided.

Acton became an 'excepted district', responsible for primary and secondary education, under the Act of 1944. By 1952 there were eight primary and one voluntary aided all-age and six secondary schools. Two were grammar schools, the county school for boys and Haberdashers' Aske's, a direct grant school, for girls, and a third, Acton central, was selective.[58] A new secondary modern school was opened in 1955 to replace an old senior school and another in 1957 to replace the central school.[59] Reorganization in 1961[60] left only two secondary modern schools. In 1963 a voluntary aided Roman Catholic secondary modern school was opened.[61] Few changes were made in primary education, the two new schools after the Second World War being a reopened Church of England school and a voluntary aided Roman Catholic school.

From 1965 Acton formed part of Ealing L.B., which reorganized all its schools in a three-tier comprehensive scheme in 1974.[62] In 1979 Acton had 8 first, 5 middle, 2 combined, and 4 high schools.

Public schools.[63] Basic historical information and numbers on the roll for existing schools have

[43] Anson, *Rel. Orders and Congs.* 390, 392.
[44] Below.
[45] *Returns relating to Elem. Educ.* [201], p. 570, H.C. (1871), lv.
[46] P.R.O., ED 16/204.
[47] Ibid. ED 7/87.
[48] Ibid. ED 16/204.
[49] *Rep. of Educ. Cttee. of Council, 1878* [C. 2342-I], p. 24, H.C. (1878-9), xxiii.
[50] Baker, *Acton*, 216; P.R.O., ED 16/204.
[51] Mdx. C.C. *Primary and Sec. Educ. in Mdx. 1900-65*, 26.
[52] *The Times*, 23 Jan. 1909.

[53] *Sec. Schs. and Evening Classes under Bd. 1902-3* [Cd. 2323], p. 289, H.C. (1905), lix.
[54] P.R.O., ED 16/204.
[55] Below.
[56] Ealing libr., Acc. 1/9.
[57] Ibid. Acc. 12/2; Acton, *Official Guide* [1928], 40.
[58] Acton, *Official Guide* [c. 1952], 12.
[59] Below.
[60] Inf. from the headmaster, Twyford high sch.
[61] Below.
[62] Below, Ealing, educ.
[63] Private schs. are separately treated below.

been supplied by head teachers. Except where otherwise stated, the remaining historical information and accommodation and average attendance figures have been taken from: files on Church of England schools at the National Society; P.R.O., ED 7/87–8; *Rep. of Educ. Cttee. of Council, 1859–60* [2681], H.C. (1860), liv(1); *1865–6* [3666], H.C. (1866), xxvii; *1866–7* [3882], H.C. (1867), xxii; *1870–1* [C. 406], H.C. (1871), xxii; *1871–2* [C. 601], H.C. (1872), xxii; *1878* [C. 2342–I], H.C. (1878–9), xxiii; *1880–1* [C. 2948–I], H.C. (1881), xxxii; *1882–3* [C. 3706–I], H.C. (1883), xxv; *1884–5* [C. 4483–I], H.C. (1885), xxiv; *1885* [C. 4849], H.C. (1886), xxiv; *1888* [C. 5804–I], H.C. (1899), xxix; *Return of Schs. 1893* [C. 7529], H.C. (1894), lxv; *1899* [Cd. 315], H.C. (1900), lxv(2); *Returns relating to Elem. Educ.* [C. 7529], H.C. (1894), lxv; *Schs. in receipt of Parl. Grants, 1898* [C. 9454], H.C. (1899), lxxiv; *1899* [Cd. 332], H.C. (1900), lxiv; *List of Schs. under Admin. of Bd. 1903* [Cd. 2011], H.C. (1904), lxxv; *1905* [Cd. 3182], H.C. (1906), lxxxvi; *Return of Non-Provided Schs.* H.C. 178–XX (1906), lxxxviii; *Public Elem. Schs. 1902–3* [Cd. 1490], H.C. (1903), li; *1906* [Cd. 3510], H.C. (1907), lxiii; *1907* [Cd. 3901], H.C. (1908), lxxxiv; *Bd. of Educ., List 21, 1919–38* (H.M.S.O.); Mdx. C.C. *List of Educ. Svces.* (1957, 1963, 1964); *Kelly's Dir. Mdx.* (1852, 1862, 1890, 1908, 1926); *Kelly's Dir. Lond.* (1880–98); Acton, *Official Guide* (1936 and later edns.).

The following abbreviations are used: a.a., average attendance; accn., accommodation; amalg., amalgamated; B, boy, boys; bd., board; bldg., building; C.E., Church of England; Cong., Congregationalist; demol., demolished; dept., department; educ., education; G, girl, girls; ho., house; J, JB, JG, JM, junior, junior boys, girls, mixed; I, infant, infants; M, mixed; mod., modern; Nat., National; parl., parliamentary; R.C., Roman Catholic; reorg., reorganized; roll, numbers on roll; S, SB, SG, SM, senior, senior boys, girls, mixed; sch., school; sec., secondary; tech., technical; temp., temporary; vol., voluntary; Wes., Wesleyan. The word 'school' is to be understood after each named entry.

ACTON COUNTY GRAMMAR, Gunnersbury Lane. First purpose-built county grammar sch. in Mdx., opened 1906 for 200 B aged 10 to 19 on 4 a. of Woodlands Ave. site, Acton hill.[64] 240 by 1908, one third from Acton. Financed by fees, Educ. Bd.'s grant, and Mdx. C.C., and managed by local higher educ. committee of C.C. Commercial training, besides arts and manual subjects, for London University and London Chamber of Commerce. Two-storeyed wing added *c.* 1934–6. Larger sch. built 1939 at Heathfield Lodge, Gunnersbury Lane; Woodlands bldgs. later annexe of tech. college.[65] Admitted G *c.* 1958 and fully co-educational by 1966. Comprehensive, renamed Reynolds high, from 1974.[66] Roll 1979: 1,040 M.[67]

ACTON GREEN C.E. I. Opened 1863 as Nat. sch. in ho. in Middle Street, later Gladstone Rd., and financed by sch. pence and rector. 1864 a.a. 56 I.[68] New sch. built 1870 on site adjoining St. Alban's church, financed by parl. grants and sch. pence. 1870 a.a. 127 M. Rented by sch. bd. 1876.[69] 1878 accn. 206 M. 1888 a.a. 193 M. JMI by 1891. Replaced by Beaumont Pk. (q.v.).[70]

ACTON GREEN MIDDLE, see Rothschild first and middle.

ACTON NAT., see St. Mary's C.E.

ACTON WELLS FIRST AND MIDDLE, School Rd., Victoria Rd. Opened 1909 on 4½-a. site[71] for 358 SM, 358 JM, 408 I, replacing Willesden Junction temp. (q.v.). 1919 a.a. 324 M, 145 I. 1927 accn. 496 M, 400 I; a.a. 469 M, 255 I. Reorg. between 1932 and 1936 for 320 SM, 364 JM, 364 I. 1938 a.a. 211 SM, 360 JM, 158 I. After 1945 SM formed Acton Wells sec. mod., which closed by 1955. JMI became combined first and middle sch. 1974. Roll 1979: 310 M.[72]

ALL SAINTS' C.E., Strafford Rd. Opened 1868 as Nat. sch. by vicar of South Acton, with 40 I. Financed by sch. pence (2d.), parl. grants, and vol. contributions. 1870 a.a. 92 I. Schoolroom added 1874 and adjoining sch. for 196 B opened 1875. Rented by sch. bd. 1876. 1877 I sch. accn. 100 G, 165 I; a.a. 166 G, 237 I.[73] Some pupils attended Osborne Rd. (q.v.) from 1880. 1888 a.a. 396 BGI. 1898 accn. 494; a.a. 414. Closed 1904.[74]

BEAUMONT PARK, Acton Lane. Opened 1891 for 300 B, 300 G, 428 I. 1891 a.a. 200 B, 225 G, 157 I. Enlarged 1898 for 540 B, 540 G, 548 I. Temp. accn. for 105 B and 60 G in iron bldg. added by 1906. 1906 a.a. 586 B, 546 G, 514 I. Temp. accn. 1911 for additional 85 G in 3 rooms rented from Acton Green Wes. mission.[75] 1919 a.a. 416 B, 450 G, 328 I. 1927 a.a. 366 B, 317 G, 279 I. Reorg. between 1927 and 1932 for 450 SG, 450 JG, 400 I. 1938 a.a. 123 SG, 193 JG, 164 I. Closed after Second World War. Bldgs. used by Priory G sec. mod. until 1961, by Cardinal Newman R.C. sec. mod. 1963–76, and Acton Green middle from 1976.

BERRYMEDE FIRST, formerly I, see Osborne Rd.

BERRYMEDE JUNIOR B, see South Acton B.

BERRYMEDE MIDDLE, Osborne Rd., South Acton. Opened 1931 for 542 JG from Osborne Rd. I (q.v.), using upper floor of Osborne Rd. bldg. 1938 a.a. 338 JG. Amalg. with Berrymede JG 1961 (see South Acton B) to form Berrymede JM in same bldgs. Middle sch., occupying both bldgs. in Osborne Rd., from 1974. Roll 1979: 300 M.

BROMYARD M SEC. MOD., see Faraday high.

CARDINAL NEWMAN R.C. HIGH, Creffield Rd. Opened 1963 as mixed vol. aided R.C. sec. mod. sch. in former Beaumont Pk. sch., taking S pupils from St. Mary's R.C., Turnham Green (q.v.). Comprehensive high sch. from 1974. Moved 1976 to former Haberdashers' Aske's bldg. in Creffield Rd.,[76] which had been extensively modernized. Roll 1979: 570 M.

[64] Ealing libr., Acc. 6/8 (Acton county sch. cttee. min. bk.).
[65] *2nd Rep. Com. for Educ. of Poor*, H.C. 547, pp. 74–5 (1819), x–B.   [66] Inf. from Mr. D. J. Kibblewhite.
[67] *Educ. Authies. Dir. and Ann.* (1979).
[68] Jolliffe, *Acton*, 79.
[69] Ealing libr., Acc. 1/24 (Acton sch. bd. min. bk.).

[70] Ibid. Acc. 5 (lease).   [71] *The Times*, 29 Nov. 1909.
[72] Threatened with closure due to low nos.: *Acton Gaz.* 21 Dec. 1978.   [73] P.R.O., ED 16/204.
[74] Ealing libr., Acc. 1/28 (Acton sch. bd. min. bk. 22 Jan. 1903).
[75] P.R.O., ED 16/204.   [76] Below, private schs.

CENTRAL, Shakespeare Rd. Opened 1905 for 340 SM, 340 JM, 403 I, with initial intake of 242 SM, 281 JM, 190 I, inc. pupils from Gunnersbury Lane (see Wes. day).[77] Weekly fees 6d. (SM), 4d. (JM), 3d. (I); one tenth of SM places free.[78] SM fees abolished 1919.[79] SM received higher grade instruction, although application for higher elementary status withdrawn on change of age structure.[80] 1908 accn. for JM increased to 400 a.a. 244 SM, 371 JM, 323 I. 1910 accn. 497 SM, 497 JM, 410 I, children over 16 being excluded.[81] 1919 a.a. 398 SM, 452 JM, 311 I. Reorg. 1924 when JMI formed Derwentwater (q.v.). 1927 accn. 480 SM, a.a. 408 SM. 1938 a.a. 365 SM. After 1945 became a selective mixed sec. mod. Closed 1957 and replaced by the Elms (see Twyford high).

DERWENTWATER FIRST AND MIDDLE, Shakespeare Rd. Opened 1924 for JM and I depts. of central sch. (q.v.), on same site. 1927 accn. 441 JM, 350 I; a.a. 417 JM, 299 I. 1938 a.a. 330 JM, 278 I. First and middle schs. from 1974. Rolls 1979: 292 M and 365 M.

EAST ACTON C.E. FIRST, East Acton Lane. Opened 1862 as Nat. sch. for 39 I in converted cottage under managers of St. Mary's C.E. Financed by parl. grants, vol. contributions, rent for a 'small bit of ground', and sch. pence (1d.). Adjoining ho. for teacher. New sch. for 92 M, 80 I built 1870 on land granted by Goldsmiths' Co. of Lond.[82] with aid of parl. bldg. grant. 1871 a.a. 37 I. 1910 accn. 64 M, 80 I.[83] 1919 a.a. 77 MI. Reorg. 1926 as East Acton J for 250 JMI, with roll of 137. Sch. used for demonstrating Montessori methods, intro. 1929.[84] Closed 1931 and replaced by John Perryn I (q.v.). Reopened 1950 for I. Extra accn. for 4 classes in huts. First sch. from 1974. Roll 1979: 177 M.

ELMS, SEC. MOD., see Twyford high.

FARADAY HIGH, Bromyard Ave. Opened 1955 as Bromyard M sec. mod., with pupils from John Perryn sec. mod. Reorg. 1961 as Faraday sec. mod. with pupils from Priory schs., and new bldg. added. Comprehensive, renamed Faraday high, from 1974. Roll 1979: 730 M.

GUNNERSBURY LANE, see Wesleyan day.

JOHN PERRYN FIRST AND MIDDLE, Long Drive, East Acton. Opened 1931 for 648 M, 336 I; 355 pupils from East Acton, Acton Wells, Derwentwater, and other schs.[85] 1932 a.a. 491 M, 325 I. Reorg. between 1932 and 1936 for 360 SM, 288 JM, 336 I. 1938 a.a. 162 SM, 217 JM, 225 I. First 4 I classes on Montessori lines.[86] SM formed M sec. mod., replaced 1955 by Bromyard (see Faraday high). First and middle schs. from 1974. Rolls 1979: 109 M and 322 M.

OSBORNE RD. I, South Acton. First sch. to be opened by sch. bd. 1880, on south side Osborne Rd.,[87] for 337 I. Pupils from All Saints' (q.v.).[88]

Sch. pence (2d.). 1880–95 a.a. 170, 1888 222. Temp. bldg. 1895 until sch. enlarged. Original bldg. enlarged 1897 and 1898.[89] 1898 a.a. 466 I. 1899 accn. 564 G, 664 I. From 1905 renamed South Acton G and I.[90] 1927 accn. 542 G, 450 I; a.a. 423 G, 390 I. Reorg. 1931 as Berrymede J sch., later middle (q.v.) on upper floor and Berrymede I for 450 on ground floor. 1938 a.a. 241 I. Became Berrymede first sch. from 1974 and moved to new bldg. in Park Rd. North. Roll 1979: 252 M.

PRIORY FIRST, formerly also B and G, Acton Lane. Opened 1882 for 360 B, 300 G. 1888 a.a. 524 G. Sch. pence (2d. and 3d.). I shared G accn. until extension built[91] to include large central hall, seating 600, also used for public assemblies. Temp. bldgs. for tech. educ., erected by Mdx. C.C., in grounds until 1894.[92] 1893 accn. 1,025 BGI. Extension built 1896 for B, including offices for Acton sch. bd.[93] 1899 accn. 1,447 BGI, a.a. 1,177. 1903 accn. 550 B, 542 G, 550 I. 1906 a.a. 576 B, 465 G, 455 I. 1927 accn. 500 B, 499 G, 400 I; a.a. 402 B, 383 G, 306 I. Reorg. between 1927 and 1932 for 500 SB, 499 SG, 400 I. 1938 a.a. 272 SB, 251 SG, 221 I. After 1945 SG formed Priory G sec. mod. and moved to Beaumont Pk. SB formed Priory B sec. mod. in original bldg. Priory G amalg. with Elms sec. mod. (see Twyford high) and Priory B with Faraday sec. mod. (q.v.) 1961. Priory I became first sch. 1974, occupying half of Priory bldgs., with youth centre in other half. Roll 1979: 180 M.

REYNOLDS HIGH, see Acton county grammar.

ROTHSCHILD FIRST AND MIDDLE, Acton Green. Temp. iron bldg. opened 1904 as Rothschild Rd. sch. for 280 I to relieve Beaumont Pk. (q.v.). 1906 a.a. 156 I. From 1909 accn. 295. 1912 a.a. 254. Closed 1912 and replaced by Rothschild sch., built on verandah system,[94] for 545 JM and 400 I on same site, taking many pupils from Beaumont Pk. and Southfield Rd. (q.v.). 1919 a.a. 438 JM, 344 I. Reorg. between 1927 and 1932 for 450 JB, 400 I. 1938 a.a. 193 JB, 224 I. After 1945 reorg. as Rothschild JM and Rothschild I on same site. Two classroom huts built in playground 1967. JM and I amalg. 1973 but reorg. separately as Rothschild first and middle schs. 1974. Middle sch. renamed Acton Green middle 1975 and moved to Beaumont Pk. bldgs. 1976. Acton Green roll 1979: 190 M. Rothschild first roll 1979: 170 M.

ST. MARY'S C.E., Oldham's Terrace, High Street. Day sch. for poor children of parish joined Nat. Soc. 1816, when 100–20 BG taught by mistress with salary and ho.[95] Schoolroom built opposite almshouses in Steyne.[96] Financed entirely by annual subscriptions 1819.[97] Separate sch. for I built 1837 at north end Oldham's Terrace. 1846–7 a.a. 43 B, 40 G, 79 I. Financed

---

[77] Ealing libr., Acc. 1/6 (Acton U.D.C. educ. cttee. min. bk.).
[78] P.R.O., ED 16/204.
[79] Ealing libr., Acc. 1/9, p. 5.
[80] P.R.O., ED 16/204.
[81] Ealing libr., Acc. 12/1 (log bk.).
[82] P.R.O., C 54/17138, no. 2.
[83] Ibid. ED 16/204.
[84] Ealing libr., Acc. 12/2 (log bk.).
[85] Ibid.
[86] Ibid.
[87] Memorial stone.
[88] Baker, *Acton*, 217.
[89] Datestone.
[90] P.R.O., ED 16/204.
[91] Baker, *Acton*, 217.
[92] Ealing libr., Acc. 1/24 (Acton sch. bd. min. bk.).
[93] Datestone.
[94] *The Times*, 27 Sept. 1912.
[95] *Nat. Soc. 5th Ann. Rep.* (1816), 46; *Educ. of Poor Digest*, 533.
[96] Vestry min. bk. (1801–22), 16 Oct. 1815.
[97] *Educ. of Poor Digest*, 533.

by subscriptions and sch. pence (1*d*.).[98] New sch. for BG, with master's ho., built 1853 at south end Oldham's Terrace, with Nat. Soc. and parl. bldg. grants. Sch. pence (1*d*.). 1854 a.a. 78 B, 41 G. 1857 a.a. 86 I. G moved into new extension built 1862.[99] 1870 a.a. 325 BGI. Rented by sch. bd. 1876. 1878 accn. 496 BGI, a.a. 392 BGI. Sch. pence raised 1883 to 6*d*. for B and 4*d*. for G.[1] 1888 a.a. 412 BGI. 1906 accn. 204 B, 155 G, 163 I; a.a. 148 B, 134 G, 174 I. 1919 accn. 310 B, 129 G, 142 I; a.a. 224 B, 110 G, 136 I. BG bldg. sold to U.D.C. 1926.[2] Reorg. 1926 for 184 JM, 122 I. 1932 a.a. 233 JMI. Closed 1932. I bldg. housed Acton Wells special sch. (q.v.) 1926–72. B and G bldg. replaced by labour exchange.

St. Mary's R.C., Turnham Green. Opened 1853 in Chiswick by parish priest for BGI, financed by sch. pence (1*d*.) and priest.[3] 1864 a.a. 27 B, 23 G, 25 I. New sch. built 1864 for 325 M in Acton Lane opposite Gladstone Rd. junction. Vol. aided by 1893, financed by parl. grants, endowment producing £44 14*s*. a year, and vol. contributions. 1893 a.a. 165 M. Trust for educ. and religious purposes created 1902. 1906 accn. 251 M, 74 I; a.a. 210 M, 67 I. 1909 accn. 123 M, 90 I, and temp. accn. for 130.[4] 1927 a.a. 284 MI. Single dept. sch. from 1932. 1938 accn. 236 M, 91 I; a.a. 229 MI. By 1952 mixed vol. sch. for all ages. S pupils formed Cardinal Newman R.C. sec. mod. (q.v.) from 1963, when JMI moved to new bldg. in Turnham Green.[5] Acton Lane bldg. demol., site forming grounds of Acton Green middle sch.

St. Vincent's R.C. first and middle, Pierrepoint Rd. Opened as private day sch.[6] but vol. aided primary sch. with intake of 350 JMI from 1963, when larger bldg. needed. First and middle sch. from 1974, with additional accn. in two huts. Roll 1979: 445 M.

South Acton B, Osborne Rd. Opened 1904[7] on north side of rd., opposite I sch., for 360 SB, 360 JB, taking pupils and staff from All Saints'. Manual centre in bldg. in grounds.[8] 1906 a.a. 474 SB, JB. 1908 a.a. 303 SB, 231 JB. 1919 accn. 400 SB, 360 JB; a.a. 335 SB, 261 JB. 1927 a.a. 255 SB, 249 JB. Closed 1931 and replaced by Berrymede JB for 640 in same bldg. 1938 a.a. 353 JB. Amalg. with Berrymede JG (q.v.) 1961.

Southfield first and middle, Bedford Pk. Opened 1906 as Southfield Rd. sch. for 378 SM, 378 JM, 383 I on separate floors of bldg. on 1½-a. site. I from Beaumont Pk., SM from Beaumont Pk. and Cobbold Rd., Hammersmith.[9] 1909 accn. 419 SM, 381 JM, 400 I. 1919 a.a. 321 SM, 336 JM, 314 I; accn. increased 1919 to 415 JM, 1922 to 451 SM. 1927 a.a. 357 SM, 281 JM, 219 I. Reorg. 1932 as Southfield sch. for 415 SB, 382 JM, 350 I. 1938 a.a. 135 SB, 285 JM, 216 I.

Reorg. after 1945 for JMI only. First and middle schs. from 1974. Rolls 1979: 122 M and 225 M.

Turnham Green R.C., see St. Mary's R.C.

Twyford high, Twyford Crescent. Opened 1957 as the Elms mixed sec. mod. in former home of Wegg family,[10] to which block was added. Pupils from central sch. and new 6th-form intake. Roll 1957: 464 SM.[11] Amalg. 1961 with Priory G sec. mod. and Acton sec. tech. to form new '7-year' sec. mod. in Elms bldgs., renamed Twyford sch. Extensions inc. teaching block early 1960s, tech. block 1971, and *c.* 15 temp. classrooms. Comprehensive high sch. from 1974, with peak attendance 1,100. Roll 1979: *c.* 800 M.

Wesleyan day, Gunnersbury Lane. Opened 1846 for 50 G in ho. in the Steyne, rented by Thomas Farmer of Gunnersbury Ho. and managed by him in connexion with Wesleyan Normal Training Institution, Westminster Financed by Farmer and sch. pence; parl. grant for teacher from 1853. Sunday and day sch., with teacher's ho. built 1857 with new Wes. chapel east side Gunnersbury Lane. 58 pupils 1863.[12] 1871 a.a. 77 M. 1878 accn. 110 M, a.a. 103 M. 1893 accn. 136 M. Rented by sch. bd. 1895 as Gunnersbury Lane bd. sch.[13] Transferred 1901 to temp. accn. in Cong. Churchfield hall, Churchfield Rd.[14] 1903 accn. 357 M, a.a. 199. 1905 a.a. 87 SM, 181 JM, 96 I, when replaced by central sch.[15]

West Acton first, Noel Rd. Opened 1937 for 300 I, with full time nursery class for 30. 1938 a.a. 204 I. First sch. from 1974. Additional accn. in huts and open-plan bldgs. 1970s. Roll 1979: 196 M.

Willesden Junction temp., Railway Cottages, Old Oak Lane. Opened 1898 for MI in iron bldg. erected by bd. behind St. Luke's mission church, leased from L. & N.W.R.[16] 1899 accn. 213 M, a.a. 193 M. Church leased during sch. hours from 1905 for additional accn.[17] 1906 accn. 123 M, 90 I; a.a. 127 M, 101 I. 1909 a.a. 198 M, 95 I. Replaced 1909 by Acton Wells (q.v.).

Special school. Acton Wells, School Rd., Victoria Rd. Opened 1915 for 65 mentally deficient children, using 2nd floor of Acton Wells council sch. Attendance 1915: 45. Moved to St. Mary's C.E. I sch. bldg., Oldham's Terrace, 1926. Roll 1949: 40, from Acton, Ealing, and Harlesden, to age 16. Roll 1972: 39.[18] Replaced by Castlebar sch., Ealing, 1972.[19]

Technical and further education. The county council provided technical education at Acton and Chiswick polytechnic[20] from 1899, to which Acton local board contributed. Designed to meet the needs of local industry, branch classes were

[98] Nat. Soc. *Church Schs. Enquiry, 1846–7*, Mdx. 2.
[99] M.R.O., Acc. 1341/2/1–5 (plans).
[1] Ealing libr., Acc. 1/32 (Acton sch. bd. min. bk.).
[2] Ibid. Acc. 19/2 (Acton U.D.C. estate bk.).
[3] Below, Chiswick, educ.
[4] P.R.O., ED 16/204.
[5] Below, Chiswick, educ.
[6] Below, private schs.
[7] P.R.O., ED 16/204.
[8] Baker, *Acton*, 230.
[9] Ealing libr., Acc. 1/28 (Acton sch. bd. min. bk. 7 May 1903).

[10] M.R.O., Hist. Notes 30/4/58; above, manors and other est.
[11] Ealing libr., Acc. 12/1 (log bk.).
[12] Hocking, *Meth. Ch. in Acton*, 5, 7.
[13] Ealing libr., Acc. 1/25 (Acton sch. bd. min. bk. 27 Dec. 1894, 24 Jan. 1895).
[14] Ibid. Acc. 1/28 (Ealing sch. bd. min. bk.).
[15] Ibid. Acc. 1/6 (Acton U.D.C. educ. cttee. min. bk.).
[16] Ibid. Acc. 1/26 (Acton sch. bd. min. bk. 22 Oct. 1897).
[17] Ibid. Acc. 5/17 (lease).
[18] Ealing libr., Acc. 9/1 (log bk.).
[19] Below, Ealing, educ.   [20] Below, Chiswick, educ.

held in Acton at the Priory schools from 1900, with 173 students in that year, and also at the central and county schools by 1911, when the total attendance in Acton was 360.[21] Acton school board, and later the technical committee of the U.D.C., also ran evening continuation schools from the end of the 19th century, for boys and girls who had left elementary school.

A junior technical school was also started, using the polytechnic until Acton technical college was opened in 1929, when it was transferred there.[22] By the 1930s it was run as a secondary technical school, taking boys at 13 years for 3-year courses leading to apprenticeships in engineering. In 1938–9 there were 312 students.[23] In 1958–9 the technical school, much reduced, moved to Acton Wells secondary modern school[24] and from 1961 it formed part of Twyford school.[25]

Acton technical college, originally 'institute', was built in 1928 on the site of Grove House, High Street, by the county council, as the first of seven colleges to expand further education in Middlesex.[26] Opened officially in 1929, it provided evening classes in science, engineering, and building trades, which had outgrown the accommodation at Acton and Chiswick polytechnic, and housed a junior technical college in the day time. In 1931 it was decided to concentrate at Acton all the more advanced further education in the county, at that time comprising courses for Higher National Certificates and the Intermediate examinations for the external London degree. Courses to final level for the B.Sc. in engineering and science subjects were soon introduced, with management subjects to gain membership of professional institutes. The college was so crowded that local schools were used by 1931 and extensions to the original buildings were made in 1932 and 1937–9. In 1939 the former county school in Woodlands Avenue was acquired. There were 3,912 students in 1938–9: 163 senior day, 147 part-time day, and 3,602 evening and weekend students. After D. Napier & Sons began to send apprentices to the college in 1936, the number of students on day release from employment rose to 321 in 1940–1 and 667 in 1944–5, increasing more rapidly thereafter.

By 1949 there were 410 full-time and 1,368 part-time day students, most of them from outside Acton. Sandwich courses started in 1955, by which date there were 100 full-time and 250 part-time teachers for nearly 5,000 students, more than half of them being evening students, one third being on day release schemes, and one tenth on full-time day courses.

In 1956 it was decided to do all the advanced teaching in new buildings in Woodlands Avenue, near the former county school, and to create two separate institutions. The Woodlands classes were formed into a regional college of technology, renamed Brunel college (below). The High Street buildings housed a local technical college, which continued with 254 full-time and 1,924 part-time students in 1957–8 and mainly undertook courses for City and Guilds certificates and the General Certificate of Education. Although it had lost its most highly qualified staff and its pre-eminence among Middlesex colleges, the college still used the former county school and acquired a former laundry building in Winchester Street in 1968, besides a disused annexe of Ealing Mead school in 1977. There were 642 full-time and 3,213 part-time students in 1978–9, when there were courses for certificates of the Business Education and Technical Education councils and in computing, mathematics, and the sciences.

Brunel college of technology opened in 1957 with departments of management and production engineering, chemistry, physics, mathematics, electronics, and electrical and mechanical engineering from Acton technical college, and became a college of advanced technology in 1962. Its buildings in Woodlands Avenue, begun in 1951 for the technical college's science departments but not completed until 1957, housed 1,200 and were later extended. Engineering courses were still taught at the technical college in High Street, plans for another block at Woodlands being superseded by the college's move in 1965 to Uxbridge common. Brunel became a university in 1967.

Thomas Huxley college opened in 1967 as Acton college of education, to prepare mature students for teaching, and was housed in the town hall. The number of students quickly increased to 300. Its name was changed in 1971, to honour the Ealing-born scientist, and the college moved into the former Brunel building in Woodlands Avenue in 1973. There were courses leading to the Certificate of Education and the B.Ed. degree of London University, besides in-service courses for teachers in west London, mainly in mathematics. The college closed in 1980, after the government had decided to cease teacher training there and Ealing L.B. had abandoned plans to merge it with Ealing technical college, which housed some of its own departments in the same building.[27]

Private Schools. The Society for Maintaining and Educating Poor Orphans of the Clergy purchased the copyhold later called Orger House in 1804, for a school, which was transferred from Thirsk (Yorks. N.R.).[28] There were 50 boys in 1809[29] and Dr. Bell's system, the basis of the National Society's system, was adopted in 1811.[30] The school was moved to St. John's Wood, Marylebone, in 1812.[31]

A boarding school used the former assembly

[21] Baker, *Acton,* 220–42, 246.

[22] Ibid. 245; J. Flaherty, 'From Tech. Coll. to Univ.: Case Study of Brunel Coll.' (Brunel Univ. M.Phil. thesis, 1976), 23.

[23] Acton, *Official Guide* (1930, 1936); Flaherty, 'Brunel Coll.' 27–8.

[24] Inf. from the principal, Acton tech. coll.

[25] Above.

[26] Following 4 paras. based on Flaherty, 'Brunel Coll.'

passim; C. Soper and G. Hutton, *New Ways in Management Training,* 12–13; inf. from the principal, Acton tech. coll.

[27] Inf. from the principal, Thos. Huxley coll.

[28] P.R.O., C 54/7842, no. 6; *Constitutions of Soc. for Orphans of Clergy* (1809), 12. Ho. identified from P.R.O., MAF 20/2/22, Bird's enfranchisement.

[29] *Constitutions,* 16, 80.

[30] *Acct. of S.P.C.K. for 1811,* 27 n.

[31] *Acct. of Soc. for Poor Orphans of Clergymen* (1817), 5.

rooms, Acton wells, by 1816,[32] and in 1819 there were two boarding schools in the parish for the children of tradesmen, and two or three other small schools.[33] They may have been the schools existing in 1826, which included two boarding schools and two preparatory schools in Acton and a preparatory school in East Acton.[34] In 1833 fee-paying pupils were about twice as numerous as the children at the National School. There were four day schools with *c.* 90 children, a boys' boarding school with *c.* 80, and two girls' boarding schools with 50 altogether.[35]

Felix Mullens ran a boys' boarding and day school by 1826 at Orger House, probably the boarding school which had 80 boys in 1833.[36] His schoolroom was used for services in 1836–7, while the parish church was being altered.[37] Mullens was still there in 1842,[38] but by 1851 had been succeeded by George Smalley, who was boarding 21 boys aged 7 to 14 years.[39] He was succeeded by a Frenchman, Stanislas Bard, who had run a day preparatory school in 1832, an academy in 1845, and a mixed boarding school in High Street in 1851. Orger House was burned down shortly before 1858, when the school apparently did not reopen.[40]

Frances Beechey ran a ladies' day and boarding school in 1826 and 1832, described as a boarding and finishing school in 1828 when it was at Acton House, West Acton.[41] Her school near the Rectory apparently had *c.* 40 boys in 1832.[42] It had probably closed by 1845, although Miss Beechey was described as an infants' school mistress in Gunnersbury Lane in 1851. In 1832 Mary Ann Fowler ran a day school at the Manor House, described as a seminary in 1845, when Ann Fowler also had a school; both had closed by 1851.[43] Sisters of the Society of the Sacred Heart from France opened their first convent in England at Berrymead Priory in 1842, where they opened a private boarding school for Roman Catholic girls and a free day school for the poor. Both convent and school moved to Roehampton (Surr.) in 1850.[44]

A commercial school was run by Frederick Geary at Acton House, Acton Vale, in 1851, when two other schoolmistresses, a French and dancing teacher, and a teacher of classics and mathematics also lived in the parish.[45] In the late 19th century the number of private schools increased: there were 12 in 1873 and 15 in 1890, 9 of them ladies' schools,[46] but most were short lived.

Acton Collegiate school, day and boarding for boys, was established in 1864 by Henry Mayner Coules, who had an academy in Mill Hill Road in 1873.[47] In the 1870s the school occupied Bank House, which had been a girls' industrial school *c.* 1865,[48] but it had moved to no. 6 Apsley Villas, Horn Lane, by 1886.[49] Coules offered mathematics, modern languages, and science, and training for the universities. The school was taken over between 1926 and 1928 by Miss C. C. Coules, who had run a ladies' school at no. 1 Apsley Villas in 1890, and had closed by 1940.[50]

Queen's College school was started in 1871 by Mary Pierce and was at no. 1 Apsley Villas, Horn Lane, in 1890 and at Shalimar, Pembridge Road, by 1901. At one time the largest private girls' school in Acton, it included a kindergarten and prepared girls for public examinations, besides offering science and cookery. It closed between 1905 and 1911.[51]

Springfield college was a boys' boarding and day school run by Henry Waymouth, who opened a collegiate school at nos. 8 and 9 Apsley Terrace, Horn Lane, *c.* 1889, moving to Hill House, Acton hill, by 1901. The school provided a commercial education and training for public school and other examinations. After its closure, between 1906 and 1911, the buildings were demolished.[52]

Acton Commercial college, a boys' boarding school, at Grove House, High Street, from 1896, was run by E. C. Sunnock, a trustee of Acton Methodist church. It provided preparatory classes for young boys and courses for careers in business, the civil service, and engineering. By 1911 the school had been taken over by John Mackay, under whom it moved to the Mall, Ealing, as Ealing college in 1925,[53] Grove House being sold to Acton U.D.C. and demolished.[54]

Helen Hopkins ran a girls' day school at no. 28 Churchfield Road West by 1890, which closed *c.* 1932.[55] Leith House, no. 10 Burlington Gardens, was a girls' day and boarding school run by Alice Mackerness in 1890. It was taken over by Mrs. Stredder by 1901, when it also had a kindergarten, and prepared girls for examinations. By 1914 Mrs. Stredder had moved her school to no. 102 Goldsmith Avenue. After the First World War it was known as Shirley House school for girls, with a preparatory department for boys. Under Miss M. Stredder in 1939, it had closed by 1955.[56]

Haberdashers' Aske's school for girls, financed

[32] Brewer, *Beauties of Eng. & Wales*, x (5), 332.

[33] *Educ. of Poor Digest*, 533.

[34] Pigot, *Lond. Dir.* (1826–7); *Com. Dir.* (1832–4).

[35] *Educ. Enq. Abstract*, 554.

[36] Pigot, *Lond. Dir.* (1826–7).

[37] Vestry min. bk. (1822–57), 21 Dec. 1837.

[38] P.R.O., IR 29/2/1.

[39] Ibid. HO 107/1699.

[40] Ibid.; Pigot, *Com. Dir.* (1832–4); *P.O. Dir. Mdx.* (1845); above, manors and other est. *Crockford's Scholastic. Dir.* (1861), 76, records Bard as still at Orger Ho.: possibly the sch. reopened elsewhere or the ho. was rebuilt. Monson, *Acton*, 29, says that the sch. was burned down in the 1860s.

[41] Pigot, *Lond. Dir.* (1826–7); *Com. Dir.* (1832–4); *Boarding Sch. and Lond. Masters' Dir.* (1828), 9.

[42] Vestry min. bk. (1822–57), 26 July 1832.

[43] Pigot, *Com. Dir.* (*1832–4*); *P.O. Dir. Mdx.* (1845); P.R.O. HO 107/1699.

[44] Anson, *Rel. Orders of G.B. and Irel.* 390, 392; *P.O. Dir. Mdx.* (1845).

[45] P.R.O., HO 107/1699.

[46] *Green's Dir. Notting Hill, Acton* (1873); *Kelly's Dir. Mdx.* (1890).

[47] F. S. de Carteret-Bisson, *Our Schs. and Colls.* (1879 boys), i. 753; *Green's Dir. Notting Hill, Acton* (1873).

[48] Baker, *Acton*, 238; rate bk. (1860s).

[49] *Ealing, Acton, Dir.* (1885–7).

[50] *Kelly's Dir. Mdx.* (1926, 1890); *Kelly's Dir. Acton* (1928, 1940).

[51] Acton Gaz. 4 Jan. 1901 (advert.); Baker, *Acton*, 238; *Kelly's Dir. Mdx.* (1890).

[52] *Kelly's Dir. N. Suburbs* (1888); *Kelly's Dir. Mdx.* (1890); Acton Gaz. 4 Jan. 1901 (advert.); Baker, *Acton*, 238.

[53] C. Hocking, *Brief Hist. of Meth. Ch. in Acton*, 5; *Paton's Schs.* (1902), 261; Baker, *Acton*, 238; Acton Gaz. 4 Jan. 1901 (advert.); Rowland, *Street Names*, 20.

[54] Ealing libr., Acc. 19/2; below, Ealing, educ.

[55] *Kelly's Dir. Mdx.* (1890); *Kelly's Dir. Acton* (1932).

[56] *Kelly's Dir. Mdx.* (1890); Acton Gaz. 4 Jan. 1901 (advert.); *Kelly's Dir. Chiswick, Acton* (1914); Acton, *Official Guide* (1924); *Kelly's Dir. Acton* (1940, 1955).

by Robert Aske's trust, was the most important girls' school in Acton, where it moved from Hoxton in 1898. Temporary premises were used[57] until new buildings, designed by Henry Stock for 350 girls, were opened in Creffield Road on the Springfield Park estate in 1901. Girls were taken from the age of 8, later 5, and prepared for university. The upper school also had a secretarial and business training department. A new wing was built in 1910 and accommodation increased to 550 places by 1924, and 600 by 1936. Playing fields of 6 a. near West Acton station had been acquired by 1936.[58] After the Second World War, the school became a direct grant secondary school for girls and in 1974 it moved to Elstree (Herts.),[59] its building being used by Cardinal Newman high school from 1976.[60]

The Sisters of Charity of St. Vincent de Paul ran a day and kindergarten school at nos. 3 and 5 (later 45 and 47) Avenue Road in 1902. Convent and school moved to no. 9 Rosemont Road in 1930 and expanded into the adjoining premises at no. 1 Pierrepoint Road in 1959. Girls were taught to the age of 16.[61] In 1964, when more accommodation was needed, the school became a voluntary aided primary school.[62]

A few new schools, mainly day and boarding schools for girls, were later added to those that had survived from before the First World War, and a very few were recognized by the L.E.A. in the 1930s. The principal ones were East Acton House high school, East Acton Lane, started c. 1928 but closed by 1939 when the house was demolished, Lancaster House school at nos. 21 and 23 Cumberland Park, started by 1928 and still there in 1940 but closed by the early 1950s, and York House school, Grafton Road, which was recognized by the L.E.A. in 1934 but closed by 1939. The Parents' National Educational Union opened Ambleside school in Creffield Road hall c. 1930, for girls to the age of 17 and boys to 10. It was recognized by the L.E.A. and survived in 1940.[63]

CHARITIES FOR THE POOR.[64] A clothing fund was established c. 1818 from clothing charities and bequests formerly distributed in money or fuel. Later gifts for food and clothing augmented the fund, which was administered with other parochial charities from 1899.

Almshouses. In 1725 almshouses were built in the Steyne on the site of a house which the parish had bought in 1681 for the poor.[65] The almshouses contained eight rooms, with seven inmates, in 1779[66] and were in disrepair by 1793,

when they were sold. Joseph Grantham thereupon granted some copyhold tenements on the west side of the Steyne, where six cottages were built for the poor[67] with the aid of sums received for inclosures of the waste.[68] In 1839 the almshouses were to be sold to contribute towards the cost of Brentford union workhouse but in 1843 the rector and overseers took charge and the rector paid for their repair.[69] The almshouses were rebuilt by public subscription as the Jubilee almshouses, nos. 1–12 the Steyne, in 1897[70] and bought by Ealing L.B. in 1967.

Frederic Ouvry gave £200 stock to the almshouses in 1880, Mrs. Sarah Mary Sibson £100 stock in 1883, and Selina Payne £1,009 stock by will dated 1893. The gifts formed an endowment fund, providing weekly pensions, from 1967, together with £10,000 paid by Ealing L.B.

Apprenticing charity. Catherine, Viscountess Conway, by will dated 1637, left £800 to the Grocers' Company of London to provide, among other purposes, £20 a year for apprenticing poor children after the death of a residuary legatee. After a dispute over arrears the vestry received a reduced income from 1706. Only boys had been apprenticed for some time in 1826, at a cost of £10 a year.

Distributive charities. Thomas Thorney, by will dated 1612, left a rent charge of 20s. On Conduit close, of which at least 6s. 8d. was for repair of the conduit and the rest for the poor. In 1826 the entire income had been spent for some time on the conduit.

Paul Freeman, by will dated 1615, and William Harraway, by will dated 1620, left sums to buy 2s. worth and 1s. of bread respectively. The money was not accounted for after 1628.

Catherine, Viscountess Conway, in addition to providing £20 for apprenticing, assigned in reversion £10 a year for bread for 21 recipients and teaching 6 children, to which her executrix Mary Harrison added £8, making the income £10 8s. Lady Conway also assigned £10 a year to the minister for alms.[71] The Grocers' Company fell into arrears with payments and in 1706 the vestry accepted £50 in lieu of £100 arrears,[72] although it later received only £22 9s. 8d. a year for all her bequests, including the apprenticing charity. Thereafter £2 12s. was paid regularly for teaching and by 1826 15s. 8d. was spent on clothing and the balance, after apprenticing, on bread for 21 parishioners weekly and on alms.

John Perryn, by will dated 1656, left a rent charge of £10 for the poor, vested in the Goldsmiths' Company of London. By 1826 it was paid into the clothing fund.

[57] *V.C.H. Mdx.* i. 297.
[58] *Acton Gaz.* 5 July 1901; Baker, *Acton*, 238–9; *Kelly's Dir. Mdx.* (1926); Acton, *Official Guide* (1924, 1936, c. 1952).
[59] *Girls' Sch. Year Bk.* (1977), 182.
[60] Above.
[61] *Rel. Orders*, 227; *Kelly's Dir. N. Suburbs* (1902); *Kelly's Dir. Acton* (1930, 1931); Acton, *Official Guide* (1939).
[62] Above.
[63] Acton, *Official Guide* (1928, 1930, 1934, 1938, 1939); *Kelly's Dir. Acton* (1940).
[64] Section based on Char. Com. files; *Char. Donations, 1786–8*, H.C. 511, pp. 758–60 (1816), xvi; *14th Rep. Com.*

Char. H.C. 382, pp. 170–7 (1826), xii; *Digest of Endowed Chars.* H.C. 433, Mdx. pp. 2–3 (1867–8), lii (1); *Endowed Chars. Mdx.* H.C. 306, p. 401 (1899), lxx; Guildhall MS. 10731/1, *Chars. Belonging to Acton* [1887].
[65] Lysons, *Environs*, ii. 20; above, local govt.
[66] Simonon, 'Poor in Acton', 83.
[67] Ibid.; Lysons, *Environs*, ii. 20; vestry min. bk. (1775–1801), 3 July 1793; P.R.O., IR 29/21/1.
[68] Vestry min. bk. (1775–1801), 3 Oct. 1792.
[69] Ibid. (1822–57).
[70] Taylor, Acton notes, 28A.
[71] P.R.O., C 90/10.   [72] Rate bk. (1701–67).

George Needler, by will dated 1638, left £40 for annual purchases of shoes and stockings. The capital was lent out to parishioners, from whom interest was last received in 1719. It was said to be vested in the Grocers' Company in 1786 and had been lost by 1826.

Henry Ramsay, by will dated 1693, left a rent charge of £10, perhaps to fulfil a similar bequest of 1601 by Mary, wife of Sir Thomas Ramsay, lord mayor of London.[73] In 1826 the sum was devoted to the clothing fund.

Sarah Crayle, by will dated 1730, left £300 to provide 40s. a year for a sermon and £6 for weekly bread doles to the poor not receiving alms, the residue to be distributed in money twice a year. In 1745 land was bought in Ealing,[74] producing £13 13s. c. 1786–8 and £30 from 1825. Bread for 14 persons was bought with £6 in 1826, when the minister received 40s. and the residue went to the clothing fund. By 1899 the principal had been invested in stock.

Ann Crayle, by will dated 1767, left £700 stock to provide £12 3s. a year for specified clothing for 6 men and 6 women, the residue to be spent on coal. In 1826 the income of £21 was paid into the clothing fund.

Edward Dickenson, by will dated 1781, left a third of the interest on £100 stock for payments to three couples married in Acton church during the previous year. The income was £45 in 1786 and £50 by 1867.

Rebecca Bulwer, by will dated 1789, left the income from £600 for eight householders, preferably Anglican communicants, and Thomas Bramley (d. 1807) left £300 for the same purpose. Twelve families then received £3 each, although by 1826 the income had fallen to £31 1s. 4d.

Elizabeth Wegg, by will dated 1799, left £100 for the poor. Her husband Samuel added £100

stock, by will dated 1802, and their son George added £300 in 1817.

John Cordy, by will dated 1799, left the income from £100 to clothe three widows. Only two women could be given the full amount of clothing in 1826.

Rebecca Cranmer, by will dated 1813, left £400 stock to provide greatcoats for six men, as did Thomas Church, by will dated 1823. Church's money had not been received in 1826, when Mrs. Cranmer's gift for clothing was augmented by the surplus income from £300 which she had left towards repairs of the family vault.

The churchwardens in 1786 held £20, of unknown origin, which was spent on cheap coal until c. 1812 and then on building the National school.

The clothing fund had an income of £85 in 1826, from the charities of Lady Conway, Perryn, Ramsay, Sarah and Ann Crayle, Cordy, and Mrs. Cranmer. It was later augmented by the following gifts: £100 stock from William Henry Church, by will dated 1832; £741 stock from Elizabeth Wegg, by will dated 1842, for food and clothing; £200 stock from Mary Tubbs, by will of c. 1852, for food; £52 stock from William Hervey, by deed dated 1860, for food and clothing.

Acton (*Middlesex*) *charities.* All the existing charities were united under a Scheme of 1899 as the Acton (Middlesex) charities, to which in 1913 was added £5 a year bequeathed to the poor by Rachel Rebecca Murton. The income from stock in 1976 was £1,224. In 1980 it produced £2 for apprenticing, £50 for nursing, and small sums for ecclesiastical purposes, the residue being spent on the poor.

CHISWICK

CHISWICK[1] parish lies in a large loop of the Thames 10 km. west of Hyde Park Corner. It is known chiefly for Chiswick House, near its centre, and for 18th- and 19th-century buildings at Chiswick village, hereafter referred to as Old Chiswick, and Strand-on-the-Green, respectively at the eastern and western ends of the loop. The greater part of the boundary follows the Thames. The eastern boundary with Hammersmith ran from the eastern end of Chiswick Eyot northward along the line of the present British Grove and part of Goldhawk Road to Stamford Brook Road. Thence the northern boundary, mainly with Acton, ran west-south-west across Stamford Brook common, to follow the course of a Roman road between Acton Green common and the Back (later Chiswick) common. West of

Turnham Green the line of the Roman road and the former boundary are followed by Chiswick High Road through Gunnersbury, a district mainly in Ealing but later with its railway station and other public buildings in Chiswick.[2] Farther west, at Old Brentford in Ealing parish, the boundary turned south-west, away from the road, to meet the river at Kew bridge.

The parish contained 1,216 a. in 1871[3] and 1,245 a. in 1881, after the addition in 1878 of a detached part of Ealing, both figures apparently excluding the tidal foreshore.[4] The detached part of Ealing formed a triangle of 29 a. called Stamford Brook grounds projecting from Chiswick's northern boundary near the east end; built over as part of Bedford Park, it is included in the present account along with that suburb's

[73] W. K. Jordan, *Chars. of Lond. 1440–1660* (1960), 102.
[74] P.R.O., C 54/5740, no. 7.
[1] The article was written in 1979. Any references to later events are dated. The help of Mrs. K. Judges, Mr. T. A. Greeves, and Mr. J. Wisdom in commenting on parts of the

article is gratefully acknowledged.
[2] O.S. Maps 6″, Mdx. XVI, SW., XXI. NW. (1873 and later edns.).   [3] Para. based on *Census*, 1881–1951.
[4] Estimated at 94 a. out of 1,314 a. in 1846: M.R.O., TA/ CHI (copy also in Chiswick libr.).

parts in Acton. The Chiswick U.D.C. Act, 1911,[5] transferred to Chiswick a small but populous area around the Star and Garter at Old Brentford, making Chiswick High Road the boundary as far as the approach to Kew bridge. In 1932 the northern boundary with Acton was adjusted to coincide with the Metropolitan District railway line, which runs more nearly east and west than the former boundary.[6] Chiswick, which had a local board of health from 1883 and became a U.D. in 1894, formed part of Brentford and Chiswick U.D. (later M.B.) from 1927 and contained 1,276 a. of the borough's 2,332 a. in 1951. From 1965, when Brentford and Chiswick joined Heston and Isleworth M.B. and Feltham U.D., Chiswick has formed the eastern extremity of Hounslow L.B.

Flood plain gravel covers nearly all the peninsular part of the parish, bordering the river at Old Chiswick along Chiswick Mall and at Strand-on-the-Green. A belt of alluvium, nowhere more than 200 m. wide, curves around the southern and south-eastern part of the loop. Brickearth covers the northern half of the parish, except where a tongue of gravel stretches north to Gunnersbury. From the Hammersmith end of Chiswick High Road, the edge of the brickearth extends south-westward to the bottom of Chiswick Lane and thence westward to the approach to Kew bridge.[7]

The land is generally flat, lying c. 6 m. above sea level but rising slightly higher in the north-west corner, along parts of Chiswick High Road, and north and west of the parish church.[8] High tide levels threatened most of the parish by 1972, when the Thames Barrier and Flood Prevention Act was passed,[9] and in 1976 ordinary tides had a high water mark of 13–14 ft., a level represented by the lowest stretches of Chiswick Mall and of the riverside path at Strand-on-the-Green.[10] Chiswick Eyot, opposite Chiswick Mall, is the most easterly of the islands in the Thames,[11] the nearest ones being Oliver's Island, facing Strand-on-the-Green, and Brentford Ait.[12] Containing 3¼ a. c. 1900, Chiswick Eyot later suffered such erosion that by 1948 its eastern tip had disappeared. Silting up of the backwater allowed it to be reached on foot at low tide[13] and in 1949 the island could be covered by a high tide. In 1978 it was to be preserved by Hounslow L.B.[14]

Bollo or Bollar brook enters the parish from Acton, west of Turnham Green, passing under the high road and, by a course no longer visible, into the grounds of Chiswick House.[15] Thither a stream also flows from a former lake near Sydney House, at the western end of the parish, through another lake at Little Sutton. From the 18th century the streams have fed a long ornamental water, created for Chiswick House and drained south-eastward by a conduit to the Thames along the present line of Promenade Approach Road. A stream ran eastward from Acton Green along the Chiswick side of the boundary towards the western branch of Stamford brook, which for a short distance formed the boundary with Hammersmith.[16]

COMMUNICATIONS. Two Roman roads from London crossed the north part of the parish and converged near Brentford.[17] The northern one, from Newgate, having crossed Hammersmith along the line of Goldhawk Road, continued west to form the northern boundary of Chiswick. Along the eastern part of that boundary there was no road in 1746, although short sections were later marked by Bath Road and Chiswick Road. Farther west Chiswick High Road, passing through Gunnersbury and curving towards the river, may represent the northern road. The southern Roman road, Akeman Street, left London along the Strand and passed through Kensington and Hammersmith to Turnham Green, where originally it may have headed west-south-west, skirting the southern edge of the common and continuing along the line of Wellesley Road. By the late 17th century the main east–west route was that of the later high road,[18] which followed the southerly Roman road to Turnham Green and thence cut due west across the common to Gunnersbury. Still known simply as the high road or Brentford Road in the 18th century, when it was turnpiked,[19] it was placed under the metropolitan turnpike roads commissioners in 1826 as the 'great western road', a description which was later to apply to a new route farther south.[20] From the late 19th century it has been called Chiswick High Road.[21]

A minor east–west route crossed the peninsular part of the parish, linking Old Chiswick with Strand-on-the-Green.[22] In 1728 it had no name[23] and by 1832 it was called Burlington Lane.[24] Shorter lanes ran southward from the high road to Old Chiswick in 1746: corresponding to the existing British Grove, Chiswick Lane, and Devonshire Road, they led respectively to the east end of the riverside road called Chiswick Mall, to its centre, and to Church Street at its west end.[25] British Grove was so called by the 1860s, as was the southern part of Devonshire Road, previously Chiswick Field Lane; Chiswick Lane, the most direct and presumably the oldest

[5] 1 & 2 Geo. V, c. 112 (Local); Chiswick libr., NC/I/lxxxvi.
[6] Chiswick libr., NC/III/lxxxviii C.
[7] Geol. Surv. Map 1″, drift, sheet 270 (1951 edn.).
[8] O.S. Maps 6″, Mdx. XXI. NW. (1873 and later edns.); J. Wisdom, 'Making of a West Lond. Suburb; Housing in Chiswick, 1861–1914' (Leicester Univ. M.A. thesis, 1976, TS. in Chiswick libr.), 26.
[9] G.L.C. leaflets in Chiswick libr.
[10] Wisdom, 'W. Lond. Suburb', 21, 24.
[11] Thorne, Environs, 105.
[12] O.S. Maps 6″, Mdx. XXI. NW. (1873 and later edns.).
[13] The Times, 10 Jan. 1948.
[14] Brentford and Chiswick Times, 4 Mar., 29 Apr. 1949; 1 Dec. 1978.
[15] Rep. on Bridges in Mdx. 191.

[16] Wisdom, 'W. Lond. Suburb', 25; O.S. Maps 6″, Mdx. XVI. SW., XXI. NW. (1873 edn.).
[17] Para. based on V.C.H. Mdx. i. 66; I. D. Margary, Roman Roads in Britain, i (1955), 50–1, 77; Rocque, Map of Lond. (1746), sheets 11, 14.
[18] J. Ogilby, Map of Mdx. (c. 1677).
[19] Robbins, Mdx. 71; 3 Geo. I, c. 14 (Priv. Act).
[20] 7 Geo. IV, c. 142; S. Lewis, Topog. Dict. Eng. (1849), iv. 402; below.
[21] Bacon, Ordnance Atlas of Lond. (1886).
[22] Following 4 paras. based on O.S. Maps 6″, Mdx. XXI. NW. (1873 and later edns.).
[23] Guildhall MS. 14236/2, f. 104.
[24] Pigot, Com. Dir. (1832–4).
[25] Rocque, Map of Lond. (1746), sheet 11.

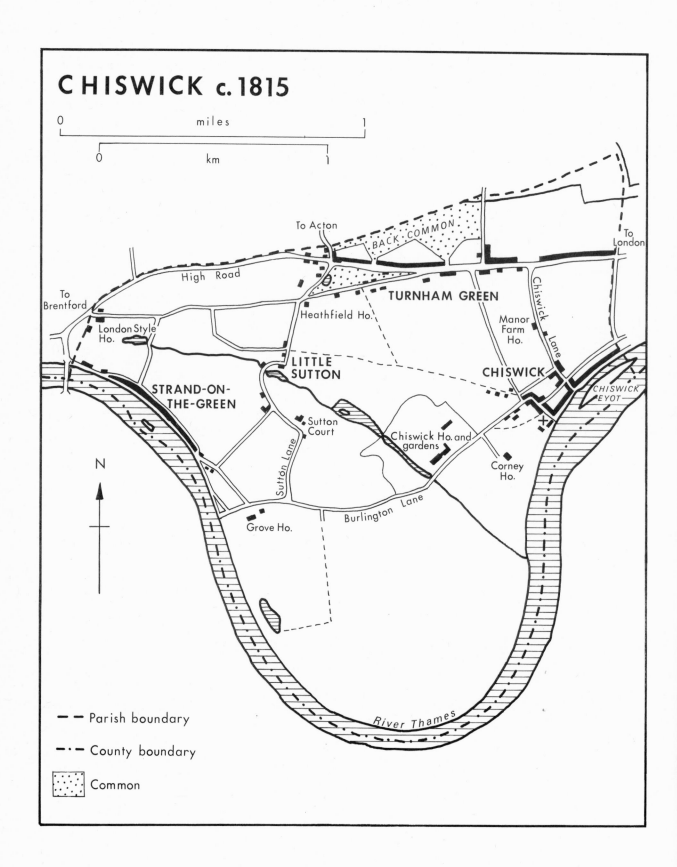

CHISWICK c.1815

0   miles   1

0   km   1

To Acton

BACK COMMON

To London

High Road

TURNHAM GREEN

To Brentford

London Style Ho.

Heathfield Ho.

Manor Farm Ho.

Chiswick Lane

LITTLE SUTTON

CHISWICK

CHISWICK EYOT

STRAND-ON-THE-GREEN

Sutton Court

Chiswick Ho. and gardens

Corney Ho.

N

Sutton Lane

Grove Ho.

Burlington Lane

River Thames

– – Parish boundary

–·– County boundary

Common

way to the village, was so called in 1747.[26] Hogarth Lane, so called by 1832,[27] led north-westward from Old Chiswick and apparently was a road in 1746;[28] although providing a short cut to Turnham Green common, it had become no more than a footpath across the duke of Devonshire's land by 1800.[29] From the high road the main northward route in the 18th century was Acton Lane, at the western end of Turnham Green common, although there were several paths to the Back common. From Turnham Green a lane also ran southward to Little Sutton, where it described a westerly loop before continuing south from the medieval manor house to join the western end of Burlington Lane; it was called Little Sutton Lane until the 1860s and Sutton Lane by 1890.[30] Strand-on-the-Green could be reached from the east along Burlington Lane or from the west by a short approach from the high road to the Kew ferry. A lane, perhaps afterwards Brook Road, in 1746 connected the later Wellesley Road with the middle of Back Lane, which ran behind the line of riverside houses[31] and c. 1908 was renamed Thames Road.[32]

The only significant changes between the mid 18th and mid 19th centuries were made in the 1820s by the duke of Devonshire. West of Chiswick Lane, and parallel with it, a carriage drive was constructed from the high road to Hogarth Lane, where it passed through the northern entrance gates of Chiswick House, and by the 1860s was called Duke's Avenue. On the other side of Chiswick House, Burlington Lane was moved farther south.[33] There were still no public roads in the central part of the parish, where the duke's parkland lay, and only tracks leading to fields south of Burlington Lane.

Apart from the addition of Sutton Court Road, which ran south from Turnham Green to Burlington Lane by 1886,[34] the main thorough-fares remained the same until after the First World War. In 1923 Chiswick U.D.C. bought 200 a. of riverside land from the duke of Devonshire as part of its plan to open up the southern tip of the parish for recreation. By 1925 a 2,000-ft. long embankment and terraced promenade lined the loop of the river, opposite Barnes, and sports grounds were under construction,[35] soon to be reached by Promenade Approach Road and Riverside Drive.

The first of several modern arterial roads, dividing one part of Chiswick from another, was planned in 1914 to improve the south-western outlet from London. Traffic was to be diverted from Chiswick High Road down Chiswick Lane to Mawson Lane, behind Old Chiswick, and thence along part of Burlington Lane to Great Chertsey Road, cut diagonally across the peninsula to the new Chiswick bridge west of Mortlake (Surr.). Work began in 1922 on a bridge over the railway south of Burlington Lane but it was not until c. 1930 that the eastern end of the lane itself was widened to form part of Great Chertsey Road[36] and not until 1933 that the bridge over the Thames was ready. Meanwhile part of the Great West Road, opened in 1925,[37] was formed from Hogarth Lane and the suburban avenues to the west as far as a new roundabout in Chiswick High Road, whence it continued across Brentford.

Another phase of road building for long-distance traffic began in 1955 with the widening and straightening of the Great West Road as part of the Cromwell Road extension. Roundabouts were built at the intersections with Devonshire Road and Sutton Court Road;[38] the names of Mawson Lane, Hogarth Lane, and its western continuations thereafter applied merely to stretches of the main road; the avenues which it crossed were bisected and later given the suffixes 'North' and 'South',[39] many being turned into cul-de-sacs and some linked by pedestrian subways, first opened in 1956.[40] From 1959 the Great West Road was carried over the roundabout near the western end of Chiswick High Road by a flyover[41] and from 1964 Chiswick flyover was linked with an elevated section of the M4 motorway.[42]

Bollo brook in 1826 passed under the high road at the west end of Turnham Green common, where a small culvert sometimes overflowed. The stream from the grounds of Chiswick House in 1746 apparently passed under Burlington Lane and in 1826 was confined to a width of 10 ft. beneath a brick bridge recently built by the duke of Devonshire.[43] Foot ferries at Old Chiswick and Kew were mentioned in 1659[44] and presumably had long been in use, since there were no medieval bridges over the Thames in Middlesex.[45] Kew ferry grew busier after Kew became a royal residence, William III being among those who probably took short cuts to the high road along Sutton Lane from Strand-on-the-Green,[46] and more traffic followed the opening of a bridge in 1759.[47] There was no other bridge nearer than Fulham in 1826, however,[48] and Chiswick ferry was still used in the 1890s.[49] Apart from the approaches to Kew bridge, on the boundary, Great Chertsey Road became the only road across the Thames from Chiswick parish, with the opening in 1933 of the 700-ft. long Chiswick bridge, designed by Sir Herbert Baker and faced with Portland stone.[50]

A coach made two return journeys daily from

[26] Guildhall Libr., map case 260.
[27] Pigot, *Com. Dir.* (1832–4).
[28] Rocque, *Map of Lond.* (1746), sheet 11.
[29] T. Milne, *Land Use Map of Lond.* (1800), plate II.
[30] *Kelly's Dir. Mdx.* (1890).
[31] Rocque, *Map of Lond.* (1746), sheet 14.
[32] *Kelly's Dir. Chiswick* (1907, 1909).
[33] *Rep. on Bridges in Mdx.* 191.
[34] Bacon, *Atlas of Lond.* (1886).
[35] *The Times*, 7 Sept. 1923; 12 June 1925.
[36] Ibid. 9 Nov. 1923; 20 June 1930.
[37] Brentford and Chiswick, *Official Guide* (1948).
[38] *Brentford and Chiswick Times*, 14, 28 Oct. 1955.

[39] Ibid. 23 Jan. 1959.   [40] Ibid. 14 Dec. 1956.
[41] Ibid. 26 Mar. 1959.
[42] *The Times*, 13 Nov. 1963; 26 Nov. 1964.
[43] *Rep. on Bridges in Mdx.* 191; Rocque, *Map of Lond.* (1746), sheet 10.
[44] P.R.O., E 134/1659 Mich. 30.
[45] W. Draper, *Chiswick*, 28–9. All references to Draper are to the 1970 edn., with preface.
[46] *Home Counties Mag.* xiii. 116.
[47] Draper, *Chiswick*, 141.
[48] *Rep. on Bridges in Mdx.* 191.
[49] O.S. Map 1/2,500, Mdx. XXI. 2 (1894–6 edn.).
[50] *The Times*, 3 July 1933.

Turnham Green to London in 1825[51] and coaches, some of them presumably stopping only in the high road en route, left every half hour by 1832.[52] Eleven omnibuses ran between Turnham Green and the Bank in 1838–9, eight of them operated from the George IV inn by George Cloud, who also operated four from Kew bridge.[53] By 1845 omnibuses left for London every quarter hour.[54]

The West Metropolitan Tramways Co., which already ran horse cars from Shepherd's Bush to Acton, in 1882 opened a route from Shepherd's Bush along Goldhawk Road to Young's Corner at the east end of Chiswick High Road. Thence horse cars ran westward along the high road to Kew bridge from 1882 and eastward to Hammersmith Broadway from 1883. Services were poor by 1894, when the West Metropolitan, whose main depot lay north of Chiswick High Road, was taken over by the new London United Tramways Co. Electric trams were introduced by the L.U.T. on the enlargement of the depot and the opening of a power station in 1901.[55]

Lack of public transport in the areas away from Chiswick High Road led to rival but abortive proposals for new routes by the L.U.T., the county council, and Chiswick U.D.C. between 1900 and 1902. Trolleybus powers were conferred on the U.D.C. by an Act of 1911, to take effect from 1913, but were not exercised,[56] the first trolleybuses arriving only in 1935[57] and surviving until 1962.[58] Motor buses operated by the London General Omnibus Co. reached Chiswick in 1911[59] and, as part of London Transport's network, later served most parts of the parish.

The first railway reached Chiswick from Surrey, cutting diagonally across the empty southern part of the parish. A branch of the London & South Western Railway Co.'s line from Waterloo to Richmond, it crossed the Thames by Barnes bridge and ran north-westward through Chiswick and Kew Bridge stations to Brentford and Hounslow. Chiswick station, designed by William Tite and opened in 1849, was renamed Chiswick and Grove Park in 1872 and Chiswick again in 1920.[60] Not until 1869 did the L.S.W.R. open a line from Kensington through Hammersmith to Turnham Green[61] and Brentford Road. South of Brentford Road station, renamed Gunnersbury in 1871, the line divided: part of it was connected by a westward curve to the old line north of Strand-on-the-Green, while part ran south across the Thames to Kew Gardens and Richmond. At Hammersmith

the station of the L.S.W.R. was close to that of the Hammersmith & City Railway Co., whence trains ran to central London. The populous northern part of the parish was also served from 1877 by the Metropolitan District Railway Co. from the City, which used the L.S.W.R.'s track from Hammersmith to Richmond, and by the Metropolitan. In 1879 the Metropolitan District, known simply as the 'District', opened a branch from Turnham Green to Ealing Broadway, with a station just across the parish boundary called Acton Green, renamed Chiswick Park and Acton Green in 1887 and Chiswick Park in 1910.[62] Early trains for workmen were provided by the L.S.W.R. and the District by 1890.[63] The District electrified its service in 1905 and opened Stamford Brook station, on the Chiswick side of the Hammersmith boundary, in 1912, after the track through Turnham Green had been widened.[64] In 1923 the L.S.W.R. was absorbed by the Southern Railway[65] and in 1933 the District's lines passed to the London Passenger Transport Board, thereafter forming part of London's Underground system.[66]

GROWTH. Articles dating from Mesolithic to Roman times have been found in the Thames, and a Roman presence is attested by coins, notably from an urn dug up at Turnham Green in 1731 and by brickwork beneath the manor house of Sutton.[67] The name Chiswick, 'cheese farm' or *wic*, occurs *c*. 1000,[68] when probably the whole parish formed part of the estates of St. Paul's.[69] Most early references, however, are to Sutton, which became the chief manor and denoted the 'south farm' or *tun*, probably in relation to Acton.[70] While the manor house of Sutton occupied a fairly central position, the hamlet, called Little Sutton by 1589,[71] remained insignificant in size compared with Old Chiswick, Turnham Green, and Strand-on-the-Green.

Chiswick and Strand-on-the-Green were riverain settlements, on gravel: Strand was a 'shore' or 'quay' and Turnham Green, which grew up farther north along the high road, possibly denoted a homestead by a turn or bend in the river.[72] The Thames has played a crucial role, symbolized in the church's dedication by 1458 to St. Nicholas, the patron saint of fishermen.[73] Both Chiswick and Strand-on-the-Green had ferries. Fishing, water traffic, and boat building were the chief occupations, before the river attracted workshops. The danger of flooding over fields in the peninsular part of the parish,

[51] Barker and Robbins, *Hist. Lond. Transport*, i. 392.
[52] Pigot, *Com. Dir.* (1832–4).
[53] Barker and Robbins, *Hist. Lond. Transport*, i. 38, 402; Pigot, *Dir. Mdx.* (1839–40).
[54] *P.O. Dir. Six Home Counties* (1845).
[55] G. Wilson, *Lond. Utd. Tramways* (1971), 17, 22, 25–6, 57–9, 63; below.
[56] Wilson, *Lond. Utd. Tramways*, 76, 137–8; 1 & 2 Geo. V, c. 112 (Local).
[57] J. R. Day, *London's Trams and Trolleybuses* (1977), 82.
[58] Lond. Transport *Bus Map* (1962); inf. from Mr. M. A. Jahn.
[59] Barker and Robbins, *Hist. Lond. Transport*, ii. 185.
[60] Ibid. i. 47, 53; J. E. Connor and B. L. Halford, *Forgotten Stations of Gtr. Lond.* (1972), 6; Pevsner, *Mdx.* 6.
[61] *Brentford and Chiswick As It Was* (1978), illus. 72.

[62] Barker and Robbins, *Hist. Lond. Transport*, i. 136, 147–8, 209–10; Connor and Halford, *Forgotten Stations*, 5–6; O.S. Map 6″, Mdx. XII. NW. (1873 edn.).
[63] M. A. Jahn, 'Railways and Suburban Development: Outer West Lond. 1850–1900' (Lond. Univ. M.Phil. thesis, 1971), 139.
[64] C. E. Lee, *Metropolitan Dist. Rly.* (1956), 8, 27, 29, 45.
[65] Barker and Robbins, *Hist. Lond. Transport*, ii. 258.
[66] Lee, *Metropolitan Dist. Rly.* 42–3.
[67] *V.C.H. Mdx.* i. 68; below, manors.
[68] A. J. Robertson, *Anglo-Saxon Charters* (1956), 144–5.
[69] Below, manors.
[70] *P.N. Mdx.* (E.P.N.S.), 90.
[71] M.R.O., Acc. 119/1.
[72] *P.N. Mdx.* (E.P.N.S.), 90.
[73] Below, churches.

which were too flat for easy drainage, kept them free from housing until the 20th century. In contrast the charm and accessibility of the riverside attracted wealthy residents, not only during the period when Chiswick could benefit from the royal family's nearby residence on the Surrey bank, at Kew.

'Chiswick town' (Old Chiswick), Turnham Green, and Strand-on-the-Green served as divisions, for the purpose of listing inhabitants, by 1590.[74] They also formed divisions for manorial and parochial government, occasionally with smaller districts added, from the 17th until the 19th century.[75] Their individual histories, with those of Little Sutton and of more recent but clearly defined suburbs, are given below.

The parish's main settlements, lying near its edges, were separated until the 19th century by fields, gardens, and parkland. Forerunners of the existing Chiswick House, which was created by the earl of Burlington (d. 1753) and enlarged by his Cavendish heirs, the dukes of Devonshire, lay between Chiswick village and, to the northwest, Little Sutton and Turnham Green. In 1979, after much intervening building had taken place, Old Chiswick and Strand-on-the-Green remained as accessible from Hammersmith and Brentford respectively as from each other, or even from Turnham Green.

In 1547 there were 120 houseling people in the parish[76] and in 1664 there were 230 houses, as many as 107 of them too poor to be assessed for hearth tax.[77] Of 167 ratepayers on the church roll in 1630, 75 lived in 'Chiswick town', 50 at Turnham Green, 31 at Strand-on-the-Green, and 11 at Little Sutton.[78] Numbers were similarly distributed in 1678,[79] although by 1706 the topographer John Bowack[80] considered that Turnham Green looked as big as Old Chiswick.[81] In 1795 the total population was thought to have doubled between 1680 and 1780 but not to have risen thereafter.[82] The balance so changed that Turnham Green had 296 families by 1801, while Old Chiswick had 201, Strand-on-the-Green 123, and Little Sutton 17.[83]

The parish had offered a country retreat for Henry VI and later for prelates in the 15th century and for courtiers and the scholars of Westminster from the 16th.[84] By 1706 its 'sweet air and situation' had brought it many noble seats,[85] although it was after the building of Chiswick House that it became most popular. The Cavendishes not only entertained the great, as their own guests,[86] but attracted sightseers: Horace Walpole in 1781 defended the duke's

practice of admitting visitors only by ticket, as had been done for the past 30 years.[87] By 1779, when Strand-on-the-Green was becoming fashionable like Old Chiswick and Turnham Green, land values had so risen that ½ a. not worth £5, presumably for agriculture, had been sold for £2,000. The vestry then revised its system of rate assessment, in order that local advantages should continue to 'lead gentlemen of expanded minds into extraordinary expenses to gratify their inclinations.'[88]

OLD CHISWICK was in 1980 the accepted name of Chiswick village, itself recorded c. 1000[89] and so perhaps named earlier than Sutton, of which it was once thought to have been an outlying hamlet.[90] From the early 17th to the 19th centuries it was known as Chiswick town or simply as 'the town'. The description, besides emphasizing that it was the main village, perhaps served to distinguish its more elegant part from a cluster of riverside cottages known by 1723-4 as Sluts Hole (in 1865 Fisherman's Corner). Inhabitants of Sluts Hole were often listed separately in 18th-century rate assessments, although their cottages, south of the church, formed the western end of the main village.[91]

The settlement apparently grew up immediately east of the church, mentioned in 1181, and away from the river.[92] Church Street there ran northward from the ferry, with a continuation across the open field which lay between the village and the high road to London and Brentford. A little to the east of Church Street and close to the river stood a stone building of c. 1100, the oldest known part of the prebendal manor house (later College House).[93] Presumably that building and its neighbours were reached by a way leading eastward from the ferry along the river bank, the forerunner of Chiswick Mall, although it is not clear how far the medieval road extended.

Londoners whose families presumably came from Chiswick included Geoffrey of Chiswick, recorded from 1247[94] and a landowner in Kent by 1264, and his contemporary Walter of Chiswick, followed by Robert, son of Gilbert of Chiswick, recorded in 1308.[95] Property in Chiswick village or parish was acquired by Londoners from the mid 15th century or earlier.[96] Henry VI's visits to Sutton may have brought some distinguished residents:[97] the chancellor Robert Stillington, bishop of Bath and Wells (d. 1491)[98] probably lived in the village, where in 1470 his 'hospice' had a great chamber by the Thames.[99] Another

[74] M.R.O., Acc. 531/66, ff. 22-8.
[75] Below, local govt.
[76] P.R.O., E 301/34, no. 123.
[77] M.R.O., MR/TH/3.
[78] Chwdns. acct. bk. (1622-35) [unpaginated], in Chiswick par. ch.
[79] Ibid. (1678-97). Nos. for 1632 and 1662 are in W. P. W. Phillimore and W. H. Whitear, Chiswick (1897), 280-1.
[80] D.N.B.
[81] Account by John Bowack, from Antiquities of Mdx., in Phillimore and Whitear, Chiswick, 14.
[82] Lysons, Environs, ii. 207.
[83] Chiswick census, 1801, in Chiswick libr.
[84] Below.
[85] Phillimore and Whitear, Chiswick, 2, 11.
[86] Below.

[87] Horace Walpole's Corresp. with Revd. Wm. Cole, ed. W. S. Lewis, ii (1937), 274.
[88] Vestry min. bk. (1777-1817), f. 11, in Chiswick libr.
[89] P.N. Mdx. (E.P.N.S.), 89.
[90] Phillimore and Whitear, Chiswick, 151-2.
[91] Chwdns. acct. bks. (1622-35, 1698-1751).
[92] Below, churches.
[93] Phillimore and Whitear, Chiswick, 69.
[94] Cal. Lib. 1245-51, 106.
[95] Cal. Close, 1261-4, 355; 1279-88, 143; 1307-13, 129; Cal. of Wills in Ct. of Husting, ed. R. R. Sharpe, i. 17-18.
[96] e.g. P.R.O., PROB 11/1 (P.C.C. 18 Rous, will of Wal. Dolman); PROB 11/6 (P.C.C. 1 Wattys, will of Ric. Copelande).
[97] e.g. Ld. Stafford, see above.   [98] D.N.B.
[99] Cal. Close, 1468-76, 130, 264, 319.

Robert Stillington was a feoffee of property in Chiswick, including the 'Counterhouse', in 1495.[1]

In the late 16th and early 17th centuries the grandest residents lived on the outskirts of the village: the Russells at Corney House to the west, and the Wardours, the earl of Somerset and their successors in a forerunner of Chiswick House, to the north.[2] What was later Chiswick Mall, however, contained the vicarage house at the bottom of Church Street by 1589–90[3] besides the old prebendal manor house, enlarged c. 1570 for Westminster school,[4] and a substantial forerunner of Walpole House.[5] They probably stood near other imposing houses, afterwards rebuilt, since in 1706 Bowack noted the interior decoration of some 'very ancient' dwellings by the river.[6] In Church Street the later Burlington Arms, so called by 1751, existed in the early 16th century.[7]

The use of Chiswick as a scholars' retreat helped to advertise its healthy reputation. Sir Edward Wardour, having moved to the smaller Turret House, claimed c. 1637 that he merely retired there during the summer vacation.[8] The village was considered royalist in 1642, when parliamentary troops came to burn the altar rails from the church but were prevented from pillaging the prebendal manor house, held by Arthur Duck, and a house belonging to the earl of Portland.[9]

A branch of the Russell family lived on the site of the existing Bedford House from c. 1664[10] but their house, like others of the 17th century, was later rebuilt. In 1706 the town, although small, was thought to be pleasantly situated and to have long contained more noblemen among its residents than any of its neighbours. Most of the houses formed a ribbon along the riverfront, stretching from the church to the parish boundary, and there were handsome buildings in Church Street. Several small traders, and many more fishermen or watermen, also lived close to the Thames.[11] Presumably most were at Sluts Hole, although the line of riverside buildings east of the vicarage was not entirely devoted to rich residents: Thomas Mawson had opened his brewery behind the houses half way along the row, near the foot of Chiswick Lane, c. 1700[12] and the brewery's Red Lion, perhaps the only inn facing the river, had been licensed by 1722.[13] The inn stood close to a draw dock, where barges were still unloaded in the late 19th century.[14]

In 1746 Old Chiswick was still mainly a riverside village, extending eastward along the gravel into Hammersmith but no farther west than Corney House, beyond which lay marshes. Church Street ran a short way inland before turning left to meet Burlington Lane, and from the churchyard a narrow way, in 1752 called Paul's Walk[15] and later Powell's Walk, provided a north-westerly short cut to the lane and Chiswick House. Roads radiated from north of the junction of Church Street with Burlington Lane, near the modern Hogarth roundabout: Chiswick Field Lane led straight to the high road, while a forerunner of Hogarth Lane led north-westward to Turnham Green, and Mawson Lane led north-eastward to meet Chiswick Lane by the brewery. Parallel with Chiswick Field Lane, Chiswick Lane led to the high road from half way along the river front, as did a forerunner of British Grove from behind its eastern end, where it joined a lane which ran behind the riverside houses from Church Street into Hammersmith. Away from the river houses lined both sides of Church Street to the point where it met Burlington Lane, a little beyond which they formed Chiswick Square. Buildings also stretched up Chiswick Lane to the corner of Mawson Lane, which ran south-west to Church Street. A few detached houses, one of them soon to be taken by William Hogarth, stood at the Old Chiswick end of the road across the common field to Turnham Green.[16]

Surviving houses recall the wealth of 18th-century residents.[17] So, from c. 1750, do views of the village, where there were many more large houses than on the waterfront at Strand-on-the-Green, although artists often preferred to show the fishermen's cottages huddled between the foreshore and the church.[18] The built up riverside had an almost urban appearance, although the name Mall, as in Hammersmith, was perhaps not adopted until the early 19th century in an attempt to suggest that the district was as fashionable as Westminster's Pall Mall.

Despite much rebuilding, the village spread very little between the mid 18th and late 19th centuries. By 1801, with 1,023 inhabitants in 172 houses, it was less populous than Turnham Green,[19] which by 1839 had the greater number of inns.[20] Chiswick Mall contained a few tall trees on a grassy verge between the road and the river in 1827.[21] Its houses retained large back gardens in the 1860s, when they also had their existing plots along the riverside verge. There was still open country, owned by the duke of Devonshire, west of the churchyard, besides the estate of the Prebend manor, including Home field, to the north. More houses stood at the south end of Hogarth Lane, beyond the village, and in Burlington Lane the Cedars, from c. 1863 the home of the landscape painter Henry Dawson (1811–78),[22] faced Corney Lodge at the end of Powell's Walk.[23] Changes in the village itself

[1] Ibid. 1485–1500, 252.   [2] Below, other est.
[3] M.R.O., Acc. 531/66, f. 13.
[4] Below, other est.   [5] Below.
[6] Phillimore and Whitear, *Chiswick*, 12.
[7] M.R.O., MR/LV7/4; Hist. Mon. Com. *Mdx.* 9.
[8] *Cal. S.P. Dom.* 1637–8, 90.
[9] Ibid. 1641–3, 372.   [10] Below, other est.
[11] Phillimore and Whitear, *Chiswick*, 11.
[12] Below, industry.   [13] M.R.O., MR/LV3/95.
[14] *Brentford and Chiswick As It Was*, illus. 46.
[15] Guildhall MS. 14219/6, f. 198.
[16] Rocque, *Map of Lond.* (1746), sheet 11.

[17] Below.
[18] Chiswick libr., local prints.   [19] *Census*, 1801.
[20] Chiswick had *c.* 7 inns and Turnham Green 11: Pigot, *Dir. Mdx.* (1839–40). Some inns, however, were located differently in later dirs.
[21] Plate facing p. 65; the riverside bldgs. are also shown in Guildhall Libr., *Panorama of Thames from Lond. to Richmond*, pub. S. Leigh [*c.* 1827].
[22] A. Dawson, *Hen. Dawson* (1891), 85, 100–2; *D.N.B.*
[23] Rocque, *Map of Lond.* (1746), sheet 11; Milne, *Land Use Map of Lond.* (1800), plate II; O.S. Map 6″, Mdx. XXI. NW. (1873 edn.).

arose mainly from industry: the Griffin brewery had expanded beside Chiswick Lane, the Lamb brewery had grown up off Church Street, and the cottages below the church were about to make way for the workshops of Thornycroft & Co., the shipbuilders.[24]

The late 19th century saw the village joined by housing both to the suburbs along the high road and to the western districts of Hammersmith. Its declining importance as a centre of parish life, already foreshadowed by the opening of churches and schools at Turnham Green and Chiswick New Town, was accelerated by its remoteness from the railways and by the rise of new suburbs, with their own services.[25] Old Chiswick thus became a residential backwater, varied by some thriving industry. It lost its most ancient buildings, with the demolition of College House and the reconstruction of the church, but expensive houses were still put up in Chiswick Mall.[26]

The departure of Thornycrofts, completed by 1909, perhaps secured the village's future as a residential area. An alleged source of pollution had gone,[27] although smaller firms moved in and extended their wharves and depots to the southwest. Church Street had several shops c. 1910,[28] in contrast with the more stately Chiswick Mall, where the Red Lion lost its licence c. 1915.[29] The closure of the Lamb brewery, in the period between the conversion of Church Street's two inns to private use, left only the Griffin as a major employer near the river. North of the village, however, the Chiswick Polish Co. and its successors gradually expanded in the angle between Burlington Lane and Hogarth Lane.[30]

The north corner of Church Street was demolished in the 1930s, when part of Burlington Lane became Great Chertsey Road, and further demolitions accompanied work on Hogarth Lane and Mawson Lane in the 1950s.[31] Heavy traffic along the widened roads helped to cut off the old village from the suburbs inland.

There have been few changes in Chiswick Mall since the First World War, apart from the rebuilding in 1936 of a hospital which had opened at Rothbury House[32] and, c. 1968, the construction near by of town houses called Miller's Court on the site of a bakery close to the Hammersmith boundary.[33] Cottages in the churchyard were pulled down in the 1930s, followed by the former schoolroom in 1951,[34] and new warehouses were built on Thornycrofts' former yard at Church wharf.[35] Old Chiswick, including Chiswick Eyot, was declared a conservation area under the Civic Amenities Act in 1969.[36] Its residential character was soon afterwards emphasized by controversial plans to replace the warehouses at Church wharf with

private flats or houses, none of which had been built by 1980.[37]

Notable inhabitants[38] not mentioned elsewhere in the article included the French born ambassador Sir Stephen Lesieur (fl. 1586–c. 1637), assessed from 1628 until 1637,[39] Leonard Mawe, bishop of Bath and Wells, who died at Chiswick in 1629, and the physician and poet Edward Baynard (b. 1641, fl. 1719), who was often there at the time of the plague in 1665. Sir Crisp Gascoyne (1700–61), lord mayor of London, and Charles Holland (1733–69), actor and son of a local baker, were both born at Chiswick. The painter Edward Penny (1714–91) died there, as did the engraver William Sharp (1749–1824), and the Anglo-Saxon scholar Benjamin Thorpe (1782–1870), a resident of Chiswick Mall. The German born painter Philip James de Loutherbourgh (1740–1812), although buried in Chiswick, lived across the boundary in Hammersmith Terrace. Jean-Jacques Rousseau lodged with a grocer named Pulleyn in Old Chiswick in 1766.[40]

Old Chiswick's main architectural distinction[41] lies in the 18th- and 19th-century residences, mainly of brown brick, which stretch along Chiswick Mall. Approached from the east, the first houses beyond Miller's Court are Cedar House, formerly Eyot Cottage, and Swan House, probably late 17th-century but largely refaced. Next to them stand Island House and Norfolk House, a taller and more elaborate pair of the early 19th century, and St. John's House of c. 1800, all three of them stuccoed. Beyond some modern buildings is the Oziers, an early 19th-century refacing of an older house, and a distinguished group formed by Morton House, Strawberry House, and Walpole House, all of brown brick with red-brick dressings. Both Morton House and Strawberry House were built c. 1700 and refronted c. 1730, the second having a late 18th-century cast iron porch on slender fluted columns. Walpole House, perhaps the finest in the row, has internal features of the 16th and 17th century, with a garden front of c. 1700, and a river front and north-west extension of c. 1730. It is said to have been the last home of Charles II's former mistress Barbara Villiers, duchess of Cleveland (1641–1709), who was buried in Chiswick church,[42] and to have supplied a lodging for the politician Daniel O'Connell (1775–1847) as a law student c. 1796. Later it was also a school, attended and made famous by Thackeray,[43] and in 1908 it was the home of the actor-manager Sir Herbert Beerbohm Tree (1853–1917).[44]

Beyond Walpole House some later buildings include the Tides and Orford House, a pair

[24] Below, trade and industry.
[25] e.g. Grove Pk., Bedford Pk.   [26] e.g. Staithe Ho.
[27] K. C. Barnaby, *100 Years of Specialized Shipbuilding* (1964), 51.
[28] *Brentford and Chiswick As It Was*, illus. 49–50.
[29] Ibid. illus. 46.
[30] Below, trade and industry.
[31] Above, communications.
[32] Below, pub. svces.
[33] *Evening News*, 6 Jan. 1973.
[34] *Brentford and Chiswick As It Was*, illus. 44.
[35] Below, industry.

[36] *Brentford and Chiswick Times*, 5 June 1969.
[37] Ibid. 14 June 1973, 13 June 1974; *Chiswick and Brentford Gaz.* 5 Feb. 1976.
[38] Para. based on *D.N.B.*
[39] Chwdns. acct. bks. (1622–35, 1636–62).
[40] G. de Beer, *Rousseau and his World* (1972), 79–81.
[41] Five paras. based on Hist. Mon. Com. *Mdx.* 8–10; Pevsner, *Mdx.* 30, 35–6; Robbins, *Mdx.* 230–3; Min. of Town and Country Planning, List of Bldgs. (1949).
[42] *D.N.B.*; C. G. Harper, *Haunted Hos.* (1927), 109–10.
[43] Below, educ.
[44] *Kelly's Dir. Mdx.* (1908).

designed in 1887 by J. Belcher. Near the entrance to Eyot Green, a modern cul-de-sac, is Greenash, designed by Belcher in 1882 in the style of Norman Shaw and, as Eyot Villa, the home until c. 1912 of the engineer Sir John Isaac Thornycroft.[45] On the west corner of Chiswick Lane part of the Griffin brewery borders Chiswick Mall for a short way, next to the old Red Lion inn. The former inn, called Red Lion House, is of c. 1700, afterwards stuccoed and given an attic. Close by are the early 19th-century Chiswick Mall Cottages. Lingard House and Thames View were built as a single house c. 1700. Said House is 19th-century and looks earlier because of a modern reconstruction.

Set back from the west end of Chiswick Mall are Eynham House and Bedford House, presumably successors of Edward Russell's building of the 1660s. Russell's house was bought by Thomas Plukenett and passed by marriage to the Woodroffes, who retained it until 1920. It then became the home of the local historian Warwick Draper (d. 1926)[46] and later of the actor Sir Michael Redgrave, who sold it in 1956.[47] The houses, originally one and with a shared pediment, are early 18th-century, but Bedford House has a south-western extension dated 1749 and both have later wings. The walled garden contains a mid 18th-century Gothic gazebo and lead cisterns dated 1622 and 1678. The neighbouring Woodroffe House is a severe building of c. 1700, with later windows, standing east of the Old Vicarage on the corner of Church Street.

On the east side of Church Street, truncated and in 1980 almost entirely residential, the side-wall of the Old Vicarage and the late 18th-century Vine House stand opposite the church. Next to Vine House is Chiswick's oldest surviving house, timber-framed and probably early 16th-century, formed out of three tenements which themselves once served as the Burlington Arms. The building is of whitewashed rubble and stucco, with exposed half timbering on the projecting upper storey; it has been much altered but retains some internal and external 17th-century plasterwork. The neighbouring Burlington Corner, of weatherboarded timber framing but with modern additions at both back and front, has reset early 16th- and mid 17th-century panelling. Beyond some converted offices by the old entrance to Lamb's brewery stands the early 18th-century Wistaria, of red brick. On the west side of the street, opposite Burlington Corner, is an early 18th-century building of brown brick with red-brick dressings, which has been divided into Holly House and Latimer House; it has later two-storeyed wings, and a wrought iron gate and screen.

Almost on the corner of Church street and Burlington Lane, an alley leads to Page's Yard, where there is a row of four 18th-century brick cottages.[48] Off Burlington Lane itself the late 17th-century Chiswick Square serves as a forecourt to Boston House, with a two-storeyed pair on the west side and a three-storeyed house on the east, all of brown brick with red dressings. Boston House itself, on the south side, is said to derive its name from Viscount Boston, a title borne by Henry d'Auverquerque, earl of Grantham (d. 1754). After the earl's move to Grove House c. 1750, Boston House passed to Lord Archibald Hamilton and to Hamilton's son-in-law Francis Greville, Earl Brooke and afterwards earl of Warwick (d. 1773). It later became a girls' school before belonging to Henry Stratton Bates from 1869 to 1889, to trustees for St. Veronica's retreat, and in 1922 to the Chiswick Products Co. and its successors,[49] which in 1980 used it mainly for staff recreation and storage.[50] The house was originally built on a half H-shaped plan but received a large early 18th-century addition to the south-west and later extensions at either end.

Modern building has left only Hogarth's 'little country box' to recall the 18th-century spread of housing from Chiswick village along Hogarth Lane.[51] A brick house with 60 rods of garden was held of the Prebend manor in 1728 by the Revd. George Andrew Ruperti, whose son George conveyed it in 1749 to the painter William Hogarth (1697–1764).[52] Although Hogarth himself died at his London house, both his mother-in-law, the widow of Sir James Thornhill,[53] and his own widow Jane died at Chiswick. Jane Hogarth was followed in 1791 by her cousin Mary Lewis, from whom the house passed in 1810 to Richard Loveday, in 1814[54] to the Revd. Francis Cary (1772–1844), the translator.[55] Much decayed by 1874, it was saved in 1891 by Alfred Dawson and again, after the failure of a public appeal, in 1902 by Lt. Col. Shipway of Grove House, who furnished it and gave it in 1907 to the county council as a Hogarth museum. After bomb damage in 1940 the museum was reopened in 1951 and taken over by Hounslow L.B. in 1965.

Hogarth's house is late 17th-century, with a low early 18th-century addition to the south. The house and its walled garden, with a mulberry tree of Hogarth's time, offer a peaceful contrast with the modern warehouses of Reckitt and Colman and heavy traffic along the lane which has become the Great West Road.

Farther east, the Great West Road has replaced Mawson Lane, named after the family which established the Griffin brewery. The Mawsons also gave their name to a terrace running south from Mawson Lane's junction with Chiswick Lane, backing on the brewery and known as Mawson Row. The corner house (no. 110 Chiswick Lane) was reputedly the home of Alexander Pope, a protégé of Lord Burlington,

---

[45] Barnaby, *100 Years of Shipbldg.* 43, 56; *Brentford and Chiswick As It Was*, illus. on back cover; *Kelly's Dir. Chiswick* (1912).   [46] M. Gilbert, *Chiswick Old and New* (1932), 36.
[47] *Evening Standard*, 21 Sept. 1956.
[48] *Brentford and Chiswick As It Was*, illus. 48.
[49] Gilbert, *Chiswick Old and New*, 37; Guildhall MSS. 14219/6, ff. 197–8, 14, f. 20; below, industry, Rom. Cathm., educ.

[50] Inf. from the librarian, Reckitt & Colman Ltd.
[51] Two paras. based on F. M. Green, *Hogarth and his Ho.* (Hounslow L.B. booklet), *passim*, in addition to the sources cited in n. 41 above.
[52] Guildhall MS. 14219/6, ff. 145, 147.
[53] *D.N.B.*
[54] Guildhall MS. 14219/8, ff. 49, 262, 299–300.
[55] *D.N.B.*

and his family from 1716 to 1719; later it was an inn, called in turn the Mawson Arms and the Fox and Hounds.[56] The inn is early 18th-century, like its neighbours (nos. 112–18, even), but has some later windows. Farther south is another brick range of the 18th century (nos. 130–4, even), with stucco refronting on the ground floor.

TURNHAM GREEN probably gave its name to Stephen of Turnham, who occurred in 1199,[57] and was itself recorded as 'the field of Turnham' between 1229 and 1237.[58] It did not grow up around a church or manor house but as a result of traffic along the high road from London to Brentford. The area described below is not merely the one around the existing common called Turnham Green but that of all the straggling settlement along Chiswick High Road, from the Hammersmith boundary to Gunnersbury.

In 1590 Turnham Green common was the name of waste land of Sutton Court manor along the high road, west of the prebendal manor.[59] Among early inns was the King of Bohemia, perhaps named after the father of Prince Rupert and mentioned in 1632.[60] Although Turnham Green had fewer ratepayers than Old Chiswick in the 17th century, there were substantial houses by 1664, when those of Lady Wortley and Lady Margaret Cholmley contained 24 and 22 hearths respectively and when the first, with College House, was assessed as the fourth largest in the parish.[61] Lady Wortley was presumably the widow of Sir Edward Wortley, who had paid rates from 1649, and a Sydney Wortley was still at Turnham Green in 1683. The Whittaker family, represented from c. 1636 to 1658 by Laurence Whittaker,[62] was living there by 1624 and had given its name[63] to a field north of the high road by 1649.[64] Viscount Shannon was a resident by 1664, as were his wife in 1678 and Lord Paston, afterwards earl of Yarmouth, who married Charlotte, Lady Shannon's daughter by Charles II, from c. 1681 to 1685.[65] A house which had belonged to Charlotte's first husband James Howard (d. 1669) was reputedly the later Bolton House, occupied by the traveller Sir John Chardin (1643–1712)[66] in 1705, when its gardens were admired by Evelyn.[67] The earl of Devonshire in 1691 occupied Arlington Garden, presumably at the west end of Turnham Green common, where in 1746 there was a seat with formal gardens[68] and later one known as Arling-

ton House. Other residents included the divine and playwright Henry Killigrew (1613–1700) in 1669,[69] the marquess of Worcester in 1672, Sir Miles Cooke in 1678, Sir John Pye, Bt., c. 1678 to c. 1685,[70] and Lady Lort.[71]

Turnham Green was thus a fashionable locality by c. 1677, when there was settlement along the south side of the high road, near the Hammersmith end.[72] By 1706 the village, with 'several good brick houses', was comparable in size to that of Chiswick[73] and by 1720 there were buildings on both sides of the high road.[74] Convenient for travel from London to the palaces at Windsor and Hampton Court and later at Kew, Turnham Green may already have been noted as a healthy place: in 1733 Sir Thomas Robinson, Bt., took lodgings there for his wife's convalescence,[75] and in the early 19th century it was thought to be well sheltered to the north by the rising ground of Ealing and Acton.[76] Besides the parish workhouse built north of the road in 1725, there were well known inns by the mid 18th century, at one of which assemblies were held.[77] With gaps on the north side opposite Devonshire Road and on the south side east of Chiswick Lane, detached buildings then intermittently lined the high road from the Hammersmith boundary to the crossroads with Acton Lane and Sutton Lane, dividing the Back or Chiswick common from Turnham Green common. Few houses stood away from the high road, except at its junction with Acton Lane and Sutton Lane, west of which stretched open country as far as London Stile. Heathfield House and some neighbouring buildings formed a group at the south-west corner of Turnham Green common, reached by Sutton Lane.[78] In the extreme north-east corner of the parish, a few inhabitants were assessed separately in the 1630s as being at Stamford Lane, and sometimes in the 18th century as at Stamford Brook. The locality, with only 4 houses in 1795, was at other times probably considered part of Turnham Green.[79]

In the late 18th century noble residents included the countess of Stafford and the marquess of Annandale, who died in 1783 and 1792 respectively,[80] besides the occupiers of Heathfield House.[81] By 1801 Turnham Green was larger than Old Chiswick, although the population, lacking the breweries and other riverside industry, was more evenly divided between trade and agriculture.[82] Houses were apparently continuous along the north side of the high road,

[56] Gilbert, *Chiswick Old and New*, 56.
[57] *Early Charters of St. Paul's* (Camd. 3rd ser. lviii), 36–7.
[58] *P.N. Mdx.* (E.P.N.S.), 90.
[59] M.R.O., Acc. 531/66, f. 8.
[60] *Brentford and Chiswick As It Was*, illus. 69; *Mdx. County Rec.* iii. 49.
[61] M.R.O., MR/TH/3.
[62] Chwdns. acct. bks. (1636–62, 1663–91); overseers' acct. bk. (1678–97).
[63] *Mdx. County Rec.* ii. 186.
[64] W.A.M. 16666.
[65] Chwdns. acct. bk. (1663–91); overseers' acct. bk. (1678–97); *Complete Peerage*, xii (2), 891.
[66] Phillimore and Whitear, *Chiswick*, 274; *D.N.B.*
[67] *Diary of John Evelyn*, ed. E. S. de Beer, v. 594.
[68] *Archaeologia*, xii. 183; Rocque, *Map of Lond.* (1746), sheet 14.
[69] *D.N.B.*; *Diary of Sam. Pepys*, ed. R. Latham and W. Matthews, ix. 557.

[70] Chwdns. acct. bk. (1663–91); overseers' acct. bk. (1678–97); G.E.C. *Baronetage*, iv. 6; Hist. MSS. Com. 75, *Downshire*, i, p. 39.
[71] Below, other est.
[72] Ogilby, *Map of Mdx.* (c. 1677).
[73] Phillimore and Whitear, *Chiswick*, 14.
[74] E. Brown, *Britannia Depicta or Ogilby Improved* (facsimile edn. 1970).
[75] Hist. MSS. Com. 42, *15th Rep. VI*, p. 107.
[76] T. Faulkner, *Hist. and Antiquities of Brentford, Ealing, and Chiswick* (1845), 461.
[77] Below, local govt., social.
[78] Rocque, *Map of Lond.* (1746), sheets 11, 14.
[79] Chwdns. acct. bks. (1622–35, 1698–1751, 1752–70); Lysons, *Environs*, ii. 207.
[80] Chwdns. acct. bk. (1752–76); *Complete Peerage*, i. 168; xii (1), 195.
[81] Below, other est.
[82] Census, 1801, in Chiswick libr.

from Windmill Road to Acton Lane, and lined the south side from Devonshire Road to the east end of Turnham Green common.[83] Those on the north side included Belmont House and the former King of Bohemia, converted into three dwellings called Bohemia House, where the Italian poet Ugo Foscolo spent his last months in 1827.[84] Those on the south side included Linden House, flanked by Afton House and Bolton House. Ralph Griffiths (1720–1803), founder of the *Monthly Review*, died at Linden House, where his grandson Thomas Griffiths Wainewright (1794–1852), the art critic and poisoner, entertained Charles Lamb and others between 1828 and 1830.[85] Farther east, substantial houses were built c. 1800 in Turnham Green Terrace, near the older Rupert House.[86]

Little business was carried on in 1832 at Turnham Green, where many Londoners had country homes or lived in retirement. In 1845 it was thought that the scattered houses around the common, where there were already a few terraces, presented a welcome variety after the unbroken line of building along the road from London, although the common would benefit from inclosure and planting. A remark that denser building was expected to take place, after it had hitherto been prevented by peculiar tenures,[87] perhaps referred to intermingling of the copyholds of Sutton Court and the Prebend manors, both of which were soon to pass to the Ecclesiastical Commissioners.[88] Already the transfer of part of Old Chiswick's school, improvements in public transport, the provision of gas along the high road, and, in 1843, the building of a church foreshadowed the emergence of Turnham Green as the main centre of administrative and commercial life.

The opening of railway stations in 1869 confirmed the importance of the area along the high road. From 1871 a furniture depository overlooked Turnham Green common, which by 1876 was surrounded by shops and houses, giving the place a 'modern look'. A few stately red-brick houses survived from the 18th century[89] but Heathfield House, perhaps the best known, had long gone; Linden House was to make way in 1878 for Linden Gardens and Bolton House, a private school like many of the older seats, was to follow in 1880.[90] Arlington House, a former home of the soldier Sir Thomas Troubridge (1815–67), was demolished in 1877.[91]

Buildings which soon disappeared included Rupert House in 1894, Belmont House, and Bohemia House in 1901.[92] Such houses were mainly replaced by middle-class avenues or, in the high road, by shops, although poorer terraces and some industry appeared to the north, near

the railway. Sanderson's wallpaper factory and the depository at the south-east corner of Turnham Green common[93] were balanced by flats, rather than more business premises, at its western end. Despite the spread of shops along Chiswick High Road and in several side streets, Turnham Green ward was mainly residential in 1901. There were some expensive houses south of Turnham Green common and particularly good shops in Chiswick High Road,[94] which perhaps also benefited from the growth of Bedford Park. Although deprived of its older residences and with several inns rebuilt, the high road was made busier by the introduction of electric trams in 1901 and the construction of public buildings, from a fire station in 1891 to a theatre in 1912.[95] Meanwhile the building of a vestry hall and its conversion into the town hall helped to make Turnham Green common, with its tall church in the middle, a dignified centre to the neighbourhood.

Apart from the building of flats south of Turnham Green common and of others over shops in the high road, Turnham Green changed little in the period between the First World War and the 1950s. Thereafter shops and offices were built in the high road and some public services rehoused, the most striking changes being on the north and south sides of Turnham Green common, with the replacement of the theatre by an eleven-storeyed office block and of the Vicarage by a fire station, and at the west end of Chiswick High Road, where an eighteen-storeyed block was built over Gunnersbury station. Although it ceased to house the civic centre in 1965, Turnham Green common retained a Victorian stateliness, with buildings which were protected by its designation as a conservation area in 1976.[96] Chiswick High Road, with its wide pavements lined with plane trees,[97] meanwhile remained a varied and attractive shopping street.

Turnham Green is best known for a 'battle' on the common in 1642, when the royalists under Prince Rupert were halted by the train bands of London. Although little more than a skirmish, the encounter was made important by the king's subsequent decision to abandon his march on the capital, so ending his hopes of a quick victory.[98]

Well known residents[99] not mentioned elsewhere included the writer Edward Weston (1703–70), editor of the *London Gazette*, in the 1740s.[1] Among those who died at Turnham Green were John Ecton (d. 1730), compiler of the *Thesaurus Rerum Ecclesiasticarum*, Thomas Bentley (1731–80), porcelain manufacturer, Thomas Morell (1703–84), classical scholar, James Ware (1756–1815), surgeon, and James Fittler (1758–1835), engraver. The author W. E.

[83] Milne, *Land Use Map of Lond.* (1800), plate II.
[84] *Brentford and Chiswick As It Was*, illus. 66, 69; C. M. Franzero, *Life in Exile: Ugo Foscolo in Lond.* (1977), 123, 126.
[85] Gilbert, *Chiswick Old and New*, 52–3; *D.N.B.*; J. Curling, *Janus Weathercock: Life of Thos. G. Wainewright* (1938), 203, 226–7.
[86] *Brentford and Chiswick As It Was*, illus. 70–1.
[87] Faulkner, *Brentford, Ealing, and Chiswick*, 461.
[88] e.g. the site of Linden Ho., enfranchised 1875, was copyhold of both mans.: Guildhall MS. 14236/16, ff. 36–49.
[89] Thorne, *Environs*, 627.
[90] Phillimore and Whitear, *Chiswick*, 246, 269, 274.

[91] *D.N.B.*; *N. & Q.* 6th ser. i. 509.
[92] *Brentford and Chiswick As It Was*, illus. 66, 69, 71.
[93] Below, trade and industry.
[94] M.R.O., *Rep. Local Inqs.* 1895–1907.
[95] *Brentford and Chiswick As It Was*, illus. 53, 64.
[96] *Brentford and Chiswick Times*, 10 June 1976.
[97] Plate facing p. 80.
[98] G. Davies, *Early Stuarts* (1959), 132; Phillimore and Whitear, *Chiswick*, 72–7.
[99] Para. based on *D.N.B.*
[1] Hist. MSS. Com. 10, *10th Rep. I*, pp. 280, 296; 20, *14th Rep. IX*, p. 132.

Henley (1849-1903) lived at no. 64 Chiswick High Road in 1887-8.[2]

Turnham Green, in contrast to Old Chiswick or Strand-on-the-Green, has only scattered reminders of its genteel past.[3] Arlington Cottage is the only survivor of the small 18th-century houses which were once characteristic of the area around Turnham Green common. Of houses which faced the south side of the common in the early 19th century, nos. 10-11 Heathfield Terrace form a pair of three storeys next to the similar but plainer nos. 12-13. Afton House, Bourne Place, at the north-east end of Duke's Avenue and in 1979 used by Chiswick memorial club, represents the larger residences built c. 1800, when Bolton House and Linden House stood immediately to the east. It has three storeys and has rusticated stucco on the ground floor. Near by in Chiswick High Road a three-storeyed pair with Coade stone dressings, also of c. 1800, serves as the presbytery of the Roman Catholic church. Farther east the south side of Chiswick High Road contains the late 18th-century no. 183, also three-storeyed. Nos. 3-21, close to the boundary at British Grove, form a uniform three-storeyed range of yellow brick and stucco, ornamented with giant pilasters. They illustrate the built up appearance of the high road c. 1835.

STRAND-ON-THE-GREEN, normally 'Strande' from 1353 until the mid 17th century,[4] was so called in 1678.[5] The name in 1979 still applied to a riverside walk, in addition to the district, serving as a reminder that the first houses and wharves had formed no more than a line along the foreshore. A rating division of the parish in the 17th century, it was the smallest of the three main settlements,[6] with no houses as large as some in Old Chiswick in 1664,[7] and in 1706 was described as a 'straggling place, inhabited chiefly by fishermen.'[8] The description was too slighting, since there were some substantial houses before 1700.[9] More than local importance had been conferred by Kew ferry, which reached the Middlesex bank at the west end of Strand-on-the-Green and which was used by William III before the plot to assassinate him near Turnham Green in 1696.[10]

The waterside path called Strand-on-the-Green ran south-eastward from Kew ferry for 600 m. along the entire length of the hamlet, dipping at the eastern end of Back Lane (later Thames Road) and rising again to turn inland and join Burlington Lane, along the line of Grove Park Road. It could be covered at high tide and never served as the towpath, which was on the Surrey bank.[11] An embankment wall protected the house fronts and by 1746 had been planted haphazardly with trees.[12] While access to the houses and workshops was from the strand, most of them also had rear entrances from Back Lane. The foreshore cannot have served as a road, as was once suggested,[13] although in the 19th century it had a 'hard' at either end and one near a malthouse by the Steam Packet. Nine alleyways led from Back Lane to the river,[14] where carts presumably crossed parts of the foreshore to unload barges at low tide. Ship Alley, made in 1911, and the much older Bell Alley, Post Office Alley, and Grove Row were still in use in 1980.[15]

Early settlement probably took place half way along the strand, where Oliver's Island diverted the main force of the river.[16] Apart from a few buildings set back near the ferry, housing in 1746 was confined between the waterside path and Back Lane but reached south-east as far as the existing Grove Park Road.[17] Of the riverside inns in 1862 the Ship and the Bull's Head had both been licensed by 1722, the Bell and Crown and the Indian Queen by 1751, and the City Navigation Barge by 1786.[18] Almshouses existed by 1655 and malthouses by c. 1700.[19]

Inland from the ferry, a few houses along the high road by 1659 formed a locality called London Stile.[20] Buildings on the Chiswick side of the road in 1746 included London Style House on the south corner of the modern Wellesley Road and, a little nearer the Star and Garter, Sydney House.[21] The first was rented from 1764 by the German-born painter John or Johann Zoffany (1733-1810), who lived there before going abroad in 1772. The second was so named because an earlier house was said to have been the one in Chiswick where Sir Philip Sidney's mother Mary had retired after her disfigurement by smallpox in 1562.[22]

The opening of the first Kew bridge in 1759 increased traffic into London and the village's popularity as a residential area. By 1796 some more large houses had arisen among the fishermen's cottages,[23] the grandest being Zoffany House and Strand Green House, and some old houses had been refronted.[24] Strand-on-the-Green remained a 'small hamlet', however, in 1816, where building formed only a narrow strip. It was still associated with fishing and river traffic,[25] although the hinterland was mainly orchards or market gardens and many structures by the Thames were maltings.[26]

[2] Gilbert, *Chiswick Old and New*, 57.
[3] Para. based on Pevsner, *Mdx.* 36-7; Robbins, *Mdx.* 234; Min. of Town and Country Planning, Provisional List of Bldgs. (1949).
[4] *P.N. Mdx.* (E.P.N.S.), 89; chwdns. acct. bk. (1636-62).
[5] Overseers' acct. bk. (1678-97). 'Strand under Green' in Rocque, *Map of Lond.* (1746), sheet 14.
[6] Above.
[7] M.R.O., MR/TH/3.
[8] Phillimore and Whitear, *Chiswick*, 14.
[9] K. Judges, *Strand-on-the-Green in 18th Cent.* (1969), 12, 15.
[10] *Home Counties Mag.* xiii. 116; Robbins, *Mdx.* 97.
[11] Para. based on inf. from Mrs. K. Judges.
[12] *Home Counties Mag.* xiii. 111-13; Rocque, *Map of Lond.* (1746), sheet 14.
[13] *Home Counties Mag.* xiii. 111-13.

[14] O.S. Map 6″, Mdx. XXI. NW. (1873 and later edns.); inf. from Mrs. K. Judges.
[15] Inf. from Mrs. K. Judges.
[16] Judges, *Strand-on-the-Green*, 15.
[17] Rocque, *Map of Lond.* (1746), sheet 14.
[18] M.R.O., MR/LV3/95; MR/LV7/4; inf. from Mrs. K. Judges.
[19] Guildhall MS. 14236/2, f. 1; below, industry.
[20] Chwdns. acct. bk. (1636-62).
[21] Rocque, *Map of Lond.* (1746), sheet 14.
[22] Gilbert, *Chiswick Old and New*, 60-1; M. Wilson, *Sir Philip Sidney* (1950), 30; Hist. MSS. Com. 77, *De L'Isle and Dudley*, ii, pp. 20, 87.
[23] W. Combe, *Hist. of R. Thames*, ii (1796), 53.
[24] Below.
[25] Brewer, *Beauties of Eng. & Wales*, x (5), 329.
[26] Milne, *Land Use Map of Lond.* (1800), plate II; below.

By the 1860s much of the waste near Kew bridge had been inclosed for wharves and there was building farther inland, including terraces in Spring Grove laid out *c.* 1850[27] across the old parish boundary. A few houses bordered the north side of Back Lane, while market gardens and orchards still covered most of the space between the lane and the new London and South Western railway line. Oliver's Island also had buildings,[28] put up after 1777 by the City of London's navigation committee and transferred in 1857 to the Thames Conservancy Board. The first City barge, bought in 1775, and its successor were often stationed there for the collection of tolls, before a dock was built on the Surrey shore for the more ceremonial *Maria Wood* of 1816.[29]

Strand-on-the-Green had six public houses: from west to east the Steam Packet, the Indian Queen, the Bell and Crown, the Ship, the City Barge, and the Bull's Head.[30] With its busy river life and irregular buildings[31] it was, and remained, popular with artists,[32] despite the railway bridge which in 1869 was carried across the Thames near the almshouses, altering the vista along the waterfront.[33]

During the next half century the scene grew less picturesque, as the weakened scouring force of the river, after the construction of a lock at Richmond, allowed grass and reeds to grow on the mud. In 1905 the Pier House laundry of 1860 began to expand north of Thames Road, as part of a move which was to leave its original riverside site as a permanent open space.[34] Near by the Indian Queen and some maltings stood empty in 1911, when a gate barred the old foreshore and when the Bell and Crown, the Ship, and maltings by Zoffany House had also closed.[35] Inland there were still gardens between Back Lane and the railway in 1894, although Waldeck and Pyrmont roads were then being laid out to the west.[36] Beyond the railway London Style House had been demolished in 1888, probably together with Sydney House, latterly renamed Stile Hall.[37] Regent Street had only been planned but housing stretched from Stile Hall Road north-eastward along the high road and across the Askew estate to Gunnersbury and Turnham Green. To the south-east Loraine Avenue and neighbouring roads linked Strand-on-the-Green with the new suburb of Grove Park.[38]

Strand-on-the-Green formed the western, largely working-class, end of Grove Park ward in 1894.[39] As such it was chosen by Chiswick U.D.C. for its first council housing, 34 houses

each of 2 flats to be built in 1903 near Back Lane in Cressey Avenue, later Mead Close.[40] Land near by had already been taken for enlarged National schools on the east side of Brooks Lane, later Brook Road. A government training centre opened east of the school in the First World War and later became the workshops of R. & J. Park.[41] Between Park's and the railway line a small recreation ground and allotments were provided,[42] leaving only cramped sites for building or rebuilding after 1935.[43] On a triangle of railway land 280 flats in the blocks known as Chiswick Village were on sale in 1936.[44]

Spared wholesale change, Strand-on-the-Green was described in 1932 as London's last remaining village.[45] Its social character so altered that by 1951 many old cottages along the waterfront had been 'resolutely prettified'.[46] Others were replaced after damage during the Second World War. The disappearance of industry, almost complete by the 1970s,[47] helped to create gaps which often were filled with small but expensive terraced houses,[48] such as the 14 on land bought from the Maritime Lighterage Co. at Magnolia wharf in 1963.[49] From 1968 Strand-on-the-Green was a conservation area, under the Civic Amenities Act, 1967.[50] Residents soon formed an amenity society and much local interest was later taken in Oliver's Island, to be leased by the Port of London Authority to the London Natural History Society,[51] and in the site of the Pier House laundry, which closed in 1973.[52]

Notable residents not mentioned elsewhere have included the comic actor Joseph or Josias Miller (1684–1738), reputedly the author of a book of jests, who died at his home at Strand-on-the-Green. The writer David Mallet (1705?–65), joint author of 'Rule Britannia', lived at Springfield House from 1735 to 1741 and then opposite Oliver's Island until 1748. The botanist Allan Cunningham (1791–1839) lived at no. 21 Strand-on-the-Green from 1814 to 1831. Mallet's daughter Dorothea Celesia (1738–90), the poet, was baptized at Chiswick church and presumably spent part of her childhood at Strand-on-the-Green.[53]

The waterfront at Strand-on-the-Green invites comparison with Chiswick Mall.[54] The first, however, has houses which are much more varied and in general less dignified than those of Old Chiswick. At Strand-on-the-Green the row, lined merely by a footpath and with no riverside gardens, appeals more because of its quaintness

[27] Guildhall Libr., La. Pr. V STR.
[28] O.S. Map 6″, Mdx. XII. NW. (1873 edn.).
[29] Thorne, *Environs*, 578; F. S. Thacker, *Thames Highway* (1968), 199–235; inf. from Mrs. Judges.
[30] *P.O. Dir. Mdx.* (1862); *Home Counties Mag.* xiii. 114.
[31] *Brentford and Chiswick As It Was*, illus. 35.
[32] Chiswick libr., NC/I/lxxiii.
[33] *Home Counties Mag.* xiii. 110; M. Binney and D. Pearce, *Railway Architecture* (1980).
[34] Inf. from Mrs. Judges.
[35] *Home Counties Mag.* 112–15; below, trade and industry.
[36] O.S. Map 6″, Mdx. XII. NW. (1894–6 edn.).
[37] Gilbert, *Chiswick Old and New*, 60–3.
[38] O.S. Map 6″, Mdx. XII. NW. (1894–6 edn.).
[39] M.R.O., *Rep. Local Inqs.* 1889–94.
[40] *Chiswick Times*, 16 Oct., 18 Dec. 1903.
[41] *Strand-on-the-Green Schs.* (centenary booklet 1974), 5.

[42] *Official Guide to Chiswick* [1911].
[43] O.S. Map 1/2,500, Mdx. XXI. 1 (1915 edn., 1935 revn.).
[44] Advert. in *Brentford and Chiswick Official Guide* [1936].
[45] Gilbert, *Chiswick Old and New*, 16.
[46] Pevsner, *Mdx.* 36.
[47] Below.
[48] Draper, *Chiswick*, preface.
[49] Below; *Brentford and Chiswick Times*, 1 Mar. 1963.
[50] Hounslow, *Guide to Local Ind.* (1978), 21.
[51] Strand-on-the-Green Soc. *Newsletter*, summer 1979.
[52] *Brentford and Chiswick Times*, 11 Oct. 1973; 10 Apr. 1975; 6, 27 Sept. 1978.
[53] *Strand-on-the-Green Schs.* 4; *D.N.B.*; inf. from Mrs. K. Judges.
[54] Para. based on Hist. Mon. Com. *Mdx.* 10; Pevsner, *Mdx.* 36; Min. of Town and Country Planning, List of Bldgs. (1949).

and the south-westerly outlook than because of its buildings' architectural distinction. Nearly all the houses are of brown brick and several have been painted or stuccoed. Those near the west end include a well preserved pair of *c.* 1700 formed by Arakne and Springfield, nos. 66 and 67, and a similar but slightly later pair formed by no. 68, Carlton House, and no. 69. Zoffany House, no. 65, is usually considered the finest in the row; it is early 18th-century and was the home of Johann Zoffany, formerly at London Style House, from 1790 until his death.[55] Nos. 52–5 constitute a well conserved terrace of five houses faced with white brick, built 1793–6.[56] Beyond the railway bridge the Bull's Head is 17th-century but much altered internally. Strand-on-the-Green House, no. 1, which was originally called Strand Green House and later the Elms, has internal walls of that period, refaced in 1788.[57]

LITTLE SUTTON, the most centrally situated of Chiswick's early settlements, was recorded as Sutton in 1181. Remote from the main lines of communication and probably owing its existence to the manor house, it was further described as Sutton (by) Chiswick in the 14th and 15th centuries, as Sutton Beauregard[58] in the 1450s[59] and as Little Sutton by 1590.[60] 'Beauregard' apparently referred to views across the Thames to the Surrey hills[61] and was used only when the Crown held the manor, which was later called Sutton Court.[62]

In the Middle Ages Sutton Lane presumably ran southward for ¼ mile from Turnham Green common, as later, before describing a westward loop and continuing south from the manor house. Little Sutton was probably the name of cottages north of the loop, where they stood on both sides of the road by 1746. At the beginning of the loop were a few more buildings, including almshouses which by 1703 backed on land stretching southward to Sutton Court itself.[63]

Ratepayers were listed separately for Little Sutton, including Sutton Court, in the 17th and 18th centuries, although they numbered only 11, out of 167 parishioners, in 1630 and 10 in 1678.[64] In 1706 the straggling hamlet did not deserve the name of a village, since it consisted only of 'a few poor houses' near Sutton Court.[65] Buildings included the Queen's Head, if the inn of that name recorded from 1722 was the one which was there in 1862.[66] Little Sutton had 11 houses in 1795[67] and 14 houses, with 17 of the parish's 637 families, in 1801. Parkland stretched around it on the east side of Sutton Lane and market gardens

on the west side in 1801, when agriculture was the sole employment.[68]

In 1845 the quietness of Little Sutton was in contrast to busy streets elsewhere,[69] presumably at Turnham Green. By the 1860s houses stretched a little farther north along Sutton Lane but they did not yet join those of any other settlement. Little Sutton House stood on the east side of the lane north-east of the almshouses, Sutton Place on the west side of the bend in the lane, and Sutton Court Lodge on the east side north-west of Sutton Court,[70] which was then a boys' school.[71]

The hamlet lost some of its character with the transfer of the almspeople to Turnham Green *c.* 1845[72] and with the closure of the Queen's Head. In 1879 the former inn was enfranchised with Little Sutton House,[73] whose estate was further enlarged in 1881 by a purchase from the duke of Devonshire.[74] The house itself was still in private occupation in 1890, as were Sutton Court and Sutton Court Lodge,[75] but by 1894 there was new housing along the west side of Sutton Lane: Sutton Place had gone and roads such as St. Mary's Grove and Gordon Road had been built up. To the east large houses and parkland survived a little longer, although the grounds of Little Sutton House and Sutton Court were already bounded by Barrowgate and Sutton Court roads.[76] The estate of Little Sutton House was offered for sale as building land in 1905,[77] when the proposed roads included Elm Wood Road[78] and Sutton Court, previously demolished, was being replaced by flats. With the building up of those two estates Little Sutton merged into the surrounding middle-class suburbs. In 1979, after the almshouses had gone, the only individual feature was the church of 1909 known as St. Michael, Sutton Court.

While there was much rebuilding in the early 19th century at Old Chiswick and Strand-on-the-Green, where riverside industries and private residences were crowded together, elsewhere the interest of the dukes of Devonshire, owners of more than half of the parish by 1847, determined the pace and quality of suburban growth. Although the family, for all its benefactions and formal patronage, took little active part in local affairs,[79] the interest was officially recognized in the duke's right to be represented on the local board of health[80] and widely commemorated in roads recalling the Cavendishes, their titles, and possessions.

The spread of building between Old Chiswick and Turnham Green was impeded not only by

[55] Gilbert, *Chiswick Old and New*, 61; *D.N.B.*
[56] *Brentford and Chiswick As It Was*, illus. 35.
[57] Inf. from Mrs. Judges.
[58] *P.N. Mdx.* (E.P.N.S.), 89.
[59] *Cal. Pat.* 1452–61, 297, 419; *Cal. Close*, 1454–61, 242.
[60] M.R.O., Acc. 531/66, f. 22.
[61] *P.N. Mdx.* (E.P.N.S.), 89.   [62] Below, manors.
[63] Rocque, *Map of Lond.* (1746), sheet 14.
[64] Chwdns. acct. bk. (1622–35); overseers' acct. bk. (1678–97).
[65] Phillimore and Whitear, *Chiswick*, 14.
[66] M.R.O., MR/LV3/95; *P.O. Dir. Mdx.* (1862).
[67] Lysons, *Environs*, ii. 207.
[68] Census, 1801 (photocopy in Chiswick libr.); Milne, *Land Use Map of Lond.* (1800), plate II.

[69] Faulkner, *Brentford, Ealing and Chiswick*, 482.
[70] O.S. Map 6″, Mdx. XXI. NW. (1873 edn.).
[71] Below, educ.
[72] Below, charities.
[73] Guildhall MS. 14236/16, ff. 251–4.
[74] Chiswick libr., NC/I/clxxxvi.
[75] *Kelly's Dir. Mdx.* (1890).
[76] O.S. Map 6″, Mdx. XXI. NW. (1894–6 edn.).
[77] Below, manors.
[78] Chiswick libr., NC/I/clxxxvi; ibid. lxvii.
[79] As president of the Royal Horticultural Soc., whose gardens were at Chiswick (below), the duke of Devonshire attended only one mtg. in 20 yrs.: H. R. Fletcher, *Story of R. Hortic. Soc. 1804–1968* (1969), 170.
[80] Below.

the grounds of Chiswick House but by the duke's lease of 33 a. to the Royal Horticultural Society in 1821.[81] The land, formerly market gardens, lay west of Duke's Avenue and immediately north of the grounds of Chiswick House. At first there was a garden for fruit and vegetables and one of *c.* 13 a. for ornamental plants which included an arboretum. Financial difficulties led to plans for closure in 1870, after the society had opened new gardens at Kensington, and a smaller area was leased from 1881, when the arboretum and many glasshouses were abandoned. From 1882 Barrowgate Road was laid out along what had been the southernmost strip of the gardens[82] but it was not until 1903 that the society finally left for Wisley (Surr.). The Chiswick grounds were then remembered not only for their place in horticulture but as a social attraction, their visitors' carriages formerly having blocked the roads from London.

The earliest concentrated building outside the old settlements took place on former market gardens[83] north-west of Old Chiswick, between Hogarth Lane and Chiswick Field Lane (later Devonshire Road). Seven streets of terraced cottages existed there by 1847,[84] were served by St. Mary Magdalen's chapel of ease from 1848,[85] and were called Chiswick New Town by the 1860s.[86] Unlike most later estates it was not built because of better communications but presumably because of the need to house workers for the nearby gardens, or for the breweries and large houses around Chiswick Mall. Chiswick New Town contained almost half of the paupers in the parish in 1851. Its cottages fronted directly on the roads, which were not made up until the 1880s, and always constituted a poor district[87] until their demolition in the 1950s.[88]

Despite the early establishment of Chiswick New Town, the parish was built up comparatively slowly. In the 1860s open country still separated the three old settlements.[89] Acton or Ealing at that time experienced their most rapid growth, whereas in Chiswick the population rose by 31 per cent, before soaring in the 1870s by 88 per cent. Chiswick's building boom began in the late 1860s, being partly attributable to the L.S.W.R.'s line of 1869, and slowed down from 1881; thereafter there were decennial rises in the population of 37, 36, and 30 per cent, the last accompanying another increase in the building of houses, until they again exceeded demand by 1911.

The first new middle-class housing, leased from 1864, was on land which had been owned in 1847 by Adam Askew. Stretching south from the high road across Turnham Green Lane, which was soon called Wellesley Road, it came to form the nucleus of a new district, served by Brentford

Road (later Gunnersbury) station, west of Turnham Green. Most of the land north of Wellesley Road had been built up by 1871, with large villas in Oxford Road and smaller ones in Cambridge Road, and to the south Grosvenor Road was soon laid out. By 1914 there were 174 houses, with a social life centred on the hall of St. James's, Gunnersbury, and the Pilot inn.

GROVE PARK, a more spacious suburb,[90] originated in the earliest and most ambitious building plans for Chiswick of the dukes of Devonshire. It arose by the river below Strand-on-the-Green, where the dukes had extended their holding westward to include Grove House and its grounds. The London and South Western railway cut off the park of Chiswick House from the duke's riverside lands to the south-west, where in the 1860s the western stretch of Burlington Lane, along the existing line of Grove Park Road, contained only a few farm buildings east of Grove House in addition to Grove End, which had been built in 1861.[91] Plans for a garden suburb to be served by Chiswick station, which had opened in 1849, were publicized in 1867[92] but discarded in favour of more piecemeal building, which started in 1871.

The first roads were Spencer, Bolton, and Hartington roads, laid out as far as Cavendish Road across the grounds south-east of Grove House. Some large detached houses were built there and Grove House itself survived, being sold by the duke for private occupation in 1895.[93] Towards Strand-on-the-Green, however, the district was less exclusive, with some small dwellings at the north end in Grove Park Terrace. Devonshire Gardens and Cavendish Road had been named but not yet built up by 1894, when there were some houses in Grove Park Road and Grove Park Gardens. A few empty plots remained in 1914, when expansion was limited beyond the railway line and to the south by the duke's Chiswick Park estate and by the sports grounds of St. Thomas's hospital, the Chiswick Park clubs, and the Polytechnic. The tendency to build more modest houses was also shown in Chiswick Park.

A lively social life, making use of the river for recreation, was planned from the first. Among the earliest buildings was the Grove Park hotel, near the station, where local societies met. Grove Park had a church from 1872, private schools by 1890, and gave its name to a large ward, including Strand-on-the-Green, in 1894.[94] As early as 1900 two large houses in Spencer Road were replaced by flats, called Burlington Court. By 1914 there was a row of new shops, a bridge over the railway instead of a level crossing, and a pleasure lake, formerly belonging to Grove House, at the south

[81] Para. based on Fletcher, *R. Hortic. Soc.* 79–80, 165–8, 217–19, 275.
[82] Wisdom, 'W. Lond. Suburb', 100.
[83] Milne, *Land Use Map of Lond.* (1800), plate II.
[84] M.R.O., TA/CHI.
[85] Below.
[86] O.S. Map 6″, Mdx. XXI. NW. (1873 edn.).
[87] Jahn, 'Rlys. and Suburban Development', 24, 118–19; Wisdom, 'W. Lond. Suburb', 28.
[88] Wisdom, 'W. Lond. Suburb', 11.
[89] O.S. Map 6″, Mdx. XXI. NW. (1873 edn.). Two paras.

based on Jahn, 'Rlys. and Suburban Development', and Wisdom, 'W. Lond. Suburb', *passim.*
[90] Subsection based on O.S. Maps 6″, Mdx. XXI. NW. (1873 and later edns.) and Wisdom, 'W. Lond. Suburb', 75–80. Many individual bldgs. are described in J. Wisdom and V. Bott, *Walk Around Grove Pk. Estate* (Grove Pk. Group and Brentford and Chiswick Local Hist. Soc. 1980).
[91] Thorne, *Environs*, 110.
[92] Gilbert, *Chiswick Old and New*, 18.
[93] Sales Cats. in Chiswick libr.; Gilbert, *Chiswick Old and New*, 46. [94] Below; Wisdom and Bott, *Grove Pk. Estate*, 8.

CHISWICK HOUSE FROM THE RIVER IN 1750

OLD CHISWICK FROM THE RIVER c. 1675

The Mall *c.* 1827

Thornycrofts' Works in 1886

CHISWICK

end of Hartington Road, besides three boat houses and a fourth near Barnes bridge. During the First World War Cubitt's Yacht Basin was formed out of the lake, for the production of concrete barges. After the war it was converted into popular houseboat moorings, with a ship repair workshop and a caravan site.[95]

Grove House in 1928 made way for the terraced houses of Kinnaird Avenue.[96] To the north-east council housing covered the St. Thomas's hospital estate after the Second World War[97] but to the south-east the land remained open except by the river along Hartington Road, where there were houses and flats of the 1930s. Hartington Court was built in 1938 on the site of Grove End. Off the southern end of the road maisonnettes at Thames Village were occupied from 1956, next to Cubitt's Yacht Basin, which held c. 50 houseboats. In 1965 expensive houses called Chiswick Staithe were completed on the site of nos. 1–15 Hartington Road,[98] and in 1969 the last houseboat dwellers were forced to leave by the Cubitt's Yacht Basin Co., which in 1975 advertised the first of 68 terraced houses, each with its own mooring.[99] In 1979 Grove Park remained a spacious suburb, with many Victorian houses, the larger ones divided, and residents covering a wide social range. Change was most evident in the three oldest roads, which none the less retained their established trees. A residents' association, the Grove Park Group, existed from 1970.

The physician and author Andrew Wynter (1819–76) died at his home, Chestnut Lodge, Grove Park. Field-Marshal Viscount Montgomery of Alamein (1887–1976) spent part of his boyhood at Grove Park, where his father rented no. 19 Bolton Road from 1902.[1]

A third estate was being built by 1871,[2] on the glebe land which had been allotted to the vicar out of Chiswick common field. Bounded by land abutting Devonshire Road to the east and the north part of Duke's Avenue to the west, it consisted of uniform terraces in and around Glebe Street. Two-thirds of the area had been built up by 1882 and nearly all, with c. 470 houses, by 1891, so extending working-class homes from Chiswick New Town to the high road.

Piecemeal building, too, was also under way by the early 1870s: in the grounds of Arlington House between Turnham Green and Askew's estate, where there were houses in Brandenburgh (later Burlington) Road by 1874,[3] and on two sites acquired by the British Land Co. north of the high road and west of Old Chiswick. Dense housing began to spread northward from the high road around the edge of the Back common, towards Turnham Green station, 79 plots by Windmill Place being auctioned in 1870 and more in 1871.[4]

BEDFORD PARK,[5] an unusually self-contained suburb, was begun in the mid 1870s, while widespread building activity continued elsewhere. Well known as the parent of England's garden suburbs, it has attracted conflicting claims both for its architecture and for its social and artistic life. Building began on land around the 18th-century Bedford House, former home of the botanist John Lindley (1799–1865),[6] and its two neighbours Melbourne House and Sydney House, facing Acton Green common. Thence housing spread over the south-eastern corner of Acton parish and eastward over a triangular detached portion of Ealing. Only a southern strip of the estate, built up comparatively late between Bath Road and Flanders Road, lay within the old parish of Chiswick. The transfer of Ealing detached in 1878, however, gave almost half of Bedford Park to Chiswick, which provided the nearest station, Turnham Green, and shopping centre, in Chiswick High Road. Bedford Park was the name of a Chiswick ward from 1894[7] and the subject of a boundary dispute in 1931, when Acton sought the transfer of some highly rated property, although residents in the Acton part themselves would have preferred to be in Chiswick.[8] In 1979 it lay within Ealing and Hounslow L.B.s.

The creator of Bedford Park was Jonathan Thomas Carr (1845–1915), a cloth merchant whose father-in-law, Hamilton Fulton, lived at Bedford House. The estate's three chief roads were the Avenue, Woodstock Road, and Bath Road, all radiating from the east end of Acton green.[9] Initially Carr acquired 24 a. in 1875 but adjoining sites were rapidly added, including part of Ealing detached on a 99-year building lease from the Ecclesiastical Commissioners in 1877.[10] Its first houses, in the Avenue, were occupied in 1876 and many in Woodstock Road were ready by 1878.[11] The Bedford Park Co. was formed in 1881, with Carr as chairman, and by 1883 there were 490 houses on 113 a. On Carr's collapse in 1886, with half of the land built up, the company's assets were largely bought by Bedford Park Estate Ltd., which finished the roads and continued to manage some property until the 1950s. Ultimately the estate came to be bounded by Gainsborough and Abinger roads to the east, Blenheim Road and Marlborough Crescent to the north, Esmond Road to the west,

[95] Inf. from Mrs. Judges.
[96] Gilbert, *Chiswick Old and New*, 46.
[97] Above.
[98] Wisdom and Bott, *Grove Pk. Estate*, 3, 10; Draper, *Chiswick*, preface.
[99] *Brentford and Chiswick Times*, 24 July, 28 Aug. 1969; *Chiswick and Brentford Gaz.* 18 Sept. 1975.
[1] *D.N.B.*; B. Montgomery, *Field-Marshal in the Family* (1973), 121.
[2] Two paras. based on Jahn, 'Rlys. and Suburban Development', and Wisdom, 'W. Lond. Suburb', *passim*.
[3] M.R.O., Acc. 1395/16. Its western neighbour, the Grange, was sold to a builder in 1889: ibid. 36.

[4] Estate maps in Chiswick libr.
[5] Subsection based on M. J. Bolsterli, *Early Community at Bedford Pk.* (1977), and T. Affleck Greeves, *Bedford Pk., the First Gdn. Suburb* (1975). The first deals mainly with the quality of life, the second (unpaginated) provides the fullest illustrated record. Much modern work is based on articles by T. A. Greeves in *Country Life*, 7, 14 Dec. 1967, 27 Nov. 1975.
[6] *D.N.B.*
[7] Below.
[8] *The Times*, 24 Mar. 1931.
[9] *Country Life*, 7 Dec. 1967, p. 1524.
[10] Guildhall MS. 12352 (40 pieces, unnumbered).
[11] Ibid.

and South Parade and Flanders Road to the south.[12]

Although Carr belonged to a Radical and artistic family, he was also a speculator whose largely commercial aims came to be obscured by Bedford Park's reputation. His chosen site lay close to a railway station, the designation 'park' could have applied to any genteel estate,[13] and the road widths and plots were narrower than those of a true garden suburb. Some of the earlier houses, not all of 'Queen Anne' red brick, were often ill finished and with woodwork too meagre for the style which they purported to revive; even their much publicized lack of basements was not new.[14] Bedford Park none the less invited public attention, both because Carr employed distinguished architects and because he provided social facilities which gave it a life of its own.

The chief architectural interest of Bedford Park lies in the extent to which it is the work of Richard Norman Shaw, estate architect from 1877 until 1880.[15] The very first houses were by H. E. Coe of Coe & Robinson or by the more adventurous E. W. Godwin,[16] who was working for Carr in 1875 but resigned because of stringent financial conditions. Shaw himself was asked first for only two designs, for a detached and a semi-detached villa, on which he produced variations. Although he gradually assumed a wider supervision, he was not responsible for planning the estate, which was laid out to preserve much of Lindley's arboretum and trees on the surrounding land. Moreover the designs were sold direct to Carr, who thus could modify them for economy or to please clients.[17] Shaw probably continued as a consultant after 1880, when he was succeeded by his aide E. J. May, who lived in Bedford Park and worked with other architects, including Maurice B. Adams, another resident.

Social life[18] centred on the club, paid for by Carr and opened in 1879. A plain building in the style of Queen Anne, it was probably designed by Shaw and enlarged by May, containing furniture by Godwin, William Morris, and G. Jackson & Sons and tiles by William de Morgan. It stood on the west side of the Avenue next to the imposing Tower House, designed by Shaw for Carr himself,[19] and in 1979 was the CAV social club. Near by the church of St. Michael and All Angels on the north side of Bath Road and the Tabard inn and the stores on the south side, all by Shaw, were opened in 1880. Chiswick school of art, next to the Tabard and designed by Adams, was opened in 1881.

The club and other public buildings were provided only after the completion of the first houses and served, like the architects' names, to sell Bedford Park to the cultured middle class. Aided by his brother J. W. Comyns Carr, art critic on the *Pall Mall Gazette*, and by Moncure

Conway, an American enthusiast who wrote in *Harper's Magazine*, Carr 'had his finger on the popular artistic magazines and built consciously for their public'.[20] His success led to the 'Ballad of Bedford Park' in 1881, which ended with a snigger at the 'boiled lobster houses',[21] and to the description 'home of the aesthetes' in 1882. Bedford Park none the less owed its reputation to more than propaganda. It proved both a convenient and a pleasant place in which to live, with leafy avenues and striking but relatively cheap houses, particularly in the 1880s when it formed a compact rural village. Above all, its public buildings made it a self-contained community rather than a mere dormitory suburb.

In the early 20th century Bedford Park attracted little public attention. As it became less fashionable, some of the larger buildings made way for three- or four-storeyed blocks of flats. Sydney House and Bedford Park Mansions were built c. 1900, the first replacing the Georgian house of that name, and Bedford House was turned into flats in 1924, when the shops called Bedford Corner were built around its garden which had extended to South Parade. In the 1930s St. Catherine's Court replaced the Tower House, which had served as a convent from 1908, and a taller block called Ormesby Lodge was built in the Avenue. In the Second World War, which brought the closure of the club, Adams's school of art was destroyed and c. 30 houses were damaged. The replacement of a house in Bedford Road by a yellow-brick home for old people led in 1963 to the formation of the Bedford Park Society, and, after the demolition of two more houses, to measures for the preservation of 356 houses in 1967.

To conventional critics Bedford Park, for all its charm, symbolized a pretentious way of life. Such was the view of G. K. Chesterton, who portrayed it as Saffron Hill in *The Man Who Was Thursday* and claimed that it attracted only the second-rate.[22] In reality there were several distinguished residents, including the architect C. F. A. Voysey (1857–1941) at no. 7 Blandford Road in 1885–6, the actress Isabella Howard Paul (1833?–1879), who died at no. 17 the Avenue, the actor William Terriss (1847–97) at no. 2 Bedford Road, the playwright Arthur Wing Pinero (1855–1934) at no. 10 Marlborough Crescent in 1885, and the historian Frederick York Powell (1850–1904) at nos. 2 and 6 Priory Gardens. The painter J. B. Yeats lived at no. 8 Woodstock Road from 1878 to 1880 and, after some years in Ireland, at no. 3 Blenheim Road from 1888 until c. 1900.[23] His son W. B. Yeats (1865–1939), who was to recall Bedford Park in his autobiography,[24] there helped to found the Irish Literary Society, parent of the Irish Literary Theatre and of Dublin's Abbey theatre, in 1893.[25] The painter Lucien Pissarro (1863–1944) lived at no. 62 Bath

[12] A plan of the estate in 1896, by Maurice B. Adams, is in Chiswick libr.

[13] M. Girouard, *Sweetness and Light, the 'Queen Anne' Movement* (1977), 160.

[14] A. Saint, *Ric. Norman Shaw* (1976), 201.

[15] W. L. Crease, *Search for Environment* (1966), 99–100.

[16] *Romantic Mythologies*, ed. I. Fletcher, 171; Girouard, *Sweetness and Light*, 160.   [17] Saint, *Shaw*, 202–3.

[18] Below, social.   [19] Saint, *Shaw*, 205–6.
[20] Ibid. 201–2.   [21] Bolsterli, *Bedford Pk.* 123–6.
[22] *Romantic Mythologies*, 169–70.
[23] *D.N.B.*; inf. from Mr. T. A. Greeves. Many residents are noted in *Bedford Pk. 1875* (exhib. catalogue by Bedford Pk. centenary cttee. and Victorian Soc.).
[24] W. B. Yeats, *Trembling of the Veil* (1922), 3.
[25] *Romantic Mythologies*, 198.

Road from 1897 to 1901.[26] At least five views of Bath Road or its neighbourhood in 1897 were painted by his father Camille Pissarro.[27]

Bedford Park was declared a conservation area by Ealing L.B. in 1969 and Hounslow L.B. in 1970.[28] Still delimited to the south by the railway and Acton Green common, it merges elsewhere into the suburbs of Acton and Hammersmith, where many streets faintly echo its style. All the public buildings survive except the school of art, whose loss, with that of the Tower House, has partly deprived the estate of its focus.[29] Bedford Park as a whole has an intimate air: its roads, mostly named after people or events of Queen Anne's time, appear deceptively narrow and winding, with their crowded trees, small front gardens, and many T-junctions. Architecturally, both in its red brick and in the decorative motifs,

of the centre of the parish remained open.[32] The attractions of Chiswick House as a retreat from London, however, dwindled as railways made the duke of Devonshire's provincial seats more accessible, while its estate increased in value as building land. The lull in building during the 1880s therefore did not prevent sales either of part of the gardens which the duke had leased to the Royal Horticultural Society or of 80 a. to the west, later known as Chiswick Park. Thomas Kemp Welch, the purchaser in 1884, intended to imitate Bedford Park, but restrictions on the type of housing delayed building on most of the land, bordering the new Sutton Court Road,[33] until the late 1890s.

By the early 1890s housing was almost continuous along the high road. The streets leading north to the Back common and the railway had

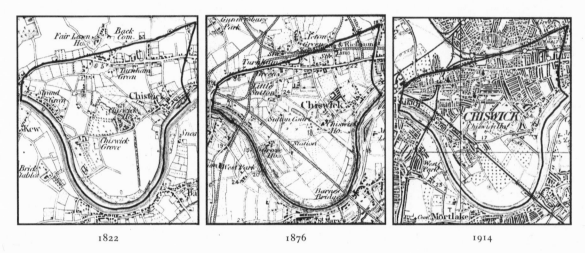

1822   1876   1914

CHISWICK: EVOLUTION OF SETTLEMENT 1822–1914

(Scale 1 inch to 1 mile)

it reflects the taste of Shaw, although there is more variety than has often been suggested, including 30 types and several individual houses.[30] Detached houses largely occupy corner sites and the only four-storeyed houses are nos. 32 and 34 Woodstock Road. The Avenue contains the side entrance to Bedford House, a much altered building whose front is hidden from South Parade by Bedford Corner. In South Parade are the yellow-brick Melbourne House and, farther west, no. 14, well known as a plain roughcast 'artist's house' of 1891, designed by C. F. A. Voysey to provide a contrast with its neighbours.[31]

While housing thus stretched northward from Old Chiswick to the high road, and westward from Turnham Green along the high road through Gunnersbury towards Brentford, much

been built up, including Belmont Road, Turnham Green Terrace, Thornton Avenue and, on the Hammersmith boundary, Goldhawk Road.[34] South of the high road there was still open land east of Devonshire Road, but housing was already advancing down Annandale Road and Chiswick Lane, towards what was soon to be an estate on some of the fields of the Prebend manor.[35] A compact area, it was known as the ABC estate, since its roads were named alphabetically from north to south, beginning with Ashbourne Grove and Balfern Grove. The plots, sold by the Ecclesiastical Commissioners in the 1870s, had been only partly built up when auctioned by the British Land Co. in 1896[36] but contained 327 houses by 1901. The population density was high, with many houses divided among poor families. Immediately to the north the old Manor Farm House was replaced by

[26] Ibid.; W. S. Meadmore, *Lucien Pissarro* (1962), 82, 94–5.
[27] L. R. Pissarro and L. Venturi, *Camille Pissarro*, ii (1939), pl. 1005–9.   [28] Inf. from Mr. T. A. Greeves.
[29] Saint, *Shaw*, 201, 206.
[30] Types are classified in Greeves, *Bedford Pk.*
[31] N. Pevsner, *Studies in Art, Architecture and Design*, ii

(1968), 142–3; Pevsner, *Mdx.* 26.
[32] Three paras. based on Jahn, 'Rlys. and Suburban Development', and Wisdom, 'W. Lond. Suburb', *passim*.
[33] Sales cats. in Chiswick libr.
[34] O.S. Map 6", Mdx. XVI. SW. (1894–6 edn.).
[35] Ibid. Mdx. XXI. NW. (1894–6 edn.).
[36] M.R.O., Acc. 891/2/9/11–12.

Wilton Avenue in 1896, as part of a separate project. To the east some houses were built along the edge of Home field but were later demolished, the field itself being preserved for recreation while middle-class housing spread over the area to the north.

In the early 20th century building continued on land already intended for housing, as at Grove Park and Bedford Park or on the Homefield estate around Airedale Avenue, which had 256 houses and 40 flats, with room for more, in 1914. In the centre of the parish the remainder of the Royal Horticultural Society's gardens, with an exceptionally large house called Devonhurst, made way for 269 middle-class houses, and by 1911 Ellesmere Road had been built up, blocking the rural views from Barrowgate Road, as had part of Park Road. North of Grove Park plots were sold in 1904 for the Riverview estate, 110 terraced houses adjoining Strand-on-the-Green, and to the east the site of Little Sutton was offered in 1905.[37] Further building on the Chiswick Park estate had led to Staveley and Chesterfield roads and their neighbours being laid out, although not built up, by 1915.[38] Housing thus stretched from Old Chiswick north-westward to Turnham Green and thence south-eastward through Little Sutton to Grove Park and Strand-on-the-Green, curving around the much reduced grounds of Chiswick House, itself an asylum from 1896. Large blocks of private flats were built in many parts: they included Sutton Court on the site of the manor house, Prebend Mansions in Airedale Avenue and the high road, Dewsbury Crescent in Chiswick Road, and flats at the north end of Grove Park Terrace.

After the First World War there was little room for building in the northern half of the parish, where almost all the market gardens had vanished and the existing commons had been preserved for recreation. South of Burlington Lane, however, in addition to land which had been acquired by private sports clubs,[39] the duke of Devonshire still owned c. 200 a. of fields and gardens. Plans to sell them to the Brentford Gas Co. were frustrated by public protest and in 1923 they were bought for recreation by the U.D.C.,[40] which retained some and leased or sold the rest.[41] Much of the peninsular part of the parish, long known as Duke's Meadows, therefore remained open.

Between 1911 and c. 1950 the building rate was about half that of the previous 40 years.[42] Chiswick Park and avenues such as Lawford and Staveley roads south-west of Chiswick House had finally been built up by 1935, while Chiswick House and its landscaped park were acquired for the public in 1929. Flat building continued, and some encroachment was made on the unbuilt land of the peninsula with new schools, sports pavilions near the river, and houses, as in Alexandra Avenue, along Great Chertsey Road. The most striking changes arose not from the spread of housing but from road widening and the cutting of Great Chertsey Road itself.[43]

The building of council houses, started in 1903 at Strand-on-the-Green,[44] continued in the period between the World Wars,[45] and increased after 1945. The sports grounds of St. Thomas's hospital, farther north than most playing fields, survived as an open space between Little Sutton and Grove Park[46] until their compulsory purchase in 1946. Brentford and Chiswick M.B. there carried out what was then its most ambitious housing scheme, for 220 flats, of which the first six, in Nightingale Close, were occupied from 1949 and a further 96 in 1952.[47] Other schemes included flats south-east of Burlington Lane in Edensor Road, where 138 were planned in 1948,[48] and tower blocks on the Hogarth estate, the first of which was named in 1953.[49] Private building in the whole borough in 1962 accounted for only one quarter of the c. 2,000 dwellings built since 1945.[50]

In keeping with a fall in the population from the peak recorded in 1931,[51] the period after the Second World War was remarkable less for the spread of housing than for the filling of small sites, for the conversion of large houses into flats, and for rebuilding. From the 1950s blocks rose along Chiswick High Road, industry tended to move away,[52] and the old parish became still more residential, with many suburbs, including those around the early villages, retaining a character of their own. Chiswick suffered more than most areas from the growth in traffic to London: the building of new roads had an even stronger impact than in the 1920s and 1930s, entailing much house demolition and helping to separate the northern and southern parts of the parish. In consequence local patriotism grew, early amenity societies were formed,[53] and the more select areas, where property values remained high, appeared still more strongly as oases of peace and some architectural distinction.

The population of the parish was 3,235 in 1801, 4,236 in 1821, and 6,303 in 1851. It rose very little in the 1850s and was only 8,508 in 1871, but had increased to 15,975 by 1881, 21,963 by 1891, 29,809 by 1901, and 38,697 by 1911. Thereafter it rose slowly to reach 40,938 by 1921 and a peak of 42,246, in the six Chiswick wards of Brentford and Chiswick, by 1931. Numbers fell to 42,207 in 1951 and 38,981 in 1961, after which date the wards were reorganized within Hounslow L.B.[54]

[37] Chiswick libr., NC/I/clxxxvi.
[38] O.S. Map 1/2,500, Mdx. XXI. 1 (1915 edn.).
[39] Below, social.
[40] *Chiswick Residents' Protest* (pamphlet 1918) in Chiswick libr.; *The Times*, 7 Sept. 1923.
[41] *The Times*, 12 June 1925; Draper, *Chiswick*, preface.
[42] Wisdom, 'W. Lond. Suburb', 11.
[43] O.S. Map 1/2,500, Mdx. XXI. 1, 2 (1935 revn.).
[44] *Chiswick Times*, 16 Oct., 18 Dec. 1903.
[45] Ibid. 28 Nov. 1919.

[46] O.S. Map 1/2,500, Mdx. XXI. 1 (1935 revn.).
[47] *Brentford and Chiswick Times*, 13, 20 Sept. 1946; 26 Aug. 1949; 29 Feb. 1952.
[48] Brentford and Chiswick, *Official Guide* (1948).
[49] *Brentford and Chiswick Times*, 11 Dec. 1953.
[50] Ibid. 17 Aug. 1962.
[51] *Census*, 1951, 1961.
[52] Below, industry.
[53] Below, social.
[54] *Census*, 1801–1961.

SOCIAL AND CULTURAL ACTIVITIES.

Houses called the Catherine Wheel and the Counter House in 1558[55] may have been taverns, as was the Bohemia in 1632.[56] The King's Head at Chiswick was among taverns known to the 'water poet' John Taylor in 1636[57] and there was the Cock and Half Moon at Turnham Green in 1680.[58] Fifteen alehouse keepers were named in 1716;[59] 17 inns were listed in 1722[60] and 27, a number probably not exceeded for over a century, in 1759. At least 5 inns in 1759 were at Turnham Green, including the Pack Horse,[61] so called by 1698,[62] whose licensee's widow in 1791 had been 'much respected by the nobility and gentry travelling the great western road'.[63] Only one inn, the Noah's Ark, was said in 1759 to be at Strand-on-the-Green.[64] There were 11 inns at Turnham Green, 7 at Chiswick, and 5 at Strand-on-the-Green in 1839–40[65] and each district had one more by 1862.[66]

An assembly room had been built at the Pack Horse by 1747.[67] Presumably it was in regular use until the 19th century, since in 1800 Edward Jenkins was licensee and in 1808, when there had been assemblies for at least 20 years, a winter ball was held at Jenkins's rooms. There were six stewards in 1807, one of whom insulted a well-connected visitor by having his subscription returned.[68]

An armed association was formed in 1798,[69] when Sir Charles Rouse-Boughton launched a successful appeal for contributions for defence.[70] Presumably the association was superseded by a volunteer corps, which was to be enrolled in 1803 and supported by subscriptions in 1804.[71] The 3rd West Middlesex militia had a stores at Turnham Green in 1862.[72] Chiswick (C) Company of the 2nd (South) Middlesex Rifle Volunteers drilled weekly during the winter in 1900 at the Hogarth schools.[73]

A clothing fund for the poor, administered by a committee presided over by the vicar, was established in 1841.[74] Perhaps it was superseded by Chiswick Philanthropic Society, formed in the 1890s,[75] which continued to raise money for charities in the old parish under new rules adopted in 1956.[76] Chiswick Memorial Club for ex-servicemen opened in 1919 in Afton House, Bourne Place, given by Daniel Mason,[77] where it remained in 1979. Chiswick Women's Aid, pro-viding refuges for battered wives, originated in meetings at no. 2 Belmont Terrace in 1971,[78] and achieved national renown.

A bowling alley lay near the south-east end of the later Devonshire Road, on part of the demesne of the Prebend manor, by 1746.[79] There were inns called the Bowling Green in 1751 and the Cricketer in 1759 and 1770.[80] Turnham Green Devonshire cricket club, so called because the duke of Devonshire accepted the presidency in 1853, played on Turnham Green common by 1856 and became Chiswick and Turnham Green cricket club by amalgamation in 1867. It was called Turnham Green cricket club from 1884,[81] after some members had founded the Chiswick Park Cricket and Lawn Tennis Co.,[82] which by 1900 had divided into separate cricket and lawn tennis clubs. New clubs by 1900 included Bedford Park for lawn tennis, Sutton Court for football, and Fairlawn Park for tennis and bowls; Grove Park had its football club in 1900[83] and a cricket and lawn tennis club by 1911. Chiswick and West London bowling and tennis club had its own grounds in Airedale Avenue in 1911.[84] They were still used in the 1960s, when cricket was played on Turnham Green common, Homefields recreation ground, and in the park of Chiswick House, while there were public tennis courts at Chiswick common, Chiswick House, and Duke's Meadows.[85]

Other sports were served by a short lived Chiswick golf club and by at least three cycling clubs, one of them for ladies, in 1900,[86] and by Chiswick rifle club, with a miniature range at no. 475 Chiswick High Road in 1911.[87] Some large firms organized their own sports clubs[88] and acquired grounds near the river,[89] as did the London Polytechnic, the Civil Service Sports Council, St. Thomas's hospital, and the Prudential Assurance Co. The Polytechnic in 1890 used a boathouse at the end of Hartington Road,[90] on land which had been acquired for it in 1888 by Quintin Hogg (1845–1903). The nearby Quintin Hogg memorial ground was opened in 1906, a stadium and an additional field for rugby were opened in 1938, the old pavilion was afterwards extended for women, and in 1979 the grounds covered over 40 a.[91] The Civil Service Sports Council in 1925 was preparing 30 a. south of Riverside Drive, where a pavilion was opened

[55] W.A.M. 16620.
[56] *Mdx. County Rec.* iii. 49.
[57] *Mdx. & Herts. N. & Q.* iv. 78.
[58] Phillimore and Whitear, *Chiswick*, 60.
[59] M.R.O., MR/LV3/4.
[60] Ibid. LV3/95.
[61] Ibid. LV7/39.
[62] *Lond. Gaz.* 25–28 Apr. 1698.
[63] *Gent. Mag.* lxi (2), 1235.
[64] M.R.O., MR/LV7/39.
[65] Pigot, *Dir. Mdx.* (1839–40).
[66] *P.O. Dir. Mdx.* (1862).
[67] *British Mag.* 16 July 1747.
[68] *Chiswick Assembly* (pamphlet 1807), in Chiswick libr.
[69] Chiswick libr., NC/II/xxvii; watercolour in Gunnersbury Pk. mus.
[70] Pamphlet, 1798, in Chiswick libr.
[71] Vestry min. bk. (1777–1817), ff. 260–1, 281–2.
[72] *P.O. Dir. Mdx.* (1867).
[73] *Chiswick Times*, 21 Dec. 1900.
[74] Chiswick libr., NC/I/lxxv.
[75] *Chiswick Times*, 9 Nov. 1906 (15th annual dinner).

[76] *Brentford and Chiswick Times*, 4 Aug. 1977; Char. Com. files.
[77] *Brentford and Chiswick Times*, 28 Aug. 1969.
[78] Erin Pizzey, *Scream Quietly or the Neighbours Will Hear* (1974), 9–10.
[79] Rocque, *Map of Lond.* (1746), sheet 11; Guildhall Libr., map case 260.
[80] M.R.O., MR/LV7/4, 39; 8/65.
[81] *Turnham Green Cricket Club, 1971* (programme in Chiswick libr.).
[82] *Kelly's Dir. Chiswick* (1928).
[83] *Chiswick Times*, 21 Dec. 1900. Lists of sports and other clubs were published regularly in the newspaper.
[84] *Official Guide to Chiswick* [1911].
[85] Brentford and Chiswick, *Official Guide* [1963].
[86] *Chiswick Times*, 21 Dec. 1900.
[87] *Official Guide to Chiswick* [1911].
[88] e.g. the Chiswick Polish Co., whose social activities were recorded in its mag. (copies in Chiswick libr.).
[89] Below, industry.
[90] *Kelly's Dir. Mdx.* (1890, 1926).
[91] Inf. from Mr. A. E. H. Winter.

by George V in 1926[92] and a much larger one in 1969.[93] St. Thomas's hospital used its land only after the First World War[94] and relinquished it for council housing, followed by a new school, in 1946.[95] Among several boating clubs by 1911 was the Ibis rowing club, with a boathouse in Hartington Road by 1890.[96] In 1979 the club was one of four main centres of the Prudential Assurance Co.'s Ibis society, which also had a 30-a. sports ground at Chiswick.[97]

A Conservative club existed by 1888 in the high road,[98] presumably at Camden House which it occupied in 1890, when there was a Radical club in Station Road.[99] In 1896, however, Camden House accommodated the Liberal and Radical club.[1] Chiswick Constitutional Club used the Chestnuts, Turnham Green, in 1900 and the Chiswick Parliament debated at Kensington House, Turnham Green Terrace, in 1911. Monthly meetings were held by the Independent Labour party in 1900.[2]

Turnham Green Literary and Scientific Society met in 1890 in Heathfield Terrace and in 1908 at the town hall, where Chiswick Scientific and Literary Society, presumably its successor, still met in 1926.[3] By 1900 Chiswick had a total abstinence council and societies, some of them run by churches, for many different pastimes, including angling, photography, and gardening.[4]

Both Grove Park and Bedford Park to some extent owed their appeal to a well publicized social life, the first being noted for activities connected with the river and the second for its artistic circles. In addition to its sporting clubs, Grove Park had its own society in the late 1870s and a literary and debating society in 1905.[5] Bedford Park, in particular, was designed to provide amusements near home.[6] Dances, concerts, and lectures were held from 1879 at the club, tennis was allowed on Sundays, and the many societies included one for amateur dramatics, formally inaugurated in 1881, whose scenery and costumes were supplied by local artists.[7] Six societies served Bedford Park in 1900, including groups for chess and natural history.[8] The club itself, supported by members' subscriptions, closed in 1939 and was a private club in 1979.[9]

The Strand-on-the-Green Association was founded in 1958, as one of the earliest amenity societies, soon followed by the Old Chiswick Protection Society[10] for Chiswick Mall, in 1963 by the Bedford Park Society, with Sir John Betjeman as patron,[11] and in 1970 by the Grove Park Group.[12] Brentford and Chiswick Local History Society, meeting at Chiswick library, was founded in 1958.[13]

Chiswick hall, in the high road, was licensed for music and dancing in 1888.[14] The Chiswick Empire theatre, originally to be called the Hippodrome,[15] was opened by Oswald (later Sir Oswald) Stoll in 1912. Larger than the Shepherd's Bush Empire, on which it was partly modelled, it stood in Chiswick High Road opposite Turnham Green common and seated 4,000.[16] Although films were to be shown at the theatre in 1932,[17] ballet and opera, besides drama and variety shows, continued to be performed there until 1959, when it was bought by Town & City Properties. Offices in the eleven-storeyed Empire House, which had been built on its site, were first occupied in 1961.[18]

Motion pictures were shown at the town hall in 1903. Chiswick's first purpose-built cinema was the Palais,[19] with elaborate plasterwork on its façade, which was open at no. 356 Chiswick High Road on part of the later Woolworths' site from 1910 until 1914.[20] The Electric theatre, on the east corner of Duke Road and Chiswick High Road, opened c. 1911, became the Coliseum in 1929 and, as the Tatler, closed in 1933,[21] whereupon it was converted into shops.[22] The slightly larger Cinema Royal, seating 450 and converted from the former Chiswick hall, opened in 1912 at no. 160 Chiswick High Road. Known from its decor as the Cave, it closed soon after renovation in 1933 and had been used as a second-hand furniture store for many years in 1979.[23] A cinema at no. 256 Chiswick High Road had its licence renewed in 1913.[24] From the mid 1930s the nearest cinemas were in Brentford or Hammersmith.[25]

Attempts to foster community spirit in Bedford Park led to the monthly publication of the *Bedford Park Gazette* in 1883–4.[26] The *Chiswick Times* was founded in 1895 by F. W. Dimbleby, who had recently acquired the *Richmond and Twickenham Times*, and was renamed the *Brentford and Chiswick Times* in 1927. It was still published weekly by the Dimbleby Newspaper Group in 1979.[27] The *Chiswick Gazette* appeared weekly, as a local edition of the

[92] *Civil Svce. Sports Jnl.* Aug. 1925; *Opening of Chiswick Ground, 1926.*
[93] *Brentford and Chiswick Times*, 5 June 1969.
[94] E. M. McInnes, *St. Thomas's Hosp.* (1963), 160.
[95] *Brentford and Chiswick Times*, 13, 20 Sept. 1946.
[96] *Kelly's Dir. Mdx.* (1890); *Official Guide to Chiswick* [1911].
[97] Inf. from the sec.
[98] *Kelly's Dir. Chiswick* (1887–8).
[99] *Kelly's Dir. Mdx.* (1890).
[1] *Chiswick Times*, 17 July 1896.
[2] Ibid. 21 Dec. 1900; *Official Guide to Chiswick* [1911].
[3] *Kelly's Dir. Mdx.* (1890, 1908, 1926).
[4] *Chiswick Times*, 21 Dec. 1900.
[5] Wisdom and Bott, *Grove Pk. Estate*, 4.
[6] Bolsterli, *Bedford Pk.* 76.
[7] Greeves, *Bedford Pk.*
[8] *Chiswick Times*, 21 Dec. 1900.
[9] Bolsterli, *Bedford Pk.* 76.
[10] Inf. from Mrs. Judges.
[11] Inf. from Mr. T. A. Greeves.
[12] Char. Com. files.
[13] *Brentford and Chiswick As It Was.*
[14] 'Cinemas in Brentford and Chiswick' (TS. in Chiswick libr.).
[15] *Official Guide to Chiswick* [1911].
[16] *Chiswick Times*, 6 Sept. 1912.
[17] *Brentford and Chiswick Times*, 24 June 1932.
[18] Ibid. 13, 20 Mar., 26 June 1959; 5 May 1961; *Brentford and Chiswick As It Was*, illus. 64.
[19] *Brentford and Chiswick Times*, 27 Oct. 1977.
[20] *Brentford and Chiswick As It Was*, illus. 67.
[21] Ibid. illus. 55; *Brentford and Chiswick Times*, 27 Oct. 1977.
[22] *Mdx. Local Hist. Council Bull.* xviii. 12.
[23] *Brentford and Chiswick Times*, 27 Oct. 1977; *Mdx. Local Hist. Council Bull.* xviii. 12.
[24] 'Cinemas in Brentford and Chiswick' (TS. in Chiswick libr.).
[25] Brentford and Chiswick, *Official Guide* [c. 1952].
[26] Bolsterli, *Bedford Pk.* 31.
[27] *Brentford and Chiswick Guide*, 6 June 1974; *Willing's Press Guide* (1979).

former *Acton and Chiswick Gazette*, owned by the Middlesex County Times Co., from *c.* 1903 to 1919 and the weekly *Chiswick Express* from *c.* 1903[28] to *c.* 1905.[29] Local news in 1979 was published in the weekly *Chiswick and Brentford Gazette*, distributed free as an advertisement.[30]

MANORS. Before the Conquest the canons of St. Paul's held 5 hides, which in 1086 constituted one manor within the vill of Fulham.[31] Their lands were divided before 1181, although the two estates of 3 hides and 2 hides were still said to form one manor in 1222.[32] The division presumably had arisen from the need to maintain the prebendary of Chiswick, first mentioned in 1103-4.[33]

The larger estate was called by 1181 the manor of *SUTTON*[34] and by *c.* 1537 *SUTTON COURT*.[35] In 1502 the bishop ordered that Sutton, with the rectory and advowson of Chiswick, was to be enjoyed by the dean of St. Paul's so long as he should keep residence. Dean Feckenham's right and his annual payments to the chapter were confirmed in 1555, when mediators found that Sutton was not part of the deanery's ancient endowment but had been 'encroached' by his predecessors.[36] Thereafter Sutton Court, which could not be leased without the dean's consent,[37] was often known as the dean's manor.[38] In 1617 some chapter officers and local tenants were found to have withheld profits from the dean, hoping that he would not be able to assert his right to a manor which had been part of the common possessions of St. Paul's.[39] Nominally the lordship remained with both dean and chapter, except during the Interregnum when it was sequestrated to the corporation of London,[40] until it passed to the Ecclesiastical Commissioners on the death of Dean Copleston in 1849.[41]

The manor probably was always farmed out, as in 1181 to Nicholas, archdeacon of London, and in 1222 to Philip of Hadham.[42] Sutton may have been held at farm by the ancestors of John de Bray, who acquired land in fee in Chiswick in 1324, 1330, and 1337.[43] His interest in the manor may have passed, with other lands of his in Chiswick, to Sir William Scrope, who granted them to Richard II.[44] The Crown held the manor of Sutton by Chiswick in 1431, granting it to the treasurer Ralph, Lord Cromwell, in 1437 and 1442,[45] and disposed of the revenues in 1457.[46] It

was said to have belonged formerly to Thomas Bray in 1469, when granted to Richard Bury,[47] and in 1470 Baldwin Bray surrendered his rights to Thomas Coveton and other clerks, who perhaps were acting for St. Paul's.[48] The dean and chapter leased Sutton in 1524 to Sir Thomas More, on whose attainder in 1535 it passed to the Crown, which granted the remainder of More's term to his widow Alice. John Lane, who denied having bought Alice's interest in Sutton Court in 1535, was granted leases by St. Paul's in 1538,[49] 1547,[50] and 1572.[51]

A 21-years' sublease was granted by Lane, of Twickenham, to John Sheppard in 1573. Under John Sheppard's will, dated 1575, the profits were to be taken during the minority of his two sons by Henry Platt, who further sublet the manor to Sheppard's widow Joan and her second husband Christopher Leyland. By 1589, when Joan was still alive, Sheppard's surviving son Robert had further subleased the manor to Robert Rowe.[52]

In 1639 the chapter granted Sutton Court for 21 years to Thomas Edgar, whose lease by 1649 had been bought by Chaloner Chute (d. 1659),[53] afterwards Speaker of the House of Commons.[54] Chute's widow Dorothy, formerly Lady Dacre, in 1661 was promised compensation for the manor, which had been assigned to her for life in 1653 but which Dr. Matthew Nicholas, on becoming dean of St. Paul's at the Restoration, had granted to his elder brother Sir Edward Nicholas,[55] the secretary of state.[56] Leases for 21 years, renewable by fine every 3 years,[57] thereafter were made by the chapter to Sir Edward in 1668, to William Ashburnham in 1672, to Thomas Belasyse, Viscount (later Earl) Fauconberg (d. 1700) from 1675, and to his widow Mary, a daughter of Oliver Cromwell, who died at Sutton Court in 1713.[58] From 1713 the lessee was Lord Fauconberg's nephew Sir Thomas Frankland, bt. (d. 1726),[59] followed briefly by Joseph Ormerod,[60] from 1728 Richard Boyle, earl of Burlington, from 1756 William Murray, later Lord Mansfield, under Burlington's will, and from 1773 John Heaton. The remainder of Heaton's final term, granted in 1799, was presumably bought by William Cavendish, duke of Devonshire, to whom in 1800 St. Paul's sold all the land but not the manorial rights.[61]

Chiswick had no separate rectory estate: the great tithes were held with Sutton Court by Sir

[28] *Kelly's Dir. Chiswick* (1902-3, 1919).
[29] Advert. in *Chiswick Illus. Almanac* (trades dir. 1905).
[30] Copies from 1972 in Chiswick libr.
[31] *V.C.H. Mdx.* i. 121.
[32] Phillimore and Whitear, *Chiswick*, 127, 137.
[33] Le Neve, *Fasti, 1066-1300, St. Paul's, Lond.* 40.
[34] Phillimore and Whitear, *Chiswick*, 137.
[35] P.R.O., C 1/851/38.
[36] W. Sparrow Simpson, *Reg. Statutorum Ecclesiae Sancti Pauli* (1873), 211, 266-7.
[37] Ibid. 268, 417.
[38] e.g. Lysons, *Environs*, ii. 186.
[39] P.R.O., E 126/2, ff. 123v.-127.
[40] M.R.O., Acc. 119/2; *Hist. St. Paul's*, ed. W. R. Matthews (1957), 168.
[41] Guildhall MSS. 14236/1-12, *passim*.
[42] *Domesday of St. Paul's* (Camd. Soc. [1st ser.], lxix), 112; Phillimore and Whitear, *Chiswick*, 137.

[43] P.R.O., CP 25(1)/149/51, no. 310; CP 25(1)/150/54, no. 28; CP 25(1)/150/57, no. 110.
[44] *Cal. Pat.* 1429-36, 5.
[45] Ibid. 1436-41, 117; 1441-6, 139.
[46] *Cal. Close*, 1454-61, 242.
[47] *Cal. Pat.* 1467-77, 155.
[48] P.R.O., CP 25(1)/152/97, no. 37.
[49] Ibid. C 1/851/38-40.
[50] M.R.O., Acc. 531/66, f. 6.
[51] P.R.O., REQ 2/233/46.
[52] Ibid. REQ 2/233/46; REQ 2/273/31.
[53] *Cal. S.P. Dom.* 1660-1, 502-3; Guildhall MS. 11816.
[54] *D.N.B.*
[55] *Cal. S.P. Dom.* 1660-1, 502-3, 597; 1661-2, 32, 101.
[56] *D.N.B.*   [57] M.R.O., Acc. 1207/2.
[58] Ibid., Acc. 531/68; *Complete Peerage*, v. 265.
[59] G.E.C. *Baronetage*, iii. 143.
[60] M.R.O., Acc. 119/12.   [61] Ibid. Acc. 531/68.

Thomas More[62] and later lessees, and were purchased in 1800 by the duke of Devonshire.[63] In 1589–90 the lessee was entitled to all tithes of corn and hay within the parish except from the demesnes of the prebendal manor, which paid only one third of the tithe of corn.[64] The great tithes were estimated to be worth £55 4s. in 1649,[65] produced £93 9s. in 1702,[66] and were commuted for a rent charge of £50 in 1846.[67]

The manor house known by 1649 as Sutton Court[68] stood near the centre of the parish, north-east of Sutton Lane.[69] Roman brickwork and 15th-century pottery were found on its site in 1905.[70] The dating of letters patent from Chiswick may record visits to Sutton by Henry VI between 1441 and 1443.[71] Several houses were acquired by John de Bray[72] but a mansion house was mentioned only in 1589, when it had a gatehouse, malthouse, and farm buildings, all in decay.[73] The buildings, including a dovecot, had been newly mended a year later, when they stood within orchards and gardens of 3 a.[74] The main house, with a large hall and with garrets over the upper floor, had grounds of 9 a. in 1649.[75] It was assessed at 30 hearths in 1664[76] and was 'fit to receive tomorrow a family of 40 or 50' in 1674, when there were 12 a. of walled garden.[77] The gardens were noted in 1691, when Lord Fauconberg possessed a maze and a bowling green,[78] and in 1725–6.[79] When part of the estates of Lord Burlington and the dukes of Devonshire, Sutton Court was occupied by undertenants, one of whom, Thomas King, largely rebuilt it before 1795.[80] Later tenants were Radcliffe Sidebotham in 1816,[81] Lt.-Col. Henry Cavendish in the 1820s,[82] Frederick Tappenden, who kept a boarding school there from c. 1845,[83] and William Compton in 1890.[84] The house, of two storeys and nine bays, with a balustrade and central pediment,[85] was demolished in 1896 and replaced c. 1905 by flats called Sutton Court,[86] which in 1979 stood on the north side of Fauconberg Road.

The prebendal estate, said in 1590 to be held of Sutton,[87] was often called in the 16th and 17th centuries CHISWICK manor[88] and from the mid 18th century the PREBEND manor of Chiswick.[89] Except during the Interregnum[90] the lordship remained with the pre-

bendaries until the death of John Smith in 1859, whereupon the manor, in reversion on the expiry of under-leases, passed to the Ecclesiastical Commissioners.[91]

The prebendaries presumably exploited the estate until Gabriel Goodman, who retained his stall on becoming dean of Westminster, decided to secure his manor house at Chiswick as a retreat, in times of sickness, for Westminster school. The transfer, begun in 1562, was completed in 1570 by a lease of the entire estate for 99 years to Westminster's receiver-general, who then joined Goodman in assigning the property to the chapter, which in 1572 in turn joined Goodman in subletting the lands while reserving the school's house.[92] Thereafter Westminster held the manor house on long leases, later for 3 lives,[93] until the remainder of the chapter's last lease was bought by the Ecclesiastical Commissioners in 1865.[94]

From 1572 the demesne lands of the Prebend manor, except the school's house, were leased out by the chapter of Westminster,[95] at first for 21 years[96] and by the early 18th century for 3 lives.[97] Leases were made to Thomas Childe in 1572, the judge Thomas Owen (d. 1598) in 1591, William Smeeth, to whom Owen had previously sublet the property, between 1592 and 1626, Henry Fryer in 1628, and the civilian Dr. (later Sir Arthur) Duck (1580–1648) between 1633 and 1640.[98] Duck's son Richard was in occupation in 1649,[99] when the manor, the school's house being reserved, was sold by parliamentary commissioners to William Angier and Edward Raddon of London.[1] The restored chapter leased the same property to Thomas Kendall and others in 1663[2] and Kendall's interest was bought by Sir Stephen Fox, already a substantial copyholder,[3] in 1684–5.[4]

After Fox's death in 1716 the manor was held by trustees under his will,[5] then by his son Stephen (later earl of Ilchester) in 1726, by Dr. Michael Hutchinson, minister of Hammersmith, from 1727, by Mrs. Mary Daniel and Joseph Ashton from 1737, by Gauntlett Fry in 1745, by Miss Susanna Sharp from 1746, and by James Fry from 1768. Alexander Weatherstone held it from 1770 to 1783, followed by his widow Ann until 1795 and by the guardians of their

[62] P.R.O., C 1/851/39. [63] M.R.O., Acc. 531/68.
[64] Ibid. 66.
[65] Guildhall MS. 11816, f. 237.
[66] M.R.O., Acc. 119/7.
[67] Ibid. TA/CHI.
[68] Guildhall MS. 11816, f. 231.
[69] M.R.O., Acc. 531/66, f. 2.
[70] Chiswick libr., NC/I/lxvii–lxviii.
[71] P.R.O., CP 25(1)/149/50, no. 310; CP 25(1)/150/54, no. 28.
[72] Cal. Pat. 1436–41, 1441–6, passim.
[73] P.R.O., REQ 2/233/46.
[74] M.R.O., Acc. 531/66, f. 2.
[75] Guildhall MS. 11816, f. 231.
[76] M.R.O., MR/TH/3, m. 1.
[77] Ibid. Acc. 1207/1. [78] Archaeologia, xii. 184.
[79] M.R.O., Acc. 119/12; 1207/2.
[80] Lysons, Environs, ii. 190.
[81] Brewer, Beauties of Eng. & Wales, x (5), 322.
[82] Chwdns. acct. bk. (1821–56).
[83] Phillimore and Whitear, Chiswick, 261–2; below, educ.
[84] Kelly's Dir. Mdx. (1890).
[85] Plate facing p. 33; advert. for sch. in Chiswick libr.

[86] Gilbert, Chiswick Old and New, 60; T. P. Singer, Short Hist. Chiswick, Sutton Ct., and Par. of St. Mic. (1935); Chiswick libr., NC/I/lxvii.
[87] M.R.O., Acc. 531/66, f. 9.
[88] e.g. W.A.M. 16654–6.
[89] Guildhall MSS. 14219/6–13. [90] Below.
[91] Guildhall MS. 14219/12, f. 248.
[92] Ho. of Kings, ed. E. Carpenter (1966), 139; Draper, Chiswick, 49–51; W.A.M. 16621; ibid. Reg. Bk. vi, ff. 53–56b.
[93] e.g. W.A.M., box RCO 41.
[94] Guildhall MS. 14219/12, ff. 248–9.
[95] Draper, Chiswick, 51–4.
[96] e.g. W.A.M., Reg. Bk. vi, f. 176; vii, f. 128b.
[97] e.g. W.A.M., box RCO 41.
[98] Draper, Chiswick, 52–4; W.A.M. 16640–1, 16649, 16654, 16656, 16658, 16661, 16663.
[99] St. Paul's MSS., box A 57.
[1] Draper, Chiswick, 73; W.A.M. 16666.
[2] Draper, Chiswick, 73; W.A.M. 16675.
[3] Guildhall MS. 14219/4.
[4] W.A.M. 16680; C. Clay, Public Finance and Private Wealth, Sir Steph. Fox (1978), 174.
[5] Para. based on ct. rolls, Guildhall MSS. 14219/4–13.

son Henry. In 1803 Henry Weatherstone, of Lower Halliford in Shepperton, sold the lease to Benjamin Welstead of Kimbolton (Hunts.) in trust for George Richards (d. 1805) of Marylebone, who left it to his nephew the Revd. Harry Welstead (d. 1819) of Stoneley Hall, Kimbolton.[6] It passed to Harry's mother Ann Welstead (d. 1827), to her younger son Charles (d. 1850), and to Charles's executors Charles Marion Welstead and Charles Holt in trust for Mary Hayton, who in 1869 was granted administration of Harry's estate. The Welsteads' final lease, which had been renewed in 1837, was acquired by the Ecclesiastical Commissioners in 1882.

The house reserved for Westminster, in 1649 first called College House,[7] was an extension of the prebendal manor house which stood east of the church[8] and which has tentatively been identified with the vicarage house mentioned in 1297.[9] Possibly Gabriel Goodman's predecessors had allowed Westminister to use the prebendal house, since Abbot John Feckenham was at Chiswick in 1558, when he employed workmen there.[10] In 1570 Goodman stipulated that his house be extended in order to accommodate the prebendary, the master and usher of Westminster grammar school, and 40 children.[11] Medieval stonework from the west part of the old manor house, previously its kitchen quarters, was used in Goodman's building, where by 1582 the entire school apparently could be lodged during an epidemic.[12] Scholars still retired to Chiswick under Dr. Richard Busby, whose premises were assessed at 24 hearths in 1664.[13] By 1705 the school's building had been divided among poor families[14] but soon afterwards was evidently repaired, being occupied by the headmaster in 1725 and intermittently by his successors until the time of William Markham, headmaster 1753–65, who used the prebendary's lodgings,[15] as did the writer James Ralph, who died there in 1762.[16] A few pupils apparently also stayed at Chiswick, since the dormitory was repaired in 1763.[17] Meanwhile the older manorial building to the east had apparently been sublet c. 1650 and later by Sir Stephen Fox.[18] It had fallen into decay in 1710 and been replaced by a brick house, which from 1770 was the childhood home of the writer Mary Berry and her sister Agnes, later

friends of Horace Walpole.[19] In 1788 the chapter of Westminster leased out its mansion house, presumably the entire range of building, for 21 years to Martin Cole, a timber merchant,[20] who in 1806 had sublet College House as a ladies' school.[21] Charles Whittingham the elder moved his Chiswick Press in 1818 from High House to College House,[22] where the printing office adjoined a two-storeyed dwelling house, with domestic offices to the east.[23] After 1852 the building was leased by the year and used as a lecture hall until its demolition in 1875, when it was replaced by the existing Suffolk House, Staithe House, the Hollies, and Thames Bank.[24]

A copyhold house with 2 a. of garden was sold in 1663 by Henry Broad,[25] a Chiswick resident in 1654,[26] to Sir Stephen Fox, who between 1682 and 1684 replaced it with a house designed by Hugh May, Comptroller of the King's works,[27] before erecting another seat on land acquired in 1691.[28] Fox's lease of the Prebend manor from 1684 probably explains why his house of 1682–4 has sometimes wrongly been called the manor house[29] and why the second, with which it has been confused, came to be named Manor Farm House.[30]

Fox's first house was assessed at 18 hearths in 1664[31] and, after rebuilding, was partly shown on Knyff's view of Lord Burlington's seat.[32] Evelyn in 1682 thought that its cramped garden did not justify the expense of its layout,[33] although it was presumably that house, rather than Fox's later one, whose garden won praise in 1691.[34] It was sold by Fox's executors to Mary, dowager countess of Northampton (d. 1719), whose son George Compton, earl of Northampton (d. 1727) had married Fox's youngest daughter Jane. Mary's heir, according to manorial custom, was her youngest son Spencer Compton (d. 1743),[35] later earl of Wilmington and First Lord of the Treasury.[36] Lord Wilmington, who also acquired Turret House in 1722 from the Wardour family,[37] was succeeded by his nephew James Compton, earl of Northampton (d. 1754),[38] whose daughter and heir was Charlotte, *suo jure* Baroness Ferrers (d. 1770), wife of George Townshend, later Marquess Townshend (d. 1807).[39] Charlotte and her husband in 1758 surrendered most of Lord Wilmington's property to Sir John Heathcote, bt., of Normanton (Rutland) (d. 1759),[40] whose

[6] W.A.M., box RCO 41.
[7] W.A.M. 16666.
[8] Para. based on Phillimore and Whitear, *Chiswick*, 63–71.
[9] Draper, *Chiswick*, 48.
[10] W.A.M. 37788A.   [11] Draper, *Chiswick*, 50.
[12] Hist. MSS. Com. 9, *Salisbury (Cecil)*, xiii. 209.
[13] M.R.O., MR/TH/3; the rooms are detailed in an inventory of 1645: W.A.M. 16665.
[14] Phillimore and Whitear, *Chiswick*, 11–12.
[15] F. H. Forshall, *Westm. Sch.* (1884), 462–4.
[16] B. Lambert, *Lond. and Its Environs*, iv (1806), 323; *D.N.B.*
[17] W.A.M. 16706.
[18] St. Paul's MSS., box A 57; W.A.M. 16680.
[19] *D.N.B.*
[20] W.A.M. 16718.
[21] Lambert, *Lond. and Environs*, iv. 323.
[22] Below.
[23] Prints in Chiswick libr., from sketch by Charlotte Whittingham Stevens. There is also a photo. of the garden front, ascribed to 1854.
[24] Gilbert, *Chiswick Old and New*, 73.

[25] Guildhall MS. 14219/4.
[26] Chwdns. acct. bk. (1636–62).
[27] Clay, *Pub. Finance and Private Wealth*, 263.
[28] Draper, *Chiswick*, 87. It is generally assumed that Fox built two new hos., although his building expenses are ascribed only to the ho. of 1682–4 in Clay, *Pub. Finance and Private Wealth*, 174, 256, 263.
[29] e.g. Lloyd Saunders, *Old Kew, Chiswick and Brentford*, 102.
[30] Draper, *Chiswick*; 87.   [31] M.R.O., MR/TH/3.
[32] Draper, *Chiswick*, 87 and illus. facing p. 62.
[33] *Diary of John Evelyn*, ed. E. S. de Beer, iv. 294.
[34] *Archaeologia*, xii. 185–6.
[35] Guildhall MS. 14219/4; *Complete Peerage*, ix. 682–3.
[36] *D.N.B.*
[37] Guildhall MS. 14219/4; below, other est.
[38] Guildhall MS. 14219/6, ff. 53–7; *Complete Peerage*, ix. 685.
[39] Guildhall MS. 14219/6, ff. 233–7; *Complete Peerage*, v. 334.
[40] Guildhall MS. 14219/6, ff. 249–51; G.E.C. *Baronetage*, v. 74.

youngest son John surrendered it to the Hon. James Douglas in 1780. Perhaps the Douglases already lived there, since the house was sometimes called Morton House:[41] James Douglas, earl of Morton, had died at Chiswick in 1768[42] and the countess of Morton paid rates in 1774–5.[43] Douglas conveyed the mansion with 7 a. of garden to Robert Stevenson in 1783[44] and the site of Turret House to William Cock, a market gardener, in 1791. Stevenson conveyed his house in 1807 to Lady Mary Coke,[45] who died there in 1811.[46] Meanwhile some land retained by Lady Ferrers, including a little in Sutton Court manor, had passed to her younger son Charles Townshend (d. 1796) and then to his brother Frederick.[47] The entire property passed to the dukes of Devonshire by purchases from Lady Mary Coke's executors, from William Cock's son William in 1814, and from Frederick Townshend's nephews George, Marquess Townshend, and the Revd. George Osborne Townshend, in 1838.[48] The mansion, of seven bays with a central pediment in Stevenson's time,[49] was demolished in 1812 and replaced by the existing great conservatory of Chiswick House.[50]

Manor Farm House,[51] itself sometimes called Manor House in the 19th century, was built by Fox on the west side of Chiswick Lane. The house was probably the house admired by William III, where the new style of architecture was extolled by Bowack and where Fox's sons Stephen, later earl of Ilchester (1704–76),[52] and Henry, later Lord Holland (1705–74),[53] were born. Eighteenth-century lessees of the Prebend manor apparently sublet the house, which c. 1786–1810 was a school under the Revd. Thomas Horne[54] and by 1849 an asylum under Dr. Thomas Harrington Tuke.[55] The building was two-storeyed and of red brick with stone dressings, with dormers in a high slate roof; the main garden front had nine bays c. 1850, when there was also an extension. Panelling was bought by the art-dealer Joseph Duveen in 1896, when the asylum moved to Chiswick House under Dr. Thomas Seymour Tuke[56] and Manor Farm House made way for Balfern Grove and neighbouring roads.

OTHER ESTATES. The *CHISWICK HOUSE* estate, to which much neighbouring property was added in the early 19th century, was chiefly copyhold of the Prebend manor,[57] Chiswick House itself being enfranchised only in 1910.[58] The estate belonged in the early 17th century to Sir Edward Wardour,[59] son of Chideock Wardour and active in local affairs.[60] After Sir Edward had moved to Turret House,[61] his former house was apparently sold to James I's disgraced favourite Robert Carr, earl of Somerset (d. 1645), who paid church rates from 1624 and whose wife died at Chiswick in 1632.[62] Later owners were Philip Howard, earl of Pembroke, in 1638 and John Poulett, Lord Poulett (d. 1649), from 1639.[63] In 1651 Poulett's sons surrendered all their property in Chiswick to their mother Elizabeth, by then the wife of John Ashburnham.[64] It was bought by the king in 1664 for his son James, duke of Monmouth,[65] and by Charles, Lord Gerard (later earl of Macclesfield), in 1668.[66] By 1677 it had passed to Richard Jones, Viscount (later earl of) Ranelagh, and by 1682 to the Speaker Edward Seymour (later Sir Edward Seymour, Bt.), who sold it in 1682 to Lord Ranelagh's uncle Richard Boyle, earl of Burlington (d. 1698).[67]

Lord Burlington was succeeded by his grandson Charles Boyle (d. 1704), whose son Richard, statesman and patron of the arts, also leased Sutton Court manor[68] and died at Chiswick in 1753.[69] The earldom then became extinct and the property passed through the marriage of the last earl's daughter Charlotte Elizabeth, *suo jure* Baroness Clifford, to William Cavendish, marquess of Hartington and later duke of Devonshire (d. 1764). It descended to William Cavendish, duke of Devonshire (d. 1811), and to William George Spencer Cavendish, duke of Devonshire (d. 1858),[70] who acquired much neighbouring property, including the Corney House and Heathfield House estates,[71] and held 655 a., covering half of the parish, in 1847.[72] Although his successors sold many sites for suburban building, which was planned as early as 1867,[73] they remained Chiswick's chief landowners in the late 19th century.[74] Some 200 a. of riverside meadow were sold to the U.D.C. in 1923 by Victor Christian William Cavendish, duke of Devonshire (d. 1938),[75] leaving Chiswick House itself with c. 66 a. to be bought by Middlesex C.C., with smaller contributions from other local authorities and subscribers who included George V. The property was leased to Brentford and Chiswick U.D., which opened the grounds in 1929 as a public park. In disrepair

[41] *Ambulator* (1820), 63.
[42] *Complete Peerage*, ix. 300.
[43] Chwdns. acct. bk. (1752–76).
[44] Guildhall MS. 14219/7, ff. 12*–14*, 353–7, 422–5.
[45] Ibid. 8, ff. 34–6, 254–5.
[46] Ibid. f. 276; *Letters of Lady Mary Coke*, ed. J. A. Home, iv (1970 edn.), pp. viii–ix.
[47] Guildhall MSS. 14236/5, f. 195; 11, f. 78.
[48] Ibid. 14219/8, ff. 276, 297; 9, f. 122; 14236/11, f. 149.
[49] Plate facing p. 33.
[50] Phillimore and Whitear, *Chiswick*, 268; Draper, *Chiswick*, 87.
[51] Para. based on Draper, *Chiswick*, 87–8.
[52] *Complete Peerage*, vii. 46.   [53] *D.N.B.*
[54] N. Hans, *New Trends in Educ. in 18th Cent.* 129; Gilbert, *Chiswick Old and New*, 54.
[55] *Lond. and Provincial Med. Dir.* (1849).   [56] Below.
[57] Guildhall MS. 14219/10, f. 156.

[58] Ibid. 15, f. 139.
[59] Phillimore and Whitear, *Chiswick*, 12.
[60] Chwdns. acct. bk. (1622–35).
[61] The seat of his descendants: P.R.O., C 5/26/201; chwdns. acct. bk. (1663–91).
[62] *Complete Peerage*, xii (1), 68; *T.L.M.A.S.* xv. 108.
[63] Chwdns. acct. bk. (1636–62).
[64] St. Paul's MSS., box B 38.
[65] *Cal. Treas. Bks.* 1660–7, 596; *Cal. S.P. Dom.* 1663–4, 539.   [66] *Cal. S.P. Dom.* 1667–8, 544, 553.
[67] Chwdns. acct. bk. (1663–91); *Complete Peerage*, x. 732.
[68] Above.
[69] *Complete Peerage*, ii. 431–3; *D.N.B.*
[70] *Complete Peerage*, iv. 346–8.   [71] Below.
[72] M.R.O., TA/CHI.
[73] Gilbert, *Chiswick Old and New*, 18.
[74] *Kelly's Dir. Mdx.* (1882, 1890).
[75] *The Times*, 7 Sept. 1923.

before the Second World War, the house was transferred in 1948 to the Ministry of Works, together with the garden buildings and statuary.[76] Restoration of the main building began in 1948 and ended in 1958.[77] Both the house, maintained by the Department of the Environment, and the grounds, leased to Hounslow L.B., were open to the public in 1979.

The 17th-century mansion, assessed at 33 hearths in 1664,[78] was probably enlarged both by the earl of Burlington (d. 1698) and by his grandson (d. 1704), who added the stables later called the Grosvenor wing.[79] The 3rd earl (d. 1753) further altered the exterior, in the Palladian style, and built a summer parlour on the south-west side, a few years before building the villa which survives as Chiswick House. His new villa stood some 18 m. to the south-west beyond a 'link' building, which was connected with the summer parlour and the villa by low walls, the western[80] or garden fronts of all three structures being aligned. Apart from the two-storeyed Grosvenor wing, which survived until 1933, the old house was pulled down in 1788, when James Wyatt was employed to add two-storeyed north and south wings to the villa, in keeping with its style. His work was demolished in 1952, revealing the link building which had been engulfed by the north wing and allowing overall restoration to the original proportions.

The surviving Chiswick House was built between 1725 and 1729 as a temple of the arts rather than a residence, Lord Burlington continuing to live in his father's seat near by. Immediately celebrated for its architecture and setting, Burlington's villa won further fame after its enlargement by Wyatt, when it served as a country annexe of Devonshire House, which had become a centre of London society under Georgiana, duchess of Devonshire (d. 1806). Charles James Fox died at Chiswick House while foreign secretary in 1806 and George Canning while prime minister in 1827.[81] Tsar Alexander I and the king of Prussia were welcomed there in 1814, Queen Victoria in 1842, and Tsar Nicholas I and the king of Saxony in 1844.[82] Under the will of the duke of Devonshire (d. 1858) Chiswick House passed for life to his sister Harriet, dowager Countess Granville (d. 1862).[83] Although later dukes did not live there, it continued to have distinguished tenants: Harriet, duchess of Sutherland, in 1867,[84] the Prince of Wales, who entertained the Shah of Persia there in 1873 and whose children were often at Chiswick,[85] and the marquess of Bute by 1881.[86] Not until the end of Lord Bute's tenancy in 1892 were the duke of Devonshire's art treasures moved to Chatsworth (Derb.) and was Chiswick

House leased as a private asylum by Dr. Thomas Seymour Tuke (d. 1917).[87] He was followed by his brother Dr. Charles Molesworth Tuke (d. 1925), whose widow remained there until 1929.[88]

Chiswick House, as restored, owes its outward appearance and its rigid internal plan to Lord Burlington, although much of the profuse interior decoration is by his close collaborator William Kent. It is modelled mainly on the 16th-century Villa Capra near Vicenza, although less closely than England's other chief Palladian work at Mereworth Castle (Kent), designed in 1723 by Burlington's mentor Colin Campbell. The main, east, front, approached from Burlington Lane, has needed little repair, unlike the north and south elevations masked by Wyatt, which have been wholly reconstructed, and the resurrected link building and the summer parlour. In the 18th century the villa was not isolated, in that it stood close to Burlington Lane and had neighbouring houses to the north, in contrast to a tree-lined vista across the meadows south of the lane as far as the Thames.[89]

The main villa is almost square and of two storeys, the lower dressed in Portland stone and the upper one rendered, and is surmounted by a lead-covered octagonal dome, flanked on either side by 4 obelisk-shaped chimney stacks. From the main front projects a two-storeyed Corinthian portico, reached by a balustraded staircase which, like one on the western front, forms a Baroque deviation from Palladian severity. Similarly, Burlington departed from his models' symmetry in the arrangement of the rooms, although on both floors they surround an octagonal hall, the lower ones corresponding to the upper ones. On the ground floor the three compartments along the western front form an apsidal-ended library entered from the hall and from lobbies to the north and south. At the north-western corner of the library a doorway leads to the link building and summer parlour. On the upper and principal floor a passage leads from the portico to the octagonal dome saloon, hung with paintings returned from Chatsworth and richly decorated, the octagonal panels lining the dome being a repetition of Kent's device for the cupola room at Kensington Palace. Around the hall are six ornate rooms and, on the west side, a gallery with a central Venetian window opening on the garden staircase and, like the library beneath, an entrance to the link building. The vases in the windows and one of the statues in the apsidal end compartments are original; eight of the ceiling panels are by Kent, the ninth and central one having been ascribed to Veronese but perhaps being the work of an

[76] J. Charlton, *Chiswick Ho.* (H.M.S.O. 1958), 15; *The Times*, 27 Aug. 1948.
[77] *The Times*, 11 Mar. 1954; 23 Feb. 1957; 24 July 1958.
[78] M.R.O., MR/TH/3.
[79] Seven paras. based on Charlton, *Chiswick Ho. passim*; Hist. Mon. Com. *Mdx.* 8; Pevsner, *Mdx.* 32–5; Robbins, *Mdx.* 232–3. There are illus. at Guildhall Libr., and M.R.O., PR 44/2–60.
[80] In order to accord with accounts in Charlton etc., the north-eastern, south-eastern (entrance), south-western, and north-western (garden) sides of the ho. are here simplified to 'north', 'east', 'south', and 'west'.   [81] *D.N.B.*

[82] Faulkner, *Brentford, Ealing and Chiswick*, 436.
[83] Guildhall MSS. 14219/10, f. 156; 11, f. 143; 14236/13, ff. 291–2; *Complete Peerage*, xii (1), 565.
[84] *Kelly's Dir. Mdx.* (1867).
[85] *The Times*, 30 June 1873; Thorne, *Environs*, 110.
[86] *Complete Peerage*, ii. 446.
[87] Phillimore and Whitear, *Chiswick*, 266; Chiswick libr., NC/I/ccx.
[88] Chiswick libr., NC/I/lxii; *Kelly's Dir. Chiswick* (1925, 1929).
[89] Plate facing p. 64; Rocque, *Map of Lond.* (1746), sheet 10.

imitator, Sebastiano Ricci. Skilful gradations in the many elaborate features of the gallery make it 'an outstanding example of grand architecture in small compass'. Similar judgements have generally been made on the villa as a whole. Lord Hervey sneered at it as a useless miniature[90] but Pope, in admiration, dedicated the fourth of his *Moral Essays* to Lord Burlington[91] and Horace Walpole aspired only to make Strawberry Hill, like Chiswick, a model of its kind.[92]

Whereas Lord Burlington's architecture was an adaptation from the Italian, with few English parallels, Kent's garden opened a new chapter in the history of landscaping.[93] While still affording vistas along straight avenues, he laid out the intervening thickets with winding paths and curved the edges of the pieces of water to produce the first ambitious design in the style of the Picturesque. Despite later changes, the main axes can still be seen: a forecourt between Burlington Lane and the portico; a grand avenue to the north-east, continued north-west on the far side of the link building to a semicircular exedra; three straight walks radiating from the exedra through a wilderness, the westernmost leading to a bridge over the canal, whence radiated further walks; three more walks radiating from an obelisk in the south-west corner of the grounds, one to the bridge, one towards the villa, and the middle one to an Ionic temple, visible from the villa, and another obelisk in a pond within an amphitheatre.

A gateway given by Sir Hans Sloane was brought from Beaufort House, Chelsea, in 1738, when Pope celebrated its move, and installed north of the summer parlour, next to the 17th-century mansion. Designed by Inigo Jones as a round-headed archway in rusticated masonry, it is linked by a wing-wall running west past the site of Lord Burlington's former orangery to the 18th-century deer-house, beyond which stands a Doric column once surmounted by a copy of the Venus de Medici. Other ornaments or buildings of Kent's time include statuary around the forecourt; urns and sphinxes in the avenue from the villa to the exedra; three Roman statues in the exedra; the rustic house at the end of the northernmost walk from the exedra; the south-western obelisk, whose base contains a Roman tombstone, reputedly one of the Arundel marbles; the Ionic temple and second obelisk; and a rusticated cascade over the southern end of the canal, with a nearby rustic bridge. Pavilions terminating the other two avenues from the exedra, one of them Lord Burlington's first essay at Chiswick, have gone, as have two sheets of

water with curving ends, which flanked the Ionic temple.

Changes were made by Capability Brown for Georgiana, duchess of Devonshire, who also had Kent's wooden bridge replaced by the existing stone one, designed in the Palladian style by Wyatt. After the acquisition of Lady Mary Coke's (formerly Sir Stephen Fox's) house to the north-east,[94] formal Italian gardens were laid out on its site, with a large greenhouse reputedly designed by Joseph Paxton, protégé of the duke of Devonshire (d. 1858). The same duke erected lodges and gates by Decimus Burton in 1835,[95] planted lime trees along Duke's Avenue, forming a drive from High Road to Chiswick House, and moved part of Burlington Lane farther south, extending the lake in place of the cascade.[96] Exotic trees and animals were displayed in the park, including an elephant, which in 1828 impressed Sir Walter Scott, and later some of England's first giraffes.[97] Wrought iron gates from Heathfield House were installed at the northern entrance in 1837 but removed to Devonshire House (London) c. 1897 and to Green Park in 1921.[98] Sales of surrounding land by the dukes in the late 19th century did not much affect the landscaped grounds, although part of the canal was drained for building[99] and by 1896 the houses of Paxton Road pressed close to the tree-lined drive. Trees in the south-west corner had been cleared to make the existing cricket field by 1915, when Park Road bordered the estate to the north. By 1935 Staveley Road formed the western boundary and there was a sports ground north-west of the conservatory.[1] Within those limits the local authority maintained the gardens and by 1979 had restored the main part to its original form.

The *GROVE HOUSE* estate originated in a tenement called the Grove, with lands in Sutton and Strand-on-the-Green. They were acquired from the feoffees of John atte Wode in 1412 by Thomas Holgill[2] and were possibly held by Robert atte Grove in 1352[3] or Robert de Grava in 1202 × 1216.[4] William Holgill, described like Thomas Holgill as esquire,[5] occurred in 1458.[6] The Barkers perhaps held the land when they were first recorded at Chiswick, in 1537.[7] Anthony Barker leased Grove farm of c. 170 a. in socage from St. Paul's in 1597 and left an interest to Anne (d. 1607), widow of William Barker of Sonning (Berks.). Anne's son Thomas Barker of the Middle Temple (d. 1630) was active in parish government and apparently was succeeded at Chiswick not by his 17-year old eldest son William[8] but by a younger son, probably Thomas, a royalist killed at Lansdown in 1643.

[90] E. Lambert, *Lond. and Its Environs*, iv (1806), 238; *Memoirs of John Ld. Hervey*, ed. R. Sedgwick, ii (1931), 574, 588.
[91] *Alex. Pope, Epistles to Several Persons*, ed. F. W. Bateson (1951), 130.
[92] *Horace Walpole's Corresp. with Sir Horace Mann*, ed. W. S. Lewis, iv (1960), 362.
[93] Plan of 1736, pub. by John Rocque in *Alex. Pope*, ed. P. Dixon (1972), plate 9.   [94] Above.
[95] H. M. Colvin, *Biog. Dict. of Brit. Architects* (1978), 173.
[96] Gilbert, *Chiswick Old and New*, 43.
[97] Violet Markham, *Paxton and the Bachelor Duke* (1935), 154.

[98] *Kelly's Dir. Mdx.* (1926); Pevsner, *Lond. and Westm.* (1962 edn.), 572.
[99] Wisdom, 'West Lond. Suburb', 25.
[1] O.S. Map 1/2,500, Mdx. XXI. 2 (1894-6 and later edns.).
[2] *Cal. Close*, 1409-13, 334-5, 348.
[3] P.R.O., CP 25(1)/150/64/293; CP 25(1)/150/65/305.
[4] *Early Charters of St. Paul's* (Camd. 3rd ser. lviii), 185.
[5] P.R.O., SC 6/185/9201; SC 6/185/9235.
[6] *Cal. Close*, 1454-61, 301.
[7] P.R.O., CP 25(2)/27/182/28 Hen. VIII East.
[8] Ibid. C 142/738/7; Phillimore and Whitear, *Chiswick*, 6; *Reg. of Adm. to Middle Temple*, i (1949), 57; chwdns. acct. bk. (1622-35).

Thomas was followed by his brother Henry,[9] who was admitted to further copyholds of Sutton Court in 1655 and whose seat was called Grove House by 1664, when he ranked with Thomas Kendall as the second largest ratepayer after Sir Edward Nicholas.[10] Further lands were added by Henry (d. 1695), who owned much property in Berkshire,[11] and by his eldest son Scory Barker, also of the Middle Temple.[12] Scory's son Henry was admitted in 1714 and was the last Barker at Grove House, where he died in 1745.[13] Although Henry had sons, he left his Chiswick lands, copyhold of both Sutton Court and the Prebend manors, to trustees, who conveyed some to Henry Barker of Wallingford (Berks.) but sold others in 1761 and 1762 to the duke of Devonshire.[14]

Grove House itself was acquired before 1750[15] by Henry d'Auverquerque, earl of Grantham (d. 1754), who was succeeded by his daughter Frances, wife of Col. William Eliott.[16] After the death of Lady Frances Eliott in 1772 the house and park were sold freehold[17] to the politician Humphry Morice (1723–85), who entertained Horace Walpole there in 1782.[18] Morice left the estate, known also as Chiswick Grove,[19] to Lavinia, widow of John Luther, on condition that she maintain an old servant and some stray animals.[20] Between 1807 and 1810[21] it passed to Robert Lowth (d. 1822), canon of St. Paul's,[22] whose widow remained there in 1830.[23] Joseph Gurney lived there in 1855[24] before its purchase in 1861 by the duke of Devonshire,[25] whose tenants included Robert Prowett in 1862 and 1867, Col. R. B. Mulliner in 1874 and 1882,[26] and Joseph Atkins Borsley by 1888.[27] Although much of the estate was built over to form Grove Park,[28] Lt.-Col. Robert William Shipway bought the house, with neighbouring lands, from Borsley and others in 1895, preserving it until after his death in 1928.[29]

Before the late 19th century Grove House stood by itself, slightly south of the existing Grove Park Road.[30] The mansion, assessed at 15 hearths in 1664,[31] had three storeys with a pedimented Ionic portico by 1792[32] but was reduced to two storeys by the duke of Devonshire, perhaps to designs by Decimus Burton.[33] Alterations carried out for Lt.-Col. Shipway revealed thin bricks which had been rendered and much decoration of the early 18th century,[34] presumably relics of the 'regular modern building' known to Bowack.[35] The grounds, stretching southward and bordering the Thames, covered 84 a. c. 1775, of which 67 a. formed an enclosed park.[36] Praised by Bowack[37] and reputedly landscaped for the earl of Grantham,[38] they were later noted for their knolls and clumps of trees.[39]

The 18th-century *CORNEY HOUSE* estate derived from a house, with marshy riverside lands described as an island, which in 1542 was conveyed in exchange by the bishop of Rochester to John, Lord Russell, afterwards earl of Bedford (d. 1555).[40] The soldier Sir William Russell, a younger son of Francis, earl of Bedford (d. 1585),[41] entertained Elizabeth I there in 1602[42] and in 1603 was created Lord Russell of Thornhaugh (Northants.). William's only son Francis (d. 1641), earl of Bedford from 1627,[43] spent much time at Chiswick,[44] where he ranked with the earl of Somerset and Lord Poulett as one of the three largest ratepayers.[45] The earl's youngest son Edward Russell, a creator of the harbour at Newhaven (Suss.),[46] sold his mansion to William Gomeldon or Gumbleton,[47] first mentioned in 1663–4,[48] and built or remodelled for himself the house in Chiswick Mall which became known as Bedford House.[49] An Act of 1667–8 after Edward's death authorized the sale of his remaining Chiswick property,[50] although Edward Russell, presumably his second son who was born at Chiswick and became earl of Orford,[51] remained a ratepayer in 1686–7.[52]

The Russells' old house apparently was rebuilt after its sale to Gomeldon[53] and eventually was bought from Robert Cary by the Hon. Peregrine

[9] *Cal. Cttee. for Compounding*, ii. 944; chwdns. acct. bk. (1636–62).

[10] Chwdns. acct. bk. (1663–91), f. 4.

[11] P.R.O., PROB 11/429 (P.C.C. 213 Irby).

[12] Guildhall MS. 14236/1, ff. 21, 28, 71, 104, 127; *Reg. Adm. M. Temple*, i. 167.

[13] Guildhall MS. 14236/3, f. 328; *Gent. Mag.* xv. 502.

[14] Guildhall MSS. 14219/6, ff. 110–12, 314–17; 14236/3, ff. 328–9; 4, ff. 14–15.

[15] Overseers' acct. bk. (1736–76), f. 236.

[16] *Complete Peerage*, vi. 81–2. Draper, *Chiswick*, 145, corrects many earlier accounts which confuse the earl of Grantham with Thos. Robinson, Ld. Grantham (d. 1770), who himself was buried at Chiswick.

[17] Newspaper cutting *c.* 1775 in Chiswick libr.

[18] *D.N.B.*; *Walpole's Corresp. with Mann*, ix. 265, 298.

[19] Rocque, *Map of Lond.* (1746), sheet 15; *Cary's Improved Map of Eng.* (1832), sheet 20.

[20] *Hist. Parl., Commons, 1754–90*, iii. 63.

[21] *Ambulator* (1807); M.R.O., Acc. 306/1.

[22] *Alum. Oxon. 1715–1886*, iii. 878; Le Neve, *Fasti, 1541–1857, St. Paul's, Lond.* 32.

[23] Chwdns. acct. bk. (1821–56), f. 395.

[24] W. Keane, *Beauties of Mdx.* (1850), 243; *Kelly's Dir. Mdx.* (1855).   [25] Draper, *Chiswick*, 146.

[26] *Kelly's Dir. Mdx.* (1862, 1867, 1874, 1882).

[27] M.R.O., Acc. 881/1.

[28] Wisdom, 'W. Lond. Suburb', 75.

[29] Sales cat. in Chiswick libr.; Gilbert, *Chiswick Old and New*, 46.

[30] O.S. Map 6″, Mdx. XXI. NW. (1873 edn.).

[31] M.R.O., MR/TH/3.

[32] Phillimore and Whitear, *Chiswick*, illus. facing p. 31.

[33] Ibid. 13; Colvin, *Dict. Brit. Architects*, 173.

[34] Phillimore and Whitear, *Chiswick*, 273 and illus. facing p. 272; *Builder*, 9 Apr. 1898.

[35] Phillimore and Whitear, *Chiswick*, 13.

[36] Newspaper cutting in Chiswick libr.

[37] Phillimore and Whitear, *Chiswick*, 13.

[38] Lysons, *Environs*, ii. 197.

[39] *Ambulator* (1800); Keane, *Beauties of Mdx.* 243–5. There were knolls and avenues by 1746: Rocque, *Map of Lond.* (1746), sheet 15.

[40] *L. & P. Hen. VIII*, xvii, p. 14; Draper, *Chiswick*, 44–5.

[41] *D.N.B.*

[42] J. Nichols, *Progresses of Queen Eliz.* iii (1823), 578–9; *Cal. S.P. Dom. 1601–3*, 246.

[43] *Complete Peerage*, xi. 239–40. Corney is not a corruption of Thornhaugh, as suggested in Draper, *Chiswick*, 45; cf. e.g. M.R.O., Acc. 531/66, f. 8; Guildhall MS. 11816, f. 233.

[44] Hist. MSS. Com. 73, *City of Exeter*, pp. 11, 138, 166; *Cal. S.P. Dom.* 1625–6, 21; 1627–8, 13; 1628–9, 189.

[45] Chwdns. acct. bk. (1636–62).

[46] *Sussex Archaeol. Collns.* lxiv. 195.

[47] Draper, *Chiswick*, 83.

[48] Chwdns. acct. bk. (1663–91).   [49] Above.

[50] 19 Chas. II, c. 4 (Priv. Act); Draper, *Chiswick*, 83, 207–9.

[51] *D.N.B.*; *Complete Peerage*, x. 77.

[52] Chwdns. acct. bk. (1663–91).

[53] Gilbert, *Chiswick Old and New*, 45; F. J. A. Skeet, *Hist. of Families of Skeet, Somerscales, Widdrington* (1906), 109–10.

Widdrington (d. 1748), a Jacobite who in 1733 married the widowed Maria, duchess of Norfolk (d. 1754).[54] Corney House was a district for the assessment of church rates in 1717–18.[55] Corney Houses constituted a group of copyhold tenements of Sutton Court, one of them the home of Samuel Richardson from 1736 to 1738 and added by Widdrington to the main property in 1745.[56] Widdrington left his Chiswick seat to his widow for life, with successive remainders to his nephews William Tempest Widdrington and John Towneley.[57] Catherine Leveson Gower in 1758 was admitted to the site of three tenements formerly called Corney House and Corney Close, which copyholds were conveyed by her heir in 1785 to John Towneley.[58] John and his son Peregrine Edward Towneley sold them in 1792 to Sir Charles Boughton-Rouse, Bt.[59] (later Rouse-Boughton).[60] Sir Charles added neighbouring plots and was described as of Corney House from 1796 to 1799.[61] Elizabeth, Viscountess Bateman, was at Corney House by 1802, when Sir Charles conveyed to her much of the land,[62] and left it on her death in 1803 to Lady Caroline Damer.[63] George, Earl Macartney, the diplomatist and colonial governor, died at Corney House in 1806[64] as the tenant of Lady Caroline, who by will dated 1827 left a life interest to Countess Macartney, who died there in 1828.[65] The estate was sold in 1830 by Lady Caroline's heir George Germain to the duke of Devonshire,[66] who in 1832 demolished the house and added its grounds to his own.[67] Corney Lodge, presumably the south-west entrance lodge built by John Towneley, stood in Corney Lane in 1871 but was not so named in the 1890s and had disappeared by 1915.[68]

The late 18th-century Corney House stood close to the Thames, south-west of Chiswick village.[69] It was altered by James Gibbs in 1748, as Norfolk House,[70] and was a plain building of five bays, with tall windows, and three dormers.[71] William Combe thought it not large but elegant, after improvements by Sir Charles Rouse-Boughton, and that earlier owners had attended chiefly to the garden. A riverside terrace had been raised by the duchess of Norfolk, with an octagonal summerhouse built by Widdrington out of the demolished Corney Houses, and was unmatched for commanding a 'polished scene of rural beauty'.[72]

At Turnham Green the forerunner of *HEATHFIELD HOUSE* was held in 1695 by Susan, widow of Sir John Lort, bt. (d. 1673). The estate, copyhold of Sutton Court, passed in 1710 to her grandson John Campbell,[73] who in 1718 conveyed it to Henry Harrison, who in 1741 conveyed it to Mary, widow of his tenant Thomas Whetham. Mary Whetham conveyed it in 1747 to James Petty, Viscount Dunkerron, who died there in 1750 and was succeeded by his infant cousin Francis FitzMaurice, earl of Kerry.[74] It was conveyed by Lord Kerry in 1762 to Matthew Hutton, by Matthew's brother James in 1765 to John Perceval, earl of Egmont (d. 1770), and by Egmont's trustee Sir Brownlow Cust, bt., in 1773 to Catherine, dowager duchess of Devonshire (d. 1777). The duchess's youngest son Lord John Cavendish sold it in 1789 to George Augustus Eliott, Lord Heathfield (d. 1790),[75] the defender of Gibraltar and a nephew of Col. William Eliott of Grove House.[76] The house was conveyed in 1792 by Francis Augustus, Lord Heathfield, to Alexander Mayersback, a London physician, and passed in 1796 to Mrs. Sarah Wildman and in 1825 to the Revd. Samuel Curteis and then to Robert How. How's trustees were admitted in 1833 and sold the unoccupied house in 1836 to John Rich and John Bertrand, who were licensed to demolish it.[77]

Heathfield House stood at the south-west corner of Turnham Green, where its site was later occupied in turn by Christ Church Vicarage and the fire station.[78] Part of the garden wall, which stretched along Sutton Lane, survived in 1897.[79] The botanist William Aiton laid out the grounds for Lord Heathfield,[80] whose house was an Italianate building: the main block of five bays contained two storeys, basement, and attics, with round-headed windows on the first floor and a pedimented porch, and was flanked by single-storeyed wings.[81] After its demolition the fine wrought iron entrance gates were bought by the duke of Devonshire for Chiswick House.[82]

ECONOMIC HISTORY. AGRARIAN HISTORY.

In 1086 the canons of St. Paul's had 3 of their 5 hides in demesne and kept 2 ploughs and 2 serfs. There was meadow for 5 ploughs, pasture for the cattle of the vill, and woodland for 150 pigs, but

[54] *Complete Peerage*, ix. 631.
[55] Chwdns. acct. bk. (1698–1751).
[56] T. C. D. Eaves and B. D. Kimpel, *Samuel Richardson* (1976), 65.
[57] Skeet, *Fam. of Widdrington*, 110.
[58] Guildhall MS. 14236/6, ff. 2–4; Burke, *Land. Gent.* (1846), ii. 1417.
[59] Guildhall MS. 14236/6, ff. 188–90.
[60] G.E.C. *Baronetage*, ii. 121–3.
[61] Guildhall MS. 14236/6, ff. 212–14, 250–1, 323.
[62] Ibid. 7, f. 32.   [63] Ibid. f. 71.
[64] *D.N.B.*; *Complete Peerage*, viii. 325.
[65] Guildhall MS. 14236/9, ff. 95–6; *Complete Peerage*, viii. 325.   [66] Guildhall MS. 14236/9, ff. 170–1.
[67] Draper, *Chiswick*, 131. The name Corney Ho. was given to a later ho. in the angle between Burlington Lane and Powell's Walk.
[68] W. Combe, *Hist. of River Thames*, ii (1796), 68; O.S. Map 1/2,500, Mdx. XXI. 2 (1871, 1894–6, and 1915 edns.).
[69] Rocque, *Map of Lond.* (1746); Guildhall Libr., map case 305 (map of 1818).

[70] Colvin, *Dict. Brit. Architects*, 341.
[71] Guildhall Libr., grangerized copy of Lysons, *Environs*, ii, illus. facing p. 196.
[72] Draper, *Chiswick*, 148–9; Combe, *Hist. Thames*, ii. 67.
[73] Guildhall MS. 14236/1, ff. 13, 109, 140; G.E.C. *Baronetage*, iii. 251.
[74] Guildhall MSS. 14236/1, f. 149; 3, ff. 266–7, 326–7, 402; *Complete Peerage*, xi. 670. Tradition has associated the ho. with the Jacobite Simon Fraser, Ld. Lovat, apparently on no stronger grounds than that Ld. Dunkerron acquired it at the time of Lovat's execution.
[75] Guildhall MSS. 14236/4, ff. 47–9, 78, 111–14; 5, ff. 122–3, 156–7, 246–8; 6, ff. 80–2.
[76] *D.N.B.*; Draper, *Chiswick*, 145.
[77] Guildhall MSS. 14236/6, ff. 179, 249; 9, ff. 274–7; 10, ff. 240–3; 11, ff. 64–9.
[78] Guildhall Libr., map case 305 (map of 1818); below.
[79] Phillimore and Whitear, *Chiswick*, 269.
[80] Lysons, *Environs*, ii. 198.   [81] Plate facing p. 33.
[82] Gilbert, *Chiswick Old and New*, 48; Pevsner, *Lond. and Westm.* 572.

the villeins had only 2 ploughs and the value had fallen from £10 T.R.E. to £8. The 40 tenants consisted of 8 villeins each with 1 virgate, 7 villeins each with ½ virgate, 7 bordars each with 5 a., and 16 cottars.[83]

In 1181 the three-hide manor of Sutton contained 330 a. of arable, 16 a. of meadow, and c. 30 a. of grown wood. There were 2 ploughs and there was pasture for 5 cows and 60 sheep.[84] In 1222 the demesne consisted of 210 a. of arable, 16 a. of meadow, c. 40 a. of wood, and enough pasture for 12 oxen, 4 stots, 10 cows, and 120 sheep.[85] The manor was leased and one of the tenants, John of Sutton, acted as assistant bailiff. Declining farms of grain were paid to St. Paul's c. 1300: the manor then owed for only 2 weeks, whereas in 1181 it was said to have owed for 16⅓ days in the time of Dean Wulman[86] (1086 × 1107).

In 1222 there were still c. 40 tenancies, including 7 of the demesne, on Sutton manor, whereas since 1086 the number had increased on most other estates of St. Paul's.[87] Services, not owed by all tenants, included ploughing in winter and Lent, sowing, harrowing, mowing, weeding, shearing, and carting.[88] In 1590 it was recommended that the demesne and parsonage should be leased out without the right to receive rents, many of which had decayed and which John Lane and other lessees of the manor had failed to collect.[89] Rents for freehold land remained negligible in 1649,[90] and some 40 tenants owed quitrents worth £13 in 1674.[91]

Copyhold lands on both Chiswick manors descended to the youngest son or brother[92] by Borough English. On Sutton Court, and presumably on the Prebend, manor copyholds were divided equally among daughters, in default of sons, and a widow was entitled to one third of her first husband's lands as dower. Tenants of Sutton Court in 1590 claimed to know nothing of heriots and to be able to sublet for 3 years without licence, but were told that heriots were payable, besides fines for underleases of more than a year, and that a full fine was due when an heir came of age, whatever his guardian might have paid.[93] In 1649 freeholders paid one year's quitrent as a relief and copyholders a sum to be agreed.[94]

A common field called Chiswick field, recorded in 1670,[95] stretched westward from the present Devonshire Road in 1746.[96] Fields of Sutton Court in 1590 included Long close northeast of the manor house and abutting Berygate (later Barrowgate) mead, Home field (unconnec-

ted with the existing open space), the Brache of 50 a., Broad field of 63 a., Little Sheeplease of 34 a. to the west abutting Great Sheeplease of 72 a., the 60-a. Strand field, apparently divided, Leylands, and Ley field.[97] Many of the fields had been divided into parcels, some of them 'now inclosed,' by 1649.[98] Names which survived in 1818 included the Brache, south-east of Burlington Lane, Leylands west of Sutton Place and Sutton Lane, and a small Strand field north-west of Grove House, with Ice House fields stretching north-eastward from Strand field towards Sutton Court.[99]

Apart from Prebend mead, c. 10 a. along the Thames south-west of the present Barnes bridge, the demesne lands of the Prebend manor lay in the north-eastern corner of the parish. In 1649 they included the 12-a. Home field north of College House at the south-east end of Chiswick Lane and adjoining the 33 a. of Thistly field, which stretched north to the London highway; Lords close and Barn close were part of Eighteen Acres on the west side of Chiswick Lane, with Churchlands to the north and, on the far side of the high road, Whitacres (Whittakers) and North field, stretching to Stamford brook on the parish boundary.[1] Both Prebend mead and Home field remained intact in 1747, when there were 5 closes in Isleworth (formerly Thistly) field, 8 in North close (formerly field), and several more around Manor Farm House in Chiswick Lane. The manor then contained c. 168 a., of which 134 a. were inclosures and c. 34 a. common, apparently excluding College House and its grounds, a riverside plot on the south side of Chiswick Mall, and Chiswick Eyot.[2] The demesne estate, apart from College House, was estimated at 120 a. in 1811, when the field-names survived,[3] and had been only slightly diminished at the time of its sale by Westminster in 1865.[4]

Arable predominated on the lands acquired by John de Bray between 1324 and 1337,[5] as on Sutton manor in 1470 and the Barkers' estate in 1537.[6] Pasture and arable together amounted to 364 a. on Sutton manor in 1590, when only c. 15 a. were meadow.[7] Much land which was arable in 1649, including Strand field and part of Leylands,[8] had been taken for market gardening by 1746; parkland also had increased, leaving Chiswick common field and the Prebend manor's Isleworth field and North close as the largest areas of arable. Lord Burlington's fields in the peninsular part of the parish south of Burlington Lane were meadow or pasture in 1746,[9] although

[83] V.C.H. Mdx. i. 121.
[84] Domesday of St. Paul's (Camd. Soc. [1st ser.], lxix), 145; printed with transl. in Phillimore and Whitear, Chiswick, 124–9, and transl. in Draper, Chiswick, 195–7.
[85] Domesday of St. Paul's, 93–8; printed with transl. in Phillimore and Whitear, Chiswick, 130–44 (which gives 'stots' as 'horses').
[86] Domesday of St. Paul's, pp. xxxvi, 93, 158.
[87] Ibid. p. xxiii.
[88] Phillimore and Whitear, Chiswick, 138–44.
[89] M.R.O., Acc. 531/66, ff. 15–16, 37.
[90] Guildhall MS. 11816, f. 230.
[91] M.R.O., Acc. 1207/1.
[92] Ibid. Acc. 531/66, f. 32; Guildhall MS. 14219/2 (note at front, ?1691); 8, f. 271.
[93] M.R.O., Acc. 531/66, ff. 32–6.
[94] Guildhall MS. 11816, f. 235b.

[95] Ibid. MS. 14219/1.
[96] Rocque, Map of Lond. (1746), sheet 11.
[97] M.R.O., Acc. 531/66, ff. 3–5.
[98] Guildhall MS. 11816, ff. 231–3.
[99] Guildhall Libr., map case 305.
[1] W.A.M. 16666 (sale); St. Paul's MSS., box A 57 (survey, ? made for sale).
[2] Guildhall Libr., map case 260.
[3] W.A.M., box RCO 41 (particulars).
[4] Ibid. (map).
[5] P.R.O., CP 25(1)/149/51/310; CP 25(1)/150/54/28; CP 25(1)/150/57/110.
[6] Ibid. CP 25(1)/152/97/37; CP 25(2)/27/182/28 Hen. VIII East.
[7] M.R.O., Acc. 531/66, f. 6.
[8] Guildhall MS. 11816, f. 232.
[9] Rocque, Map of Lond. (1746), sheets 10, 11, 14, 15.

many were arable in 1800, by which date gardens and parkland had made more inroads on agricultural grassland farther north.[10] Corn was still grown on *c.* 300 a. in 1795, when *c.* 200 a. were grassland and *c.* 280 a. were market gardens.[11] Arable accounted for only *c.* 136 a. in 1846, *c.* 349 a. being meadow or pasture, 336 a. market gardens, 97 a. plantations, and 71 a. osier beds.[12] As farmland dwindled in the early 20th century, field crops again predominated: permanent grass accounted for *c.* 100 a. in 1900, most of it being pasture, for 15 a. in 1910, and for 6½ a. in 1920, while crops were grown on 408 a. in 1900, *c.* 232 a. in 1910, and 215 a. in 1920. Cultivation, however, was of vegetables rather than corn.[13]

Grazing rights were enjoyed by all tenants in 1590 on the demesne of Sutton Court, except on gardens and orchards,[14] the fields being called Lammas lands in 1649.[15] Lammas grazing was said to impoverish the soil in 1794, necessitating heavy manuring.[16] The rights extended from Lammas to Candlemas on meadowland and from harvest time until resowing on arable in 1806, when an Act was passed to extinguish them on 68 a. of the duke of Devonshire. The Act, which was not to affect waste lands,[17] was apparently supplemented or superseded by another, for 141 a., in 1814. No award apparently has survived,[18] although one was made in 1840.[19]

Waste land called Turnham Green, along the highway from London, belonged to both manors.[20] By the mid 18th century roadside building had already divided it into northern and southern parts,[21] which increasingly came to be exploited for turf or loam and used for sand or dung heaps.[22] The northern or Back common covered *c.* 24 a. and the southern or Front common 12 a. in 1846.[23] Further encroachments, including the building of Christ Church, left Chiswick (formerly the Back) common with *c.* 11 a. and Turnham Green (formerly the Front) common with 7½ a. in 1911, when Stamford Brook common in the extreme north-east corner of the parish covered 2½ a.[24] Horses and geese still grazed on Turnham Green common *c.* 1885.[25] Under the Metropolitan Commons Act, 1866,[26] all waste lands were acquired by the local board[27] and thereafter preserved for recreation.[28]

Wheat, barley, and oats were due from Sutton manor in 1181,[29] and both were sold in 1407–8.[30] Wheat was sown on 37 a., rye and maslin on 18 a., oats on 18 a., and barley on 12 a., while 64 a. lay fallow, when Sir Thomas More leased the manor, also containing an unspecified amount of meadow, in 1524.[31] Crops were grown in almost the same amounts, although oats covered only 8 a., in 1590.[32] The crop rotation in 1794 was of vetches, or peas and beans, followed by turnips, sold to London cow-keepers, and then by wheat and barley or oats. The soil varied widely in richness: Chiswick, Fulham, and Chelsea produced exceptionally fine barley both for cattle food and, from its whiteness and thin skin, for malting, although it had recently become less profitable than vegetables. The Lammas lands had to be manured rather than restored by a clover lay, lest graziers take advantage of any clover crop, and riverside fields, often flooded and too level for easy drainage, produced poor hay.[33] Some 26 a. of grassland were mown and 74 a. used as pasture in 1900, when the only 'corn' crops were *c.* 16 a. of peas or beans; in 1917 37 a. were mown for hay and 74 a. for clover.[34] Osiers, cut by basket makers, were recommended for more widespread planting in 1794[35] and were grown on Chiswick Eyot by 1800 and Prebend mead by 1811.[36] They fringed many of the riverside fields *c.* 1827,[37] grew inland east of Little Sutton in 1846,[38] and were still cut on the eyot in 1927.[39]

Sheep shearing was a service due from several tenants of Sutton manor in 1222.[40] Wool was sold in 1407–8,[41] there were 315 sheep and 125 lambs in 1535,[42] and Great Sheeplease in 1590 contained a 'long sheephouse'.[43] Stock on the manor included 9 oxen in 1524[44] and 1590.[45] Fines were laid down for illicit pasturing of horses and cattle in 1650, when hogs were to be ringed,[46] and on the Prebend manor for a wide range of livestock in 1810, when stallions, hogs, goats, and geese were not commonable.[47] Hogs, which were to be ringed in 1650, became an increasing nuisance in the late 18th century.[48] There were 26 horses, 17 cattle, 159 pigs, and no sheep in 1900, as many as 290 pigs in 1910, and still 18 horses, 5 cattle, and 175 pigs in 1920, but only 1 horse and a few pigs by 1930.[49] A pound on the Prebend manor was decayed by 1810, when a new keeper was appointed,[50] and presumably was rebuilt in Home

---

[10] Milne, *Land Use Map of Lond.* (1800), plate II.
[11] Lysons, *Environs*, ii. 185.   [12] M.R.O., TA/CHI.
[13] P.R.O., MAF 68/1846; MAF 68/2416; MAF 68/2980.
[14] M.R.O., Acc. 531/66, f. 33.
[15] Guildhall MS. 11816, f. 235b.
[16] Foot, *Agric. of Mdx.* 23.
[17] 46 Geo. III, c. 111 (Local and Personal) (copy in Chiswick libr.).
[18] 54 Geo. III, c. 69 (Local and Personal); W. E. Tate and M. E. Turner, *Domesday of Eng. Enclosure Acts* (1978), 174.
[19] Guildhall MS. 14219/10, f. 156.
[20] M.R.O., Acc. 531/66, f. 8.
[21] Rocque, *Map of Lond.* (1746), sheets 11, 14.
[22] e.g. Guildhall MSS. 14236/6, f. 116; 8, f. 247; W.A.M., box RCO 41.
[23] M.R.O., TA/CHI.
[24] *Official Guide to Chiswick* [1911].
[25] *Brentford and Chiswick As It Was*, illus. 61.
[26] 29 & 30 Vic., c. 122.   [27] *Kelly's Dir. Mdx.* (1908).
[28] *Chiswick Times*, 19 Jan. 1912.
[29] Phillimore and Whitear, *Chiswick*, 129.
[30] St. Paul's MSS., box A 64 (bailiffs' accts.).

[31] P.R.O., C 1/851/39.
[32] M.R.O., Acc. 531/66, f. 8.
[33] Foot, *Agric. of Mdx.* 22–4, 70–1.
[34] P.R.O., MAF 68/1846; MAF 68/2815.
[35] Foot, *Agric. of Mdx.* 71.
[36] Milne, *Land Use Map of Lond.* (1800), plate II; W.A.M., box RCO 41.
[37] Leigh, *Panorama of Thames* [*c.* 1827].
[38] M.R.O., TA/CHI; Wisdom, 'W. Lond. Suburb', 25.
[39] *Brentford and Chiswick As It Was*, illus. 47.
[40] Phillimore and Whitear, *Chiswick*, 142–3.
[41] St. Paul's MSS., box A 64.
[42] P.R.O., C 1/851/38.
[43] M.R.O., Acc. 531/66, f. 4.
[44] P.R.O., C 1/851/39.
[45] M.R.O., Acc. 531/66, f. 8.
[46] St. Paul's MSS., box B 38.
[47] Guildhall MS. 14219/8, ff. 270–1.
[48] St. Paul's MSS., box B 38; vestry min. bk. (1777–1817), ff. 17, 101.
[49] P.R.O., MAF 68/1846; MAF 68/2416; MAF 68/2980.
[50] Guildhall MS. 14219/8, ff. 270–1.

High Road at Turnham Green, looking west

Cubitt's Yacht Basin, Hartington Road

CHISWICK

EALING: TOWN HALL

BEDFORD PARK: SCHOOL OF ART

field by Chiswick Lane, where it survived, disused, in 1894.[51]

The buildings and layout of Sutton Court farm, apparently new, were considered a model in 1794.[52] Much the largest 19th-century agricultural holding was the Jessops' Grove farm. Its buildings stood east of Grove House, with 310 a. covering most of the parish south-west of Burlington Lane, in 1846, when Joseph Jessop, who recently had succeeded his father Joseph, was the duke of Devonshire's leading tenant in Chiswick.[53] Jessop employed 54 men at Grove farm in 1851.[54] Either he or a namesake was listed as a market gardener in 1862[55] and was still at Grove Park farm, a more isolated farmhouse, in 1887.[56] Known as Smith's farm,[57] it was one of the parish's 17 agricultural holdings in 1900 and 5 in 1920, presumably the only one of more than 150 a. The fields had gone by 1930, when there were only 2 smallholdings,[58] but the farmhouse survived in 1948[59] to be replaced by Chiswick school.[60]

NURSERIES AND MARKET GARDENS. Many people described as agricultural workers in the early 19th century were employed in horticulture, particularly in fruit growing, since Chiswick and neighbouring parishes to the east and west were then seen as the 'great garden' of London.[61] Gardens and orchards had covered most of the north-western part of the parish, between the high road and Sutton Lane, by 1746[62] and had spread eastward, south of Turnham Green, by 1800,[63] when they included ground which was to be leased from 1821 to the Royal Horticultural Society.[64] Market gardeners were blamed for continual depredations on the common in 1811[65] and their demand for baskets stimulated the planting of osiers.[66] Thefts of vegetables, recorded from 1798, caused many market gardeners to employ their own watchmen in 1827-8.[67]

At Strand-on-the-Green nurseries were occupied by George Masters before 1722 and by Nicholas Parker (d. 1726), who was noted for his fruit trees. Both gardens may have passed to Parker's relative Henry Woodman (d. 1758), whose widow stayed in business until 1780. At Turnham Green 8 a. near the later Thornton Avenue probably formed the nursery of James Scott c. 1740-60 and from 1785 that of Richard Williams, who specialized in heathers, introduced exotic plants, and marketed the improved 'William' pear.[68]

Twenty-three market gardeners or nurserymen were listed in 1826-7, most of them at Turnham Green or Strand-on-the-Green,[69] and in 1862, largely in Brentford (later Chiswick High) Road or around Acton Green common (later Chiswick common).[70] Long-lived firms included that of Richard Williams's successor Robert Glendinning, whose widow retained it in 1867,[71] of William Cock at Chiswick village by 1801 and until 1862 or later,[72] of the Jefferys family by 1826 and until 1890 or later at the corner of Gunnersbury Lane (later Avenue) and Chiswick High Road,[73] and of Edward Dean at Strand-on-the-Green by 1826 and until c. 1878.[74] The Sutton Court nursery of the Fromow family, at the corner of Wellesley Road and Sutton Lane, was established in 1828. As William Fromow & Sons, the firm moved its office to the north side of Wellesley Road in 1888, retaining its original nursery ground until 1932 and land in Acton Lane, acquired by 1887, until 1970.[75]

Market gardeners catered mainly for London until Brentford market was established to serve local growers in 1890. By that date building had reduced the number of businesses to c. 8, and in 1894 Chiswick was no longer among Middlesex's ten leading horticultural parishes,[76] although there were still 110 a. of orchard in 1900, in addition to 38 a. of small fruit, and 100 a. in 1920.[77] Two holdings, covering 3 a., survived in 1947,[78] one of them probably the Jersey nursery, in Bolton Road, which closed in 1958.[79]

WOODS. Some woodland of Sutton manor had been assarted by 1181 and more by 1222, when there was a woodward.[80] Old Holt wood was leased with Sutton in 1524[81] and was thought to belong entirely to that manor in 1590, although claimed by the prebendary of Chiswick. In 1590 it covered c. 200 a., extending from Acton into Willesden, and had been so thinned of great trees as to consist of 'scrubbed oaks full of thorns, bushes, and furze'. Copyholders were then felling trees and grubbing up the undergrowth without licence.[82] Timber and pollards in Sutton manor were valued at £120 in 1649, more than a quarter of the improved value of the copyholds,

[51] Chiswick libr., prints; W.A.M., box RCO 41 (map of 1865).
[52] Foot, Agric. of Mdx. 79.
[53] M.R.O., TA/CHI; Guildhall MSS. 14236/12, ff. 35, 51, 107.
[54] P.R.O., HO 107/1699/134/4.
[55] Kelly's Dir. Mdx. (1862).
[56] Kelly's Dir. Chiswick (1887-8). The late 19th-century Grove Park Fm. stood south of Burlington Lane, by the later Promenade Approach Rd.: O.S. Map 1/2,500, Mdx. XXI. 2 (1894-6 and later edns.).
[57] Brentford and Chiswick As It Was, illus. 59.
[58] P.R.O., MAF 68/1846; MAF 68/2980.
[59] O.S. Map 1/2,500, Mdx. XXI. 2 (1948 revn.).
[60] Brentford and Chiswick As It Was, illus. 59.
[61] T. Baird, View of Agric. of Mdx. (1793), 11.
[62] Rocque, Map of Lond. (1746), sheet 11.
[63] Milne, Land Use Map of Lond. (1800), plate II.
[64] Above.
[65] W.A.M., box RCO 41 (memorial, and parts. of Prebend man., 1811).

[66] Foot, Agric. of Mdx. 71; Robbins, Mdx. 52.
[67] Chiswick assoc., patrolmen's notebk. in Chiswick libr.; Rep. of Sel. Cttee. on Police of Metropolis, H.C. 533, p. 228 (1828), vi; ex inf. Mr. J. Wisdom.
[68] T.L.M.A.S. xxiv. 182; xxvi. 297.
[69] Pigot, Lond. Dir. (1826-7).
[70] P.O. Dir. Mdx. (1862).   [71] Ibid. (1867).
[72] P.R.O., HO 107/1699/134/4; P.O. Dir. Mdx. (1862).
[73] Pigot, Lond. Dir. (1826-7); Kelly's Dir. Mdx. (1890); Brentford and Chiswick As It Was, illus. 62.
[74] Pigot, Lond. Dir. (1826-7); P.O. Dir. Mdx. (1878).
[75] Brentford and Chiswick As It Was, illus. 57; Pigot, Com. Dir. (1832-4); Kelly's Dir. Chiswick (1887-8).
[76] L. G. Bennett, Horticultural Ind. of Mdx. (1952), 15, 20, 30; Kelly's Dir. Mdx. (1890).
[77] P.R.O., MAF 68/1846; MAF 68/2980.
[78] Bennett, Horticultural Ind. 38.
[79] Brentford and Chiswick Times, 27 June 1958.
[80] Phillimore and Whitear, Chiswick, 127, 144.
[81] P.R.O., C 1/851/39.
[82] M.R.O., Acc. 531/66, ff. 6-7, 33.

and all woods were reserved by St. Paul's, the lessee being allowed firebote, cartbote, ploughbote, and hedgebote for his own fires and for repairs.[83] Woods were still reserved, with similar rights for the lessee, in the 18th century.[84]

Timber in the Prebend manor, apart from trees around Home field, was said in 1760 to have been regularly reserved to Westminster in underleases of the manor. Westminster's own right, however, had not been made clear in a lease by the prebendary of Chiswick, who objected when Susanna Sharp, as underlessee, claimed the right to make repairs and felled some decayed elms, only to sell them for more seasoned timber. By that date there was no woodland in the parish, except ornamental groves, and the felled trees were in hedgerows or along the roadside.[85]

MILLS. Sutton Court manor had a mill, presumably a watermill, 'next Sutton' in 1458 but none in 1590.[86] A windmill and cottage stood on part of the waste of the Prebend manor at Turnham Green c. 1650,[87] presumably north of the high road as c. 1677,[88] near the later Windmill Road.

FISHING. The canons of St. Paul's were entitled to 5s. a year for the fishery or to every tenth fish of Sutton manor in 1181.[89] By an agreement of 1234 with the prior of Merton (Surr.), who had enjoyed fishing rights at Brentford since c. 1170,[90] the men of Sutton and Chiswick could place 40 weirs for catching barbels and lamperns, paying 23s. a year to the prior.[91] In 1458 tithes of fish were owed by four farmers of the water[92] and in 1590 the underlessee of the fishing rights, with a house and Corney or Cornhithe acres, owed 30s. and 3 salmon a year.[93] The farmer still derived a royalty of 4 salmon, worth 40s., in 1649[94] and 2 salmon and £5 a year in 1674.[95]

No weir was maintained by Sutton manor in 1590, although one was then mentioned as having been at Strand-on-the-Green when St. Paul's had made its agreement with the prior of Merton.[96] Presumably it was at Strand-on-the-Green that Thomas Holgill of the Grove erected weirs to the detriment of local fishermen c. 1412[97] and that the Barkers acquired free fishing with their estate in 1537.[98]

Chiswick village had many fishermen and watermen in Bowack's time. Strand-on-the-Green, seen purely as a fishing hamlet until the late 18th century,[99] furnished fishermen as models for Zoffany's painting of the Last Supper

in St. George's church, Brentford.[1] Fishing was precarious in 1821, when apprenticing was discouraged,[2] and presumably suffered from the pollution experienced at Brentford.[3] At Strand-on-the-Green there were at least 15 fishermen and 2 others who were paupers in 1851. At Chiswick village there were then 4 fishermen in Fisherman's Place,[4] which was soon to be replaced by Thornycrofts' yard.

TRADE AND INDUSTRY. Tradesmen or craftsmen of Chiswick included tailors, a baker, a butcher, a bricklayer, and a cobbler between 1612 and 1618.[5] More people lived by trade, craft, or manufacture than off the land by 1801, when those in the first three categories were twice as numerous as agricultural workers in Old Chiswick and numbers were almost equal in Turnham Green.[6] Those in trade or manufacture, which presumably included fishermen and watermen, rose from 287 families in 1811 to 531 by 1831, while those employed chiefly in agriculture rose only from 274 to 277.[7] By 1832-4 the parish had a wide range of shopkeepers and craftsmen: 22 grocers or dealers in sundries and 5 grocers and cheesemongers, 11 carpenters and undertakers, 8 bricklayers or plasterers, 8 bakers, 7 coal merchants, 6 butchers, 6 cobblers, and 6 blacksmiths. There were more businesses at Turnham Green, including most of those connected with transport, than at Old Chiswick or Strand-on-the-Green. Less common services included those of a bookseller and stationer, a dancing teacher, and a greengrocer at Turnham Green, a drawing master at Old Chiswick, and a hairdresser at both places.[8]

Brickearth, plentiful in the northern half of Chiswick, was the subject of special payments to St. Paul's in a lease of Sutton Court manor in 1731.[9] Its extraction, however, was more important in neighbouring parishes: the 18th- and 19th-century brick and tile kilns of the Trimmer family, near Kew bridge, were approached from Brentford,[10] and there were large brick fields near Stamford brook, in Hammersmith.[11]

Brewing, in 1979 perhaps still the best known local activity, was among the earliest. Payments for making malt (maltsilver) were owed by nearly half of the tenants of Sutton manor in 1222.[12] The Russells owned a brewhouse in 1588,[13] the manor house had a long malthouse in 1589[14] and retained its own brewery in 1725,[15] and Edward Russell had a new brewhouse behind Bedford House in 1661.[16] The river, providing access and

[83] Guildhall MS. 11816, f. 234.
[84] M.R.O., Acc. 531/68.
[85] W.A.M. 16702-4, 16708; Rocque, Map of Lond. (1746).
[86] Phillimore and Whitear, Chiswick, 111; M.R.O., Acc. 531/66.
[87] St. Paul's MSS., box A 57.
[88] Ogilby, Map of Mdx. (c. 1677).
[89] Phillimore and Whitear, Chiswick, 127.
[90] Below, Ealing, econ.
[91] Early Charters of St. Paul's (Camd. 3rd ser. lviii), 260.
[92] Phillimore and Whitear, Chiswick, 110-11.
[93] M.R.O., Acc. 531/66, ff. 8, 37.
[94] Guildhall MS. 11816, f. 230.
[95] M.R.O., Acc. 1207/1.
[96] Ibid. Acc. 531/66, f. 9.
[97] P.R.O., SC 6/185/9201; SC 6/185/9235.
[98] Ibid. CP 25(2)/27/182/28 Hen. VIII Easter.

[99] Phillimore and Whitear, Chiswick, 11, 14; Combe, Hist. Thames, ii. 53.
[1] Robbins, Mdx. 337.
[2] Select vestry min. bk. (1820-2), f. 111.
[3] Below, Ealing, econ.
[4] P.R.O., HO 107/1699/134/4.
[5] Mdx. Sess. Rec. i. 80, 118, 273; ii. 333; iii. 161; iv. 129.
[6] Photocopy of census in Chiswick libr.
[7] Census, 1811-31.
[8] Pigot, Com. Dir. (1832-4).
[9] M.R.O., Acc. 531/68.
[10] Below, Ealing, trade and industry.
[11] O.S. Map 6", Mdx. XVI. SW. (1873 edn.).
[12] Phillimore and Whitear, Chiswick, 141-4.
[13] Inf. from Mrs. D. Yarde.
[14] M.R.O., Acc. 531/66.
[15] Guildhall MS. 11816, f. 231; M.R.O., Acc. 1207/2.
[16] Inf. from Mrs. Yarde.

an outlet for waste, played a large part in the growth of brewing and of later factory industries. A brewer of Chiswick was recorded in 1617[17] and a malthouse at Strand-on-the-Green was burnt down in or before 1708.[18] By 1736 there were at least 5 malthouses, 2 of them at Strand-on-the-Green and one at Turnham Green.[19] At Strand-on-the-Green there was a large one in Back Lane, rebuilt after 1708 and with three kilns c. 1827, which had access to the Thames through Grove Row, and another on the site of nos. 46–7, with two kilns.[20] In 1826–7 the parish's three maltsters were all at Strand-on-the-Green,[21] where William Jupp of Brentford had extensive maltings by 1862. Two kilns behind the former barley house at nos. 46–7 were the last relics of brewing there in 1980.[22]

The Griffin brewery at Old Chiswick of Fuller, Smith & Turner has grown around the brewhouse behind Bedford House, acquired in 1680 by Thomas Plukenett, and a nearby copyhold of the Prebend manor, converted into a brewhouse by the undertenant Thomas Urlin or Erland (d. 1682) between 1664 and 1671. Thomas Mawson (d. 1714), in Chiswick by 1685, became undertenant and in 1699 tenant of Urlin's premises, acquiring the George inn, later the George and Devonshire, in 1700 and the Bedford House brewhouse in 1701. The business was probably managed by his eldest son Thomas before its lease in 1740 to William Harvest of Brentford and later to Matthew Graves, who also leased many local inns.[23] Known as the Griffin Hock brewery in 1745, it eventually helped to enrich Thomas Mawson's younger son Matthias (1683–1770), bishop of Ely and benefactor of Corpus Christi College, Cambridge.[24] Matthias's niece Amy married Charles Purvis, who in 1791 sold the brewery to John Thompson of Chiswick, whose sons Douglas and Henry in 1829 took another partner, Wood, and secured new capital from John Fuller of Neston Park (Wilts.). Control passed to Fuller's son John Bird Fuller, who in 1846 recruited Henry Smith, formerly of Ind & Smith of Romford (Essex), and Smith's head brewer John Turner.[25] Thereafter the three families remained in partnership, forming the existing limited company in 1929. By 1978 Fuller's had 110 public houses, mostly within 15 miles of Chiswick, in addition to off-licence shops, and sold over a wide area as one of London's two surviving independent brewers.[26] Some 300 people were employed by the company in 1979.[27]

Mawson's copyhold brewhouse abutted on a passageway behind Chiswick Mall leading westward from Chiswick Lane to Bedford House,[28] where the brewery has always had its main entrance. A slip of land between the copyhold brewhouse and the freehold one behind Bedford House was bought in 1707.[29] The property thereafter expanded to form a square block bounded on the north by Mawson Lane and containing in Chiswick Lane the early 18th-century terrace called Mawson Row, which included the surviving Fox and Hounds. A block to the south, including the Red Lion in Chiswick Mall and some cottages, was later acquired and used mainly for bottling and storage.[30] In 1978 rebuilding and re-equipment were in progress at the Griffin brewery. From 1924 the company maintained a 5-a. sports ground which it leased from the council in Riverside Drive.[31]

The Lamb brewery at Old Chiswick was leased in 1790 to John Sich and William Thrale, brewers who already had acquired the Feathers inn, and conveyed in 1795 to Sich.[32] In 1809 he formed a partnership with John Sich the younger and Henry Sich, who in 1819 also became coal merchants[33] and whose brewery in 1832 was considered comparable in scale to that of Fuller.[34] Their premises, copyhold of the Prebend manor, lay north of the Vicarage on the east side of Church Street and in 1887 included the Burlington Arms, with the Lamb to the north next to the brewery itself.[35] The firm had acquired several inns before it was taken over in 1920 by the Isleworth Brewery Co., which itself soon passed to Watney, Combe, Reid & Co.[36] The Lamb and, in 1923, the Burlington Arms lost their licences,[37] the first becoming known as Burlington Corner and later as Lamb Cottage, the second as the Old Burlington.[38] The Sich family, whose members occupied many large houses in Old Chiswick in the 19th century,[39] was still represented there in 1977 by Sir Rupert Sich of Norfolk House.[40]

The origins of the Chiswick Press lay in a paper-pulp factory started in 1809 by the printer Charles Whittingham (1767–1840),[41] who had bought a patent for extracting the tar from old ropes.[42] By 1816 his was the 'principal manufactory' in the parish, with claims to produce material for the finest paper in the country.[43] Meanwhile the neighbouring High House in Chiswick Mall had been leased to Whittingham in 1810 and equipped as a printing works, from which the first imprint of the Chiswick Press was issued in 1811. Whittingham moved to the larger

[17] Mdx. Sess. Rec. iv. 160.
[18] Cal. Mdx. Sess. Bks. 1689–1709, 333.
[19] Overseers' acct. bk. (1736–66), ff. 6–7, 12.
[20] Judges, Strand-on-the-Green, 13, 15.
[21] Pigot, Lond. Dir. (1826–7); three malt hos. were named and a fourth was depicted in Leigh, Panorama [c. 1827].
[22] P.O. Dir. Mdx. (1862); Judges, Strand-on-the-Green, 15.
[23] M.R.O., Acc. 891/2/1/73–4; inf. from Mrs. Yarde.
[24] Fuller, Smith & Turner, Brewers' Handbk. [c. 1972], 17; D.N.B.
[25] Fuller, Smith & Turner, Brewers' Handbk. 17–19; M.R.O., Acc. 891 (summary).
[26] Hounslow: Guide to Local Ind. (1978), 42, 65.
[27] Inf. from Fuller, Smith & Turner.
[28] M.R.O., Acc. 891/2/1/73.   [29] Inf. from Mrs. Yarde.
[30] Guildhall MS. 14219/15 (plan, 1912).

[31] Brentford and Chiswick Times, 8 Aug. 1968; 7 July 1977; inf. from Fuller, Smith & Turner.
[32] M.R.O., Acc. 1214/1479; Acc. 1348/1–2.
[33] Ibid. Acc. 1214/1436–7.
[34] Pigot, Com. Dir. (1832–4).
[35] Guildhall MS. 14219/14, ff. 5–7 (inc. plan).
[36] Brentford and Chiswick Times, 17 Oct. 1974; Story of Watneys, ed. W. P. Serocold (1949), 28–9; M.R.O., Acc. 1214.
[37] Guildhall MS. 14219/15, ff. 203–4 (inc. plan); Chiswick Times, 28 Sept. 1923.
[38] Min. of Town and Country Planning, List of Bldgs. (1949).   [39] Kelly's Dir. Chiswick, passim.
[40] Who's Who, 1977.   [41] D.N.B.
[42] A. Warren, The Chas. Whittinghams (Grolier Club of New York, 1896), 43–4.
[43] Brewer, Beauties of Eng. and Wales, x (5), 327.

College House in 1818 and on his death there was succeeded by his nephew and namesake (1795–1876). Books were printed from 1840 to 1848 at Chiswick and at Took's Court, off Chancery Lane (London), where the nephew had started his own press, and from 1849 at Chiswick alone. The Chiswick Press retained its name after a final move to Chancery Lane in 1852 and the younger Charles Whittingham's retirement in 1860.[44] The books, which set a new standard in English printing, were noted in particular for their engravings of woodcuts and soon became collectors' pieces.[45] They were produced on iron hand presses, of which probably the earliest example in England, from Chiswick, is at Gunnersbury Park Museum.[46]

A laundry was opened by a French immigrant, Camille Simon, on the river's edge at the west end of Strand-on-the-Green in 1860, moving to the north side of Thames Road in 1905 and 1914. As Pier House Laundry it became one of the largest in London, managed by the Simon family, with 200 employees before the introduction of automation and 19 collection shops at the time of its closure in 1973.[47] The premises, covering 1½ a., were then sold[48] and in 1980 were being cleared for new offices and craft industries, although the brick façade of the main building was preserved.[49] A chemical manufacturing plant called Camille Simon, which had been started as a subsidiary business on the same site, moved in 1973 to the north of England.[50] Most of the other laundries advertised in 1890 as being in Chiswick lay beyond the boundary, in and around Acton Lane. Three in British Grove, on the Hammersmith boundary, included the Royal Chiswick Laundry,[51] which closed between 1964 and 1975.[52]

The most momentous industrial achievements at Chiswick were those of the naval architect John Isaac Thornycroft (1843–1928).[53] Launch building started in 1864,[54] when his father Thomas Thornycroft (1815–85), the sculptor and amateur engineer,[55] was first admitted to a site south of the churchyard which was to become Church wharf.[56] There J. I. Thornycroft designed and, in partnership with his brother-in-law John Donaldson from 1873, produced high-speed launches, including the *Sir Arthur Cotton*, claimed in 1874 to be the fastest vessel in the world. Torpedo-boats formed the main output in the 1880s, 222 being built for the British and foreign navies between 1874 and 1891,

followed from 1893–4 by the first torpedo-boat destroyers. Trials and launchings were a popular sight until difficulties in negotiating bridges downstream led to a decision to acquire a yard at Woolston, near Southampton, in 1904.[57] Thornycrofts, a limited company from 1901, built its last naval vessels at Chiswick in 1905–6 and had finally left by 1909.[58] A small factory making steam waggons for the company had already moved in 1899, to Basingstoke, although experimental work on diesel and petrol engines continued at the Chiswick yard until its closure.[59] Church wharf was occupied by Gwynne's Engineering Co., afterwards Gwynne Cars, in the 1920s[60] and later was divided and used partly for storage. The original buildings were bombed in the Second World War[61] and were replaced by Reckitt & Colman.[62] Thomas Thornycroft was buried in the nearby churchyard[63] and J. I. Thornycroft, knighted in 1902, lived for many years at Eyot Villa in Chiswick Mall.[64]

Traditional boat building was already carried on mainly at Strand-on-the-Green, before Thornycrofts' expansion at Old Chiswick.[65] Strand-on-the-Green in 1851 had at least 10 barge builders or shipwrights.[66] In 1890 there were still 4 boat builders there, besides Robert Talbot & Sons,[67] who built c. 300 barges between 1858 and 1908. Talbots by 1908 were working for the Maritime Lighterage Co.,[68] a London firm whose Magnolia wharf at Strand-on-the-Green was closed in the 1950s[69] and sold for building in 1961.[70] A 'grid' for boat repairs survived in 1980 by the river bank opposite Picton House, no. 45 Strand-on-the-Green.[71]

The Army & Navy Stores depository was built in 1871 at the south-east corner of Turnham Green common, on the site of one of three blocks of buildings formerly used by the militia. A computer centre was opened in 1969 on one floor of the depository, which had been recently modernized, and the rest was still used for storage in 1980. The militia's other blocks, destroyed in the Second World War, were rebuilt as a post office and as a warehouse, leased from 1966 to the Pantechnicon.[72]

Arthur Sanderson & Sons had a paper staining works by 1884,[73] presumably in Heathfield Terrace, Turnham Green, where it still existed in 1890, when the firm also had a wallpaper factory near by in Barley Mow Lane.[74] A new factory was built on the north side of the lane in 1902; partly faced with glazed white bricks, it was

[44] *D.N.B.*

[45] Warren, *Chas. Whittinghams*, 10, 48–50, 85, *passim*; G. Keynes, *Wm. Pickering, Publisher*, 22–4. A colln. of most works of the Chiswick Press is at Chiswick libr.

[46] *Hist. Gunnersbury Pk. and Mus.* (booklet, 1974 edn.).

[47] *Brentford and Chiswick Times*, 1 April 1960; 4 Oct. 1973.

[48] Ibid. 11 Oct. 1973.

[49] Inf. from Mrs. K. Judges.

[50] *Brentford and Chiswick Times*, 4 Oct. 1973.

[51] *Kelly's Dir. Mdx.* (1890).

[52] *P.O. Dir. Lond.* (1964, 1975).

[53] *D.N.B.* 1922–30.

[54] Barnaby, *100 Years of Shipbldg.* 19.

[55] *D.N.B.*

[56] Guildhall MS. 14236/15, ff. 345–50. A plan of the premises in 1878 is in ibid. 16.

[57] Barnaby, *100 Years of Shipbldg.* 23–4, 30, 35, 38, 40, 47–9.

[58] Ibid. 44, 51, 64.

[59] J. E. Martin, *Industrial Geog. of Gtr. Lond.* (1966), 39.

[60] *Kelly's Dir. Chiswick* (1923, 1930).

[61] Barnaby, *100 Yrs. of Shipbldg.* 54.

[62] Below.

[63] *D.N.B.*

[64] *P.O. Dir. Mdx.* (1878); *Kelly's Dir. Chiswick* (1912).

[65] Pigot, *Dir. Mdx.* (1839–40).

[66] P.R.O., HO 107/1699/134/4.

[67] *Kelly's Dir. Mdx.* (1890).

[68] Chiswick libr., NC/I/lxxiii.

[69] *P.O. Dir. Lond.* (1952, 1959).

[70] *Brentford and Chiswick Times*, 1 Mar. 1963.

[71] Inf. from Mrs. Judges.

[72] Inf. from Army & Navy Stores dep.

[73] *P.O. Dir. Lond.* (*Suburban, North*), 1884.

[74] *Kelly's Dir. Mdx.* (1890).

the only factory designed by C. F. A. Voysey.[75] There were *c.* 250 employees by 1896 and 700–800 by 1928, when there was a fire,[76] followed by Sandersons' move to Perivale.[77] Their former building on the south side of Barley Mow Lane, known as the Devonshire works, was used for light engineering in the 1960s by Evershed & Vignoles of Acton Lane. From 1971 it stood empty until restored by the Cornhill Insurance Co. as the Barley Mow Workspace, for individuals or small firms of designers or craftsmen, the first of whom arrived in 1976.[78] Their building on the north side of Barley Mow Passage, Voysey House, was acquired from the Sun Alliance Insurance Group by the National Transit Insurance Co. in 1969.[79]

The Chiswick Soap Co., founded by the Mason family,[80] had a works on the north side of Burlington Lane, opposite Chiswick Square, by 1878.[81] The firm, well known for its 'Cherry Blossom' and other shoe and household polishes, became a public company in 1916, with some directors from Reckitts of Hull. It was called the Chiswick Polish Co. by 1926[82] and Chiswick Products from 1930, on amalgamation with the Nugget Polish Co.,[83] until its acquisition by Reckitts' successor, Reckitt & Colman, in 1954.[84] Eventually it occupied a large site in the triangle between Burlington Lane (later Great Chertsey Road) and Hogarth Lane, stretching west across the grounds of the Cedars, which survived in 1916, to the backs of the houses in Paxton Road.[85] Buildings included an administrative block of the 1920s, extended eastward in 1958, in Great Chertsey Road, a central polish works of *c.* 1930, demolished in 1976, and an engineer's shop, offices, manufacturing area, and warehouses of the 1960s along Hogarth Lane. Boston House was bought for the female staff in 1922[86] and a printing works and cardboard box factory, with its chimney disguised as a clock tower, had been built by 1930 in Duke's Meadows.[87] At Church wharf, where imported waxes were brought by barge, a new warehouse was built after the Second World War. Reckitt & Colman employed some 1,500 people in Chiswick, mainly in making polishes, shortly before it moved all production to Hull in 1972. The printing works was then sold to Hounslow L.B., which replaced it with a housing estate. The industrial premises stood empty in 1979, although *c.* 250 were still employed there and in

the offices, which the company retained as its corporate headquarters.

West Metropolitan Tramways from 1887 had its main depot at Chiswick,[88] where in 1901 London United Tramways opened its headquarters, with a large power house and tram depot, on 4 a. north of the high road. The power house was built of brick with elaborate freestone dressings, to the design of W. Curtis Green, and had a 260-ft. high steel smoke-stack[89] which was later demolished. Although largely superseded by Lots Road (Chelsea) power station from 1919, the Chiswick installation remained in use as Goldhawk substation until 1962[90] and the building itself was to be preserved by London Transport in 1976. Coaches of British European Airways had then been using the depot at least since 1947 but were to make way for motorbuses from Belmont Road, Turnham Green,[91] where the London General Omnibus Co. had owned a stable, later a garage, since *c.* 1900.[92]

Off the western end of Chiswick High Road, in Gunnersbury, the London General Omnibus Co. opened its central overhaul works, to employ 2,000 men, in 1921–2.[93] Originally designed to maintain 4,000 vehicles, the factory included a training school from 1925 and was restricted to engineering after London Transport opened its Aldenham works, for maintenance, near Elstree in 1956.[94] In 1979 London Transport employed over 2,680 at its Chiswick works and adjoining departments and *c.* 200 at the Turnham Green garage.[95]

A covered market was opened by the U.D.C. in 1926, to accommodate street traders in Chiswick High Road. It stood on the south side, next to Linden House, and was used by the fire services from 1937.[96]

After the Second World War companies included J. Coales & Son, transport contractors, in Chiswick Common Road, and LEP Transport, London cargo agents, with wharves in Corney Road from 1922.[97] In 1978 much employment was provided by offices and by shops, many of them still small family businesses, in and around Chiswick High Road.[98]

Office blocks included Empire House, first occupied in 1961, on the site of the Chiswick Empire.[99] The largest was an L-shaped 18-storeyed block of granite-faced concrete, erected for the British Transport Commission over Gunnersbury station, which itself was rebuilt,

[75] *Industrial Monuments in Gtr. Lond.* (Thames Basin Archaeol. Observers Group, 1969), 35; *C. F. A. Voysey* (Brighton Mus. exhib. catalogue, 1978), illus. on p. 52.

[76] *Chiswick Times*, 10 July 1896; *Brentford and Chiswick Times*, 12 Oct. 1928; *Century of Sanderson, 1860–1960*, 1.

[77] *V.C.H. Mdx.* iv. 125.

[78] *P.O. Dir. Lond.* (1964); *Brentford and Chiswick Times*, 25 Mar. 1976.

[79] Inf. from Nat. Transit Insurance Co. Ltd.

[80] Para. based on inf. from the librarian, Reckitt & Colman Ltd.

[81] *Kelly's Dir. Mdx.* (1878).   [82] Ibid. (1926).

[83] *Brentford and Chiswick Times*, 17 Jan. 1930.

[84] *Reckitt & Colman Today* [1972], 2.

[85] O.S. Maps 1/2,500, Mdx. XXI. 2 (1894–6 and later edns.).

[86] Gilbert, *Chiswick Old and New*, 37.

[87] *Brentford and Chiswick Times*, 26 Sept. 1930.

[88] Ex inf. Lond. Transport; Wilson, *Lond. Utd. Tramways*, 25–6.

[89] Barker and Robbins, *Hist. Lond. Transport*, ii. 33; Wilson, *Lond. Utd. Tramways*, 58–9; Chiswick libr., NC/I/lxiva (*Souvenir of Inauguration* 1901).

[90] Inf. from Lond. Transport.

[91] Ibid.; *Brentford and Chiswick Times*, 29 July, 5 Aug. 1976.

[92] *Kelly's Dir. Chiswick* (1901–2 and later edns.).

[93] *Hist. Lond. Transport*, ii. 222; *Acct. of Chiswick Works of L.G.O.C.* (1922) in Chiswick libr.

[94] *Hist. Lond. Transport*, ii. 340; V. Sommerfield, *London's Buses* (1933), 88; *V.C.H. Mdx.* v. 120.

[95] Inf. from Lond. Transport.

[96] Draper, *Chiswick*, preface.

[97] Inf. from LEP Transport Ltd.; *P.O. Dir. Lond.* (1964).

[98] *Hounslow: Guide to Local Ind.* (1978), 81–2.

[99] Draper, *Chiswick*, preface.

between 1964 and 1966. Designed to hold 1,500 workers, it became the headquarters of IBM United Kingdom, the computer manufacturers.[1]

LOCAL GOVERNMENT. MANORIAL GOVERNMENT.

In 1294 the chapter of St. Paul's claimed view of frankpledge, the assize of bread and of ale, infangthief, outfangthief, gallows, tumbril, pillory, and fugitives' chattels in Chiswick and Sutton, as on other Middlesex estates. St. Paul's was found to have enjoyed all the rights from time immemorial except gallows, which it had only in Finsbury.[2]

Separate courts were held for Sutton Court and for the Prebend manor by 1590[3] and presumably much earlier. A few court rolls for Sutton Court survive from between 1635 and 1672[4] and court books from 1668 until 1950.[5] Court books for the Prebend manor, concerned almost entirely with land transactions, survive for 1670–3 and from 1691 until 1937.[6] For Sutton Court a court leet and court baron were held at the manor house at Lady Day and Michaelmas in 1649.[7] Later a view of frankpledge, followed by a court baron, was normally held by St. Paul's in June or July, with special courts baron which became more frequent from the mid 18th century.[8] Courts baron alone were held from 1853, ceasing after 1900.[9] For the Prebend manor in the 18th century there were general courts in the name of Westminster's lessee at least once a year and special courts, held from 1747 at various inns[10] and from 1783 usually at the Roebuck.[11] Sessions of the Prebend manor court in Chiswick ceased after 1882.[12]

A constable and two aletasters were elected at the view of frankpledge in the 17th and early 18th centuries.[13] Two constables were chosen from 1729, whereupon the election of aletasters lapsed,[14] and three from 1791.[15] In 1787 the magistrates declined to swear in a third constable, who had been nominated by the vestry, until he had been returned at the manorial court.[16] A headborough was named only from 1787 until 1840 and aleconners were again chosen from 1795 until 1840.[17] In 1824 and from 1831 to 1843 two constables were elected, normally one each for Turnham Green and Strand-on-the-Green.

From 1845 there were constables for Chiswick and Turnham Green, and a third, also styled headborough, for Christ Church, Turnham Green, until the last recorded elections in 1855.[18] At courts of the Prebend manor the only election was in 1811, when the customs were restated and a combined bailiff, common keeper, and pound keeper was appointed.[19]

PARISH GOVERNMENT TO 1836. There were two churchwardens in 1580,[20] chosen annually in vestry by 1622, together with two sidesmen and two surveyors of the highways.[21] Two overseers for the poor were named annually by 1663, when the vestry also named the constable.[22] By 1777 one churchwarden was chosen by the vicar and the other by the parish. There was a salaried collector of poor rates from 1788[23] and an assistant overseer from 1820, when a select vestry was formed.[24] Other salaried officers included a vestry clerk from 1622,[25] a beadle by 1702,[26] and a woman pew opener before 1784;[27] aleconners were paid, although not appointed, by the parish in the 1820s.[28] The beadle also acted as sexton by 1795[29] and, to retain both posts, was required to do no other work in 1825.[30] There are churchwardens' accounts for most years from 1622,[31] overseers' accounts for 1678–97, 1736–66, and 1810–16,[32] vestry minutes from 1777,[33] and select vestry minutes from 1820.[34]

The vestry met at the church in 1622, when it included the vicar, Edward Wardour, and Thomas Barker. Members of the Barker family often attended thereafter, as did successive incumbents. Others present included Arthur Duck and Chaloner Chute, both of them lessees of the Prebend manor, the brewer Thomas Mawson and, in 1794, John Zoffany.[35] Select vestries normally met weekly at the workhouse.[36] From 1631 church rate payers were listed by districts: Chiswick village or 'the town', Little Sutton, the Strand, Turnham Green, and Stamford Lane. Sluts Hole, Corner or Corney House, which included Grove House, and Sutton Court also formed districts by 1724.[37]

Apart from church rates and poor rates, the parish in 1629 had a small income from tenants of the church house and lands.[38] Church rates were fixed annually and varied between 3d. and 6d. in

[1] *Brentford and Chiswick Times*, 13 Mar. 1964, 25 Feb. 1966; *Taywood News*, Jan.–Feb. 1966 (pamphlet by Taylor-Woodrow Ltd. in Chiswick libr.).
[2] *Plac. de Quo Warr.* (Rec. Com.), 476.
[3] M.R.O., Acc. 119/1 (Sutton Ct.).
[4] St. Paul's MSS., box B 38.
[5] Ibid. W.C.5 [1668–93]; Guildhall MSS. 14236/1–19 [from 1694].
[6] Guildhall MSS. 14219/1–15.
[7] Ibid. 11816, f. 253 b.
[8] Ibid. 14236/1–19 *passim*.
[9] Ibid. 14236/13, f. 46; 18, f. 317.
[10] Ibid. 14219/1–15 *passim*.   [11] Ibid. 14219/7.
[12] Ibid. 14219/13, f. 199.
[13] St. Paul's MSS., box B 38; St. Paul's MS. W.C. 5; Guildhall MSS. 14236/1–2, *passim*.
[14] Guildhall MS. 14236/2, f. 123.
[15] Ibid. 6, f. 143.
[16] Vestry min. bk. (1777–1817), f. 53.
[17] Guildhall MSS. 14236/6, ff. 32, 238; 11, f. 241.
[18] Ibid. 9, f. 237; 10, f. 181; 11, f. 358; 12, f. 51; 13, f. 113.
[19] Guildhall MS. 14219/8, f. 270.
[20] Ibid. 9537/4.

[21] Chwdns. account bk. (1622–35) [unpag.].
[22] Ibid. (1663–91).
[23] Vestry min. bk. (1777–1817), ff. 1, 60.
[24] Select vestry min. bks. (1820–2), ff. 1–2; (1822–5), f. 77.
[25] Chwdns. acct. bk. (1622–35).
[26] Ibid. (1698–1751) [unpag.].
[27] Vestry min. bk. (1777–1817), f. 37.
[28] Select vestry min. bk. (1822–5), f. 77.
[29] Vestry min. bk. (1777–1817), f. 115.
[30] Select vestry min. bk. (1822–5), ff. 211, 213–14.
[31] Acct. bks. for 1777–1803 and 1856–71 are at Chiswick libr. and the others at the ch. Accts. for 1622 and 1629 are printed in Phillimore and Whitear, *Chiswick*, 160–5, 282–8.
[32] Acct. bks. for 1736–66 are at Chiswick libr. and the others at the ch.
[33] At Chiswick libr.
[34] Min. bks. for 1820–2 and 1825–8 are at Chiswick libr. and the others at the ch.
[35] Chwdns. acct. bks. (1622–35, 1636–62, 1663–91, 1698–1751); vestry min. bk. (1777–1817), f. 103.
[36] Select vestry min. bks. *passim*.
[37] Chwdns. acct. bks. (1622–35, 1698–1751).
[38] Ibid. (1622–35); below, charities.

the £ in the late 18th century.[39] Poor rates, fixed yearly or half yearly, ranged from 4*d.* to 8*d.* between 1696 and 1698 but were often 2*s.* in the mid 18th century.[40] In 1777 it was decided to assess property in proportion to yearly value rather than to purchase price.[41] Sums spent on the poor were £894 in 1776 and, on average, £786 from 1783 to 1785.[42] Expenditure was £2,121 in 1803,[43] as high as £3,240 in 1816,[44] and £2,158 in 1821; a reduction by one third, to £1,397, by 1831 was ascribed to the establishment of a select vestry.[45]

Poor relief was to be considered every month by the parish officers in 1659.[46] Payments in 1678 were divided between pensioners, 18 of whom received from 1*s.* to 2*s.* 6*d.* a week, and 'chance poor', who were given small sums, nursing, clothing, and, in one case, a boat.[47] Three and a half dozen badges were bought in 1697–8[48] and paupers who had not served any parish office were to be badged in 1779.[49] A workhouse was said to have been built in 1725;[50] it existed by 1736[51] and was enlarged in 1785. It stood near the Back common at Turnham Green, where it was hoped to acquire land near by in 1794 and 1801. The workhouse poor apparently were farmed out by 1790, when an additional sum was paid to make up for falling profits from their labour. The vestry itself scrutinized tradesmen's tenders for supplying the workhouse in 1795,[52] as did the select vestry, which employed a salaried master and mistress, or matron, in 1823.[53] Damages were to be sought from Hammersmith in 1781, after its beadle had driven a dying pauper into Chiswick.[54]

LOCAL GOVERNMENT AFTER 1836. Chiswick in 1836 became part of Brentford poor law union,[55] which sold the parish workhouse in 1838[56] and afterwards used the new union workhouse in Twickenham Road, Isleworth.[57] The parish lay within the Metropolitan Police district from 1840[58] and had a burial board from 1852.[59] Under the Chiswick Improvement Act, 1858, commissioners were elected with powers to construct a wharf, levy rates, and borrow money for lighting, paving, and sewerage.[60] The 19 commissioners included a nominee of the duke of Devonshire and were served by a salaried clerk.[61] They met about twice a month, at first at the Roebuck, then at Chiswick hall in Chiswick Mall until 1868, at the boys' National school in

the churchyard until 1873, and thereafter at the new vestry hall by Turnham Green.[62] In 1869 the commissioners adopted sections of the London Government Act, 1858, in order to control the siting and quality of new housing.[63] The vestry meanwhile had reached a compromise with the Metropolitan Board of Works over non-payment of sewer rates between 1857 and 1859.[64] It also successfully opposed an attempt to attach much of Chiswick to Chelsea in 1868, decided to adopt the Vestries Act in 1872, and consequently to pay for a hall at Turnham Green in 1874.[65]

Stamford Brook grounds, at the time of its transfer to Chiswick in 1878, was being built up to form part of Bedford Park. Residents of the new suburb formed a vigilance committee, concerned mainly with sanitation, in 1881 and a more general Bedford Park committee in 1883.[66]

A local board was formed for Chiswick in 1883, under the Public Health Act, 1875.[67] It met twice a month at the vestry hall[68] and consisted of 19 members, one of them to be nominated by the duke of Devonshire so long as he should hold 500 a. in the parish, although the duke did not exercise his right after 1891.[69] The local board took over the burial board's powers[70] and also formed committees for works, audit and finance, lighting, and special purposes in 1888, when its officers included a clerk and solicitor, an engineer and surveyor, a medical officer of health, and a sanitary inspector.[71]

BOROUGH OF BRENTFORD AND CHISWICK. *Parted saltirewise argent and gules, in chief the figure of St. Nicholas proper, in base two bars wavy azure, and in fess two seaxes with points upward and edges inward, their blades proper and their hilts or* [Granted 1932]

Chiswick U.D.C. superseded the local board under the Local Government Act, 1894, its district being divided between Chiswick (including Strand-on-the-Green) and Turnham Green wards. Six wards, with three members each, were created in 1901: Bedford Park, Chiswick Park, Grove Park, Gunnersbury, Old Chiswick, and Turnham Green.[72] The council,

[39] Chwdns. acct. bk. (1776–1803), *passim.*
[40] Overseers' acct. bks. (1678–97, 1736–66), *passim.*
[41] Vestry min. bk. (1777–1817), f. 11.
[42] *Abstract of Returns by Overseers, 1787,* H.C. 1st ser. ix, p. 628.
[43] *Rep. Com. Poor Laws,* H.C. 44, p. 86*f* (1834), xxxv.
[44] *Rep. Sel. Cttee. on Poor Rate Returns,* H.C. 748, p. 100 (1821), iv.
[45] *Rep. Com. Poor Laws,* 86*f.*
[46] Chwdns. acct. bk. (1636–62).
[47] Overseers' acct. bk. (1678–97), ff. 5v.–6v.
[48] Ibid. f. 204.
[49] Vestry min. bk. (1777–1817), f. 15.
[50] Lysons, *Environs,* ii. 222.
[51] Overseers' acct. bk. (1736–66), f. 16.
[52] Vestry min. bk. (1777–1817), ff. 41, 71, 93–4, 128, 188.
[53] Select vestry min. bk. (1822–5), ff. 30, 77, and *passim.*
[54] Vestry min. bk. (1777–1817), f. 23.
[55] *Poor Law Com. 2nd Rep.* H.C. 595-I, p. 533 (1836), xxix.

[56] P. D. Butler, 'Par. Life in Chiswick 1777 to 1858' (TS. thesis, 1960) in Chiswick libr.   [57] *V.C.H. Mdx.* iii. 121.
[58] *Lond. Gaz.* 13 Oct. 1840, p. 2250.
[59] Draper, *Chiswick,* 172.
[60] 21 & 22 Vic. c. 69 (Local and Personal).
[61] Chiswick improvement cttee. min. bk. i (1858–72), ff. 2, 4, in Chiswick libr.   [62] Ibid. i–iv (1858–83), *passim.*
[63] *Lond. Gaz.* 23 Nov. 1869, p. 6293.
[64] Butler, 'Par. Life in Chiswick', 57–8.
[65] 'Opening of enlarged town hall, 1901' (programme in Chiswick libr.), 16, 18.   [66] Bolsterli, *Bedford Pk.* 79.
[67] 'Opening of town hall, 1901', 18.
[68] *Kelly's Dir. Mdx.* (1890).
[69] M.R.O. *Rep. Local Inqs.* 1889–97, 73–5.
[70] 'Opening of town hall, 1901', 18.
[71] Chiswick local bd. *Ann. Reps.* (1888–94) in Chiswick libr.
[72] M.R.O. *Rep. Local Inqs.* 1895–1907; Chiswick libr., NC/I/lxxxvi (map of wards, 1905).

which met monthly,[73] secured an Act to build a river wall and carry out other improvements and to enlarge Grove Park, by a transfer from Brentford U.D., in 1911.[74] Chiswick's wards remained unchanged in 1927, when Brentford added its own east, central, and west wards to form Brentford and Chiswick U.D., which was incorporated as a municipal borough in 1932.[75] The borough retained its 9 wards[76] until it joined Heston and Isleworth M.B. and Feltham U.D. in 1965, forming the eastern part of the London Borough of Hounslow.[77] Whereas Conservatives had controlled Brentford and Chiswick B.C.,[78] the Labour party controlled Hounslow except between 1968 and 1971.[79]

LONDON BOROUGH OF HOUNS-LOW. *Parted fesswise azure and gules a fess wavy argent charged with two others wavy azure, in chief two wings argent joined together and charged with a sword or with point upward, and in base a lion rampant guardant parted fesswise or and argent* [Granted 1965]

The offices of the local board and of the U.D. were at the vestry hall on the south side of Turnham Green. Designed by W. J. Treherne, it was an Italianate building of yellow brick with stone dressings and included a hall seating 700.[80] Enlargements were planned by the overseers in 1896 before it was vested in the U.D.C., which temporarily used Sutton Court while enlarging the vestry hall, reopened as the town hall in 1901.[81] After the establishment of Hounslow L.B. the premises were used chiefly for the registration of births, deaths, and marriages.

Under the Redistribution of Seats Act, 1885, Chiswick formed part of the Ealing division of Middlesex.[82] A Conservative or Unionist was returned, often unopposed, until the formation of Brentford and Chiswick parliamentary constituency in 1919. Unionists were elected in the period between the World Wars but thereafter the seat remained marginal, returning a Labour member in 1945, 1966, and 1970, and a Conservative at other elections. From 1974 Chiswick has formed part of Brentford and Isleworth, represented by a Conservative.[83]

PUBLIC SERVICES. Nursing was provided for the poor by 1660, when the vestry sent one patient to St. Bartholomew's hospital and another to St. Thomas's hospital (Southwark) and when a doctor gave individual treatment.[84] A salary for medical attendance at the workhouse was paid before 1823, the recipient being described as 'house surgeon' in 1825.[85] The vestry considered providing a place for diseased paupers in 1793[86] but apparently did nothing, as a room at the workhouse had to be adapted for the sick in 1822.[87] Concerned at the number of inmates suffering from venereal disease, the parish subscribed annually to the Lock hospital (Westm.) from 1823.[88] Payments were also made to St. George's hospital (Westm.) in 1829.[89]

The Sisterhood of St. Mary and St. John cared for the incurable at St. Mary's convent, which was founded in Kensington in 1868 and moved to Burlington Lane in 1897. Sisters of the Society of St. Margaret took over the convent and its adjoining St. Joseph's hospital in 1910 and still managed them in 1979. The hospital had 48 beds for women and children in 1921, when a small nursing home for paying patients had also opened, and 36 beds for women in 1979.[90]

Chiswick Nursing Home and Institution, at nos. 449 and 451 High Road in 1908, was presumably a private establishment.[91] Chiswick isolation hospital, opened in Clayponds Lane, South Ealing, in 1904,[92] became a maternity hospital, serving both areas, in 1921.[93] A cottage hospital, endowed by Daniel Mason, opened in 1911 in Burlington Lane and moved in 1912 to a new building adjoining Rothbury House, Chiswick Mall. It was used for maternity cases in 1926, when nurses' accommodation was built and Rothbury House became an administrative block, and rebuilt in 1936.[94] As Chiswick hospital, a branch of the West Middlesex hospital at Isleworth, it was administered by the South-West Metropolitan Regional Hospital board under the National Health Act, 1948, and had 66 beds c. 1963.[95] The hospital was temporarily closed from 1975, when it was to be adapted as a psychiatric unit, and in 1979 lay within the Ealing, Hammersmith and Hounslow area of the North-West Thames Regional Health Authority.[96] There was a dispensary at no. 8 Heathfield Terrace, Turnham Green, in 1926 and a new health centre in Fisher's Lane north of the high road was in partial use from 1977.[97]

[73] *Kelly's Dir. Mdx.* (1908).
[74] 1 & 2 Geo. V, c. 112 (Local).
[75] *Census*, 1901–31; Brentford and Chiswick B.C. *Intro. to material illustrating hist. of Brentford and Chiswick* (1957), 19.
[76] Brentford and Chiswick, *Official Guide* [1963], 55.
[77] Lond. Govt. Act, 1963.
[78] Election results in *The Times*, 2 Nov. 1934, 3 Nov. 1936, 14 May 1949, 12 May 1950.
[79] Ibid. 9 May 1964, 10 May 1968, 14 May 1971, 4 May 1974, 6 May 1978.
[80] *Kelly's Dir. Mdx.* (1890).
[81] *Chiswick Times*, 2 Feb. 1900; 'Opening of town hall, 1901', 20.
[82] 48 & 49 Vic. c. 23.
[83] *Whitaker's Almanack* (1890 and later edns.).
[84] Chwdns. acct. bk. (1636–62); overseers' acct. bk. (1678–97), f. 6.

[85] Select vestry min. bk. (1822–5), ff. 27, 190.
[86] Vestry min. bk. (1777–1817), f. 89.
[87] Select vestry min. bk. (1820–2), f. 187.
[88] Ibid. (1822–5), f. 30.
[89] Ibid. (1828–32), f. 44.
[90] *Official Year Bk. of Ch. of Eng.* (1910 and later edns.); inf. from St. Joseph's hosp.
[91] *Kelly's Dir. Mdx.* (1908).
[92] Draper, *Chiswick*, 177.
[93] Below, Ealing, pub. svces.
[94] Draper, *Chiswick*, 179; *Kelly's Dir. Mdx.* (1926); *Brentford and Chiswick Times*, 27 Sept., 4 Oct. 1912; 6 Mar. 1936.
[95] Brentford and Chiswick, *Official Guide* (1948) [1963].
[96] *Brentford and Chiswick Times*, 20 Feb., 26 Mar. 1975; *Hospitals Year Bk.* (1978).
[97] *Kelly's Dir. Mdx.* (1926); *Brentford and Chiswick Times*, 10, 17 Nov. 1977.

Policing until the late 18th century was presumably left to the parish constables and the watch, who in 1680 stopped the earl of Pembroke's coach as it crossed Turnham Green but then failed to detain the earl after he killed a prominent resident.[98] By 1798 there was a Chiswick association for the protection of persons and property, whose 40 members in 1808 were headed by the duke of Devonshire. Subscribers paid 1 guinea initially and thereafter at least 5s. a year towards a fund, which was used to advertise rewards and defray the cost of prosecutions.[99] The association had been revived by 1827, when the richer districts paid for their own policing.[1] In 1828 there were horse patrols, apparently along the high road, where many crimes took place, and foot patrols over a wider area. Two parish constables worked during the day and as many as 4 patrolmen and 6 watchmen were employed privately at night, being responsible to the assistant overseer at the workhouse.[2] Chiswick was included in the Metropolitan Police Area from 1829[3] and lay within T division, with a station in High Road west of Windmill Place by 1871. It was superseded by one on the east corner of Windmill Place, manned by 73 policemen in 1890[4] and 131 in 1926.[5] A new police station, replacing buildings at the corner of Linden Gardens and High Road, was opened in 1972.[6]

A parish fire engine was to be repaired in 1781[7] and was the responsibility of the sexton and beadle in 1804,[8] being kept then or later in a shed near the church.[9] The local board employed a volunteer fire brigade, with contingents for Turnham Green and Chiswick, in 1888 and opened a new fire station, mortuary, and parish depot on the south side of the high road in 1891. The station had a new steam engine in 1891[10] and a motor fire escape and ambulance in 1911, when it was claimed to be one of the best equipped near London.[11] From 1937 the fire services in Chiswick High Road used a former market near by and the adjoining Linden House, before moving to a station which had replaced Christ Church Vicarage, Heathfield Gardens, in 1963.[12]

Water was to be supplied by the Grand Junction Waterworks Co. under an Act of 1861[13] and was obtained partly from that company but mainly from the West Middlesex Water Co. in 1888. A constant supply, as promised by the

West Middlesex Water Co. by 1895, had been provided for nearly every house by 1897.[14] Under the Metropolis Water Act, 1902, both companies were superseded in 1903 by the Metropolitan Water Board.[15]

Sewerage was perhaps the chief problem facing the improvement commissioners, whose successors in 1888–9 took pride in their having carried out an expensive scheme for sewage disposal.[16] The works and filter beds lay close to the Thames and south of Corney Lane, where a power station was later built.[17] From 1936, under the West Middlesex Sewerage and Sewage Disposal Scheme, the area was served by trunk sewers to the central works at Mogden, in Isleworth.[18]

Gas was to be supplied along Chiswick High Road by the new Brentford Gas Co. in 1821.[19] The company was taken over in 1926 by the Gas Light and Coke Co.,[20] which in 1948 still supplied gas from its Brentford works and by 1963 had been superseded by the North Thames Gas Board.[21] Many shopkeepers in the high road favoured electric lighting by 1890.[22] The Aberystwyth and Chiswick Electricity Supply Corporation agreed with the U.D.C. to supply electricity in 1898[23] and continued to do so until its Chiswick area was bought by the council in 1935.[24] After nationalization, services were maintained by the Southern Electricity Board.[25]

After adopting the Public Libraries Act, the local board opened a lending library in 1891.[26] A new building in Duke's Avenue was presented to the U.D.C. by Messrs. Sanderson in 1897 and was extended in 1901[27] and again, having been damaged by a fire from Sanderson's factory, in 1930. Exhibits from a small museum were moved to Gunnersbury House after the Second World War but the library retained its collections of books issued by the Chiswick Press and material on Hogarth in 1979.[28]

Waste lands along the high road were acquired by the local board under the Metropolitan Commons Act, 1866, and laid out for recreation, forming Turnham Green common and Chiswick (formerly the Back) common.[29] Homefields and adjoining land east of Chiswick Lane, totalling 10 a., were bought by the U.D.C. from the Ecclesiastical Commissioners in 1898, with help from the county council.[30] The U.D.C. administered Homefields recreation ground, 7½ a. of Turnham Green common, c. 11 a. of Chiswick

[98] Phillimore and Whitear, *Chiswick*, 57–62.
[99] Framed adverts. (1798, 1799, 1808) in Chiswick libr.
[1] Chiswick assoc., patrolmen's notebk. 1827–8, in Chiswick libr.; inf. from Mr. J. Wisdom.
[2] Ibid.; *Rep. of Sel. Cttee. on Police of Metropolis*, H.C. 533, pp. 217, 219, 406–7 (1828), vi.   [3] 10 Geo. IV, c. 44.
[4] O.S. Map 1/2,500, Mdx. XXI. 2 (1871 and 1894–6 edns.); *Kelly's Dir. Mdx.* (1890).
[5] *Kelly's Dir. Mdx.* (1926).
[6] Draper, *Chiswick*, preface.
[7] Vestry min. bk. (1777–1817).   [8] Ibid. f. 272.
[9] Draper, *Chiswick*, 167.
[10] Chiswick local bd. *Ann. Rep.* (1888–9), 45–6; (1891–2), 30, 49.
[11] *Official Guide to Chiswick* [1911], 16; Draper, *Chiswick*, 177.
[12] O.S. Map 1/2,500, Mdx. XXI. 2 (1935 and 1948 revns.); Draper, *Chiswick*, preface.   [13] 24 & 25 Vic. c. 151.
[14] Chiswick local bd. *Ann. Rep.* (1888–9), 38; Chiswick U.D.C. *Ann. Rep.* (1894–5), 11; (1896–7), 93.

[15] L. J. Flowerdew and G. C. Berry, *London's Water Supply, 1903–53*, 15–16 and map facing p. 22.
[16] Chiswick improvement cttee. min. bks. (1858–83), *passim*; Chiswick local bd. *Ann. Rep.* (1888–9), 23; Chiswick libr., NC/I/lxviii (plan of sewerage and lighting, 1905).
[17] O.S. Map 6″, Mdx. XXI. NW. (1894–6 edn.).
[18] C. Radcliffe, *Mdx.* (2nd edn. c. 1951), 148–9.
[19] 1 & 2 Geo. IV, c. 69 (Local).
[20] *V.C.H. Mdx.* iv. 249.
[21] Brentford and Chiswick, *Official Guide* (1948); ibid. [1963].
[22] Chiswick local bd. *Ann. Rep.* (1891–2), 29.
[23] Chiswick U.D.C. *Ann. Rep.* (1898–9), 16.
[24] *The Times*, 16 Mar. 1935; 26 June 1935.
[25] Brentford and Chiswick, *Official Guide* [1963].
[26] Chiswick local bd. *Ann. Rep.* (1890–1), 8; (1891–2), 56.
[27] *Kelly's Dir. Mdx.* (1908).
[28] Draper, *Chiswick*, preface.
[29] *Kelly's Dir. Mdx.* (1908).
[30] Chiswick U.D.C. *Ann. Rep.* (1896–7), 12; (1898–9), 15.

common, 2½ a. of Stamford Brook common, and 1 a. at Strand-on-the-Green in 1911, when it planned to buy c. 11 a. by the river at Grove Park.[31] Land bought from the duke of Devonshire was consecrated as a cemetery in 1888,[32] a chapel being built in 1898,[33] and the grounds of Chiswick House formed a public park of c. 66 a. from 1929.[34] Additional open space in the southern part of the parish was used by schools or for private sports grounds.[35]

Open-air swimming baths beside Duke's Meadows, in Edensor Road, were open in 1911, when the council claimed to have pioneered mixed bathing.[36] Fashionable with Londoners in the 1920s, they were extended in 1931.[37]

CHURCHES. In 1181 the canons of St. Paul's had a church for their manor of Sutton,[38] where there was a vicar by 1241.[39] As a peculiar of St. Paul's, the church was normally exempt from episcopal jurisdiction both before and after the Reformation.[40] It served the whole parish until the establishment of its first daughter church, at Turnham Green, in 1845.[41]

Vicars were presented by the chapter of St. Paul's,[42] until in 1502 part of their Chiswick estate was formally assigned to the dean so long as he should be a residentiary.[43] As lord of Sutton Court and rector, except during the Interregnum, the dean reserved the advowson when leasing the manor from the 16th[44] until the late 18th century.[45] Thereafter the patronage has been exercised by the chapter.[46]

St. Paul's apparently had appropriated the church and farmed it by 1181, having endowed it with glebe, tithes from the tenants except hay, and ⅓ of the tithes of the two demesnes.[47] The vicar, who may have had the hay tithes in 1181, received one mark a year from the chamberlain in 1252, in addition to altar dues,[48] and 1297.[49] The vicarage was not wealthy, being assessed at £5 in 1291[50] and valued at £9 18s. 1d. in 1535.[51] In 1458 many tithes were withheld, including tithes

of sheaves by the lessee of Sutton and various small tithes by the lessee of the prebendal estate.[52] When the rectory as a whole was thought to be worth £40 in 1549, the vicar had only £10.[53] Small tithes were paid to the vicar in 1589–90[54] and amounted to £25 a year in 1650, when the house was valued at £3 and the glebe, which was leased, at £27.[55] An allowance of £60 a year was made to the minister out of the impropriated tithes in 1658.[56] Lord Fauconberg, as lessee of Sutton Court manor, successfully claimed tithes of pulse and hay which had been paid to the vicar.[57] Later lessees, at least from 1731, paid an extra £10 annual rent to augment the living.[58] The gross income was £601 in 1835,[59] and had risen to £686 by 1851,[60] after £420 a year had been awarded in 1846 in lieu of small tithes.[61]

The glebe comprised 16½ a. of arable and 1 a. of meadow in 1181,[62] 12 a. of arable and 1 a. of meadow in 1252,[63] and 14 a. of arable and 1 a. of meadow in 1297.[64] It was estimated at 20 a. of arable in 1458,[65] at 15 a. in Chiswick field, a further 4 a. of arable, 1 a. of meadow, and a ½-a. close in 1589–90[66] and 22 a. in 1649.[67] Probably the same land was held by the vicar in 1846; the glebe then amounted to c. 20 a., of which c. 19 a. were market garden west of the later Devonshire Road.[68] The land remained glebe in 1887,[69] although Glebe Street and neighbouring roads had already been built there.[70]

A vicarage house had been repaired by 1297.[71] It has been suggested that it was the medieval prebendal manor house,[72] although prebendaries apparently had no interest in the vicarage. By 1590 the vicar held 'the corner house on the east side of the street towards the Thames',[73] presumably the house which was dilapidated in 1650,[74] rebuilt in brick in 1658, and repaired in 1698.[75] It was replaced in the 18th century by a three-storeyed, stuccoed building, later extended to the north and with a bow window facing Chiswick Mall, which remained the Vicarage until 1974.[76] The vicar was excused all parish rates on his house in 1792, in return for waiving

[31] Official Guide to Chiswick [1911], 18.
[32] Chiswick local bd. Ann. Rep. (1888–9), 43.
[33] Chiswick U.D.C. Ann. Rep. (1898–9), 17.
[34] J. Charlton, Chiswick Ho. (guidebk. 1958), 15; Brentford and Chiswick, Official Guide (1948), 30.
[35] Above, social.
[36] Official Guide to Chiswick [1911], 24.
[37] The Times, 4 May 1931; Brentford and Chiswick Times, 26 Aug. 1949.
[38] Domesday of St. Paul's (Camd. Soc. [1st ser.], lxix), 151; printed with transl. in Phillimore and Whitear, Chiswick, 124–9, and transl. in Draper, Chiswick, 195–7.
[39] Hist. MSS. Com. 7, 8th Rep. I, Queen Anne's Bounty, p. 632b.
[40] V.C.H. Mdx. i. 139; Guildhall MS. 9557, f. 29.
[41] Below. St. Jas., Gunnersbury, serving part of Chiswick west of Gunnersbury sta., is treated with Brentford chs. under Ealing.
[42] Hennessy, Nov. Rep. 124.
[43] Sparrow Simpson, Registrum Sancti Pauli, 211.
[44] M.R.O., Acc. 531/66, f. 6.
[45] Guildhall MS. 11816, ff. 235, 238; M.R.O., Acc. 531/68.
[46] Rep. Com. Eccl. Revenues, 640; Crockford (1973–4).
[47] Draper, Chiswick, 195–6.
[48] Phillimore and Whitear, Chiswick, 101.
[49] Visitations of Chs. belonging to St. Paul's (Camd. Soc. N.S. lv), 58; printed with transl. in Phillimore and Whitear, Chiswick, 101–5.
[50] Tax. Eccl. (Rec. Com.), 19.

[51] Valor Eccl. (Rec. Com.), i. 434.
[52] Phillimore and Whitear, Chiswick, 110–11.
[53] P.R.O., E 301/34, no. 143.
[54] M.R.O., Acc. 531/66, f. 2.
[55] Home Counties Mag. i. 224.
[56] Phillimore and Whitear, Chiswick, 86.
[57] P.R.O., E 126/13, ff. 281–2.
[58] M.R.O., Acc. 531/68.
[59] Rep. Com. Eccl. Revenues, 641.
[60] P.R.O., HO 129/134/4/1/2.
[61] M.R.O., TA/CHI.
[62] Draper, Chiswick, 196.
[63] Phillimore and Whitear, Chiswick, 101.
[64] Ibid. 105.
[65] Ibid. 111.   [66] M.R.O., Acc. 531/66, f. 13.
[67] Guildhall MS. 11816, f. 237.
[68] M.R.O., TA/CHI; see also Guildhall Libr., map case 305 (map of 1818).
[69] Return of Glebe Lands, H.C. 307, p. 84 (1887), lxiv.
[70] P.R.O., ED 7/88.
[71] Phillimore and Whitear, Chiswick, 105.
[72] Draper, Chiswick, 48.
[73] M.R.O., Acc. 531/66, f. 13.
[74] Home Counties Mag. i. 224.
[75] Chwdns. acct. bk. (1636–62); Phillimore and Whitear, Chiswick, 4; C. Brooke Coles, Chiswick Par. Ch. (booklet c. 1965), 12.
[76] Brooke Coles, Chiswick Par. Ch. 12; Pevsner, Mdx. 36; inf. from the chwdn.

his fees at paupers' burials.[77] In 1979 he lived in a smaller house next to the Old Vicarage, which had been divided and sold.[78]

The first recorded vicar John Belemains or Belemus (d. 1252) was also prebendary of Chiswick in St. Paul's cathedral.[79] No later vicar held that prebend, although other prebends in the cathedral were held by Thomas Spateman, vicar 1732–61, Thomas Hughes, 1808–9,[80] E. C. Rich, 1934–45, and G. A. Lewis Loyd, 1954–74.[81]

There were altars in 1297 to St. Catherine, St. Margaret, St. Mary Magdalene, and St. Mary the Virgin, at the last of which a perpetual light was to be endowed.[82] No lights were recorded later. In 1458 the vicar's 20 a. were supposed to support a boy to assist at daily services; the vicarage was leased and there was a parish priest to celebrate on feast days.[83] In 1644 Beriah Packington was sequestrated in favour of 'an honest preaching minister'.[84] There was an assistant curate in 1673[85] and normally at least one from the mid 19th century. The curate in 1737 was Thomas Hartley (1709?–84), translator of Swedenborg.[86] Arthur Coham, vicar 1761–81, was also a canon of Salisbury and archdeacon of Wiltshire.[87] James Trebeck, vicar 1781–1808, was active in local affairs[88] while also rector of St. Michael, Queenhithe (Lond.), another living of St. Paul's.[89] In 1787 he presided over a vestry which attacked gambling and tried to enforce Sunday observance on shopkeepers.[90] As a place of fashion, Chiswick by 1784 had an afternoon lecturer, chosen by the vestry with the vicar's consent.[91] One lecturer was Henry Francis Cary (1772–1844), translator of Dante[92] and from 1814 tenant of Hogarth's former house.[93]

In 1851, when 250 out of the 1,300 sittings were free, there was a morning attendance of 517 and an afternoon attendance of 334, on each occasion including c. 60 Sunday school children.[94] In 1866, when the chapel of St. Mary Magdalene was served from the mother church, and in the 1970s, after the demolition of St. Mary Magdalene, the vicar of Chiswick had three assistant curates.[95] Attendances in 1903 were 503 in the morning and 461 in the evening.[96] An Anglo-Catholic tradition was maintained in 1979.[97]

The church of *ST. NICHOLAS*, at the south-east end of Church Street, had no dedication in 1252[98] but, presumably because it was near the river,[99] had been dedicated to the patron saint of fishermen by 1548.[1] It consists of a chancel, north vestry, north and south chapels, nave with north and south aisles and porches, and three-stage west tower,[2] with an embattled parapet and spirelet. The tower, of Kentish ragstone with freestone dressings, was built by William Bordall, vicar 1416–35, according to a lost brass[3] and a 17th-century tablet. The older body of the church was largely rebuilt in the 15th or 16th century, the chancel roof having been in bad repair in 1252, mended by 1297, and again in poor condition in 1458. Part of the fabric was derelict c. 1650, when a south aisle was built,[4] and Sir Stephen Fox in 1711 claimed to have paid for expensive repairs.[5] Galleries were added when new aisles of brick, with round-headed windows, were built on the south side in 1772 and the north in 1817.[6] Apart from the tower, the entire church was rebuilt between 1882 and 1884 in the Perpendicular style by J. L. Pearson, the main cost being borne by Henry Smith.[7] A cramped site, between the tower and Church Street, led Pearson to design the nave with a breadth nearly equal to its length.

Fittings include a screen, extended in 1909 to form the south aisle chapel, and pulpit, both by W. D. Caroë. The south wall of the chapel contains glass from the east window of the old church, probably 18th-century[8] and said to come from Cologne cathedral, the chancel contains a window attributed to W. Burges, also from the old church, and some of the other windows are by Clayton & Bell. There are brass inscriptions to Mary (d. 1599), wife of Richard Barker, and Anne [d. 1607], widow of William Barker, both of which were moved in 1882.[9] Other monuments include a pavilion with kneeling effigies in alabaster of the naturalist Sir Thomas Chaloner (d. 1615)[10] and his wife, a wrongly dated plaque to William Bordall erected in 1631 by Francis Russell, earl of Bedford, and memorials to the actor Charles Holland (d. 1769) by W. Tyler, to the porcelain manufacturer Thomas Bentley (d. 1780)[11] by Thomas Scheemakers, and to Thomas Tomkins (d. 1816) by Sir Francis Chantrey.[12]

The churchyard, which was enlarged by John de Bray in 1349,[13] was later used for the burial of

[77] Vestry min. bk. (1777–1817), f. 77.
[78] Inf. from the chwdn.
[79] Brooke Coles, *Chiswick Par. Ch.* 27; Le Neve, *Fasti, 1066–1300, St. Paul's, Lond.* 42, 84.
[80] Le Neve, *Fasti, 1541–1857, St. Paul's, Lond.* 31, 54.
[81] *Crockford* (1935, 1965–6).
[82] Phillimore and Whitear, *Chiswick*, 104–5.
[83] Ibid. 110–11.
[84] *Walker Revised*, 261; *Home Counties Mag.* i. 224.
[85] Guildhall MS. 9537/20, f. 33.
[86] *D.N.B.*
[87] W. H. Jones, *Fasti Ecclesiae Sarisberiensis*, i (1879), 177.
[88] Vestry min. bk. (1777–1817), *passim*.
[89] A. H. Stenning and G. F. Russell Barker, *Rec. of Old Westminsters*, ii (1928), 926.
[90] Vestry min. bk. (1777–1817), f. 55.
[91] Ibid. ff. 35, 121, 164.
[92] *D.N.B.*
[93] Guildhall MS. 14219/8, ff. 299–300.
[94] P.R.O., HO 129/134/4/1/2.
[95] *Clergy List* (1866 and later edns.); *Crockford* (1973–4).
[96] Mudie-Smith, *Rel. Life*, 435.
[97] Inf. from the Revd. A. Long.
[98] *Camd. Misc.* ix (Camd. Soc. N.S. liii), 8; printed with transl. in Phillimore and Whitear, *Chiswick*, 98–101.
[99] Brooke Coles, *Chiswick Par. Ch.* 4.
[1] *Visitations of Chs. belonging to St. Paul's*, 110; printed with transl. in Phillimore and Whitear, *Chiswick*, 106–11.
[2] *T.L.M.A.S.* xviii (2), no. 14. Rest of para. and next para. based on Brooke Coles, *Chiswick Par. Ch.*
[3] J. Weaver, *Antient Funeral Monuments* (1767), 296.
[4] Bowack's account in Phillimore and Whitear, *Chiswick*, 3.
[5] W.A.M. 16680.
[6] Faulkner, *Brentford, Ealing and Chiswick*, 310. Several views of the ch., from 1750, are in Guildhall Libr., granger-ized copy of Lysons, *Environs*, ii, between pp. 198 and 199.
[7] Plans of the ch., before and after 1882, are in Chiswick libr.
[8] Hist. Mon. Com. *Mdx.* 7.
[9] *T.L.M.A.S.* xvii. 207–9. [10] *D.N.B.*
[11] Ibid.
[12] Gunnis, *Dict. Sculptors*, 95, 344, 404.
[13] *Cal. Pat.* 1348–50, 277.

many non-parishioners[14] and was further extended in 1805 and, by the dukes of Devonshire, in 1838 and 1871.[15] It stands higher than the road and contains a 13th-century coffin lid of Purbeck marble, a table tomb of Thomas Carey (d. 1694) and another reputedly designed by William Kent for Lord Burlington's bricklayer Richard Wright (d. 1734), an urn on a tall pedestal above the grave of William Hogarth, the small mausoleum of P. J. de Loutherbourg (d. 1812)[16] by Sir John Soane, and the former tomb of the Italian poet Ugo Foscolo (d. 1827), besides the tombs of William Kent, Charles Holland, and the painter J. A. M. Whistler.[17]

There are eight bells, (iii) to (vii) by Knight of Reading having been hung in 1656,[18] presumably in place of the five bells recorded in 1552. Most of the plate, perhaps including items recorded in 1552,[19] was stolen in 1785[20] and replaced in 1786[21] by two silver flagons, a cup, and spoon, given by the duke of Devonshire, and four dishes, one of them given by Georgiana, duchess of Devonshire. The church retained the plate, with later pieces and a silver cup ascribed to 1747, the gift of Robert Stevenson,[22] in 1979. The registers begin in 1678.[23]

ALL SAINTS' mission church, Chiswick Lane.[24] Attendance 1903: 148 a.m.; 157 p.m. Red brick bldg. 1901, seating 400.[25] Run by London Diocesan Home Mission 1926, closed by 1935.[26]

CHRIST CHURCH, Turnham Green. Dist. formed 1845 from Chiswick.[27] Patron from 1858 bp. of London.[28] One asst. curate 1866 and 1935, none in 1947. Attendance 1851: 468 a.m. (inc. Sunday sch. 138); 416 p.m. (inc. Sunday sch. 36);[29] 1903: 527 a.m.; 585 p.m. Bldg. of flint with stone dressings in early Gothic style, on former common land:[30] W. tower, spire, nave, N. and S. aisles, N. and S. transepts 1843 by G. G. Scott and W. B. Moffatt, seating 930;[31] chancel and NE. chapel 1887 by J. Brooks. Mission in Nat. sch., High Rd., attendance 1903: 340 a.m.

ST. MARY MAGDALENE, Bennett St. Chapel blt. 1848 at expense of J. C. Sharpe. Served from Chiswick 1862, gratuitously by a min. 1867.[32] Dist. formed 1894 from Chiswick.[33] Patron V. of Chiswick, from 1898 dean and chapter of St. Paul's.[34] No asst. curate 1926, two

in 1935. Attendance 1851: 93 a.m. (inc. Sunday sch. 82); 121 p.m. (inc. Sunday sch. 36);[35] 1903: 257 a.m.; 249 p.m. A. Tooth, min. 1867, later imprisoned for ritualism.[36] Stone bldg. 1848 by J. C. Sharpe, seating 300. Rebuilt with chancel, SE. chapel, nave, N. aisle, and NW. bell-turret 1894 by Newman & Newman, seating 500.[37] Damaged in Second World War, demol. with Chiswick New Town, and replaced by St. Nicholas's church hall 1956.[38] Benefice united with St. Nicholas 1954.[39]

ST. MICHAEL, Elmwood Rd., known as St. Michael, Sutton Court.[40] Dist. assigned from Chiswick and Christ Church, Turnham Green, 1906 and 1907.[41] Bldg. funds from sale of St. Michael, Burleigh St. (demol. 1906), a chapel of ease to St. Martin-in-the-Fields. Patron V. of St. Martin-in-the-Fields, whose son was first V. of St. Michael's. Iron church in Elmwood Rd. built 1908 and used as hall from 1909. Red brick bldg. in a Tudor style 1909 by W. D. Caroë, seating c. 350: chancel, SE. chapel, timber E. tower, nave, N. and S. aisles. Lectern, font, and other fittings from St. Michael, Burleigh St.

ST. MICHAEL AND ALL ANGELS, Bath Rd., Bedford Pk. Dist. formed 1879 from Chiswick, All Saints, S. Acton, and St. George, Old Brentford. Patrons benefactors Revd. Alfred Wilson and J. T. Carr for first turn, bp. of London thereafter.[42] One asst. curate 1905 and 1955–6, none in 1961–2. Attacked as High Church 1880.[43] Attendance 1903: 409 a.m.; 205 p.m. Iron church N. end Chiswick Lane used 1876–8.[44] Red brick bldg. with stone dressings and white timberwork, the lower part in a Perpendicular style. Raised chancel, SE. chapel, timber E. bellcot, nave, and S. aisle 1879, by R. Norman Shaw; N. aisle 1889, SW. chapel 1909, by Maurice B. Adams.[45] Glass in SE. chapel 1915, by M. Travers. Mission in Back Common Rd., attendance 1903: 27 p.m. Vicarage 1880, by E. J. May.

ST. PAUL, Grove Park Rd. Dist. formed 1872 from Chiswick and Christ Church, Turnham Green.[46] Patron V. of Chiswick.[47] One asst. curate 1905 and 1926, two in 1961–2 and 1965–6, none in 1973–4. Attendance 1903: 324 a.m.; 212 p.m. Iron church used 1870–2. Stone bldg. in a Gothic style 1872 by H. Currey, blt.

[14] Lysons, *Environs*, ii. 208.
[15] Vestry min. bk. (1777–1817), ff. 292, 306; plaques on walls.   [16] *D.N.B.*
[17] See also TS. list of tombs in Chiswick libr.
[18] Brooke Coles, *Chiswick Par. Ch.* 24.
[19] *T.L.M.A.S.* xxv. 297.
[20] Draper, *Chiswick*, 93–4.
[21] Vestry min. bk. (1777–1817), f. 43.
[22] Freshfield, *Communion Plate*, 7.
[23] Marriages 1678–1800 are in Phillimore and Whitear, *Chiswick*, 181–243. In 1979 the regs. were at the church.
[24] For the 19th- and 20th-century churches below, inf. about asst. curates is from *Clergy List* (1859 and later edns.); *Crockford* (1926 and later edns.); architectural descriptions based on *T.L.M.A.S.* xviii (2); attendance figs. 1903 from Mudie-Smith, *Rel. Life*, 435. For abbreviations see above, p. 37 n. 68.
[25] *Kelly's Dir. Mdx.* (1908).
[26] *Crockford* (1926, 1935).
[27] *Lond. Gaz.* 20 Apr. 1845, p. 1292.
[28] Hennessy, *Nov. Rep.* 124.
[29] P.R.O., HO 129/134/4/1/1.
[30] Guildhall MS. 14236/19, ff. 131–2.

[31] P.R.O., HO 129/134/4/1/1.
[32] *Kelly's Dir. Mdx.* (1852, 1862, 1867).
[33] *Lond. Gaz.* 28 Aug. 1894, p. 4994.
[34] *Return of Parishes Divided, 1891–6*, H.C. 302, p. 10 (1897), lxvii (6).
[35] P.R.O., HO 129/134/4/1/3.
[36] O. Chadwick, *Victorian Ch.* ii (1970), 348; *The Times*, 23 Jan. 1877.
[37] *Return of Pars. Divided, 1891–6*, 10.
[38] Foundation stone of hall; inf. from Mr. J. Wisdom.
[39] Coles, *Chiswick Par. Ch.* 27.
[40] Para. based on T. P. Singer, *Short Hist. Chiswick, Sutton Ct., and Par. of St. Mic.* (booklet 1935) and inf. from the vicar.
[41] *Kelly's Dir. Mdx.* (1926).
[42] *Lond. Gaz.* 31 Oct. 1879, p. 6180.
[43] Bolsterli, *Bedford Pk.* 65.
[44] Hist. notice in ch.
[45] Cuttings in Chiswick libr.; inf. from Mr. G. E. T. Holloway. 'The best ch. roof Shaw designed': Saint, *Ric. Norman Shaw*, 210.
[46] *Lond. Gaz.* 13 Aug. 1872, p. 3610.
[47] Hennessy, *Nov. Rep.* 125.

largely at expense of duke of Devonshire and seating 500–600:[48] chancel, lady chapel (converted to vestry room after damage in Second World War),[49] nave, N. and S. aisles, W. bellcot.

ROMAN CATHOLICISM. Only one recusant was reported at Chiswick in 1577.[50] Five recusants in 1628 included Sir William Foster, Edward Leigh, and William Saunders.[51] Leigh and Saunders were later described as gentlemen and they or members of their families thereafter were repeatedly indicted until 1640.[52] The three papists listed in 1706 included Sir Richard Beeling or Bellings, who stayed only during the summer months[53] and who in 1711 leased the old prebendal manor house from Sir Stephen Fox.[54] A Mr. Thompson and his two servants were listed as recusants in 1708,[55] as were Sir Richard Beeling, his family, and seven other men c. 1714.[56]

Late 18th-century Roman Catholics included Henry Widdrington (d. 1774) of Turnham Green, heir of the attainted Jacobite William, Lord Widdrington (d. 1743),[57] Charles Tempest, a Jesuit who died at Chiswick in 1768,[58] and John Towneley of Corney House, who had a chapel there in 1791.[59] From 1799 local children were taken for baptism to Brook Green, Hammersmith, from where Chiswick continued to be served until 1848.[60]

An influx of Irish labourers, many of them gardeners, led to the opening of a day school and chapel in Windmill Place, Turnham Green.[61] The building, of 1848, was attended by 200 worshippers in the morning and 70 in the evening on census Sunday 1851, when its upper storey accommodated the schoolmaster and mistress.[62] The mission was said to serve over 1,000 in 1852, when it also used a small chapel in Acton,[63] and to be the poorest in the diocese in 1855. The Acton chapel, dedicated to Our Lady of Grace, had closed by 1856[64] and the Turnham Green mission was known as St. Mary's by 1858.[65] Its successor and other Roman Catholic places of worship are described below.

St. Joseph's, Grove Pk., originated in services at no. 1a Bolton Rd., bought c. 1944[66] as chapel of ease to Our Lady of Grace and St. Edward.[67] Red brick building with pantiled roof on adjoining site, seating 200,[68] registered 1961.[69]

St. Mary's church opened 1864[70] on land bought by 1855 at W. corner Duke's Ave. and Chiswick High Rd.,[71] replacing Windmill Place chapel. Low building in Gothic style, with sanctuary to S.; demolished 1885.[72]

Our Lady of Grace, on site of St. Mary's and known as Our Lady of Grace and St. Edward by 1903,[73] registered 1886.[74] Attendance 1903: 864 a.m.; 392 aft.[75] Deep red brick bldg. in Italianate style, with sanctuary to S., by Kelly & Birchall. Campanile added as war mem. c. 1936; restoration after war damage 1955. Seated 400, 1978.[76]

Chiswick Ho. oratory blt. by marquess of Bute, tenant, c. 1881.[77]

Sisters of Mary Immaculate acquired no. 10 Chiswick Lane as Regina Pacis convent 1968. Kindergarten opened 1969 and hall added 1972.[78]

Sisters of Nazareth apparently acquired St. Veronica's retreat, Chiswick Sq., between 1911 and 1913. Renamed Nazareth House until sisters'[79] move to Finchley 1921.[80]

Sisters of Perpetual Adoration occupied Tower House, no. 4 Chiswick Lane, as convent of Marie Réparatrice, c. 1901–51.[81] Adoratrices (? same community) registered ground floor of no. 34 Barrowgate Rd. as convent chapel 1963–71.[82]

Sisters of Verona acquired no. 4 Chiswick Lane 1951, added wing 1959, and used it as order's training centre 1978. Girls' hostel and nursery school opened at no. 2 Chiswick Lane 1951.[83]

St. Veronica's retreat by 1893–4 in former Boston Ho., Chiswick Sq.,[84] which had been acquired 1889 by Cardinal Manning and other trustees,[85] was conducted by Revd. Robt. Clarke 1900. Probably replaced by Sisters of Nazareth c. 1912.[86]

PROTESTANT NONCONFORMITY. Thomas Case, formerly rector of St. Giles-in-the-Fields, and William Low, who had been ejected as a preacher at Hereford, were both licensed as Presbyterians when at Chiswick in 1672.[87] George Fox made several visits to

[48] Kelly's Dir. Mdx. (1890).
[49] Inf. from the vicar.
[50] Catholic Rec. Soc. xxii. 48.
[51] Mdx. County Rec. iii. 20.
[52] Ibid. 144, 147, 153 and passim.
[53] Guildhall MS. 9800.
[54] W.A.M. 16680.
[55] M.R.O., MR/RR 11/4.
[56] Ibid. 19/13. Beeling was listed as Bellingham.
[57] Complete Peerage, xii (2), 629–30.
[58] G. Anstruther, Seminary Priests, iv (1977), 276.
[59] M.R.O., MR/RH 4–5.
[60] [M.D. Groarke], Par. Hist. of Our Lady of Grace, Chiswick (1967), 7, 27, in Chiswick libr.
[61] Ibid. 9.
[62] P.R.O., HO 134/4/1/6.
[63] Catholic Dir. (1852).
[64] Ibid. (1855, 1856).
[65] G.R.O. Worship Reg. no. 8464.
[66] Inf. from the parish priest.
[67] Catholic Dir. (1951).
[68] Inf. from the parish priest.

[69] G.R.O. Worship Reg. no. 68052.
[70] Par. Hist. of Our Lady of Grace, 14; G.R.O. Worship Reg. no. 16114.
[71] Catholic Dir. (1855).
[72] Cuttings in Chiswick libr., local prints.
[73] Mudie-Smith, Rel. Life, 436.
[74] G.R.O. Worship Reg. no. 29525.
[75] Mudie-Smith, Rel. Life, 436.
[76] Par. Hist. of Our Lady of Grace, 17–22; inf. from the Revd. P. L. Gilburt.
[77] Par. Hist. of Our Lady of Grace, 13.
[78] Inf. from Sister Stefanina.
[79] Gilbert, Chiswick, 37; Kelly's Dir. Chiswick (1911, 1913, 1920–1). [80] V.C.H. Mdx. vi. 87.
[81] Kelly's Dir. Chiswick (1901–2 and later edns.); inf. from the regional superior, Verona Sisters.
[82] G.R.O. Worship Reg. no. 69079.
[83] Inf. from the regional superior.
[84] Kelly's Dir. Chiswick (1893–4).
[85] Guildhall MS. 14219/14, f. 20.
[86] Catholic Dir. (1900); Kelly's Dir. Chiswick (1911, 1913).
[87] Calamy Revised, 104, 329.

Chiswick, where he helped to find a schoolhouse for Anne Travers, between 1685 and 1690.[88] Meetings were held at the house of Obadiah Marriot, a minister, in 1689 and 1691.[89]

A building at Turnham Green was registered in 1809 by dissenters,[90] including one who in 1817 registered the boys' school near the Windmill as a place of instruction for Independents.[91] Part of Belmont House academy, also at Turnham Green, was registered for worship in 1821.[92] There were apparently two protestant nonconformist chapels, both of them Independent, in 1851, when neither had a congregation as large as that of the Roman Catholic mission.[93] By 1890 most of the leading denominations had acquired premises[94] and by 1903 the largest sect was the Baptists, with 903 attendances on one Sunday; varying Methodist worshippers then totalled 479, attenders at an evangelistic mission in Fraser Street numbered 333, and Congregationalists 318.[95] Arrivals in the period between the World Wars included Christian Scientists, Seventh Day Adventists, and Mormons. Falling attendances among the older congregations led to the closure of several churches, in Chiswick and elsewhere, after the Second World War.[96]

CONGREGATIONALISTS.[97] Independents, said to have formed mtg. 1812, leased bldg. near S. side Chiswick Lane as chapel and Sunday sch. 1831. Replaced 1841 by pedimented bldg., with round-headed windows, containing chapel seating 350 and schoolroom overhead.[98] Attendance 1851, when known as Chiswick dissenting chapel: 192 a.m.; 28 aft.; 114 p.m.[99] After numbers had dwindled, chapel acquired by Bapts. 1866.[1]

Strand chapel, Strand-on-the-Green, blt. 1833 and used on weekdays as British sch. Attendance 1851, when it seated c. 92 and served a neighbourhood 'destitute . . . of religious obligation': 50 a.m.; 44 aft.; 30 p.m.[2] Closed by 1903.

Turnham Green or Gunnersbury Cong. church originated in mtgs. in lecture hall from 1873. Hall burnt down 1875, plot bought S. side Chiswick High Rd.,[3] and new church reg. 1882.[4] Attendance 1903: 157 a.m.; 161 p.m. Church, of stock brick with stone dressings in the Early English style, seated c. 450 and inc. classrooms on lower floor.[5] From 1963 church leased as a

store and in 1978 awaited demolition (between nos. 345 and 347). Services held in a hall 1963–74; cong. joined Brentford Cong. ch. (q.v.) and Presbs. 1972 as Chiswick United Reformed church.[6]

METHODISTS. Chiswick Meth. church, Sutton Court Rd., originated in mtgs. of Hammersmith Wes. circuit in Chiswick by 1845, in shops off High Rd. c. 1865 and c. 1876. Yellow-brick Sunday sch. chapel blt. 1880 on land given by duke of Devonshire.[7] Attendance 1903: 102 a.m.; 95 p.m. Red-brick church with stone dressings, in a Perpendicular style and with NE. tower, built N. of sch. chapel 1909, seating c. 800. Damaged in Second World War. Remained in use with older chapel as hall 1978.[8]

Strand-on-the-Green Wes. mtg. bef. 1880,[9] in mission room in Back Lane by 1887–8, mission ho. by 1901–2.[10] Attendance 1903: 70 p.m. Hammersmith circuit 1908. Closed by 1909.[11]

Primitive Meths. in former Cong. and Bapt. chapel in Chiswick Lane 1882 (demol. 1884),[12] in hall in Fisher's Lane 1884.[13] Attendance 1903: 95 a.m.; 117 p.m. Richmond circuit 1908.[14] Closed by bombing in Second World War.[15]

BAPTISTS. Chiswick Bapt. church originated in acquisition of former Cong. chapel in Chiswick Lane 1866. Moved to iron chapel E. side Annandale Rd. 1882 on land bought by J. T. Olney of Metropolitan Tabernacle,[16] seating 200[17] before extension 1893. Moved to rented hall in Turnham Green Terrace 1896 and to new church in Annandale Rd. 1897.[18] Attendance 1903: 235 a.m.; 276 p.m. Red-brick church with stone dressings, in a Gothic style, seating 625.[19] Remained in use 1978.

Gunnersbury Bapt. church,[20] begun in iron chapel of 1873, replaced by church S. side Wellesley Rd., opened 1877 and reg. by Union of Protestant Dissenters as Trinity Martyrs' Mem. church 1879.[21] Declared Bapt. 1885, in charge of London Bapt. Assoc. 1887. Attendance 1903: 151 a.m.; 241 p.m. Red-brick church with stone dressings in an Early English style, seating 650 from 1890.[22] Remained in use 1979, not in membership with Bapt. Union.[23] Lecture hall in Sutton Lane, blt. 1881 and reg. for worship 1897,[24] replaced by hall adjoining church in Wellesley Rd. 1931.

[88] *Short Jnl. and Itinerary Jnls. of Geo. Fox*, ed. N. Penney, 123, 127, 134, 145, 197, 208.
[89] *Calamy Revised*, 561; M.R.O., MJ/SBB 490/64.
[90] Guildhall MS. 9580/3.
[91] Ibid. 4. [92] Ibid. 6.
[93] P.R.O., HO 129/134/4/1/3; HO 129/134/4/1/4; HO 129/134/4/1/5.
[94] *Kelly's Dir. Mdx.* (1890).
[95] Mudie-Smith, *Rel. Life*, 435–6. [96] Below.
[97] For abbreviations used in the accounts of protestant nonconformist churches, see p. 40 n. 51. All attendance figs. 1903 are from Mudie-Smith, *Rel. Life*, 435–6.
[98] A. W. Savage, *Chiswick Bapt. Ch. 1866–1966*, 9–11.
[99] P.R.O., HO 129/134/4/1/5.
[1] *Chiswick Bapt. Ch.* 11, 13.
[2] P.R.O., HO 129/134/4/1/4.
[3] Cuttings in Chiswick libr., local prints.
[4] G.R.O. Worship Reg. no. 26144.
[5] *Kelly's Dir. Mdx.* (1890, 1908).
[6] *Brentford and Chiswick Times*, 29 Feb. 1969; 21 Sept. 1972; 24 Jan., 28 Feb. 1974.
[7] *Sutton Ct. Wes. Ch. Handbk. of Old Eng. Fair* (1923), in Chiswick libr.; inf. from Mr. W. P. Roe.
[8] *Meth. Ch. Sutton Ct. Rd. Jubilee Handbk.* [1959], 11–13; inf. from Mr. W. P. Roe.
[9] *Meth. Ch. Sutton Ct. Rd. Jubilee Handbk.* 10.
[10] *Kelly's Dir. Chiswick* (1887–8, 1901–2).
[11] *Kelly's Dir. Mdx.* (1908); *Kelly's Dir. Chiswick* (1909).
[12] Savage, *Chiswick Bapt. Ch.* 20.
[13] G.R.O. Worship Reg. no. 27721.
[14] *Kelly's Dir. Mdx.* (1908).
[15] *Meth. Ch. Sutton Ct. Rd. Jubilee Handbk.* 10.
[16] Savage, *Chiswick Bapt. Ch.* 11–12, 18–20.
[17] *Kelly's Dir. Mdx.* (1890).
[18] Savage, *Chiswick Bapt. Ch.* 25–7.
[19] *Kelly's Dir. Mdx.* (1908).
[20] Para. based on inf. from Mr. R. S. Jewell.
[21] G.R.O. Worship Reg. no. 24669.
[22] *Kelly's Dir. Mdx.* (1890).
[23] *Bapt. Union Dir.* (1977–8).
[24] G.R.O. Worship Reg. no. 35860.

REFORMED EPISCOPALIANS. Emmanuel Reformed Episcopal church reg. 1883[25] by branch of Protestant Episcopal Church of America,[26] as iron bldg. N. side Wellesley Rd., seating 550. Larger iron church in use from 1890,[27] when old bldg. became sch. room.[28] Attendance 1903: 129 a.m.; 98 p.m. Regular services ceased c. 1940. Church demol. 1949[29] and replaced by flats called Wellesley Court by 1978.

SALVATION ARMY. Chiswick hall, High Rd., reg. 1890. Still used 1895-6 but replaced by 1900 by Shaftesbury institute (later hall), William Street.[30] Attendance 1903: 24 a.m.; 42 p.m. Army moved by 1914 and reg. Clifton hall, Clifton Gardens, 1916, leaving between 1940 and 1964.[31]

OTHER DENOMINATIONS AND UNSPECIFIED MISSIONS. Undesignated Christians reg. no. 45 William Street 1861 but no longer used in 1895.[32]

Chiswick Mission, originally coffee-stall of R. T. Smith for Thornycrofts' workmen, later in Furze Street and then in Fraser Street, where iron bldg. reg. by unsectarian mission 1882 and brick bldg. reg. 1891.[33] Attendance 1903: 163 a.m.; 170 p.m. Yellow-brick bldg. with rendered gable end in Fraser Street still used 1978.

Plymouth Brethren used Clifton hall, Clifton Gardens, 1890[34] but apparently had left by 1903.

Shaftesbury ragged sch., William Street, reg. for unsectarian worship 1886. Replaced 1895 by Shaftesbury institute,[35] presumably bldg. used by Salvationists 1903.[36]

Robert Raikes mem. schs. mission and lecture hall, Sutton Lane, reg. by unspecified dissenters 1882 to 1895.[37]

Society of Friends first met at Chiswick Mission 1906, then in Fisher's Lane 1907 and Turnham Green Terrace.[38] Reg. nos. 15-17 Essex Place 1913 to 1924.[39]

Christian Scientists, previously in Twickenham, rented hall in Turnham Green Terrace 1920, called Tenth Church of Christ, Scientist, 1921 and First Church of Christ, Scientist, 1924. New church in Marlborough Rd. founded 1931 and reg. 1932; bldg., finished after Second World War, seated c. 100 1978.[40]

Chiswick Seventh Day Adventist church, S. side Bath Rd. but postal address Stamford Brook Rd. (Hammersmith), opened 1916, reg. 1932 and 1937, and burnt down 1971. Larger church of red brick and glass, seating 280, officially opened on same site 1974 and attended mainly by West Indians 1978.[41]

Crusader hall, blt. E. side Sutton Court Rd. 1926, replaced temporary accommodation and seated 150-200. Also used by Pentecostalists 1979.[42]

Church of Jesus Christ of Latter Day Saints reg. Ivy hall, Cambridge Rd., 1937, replacing it 1941 with no. 58 Wellesley Rd. and 1944 with room at no. 1A Chiswick Common Rd., which it had left by 1964.[43]

JUDAISM. Worshippers used Mulberry House, a Jewish orphanage at the corner of Barrowgate and Sutton Court roads, from 1953 and the hall of Christ Church in 1956.[44] Chiswick and District synagogue was affiliated to the United Synagogue from 1957,[45] registered at no. 64 Barrowgate Road in 1960,[46] and attended by c. 100 families in 1966.[47]

BUDDHISM. In 1964 a small relic of Buddha was enshrined[48] at no. 5 Heathfield Gardens, where in 1965 rooms were registered as the London Buddhist Vihara.[49] A single-storeyed library and meditation room were opened at the rear of the building in 1975.[50]

EDUCATION. A schoolhouse repaired in 1642-3 and 1663-4 probably was also used for vestry meetings, since it was to make way for a new vestry room by the church gate in 1691.[51] Presumably it had no successor until a charity school, also near the church, was founded in 1707.[52] Aided by legacies,[53] the school expanded until in 1813[54] the boys were rehoused at Turnham Green and in 1819, when it was a National school, the vicar claimed that Chiswick offered sufficient education for the poor.[55] Dissenters' schools, of which there were two by 1833,[56] proved short lived but perhaps prompted the foundation and enlargement of National schools for Turnham Green and Strand-on-the-Green, as did the opening of Turnham Green Roman Catholic school c. 1848.[57] From 1857 all

[25] Ibid. 27349.   [26] Chiswick Times, 20 Dec. 1895.
[27] Kelly's Dir. Mdx. (1890); G.R.O. Worship Reg. no. 31980.
[28] Chiswick Times, 20 Dec. 1895.
[29] Brentford and Chiswick Times, 4 Feb., 1 Apr. 1949; Chiswick libr., local prints.
[30] G.R.O. Worship Reg. no. 32347; Kelly's Dir. Chiswick (1895-6, 1899-1900).
[31] G.R.O. Worship Reg. nos. 39950, 46926.
[32] Ibid. 12107.
[33] Brentford and Chiswick Times, 28 Jan. 1966; G.R.O. Worship Reg. nos. 26612, 32706.
[34] Kelly's Dir. Mdx. (1890).
[35] G.R.O. Worship Reg. nos. 29383, 35051.
[36] Above.
[37] G.R.O. Worship Reg. no. 26371.
[38] Chiswick Times, 11 Jan. 1924.
[39] G.R.O. Worship Reg. no. 45913.
[40] Ibid. 48289, 49299, 53855; pamphlet for dedication svce. 1973; inf. from the clerk.

[41] G.R.O. Worship Reg. nos. 53703, 57454; inf. from the public relations sec.
[42] Inf. from Mr. R. W. Elgar.
[43] G.R.O. Worship Reg. nos. 57805, 59880, 60792.
[44] Brentford and Chiswick Times, 4 Mar. 1966.
[45] A. Newman, Utd. Synagogue, 1870-1970 (1976), 222.
[46] G.R.O. Worship Reg. no. 67866.
[47] Brentford and Chiswick Times, 4 Mar. 1966.
[48] The Times, 13, 19 Oct. 1964.
[49] G.R.O. Worship Reg. no. 69940.
[50] Chiswick and Brentford Gaz. 3 Apr. 1975.
[51] Chwdns. acct. bks. (1636-62, 1663-91).
[52] Individual schools are treated below.
[53] Char. sch. acct. bk. (1706-88) in Chiswick libr.
[54] Faulkner, Brentford, Ealing and Chiswick, 344.
[55] Educ. of Poor Digest, 534. The boys' branch of Chiswick Nat. schs. at Turnham Green has sometimes been confused with the later Turnham Green Nat. sch.
[56] Educ. Enq. Abstract, 557.
[57] Nat. Soc. files.

three of the parish's main settlements were served by National schools, which in the late 1860s catered for *c.* 1,000 children.[58]

A school board was elected in 1872, when, being predominantly Anglican,[59] it took over all the National schools with very little opposition. Although there was then no shortage of places, the spread of housing had led to overcrowding by 1876. Provision for the most populous areas started with the lease in 1874 of part of the new Glebe estate, where a school was opened in 1877, and continued at Turnham Green and Chiswick until a new school was opened in Hogarth Road in 1884. Overcrowding recurred in the 1890s at Strand-on-the-Green, where attendance was poor and where the school was enlarged, and Turnham Green, but the board's standards were generally held to be high.[60] From 1893 the endowments of Chiswick National school formed an educational charity, a branch of the parochial charities, to support a Sunday school.[61]

Chiswick U.D. became an autonomous part III authority, responsible for elementary education, under the Education Act of 1902. The school board accordingly was replaced in 1903 by the U.D.C.'s education committee, which was rebuked by the Board of Education for the lack of places.[62] Alleviation started with the opening of Belmont school in 1905 and was such that there was little overcrowding in the period between the World Wars, except briefly at the new Hogarth and Beverley Road infants' schools in the 1920s, before their extension. Between 1921 and 1931 the committee (from 1927 for Brentford and Chiswick) reorganized the boys' and girls' departments at Belmont, Hogarth, and Strand-on-the-Green schools into senior and junior mixed schools, on the lines of the Hadow Report. The area's first county secondary school was opened in 1916 and followed by Brentford and Chiswick's own central schools, in Staveley Road, in 1927.[63]

Under the Act of 1944 Brentford and Chiswick became an 'excepted district', responsible for both primary and secondary education. After primary schools for new estates had been opened in 1952, the Chiswick part of the borough in 1957 contained 10 primary schools: 2 junior mixed schools (Belmont and Strand-on-the-Green), 1 junior boys' and 1 junior girls' school (Hogarth), 2 junior mixed and infants' (the new Grove Park and Cavendish), and 4 infants' (Belmont, Beverley Road, Hogarth, and Strand-on-the-Green). There were also 5 secondary schools: a mixed secondary modern (Hogarth), boys' and girls' secondary moderns (Staveley Road), and boys' and girls' grammar schools (Chiswick County).[64] By 1964 Hogarth junior schools had been united, Hogarth senior school had closed,

and the transfer of St. Mary's R.C. school from Acton had brought Chiswick its sole voluntary aided school, although there were four such schools in Brentford.[65]

Hounslow L.B. succeeded as the education authority in 1965 and adopted a comprehensive scheme which in 1968 led to the amalgamation of the secondary modern and grammar schools.[66] In 1979, in addition to the comprehensive Chiswick school, there were 8 primary schools, 4 of them for juniors and infants, 2 for juniors alone, and 2 for infants alone.[67]

Public schools.[68] The general sources are those indicated above, p. 44, and the same abbreviations are used.

BELMONT PRIMARY, Belmont Rd. Opened 1905 as council schs. for BGI to replace Turnham Green Nat. 1919 accn. 354 B, 354 G, 396 I, a.a. 327 B, 325 G, 322 I. Also served as central sch. bef. opening of Staveley Rd. (q.v.) 1927. Reorg. 1931 for SM, JM, I. 1938 accn. 320 SM, 394 JM, 350 I, a.a. 159 SM, 245 JM, 183 I. SB, SG moved 1948 to Staveley Rd. JM and I amalg. 1969. Roll 1979: 159 and nursery class.

BEVERLEY RD. I. Opened 1926 on site of All Saints' ch.[69] as council sch. for 400 I. 1938 accn. 450, a.a. 262. Amalg. 1978 with Hogarth I (q.v.).

CAVENDISH PRIMARY, Edensor Rd. Opened 1952 for JMI. Roll 1979: 190.

CHISWICK BRITISH, Chiswick Lane. Opened by ? 1833 as Lancasterian sch. with 155 BG.[70] New bldg. 1836, blt. with parl. grant and vol. contributions, financed 1845 by vol. contributions and school pence (2*d.*).[71] Closed between 1852 and 1862.

CHISWICK COUNTY, Burlington Lane. Opened as county grammar schs. 1916 SG, 1926 SB. Co-ed. grammar sch. 1966. Amalg. 1968 with Staveley Rd. schs. as Chiswick sch. (q.v.).

CHISWICK NAT. Opened 1707[72] in churchyard as charity sch. for 25 B and 10 (later 25) G.[73] Trustees, first headed by Sir Stephen Fox and Sir John Chardin,[74] from 1717 inc. all subscribers of 40*s.* or more a year.[75] Financed by subscriptions, inc. from dukes of Devonshire from 1762,[76] sermons, and legacies: rent charge of £37 10*s.* in 1819 under will (pr. 1721) of Dorothy, Lady Capel, sums left by various donors recorded in 1785 but not thereafter, and interest on £100 from Robert Horley by will dated 1800 and £100 from Mrs. Elizabeth Blackshaw by will dated 1805. B in vestry room 1795 and G in schoolroom blt. *c.* 1792.[77] B moved to new schoolroom with master's ho. at Turnham Green on land given by duke of Devonshire 1813, when sch. of industry and Sunday sch. attached and G sch. repaired.[78] Union with Nat. Soc.[79] and Dr.

[58] R. Housden, 'Hist. of Educ. in Chiswick from the mid 19th cent. to 1902' (TS. thesis, 1974) in Chiswick libr.

[59] Ibid. 17–18; Nat. Soc. files.

[60] Housden, 'Educ. in Chiswick', 22–9. [61] Char. Com. file.

[62] Mdx. C.C. *Primary and Secondary Educ. in Mdx. 1900–65*; Housden, 'Educ. in Chiswick', 34–6.

[63] *Bd. of Educ., List 21, 1919–38* (H.M.S.O.).

[64] Mdx. C.C. educ. cttee. *List of Schs.* (1957).

[65] Ibid. *List of Educ. Svces. and Establishments* (1964).

[66] Hounslow L.B. *Secondary Schs. maintained by Council* (1971). [67] Ex inf. the educ. offr., Hounslow L.B.

[68] Private schs. are separately treated below.

[69] *Brentford and Chiswick As It Was*, illus. 52.

[70] *Educ. Enquiry Abs.* 557.

[71] Faulkner, *Brentford, Ealing and Chiswick*, 454–5.

[72] Char. sch. acct. bk. (1706–88). Trustees were chosen in Feb. 1706–7. [73] *2nd Rep. Com. Char.* 76.

[74] Char. sch. acct. bk. (1706–88), f. 4.

[75] Memo. (loose) in bk. of subscriptions for N. aisle of ch., in Chiswick par. ch. [76] Char. sch. acct. bk. (1706–88).

[77] Lysons, *Environs*, ii. 221.

[78] Char. sch. acct. bk. (1706–88, 1786–1842); *2nd Rep. Com. Char.* 76, 145–6, 302; Faulkner, *Brentford, Ealing and Chiswick*, 344. [79] *2nd Rep. Com. Char.* 76.

Bell's system adopted by 1819: 130 B, inc. 25 clothed; 90 G, inc. 35 clothed.[80] Sch. for I established bef. 1848 by J. C. Sharpe.[81] B sch. enlarged 1836, G sch. rebuilt 1838.[82] Further bequests 1826, 1849; parl. grant for G 1857,[83] for B 1860.[84] a.a. 1866: 276 BGI. Called Chiswick Nat. char. schs. to 1852,[85] bd. sch. from 1872; GI replaced by (Chiswick) Glebe 1877, B by Hogarth J 1884.[86] Bldg. in churchyard repaired c. 1923, demol. 1951.[87]

CHISWICK SCH., Burlington Lane. Opened 1968 as SM comprehensive formed by amalg. of Chiswick County (see above) with Staveley Rd. sec. mod. (q.v.). 1979 lower sch. in Staveley Rd., upper sch. in Burlington Lane. Roll 1979: 1,650 BG.

GLEBE, Glebe Street. Opened 1877 as Chiswick Glebe bd. sch. for 625 GI. G moved 1884 to Hogarth Rd.[88] By 1898 accn. 702, a.a. 620; 1919 accn. 651, a.a. 505. Closed 1926.

GROVE PARK PRIMARY, Nightingale Close. Opened 1952 for JMI. Roll 1979: 210.

HOGARTH J, Duke Rd. Opened 1884 as Hogarth Rd. bd. schs. to replace Chiswick B Nat. and take G from Glebe.[89] By 1898 accn. 824 B, a.a. 843; 948 G, a.a. 639. Called Hogarth schs. by 1919. Reorg. for SB, JB 1921, SG, JG 1927/32. 1927 accn. 872 B, a.a. 740; 948 G, a.a. 748; 1938 accn. 776 B, a.a. 447; 800 G, a.a. 425. Reorg. as JM in new bldg. next to Hogarth I sch. 1958, old blgs. becoming a youth centre and St. Mary's R.C. sch. Roll 1979: 213 JM.

HOGARTH I, Devonshire Street. Opened 1920 in Hogarth Lane. 1927 accn. 200, a.a. 194; 1938 accn. 250, a.a. 164. New bldg. 1956, old one being demol. for rd. widening. Amalg. with Beverley Rd. I 1978. Roll 1979: 196 I and nursery class.

ST. MARY MAGDALENE NAT. Established by deed 1859. Nothing further known.[90]

ST. MARY'S R.C. PRIMARY, Duke Rd. JI moved 1964 from Acton Lane (Acton)[91] to former Hogarth J sch. Roll 1979: 275.

STAVELEY RD. Opened 1927 as central schs.[92] 1938 accn. 320 SB, 320 SG, a.a. 146 SB, 183 SG. Later sec. mod. schs. for 400 SB, 400 SG. Amalg. 1968 with Chiswick County grammar sch. as Chiswick sch. (q.v.).[93]

STRAND-ON-THE-GREEN BRITISH. Opened ? 1829, with 80 BG 1833.[94] New bldg. 1833, used also as Cong. chapel 1851.[95] Closed by ? 1857, bldg. thereafter housing Strand-on-the-Green (Nat.) J and I (q.v.).

STRAND-ON-THE-GREEN J and I, Thames Rd. Opened 1857 in yard of Ship inn as Nat. sch. for GI.[96] Bd. sch.; also B, from 1872. Moved 1874. 1880 accn. 211, a.a. 100; 1894 accn. 447, a.a. 278; 1906 accn. 629, a.a. 671. New bldg. for B 1912.[97] 1919 accn. 420 B, 396 G, 357 I, a.a. 348 B, 317 G, 281 I. Reorg. 1930 for SM, JM, I. 1938 accn. 280 SM, 350 JM, 338 I, a.a. 131 SM, 274 JM, 230 I. SM moved to Staveley Rd. 1946, 1947.[98] Rolls 1979: 165 J; 160 I and nursery class.

TURNHAM GREEN NAT. Opened before 1845 by Fred. Gibson[99] for 100 I in hired bldg. New schoolroom and ho. 1848 on waste land north side Chiswick High Rd. erected with parl. grant and financed by subscriptions, sermons, and school pence.[1] B and I schs. by 1860. 1866 a.a. 57 B, 105 I. Sch. for G south side Chiswick High Rd. by 1867.[2] Bd. schs. from 1872. 1880 accn. 125 B, 375 GI, a.a. 92 B, 148 GI; 1894 accn. 125 B, 522 GI, a.a. 102 B, 520 GI. B closed 1897, GI c. 1905.

TURNHAM GREEN R.C., Windmill Place. Opened by 1848,[3] reopened 1853 for BGI in bldg. of 1850 with 3 schoolrooms and ho. for teacher. Managed by priest of Turnham Green R.C. mission. Financed 1864 by vol. contributions and school pence,[4] by 1866 parl. grant. 1866 a.a. 105. 1882 accn. 328, a.a. 127. Closed by 1894.

Adult and technical education. Evening classes were held at Chiswick National school in 1869.[5] They apparently ceased on the establishment of a school board but were resumed in 1891 and were attended by 79 in 1892. Under the Technical Instruction Act, 1889, day and evening classes within a scheme drawn up by Middlesex C.C. were offered in 1895 at Chiswick School of Art, which had opened in Bath Road, Bedford Park, in 1881, in a building designed by Maurice B. Adams.[6] Subjects included laundry work, carpentry, and plumbing in 1897, when there was a Chiswick technical committee, presumably appointed by the U.D.C.[7]

Acton and Chiswick Polytechnic was formed in 1899, when Middlesex C.C. took over the school of art. After more rooms had been added in 1908 it was the largest polytechnic in Middlesex, supported also by the two U.D.C.s and attended in 1909 by 2,282 students, including 571 at branch classes in Acton and Chiswick.[8] The buildings were further extended in 1953–4 and formed part of Hounslow Borough College from 1965. Some 300 full-time and 150 part-time students attended in 1979.[9]

[80] *Educ. of Poor Digest*, 534.
[81] Chiswick libr., NC/I/lxxv.
[82] Faulkner, *Brentford, Ealing and Chiswick*, 345.
[83] *Gen. Digest of Endowed Chars*. H.C. 433, pp. 6–7 (1867–8), lii (1); *Mins. of Educ. Cttee. of Council, 1857* [2380], p. 139, H.C. (1857–8), xlv.
[84] *Rep. of Educ. Cttee. of Council, 1860–1* [2828], p. 644, H.C. (1861), xlix (1).
[85] Acct. bk. (1842–79) in Chiswick libr.
[86] Housden, 'Educ. in Chiswick', 22, 24–5.
[87] Draper, *Chiswick*, 176 and preface.
[88] Housden, 'Educ. in Chiswick', 24.
[89] Ibid.
[90] *Endowed Chars. Mdx.* H.C. 306, pp. 4–5 (1899), lxx.
[91] Above, Acton, educ.
[92] Draper, *Chiswick*, preface.
[93] Hounslow L.B. *Sec. Educ.* (1971).

[94] *Educ. Enquiry Abs.* 557.
[95] P.R.O., HO 129/134/4/1/4.
[96] Ibid., ED 7/87; inf. from Mrs. K. Judges.
[97] P.R.O., ED 7/87.
[98] *Strand-on-the-Green Schs.* (centenary booklet 1974), 10.
[99] Faulkner, *Brentford, Ealing and Chiswick*, 345.
[1] Nat. Soc. files.
[2] O.S. Map 1/2,500, Mdx. XXI. 2 (1867 edn.).
[3] Nat. Soc. files.
[4] P.R.O., ED 7/87.
[5] *Rep. of Educ. Cttee. of Council, 1869–70* [C. 165], p. 611, H.C. (1870), xxii.
[6] Housden, 'Educ. in Chiswick', 31–2 (inc. amendments); W. King Baker, *Acton* (1912), 240.
[7] *Chiswick Times*, 19 Apr. 1895; 17 Sept. 1897.
[8] Baker, *Acton*, 240–2.
[9] Inf. from the principal.

Private schools.[10] Several large houses served in the 18th and 19th centuries as private schools, where *c.* 450–500 were educated in 1819.[11] There were 22 fee-paying boarding schools in 1835[12] and roughly the same number of private schools throughout the century, although by 1890 many were for day pupils.

An expensive boarding academy was that of Maurice Margarot, which *c.* 1780 contained a French chapel and where young nobles and gentlemen were taught French, classics, and geography, with Portuguese and several fashionable accomplishments as extra subjects. Described as at Turnham Green, 'near Lord Egmont's',[13] it may possibly have been a forerunner of Afton college, said to have been founded in 1748 and with 75 boys in 1872, when its previous history was not recorded.[14]

Dr. William Rose (1719–86), translator of Sallust, kept a successful academy at Chiswick from 1758 until his death. A friend of Dr. Johnson, who disapproved of his leniency, Rose was assisted in his last years by his son-in-law Dr. Charles Burney (1757–1817), the classical critic, who moved to Hammersmith in 1786. Rose's pupils included his son Samuel (1767–1804), the friend of Cowper, Irwin Eyles (1751?–1817), oriental traveller, Henry Angelo (1760–1839?), fencing master, and probably Samuel Shepherd (1760–1840), lawyer, and Sir Richard Phillips (1767–1840), author and publisher.[15] Rose's academy was probably the later Bradmore House in Chiswick Lane, still a school under Edmund Brasier in 1832 and 1851[16] and under William John Stafford in 1890 but demolished by 1904.[17]

At Manor Farm House in Chiswick Lane a boarding academy was kept from *c.* 1786 by the Revd. Thomas Horne (1737–1824),[18] who taught 82 boys in 1801.[19] Pupils included his son William (1774–1860), later Sir William, the attorney-general, John Copley (1772–1863), later Lord Chancellor as Lord Lyndhurst, who thought Horne a good classical scholar, and the philanthropist Anthony Ashley Cooper (1801–85), later earl of Shaftesbury,[20] who remembered a large and brutal school which had given him an early horror of oppression.[21] Horne's son Thomas was master from 1824 until 1835 but by 1845 the school had been turned into an asylum.[22]

College House, no longer used by Westminster school, was a boarding school under Mary Solieux, with 56 inmates in 1801, before its acquisition for the Chiswick Press.[23] At Walpole House, also in Chiswick Mall, a school was kept

by the Revd. John Turner and attended by his wife's great nephew William Makepeace Thackeray (1811–63) from 1818.[24] It was probably the original of Miss Pinkerton's academy in *Vanity Fair*, which Thackeray placed in Chiswick Mall, although his illustration,[25] showing massive gate piers and another house opposite, gave some support to a claim that he had been describing Boston House.[26]

Sutton Court, advertised as in 9 a. and convenient for London,[27] was a boarding school under Frederick Tappenden by 1845. It had a resident French teacher and 17 boys in 1851,[28] apparently had expanded by 1872, when younger boys were prepared for public school and elder ones for the professions,[29] and was an expensive preparatory school by 1879.[30] Frederick Tappenden had left Sutton Court by 1886 and Charles Tappenden, probably his son, was principal of the purpose-built Gunnersbury college in 1890.[31]

Many well established boys' schools closed in the 19th century. Belmont House, Turnham Green, was kept in 1832 by the Revd. Thomas Crabb, in 1845 by Benjamin Clements, and in the 1870s by J. Russell Cloutte, who prepared boys for the services and professions. Walpole House, in 1872 under John Wilson Allen and in 1879 under Thomas Corfield Allen, was said to have been founded in 1845, although J. W. Allen had a school in Chiswick Mall by 1832. Bolton House, in the high road under T. G. Dyne in 1845 and 1861, was still the name of a boys' preparatory school, in Grove Park Terrace, in 1890. Chiswick Collegiate school, for boarders and day boys like Walpole House, existed from 1847 until 1879 or later.[32] Ivy House, Turnham Green, was kept in 1861 by the Revd. John Bonus, a Roman Catholic, and advertised for foreigners. Longer lived girls' schools included Boston House, under Mrs. Nethercliff in 1845 and 1861 and offering a refined education to university entrance for boarders and day pupils in 1884.[33] St. Agnes's orphanage in 1878 briefly opened a Church of England school for *c.* 60 girls by renting the old charity school building in the churchyard.[34]

There were still *c.* 20 private schools in 1908, several of them founded for the new suburbs. Grove Park in 1890 was served by a girls' school in Spencer Road, perhaps one which survived under Miss I. Eley in 1926, and by boys' and kindergarten schools in Grove Park Terrace. Bedford Park school, an early mixed school with

[10] Section based on: Pigot, *Com. Dir.* (1832–4); *P.O. Dir. Six Home Counties* (1845); *Crockford's Scholastic Dir.* (1861); *Kelly's Dir. Mdx.* (1890, 1908, 1926).

[11] *Educ. of Poor Digest*, 534.

[12] *Educ. Enq. Abstract*, 558.

[13] Draper, *Chiswick*, 134–5; Guildhall Libr., Pr. V TUR.

[14] F. S. de Carteret-Bisson, *Our Schs. and Colls.* (1872), 304.

[15] N. Hans, *New Trends in Educ. in 18th Cent.* (1951), 129; *D.N.B.*

[16] P.R.O., HO 107/1699/134/4.

[17] Chiswick libr., NC/I/iii.

[18] Hans, *Educ. in 18th Cent.* 129.

[19] Census return 1801, copy in Chiswick libr.

[20] *D.N.B.*

[21] J. L. Le B. and L. B. Hammond, *Lord Shaftesbury* (1969 edn.), 2–3.

[22] Hans, *Educ. in 18th Cent.* 129; above.

[23] Census return 1801, copy in Chiswick libr.; Draper, *Chiswick*, 76.

[24] L. Stevenson, *Showman of Vanity Fair* (1947), 8; *V.C.H. Mdx.* i. 245.

[25] W. M. Thackeray, *Vanity Fair* (centenary edn. 1910), i, illus. facing p. 9.

[26] Draper, *Chiswick*, 163–4; Gilbert, *Chiswick Old and New*, 67; plaque on Boston Ho.

[27] Advert. in Chiswick libr.

[28] P.R.O., HO 107/1699/134/4, ff. 556–7.

[29] Bisson, *Our Schs. and Colls.* (1872), 304.

[30] Ibid. i (1879), 575.

[31] M.R.O., PR 44/197; *Kelly's Dir. Mdx.* (1890).

[32] Bisson, *Schs. and Colls.* i (1879), 575–6.

[33] Bisson, *Schs. and Colls.* ii (1884), 501.

[34] P.R.O., ED 7/87.

no religious instruction, and the more conventional Bedford Park high school both opened in 1884.[35] In addition to professors of music and languages, Bedford Park in 1890 had Chiswick high school at Sydney House and Bedford Park high school near by in Priory Road, Acton. The first, a mixed secondary school under Miss Alice Woods,[36] was presumably the former Bedford Park school and unconnected with Chiswick high school for girls or Chiswick girls' school, both of which existed by 1926. It amalgamated in 1895 with Bedford Park high school to form Chiswick and Bedford Park high school,[37] at no. 9 Queen Anne's Gardens in 1908 and at Priory House, Priory Avenue, in 1909. A girls' school at Priory House, called Bedford Park college, was bought c. 1932 by Mme Fellowes, who transferred pupils there from Haslemere school in the Avenue. Her new school, renamed Chiswick and Bedford Park high, later preparatory, school, was managed by her daughters in 1979, when it contained 200 boys and girls to the age of eleven.[38]

No other private schools survived in 1979. A ladies' school under Miss M. C. Martin at no. 26 Oxford Road by 1890 may have been the later Oxford college, at no. 367 High Road from 1916; the school had 70–80 pupils aged 3 to 16 and was said to be over 100 years old on its closure in 1973, which was followed by the building's conversion into the headquarters of Brentford and Isleworth Labour party.[39] Gunnersbury preparatory school for boys, in Burnaby Gardens by 1900, was later claimed to date from 1820[40] and survived c. 1952, when it was one of Chiswick's three best known independent schools. The others were St. Margaret's, opened in 1932 in Sutton Court Road and in 1957 containing over 100 girls, many with well known parents, and the adjoining Compton House, for boys.[41] Both schools, in Sutton Court Road, closed in 1962.[42] Arlington Park college, Sutton Lane, opened in 1890, prepared boys for university, and survived until the Second World War, as did Sutton girls' school, with a boys' preparatory department, in Sutton Lane from 1903 and later in Marlborough Road.[43]

CHARITIES FOR THE POOR.[44] Apart from the almshouses in Sutton Lane, benefactions of unknown origin included 2 a. known as the poor's land in Chiswick field. Producing £3 a year before inclosure, they were then replaced by a plot at the corner of Duke Road and Hogarth

Lane[45] which was let for market gardens at £25 a year by 1893. A rentcharge left by Thomas Barker by will proved 1643 was probably never paid. Sums left for coal by 1622 and 1659 may have been only gifts; in 1659 money, which had been misspent on the church, was to be used as the donors had wished,[46] but it was not recorded again. In 1826 rent from the poor's land had for long been wrongly included in the overseers' general accounts. The five oldest distributive charities, apart from Quaife's, were disbursed in money before forming a bread and coal fund from c. 1818. Nearly all the distributive charities from 1893 constituted a branch of the parochial charities devoted to the almshouses, none of which had originally been endowed.

Almshouses. A church house and other rooms in the churchyard served as lodgings for poor people, chosen by the vestry, in 1629.[47] Probably nothing was done after Chaloner Chute, by will proved 1661, desired the building and endowment of a hospital as he had elsewhere directed,[48] but almshouses in Sutton Lane were built before 1676 by William Ashburnham. Lord Fauconberg and his widow, by wills proved 1700 and 1713, left money for mourning gowns to women in the hospital at Little Sutton, presumably the almshouses which were maintained by Ashburnham's successors as lessees of Sutton Court manor and which accordingly came to be known as the duke of Devonshire's almshouses.[49] Six tenements of c. 1700, single-storeyed and with attics, survived in Sutton Lane until 1957,[50] when they made way for flats called Sutton Close.[51] The inmates were moved to Essex Place, Turnham Green, before 1822, when the almshouses there were enlarged; those almshouses were demolished in 1885.[52]

At Strand-on-the-Green there was a parish house in 1655 and almshouses in 1658.[53] The thatched buildings thereafter were often repaired by the vestry,[54] until some parishioners paid for four new almshouses between 1721 and 1724.[55] Repaired in 1816, apparently for six inmates,[56] they were extended and converted into three under a Scheme of 1934 with the aid of £801 from the estate of Hopkin Morris, in whose memory they were renamed the Hopkin Morris homes of rest. After the trustees of Chiswick parochial charities had proposed to sell them for demolition in 1971, the almshouses, a single-storeyed brick range backing onto Grove Row, were bought in 1973 and meticulously restored in 1974 by Hounslow L.B.[57]

[35] Bolsterli, *Bedford Pk.* 81.
[36] *V.C.H. Mdx.* i. 257.
[37] Bolsterli, *Bedford Pk.* 82.
[38] Inf. from the directors, Chiswick and Bedford Pk. Prep. Sch. Ltd.
[39] *Brentford and Chiswick Times*, 26 July, 2 Aug. 1973.
[40] *Chiswick Times*, 6 July 1900; *Brentford and Chiswick Times*, 25 Mar. 1949.
[41] Brentford and Chiswick, *Official Guide* [c. 1952]; *Brentford and Chiswick Times*, 26 July 1957.
[42] *Brentford and Chiswick Times*, 27 Apr. 1962.
[43] Chiswick, *Official Guide* (1909); *Chiswick and Turnham Green* [1913]; *Kelly's Dir. Chiswick* (1940).
[44] Section based on Char. Com. files; *14th Rep. Com. Char.* H.C. 382, pp. 177–80 (1826), xii; *Digest of Endowed Chars.* H.C. 433, Mdx. pp. 6–7 (1867–8), lii (1); *Endowed Chars. Mdx.* H.C. 306, pp. 4–5 (1899), lxx; 'Chiswick Benefactions

1776' (MS. acct. bk. 1776–1886) in Chiswick libr.
[45] M.R.O., TA/CHI.
[46] Chwdns. acct. bks. (1622–35, 1636–62).
[47] Chwdns. acct. bk. (1622–35).
[48] Draper, *Chiswick*, 70; P.R.O., PROB 11/303 (P.C.C. 19 May).
[49] Draper, *Chiswick*, 79; inf. from Mrs. K. Judges.
[50] Hist. Mon. Com. *Mdx.* 12; Draper, *Chiswick*, preface.
[51] *Brentford and Chiswick As It Was*, illus. 58.
[52] Inf. from Mrs. K. Judges.
[53] Chwdns. acct. bk. (1636–62); inf. from Mrs. K. Judges.
[54] e.g. chwdns. acct. bk. (1698–1751).
[55] Draper, *Chiswick*, 139.
[56] Inf. from Mrs. K. Judges; Faulkner, *Brentford, Ealing and Chiswick*, 344.
[57] *Brentford and Chiswick As It Was*, illus. 37; *Brentford and Chiswick Times*, 30 Sept. 1976; plaque on bldg.

Six almshouses, under the Scheme of 1934, were built at the corner of Edensor Road and Alexandra Avenue. Rebuilding was planned in 1971 and later carried out by the trustees of Chiswick parochial charities, with money from the sale of the Hopkin Morris homes. Eighteen flats, each for two people, were opened, as Whittington Court, in 1976.[58]

Distributive charities. Henry Fryer, by will dated 1631, left part of a rentcharge to the poor of Chiswick, who were later awarded £25 a year. In 1698 the income met a wide range of expenses, including an apprenticeship and medical care.[59] The churchwardens spent it on a customary payment to the parish clerk and on gifts of from 2s. 6d. to £1 1s. to 88 recipients in 1777-8 and on almost twice as many gifts, some of only 1s. or in kind, in 1778-9. Although providing bread and coal in 1826, it was again distributed in money by 1868.

Mary Quaife, by will dated 1730, left £400 stock for the poor, subject to her sister's life interest. The stock was soon afterwards sold for £430 1s., which the vicar transferred to the parish officers in order that they could discharge a debt to Thomas Mawson over the new workhouse. In 1826, as advised by the Charity Commissioners, the vestry had agreed to buy stock worth £430 1s. out of the poor rates and return it to the vicar. In 1867-8 the income of £14 18s. 5d. was distributed in bread.

Elizabeth Lutwyche, by will proved 1776, left £200 for gifts to the poor at Christmas. The income of £7 6s. 6d. on stock worth £244 5s. 6d. was spent on fuel in 1867-8.

Anna Maria Reynolds, by will dated 1803, left £500 for the poor. The income of £25 2s. 6d. on stock worth £837 10s. provided fuel in 1867-8.

Elizabeth Blackshaw, by will proved 1811, left £100 stock for gifts to the poor at Christmas. The income of £3 provided fuel in 1867-8.

Compensation money from Thomas Whipham for permission to inclose a wastehold at Strand-on-the-Green in 1815 was spent on stock worth £59 0s. 2d. The income of £2 7s. 2d. provided fuel in 1867-8.

Edward Waistell, by will dated 1812, left £200 for gifts to poor householders not receiving parish relief. Stock worth £244 3s. 8d. in 1826 produced £9 15s. 4d., which furnished gifts of from 2s. to £1, and £7 6s. 6d. in 1867-8, when it was still distributed in money.

Charles Whittingham, by will proved 1840, left £1,000 for coal. In 1867-8 £33 6s. 8d. was spent, from stock worth £1,111 2s. 3d.

Sarah Sermon of Isleworth,[60] by will proved 1849, left £666 13s. 4d., producing £20 which was distributed in money in 1867-8.

Sarah Wilhelmina Brande, by will proved 1856, left £250 for the poor and £500 to maintain her family's vault, any surplus to be spent on lying-in women in accordance with the objects of a maternity society already established. Stock worth £450 in 1867-8 produced £13 10s., which was distributed in money.

David Goodsman, by will proved 1870, left a sum represented by £531 4s. 2d. stock in 1899, when distributions were made in kind.

Chiswick parochial charities. A Scheme of 1893 provided for 12 trustees to administer the parochial charities, which were divided into four branches: the educational charities, the almshouse charities, including the poor's land and all the distributive charities except Sermon's and Brande's, the eleemosynary charity of Mrs. Sermon, and the lying-in charity of Mrs. Brande. Income from the almshouse charities was to be spent on the buildings and on paying 5s.-8s. a week to almspeople who had lived in Chiswick for at least five years, their number to be decided by the trustees. Investments were later increased after sales of the poor's land in 1898 for £1,200 and the site in Essex Place in 1905 for £175, and the redemption of Fryer's rentcharge for £1,000. In 1934 the educational branch was separated from the others and from 1960 almspeople might be required to make contributions of up to 5s. a week. The almshouse branch had an investment income of £503 in 1973-4, when the eleemosynary charity had £22, mostly distributed at Christmas, and the lying-in charity £25, largely paid in a grant to the Hounslow branch of WEL-CARE.

EALING AND BRENTFORD

EALING,[1] which in 1904 claimed to be the 'queen of the suburbs',[2] was a roughly rectangular parish whose centre lay 10 km. west of Hyde Park Corner.[3] Its southern part, formerly called Lower Side in contrast with Upper Side or the northern part, included Old Brentford, containing most of the township of Brentford and constituting a chapelry from the 1760s and a

parish from 1828. New Brentford, to the west, was a medieval chapelry formed out of the southern end of Hanwell parish and had its own government by the early 17th century. Ealing local board district was formed in 1863 without Old Brentford, which joined New Brentford to form a separate district in 1874.[4] The present account includes both Old and New Brentford

[58] *Brentford and Chiswick Times*, 30 Sept. 1976.
[59] Acct. bk. for Fryer's Char. (1698-1776), in Chiswick libr. Some later expenses are in 'Chiswick Benefactions 1776'.
[60] *V.C.H. Mdx.* iii. 138.
[1] The article was written in 1979. Any references to later events are dated. The help of Mr. J. M. Lee and Mr. P.

Hounsell in commenting on parts of the article is gratefully acknowledged.
[2] *Ealing, Country Town Near Lond.* (1904), 1.
[3] First 2 paras. based on O.S. Maps 6", Mdx. XV. NE., SE., XVI. NW., SW., XX. NE., XXI. NW. (1873 and later edns.).
[4] Below, local govt.

but excludes a small detached portion of Ealing, south-east of Acton and known as Stamford Brook grounds, which was transferred in 1878 to Chiswick.

The southern boundary of the old parish followed the Thames eastward from Lot's meadow, east of Town meadow, to include Lot's Ait but not Brentford Ait (Surr.). From a point slightly east of Kew bridge it turned inland to Chiswick High Road, which it followed eastward before turning north and then east to Bollo Bridge Lane. The eastern boundary, with Acton, ran along Bollo Bridge Lane and east of Ealing common and Hanger Lane to a detached part of Hanwell, included in the present account, north-east of Hanger Hill. Thence it turned westward almost to Hanger Lane and followed it to the river Brent, which formed the northern boundary with Harrow, Perivale, and Greenford. The western boundary, with Hanwell, ran southward to the west of the modern Argyle Road and Northfield Avenue to meet Boston Manor Road near Boston House, whence it continued to the Half Acre, Brentford High Street, and the Thames. New Brentford consisted of a narrow strip between the Brent on the west and the Half Acre and Boston Lane on the east, except where the boundary curved east of the lane to include Boston Farm. The division between New Brentford and the rest of Hanwell lay roughly along the line of the railway west of Boston Manor station.

Ealing parish, with Old Brentford, contained 3,821 a. in 1881,[5] after the loss of 29 a. at Stamford Brook grounds. New Brentford then contained 216 a. In 1901 Ealing M.B. contained 2,947 a. and Brentford U.D. 1,091 a. During the 1920s Ealing M.B. was enlarged to 9,133 a. by the addition of neighbouring areas to the north and west, and from 1927 Brentford formed three wards of Brentford and Chiswick U.D., later M.B. In 1965 Ealing M.B. joined Acton and Southall M.B.s to form Ealing L.B., and Brentford and Chiswick became part of Hounslow L.B.

Much of the land is flat, rising gently from the Thames to reach 23 m. at the centre of the parish and 30 m. near Uxbridge Road. North of the road it rises more steeply before sloping down towards the Brent. The ridge of high ground, with Castlebar Hill at its western end, reaches c. 60 m. at Hanger Hill in the north-eastern corner of the parish.[6]

In the north part some alluvium, bordered by flood plain gravel, lies along the Brent. Most of the higher ground is covered by London Clay, with Claygate Beds on the slopes of Hanger Hill and Boyn Hill gravel on the east side of Castlebar Hill. Brickearth lies along Uxbridge Road,

except where a band of Taplow gravel stretches north across the road east of Ealing common and east of Ealing Dean. The Taplow gravel extends across the parish north of Gunnersbury park from Acton to the Brent except at Little Ealing, where a tongue of brickearth runs from Uxbridge Road. Farther south is more brickearth, with flood-plain gravel at Old Brentford and a strip of alluvium along the Thames and at the mouth of the Brent.[7]

Two streams, later hidden by housing, ran southward on either side of Ealing village in the mid 19th century. The easterly one, from water in the grounds of Elm Grove, fed some small ponds in the fields east of South Ealing Road and larger ones near Clayponds Lane before flowing under Brentford High Street to the Thames. The westerly stream ran from Castlebar Hill east of Northfield Avenue to Little Ealing, where it fed ponds at Ealing Park; farther south it followed the line of Brook Road before passing under Brentford High Street and entering the Thames near Ferry Lane.[8]

COMMUNICATIONS. Two roads from London ran across the parish. The more northerly was Uxbridge Road, which probably dated from the early Middle Ages.[9] From Acton it headed north-west over Ealing common to Haven Green, at the north end of Ealing village, and thence west-south-west to Hanwell.[10] In the south part of the parish the Roman road to Silchester ran close to the Thames, forming Brentford High Street.[11] Its modern alignment existed by the late 14th century, although modified when the bridge over the Brent was rebuilt in 1446 and 1824,[12] and money was collected for repairs to the road from 1360 to 1393.[13] Narrow and crowded, the high street was notorious for its bad state[14] before and after the establishment of Brentford turnpike trust in 1717. The Old Brentford stretch was relinquished to Ealing's highway trustees in 1769 and the New Brentford stretch to the metropolitan turnpike roads commissioners in 1826.[15] Between those two east–west routes a third, Pope's Lane, was so called by 1423[16] and briefly called Folly Lane c. 1746; it branched west from Gunnersbury Lane, which led from Acton, running south of Ealing village and continuing west as Little Ealing Lane.[17]

A north–south track may have led from Perivale through Ealing to Brentford, probably the lowest permanent ford over the Thames, in pre-Roman times.[18] Later a road led north from Old Brentford along the line of South Ealing Road, called Drum Lane in 1746,[19] through the centre

[5] Para. based on *Census*, 1881–1951.
[6] O.S. Maps 6″, Mdx. XV. NE., SE., XVI. NW., SW., XX. NE., XXI. NW. (1873 and later edns.).
[7] Geol. Surv. Maps 1″, drift, sheets 256, 270 (1951 edn.).
[8] O.S. Maps 6″, Mdx. XV. NE., SE., XVI. NW., SW., XX. NE., XXI. NW. (1873 and later edns.); Bacon, *Atlas of Lond.* (1886); Gtr. Ealing Local Hist. Soc. *Broadsheet*, 10 Oct. 1960.   [9] *V.C.H. Mdx.* iii. 221.
[10] Rocque, *Map of Lond.* (1746), sheet 14.
[11] R. Canham, *2,000 Yrs. of Brentford* (1978), 150.
[12] *V.C.H. Mdx.* iii. 86.
[13] e.g. *Cal. Fine R.* 1356–68, 380; *Cal. Pat.* 1364–7, 104,

234, 292; *Abbrev. Rot. Orig.* (Rec. Com.), ii. 296; *T.L.M.A.S.* xxi (1), 60.
[14] *Mdx. Sess. Rec.* i. 138; M.R.O., Acc. 890, pp. 147, 150–1, 169; Cal. Mdx. Sess. Bks. xi. 88.
[15] J. Ryan, 'Assessment of Brentford turnpike trust old dist. 1767–1812' (TS., undated, in Chiswick libr.).
[16] *P.N. Mdx.* (E.P.N.S.), 91.
[17] Rocque, *Map of Lond.* (1746), sheet 14.
[18] Robbins, *Mdx.* 69.
[19] Rest of para. based on Rocque, *Map of Lond.* (1746), sheet 14, and O.S. Map 6″, Mdx. XV. NE., SE., XVI. NW., SW., XX. NE., XXI. NW. (1873 edn.).

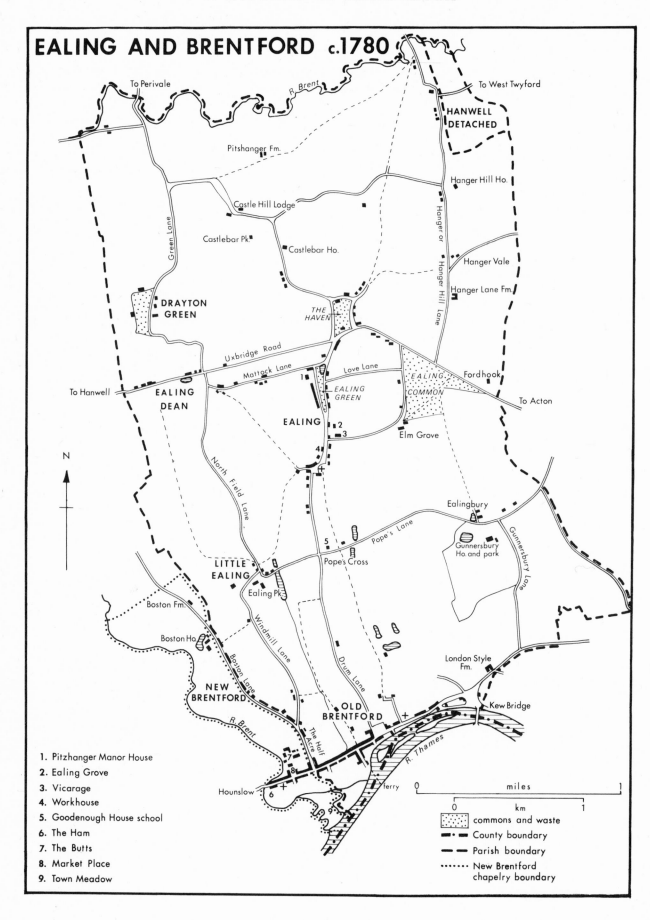

EALING AND BRENTFORD c.1780

To Perivale

R. Brent

To West Twyford

HANWELL
DETACHED

Pitshanger Fm.

Hanger Hill Ho.

Green Lane

Castle Hill Lodge

Castlebar Pk.

Castlebar Ho.

Hanger or Hanger Hill Lane

Hanger Vale

Hanger Lane Fm.

DRAYTON
GREEN

THE
HAVEN

Uxbridge Road

Mattock Lane

Love Lane

1

EALING
GREEN

EALING
COMMON

Fordhook

To Hanwell

EALING
DEAN

EALING

2

3

Elm Grove

To Acton

N

4

North Field Lane

Ealingbury

Pope's Lane

Gunnersbury Lane

5

Pope's Cross

Gunnersbury
Ho. and park

LITTLE
EALING

Ealing Pk.

Boston Fm.

Windmill Lane

Drum Lane

London Style
Fm.

Boston Ho.

Boston Lane

NEW
BRENTFORD

OLD
BRENTFORD

Kew Bridge

R. Brent

The Half
Acre

R. Thames

Hounslow

8

7

ferry

9

6

1. Pitzhanger Manor House
2. Ealing Grove
3. Vicarage
4. Workhouse
5. Goodenough House school
6. The Ham
7. The Butts
8. Market Place
9. Town Meadow

| 0 | miles | 1 |
| 0 | km | 1 |

commons and waste
County boundary
Parish boundary
New Brentford
chapelry boundary

of the parish and past Ealing green, where it formed the main street of Ealing village, to join Uxbridge Road near the Haven or Haven Green. Beyond Haven Green a road zigzagged north-westward past Castlebar Hill, where it was called Perryfield Lane in 1746, to cross the Brent into Perivale, while another, Dog Kennel Lane in 1746, branched eastward from it to Hanger Hill. In the east part of the parish Gunnersbury Lane led north from Chiswick High Road to meet Pope's Lane west of Gunnersbury House. There it turned east to meet Bollo Bridge Lane at the Acton boundary, while by 1746 an unnamed track continued northward along the line of Gunnersbury Avenue to Ealing common and Uxbridge Road. In the west part of the parish the Half Acre led north between Old and New Brentford before dividing into Boston Lane, leading to Hanwell and so called by 1408,[20] and Windmill Lane, leading to Little Ealing. The lanes were later called Boston Road and Windmill Road, the southern stretch of Boston Road being renamed Boston Manor Road in the 20th century.[21] From Little Ealing Northfield Lane, later Northfield Avenue, led to Uxbridge Road at Ealing Dean, whence another lane, called Green Lane in 1777,[22] continued north through Drayton Green to Perivale.

Major changes in the 20th century included the widening of Brentford High Street for electric trams in 1901 and its bypassing to the north by the Great West Road, opposed by the town's manufacturers but opened in 1925.[23] The southern stretch of Gunnersbury Lane and its continuation across Ealing common, renamed Gunnersbury Avenue, from the 1920s formed part of the North Circular Road, which continued northward along Hanger Lane. The main road called Western Avenue crossed the north end of Hanger Lane from 1930.[24] An elevated section of the M4 motorway, along the line of the Great West Road north of Brentford, was begun in 1962 and linked to Chiswick flyover in 1964.[25]

Perivale was approached by a ford in 1777;[26] a footbridge existed in 1819,[27] and a road bridge by 1865.[28] Farther east Hanger Lane crossed the Brent by Alperton bridge, also known c. 1680 as Vicar's or Vicarage bridge.[29] It was a wooden structure, repeatedly mended in the 1790s and whose repair was disputed in 1818 between the lords of Ealing and Harrow, who finally agreed to share the cost.[30]

At New Brentford there was a bridge across the Brent by 1224, when pontage was granted for its upkeep,[31] as in 1280,[32] 1293-4,[33] 1331, and 1369.[34] The wooden bridge was replaced in 1446 by a stone one, farther north and separated from it on the Hounslow side by the chapel of St. Michael and All Angels.[35] The maintenance of the new bridge was in 1450 charged partly on the abbot of Westminster, who had a fishery in the river there.[36] The bridge, of three arches in 1542 and 1635,[37] was dangerous in 1617-18, particularly because of its low parapet,[38] and in 1623 the lords of Isleworth and Boston were indicted for not repairing it;[39] by 1635 rates were levied for that purpose[40] and from 1691 the county contributed regularly to its upkeep.[41] A footbridge for which money was left in 1678[42] may not have been built. Heavy traffic in summer was blamed for the road bridge's disrepair in 1707, when posts were erected to reserve it for pedestrians,[43] and in 1712 vehicles used it only when the river was too high to ford. Rebuilt in 1742 by Charles Labelye,[44] it remained difficult to approach and too narrow,[45] despite improvements on the west side in 1807 and to the bridge itself in 1811.[46] A new bridge was built for the county by Robert Sibley in 1824;[47] the eastern approach was widened in 1826[48] and there had been a further widening by 1909.[49] A footbridge over the Brent from the Ham to Old England in 1635[50] may have been the bridge of Sir John Thynne mentioned in 1584[51] and the precursor of one surviving in 1979.

High Street also crossed two streams in Old Brentford. A stone bridge near the boundary with New Brentford in 1578[52] was ruinous in 1630, when the lord of Ealing was responsible,[53] but was apparently rebuilt and called the new bridge in 1663.[54] It was widened for pedestrians c. 1672.[55] Cotman bridge, mentioned in 1436[56] and probably near Ealing Road,[57] was also the responsibility of the lord of Ealing.[58]

[20] P.N. Mdx. (E.P.N.S.), 32.
[21] Kelly's Dir. Mdx. (1890, 1926).
[22] M.R.O., Acc. 649/6 (map of Ealing par. by A. Bassett, 1777); B.L. Maps K.29.9.a. Copies of revised versions dated 1822 and 1836 are in M.R.O., F 51 A, B, the originals being in Ealing libr. and Chiswick libr.
[23] Robbins, Mdx. 226; Mdx. C.C. (Western Rd. and Improvements) Petition against Bill (1914), in Chiswick libr.
[24] Robbins, Mdx. 239; V.C.H. Mdx. iv. 123.
[25] Contract Jnl. 10 Oct. 1963 and other cuttings in Chiswick libr.; above, Chiswick, communications.
[26] M.R.O., Acc. 649/6.
[27] K. J. Allison and E. D. G. Holt, Ealing in 18th and 19th Cent. (Ealing Local Hist. Soc. 1966), 23.
[28] O.S. Map 6″, Mdx. XV. NE. (1868 edn., surveyed 1864-5).
[29] C. H. Keene, Field-Names of Ealing L.B. (1976), 4; V.C.H. Mdx. iv. 172.
[30] Guildhall MS. 12357; Rep. on Bridges in Mdx. 195.
[31] Rott. Litt. Claus. (Rec. Com.), i. 589-90.
[32] Cal. Pat. 1272-81, 418.
[33] P.R.O., JUST 1/543, rot. 51.
[34] Cal. Pat. 1330-4, 81; 1367-70, 325.
[35] Ibid. 1446-52, 29.
[36] M. Sharpe, Bygone Hanwell (1924), 83.

[37] Leland, Itin. ed. Toulmin Smith, i. 107; VCH Mdx. iii. 90.   [38] Cal. Mdx. Sess. Bks. iv. 336.
[39] Mdx. County Rec. ii. 237.
[40] Cal. S.P. Dom. Addenda, 1625-49, 508.
[41] Mdx. County Rec. Sess. Bks. 1689-1709, 40, 274, 286, 296-7, 310, 328.
[42] Home Counties Mag. v. 219; see also M.R.O., Acc. 890 (1672).
[43] Mdx. County Rec. Sess. Bks. 1689-1709, 317.
[44] Robbins, Mdx. 77.   [45] Plate facing p. 144.
[46] Ryan, 'Brentford turnpike trust'; Lysons, Environs (Suppl.), 105; Brewer, Beauties of Eng. & Wales, x (5), 605.
[47] F. Turner, Hist. Brentford (1922), 54; Ryan, 'Brentford turnpike trust'; Colvin, Biog. Dict. British Architects, 542.
[48] Ryan, 'Brentford turnpike trust'.
[49] J. Tavenor-Perry, Memorials of Old Mdx. (1909), 279.
[50] V.C.H. Mdx. iii. 90; see also B.L. Add. MS. 33767 (1669).
[51] P.R.O., E 134/26 Eliz. I Easter/6.
[52] Guildhall MS. 10312/94, rot. 3d.
[53] P.R.O., SC 2/190/7, rot. 5.
[54] Guildhall MS. 10312/99, rot. 10d.
[55] M.R.O., Acc. 890, p. 150.
[56] Guildhall MS. 10312/71, rot. 2d.
[57] Ibid. 94, rot. 44.   [58] Ibid. 71, rot. 2d.

The lowest permanent ford over the Thames until Roman times was probably at Old England, later covered by Brentford dock.[59] Residents of Old Brentford claimed free passage on a ferry to Kew from time immemorial until John Hale's appointment as keeper in 1536. Hale charged ½d. for horsemen and ¼d. for pedestrians, prevented the use of other boats, and suppressed a rival ferry. He claimed that earlier kings had appointed ferrymen,[60] and his own ferry survived as the only one to carry horses and vehicles until 1659, when it was called Kew or King's ferry. By 1659, after fares had been raised, a cheaper service was offered by Robert Tunstall, who previously had taken some pedestrians.[61] The newer ferry was farther east, probably at the Hollows,[62] and presumably closed after the opening of the first Kew bridge. The older one may always have been at Ferry Lane, where it remained until 1939.[63]

The first Kew bridge was built by Robert Tunstall, owner of the ferry, under an Act of 1757.[64] Of timber and with 11 arches, it was opened at the east end of Old Brentford in 1759 and replaced by a stone bridge, built by another Robert Tunstall, in 1789. A new bridge built for Middlesex and Surrey councils was opened in 1903.[65]

The river Brent, with its weirs and mills, was probably unnavigable until work started on the Grand Junction canal, from Brentford to Braunston (Northants.), in 1793. Apart from its wider bends, the river was canalized along the south-western boundary of New Brentford. Construction had reached Uxbridge by 1794 and was completed in 1805.[66] The canal formed part of the Grand Union canal from 1929.[67]

There was a daily postal service from Westminster to Ealing village and Little Ealing in 1692 and 1732.[68] By 1825 two short-stage coaches between them made three return journeys a day,[69] and in 1832 there were four daily departures from the New inn. Many more coaches passed through the parish along Uxbridge Road, presumably accounting for Ealing's half-hourly service recorded in 1826.[70] Brentford had twice daily postal deliveries from Westminster in 1692.[71] Coaching was probably already important in 1750,[72] and 11 short-stage coaches made 14 return journeys to London in 1825, when two return journeys were also made from Kew bridge.[73] Longer-distance coaches called every half hour in 1791, 1826, and, at the

Castle inn, in 1832.[74] Thomas and John Ives were licensed to run three omnibuses from Ealing to London in 1838[75] and, with six departures a day, had replaced the short-stage coaches by 1845. Coaches and omnibuses then ran from Brentford every 20 minutes to London and every half hour to Hounslow.[76]

Despite its name, the Southall, Ealing & Shepherd's Bush Tram-Railway Co. operated no farther west than Acton from 1874. Its successor the West Metropolitan Tramways Co. from 1883 ran horse trams along Chiswick High Road to Kew bridge, where London United Tramways introduced London's earliest regular electric working in 1901. The first trams to penetrate the parish were electric trams of the L.U.T., on the extensions in 1901 of the lines from Acton along Uxbridge Road, Ealing, to Hanwell and Southall and from Kew bridge along Brentford High Street to Hounslow.[77] Although Ealing vestry had approved of a suggested tramway between Ealing and Brentford in 1871,[78] many residents later opposed electrification.[79] It was only in 1906 that the two routes were linked by a line from Hanwell to Brentford. Under the London Passenger Transport Board, trolleybuses replaced trams along Brentford High Street in 1935 and on the routes through Ealing to Hanwell and from Hanwell to Brentford in 1936.[80] They continued to run daily through Ealing until c. 1960 and Brentford until 1962.[81]

A motor bus route of the London General Omnibus Co. terminated at Ealing and at East Ham (Essex) in 1911 and motor buses reached Hounslow in 1914.[82] Later, as part of London Transport's network, they served most of Ealing M.B. and Brentford.[83]

The G.W.R.'s main line to Slough and the west country opened in 1838, with its first station out of Paddington near the south-east corner of Haven Green common. The station, later called Ealing Broadway[84] and at the line's nearest point to Uxbridge Road, thereafter served much of the northern part of the parish. Farther west on the same line Castle Hill station was opened in 1871 to serve Ealing Dean and was renamed West Ealing in 1899.[85] A link with the G.W.R.'s new main line to Birmingham was opened in 1904, with a loop from West Ealing running north, close to the Hanwell boundary, through stations at Drayton Green, from 1905, and Castlebar

[59] Robbins, *Mdx.* 69.
[60] *L. & P. Hen. VIII*, xi, p. 566; P.R.O., STAC 2/6/60-1.
[61] P.R.O., E 134/Mich. 1659/30.
[62] *Cal. S.P. Dom.* 1659-60, 128.
[63] Turner, *Brentford*, 107; *Evening News*, 24 July 1939.
[64] Brentford and Chiswick Boro. *Intro. to Brentford and Chiswick* (1957); 31 Geo. II, c. 46 (Priv. Act).
[65] *Intro. to Brentford and Chiswick* (1957); *Home Counties Mag.* ii. 151-2; *Brentford and Chiswick As It Was*, illus. 32.
[66] E. C. R. Hadfield, *Canals of East Midlands* (1970), 110-11.
[67] *Brentford and Chiswick As It Was*, illus. 3.
[68] Gtr. Ealing Local Hist. Soc. *Local Historian*, i (1961), 58; Ealing Local Hist. Soc. *Local Historian* (1964), 14-15.
[69] Barker and Robbins, *Lond. Transport*, i. 391.
[70] Pigot, *Lond. Dir.* (1826-7); ibid. *Com. Dir.* (1832-4).
[71] Ealing Local Hist. Soc. *Local Historian* (1964), 14-15.
[72] *T.L.M.A.S.* xxiii. 178.
[73] Barker and Robbins, *Lond. Transport*, i. 391-2.

[74] *Univ. Brit. Dir.* (1791); Pigot, *Lond. Dir.* (1826-7); Pigot, *Com. Dir.* (1832-4).
[75] Barker and Robbins, *Lond. Transport*, i. 396.
[76] *P.O. Dir. Six Home Counties* (1845).
[77] Barker and Robbins, *Lond. Transport*, i. 196, 258-9, ii. 33.
[78] Allison and Holt, *Ealing in 18th and 19th Cents.* 48.
[79] M. A. Jahn, 'Railways and Suburban Development: Outer West Lond. 1850-1900' (Lond. Univ. M.Phil. thesis, 1971), 148.
[80] Barker and Robbins, *Lond. Transport*, ii. 31-2, 100-1, 300-1.
[81] Ealing Boro. *Official Guide* [1961]; Lond. Transport, *Bus Map* (1960, 1962); inf. from Mr. M. A. Jahn.
[82] Barker and Robbins, *Lond. Transport*, ii. 169, 185.
[83] Ealing Boro. *Official Guide* (1950 and later edns.).
[84] Robbins, *Mdx.* 78, 238-9.
[85] T. B. Peacock, *Gt. Western Suburban Svces.* (1948), 44, 47.

Park.[86] The Birmingham line itself crossed the north-eastern corner of the parish, where Brentham halt received suburban services from 1911 until its supersession by Hanger Lane station.[87]

Brentford, in 1950 renamed Brentford Central,[88] and Kew Bridge stations opened in 1849 on the L. & S.W.R.'s loop line through Chiswick to Hounslow, so connecting Brentford with Waterloo. The line was joined near Kew Bridge in 1853 by the North & South-Western Junction Railway Co.'s line from Acton, itself connected to Kew Bridge station in 1862.[89] Beyond the town the line to Hounslow was crossed by the Great Western & Brentford Railway Co.'s single track branch from Southall past Brentford goods yard, in Isleworth parish, to Brentford dock. Opened for freight in 1859 and for passengers to Brentford End in 1860, the branch was acquired by the G.W.R., which had leased it, in 1872 and was converted to a double track in 1876.[90] It closed in 1964, passenger services having ceased in 1942, whereupon the tracks south of the goods yard were lifted and the railway bridge beyond the western end of Brentford High Street was demolished.[91] The L. & S.W.R.'s Brentford Road, later Gunnersbury, station lay in Chiswick parish.[92]

Services to both Paddington and Waterloo were poor in the 1850s. Although those from Ealing became much more popular from 1863, when they connected with the new Metropolitan Railway's line from Paddington to the City, there was a strong local demand for improvements c. 1872. The G.W.R. did not introduce third class return tickets until 1875 or an early train to Paddington until 1876, and it provided only a few workmen's trains in the 1890s. The general service was more frequent from 1878, however, after the main line had been widened.[93]

Ealing was better served in 1879, when the Metropolitan District Railway opened a branch from Turnham Green through Mill Hill Park, later Acton Town, and Ealing Common, called Ealing Common and West Acton 1886–1910. Its terminus, at Ealing Broadway, stood slightly north of the G.W.R.'s station.[94] Although no railway linked Ealing village with Brentford, from 1883 the District's trains worked another east–west line, across the centre of the parish from Mill Hill Park to Hounslow. There were stations at South Ealing and at Boston Road, which was renamed Boston Manor in 1911. The intermediate Northfield halt was opened in 1908 and renamed Northfields and Little Ealing from 1911 and Northfields from 1932.[95] Workmen's trains were provided by the District from 1890, although too sparsely to satisfy the local authority.[96]

The north-eastern side of the parish received the District's first electrified service in 1903, when the South Harrow branch was opened. From a junction with the existing District line to Ealing Broadway at Hanger Lane, the Ealing & South Harrow railway ran northward, with stations at North Ealing and Park Royal. District services to Hounslow and between Ealing and Whitechapel were electrified in 1905.[97] Yet another service to London from Ealing Broadway, authorized in 1905 for the Ealing & Shepherd's Bush Railway, a G.W.R. promotion, was opened in 1920 by Central London trains.[98] It later formed part of London Transport's Central line, while the District's service from Ealing Broadway formed part of the District line and that to South Harrow part of the Piccadilly line from 1932; services to Hounslow received both District and Piccadilly trains from 1932 to 1964 and thereafter only those of the Piccadilly. With the opening of the Piccadilly line most stations were rebuilt, notably Ealing Common, by Charles Holden c. 1930, and Northfields, by Holden and S. A. Heaps in 1933.[99] South Ealing's 'temporary' booking hall of 1931 was still used in 1980, as was North Ealing's original District station. Park Royal station was moved in 1931 to Western Avenue, where the existing building with its shops and flats dates from 1936. At Ealing Broadway rebuilding started in 1962 after the merging of the old G.W.R. and District stations, the second of which had already been rebuilt c. 1910 and whose booking hall, converted into shops, survived in 1980.[1]

A westward extension of the Central line from North Acton was opened in 1947 beside the main line to Birmingham. Brentham halt was replaced by Hanger Lane station, completed in 1949, at the junction of Hanger Lane and Western Avenue.[2]

The Thames was used by travellers from Brentford to London, including Samuel Pepys in 1665.[3] Boats provided a convenient service in 1691[4] and a daily water conveyance, presumably for passengers, was still offered in 1845.[5] Under the Thames Navigation Act, 1777, tolls were collected by the navigation committee of the City of London, which in 1857 handed over government of the river to the Thames Conservancy Board, itself superseded in 1908 by the Port of London Authority.[6]

[86] Ibid. 44; Baker and Robbins, *Lond. Transport*, ii. 158.

[87] Peacock, *Gt. Western Suburban Svces.* 44; below.

[88] Connor and Halford, *Forgotten Stations*, 5.

[89] Barker and Robbins, *Lond. Transport*, i. 47, 136.

[90] H. P. White, *Regional Hist. Rlys. of G.B.* iii (1963), 117; *Mdx. Independent*, 20 Oct. 1951.

[91] *Brentford and Chiswick As It Was*, illus. 1; Connor and Halford, *Forgotten Stations*, 16; inf. from Mr. P. Hounsell. A single track served the goods yard in 1980.

[92] Above, Chiswick, communications.

[93] Jahn, 'Rlys. and Suburban Development', 28, 43, 75, 78–9.

[94] *Ealing As It Was* (Ealing L.B. Libr. Svce. 1980), illus. 38.

[95] Barker and Robbins, *Lond. Transport*, i. 209, 212;

Connor and Halford, *Forgotten Stations*, 5, 7, 11; C. E. Lee, *Metropolitan Dist. Rly.* (1956), 10, 48.

[96] Jahn, 'Rlys. and Suburban Development', 145.

[97] Lee, *Metropolitan Dist. Rly.* 45; Barker and Robbins, *Lond. Transport*, ii. 107–8.

[98] Barker and Robbins, *Lond. Transport*, ii. 243–4.

[99] Ibid. 252–3; Pevsner, *Mdx.* 42; C. E. Lee, *District Line* (1973), 29–30; A. A. Jackson and D. F. Croome, *Rails Through the Clay* (1962), 215–17.

[1] Inf. from Mr. P. Hounsell; *Ealing As It Was*, illus. 39.

[2] Jackson and Croome, *Rails Through the Clay*, 317–18.

[3] *Diary of Sam. Pepys*, ed. R. C. Latham and W. Matthews, vi. 199.   [4] G. Miege, *New State of Eng.* (1691).

[5] *P.O. Dir. Six Home Counties* (1845).

[6] 17 Geo III, c. 18; inf. from Mrs. K. Judges. See also above, Chiswick, Strand-on-the-Green.

GROWTH OF EALING.[7] Early settlement is attested by finds of Palaeolithic articles, chiefly around Ealing common and the main railway line, Neolithic implements, coins of the Iron Age, and Romano-British burials at Hanger Hill.[8] Although no Anglo-Saxon settlement is recorded, the name Ealing denotes the Gillingas, or Gilla's people, of c. 700.[9]

Ealing village and the medieval church lay at the centre of the parish, between two streams and south of Uxbridge Road. Smaller hamlets arose to the west at Ealing Dean and to the south-west at Little Ealing, both of them between the more westerly stream and the Brent.[10] South-east of Ealing village lay the manor house of Gunnersbury. North of Uxbridge Road the heavy clay land was less attractive to early settlement. Hanger Hill was so called from a *hangra* or 'wooded slope', where a wood existed in 1393 and 1539, as was the farm at Pitshanger, whose name occurred in 1222.[11] Drayton Green, close to Ealing Dean, and Haven Green, an extension of Ealing village, were the only settlements north of Uxbridge Road in the early 19th century.[12] There was then a contrast between the large estates north of the road, with their farms and parkland, and the more populous area to the south, with its market gardens joining those of Brentford.[13]

There were 85 households in Ealing and its surrounding hamlets, excluding Old Brentford, in 1599 and 116 by 1664. Ealing village was as large as the other hamlets combined in 1675.[14] The relative sizes of the hamlets in the 18th century cannot be assessed,[15] but the northern part of the parish as a whole was much less populous than Old Brentford or Lower Side, which had 259 households in 1664,[16] and was to remain so until 1861.[17] Ealing and Little Ealing in 1746 were described merely as very pleasant villages near Brentford,[18] although Ealing was noted for its royal and noble residents in the 18th and early 19th centuries, before becoming a spacious upper middle-class suburb from the 1860s.[19]

EALING village, where there was a church by c. 1127,[20] was also known in 1274 and 1393 as Church Ealing[21] and from 1593 as Great Ealing.[22] It was linear in shape, extending northward from the church along a street, much of it bordered by a narrow green, almost to Uxbridge Road. The village, with no medieval manor house and with no inn in 1599,[23] won little notice from travellers until the late 18th century, although in assessments of 1711 and later it was sometimes described as Ealing town.[24] Objects found in Grange Road and at the north end of Ealing green suggest that by 1700 buildings stretched the length of the modern St. Mary's Road. The finds from Grange Road may have come from Ealing House, which, with the adjoining Ealing Grove, originated in an estate of the late 16th century.[25]

By 1746 there had been little building south of the church, except a boys' school in South Ealing Road, but houses stood on either side of St. Mary's Road, those at the northern end facing each other across Ealing green. There was a pond on the green near the entrance to Mattock Lane, Maddock Lane in 1766, south of Ashton House or its forerunner. The village was extended still farther north by some buildings at the corner of Uxbridge Road. The high road itself was almost empty, apart from the Feathers and, to the east, the Bell. Beyond the Feathers, north of the road, houses stood on the north and east sides of the Haven or Haven Green,[26] an area normally assessed separately from Ealing village in the 18th century.[27]

Eminent residents, in addition to the occupiers of neighbouring estates mentioned below, included Earl Rivers and Lady Russell as early as 1704.[28] The novelist Henry Fielding (1707-54) from 1752 had a country house at Fordhook, north of Uxbridge Road near the Acton boundary, since the air was the 'best in the kingdom'.[29] Of two storeys and attics, with a stuccoed front of five bays,[30] Fordhook was a farmhouse in 1795[31] and the home of Byron's widow Lady Noel-Byron in 1835.[32] Noted for its gardens in 1845, it was pulled down after 1903.[33]

Although the parish became increasingly fashionable during the 18th century, housing in Ealing village spread very little between 1746 and 1822. By 1777 there were a few buildings in Mattock Lane and by 1822 some more in Love Lane, later the Grove, besides the Coach and Horses and a few other buildings, including almshouses, in Uxbridge Road.[34] The handsome villas noted from the 1790s included many that were outside the village,[35] which in 1816 bore a 'desirable air of retirement and country quiet.' There were however some dignified residences around the green, including one of c. 1770 later

[7] Old Brentford, with New Brentford, is described separately below.
[8] C. H. Keene, *Field Monuments of Ealing* (Ealing L.B. Technical Svces. Group, 1975), 11-15 and maps; *V.C.H. Mdx.* i. 18, 69.
[9] *V.C.H. Mdx.* i. 78; *P.N. Mdx.* (E.P.N.S.), 90.
[10] Gtr. Ealing Local Hist. Soc. *Broadsheet*, Oct. 1960.
[11] *P.N. Mdx.* (E.P.N.S.), 91-2.
[12] M.R.O., F 51 A, B.
[13] Jahn, 'Rlys. and Suburban Development', 21.
[14] K. J. Allison, *Elizabethan 'Census' of Ealing* (Ealing Local Hist. Soc. 1962), 7-9.
[15] There were changes in the areas assessed for poor rates: M.R.O., D.R.O. 37/B1/1, B2/4.
[16] Allison, *Elizabethan Census*, 8.
[17] K. J. Allison and E. D. G. Holt, *Ealing in 18th and 19th Cent.* 1.   [18] S. Simpson, *Agreable Historian*, ii (1746), 620.
[19] Jahn, 'Rlys. and Suburban Development', 22.
[20] Below, churches.

[21] *P.N. Mdx.* (E.P.N.S.), 90.
[22] Norden, *Spec. Brit.* 19; Camden, *Magna Britannia*, iii (1724), 48.
[23] Allison, *Elizabethan Census*, 8, 10.
[24] M.R.O., D.R.O. 37/B1/1.
[25] Keene, *Field Monuments*, 20 and map; below, other est.
[26] Rocque, *Map of Lond.* (1746), sheet 14.
[27] M.R.O., D.R.O. 37/B1/1, B2/4.   [28] Ibid. B1/1.
[29] W. L. Cross, *Hist. of Hen. Fielding*, ii (1918), 290; *D.N.B.*
[30] Guildhall Libr., grangerized copy of Lysons, *Environs*, ii (2), illus. between pp. 228 and 229.
[31] Lysons, *Environs*, ii. 228.
[32] *Complete Peerage*, ii. 457; viii. 226.
[33] *P.O. Dir. Six Home Counties* (1845), s.v. Acton; *Ealing As It Was*, illus. 58.
[34] Rocque, *Map of Lond.* (1746), sheet 14; M.R.O., Acc. 649/6; M.R.O., F 51 A.
[35] *Ambulator* (1793, 1796, 1800).

altered by Sir John Soane and known as Pitz-hanger Manor House.[36] Several smaller houses also were rebuilt, many surviving in 1979.[37]

The railway station, opened in 1838, was thought in 1845 to have brought many visitors to a pretty but previously little known place,[38] and already to have stimulated building to the north.[39] Within the old village the Park was laid out by Sidney Smirke as a residential side street off the east side of St. Mary's Road in 1846,[40] when it was also agreed to build on 9 a. belonging to Ashton House between Mattock Lane and Uxbridge Road. Some large villas there constituted Ealing's first successful building scheme on such a scale, although completion proved slow: Ashton House itself survived in the mid 1860s, when much of the Uxbridge Road frontage but only part of Mattock Lane had been built up. Meanwhile at the south end of the village smaller houses were being planned around Ranelagh Road on the Old Rectory estate, which had been bought c. 1852 by the Conservative Freehold Land Society, the first land society to obtain a foothold in Ealing. Progress was slow, only c. 20 houses being ready by the mid 1860s, presumably because the railway station was too far away.[41]

The northern end of the village, close to the railway, grew more rapidly, although a poor train service may have slowed building on the Ashton House estate and along the northern side of Uxbridge Road, where Christ Church had been erected in 1852-3. The road between Ealing green and Uxbridge Road was called High Street by 1873, when continuous building lined its eastern side, opposite the grounds of Ashton House.[42] High Street's western side was built up near Uxbridge Road in the 1870s and farther south in the 1880s.[43] The street consisted mainly of shops in 1877, when they extended to the stretch of Uxbridge Road called the Broadway and were about to be built along a more easterly stretch, the Mall.[44] East of High Street, buildings put up by John Galloway in Oxford Road included a block on the corner of the Broadway.[45]

A spate of building in the late 1870s and early 1880s saw Uxbridge Road lined with houses in both directions, the section near the station being dignified with shops, local offices, and, in 1889, a town hall.[46] The town extended to Ealing common by 1886, when large detached houses lined North Common Road, although on the east the common was still bordered by open country.[47] North Common Road, like the municipal offices and, earlier, Christ Church, was built on land belonging to the Wood family, whose estate included both sides of Uxbridge Road from Haven Green to the eastern boundary, besides frontages towards West Ealing.[48] New housing was still mainly for the middle or upper middle classes, following the example set elsewhere on the Woods' estate, although standards were less strict than in the 1850s. Farther south humbler housing was provided west of St. Mary's and South Ealing roads on the Beaconsfield estate of c. 1880, from Disraeli Road as far south as Venetia Road, which was close to the new South Ealing station.[49] Although building did not yet extend beyond the railway, a stretch of South Ealing Road on either side of the line was called Station Parade in 1886.[50] Housing also stretched eastward from St. Mary's Road over the Grange estate, along Warwick Road by 1883 and the south part of Windsor Road from 1889.[51] The western roads were short ones, leading to the future Walpole park, opened in 1901, and Lammas park, acquired in 1881, which together helped to preserve the old north-south line of the village.[52]

In 1893 most business premises were in High Street, the Broadway, and the Mall, or in Spring Bridge Road, leading to the west side of Haven Green, and the Parade, a row of shops near the station at the south-east corner of Haven Green.[53] The almshouses made way for shops on the south side of the Mall in 1902.[54] Bond Street, leading due north from Ealing green to Uxbridge Road, was under construction in 1904, when Ashton House was finally pulled down.[55] Shopping parades were built in 1905 both there and along the south side of the stretch of Uxbridge Road known as New Broadway,[56] where electric trams had run since 1901.[57] So was created an urban centre along Uxbridge Road and its shorter offshoots, in contrast with the much quieter old village along Ealing green and St. Mary's Road.

Growth around Uxbridge Road was largely to serve new suburbs to the north, themselves the product of better public transport. In the 20th century rebuilding and infilling continued along the main road, where most of the town's shops and restaurants were said to be modern in style in 1954[58] and where some imposing office blocks were built towards the west from the 1960s.[59] In the 1970s there were large modern stores on the south side of the Broadway, a street which also retained a refronted parade of 1883 and which had been altered much more than the Mall. Meanwhile at Haven Green some houses on the north side made way in the 1930s for the five-storeyed block of 160 flats called Haven Court. In St. Mary's Road the technical college was built in

[36] Brewer, *Beauties of Eng. & Wales*, x (5), 334; below, manors.
[37] Pevsner, *Mdx.* 43; Min. of Town and Country Planning, List of Bldgs. (1948).
[38] *P.O. Dir. Six Home Counties* (1845).
[39] T. Faulkner, *Hist. and Antiquities of Brentford, Ealing and Chiswick* (1845), 270.
[40] Pevsner, *Mdx.* 43.
[41] Jahn, 'Rlys. and Suburban Development', 24, 32-4.
[42] O.S. Map 6″, Mdx. XV. SE. (1873 edn.).
[43] Inf. from Mr. P. Hounsell; M.R.O., Acc. 1386/1069-81; date on pavement in Lamertons' bldg.
[44] *Brentford, Ealing Dir.* (1877); *Ealing Illustrated* (1893), 5; *Ealing As It Was*, illus. 26.
[45] Date on Midland Bank bldg.

[46] Jahn, 'Rlys. and Suburban Development', 108; M.R.O., 6″, Mdx. XV. SE. (1894-6 edn.).
[47] Bacon, *Atlas of Lond.* (1886).
[48] Inf. from Mr. P. Hounsell; below, manors.
[49] Jahn, 'Rlys. and Suburban Development', 108; M.R.O., Acc. 549/14; Acc. 1369/1.
[50] Bacon, *Atlas of Lond.* (1886).
[51] Gtr. Ealing Local Hist. Soc. *Local Historian*, iii. 40.
[52] O.S. Map 6″, Mdx. XV. SE. (1894-6 edn.).
[53] *Ealing Illustrated*, 5.   [54] *Ealing As It Was*, illus. 26, 29.
[55] *Ealing: Country Town Near Lond.* (1904), 19.
[56] Dates on bldgs.
[57] *Souvenir of Opening of L.U.T.* (1901), 41-2.
[58] Ealing Boro. *Official Guide* [1954].
[59] Plate facing p. 193.

1929 opposite Cairn Avenue, itself laid out by 1934 on the site of a house called the Owls, but otherwise little change took place in the old village or the Victorian avenues which branched off it on either side.[60]

The Broadway and its neighbourhood was by far the busiest of Ealing L.B.'s shopping centres in the early 1970s, with a turnover twice that of Acton or Southall. Rebuilding south of the Broadway and east of High Street was suggested in the 1950s, approved by the council in 1969, and planned to begin in a modified form in 1980, by which date several small streets behind the shops and north of the Grove had been demolished. The new scheme included shops, offices, flats, car parks, and a pedestrian precinct.[61]

In 1980 a conservation area stretched from Pitzhanger Manor House to St. Mary's church[62] where the line of old Ealing village along the west side of the road contained several brown-brick houses of the 18th and early 19th century.[63] Those along Ealing green include the 18th-century St. Mary's, the 19th-century pair formed by Pine Cottage and Thorpe Lodge, and a group of c. 1800 formed by St. Aidan and the neighbouring terrace of Morgan House, Wrexham Lodge, the Willow House. Farther south in St. Mary's Road stand the larger Ealing Court Mansions and Westfield House (no. 94), both of the early 19th century. The second faces the small St. Mary's Square, crossed by heavy traffic, where humbler buildings, including the former fire station, mark the southern limit of the 19th-century village. In Church Lane, leading west from the square, nos. 1 and 17 are 18th-century cottages. At the north-east end of the village, the Mall contains a pair of stuccoed early 19th-century houses, nos. 42–3, next to some shops.

LITTLE EALING, so called by 1650,[64] lay 1 km. south-west of the parish church. Equidistant from Uxbridge Road and Brentford, it was linked with them by Northfield Lane (later Avenue) and Windmill Lane respectively and grew up where they met Little Ealing Lane from the east.[65] The manor house of Coldhall was once thought to have stood farther east beside South Ealing Road, but more probably it was near the lanes' junction on the west side of Northfield Lane.[66] By 1664 the largest house was probably Place House, south of the junction and later called Ealing Park.[67]

Until the late 19th century Little Ealing was only a small hamlet, with 14 householders assessed for church rates in 1704 and 1719,[68] 19 in

1750, and 14 in 1766.[69] Its population was 129 in 1841.[70] Buildings included the early 18th-century Rochester House,[71] at the corner of Little Ealing Lane and close to the Plough, perhaps the inn so called in 1722 and said in 1898 to be the parish's oldest building.[72] All the houses were close to the lanes' junction in 1746[73] and remained so in the 1860s.[74] A residence inherited from King Gould in 1756 by his son Charles (1726–1806), later a baronet and Judge Advocate-General,[75] may have been replaced by a nursery garden of Hugh Ronalds, west of the south end of Northfield Lane, before 1822.[76] Charles Gould sold much Ealing property, changed his name to Morgan, and moved to Monmouthshire; on the other hand his heirs still paid rates in Little Ealing, where his house was said to stand empty in 1898.[77]

Ealing Park and 70 a. were sold for building in 1882.[78] The house, as a convent, retained some of its landscaped grounds in the 1890s,[79] and Little Ealing was still a quiet hamlet in 1898.[80] To the south, however, Murray and Whitestile roads had been laid out by the British Land Co. by 1883[81] and some houses stood in Darwin Road by 1896, foreshadowing the joining up of the village and northern Brentford. Soon the spread of housing around South Ealing station reached Little Ealing, where the old Plough was demolished in 1905[82] and a school was built east of Rochester House. A few small shops were built on the east side of Northfield Avenue, between the Plough and Julien Road, c. 1909.[83]

By 1920 the grounds of Ealing Park had been mostly covered with terraced or semi-detached houses, as had all the land stretching eastward to South Ealing Road and northward to the District railway line. Some open ground survived on the west side of Northfield Avenue, near Niagara House, but much of the avenue had been built up beyond the railway, where the naming of a halt as Northfields and Little Ealing signified the end of the village's separate identity. By 1934 Niagara House had gone and there were more shops and a cinema on the west side of Northfield Avenue. The last adjoining open spaces, to the west, had been taken for sports grounds and for housing which stretched along Swyncombe Avenue to Boston Manor Road.[84]

Both the former Ealing Park[85] and Rochester House survived in 1980. Rochester House was presumably built for John Pearce (d. 1752), a London distiller who bought land at Little Ealing c. 1712, and named after his son Zachary Pearce, bishop of Rochester (1690–1774), who died there.[86] A residence of the exiled General Charles-

[60] O.S. Map 6″, Mdx. XV. SE. (1920, 1934 edns.).
[61] *Ealing Central Area* (Ealing L.B. Technical Svces. Group, 1979).
[62] Ealing L.B. *Official Guide* [1973–4].
[63] Para. based on Pevsner, *Mdx.* 43; Min. of Town and Country Planning, List of Bldgs. (1948).
[64] *P.N. Mdx.* (E.P.N.S.), 92.
[65] O.S. Map 6″, Mdx. XV. SE. (1873 edn.).
[66] Below, manors.   [67] Below, other est.
[68] M.R.O., D.R.O. 37/B1/1.
[69] Ibid. B2/4.
[70] *Census*, 1841.   [71] Below.
[72] M.R.O., MR/LV3/95; E. Jackson, *Annals of Ealing* (1898), 163.

[73] Rocque, *Map of Lond.* (1746), sheet 14.
[74] O.S. Map 6″, Mdx. XV. SE. (1873 edn.).
[75] *D.N.B.*
[76] M.R.O., Acc. 649/6; F 51 A.
[77] Ealing Local Hist. Soc. *Local Historian* (1966), 4–7.
[78] Jahn, 'Rlys. and Suburban Development', 97.
[79] Rest of para. and following para. based on O.S. Map 6″, Mdx. XV. SE. (1894–6 and 1920 edns.).
[80] Jackson, *Ealing*, 221.
[81] Jahn, 'Rlys. and Suburban Development', 112.
[82] Photo. in Chiswick libr.
[83] Date on bldgs.
[84] O.S. Map 6″, Mdx. XV. SE. (1920, 1934 edns.).
[85] Below, other est.   [86] *D.N.B.*

François Dumouriez[87] from 1804 to 1818, it later became a school and in 1980 housed the Institution of Production Engineers. It is a three-storeyed brown-brick building, with a late 18th-century extension to the south-west.[88]

EALING DEAN, perhaps so called from 'valley' or *denu*, was recorded from 1456 and was known earlier, from 1234, as West Ealing.[89] It grew up along Uxbridge Road 1·5 km. west of the north end of Ealing village beyond the 7-mile stone, where a crossroads was formed by the junction of the high road with Northfield Lane and Drayton Green Lane.[90] Ealing Dean's householders probably included at least half of the 25 assessed at Drayton in 1710 and the 34 at 'Drayton and the roadside' in 1719; eleven were assessed at the roadside alone in 1766.[91]

In 1746 and 1822 buildings stood only on the north side of Uxbridge Road, west of the crossroads. They included the Green Man, licensed by 1722, and the Old Hat, by 1759 the name of two inns, farther west.[92] One of the Old Hats was also called Halfway House by 1845[93] and the other in the 1880s was claimed to have existed for 300 years.[94]

The G.W.R.'s main line from 1838 marked off a strip of land between itself and Uxbridge Road, where the working-class cottages of Stevens Town were built at Ealing Dean between 1840 and 1860.[95] As part of the district of Christ Church at Haven Green, they probably formed the neighbourhood which in 1864 was said to be attracting large numbers of the poor, whose low standards threatened to reduce it to the condition of Brentford.[96]

In 1873 the buildings along the north side of the main road, in front of Stevens Town, still faced fields, market gardens, the parish allotments beside Northfield Lane, and a solitary inn. East of the crossroads, however, there was building on both sides of Uxbridge Road and also at the west end of Mattock Lane, where St. John's church was built in 1876. Houses, with a few gaps, lined most of Uxbridge Road between Ealing Dean and the town[97] and spread rapidly between the road and the railway after the opening of Castle Hill, later West Ealing, station in 1871.[98] The northern part of the parish's only working-class housing of that date was built east of Stevens Town c. 1880. Serious overcrowding was said to exist in the following decade, when Ealing Dean had c. 8,000 people in 700 cottages.[99] By 1886 building stretched continuously along Uxbridge Road towards Ealing and also filled the short roads such as Broughton

Road which branched off it towards the railway.[1]

The last part of Ealing Dean to be built up was on the south side of Uxbridge Road west of the crossroads. There were a few houses near the Hanwell boundary at the top of Coldershaw and Grosvenor roads in 1886[2] and many more, as far east as Seaford Road, by 1896.[3] St. James's church was built for the western end of the suburb in 1903–4, by which date a stretch of Uxbridge Road served as a shopping centre half way between Ealing and Hanwell.[4] Some rebuilding took place there in the 1930s, when the stretch was known as the Broadway, West Ealing, and Stevens Town was rebuilt in the 1960s. By 1979 the Broadway was the second busiest shopping area in the borough.[5] Only between Seaford Road and the crossroads did open spaces survive, in the form of Dean gardens and the allotments which in 1980 still gave a rural air to the north end of Northfield Lane.

The Ealing-born novelist Nevil Shute (1899–1960) was the son of Arthur H. Norway, who lived at no. 16 Somerset Road by 1890.[6]

DRAYTON GREEN, near to the Hanwell boundary, was called Drayton in 1387 and later often Drayton in Ealing, to distinguish it from the separate parish of West Drayton.[7] Although often taxed in the 18th century with houses along Uxbridge Road at Ealing Dean,[8] Drayton Green remained a distinct hamlet until the spread of building in the late 19th century.

The hamlet grew up near the site of a house, perhaps once moated,[9] at the northern end of a green.[10] In 1636 the green consisted of a rectangle bisected by the way later called Drayton Green Lane, which was bordered by narrower strips of waste for much of its course northward to Perivale ford. About a dozen buildings stood on the northern, eastern, and western sides of the green, including David Walter's Drayton House by the road at the north end and William Baringer's house next to some cottages on the east side. Most of the surrounding land was held by Walter, who was to be assessed on 11 hearths in 1664,[11] or Baringer.

Drayton Green, remained a small hamlet, where in 1766 only 8 householders were assessed for church rates[12] and where buildings in 1822 occupied much the same positions as in 1636.[13] The G.W.R. line ran close to the south end of the green from 1838 and perhaps helped to keep it separate from Ealing Dean. In the mid 1860s the surroundings were still open, whereas building had spread along most of the north side of

[87] *Dictionnaire de Biographie Française*, xii.
[88] Min. of Town and Country Planning, List of Bldgs. (1948); Hist. Mon. Com. *Mdx.* 15; below, educ.
[89] *P.N. Mdx.* (E.P.N.S.), 92.   [90] M.R.O., F 51 A.
[91] M.R.O., D.R.O. 37/B1/1, B2/4.
[92] Rocque, *Map of Mdx.* (1746), sheet 14; M.R.O., F 51 A; M.R.O., MR/LV3/95, LV7/39.
[93] *P.O. Dir. Six Home Counties* (1845).
[94] Jackson, *Ealing*, 158–9.
[95] Jahn, 'Rlys. and Suburban Development', 38.
[96] M.R.O., D.R.O. 37/A11/1.
[97] O.S. Map 6″, Mdx. XV. SE. (1873 edn.).
[98] M.R.O., D.R.O. 37/A12/1.
[99] Jahn, 'Rlys. and Suburban Development', 95–6, 118.

[1] Bacon, *Atlas of Lond.* (1886).   [2] Ibid.
[3] Rest of para. based on O.S. Map 6″, Mdx. XV. SE. (1894–6 and later edns.).
[4] *Ealing: Country Town Near Lond.* 19; *Ealing As It Was*, illus. 67.
[5] Inf. from Mr. P. Hounsell; *Ealing Central Area* (1979).
[6] *D.N.B.*; *Kelly's Dir. Mdx.* (1890).
[7] *P.N. Mdx.* (E.P.N.S.), 91.
[8] M.R.O., D.R.O. 37/B1/1.
[9] Keene, *Field Monuments*, 18 and map.
[10] Para. based on P.R.O., MPA 7.
[11] K. J. Allison, *Ealing in 17th Cent.* (Ealing Local Hist. Soc. 1963), no. E. 157.
[12] M.R.O., D.R.O. 37/B2/4.   [13] M.R.O., F 51 A.

Uxbridge Road. A house on the green, west of the lane, was called Manor House, although Drayton had never been a manor, and a farmhouse, later called Drayton Farm, lay to the north. A residence set back from the east side of the green was called Drayton House, with grounds stretching southward to a lodge by the railway.[14]

To the east Argyle and Sutherland roads were laid out in 1870, when the G.W.R. was about to open Castle Hill, later West Ealing, station.[15] Housing was approaching along those roads by 1886,[16] although Drayton Green itself remained unchanged in 1896.[17] The iron church of St. Luke stood north-east of the green, at the corner of the new Courtfield Gardens and Lynton Avenue, from 1901.[18] At that time the east side of the green was built up, Drayton House being replaced by a school which opened in 1908,[19] while the hamlet was hemmed in to the west by the G.W.R.'s depot and the loop line through Drayton Green station, opened in 1905. Semi-detached houses had encroached on the north-eastern corner of the green by 1908, when its remaining 4 a. were fenced and improved as an open space.[20] Manor House survived until after 1920, by which date there was building over all the grounds of Drayton House around Drayton Avenue.[21]

Away from the old hamlets, building in the northern half of the parish in the late 19th century followed the sale of large estates.[22] Activity was often delayed, however, by problems over drainage, caused partly by the London Clay and partly by the fact that the authority of Ealing's local board of health, set up in 1863, was not extended to the northern boundary until 1873. A modest beginning was the Ecclesiastical Commissioners' sale in 1852 of 5 a. of glebe at Castlebar Hill, where two houses were built in 1853 and most plots had been let by the early 1860s. Houses formed an isolated row in the later Castlebar Road in the mid 1860s, when building was about to start nearby in Eaton Rise, which was laid out by John Galloway.[23]

The most ambitious building scheme was that of Henry de Bruno Austin,[24] lessee of Castle Hill Lodge,[25] who in 1864 began to build on 190 a. between the G.W.R. line and the northern boundary, on both slopes of the western end of the Hanger Hill ridge. The land included 107 a. leased from C. P. Millard of Pitshanger, Brent, and Drayton Green farms and 65 a. from F. C. Swinden of Castle Hill Park, but not Castle Hill Park itself. Several roads had been laid out north of Castle Hill by 1866, where Kent Gardens was lined with large semi-detached houses and Cleveland Gardens, to the west, had a few 10-bedroomed villas. Austin went bankrupt in 1872 and building on the most southerly part of his estate, near Castle Hill station, was delayed until

its purchase by a land company in 1882. The rest of his land, where avenues had been laid out around St. Stephen's church, consecrated in 1876, remained empty in the 1890s. Building was also delayed on the adjoining estates of Castlebar Park, where St. Stephen's Road was laid out in 1874 but plots were not marked out until c. 1880, and Castle Hill Park, partly divided in 1870 but built up only gradually from 1880. Such delays in fulfilling the extensive plans of the 1860s made the early growth of north Ealing 'the most notable failure in outer west London'.

The largest landowner c. 1850 was the Wood family, with over 920 a. in Ealing and northern Acton, including the compact 750-a. Hanger Hill estate, land along Uxbridge Road, and smaller pieces near the Perivale boundary. The antiquary John Bowyer Nichols (1779–1863) was an early resident at Hanger Hill.[26] Although the first villas in Uxbridge Road were finished in the 1850s, most of the Woods' land was built up only after c. 1877, when activity was so intense that in 1878 six times as many houses were completed in Ealing as in 1876. Craven, Culmington, and Madeley roads recall the Shropshire associations of Edward Wood (d. 1904), of Culmington Manor, Craven Arms (Salop).[27] Just as the first villas in Uxbridge Road had been intended for buyers who kept their own carriages, so most of the Woods' property north and west of Ealing town was intended for the upper middle class. Probably the area's assured social status explained the successful sale of houses in Mount Park Crescent, Madeley Road, and similar avenues in the 1880s. Most of the Hanger Hill estate, however, was not built up in 1899, when Wood complained that progress had been impeded by the construction of the South Harrow railway.[28]

Meanwhile cheaper housing was being built in Arlington Road and its neighbours north of Castle Hill station and, more widely, south of Uxbridge Road. The Beaconsfield estate on the west side of old Ealing village was the forerunner of extensive lower middle-class housing around South Ealing station and Little Ealing, where such houses may have hindered the sale of larger ones on the British Land Co.'s property around Whitestile Road.

In the mid 1890s[29] building joined the new urban centre at the north end of Ealing village to both Ealing Dean and the western end of Ealing common. It was also approaching Drayton Green and from Haven Green it stretched westward along Gordon Road, northward, and north-eastward. Farther north some houses stood in Castlebar Park, Mount Avenue, and Montpelier Road. There remained empty roads around St. Stephen's church, however, and the fringes of the parish were still rural: near Brentside farm in the north-western corner, Woodbury and Pits-

---

[14] O.S. Map 6″, Mdx. XV. SE. (1873 edn.).
[15] Jahn, 'Rlys. and Suburban Development', 62.
[16] Bacon, *Atlas of Lond.* (1886).
[17] O.S. Map 6″, Mdx. XV. SE. (1894–6 edn.).
[18] Below, churches.
[19] *Mdx. County Times,* 1 Mar. 1913.
[20] C. Jones, *Decade of Progress, 1901–11,* 42 and map.
[21] O.S. Map 6″, Mdx. XV. SE. (1920 edn.).

[22] Following 4 paras. based on Jahn, 'Rlys. and Suburban Development', *passim.* [23] M.R.O., Acc. 1386/1053–68.
[24] *Ealing As It Was,* illus. 60. [25] M.R.O., Acc. 1028/64–5.
[26] D.N.B.; *Gent. Mag.* cliii (2), 794.
[27] Inf. from Mr. P. Hounsell.
[28] Ibid.; M.R.O., Acc. 234/1–2.
[29] Para. based on O.S. Maps 6″, Mdx. XV. NE., SE., XVI. NW., SW., XX. NE., XXI. NW. (1894–6 edn.).

hanger farm north of Pitshanger Lane, Hanger Hill House in the north-east, and Fordhook at the eastern end of Ealing common. South of Uxbridge Road housing branched to east and west from the old line of Ealing village but open country lay beyond on either side. Housing was approaching Little Ealing, in the south-west, from both Ealing and Brentford, whereas the south-eastern corner of the parish remained open. Gunnersbury Lodge stood north of Gunnersbury Lane, with Manor House to the west and the two seats of Gunnersbury Park and Gunnersbury House to the south, overlooking parkland and fields which stretched south to Chiswick High Road. A few buildings, including St. James's church, stood on the Ealing side of the high road and many more, constituting the suburb called Gunnersbury, on the Chiswick side.

The prosperous middle-class character of Ealing as a whole was widely advertised and strenuously defended. Unlike neighbouring authorities, the local board did not encourage cheap railway fares and its successor, the U.D.C., opposed all projected tramways after 1885.[30] Promotional literature, often financed by tradesmen, presented Ealing as more of a separate town in its own right than any other outlying suburb, offering in 1893, amidst 'charming rusticity', 'every advantage of modern civilization'. Few of the shops were mere branches of London stores, the main streets did not peter out in cheaper ones, and there were many fashionable promenades, clubs, hotels, and entertainments.[31] A low death-rate was repeatedly stressed and in 1904 ascribed to the gravel subsoil, high housing standards, and good sewerage. Potential residents were also lured by the private schools, which for long had produced famous pupils, by modest local rates, and the absence of industry. Pride was taken in being free of such 'nuisances' as non-parochial cemeteries or asylums and even in the fact that criminals were sent for trial to Brentford.[32] In 1901 Ealing had a higher proportion of female domestic servants than any suburb except Hampstead and Kensington.[33]

Renewed building activity from the late 1890s weakened some of the claims that Ealing was an exclusive suburb. By 1904 it was admitted that cheaper houses were spreading, although large ones were still going up and the rich had not been driven away.[34] In 1911 the whole borough was described, with exaggeration, as a garden suburb, since 12,000 trees had been planted since 1873.[35] It would have been true to say that the prosperous areas retained their identity, with the result that Ealing was still predominantly middle-class in 1911.[36]

In the northern part of the parish many plots were filled after 1896, during a building boom which reached its peak in 1903. Houses were at

last built in Egerton Gardens and other roads around St. Stephen's church.[37] Already there was rebuilding on desirable sites, such as that of no. 17 Ealing Common, which made way for an ornate five-storeyed block of flats.[38] Most building, however, was in the south and west parts, notably on market gardens south of Ealing Dean, and was for clerks and other lower middle-class occupants.[39] Council houses were built on part of 6½ a. off South Ealing Road, bought in 1899, where 131 cottages and flats in North and South roads were first occupied in 1902.[40]

Six working men combined in 1901 to buy plots for 9 houses in Woodfield Road, east of Pitshanger Farm.[41] Encouraged by Henry Vivian, Ealing Tenants Ltd. was formed as a co-partnership, also in 1901, to build terraces in Woodfield Avenue, Woodfield Crescent, and Brunner Road, with support from Leopold de Rothschild and others. So originated the first true garden suburb and a national movement, similar tenants' associations being formed at Letchworth (Herts.) and Sevenoaks (Kent) in 1905 and later at Hampstead.[42] Land, much of it formerly part of Pitshanger farm, was bought piecemeal until Brentham, as the estate was called, covered 60½ a., where the last of 700 planned houses were finished in 1914–15. Ealing Tenants having been absorbed by Co-Partnership Tenants before 1930, the estate was sold to Liverpool Trust Ltd. in 1936 and to Bradford Property Trust in 1940. A few houses had been sold privately by 1936 but despite further sales a third of the property was still rented in 1964.

The garden estate proper was begun in 1907, when Barry Parker and Raymond Unwin advised on the layout. They designed the distinctive nos. 1–7 Winscombe Crescent and were followed by F. Cavendish Pearson, whose work included Neville, Ludlow, and Meadvale roads, and then by G. L. Sutcliffe, whose last work was in Fowlers Walk. During the 1930s and after the Second World War there was some private infilling, and several of the original properties lost their privet hedges and acquired garages. Brentham nonetheless retained its character in 1969, when it was designated a conservation area.[43]

The establishment of Brentham combined with the building up of older roads on the northern side of the Hanger Hill ridge to create a small shopping centre along the north side of Pitshanger Lane. St. Stephen's school had been opened there in 1882, St. Barnabas's church was begun in 1914, and many shops stood between the two sites by 1908. In 1979 they served a district separated from the rest of Ealing by the Hanger Hill ridge and from more modern suburbs to the north by recreational land along the Brent.

[30] Jahn, 'Rlys. and Suburban Development', 163.
[31] Ealing Illustrated, 3.
[32] Ealing: Country Town Near Lond. 4, 6, 15; Ealing Illustrated, 4–7, 10–11.
[33] Jahn, 'Rlys. and Suburban Development', 156.
[34] Ealing: Country Town Near Lond. 20.
[35] Ealing Local Hist. Soc. Local Historian (1964), 39.
[36] Jahn, 'Rlys. and Suburban Development', 156.
[37] Ibid. 153–4.   [38] Bldg. News, lxxxii. 307.

[39] O.S. Map 6", Mdx. XV. SE. (1894–6 edn.); Jahn, 'Rlys. and Suburban Development', 153.
[40] Kelly's Dir. Mdx. (1908); Jones, Decade of Progress, 67.
[41] Following 2 paras. based on Ealing Local Hist. Soc. Local Historian (1964), 39–42; M. Tims, Ealing Tenants Ltd. (Ealing Local Hist. Soc. 1966); Brentham, England's Garden Suburb (Brentham Soc. 1977).
[42] V.C.H. Mdx. v. 13.
[43] Ealing L.B. Official Guide [1973–4].

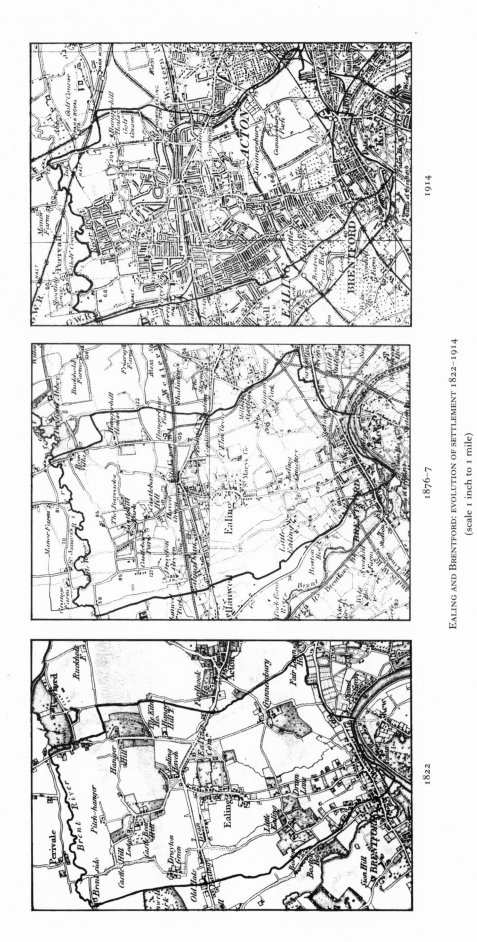

EALING AND BRENTFORD: EVOLUTION OF SETTLEMENT 1822–1914

(scale 1 inch to 1 mile)

Between the World Wars building covered most available plots and was carried to the edges of the borough, except where open spaces had been preserved.[44] In the north-west corner the Cleveland estate off Argyle Road was planned in 1924.[45] Semi-detached houses in Avalon Road ran from Vallis Way to the Crossway by 1928 and to Ruislip Road by 1932, while Cavendish Avenue ran along the Hanwell boundary by 1939. In the north-east corner Kingfield, Mulgrave, and neighbouring roads had been built up east of Brentham by 1935 and detached houses were built before and after the Second World War in avenues east of Hanger Lane. South of Uxbridge Road housing stretched from Ealing Dean or West Ealing southward to Little Ealing, except where allotments survived at the north end of Northfield Avenue: Camborne Avenue and Leyborne Avenue, projected in 1920, had been built up by 1934. In the south-eastern corner of the borough, building drew closer to Gunnersbury park. Sunderland and Durham roads in 1920 led from South Ealing Road only as far as Roberts Alley, later Olive Road, but by 1934 they stretched eastward along Maple Grove and its neighbours between the District railway and Pope's Lane. Infilling included Ealing Village, where 128 flats in four-storeyed blocks, apart from the gatehouse, formed a cheaply built private estate on a previously neglected strip of ground near the railway north-east of Ealing Broadway station.[46]

By 1951 there was so little land available that it was not thought possible to house all applicants within the borough.[47] Council houses multiplied from 3,484 before the Second World War to 8,639 by 1965[48] but most building took place beyond the old parish, notably at Northolt. Many older houses in and around Ealing town had been subdivided by 1951,[49] as others were thereafter. There remained a contrast between the leafy avenues north of the main railway line and east of the old village around the common, on the one hand, and the denser housing of West and South Ealing. The area north and north-east of the town, in particular, remained exclusive, with blocks of private flats interspersed among the large Victorian villas. Characteristic of such high-density but expensive building were two ten-storeyed towers begun in 1963 on the north side of St. Stephen's Road.[50]

The population of Ealing parish, including Old Brentford, rose slowly from 5,035 in 1801 to 7,783 in 1831, after a recent influx of market garden workers, and 9,828 in 1851.[51] Old Brentford chapelry, with 6,057 inhabitants, remained more populous than the rest of Ealing in 1851 but thereafter Brentford's growth rate declined:[52]

increases in the ancient parish to 11,963 in 1861, 18,189 by 1871, 25,436 by 1881, and 35,648 by 1891 resulted mainly from growth around Ealing itself. Separated from Brentford, Ealing M.B. had 33,031 inhabitants in 1901, 61,222 in 1911, and 67,755 in 1921, before the absorption of Hanwell and other areas. The population of the enlarged borough fell slightly between 1951 and 1961, from 187,323 to 183,077, as in neighbouring districts.

GROWTH OF BRENTFORD. The town grew up as Old Brentford in Ealing parish and New Brentford in Hanwell. It was united under a local board of health in 1874 and from 1894 lay within Brentford U.D., later said to consist of 1,091 a. from Old Brentford and 217 a. from New Brentford.[53] Despite Brentford's antiquity, there were no substantial grounds for the claim that it was the county town, first made in 1789: the county court had sometimes sat there, as in 1378 and 1608, and Middlesex's parliamentary elections took place there in the 18th and 19th centuries.[54]

The name Brentford was recorded from 705 and has generally been assumed to refer to the ford over the Brent or 'holy water', although it may have referred to the crossing of the Thames. The Ham was an Anglo-Saxon name, denoting a *hamm* or piece of flat land beside the river. The parts of the settlement in Ealing and Hanwell respectively were distinguished as East Brentford and West Brentford by 1294 and as Old and New Brentford by c. 1500.[55] New Brentford, whose buildings met those of Old Brentford at the Borough,[56] c. 1170 was called Bordwadestone, presumably Bord's *tun* or farm,[57] and some early 13th-century references to Brentford were to Old Brentford alone.[58] Bordwadestone or Bordestone came to be the name of a manor, from the 16th century called Boston, whose boundary in 1749 was taken as that of St. Lawrence's or New Brentford parish. Brentford End was the name of a settlement on the west bank of the Brent, in Isleworth.[59]

A Neolithic site, perhaps of a flint workshop, has been identified at New Brentford.[60] The hypothesis that an important Roman north–south route forded the Thames at Brentford is unproven:[61] stakes along the foreshore at Old England, which later was largely covered by a rail head dock, and to the west at Brentford End were perhaps used to defend the ford. They are the only material evidence that Julius Caesar's crossing in 54 B.C. was at Brentford.[62]

From the late 1st century A.D. Brentford was a settlement on the road from London to the west. Habitations, mainly on the high ground north of the modern High Street, stretched from Old

[44] Para. based on O.S. Maps 6″, Mdx. XV. NE., SE. (1920, 1934–5 edns.).
[45] Ealing libr., sales cats.
[46] Plate facing p. 193.
[47] *Ealing, 1901–51*, ed. F. W. Scouse, 35.
[48] *Boro. of Ealing Year Bk.* (1949–50, 1965–6).
[49] *Ealing, 1901–51*, 35.
[50] *Contract Jnl.* 6 June 1963.
[51] Para. based on *Census*, 1801–1961.
[52] Jahn, 'Rlys. and Suburban Development', 174.
[53] *Census*, 1921; below, local govt.

[54] P.R.O., C 88/50; C 88/225; Canham, *Brentford*, 8; below.
[55] *P.N. Mdx.* (E.P.N.S.), i, 31–2, 200.
[56] Guildhall MSS. 11765, 11766.
[57] *Letters and Charters of Gilb. Foliot*, ed. A. Morey and C. N. L. Brooke (1967), 492; *P.N. Mdx.* (E.P.N.S.), 32.
[58] e.g. *Cur. Reg. R.* ix. 185–6, 190.
[59] Canham, *Brentford*, 3, 5.
[60] Canham, *Brentford*, 20, 24, 36–40, 147.
[61] Sharpe, *Bygone Hanwell*, 4–5; Canham, *Brentford*, 3.
[62] Canham, *Brentford*, 9, 147–8; *V.C.H. Mdx.* i. 65.

Brentford for 400 to 600 m. to a point west of St. Lawrence's church, close to the Brent.[63] There was Roman settlement also on the west bank of the Brent[64] and Romano-British huts, presumably of fishermen, existed at Old England and on the Thames foreshore in front of Syon House, Isleworth.[65] Agriculture was practised but apparently there was little material wealth and in late Roman times all the sites that have been excavated, except one west of the church, were deserted.[66] A single site, at Old Brentford, revealed Saxon occupation. Since the line of the Roman road did not survive,[67] Brentford seems to have been abandoned soon after the Romans left.

The kings of Wessex and Essex met at Brentford in 705,[68] Offa, king of Mercia, held a council there in 780,[69] and Archbishop Jaenbeorht held a synod there in 781.[70] The strategic importance of the ford over the Thames was shown by the battle of Brentford, fought on the south bank between King Edmund Ironside and King Canute, in 1016.[71] No trace of late Saxon occupation, however, has been found.[72]

Old Brentford was probably included with Ealing in the grant of Fulham c. 704 to the bishop of London[73] and New Brentford was part of the abbot of Westminster's manor of Hanwell by 1157.[74] Both Old and New Brentford were probably included with their parent manors in Domesday Book,[75] and the fact that neither became a parish suggests that they were not populous in the 11th and 12th centuries. In addition to the royal fishery in the Thames recorded from 996 and an episcopal fishery from 1257, three other fisheries were held by tenants by 1423.[76] Gervase of Brentford in 1220 held 5 virgates of villein land at Old Brentford.[77] In 1383 open fields stretched north and south of the highway. Besides Sergeaunts free tenement there were between 9 and 13 villein holdings along the road. Several lay to the east, near London Style on the Chiswick boundary, and others near the Borough, where there was a gravel pit.[78] Although the original holdings had been broken up by 1383, no new dwellings were recorded in the early 15th century. Tenants then held less land than those elsewhere in Ealing manor,[79] but apparently not because of any urban activities.[80]

At New Brentford the estate which later became the manor of Boston had been subinfeud-

ated by c. 1170, when the lord founded St. Lawrence's hospital and chapel near his house south of High Street.[81] To the north some land was kept in demesne; also to the north and to the west lay commons, while to the south there were probably marshy meadows, leaving little space for tenants' holdings.[82] Thirteenth-century settlement has been uncovered on only one site, immediately west of the church.[83] Increasing traffic, however, was indicated by grants of pontage in 1224 on merchandise and in 1280 towards Brentford bridge,[84] and may also have prompted the grant of a market and fairs in 1306.[85] Dealings in property, sometimes by craftsmen, became more common from c. 1300[86] and several sites south of High Street were occupied during the 14th century.[87] Pavage was repeatedly levied for the highway from 1360[88] and another hospital, serving poor wayfarers, existed by 1393.[89] The first named inns occurred in 1384 and 1436.[90] The foundation of Syon abbey in 1415 and of a third hospital immediately west of the rebuilt bridge in 1446[91] contributed to the emergence of Brentford End by the early 16th century[92] and perhaps also to neighbouring New Brentford; in 1502 Syon abbey gave a Brentford brickmaker a large order.[93] About 1528 New Brentford, an urban area almost entirely dependent on imported food,[94] was rich enough to support its own priest by subscription.[95]

There were side streets and still some gaps in the roadside settlement c. 1530.[96] High Street and its buildings ran across the Ham, a common recorded from 1436.[97] Part of the Ham north of High Street was the site of the butts required by Henry VIII[98] and was usually known as the Butts from 1596.[99] Common continued to surround New Brentford on three sides until a neck of waste between High Street and the Brent was occupied in the 16th and 17th centuries.[1] Building apparently then severed the Ham from the Butts, and in 1635 the George and other buildings occupied sites stretching from High Street to the river.[2]

Behind two leading inns, the Three Pigeons or Three Doves, formerly the Crown, and the Red Lion, an orchard was converted c. 1560 into a market place. Several times extended,[3] Market Place was surrounded by inns: the Three Pigeons, which ultimately stretched to the Brent, was at the south-west corner,[4] the White Horse by 1603

[63] Canham, *Brentford, passim*, esp. 148.
[64] *T.L.M.A.S.* xxvii. 179–205.
[65] Canham, *Brentford*, 14, 32.
[66] Ibid. 29, 148–50. [67] Ibid. 30–1, 150.
[68] *Cart. Sax.* ed. Birch, i, pp. 169–70.
[69] *Cod. Dipl.* ed. Kemble, i, p. 172.
[70] Ibid. pp. 173–4.
[71] F. M. Stenton, *Anglo-Saxon Eng.* (1971), 391.
[72] Canham, *Brentford, passim*, esp. 17.
[73] Below, manors.
[74] *V.C.H. Mdx.* iii. 224.
[75] Below, manors; *V.C.H. Mdx.* iii. 224.
[76] Below, econ., fishing.
[77] *Cur. Reg. R.* ix. 185–6, 190, 323.
[78] Guildhall MSS. 11765, 11766; Canham, *Brentford*, 30.
[79] Guildhall MSS. 11765, 11766.
[80] Below, econ., trade and industry.
[81] *Letters of Gilb. Foliot*, 492.
[82] There were no open fields: below, econ., agrarian.
[83] Canham, *Brentford*, 18, 22.
[84] Above, communications.

[85] Below, econ., markets and fairs.
[86] e.g. P.R.O., CP 25(1)/149/49/261; CP 25(1)/150/59/151; CP 25(1)/150/54/47; CP 25(1)/150/55/74; *Cal. Close, 1330–9*, 399.
[87] Canham, *Brentford*, 22.
[88] Above, communications.
[89] *T.L.M.A.S.* xxi. 60.
[90] Below, social.
[91] *V.C.H. Mdx.* i. 182, 204. [92] Ibid. iii. 90.
[93] Below, econ., trade and industry.
[94] Below, econ., agrarian.
[95] Below, churches.
[96] Canham, *Brentford*, 19.
[97] P.R.O., C 260/23/105.
[98] Ibid. E 134/26 Eliz. I East./6.
[99] Ibid. REQ 2/168/53; ibid. C 7/324/54(1611).
[1] Canham, *Brentford*, 19.
[2] Canham, *Brentford*, 6–7 and fig. 2.
[3] Below, econ., markets and fairs.
[4] See M.R.O., Acc. 891/2/9/4 (plan, 1838); *Brentford and Chiswick As It Was* (1978), illus. 6.

at the north-west, the White Hart to the east, and the Red Lion at the south-east.[5] Immediately to the east the Harrow, later the Castle, occupied a site reaching from High Street to the Butts.[6] Market Place was shown as the first departure from the linear plan in 1635, when building extended along both sides of High Street as far as the Hollows, Kew Bridge Road.[7] While busy road traffic was suggested by the large number of inns,[8] wharfs and a timber yard[9] and references to watermen[10] also pointed to growing traffic on the Thames. In the Civil War, fishing and the expanding market gardens at Brentford suffered depredation.[11]

In 1664 there were 136 houses at New Brentford, most of them small: 73 had 2 hearths or less, of which 29 were not chargeable for hearth tax, 19 had 3 hearths, 15 had 4, 9 had 5, and 7 had 6 hearths. The 6 with 10 or more hearths included the manor house, at least one inn, and an unoccupied house.[12] New Brentford was hard hit by the plague in 1665, when 103 burials took place,[13] but recovered quickly and grew, perhaps partly because of the uncertificated paupers recorded from 1676.[14] In 1672 there were 153 houses, those of all sizes having increased in number. Most of the humbler ones lay south of High Street, where the 105 houses included 55 with 2 hearths or less and another 38 with less than 5. The largest houses stood north of High Street,[15] as they still did after the total number had risen to c. 237 houses in 1764 and c. 270 in 1795.[16]

The survival of common to the west and north helped to concentrate early growth south of High Street, although the land there was more often flooded, as in 1682.[17] Houses later encroached on the Ham, until they lined the whole approach road to the bridge in 1777,[18] while existing plots fronting High Street were divided and cottages were built in yards behind, forming narrow alleys. By 1688 a gateway with a dwelling overhead gave access to Catherine Wheel Yard, later Road, with four cottages and access to the river.[19] By 1719 an inn called the Boar's Head had been divided into 4, with at least 8 other cottages extending to the Ham; another 5 stood in Reindeer Yard, another 4 behind 4 houses in High Street, and a further 10 behind 2 others. By 1720 inns called the Three Tuns and the Plough had been divided. Jack of Newbury's Alley existed

west of the church, with 5 and later 6 houses.[20] Such infilling continued in spite of the spread of warehouses and malthouses associated with the busy corn market. Cottages in the alleys were smaller than the shops in High Street, where 60 branches of trade catered for travellers and the hinterland by 1720.[21] New Brentford won praise for its shops and pavements, little inferior to those of London, in 1774,[22] when the back alleys passed unremarked. There were then three large coaching inns: the Harrow, the Red Lion, and the Three Pigeons, which in 1787 had stabling for 100 horses.[23]

North of High Street and Market Place, the Butts extended from the Half Acre in the east to the Brent in the west and was bounded to the north by Butts closes, part of the Boston manorial demesne. The Butts was relatively narrow at the eastern end, where a large garden limited building on the western side of the Half Acre to three houses as late as 1786[24] and where there were long plots behind the premises fronting High Street.[25] Farther west, the Butts widened southward into a large square beside the Brent and was thus L-shaped. A house in the angle of the L was alienated by the lord of Boston in 1663,[26] and by 1713 there were five neighbouring houses, two facing west and three north.[27] Butts closes were granted by Goldsmith in 1663 to William Parish, innkeeper of New Brentford,[28] who leased the eastern part as market gardens[29] and divided the rest into large plots. The most westerly plot fronting the Butts was let in 1685[30] and built on by 1691;[31] two plots to the east were let in 1688,[32] when five adjacent plots had been leased.[33] Some of them were probably sites for the new houses at the Butts recorded in 1690.[34] At the rear the westernmost plot was let in 1688[35] and Brent House was built c. 1694.[36] Presentments of a gravel pit, sawpits, and heaps of timber suggest continued building on the Butts c. 1700,[37] where other houses were erected between 1714 and 1719.[38] The soil was granted to Parish in 1663, perhaps with the intention of preserving an open space,[39] as ultimately happened. Boston manorial court resisted encroachments by residents but in 1700 permitted the planting of ornamental lime trees.[40] The Butts was a 'pleasant airy place' in 1746,[41] despite its regular use for markets by 1679[42] and parliamentary elections from 1701,[43] and increasing traffic between the Half Acre and

[5] Chiswick libr., cuttings; *Brentford and Chiswick As It Was*, illus. 7.
[6] Chiswick libr., letter (1747).
[7] Canham, *Brentford*, fig. 2.
[8] Below, social.
[9] Canham, *Brentford*, fig. 2.
[10] Below, econ., trade and industry.
[11] Below, econ., nurseries, fishing.
[12] M.R.O., MR/TH/6, mm. 9d.–10.
[13] Lysons, *Environs*, ii. 52.
[14] M.R.O., Acc. 890, pp. 232, 334 sqq.
[15] Ibid. MR/TH/25; Canham, *Brentford*, 7, 152.
[16] Lysons, *Environs*, ii. 52.
[17] Canham, *Brentford*, 152; Faulkner, *Brentford, Ealing and Chiswick*, 147–8.
[18] M.R.O., Acc. 649/6.
[19] P.R.O., PROB 11/393 (P.C.C. 145 Exton, will of Hen. Bright).
[20] Boston man. ct. bk. (1692–1842).
[21] Below, econ., trade and industry.
[22] *Diary of John Yeoman*, ed. M. Yearsley (1934), 47.

[23] Chiswick libr., sales cat.
[24] Boston man. ct. bk. (1692–1842).
[25] M.R.O., Acc. 257/3.
[26] P.R.O., C 93/30/18.
[27] M.L.R. 1713/5/167–9.
[28] P.R.O., C 93/30/18.
[29] M.R.O., Acc. 257/10.
[30] Ibid. 12; ibid Acc. 309/1.
[31] Ibid. Acc. 309/1.   [32] Ibid. Acc. 257/13–15.
[33] Ibid. 20.
[34] P.R.O., PROB 11/404 (P.C.C. 49 Vere, will of Wm. Baldwin).
[35] M.R.O., Acc. 257/20.   [36] Ibid. 21.
[37] Boston man. ct. bk. (1692–1842), f. 10.
[38] Ibid. ff. 16–17 sqq.
[39] Chiswick libr., letter of James Clitherow (1797).
[40] Boston man. ct. bk. (1692–1842), f. 11; Faulkner, *Brentford, Ealing and Chiswick*, 141.
[41] Simpson, *Agreeable Historian*, ii. 613.
[42] Brentford libr., New Brentford MS. 17513, f. 49v.
[43] Faulkner, *Brentford, Ealing and Chiswick*, 121–3; below.

Market Place, which was cutting up the surface by 1797.[44]

The select character of the area around the Butts, with Brentford's proximity to Kew Palace, explain the erection at the corner of the Half Acre and the later Clifden Road of Clifden House. A three-storeyed brick mansion with seven bays and a central pediment, containing fine ceilings and woodwork, it was built in the mid 18th century and occupied from 1799 by Henry Agar, Viscount Clifden.[45] New Grove Mansions, in the style of the Greek Revival, was built immediately to the south c. 1800.[46] The Butts backed on orchards, which resembled the 'seat of paradise' in 1774,[47] and Brentford itself was considered 'almost a garden' in 1794.[48]

By 1635 building lined both sides of High Street as far east as the modern Kew bridge.[49] Old Brentford, with 259 houses, was far more populous than New Brentford in 1664 and, with 135 not chargeable for hearth tax, was also much poorer.[50] Houses continued to multiply, while the linear pattern persisted, with increasing emphasis on the waterfront. To the north a back lane skirted the fields by 1575:[51] many tenements in High Street extended back to it[52] and there may already have been some infilling. South of High Street the whole riverside was taken for wharfs, reached by passages such as Smith Hill, a public way by 1581,[53] Ferry Lane, and Spring Gardens. The passages were lined with cottages and inns, among them the Goat and the Salutation in Ferry Lane, recorded in 1636[54] and 1751.[55] Where road and river lay close together, tenements often had access to both, such as the One Tun and the Half Moon and Seven Stars.[56] The fields south of High Street, like those near Ferry Lane, were inclosed and built on piecemeal.[57] Old Brentford was said in 1769 to be populated chiefly by poor fishermen and watermen[58] and in 1774 to have more trade than New Brentford because the river came up to everyone's doors.[59] Many small alehouses presumably catered for such inhabitants, among them the Mermaid, recorded from 1651,[60] the Anchor from 1674,[61] the Barge from 1751,[62] the Tackle Block from 1758,[63] and the Waterman's Arms from 1790.[64] Travellers were served by the larger coaching inns at New Brentford and from c. 1750

by those at the east end of Old Brentford in Kew Bridge Road, including the Star and Garter and the Wagon and Horses.[65] Old Brentford's growth stimulated the opening in 1762 of George chapel, built by local subscribers led by the Trimmer family.[66] Chronic poverty led to Mrs. Sarah Trimmer's successive schemes for educating the poor from 1786.[67] Many 18th-century travellers saw only the handsome shops, Market Place, the Butts, orchards and market gardens, and a few aristocratic houses at Old Brentford.[68] Heavy traffic on the highway, however,[69] churning up mud or creating dust,[70] had already given much of Brentford a reputation for dirtiness.[71] Most inhabitants lived in weatherboarded cottages, crammed into yards and alleys such as Spring Gardens and sometimes constituting districts such as Troy Town. Many cottages were ramshackle huts in 1765[72] and not liable for rates in 1786.[73] From the Surrey side of the Thames they were an eyesore: hence the remarks that Brentford in 1765 was the 'ugliest and filthiest place in England'[74] and that in 1807 Kew Palace looked on to the worst part of Old Brentford.[75] That was before industrial growth had added to Brentford's unsavoury character.

The late 18th century saw the expansion of the older extractive and corn-based industries, notably the potteries, brickworks, and breweries. The construction of the Grand Junction canal attracted a new flour mill to Catherine Wheel Yard and a turpentine factory to the Ham.[76] At New Brentford, still constricted to north and south, new housing was provided on the Ham[77] and by further infilling: there were 272 houses in 1801 and 389 by 1851, when there was little further room.[78] At Old Brentford the potter Daniel Turner had put up 14 cottages between High Street and the back lane by 1778, presumably the Pot House Row of 1786,[79] and the first 9 cottages of Union Court had been built on a similar site by 1813.[80] There were 13 cottages at Troy Town, 22 at Smith Hill, and 4 in Spring Gardens, Old Brentford, in 1786.[81]

Although some businesses failed, the distillery, breweries, maltings, soap works, and timber yard expanded along the waterfront, and waterworks and gasworks were built at the east end of the town. Displacing housing and shops on both

[44] Chiswick libr., letter of James Clitherow.
[45] Pevsner, *Mdx.* 29; Briggs, *Mdx. Old and New*, 253; *Brentford and Chiswick As It Was*, illus. 13.
[46] Pevsner, *Mdx.* 29; Min. of Town and Country Planning, List of Bldgs. (1949).
[47] *Diary of John Yeoman*, 41.
[48] Foot, *Agric. of Mdx.* 16.
[49] Canham, *Brentford*, fig. 2.
[50] M.R.O., MR/TH/3.
[51] Guildhall MS. 10312/92, rot. 34d.; see also ibid. rot. 40.
[52] M.R.O., Acc. 891/2/1/1.
[53] Guildhall MS. 10312/92, rot. 43.
[54] *Mdx. & Herts. N. & Q.* iv. 78.
[55] M.R.O., Acc. 891/2/3/120.
[56] Ibid. 143.
[57] P.R.O., C 7/501/39.
[58] M.R.O., Hist. Notes N/D4.
[59] *Diary of John Yeoman*, 47; see also *New Present State of Eng.* (1750), i. 158.
[60] M.R.O., Acc. 891/2/5/519.
[61] P.R.O., C 6/232/6.
[62] M.R.O., MR/LV7/15.
[63] Ibid. Acc. 891/2/8/1.   [64] Ibid. MR/LV9/189.

[65] M.R.O., MR/LV7/15.   [66] Below, churches.
[67] Below, educ.
[68] e.g. those inhabited by Edward Leigh, Lord Leigh, 1769–74, the ctss. of Glasgow 1777–9, and Lady St. John 1781: M.R.O., D.R.O. 37/B2/5.
[69] Above, communications; W. Camden, *Britannia*, ed. R. Gough (1789), ii. 14.
[70] *Diary of John Yeoman*, 47.
[71] I. Doddridge, *Like Will to Like* (1728); James Thomson, *Castle of Indolence*, ed. A. D. McKillop (1961), 119; Boswell, *Life of Johnson* (O.U.P. 1953), 1210.
[72] Chiswick libr., Brentford survey (photos.); cutting (1765); Hist. Mon. Com. *Mdx.* 7.
[73] M.R.O., D.R.O. 37/B1/2.
[74] Chiswick libr., cutting (1765).
[75] *Ambulator* (1807).
[76] Below, trade and industry.
[77] Boston man. ct. bk. (1692–1842).
[78] *Census*, 1801–51; below.
[79] Cf. M.R.O., D.R.O. 37/B1/2; Guildhall MS. 10465/93, pp. 88–90.
[80] Guildhall MS. 10465/55, pp. 72–4.
[81] M.R.O., D.R.O. 37/B1/2.

sides of High Street,[82] such industries demanded labour and so led to more house building: 18 cottages were built by Thomas Shackle between 1818 and 1825 at Running Horse Yard, between High Street and the back lane,[83] 5 more were built at Union Court before 1840,[84] and 17 to the north of two High Street houses between 1824 and 1837.[85] Building included work on 25 plots west of Ealing Road and 19 east of the new North Road by 1840,[86] besides the 8 cottages of Bridge Terrace at the northern approach to Kew bridge by c. 1826.[87] Nonetheless there was a shortage of housing in 1849.[88]

Drinking, swearing, and gambling were commonplace by 1819[89] and were attacked by the new nonconformist chapels and by the established church: a new infants' school advocated in 1831 was found in 1834 to be making it easier for mothers to work and hence neglect their children.[90] Later industrial expansion coincided with the decline of coaching traffic, when the victualling and retail trades were depressed, causing some closures and further accentuating Brentford's working-class character. In 1843 the rapidly growing population was overwhelmingly one of labourers in industry, fishing, and market gardening, liable to intermittent unemployment.[91]

Brentford town, dignified by a new magistrates' courthouse in Market Place c. 1850,[92] was treated as a distinct entity in the census of 1851.[93] It then contained a total of 1,750 houses, a figure which had nearly doubled by 1921, when the U.D. contained 3,261 dwellings and when further building was in train. New Brentford, with 389 houses in 1851 and 408 in 1891, grew very little until the 1920s, building being confined to the High Street area by industries along the waterfront and by Boston Manor to the north. Meanwhile at Old Brentford, where at first there was more space and where much land came on the market in 1872 and c. 1885, the houses increased from 1,361 in 1851 to 2,224 in 1891, by which date its population was three times that of New Brentford. Small brick terraces were erected, much superior to the flimsy dwellings crowded into the yards behind High Street, and from 1892 systematic slum clearance accompanied new building. The building of the Great West Road in the 1920s brought more estates on to the market and further industrial growth north of the town. Much parkland remained but most of the area was built over and middle-class districts emerged near the parks in the north-east and north-west corners of Brentford.

Until c. 1883 there was little building in the St. George's district of Old Brentford east of Ealing Road than in the St. Paul's district farther west. Infilling continued, as at Hales Yard,[94] until 1913 or later, when terraces were built in Catherine Place, parallel to Paradise Place and north of Albany Road.[95] More dwellings, however, were in new streets. Plots in Orchard Road, Old Brentford, were being offered in 1851 by the National Freehold Land Society.[96] Brook Road was laid out northward from behind High Street and, with the older Distillery, Pottery, and North roads to the east, was partly built up by 1872.[97] All four were linked by cross roads, of which only New Road near the L. & S.W.R. line, with 53 dwellings in 15 blocks, had been largely built up in 1872, when surrounding land was sold in lots.[98] There was still space to the south in 1883, when it was secured for St. Paul's recreation ground. In 1883 25 a. were laid out for building between Ealing and Pottery roads and the British Land Co. was laying out c. 77 a. between Ealing and Windmill roads.[99] Market gardens on the Hope-Edwardes estate between the waterworks and the L. & S.W.R. line were leased for working-class housing by 1885, when construction was under way.[1]

The town's working-class character was confirmed in the late 19th century. The gasworks, stretching along both sides of High Street, Old Brentford, for c. 400 m., were reputed the largest and most repulsive concern, likened to the fabled Cyclops and dubbed 'king of Brentford'.[2] In 1867 no town in England was thought to have more poverty in relation to its size and in 1882 it was considered as wretched as any place, not excluding London's east end. Limited space kept rents high and the worst slums overcrowded,[3] many weatherboarded cottages in the yards being dilapidated and none having proper sanitation.[4] After the 18 hovels of Canon Alley had at last been condemned in 1878, they needed almost complete reconstruction to bring them up to standard.[5] In 1877 Bailey's Row, Old Brentford, and the 18 Prospect Cottages behind the King's Arms were nearly as bad.[6] In 1853 Brentford was considered a byword for immorality among both sexes[7] and in 1867 the worst vice was seen as drunkenness, encouraged by the large number of

[82] Below, trade and industry.
[83] M.R.O., Acc. 638/159–61.
[84] Guildhall MS. 10465/155, pp. 72–4.
[85] Ibid. 150, pp. 105–6.
[86] M.R.O., Acc. 634/6, 7, 8A; Acc. 891/1/5/298.
[87] Ibid. Acc. 891/2/12/2; ibid. Acc. 891/2/5/681, 684, 686–8.
[88] Ibid. Acc. 880/10, p. 330.
[89] J. Smith, *Marvellous Mercy Displayed in Life of Author* (1862), esp. pp. 11, 16.
[90] F. E. Thompson, *Two Sermons in St. George's Chapel, Old Brentford* (1831); *Rep. of Sel. Cttee. for Educ. of Poor*, H.C. 572, pp. 217, 219 (1834), ix.
[91] *Jnl. Statistical Soc. of Lond.* vi. 126–7.
[92] *Brentford and Chiswick As It Was*, illus. 6.
[93] Para. based on following paras. and *Census*, 1851–1931.
[94] M.R.O., Acc. 638/267.
[95] Chiswick libr., council papers.
[96] M.R.O., Acc. 1285/1; Chiswick libr., deed.

[97] Chiswick libr., sales cat.; *Brentford, Kew, Isleworth and Spring Grove Dir.* (1872).
[98] *Brentford, Kew Dir.* (1872); Chiswick libr., sales cat.
[99] Chiswick libr., council papers; *The Independent*, 28 Mar. 1883.
[1] *Mdx. Independent*, 25 Apr. 1885; *Mdx. County Times*, 16 May 1885; see also 'Archimedes', *Rep. on Drainage to Brentford local bd.* (1881).
[2] F. Watt, 'Brentford Old Town' (cutting in Chiswick libr.); R. Henrey, *The King of Brentford* (1946); see also D. Maxwell, *Pilgrimage of the Thames* (1932), 88.
[3] Brentford cent. ragged schs. and town mission, *Rep.* (1867); M.R.O., D.R.O. 37/A12/2.
[4] Brentford local bd. min. bk. (1874–8), pp. 124, 365, 397.
[5] Ibid. p. 150; see also *The Times*, 22 Sept. 1873.
[6] Brentford local bd. min. bk. (1874–8).
[7] J. A. Emerton, *Sermon on Educ. of Poor* (1853). See also Brentford cent. ragged schs. and town mission, *Rep.* (1867); Brentford U.D. *Reps. of M.O.H.* (1901, 1903).

inns.[8] Many working mothers neglected their children[9] and a high infant mortality was attributed to malnutrition.[10]

Lack of a sewerage system was condemned in the national press in 1873, when Brentford was associated with everything 'stagnant and disgraceful' and again labelled the filthiest place in England.[11] That mortality was no worse was ascribed in 1878 to the natural healthiness of the site.[12] With the spread of new housing around St. Paul's and the blighting influence of the gasworks farther east, St. George's had become the poorest area in Old Brentford by 1865.[13] It probably remained superior to parts of New Brentford, such as the Ham, inhabited by the very poorest and often flooded.[14] At New Brentford there was also a fluctuating population of barge dwellers.[15]

Social problems were first tackled by the churches and the Ragged School Union. After the foundation of Brentford local board a sewerage system was constructed and some of the worst slums were condemned.[16] Municipal activity increased in the 1890s, when the public baths and isolation hospital were opened. An imposing vestry hall, later a county courthouse, was built in the Half Acre in 1899.[17] High mortality, especially infant mortality of 197 per 1,000 and rather more in New Brentford, prompted a regular attack on slums from 1892.[18] Infant mortality had scarcely changed by 1901 but by 1912 had dropped to 74 per 1,000; meanwhile mortality overall fell from 21 to 8.[19] Slum clearance was impeded by lack of alternative accommodation,[20] until in 1899 the U.D.C. started four schemes for 762 council houses east of Ealing Road on either side of the L. & S.W.R. line.[21]

At the eastern end of the town a drinking fountain was set up in 1877 near Kew bridge, where open markets caused much traffic congestion before an enclosed site was provided in 1893. The area became still busier with the opening of the L.U.T.'s terminus in 1901 and of the rebuilt Kew bridge in 1903, soon followed by the building of a covered market.[22]

Widening of High Street and the Half Acre, before the arrival of tramways in 1905, swept away many old buildings, including ancient inns. Although the yards behind changed less than had been hoped,[23] some progress was made there, in particular with the demolition of all of Running

Horse Yard, Moore's Alley, Eaton Court, and Eaton Buildings in 1911–12. Some of the worst slums in Troy Town were cleared in 1910.[24] A further 465 houses had been cleared by 1914[25] and still more by 1927, when labyrinths of tenements were a mere memory and Brentford was no more unhealthy than its neighbours.[26] Much housing, however, remained untouched.

After the First World War slum clearance was again delayed by lack of accommodation for those displaced. An influx of workers for the new factories along the Great West Road exacerbated the housing problem. Brentford U.D.C.'s 146 houses in Ealing and Whitestile roads comprised almost all the building between 1920 and 1924,[27] but thereafter private activity resumed. Much of northern New Brentford was built up by A. J. A. Taylor's Boston Land and Investment Co.[28] Messrs. Steele planned 40 houses in Boston Manor Road and the Ride in 1924, a further 430 were planned for the Gunnersbury Park estate farther east in 1925, and in 1925–6 private builders were responsible for all the 277 new houses.[29]

Expansion was made possible by the Clitherow, Rothschild, and Hope-Edwardes families, who sold up as the Great West Road neared completion. Widely spaced factories along the road were later seen, nostalgically, as symbols of economic self-confidence, forming an industrial Arcadia.[30] Some of the land was secured for middle-class housing near Gunnersbury Park and Boston Manor, and much remained open, notably Boston Manor park (407 a.), Gunnersbury park (183 a.), and Carville Hall park (161 a.).[31] Brentford U.D.C., which had wanted to build on Gunnersbury park, erected 118 houses in Lionel Road in 1928–9[32] and 428 on the Syon estate at Brentford End.[33] In 1930 Brentford and Chiswick U.D.C. owned 1,520 houses and flats, when 600 more were needed if the remaining alleys and courts were to be cleared. Only 261 more dwellings had been demolished by 1938 and there were 1,548 council houses in the borough in 1937, when land was in short supply.[34] A few small blocks of flats were erected in the late 1930s.[35]

Growth continued until the Second World War, by which time Brentford was completely built up. The old market declined, however, finally closing in 1933,[36] and by 1929 the town

[8] Brentford cent. ragged schs. and town mission, *Rep.* (1867).
[9] Ibid.; see also Brentford U.D. *Rep. of M.O.H.* (1898); Brentford local bd. *Rep. of M.O.H.* (1893).
[10] Brentford U.D. *Rep. of M.O.H.* (1901).
[11] *Brentford Advertiser*, 4 Oct. 1873.
[12] Brentford local bd. min. bk. (1874–8), pp. 515–16.
[13] *Ealing Post*, 3 June 1865; St. Mary's Ealing *Monthly Church Paper*, May 1884.
[14] Chiswick libr., cuttings (1928, 1930).
[15] C. G. Harper, *Thames Valley Villages* (1910), ii. 231; Henrey, *King of Brentford*, 13.
[16] Below, pub. svces.
[17] Below, local govt., pub. svces.
[18] Brentford local bd. *Rep. of M.O.H.* (1892).
[19] Ibid. (1892–4); Brentford U.D. *Reps. of M.O.H.* (1895–1912).
[20] Brentford U.D. *Rep. of M.O.H.* (1896).
[21] Brentford U.D. *Surveyor's Rep. to Artizans' Dwellings Cttee.* (1899).
[22] *Brentford and Chiswick As It Was*, illus. 27, 30.

[23] Above, communications; photos. in Chiswick libr.; Brentford U.D. *Rep. of M.O.H.* (1905); cutting (Dec. 1907).
[24] Brentford U.D. *Rep. of M.O.H.* (1911–12); Chiswick libr., plans (1907) and sales cat. (1910); M.R.O., Acc. 638/192; Harper, *Thames Valley Villages*, ii. 233.
[25] Brentford U.D. *Reps. of M.O.H.* (1912–14).
[26] Chiswick libr., cutting in scrapbk.
[27] e.g. Brentford U.D. *Reps. of M.O.H.* (1921–5).
[28] D. M. Yarde, 'Manor of Boston' (TS. in Chiswick libr.), 18.
[29] Brentford U.D. *Reps. of M.O.H.* (1925–6); *Rep. of Housing and Town Planning Cttee.* 4 Nov. 1924, 1 Dec. 1925.
[30] *Observer*, 31 Aug. 1980.
[31] Brentford and Chiswick U.D. *Petition for Incorp.* (1931). [32] Ibid. *Abs. of Accts.* (1928–9).
[33] *Brentford and Chiswick Times*, 8 Apr. 1938; Brentford and Chiswick boro. *Rep. of M.O.H.* (1935).
[34] Brentford and Chiswick U.D. *Rep. of M.O.H.* (1930); Brentford and Chiswick boro. *Reps. of M.O.H.* (1937–8).
[35] Brentford and Chiswick boro. *Statement of Housing Estates* (1946). [36] Below, econ.

had clearly been supplanted as a shopping centre by neighbouring suburbs.[37] After the Second World War many factories in the Great West Road were turned into warehouses or offices, while by 1954 Brentford's shops were described as squalid and there was almost no public entertainment.[38] Among older industries the waterworks, the soap factory, Brentford dock, and the huge gasworks all closed in the 1950s and 1960s, before the large market was moved from its covered site near Kew bridge in 1974.[39] Falling employment reduced the demand for housing and gave opportunities for large-scale rebuilding.

In 1954 Brentford formed three distinct districts. In the north were modern houses, municipal and private, and factories in the Great West Road. Immediately south of the railway were streets of terraces dating from c. 1870–1920. Farther south lay the old town, comprising the docks area, High Street and the yards behind, and St. George's district, which included many slums.[40] Buildings south of High Street were in very bad repair; those north of High Street included many awaiting demolition, among them some tall weatherboarded 18th-century shops.[41] Even the late 19th-century terraces near High Street had become slums.[42]

Piecemeal demolition continued, Troy Town finally being cleared in 1958.[43] A plan for the wholesale rebuilding of High Street in 1947 proved too costly but in 1959 a phased scheme was started along the northern side from St. Paul's Road to North Road, also taking in Albany, Ealing, Pottery, Distillery, North and Walnut Tree roads. By 1959 118 families had already been rehoused[44] and by 1978 the whole northern frontage of High Street had been rebuilt, with clusters of small shops, and the terraced streets behind replaced by council houses and flats on new alignments. Work was still in progress east of Ealing Road and there were empty plots in St. Paul's Road. Modern buildings included a county courthouse west of Alexandra Road, used from 1963 in place of the former vestry hall in the Half Acre, which itself was replaced by a police station in 1966.[45]

The decline of large industries made more land available. A plan of 1959 for comprehensive rebuilding on the waterworks site[46] came to nothing, but land was appropriated from 1966 by Hounslow L.B. for tower blocks containing 528 flats.[47] In 1978 the north side of Green Dragon Lane had been cleared and Brentford dock replaced by a housing estate of the G.L.C., where the building of flats was far advanced. Although the closure of the gasworks had stimulated plans to make use of the waterfront, the long narrow strip between road and river was still vacant. Brentford was called depressed and depressing in

1975.[48] Much remained to be done in western and southern New Brentford and at Kew bridge in 1978, when the town had ceased to be a centre of industry or trade and was inhabited mainly by council tenants, who worked elsewhere and often shopped in Ealing or Chiswick.

The scene in 1978 was of decaying slums and empty sites, juxtaposed with the select Butts and new municipal housing. Near Brentford bridge little weatherboarded houses awaited clearance; to the south the Ham was a wasteland beside car-repair workshops and the redundant St. Lawrence's church. There was little activity along the banks of the Brent or most of the Thames waterfront. The alleys, no longer lined with cottages and sometimes overgrown, led to wharfs that were often deserted, the few exceptions including DRG's new warehousing in Ferry Lane and the Thames & General Lighterage Co.'s barge repair yards. High walls and factories lined the southern side of High Street. On the northern side older properties survived west of Market Place, while chiefly modern building stretched as far east as North Road. Beyond, Mrs. Trimmer's school and the former St. George's church, the gasholders, and the waterworks buildings were all undisturbed, as were the shabby Kew Bridge Road and the disused Brentford Market.

Behind Market Place the elegance of the Butts was marred by the use of its central space as a car park. Large Victorian houses to the north looked less well kept than those in the Butts, and Clifden House, pulled down in 1954, had made way for flats. Brentford football ground was still surrounded by terraced streets but many similar terraces had disappeared with rebuilding. Near High Street St. Paul's recreation ground, amid terraced housing and school buildings, was an isolated open space. Carville Hall, a low brick 19th-century house in a deserted park, adjoined the Great West Road to the south. The road itself, with its flyover on stilts, lined by factories and generally noisy and windy, formed a barrier between northern and southern Brentford. The northern part had large open spaces and less dense housing: to the west middle-class houses in Boston Manor Road resembled those of Hanwell; in the centre council houses and dingy shops in Ealing Road were hardly distinguishable from those of South Ealing; and to the east tree-lined avenues and large houses near Gunnersbury park extended northward towards those nearer Ealing common. While southern Brentford was still distinct, northern Brentford thus merged with its neighbours.

Notable buildings survive mainly in the Butts.[49] On the south side at the eastern end is St. Raphael's convent, a three-storeyed 18th-century

[37] Chiswick libr., cutting; see also *Brentford and Chiswick Times*, 3 Dec. 1937.

[38] K. F. Dalton, 'Brentford: County Town' (TS. at Chiswick libr.); Watt, 'Old Brentford Town'.

[39] Below, econ.

[40] Dalton, 'Brentford'; see also M.R.O., MCC/E correspondence file 168 (H.M.I. reps.).

[41] M.R.O., PR 247/14-15, 17, 28, 30-2 (photographic survey); the shop front of 1798 of Rattenbury & Co. is in the Mus. of Lond.   [42] Dalton, 'Brentford'.

[43] *Brentford and Chiswick Times*, 28 Dec. 1962.

[44] *Brentford Yesterday, Today, and Tomorrow Exhib.* (1959).

[45] *Brentford and Chiswick As It Was*, illus. 9.

[46] *Brentford Yesterday* (1959).

[47] Hounslow L.B. *Ann. Reps. of Housing Dir.* (1965-8).

[48] P. Howard, *London's River* (1975), 46.

[49] Following 2 paras. based on Pevsner, *Mdx.* 28-9; Min. of Town and Country Planning, List of Bldgs. (1949); Hist. Mon. Com. *Mdx.* 6.

house of yellow brick, much extended. To the west are four 18th-century cottages, nos. 16 to 22, of which the first two have been refaced. Other houses date from *c.* 1690 or later, are of brown brick with red-brick dressings, and mainly consist of two storeys with attics. They include, in the angle of the **L**, the double fronted nos. 24 and 26, formerly the cottage hospital, which also have basements. The three-storeyed no. 40 and the row formed by nos. 42 to 46, also on the south side, are 18th-century. The north side of the Butts includes pairs formed by Chatham House and Beaufort House (nos. 15 and 17) and the partly refaced Cobden House and Linden House (nos. 21 and 23). In Upper Butts, leading north-ward to Church Walk, are the early 18th-century Llan Helen (no. 1) and the Cedars, which is slightly later and has been rendered and reroofed.

A three-storeyed 18th-century house of brown brick, converted into flats by 1948, survives as no. 80 on the south side of High Street. Farther west near the Brent are the shells of the 18th-century nos. 154–6 and the early 19th-century nos. 157–8, apparently awaiting demolition. On the east side of Boston Manor Road, over-shadowed by the flyover, some restored 18th-century houses serve as offices. All are of brown brick with red-brick dressings, no. 67 being three-storeyed, nos. 69 and 71 representing a divided house of two storeys with attics, and nos. 73 and 75 forming a three-storeyed pair with basements.

Six Protestants were burned at Brentford in 1558.[50] At the battle of Brentford in 1642 Lord Ruthven's royalists drove two parliamentary divisions out of the town and then plundered it, before withdrawing in the face of larger forces at Turnham Green.[51] From 1701 the Butts was the scene of the county's elections, of which the most tumultuous were those contested in 1768 and 1769 by John Wilkes, giving rise to inns being called the Number 45 and the Wilkes's Head, and in 1802 by Sir Francis Burdett, when large profits were made by innkeepers. Additional polling stations were provided in 1832, although declara-tions of the poll were still made at the Butts until 1885.[52]

Lord Ruthven, who was also earl of Forth, was created earl of Brentford in 1644 and died without male heirs in 1651. William III's general Frederick Schomberg (1615–90) in 1689 was created duke of Schomberg and earl of Brent-ford, which titles became extinct in 1719. The barony of Brentford, with the earldom of Darlington, was conferred for life on George I's mistress Baroness von Kielmansegge (d. 1725) in 1722. The statesman William Joynson-Hicks (1865–1932) was created Viscount Brentford in 1929.[53]

The population of New Brentford was 1,443 in 1801 and 2,063 in 1851, when that of Old Brentford was 6,057. Brentford town, including some houses in Isleworth parish, was estimated to have 8,870 inhabitants in 1851 and 11,091 in 1871. Brentford U.D. had 15,171 inhabitants in 1901 and 17,032 in 1921 and the three Brentford wards of Brentford and Chiswick U.D. had 20,372 in 1931.[54]

SOCIAL AND CULTURAL ACTIVITIES.
Inns[55] in Old and New Brentford greatly out-numbered those in Ealing village or elsewhere in the parish, both before and after the decline of the coaching trade. Some were variously described as being in either Ealing or Old Brentford, while some in New Brentford were listed with those in Hanwell.

At Brentford there were taverns in 1304.[56] The Bell was recorded in 1384[57] and the Crown, the Angel, and the Horseshoe in 1436.[58] Henry VI in 1446 held a chapter of the Garter at the Lion,[59] presumably the later Red Lion. Other inns included the White Horse, by 1603, and the Three Pigeons,[60] which was mentioned in Ben Jonson's *The Alchemist* of 1610 and had a loose reputation.[61] The Three Pigeons was later kept by the actor John Lowin (1576–1659)[62] and noted by the 'water poet' John Taylor in 1636, as were the Half Moon, the Lion, the Goat, the George, and the Swan.[63] Samuel Pepys in 1665 stopped at a waterside inn, perhaps the Wagon and Horses.[64] There were at least 10 inns in New Brentford alone in 1614.[65] By 1722 probably 12 of Hanwell's inns were in New Brentford and at least 12 of Ealing's were in Old Brentford. The maximum number for the whole town-ship may have been *c.* 40 in 1770, when New Brentford alone had 17 inns; it had 13 in 1800 and 9 in 1815, when Old Brentford had 25 and 21 respectively. There were 28 inns listed at Brentford in 1832–4 and, despite closures reported in 1843,[66] as many as 36 in 1890, most of them in High Street.

Ealing apparently had 2 victualling houses in 1599.[67] Apart from Old Brentford, the parish as a whole may have had as many as 19 inns in 1722, most of them presumably in Ealing village but some of them in the hamlets, such as the Plough at Little Ealing, or along Uxbridge Road, such as the Old Hat.[68] Apart from Old Brentford, Ealing had 15 inns in 1800, 13 in 1815, 14 in 1832–4, and 12 in 1890. A coffee house existed at Brentford in 1717 and 1733, the first being associated with the Harrow, later the Castle, inn and the second being opposite the Magpie and Crown and so presumably in High Street.[69]

An armed association for Ealing and Brentford

[50] J. Strype, *Eccl. Memorials*, iii (2) (1822), 556.
[51] Robbins, *Mdx.* 94–5, 225–6.
[52] Ibid. 226; Lysons, *Environs*, ii. 40; Canham, *Brentford*, 8; *Annual Reg.* (1802), 425.
[53] *D.N.B.*; *Complete Peerage*, ii. 299; iv. 81; xi. 525–9.
[54] *Census*, 1801–1931.
[55] Following 3 paras. based on M.R.O., MR/LV3/95, LV8/65–6, LV10/90–1, LV15/4–5; Pigot, *Com. Dir.* (1832–4); *Kelly's Dir. Mdx.* (1890).
[56] P.R.O., C 260/15/21.   [57] *Cal. Pat.* 1381–5, 400, 478.
[58] *Cal. Close*, 1435–41, 62; P.R.O., C 143/450/30.

[59] J. Anstis, *Reg. of Order of Garter*, i (1724), 129.
[60] Jackson, *Ealing*, 109, 133–5.
[61] *Alchemist*, ed. H. C. Hart (1903), 225.   [62] *D.N.B.*
[63] *Mdx. & Herts. N. & Q.* iv. 78.
[64] Jackson, *Ealing*, 134; *Diary of Sam. Pepys*, vi. 199.
[65] A. J. Howard, 'Boston Manor and the Clitherow family' (TS. thesis, 1969, in Chiswick libr.), 59–64.
[66] *Jnl. Statistical Soc. of Lond.* vi. 126.
[67] Allison, *Elizabethan Census*, 10.
[68] Jackson, *Ealing*, 158–9, 163.
[69] Boston man. ct. bk. (1692–1842), ff. 21, 44.

was formed in 1798[70] and was succeeded in 1803 by a volunteer corps, organized by committees for Upper Side, Lower Side, and New Brentford, which was disbanded in 1806. Another volunteer corps, the 30th Middlesex, drawn from Acton, Hanwell, and Ealing, was formed in 1857-8.[71] A company of the 8th Middlesex Rifle Volunteers drilled at Churchfield Road, Ealing, in 1887, as did its successor, belonging to the 2nd Volunteer Battalion of the Duke of Cambridge's Own (Middlesex) Regiment in 1890. There was also a drill hall in Ealing Road, Brentford, by 1901.[72]

Philanthropic societies were formed comparatively early in Brentford, where in 1657 contributions were made to a watermen's chest,[73] a body which held some property in 1728.[74] Freemasons met by 1799 at the Castle inn.[75] Brentford and Ealing savings bank, intended also to serve Acton, Hanwell, and Heston, was founded in 1818, as was the dispensary, and used Brentford town hall in 1856.[76] A visiting society for the sick and lying-in poor of Old Brentford was founded in 1832, a mechanics' institution, with lectures and a library, in 1835, and a visiting society for New Brentford in 1838. A branch of the S.P.C.K. opened in 1842.[77] Brentford Philanthropic Society was established in 1867, surviving in 1978,[78] and St. George's had a clothing and coal club by 1876.[79]

Ealing had a mechanics' institution, with a library, by 1845.[80] The vicar of St. Mary's, E. W. Relton, in 1853-4 administered a society for the sick, besides a district visiting society and a lying-in society. The first two had apparently merged by 1854-5, when the society was responsible for a soup kitchen, a coal fund, a provident fund, and a children's shoe club, and when the Sunday school opened a lending library.[81] Ealing Philanthropic Institution, presumably inspired by Brentford's example, was started in 1868, apparently dissolved after 1870 but refounded in 1881; it met for many years in a hall behind the King's Arms and survived in 1978.[82] The vicar of Christ Church formed a friendly society and working men's club in 1868 and several churchmen helped to sponsor the St. Mary's coffee tavern, with a reading room and youth room at the corner of Warwick Road, in 1880.[83]

In 1621 the people of New Brentford had long been accustomed to feast in the church house at Whitsun and 'liberally to spend their moneys' in aid of a common fund. There was a maypole in 1623 and sums were also raised from hocking, 'risling', and 'pigeon holes', games which continued to be held until 1642.[84] There was an enclosed bowling alley by the Ham at New Brentford in 1635.[85] Ealing in 1774 was the scene of a cricket match against Norwood and Southall,[86] and in 1776 it had a toxophilite society, which met weekly during the summer in 1795,[87] and in 1792 a bowling green opposite the Old Hat inn,[88] which was also a meeting place for pigeon shooters.[89] There were horse races at Brentford in 1736[90] and pony races at Ealing in 1819 and steeplechases there in 1851.[91] More races near Ealing village, started in 1865, continued against local opposition in 1882.[92] In the 1860s an inn called the Cricketer stood near the south-west corner of Ealing common.[93] Ealing village cricket club was founded in 1864[94] and perhaps used a ground near the Green Man in 1866.[95] It amalgamated in 1874 with Ealing cricket club, which from 1871 leased land near the Royal India asylum in Corfton Road, where the existing two-storeyed pavilion was opened in 1900.[96] Ealing Dean cricket club played at Uxbridge Road by 1907.[97] At Brentford the police and the gasworks' employees ran their own cricket clubs in 1888, when Boston Park club had its ground in Ealing Road.[98]

Brentford football club was formed in 1888 as a sports club of the Wesleyan chapel and opened its existing ground at Griffin Park in 1905, where the main stands were built in 1927-8. The club, champion of the 2nd division of the Southern League in 1901, played in the 1st division before joining the new 3rd division of the Football League in 1920. It was promoted to the 2nd division in 1933 and later to the 1st division, from which it was relegated in 1947.[99]

In the 1860s there were several bathing ponds in the fields east of St. Mary's Road and Ealing Road, the largest being south of Elm Grove.[1] Presumably they were superseded by the public baths, opened in 1884.[2] Swimming clubs for Ealing and Ealing Dean were among the oldest sports clubs in 1925, together with those for cricket, rugby, and association football. Badminton was played in the winter at the public baths and in 1926 there were croquet and bowling clubs.[3] Ealing lawn tennis club, with courts off Madeley Road, was founded in 1882[4] and the

[70] M.R.O., D.R.O. 37/B1/2/1; T. Rowlandson, *Loyal Volunteers of Lond.* (1799), no. 26.
[71] Faulkner, *Brentford, Ealing and Chiswick*, 223-4, 228; C. Jones, *Ealing, from Village to Corporate Town* (1902), 129-33.
[72] *Kelly's Dir. Ealing* (1887-8, 1901-2); *Kelly's Dir. Mdx.* (1890, 1908).
[73] Guildhall MS. 10312/38, rot. 10d.
[74] M.L.R. 1728/1/353.
[75] M.R.O., MR/SF/1799/56.
[76] Faulkner, *Brentford, Ealing and Chiswick*, 80 (rules in grangerized copy in Chiswick libr.); *Brentford and Chiswick Bank for Savings* (1866).
[77] Faulkner, *Brentford, Ealing and Chiswick*, 78-9, 132, 136.
[78] *Ann. Reps.* in Chiswick libr.
[79] M.R.O., D.R.O. 37/A12/2.
[80] *P.O. Dir. Six Home Counties* (1845).
[81] M.R.O., D.R.O. 37/A12/1.
[82] Holt's local hist. notes (TS.).
[83] M.R.O., D.R.O. 37/A12/1.

[84] Faulkner, *Brentford, Ealing and Chiswick*, 81-4; Brentford libr., New Brentford MS. 17512.
[85] *V.C.H. Mdx.* iii, plate facing p. 90.
[86] Robbins, *Mdx.* 145.
[87] Jones, *Ealing*, 128-9; *Ealing Local Historian* (1966), 1-3.
[88] M.R.O., D.R.O. 37/D1/2.
[89] Robbins, *Mdx.* 144.
[90] Newspaper cutting at Chiswick libr.
[91] Posters at Ealing libr.
[92] E. Walford, *Gtr. Lond.* i [1882], 23.
[93] O.S. Map 6", Mdx. XVI. SW. (1873 edn.).
[94] *Ealing Cricket Club, 1970* (centenary handbk.), 28.
[95] P.R.O., MAF 9/167/7185.
[96] *Ealing Cricket Club, 1970*, 24-5, 33-4.
[97] *Kelly's Dir. Ealing* (1907).
[98] *County of Mdx. Independent Dir. Brentford* (1888).
[99] *Brentford F.C. Handbk.* (1951-2).
[1] O.S. Map 6", Mdx. XVI. SW. (1873 edn.).
[2] Below, publ. svces.
[3] *Ealing* (1925); *Kelly's Dir. Mdx.* (1908, 1926).
[4] Notice on pavilion.

Magpie club, at Castlebar Hill, by 1896. Tennis later gave rise to several local clubs: six were listed in 1926, in addition to one founded by St. John's church in 1923, hard courts in Uxbridge Road, and courts at the private West Side Country Club in Eaton Rise.[5] Brentford had a lawn tennis club, apparently short lived, and a gymnastic society which met at the Star and Garter in 1888, and a rowing club for the gasworks' employees in 1907.[6]

Golf was provided in 1908 by the Castlebar and Hanger Hill clubs, the first of which had been founded in 1898 and was later called Ealing golf club. Hanger Hill golf club closed in 1933 and its clubhouse, formerly Hanger Hill House, was later demolished.[7]

Societies at Ealing included a literary and scientific institution by 1855[8] and St. Mary's association for literary and social recreation in 1884.[9] From 1888 there were varied meetings at the new Victoria hall behind the municipal buildings or at the smaller Prince's room or lecture room beneath. Choral, orchestral, philharmonic, photographic, and scientific societies existed by 1907, an arts club was founded in 1910, and by 1925 there was a debating society, besides a literary society at Ealing Green.[10] Political groups included a Liberal association by 1880,[11] with premises on the Green in 1890, a Conservative association in Uxbridge Road by 1890, and a constitutional club, also in Uxbridge Road, by 1908.[12] Among more recent groups is Ealing Civic Society, a conservation and amenity society formed in 1967.[13] Brentford lacked Ealing's artistic societies, although in 1853 a literary and scientific institution met at the town hall.[14] There was a Conservative association in 1882[15] and a Liberal and Radical club at no. 334 High Street, also used by the Irish National League of Great Britain, by 1888.[16]

Both sporting and cultural activities were planned for the Brentham estate, where 12 a. were reserved as playing fields.[17] A cricket pavilion was opened there in 1908, followed in 1911 by the Institute,[18] with a lending library and lecture rooms, in Meadvale Road. Social interests later predominated and in 1947 the building and grounds were bought by members from Bradford Property Trust as a private club.

An amphitheatre at Brentford was advertised in 1826.[19] A hall in Walnut Tree Road was leased in 1886 by T. W. Beach and soon known as Brentford theatre, later being used as a cinema and surviving until 1930.[20] The Q theatre was opened in 1924 by Jack De Leon in the former Prince's hall and was the scene of early works by several well known playwrights before its closure in 1956.[21] In 1980 the St. Lawrence, Brentford, Trust, consisting of the Brentford Community Association and the New Hope Theatre Co., was converting the former church into a theatre and communal centre.[22] Cinemas at Brentford included the Queen's hall in the Half Acre from 1913 to 1957, the Prince's hall in the garden of the Star and Garter, and the Brentford, later the Coronet, at no. 275 High Street from 1912 to c. 1930. The former Coronet was a garage in 1934 and used by the Press Plating Co. in 1964.[23]

A hall of variety was Ealing's sole place of entertainment in 1832. It stood next to the New inn in St. Mary's Road and may have been the Royal Standard theatre of 1850 and the assembly rooms of the 1860s. A concert hall in the Broadway, adjoining an older building, was opened in 1881. Known as the Lyric hall by 1883, it was replaced in 1899 by the Lyric restaurant and the New or Ealing theatre,[24] later called Ealing Hippodrome.[25] The Questors theatre originated in a group founded in 1929, which used a former chapel in Mattock Lane from 1933, formed a limited company in 1949, and opened a new theatre in 1964.[26]

Films were shown in 1910 at an electric theatre in the Broadway and at the Hippodrome,[27] which was called the Palladium from 1922 and closed in 1957, being replaced by shops.[28] The Walpole picture palace in Bond Street was converted from a former skating rink in 1912 and, having closed in 1972, was under threat of demolition in 1980.[29] The Kinema, West Ealing, opened in 1913 on the site of Ealing cottage hospital at the corner of Northfield Avenue and Uxbridge Road, was rebuilt in 1928, and called the Lido from 1931; it was used partly for bingo from c. 1969 but survived as a double cinema, Studios 1 and 2, in 1980.[30] The Northfield cinema, on the east side of Northfield Avenue, was open by 1914 and renamed the Elite in 1924. The Avenue theatre, on the opposite side of the road, replaced it in 1932; popularly known as Spanish City, because of its architecture, it became an Odeon cinema c. 1938 and survived in 1980.[31] The Forum, Uxbridge Road, was built in 1934 in a quasi-Egyptian style; later part of the ABC chain, it was divided into

[5] Kelly's Dir. Ealing (1896–7); Kelly's Dir. Mdx. (1926); St. John's, W. Ealing (centenary booklet 1976), 19.
[6] County of Mdx. Independent Dir. Brentford (1888); Kelly's Dir. Ealing (1907).
[7] Golf in Ealing L.B. (TS. in Ealing libr.); V.C.H. Mdx. iv. 123; below, manors.
[8] P.O. Dir. Six Home Counties (1855).
[9] M.R.O., D.R.O. 37/A12/2.
[10] Kelly's Dir. Ealing (1907); Ealing (1925); Ealing, 1901–51, ed. Scouse, 85.
[11] The Times, 22 July 1880.
[12] Kelly's Dir. Mdx. (1890, 1908).
[13] Char. Com. files.
[14] Mason's Dir. Brentford (1853).
[15] The Times, 4 May 1882.
[16] County of Mdx. Independent Dir. Brentford (1888).
[17] Para. based on Ealing Local Hist. Soc. Local Historian (1964), 42; Brentham, 13, 24.
[18] Jones, Decade of Progress, 80.
[19] M.R.O., Acc. 880/5, p. 289.

[20] 'Cinemas in Brentford and Chiswick' (TS. in Chiswick libr.).
[21] Newspaper cuttings in Chiswick libr.
[22] Inf. from the chairman, St. Lawr., Brentford, Trust.
[23] 'Cinemas in Brentford and Chiswick'; Brentford and Chiswick Times, 27 Oct. 1977; Mdx. Local Hist. Council Bull. xviii. 5.
[24] Ealing libr., Holt's local hist. notes (cutting, ? from Mdx. County Times, 1957); Ealing As It Was, illus. 36.
[25] Mdx. Local Hist. Council Bull. xviii. 21.
[26] B. D. Steam, 'Urban Leisure: Study of a Lond. suburb' (TS. thesis 1966 in Ealing libr.), 8; Questors (40th anniv. booklet, 1969).
[27] Mdx. Local Hist. Council Bull. xviii. 21.
[28] Holt's local hist. notes.
[29] D. Atwell, Cathedrals of the Movies (1980), 9–10.
[30] Mdx. County Times, 28 June 1913; 30 Oct. 1928; 3 Oct. 1931; Kelly's Dir. Ealing (1969–70).
[31] Kelly's Dir. Ealing (1914, 1924, 1938); Mdx. County Times and Gaz. 5 Sept. 1932; Atwell, Movies, 135–7.

three auditoria in the 1970s and survived in 1980. The Ritz, at the junction of Hanger Lane and Western Avenue, opened in 1938 and later belonged to the Odeon and then the Classic chains. In 1980 it had for some years been a cinema club, the Paradise.[32]

Numerous antiquities collected by Thomas Layton (1819–1911)[33] were left to Brentford library, with his house, no. 22 Kew Bridge Road, to form a Layton museum. The collection included objects of the Stone Age and later from the Thames[34] and c. 11,000 volumes and 3,000 prints, which after a Chancery ruling of 1913, were kept at Brentford library and St. George's church. Since the endowment proved inadequate, the archaeological finds were transferred in 1963 to the London Museum while the books were temporarily stored, from 1968, at the former Chiswick town hall.[35] The Musical museum was founded by F. W. Holland in 1963 as the British Piano museum, a charitable trust, in the former St. George's church. Its collection, including a library of rolls, was formed around reproducing pianos, to which were added other large automatic musical instruments.[36] A museum of steam engines connected with water supply, maintained by the Kew Bridge Engines Trust, in 1980 occupied part of the old Grand Junction Waterworks Co.'s premises in Kew Bridge Road.[37]

The weekly Ealing Post and General Advertiser was first published in 1863 by J. E. Acworth, sub-postmaster and owner of a circulating library, who from 1857 had printed the parish magazine. Intended also to serve Brentford, Acton, and Hanwell, his newspaper was renamed the Middlesex County Times in 1868 and moved from its original offices at no. 63 Broadway to no. 61 in 1878. After it had bought the more recent Acton Gazette, its local monopoly was briefly challenged by the Conservative West Middlesex Standard, which it took over in 1889, and, in the north part of the parish, by the Ealing Advertiser of 1882, published from Southall. Middlesex County Times Ltd. was formed in 1892 and later acquired the Chiswick Gazette. Meanwhile the Ealing Gazette and Ealing Guardian were both founded in 1898, although the second proved short lived. In 1923 the Ealing Gazette combined with Southall and Hanwell editions of John King's Uxbridge Gazette to form the West Middlesex Gazette, which in 1941 merged with the Middlesex County Times, whose Ealing edition from 1974 was published as the Ealing Gazette. In 1980 the Middlesex County Times

group also published the Mid-Week Gazette, started in 1969. The Ealing and District Weekly Post, previously the Ealing Weekly Post, appeared for a few years until 1974. At Brentford, where Chiswick newspapers circulated, the Brentford Independent was published in 1883–4 and continued as the County of Middlesex Independent from 1885 until 1942 and then as the Middlesex Independent until 1964. Its successor, the Hounslow, Brentford, Chiswick Post, closed in 1971.[38]

MANORS. The manor of EALING or EALINGBURY was presumably the 10 hides at Ealing granted in 693 × 704 by Ethelred, king of Mercia, to the bishop of London for the augmentation of monastic life in London.[39] Only in 704 × 709 was the bishop granted 50 hides in Fulham,[40] of which Ealing was probably thought to form part at the time of Domesday Book.[41] Ealing and Acton were said to be members of Fulham in 1294[42] and in 1388 the tenants of Ealing owed 11s. 10d. of the 33s. 4d. common fine due from Fulham and its members,[43] although the issues were accounted for separately.[44] In 1588 the tenants denied that Ealing had ever been part of Fulham: while admitting that their courts were usually held there, they pointed out that their business and officers were separate, and that courts were occasionally held at Ealing.[45] The tenure of the bishop was interrupted only during the Interregnum, when the manor was sold in 1647 to Col. Edmund Harvey and belonged from 1654 to 1658 to Alderman Francis Allen, and in 1659–60 to the regicide Sir John Barkstead (d. 1662),[46] as Lord Barkstead.[47]

The bishop farmed the royalties from at least 1749: the farmer, who was also the gamekeeper, paid partridges and pheasants as part of the rent.[48] The 648 a. of demesne in 1840 lay mostly in the east part of the parish and south of Uxbridge Road, with the largest block south and east of Gunnersbury Park; some was interspersed with other estates and some was included in Ealing and Gunnersbury parks.[49]

The manor house was called Ealingbury in 1422,[50] Ealingbury House in 1813,[51] and Ealingbury or Gunnersbury Manor House in 1835.[52] North-west of the junction of Gunnersbury Lane and Pope's Lane,[53] it was said to have been a fine house with well appointed outbuildings but was sacked in 1642 and was uninhabitable in 1647.[54] Thereafter it was either rebuilt or remodelled: in 1898, despite recent alterations, it was considered

[32] Atwell, Movies, 109; Mdx. County Times, 16 April 1938.
[33] Proc. Soc. Antiq. (2nd ser.), xxiv. 232; rest of para. based on R. J. Jones, 'Thos. Layton and Layton Colln.' (TS. at Chiswick libr.) and Lond. Archaeologist, iii (4), 90–6.
[34] Archaeologia, lxix. 1–30.
[35] Inf. from Hounslow L.B. ref. libr.
[36] Leaflet and newspaper cuttings at Chiswick libr.; inf. from Mr. F. W. Holland.   [37] Inf. on bldg.
[38] Mdx. County Times and Gaz. 16 Mar. 1963 (centenary issue); B.L. Newspaper Cat.; Willing's Press Guide (1980).
[39] Eng. Hist. Docs. i, ed. D. Whitelock (1955), 448.
[40] P. J. Taylor, 'Estates of Bishopric of Lond. from 7th to early 16th cent.' (Lond. Univ. Ph.D. thesis, 1976), 29.
[41] V.C.H. Mdx. i. 105; vi. 55.
[42] Plac. de Quo Warr. (Rec. Com.), 475.
[43] Taylor, 'Estates of Bishopric of Lond.' 19.

[44] e.g. P.R.O., SC 6/1140/18, m. 1.
[45] Cts. were normally held at Fulham from at least 1445; below, local govt.
[46] Jackson, Ealing, 4; Cal. Cttee. for Compounding, v. 3266; Guildhall MSS. 10312/38, rott. 3 and d., 9; 10312/39, rot. 1; P.R.O., C 8/161/72.
[47] Barkstead sat in the Protectorate House of Lords: Complete Peerage, iv. 594–5.
[48] Guildhall MS. 10243, p. 85.
[49] M.R.O., TA/EAL; see also M.R.O., Acc. 26/5.
[50] Guildhall MS 11766, f. 9.
[51] Ibid. 12688.   [52] Ibid. 12359.
[53] Keene, Field Monuments, 18; compare Guildhall MS. 12688; M.R.O., Acc. 26/10–11.
[54] Guildhall MS. 10464A, f. 41; Cal. Cttee. for Compounding, iv. 3154.

to be substantially of the late 17th century except the cellars, which were older, and was a large red-brick and tiled house of three storeys, with pedimented windows, described as the ideal country house.[55] Modernized in 1935,[56] it was later demolished.

The demesne was already leased in 1381, when John Eustace was farmer in succession to his father Robert.[57] In 1539 the lessee was William Honyng of London,[58] servant of Sir Thomas Wriothesley, Secretary of State, under a lease to John Langton. Honyng obtained a new lease,[59] which included the woods, in 1545.[60] In 1547 the bishop granted a 200-year lease of Ealing and Fulham to Edward, duke of Somerset, on whose attainder it was forfeited to the Crown. The lease was granted in 1600 to Simon Willis, who divided the estate in 1601: he assigned the lands north of Uxbridge Road, Ealing, to Thomas Fisher, skinner of London, and the larger part, including those lands in Ealing south of Uxbridge Road, to Thomas, later Sir Thomas, Penruddock.[61] The Penruddocks' possession was disputed in 1615 by Thomas, son of Anthony Mason, a former tenant,[62] perhaps as beneficiary under an earlier lease.

The descent of Fisher's share is not known. Penruddock's estate descended in his family, except when sequestrated in the Interregnum,[63] until Edward Penruddock devised it to his brother-in-law Joseph Cage. By will dated 1700, Joseph left it to his son John Cage, a minor, whose administrators assigned it in 1717 to Richard Webb, later of Cavenham (Suff.).[64] In 1735 the bishop granted three new leases to Webb, Sir William Halton, Bt. (d. 1754), and Anne and Mary Brand.[65] Thereafter the estate leased out in 1547 was repeatedly divided, until there were seven separate leases of the demesne in Ealing by 1840.[66]

The estate leased in 1735 to Richard Webb consisted of 285 a. in Fulham and 376 a. in Ealing,[67] most of it south of Uxbridge Road. In 1749 the issues were divided into five, two shares for Richard's brother William, the lessee, and one share for Richard Long of Cavenham.[68] The lease was held by Long from 1756 and his trustees from 1777,[69] until in 1798 the estate was divided between his sons-in-law George Hardinge and Richard Vachell.[70] Hardinge assigned his share by 1806 to Peter Thorne of Ealing, who relinquished lands outside Ealing in 1813[71] but

retained the manor house and 245 a., most or all of which were sold in 1822 to William Booth (d. 1833) of Brentford, distiller. The bulk was again sold in 1835 to George Robinson of Kew (Surr.)[72] who held episcopal leasehold estates of 276 a. in 1840,[73] including some from Vachell's share. Vachell's 365 a. of leasehold, including 125 a. in Ealing, were for sale in 1829: London Style farm of 96 a. was sold to Samuel Ware, while 29 a. were sold to William Booth but acquired in 1835 by Robinson, himself lessee of London Style farm from 1841.[74] After Robinson's death in 1852 his estate was held by his sons until 1861 when the lease of 331 a. surrounding Gunnersbury Park, including the manor house and London Style farm, was assigned to Baron Lionel Nathan de Rothschild, who bought the freehold.[75]

The land leased in 1739 to Sir William Halton consisted of 61 a. near Little Ealing, 34 a. north of Uxbridge Road, 24 a. at Stamford Brook, and 40 a. at Fulham.[76] It was held by trustees until 1806, when the lessee was William Halton, a Canadian,[77] but was broken up in 1813, when four separate leases were granted: the largest estate was Little Ealing farm of 54 a., leased to Jonathan Knevett.[78]

In 1739 Anne Brand, widow, and her daughter Mary Brand of Edwardstone (Suff.) were leased a mansion house and 101 a., formerly woodland, on Hanger Hill west of Hanger Lane. The lease was renewed for John Williams in 1746, for King Gould in 1754, and in 1761 for William Tanner of St. Marylebone, who immediately assigned it to Richard Latham. It was auctioned in 1769 and renewed in 1775 to Richard Wood,[79] who held Hanger House and land west of Hanger Lane in 1777.[80] The lands formed the nucleus of the Wood family's large estate on both sides of Hanger Lane. Richard Wood was dead by 1785, when his youngest son James was admitted to 6 a. of copyhold,[81] and the leasehold estate had passed by 1790 to Thomas Wood[82] who was rated on a new house and c. 240 a.,[83] and by 1811 to William Wood (d. 1817), who had acquired 100 a. of copyhold from Jonathan Gurnell in 1787.[84] The estate was later held by William's trustees and from 1844 under the will of Edward Wood (d. 1844).[85] From 1838 or earlier the tenant for life was George Wood (d. 1864), who held 501 a. in 1840, including 167 a. of leasehold.[86] The Woods bought the freehold of the land held by

[55] Jackson, *Ealing*, 88–90 and illus. facing p. 89.
[56] *Mdx. County Times*, 20 Apr. 1935; but see C. M. Neaves, *Hist. Gtr. Ealing* (1930), 63.
[57] Guildhall MS. 11765, f. 29.
[58] *L. & P. Hen. VIII*, xiv (2), p. 80.
[59] St. Paul's MS. C (Sampson), ff. 144v.–5.
[60] Ibid. ff. 172–3v.
[61] Guildhall MS. 10234/2, pp. 836–8. Sir Thos. was related to the Penruddocks of Compton Chamberlayne (Wilts.): *Vis. Wilts.* (Harl. Soc. cv), 149.
[62] P.R.O., C 2/Jas. I/M 12/20; C 2/Jas. I/P 21/50; STAC 8/228/18.
[63] Ibid. E 367/2674.
[64] M.L.R. 1713/4/123–4; 1717/1/141; 1717/5/27.
[65] Guildhall MS. 10237, f. 12.
[66] M.R.O., TA/EAL.
[67] Guildhall MSS. 10239, 12337.
[68] M.R.O., Acc. 26/2.
[69] Ibid Acc. 26/7, 12; Guildhall MS. 10240.

[70] M.R.O., Acc. 26/5; Guildhall MS. 10240.
[71] Guildhall MSS. 10239, 10240.
[72] Ibid. MSS. 12359, 12337.
[73] M.R.O., TA/EAL.
[74] Guildhall MSS. 12328, 12337–8, 12359.
[75] Ibid. MS. 12337.
[76] Ibid. MSS. 12340, 10234/2.
[77] Ibid. MSS. 10242–3, 12340.
[78] Ibid. MSS. 10241–2, 12359.   [79] Ibid. MS. 12351.
[80] B.L. Maps K.29.9.a.
[81] Guildhall MS. 10465/100, pp. 40–2.
[82] Ibid. MS. 10242.
[83] M.R.O., D.R.O. 37/D1/2; *Ambulator* (1792).
[84] Guildhall MSS. 10465/102, pp. 88–100; 10465/132, pp. 438–45; 12351.
[85] Ibid. MSS. 10465/160, pp. 346 sqq.; 10465/163, pp. 422–34; 12350.
[86] M.R.O., TA/EAL; M.R.O., D.R.O. 37/A12/1; Guildhall MS. 10465/153, pp. 88–91.

lease in or after 1854, and the copyhold was enfranchised in 1862.[87] In 1899 the Wood estate included 560 a. east of Hanger Lane, much of it in Acton parish; Hanger Hill House and 145 a. were leased to Sir Montague Nelson, tenant from 1874 and chairman of Ealing U.D.C.[88] George Wood's son Edward (d. 1904) moved to Shropshire in the 1870s and was succeeded by his son Lt.-Col. Charles Peevor Boileau Wood (d. 1932), who in 1906 sold most or all of the land to the Prudential Assurance Co.[89] Hanger Hill House, a large three-storeyed building of the 18th century, was used by Hanger Hill golf club from 1901 and survived until 1935 or later.[90]

COLDHALL or *WEST EALING* manor at Little Ealing was probably held of Ealing manor. It was recorded from 1377 when John Torngold, alderman of London, died seised of Coldhall and his daughter Alice was heir.[91] It may have been held in 1408 by William and Agnes Powe, who exchanged it for a pension with John Spartgrave of Spargrove (Som.),[92] perhaps in connexion with his marriage: in 1415 Powe was executor of Spartgrave, who left the manor to his wife Agnes, daughter Agnes, and their heirs.[93] Presumably it was the younger Agnes who married Sir Nicholas Stukeley and later one Montgomery: her son Thomas Montgomery inherited her copyhold estate and perhaps Coldhall,[94] which was sold in 1496 by Henry Barnes and his wife Anne, with 250 a. and rent, to Richard Awnsham or Amondesham, alderman of London,[95] who had been accumulating land in Ealing since 1482 or earlier.[96] Coldhall descended with other manors in Heston until 1643, when it passed to Robert Awnsham's sisters Jane, wife of Henry Mildmay, and Margaret, later wife of Gideon Awnsham.[97] Their tenure was disturbed by litigation[98] until in 1667, by authority of parliament, they sold Coldhall to William Dennington (d. 1681) of the Inner Temple.[99] Each of Dennington's three sisters and coheirs received some land in Ealing but Coldhall itself was assigned in 1688 to his sister Anne and her husband Thomas Watts, mercer of London,[1] who in 1701 sold it to John Loving of Place House. Loving also bought Twyfords in 1708[2] and sold Holly House in 1722 and Coldhall and Twyfords in 1728 to Charles Lockyer of Ilchester

(Som.), M.P., who had made at least nine other purchases by 1735.[3] Lockyer was succeeded in 1752 by his illegitimate son John Lockyer or Green,[4] who left the estate in 1762 to his widow Elizabeth and daughter Elizabeth. The elder Elizabeth was admitted to the copyhold estate in 1764[5] and the younger, who had married Henry Burgoyne Sharp, to 134 a. of copyhold in 1774:[6] the total estate including Coldhall totalled *c.* 330 a. *c.* 1774[7] and 302 a. in 1817, when some had been sold.[8] In 1819, following Sharp's death, the copyhold estate was held jointly by Francis Brodrip's trustees and Lockyer Sharp.[9] Frederick Sharp was admitted in 1828 and on his death, trustees were admitted in 1835.[10] Much had been sold, perhaps including Coldhall, by 1840, when the total estate of the executors of Brodrip and William Sharp was only 174 a.[11] Coldhall later belonged to the Meacock family: in 1886 it was sold by John and William Meacock,[12] perhaps already to Blondin (Jean François Gravelet) the tightrope walker, who renamed the house Niagara and died there in 1897.[13] The manor house, mentioned in 1693,[14] probably stood beside the modern Northfield Avenue, Little Ealing,[15] near Niagara and Blondin avenues.

GUNNERSBURY manor was held of the bishop of London in 1378 for fealty, suit of court, and rents, and included 228 a. land and £1 7s. rent from tenants.[16] The manor may have been the ½ carucate and 2 marks rent in which Maud, widow of Lawrence del Brok, claimed dower against Joan of Somery in the late 13th century.[17] In 1347 John of Ceppeham granted two-thirds of the manor to John de Bray and Joan his wife for life, with the reversion of the third held in dower by Maud, widow of Thomas of Gloucester.[18] John of Ceppeham was dead by 1364, when his son John granted the reversion to Geoffrey Scrope.[19] Lands including Gunnersbury, late of John of Northwich, goldsmith, were conveyed in 1373 by feoffees to those of Edward III's mistress Alice Perrers.[20] Alice forfeited them but her husband William of Windsor was granted Gunnersbury in 1380, to hold to the use of her and her heirs.[21] It was held by Thomas Charlton and Alice his wife, apparently in her right, in 1390, when it was settled in trust,[22] presumably to Alice's use. The estate was held by her son

---

[87] P.R.O., MAF 9/167/4146; Guildhall MSS. 12350-1.
[88] M.R.O., Acc. 234/1-2; *Mdx. County Times*, 26 June 1897.   [89] Inf. from Mr. P. Hounsell.
[90] *Ealing As It Was*, illus. 53; *Mdx. County Times*, 20 Apr. 1935; photos. in Ealing libr.
[91] *Cal. of Wills in Ct. of Husting*, ii (1), 199; Guildhall MS. 9171/1, f. 5v.
[92] P.R.O., CP 25(1)/151/84/58.
[93] Guildhall MS. 9171/2, f. 326; see also *Feud. Aids*, vi. 489.
[94] Guildhall MS. 10765, f. 106v.
[95] P.R.O., CP 25(2)/152/101/Mich. 12 Hen. VII.
[96] Guildhall MS. 10312/87, rot. 12d.
[97] *V.C.H. Mdx.* iii. 110-11; P.R.O., C 142/698/62.
[98] e.g. ibid. C 5/56/4; C 5/99/80; C 5/436/43; C 5/438/91; C 5/475/12; C 7/434/86; C 8/286/15; 18 & 19 Chas. II, c. 12 (Priv. Act).
[99] M.R.O., Acc. 562/1; P.R.O., C 6/471/70.
[1] M.R.O., Acc. 562/1, 9; Lysons, *Environs*, ii. 227.
[2] M.R.O., Acc. 562/1.
[3] M.L.R. 1728/1/77-80; M.R.O., Acc. 562/1.
[4] Guildhall MS. 10465/68, pp. 35 sqq.; *Hist. Parl., Commons, 1715-54*, ii. 222-3.

[5] Guildhall MS. 10465/78, pp. 262 sqq.
[6] Ibid. 89, pp. 225 sqq.
[7] Ealing libr., survey (1774).
[8] Ibid. survey (1817).
[9] Guildhall MS. 10465/134, pp. 262 sqq.
[10] Ibid. 153, pp. 70 sqq.
[11] M.R.O., TA/EAL.
[12] *Mdx. County Times*, 15 May 1886; see also ibid. 2 Jan. 1892.
[13] Jackson, *Ealing*, 98; *The Times*, 23 Feb. 1897; *Ealing As It Was*, illus. 47.
[14] P.R.O., C 8/455/35.
[15] M.L.R. 1728/1/77. It was probably not at Pope's cross in South Ealing Lane, *pace* Keene, *Field Mons. of Ealing*, 18.
[16] *Cal. Inq. Misc.* iv, p. 12; Guildhall MSS. 11766, f. 9; 10312/87, rot. 87.
[17] P.R.O., CP 40/10, rot. 20.
[18] Ibid. CP 25(1)/150/62/236.
[19] *Cal. Close*, 1364-8, 61.
[20] Ibid. 1369-74, 535-6; see also P.R.O., E 159/191, recorda Hil. 2 Hen. V, rot. 1 and d.
[21] *Cal. Pat.* 1377-81, 503.
[22] P.R.O., CP 25(1)/151/79/106.

Henry Frowyk in 1422[23] and remained with the Frowyks until the death of another Henry Frowyk in 1520, when it was allotted to his sister Elizabeth, wife of the judge Sir John Spelman,[24] descending in the Spelman family with Flambards in Harrow.[25] It was held by the judge John, later Sir John, Maynard (d. 1690) by at least 1656[26] and then in turn by his widow Mary, countess of Suffolk (d. 1721), and his great-grandson John Hobart, Lord Hobart, later earl of Buckinghamshire (d. 1756). In 1739, after a private Act, Hobart sold Gunnersbury to Henry Furnese, M.P. (d. 1756),[27] whose sister Elizabeth Pearce sold it in 1761 to Princess Amelia (d. 1786), daughter of George II.[28] Lavish entertainments were given by the princess,[29] who extended the estate by purchase and lease to 236 a. but ordered it to be sold in lots on her death.[30] The main part, comprising the house and c. 95 a., was bought by Col. Gilbert Ironside in 1788, passed to Walter Stirling in 1792, and was sold by Andrew Stirling to Henry Crawford in 1794.[31] Crawford sold it to Mr. Morley, a floor-cloth manufacturer, by 1800, when demolition of the house and partition of the estate were impending.[32]

The north-east corner of the estate, in the angle of Pope's Lane and Gunnersbury Avenue, was bought by Stephen Cosser (d. 1806), who erected the smaller of the two Gunnersbury seats, called Gunnersbury House.[33] On his death it was bought by Alexander Morrison (d. 1828), whose widow Jane, countess of Carnwath, sold it to Thomas Farmer c. 1833.[34] Trustees of Mrs. Elizabeth Atkinson (née Farmer) sold it in 1889 to Leopold de Rothschild (d. 1917),[35] youngest son of Baron Lionel Nathan de Rothschild (d. 1879). The bulk of the estate sold c. 1800, 76 a., was bought by Alexander Copeland (d. 1834), who erected the larger mansion, Gunnersbury Park.[36] It had been acquired by Nathan Mayer de Rothschild by 1836,[37] passed to his wife Hannah, who held 109 a. in 1840,[38] to his son Baron Lionel Nathan de Rothschild, who bought 331 a. nearby in 1861 from the bishop of London,[39] and to the latter's three sons. Baron Nathaniel Mayer de Rothschild and Leopold de Rothschild bought their brother's share in 1894 and Leopold (d. 1917) became sole owner in 1901. His son Lionel Nathan sold some land for building[40] and

in 1925 sold the remaining 199 a. to Ealing and Acton councils, 186 a. for a park and 13 a. for housing.[41]

No manor house was mentioned in 1378[42] but one evidently existed by c. 1464 when Sir Thomas Frowyk (d. 1506) was born at Gunnersbury.[43] In 1593 there was an ancient house, formerly of the Frowyks and conveniently situated near woodland and water, which was leased to the Corbet family.[44] It was presumably the residence of John Maynard until his house was rebuilt c. 1658 by John Webb (d. 1672), nephew of Inigo Jones, with assistance from Edward Marshall (d. 1675).[45] Webb's was a red-brick three-storeyed building of seven bays with a Corinthian portico on the north front,[46] described in 1736 as a great and ancient fabric expensive to repair.[47] The gardens, reputedly laid out by William Kent for Henry Furnese,[48] were improved by Princess Amelia, who erected the bath-house and chapel. The house had been demolished by 1807.[49]

Gunnersbury Park and Gunnersbury House stand side by side on a terrace, respectively to west and east. Gunnersbury Park, the larger, was built in 1811 and rebuilt c. 1836 by Sydney Smirke (d. 1877):[50] white and stuccoed, it consists of two-storeyed wings and a three-storeyed central block with Roman Doric portico. Gunnersbury House was built by 1806 and altered by W. F. Pocock between 1837 and 1850:[51] an ornate two-storeyed stuccoed house with semicircular terminal bays, it has housed Gunnersbury Park museum since 1929.[52] The gardens, much admired in the 19th century,[53] contain several ponds and extensive sports grounds. In 1977 the orangery, reputedly by Smirke,[54] was derelict and the bath-house had been demolished. The Temple, an 18th-century Roman Doric structure, was restored in 1975.[55]

PITSHANGER manor was described as a free tenement in 1423, when it was held of Ealing manor for rent, relief, and aid.[56] The demesne consisted of c. 140 a. stretching northward from Hanger Hill to the Brent.[57] Members of the Putelshanger or Pitshanger family occurred from 1229 and in 1293-4 Robert of Pitshanger fraudulently claimed woodland at Ealing from the bishop.[58] The manor was held by William,

[23] Guildhall MS. 11766, f. 9.
[24] Ibid. 10312/87, rot. 18; P.R.O., CP 25(2)/51/367/22 Hen. VIII; above, Acton, manors and other est.
[25] *V.C.H. Mdx.* iv. 209.
[26] M.R.O., Acc. 890; *D.N.B.*
[27] 10 Geo. II, c. 4 (Priv. Act); M.L.R. 1740/1/7-9; *Hist. Parl., Commons, 1715-54*, ii. 55-6.
[28] M.R.O., D.R.O. 37/B2/4; see also M.R.O., Acc. 1281/2.
[29] *Horace Walpole's Corresp.* ed. W. S. Lewis, 23 (Sir Horace Mann, vii), 48; 33 (Ctss. of Upper Ossory, ii), *passim*.
[30] Ealing libr., sales cat. (1785); Chiswick libr., sales cat. (1787); Faulkner, *Brentford, Ealing and Chiswick*, 254, 258.
[31] M.R.O., D.R.O. 37/D1/2; *Ambulator* (1796); Lysons, *Environs*, ii. 226.
[32] *Ambulator* (1800); Lysons, *Environs* (Suppl.), 128.
[33] Lysons, *Environs* (Suppl.), 128.
[34] Faulkner, *Brentford, Ealing and Chiswick*, 257.
[35] *Some Hist. Notes on Gunnersbury Pk.* [c. 1951] in Chiswick libr.
[36] Lysons, *Environs* (Suppl.), 128.
[37] Allison and Holt, *Ealing in 18th and 19th Cent.* 31.
[38] M.R.O., TA/EAL.
[39] Above. [40] M.R.O., Acc. 638/240.
[41] TS. in Chiswick libr.; *The Times*, 12 Oct. 1925.

[42] *Cal. Inq. Misc.* iv, p. 12. [43] *D.N.B.*
[44] Norden, *Spec. Brit.* 21.
[45] Colvin, *Biog. Dict. of Brit. Architects*, 378, 658.
[46] C. Campbell, *Vitruvius Britannicus* (1717), i. 4, 17-18; *Prospect of Ealing* (views pub. by Ealing libr. 1972), plate 3. Below, plate facing p. 128. A plan of the main floors is in Guildhall Libr., grangerized copy of Lysons, *Environs*, ii (2), between pp. 226 and 227.
[47] 10 Geo. 11, c. 4 (Priv. Act).
[48] Lysons, *Environs*, ii. 226.
[49] *Ambulator* (1782, 1796, 1807).
[50] Pevsner, *Mdx.* 29.
[51] Gunnersbury Pk. Mus., TS. notes.
[52] R. G. L. Rivis, *Gunnersbury Pk. Mus. 1927-55* (1960).
[53] *Hist. Gunnersbury Pk. and its Mus.* (official brochure, after 1965); Keane, *Beauties of Mdx.* (1850), 88-9; *Country Life*, 24 Nov. 1900, 656-9.
[54] *Hist. Gunnersbury Pk. and Mus.*
[55] *Gaz. & Post*, 17 Apr. 1975; Hounslow L.B. *Hounslow's Historic Bldgs.* (1968).
[56] Guildhall MS. 11766, f. 9.
[57] P.R.O., C 8/126/18; M.R.O., TA/EAL.
[58] *Early Charters of St. Paul's* (Camd. 3rd ser. lviii), 268, 270, 272, 274; P.R.O., JUST 1/543 rot. 19.

son of Thomas Bray, in 1423[59] and descended in the Bray family to Catherine Welby (*née* Bray) in 1508,[60] perhaps the Catherine on whom Pitshanger was settled jointly with her husband John Hall in 1537, with remainder to her son Thomas Webb.[61] It descended to her son George Hall and was held in 1553 by Edward Bayshe,[62] who conveyed it in 1563 to Gilbert Gerard, later Sir Gilbert Gerard, Master of the Rolls, and Gilbert Sherrington,[63] apparently to Gerard's use. Pitshanger belonged to Thomas Stevens in 1575, passed to his son Henry in 1579,[64] and was conveyed by Uriah and Anne Babington in 1596 to Arthur, later Sir Arthur, Atye,[65] who held the manor, 3 houses, with gardens and barns, and 331 a. in Ealing at his death in 1605.[66] Atye's son Robert was succeeded in 1612 by his daughter Eleanor, a minor.[67] The manor was held by Richard Lee of Kingston from 1620 or earlier until 1663,[68] when he left it to Thomas and Margaret Edwards. It descended to Thomas Edwards (1699–1757), critic, whose nephew sold it to King Gould (d. 1756). Charles Gould (1726–1806), Judge Advocate General and from 1792 Sir Charles Morgan, Bt., sold it and Botelers farm to Thomas Gurnell, who settled it in 1780 on his son Jonathan and prospective daughter-in-law Susannah Swinden,[69] whose second husband was Admiral Peyton. Her daughter Mary Anne, wife of Henry Armstrong, held 429 a. until her death in 1858.[70] In 1862 the estate belonged to C. P. Millard.[71]

The manor house, usually called Pitshanger farmhouse, stood near the centre of the modern Meadvale Road. A plain house of brick and tile, it was demolished in 1908.[72] The so-called Pitzhanger Manor House, Ealing Green, in 1979 the public library, stands on former copyhold land of Ealing manor.[73] The latter house, consisting of a three-storeyed central block with two-storeyed wings, was built *c.* 1770 for Thomas Gurnell by George Dance the younger and sold in 1799 by Susannah Peyton to John, later Sir John, Soane (1753–1837), architect, who largely rebuilt it in 1801–2. It belonged to Eric Mackay, Lord Reay (d. 1847), from 1832[74] and was inhabited by the daughter of Spencer Perceval from 1844 until 1900,[75] when it was sold to Ealing U.D.C. Soane retained only the south wing of Dance's house, rebuilding the central block and replacing the

north wing by sham ruins. Although modest in size, his villa is designed on a grandiose scale. The centre block, of Portland stone and brick, is of three bays and two storeys, fronted by monumental Ionic pillars topped by statues of Coade stone.[76] The house was adapted as a library by extending Dance's wing westward, and by additions on the north side which were replaced by the modern wing in 1938.[77]

The manor of *BOSTON, BURSTON*, or *BORDESTON* was conterminous with the township of New Brentford. In 1157 the abbot of Westminster held 3 hides in Brentford, Hanwell, and nearby.[78] By 1179 the vill had been sub-infeudated to Ralph Brito,[79] whose son Robert had granted it by 1194 to Geoffrey Blund.[80] After 1216 he granted a quitrent from it to his son-in-law Henry, son of Rainier, who later held Boston. By 1294 it was held by the prioress of St. Helen's, Bishopsgate, as tenant of Westminster, which claimed Boston as part of its liberty[81] and was sued by the nuns for distraining the plough animals of their tenants.[82] In 1535 the sacrist of Westminster still received an annual rent from Brentford.[83] The lordship was retained by the priory until its surrender in 1538, when Boston passed to the Crown and became part of the new honor of Hampton Court.[84] The manor had been leased for 80 years in 1534 to John Rollesley, presumably a kinsman of the prioress Mary Rollesley. His lease was confirmed in 1542[85] and the residue of his term was granted to Jerome Hawley, a clerk of the Petty Bag, in 1567.[86]

Boston was granted in 1547 to Edward Seymour, duke of Somerset, but reverted to the Crown on his forfeiture and was granted in 1572 to Robert Dudley, earl of Leicester, who immediately conveyed it to Sir Thomas Gresham (1519?–79), founder of the Royal Exchange and lord of Osterley. On Gresham's death Boston was held in turn by his widow Anne (d. 1596) and Sir William Reade (d. 1621), her son by a former husband. In 1606 Reade settled it on his bride Mary Goldsmith,[87] who later married Sir Edward Spencer of Althorp (Northants.), a Royalist during the Civil War.[88] Having bought out the claims of Reade's heirs,[89] Mary left Boston in 1658 to her kinsman John Goldsmith (d. 1670),[90] whose trustee sold it in 1670 to James Clitherow (d. 1682). Boston descended in the Clitherow

[59] Guildhall MS. 11766, f. 9.
[60] Ibid. MS. 10312/85, rot. 2d.
[61] P.R.O., CP 25(2)/27/183/Trin. 29 Hen. VIII.
[62] Ibid. SC 2/189/24, rott. 1, 5d.
[63] Ibid. CP 25(2)/171/5 Eliz. I Trin.; *D.N.B.*
[64] Ibid. PROB 11/61 (P.C.C. 14 Bakon); Guildhall MS. 10312/94, rot. 18.
[65] P.R.O., CP 25(2)/173/38 Eliz. I Trin.
[66] Ibid. WARD 5/30/431.
[67] Ibid. WARD 5/30/432.
[68] Ibid. C 8/126/18; Guildhall MS. 10312/99, rot. 8.
[69] *D.N.B.* svv. Edwards; Gould; M.R.O., Acc. 1028/29; below, other est.
[70] Mrs. Basil Holmes, *Home of Ealing Free Libr.* (1902), 13; M.R.O., TA/EAL.
[71] P.R.O., MAF 20/64/959; Guildhall MS. 10465/177, pp. 250–1.
[72] Tims, *Ealing Tenants Ltd.* 14–15; photos. at Ealing libr.
[73] Guildhall MS. 10465/115, pp. 213B–215B. Rest of para. based on Pevsner, *Mdx.* 41–2; A. T. Bolton, *Pitzhanger Man., Ealing Green, 1800–11* (1918); Holmes, *Ealing Free Libr.*

[74] Guildhall MS. 10465/147, pp. 223–30; *Complete Peerage*, x. 757.   [75] Jones, *Ealing*, 69.
[76] Gunnis, *Dict. Sculptors*, 108; *Prospect of Ealing*, plate 3; below, plate facing p. 128.
[77] Below, pub. svces.; inf. from Mr. P. Hounsell.
[78] Westm. Abbey, Westm. Domesday, f. 36. Next 3 paras. based on A. J. Howard, 'Boston Manor and the Clitherows' (TS. thesis, 1969).
[79] *Letters of Gilb. Foliot*, 491–2.
[80] *Pipe R. 6 Ric. I* (P.R.S. n.s. v), 182.
[81] P.R.O., JUST 1/543, rot. 39; JUST 1/544, rot. 51d.
[82] Ibid. CP 40/43, rot. 106; CP 40/45, rot. 39d.
[83] *Valor Eccl.* (Rec. Com), i. 412.
[84] *L. & P. Hen. VIII*, xv, p. 214.
[85] J. E. Cox, *Annals of St. Helen's Bishopsgate* (1876), 14–15.
[86] *Cal. Pat. 1566–9*, 9.
[87] P.R.O., C 142/396/137.
[88] *Cal. S.P. Dom. 1642–56*, i. 171.
[89] Lysons, *Environs*, ii. 45.
[90] P.R.O., PROB 11/287 (P.C.C. 52 Pell, will of Dame Mary Spencer).

family until 1923, when the estate was sold by the trustees of the late Col. E. J. Stracey-Clitherow. Most of the land was built over, but Brentford U.D. bought Boston House and 20 a. as a park, opened in 1924.[91]

The Boston demesne consisted of 230 a. in 1712,[92] and the lords also held copyhold land in Ealing between Boston Manor and Windmill roads, amounting to 62 a. in 1659 and 80 a. in 1840.[93] Ralph Brito lived in a house by St. Lawrence's church,[94] but the site of a manor house mentioned in 1377 and 1584 was not recorded.[95] The existing Boston House in Boston Manor Road was erected by Mary Reade in 1622–3 in a curve of the river Brent and, after a fire, was extensively repaired by James Clitherow c. 1671.[96] A three-storeyed red-brick house, with three gables on the longer sides and two on the shorter, it has a large Jacobean stone porch and contains three ornate plaster ceilings and an elaborate fireplace.[97] It also contained a collection of paintings, dispersed in 1922.[98] The house was restored in 1960 and since 1963 has been leased to the National Institute of Housework.[99]

OTHER ESTATES. At Castlebar Hill Richard Barenger in 1423 held c. 90 a. of copyhold, including 53 a. called Absdonsland, to which Simon Barenger was admitted in 1560.[1] Absdonsland, then 72 a., passed in turn to Anne Perrott and her son Thomas, who surrendered it in 1574 to Christopher Rythe,[2] by whom it was settled in 1585 on Joan Southcott, widow.[3] Edward More surrendered it in 1627 to his wife Philippa, who settled it in 1641 on his son John.[4] The estate was acquired from George and Rebecca Lamplowe by Sir William Bateman, the purchaser of other property in Ealing, in 1650 and descended in 1664 from Bateman's widow to his son Sir William,[5] whose youngest son Charles settled it on his son William in 1719.[6] It descended in turn to William Bateman (d. c. 1797) and his children William (d. 1820) and Mary Bateman (d. 1833), all three of them lunatics,[7] and included 160 a. in Ealing when it was disputed among Mary's heirs.[8] Francis Swinden bought out other claimants in 1854, with a view to leasing the estate for building.[9] The three-

storeyed mansion, called Castlebar House or *CASTLEBAR PARK* in 1824,[10] stood on the south side of Castlebar Hill. First mentioned in 1641,[11] it was difficult to let by 1818[12] and dilapidated in 1855, when Swinden allowed for its demolition in a lease.[13] Among tenants were Isabella Cunningham, countess of Glencairn (d. 1796), in 1806,[14] Lt.-Gen. Sir Frederick Augustus Wetherall (1754–1842) in 1818, and Sir Jonathan Miles in 1819.[15]

A forerunner of Castle Hill Lodge, north of Castlebar Hill, was sold by Charles Gould in 1763 to Capt. James Cusack. In 1764 it was acquired by John Scott,[16] who combined 5 freehold closes and 10 a. leased from the Isleworth charity trustees[17] to form an estate of c. 27 a. The house had been enlarged or rebuilt by c. 1773,[18] when the estate was bought by Francis Burdett. During the tenure of the Burdetts, Stebbing Shaw (1762–1802), topographer, was tutor there to the politician Sir Francis Burdett, Bt. (1770–1844).[19] In 1791 the house was bought by Henry Beaufoy (d. 1795), who improved it and whose brother sold it in 1795 to Mrs. Maria FitzHerbert (1756–1837),[20] morganatic wife of the prince of Wales.[21] She sold it in 1801 to Edward Augustus, Duke of Kent (1767–1820),[22] who called it *CASTLE HILL LODGE* and commissioned improvements by Wyatt[23] but lived elsewhere from 1812.[24] After attempted sales in 1820 and 1827 the estate was bought in 1829 by Gen. Sir F. A. Wetherall, the duke's former aide-de-camp.[25] The general's son, Adm. Frederick Augustus Wetherall (d. 1856), was succeeded by his son Frederick Henry Pakenham Wetherall,[26] the house being leased from 1856 to Henry Austin.[27] The property was called the Kent House estate in 1870, when F. H. P. Wetherall sold the house to Thomas Harrison and the rest of the land to Alfred Prest, Ebenezer J. Pearce, and Charles Jones, for building.[28] Some of the land was later bought by Harrison, who sold it in 1880 to the British Land Co.[29]

Two-storeyed and in the Grecian style, Castle Hill Lodge was long and low in 1816, when its principal, north, front featured an Ionic portico beneath a pediment. Lacking woodland and water, it was considered a pleasant but not a first-class seat.[30] Fittings were sold in 1820 and further

[91] Burke, *Landed Gentry* (1952); *The Times*, 12 July 1923; 18 Jan. 1924; Brentford and Chiswick, *Official Guide* (1948).
[92] Chiswick libr., Boston manor ct. bk. 1692–1842 [survey].
[93] Guildhall MS. 10312/39, rot. 5d.; M.R.O., TA/EAL; B.L. Maps K.29.9.a.
[94] *Letters of Gilb. Foliot*, 492.
[95] P.R.O., E 134/26 Eliz. I Easter/6; Guildhall MS. 9171/1, f. 51v.   [96] P.R.O., C 10/152/169.
[97] Hist. Mon. Com. *Mdx.* 5–6; Pevsner, *Mdx.* 29–30; *Country Life*, 18 Mar. 1965.
[98] Turner, *Brentford*, 225.
[99] Brentford and Chiswick Boro. *Reopening of Restored Boston Man. Ho.* (1963).
[1] Guildhall MS. 11766, f. 13; P.R.O., SC 2/189/26, rot. 7 and d.
[2] Guildhall MS. 10312/92, rot. 42.
[3] Ibid. 96, rot. 4d.
[4] P.R.O., SC 2/190/11, rot. 10.
[5] Guildhall MSS. 10312/100, rot. 9; 101, rott. 5d.–6.
[6] Ibid. MS. 10465/6; M.R.O., Acc. 828/4.
[7] Guildhall MS. 10465/149, pp. 215–17; M.R.O., Acc. 828/4.

[8] M.R.O., TA/EAL; ibid. Acc. 828/21.
[9] Ibid. Acc. 828/15.
[10] Ibid. Acc. 526/11.
[11] P.R.O., SC 6/190/11, rot. 10.
[12] M.R.O., Acc. 828/3.
[13] P.R.O., MAF 20/64/159; M.R.O., Acc. 828/24.
[14] M.R.O., Acc. 828/6.
[15] Ibid. 3.
[16] Ibid. Acc. 1028/1, 5, 6.
[17] Ibid. 6, 12, 84.   [18] Ibid. 16–18.
[19] *D.N.B.* s.v. Shaw.
[20] M.R.O., Acc. 1028/25–6, 30–2.
[21] *D.N.B.*
[22] M.R.O., Acc. 1028/35–6.
[23] Ibid. 44 (sales cat.).
[24] Ibid. Acc. 1028/43.
[25] Ibid. 53; above.
[26] M.R.O., Acc. 1028/66–7.
[27] Ibid. 64–5.
[28] Ibid. 70, 73–83; Jones, *Ealing*, 141; Ealing libr., Wetherall colln.
[29] Ealing libr., copy of abs. of title.
[30] Brewer, *Beauties of Eng. & Wales*, x (5), 336–7.

Pitzhanger Manor House *c.* 1808

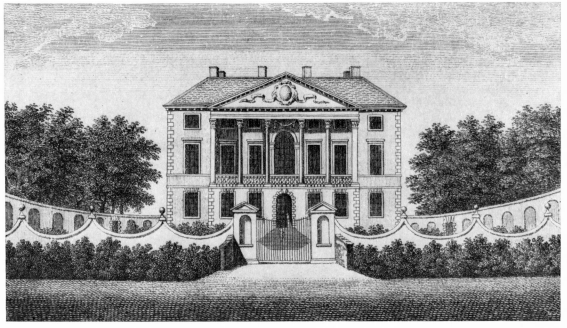

Gunnersbury House *c.* 1780

EALING

Brentford: Market House and Market Square in 1848

West Twyford: St. Mary's Church and Manor House *c.* 1800

materials were removed in 1827.[31] No house apparently survived in 1840 but a new one had been built by 1845.[32] As Kent House it was still occupied by Henry Gibbons in 1890 and 1908,[33] becoming St. David's Home in 1918.[34]

Gen. Wetherall, tenant of the Batemans' seat until 1818,[35] in 1817 bought the lease and in 1824 the freehold of *CASTLEBAR HOUSE*, east of Castlebar Hill and newly built in 1790 when leased by John Wey to Richard Meux (d. 1813), brewer.[36] In 1840 Wetherall held *c.* 47 a. of freehold, copyhold, and leasehold,[37] including Castle Hill Lodge. The residue passed to his son Gen. Sir George Augustus Wetherall (1788–1868), who devised it to his sons Maj.-Gen. Sir Edward Wetherall (d. 1869) and the Revd. A. W. Wetherall, the second of whom intended to sell it in 1870.[38] Castlebar House belonged to Mr. Bartholomew in 1897, when it was acquired as a Benedictine monastery. It was used as a girls' school successively by Visitation nuns, by nuns of the Holy Child Jesus 1901–10, and by Augustinian nuns 1912–15. In 1976 it was a Roman Catholic men's club and youth club. The principal front of the classical 18th-century house had faced the garden and only three bays had faced the road until *c.* 1830, when an extension by two bays gave an asymmetrical appearance.[39]

John Twyford settled three customary tenements and two crofts on his daughter Isabel and her husband Richard Hayward in 1456.[40] Their daughter Isabel married Thomas Clavell, who held most of the estate in 1492.[41] It descended to his grandson John Clavell, on whom his great-grandmother Isabel Hayward settled a homestead and croft in 1518[42] and whose coheirs in 1547 were his three sisters Agnes Alderton, later Hore, Elizabeth Cogges, and Alice, later wife of John Living.[43] Following Elizabeth's death without issue, her sisters sold the estate of *c.* 160 a. in 1584 to William, later Sir William, Fleetwood, recorder of London,[44] who in 1588 sold it to Edward Boteler,[45] who as Sir Edward Boteler of Birchanger (Essex), settled copyhold property on his son John and his wife Jane in 1608.[46] Probably it was the house and 156 a. called Botelers farm near Drayton Green and Drayton Lane, which they surrendered in 1610 to the lawyer John, later

Sir John, Walter (1566–1630).[47] Sir John's youngest son David was admitted in 1635[48] and lived in *DRAYTON HOUSE* at the north end of Drayton Green.[49] The estate descended to Sir William Walter, Bt. (d. 1694). In 1698, in accordance with his will, Botelers farm was settled on his second wife Mary and their son Robert, later Sir Robert (d. 1731).[50] It passed to John Mead, to his widow Jane, and then to his son John, whose grandson Grantham Mead, merchant of London, was admitted in 1712.[51] Mead surrendered Botelers farm in 1747 to King Gould,[52] who held at least 225 a. of copyhold and Pitshanger manor at his death in 1756. His son Charles[53] sold Botelers farm with Pitshanger to Thomas Gurnell in 1765 but retained land west of Northfield Avenue and a house at Little Ealing,[54] which may however have been Coldhall manor house and leased out.[55]

PLACE HOUSE, Little Ealing Lane, was reputedly sequestrated as recusants' property during the Interregnum[56] and had nine hearths in 1664.[57] It belonged to John Loving (d. 1693) and descended to his son and namesake, who successfully asserted his claim to a pew in Ealing church and his independence of Coldhall manor in 1693.[58] In 1729 Loving sold the house to Sir Richard Ellis, Bt. (d. 1742),[59] whose widow Sarah sold 33 a. of copyhold to King Gould before her marriage in 1745 to Sir Francis Dashwood, Bt., later Lord Le Despenser (d. 1781).[60] The Dashwoods either sold the house or let it on a 1,000-year lease in 1746 to Richard, later Sir Richard, Lyttelton, who in 1760 with his wife Rachel, dowager duchess of Bridgwater, assigned the lease to Francis Greville, Earl Brooke and earl of Warwick (d. 1773),[61] who assigned it in 1765 to Lord James Manners.[62] In 1765 and 1777 the tenant of at least part of the estate was the statesman Thomas Thynne, Viscount Weymouth and later marquess of Bath (1734–96).[63] Manners sold the estate in 1789 to Cuthbert Fisher,[64] whose widow was owner in 1811, when the estate had been renamed *EALING PARK*.[65] Mrs. Fisher was succeeded by 1824 by her husband's devisee Jacob Jeddere, who took the name Fisher[66] and had died by 1834.[67] In 1840 Ealing Park belonged to the surgeon William Lawrence, later a baronet (1783–1867), whose 89-a. estate

[31] M.R.O., Acc. 1028/53; sales cat. (1827) at Ealing libr.
[32] M.R.O., TA/EAL; Faulkner, *Brentford, Ealing and Chiswick*, 259.
[33] Jones, *Ealing*, 141; *Kelly's Dir. Mdx.* (1890, 1908).
[34] Inf. from Mr. P. Hounsell; below, public svces.
[35] M.R.O., Acc. 828/3.
[36] Ibid. Acc. 224/6; Acc. 1028/89; D.R.O. 37/D1/2.
[37] Ibid. TA/EAL.
[38] Ibid. Acc. 224/6; *D.N.B.*
[39] Ealing libr., TS. notes; *Prospect of Ealing*, plate 5.
[40] Guildhall MS. 10312/87, rot. 13d.
[41] Ibid. rot. 13d.; P.R.O. SC 2/189/11, rot. 2d.
[42] Guildhall MS. 10312/87, rot. 13d.
[43] Ibid. 42, rot. 1 and d.
[44] Ibid. 95, rott. 2 and d., 11, 14d.
[45] P.R.O., SC 2/189/287, rott. 2–3.
[46] Ibid. SC 2/189/32, rot. 9.
[47] Ibid. SC 2/189/34, rot. 6 and d.; *D.N.B.*
[48] P.R.O., SC 2/190/9, rot. 1d.
[49] Ibid. MPA/7. It may have been the Manor Ho. of the 1880s, when there was a mid 19th-cent. Drayton Ho. east of the green: O.S. Map 6″, Mdx. XV. SW. (1873 edn.); *Ealing As It Was*, illus. 56.
[50] 10 Wm. III, c. 42 (Priv. Act); Guildhall MS. 10465/13; G.E.C. *Baronetage*, ii. 142.
[51] Guildhall MS. 10465/51.
[52] Ibid. 63, pp. 49–50.
[53] Ibid. 71, pp. 239 sqq.; M.R.O., Acc. 276/138.
[54] Guildhall MS. 10465/80, pp. 250–4; Gtr. Ealing Local Hist. Soc. *Local Historian*, i (1966), 4–7; B.L. Maps K.29.9.a.
[55] Ealing libr., survey (*c.* 1774).
[56] P.R.O., C 8/455/35.
[57] Allison, *Ealing in 17th Cent.* no. E 15.
[58] Ibid.; M.R.O., Acc. 526/83.
[59] M.L.R. 1730/1/116–17; G.E.C. *Baronetage*, iii. 71.
[60] Guildhall MS. 10465/104, pp. 328 sqq.; G.E.C. *Baronetage*, v. 3.
[61] Guildhall MSS. 10465/61, pp. 49–51; 75, pp. 228–31; M.L.R. 1766/2/361.
[62] M.L.R. 1765/6/332–5; Guildhall MS. 10465/80, pp. 254–9.
[63] M.L.R. 1765/6/332; B.L. Maps K.29.9.a; *D.N.B.*
[64] Guildhall MS. 10465/138, pp. 75–8.
[65] Lysons, *Environs* (Suppl.), 129.
[66] Guildhall MS. 10465/139, pp. 122 sqq.
[67] Ibid. 149, pp. 52 sqq.

lay mainly between Boston Road, Little Ealing Lane, and Ealing Road[68] and whose wife Louisa Trevor (d. 1855), a leading social figure, made the gardens.[69] After her death Ealing Park was leased by 1863 to J. Wainright, and then to James Budgett, before its sale by Sir Trevor Lawrence, Bt. (d. 1913).[70] Acquired in part in 1882 by the British Land Co.,[71] much of the grounds had been built over by 1898, when the house was a convent of the Ladies of Nazareth;[72] by 1912 it was a convent of the Sisters of Charity.[73] Built in the late 18th century and soon extended, the house is two-storeyed and of nine bays, with a pedimented central projection and, on the east front, a single-storeyed Ionic colonnade.[74]

The *ELM GROVE* estate, earlier called Hicks on the Heath, lay on the west of Ealing common, of which it may once have been part. A copyhold toft and 20 a. of woodland called Hickes atte Hethe, late of Richard atte Hethe, were leased in 1458 to John Merryweather and others, who immediately assigned them to Thomas and Henry Frowyk.[75] The estate apparently descended with Gunnersbury until Henry Frowyk's death in 1520, when it reverted to the lord, who farmed it in 1520 to John Basset.[76] In 1578 Christopher Rythe held Hickes atte Hethe, which he surrendered in 1584 to Joan Southcott, with Abdonsland.[77] It belonged in 1613 to Edward More[78] and in 1667 to Thomas Talbot,[79] who surrendered it in 1670 to Sarah Baker of Holborn.[80] Robert Newdigate, admitted in 1677,[81] was succeeded in 1684 by Sir William Trumbull (1639–1716), Secretary of State, who leased it c. 1688 to the lawyer and politician Dr., later Sir Charles, Hedges (d. 1714)[82] and sold it in 1696 to Samuel Cox.[83] In 1721 the Hon. George Watson was owner or occupier,[84] between 1730 and 1753 it belonged to Charles Scholes,[85] and in 1764 William Turner surrendered it to Anne Cotesworth.[86] She surrendered it in 1769 to William Birch,[87] who had let it by 1777 to Dr. John Egerton, bishop of Durham (1721–87), to whom he surrendered it next year.[88] The bishop's son John Egerton sold it in 1787 to Frederick Augustus Barnard,[89] who sold it in 1795 to George Kinnaird, Lord Kinnaird (d. 1805). Kinnaird devised it to his wife Elizabeth (d.

1806), who devised it to their daughters, several of whom were minors. Under an Act of 1808 the estate, described as the mansion called Elm Grove and 35 a., was sold[90] to Spencer Perceval (1762–1812), prime minister, on whose assassination it was held by his widow Jane, who later married Sir Henry Carr. In 1821 the estate was settled on Lady Carr and her son Spencer Perceval (d. 1859),[91] and on Lady Carr's death in 1864 it passed to her daughter-in-law Anna Elizabeth Perceval, who enfranchised it.[92] The house was occupied by Dr. W. R. Vines as a boys' school c. 1861,[93] by the Revd. Charles Scott in 1864,[94] and by the Royal India Asylum 1870–92.[95] After Leopold de Rothschild had bought the estate for building, Elm Grove was demolished in 1894.[96] The house, first mentioned in 1696,[97] was improved by Frederick Barnard[98] and was a large, plain, stuccoed building of three storeys and attics.[99]

From 1734 Thomas Barratt of Old Brentford (d. 1762)[1] was building up a substantial copyhold estate on both sides of Boston and Ealing roads, mainly from open field strips. In 1760 he settled some on his daughter Anne and her husband Thomas Edwards, later Sir Thomas Edwardes, Bt. (d. 1790), and by will dated 1760 left the rest to Anne and her issue. On Sir Thomas's death all descended to his daughter Ellen Hester Mary (d. 1836)[2] and in 1794 was settled on her and her husband John Thomas Hope.[3] In 1840 J. T. Hope held 155 a., mainly at Brentford but some north of Haven Green.[4] Part was enfranchised in 1849 and 1851, when the tenant for life was Frederick Hope.[5]

The adjoining houses and estates of *EALING HOUSE* and *EALING GROVE*, east of St. Mary's Road, originated in the freehold and copyhold capital messuage and house held in 1593 by Joan, widow of William Frost.[6] Following her marriage to Matthew Grey, Joan sold her estate in 1598 to Thomas Soame,[7] who was admitted in 1605 to the copyhold estate consisting of Crowchmans tenement, Cooper's homestead, and 55 a.[8] A second house already stood on an adjoining orchard by 1616, when a wall was erected around it,[9] suggesting, with later evidence,[10] that it was the future Ealing House

[68] M.R.O., TA/EAL; *D.N.B.*
[69] Keane, *Beauties of Mdx.* 25–30; Walford, *Gtr. Lond.* i. 23.
[70] Jones, *Ealing*, 142.
[71] Jahn, 'Rlys. and Suburban Development', 97.
[72] Jackson, *Ealing*, 223–4.
[73] *Mdx. County Times*, 21 Dec. 1912.
[74] Pevsner, *Mdx.* 43; Guildhall Libr., grangerized copy of Lysons, *Environs*, ii (2), illus. between pp. 228 and 229.
[75] Guildhall MS. 11765, ff. 106–7v.
[76] Ibid. MS. 10312/87, rot. 18.
[77] Ibid. 94, rot. 8; 96 rot. 4d.; above.
[78] P.R.O., SC 2/190/5, rot. 12.
[79] Guildhall MS. 10312/103, rot. 12.
[80] Ibid. 106, rot. 8.
[81] Ibid. 115, m. 4d.
[82] Lysons, *Environs*, ii. 228; *D.N.B.*
[83] Guildhall MS. 10465/12.
[84] Lysons, *Environs*, ii. 228.
[85] Guildhall MSS. 10465/51; 52; 68, p. 248.
[86] Ibid. 79, pp. 263–4.
[87] Ibid. 84, pp. 64 sqq.
[88] B.L. Maps K.29.9.a; Guildhall MS. 10475/93, pp. 93–6; *D.N.B.*

[89] Guildhall MS. 10465/102, pp. 253 sqq.
[90] Elm Grove Estate Act, 47 Geo. III, Sess. 2, c. 30 (Local and Personal, not printed); Neaves, *Hist. Gter. Ealing*, 85.
[91] Guildhall MS. 10465/136, pp. 334 sqq.
[92] P.R.O., MAF 9/167/8562; MAF 9/167/9387.
[93] M.R.O., D.R.O. 37/A12/1; Jackson, *Ealing*, 205.
[94] M.R.O., D.R.O. 37/B2/7.
[95] *Kelly's Dir. Mdx.* (1890); *Prospect of Ealing*, note for plate 4.
[96] M.R.O., Hist. Notes 25/8/71; Jackson, *Ealing*, 205.
[97] Guildhall MS. 10465/12.
[98] *Ambulator* (1807).
[99] *Prospect of Ealing*, plate 4.
[1] *Gent. Mag.* xxxii. 552.
[2] Guildhall MS. 10465/106, pp. 395 sqq.; B.L. Maps K.29.9.a; G.E.C. *Baronetage*, iv. 98.
[3] Guildhall MS. 10465/166, pp. 553 sqq.
[4] M.R.O., TA/EAL.
[5] P.R.O., MAF 20/64/959; Guildhall MS. 10465/166, p. 557.
[6] P.R.O., REQ 2/144/44.
[7] Ibid. SC 2/189/27.
[8] Ibid. SC 2/189/29, rot. 15.
[9] Ibid. C 2/Jas. I/S 14/55.
[10] M.R.O., F 111.

and that Crowchmans was the future Ealing Grove. The two houses probably descended in the Soame family until the Interregnum, when they were divided.

Ealing House, already so called, and *c.* 40 a., including land leased from the rector, were sold in 1657 by John Wadlowe and other Londoners to Sir John Barkstead,[11] whose widow in 1663 surrendered the estate to Nicholas Bonfoy, merchant of London.[12] On the death of Bonfoy's widow, their son Hugh was admitted in 1691 and surrendered it to Richard Lascelles, goldsmith of London.[13] In 1715 William Kingsford and Joseph Denys sold the estate to the lawyer Sir James Montagu (1666–1723)[14] whose widow sold it in 1724 to Sir Thomas Gery, master in Chancery.[15] Gery's widow sold it to Nathaniel Oldham of Holborn,[16] who conveyed it in 1735 to Thomas Bale,[17] who sold it in 1747 to Hugh Bethel. Hugh's brother Alderman Slingsby Bethel was admitted in 1748[18] and sold it in 1751 to Richard Coope,[19] who surrendered it in 1753 to Lt.-Gen. John Huske (1692?–1761). Huske, who died there,[20] devised it to William Adair, who devised it in 1780 to trustees.[21] In 1803 it was acquired for Anne, dowager countess of Galloway, who released it in 1813 to Col. Patrick Douglas.[22] He sold it in 1817, probably to Mason Gerard Streetford,[23] and in 1830 William Johnson surrendered it to his brother John (d. 1848), who devised it to his widow for sale. Bought in 1851 by Ambrose Brown of London and Robert Shorter of Ealing,[24] it belonged in 1860 to the Ragged School trust.[25] Ealing House had a gatehouse by 1657 and was of brick, containing two storeys with projecting mullioned windows and attics in a steeply pitched roof, in 1795, before alterations.[26]

Ealing Grove, formerly Crowchmans tenement, adjoined Ealing House to the north and Grove Road to the south. It was leased from 1608 to Sir William Fleetwood[27] and later to John Maynard. In 1657 Sir Thomas Soame and his eldest son Stephen surrendered it, another house, and 27 a. to Joseph and Sarah Wadlowe, who surrendered it in 1675 to Robert Welstead, goldsmith of London.[28] The soldier Richard Savage, Earl Rivers, lived at Ealing Grove for several years and died there in 1712,[29] leaving it to his illegitimate daughter Bessy, wife of

Frederick Nassau de Zuylestein, earl of Rochford, owner in 1722.[30] Their son Richard Savage Nassau sold it in 1746, probably in trust for Sir Hildebrand Jacob.[31] Mary Swift and Amy Peters were admitted to the copyhold estate in 1750 and Capt. Edward Hughes, R.N., in 1754; Hughes and Charles Guild conveyed the estate in 1755 to Joseph Gulston, M.P. (d. 1766),[32] whose son Joseph (1744?–86), the collector, sold Ealing Grove to George Spencer, duke of Marlborough (d. 1817), in 1775.[33] It was bought from him by John Campbell, duke of Argyll (d. 1806), who sold it in 1791 to James Baillie (d. 1793). Baillie devised Ealing Grove to his wife Colin for life, but she immediately conveyed it to their eldest son Alexander.[34] The tenant from 1799 to 1802 was Edward Harley, earl of Oxford (d. 1848).[35] Under an Act of 1805 the estate, described as a mansion house and 64 a.,[36] was sold by 1811 to Charles Wyatt, still the owner in 1845.[37] The house was converted into an Italianate villa, at great expense, by Joseph Gulston the younger[38] and *c.* 1800 was a three-storeyed classical mansion of nine bays, with a pedimented central projection, set among trees.[39]

ECONOMIC HISTORY. Agrarian history.

The demesne of Ealing manor lay mainly in the east part of the parish, stretching from London Stile northward to Hanger wood. The submanor of Pitshanger, with its 140 a. of demesne, was in the extreme north, Coldhall at West Ealing, Gunnersbury in the east, and Boston manor at New Brentford.[40] The demesne of Ealing manor was exploited directly by the bishop between 1303 and 1339[41] but farmed by 1363[42] and the demesne of Boston was farmed by 1377,[43] whereas that of Gunnersbury was still in hand in 1378.[44] The fields of all five manors seem to have been separate: only the demesne of Coldhall and parts of Ealing demesne were distributed in open-field strips.[45]

Crops were sown on 169 a. of Ealing demesne in 1303 but on only 88½ a. in 1318 and 97½ a. in 1339. The main crop was rye, sown on 112 a., in 1303, but none was planted in 1318 or 1339. Maslin and wheat were sown on 35 a. and 22 a. respectively in 1303, 68 a. and 20 a. in 1318, and 80½ a. and 17 a. in 1339. There were 120 bu. of rye

[11] Ibid.
[12] Guildhall MS. 10312/99, rot. 10 and d.
[13] P.R.O., PROB 11/404 (P.C.C. 49 Vere); Guildhall MS. 10465/9.
[14] M.L.R. 1715/5/58–60; *D.N.B.*
[15] M.L.R. 1724/5/160–2.
[16] Guildhall MS. 10465/51.
[17] M.L.R. 1735/2/409–10; Guildhall MS. 10465/51.
[18] Guildhall MS. 10465/63, pp. 120–2.
[19] M.R.O., Acc. 112/2.
[20] Ibid. 4; Guildhall MS. 10465/76, pp. 32–3; *D.N.B.*
[21] Gtr. Ealing Local Hist. Soc. *Local Historian* (1963), 35; Guildhall MSS. 10465/76, pp. 55–9; 106, pp. 94–6.
[22] M.R.O., Acc. 112/7.
[23] Guildhall MS. 10465/132, pp. 401–5.
[24] Ibid. 166, pp. 215 sqq.
[25] P.R.O., C 54/16807, no. 1.
[26] M.R.O., F 111; grangerized copy of Lysons, *Environs*, iii. 228.
[27] P.R.O., C 2/Jas. I./S14/55.
[28] Guildhall MS. 10312/110, rot. 5.   [29] *D.N.B.*
[30] Lysons, *Environs*, ii. 228; *Complete Peerage*, xi. 53.

[31] M.R.O., Acc. 276/119; Guildhall MS. 10465/61, pp. 65–8; M.L.R. 1745/3/173.
[32] M.L.R. 1755/2/572.
[33] *D.N.B.*; *Hist. Parl.*, *Commons*, 1754–90, ii. 560–2.
[34] Ealing Grove Act, 45 Geo. III, c. 90 (Local and Personal); Guildhall MS. 10465/106, pp. 423 sqq.
[35] B.L. Maps K.29.9.d; M.R.O., D.R.O. 37/A8/1.
[36] Ealing Grove Act, 45 Geo. III, c. 90 (Local and Personal).
[37] Guildhall MS. 10465/131, pp. 542–3; Chiswick libr., grangerized copy of Faulkner, *Brentford, Ealing and Chiswick*; Lysons, *Environs* (Suppl.), 129.
[38] *Hist. Parl.*, *Commons*, 1754–90, ii. 561.
[39] B.L. Maps K.29.9.d; below, plate facing p. 33.
[40] Above, manors.
[41] *Accts. of Executors of Ric. Bp. of Lond. 1303 and Thos. Bp. of Exeter 1310* (Camd. Soc. N.S. x), 61–2; P.R.O., E 154/1/47.
[42] Taylor, 'Estates of Bishopric of Lond.' 305.
[43] *Cal. of Wills in Ct. of Husting*, ii (1), 199.
[44] *Cal. Inq. Misc.* iv, p. 12.
[45] M.R.O., TA/EAL.

and 14 bu. of maslin in the granary in 1303 and the granary and grange together contained 571 bu. of rye, 914 bu. of oats, 12 bu. of wheat, 40 bu. of peas but no maslin in 1339, when there were 2 ploughs, several carts, 4 stots and 12 oxen.[46] The farmers sent 36 bu. of wheat and 72 bu. of rye to Fulham in 1392–3 and 112 bu. of oats in 1410.[47] Of the 140 a. of arable on Gunnersbury demesne in 1378, only 60 a. were sown, suggesting a two-field system: wheat was sown on 31 a. and rye on 29 a., but the value of the crops was reduced by flooding.[48]

Livestock was prominent on Gunnersbury manor in 1378, when 80 a. of the demesne were pasture and 4 a. meadow,[49] and also on Ealing manor. A switch to stock farming may explain the sharp fall in the sown area by 1318,[50] and the large store of oats in 1339 was probably needed for the 2 bulls, 27 cows, and 3 yearling calves, which the bishop kept in addition to draught animals, 190 sheep, and poultry.[51] A new byre was built in 1363–4, when another was repaired.[52] The sheep had gone in 1382, when a new lease of the demesne included 2 carthorses, 4 stots, 4 oxen, a bull, and 19 cows,[53] but in 1392–3, when a new lease was due, the bishop bought a further 200 sheep,[54] which remained in 1397[55] and had disappeared by 1409.[56] There were repairs to the dairyhouse in 1399–1400[57] and again to it, the byre, and the grange in 1409–10.[58] The bishop sold the stock to the farmer in 1411[59] and thereafter no animals were included in leases.

There were five free tenements on Ealing manor in 1423: Absdons in the north, Baldswells at Drayton, Abyndons and Denys at Ealing village, and Sergeaunts at Old Brentford. It is likely that there had once been 32 copyhold tenements,[60] including at least 19 virgates of 20 rateable acres and 9 half virgates.[61] When the holdings were created the copyhold land presumably amounted to not more than 540 a., a total increased before 1423 by land at Castlebar Hill. Later additions were made at the expense of heath and woodland: Hicks on the Heath was a new tenement carved from the waste in the 15th century.[62] Of the 28 holdings whose acreage is known, 9 were at Ealing, 9 at Drayton, 9 at Old Brentford, and 1 at West Ealing.[63]

No open fields were recorded at New Brentford and little is known of the fields of Gunnersbury, Coldhall, and Pitshanger manors.[64] There were many fields of varying sizes on Ealing manor, the main ones apparently being Windmill or New Brentford field, Old Brentford field, and Popes field in the south part, Westfield immediately west of Ealing village, and Great and Little

Northfield in the extreme west. The lands of individual tenements were scattered, Old Brentford tenements not being confined to land near Old Brentford, thereby probably contributing to the very active land market in existence by 1383. Several, if not most, holdings were no longer held in 1395 by the families after which they were named.[65] Only 7 holdings survived intact in 1423, when 4 were held by eponymous families. There were then 47 copyholders with estates ranging from 1 a. to the 3 tenements of Joan Virly and 2 each held by 5 other tenants. By 1438 there were 64 copyholders and by 1445, when only Thomas in the Hale had two tenements, there were 70.[66] The brief existence of some large estates was due partly to the grant of escheated lands only for one life and partly to inheritance by Borough English, which favoured the youngest son and so prompted tenants to divide their lands to provide for elder sons. Another factor was the demand for land by Londoners, who had acquired only manors in the 14th century: the first Londoner holding copyhold land appeared in 1400.[67]

The large acreage of open field and the comparatively small commons suggest that the early medieval tenants were predominantly arable farmers. Tenants left much stock between 1399, when John atte Cote owned at least 38 sheep,[68] although early 16th-century wills did not indicate the relative importance of animal husbandry.[69] Presumably it was to stock rearing that most farmers had turned from grain production by c. 1528, although it is not known whether the harvest then had been exceptional. Only 18 households in the parish had stocks of grain, 14 of them at Ealing or Drayton and only 4 in Lower or Old Brentford Side, and a further 5 had stocks at New Brentford. Some of the households, moreover, had too little grain for their own bread or for seed. Not enough corn was grown either at Ealing or at New Brentford, which produced less than a tenth of its needs, to keep the population in bread. All households with grain ate wheaten bread, sometimes supplemented with rye: 261 qr. of wheat were in stock, compared with only 12½ qr. of rye, but there were also 85 qr. of barley and as many as 464 qr. of oats. The move from cereal farming was most marked at Old Brentford: there were 648 qr. of grain in Upper Side and only 52 qr. in Lower Side, less than half the 121 qr. grown in the much smaller township of New Brentford.[70]

Inclosure accompanied the change from arable farming. By the late 18th century little remained of the open fields and in 1840 there were strips only in the West field, North, Brentford,

[46] *Accts. of Executors of Ric. Bp. of Lond.* 61–2 (accts. 9 Dec. 1303); St. Paul's MSS., box B 76, rott. 1–2 (accts. 24 Aug.–12 Nov. 1318); P.R.O., E 154/1/47 (inventory 12 Dec. 1339).
[47] St. Paul's MSS., box B 89; P.R.O., SC 6/1138/9.
[48] *Cal. Inq. Misc.* iv, p. 12.
[49] Ibid.   [50] Above.
[51] P.R.O., E 154/1/47.
[52] St. Paul's MSS., box B 89, m. 2.
[53] Guildhall MS. 11765, f. 29.
[54] St. Paul's MSS., box B 89.
[55] P.R.O., SC 6/1138/7, m. 1.
[56] Ibid. SC 6/1138/9d.
[57] Ibid. SC 6/1138/7.
[58] Ibid. SC 6/1138/9, m. 1.

[59] Ibid. SC 6/1138/10.
[60] Guildhall MS. 11766, ff. 13–23 (1423 rental).
[61] Ibid. ff. 13–23; P.R.O., SC 6/1138/18.
[62] Above, other est.
[63] Guildhall MS. 11766, ff. 13–23.
[64] Para. based on ibid. ff. 13–23; 11765.
[65] P.R.O., SC 6/1138/18.
[66] Guildhall MSS. 11766, ff. 29–43 (1438 rental); 11765, ff. 79–92 (1445 rental).
[67] Guildhall MS. 11765, f. 37v.
[68] Ibid. MS. 9171/1, f. 425.
[69] Ibid. 2, f. 163; 5, f. 357; 6, ff. 128, 319; 8, ff. 22, 196; 9, f. 86.
[70] Gtr. Ealing Local Hist. Soc. *Local Historian* (1962); P.R.O., E 36/207, f. 48 and v.

Suswells, and Brencot fields.[71] The 15th-century consolidation of holdings may have contributed to inclosure and from the early 16th century the growing activity of Ealing manor court revealed tension between arable and pastoral interests. In 1553 animals were allowed to graze in open fields from Lammas to Candlemas,[72] but at other times were to be kept out with fences.[73] At Old Brentford in 1511 and later animals were forbidden to enter the fields until Michaelmas.[74] Detailed orders were frequently made,[75] but in 1697 it was stated merely that no beasts were allowed in common grain fields until after they were rid and no sheep until a fortnight later.[76]

Refusals to open land for common grazing occurred at Hicks on the Heath in 1520, 1566, and 1578,[77] and Elwickfield in 1604,[78] and general orders were often issued. Part of the problem arose from inclosure: in 1605 nobody was to inclose common field land without the consent of other tenants and large fines were prescribed. Orchards proved a more permanent obstruction: a brick wall surrounded one open-field orchard in 1616, others were recorded later.[79] Lammas rights survived over much of Ealing until the 19th century, over London Style farm in 1833 and still later over Walpole park, although they were not always exercised.[80] They had to be bought out,[81] like the similar rights over the Town Meadow and Old England at New Brentford in 1857.[82]

For grazing, 100 a. of pasture commons and the common fields were treated jointly. A stint was necessary by 1474,[83] offenders were frequently prosecuted, and those exercising rights of common were limited: inhabitants of Acton were repeatedly excluded from 1520[84] and in 1545 those of New Brentford and Gunnersbury were excluded from Old Brentford field.[85] From 1582 rights were denied to strangers,[86] from 1615 to lessees of land in Ealing,[87] from 1630 to servants of inhabitants,[88] and from 1652 to out-parishioners.[89] Inhabitants of Old Brentford were denied access to Haven Green common, residents of Ealing village were shut out of Old Brentford field in 1524,[90] and tenants using Ealing common were restricted in 1525 and 1561.[91] The stint was $1\frac{1}{2}$ sheep per acre of

common field arable and 3 sheep per acre of common field meadow in 1611; owners of land in Ealing that was not commonable might pasture no more than 4 sheep and 2 kine and inhabitants of new cottages on the waste had no rights.[92] From 1630 until 1697 or later only those paying scot and lot were entitled to common grazing.[93] Repeated offences indicated a severe shortage of pasture.

The shift from cereal farming apparent c. 1528 continued only slowly: 37 per cent of Ealing's farmland was still arable in 1799.[94] The lessee of Ealing demesne in 1533 left livestock, ploughs, carts, harrows, and corn to his executors,[95] and other 16th-century testators left ploughs, draught animals, and corn.[96] At least two, in 1563[97] and 1583, practised mixed farming.[98] It is not clear whether the grassland which replaced arable was for grazing or mowing. By 1590 the Brentford fields were evidently under grass for mowing.[99] The Boston home farm employed a dairy maid, a hog boy, and a poultry maid in 1659.[1] Market gardening, increasing from the late 16th century in Old Brentford and southern New Brentford but also to some extent in Ealing, was later claimed to have taken over arable rather than pastoral land.[2]

A Gunnersbury estate in 1785 contained $93\frac{1}{2}$ a. of pasture and meadow and 131 a. of arable.[3] That was a much higher proportion of arable than in Ealing parish as a whole, since in 1799 only 1,027 a. were under the plough: 1,377 a. were grassland, 289 a. were market gardens, and 85 a. were gentlemen's gardens.[4] By 1814 arable had fallen to 800 a. while meadow and pasture had risen to 1,600 a.[5] Market gardens, whose rents were falling,[6] covered 469 a. by 1840 when arable remained stable at 834 a. but grassland had also apparently grown to 1,976 a.[7] At New Brentford in 1837 there were 121 a. of meadow and pasture and 37 a. of arable and market gardens.[8] Arable at Ealing and New Brentford decreased sharply to 307 a. in 1869 and 74 a. in 1887, and had disappeared by 1927. Meanwhile, despite inroads by building, the relative importance of grassland and market garden increased: Ealing and Brentford still had 1,812 a. under grass in 1887, 994 a. in 1907, and 156 a. in 1927.

[71] M.R.O., TA/EAL.
[72] P.R.O., SC 2/189/24, rot. 4.
[73] Guildhall MS. 10312/94, rot. 44; Jackson, *Ealing*, 94.
[74] Guildhall MS. 10312/87, rot. 12; P.R.O., SC 2/189/20, rot. 1.
[75] e.g. P.R.O., SC 2/190/7, rott. 2d., 7; Guildhall MSS. 10312/39, rot. 1d.; 102, rot. 9d.; 103, rot. 7d.
[76] Jackson, *Ealing*, 94.
[77] Guildhall MSS. 10312/87, rot. 18; 94, rot. 3.
[78] P.R.O., SC 2/189/29, rot. 9; ibid. SC 2/189/30, rot. 6d.
[79] Ibid. C 2/Jas. I/S14/55; Chiswick libr., deed (1745); M.R.O., Acc. 276/73 (1657).
[80] Guildhall MS. 12359; Jones, *Ealing*, 77–8.
[81] Allison and Holt, *Ealing in 18th and 19th Cent.* 44 sqq.
[82] New Brentford MS. 17825.
[83] Guildhall MS. 10312/80, rot. 2.
[84] Ibid. 87, rot. 18; P.R.O., SC 2/189/24, rot. 1; SC 2/189/26, rot. 17.
[85] P.R.O., SC 2/189/22, rot. 5d.
[86] Guildhall MS. 10312/95, rot. 27d.; see also P.R.O., SC 2/189/29, rot. 14.
[87] P.R.O., SC 2/190/2, rot. 17.
[88] Ibid. SC 2/190/7, rot. 2d.
[89] Ibid. SC 2/190/15, rot. 2.

[90] Guildhall MS. 10312/87, rot. 30.
[91] Ibid.; P.R.O., SC 2/189/26, rot. 17.
[92] P.R.O., SC 2/189/34, rot. 10.
[93] Ibid. SC 2/190/7, rot. 7; Jackson, *Ealing*, 94.
[94] M.R.O., D.R.O. 37/A8/1.
[95] Guildhall MS. 9171/10, f. 212.
[96] Ibid. 15, ff. 45, 55, 163, 361.
[97] Ibid. 15, f. 194.
[98] P.R.O., PROB 11/65 (P.C.C. 36 Rowe).
[99] Ibid. SC 2/189/27, rot. 5.
[1] Ibid. PROB 11/287 (P.C.C. 52 Pell).
[2] *Jnl. Stat. Soc. of Lond.* vi. 126.
[3] Ealing libr., sales cat.
[4] *Jnl. Stat. Soc. of Lond.* vi. 126, based on M.R.O., D.R.O. 37/A8/1.
[5] *Jnl. Stat. Soc. of Lond.* vi. 126; no fig. for market gardening.
[6] Ibid. 125; *6th Rep. Com. Char.* H.C. 12, p. 370 (1822), ix.
[7] M.R.O., TA/EAL.
[8] Ibid. TA/BRE. Rest of para. based on P.R.O., MAF 68/193; MAF 68/535; MAF 68/1105; MAF 68/1675; MAF 68/2245; MAF 68/2815; MAF 68/3358. Returns relate to boros. from 1937.

Fears in 1842 that declining traffic at Brentford would destroy the market for hay proved unfounded:[9] the area under hay reached a peak of 1,044 a. of mowing grass compared with 676 a. of grazing grass by 1887. The position was later reversed, until in 1927 there were 4 a. under hay and 152 a. of pasture.

About 1790 small tithes in Ealing were assessed on 119 cows and 1,170 sheep. The sheep were in 11 flocks, of from 30 to 200, and the cattle belonged to 29 owners, the largest herd numbering 14.[10] Cattle, 570 in 1808 and 800 in 1845, were kept by Smith & Harrington, distillers, because there were no cowkeepers near Brentford to take their grains.[11] In 1843 there were 269 agricultural horses, 324 grazing cattle, 279 cows, and 2,822 sheep in Ealing parish.[12] The number of horses at Ealing and Brentford fell to 242 in 1869, 162 in 1887, 81 in 1907, and 13 in 1927, while the number of cattle fell slightly to 506 in 1869 and then rose to 612 in 1887, before declining to 285 in 1907 and 44 in 1927. The increase before 1887 apparently consisted of milk cows, kept by firms such as Cotching, Son & Co. at their model Hanger Lane farm dairy near Ealing common in 1893.[13] By 1907 milk cattle were less important: 170 cows were in milk or calf and 104 were not. Sheep dwindled to 628 in 1869, 387 in 1887, and 158 in 1907, but recovered to 790 in 1917 and 450 in 1927. There were 166 pigs in 1869, 152 in 1907, and 100 in 1927; 105 pigs kept at the Fox and Hounds, Brentford, in 1873 and 100 kept in Clayponds Lane, South Ealing, in 1911 were removed as a danger to health.[14] In 1927 there were still 152 a. of pasture, with 13 horses, 44 cattle, and 450 sheep, besides 100 pigs, 223 hens, and a few ducks.

NURSERIES AND MARKET GARDENS. Ealing had an orchard in 1540[15] and others in 1577–8[16] and 1584.[17] Numbers thereafter increased, orchards often being taken out of open fields, by 1616 in Crowchmans field,[18] in 1680–1 in Popes field,[19] and in 1738 in Little North field.[20] Some lay as far north as the centre of the parish.[21] River Long field and adjoining closes at West Ealing contained 1,008 fruit trees in 1767, including 850 apple trees, 63 plum, and 63 cherry.[22]

Most orchards were around Brentford. At Old Brentford there was an orchard in 1578[23] and at New Brentford there was apparently an orchard c. 1557 on what became the new market place c. 1580.[24] Two adjoining orchards were added to the market place c. 1620 and 1635,[25] and others at New Brentford were recorded c. 1603 and in 1611.[26] In 1642 it was claimed that royalist soldiers had greatly damaged the nurseries at Brentford, taking as much as 300 bu. of apples from a single man.[27] Orchards near the Butts were mentioned in 1656, 1668, and 1672.[28] At Old Brentford an orchard was planted in 1665 beside the Green Dragon to supply the choicest fruits to London,[29] and others existed by 1669[30] and 1674.[31] In 1670 the 3-a. Great Orchard at Old Brentford was stocked with 35-year old trees: in 1673 the lessor complained that 300 had been destroyed and the lessee claimed to have replaced old stock with apple, pear, codling, and quince trees.[32] Orchards south of High Street in Old Brentford and New Brentford were recorded in 1699 and 1707.[33] In 1702 John Gillett, gardener of Ealing, left 3 a. lately converted to garden ground and a further 3 a. of garden in the open fields of Ealing.[34] In 1711 his widow leased 5 a. in Boston Road, already planted with mulberries, for apple and cherry trees and asparagus and strawberries.[35] By 1774 there were orchards all the way from Brentford to Ealing.[36]

Several Brentford gardeners achieved distinction. The stocking of all varieties of tree in 1721 by 'Mr. Green'[37] may have related to the nursery of the Greening family of Leominster (Herefs.) and Brentford, which between 1733 and 1742 helped to lay out or supply gardens for the duke of Marlborough and Lords Weymouth and Cornwallis.[38] Benjamin, elder brother of Horne Tooke, was credited with the introduction of the pine strawberry,[39] Mr. Bell of Brentford raised plants from seeds from the Crimea c. 1793,[40] and Nathaniel Swinden, author of The Beauties of Flora Displayed (1778), was active at Brentford End and Old Brentford c. 1768–1805[41] and a member of a family of local gardeners dating from 1681 or earlier.[42] Best known, however, were Hugh Ronalds & Sons of New Brentford. Hugh Ronalds the elder (d. 1788) occurred in rate-books c. 1754,[43] lived at the Butts by 1760,[44] and was a nurseryman and seedsman in 1786.[45]

[9] Guildhall MS. 12359.
[10] M.R.O., D.R.O. 37/A8/2. The account for 1799 gives much smaller figs. and is probably less complete: ibid. A8/1.
[11] Rep. Sel. Cttee. on Sugar and Molasses, H.C. 83, p. 23 (1806–7), ii; P.O. Dir. Six Home Counties (1845).
[12] Jnl. Stat. Soc. of Lond. vi. 120. Rest of para. based on P.R.O., MAF 68/193; MAF 68/535; MAF 68/1105; MAF 68/1675; MAF 68/2245; MAF 68/2815; MAF 68/3358. All figs. relate to Ealing and New Brentford.
[13] Ealing Illustrated (1893), 41; Illustrated Lond. (1893), 271; Cotching, Son & Co. (pamphlet at Ealing libr.).
[14] The Times, 22 Sept. 1873; Brentford U.D.C. Rep. of M.O.H. (1911).
[15] P.R.O., C 1/1018/16.
[16] Guildhall MS. 10312/93, rot. 3.
[17] Ibid. 94, rot. 3d.
[18] P.R.O., C 2/Jas. I/S 14/55.
[19] Ibid. E 134/32 Chas. II/Trin./8.
[20] M.R.O., Acc. 562/1.
[21] P.R.O., C 8/59/46; M.R.O., Acc. 538/1st dep./41/1; Acc. 513.
[22] Ealing libr., photocopy of survey.
[23] Guildhall MS. 10312/94, rot. 3d.

[24] P.R.O., C 2/Eliz. I/H 22/34.
[25] Ibid. C 5/390/123.
[26] Ibid. C 2/Jas. I/N 5/17; C 7/324/54.
[27] True Relation of Barbarous Passages of King's Army at Old Braineford (1642).
[28] P.R.O., C 7/324/54; C 8/414/85; M.R.O., Acc. 257/10.
[29] P.R.O., C 8/282/33.
[30] M.R.O., Acc. 1376/1; see also P.R.O., C 10/491/54.
[31] P.R.O., C 7/246/33.
[32] Ibid. C 10/115/146.
[33] Ibid. C 5/202/54; C 7/313/27.
[34] M.R.O., Acc. 276/98.   [35] Ibid. 100.
[36] Diary of John Yeoman, 32.
[37] R. Bradley, Works of Nature (1721), 185.
[38] P.R.O., C 108/353.
[39] Thorne, Environs, 58.   [40] T.L.M.A.S. xxiv. 184.
[41] Ibid.; J. H. Harvey, 'Hort. Hist. in Hounslow' (TS. 1971) in Chiswick libr.
[42] P.R.O., E 134/32 Chas. II Trin./8; G.L.R.O.(L) N/C/134/1/1.
[43] New Brentford MS. 17516.
[44] 'Hugh Ronalds, Nurseryman' (TS. in Chiswick libr.).
[45] T.L.M.A.S. xxvi. 300.

By 1774 he occupied a house adjoining the Vicarage called Lamberts,[46] probably Noy's House, with 2 a. between the church, the Ham, and the Brent,[47] which was the firm's chief nursery in 1841.[48] Ronalds occupied Butts closes of 9½ a. between the Butts and Boston Manor Road in 1774,[49] and his firm in 1839 also occupied Isleworth nursery.[50] Hugh Ronalds the younger (d. 1833) was noted for fruit trees, growing 300 varieties of apple in 1829,[51] and commemorated in his *Pyrus Malus Brentfordiensis* (1831). He supplied many plants to Kew Gardens from 1801 to 1816[52] and his firm provided 14,000 shrubs for Kensal Green cemetery.[53] Robert Ronalds (d. 1880) still occupied the nursery by St. Lawrence's church in 1863.[54]

In 1819 there were c. 3,000 a. of market garden in the parishes around Brentford,[55] which itself in 1850 was almost all market garden.[56] There was little at New Brentford in 1837[57] but most of Ealing's 469 a. of market garden in 1840 were nearby.[58] Brentford was the 'great fruit and vegetable garden of London' in 1843, when it was common to grow a low crop under the trees.[59] Such was the practice in 1833 on London Style farm in the extreme south-east, at 96 a. the largest market garden in Ealing: 18½ a. of fruit trees had green vegetables underneath, 3 a. had asparagus, and 10 a. had soft fruit; vegetables and soft fruit were also grown independently.[60] In 1844 a lessee covenanted to leave 960 raspberry, currant, and gooseberry bushes beneath the apple and pear trees on a 9½-a. market garden.[61] Much labour was needed: it was estimated that 35–40 people per acre were employed during the fruit season in 1819[62] and 30 per acre in 1843. Many of the workers were women, who in 1843 were twice as numerous as men.[63]

Market gardens formed 23 per cent of the 2,900 a. of farmland at Ealing and New Brentford in 1887.[64] As the cultivated area contracted, the proportion of market garden rose to 38 per cent in 1907 and 65 per cent in 1927. There were 275 a. of orchard, of which 117 a. had soft fruit under the trees, in 1887 and 152 a. of orchard, of which 90 a. had soft fruit below, besides 74 a. of soft fruit grown separately, in 1907. There were 164 a. of orchard and 88 a. of soft fruit in 1917 but only 66 a. of orchard and 5 a. of soft fruit in 1927. Green vegetables covered 405 a. in 1887, 294 a. in

1917, and only 50½ a. in 1927. Root crops were important until 1887, and as many as 347 a. in 1877 and 389 a. in 1887 produced unspecified 'green crops'. Cabbages were widely grown by 1897 and rhubarb in 1917.

Market gardening was concentrated at Old Brentford by the period 1907–27, when the area was entered separately. Between 83 and 85 per cent of Old Brentford's cultivated acreage was market garden, compared with 20 to 36 per cent in the Upper Side of Ealing and an insignificant proportion at New Brentford up to 1917; in 1927, however, 49 a. of orchard and 5 a. of soft fruit survived among the 62 a. cultivated at New Brentford. Well known gardeners included Robert Addey of Ealing Road, who grew c. 15 cwt. of mushrooms each week in season.[65] Informal dealing at Kew Bridge Road led in 1893 to the building of an enclosed market[66] and as late as 1903 many gardeners' wagons left High Street for Covent Garden, whence they returned with manure.[67]

MILLS. Ealing demesne in 1318 had a windmill,[68] which was rebuilt in 1363–4.[69] The new one was destroyed in or before 1409 and was still out of order in 1418–19,[70] but may have been repaired by 1431, when it was again broken.[71] Another windmill stood in Old Brentford near Boston Manor Road in 1698 and 1703[72] and had given the name Windmill field to the former New Brentford field by 1670.[73] A watermill had been built over a common sewer at Old Brentford by 1564.[74]

In 1377 there was a horsemill on Boston manor.[75] In 1738 the lord leased the right to a mill on the Brent.[76] Presumably it was that mill, recorded from 1746,[77] which stood at the west end of the Butts from 1777[78] until its demolition in 1905.[79] It was one of five mills existing in 1792: others were associated with malthouses south of High Street and the turpentine and starch works.[80] Mills at Old Brentford also served the distillery,[81] malthouses, and breweries.

FISHING. In 996 King Ethelred granted half of a fishery in the Thames at Brentford to the church of St. Peter and St. Paul, Winchester.[82] Although the pope confirmed the rights of

[46] Chiswick libr., Boston man. ct. bk. (1692–1842).
[47] M.R.O., TA/BRE; Boston man. ct. bk. (1692–1842).
[48] *The Times*, 18 Jan. 1841; Faulkner, *Brentford, Ealing and Chiswick*, 150.
[49] Boston man. ct. bk. (1692–1842); cf. M.R.O., TA/BRE; *Jnl. of Kew Gild for 1972*, ix (77), 127–9.
[50] M.R.O., Hist. Notes 2/11/1972.
[51] *Loudoun Gardeners Mag.* v. 736–7.
[52] Ibid. x. 96; P.R.O., LS 10/5, esp. pp. 52, 92–3; *Jnl. of Kew Gild*, viii. 691.
[53] *Jnl. of Kew Gild*, ix (77), 127–9.
[54] New Brentford MS. 17825; M.R.O., Hist. Notes 9/11/1972.
[55] J. Dugdale, *New Brit. Traveller* (1819), iii. 468.
[56] *Ec. Jnl.* lvii. 328.
[57] M.R.O., TA/BRE.   [58] Ibid. TA/EAL.
[59] *Jnl. Stat. Soc. of Lond.* vi. 125.
[60] Guildhall MS. 12359.   [61] Ibid. 12843.
[62] Dugdale, *New Brit. Traveller*, iii. 468.
[63] *Jnl. Stat. Soc. of Lond.* vi. 125; cf. F. M. Eden, *State of the Poor* (1797), 419; Brentford loc. bd. *Rep. of M.O.H.* (1893).

[64] Next two paras. based on P.R.O., MAF 68/535; MAF 68/1105; MAF 68/2245; MAF 68/2815; MAF 68/3358.
[65] *Gardeners Chron.* 18 June 1898.
[66] *Brentford and Chiswick As It Was*, illus. 27.
[67] Brentford U.D.C. 'High Street, Brentford: Petition to Local Govt. Bd.' (draft at Chiswick libr.).
[68] St. Paul's MSS., box B 76.
[69] Ibid. B 89.
[70] Ibid. B 89; B 90; P.R.O., SC 6/1138/9.
[71] St. Paul's MSS, box B 90.
[72] M.R.O., Acc. 891/2/6/806.
[73] Guildhall MS. 10312/106, rot. 7.
[74] Ibid. 91 rot. 5d.
[75] *Cal. Wills. Ct. Husting*, ii (1), 199; Guildhall MS. 9171/1, f. 51v.
[76] Boston man. ct. bk. (1692–1842), 1774 rental.
[77] New Brentford MS. 17517–18.
[78] B.L. Maps K.29.9.a.
[79] Chiswick libr., photo.
[80] New Brentford MS. 17518; below.
[81] Guildhall MS. 10465/106, p. 127.
[82] *Cod. Dipl.* ed. Kemble, vi, pp. 134–6.

Winchester cathedral priory in 1205,[83] they apparently fell into disuse. In 1162 the sheriff of Surrey accounted for the king's fishery at Brentford[84] and by 1173 Henry II had granted it to the prior of Merton (Surr.).[85] In 1252 fishing was permitted only as in the time of the king's ancestors.[86] After suing the chapter of St. Paul's in 1233,[87] the prior conceded limited rights to St. Paul's and its tenants of Sutton manor, Chiswick, at a distance from his own weirs at Brentford and Mortlake.[88] In 1241 the sheriffs of Middlesex and Surrey were to seize the tackle of those infringing the prior's fishery, and in 1242 a net was to be restored to Robert de Beauchamp.[89] Merton's fishing rights were confirmed in 1340.[90]

The bishop of London as lord of Ealing had a fishery at Old Brentford by 1257, when the king ordered the keepers *sede vacante* to provide 8,000–10,000 lampreys and other fish.[91] The fishery was called Brentford weir by 1424. Then and in 1470 it included a weirditch and adjoining meadow,[92] which in 1517–18 was described as 10 perches square within the Thames and was presumably an islet.[93] In 1339 the bishop owned a boat for the fishery at Brentford.[94] In 1313 and 1470 he covenanted to provide the lessee with materials each year for repairs.[95] In 1262–3 the fishery yielded 13s. 4d. in half a year.[96] It had been destroyed by rebels in 1458 but was repaired by 1464.[97] It was not recorded after 1509, when it had not been leased for a long time.[98]

A common fishery in the Brent had been appropriated by Thomas Maidstone in 1381.[99] The abbot of Westminster was said to have a fishery there in 1450[1] and the chapel of All Angels held one from Brentford bridge to the Thames at the Dissolution. The chapel's fishery was granted in 1547 to Edward Seymour, duke of Somerset,[2] and presumably reverted to the Crown on his attainder. In 1583–4 it was claimed that the fishery had been held in turn from c. 1550 by Sir John Thynne, Mr. Godwin, and Mr. Buckfolde, who leased it to inhabitants of Isleworth; they fished both sides of the river until the lessee of Boston manor, claiming the fishing on the Brentford side, took away their equipment.[3] In 1585 the fishery of the former chapel was conveyed to Henry Buckfolde, Thomas Allycock, and others,[4] and in 1598 Allycock conveyed it to Henry Butler.[5] Fishing rights in the Brent were men-

tioned in the 17th century[6] and rights perhaps once belonging to Boston manor were alienated by James and Henry Hawley in 1738.[7]

In 1423 tenants of Ealing manor rented three fisheries in the Thames, one of them attached to Sergeaunts free tenement[8] and presumably among those conveyed in 1521 to John and Alice Pattishall.[9] About 1712 a fisherman of Old Brentford held several lodges on the Thames, where he caught eels.[10] Thomas of Brentford, fishmonger, held property in London in 1327[11] and a London fishmonger rented land by the Brent at Old Brentford in 1466.[12] Royalists were accused of burning boats and cutting nets there in 1642.[13] Ealing parish paid in 1723 to replace the boat and tackle of an Old Brentford fisherman.[14] Pollution from Brentford gasworks had destroyed most of the fish by 1828, when many fishermen's apprentices were idle.[15] In 1845 it was claimed that the number of families supported by fishing had fallen from 100 to 20 over fifty years, with disturbance by steamboats and increasing sewage.[16] In 1848 it was also claimed that there had been no fish for ten or twelve years, because of the steamboats and gasworks.[17]

MARKETS AND FAIRS. At the request of Queen Margaret a weekly market and a fair for six days at New Brentford on the feast of St. Lawrence (10 August) were granted to the priory of St. Helen, Bishopsgate, in 1306.[18] All the prioress's rights were leased in 1534 to John Rollesley, by whom the market was conveyed to Hugh Eston, who obtained confirmation from Elizabeth I. Eston conveyed his interest to Jerome Hawley, lessee of Boston manor, who brought a lawsuit over the market between 1579 and 1587[19] and whose family apparently paid no rent to the Crown until both market and fair were abolished in 1610. A new licence was issued to James Hawley, after local protests, and a weekly market and six-day fairs on 1 May and 1 September were granted in 1635 and confirmed in 1666.[20]

Stallholders were restricted by the narrowness of New Brentford's High Street until Eston moved them north to an orchard which he had acquired behind the Crown. The square which became Market Place existed there by 1635 and was later enlarged and furnished with a market house.[21] New Brentford was called Great or

[83] *Cal. Papal Reg.* i. 21, 201.
[84] *Pipe R.* 9 Hen. II (P.R.S. vi), 62.
[85] *Cal. Chart.* 1327–41, 472.
[86] *V.C.H. Mdx.* ii. 267; *Cal. Chart.* 1226–57, 382.
[87] *Cur. Reg. R.* xv, no. 57.
[88] P.R.O., CP 25(1)/146/9/114.
[89] *Cal. Close,* 1237–42, 293, 392–3.
[90] *Cal. Chart.* 1327–41, 472.
[91] *Cal. Close,* 1256–9, 153.
[92] Guildhall MSS. 10312/67, rot. 4d.; 11765, ff. 126v.–27.
[93] Ibid. MS. 10123/2, under fishery and lands in lord's hands. [94] P.R.O., E 154/1/47, m.3.
[95] Hist. MSS. Com. 8, *9th Rep.* i, p. 34; Guildhall MS. 11765, ff. 126v.–27.
[96] P.R.O., E 372/108, rot. 15d. [97] Ibid. SC 6/1140/24.
[98] Ibid. SC 6/Hen. VIII/2109.
[99] *Pub. Wks. in Med. Law,* ii (Seld. Soc. xl), 7, 10.
[1] Sharpe, *Bygone Hanwell,* 83.
[2] *Cal. Pat.* 1547–8, 173.
[3] P.R.O., E 134/Easter 26 Eliz. I/6.
[4] Ibid. CP 25(2)/172/27 Eliz. I East. no. 4.
[5] Ibid. CP 25(2)/173/40–1 Eliz. I Mich. no. 5.

[6] Ibid. E 308/3/21/40, no. 143. [7] M.R.O., Acc. 308/4A.
[8] Guildhall MS. 11766, ff. 20v., 21v., 22.
[9] P.R.O., CP 25(2)/27/179/28. [10] Ibid. C 8/1643/12.
[11] *Cal. Mem. R.* 1327–8, no. 1434; *Cal. of Wills. in Ct. of Husting,* i. 465.
[12] Guildhall MS. 11765, p. 118.
[13] *True Relation of Barbarous Passages of King's Army at Old Braineford* (1642).
[14] R. H. Lightning, *Ealing and the Poor* (Ealing Local Hist. Soc. 1966), 30.
[15] *Rep. of Sel. Cttee. on Police of Metropolis,* H.C. 533, p. 266 (1828), vi.
[16] Faulkner, *Brentford, Ealing and Chiswick,* 8.
[17] P. Howard, *London's River* (1975), 45.
[18] *Cal. Chart. R.* 1300–26, 81.
[19] *Cal. Proc. in Chancery* (Rec. Com.), ii. 74–5; P.R.O., C 2/Eliz. I/H22/34.
[20] Faulkner, *Brentford, Ealing and Chiswick,* 92; P.R.O., C 78/1289/20; C 5/390/123; C 66/3083/5.
[21] P.R.O., C 2/Eliz. I/H22/34; Faulkner, *Brentford, Ealing and Chiswick,* 92–3; Canham, *Brentford,* 2, 6; *Brentford and Chiswick As It Was,* illus. 6; below, plate facing p. 129.

Market Brentford by 1593[22] and trade thereafter prospered with the growth of traffic to London by road and river, while Brentford fair was mentioned in Samuel Butler's *Hudibras* of 1663. The old market house was replaced *c.* 1850 by a town hall and market house, in front of which markets continued to be held.[23] Suppression of the fair was sought before 1845[24] and Brentford Town Hall and Market House Co. in 1890 was accused of often allowing the market to be used for 'semi-fair purposes'.[25] The county council acquired the licence in 1891 and, after pressure from the U.D.C. and its successor, the fair was finally abolished in 1932 and the market in 1933.[26]

In the late 19th century market gardeners set up stalls in the roadway north of Kew bridge, causing such traffic congestion that in 1893 the local board bought 2 a. of the Gunnersbury House estate for a market, which opened on the north side of Chiswick High Road in 1893. A large building of yellow brick with terracotta dressings was built in 1905, after the site had been extended, and, as Brentford Market, remained in use until 1974, when the traders moved to Southall. In 1980 the former covered market served as a skateboard park.[27]

At Ealing a fair was held on the green in 1822, when William Cobbett was diverted by crowds of Cockneys on their way there.[28] The fair, of unknown origin, was held from 24 to 26 June[29] until its suppression in 1880.[30]

TRADE AND INDUSTRY: EALING. Inhabitants had business connexions with Londoners by 1344, when a London goldsmith owed money to John of Bristol of Ealing, himself a debtor to citizens in 1346 and 1353 and to Queen Philippa's butler in 1350.[31] More dealings were recorded in 1360, with a Londoner,[32] and in 1410, with men from Westminster and Holborn. Four out of five Ealing tradesmen executed in 1443 were also of London; one was also of King's Lynn (Norf.), another of Bury St. Edmunds (Suff.), and a third of Horndon-on-the-Hill (Essex). In 1469 an Ealing fisherman had dealings with an Enfield maltman.[33]

There was a tailor in 1293-4[34] and from 1388 apparently always a carpenter.[35] A ploughwright was recorded in 1408, a chapman in 1410, a smith in 1414, a tanner in 1437,[36] a painter, a scrivener,

and a baker in 1443,[37] and a thatcher in 1455.[38] In the 1650s there were references to a butcher, a miller, a fellmonger, a cordwainer, a cheesemonger, a tallowchandler, three tailors, and a brickmaker,[39] in 1668 to a sawyer, a bricklayer, and a brewer, and in 1670 to a hempdresser. By 1704 there was a barber.[40] All were individual craftsmen in a predominantly agricultural parish; the only industries were small-scale brewing and brickmaking and tilemaking.

Lewis Furnell had a brewhouse at Ealing in 1728[41] but in 1733 only a malthouse remained.[42] Other malthouses occurred between 1780 and 1796, at Gunnersbury,[43] and in 1739.[44] A house at Ealing village, leased to T. P. Oakley in 1806, had been converted by 1810 into the Lion brewery, which had failed by 1822.[45] Another brewhouse, late of Dr. Nicholas, existed on the rectory estate in 1838.[46] William Griffiths was a brewer at Ealing Dean in 1845 and 1855[47] and David Nolden in Ealing Road in 1853.[48]

There were frequent references to brickearth and in 1668 there was a brickworks in the open fields.[49] A kiln stood in tilekiln close east of Hanger Lane from 1654 until at least 1761;[50] it was omitted from leases after 1804[51] and a pond occupied most of the field in 1810.[52]

Late 19th-century growth was mainly residential, and new firms were all small, including W. J. Cocks's bicycle factory at no. 32 High Street in 1893[53] and a mineral water works at Gower House, St. Mary's Road, in 1894.[54] In 1901 the largest employers of men were the building trade, with 1,458, and the transport industry, with 995. There were 495 clerks and still 405 workers in agriculture.[55] Numbers in the building industry rose to 1,935 in 1911 but fell back to 1,458 in 1921, while those in transport increased steadily to 2,161 in 1921. By then 2,774 clerks formed the largest single group, although they were less prominent than in some suburbs, such as Hornsey.[56] Other important trades in 1921 were related to interior decoration and clothing. Women worked mainly in domestic service and laundries. Servants numbered 4,616 in 1901, 5,545 in 1911, and 4,004 in 1921. Laundries, including the Ealing Park laundry of Darwin Road, which advertised its drying grounds *c.* 1903, employed 387 in 1901 and *c.* 500 in 1911.[57] Of the 16,589 residents who worked elsewhere in 1921, 11,479 travelled to the City,

[22] Norden, *Spec. Brit.* 16.
[23] Canham, *Brentford*, 6; S. Butler, *Hudibras*, ed. J. Wilders and H. de Quehen (1973), 2nd pt. Canto III, l. 995.
[24] Faulkner, *Brentford, Ealing and Chiswick*, 93.
[25] *Rep. Com. on Mkt. Rights and Tolls* [C. 6268-VIA], p. 344, H.C. (1890-1), xl.
[26] *Brentford and Chiswick As It Was*, illus. 6.
[27] Ibid. illus. 27, 30; Canham, *Brentford*, 10.
[28] Wm. Cobbett, *Rural Rides*, ed. G. D. H. and M. Cole, i (1930), 84.
[29] Gtr. Ealing Local Hist. Soc. *Local Historian* (1961), 10, 28-9.
[30] *Kelly's Dir. Mdx.* (1890).
[31] *Cal. Close*, 1343-6, 359; 1346-9, 44; 1349-54, 54, 217.
[32] *Cal. Pat.* 1358-61, 426.
[33] *Cal. Close*, 1409-13, 88; 1441-7, 98; 1454-61, 480.
[34] P.R.O., JUST 1/543, rot. 57.
[35] Guildhall MSS. 11765, ff. 31, 33v., 37, 41v.; 11766, f. 14v.
[36] Ibid. 11765, ff. 43-4, 47, 78.
[37] *Cal. Close*, 1441-7, 98.

[38] Guildhall MS. 9171/8, f. 159v.
[39] *Mdx. County Rec.* iii. 240; M.R.O., Acc. 890, p. 60; *Mdx. Par. Regs.* iv. 8, 13; viii. 20, 22.
[40] M.R.O., Acc. 890, pp. 100, 108, 132, 516.
[41] Guildhall MS. 10465/44.
[42] Ibid. 49.
[43] M.R.O., D.R.O. 37/B1/2.   [44] Ibid. 1.
[45] *6th Rep. Com. Char.* H.C. 12, p. 273 (1822), ix; M.R.O., D.R.O. 37/D1/3.
[46] Guildhall MS. 1568A.
[47] *P.O. Dir. Six Home Counties* (1845, 1855).
[48] *Mason's Dir. Brentford* (1853).
[49] P.R.O., C 10/112/56.
[50] Ibid. C 10/21/104; Guildhall MS. 12350.
[51] Guildhall MS. 12350.
[52] Ibid. MS. 12359.
[53] *Illustrated Lond.* (1893).   [54] Ealing libr., plan.
[55] *Census*, 1901. Para. based on *Census*, 1901-21.
[56] *V.C.H. Mdx.* vi. 111.
[57] London United Tramways, *By Tube and Electric Car to Hampton Ct.* (n.d.); *Ealing: Country Town near Lond.* (1904).

Westminster, and other parts of London, and 4,194 to Acton, Brentford, or elsewhere in Middlesex. Of 4,715 workers who commuted into Ealing, presumably most were employed in domestic service or shops.

Twentieth-century Ealing came to be largely hemmed in by industry along Western Avenue and the Great West Road, at Park Royal, Acton, and Brentford. Since the First World War several firms have moved into Ealing without seriously affecting its generally residential character.

W. Ottway and Co., scientific instrument makers, occupied workshops, warehouses, and offices off New Broadway by 1908.[58] They manufactured components and sighting equipment for the Ministry of Defence in 1966, as a subsidiary of the Hilger & Watts group, but closed in 1968.[59]

Wolf Electric Tools, founded in 1900, opened the Pioneer works in Hanger Lane in 1935 and acquired extra office and factory space on an adjoining site in 1976. The firm, innovators in making certain portable electric tools, in 1978 had 850 people at the works, which was also its headquarters.[60]

Film production began in Ealing in 1904, when William George Barker bought West Lodge, Ealing Green, with 3 a. adjacent to Walpole park. Studios, said to be the largest in England,[61] were built by Barker Motion Picture Photography Ltd. and in 1920 acquired by General Film Renters, which leased them to various companies. The site was bought in 1929 by Union Studios, which quickly failed,[62] and then by Associated Talking Pictures, which built a sound studio in 1931 and turned a house on Ealing Green into offices and the main entrance.[63] Michael Balcon became head of production in 1938 and the company, called Ealing Studios Ltd., made films which included, after the Second World War, the famous Ealing comedies. The studios were sold in 1955 to the B.B.C., which still used them in 1980, while Balcon bought Nile Lodge in Queen's Walk as his headquarters and produced further Ealing comedies elsewhere until 1958.[64] B.B.C. Enterprises had offices in Villiers House, Haven Green, in 1980.

Several large companies had offices in Ealing in 1980. Those in Uxbridge Road included Percy Bilton at Bilton House, Transworld Publishers (Corgi books) at Century House, no. 61, Consolidated Pneumatic Tools Co. at no. 97, and Curry's, the electrical retailers, at no. 46. Taylor Woodrow occupied Western House, at the corner of Western Avenue and Hanger Lane.[65]

TRADE AND INDUSTRY: BRENTFORD. One inhabitant owed money to a Londoner in 1367[66] and another to a Salisbury man in 1383. Others stood surety to a man from Sittingbourne (Kent) in 1390 and to an Uxbridge chapman in 1441,[67] and from 1469 many had dealings with Londoners.[68] In 1501 a yeoman had property at Holborn, Knightsbridge, and Brentford,[69] in 1510 a London grocer was also of Brentford,[70] and in 1591 a haberdasher traded at both London and Brentford.[71]

The main road and the two rivers produced distinctive occupations. The road was lined with inns and served by local carters, carriers, and later stagecoachmen.[72] The rivers gave rise to basket makers, fishermen, and watermen. Osiers were cultivated on aits in the Thames by 1397,[73] the Godwins in early 18th-century New Brentford[74] and the Bowdens from 1791 to 1843 being the leading basket makers.[75] Fishing and water transport, sufficiently common in 1666 to justify the appointment of a pressmaster,[76] were the chief occupations in 1733,[77] although there had long been many others. A baker occurred in 1255,[78] a draper in 1384,[79] a ploughwright in 1410,[80] a mason in 1423,[81] a cardmaker in 1429,[82] and a butcher in 1497.[83] By c. 1600 trades included those of tanner, chapman, baker, tiler, miller, and shoemaker;[84] between 1606 and 1628 a chandler, clothmaker, cordwainer, saddler, poulterer, butcher, brewer, glover, merchant, and vintner were also recorded.[85] Other occupations included those of a cooper in 1642,[86] mealman in 1653,[87] hempman and bricklayer in 1654, fellmonger, wharfinger, weaver, glazier, shipwright,[88] tobacco pipemaker, surgeon, clockmaker, hempmaker, distiller, apothecary, and lodesmith by 1670,[89] woollen draper, gunsmith, bargeman, tobacconist, and cowleech by 1678,[90] and flaxdresser, upholsterer, scrivener, pattenmaker, barber, haberdasher, excise officer, coalfactor, stationer, and stonecutter by 1719.[91] In 1720 there were 60 different trades at New Brentford alone, including those of stagecoachman, hatter,

[58] M.R.O., Acc. 676/2 [767]; *Kelly's Dir. Mdx.* (1908).
[59] Ealing L.B. *Official Guide* [1968].
[60] 'Wolf: short hist. of Co. 1900–77'; inf. from Wolf Electric Tools Ltd.
[61] *Brit. Jnl. of Photography*, 30 Jan., 12 Mar., 9 Apr., 25 June 1976; R. Low, *Hist. Brit. Film, 1914–18* (1950), 66.
[62] R. Low, *Hist. Brit. Film, 1918–29* (1971), 136, 195, 218.
[63] B. Dean, *Minds Eye* (1973), 142–9; *Kinematograph Weekly*, 4 Oct. 1951 (suppl. on Ealing Studios).
[64] *Kemp's Dir. Ealing* (1957); M. Balcon, *Mic. Balcon Presents* (1969), 116–17, 184, 191.
[65] Inf. from Mr. P. Hounsell.
[66] *Cal. Pat.* 1385–9, 294.
[67] *Cal. Close*, 1381–5, 306; 1389–92, 166; 1435–41, 453.
[68] Ibid. 1468–76, 77, 95, 202; *Cal. Pat.* 1485–94, 184.
[69] *Cal. Pat.* 1494–1509, 207.
[70] *L. & P. Hen. VIII*, i (1), p. 246.
[71] P.R.O., REQ 2/250/19.
[72] Below.
[73] Guildhall MS. 11765, f. 34v.
[74] Boston manor ct. bk. (1692–1842).

[75] M.R.O., D.R.O. 37/B1/2, 3.
[76] *Cal. S.P. Dom.* 1665–6, 468.
[77] Lightning, *Ealing and the Poor*, 2.
[78] *Cal. Close*, 1254–6, 91.
[79] *Cal. Pat.* 1381–5, 400.
[80] Guildhall MS. 9171/2, f. 181.
[81] P.R.O., KB 29/57, Mich. rot. 3.
[82] Ibid. KB 29/62, Mich. rot. 7.
[83] Guildhall MS. 9171/8, f. 141.
[84] *Mdx. County Rec.* i. 102, 103; P.R.O., E 134/26 Eliz. I East./6; ibid. REQ 2/168/53.
[85] *Mdx. County Rec.* ii. 17; *Mdx. Sess. Rec.* i. 80, 231, 234; ii. 143; iii. 141, 293; iv. 260, 336; *Acts of P.C.* 1625, 67.
[86] *Mdx. County Rec.* iii. 175.
[87] *Mdx. Par. Regs.* viii. 19.
[88] Ibid. 20–2; P.R.O., E 134/1659/Mich./30.
[89] M.R.O., D.R.O. 37/A1/3; ibid. Acc. 890, pp. 103–4, 127, 132; Guildhall MS. 10116/2/3.
[90] M.R.O., Acc. 890, pp. 149, 176, 236, 255.
[91] Ibid. 310, 374, 510, 567; Boston man. ct. bk. (1692–1842).

milliner, pewterer, and bodicemaker,[92] and, as in 1774,[93] many shops. Brentford had 10 academies, 14 bakers, 18 bootmakers, 17 coalmerchants, 13 market gardeners, and 29 victuallers in 1826[94] and 62 listed trades in 1834.[95]

Many of the earliest industries, mentioned more fully below, were extractive. They included gravel digging,[96] lime burning, brickmaking, and tilemaking, and all owed their growth to river or canal transport. Tanning also required a plentiful supply of water and the gunpowder whose storage caused alarm in 1700[97] was presumably brought to Brentford by boat. The growth of malting and allied trades from the late 17th century depended on the existence of New Brentford's corn market. From the mid 18th century granaries proliferated[98] and extractive industries expanded until in 1791 there was a large distillery, a large flour mill, and extensive brick, tile, and pottery works. The main road was important[99] and so too, from the 1790s, was the Grand Junction Canal. The same industries were employing great numbers in 1800.[1] By 1816, however, the brick and pottery works were depressed[2] and in 1819 recent industries, presumably Corson's turpentine works and Johnson's starch mill, were said to have disappeared.[3] Almost immediately new industries were introduced including a gasworks[4] and the Grand Junction waterworks,[5] and in 1826-7 Montgomery's sawmills and the soap factory were noted.[6] The distillery, gasworks, and soap works attracted more attention than the kilns, breweries, and malthouses in 1845.[7] Most industry had moved out of New Brentford and the distillery at Old Brentford had closed by 1859, but Brentford dock was opened and the gasworks was increasingly dominating High Street. New factories included Beach's jam factory, the Star Chemical works at the Ham by 1872,[8] a foundry north of High Street in 1912,[9] the York Mineral Water Co. in 1909,[10] Water Softeners Ltd. in 1911,[11] and by 1921 an indiarubber factory employing 344 people.[12] Since most were small businesses, the chief firms in 1898 were much as in 1859.[13] All the lesser breweries had closed by 1908, Montgomery's timberyard by 1911, and the Royal brewery in 1923, leaving only the gasworks and the waterworks and firms mostly with under 50 employees by 1933.[14]

Closures were counterbalanced by the opening of factories along the Great West Road. Hudson Essex Motor Co.'s factory was authorized in 1925,[15] the Firestone Tyre Co.'s works opened in 1929,[16] the factories of Trico-Folberth, Smith's potato crisps,[17] Sperry Gyroscope, and R. B. Pullin soon afterwards, and Macleans by 1938.[18] By 1938 Brentford had manufacturing chemists and makers of scientific instruments, motor cars, aeroplane accessories, and other products, providing virtually full employment.[19] The turnover of firms was extremely rapid: Beechams, the Jantzen Knitting Co., the Raleigh Cycle Co., and the British Oxygen Co. (B.O.C.) had premises in the Great West Road in 1954,[20] by which date manufacturers were being replaced by warehouses and offices, which employed many fewer local people.[21] Few factories remained in 1978, when buildings included the large headquarters of Mowlem, Honeywell Information Systems, and Beechams, the offices of Brentford Nylons,[22] and the distributive centres of Mercedes-Benz (G.B.), Honda, Agfa Gevaert, Peugeot Automobile U.K., and Fiat. The central portion of Wallis, Filbert & Partners' white Firestone factory, which 'for sheer panache had no equal in Britain', was demolished in 1980.[23]

Brentford gasworks closed in 1964, followed by the Grand Junction waterworks, Brentford dock, and the Brentford Soap Co., leaving no large-scale industry in Brentford town itself. Remaining firms, such as the Grafton Paper Manufacturing Co. in Brook Lane,[24] were relatively small. By the late 19th century Brentford had also been supplanted as a retail centre of more than local importance.

Water freight was presumably received at Brentford long before the first watermen were recorded in 1613.[25] Fruit, bricks,[26] and probably fish were shipped to London in the 17th century, the return cargoes including dung by 1609, when there was a dung wharf,[27] and coal, used by 1679 for brickmaking.[28] By 1733 water carriage was a leading occupation.[29] In 1782 corn was an important cargo[30] and in 1791 boats carried market produce to Hungerford (Berks.) and Queenhithe (Lond.) by every tide.[31] Coal, in the absence of local wood, was probably also used for lime, tile, and pottery kilns and for malting. In 1791 coke powered William Johnson's starch mill[32] and

[92] Boston man. ct. bk. (1692-1842), 1720 rental.
[93] Diary of John Yeoman, 47.
[94] Pigot, Lond. Dir. (1826-7).
[95] Pigot, Com. Dir. (1834); see also Univ. Brit. Dir. (1791).
[96] Guildhall MS. 11766, f. 16.
[97] Cal. S.P. Dom. 1699-1700, 396.
[98] Based on New Brentford MS. 17516.
[99] Univ. Brit. Dir. (1791).
[1] Ambulator (1800).
[2] Brewer, Beauties of Eng. & Wales, x (5), 346.
[3] Dugdale, New Brit. Traveller, iii. 484.
[4] Below, pub. svces.
[5] Ibid. Following 3 paras. based on inf. given in detail below.
[6] Pigot, Lond. Dir. (1826-7).
[7] P.O. Dir. Six Home Counties (1845).
[8] Brentford, Kew, Isleworth and Spring Grove Dir. (1872).
[9] Brentford U.D. Rep. of M.O.H. (1912).
[10] M.R.O., Acc. 891/2/9/5.
[11] Ibid. Acc. 1285/33.
[12] Census, 1921.

[13] Jackson, Ealing, 134; P.O. Dir. Six Home Counties (1859).
[14] D. H. Smith, Ind. of Gtr. Lond. (1933), 82.
[15] Brentford U.D. Rep. Housing Cttee. 3 Mar. 1925.
[16] Robbins, Mdx. 57.
[17] Petit. for Incorp. as Mun. Boro. (1931).
[18] Beechams in Brief [1971].
[19] Brentford and Chiswick Boro. Rep. of M.O.H. (1938).
[20] K. F. Newton, 'Brentford' (TS. in Chiswick libr.), 49.
[21] Mdx. Educ. Cttee., Brentford and Chiswick Youth Employment Cttee. Rep. 1953-4.
[22] Brentford and Chiswick Times, 31 Mar. 1977.
[23] Sunday Telegraph and Observer, 31 Aug. 1980.
[24] Inf. from the managing dir.
[25] Mdx. Sess. Rec. i. 36, 118, 232, 306.
[26] Below; P.R.O., C 8/338/156.
[27] P.R.O., SC 2/189/32, rot. 14.
[28] Ibid. C 8/338/156.
[29] Lightning, Ealing and the Poor, 2.
[30] Ambulator (1782).
[31] Univ. Brit. Dir. (1791).
[32] Below.

from 1821 it was processed at Brentford gas-works.[33] Several coal warehouses existed from the 1790s,[34] when coal from the Midlands probably supplanted that brought via London. In 1841 boats wrecked at Brentford included 2 from Tipton (Staffs.) loaded with coal, 2 others from Tipton with coal and peas, 2 from Bloxwich (Staffs.) with hoop iron, and 2 from Stourbridge (Worcs.) with wheat. There were also 3 large coal barges at Brentford End, 5 large barges with wheat and linseed, and a barge with slate and stone from Nuneaton (Warws.); other craft came from Wolverhampton, Brierley Hill (Staffs.), and Tipton.[35] In 1879 a wide boat, 27 narrow canal boats, and 4 tugs, were registered at Brentford, the narrow boats mainly for use on the Grand Junction canal, on which 6 would go to Birmingham, 1 to South Staffordshire, and 2 to Oxford; 8 carried general merchandise, 2 iron, 3 grain, 2 coal, 12 building material, and 2 ammunition.[36] As many as 35 canal boats were recorded at Brentford in 1891 and 36 in 1911, but only 9 in 1921.[37] Water traffic in 1930 was declining every year. In 1975 the barges of the Thames & General Lighterage Co., the largest company on the Thames, travelled mainly between Brentford and London docks.[38] The Grand Union canal at Brentford was then still heavily used for freight.[39]

Wharves, such as the Hollows,[40] were first recorded in the 17th century and ultimately lined the whole waterfront. They became increasingly elaborate and permanent, such as T. B. Rowe's canal basin.[41] Town Meadow dock, rented by Brentford U.D.C. in 1875 and bought soon afterwards,[42] was unused in 1929; a plan to renovate it in 1930 was opposed by Clements Knowlinge, whose Goat, Victoria, and Ferry wharves could handle most craft but were frequently idle.[43] Tunnel Cement, a subsidiary of Portland Cement, distributed cement from Essex in the 1950s,[44] and Clements Tough, a subsidiary of the Dickenson Rob Group, in 1977 still provided handling and warehousing at Ferry Lane.[45] In 1978 many other wharves at Brentford were disused.

Brentford dock was erected by the G.W.R. to the designs of I. K. Brunel and opened in 1859,[46] to connect river and canal traffic with the railways. The site in Isleworth and New Brentford, bought in 1855 from James Montgomery, timber merchant, consisted of Old England, on the western bank of the Brent and eastern bank of the Grand Junction canal at their junction with the Thames, together with land west of the canal and east of the Brent.[47] Brunel's covered wooden dock was destroyed by fire in 1920 and replaced by 1923 by a steel and iron structure. From 1918 the Thames frontage was adapted for boats of up to 300 tons and in 1923 craft ranged from heavy down-river barges to light canal boats, including sailing barges. There were customs and weighing facilities, a coal-tip, and 3 sidings and 1,000 waggons to serve the south and west of England, South Wales, and the Midlands.[48] A great variety of goods, together with coal for ships in the Pool of London, was still handled in 1964, when the dock was closed.[49]

Boat building was attested by a shipwright at Old Brentford in 1659[50] and by the devise of a copyhold boatyard there in 1731.[51] In 1853 Mr. Sims had a barge building yard at the Ham, New Brentford,[52] and in 1898 Messrs. Radford had a barge and waggon works at the confluence of the Thames and Brent.[53] Works were built at Old Brentford for the Thames (later Thames & General) Lighterage Co. in 1881[54] and enlarged in 1926 by slipways on Lot's Ait.[55] A 34-ton tug to tow strings of 7 barges from London docks to Brentford was built there in 1958[56] and although boat building ceased c. 1965[57] the yard in 1978 remained an active maintenance yard for the company. E. C. Jones & Son were building Bantam boats, small tugs to manœuvre barges in confined spaces, in 1953[58] and survived in 1978.

Tanning was recorded in 1591[59] and 1714.[60] A tanyard on the Brent, west of Market Place and north of St. Lawrence's church, was continuously occupied between 1720 and 1853.[61] James Band, from a family of Bermondsey tanners, established his own firm of parchment makers at a tannery in Boston Road near Park chapel in 1845. The firm moved c. 1910 to Plough Yard, the premises being extended during the Second World War. There were 70 employees c. 1960 and 80 c. 1975 but only 15 in 1978, by which date they also produced chamois leather and all kinds of vellum.[62]

Soap making was practised at Old Brentford c. 1603, when tenants were not to put soap-ash on the waste.[63] William Seagar managed a soap works there from 1764 or earlier[64] until c. 1792, when it passed to Roger Griffin and Peter Warren.[65] Another firm, in which Griffin, Alexander Corson, and others were partners,

[33] Below, pub. svces.
[34] M.R.O., D.R.O. 37/B1/2.
[35] *The Times*, 18, 19 Jan. 1841.
[36] Chiswick libr., canal boat certs. (1879).
[37] *Census*, 1891-1921.
[38] *Gazette & Post*, 10 Apr. 1975.
[39] H. McKnight, *Shell Bk. of Inland Waterways* (1975), 286.   [40] M.R.O., Acc. 526/6.
[41] Ibid. Acc. 638/288; Acc. 538/1/46/1.
[42] Brentford loc. bd. min. bk. (1874-8), pp. 76, 587.
[43] Chiswick libr., scrapbk. of cuttings.
[44] Newton, 'Brentford', 42.
[45] *Brentford and Chiswick Times*, 28 July 1977.
[46] *D.N.B.*; *P.O. Dir. Six Home Counties* (1859); 'Brentford Dock' (TS. at Chiswick libr.).
[47] M.R.O., Acc. 638/76.
[48] Chiswick libr., cutting (1923) from G.W.R. staff mag.
[49] *Brentford and Chiswick Times*, 20 Mar. 1969; Chiswick libr., letter of goods agent.

[50] P.R.O., E 134/1659/Mich./30.
[51] Guildhall MS. 10465/48.
[52] New Brentford MS. 17825.
[53] M.R.O., Acc. 638/288.
[54] *T.L.M.A.S.* ix. 387.
[55] Brentford U.D.C. *Rep. Housing Cttee. 2 Mar. 1926*.
[56] Chiswick libr., cutting.
[57] *Gazette & Post*, 10 Apr. 1975.
[58] Brentford and Chiswick Boro. *Official Guide* [1953].
[59] P.R.O., REQ 2/183/57.
[60] M.R.O., Acc. 890.
[61] *Mason's Dir. Brentford* (1853). Chiswick libr., Boston man. ct. bk. (1692-1842); *The Times*, 18 Jan. 1841.
[62] *Introducing H. Band & Co.* (undated pamphlet at Chiswick libr.); *Brentford and Chiswick As It Was*, illus. 4; inf. from Mr. H. C. Band.
[63] P.R.O., SC 2/189/29, m. 14.
[64] Guildhall MS. 10465/106, pp. 110-11.
[65] M.R.O., D.R.O. 37/D1/2.

went bankrupt by 1796.[66] Lawrence Rowe acquired land in 1800 near Ferry Lane,[67] presumably to the west,[68] and by 1827 Brentford was the main centre of hard soap production in south-eastern England.[69] A prominent landmark c. 1827[70] and described as very extensive in 1845,[71] T. B. Rowe & Co.'s Thames Soap Works occupied a large site between Ferry Lane, Town Meadow, and the Thames in 1888.[72] The factory was acquired by Messrs. Lever in 1916 and closed in 1933. Employees then opened the Brentford Soap Co. at the former Beehive brewery in Catherine Wheel Yard, New Brentford, where 150 worked by 1958[73] and which, after a fire, reopened temporarily in 1961.

A brickmaker of New Brentford contracted in 1502 to supply 400,000 bricks to Syon abbey.[74] In 1671 bricks were shipped to London[75] and in 1687 an Ealing brickmaker had 180,000 bricks in stock.[76] In 1774 hundreds of loads had been stockpiled and so much brickearth had been dug around Brentford that the surrounding fields were stated, wrongly, to be exhausted.[77] Brickmaking was often carried on with tilemaking: in 1679 tile kiln close adjoined Ferry Lane, Old Brentford,[78] and in 1731 there was a tile kiln south of Old Brentford High Street.[79] The Barrett family, brickmakers in 1729 and 1748, were noted for pantiles.[80] The partnership of Trimmer and Clarke, which managed a tile kiln in 1776,[81] already existed in 1742,[82] presumably for the same purpose, and had an extensive business in 1791.[83] Conducted from 1786 by Samuel Clarke and from 1807 by John Clarke, the old tile kiln, together with a new one, was run from 1800 by Messrs. Trimmer,[84] who had their own tile kilns from at least 1772 until 1835 over the boundary in Chiswick, with access from Kew Bridge Road.[85] By 1834 part of the business had been taken over by George Robinson,[86] who had acquired the rest by 1845[87] and managed the tile kiln and brickfield by the Potomac pond in Gunnersbury park until at least 1861.[88] Bricklayers, working only in the summer, were said to

be well paid and responsible for increasing crime in 1828.[89]

Potters were working in New Brentford in 1691, 1693, and 1699.[90] Thomas Edwardes owned a pottery at Bull Lane, Old Brentford, in 1766, which was let to Messrs. Johnson and Turner from 1770, to Daniel Turner alone from 1772 to 1781, and then to members of his family until c. 1820.[91] The business expanded greatly between 1774[92] and 1791[93] but the stock was auctioned in 1820, probably because of the failure of T. W. Turner (d. 1833).[94] It had been taken over by 1823 by Trimmers[95] and by 1840 by George Robinson,[96] who had relinquished it by 1849,[97] and was managed by George Wood in 1853[98] and J. T. Greenwood in 1870-2.[99]

Another pottery at Old Brentford was managed by Daniel Roberts from 1773 and a Mr. Shepherd in 1790.[1] James Ashford ran Coleshole pottery, Old Brentford, in 1853[2] and James Collier was a tile and pottery maker in 1859[3] and 1870.[4] Garden pots were still made by traditional methods c. 1946.[5]

Lime burning was practised in 1659 by Robert Tunstall, whose kiln near the Hollows, Old Brentford, supplied builders and farmers in both Middlesex and Surrey[6] and was probably the one mentioned in 1669.[7] Robert Tunstall, cooper, owned several lime kilns at the Hollows, Old Brentford, in 1679[8] and a namesake in 1790 leased two lime kilns, probably at the Hollows, to James Trimmer,[9] described as a lime burner in 1791.[10] Mr. Watkins was a lime merchant of Brentford in 1845.[11]

Timber was bought at Brentford by Westminster abbey in 1607.[12] A timber yard between High Street and the Brent, New Brentford, in 1638 and 1667[13] had disappeared by 1693,[14] having been leased by Robert Tunstall, cooper, who himself kept 100 loads of timber in stock in 1667.[15] Another timber yard, recorded in 1690, was occupied in turn by William Baldwin, carpenter and builder of houses in the Butts, and Robert Mundy.[16] Yet another yard faced the Half

---

[66] Ibid. Acc. 909/313; cutting (1796) at Chiswick libr.
[67] Guildhall MS. 10465/139, p. 553.
[68] M.R.O., F 51.
[69] Acct. of Soap made 1826-7, H.C. 492, p. 3 (1826-7), xviii.
[70] Guildhall Libr., Panorama of Thames from Lond. to Richmond, pub. S. Leigh (c. 1827).
[71] P.O. Dir. Six Home Counties (1845).
[72] M.R.O., Acc. 638/288. For what follows, see 'Hist. of Manufacture of Soap in Brentford 1767-1962' (TS. at Chiswick libr.).
[73] Mdx. Educ. Cttee., Brentford and Chiswick Youth Employment Cttee. Rep. 1958-9; Brentford and Chiswick Times, 6 Sept. 1957.
[74] P.R.O., E 315/36/146.
[75] M.R.O., Acc. 890, p. 161.
[76] P.R.O., C 8/338/156.
[77] Diary of John Yeoman, 48.
[78] Guildhall MS. 10312/114, rot. 6.
[79] M.R.O., Acc. 942/1.
[80] Cal. Mdx. Sess. Bks. xiv. 129; Robbins, Mdx. 50.
[81] M.R.O., D.R.O. 37/B1/3.
[82] Ibid. B2/2.
[83] Univ. Brit. Dir. (1791).
[84] M.R.O., D.R.O. 37/B1/2.
[85] Guildhall MSS. 10465/94, pp. 290 sqq.; 150, p. 93; Chiswick libr., deed with plan (1819).
[86] Pigot, Lond. Dir. (1834); compare ibid. (1826-7).
[87] P.O. Dir. Six Home Counties (1845); Faulkner, Brentford, Ealing and Chiswick, 168.

[88] Guildhall MS. 12337 (plan).
[89] Rep. of Sel. Cttee. on Police of Metropolis, 226.
[90] New Brentford MSS. 17513, f. 91; 17514, f. 38; Boston man. ct. bk. (1692-1842).
[91] M.R.O., D.R.O. 37/B2/4, 5; B1/2, 3.
[92] Diary of John Yeoman, 16.
[93] Univ. Brit. Dir. (1791).
[94] New Times, 14 Dec. 1820; Chiswick libr., cuttings.
[95] M.R.O., D.R.O. 37/B1/3.
[96] Ibid. TA/EAL.
[97] M.R.O., D.R.O. 37/B1/4.
[98] Mason's Dir. Brentford (1853).
[99] Brentford, Kew, Isleworth and Spring Grove Dir. (1872).
[1] M.R.O., D.R.O. 37/B1/2.
[2] Mason's Dir. Brentford (1853).
[3] P.O. Dir. Six Home Counties (1859).
[4] P.O. Dir. Mdx. (1870).
[5] Henrey, King of Brentford (1946), 41-2.
[6] P.R.O., E 134/1659 Mich./30.
[7] Guildhall MS. 10312/105, rot. 10d.
[8] M.R.O., Acc. 250/3.
[9] Ibid. D.R.O. 37/D1/2.
[10] Univ. Brit. Dir. (1791).
[11] M.R.O., Acc. 880/9.
[12] W.A.M. 41200.
[13] P.R.O., C 8/152/127; M.R.O., Acc. 891/2/1/92.
[14] M.R.O., Acc. 891/2/1/67.
[15] Ibid. 92; Cal. S.P. Dom. 1667-8, 50, 72 (which wrongly says 'Dunkin').
[16] P.R.O., PROB 11/404 (P.C.C. 49 Vere).

Acre, New Brentford, in 1717[17] and a new one was established near the Butts and Windmill Lane by 1735.[18]

A wharf between the Brent and High Street, Old Brentford, was later said to have been a timber yard from c. 1750.[19] It belonged by 1790 to the Shairpe family,[20] who leased it in 1806 to William Anthony and James Montgomery and in 1818 to Montgomery alone, then described as timber merchant of Old Brentford.[21] Montgomery, who in 1826 also dealt in coal,[22] occupied 2¾ a. in 1840[23] and bought the freehold in 1853.[24] In 1845 he had a spacious wharf and sawmills, employing many people and with a range of buildings and stock greater than any other in Middlesex.[25] The business continued as James Montgomery & Son until 1911, when the site was sold to Water Softeners Ltd.[26]

A timber yard by the Brent was managed by Messrs. Joseph and Dawson in 1841[27] and another at the Hollows, between High Street and the Thames, Old Brentford, was offered for sale in 1907.[28]

Malthouses, breweries, and distilleries, relying on Brentford's corn market, were noteworthy from the late 17th century, some maltsters being also dealers in corn and coal. New Brentford had the greater number of businesses but the larger firms were at Old Brentford.

Most of New Brentford's malthouses were attached to inns, including ones at Catherine Wheel Yard in 1679,[29] at the Royal Oak, Market Place, in 1702, and at White Horse Yard, off Market Place, in 1702[30] and 1738.[31] The latter was disused in 1768[32] and many malthouses operated only briefly, since four were vacant in 1741 and three in 1750.[33] Some families managed several malthouses: the Lowe family had three c. 1690–1705;[34] the Banks family had one in 1743 and two, probably south of High Street, between 1772 and 1812, besides four at Old Brentford between 1790 and 1817;[35] and the Jones family's coal, corn, and malting business, based on Catherine Wheel Yard until 1821, included at least two malthouses from 1779, one at Plough Yard and another at the Black Boy and Still inn.[36] In 1791 Thomas Jullion, jeweller, and Thomas Whitbread ran distilling and rectifying businesses.[37]

A brewhouse by the Thames at Old Brentford in 1685 was acquired in 1696 by John Clarke, distiller, of London[38] and later of Old Brentford.[39] A distillery and malthouse on the site were surrendered by William Lonsdale in 1735,[40] occupied by four partners, including Percival Hart and Daniel Roberts, from 1763,[41] by Hart's son-in-law David Roberts from 1773,[42] and by him in partnership with Thomas Smith and Thomas Harrington from 1792.[43] Another Thames-side brewhouse at Old Brentford acquired by maltsters in 1740 was occupied by Hart in 1760.[44] After his death a malthouse stood on the site,[45] which was occupied from 1773 by David Roberts,[46] whose premises in 1777 covered a large area between High Street and the Thames.[47] In 1790, besides the premises south of High Street, Roberts, Smith, and Harrington also had land to the north, where their principal distillery stood. Considerable by 1791,[48] the distillery was the fourth largest in England in 1802.[49] In 1817 it was sold to Messrs. Booth of Clerkenwell, who by 1819 had also acquired Moses Banks's four malthouses and other property from Smith and Harrington.[50] Despite a major fire in 1837[51] the distillery in 1845 was described as one of the most complete in the world, producing nearly a million gallons of spirit every year.[52] Sold in 1851 to Messrs. Haig, it was still operating on a large scale in 1855 but apparently had ceased production by 1859.[53] From 1864 parts of the site were used for housing.[54]

A distillery and malthouse south of Old Brentford High Street in 1735 were settled in trust on Abraham Harvest and his wife Anne Trimmer in 1748[55] and owned by Abraham Trimmer, brewer, in 1790.[56] There were two malthouses on the site in 1796, which were worked from c. 1814 by John Newton,[57] the purchaser in 1801 of a brewery by the Thames at Old Brentford; that brewery had been Francis Harvest's in 1735 and Thomas Stump's since 1774.[58] Newton's brewery was sold in 1817 to Messrs. Thompson of Chiswick and passed in 1825 to John Hazard,[59] probably

[17] Boston man. ct. bk. (1692–1842).
[18] M.R.O., Acc. 308/2.
[19] Faulkner, *Brentford, Ealing and Chiswick*, 164.
[20] M.R.O., D.R.O. 37/D1/2.
[21] Ibid. Acc. 638/52.
[22] Pigot, *Lond. Dir.* (1826–7).
[23] M.R.O., TA/EAL.
[24] Ibid. Acc. 638/73.
[25] *P.O. Dir. Six Home Counties* (1845); Faulkner, *Brentford, Ealing and Chiswick*, 163–4.
[26] M.R.O., Acc. 1285/27.
[27] *The Times*, 18 Jan. 1841.
[28] M.R.O., Acc. 891/2/9/8.
[29] New Brentford MS. 17513, f. 49v.
[30] Chiswick libr., deed.
[31] M.R.O., Acc. 308/2.
[32] Chiswick libr., deed.
[33] New Brentford MS. 17516.
[34] Ibid. 17514.
[35] Ibid. 17516–18; M.R.O., D.R.O. 37/B1/2; D1/2.
[36] Chiswick libr., sales cat. (1821); M.R.O., Acc. 891/2/4/92; Acc. 891/2/9/6.
[37] *Univ. Brit. Dir.* (1791).
[38] Guildhall MS. 10465/5, 11, 12.
[39] Boston man. ct. bk. (1692–1842), f. 15.

[40] Guildhall MS. 10465/51.
[41] Ibid. 78, pp. 243–7.
[42] M.R.O., D.R.O. 37/B2/5.
[43] Guildhall MS. 10465/108, pp. 48 sqq.
[44] Ibid. 64, pp. 176–8; 75, pp. 221–3.
[45] Ibid. 89, pp. 224–5.
[46] M.R.O., D.R.O. 37/B2/5.
[47] B.L. Maps K.29.9.a.
[48] M.R.O., D.R.O. 37/D1/2; *Univ. Brit. Dir.* (1791).
[49] *Accts. on Distilling in G.B. & Irel. 1802–3*, H.C. [122], p. 1037 (1803), viii.
[50] M.R.O., D.R.O. 37/B1/2.
[51] J. F. D. Balfour, Ld. Kinross, *Kindred Spirit* (1959), 36 sqq.; Chiswick libr., photocopy of cutting.
[52] *P.O. Dir. Six Home Counties* (1845); Faulkner, *Brentford, Ealing and Chiswick*, 164–5.
[53] *P.O. Dir. Six Home Counties* (1851–9).
[54] Chiswick libr., deeds; T. E. Platten, *Memories of Old Brentford* (1877), 30.
[55] Guildhall MS. 10465/51, 63.
[56] M.R.O., D.R.O. 37/D1/2.
[57] Ibid. B1/2.
[58] Ibid. D1/2; ibid. Acc. 276/163; Acc. 891/2/1/382; Guildhall MSS. 10465/52; 10465/140, pp. 76 sqq.
[59] M.R.O., D.R.O. 37/B1/2; ibid. Acc. 891/2/5/291; Guildhall MS. 10465/140, pp. 76–81.

already a partner of Booth & Co. The name was apparently changed from the British to the Red Lion brewery and in 1832, after a visit by William IV, to the Royal brewery.[60] The business was sold to Messrs. Carrington and Whitehurst in 1851[61] and run by Montagu Ballard from 1880 until 1923, when brewing ceased.[62] About 1926 the building was replaced by extensions to the gasworks.[63]

The Grand Junction brewery, Catherine Wheel Yard, New Brentford, was worked from 1826 by James Crooks,[64] in 1845–8 by William Gearey,[65] in 1853 by Sophia and Charles Gearey, and in 1862 and 1866 by George Gearey.[66] The buildings apparently were taken over by William Gomm, mentioned in 1843,[67] whose Beehive brewery was in High Street in 1853[68] but later in Catherine Wheel Yard. W. Gomm & Son advertised ten brews in 1893[69] and operated until 1900 or later.[70] Their business had been acquired by Fuller, Smith & Turner by 1908, when the Catherine Wheel Yard premises were for sale.[71]

Breweries in Boston Manor Road included Thomas Tearle's Star brewery in 1848[72] and the Metropolitan and Provincial Joint Stock Brewery Co. in 1853.[73] Thomas Lawrence's Boston brewery, almost opposite Boston House,[74] functioned from 1862 or earlier until 1896[75] but evidently had been taken over by Fuller, Smith & Turner by 1900.[76] High Street contained David Allen's Albion brewery between 1851 and 1866, and Richard Hunt's Harefield brewery in 1853.[77]

The leading 19th-century maltsters were Messrs. Jupp. In 1802 William Jupp occupied a single malthouse at Old Brentford, first mentioned in 1780,[78] and in 1855 the premises, east of Ferry Lane and north of Goat Wharf, were very extensive.[79] The firm had other malthouses near Kew bridge in 1877, when it planned to rebuild them,[80] and from at least 1826 until 1896 Jupp & Sons were also coal and corn merchants.[81]

Starch making was recorded in 1603.[82] Dr. William Johnson's premises in Catherine Wheel Yard in 1791 included steam mill, coke house, starch house, and laboratory piggeries.[83] The business may have existed in the 1770s[84] and was much admired[85] but proved unsuccessful, often changing hands.[86] Described as Messrs. Burrell's starch manufactory in 1811,[87] it was not recorded after 1812.[88] Richard Thoroughgood and John Wallace had another starch factory at Old Brentford in 1791.[89]

Mrs. Sumner had a printing office at Brentford in 1774.[90] Philip Norbury of High Street, New Brentford, was rated from 1769[91] and printed sermons in 1775.[92] The family firm continued to print until at least 1859[93] as part of a business which, in 1848, included the selling of stationery, medicines, and perfumery, besides a circulating library and the post office.[94] Other printers were W. H. Jackson, in High Street in 1872,[95] the Brentford Publishing Co., Albany Road, between 1901 and 1956,[96] and Walter Pearce & Co. in 1939.[97]

Alexander Corson, surgeon, leased a turpentine works, laboratory, and warehouse in Catherine Wheel Yard in 1792.[98] He had occupied the laboratory before 1791, when he was granted more land on the west of the Ham,[99] and a counting house, mill house, and distillery stood on the site in 1792.[1] On the failure of his soap making concern,[2] the Ham premises were sold in 1797[3] and thereafter often changed hands.[4] Turpentine was still made in 1813.[5]

T. W. Beach moved from Isleworth to Brentford in 1867, leased a jam factory at Walnut Tree Road, Old Brentford, in 1886, and formed a limited company with three factories in Middlesex and Worcestershire in 1887. His sale of jam made from whole fruit in glass bottles earned the description 'father of the jam trade' in 1902. Beach's sons assigned the lease on the Brentford factory in 1930.[6]

The firm of Trico-Folberth was formed in 1928 and established in a new factory in the Great West Road in 1930, making windscreen wipers

[60] Balfour, *Kindred Spirit*, 21–3; M.R.O., Acc. 880/6.
[61] *P.O. Dir. Six Home Counties* (1851); Guildhall MS. 10465/166, pp. 19–23.
[62] *Royal Brewery, Brentford* (pamphlet c. 1904); M.R.O., Acc. 638/257; Balfour, *Kindred Spirit*, 23; *Mdx. Chron.* 2 June 1923.
[63] *Brentford and Chiswick As It Was*, illus. 25.
[64] Pigot, *Lond. Dir.* (1826–7, 1834).
[65] *Whetstone's Dir. Richmond* (1848); *P.O. Dir. Six Home Counties* (1845).
[66] *Mason's Dir. Brentford* (1853); *P.O. Dir. Mdx.* (1862, 1866).
[67] M.R.O., D.R.O. 37/B1/4.
[68] *Mason's Dir. Brentford* (1853).
[69] *Mdx. Independent*, 27 May 1893.
[70] M.R.O., MR/LV31/7.
[71] Ibid. Acc. 891/2/9/3.
[72] *Whetstone's Dir. Richmond* (1848).
[73] *Mason's Dir. Brentford* (1853).
[74] O.S. Map 6″, Mdx. XIX. NE. (1894–6 edn.).
[75] *Brentford, Kew, Isleworth and Spring Grove Dir.* (1872); *P.O. Dir. N. Suburbs* (1896); *P.O. Dir. Mdx.* (1862, 1866).
[76] M.R.O., MR/LV31/7.
[77] *Mason's Dir. Brentford* (1853); *P.O. Dir. Mdx.* (1862, 1866); *P.O. Dir. Six Home Counties* (1851).
[78] M.R.O., D.R.O. 37/B1/2; B2/5.
[79] Ibid. B1/5; *P.O. Dir. Six Home Counties* (1855).
[80] Brentford loc. bd. min. bk. (1874–8), p. 346.
[81] *P.O. Dir. N. Suburbs* (1896); Pigot, *Lond. Dir.* (1826–7).
[82] *Mdx. County Rec.* i. 261.
[83] New Brentford MS. 17818.
[84] Johnson was then described as Dr. Wal. Johnson: *T.L.M.A.S.* xxiii. 181 n. He was also confused with Dr. Rob. Wallace Johnson, e.g. Lysons, *Environs*, ii. 58.
[85] e.g. Lysons, *Environs*, ii. 58.
[86] New Brentford MS. 17786.
[87] Lysons, *Environs* (Suppl.), 106.
[88] New Brentford MS. 17786.
[89] *Univ. Brit. Dir.* (1791); M.R.O., D.R.O. 37/D1/2.
[90] *Diary of John Yeoman*, 41.
[91] New Brentford MS. 17517.
[92] G. Costard, *Two Sermons in Twickenham Par. Ch.* (1775).
[93] *P.O. Dir. Six Home Counties* (1859); see also books printed by the Norburys at Chiswick libr.
[94] *Whetstone's Dir. Richmond* (1848).
[95] *Brentford, Isleworth, Kew and Spring Grove Dir.* (1872).
[96] *Adventures of Thos. Williams of St. Ives*, ed. F. Turney (1901); Brentford Printing and Publishing Co. Ltd. *Calendar* (1956).
[97] Lockhart Law, *Famous Cities of Iron* (1939).
[98] New Brentford MS. 17818.
[99] Boston man. ct. bk. (1692–1842).
[1] New Brentford MS. 17828.
[2] Above.
[3] M.R.O., Acc. 909/3B.
[4] Boston man. ct. bk. (1692–1842).
[5] D. Hughson, *Lond.* vi (1813), 523.
[6] 'Cinemas in Brentford and Chiswick' (TS. in Chiswick libr.); cuttings in Chiswick libr.

and other motor accessories. It had 700 employees in 1948[7] and survived in 1963[8] but not in 1975.[9]

The Sperry Gyroscope Co. was formed in 1915 and moved from Shepherd's Bush (Hammersmith) to the Great West Road in 1931, with 250 employees.[10] There were c. 2,500 employees when it moved to Feltham c. 1950.[11]

R. B. Pullin & Co. was founded in 1932 and moved in 1935 to Phoenix works in the Great West Road. The company made electrical equipment and precision instruments in 1948[12] and extended the buildings in 1958.[13] Taken over as part of the industrial division of Rank Precision Industries by 1968,[14] it had 800 employees in 1972.[15] It was called Rank Pullin Controls in 1978, when there were 500 employees[16] and the works also housed a film library and laboratories.

The Permutit Co. originated in the amalgamation of two firms in 1914 and moved in the 1930s to Permutit House, Gunnersbury Avenue, where it made water softeners and purifiers. The engineering workshops were moved c. 1955 and the offices to Isleworth in 1966, leaving only the laboratories at Permutit House in 1978.[17]

The British Oxygen Co. occupied buildings on the north side of the Great West Road in 1938 and 1940, where in 1978 Great West House was the headquarters of the company's gases division, employing 150 in making medical gases.[18]

Beechams Ltd., the international pharmaceutical, cosmetic, and food group, established laboratories in the Great West Road in 1944. Its Lucozade factory moved there by 1951[19] and Beechams' main offices followed in 1955, occupying premises used since 1947 as the headquarters of B.O.A.C.[20] In 1978 the building housed only research and administrative staff.[21]

The Strand Glass Co., renamed Strand Glassfibre in 1966, operated from no. 79 High Street before moving to the Brentway trading estate c. 1968. It employed 140 people in distributing materials in 1978.[22]

Polco Products was founded in 1956 at Covent Garden (Westm.) to make or import motor car accessories, notably vacuum cleaners. The firm moved to the Brent works, Catherine Wheel Yard, in 1972 and had 37 staff in 1978.[23]

LOCAL GOVERNMENT. MANORIAL GOVERNMENT.

In 1294 the bishop of London claimed to have in Ealing, as a member of his manor of Fulham, view of frankpledge, infangthief, outfangthief, chattels of fugitives, tumbril, pillory, gallows, and the assize of bread and of ale.[24] Courts baron for Ealing were normally held twice a year from 1383 until the mid 19th century, meeting at Fulham from 1445 or earlier.[25] The spring court was also a view of frankpledge, and other courts baron were held occasionally. There were separate aletasters for Ealing and Old Brentford in 1383, and the number of chief pledges was large and fluctuating. A constable occurred in 1492, a constable for Old Brentford and a constable and chief pledge for Little Ealing in 1509, and a constable for Great Ealing and a constable and chief pledge for West Ealing in 1512. From 1522 until 1834 or later one constable, two chief pledges, later called headboroughs, and one aletaster were elected annually for each of Ealing and Old Brentford wards. The vestry paid the expenses of constables and headboroughs in 1798 and 1806.[26]

Between 1791 and 1920 the homage of Ealing manor acted as a standing committee out of court, regulating manorial business and convening public meetings of copyholders.[27] Its continued vitality stemmed from control of the uninclosed waste, which the lord by 1697 could not alienate without consent.[28] The copyholders maintained the commons as an amenity and spent income from any grants of the waste on charitable purposes.

New Brentford lay within Boston manor. Westminster abbey in 1294 claimed that the manor was part of the liberty where it exercised extensive rights, including view of frankpledge and the assize of bread and of ale, although those rights, with tumbril, were also claimed by the priory of St. Helen, Bishopsgate.[29] A view of frankpledge and court for Brentford were held at Westminster in 1364 and 1365, in June,[30] and a solitary roll recorded a view of frankpledge and court baron in 1614.[31] In the late 17th and early 18th century a court for Boston 'with West Brentford' was usually held in April, often at the Red Lion or the Three Pigeons. Meetings, described sometimes as those of a court leet with view of frankpledge followed by a court baron, later became less frequent: there were 10 between 1743 and 1805 and 4, all at the Three Pigeons, between 1811 and the last recorded court in 1842.[32] There was a constable and a bailiff in 1378.[33] Officers elected in 1614 and 1692 were 2 constables, 2 headboroughs, 2 aleconners, 2 flesh

[7] Brentford and Chiswick Boro. *Ind. of Brentford and Chiswick* [1948]; Newton, 'Brentford', 46.
[8] Brentford and Chiswick Boro. *Official Guide* [1963].
[9] *P.O. Dir. Lond.* (1975).
[10] Brentford and Chiswick Industrial Exhib. *Official Cat.* (1950).
[11] Mdx. Educ. Cttee., Brentford and Chiswick Youth Employment Cttee. *Rep. 1949–50.*
[12] Brentford and Chiswick Boro. *Ind. of Brentford and Chiswick* [1948].
[13] *Architects Jnl.* 28 Aug. 1958; *Builder,* 8 Aug. 1958,
[14] Hounslow L.B. *Official Guide and Ind. Review* [1968].
[15] Ibid. (1972).
[16] Inf. from Rank Pullin Controls.
[17] Hounslow L.B. *Official Guide and Ind. Review* [1968].
[18] Inf. from the records officer, B.O.C. International Ltd.
[19] Mdx. Educ. Cttee., Brentford and Chiswick Youth Employment Cttee. *Rep. 1950–1.*

[20] *Daily Mail,* 1 Feb. 1947; *Builder,* 19 Aug. 1955; *Beechams in Brief* [c. 1971].
[21] Inf. from Beecham Group Ltd.
[22] Inf. from Strand Glassfibre Ltd.
[23] Inf. from Polco Products Ltd.
[24] *Plac. de Quo Warr.* (Rec. Com.), 475.
[25] Para. based on ct. rolls and bks. for manor of Fulham including Ealing or for Ealing separately: Guildhall MSS. 10312/36–117 (1383–1682); ibid. 10465/1–228 (1681–1951); P.R.O., SC 2/188/65–81 (1384–1462); SC 2/189/1–34 (1469–1612); SC 2/190/1–16.
[26] Allison and Holt, *Ealing in 18th and 19th Cent.* 2.
[27] Para. based on M.R.O., Acc. 538/1/46/1. [28] Ibid. 2.
[29] P.R.O., JUST 1/543, rot. 39; JUST 1/544, rot. 51d.
[30] W.A.M. 50699–700.
[31] P.R.O., WARD 2/44/2; Howard, 'Boston Man.', app. I.
[32] Chiswick libr., Boston man. ct. bk. (1692–1842).
[33] *Cal. Close,* 1377–81, 211.

St. Lawrence's Chapel in 1796

Brentford Bridge in 1802

BRENTFORD

St. Mary's Church in 1809

St. Mary's Church in 1890

EALING

and fish tasters, a leather searcher, a leather sealer, and a registrar; from 1692 there was also a pinder. A bailiff and 2 affeerors were added in 1786 and all the offices were filled as late as 1792.[34] A court baron was held for Coldhall or West Ealing manor from 1504 to 1722.[35]

PARISH GOVERNMENT TO 1836.[36] Ealing vestry met from two to four times a year between 1704 and 1715, with from 5 to 19 attenders.[37] In the early 19th century it was thinly attended, except on special occasions, and met at the Cross House, north of Ealing church, possibly the former church house.[38] A new Cross House, often called simply the vestry room, was built in St. Mary's churchyard in 1840 and replaced in 1880 by the vestry hall in Ranelagh Road.

Churchwardens and overseers were recorded in 1599[39] and two surveyors of the highways in 1654.[40] There were separate overseers for Upper Side (Ealing) and Lower Side (Old Brentford) by 1675,[41] one churchwarden and one overseer being elected for each from 1798 and two overseers for each from 1834. An assistant overseer was employed in 1812. Highway trustees, under an Act of 1767, were elected by the vestry, with which they were often at variance. The office of vestry clerk, filled by Thomas Jullion from 1796 until 1834, lapsed in 1836 but may have existed in an honorary capacity until its revival shortly before Ealing adopted the Vestry Clerk's Act in 1869.[42] There was a beadle by 1797, whose duties were defined in 1808 and 1833, and a parish clerk in 1654,[43] whose office in 1802 was combined with that of sexton. A separate parish clerk was appointed for Old Brentford in 1829 and in 1839 two unpaid sextons were appointed, one for each ward. Other officers included the keeper of the church clock in 1806, the overseers' messenger in 1836, and the bellringer in 1865.

Poverty was not serious in 1599, when the impotent poor were supported by a weekly rate distributed by the churchwardens and overseers. Able-bodied paupers were set to work, with the aid of £5 which had been collected, and the parish officers knew of no vagabond who had not been apprehended.[44]

The poor of each ward[45] were relieved by its overseer until 1814, when they were administered jointly by the assistant overseer. By 1698 poverty was causing concern[46] and in 1724–5 the vestry ordered that casual relief was to cease and that no outsiders should settle without certificates. The

building of a workhouse did not eliminate outdoor relief. Paupers increased greatly during the 18th century, as did the poor rates, which stood at 4s. or 5s. in the £ in the 1790s and even higher later. There were 20 regular pensioners between 1789 and 1792 and 141, including 59 widows, in 1832. After 1750 there were increases in settlement litigation and in the apprenticing of poor boys, generally with small premiums. Bread was distributed at times of dearth, and in 1832 paupers were helped to emigrate.[47]

A workhouse and stock for the poor to work on were to be provided in 1698, whereupon a house for 8 poor was acquired in 1701. After abortive plans for its extension, a new workhouse was built west of St. Mary's Lane in 1728. Its supplies were arranged by the vestry,[48] which often dismissed the master. The inmates were employed at spinning and later at casual labour, but their work was never profitable: tools were lacking, men were outnumbered by women, and women by children. There were 30 beds in 1743–4 but before 1750 the number of inmates reached 64 on occasion. There were 48 inmates in 1754, 17 in 1760, 86 in 1779, 142 in 1785, and 175 in 1801. In 1797 the workhouse was badly overcrowded. In 1803, when there were 150 inmates for 55 beds, the parish vainly promoted a Bill to take over 14 a. of common at Ealing Dean for a workhouse,[49] and in 1812 the existing workhouse was enlarged. Its state was found acceptable in 1820[50] and again in 1836, when it could accommodate 360 and had only 84 inmates. The buildings were sold in 1839[51] but partly survived in 1979. Sums spent on the poor rose steeply from £720 in 1776 to an average of £1,316 from 1783 to 1785;[52] they were £2,886 in 1834–5 and £2,003 in 1835–6.[53]

New Brentford was governed separately from the rest of Hanwell by 1621, when the vestry of the chapelry decided to make its own officers more accountable. Two chapelwardens, one of them nominated by the minister, 2 overseers of the poor, also called collectors before 1641, and 2 surveyors of the highways were elected annually, usually at a meeting in the chapel in April.[54] There was a sexton, paid quarterly, by 1694, a uniformed beadle by 1752, and a salaried vestry clerk[55] and a salaried organist in 1814. The vestry also elected constables and headboroughs from 1815.[56] Chapelwardens' accounts, including orders of the vestry, exist for 1615–1814,[57] together with overseers' accounts ('poor's books')

[34] P.R.O., WARD 2/44/2; Boston man. ct. bk. (1692–1842).
[35] M.R.O., EMC 126.
[36] Chwdns. acct. bks. (1721–75, 1797–8, 1820–30) and vestry min. bks. (1797–1885, 1895–1927) are at Ealing town hall.
[37] Next two paras. based on Allison and Holt, Ealing in 18th and 19th Cent., which includes abstracts from the vestry min. bks.
[38] Mdx. County Times, 22, 29 Mar., 12 Apr. 1952.
[39] Allison, Ealing Census, 10.
[40] M.R.O., Acc. 890, p. 22.
[41] Jackson, Ealing, 40.
[42] Lond. Gaz. 24 Sept. 1869, p. 5194.
[43] M.R.O., Acc. 890, p. 19; vestry min. bk. (1832–60), pp. 66–7.
[44] Allison, Ealing Census, 10.
[45] Next two paras. based on Lightning, Ealing and the

Poor. Poor rate bks. (1674–1862, with a few gaps), highway rate bks. (1767–1874), and workho. acct. bks. (1728–1836, with gaps) are at Ealing town hall.
[46] Jackson, Ealing, 150.
[47] Allison and Holt, Ealing in 18th and 19th Cent. 27.
[48] e.g. vestry min. bk. (1832–60), pp. 32–3.
[49] Allison and Holt, Ealing in 18th and 19th Cent. 16–17; Ealing Workho. Bill at Ealing libr.
[50] Allison and Holt, Ealing in 18th and 19th Cent. 21, 23.
[51] M.R.O., BG/B/1, pp. 13 sqq.
[52] Abstract of Returns by Overseers, 1787, H.C. 1st ser. ix, p. 628.
[53] Poor Law Com. 2nd Rep. H.C. 595–II, pp. 214–15 (1836), xxix.
[54] Brentford libr., New Brentford MS. 17512.
[55] Ibid. MSS. 17514, 17516, 17518.
[56] Ibid. MS. 17825.
[57] Ibid. MSS. 17512–18.

for 1617–61 and 1714–1808,[58] vestry minutes for 1814–64, and constables' accounts for 1688–1710.[59]

The chapelwardens' funds were spent partly on the poor in the early 17th century, being supplemented by money raised at the Whitsuntide games,[60] although there was already a separate poor rate.[61] New Brentford was comparatively backward in its poor relief in 1733,[62] when pauper children were boarded out with the master and mistress of the charity school. A poor house on the Ham common was to be inspected regularly by the beadle in 1753, when the vestry also rented other houses for the poor, and was adapted as a workhouse in 1757, when those who refused to enter were to have their pensions stopped.[63] The workhouse, with a maximum of 27 inmates in 1758–9 and 32 in 1760–1,[64] was usually managed directly by the vestry, which considered quarterly tenders from local tradesmen. The poor were farmed, however, from 1796 to 1807 and again from 1832;[65] out pensions, at first disguised as casual relief, were resumed from 1785–6.[66] Money spent on the poor of New Brentford totalled £334 in 1776, an average of £383 from 1783 to 1785,[67] £907 in 1834–5, and £817 in 1835–6.[68] Originally leased, the workhouse was conveyed to the chapelry in reversion by James Clitherow in 1796. A confinement room for riotous inmates was to be added in 1787 and the building was ordered to be sold in 1838.[69]

LOCAL GOVERNMENT AFTER 1836. Both Ealing and New Brentford were included in Brentford poor law union in 1836.[70] The parish continued to elect trustees of the highways,[71] who were consulted by a committee of the vestry in 1859 before it recommended adoption of the Local Government Act, 1858.[72] Six inspectors were appointed in 1851, after adoption of the lighting provisions of the Lighting and Watching Act, 1833, for Ealing village, and a further nine were appointed in 1857, for the lighting of an area farther south.[73] Agitation for a local board of health was repeatedly frustrated by Old Brentford, with the result that in 1863 the highway trustees were superseded by a local board only in that part of Upper Side extending a furlong north of the G.W.R. line. Northern Ealing, being rural, was not included until 1873, when the board's membership was raised from 9 to 12.[74]

In 1894 Ealing became a U.D.C. and in 1901 the first municipal borough in Middlesex, with 6

aldermen and 18 councillors representing 6 wards: Drayton, Castlebar, and Mount Park north of Uxbridge Road, Lammas, Manor, and Grange to the south.[75] Ealing absorbed Hanwell U.D. and Greenford U.D., which included Perivale and West Twyford, in 1926, and Northolt in 1928. There were 15 wards in 1950, represented by 45 councillors and 15 aldermen,[76] and 16 wards from 1960 with 48 councillors and 16 aldermen. A Bill to achieve county borough status was defeated in 1952[77] and Ealing, Acton, and Southall boroughs united in 1965 to form Ealing L.B. The council consisted of 10 aldermen and 60 councillors, representing 20 wards.[78] Conservatives, who had dominated Ealing M.B.,[79] won control of Ealing L.B. from Labour between 1968 and 1971 and again in 1978.[80]

BOROUGH OF EALING. *Parted chevronwise gules and argent, in dexter chief two crossed swords and in sinister chief three seaxes all proper pommelled and hilted or; and in the base an oak tree eradicated proper*

[Granted 1902]

Ealing local board first met at Cross House. The officers worked above a shop in High Street[81] and consisted of a clerk and the local historian Charles Jones (d. 1913), who, as engineer and surveyor, planned much of suburban Ealing.[82] They moved c. 1866 to the corner of Railway Approaches and the Broadway, and later offices and an engine house, designed by Jones, were built on the corner of the Mall, where the offices survived in 1980 as the National Westminster Bank. The existing town hall in Uxbridge Road,[83] of stone and designed in the Gothic style by Jones, was opened in 1889 and greatly extended in 1930 and later by G. H. Fellowes Prynne.[84] In 1979 it housed the main municipal offices of Ealing L.B. except those of the engineer, surveyor, and architect, which were at no. 24 Uxbridge Road, those of the chief education officer at Hadley House (nos. 79–81), and the children's department, at no. 26 Castlebar Road.

New Brentford had three surveyors of the highways in 1853.[85] From 1874 Brentford as a whole was governed by its own 12-member

[58] Ibid. 17608–17; acct. bks. 1722–9 and 1826–42 in care of vicar.
[59] New Brentford MSS. 17825, 17785.
[60] Ibid. MS. 17512; above, social. For details of poor relief 1720–1834 see *T.L.M.A.S.* xxiii. 174–89.
[61] New Brentford MS. 17608.
[62] *T.L.M.A.S.* xxiii. 176.
[63] New Brentford MS. 17516.
[64] Ibid. 17618 (poor ho. accts. 1757–69).
[65] *T.L.M.A.S.* xxiii. 184.   [66] Ibid. 183.
[67] *Abstract of Returns by Overseers, 1787*, 142.
[68] *Poor Law Com. 2nd Rep.* 212–13.
[69] New Brentford MSS. 17516–18, 17825; *6th Rep. Com. Char.* 351.
[70] *Poor Law Com. 2nd Rep.* 533.
[71] e.g. vestry min. bk. (1832–60), pp. 116, 177.
[72] Ibid. p. 330.
[73] Ibid. pp. 285, 314; below, pub. svces.

[74] Jackson, *Ealing*, 289 sqq.; *Lond. Gaz.* 17 Mar. 1863, p. 1517; 14 Apr. 1863, p. 2019; 36 & 37 Vic. c. 1 (Local Act).
[75] Jones, *Ealing*, 166–7.
[76] Ealing Boro. *Year Bk. and Diary* (1949–50, 1960–1).
[77] *The Times*, 2, 15 Nov. 1951; 498 *H.C. Deb.* 5th ser. 477–534.
[78] Lond. Govt. Act, 1963, c. 33; Ealing L.B. *Official Guide* [1966].
[79] *The Times*, 2 Nov. 1934; 3 Nov. 1936; 14 May 1949; 12 May 1950.
[80] Ibid. 9 May 1964; 11 May 1968; 14 May 1971; 4 May 1974; 6 May 1978.
[81] Jones, *Ealing*, 38; Jackson, *Ealing*, 292–3.
[82] *The Times*, 18 July 1913; *Ealing As It Was*, illus. 20.
[83] Jones, *Ealing*, 38 sqq., 177; Jackson, *Ealing*, 293–4; *Ealing As It Was*, illus. 29.
[84] *Ealing As It Was*, illus. 22; *Builder*, cxl (24 Apr. 1931); Robbins, *Mdx.* 239.   [85] *Mason's Dir. Brentford* (1853).

local board of health, which was superseded by Brentford U.D.C., itself united with Chiswick U.D.C. in 1927. The local board's offices were at the market house, also the seat of the county court and petty sessions, in 1890, as were those of the U.D.C. in 1908.[86] From 1907 the courts sat at the vestry hall in the Half Acre, built in 1899, and later, before amalgamation with Chiswick, the council used Clifden House, Boston Manor Road. Clifden House was demolished in 1953 and the former vestry hall in 1963.[87]

LONDON BOROUGH OF EALING.
Argent, an oak tree proper fructed or growing out of a grassy mount; on a chief gules three Saxon crowns or
[Granted 1965]

The Redistribution of Seats Act, 1885, established the Ealing parliamentary division of Middlesex, which included Ealing Upper Side, Acton, Chiswick, Greenford, and Perivale.[88] It always returned a Conservative or Unionist, as did the separate constituency of Ealing between the World Wars.[89] In 1945 Ealing M.B. was divided into Ealing East, which included most of the former Upper Side and elected a Conservative, and Ealing West, containing most of the newer additions. Under the Representation of the People Act, 1948, it was again reorganized as Ealing South, containing all Upper Side except Mount Park ward, and Ealing North, which covered the rest. Ealing South was represented by a Conservative from 1950 until 1974 and Ealing North by a Labour member, except between 1955 and 1964. Further reorganization in 1974 divided Ealing L.B. into Southall, thereafter represented by Labour, Ealing North, represented by Labour until 1979, and Acton, which returned a Conservative. That part of Ealing which lay within the local government district of Brentford from 1885 was in the Brentford division, which also included Hanwell, Isleworth, Norwood, and Twickenham,[90] and normally returned a Conservative before the creation of Brentford and Chiswick constituency.[91]

PUBLIC SERVICES. There was a common well at Ealing in 1506.[92] Water was piped to Richard Meux's house from a pond in the early 19th century[93] and, although the Grand Junction Waterworks Co. had laid pipes to Ealing by 1850,[94] most households still depended on shallow wells in 1863.[95] The Grand Junction Waterworks Co. had been authorized in 1835 to build a pumping station near Kew bridge,[96] where the works included a 150-ft. chimney by 1845.[97] Its water, drawn from the Thames at Hampton from the 1850s,[98] supplied Acton, Chiswick, and the south part of Ealing parish under an Act of 1861[99] and the whole of Ealing by 1890.[1] Fox reservoir, with a capacity of 3 million gallons, was erected north of Hill Crest Road, Hanger Hill, in 1888 and a neighbouring reservoir for 50 million gallons was constructed c. 1889.[2] The company was superseded by the Metropolitan Water Board under an Act of 1902 and Fox reservoir, disused by 1946, was filled in during the 1970s.[3]

Ealing's ditches were so offensive in 1809 that the copyholders voted £300 for improvements to be effected by the highway trustees.[4] Several schemes were debated from 1854 and a sewer rate was levied by the vestry for the metropolitan commissioners of sewers from 1857 to 1860 but probably no work was done before the establishment of Ealing local board.[5] A sewage farm for the southern district was opened at South Ealing Road in 1863 and extended in 1868, 1874, and 1881, and a 22-a. farm for the northern district was constructed beside the Brent in 1872.[6] Under Brentford's drainage and sewerage works, completed in 1884, sewage was collected in the Town meadow and pumped to South Ealing Road. There the sewage was treated, the sludge being dried in filter presses and the effluent discharged into the Thames through a culvert along Clayponds Lane.[7] Although the northern works were sometimes flooded,[8] Ealing was credited with the first efficient scheme in the Thames Valley that prevented pollution of the Thames.[9] In 1936 the West Middlesex Sewerage and Sewage Disposal Scheme was inaugurated, with central works at Mogden in Isleworth, and the Ealing works were superseded.[10]

Ealing had an engine house in 1781 and parish fire engines in 1782 and 1784.[11] An engine was acquired for Upper Side in 1835[12] and kept near St. Mary's church in 1853,[13] but was obsolete c. 1863. A volunteer fire brigade used two manual engines in 1870[14] and a house in Broadway was

[86] *Kelly's Dir. Mdx.* (1890, 1908, 1926).
[87] *Brentford and Chiswick As It Was*, illus. 9, 13.
[88] 48 & 49 Vic. c. 23.
[89] Rest of para. based on C. Hankinson, *Political Hist. of Ealing 1832–1971* (1971); *Whitaker's Almanack* (1890 and later edns.).
[90] 48 & 49 Vic. c. 23.
[91] Above, Chiswick, local govt.
[92] P.R.O., SC 2/189/15, m. 1d.
[93] M.R.O., Acc. 1028/89.
[94] *Mdx. County Times*, 4 Aug. 1888.
[95] Jackson, *Ealing*, 291.
[96] H. W. Dickinson, *Water Supply of Gtr. Lond.* (1954), 100.
[97] *P.O. Dir. Six Home Counties* (1845).
[98] Dickinson, *Water Supply*, 100.
[99] 24 & 25 Vic. c. 151.

[1] *Kelly's Dir. Mdx.* (1890).
[2] *W. Lond. Sketcher*, 1 Apr. 1889.
[3] Cuttings and photos. at Ealing libr.
[4] M.R.O., Acc. 538/1/46/1.
[5] Allison and Holt, *Ealing in 18th and 19th Cent.* 9; vestry min. bk. (1832–60), pp. 316, 319.
[6] C. Jones, *20 Years Devel. of a Lond. Suburb* (1884), 4–8; Jones, *Ealing*, 181–2.
[7] *Kelly's Dir. Mdx.* (1890).
[8] e.g. Ealing U.D. *Rep. of M.O.H.* (1903).
[9] Jackson, *Ealing*, 291; *Mdx. County Times*, 4 Aug. 1883.
[10] C. Radcliffe, *Mdx.* (2nd edn. c. 1951), 148–9; Mdx.C.C. *West Mdx. Main Drainage Scheme Inauguration* (1936).
[11] M.R.O., D.R.O. 37/B1/2, 3.
[12] Allison and Holt, *Ealing in 18th and 19th Cent.* 10, 30.
[13] *Mason's Dir. Brentford* (1853).
[14] M.R.O., D.R.O. 37/A12/5.

thereafter manned by professional firemen.[15] A fire station was built at Longfield Avenue in 1888 and extended in 1901-2, when, as in 1908, another station near St. Mary's church was manned by volunteers.[16] In 1933 a central station was built on the corner of Uxbridge and St. Leonard's roads,[17] where it survived in 1979. At New Brentford two engines, kept under the chapel belfry, had suffered from inexpert handling in 1738.[18] There was an engine house in the Ham by 1853,[19] a volunteer fire brigade from 1868,[20] and a fire station in High Street in 1908 and 1926.[21]

Land at New Brentford for a cage, stocks, and whipping post was sought in 1720.[22] A cage was to be built or rebuilt in 1753; a watch box for the beadle was to be set up near the market house and a new stocks provided in 1787.[23] There was a cage at Ealing in 1781[24] and the copyholders built a watch house in 1804.[25] Both Ealing and Brentford had cages in 1813.[26] Ealing, with the township of New Brentford, lay within the Metropolitan Police Area from 1829.[27] The Ealing cage adjoined the engine house near the church.[28] Premises in Uxbridge Road were to be leased for the police in 1836 and were replaced by a new station in 1875 at no. 5 High Street, itself superseded in 1965 by one at nos. 67-9 Uxbridge Road.[29] At Brentford the cage stood on the corner of Ferry Lane and High Street in 1839[30] and there was a police station at no. 42 High Street by 1890.[31] A new station on the site of the vestry hall was opened in 1966.[32]

Lighting in Brentford High Street was to be provided in 1767.[33] Gas[34] was first supplied in 1821 by J. and E. Barlow, who built a works on the north side of the street, in Old Brentford, and were to light the turnpike road to Kensington. They were superseded later in 1821 by Felix Booth's new Brentford Gas Co., which was to serve Brentford, Chiswick, and neighbouring parishes to east and west.[35] Brentford itself was 'well lighted' in 1832[36] but it was not until demand rose after 1840 that daytime supplies were available and that the company extended its area northward to Ealing, in 1846, and Acton, in 1850. The lighting provisions of the Lighting and Watching Act, 1833, were adopted in 1851 for Ealing village, from the boys' National school northward to the Feathers in Uxbridge Road,[37]

and were extended in 1857 as far south as Gunnersbury Lane and Little Ealing.[38] Brentford gasworks, supplemented by another at Southall from 1869,[39] often drew adverse comment for polluting both the river and the air.[40] After taking over neighbouring concerns, Brentford Gas Co. was itself taken over in 1926 by the Gas Light and Coke Co., which on nationalization in 1949 was succeeded by the North Thames Gas Board.[41] Production ceased at the works, which had been gradually extended on both sides of High Street, in 1963.[42]

Applications by two companies in 1888 to supply electricity to Ealing were opposed by the local board, which itself obtained powers in 1891.[43] A works by Messrs. Bramwell & Harris was opened off South Ealing Road in 1894. Built to a new design, to use waste heat and effluent from the adjoining sewage farm, it was extended in 1897[44] and 1923.[45] From 1950, after nationalization and the closure of the works, electricity was supplied by the Southern Electricity Board.[46] Under an Act of 1905 Brentford was served by the Brentford Electricity Supply Co.[47]

A burial board appointed for Ealing and Old Brentford in 1858 acquired 8 a. east of South Ealing Road[48] in 1860, which were laid out as a cemetery in 1861. Chapels for Anglicans and dissenters, forming a single building, had been built by 1873 and the area had been extended to 21 a. by 1890.[49]

A parish nurse was employed for Ealing in 1727-8 and a surgeon or apothecary from 1760.[50] Ealing Provident dispensary was opened in 1869 at Minton Lodge, Ealing Dean, and had a branch dispensary at Ealing Green between 1888 and 1906. Ealing cottage hospital opened at Minton Lodge in 1871 and was enlarged in 1873 and, to 16 beds, in 1886. It was rebuilt in 1893 with 19 beds and a dispensary and replaced in 1911 by the new King Edward Memorial hospital, Mattock Lane, itself enlarged from 40 to 70 beds by 1915. Extensions between 1927 and 1937 increased the beds to 145 and nearby houses raised the total to 160 by 1945.[51] King Edward's was included in the National Health Service from 1948, was managed by the North-West Metropolitan Regional Hospital Board in 1950,[52] and lay within the Ealing, Hammersmith, and Hounslow area of the North-West Thames

[15] Jones, *Ealing*, 126.
[16] Ibid. 127, 180; *Kelly's Dir. Mdx.* (1908).
[17] *The Times*, 24 Oct. 1933.
[18] New Brentford MS. 17516.
[19] *Mason's Dir. Brentford* (1853).
[20] M.R.O., D.R.O. 37/A12/5.
[21] *Kelly's Dir. Mdx.* (1908, 1926).
[22] Boston man. ct. bk. (1692-1842), f. 34.
[23] New Brentford MSS. 17516-17.
[24] M.R.O., D.R.O. 37/B1/2.
[25] Ibid. Acc. 538/1/46/1.
[26] Allison and Holt, *Ealing in 18th and 19th Cent.* 10.
[27] 10 Geo. IV, c. 44.
[28] M.R.O., TA/EAL.
[29] Inf. from P. C. Jephcote; *Ealing As It Was*, illus. 43.
[30] M.R.O., TA/EAL.
[31] *Kelly's Dir. Mdx.* (1890).
[32] *Brentford and Chiswick As It Was*, illus. 9.
[33] 7 Geo. III, c. 75.
[34] Para. based on M.R.O., Acc. 880 and inf. from Mr. E. Kenward.
[35] 1 & 2 Geo. IV, c. 69 (Local and Personal).

[36] Pigot, *Com. Dir.* (1832-4).
[37] Allison and Holt, *Ealing in 18th and 19th Cent.* 35.
[38] Vestry min. bk. (1832-60), pp. 285, 314.
[39] *V.C.H. Mdx.* iv. 47.
[40] e.g. Thorne, *Environs*, 58.
[41] M.R.O., Acc. 638; Acc. 880/114-21.
[42] *Brentford and Chiswick As It Was*, illus. 1, 24.
[43] Jackson, *Ealing*, 296-7; 54 & 55 Vic. c. 50 (Local).
[44] Jones, *Ealing*, 123-4; Jackson, *Ealing*, 296-7; *Electrical Engineer*, 28 Sept. 1894.
[45] *The Times*, 15 Apr. 1924.
[46] Ealing Boro. *Official Guide* (1950 and later edns.).
[47] 5 Edw. VII, c. 192 (Local).
[48] Allison and Holt, *Ealing in 18th and 19th Cent.* 38; Jackson, *Ealing*, 298; Ealing par. *New Burial Ground: Letter from Vicar* (1860); Guildhall MS. 12337.
[49] *Kelly's Dir. Mdx.* (1890); O.S. Map 6", XV. SE. (1873 edn.).
[50] MS. agreement at Ealing libr.
[51] *67th Ann. Rep. of K. Edw. Hosp.* (1937); C. M. Tippett, *Short Hist. of K. Edw. Mem. Hosp.*, Ealing (1976).
[52] *Ealing 1901-51*, ed. Scouse, 79.

Regional Health Authority in 1978, when it had 128 beds.[53] It was superseded by a new hospital in Hanwell in 1979.[54]

Ealing isolation hospital, South Ealing Road, opened in 1884 and was extended to provide 12 permanent beds and 12 in a temporary wing by 1902 and 55 beds by 1911.[55] In 1921, following the formation of the Ealing and Chiswick joint hospital committee, it became the isolation hospital for both Ealing and Chiswick, to which Brentford isolation hospital was also annexed; from c. 1937 it included the former Clayponds maternity hospital,[56] which had been established in 1904 as an isolation hospital for Chiswick in Clayponds Lane, close to Ealing's isolation hospital, and became the maternity hospital for both Ealing and Chiswick in 1921. After its replacement by Perivale maternity hospital the buildings were annexed to Chiswick and Ealing isolation hospital,[57] which in 1978, with 128 beds, formed a branch of King Edward Memorial hospital.[58]

In 1932 no. 10 Castlebar Hill was given by Sir John Smith Young to the Central London Throat hospital, later the Royal National Throat, Nose and Ear hospital, and was named the Dame Gertrude Young Memorial convalescent home. It had 26 beds for post-operative patients in 1961, was used by the North-West Metropolitan Regional Hospital Board as a geriatric hospital in 1964, and became a hostel for patients awaiting operation in 1976–7. No. 8 Castlebar Hill, acquired in 1953, contained 10 parents and 7 deaf children in 1978. No. 6, acquired in 1960 for infants with hearing and speech defects, accommodated 12 children in 1978.[59]

The East India Co.'s asylum for insane employees was moved by the India Office in 1870 from Hackney to Elm Grove, Ealing, which was renamed the Royal India Asylum. The asylum was closed in 1892 and its 75 inmates were transferred elsewhere.[60]

The Sisters of Charity opened Kent House, Castlebar Hill, in 1920 as St. David's Home for disabled ex-servicemen, which was substantially extended between 1925 and 1929.[61]

At New Brentford a doctor's bill was paid by the overseers in 1714.[62] Attendance for accidents was considered too costly in 1822 and tenders for treating the poor were sought in 1835.[63] A dispensary was established in 1818 opposite St. Lawrence's church in High Street. A house at the entrance to the Butts was acquired in 1891 as a dispensary, cottage hospital, and nurses'

home, and was so used until the opening of Brentford hospital in Boston Manor Road in 1928. Brentford hospital closed in 1977, when it was to be converted into an old people's home.[64]

Brentford isolation hospital, Pottery Road, Clayponds Lane, was opened between 1890 and 1908 and later annexed to Chiswick and Ealing isolation hospital.[65]

Ealing adopted the Public Libraries Act, 1855, and opened a library at Ashton Villa, the Green, in 1883.[66] The library moved in 1888 to premises near the town hall and in 1902 to Pitzhanger manor house,[67] which had been adapted as the central library and which was extended in 1940. West Ealing branch library opened in 1903 at Melbourne Avenue, Pitshanger library in 1948 in shops in Pitshanger Lane, Hanger Hill library in 1955 in a shop at no. 11 Abbey Parade,[68] moving in 1963 to Fernlea House, Hanger Lane, and Northfields library in 1960 in Northfield Avenue. Hanger Hill library closed in 1980.[69]

Brentford adopted the Public Libraries Act in 1889.[70] A library opened at Clifden House in 1890 and moved to its existing premises next door, opened by Andrew Carnegie, in 1904.[71]

Public baths for Ealing were built in Longfield Avenue in 1884 and had been enlarged by 1908, when there were also slipper baths in Williams Road.[72] There were swimming baths at both sites and at Murray Road in 1965.[73] Baths by the Brent, to replace those in Longfield Avenue, were being built in 1980.[74] Brentford public baths, Clifden Road, were opened in 1896[75] and still used in 1965.[76]

Open spaces administered by Ealing M.B. in 1904 totalled c. 117 a. They consisted of Ealing common of 47 a., Haven Green of 7 a., Lammas park, bought by the local board in 1881, of 25 a., Walpole park, opened in 1901, of 30 a., and Drayton Green and Ealing Green commons, each of 4 a. In the north Pitshanger park of c. 26 a. and Hanger Hill park of 5 a. had been added by 1911, as had Dean gardens, 3 a. converted from allotments at West Ealing.[77] By 1960 Ealing M.B., after its absorption of Greenford and neighbouring parishes, contained more than 1,100 a. of open space, excluding the 186 a. of Gunnersbury park which Ealing controlled jointly with Acton and with Brentford and Chiswick.[78] At Brentford 38 a. around Boston House were bought by Brentford U.D.C. and opened in 1924 as Boston Manor park.[79]

[53] *Hospitals Year Bk.* (1978).
[54] Inf. from Mr. P. Hounsell.
[55] Jones, *Ealing*, 54–5; Jones, *Decade of Progress*, 52.
[56] Brentford, Chiswick and Ealing hosp. cttee. *Official Opening of Clayponds Isolation Hosp.* (1937).
[57] Ibid.
[58] *Hospitals Year Bk.* (1978).
[59] Inf. from the hosp. sec.
[60] A. Faringdon, *Rec. of E. India Coll.*, Haileybury (1976), 127–8.
[61] Inf. from the matron; L. Water, *Story of St. David's* (1977).
[62] New Brentford MS. 17609.
[63] Ibid. 17825.
[64] *Brentford and Chiswick As It Was*, illus. 10.
[65] *Kelly's Dir. Mdx.* (1890, 1908); above.
[66] *Mdx. County Times*, 4 Aug. 1883; Jackson, *Ealing*, 295.

Para. based on 'Ealing L.B. Pub. Librs.' (TS. at Ealing libr.).
[67] Above, manors.
[68] Ealing libr. *Selborne Soc. Libr.* (1958).
[69] Inf. from Mr. P. Hounsell.
[70] Turner, *Brentford*, 154.
[71] *Kelly's Dir. Mdx.* (1890); *Brentford and Chiswick As It Was*, illus. 13.
[72] *Kelly's Dir. Mdx.* (1908).
[73] *P.O. Dir. Lond.* (1965).
[74] Inf. from Mr. P. Hounsell.
[75] *Brentford and Chiswick As It Was*, illus. 15.
[76] *P.O. Dir. Lond.* (1965).
[77] *Ealing: Country Town Near Lond.* 7–9; Jones, *Decade of Progress*, 41.
[78] Ealing Boro. *Official Guide* [c. 1960].
[79] *Kelly's Dir. Mdx.* (1926); Chiswick libr., grangerized copy of Turner, *Brentford*, facing p. 104.

CHURCHES: EALING. The church at Ealing was in the gift of the bishop of London *c.* 1127, when he gave the great tithes to Canon Henry for keeping St. Paul's cathedral school.[80] Later the school was kept by the chancellor of St. Paul's, to whom the bishop appropriated the church in 1308 on condition that he acted as reader of theology at the school. The patronage of the vicarage was reserved to the bishop in 1308 and thereafter remained with him, except during the Interregnum.[81] The church served the whole parish[82] until part of Ealing was assigned to St. George's, Old Brentford, in 1828 and a new district was formed for Christ the Saviour in 1852.

A vicarage was ordained, with a pension of £10, in 1308.[83] A revised arrangement in 1315 assigned to the vicar the house where he lived, part of the glebe, the small tithes, and the offerings; the rector received the great tithes, the rectory house, and most of the glebe.[84] The vicarage was worth £13 6s. 8d. in 1535,[85] £60 in 1650,[86] and between £600 and £700 in 1853.[87] There were 40 a. of vicarial glebe in 1650,[88] part of which was sold *c.* 1900.[89] The small tithes were worth £25 in 1650[90] and £663 in 1799,[91] and were redeemed for £600 rent charge in 1840.[92] In 1530 tithes were assessed by custom as at Hayes[93] and after a dispute in 1708 it was confirmed that there was a modus on cows and calves and that some fodder crops were not tithable.[94] Most of the tithes were compounded in 1799.[95]

The vicarage house of 1315[96] was presumably where its successor stood in 4¾ a. between the Park and Grange and St. Mary's roads in 1915.[97] A red-brick house, said to be 250 years old in 1900,[98] was improved by Colston Carr, vicar 1797–1822, and was commodious in 1816 and 1845.[99] Standing south of the church, it had decayed by 1900 and was rebuilt to an expensive design by W. A. Pite.[1] In 1939 part of the site was sold[2] and in 1969 a new Vicarage was built at no. 11 Church Place, on part of the old burial ground.[3] A church house, recorded from 1492,[4] was leased out in 1611[5] and accommodated the assistant curate in 1797.[6]

Walter, son of the bishop of London, owed 10 marks to Henry I for his judgement concerning Ealing church[7] and may have been rector. Some medieval vicars were pluralists[8] but in the 15th and 16th centuries most were resident at least occasionally.[9] Robert Cooper, vicar from 1638, was replaced *c.* 1645[10] and Thomas Gilbert, vicar 1651–60, a Scottish Congregationalist, was ejected and remembered as proto-martyr of nonconformity.[11] William Beveridge, vicar 1661–73, was later bishop of St. Asaph. William Hall, vicar 1702–16, seldom resided;[12] Dr. Thomas Mangey, vicar 1730–54, a prolific writer,[13] resided more often in his later than in his earlier years;[14] Charles Sturgess, vicar 1773–97, did so for only part of the year.[15] Later vicars were normally resident: Sir Herbert Oakley, Bt. (d. 1845), vicar 1822–34, pioneered modern methods of parochial organization,[16] which E. W. Relton, vicar 1856–86, and his successors greatly extended.[17] From 1719 there was usually an assistant curate.[18] St. Mary's often had two in the 20th century and as many as four in 1907 and 1973–4, but only one in 1980.[19]

The churchwardens held 1 a. in Old Brentford in 1423.[20] Other benefactions[21] included those of Thomas Curtis, vicar 1451–78, who gave a cottage, garden, 5½ a., and an orchard to maintain an obit, and William Turner, vicar 1478–99, who gave 4 a. later called Churchbread for an obit and poor relief.[22] Before 1533 John Buckmaster surrendered a cottage to William Needler to provide an obit, for which in 1541 Needler left a rent charge of 7s. In 1547, in addition to the three obits, there was 1 a. given by one Needler for a lamp and property endowing an unobserved obit of the Ingram family.[23] After the chantry lands had passed to the Crown, those of Turner and Curtis were sold in 1548 to Thomas Tanner and Henry Butcher.[24] In 1629 John Bowman, chancellor of St. Paul's and rector of Ealing, left £40 a year to endow four afternoon sermons at

[80] *Early Charters of St. Paul's* (Camd. 3rd ser. lviii), 216–17.
[81] *Cal. Pat.* 1307–13, 149–50.
[82] Except that in 1297 the manor of Gunnersbury was recorded as belonging to Twyford chapel: below, W. Twyford, church.
[83] *Cal. Pat.* 1307–13, 149.
[84] Ibid. 1313–15, 277–8; *Reg. Baldock, Segrave, Newport and Gravesend* (Cant. & York Soc. vii), 88–91; Hist. MSS. Com. 8, *9th Rep. I*, p. 40.
[85] *Valor Eccl.* (Rec. Com.), i. 434.
[86] *Home Counties Mag.* i. 223.
[87] M.R.O., D.R.O. 37/A12/1 (cover).
[88] *Home Counties Mag.* i. 223.
[89] Gunnersbury Pk. mus., scrapbk. Sabin 62/11/80.
[90] *Home Counties Mag.* i. 223.
[91] M.R.O., D.R.O. 37/A8/1.
[92] Ibid. TA/EAL.
[93] *V.C.H. Mdx.* iv. 34.
[94] P.R.O., E 126/19, ff. 56v.–7, 222 and v.
[95] M.R.O., D.R.O. 37/A8/1.
[96] *Cal. Pat.* 1313–15, 277.
[97] M.R.O., D.R.O. 37/A9/1.
[98] *Mdx. County Times*, 20 Apr. 1935; Gunnersbury Pk. mus., scrapbk. Sabin 62/11/80 (appeal leaflet); see also Jackson, *Ealing*, 216.
[99] Brewer, *Beauties of Eng. & Wales*, x (5), 335; Faulkner, *Brentford, Ealing and Chiswick*, 231.
[1] W. E. Oliver, *20 Years' Retrospect, 1886–1906*.

[2] *Mdx. County Times*, 21 Jan. 1939.
[3] Inf. from the vicar.
[4] P.R.O. SC 2/189/11, rot. 2.
[5] M.R.O., D.R.O. 37/A1/1.
[6] Lysons, *Environs*, ii. 51.
[7] Pipe R. 1130 (P.R.S. i), 146.
[8] Newcourt, *Rep.* i. 763–4.
[9] Guildhall MSS. 9171/9–10, 14–15.
[10] *Walker Revised*, ed. A. G. Matthews, 259. Probably dead by 1648, although often said to have been reinstated in 1660, e.g. Faulkner, *Brentford, Ealing and Chiswick*, 179.
[11] E. Calamy, *Nonconformist's Memorial*, ed. S. Palmer (1802), ii. 446; *D.N.B.*
[12] Jackson, *Ealing*, 43.
[13] *D.N.B.*; Faulkner, *Brentford, Ealing and Chiswick*, 179–80.
[14] Jackson, *Ealing*, 44.
[15] Guildhall MS. 9557A, p. 35.
[16] *D.N.B.*
[17] Above, social.
[18] Guildhall MSS. 9550, 9557A.
[19] *Crockford* (1907 and later edns.).
[20] Guildhall MS. 11766, f. 19v.
[21] e.g. ibid. 9171/1, f. 425; 8, f. 196; P.R.O., PROB 11/14 (P.C.C. 41 Holgrave, will of Hen. Frowyk).
[22] P.R.O., E 301/34, no. 156.
[23] Guildhall MS. 9171/10, f. 212; P.R.O., SC 2/189/21, rot. 5; ibid. E 301/34, no. 156.
[24] P.R.O., E 318/26/1461.

Ealing church, to be delivered by a licensed lecturer.[25] The lectureship was held by the vicar in 1869, when it was intended that the stipend should be spent on an assistant curate.[26] Seven parishioners were excommunicated by the vicar for recusancy and incontinence[27] in 1613 and services were disturbed in 1653 and 1655.[28] E. W. Relton preached frequently against Rome, yet in 1866 he saved a new reredos; the reredos was considered Romanist, as were other ornaments in the new church, particularly a cross in the chancel.[29] There were attendances of 350 in the morning and 300 in the afternoon on census Sunday 1851[30] and of 733 in the morning and 610 in the afternoon on one Sunday in 1903.[31]

The church of *ST. MARY*, called St. Mary of the Assumption in 1446,[32] stands at the south end of St. Mary's Road, at least the second building on the site. A church stood there in the late 14th century and included a nave, chancel, and north chapel or Little Ealing aisle;[33] there was also a chapel of St. Anne, containing an image of the Holy Trinity in 1504, where the Frowyks were buried.[34] A bell tower, mentioned in 1490, was rebuilt or enlarged c. 1495.[35] There were lights in 1408 to St. Mary, described in 1464 as Our Lady of Pity, St. Catherine, and St. Nicholas,[36] in 1419 to the Holy Cross,[37] from 1468 to St. Christopher, in 1471 to St. Anthony, and from 1473 to All Souls.[38] There was a rood by 1445[39] and a feretory by 1490.[40] The church required frequent repair in the 1650s[41] and was so ruinous c. 1675 that services were held elsewhere for several years. Worshippers moved to a wooden tabernacle in 1726 and the steeple fell in 1729, destroying the church.[42]

A brief for rebuilding was obtained in 1733[43] and the shell of the fabric was complete in 1739, when an Act permitted borrowing on security of the rates.[44] Opened in 1740,[45] the new church was of brick to a plain design by James Horne and seated 1,070 in 1828.[46] It was simple in plan, with no chancel and the west tower and north-west vestry standing in the body of the church. A double row of windows lit galleries along three sides.[47] A cupola was added to the tower in 1754 but removed in 1838,[48] and the seating was increased c. 1810 and again in 1824, when there were extensive repairs.[49] The church was still regarded favourably in 1822[50] but seen as unsightly in 1861, when repairs and more seating were needed.

The existing church, of brown brick with coloured brick and stone dressings, consists of an apsidal aisled chancel with ambulatory, north organ chamber and vestries, clerestoried nave with processional aisles, south baptistery, north porch, west tower, and west porch. The 18th-century church was remodelled and extended between 1865 and 1873 in a Venetian style by S. S. Teulon. The roof was raised, window tracery, stained glass, and buttresses were inserted, and the chancel and many other parts were added. Only a projected west spire was omitted.[51] In 1920 a new chapel was dedicated[52] and in 1935 the vestries were enlarged.[53] The church was restored in 1955[54] and the church lounge was added on the south in 1959 and much enlarged as the parish centre in 1977–8,[55] when Ealing L.B. bought the parish hall of 1884 in Warwick Road.[56] Modern architectural assessments of the church are unfavourable.[57]

The ancient pillared font was replaced in 1743.[58] There is a brass of c. 1490 to Richard Amondesham or Awnsham and an alabaster tablet to Richard Taverner (d. 1638).[59] Other monuments include those to Oliver Stapleton (d. 1811) by T. and G. Marshall, to Thomas Smith (d. 1823) by Sarah Holmes of Brentford, to Richard Gray (d. 1825) by William Pistell, to Sir Jonathan Miles (d. 1821) by Charles Regnart, to Henry Beaufoy (d. 1795) by Richard Westmacott the elder, and to Charles Hutchinson (d. 1828) by Sir Richard Westmacott.[60] Among those buried in the church or churchyard were John Oldmixon (1673–1742) and Robert Orme (1728–1801), historians, Dr. William King (1685–1763), Jacobite and principal of St. Mary Hall, Oxford, Sir Frederick Morton Eden, Bt. (1766–1809), writer on the poor, and John Horne Tooke (1736–1812), philologist and radical politician, who was commemorated by an American monument erected in the church in 1919.[61] There were three silver chalices in 1552,

[25] *6th Rep. Com. Char.* H.C. 12, pp. 370–2 (1822), ix.
[26] M.R.O., D.R.O. 37/F2/1.
[27] Jackson, *Ealing*, 32 and illus. betw. pp. 32 and 33.
[28] M.R.O., Acc. 890, p. 14; *Mdx. County Rec.* iii. 240.
[29] M.R.O., D.R.O. 37/A12/3/1 (cutting); Allison and Holt, *Ealing in 18th and 19th Cent.* 43.
[30] P.R.O., HO 129/134/3.
[31] Mudie-Smith, *Rel. Life*, 429.
[32] Guildhall MS. 9171/4, f. 199v.
[33] M.R.O., D.R.O. 37/A1/1, 3; P.R.O., C 8/455/35.
[34] P.R.O., PROB 11/7, 14, 20 (P.C.C. 18 Logge, 41 Holgrave, 5 Maynwaring); M.R.O., D.R.O. 37/B2/1.
[35] Guildhall MS. 9171/8, ff. 85, 88, 201.
[36] Ibid. 1, f. 128; 5, f. 357.
[37] Ibid. 3, f. 27v.
[38] Ibid. 6, ff. 34, 86v., 128.
[39] Ibid. 4, ff. 175v., 199v., 160v.
[40] Ibid. 8, ff. 22, 85.
[41] M.R.O., Acc. 890, pp. 12, 48, 49, 60.
[42] Jackson, *Ealing*, 41–6.
[43] M.R.O., Cal. Mdx. Sess. Bks. xv. 39–41.
[44] 12 Geo. II, c. 7.
[45] Brewer, *Beauties of Eng. & Wales*, x (5), 341.
[46] *Lond. Gaz.* 18 Nov. 1828, p. 2203.
[47] M.R.O., D.R.O. 37/B2/1–2; below, plate facing p. 145. For plans and elevations see B.L. Maps K. 29.9.b. 1–9.

[48] Jackson, *Ealing*, 64; Allison and Holt, *Ealing in 18th and 19th Cents.* 32.
[49] Allison and Holt, *Ealing in 18th and 19th Cents.* 7, 19, 24; M.R.O., D.R.O. 37/B1/3.
[50] *Ambulator* (1820); see also ibid. (1774); *Diary of John Yeoman*, 32.
[51] M.R.O., D.R.O. 37/A11/1; B2/6, 23–4; Thorne, *Environs*, 158; Jackson, *Ealing*, 239–43; T. S. Rosoman, 'S. S. Teulon and St. Mary's Ch., Ealing' (Ealing Coll. of Higher Educ. B.A. thesis, 1978, in Ealing libr.); below, plate facing p. 145.
[52] M.R.O., D.R.O. 37/B2/26; *The Times*, 3 May 1920.
[53] *The Times*, 8 Oct. 1934; datestone; M.R.O., D.R.O. 37/B2/29.   [54] *T.L.M.A.S.* xviii (2), no. 21.
[55] Inf. from Mr. J. Wolton; see also St. Mary, Ealing, Act 1966, c. 21.
[56] *St. Mary's Monthly Ch. Paper*, Nov. 1883; M.R.O., D.R.O., 37/A12/2; *Architect*, 15 Feb. 1879; inf. from Mr. J. Wolton.
[57] e.g. Robbins, *Mdx.* 176; Pevsner, *Mdx.* 40.
[58] *Mdx. & Herts. N. & Q.* iv. 175; Faulkner, *Brentford, Ealing and Chiswick*, 60.
[59] Pevsner, *Mdx.* 40; Hist. Mon. Com. *Mdx.* 15.
[60] Gunnis, *Dict. Sculptors*, 208, 256, 306, 318, 423, 427.
[61] Brewer, *Beauties of Eng. & Wales*, x (5), 341–2; *D.N.B.*; inf. from the vicar.

besides other goods,[62] but in 1885 there was only a silver bowl and cover;[63] the church later acquired 16th-, 17th-, and 18th-century silver.[64] There were 5 bells in 1552;[65] 5 were melted down in 1739, when 8 were hung, and there were still 8 in 1955.[66] The registers begin in 1582.[67]

Most of Lower Side was in the district assigned to St. George's, Old Brentford, in 1828.[68] Consequently there were only 650 attendances from the rest of the old parish at St. Mary's in 1851.[69] There were 10,289 worshippers at ten churches and mission churches in 1903, when Ealing had one of the highest attendances in and around London. Seven churches were already permanent and ultimately there were to be twelve, besides several longstanding missions. Such large districts were assigned in 1852 to Christ Church and in 1876 to St. John's that St. Mary's had relatively few daughter churches, whereas Christ Church had four and St. Stephen's and St. John's three each. Ealing Ruri-Decanal Association, founded in 1859, helped to establish new churches by making grants and lending iron churches.[70] By 1916 there were eleven permanent churches, eight of them in central Ealing between the Piccadilly and G.W.R. lines and five in the small area between Ealing village, the Broadway, and Ealing common. Ealing was still the 'most Sabbath-loving suburb in London' in 1926,[71] but the only foundation after the First World War was Ascension church, in the north part of the parish. In the Second World War St. Saviour's was bombed and several missions failed to survive. In 1903 by far the best attended churches were St. Saviour's and St. John's, respectively Anglo-Catholic and Evangelical but both in working-class areas, whereas in 1978 it was churches in the poorer districts which showed signs of retreat.

ALL SAINTS, Elm Grove Rd., Ealing common. Built on site of former Elm Grove, given by Leopold de Rothschild, by bequest of Miss Frederica Elizabeth Perceval in memory of Spencer Perceval (1762–1812), prime minister. Chapel of ease of St. Mary's until dist. assigned 1948. Patron bp. of London. Stone bldg. in mixed Gothic style 1905 by W. A. Pite: chancel, N. chapel, S. organ chamber and vestries, aisled and clerestoried nave, N. and S. porches, NW. tower, apsidal W. baptistery.[72]

ASCENSION church, Beaufort Rd., Hanger Hill. Served by London Diocesan Home Mission until parish formed 1948. Patron bp. of London. Iron church used c. 1937–9. Buff brick bldg. in a Georgian style 1939 by Seely & Paget: apsidal sanctuary with ambulatory, chancel beneath lantern tower, N. and S. vestries, aisled nave with dormers in roof.[73]

ST. BARNABAS,[74] Pitshanger Lane. Mission of St. Stephen's from 1907 until dist. assigned 1917. Patron bp. of London. Iron church, later hall, at corner of Castlebar Rd. built 1908 and destroyed 1942. Dark red brick bldg. in French Gothic style 1914–16 by E. C. Shearman at corner of Denison Rd., seating 1,000:[75] apsidal chancel with ambulatory, N. vestries, apsidal S. chapel, clerestoried nave with processional aisles and galleried N. and S. transepts, W. organ gallery over baptistery; two-storeyed NW. and SW. porches are lower stages of uncompleted towers.[76] Damaged by fire 1962. High Church 1978.

CHRIST THE SAVIOUR,[77] Ealing Broadway, built as Christ Church[78] at expense of Miss Rosa Frances Lewis (d. 1862) of Castle Hill Ho. Dist. assigned 1852.[79] Patron Miss Lewis, with remainders to W. E. Hilliard, who presented his brother 1859,[80] and, from 1864, bp. of London. Three asst. curates 1896, one in 1926, two in 1947, one in 1973–4. Attendance 1903: 461 a.m.; 447 p.m. First V., William Lambert, suspended for immorality 1856. Move towards Anglo-Catholicism begun by W. Templeton King, V. 1895–1929. Bldg. of Kentish rag with Bath stone dressings in early Decorated style 1850–2 by G. G. (later Sir Geo. Gilbert) Scott: aisled chancel, SE. chapel, aisled and clerestoried nave, S. porch, W. tower with spire. Redecorated by G. F. Bodley 1903–8, N. vestry 1904. NE. chapel 1919 by C. G. Hare, from former chancel aisle. Church restored 1946–52. High Church 1978. Renamed on reunion of benefice with St. Saviour 1952. Vicarage ho. by Scott c. 1865,[81] demol. 1930.

GOOD SHEPHERD church, at corner of South Ealing and Temple rds. Mission church and institute of St. Mary's, for S. part of parish, but with own min. 1906. Services in hall 1905 by W. A. Pite, seating 300.[82] Hall sold to Assyrian church 1978.[83]

ST. JAMES,[84] Ealing Dean. Mission church of St. John's from 1890 until dist. assigned 1905.[85] Patron bp. of London. One asst. curate

[62] *T.L.M.A.S.* xxiii. 298–9.
[63] Guildhall MS. 9537/20.
[64] Freshfield, *Communion Plate*, 11–12; Hist. Mon. Com. *Mdx.* 15.   [65] *T.L.M.A.S.* xxiii. 299.
[66] Jackson, *Ealing*, 61 sqq.; *T.L.M.A.S.* xviii (2), no. 21. See also Faulkner, *Brentford, Ealing and Chiswick*, 213.
[67] In 1980 at M.R.O. Marriages 1582–1837 are printed in Phillimore, *Mdx. Par. Regs.* viii.
[68] For the 19th- and 20th-century churches below, inf. about most patrons and asst. curates is from *Clergy List* (1866 and later edns.); *Crockford* (1896 and later edns.); architectural descriptions based on *T.L.M.A.S.* xviii (2); *Ealing Churches* (Ealing Museum, Art and Hist. Soc. 1977); attendance figs. 1903 from Mudie-Smith, *Rel. Life*, 429. For abbreviations see above, p. 37 n. 68.
[69] Para. based on inf. given in detail below and Mudie-Smith, *Rel. Life*, 429.
[70] Ealing Ruri-Decanal Assoc. *Rep.* (1883); *Guardian*, 23 Nov. 1859.
[71] *The Times*, 26 Oct. 1929; 15 Feb. 1930.

[72] All Saints', Ealing Common, *Year Bk. 1952 and Ch. Hist.* (booklet).
[73] Robbins, *Mdx.* 241; *The Times*, 22, 24 July 1939; datestone; inf. from the vicar.
[74] Para. based on *St. Stephen's, W. Ealing* (jubilee booklet 1976); *St. Barnabas Golden Jubilee Souvenir* (1966); *T.L.M.A.S.* xviii (2), no. 24.
[75] *Kelly's Dir. Mdx.* (1926).
[76] *The Times*, 5 June 1916.
[77] Para. based on Jackson, *Ealing*, 247–50; *Christ Church— Christ the Saviour, 1852–1952* (centenary booklet); *The Times*, 1, 2 July 1852.   [78] M.R.O., D.R.O. 37/A12/1.
[79] *Lond. Gaz.* 19 Oct. 1852, pp. 2722–3.
[80] M.R.O., D.R.O. 37/A11/1.
[81] Ibid. Acc. 1083/2; D.R.O. 37/A11/1.
[82] Ealing Par. Ch. with All Saints' *Mission Hall of Good Shepherd and Temple Institute* (bazaar programme 1906); Oliver, *20 Yrs. Retrospect.*   [83] Inf. from Mr. J. Wolton.
[84] Para. based on Jackson, *Ealing*, 257–8; *Builder*, 25 Feb. 1905.   [85] *Lond. Gaz.* 21 Mar. 1905, pp. 2172–3.

1926 and 1935, none in 1947. Attendance 1903: 168 a.m.; 183 p.m. Iron church in Alexandra Rd. used until 1904. Red-brick bldg. with stone dressings in early Gothic style 1903-4 by W. Pywell in St. James's Ave., seating c. 770: chancel, NE. chapel, nave with N. and S. aisles. Suspended benefice, served from St. John's, from 1977.[86]

ST. JOHN,[87] Ealing Dean. Mission church of Christ Church from 1865 until dist. assigned from Christ Church and St. Mary's 1876.[88] Patron bp. of London. One asst. curate 1896, two in 1907 and 1935, none in 1947, four in 1977-9. Attendance 1903: 1,116 a.m.; 1,058 p.m. Evangelical tradition established under Julius Summerhayes, curate and V. 1867-1903, and son Julius James Summerhayes, V. 1903-39. Temp. church in St. John's Rd. used until 1867, thereafter wooden church at corner of Mattock Lane and Churchfield Rd., enlarged 1868 and 1870 to seat 750, used until 1876. Yellow brick bldg. in early Gothic style 1876 by E. H. Horne, on island site at junction of Mattock Lane with Broomfield Place and Broomfield Rd.: chancel, central tower, N. and S. transepts, aisled and clerestoried nave. Repaired 1878-83[89] but badly damaged by fire 1920, when services were held in Griffith Davies memorial hall, built 1917. Church repaired by F. Hall-Jones[90] 1923. Damaged by lightning 1928,[91] W. end remodelled as church lounge 1970, on sale of Griffith Davies and Jubilee (1929) halls, and crypt remodelled for recreation 1973, on sale of Peal and Summerhayes memorial hall, built 1904. Northfield mission hall, at corner of Northfield Ave. and Dudley Gdns., opened 1901[92] and used as Sunday sch. 1977. Attendance 1903: 79 p.m.

ST. LUKE, at corner of Lynton Ave. and Courtfield Gdns., Drayton Green. Mission church of St. Stephen's from 1901. Attendance 1903: 159 a.m.; 86 p.m. Iron church was sold 1952 and became Ealing Liberal synagogue.[93]

ST. MATTHEW,[94] North Common Rd., Ealing common. Dist. assigned from St. Mary's and Christ Church 1885.[95] Patron bp. of London. One asst. curate 1907, none in 1926. Attendance 1903: 638 a.m.; 253 p.m. Iron church in Grange Pk. used from 1872. Brown and red brick bldg. in early Gothic style by Alfred Jowers, on site given by Edward Wood, seating 935,[96] built 1883-4, not oriented: apsidal chancel, apsidal NW. organ chamber and vestries and NE. chapel, aisled and clerestoried nave, base of unfinished SW. tower, W. porches. Shared with Polish Roman Catholics 1978.[97]

ST. PAUL, Northcroft Rd., Northfields. Dist. assigned from St. John's 1907. Patron bp. of London. One asst. curate 1947. Yellow brick bldg. with stone dressings in late Gothic style 1906-7 by F. Hall-Jones and E. S. Cummings: chancel, N. vestries and organ chamber, apsidal S. chapel, aisled nave, S. porches, N. porch. Seating reduced from 850 to 650 by 1978.[98]

ST. PETER,[99] Mount Park Rd. Mission church of Christ Church from 1882 and dedicated to St. Andrew until 1889. Dist. assigned 1894.[1] Patron V. of Christ Church, then bp. of London. One asst. curate 1896, two in 1955-6, one in 1973-4. Attendance 1903: 584 a.m.; 283 p.m. Iron church, seating 1,044 in 1898, on land given by John Clark Record, used 1882-93. Yellow brick and Box stone bldg. in a Decorated style, designed by J. D. Sedding 1889 and built by H. Wilson 1892-3: chancel, N. organ chamber over vestries, S. chapel, aisled nave with triforium and gallery, W. baptistery and entrance under large window; roof turrets, linked by depressed arches, repeat arcades within. E. end of chancel, with tower and spire, not built. Seating reduced to 540 by 1978. High Church 1978.

ST. SAVIOUR,[2] the Grove. Mission church of Christ Church from 1881 until dist. assigned 1916. Patron bp. of London. Three asst. curates 1947, none in 1955-6. Attendance 1903: 1,397 a.m.; 1,131 p.m. Anglo-Catholic tradition under A. C. Buckell, curate and V. 1897-1936. Brick bldg. with stone dressings[3] begun 1897 by G. H. Fellowes Prynne: chancel, aisled nave, baptistery. Bombed 1940, services thereafter held in parish hall called Little St. Saviour's until union with Christ Church 1951. Crenellated gateway and clergy ho. by Fellowes Prynne 1909.[4]

ST. STEPHEN,[5] Castle Hill. Dist. assigned 1876 from Christ Church.[6] Patron bp. of London, from c. 1940 chapter of St. Paul's. One asst. curate 1896, three in 1907, two in 1926 and 1973-4, none in 1977-9. Attendance 1903: 570 a.m.; 303 p.m. Iron church 1867-76. Bldg. of ragstone, with ashlar dressings, in Decorated style, eventually seating 686: chancel, nave, and N. aisle 1875-6 by J. Ashdown; S. aisle, S. transeptal chapel, and S. organ chamber completed 1880 by A. Rovedino; NW. tower and spire 1888-91 by Sir Arthur Blomfield. Church repaired 1951, 1953, and modernized 1966 but unsafe 1978 and closed by 1979, when hall was used for worship.[7]

CHURCHES: BRENTFORD. Ecclesiastical synods were held at Brentford in the 8th century,[8] apparently before there was a church. Between 1175 and 1179 Ralph de Brito founded St.

[86] Inf. from the vicar, St. John's, Ealing Dean.
[87] Para. based on Jackson, *Ealing*, 253-6; *St. John's, W. Ealing* (centenary booklet 1976).
[88] *Lond. Gaz.* 27 Oct. 1876, pp. 5704-6.
[89] St. John's Ch. *Bldg. Fund Rep.* (1883).
[90] Neaves, *Ealing*, 89.
[91] *The Times*, 22 May 1928.   [92] Datestone.
[93] *St. Stephen's, W. Ealing* (jubilee booklet 1976); photo. in Ealing libr.; below, Judaism.
[94] Para. based on Jackson, *Ealing*, 261-3; *St. Matthew's, Ealing Common, 1884-1934* (jubilee programme).
[95] *Lond. Gaz.* 2 Jan. 1885, p. 12.
[96] M.R.O., D.R.O. 37/A12/2.   [97] Notice at ch.

[98] W. H. Findell, *Glory of this Ho.* (St. Paul's jubilee booklet 1957); inf. from the vicar.
[99] Para. based on Jackson, *Ealing*, 264-7; *Builder*, 16 Nov. 1889; Pevsner, *Mdx.* 41; Robbins, *Mdx.* 241; inf. from Mr. D. H. Wells.   [1] *Lond. Gaz.* 27 July 1894, p. 4291.
[2] Para. based on Jackson, *Ealing*, 251-2; *Christ Ch. 1852-1952*.   [3] M.R.O., Acc. 938/2/150 (postcard).
[4] Datestone; *Builder*, 7 May 1910; *The Times*, 2 Nov. 1909.
[5] Para. based on Jackson, *Ealing*, 258-61; *St. Stephen's Ch. W. Ealing* (jubilee booklet 1976).
[6] *Lond. Gaz.* 27 Oct. 1876, pp. 5703-4.
[7] Inf. from the vicar of St. Mary's.
[8] *Cart. Sax.* ed. Birch, i. 336.

Lawrence's hospital, New Brentford, in honour of the royal family, his lord Richard de Lucy (d. 1179), and his own kin. Beside it he founded St. Lawrence's chapel, served by a chaplain, and a burial ground. All offerings and tithes were reserved to the rector of Hanwell, who was also to receive an annual payment of wax from the chaplain. The townspeople of New Brentford were to worship at Hanwell on the four principal feasts and to be buried there, except the infirm, chaplains, and their servants.[9] There was no further reference to the hospital until c. 1563, and then perhaps only to a later almshouse,[10] but the chapel survived. The chaplain, normally called the curate from 1500,[11] was paid by residents for his services c. 1529, because of their distance from the parish church.[12] He enjoyed some tithes by the mid 17th century,[13] when New Brentford, already governed by its own vestry, was thought fit to be made a separate parish.[14]

Ralph de Brito made no known provision for appointments but apparently the chapel was served by the rector of Hanwell or his nominees: chapel and church were treated together in surveys of livings from 1291[15] and joint presentations were made by 1335.[16] It was claimed that appointments were customarily made by the township in 1707, when the rector successfully named his own candidate.[17] The rector held monthly services until 1744, when New Brentford became a perpetual curacy, often called a vicarage, in his gift.[18] The presentation of 1760 was sold[19] and two later ones were delegated to Dr. J. A. Emerton, principal of Hanwell college, because of difficulty in finding candidates.[20] In 1961 the parish of St. Lawrence, New Brentford, was amalgamated with St. George's and St. Paul's, Old Brentford, in the united parishes of Brentford, with the bishop of London as patron.[21]

New Brentford, previously valued with Hanwell, was worth £75 10s. in 1650.[22] The curacy was worth £150 in 1763, £283 in 1828, and £292 after rates in 1851.[23] Originally the chaplain was to be supported by the inmates of the hospital.[24] The householders of New Brentford paid him 1s. 4d. weekly until 1529, when an endowment of £3 9s. 4d. was left by Henry Redman and executed by his widow's gift of a house, later the George inn, which was also subject to other charges. On the dissolution of the chantries the payment became a rent charge of £6, to be divided equally between the curate and the parish but normally paid entirely to the curate from 1647 until at least 1851.[25] The curate also received some tithes, perhaps from the mid 16th century:[26] in 1647 they amounted to £12 10s. and in 1654 a larger share of the rector's income was sought,[27] probably in vain. In 1714 the rector managed to assert his right to the hay tithes from Boston manorial demesne[28] but in 1744 he gave up the small tithes of New Brentford, all hay tithes except those from Boston demesne, and all offerings. Evidently there was a further dispute over hay tithes in 1790.[29] In 1837, when 52 a. in New Brentford were not tithable, the rector was allotted £60 and the vicar of New Brentford £85 in tithe rent charges.[30] In 1694 the pew rents of a new gallery were assigned to the curate[31] and in 1764 a successor was assigned pews in the new church,[32] worth £98 in 1851.[33] The living was augmented by £60 in 1647 and £100 in 1657 but payment may not have survived the Restoration.[34] Queen Anne's Bounty supplemented it by 1721 and endowed it in 1747 with land at Heston and in Surrey,[35] which yielded £71 a year in 1851.[36] In 1843 the cure was so poor and the charity required of incumbents so heavy that only rich men could be presented.[37]

The medieval hospital may have been the almshouse which c. 1563 lay west of the church and was said to have been the gift of a former manorial lessee.[38] Perhaps the almshouse was also the church house, towards which money was given in 1531.[39] A church house stood immediately east of the church in High Street in 1611 and 1621[40] and later was said to stand in the churchyard.[41] It had customarily been inhabited by the curate or the poor in 1646, when the lord leased it to the township for those purposes.[42] In 1647 the curate apparently was excluded and in 1655 he was consequently allowed £4 towards his rent.[43] The house was used as a school in 1672[44] and rebuilt in 1698, when the freehold was

[9] Letters of Gilb. Foliot, 491–3; V.C.H. Mdx. iii. 230. Maurice of Berkeley's foundation was apocryphal: Faulkner, Brentford, Ealing and Chiswick, 43; J. Clitherow, 'Agreement between Hanwell ch. and New Brentford chapel, 1790' (TS. in Ealing libr.).

[10] New Brentford MS. 17518; P.R.O., E 134/26 Eliz. I Easter 6; below.

[11] Guildhall MS. 9171/8, f. 201v.

[12] Faulkner, Brentford, Ealing and Chiswick, 44.

[13] Below.

[14] Above, local govt.; Home Counties Mag. iii. 33.

[15] Tax. Eccl. (Rec. Com.), 17; Feud. Aids, iii. 377.

[16] Newcourt, Rep. i. 626–7.

[17] New Brentford MS. 17514; see also Faulkner, Brentford, Ealing and Chiswick, 49, 68.

[18] Faulkner, Brentford, Ealing and Chiswick, 50; Clitherow, 'Agreement'; V.C.H. Mdx. iii. 230.

[19] D.N.B. (s.v. J. Horne Tooke).

[20] J. A. Emerton, Discipline of Church (1843).

[21] Lond. Dioc. Bk. (1970).

[22] Home Counties Mag. iii. 33.

[23] Guildhall MSS. 9557, 9560; P.R.O., HO 129/134/3/1/1.

[24] Letters of Gilb. Foliot, 492.

[25] 6th Rep. Com. Char. H.C. 12, p. 346 (1822), ix; New Brentford MS. 17512; Faulkner, Brentford, Ealing and Chiswick, 44–6; P.R.O., HO 129/134/3/1/1.

[26] Faulkner, Brentford, Ealing and Chiswick, 49; Clitherow, 'Agreement'.

[27] Cal. S.P. Dom. 1654, 342; see also V.C.H. Mdx. iii. 230.

[28] V.C.H. Mdx. iii. 230.

[29] Clitherow, 'Agreement'.

[30] M.R.O., TA/BRE; Faulkner, Brentford, Ealing and Chiswick, 139–40.

[31] Faulkner, Brentford, Ealing and Chiswick, 50.

[32] New Brentford MS. 17517.

[33] P.R.O., HO 129/134/3/1/1.

[34] Home Counties Mag. iii. 33; L.J. x. 34–5; Cal. S.P. Dom. 1654, 342; 1657–8, 81; Faulkner, Brentford, Ealing and Chiswick, 47–9.

[35] Faulkner, Brentford, Ealing and Chiswick, 50; Clitherow, 'Agreement'; C. Hodgson, Queen Anne's Bounty (1845), p. cccxiv.

[36] P.R.O., HO 129/134/3/1/1.

[37] Emerton, Discipline of Church, 25.

[38] New Brentford MS. 17518; P.R.O., E 134/26 Eliz. I Easter 6.

[39] Guildhall MS. 9171/10, f. 171.

[40] Mdx. Par. Regs. viii. 1; Lysons, Environs, ii. 54.

[41] New Brentford MS. 17514.

[42] Faulkner, Brentford, Ealing and Chiswick, 50; New Brentford MS. 17649.

[43] Neaves, Gt. Ealing, 204; New Brentford MS. 17512.

[44] New Brentford MS. 17513.

acquired for the curate,[45] who leased it out in 1716 and lived elsewhere in New Brentford *c.* 1726.[46] The parish repaired the house in 1773[47] and again in 1803, when it was offered to the vicar or, in his absence for six months, to his assistant curate. The house was leased to another tenant when the vicar refused those terms, but on his successor's acceptance it was permanently annexed as the Vicarage in 1805.[48] After more repairs in 1817, it was dilapidated and again in dispute in 1822.[49] A house adjoining it to the east was said to have belonged to the attorney-general Sir William Noy (1577–1634);[50] Noy's house was acquired in 1889 and both were replaced by a new Vicarage.[51] The clerk's house in the churchyard was uninhabitable in 1743 and may then have been demolished.[52]

There was a chaplain *c.* 1179[53] and royal gifts were made in 1226 and 1246 to recluses of Brentford.[54] About 1330 the curate of Brentford was killed in a brawl[55] and *c.* 1540 another was a drunkard.[56] Curates in the 14th and 15th centuries probably lived in New Brentford[57] and augmentation of the living in 1647 was intended to encourage residence.[58] Both Dr. Chilcot, curate 1726–69, and Dr. Stoddart, vicar 1837–42, were pluralists but resident;[59] Chilcot, like the curate in 1598, kept a local school.[60] John Horne Tooke, vicar 1760–73,[61] was sometimes non-resident and in 1822 Sir Robert Peat, vicar 1808–37, had been absent without licence for six months.[62] There was a parish clerk by 1433.[63]

Joan Redman gave property towards the salary of the curate and also for an obit, which was observed in 1547.[64] Her other bequests of 1531 included a cow, pewter vessels for weddings of the poor, and money towards the church house,[65] which was used for drinkings in support of the poor in 1621.[66] Richard Byfield (d. 1664), later ejected from the rectory of Long Ditton (Surr.), was lecturer at Brentford in 1643.[67] The augmentation of 1657 was annexed to an afternoon lecturer,[68] who later was supported by voluntary subscriptions until at least 1845.[69] There were two Sunday services, monthly communions, and

catechisms in Lent between 1770 and 1828.[70] Worshippers in 1806 were enjoined to stand, rather than sit, during hymns, to take communion, and to kneel during prayers.[71] There were attendances of 487, including 190 Sunday school children, in the morning and 387, again including Sunday school children, in the afternoon on census Sunday 1851, and of 163 in the morning and 124 in the afternoon on one Sunday in 1903.[72]

The existing church of *ST. LAWRENCE*, New Brentford, on the south side of High Street, is at least the second one on the site. Nothing is visible of the 12th-century chapel and only the 15th-century tower, of Kentish ragstone with Reigate stone dressings, remains from before a rebuilding of 1764.[73] The existing tower, which presumably replaced the bell tower mentioned in 1373,[74] stood at the west end of a three-bay nave and two-bay chancel, which had been enlarged by a north chapel before 1496 and a north aisle and north porch with a chamber overhead by 1500.[75] There were lights to St. Mary in 1378, St. Lawrence, St. Michael, and St. Katherine by 1396, and St. Nicholas by 1475,[76] and there was a roodloft by 1496.[77] A gallery existed in 1632, another was added in 1694, the west gallery was altered in 1712, and there were north and west galleries in 1762.[78] The church was repaired in 1673[79] and the tower in 1757,[80] but in 1762 both walls and roof were decayed,[81] whereupon services were moved to the Red Lion inn during rebuilding.[82]

The new church, designed by Boulton Maynwaring and built by Thomas Hardwick the elder,[83] abutted west on the tower and north-east on the Vicarage, like its predecessor, but extended much farther south. Built of brick, it consisted of a recessed chancel, north-east vestry, and nave with galleries on three sides.[84] The original intentions to enclose the tower in the nave and to avoid any ornament were not observed.[85] The church, seating *c.* 500, was too small by 1797[86] but it was not until 1874 that the replacement of the galleries by a south aisle provided 50 extra seats. A north-east organ

[45] Ibid. MSS. 17514, 17560–1.
[46] Ibid. MS. 17514; Guildhall MS. 9550.
[47] New Brentford MS. 17517.
[48] Ibid. 17518; Faulkner, *Brentford, Ealing and Chiswick*, 51.
[49] New Brentford MS. 17825; *6th Rep. Com. Char.* 352.
[50] Faulkner, *Brentford, Ealing and Chiswick*, 147; *D.N.B.*
[51] *W. London Sketcher*, 1 May 1889; cutting in Chiswick libr.; F. A. Turner, *Brentford Literary and Hist. Sketches* (1898), 68.
[52] New Brentford MS. 17516.
[53] *Letters of Gilb. Foliot*, 492.
[54] *Rot. Litt. Claus.* (Rec. Com.), ii. 93; *Cal. Close*, 1242–7, 400, 491.
[55] *Cal. Pat.* 1327–30, 494.
[56] P.R.O., C 1/1056/25.
[57] e.g. Guildhall MSS. 9171/1, f. 8v.; 3, ff. 103v., 324.
[58] *L.J.* x. 35.
[59] Faulkner, *Brentford, Ealing and Chiswick*, 70; Guildhall MS. 9550.
[60] Guildhall MSS. 9537/9, f. 154v.; 9550.
[61] *D.N.B.*
[62] *6th Rep. Com. Char.* 352; *D.N.B.*
[63] Guildhall MS. 9171/3, f. 324.
[64] P.R.O., E 301/34, no. 118.
[65] Ibid.; Guildhall MS. 9171/10, f. 171v.
[66] Lysons, *Environs*, ii. 54.

[67] *Calamy Revised*, 96–7.
[68] *Cal. S.P. Dom.* 1657–8, 206.
[69] Faulkner, *Brentford, Ealing and Chiswick*, 51.
[70] Guildhall MSS. 9558, 9557.
[71] *Psalms and Hymns for Chapel of New Brentford* (1806).
[72] P.R.O., HO 129/134/3/1/1; Mudie-Smith, *Rel. Life*, 425.
[73] Hist. Mon. Com. *Mdx.* 4.
[74] Guildhall MS. 9171/1, f. 8v.
[75] New Brentford MS. 17644 (plan on cover); Guildhall MS. 9171/9, f. 91v.
[76] Guildhall MSS. 9171/1, ff. 51v., 351v.; 6, f. 187.
[77] Ibid. 9, f. 57v.; P.R.O., PROB 11/11 (P.C.C. 3 Horne).
[78] Faulkner, *Brentford, Ealing and Chiswick*, 72; New Brentford MSS. 17512, 17644 (plan).
[79] Guildhall MS. 9537/20.
[80] New Brentford MS. 17516.
[81] Ibid. MS. 17644.
[82] Guildhall MS. 11189.
[83] Ibid.; New Brentford MS. 17517; Colvin, *Dict. Brit. Architects* (1978), 388.
[84] New Brentford MSS. 17517 (plan), 17644; Guildhall Libr., grangerized copy of Lysons, *Environs*, ii(1), between pp. 58 and 59; Guildhall Libr., Pr. W V/BRE; below, plate facing p. 144.
[85] New Brentford MSS. 17517, 17644 (plan).
[86] Ibid. MSS. 17518, 17644, 17825.

chamber was built and the chancel was refurnished at that time[87] and wooden Gothic arcades were inserted in 1889.[88] Disused from 1911,[89] the church was dilapidated by 1979, when it was leased to the St. Lawrence, Brentford, Trust. Many fittings were then removed, while the fabric was restored to serve as a theatre.[90]

Fittings formerly included a plain font of c. 1500, a 15th-century panel with the Berkeley family's arms,[91] and a brass to William Clavell (d. 1496).[92] The oldest surviving brass commemorates Henry Redman (d. 1528), the king's master mason, and his family.[93] In 1834 the chancel walls were covered with tablets and monuments;[94] many, from the 17th century or later, commemorated the Hawley and Clitherow families, including one to Ann Clitherow (d. 1801) by John Bacon the younger.[95] Among other memorials are figures of Faith and Hope for William Howell Ewin (d. 1804), the usurer, and his sister Sarah Howell (d. 1808) by John Flaxman,[96] kneeling wall figures for John Middleton (d. 1624) and his wife, a neo-Greek tablet by J. J. P. Kendrick for Thomas Hardwick the younger (d. 1829), the architect,[97] and tablets for John Howard (d. 1818) by Sarah Holmes of Brentford and for the Revd. William Cook (d. 1810) in Coade stone.[98] There was only one chalice in 1669 and 1685[99] but the plate later included a silver chalice and paten of 1689, a silver flagon of 1709 by D. Willaume, and other pieces of the 18th century and later.[1] The six bells in 1955 included one by William Culverden c. 1510.[2] The registers begin in 1570.[3]

ST. FAITH,[4] Windmill Rd., Old Brentford.

Mission church of St. Paul's until dist. assigned 1907.[5] Patron bp. of London. Attendance 1903: 94 a.m.; 148 p.m. Ho. in Windmill Rd. used from 1901, then temp. church by 1903. Bldg. of red brick and stone dressings in early Decorated style 1907 by G. F. Bodley and C. G. Hare: chancel, N. chapel, aisled and clerestoried nave with N. porch, SW. bell turret. Fittings inc. font and altar from chapel of St. James's Palace, Westm. Seating reduced from c. 600 to c. 400 by 1977.

ST. GEORGE,[6] Kew Bridge Rd., Old Brentford.

Founded as an unconsecrated chapelry with subscriptions first raised 1762 from 57 prominent inhabitants.[7] Under construction, as George chapel, 1766.[8] Min. apparently chosen by V. of Ealing 1763 and 1784, although chapel maintained by proprietors until 1820 when it was bought with money raised from sale of waste lands. Min., perhaps normally non-resident, received £30 in 1774, £35 in 1790, and also pew rents in 1797.[9] Income, after augmentation in 1828, £135 c. 1830,[10] excluding £40 from lectureship founded 1630 by John Bowman.[11] Two Sunday services with sermons, up to 50 communicants in 1790.[12] Consecrated as St. George's church 1828. Dist. assigned 1828 and later, 1865–79, inc. Ealing detached at Stamford Brook.[13] Patron V. of Ealing.[14] One asst. curate 1881 and 1935, none 1947. Attendance 1851: 700 (inc. Sunday sch. 300) a.m.; 500 p.m.;[15] 1903: 229 a.m.; 392 p.m. Brick bldg. in domestic style c. 1766 by J. J. Kirby: pedimented S. front, with entrance in projecting centre, square- and round-headed windows, cupola.[16] Seating enlarged to 400 1828, perhaps by galleries,[17] and to 651 by 1851, when bldg. was too small. Church, in shadow of gasworks, dilapidated 1863 and demol. 1886.[18] New site bought 1852[19] but used for St. Paul's iron church 1861 and another site bought 1881 but made superfluous by St. James's Gunnersbury. Ragstone bldg. in early Decorated style on old site by A. W. Blomfield, seating 600: chancel, SE. chapel, N. organ chamber, nave, S. aisle, base of octagonal SW. tower 1886–7; tower, without projected spire,[20] 1913. Fittings from old chapel inc. painting of Last Supper by Zoffany c. 1770,[21] later moved to St. Paul's. Vicarage S. of High St. at Bull Wharf Ho. provided 1866.[22] Benefice sequestrated 1958 and united with St. Lawrence's and St. Paul's 1961. Church closed 1959[23] and used as musical museum from 1963.[24]

ST. JAMES, Chiswick High Road, Gunnersbury.

Mission church of Christ Church, Turnham Green, in Chertsey Rd. before move 1884 to Blenheim Rd., Chiswick, where served by London Diocesan Home Mission.[25] Dist.

[87] New Brentford MS. 17636.
[88] Pevsner, Mdx. 28; T.L.M.A.S. xviii (2), no. 10.
[89] Brentford and Chiswick Times, 22 Aug. 1968.
[90] Inf. from the chairman, St. Lawr., Brentford, Trust; The Times, 9 Dec. 1980. [91] Hist. Mon. Com. Mdx. 4.
[92] J. Weever, Ancient Funeral Monuments (1767 edn.), 296.
[93] T.L.M.A.S. xvii. 51 sqq. [94] Pigot, Com. Dir. (1832–4).
[95] Brewer, Beauties of Eng. & Wales, x (5), 600; Hist. Mon. Com. Mdx. 4; Gunnis, Dict. Sculptors, 29.
[96] D.N.B.; Gunnis, Dict. Sculptors, 151.
[97] Pevsner, Mdx. 28; D.N.B.; Gunnis, Dict. Sculptors, 227.
[98] Gunnis, Dict. Sculptors, 109, 208.
[99] Faulkner, Brentford, Ealing and Chiswick, 67; Guildhall MS. 9537/20. [1] Freshfield, Communion Plate, 5–6.
[2] T.L.M.A.S. xviii (2), no. 10; Hist. Mon. Com. Mdx. 4.
[3] T.L.M.A.S. xviii (2), no. 10. In 1980 they were at St. Paul's ch.
[4] Para. based on inf. from the vicar. For the 19th- and 20th-century churches below, inf. about patrons and asst. curates is from Clergy List (1866 and later edns.); Crockford (1896 and later edns.); archit. descriptions based on T.L.M.A.S. xviii (2); attendance figs. 1903 from Mudie-Smith, Rel. Life, 424. For abbreviations see above, p. 37 n. 68.
[5] Kelly's Dir. Mdx. (1926).
[6] Para. based on Faulkner, Brentford, Ealing and Chiswick, 128–30. [7] M.R.O., Acc. 728/1.
[8] Guildhall MS. 9558, f. 433; H. W. Simpson, Sermon at Consecration of St. Geo.'s Chapel (1828).
[9] Guildhall MSS. 9557A, pp. 35, 43; 9558, f. 433; Lysons, Environs, ii. 233.
[10] P.R.O., C 54/10538, no. 18; Hodgson, Queen Anne's Bounty, p. cccxiv; Mdx. Independent, 20 May 1885.
[11] M.R.O., D.R.O. 37/A12/3/1 (cuttings); below, charities. [12] Guildhall MS. 9558, f. 433.
[13] Lond. Gaz. 21 Nov. 1865, p. 5506; 31 Oct. 1879, pp. 6179–80. [14] Ibid. 18 Nov. 1828, pp. 2203–4.
[15] P.R.O., HO 129/134/3/2/2.
[16] Faulkner, Brentford, Ealing and Chiswick, 128–30 and plate facing p. 176. Illus. also in Guildhall Libr., Pr. W V/BRE.
[17] Lond. Gaz. 18 Nov. 1828, p. 2204; Faulkner, Brentford, Ealing and Chiswick, 128–9.
[18] M.R.O., D.R.O. 37/A11/1; 700 sittings according to P.R.O., HO 129/134/3/2/2; St. Geo., Brentford, Par. Mag. July 1885, May 1886.
[19] Rest of para. based on M.R.O., D.R.O. 37/A11/1 (scrapbks.).
[20] Mdx. County Times, 3 July 1886. [21] D.N.B.
[22] Guildhall MS. 10236; M.R.O., Acc. 638/221.
[23] Brentford and Chiswick Times, 20 Mar. 1959, 3 Sept. 1970; St. Geo., Brentford, Par. Mag. Jan. 1959.
[24] Above, social.
[25] M.R.O., D.R.O. 37/A12/2 (statement of accts. and cutting); above, Chiswick, churches.

assigned from St. George's, Christ Church, Turnham Green, and All Saints', S. Acton, 1888.[26] Patron V. of St. George's, then V. of united parishes of Brentford. One asst. curate 1965–6, none 1977–9. Attendance 1903: 186 a.m.; 172 p.m. Kentish ragstone bldg. in Early English style, on site given by Rothschild fam. on Ealing side of Chiswick High Rd., 1887 by T. Chatfeild Clarke: chancel, N. transeptal chapel, vestries, organ chamber, aisled and clerestoried nave, W. baptistery and porches.[27] Seating reduced from 750 in 1926 to 350 by 1978.[28]

ST. PAUL, St. Paul's Rd., Old Brentford. Iron church for W. part of Old Brentford provided by Ealing Ruri-Decanal Assoc. on site for projected new St. George's church.[29] Dist. assigned 1864.[30] Patron Crown and bp. of London alternately, bp. of London alone by 1915. Two asst. curates 1881, one 1896, none 1926. Attendance 1903: 494 a.m.; 318 p.m. Ragstone bldg. on new site in early Decorated style 1867–8 by H. Francis, seating 700: chancel, N. vestry, aisled and clerestoried nave, S. porch, SW. tower with spire. Chapel in N. aisle 1909 and additions 1918. Restoration, after bomb damage, by M. Farey 1953.[31] Chapel of ease of St. Lawrence's 1952[32] and principal church of united parishes of Brentford from 1961.[33]

ROMAN CATHOLICISM. Sir Christopher Roper and his wife and another family were recusants at Ealing between 1613 and 1617.[34] At New Brentford one family was repeatedly presented between 1606 and 1623 and two others were presented between 1623 and 1636.[35] Archibald Campbell, earl of Argyll, was a recusant there in 1638; in 1640 two recusants at New Brentford were presented and two at Ealing, John Penruddock and Woolsey, wife of George Brent.[36] Brent was described as a church papist in 1642.[37] Ealing parish had no recusants in 1706; a small group of suspected papists at New Brentford included Mary Thompson, who practised physic[38] and was the only papist recorded in Elthorne hundred in 1711, when she was required to move farther from London.[39] Apart from two papists at New Brentford in 1767,[40] none was recorded at Ealing or Brentford until the mid 19th century.

A Roman Catholic church at Brentford was opened in 1856 to serve Irish labourers on the

G.W.R. line.[41] It is described below, with other churches opened at Ealing in 1893, North Ealing in 1899, Northfields in 1922, and Gunnersbury in 1931. Ealing abbey, opened in 1896, was one of several convents associated with schools. In 1978 Ealing and Brentford were centres of Roman Catholic education.[42]

St. Benedict's abbey, Ealing, at corner of Charlbury Grove and Marchwood Crescent, dates from acquisition of house by Downside abbey 1896.[43] St. Benedict's church opened 1899.[44] Attendance 1903: 328 a.m.; 94 p.m.[45] Cruciform Perpendicular church by Frederick and Edward Walters finished 1935 but E. end destroyed 1940 and not rebuilt until 1962. As Ealing priory, community became independent of Downside 1947 and became an abbey 1955.[46]

St. Dunstan's, Gunnersbury, opened in hall on E. side of Gunnersbury school in Gunnersbury Ave. 1931.[47] Seated 250 in 1978.[48]

Holy Family church, Vale Lane, on Acton boundary, built and opened 1967. Modern style, with lower walls of yellow brick surmounted by sloping walls of aluminium.[49]

St. John the Evangelist's church, Brentford, founded 1856; used former Baptist chapel at Market Place from 1857 or earlier.[50] Unpretentious church at Boston Park Rd. opened 1866.[51] Attendance 1903: 329 a.m.; 150 p.m.[52] Seated 300, 1978.[53]

Mission of St. Joseph and St. Peter in private house in Windsor Rd., Ealing, from 1893, moving to house in Mattock Lane, property of Revd. Richard O'Halloran, 1897.[54] Attendance 1903: 65 a.m.; 43 p.m.[55] O'Halloran tried to remain independent of Cardinal Vaughan[56] and in 1915 registered a different building for 'unattached Catholics'.[57] Building in Mattock Lane passed to Crown on his death without heirs 1925 and later became Questors theatre.[58]

St. Peter and St. Paul, Camborne Ave., founded 1922 as chapel of ease to Hanwell.[59] Separate parish from 1926. Services in hut in Leyborne Ave.[60] until first stage of existing church opened 1931.[61] Church, completed after 1951, seated *c*. 450 in 1978.[62]

St. Mary's convent, New Brentford, opened 1880 for Poor Servants of Mother of God in two 18th-century houses and gradually extended to cover whole corner of the Butts and the

[26] *Lond. Gaz.* 14 Aug. 1888, p. 4355.
[27] *The Times*, 9 Nov. 1887.
[28] *Kelly's Dir. Mdx.* (1926); inf. from the vicar.
[29] M.R.O., D.R.O. 37/A11/1.
[30] *Lond. Gaz.* 12 July 1864, p. 3485.
[31] M.R.O., D.R.O. 37/A11/1; *The Times*, 16 Jan. 1909.
[32] *Crockford* (1973–4).
[33] *Lond. Dioc. Bk.* (1970).
[34] Jackson, *Ealing*, plate between pp. 12 and 13; *Mdx. Sess. Rec.* iv. 91; i. 246; ii. 124, 296; *Mdx. County Rec.* ii. 126.
[35] *Mdx. County Rec.* i. 130; ii. 17, 84, 127, 144, 146, 237; iii, passim; *Mdx. Sess. Rec.* i. 106, 452; iv. 142, 190.
[36] *Mdx. County Rec.* iii. 143, 153–4.
[37] Faulkner, *Brentford, Ealing and Chiswick*, 23.
[38] Guildhall MSS. 9800A/2; 3498/11.
[39] Ibid. MS. 3498/12.   [40] Ibid. MS. 9557.
[41] B. W. Kelly, *Hist. Notes on Eng. Catholic Missions* (1907), 95.
[42] Below, educ.   [43] Scouse, *Ealing 1901–51*, 60.
[44] G.R.O. Worship Reg. no. 37474.

[45] Mudie-Smith, *Rel. Life*, 430.
[46] *Westm. Cathedral Chron.* Sept. 1962; *Ealing Abbey Ch.* (leaflet).
[47] Stone on bldg.; G.R.O. Worship Reg. no. 53369.
[48] Inf. from the rector.
[49] *Ealing Churches*, no. 7; G.R.O. Worship Reg. no. 71240.
[50] G.R.O. Worship Reg. no. 7951.
[51] Ibid. 17295.
[52] Mudie-Smith, *Rel. Life*, 425.
[53] Inf. from the rector.
[54] G.R.O. Worship Reg. no. 36219; Ealing Local Hist. Soc. *Local Historian* (1964), 47; *Kelly's Dir. Ealing* (1897–8).
[55] Mudie-Smith, *Rel. Life*, 430.
[56] G. Bell, *Randall Davidson*, i. 404–5.
[57] G.R.O. Worship Reg. no. 46645.
[58] *Mdx. County Times*, 4 May 1935 (jubilee suppl.); above.
[59] *Mdx. County Times*, 4 May 1935 (jubilee suppl.).
[60] G.R.O. Worship Reg. no. 50286.
[61] Ibid. 53223; inf. from the rector.
[62] Scouse, *Ealing 1901–51*, 61; inf. from the rector.

Half Acre. Contained laundry, school c. 1900, orphanage until 1949, and home for mentally retarded girls from 1924. Chapel opened for public worship 1914 and replaced in 1950s.[63]

Visitation nuns from Westbury (Som.) used Castlebar House 1895-7.[64] English canonesses regular of the Lateran established a priory there before moving in 1914 to the Elms, Hillcrest Road.[65]

PROTESTANT NONCONFORMITY. A separatist church at New Brentford was claimed to be maintaining its own poor in 1654,[66] and Quakers were recorded at Brentford in 1659.[67] After the Restoration, particularly after the Five Mile Act of 1666, there was a colony of ejected ministers at Brentford. One of them ministered to a congregation formerly of Thomas Gilbert, former vicar of Ealing, which sometimes numbered 40 in 1663. Teachers included Philip Taverner and Ralph Button (d. 1680), who were consequently imprisoned, and Thomas Pakeman (d. 1691). Others were imprisoned with Button for worshipping together in private.[68] John Jackson (d. 1693), who came to Brentford after 1666,[69] may have conducted services before he was licensed in 1672 and continued to hold them until c. 1689, latterly with John Doddridge.[70]

There was thus a tradition of nonconformity and at least one established meeting at Brentford before the Toleration Act, 1689. Several meetings started immediately afterwards both at Brentford and Ealing and more were to follow,[71] most of them short lived but at Brentford probably including permanent congregations of Congregationalists, of Baptists from 1692, of Quakers from 1706, and of Methodists from 1760. Ealing Green Congregational church was founded c. 1800 and at Brentford there were two Baptist churches from 1818 and two Congregationalist ones from 1829. Congregations at Brentford included members far afield, before daughter churches were established in surrounding parishes in the early 19th century. In 1851 there were eight meetings at Brentford and Ealing, with 1,129 worshippers in the morning, 345 in the afternoon, and 969 in the evening on census Sunday. Three meetings were of Congregationalists, two of Baptists, two of Methodists, and one of Mormons. The Congregationalists, with 1,102 attendances, outnumbered both the Baptists with 812 and the Methodists with 480, although at Brentford the Baptists were the leading denomination. Ealing Green Congregational church, the only meeting recorded at Ealing, was the best attended.

At Brentford the late 19th century saw the foundation of another Baptist church, the closure of a Congregationalist chapel, and the arrival of Salvationists, Brethren, and the London City Mission. The Baptists advanced, having 872 attendances on one Sunday in 1903, and the Congregationalists declined, with only 315 attendances; Methodist attendances had reached 715 but the other denominations were small. Overall attendances rose slightly from 1,906 in 1851 to 2,305 in 1903. They had changed little by 1978, when there remained three Baptist churches, a United Reformed church, one Methodist church, and two meetings of the London City Mission.

At Ealing, in contrast, the number of meetings had increased to nine by 1903, when attendances had grown eleven-fold to 5,676, more than half the total recorded at Anglican churches. The principal denominations were the Baptists with 2,130 attendances, the Methodists with 1,370, the Congregationalists with 817, the Presbyterians with 690, and the Brethren with 444, but there were also Quakers, Salvationists, and others. As building spread, more meetings of Presbyterians, Congregationalists, Methodists, Brethren, and smaller denominations were established, mainly before the Second World War, and daughter churches were founded in adjoining parishes. In spite of some decline, particularly among the Congregationalists, there were 25 places of nonconformist worship in 1978, including three Methodist, two Baptist, four Presbyterian, and four of Brethren.

SOCIETY OF FRIENDS.[72] Quakers, at Brentford 1659,[73] had mtg. there 1706[74] and reg. ho. and barn near Goat inn, Ferry Lane, Old Brentford, 1707.[75] William Penn (d. 1718) lived at Brentford 1706-10.[76] Numbers at New Brentford increasing c. 1770.[77] Moved to Brentford End, Isleworth, 1785 but still called Brentford mtg.[78]

Ealing Quakers' attendance at Y.M.C.A. 1903: 14 a.m. Thereafter met regularly at Y.M.C.A., Uxbridge Rd., 1905-7, at Y.M.C.A., Bond Street, 1908-28, at no. 49 Uxbridge Rd., 1929-51, at no. 20 Florence Rd., 1952-3, at Y.M.C.A., Uxbridge Rd., 1953-4, and from 1954 at modern hall seating 100 at no. 17 Woodville Gdns. Acton mtg. joined them 1940.[79]

BAPTISTS. Anabaptists met at Brentford 1692.[80] Another mtg. reg. at ho. of Nathaniel Swinden in Ealing parish 1710[81] may have been licensed mtg. mentioned 1770,[82] mtg. ho. rented by Francis Swinden 1790-2,[83] and one at Old Brentford 1797 and 1816.[84] May also have been chapel later

63 Inf. from the sister superior.
64 *Catholic Dir.* (1896, 1897).
65 *Mdx. County Times*, 16 Apr. 1932; inf. from the revd. mother.
66 M.R.O., Acc. 890, p. 26.
67 *Cal. S.P. Dom.* 1658-9, 358-9.
68 *D.N.B.* (s.v. Button, Ralph; Owen, John, D.D.; Pakeman; Sangar; Sylvester, Mat.); *Calamy Revised*, ed. Matthews, 11, 95, 166, 290-1, 379, 427, 476.
69 *Trans. Cong. Hist. Soc.* ii. 97.
70 *Calamy Revised*, ed. Matthews, 166-7, 290-1.
71 P.R.O., RG 31/3, Lond. dioc. returns; Guildhall MSS. 9580/1-9, 9557. Rest of para. and following 2 paras. based on detailed inf. below.

72 For abbreviations used in the accounts of protestant nonconformist churches, see p. 40 n. 51. All attendance figs. 1903 are from Mudie-Smith, *Rel. Life*, 425-6 (Brentford) and 429-30 (Ealing).   73 *Cal. S.P. Dom.* 1658-9, 358-9.
74 *V.C.H. Mdx.* iii. 131.   75 Guildhall MS. 9579.
76 *D.N.B.*   77 Guildhall MS. 9557, p. 37.
78 *V.C.H. Mdx.* iii. 131.
79 G.R.O. Worship Reg. no. 64708; inf. from Mr. G. R. Howe.   80 Robbins, *Mdx.* 115.
81 P.R.O., RG 31/3, Lond. dioc. returns.
82 Guildhall MS. 9557, p. 35.
83 M.R.O., D.R.O. 37/D1/2.
84 Lysons, *Environs*, ii. 233; Brewer, *Beauties of Eng. & Wales*, x (5), 346.

claimed to have been at Troy Town, Old Brentford,[85] and preaching ho. of Thomas Wood recorded at Spring Gdns., Old Brentford, 1786–1805.[86] No direct connexion with later Bapt. chapels.

Park chapel, at corner of Boston Manor and Great West rds., New Brentford. Mtg. founded 1799 by min. at Hammersmith in ho. in Market Place,[87] later in min.'s ho. as Particular Bapts., and moved 1808 to chapel NW. of Market Place 1808,[88] which was enlarged to seat 190 after foundation of Sunday sch. 1817. Supported by Hammersmith mtg. 1824–9. Attendance 1851: 77 a.m. (inc. Sunday sch. 21); 35 children afternoon; 100 evening.[89] Services in town hall from c. 1851 until 1855, when surviving chapel seating 500 opened.[90] Attendance 1903: 190 a.m.; 426 p.m. Classrooms added 1869 replaced 1936 by hall, where services held 1940 until 1950 reopening of bomb-damaged church, seating 400 in 1978.[91] Seceders founded W. Ealing Bapt. church 1864 and Ealing Rd. Bapt. church c. 1893, the second reuniting with Park chapel between 1903 and 1923. Albany (Independent) and Park chapels amalgamated 1879.

North Rd. Bapt. church, Old Brentford, said to descend from earlier chapel at Troy Town.[92] Thomas Dewell, who reg. mtg. of Independents in bldg. opposite Moon and Seven Stars inn,[93] Old Brentford, was trustee of mtg. of Bapts., later Particular Bapts., established in outhouse on E. side of North Rd. 1819.[94] No min. from 1820 until 1825, when John Andrews Jones (d. 1868), pamphleteer, was appointed.[95] In 1837 Zoar chapel was founded at Hounslow.[96] Surviving bldg. on W. side of North Rd. opened 1840[97] and enlarged 1854, when min. seceded to Brethren. Attendance 1851: 200 a.m. (inc. 90 Sunday sch.); 90 children afternoon; 220 evening.[98] Attendance 1903: 201 a.m.; 157 p.m. Church bombed 1940 and restored 1954, with sittings reduced to 200.

West Ealing, formerly Ealing Dean, Bapt. church founded 1864 by Particular Bapts. from Park chapel, Brentford. Mtgs. first at small drill hall of 30th Mdx. Volunteers, Uxbridge Rd.,[99] and from 1865 at surviving church seating 450, in Chapel Rd., W. Ealing. Attendance 1903: 334 a.m.; 358 p.m. Bldg. enlarged 1927 and repaired, after war damage, 1953; adjoining Sunday schs. of 1897 enlarged 1913. Seated 300 in 1978.[1]

Haven Green Bapt. church, Castlebar Rd., founded 1880 by Lond. Bapt. Assoc. Seated 872 but overcrowded 1893.[2] Attendance 1903: 576 a.m.; 862 p.m. Sunday sch. and hall added 1910, church renovated 1928, and room at rear demol. 1974.[3] Seated 930 in 1978. Daughter churches founded at Greenford by 1931 and N. Hanwell 1938.[4]

Pastor and other seceders from Park chapel 1893 met by 1896 in iron tabernacle at Ealing Rd., Old Brentford. Attendance 1903: 55 a.m.; 63 p.m. Later in 1903, after min.'s departure, members reunited with Park chapel and tabernacle sold. Existing bldg. beside tabernacle used by Meths. 1914[5] but reg. as Park chapel mission church 1919[6] and independent as Ealing Rd. Bapt. church 1923. Tabernacle demol. 1945.[7]

South Ealing Bapt. church existed at Junction Rd. by 1921 and had closed by 1961.[8]

CONGREGATIONALISTS. John Jackson held services at Brentford in 1672, when licensed to hold them at his ho., and until c. 1689.[9] Apparently succeeded by John Walker, who kept mtg. ho. at Old Brentford 1690[10] and became min. of Brentford Cong. church 1694, when Protestant dissenters reg. leasehold mtg. ho. in Ferry Lane. Church served wide area[11] and attracted many legacies, notably those of John Sanders c. 1731, John Brice c. 1778, one Ormerod, and Revd. Timothy Hargreaves (d. 1793);[12] income from endowments was £51 in 1840 and £1,791 was invested in stock 1868.[13] Existing bldg. opened at E. end of the Butts 1783 as the 'new temple', but called Boston Rd. chapel by 1845.[14] Members, Cong. or Independent by 1851, united with Albany chapel 1840 and again 1875. Attendance 1851, when seating for 400: 240 a.m. (inc. 110 Sunday sch.); 130 children afternoon; 180 evening.[15] Attendance 1903: 135 a.m.; 180 p.m. After bomb damage 1944 church was restored with reduced accommodation, seating 160 in 1978. Joined Presbs. as Brentford United Reformed church 1972.[16]

Independents reg. Old Mtg. Ho. at the Borough, Old Brentford, 1798, first floor of ho. opposite Moon and Seven Stars, Old Brentford, 1818, and bldg. near Ealing Rd., Old Brentford, 1819.[17]

[85] Old Brentford Bapt. Mtg. (booklet 1854).
[86] Guildhall MSS. 10465/112, p. 65; 160, pp. 8–9; M.R.O., D.R.O., 37/B1/2.
[87] Para. based on H. Wickenden, Short Hist. Park Chapel, Brentford (jubilee booklet 1955), and inf. from the sec.
[88] Guildhall MSS. 9580/2, 3.
[89] P.R.O., HO 129/134/3/1/8.
[90] Ibid. C 54/14774, no. 4.
[91] Inf. from Mr. H. Wickenden.   [92] Above.
[93] P.R.O., RG 31/3, Lond. dioc. returns; M.R.O., Acc. 634/6.
[94] Guildhall MS. 9580/5; M.R.O., Acc. 634/8a–b, 6. Para. based on L. Lupton, Old Brentford Bapt. Mtg. (booklet 1954).
[95] D.N.B.
[96] V.C.H. Mdx. iii. 132–3.
[97] M.R.O., Acc. 634/6, 8a–b; Guildhall MS. 9580/8; P.R.O., C 54/12476, no. 1.
[98] P.R.O., HO 129/134/3/3/9.
[99] G.R.O. Worship Reg. no. 16402; W. Ealing Bapt. Church Centenary 1864–1964 (booklet).

[1] W. Ealing Bapt. Ch. 1864–1964; inf. from the min.
[2] Jackson, Ealing, 274–5.
[3] Haven Green's 50 Years: Jubilee Story (1931); inf. from the min.
[4] V.C.H. Mdx. iii. 234.
[5] Wickenden, Park Chapel; G.R.O. Worship Reg. no. 35675; leaflet at Ealing Rd. Bapt. church.
[6] G.R.O. Worship Reg. no. 47659.
[7] Ealing Rd. Bapt. church leaflet.
[8] G.R.O. Worship Reg. no. 48353.
[9] Above.
[10] Mdx. County Rec. Sess. Bks. 1689–1709, 24.
[11] Rest of para. based on Brentford Cong. Ch. 1694–1972 (leaflet).
[12] G.L.R.O., N/C/34/2; will at Chiswick libr.
[13] Digest Endowed Chars. Mdx. H.C. 433, p. 12 (1867–8), lii (1).
[14] Faulkner, Brentford, Ealing and Chiswick, 133.
[15] P.R.O., HO 129/134/3/3/7.
[16] Inf. from the min.
[17] Guildhall MSS. 9580/2, p. 17; 9580/4–5.

Albany chapel, S. of Albany Rd., Old Brentford, opened 1829 by Independents,[18] who, with no settled pastor, moved to Boston Rd. chapel 1840. Albany chapel again used for worship from 1842[19] and was interdenominational 1851, when pastor of Boston Rd. chapel reported attendance of 40 a.m.[20] Threatened with closure 1862[21] but again reg. 1864 by Independents,[22] who united with Boston Rd. chapel 1875 and closed Albany chapel 1879.[23] Bldg. used for interdenominational worship 1882.[24]

Ealing Green Cong. church said to originate in mtgs. in cottage at Ealing c. 1800, which may have been chapel near Red Lion 1816.[25] Chapel opened in the Grove 1822, with permanent min. from 1834,[26] rebuilt to seat 430 in 1848. Attendance 1851: 265 a.m. (inc. 109 Sunday sch.); 267 p.m.[27] Grove chapel, later St. Saviour's sch., replaced by bldg. E. of Ealing green 1860. Hall added and church enlarged, to seat 760, by 1895. Attendance 1903: 386 a.m.; 235 p.m. Bldg. known as 'big church' from 1926, when rooms were added and 'little church' was opened for children.[28] Used since 1972 by both United Reformed and Meth. churches,[29] Meths. being more numerous 1978.[30]

West Ealing Cong., from 1972 United Reformed, church was formed in 1900, with services at no. 70 the Avenue from 1901 and at hall in Argyll Rd. from 1903.[31] Attendances 1903: 108 a.m.; 88 p.m. After First World War hall adapted as permanent church and another hall and classrooms added. Church, seating 200, closed between 1951 and 1976.[32]

PRESBYTERIANS. St. Andrew's Presb., from 1972 United Reformed, church was formed by Scottish members of Ealing Green Cong. church, who met from 1875 in iron bldg. seating 300 opposite Christ the Saviour church in Broadway. New church at corner of Mount Park and Aston rds. 1887, with seating increased from 550 to 800 in 1890s.[33] Attendance 1903: 390 a.m.; 300 p.m. Seated 480 in 1978.[34] Daughter churches established at Wembley 1898 and Elthorne Pk., Hanwell, 1906.

St. Aidan's Presb., from 1972 United Reformed, church, Northfields, replaced Elthorne

Pk. Presb. church, Hanwell, 1922. Bldg., at corner of Leybourne Ave. and St. Aidan's Rd., seats 200.[35]

Members of Presb. Church of Wales met at Y.W.C.A., Uxbridge Rd., 1903-4 and at Swift's assembly rooms from 1904 until 1909, when Welsh Presb. church, Ealing green, was opened. Church flourished during 1930s but shared min. with Hammersmith (closed 1972) from 1961 and Walham Green, Fulham, from 1969.[36]

An International Presb. church reg. at no. 52 Cleveland Rd., Ealing, 1975.[37]

METHODISTS. John Wesley frequently visited Brentford,[38] where a Meth. group existed 1745 and 1748 but had almost disappeared by 1750. New cong. met in large bldg., perhaps near St. George's church, 1760 and had almost died out 1786, but revived with well attended mtgs. by 1790.[39] Former Presb. chapel at Ferry Lane, Old Brentford, used from 1783,[40] and new Wes. mtg. ho. N. of High St. near modern St. Paul's Road, from 1811.[41] Attendance 1851: 230 a.m. (inc. 145 Sunday sch.); 120 p.m. Church, seating 536 in 1851,[42] rebuilt c. 1865 and replaced by ornate Gothic bldg. at corner of Windmill and Clifden rds. 1890,[43] with spire added 1903.[44] Attendance 1903: 273 a.m.; 324 p.m. Church restored 1951 after bomb damage[45] and replaced 1964, after union with Jubilee chapel (q.v.), by Clifden Rd. Meth. church[46] on part of site in Clifden Rd.

Primitive Meths. reg. private ho. at Ealing 1825[47] and schoolroom at New Brentford 1843.[48] Met 1847-95 in committee room seating 70 at Ferry Lane, Old Brentford. Average attendance 1851: 25 a.m.; 25 afternoon; 70 evening.[49]

Land conveyed 1869 for Primitive Meth. chapel in a new road,[50] apparently Distillery Rd., Old Brentford. Jubilee chapel, New Rd., Old Brentford, was founded 1897 by Primitive Meths. who used two other halls in New Road 1884-95 and 1890-99 respectively.[51] Attendance 1903: 89 a.m.; 106 p.m. Replaced by new Meth. church in Clifden Rd. 1964.[52]

Ealing Broadway Wes. Meth. church originated in services at no. 1 Milford Villas, the Mall, 1864.[53] Sch. chapel seating 300 built in Windsor Rd. 1865[54] and adjoining church seating 1,000

[18] P.R.O., C 54/10889, no. 1; Faulkner, *Brentford, Ealing and Chiswick*, 135. There is a burial and baptism reg. 1831-7: P.R.O., RG 4/370.
[19] Faulkner, *Brentford, Ealing and Chiswick*, 134-5; G.L.R.O., N/C/34/1/1.
[20] P.R.O., HO 129/134/3/2/11.
[21] M.R.O., D.R.O. 37/A11/1, p. 77.
[22] G.R.O. Worship Reg. no. 16167.
[23] *Brentford Cong. Ch. 1694-1972*; Wickenden, *Park Chapel*.
[24] Nat. Soc. files.
[25] M.R.O., Acc. 956/1.
[26] Para. based on Jackson, *Ealing*, 268-71; *100 Years on Ealing Green 1860-1960* (jubilee booklet).
[27] P.R.O., HO 129/134/3/2/6; *Lond. Gaz.* 28 Nov. 1848, p. 4336.
[28] Inf. from Mr. N. M. Eggleton.
[29] G.R.O. Worship Reg. no. 36249.
[30] Ealing and Acton circuit, *Plan and Dir.* (1978).
[31] Para. based on W. Ealing Cong. Church, *Jubilee, 7 June 1953* (pamphlet).
[32] *Cong. Year Bk.* (1951); G.R.O. Worship Reg. no. 44160.
[33] Jackson, *Ealing*, 272-4; *1875-1975: St. Andrew's Utd. Reformed Church Ealing* (booklet 1975).
[34] Inf. from the church sec.

[35] *1875-1975: St. Andrew's Church*; inf. from the sec.
[36] G.R.O. Worship Reg. no. 43637; inf. from Mrs. E. A. Davies.
[37] G.R.O. Worship Reg. no. 74072.
[38] *Works of John Wesley* (1872 edn.), i-iv, *passim*.
[39] Ibid. i. 483; ii. 126, 217, 523; iv. 353, 445, 475, 479, 480; Turner, *Brentford*, 210.
[40] *Brentford Cong. Church 1654-1972* (leaflet); G.L.R.O., N/C/39/2, pp. 74-5.
[41] P.R.O., C 54/9299, no. 13; M.R.O., TA/EAL.
[42] P.R.O., HO 129/134/3/2/4.
[43] *Lond. Gaz.* 4 July 1865, p. 3360; Brentford Wesl. Meth. circuit, *Year Bk. 1928*.
[44] Photos. in Chiswick libr.
[45] Appeal leaflet in Chiswick libr.
[46] G.R.O. Worship Reg. no. 69763; below.
[47] Guildhall MS. 9580/6.   [48] Ibid. 8.
[49] G.R.O. Worship Reg. no. 416; P.R.O., HO 129/134/3/2/5.   [50] P.R.O., C 54/16990, no. 14.
[51] G.R.O. Worship Reg. nos. 27722, 32195, 36133; datestone.
[52] G.R.O. Worship Reg. no. 36133; above.
[53] Jackson, *Ealing*, 271.
[54] *Mdx. County Times*, 2 June 1866; G.R.O. Worship Reg. no. 16898.

added on corner with the Mall 1869.[55] Attendance 1903: 364 a.m.; 381 p.m. Sch. chapel replaced by hall 1925.[56] Bldg. compulsorily sold 1970[57] but survived 1978; members moved 1972 to Ealing Green United Reformed.[58]

West Ealing Primitive Meth. church, Uxbridge Rd., built 1900 with seating for 450 on site of temporary chapel used since 1861.[59] Attendance 1903: 237 a.m.; 378 p.m. Closed 1959, when cong. moved to Kingsdown Meth. church, and sold 1963.[60]

Kingsdown Wes. Meth. church, at corner of Northfield and Kingsdown aves., originally in sch. chapel seating 400 and opened 1908.[61] Permanent church built beside it 1929 at expense of T. W. Moullin and called Moullin Memorial Meth. church. Renamed Kingsdown 1959 after amalgamation with W. Ealing Meth. church. Sch. chapel replaced by hall 1964. Church, altered 1963, seated 220 in 1978.[62]

Pitshanger Wes. Meth. church, at corner of Pitshanger Lane and Lindfield Rd., N. Ealing, built 1913 for members who had worshipped since 1910 at private ho. in Pitshanger Lane. Intended as temporary bldg. but extended 1929 and reconstructed 1955,[63] before replacement 1977-8 by new church on same site. Adjoining hall of 1950 used for services during rebldg.[64]

Meth. church in Ealing Rd., Old Brentford, built 1914 but called Ealing Rd. Bapt. church by 1923.[65]

BRETHREN. C. H. Coles, pastor of North Rd. Bapt. church, seceded with others 1854 to found mtg. of Brethren,[66] perhaps group which met 1903 at no. 93 High St. Attendance 1903: 19 a.m.; 26 p.m.

Brethren met at Gospel hall (later Grove hall), on N. side of the Grove, Ealing c. 1875.[67] Attendance 1903: 83 a.m.; 75 p.m. Mtg. survived 1978 and established daughter church at Greenford 1929.[68]

Brethren met at Sunnyside Room, Disraeli Rd., Ealing 1903. Attendance 1903: 148 a.m.; 138 p.m. Room had been converted to a dwelling by 1977.

Brethren met at Dean hall, Williams Rd., Ealing Dean, from 1912[69] and at Southfield hall, on S. side of Pope's Lane, S. Ealing, from 1928.[70] Both groups survived 1978.

Florence hall, one-storeyed structure in garden of no. 8 Florence Terrace, the Mall, reg. 1933 but disused 1964.[71]

Exclusive Brethren from Dean hall mtg. worshipped at room in Green Man Passage, W. Ealing, 1933-78.[72]

SALVATION ARMY. Barracks at Ealing in Baker's Lane by 1889.[73] Attendance 1903: 55 a.m.; 166 p.m. Moved 1909 to surviving citadel at corner of Leeland Rd. and Leeland Terrace, W. Ealing.[74] Another barracks reg. at no. 5 Green View, High St., Ealing, between 1891 and 1895.[75]

At New Brentford Salvationists sought premises 1887[76] and opened gospel hall in Market Place 1894.[77] Attendance 1903: 16 a.m.; 50 p.m. Moved 1903 to hall over post office in Market Place,[78] 1909 to hall at no. 34 High St. acquired in previous year,[79] and 1915 back to hall over post office. Closed by 1925.[80]

MORMONS. Latter Day Saints reg. Potter's auction room in High St., Old Brentford, 1851.[81] Average Sunday sch. attendance 1851: 6 a.m.; 10 afternoon; 12 evening.[82]

CHRISTIAN SPIRITUALISTS. Ealing National Spiritualist church originated in mtg. 1906 at Horn Lane, Acton. Moved 1908 to New Broadway, Ealing, and 1923 to former Salvation Army barracks in Baker's Lane, replaced by church at nos. 8 and 9 Baker's Lane 1936-7.[83]

Three rooms at no. 12 Somerset Rd., W. Ealing, reg. by 1964 as Lileth Spiritualist church and healing sanctuary,[84] which survived 1978.

OTHER DENOMINATIONS AND UNSPECIFIED MISSIONS. The Blue Ribbon Gospel Army reg. hall in Baker's Lane, Ealing, 1885. Reg. cancelled 1925.[85]

Elim Foursquare Gospel Alliance worshipped at Cranmer hall social bldg. 1930-4. Moved to tabernacle, formerly Elite picture palace, in Northfield Ave., W. Ealing, which seated over 300 in 1978.[86]

Crusaders opened surviving Crusader hall in Woodgrange Rd., Ealing, 1935.[87]

Seventh Day Adventists reg. Shaftesbury hall, at no. 5A New Broadway, Ealing, 1936. Reg. cancelled 1954.[88]

Jehovah's Witnesses in 1939 opened Kingdom hall at no. 40B Uxbridge Rd., Ealing, which was

[55] Jackson, *Ealing*, 272; Jones, *Ealing*, 104; P.R.O., C 54/16566, no. 4.
[56] *Ealing Broadway Meth. Church Centenary 1869-1969* (booklet).
[57] *Mdx. County Times*, 24 July 1970.
[58] G.R.O. Worship Reg. no. 19116; notice at church (1977); *County Times & Gazette*, 6 Oct. 1972.
[59] G.R.O., Worship Reg. nos. 14155, 37697; Jones, *Ealing*, 104.
[60] Inf. from Mr. H. Beaumont.
[61] G.R.O. Worship Reg. no. 42949; Moullin Mem. Meth. Church *Jubilee Fair* (booklet 1958).
[62] G.R.O. Worship Reg. no. 51870; inf. from Mr. H. Beaumont.
[63] Pitshanger Meth. Church *Reopening and Rededication of Church* (1955).
[64] Inf. from the sec.
[65] Above, Bapt.
[66] Lupton, *Old Brentford Bapt. Mtg.*
[67] G.R.O. Worship Reg. no. 26363; inf. from Mr. G. B. Fyfe.
[68] *V.C.H. Mdx.* iii. 218.
[69] G.R.O. Worship Reg. no. 45124.
[70] Ibid. 51348.
[71] Ibid. 54572.
[72] Ibid. 54645.
[73] Ibid. 31648.
[74] Datestone.
[75] G.R.O. Worship Reg. no. 32787.
[76] Newspaper in Chiswick libr.
[77] G.R.O. Worship Reg. no. 34357.
[78] G.R.O. Worship Reg. no. 40085.
[79] Ibid. 43470; M.R.O., Acc. 638/216.
[80] G.R.O. Worship Reg. no. 46591.
[81] Guildhall MS. 9580/9, p. 85.
[82] P.R.O., HO 129/134/3/3/10.
[83] G.R.O. Worship Reg. nos. 49557, 57225; inf. from the sec.
[84] G.R.O. Worship Reg. no. 69436.
[85] Ibid. 28913.
[86] Ibid. 55647; inf. from the min.
[87] G.R.O. Worship Reg. no. 56048.
[88] Ibid. 57805.

disused 1947.[89] Opened Kingdom hall, formerly St. Mary's girls' sch., W. of Ealing green 1950.[90]

Christian Scientists reg. first floor of nos. 11 and 12 the Green, High St., Ealing, 1939. Reg. cancelled 1961, on move to Hanwell.[91]

The Sutcliffe School of Radiant Living, established since 1934 at Westm., reg. Harmony hall, upstairs room at no. 64 St. Mary's Rd., Ealing, 1940. Reg. cancelled 1964.[92]

Children of God reg. classroom at Ealing college, the Mall, 1947. Reg. cancelled 1954.[93]

Undesignated Christians reg. existing Mount Ave. room, behind no. 38 Mount Ave., N. Ealing, 1951.[94]

Ealing Pleasant Sunday Afternoon Society had hall and institute at Green Man Passage, W. Ealing, reg. for worship 1970.[95]

Christadelphians used hall at corner of Ranelagh and Blandford rds., Ealing, 1977.

Assyrian church opened former Good Shepherd hall, Ealing Rd., as Assyrian hall 1978.[96]

UKRAINIAN ORTHODOX CHURCH. A room on the third floor of no. 11 Creffield Road, Ealing Common, was registered as St. Andrew's chapel of the Ukrainian Orthodox Autocephalous Church by the vicar for Great Britain in 1959.[97]

JUDAISM. Although the Rothschilds were practising Jews, as were other families at Ealing by 1910, there was no synagogue until the foundation in 1919 of Ealing and Acton Hebrew Congregation, which was affiliated to the United Synagogue. Meeting first at a private house, then at the Y.M.C.A. in Bond Street, and from 1921 at no. 75 Uxbridge Road, it moved in 1924 to no. 15 Grange Road. There it was registered as Ealing and Acton associate synagogue, which by 1978 had become a district synagogue. The synagogue was enlarged in 1931 and a new hall was added in 1938 and extended in 1962.[98]

Ealing Liberal synagogue, affiliated to the Union of Liberal and Progressive Synagogues, was established in 1943[99] and acquired the former St. Luke's church for worship in 1952.[1]

EDUCATION.[2] New Brentford charity school (St. Lawrence's) opened in 1703. It served several parishes, closed temporarily in 1714 when Ealing's children withdrew, and later probably took no more than 20 children a year. Many more were taught after 1786, when Old Brentford Sunday schools opened, followed by a girls' and a short-lived boys' school. Another Sunday school

founded at New Brentford in 1810 apparently led to the enlargement of the boys' charity school and opening of a girls' school there in 1815. In 1819 309 pupils attended Old and New Brentford charity schools. Infants' schools were opened at Old Brentford in 1837 and at New Brentford in 1840, and a British school was opened in 1834. In 1843 92 pupils attended daily at Brentford: 15 at a common day school, 94 at 5 middle day schools, 114 at dame schools, and 759 at public elementary schools, 272 of them at the British school.[3]

Ealing children attended New Brentford charity school from 1703 until their own opened c. 1714. A girls' school was endowed in 1712 and a boys' in 1719, but in 1724 a single school (St. Mary's) contained boys and girls and apparently it was only in 1782 that separate schools were established.[4] The boys' school was much enlarged in 1817 and c. 1820, when there were 176 children in the two schools. An infants' school opened in 1837 and Ealing had 339 daily pupils in 1843: 50 at dame schools, 34 at common day schools, 36 at middle day schools, and 242 at charity and National schools.[5]

A rising demand for places after 1843 was met partly by existing schools, notably Brentford British school. The Ragged School Union had Sunday schools at Brentford from 1854 and from 1867 a free day school, which was replaced by St. Paul's schools in 1873. At Ealing the growth of the Ealing Dean and Grove districts led to the opening of a separate infants' school in 1857 and Ealing British school in 1859, the rebuilding of the girls' school in 1862, and the opening of St. John's National, Christ Church National, and the Wesleyan schools by 1874.

From 1871 demands for a school board, particularly by nonconformists,[6] were resisted by the Revd. E. W. Relton and other Anglicans. All schools charged fees, those of the Wesleyan and British schools being the highest;[7] many places therefore were not filled at Brentford, where the failure of some poor children to transfer to the new St. Paul's school resulted in a revival of the Ragged school. Under the Education Act of 1876 Ealing educational association was formed instead of a school board in 1877 to meet current deficits and pay for building extensions. Nominally interdenominational but dominated by Anglicans, it survived the opposition of the British school managers, since the ratepayers were overwhelmingly opposed to a board.[8] Apart from an unsuccessful voluntary rate in 1880, funds were raised by subscription until 1895, when Old Brentford became a separate civil parish. Rates levied for the association by Ealing council from 1896 were criticized because the demands did not indicate that they were volun-

[89] G.R.O. Worship Reg. no. 58730.
[90] Ibid. 62730.
[91] Ibid. 58664, 68435.
[92] Ibid. 55533, 59221.
[93] Ibid. 61603.
[94] Ibid. 63131.
[95] Ibid. 72286.
[96] Inf. from Mr. Jack Wolton.
[97] G.R.O. Worship Reg. no. 67393.
[98] G.R.O. Worship Reg. no. 49012; *Ealing and Acton Dist. Synagogue* (jubilee booklet 1969).
[99] *Jewish Year Bk.* (1980).

[1] G.R.O. Worship Reg. no. 63882.
[2] Following 8 paras. based on accounts of individual schs. below.
[3] *Jnl. Stat. Soc. of Lond.* vi. 128.
[4] J. M. Craddock, 'Ealing: 2nd Educ. Era' and 'Short Hist. of Educ. of Poor in Ealing' (TSS. in Ealing libr.).
[5] *Jnl. Stat. Soc. of Lond.* vi. 128.
[6] Para. based on Craddock, 'Ealing: 2nd Educ. Era' and 'Educ. of Poor'.
[7] *Brentford Advocate*, 13 Sept. 1873.
[8] e.g. Ealing Educ. Assoc. *Rep.* (1881). Several reps. are in M.R.O., D.R.O. 37/A12/2.

tary, and by 1901 only one-third was collected. Average attendance under the association rose from 754 in 1878 to 2,388 in 1902 at Ealing.[9] By the late 1890s there may have been overcrowding but a request by the Board of Education for extra places in 1901 was ignored, as responsibility under the Education Act of 1902 was to pass to Ealing M.B., which duly became an autonomous part III authority.[10] At Brentford a census in 1898 revealed that 574 children of school age were not at school.[11] There were 716 absentees in 1901,[12] when Old Brentford school board was established. It achieved nothing before being superseded in 1903 by the county council.[13]

Ealing had too few places in 1903, when the population was growing rapidly. In addition to temporary schools, permanent ones were built by the borough engineer Charles Jones: Little Ealing, Northfields, Drayton Grove, Lammas, and North Ealing,[14] the first four containing large boys', girls', and infants' schools on a single site. Plans for a school on Ealing Dean common were dropped after local opposition.[15] Few places were needed in North Ealing, where most children were educated privately,[16] and elsewhere the council charged fees, which at Drayton Grove were higher than the Board of Education would permit.[17] After the First World War only Grange school replaced the voluntary schools as they closed. From 1931 school building was concentrated in the expanding north and west parts of the borough; although Jones's buildings were seen as outmoded by 1938,[18] it was only from 1952 that they were replaced. North Ealing's Montpelier school was still opposed as unnecessary in 1957.[19]

At Brentford all new needs between 1903 and 1914 were met by Ealing Road primary school. After the First World War, notwithstanding the closure of St. Lawrence's and Rothschild schools, only Lionel Road school was built. The opening of Green Dragon school in 1972 permitted the closure of Ealing Road and St. George's schools.

The county council established secondary schools for boys in 1913 and girls in 1926 at Ealing, where a selective central school was opened in 1925. Following the Hadow report, four of Ealing's council schools acquired a single-sex senior department and after the Education Act of 1944 the former central school became a grammar school. Secondary classes elsewhere used converted premises and the only change before the introduction of the comprehensive system was the transfer of two of the smaller secondary schools to the new Ealing Mead school in 1962. At Brentford the boys' and girls' senior

schools and Gunnersbury Roman Catholic grammar school were the only secondary schools.

Ealing M.B. became an 'excepted district', responsible for primary and secondary education, under the Act of 1944, as did Brentford and Chiswick M.B. From 1965 they lay within Ealing and Hounslow L.B.s. When Hounslow adopted a comprehensive scheme in 1971, secondary and grammar schools were amalgamated but the structure was otherwise unchanged. When Ealing adopted a scheme in 1974, it established first schools for children aged 5–8, middle schools for those aged 8–12, and high schools for those aged 13 and over. The rearrangement entailed building extensions to some first and middle schools. The remaining secondary departments in older three-department schools were eliminated and Ealing Mead school was closed. The former county schools survived as high schools and Walpole school merged with Bordeston school, Hanwell, on a split site. A small educational foundation, formed from part of John Bowman's charity in 1904, had an income of c. £35 in 1973.[20] For Old Brentford the educational foundation established from the charities of Need and Taylor in 1856 had an income of c. £263 in 1979, spent largely on school libraries.[21]

Public schools.[22] The general sources are those indicated above, p. 44, and the same abbreviations are used.

BOSTON MANOR HO. COUNTY I, Boston Manor Pk., Brentford. Opened 1940 at Boston Manor Ho., moved temporarily to St. Paul's sch. 1944. 67 I in 1955, 37 in 1957. Closed 1961.[23]

BRENTFORD BRITISH, see Rothschild.

BRENTFORD CANAL BOATMEN'S. Opened c. 1896 at mission in Isleworth,[24] moved c. 1904 to the Butts,[25] 1932 to two rooms at Brentford sr. schs., 1950 to former St. Lawrence's sch. in the Ham.[26] Irregularly attended by children of all ages. 1898 roll 500, a.a. 13.[27] 1950 roll 100, maximum attendance 18.[28] Closed by 1957.

BRENTFORD CENTRAL RAGGED, Old Spring Gardens. Opened 1867 as free day sch. in former British sch., where evening mtgs., held at various schs. since 1854, had been held on Sundays since 1860.[29] 1867 a.a. 117. 1871 a.a. 264.[30] Replaced by St. Paul's sch. 1873.[31]

BRENTFORD SCH. FOR G, Clifden Rd. Opened 1968 as comprehensive sch. in former Brentford sec. mod.[32] Extended after 1971. Roll 1978: 1,080 SG.

BRENTFORD SEC. MOD., Clifden Rd. Opened 1930 on single site as separate schs.[33] 1930 accn.

[9] *Rep. of Educ. Cttee. of Council, 1878* [C. 2342–I], p. 947, H.C. (1878–9), xxiii; *List of Schs. under Admin. of Bd. 1902* [Cd. 1277], p. 167, H.C. (1902), lxxix.
[10] Mdx. C.C. *Primary and Sec. Educ. in Mdx. 1900–65.*
[11] M.R.O., SB/OB/1, p. 15.
[12] Ibid. p. 49.   [13] Ibid. (min. bk.).
[14] Jones, *Decade of Progress*, 16 sqq.
[15] Plan and cuttings (1906) in Ealing libr.
[16] *Ealing, 1901–51*, ed. Scouse, 32.
[17] E. P. H. Pugh, *Drayton Schs. 1908–58* (1958), 3.
[18] Cuttings in Ealing libr.
[19] Inf. from the headmaster; see also Ealing Boro. *Rep. of Development Plan Subcttee. 1946–7.*   [20] Char. Com. files.
[21] Below, charities; inf. from chief executive's office, Hounslow L.B.

[22] Private schs. are treated separately below.
[23] M.R.O., MCC/E correspondence file 168; Yarde, 'Boston Manor', 20–1.
[24] *2nd Ann. Rep. of Canal Boatmen's Mission and Day Sch. 1897–8.*   [25] *10th Ann. Rep. 1905–6.*
[26] *Mdx. Independent*, 29 Sept. 1950.
[27] *2nd Ann. Rep. 1897–8.* See also *Living Lond.* ed. G. R. Sims (1901), ii. 66.
[28] *Mdx. Independent*, 29 Sept. 1950.
[29] Craddock, 'Ealing: 2nd Educ. Era'; Brentford cent. ragged schs. and town mission, *Rep.* (1867).
[30] *Brentford Cent. Ragged Schs.* (1871).
[31] *Brentford Advocate*, 13 Sept. 1873.
[32] Hounslow L.B. *Sec. Schs. Maintained by Council* (1971).
[33] Brentford and Chiswick U.D. *Rep. of M.O.H.* (1930).

320 SB, 320 SG, a.a. 247 SB, 247 SG. 1936 accn. 360 SB, 440 SG, a.a. 241 SB, 301 SG. Extended 1954 but overcrowded 1955.[34] Became Brentford Sch. for G 1968, when B moved to Syon sch., Isleworth.[35]

BRENTFORD TEMP. I, Upper Butts. Opened 1907 for 120. 1919 accn. 120, a.a. 64. 1927 accn. 120, a.a. 120. Closed 1932.

BRENTFORD, NEW, NAT., see St. Lawrence's.

BRENTFORD, OLD, NAT., see St. George's.

CHRIST CHURCH C.E. MIDDLE, New Broadway.[36] Opened 1872 for B, 1886 for G.[37] Former I sch. for St. Mary's and Christ Church known as Christ Church I sch. 1878–1930, then as St. Saviour's. 1906 accn. 251 B, 234 G, 272 I, a.a. 217 B, 171 G, 113 I. 1919 accn. 203 B, 187 G, 254 I, a.a. 125 B, 135 G, 80 I. Reorg. 1921 for SB, JG. Again reorg. 1925, 1926, and 1930 for JM.[38] 1932 accn. 350 JM, a.a. 379. 1936 accn. 328 JM, a.a. 226. Middle sch. from 1974. Roll 1977: 325.

COMPTON FIRST, Cavendish Ave. Opened 1972 for JMI. First sch. from 1974. Roll 1978: 160.

DRAYTON TEMP., Alexandra Rd. Opened 1904 as St. James's JMI in former iron church. 1906 accn. 300, a.a. 251. Replaced by Drayton Grove sch. 1908.[39]

DRAYTON FIRST, Drayton Grove.[40] Opened 1908 for BGI. 1919 accn. 300 B, 300 G, 336 I, a.a. 315 B, 275 G, 221 I. Reorg. 1936 for SB, JM. 1938 accn. 320 SB, 400 JM. I added 1939.[41] SB closed between 1957 and 1963. First sch. from 1974. Roll 1978: 159.

EALING BRITISH, see Joseph Lancaster.

EALING CENTRAL, see Walpole.

EALING COUNTY B, Ealing Green. Opened 1913 for 330 SB on site of the Hall,[42] as sec. sch. with art and technical classes. Later called Ealing grammar sch. for B. Extended 1936,[43] 1961, 1964. Became Ealing Green high sch. 1974.

EALING COUNTY G, Queen's Drive. Opened 1926 for SG in the Park.[44] Later called Ealing grammar sch. for G. Moved c. 1965 to Queen's Drive. Became Ellen Wilkinson high sch. 1974.

EALING DEAN, see St. John's.

EALING DRILL HALL TEMP. Opened 1904 for 320 I, closed 1905.

EALING GREEN HIGH, Ealing Green. Opened 1974 as SB comprehensive in former Ealing county grammar sch. Roll 1977: 690 SB.

EALING MEAD, Almond Ave. Opened 1962 as SB sec. mod., replacing Little Ealing sec. mod.[45] Closed 1974.[46]

EALING NAT., see St. Mary's.

EALING RD. Opened 1903–4 for BGI. 1906 accn. 370 BG, 300 I, a.a. 305 BG, 234 I. 1919 accn. 480 BG, 300 I, a.a. 382 BG, 226 I. Reorg.

1932 for JMI. 1938 accn. 440 JM, 300 I, a.a. 282 JM, 116 I. Closed 1975.[47]

EALING WESLEYAN, Broadway.[48] Opened 1874 for BG and probably I next to Meth. church. 1878 accn. 208, a.a. 88. Charged high fees, was refused grant 1891,[49] and was described as middle-class elementary 1893. Extended c. 1879 and rebuilt c. 1893. 1898 accn. 283, a.a. 275. 1906 accn. 215 BG, 68 I, a.a. 272 BGI. 1919 accn. 212 BG, a.a. 200 BG. Closed 1921, when pupils moved to Joseph Lancaster.

EALING, LITTLE, see Little Ealing.

EALING, NORTH, FIRST AND MIDDLE, Pitshanger Lane. Opened 1911 for G from St. Stephen's C.E. and I.[50] 1919 accn. 400 GI, a.a. 33. B from St. Stephen's 1921. 1926 accn. 143 B, 400 GI, a.a. 112 B, 286 GI. Reorg. for JMI and extended c. 1935 on closure of B sch. 1938 accn. 460, a.a. 450. Combined first and middle sch. from 1974. Roll 1978: 520.

EALING, SOUTH, TEMP., Junction Rd. Opened 1914 for JMI. From 1922 called S. Ealing Good Shepherd hall temp. sch. 1919 accn. 300 JMI, a.a. 134. 1922 accn. 150, a.a. 131. Closed 1927.

ELLEN WILKINSON HIGH, Queen's Drive. Opened 1974 as comprehensive high sch. in former Ealing county G sch. Roll 1978: 1,100 SG.

ELTHORNE HIGH, see Walpole.

FIELDING FIRST AND MIDDLE, Wyndham Rd. Opened 1953 as separate JM and I schs.,[51] amalgamated 1967.[52] First and middle schs. from 1974. Rolls 1977–8: 210 and 265.

GRANGE FIRST AND MIDDLE, Church Place. Opened 1925 for JM, 1927 and 1931 for I, 1931 for SG.[53] 1927 accn. 420 JM, a.a. 380. 1932 accn. 296 SG, 400 JM, 400 I, a.a. 166 SG, 386 JM, 316 I. First and middle schs. from 1974, when SG moved to Ellen Wilkinson. Rolls 1978: 320 and 258.

GREEN DRAGON, North Rd., Brentford. Opened 1975 as JMI schs., replacing Ealing Rd. sch. Rolls 1977: 280 I, 290 JM.

GUNNERSBURY R.C., Gunnersbury Ave. Opened c. 1919 as sec. sch. in Boston Pk. Rd.,[54] moved to Gunnersbury Ave. 1932,[55] and extended c. 1938 after bequest from Patrick Murphy (d. 1934).[56] Received grant 1939[57] and became vol. aided grammar sch. 1944, J sch. closing 1947. 180 B in 1932, 331 in 1947, 374 in 1956.[58] Comprehensive from 1971, with lower sch. in Gunnersbury Ave. and upper sch. in new bldgs. at the Ride. Rolls 1977: 360 and 700 SB.

GURNELL MIDDLE, Hathaway Gardens. Opened 1974 as middle sch. Roll 1977: 275.

[34] M.R.O., MCC/E correspondence file 168.
[35] *Brentford and Chiswick As It Was*, illus. 20.
[36] Para. based on Nat. Soc. files; Jackson, *Ealing*, 278, in addition to the usual sources.
[37] Craddock, 'Ealing: 2nd Educ. Era'.
[38] *Christ Church—Christ the Saviour* (booklet).
[39] Pugh, *Drayton Schs.* 1.
[40] Para. based on Pugh, *Drayton Schs.* in addition to the usual sources.
[41] Ealing Boro. *Educ. in Ealing, 1877–1945*.
[42] *The Times*, 30 Oct. 1913.
[43] Mdx. Educ. Cttee. *Opening of Extension* (1936).
[44] *The Times*, 3 Feb. 1926.
[45] Inf. from the headmaster, Little Ealing middle sch.
[46] Inf. from the headmaster, Ealing Green high sch.

[47] Inf. from the headmaster, Green Dragon J sch.
[48] Para. based on P.R.O., ED 7/87; Jackson, *Ealing*, 281–2; *Ealing Broadway Meth. Church 1869–1969* (centenary booklet), in addition to the usual sources.
[49] Craddock, 'Educ. of Poor', 21, 32.
[50] P.R.O., ED 7/87.
[51] *Case Against Reorg. of Ealing Schs.* (1969).
[52] Ealing L.B. *List of Educ. Establishments* (1966).
[53] P.R.O., ED 7/87; Ealing Boro. *Educ. in Ealing, 1877–1945.* [54] *Brentford and Chiswick Times*, 26 Nov. 1937.
[55] *The Times*, 21 Jan. 1932.
[56] *Mdx. County Times*, 25 May 1935; M.R.O., MCC/E correspondence file 139 (Gunnersbury R.C.).
[57] M.R.O., MCC/E correspondence file 139.
[58] Ibid. files 139, 139A, 168.

JOSEPH LANCASTER, Lancaster Rd.[59] Opened 1859 as Ealing British sch. for BGI.[60] Charged high fees and soon won good reputation. 1865 a.a. 103. 1871 a.a. 219. Extended *c.* 1880, *c.* 1887, 1895. Taken over by council as Joseph Lancaster sch. *c.* 1904. 1906 accn. 293 BG, 136 I, a.a. 326 BG, 131 I. 1919 accn. 248 BG, 123 I, a.a. 326 BGI. Replaced by Grange sch. 1925.

LAMMAS TEMP. Opened 1904 for 312 M, closed 1905.

LAMMAS, Cranmer Ave. Opened 1910 for BGI.[61] 1919 accn. 398 B, 400 G, 460 I, a.a. 356 B, 365 G, 318 I. B and G formed Ealing central (later Walpole) sch. 1925, I remained until reorg. *c.* 1932 for JMI. 1938 accn. 370, a.a. 317. I moved to Fielding sch. 1953, when bldgs. occupied by Walpole sch.[62]

LIONEL RD., Brentford. Opened 1931 for JMI. Extended 1934, 1939.[63] 1932 accn. 300, a.a. 186. 1936 accn. 500, a.a. 380. Roll 1978: 249.

LITTLE EALING FIRST AND MIDDLE, Little Ealing Lane. Opened 1905 for BGI.[64] Extended before 1919 and in 1950s. 1919 accn. 440 B, 440 G, 486 I, a.a. 367 B, 371 G, 315 I. Reorg. 1932. 1936 accn. 394 SB, 390 JM, 380 I, a.a. 324 SB, 327 JM, 270 I. SB moved to Ealing Mead 1962. First and middle schs. from 1974. Rolls 1977: 240 and 344.

MONTPELIER FIRST AND MIDDLE, Helena Rd. Opened 1957 for JMI. First and middle schs. from 1974. Rolls 1978: 230 and 300.

MOUNT CARMEL R.C. FIRST AND MIDDLE, Little Ealing Lane. Opened 1968 for JMI. Combined first and middle sch. from 1974. Part of former Lourdes Mount private sch. taken over as annexe 1974 and used mainly by middle sch. 1977. Roll 1977: 364.

NORTHFIELDS FIRST AND MIDDLE, Balfour Rd. Opened 1905[65] for 400 B, 400 G, 446 I. 1919 accn. 440 B, 440 G, 486 I, a.a. 352 B, 317 G, 326 I. Reorg. 1932 for SG, JMI. 1936 accn. 314 SG, 440 JM, 380 I, a.a. 241 SG, 366 JM, 268 I. JMI moved by 1938. First and middle schs. from 1974. Rolls 1978: 190 and 180.

ROTHSCHILD, High Street, Brentford. Opened 1834 for BG as Brentford British sch. in Old Spring Gardens near One Tun Alley.[66] 1850 a.a. 250.[67] Moved 1859 to N. side of High Street.[68] Financed by subscriptions, especially from Rothschild family, and considered one of best schs. in London 1872.[69] Extended twice in 1880s and *c.* 1902. 1906 accn. 358 B, 190 G, 166 I, a.a.

278 B, 215 G, 113 I. Renamed Rothschild sch. by 1906 and taken over by Ealing M.B. 1919 accn. 282 B, 282 G, a.a. 240 B, 240 G. Closed 1930, on opening of Brentford sec. mod. sch. Bldg. demol. *c.* 1936 and replaced by health centre 1938.[70]

ST. GEORGE'S C.E., Clayponds Lane, Brentford. Originated in Sunday schs. near St. George's church and in sch. of industry.[71] Sunday schs. founded 1786 by vicar of Ealing and author Mrs. Sarah Trimmer (1741–1810) modelled on those of Robert Raikes.[72] 300 BG 1788. 60 B and 100 G 1796–1811. Closed 1824 but revived 1833 and 1839–80. 1843 a.a. 240.[73] Sch. of industry, later Green sch., founded 1787 by Mrs. Trimmer, had 40 G until 1810, 85 G 1811, and over 100 G 1834, when run by her daughters. Sch. of industry for B opened by 1796 but failed by 1807.[74] Nat. sch. for *c.* 100 I opened 1831, moving 1837 to bldg. for 178 W. of North Rd.[75] 1878 a.a. 149. 1893 a.a. 220. Moved 1893 to new bldg. for 480 BGI at corner of Clayponds Lane and Green Dragon Lane.[76] 1906 accn. 152 B, 152 G, 176 I, a.a. 152 B, 150 G, 184 I. 1919 accn. 144 B, 144 G, 151 I, a.a. 85 B, 129 G, 165 I. Bldgs. improved 1926, when renamed St. George's primary sch.,[77] 1933, and 1937. 1927 accn. 288 JM, 151 I, a.a. 231 JM, 114 I. 1938 accn. 354 JMI, a.a. 203. Roll 1977: 60 JMI. Closed 1978.[78]

ST. GREGORY'S R.C. FIRST AND MIDDLE, Woodfield Rd. Opened 1953 for JMI as overflow for R.C. schs. in Greenford and Hanwell. Combined first and middle sch. from 1975. Roll 1978: *c.* 500.

ST. JOHN'S FIRST AND MIDDLE, Felix Rd.[79] Opened 1862 for BG in iron hall as Ealing Dean sch.[80] Hall moved to Felix Rd. and used as Nat. sch. for 60–70 I 1872, when sch. for 180 BG added. 1878 accn. 211 BGI, a.a. 127. Mixed sch. bldg. used for I 1882, when new mixed sch. built. 1885 accn. 522 BGI, a.a. 380. 1906 accn. 333 B, 333 G, 273 I, a.a. 427 B, 395 G, 288 I. 1919 accn. 298 B, 298 G, 234 I, a.a. 269 B, 269 G, 160 I. Transferred to Ealing M.B. 1932 and became JMI sch.[81] Bldgs. replaced 1973. Combined first and middle sch. from 1974. Roll 1977: 400.

ST. JOHN'S R.C., Boston Park Rd., Brentford. Opened by 1866 in the Butts. 1865–6 a.a. 75. 1885 accn. 211, a.a. 151. Moved 1901 to Brook Rd.[82] 1906 accn. 142 BG, 124 I, a.a. 14 BG, 108 I. 1919 accn. 182 BG, 85 I, a.a. 172 BGI. Extended 1928.[83] 1932 accn. 284 BGI, a.a. 249. Pupils aged 5–15[84] until seniors moved

[59] Para. based on Jackson, *Ealing*, 280–1, and Ealing Local Hist. Soc. *Local Historian* (1964), in addition to the usual sources.   [60] P.R.O., ED 7/87; ibid. C 54/15502, no. 10.
[61] Ibid. ED 7/87.
[62] *Case Against Reorg. of Ealing Schs.* (1969).
[63] Brentford and Chiswick U.D. *Ann. Rep. of M.O.H.* (1931); M.R.O., MCC/E correspondence file 168.
[64] P.R.O., ED 7/87.   [65] Ibid.
[66] Faulkner, *Brentford, Ealing and Chiswick*, 135; P.R.O., C 54/11055, no. 17; Guildhall MS. 10465/149, pp. 68–9.
[67] *Mins. of Educ. Cttee. of Council, 1848–50* [1215], p. ccxiv, H.C. (1850), xliii.
[68] P.R.O., C 54/15331, nos. 15–16; Brentford Brit. sch. min. bk. (1844–73) in Chiswick libr.; Turner, *Brentford*, illus. (grangerized copy in Chiswick libr.).
[69] *Rep. of Educ. Cttee. of Council, 1872* [C.812], p. 64, H.C. (1873), xxiv.
[70] *Brentford and Chiswick As It Was*, illus. 20.
[71] For the early schs., see D. M. Yarde, *Life and Works of Sarah Trimmer* (Hounslow and Dist. Hist. Soc. 1972).

[72] *D.N.B.*
[73] *Ambulator* (1796 and later edns.); *Jnl. Stat. Soc. of Lond.* vi. 130; St. George's par. notes 1880.
[74] *Ambulator* (1796 and later edns.); Lysons, *Environs*, ii. 240; Brewer, *Beauties of Eng. & Wales*, x (5), 347; *Rep. of Sel. Cttee. on Educ.* H.C. 572, pp. 215–16 (1834), ix.
[75] St. George's ch. *Rep. of I Sch.*, *Old Brentford, 1836–7*; *I Sch.* (appeal leaflet, 1837); Guildhall MS. 10465/152, pp. 295 sqq.; Nat. Soc. files; Colvin, *Dict. Brit. Architects*, 40.
[76] Nat. Soc. files.
[77] Ibid.
[78] *Mdx. Chron.* 13 Jan. 1978.
[79] Para. based on Jackson, *Ealing*, 278–9, in addition to the usual sources.
[80] M.R.O., D.R.O. 37/A11/1; *Christ Church, Money Required for Char. Purposes* (1863).
[81] Nat. Soc. files.
[82] *Brentford and Chiswick Times*, 8 Apr. 1938.
[83] Brentford and Chiswick U.D. *Rep. of M.O.H.* (1928).
[84] M.R.O., MCC/E correspondence file 168.

c. 1957, leaving sch. still overcrowded with 272 JMI in 1962. Moved to Boston Pk. Rd. 1968. Roll 1978: 256 JMI.

ST. LAWRENCE'S C.E., Brentford. Opened 1703 as char. sch. for BG. Financed by subscriptions, mainly from Ealing and Isleworth, and closed on opening of Ealing char. sch. 1714.[85] Curate J. Le Hunt retained 10 B and reopened sch. in own ho. 1715,[86] soon replaced by schoolroom for 20 B in the Butts.[87] Financed by subscriptions, sermons, and legacies, inc. rent charge of £37 10s. in 1819 under will (proved 1721) of Dorothy, Lady Capel, and £30 a year under will (dated 1810) of Mrs. Alithea Mary Stafford.[88] Parish children boarded 1735 and later employed, master being part-time tradesman.[89] 23 B and 13 G clothed and educ. 1811.[90] After merging with Sunday sch. of *c.* 1810,[91] new sch. ho. for 200 B opened in the Ham 1815, when bldg. in the Butts became sch. for G.[92] Dr. Bell's system adopted by 1819, when 146 B and 71 G.[93] Nat. schs. by 1835.[94] G moved 1840 to new sch. in Half Acre, paid for by legacies and Clitherow family;[95] bldg. in the Butts then used by I[96] until their move to Half Acre *c.* 1860.[97] 1870 accn. 457 BGI, a.a. 270. Extended *c.* 1885 and rebuilt 1893.[98] 1880–1912 a.a. *c.* 340.[99] 1919 accn. 207 B, 112 G, 131 I, a.a. 98 B, 94 G, 64 I. Closed 1931.

ST. LAWRENCE'S WITH ST. PAUL'S, see St. Paul's.

ST. LUKE'S C.E., Drayton Green. Opened 1902–3 for I in St. Luke's iron church.[1] 1906 accn. 110, a.a. 71. Replaced by Drayton sch. 1908.[2]

ST. MARY'S C.E. G, Ealing Green. Jane (d. 1712), widow of Sir William Rawlinson,[3] left £500 to clothe and educ. 20 G but there was no separate foundation until 13 a. near church were bought and leased out under Chancery decree of 1787. Sch. ho., with accn. for mistress, bought W. of Ealing Green 1795. 20 G clothed and educ. 1819, when Nat. system to be adopted.[4] 60 G educ. 1821 and 1857. I sch. added 1837 but moved 1857, when teaching was poor.[5] Sch. rebuilt 1862[6] and extended 1894.[7] 1906 accn. 145, a.a. 174. 1919 accn. 128, a.a. 121. Reorg. 1921 for 128 SG and transferred to Ealing M.B. Closed 1926.

ST. MARY'S C.E. B, South Ealing Rd.[8] Opened *c.* 1714 as char. sch.[9] Sch. ho. built 1719 and used by B and G.[10] Boys' sch. ho., with accn. for master, built 1782. Financed by subscriptions, sermons, and legacies,[11] inc. rent charge of £37 10s. in 1819 under will (proved 1721) of Dorothy, Lady Capel, and £30 a year under will (dated 1810) of Mrs. Alithea Mary Stafford. 20 B clothed and educ. until 1817, when Nat. system adopted and schoolroom built for 100. 106 B educ. 1819,[12] 115 in 1845. Sch. rebuilt 1874 and extended 1890. I sch. added 1887. 1906 accn. 237 B, 120 I, a.a. 220 B, 235 I. 1919 accn. 187 B, 94 I, a.a. 173 B, 66 I. Reorg. 1921 for SB and I, 1922–3 for JM. 1927 accn. 272, a.a. 250. Closed 1939.[13]

ST. PAUL'S C.E., St. Paul's Rd., Brentford. Opened 1873 for 522 BGI.[14] Extended 1883, with places for 200 I, and 1898.[15] 1906 accn. 248 B, 210 G, 322 I, a.a. 236 B, 209 G, 310 I. 1919 accn. 144 B, 171 G, 284 I, a.a. 140 B, 162 G, 236 I. Bldgs. condemned 1920.[16] Reorg. *c.* 1925 for M and I, 1930 for separate JM and I, 1932 for JMI. 1932 accn. 329 JM, 264 I, a.a. 308 JM, 154 I. Called St. Lawrence's with St. Paul's sch. 1953 on union of benefices. Extended 1966. Roll 1977: 210.

ST. SAVIOUR'S C.E. FIRST, the Grove. Opened 1861 as Nat. I sch. for St. Mary's and Christ Church in former Cong. chapel, I having been taught 1837–57 at charity (St. Mary's G) sch. and afterwards in overcrowded temp. premises.[17] Became Christ Church I sch. 1878.[18] Reorg. 1930 as St. Saviour's C.E. I sch. 1932 accn. 250, a.a. 173. Extended 1962 and 1974. First sch. from 1974. Roll 1978: 300.

ST. STEPHEN'S C.E., Pitshanger Lane. Opened after 1867 for BG in stables of Kent Ho. Moved 1882 to Pitshanger Lane.[19] 1906 accn. 146 BG, a.a. 92. G moved to N. Ealing sch. 1911.[20] 1919 accn. 143 B, a.a. 124. Closed when B moved to N. Ealing 1921.

WALPOLE, Cranmer Ave. Opened 1925 as Ealing central sch. 1926 accn. 320 B, 320 G, a.a. 245 B, 240 G. Reorg. 1937 as Ealing modern sch.[21] 1938 accn. 640 SM, a.a. 413. Extended 1945 as Walpole grammar sch., took over former Lammas I sch. 1953 and Little Ealing sec. mod. 1962.[22] Formed Elthorne high sch. with

[85] Turner, *Brentford*, 207–8; New Brentford MS. 17798.
[86] MSS. in Chiswick libr.
[87] M.L.R. 1718/4/54; *2nd Rep. Com. Educ. of Poor*, H.C. 547, p. 100 (1819), X-B.
[88] *2nd Rep. Com. Educ. of Poor*, 100–1; *Digest of Schs. and Chars. for Educ.* H.C. 435, p. 177 (1843), xviii.
[89] New Brentford MS. 17515; *T.L.M.A.S.* xxiii. 176.
[90] Lysons, *Environs* (Suppl.), 105.
[91] T. T. Haverfield, *Sermon Occasioned by Death of Mrs. Trimmer* (1811).
[92] Brewer, *Beauties of Eng. & Wales*, x (5), 804; P.R.O., C 54/9747, no. 8; C 54/9815, no. 3; *Educ. of Poor Digest*, 534; Boston man. ct. bk. in Chiswick libr.
[93] *Educ. of Poor Digest*, 534. [94] *Educ. Enq. Abstract*, 556.
[95] Nat. Soc. files; P.R.O., C 54/12291, no. 3; Faulkner, *Brentford, Ealing and Chiswick*, 76–7.
[96] Faulkner, op. cit. 75; *P.O. Dir. Six Home Counties* (1845).
[97] M.R.O., CMD. 2/145; New Brentford MS. 17808; P.R.O., C 54/15546, no. 3.
[98] *Rep. of Educ. Cttee. of Council, 1887* [C. 5467-I], p. 612, H.C. (1888), xxxviii; Nat. Soc. files.
[99] *Rep. of Educ. Cttee. of Council, 1893* [C. 7437-I], p. 912, H.C. (1894), xxix; Mdx. educ. cttee. Brentford division, *Returns of Attendance* (Apr. 1912).

[1] Pugh, *Drayton Schs.* 1.
[2] Ealing Boro. educ. cttee. *Rep. of Sec.* (1907–8).
[3] Jackson, *Ealing*, 71.
[4] Lysons, *Environs*, ii. 239; ibid. (Suppl.), 132–3; *2nd Rep. Com. Educ. of Poor*, 81–2.
[5] M.R.O., D.R.O. 37/G1/1, pp. 8, 74, 76; Faulkner, *Brentford, Ealing and Chiswick*, 210.
[6] M.R.O., D.R.O. 37/A12/1.
[7] Jackson, *Ealing*, 276.
[8] Para. based on ibid. 276–8, in addition to the usual sources.
[9] Lysons, *Environs*, ii. 238; ibid. (Suppl.), 132.
[10] Craddock, 'Educ. of Poor'.
[11] Many educ. chars. are listed in Jackson, *Ealing*, 285–6.
[12] *2nd Rep. Com. Educ. of Poor*, 80.
[13] Craddock, 'Ealing: 2nd Educ. Era'.
[14] Nat. Soc. files; M.R.O., CMD 2/145.
[15] Nat. Soc. files. [16] Ibid.
[17] Ibid.; M.R.O., D.R.O. 37/G1/1, pp. 70 sqq.; P.R.O., C 54/15627, no. 17.
[18] Jackson, *Ealing*, 278.
[19] Ibid. 280.
[20] *St. Stephen's Church* (1976).
[21] Scouse, *Ealing, 1901–51*, 69.
[22] Ibid.; *Case Against Reorg. of Ealing Schs.* (1969).

Bordeston sec. mod., Hanwell, from 1974. New bldgs. on Bordeston site under construction 1978. Roll 1978: 1,140 SM.

Special schools.[23] ASTON, see Cavendish.

CASTLEBAR, Hathaway Gardens. Opened 1972 for multi-handicapped BG aged 4–13. Roll 1977: 120.

CAVENDISH, Cavendish Ave. Opened 1960 as Aston sch., Aston Rd., for emotionally disturbed BG aged 3–16. Moved 1971 to new Cavendish sch. Roll 1977: 31.

ST. MARY'S RD. GIRLS' HOME. Opened at Ealing Ho. 1867, having moved from Acton, by Nat. Refuges for Homeless and Destitute Children. G educ. and trained in household work. Extended 1870 for G under age of 9.[24] Financed by subscriptions,[25] but parl. grant paid by 1884–5, when accn. 140, a.a. 78. 1906 accn. 140, a.a. 85. 1919 accn. 105, a.a. 76. Moved to Esher (Surr.) 1930.[26]

SPRINGHALLOW, Aston Rd. Opened 1971 for autistic BG aged 3–16 in former Aston sch. A unit of Cavendish sch. until 1976. Roll 1978: 22.

Adult and technical education.[27] Evening classes for adults were held in 1842[28] and during the winter from 1859 to 1863 or later, when half of the master's salary was borne by the boys' National school and half by subscriptions.[29] Ealing college of higher education derived from art classes held from *c.* 1884 and science classes added by 1895. At first they took place at Ealing free library,[30] by 1901 at the Hall, Ealing Green, and from 1913 at Ealing county school for boys. In 1929 they moved to the surviving building provided by the county council at the corner of St. Mary's and Warwick roads, which housed a school of arts, a technical institute, and evening intermediate schools. After several changes of name the building was called Ealing technical institute (later college) and school of art in 1937, Ealing technical college in 1961, and Ealing college of higher education in 1977. There were *c.* 220 full-time students in 1946, 450 full-time, 700 part-time, and 7,000 evening students in 1956,[31] and 1,800 full-time and 3,400 part-time students in 1977–8. New buildings were added in 1953, 1962, and 1966, when the college also took over the former girls' county school.

Private schools.[32] In 1599 Thomas Haward taught 18 boys, mostly gentlemen's sons aged 6–17, at his father's house in Ealing.[33] In the 17th century and early 18th several schoolmasters were licensed.[34]

The Revd. William Dodd (1729–77), the forger, taught a few boys at his London house from 1766.[35] He rented a house at Pope's Cross near the west end of Pope's Lane, wrongly identified as Coldhall manor house, in 1769[36] but had moved to Whitton in Isleworth by 1773.[37] Pupils included Philip Stanhope (d. 1815), who in 1773 succeeded his godfather the letter writer as earl of Chesterfield.[38] The same house became known as Goodenough House, where a school was kept by the Revd. Samuel Goodenough (1743–1827), later bishop of Carlisle, from 1772 until 1798[39] and thereafter by his nephew William Goodenough until 1818.[40] Pupils included the prime minister Henry Addington, Viscount Sidmouth (1757–1844), in 1773–4,[41] the diplomat and collector Thomas Bruce, earl of Elgin (1766–1841),[42] the antiquary Barré Charles Roberts (1789–1810) from 1799 to 1805,[43] and the soldier Sir Robert Walpole (1808–76).[44] Among later principals were the Revd. William Moseley from 1820 to 1832,[45] George Mowbray Gilbert, with 42 boys in 1851,[46] and Frank Howard in 1853.[47] Goodenough House was demolished in 1858 and replaced by the Limes.[48]

The Revd. Charles Wallington kept a boys' boarding school at Haven Green, wrongly thought to have been at Ealing House, where he lived from 1783 to 1822[49] and was succeeded by the Revd. B. Greenlaw from 1823 to 1828.[50] The novelist Edward Bulwer-Lytton, Lord Lytton (1803–73), was a pupil.[51]

Great Ealing school was founded in 1698.[52] A Mr. Pierce was succeeded as master in 1768 by his son-in-law the Revd. Richard Badcock Shury, rector of Perivale, whose son-in-law the Revd. David Nicholas became headmaster in 1791. Nicholas (d. 1829) and his sons the Revd. George, who left in 1837, and the Revd. Francis Nicholas spent large sums on buildings and achieved a wide reputation.[53] The school, in a house known as the Old Rectory near the church, had 200 boys in 1811[54] and 365 in 1820.[55] The curriculum was that of a public school,[56] and Louis-Philippe, later king of the French, taught

[23] Inf. on special schs. has been supplied by the head teachers.
[24] *Mdx. County Times*, 30 July 1870.
[25] Jackson, *Ealing*, 284–5.
[26] *Mdx. County Times*, 26 July 1930.
[27] Para. based on inf. from Mr. A. W. Slater.
[28] *Mins. of Educ. Cttee. of Council, 1842–3* [520], p. 143, H.C. (1843), xl.
[29] M.R.O., D.R.O. 37/A12/1.
[30] Jones, *Ealing*, 137; Jackson, *Ealing*, 295.
[31] *Popular Pictorial*, Feb. 1956.
[32] Following subsection drafted by Mr. P. Hounsell.
[33] P.R.O., E 163/24/35; Allison, *Elizabethan Census of Ealing*, 13–14.
[34] Guildhall MS. 10116.
[35] *D.N.B.*; W. Dodd, *Thoughts from Prison* (1793), 9.
[36] M.R.O., Acc. 938/10 deposit/1; Jackson, *Ealing*, 98.
[37] G. Howson, *Macaroni Parson* (1973), 73.
[38] *D.N.B.*; *Letters of Earl of Chesterfield*, ed. B. Dobrée, vi (1932), 2703, 2713, 2717, 2916.
[39] Ealing rate bk. (Mar. 1773); *D.N.B.*

[40] Jackson, *Ealing*, 98; rate bk. (1818).
[41] P. Ziegler, *Addington* (1965), 24–5.
[42] *D.N.B.*; Wilts. R.O. Acc. 1300 (letters of Geo. Bruce-Brudenell).
[43] *D.N.B.*; *Letters of B. C. Roberts* (1874), p. xi.
[44] *D.N.B.*
[45] Rate bks. (1820, 1832); Pigot, *Lond. Dir.* (1826–7).
[46] Census, 1851 (copy in Ealing libr.).
[47] *Mason's Dir. Ealing* (1853).
[48] Jackson, *Ealing*, 101; O.S. Map 6″, Mdx. XV. SE.
[49] Jackson, *Ealing*, 211; Jones, *Ealing*, 143–4; rate bks. (1783, 1822).
[50] Rate bks. (1823, 1828); Pigot, *Lond. Dir.* (1826–7).
[51] *Life of Edw. Bulwer Lytton by his Son*, i (1883), 130 f.
[52] Date in prize bk. of 1875 in Ealing libr.
[53] Jackson, *Ealing*, 172–3; Gtr. Ealing Local Hist. Soc. *Local Historian* (1961), 30; Pigot, *Lond. Dir.* (1826–7, 1839).
[54] Lysons, *Environs* (Suppl.), 130; illus. in Jackson, *Ealing*, 154.
[55] H. C. Banister, *G. A. MacFarren, Life and Works* (1892), 10.
[56] *T.L.M.A.S.* xvii. 107–8.

geography and mathematics there in the early 19th century.[57] Pupils included the soldier Sir Robert Sale (1782–1845),[58] the publisher Charles Knight 1803–5,[59] John Henry Newman (1801–90),[60] the composer Sir George MacFarren (1813–87),[61] and the Ealing-born scientist T. H. Huxley (1825–95).[62] After the school had moved to the Owls, built 1846–7, on the west side of St. Mary's Road, the Old Rectory made way for Ranelagh Road and part of the grounds were added to the churchyard.[63] The school was directed by Dr. Ebenezer Pearce in 1861,[64] the Revd. Edward Hedges in 1868, Charles Morgan in 1874,[65] and Dr. John Chapman, the Jewish educationalist, from 1881.[66] Under Morgan it was a day school, with subjects including book-keeping and physical science.[67] After its closure in 1908 the Owls was replaced by Cairn Avenue and Nicholas Gardens.[68]

Ealing's private schools increased in the 19th century, from 9 'academies' in 1826 to 14 private schools in 1871, 22 in 1880, and 29 in 1900. There were still 26 in 1949 and 14 in 1979.[69] Brentford had comparatively few, 5 being listed in 1832, 6 in 1845, and 5 in 1890, none of them apparently long lived.[70]

Ealing Grove school, near Ealing green,[71] was founded in 1834 by Lady Noel-Byron, of Fordhook House. Interested in combining learning with practical skills,[72] she had visited Philipp Emanuel de Fellenberg at Hofwyl (Switzerland)[73] and appointed as first headmaster E. T. Craig, who had an Owenite background.[74] The curriculum eschewed corporal punishment and included drawing, carpentry, and gardening, with much use of equipment favoured by de Fellenberg and Pestalozzi. Boys from the age of 6, mostly poor, were taken for 2d. a week and boarders from the age of 12.[75] Despite a change of emphasis, advanced methods were still used when Lady Byron moved in 1842.[76] The school closed in 1852.[77]

C. N. Atlee, master of St. Mary's National school until 1835 and of Ealing Grove 1835–52,

opened Byron House school, in the Park, in 1859[78] and had 87 boys, aged 8–17, in 1861.[79] Atlee's son Charles continued it from 1866[80] until 1886, when it was acquired by Dr. B. Brucesmith,[81] who in 1896 renamed it Ealing Grammar school and prepared boarders and day boys for the main public examinations.[82] It had 200 boarders in 1912,[83] and closed in 1917.[84]

Ealing college originated in Church House boys' school, founded in 1820 at the corner of Church Lane and St. Mary's Road.[85] Headmasters included Thomas Lovegrove in 1839,[86] William Quicke by 1851,[87] and William Rowlatt, under whom the school apparently declined, from 1864 to 1872.[88] Charles Taylor then took over and modernized the school, tripling the numbers by 1876. He moved it to new premises in the Mall at the corner of Hamilton Road, opened in 1880 as Ealing college, leaving Church House to be demolished in 1882.[89] It was called Hermosa school after Taylor's departure in 1886 and the Proprietary school from 1894 until its closure in 1901.[90] Girton House school for girls occupied the building from 1905 to 1923[91] and Acton college moved there in 1925, when it was renamed Ealing college. In 1943 it was divided, the lower school moving to the former Hillsborough preparatory school in Creffield Road and the upper to the former Castle Hill school at no. 83 the Avenue in 1957. After transferring to no. 70 the Avenue, previously Wynnstay school, in 1961,[92] the lower school closed in 1973.[93] The upper school had 340 boys on the roll in 1978.[94]

Thorn House academy was founded in 1836 by William Henry Ray in the former master's house of Great Ealing school.[95] There were 36 boarders, aged 6 to 15, in 1851 and 77, aged 8 to 19, in 1871.[96] Under the Revd. Richard Mulcaster, Ray's successor from 1874, Thorn House was called a collegiate and commercial school.[97] Later headmasters were F. Bynoe by 1881, H. P. Greaves by 1887,[98] and Samuel Dyer, who in 1890 moved it to Warwick Road as the short lived Harlingen school.[99] In 1893 the original premises

[57] Jackson, *Ealing*, 174.
[58] *D.N.B.*
[59] C. Knight, *Passages of a Working Life*, i (1864), 54–5.
[60] *Letters and Diaries of J. H. Newman*, ed. I. Ker and T. Gornall, i (1978), 4–28.
[61] Banister, *MacFarren*, 10.
[62] Jackson, *Ealing*, 195. Thackeray, said to have been a pupil, e.g. Jackson, *Ealing*, 186–8, was at sch. in Chiswick: above, Chiswick, educ.
[63] Jackson, *Ealing*, 161, 175; *Ealing As It Was*, illus. 9.
[64] Census, 1861 (copy in Ealing libr.).
[65] *Mdx. County Times*, 23 May 1868; 29 Aug. 1874.
[66] *Jewish Chron.* 20 Apr. 1917; *Jewish Encyclopaedia*, 1902, iii. 666.
[67] *Mdx. County Times*, 29 Aug. 1874.
[68] Gtr. Ealing Local Hist. Soc. *Local Historian* (1961), 32.
[69] Pigot, *Lond. Dir.* (1826–7); Census (1871); *P.O. Dir. W. Suburbs* (1880); *Kelly's Dir. Ealing* (1900–1); *Ealing Blue Bk.* (1949–50); *Schools* (1979).
[70] Pigot, *Com. Dir.* (1832–4); *P.O. Dir. Six Home Counties* (1845); *Kelly's Dir. Mdx.* (1890, 1908, 1926). Old Brentford schs., however, were sometimes listed under Ealing, e.g. *Educ. Enq. Abstract.*
[71] Jackson, *Ealing*, 159.
[72] E. C. Mayne, *Life and Letters of Lady Noel-Byron* (1929), 329.
[73] W. A. C. Stewart and W. P. McCann, *Educ. Innovators, 1750–1880* (1967), 155.

[74] Ibid. 159; *Vocational Aspects of Sec. and Further Educ.* xv, no. 31 (1963), 135–50.
[75] Stewart and McCann, *Educ. Innovators*, 162; *American Annals of Educ. and Instruction*, vi (1836), 75–8.
[76] *Mins. of Educ. Cttee. of Council 1842–3* [520] pp. 141–3, H.C. (1843), xl; *D.N.B.*
[77] Stewart and McCann, *Educ. Innovators*, 169.
[78] Ibid. 167–8; *Mdx. County Times*, 2 June 1866.
[79] Census, 1861.
[80] *Mdx. County Times*, 2 June 1866; Census, 1871.
[81] D. J. E. Sykes, *Ealing and Its Vicinity* (1895), 34.
[82] *Mdx. County Times*, 4 Jan. 1896.
[83] Ealing Boro. *Official Guide* (1912). Brucesmith also had a sch. in Essex: *Mdx. County Times*, 4 June 1924.
[84] *Mdx. County Times*, 21 July 1917.
[85] *Ealing Coll. 1820–1970*, comp. I. R. Dowse, 19.
[86] Pigot, *Com. Dir.* (1839).   [87] Census, 1851.
[88] *Ealing Coll.* 20; Census, 1861, 1871.
[89] *Ealing Coll.* 20–1; *Mdx. County Times*, 22 April 1876.
[90] *Ealing Coll.* 25, 29, 54.
[91] *Kelly's Dir. Ealing* (1905–6, 1923).
[92] *Ealing Coll.* 35–7.
[93] *Mdx. County Times*, 24 July 1973.
[94] Inf. from the headmaster.
[95] *Mdx. County Times*, 29 Aug. 1874.
[96] Census, 1851, 1871.
[97] *Mdx. County Times*, 29 Aug. 1874.
[98] *Cordingley's Dir.* (1881); *Kelly's Dir. Ealing* (1887–8).
[99] *Mdx. County Times*, 4 Jan., 23 Aug. 1890.

were occupied by St. Mary's college, which emphasized science[1] and closed in 1895, the building becoming a Liberal club until its demolition in 1902.[2]

Ealing Deanery middle-class school was promoted by Ealing Ruri-Decanal Association, to give prominence to religious instruction.[3] In face of opposition[4] the school opened in Brentford High street in 1864, with both day pupils and boarders.[5] Never self-supporting, the school closed in 1879.[6]

Girls' schools, which included Mrs. Robinson's school for ladies in 1790,[7] proliferated in the late 19th century. One at no. 9 Bonchurch Villas, the Grove, in 1866[8] had moved by 1874 to Grosvenor House, no. 46 Windsor Road,[9] where in 1882 there was a ladies' collegiate school with a kindergarten.[10] It moved to the Hawthorns, no. 19 Ealing Common, in 1883,[11] had day girls and boarders in 1908,[12] and closed in 1912.[13]

Princess Helena college moved in 1882 from Regent's Park (St. Marylebone) to new buildings in 9 a. in Montpelier Road.[14] Founded in 1820 as the Adult Orphans Institution, to train governesses, it had changed its name in 1876 when partly evolving into a high school.[15] There was accommodation for 55 boarders and 100 day girls,[16] with a kindergarten which also took boys. Scholarships continued to be awarded to orphans in 1889.[17] The school moved in 1936 to Temple Dinsley (Herts.)[18] and in 1979 the site was occupied by Helena Court and Montpelier school.

Notting Hill and Ealing high school for girls, opened by the Girls' Public Day School Trust as Notting Hill and Bayswater high school,[19] moved in 1931 to Ealing, where many pupils lived. It took over some girls from Girton House, whose building at no. 2 Cleveland Road it occupied. The reorganized junior school opened at Redlands, no. 20 St. Stephen's Road, in 1935. The school was grant-aided under the Education Act, 1944,[20] until 1976. New buildings included a library in 1970 and science block in 1979. There were 643 girls aged 5–18 in 1978.[21]

Harvington school, until 1916 called Heidelberg college,[22] had opened by 1893 as a girls' day and boarding school at no. 67 Gordon Road. In 1908 it was at nos. 24 and 26 Castlebar Road,[23] where it remained in 1979.

Durston House, a boys' preparatory school, was founded in 1886 at no. 14 Castlebar Road,[24] under B. C. and R. M. Pearce, sons of Ebenezer Pearce of Great Ealing school.[25] Only day boys were taken after 1892.[26] Durston House retained expanded premises in Castlebar Road in 1978, with 200 boys.[27]

Hamilton House, opened in 1905[28] in Hamilton Road, had moved by 1908 to Florence Road[29] and specialized in preparing boys for the Royal Naval College, Osborne. From 1973 numbers rose,[30] the juniors moving in 1974 to the former lower school of Ealing college at no. 70 the Avenue.[31] In 1978 it took girls aged 4–9 and boys aged 4–14.[32]

Lourdes Mount school for girls was started in 1923 by Sisters of the Sacred Heart of Mary at Rochester House, Little Ealing Lane,[33] which earlier housed Mrs. Robinson's girls' school in 1839, Dr. Northcott's military college from 1872, the Metropolitan Board asylum 1903–5, and Marylebone school for orphan girls 1910–22.[34] Lourdes Mount, with 300 children in 1958, closed in 1971 on amalgamating with the convent of the Sacred Heart of Mary, Hillingdon.[35] Rochester House was bought by the Institution of Production Engineers in 1974.[36]

The convent of the Augustinians ladies' school opened in 1915 in new buildings in Hillcrest Road. Originally a day and boarding school for girls, with a day school for small boys, it was extended in 1932[37] and had 325 day girls, aged 4–18, in 1978.[38]

St. Anne's convent school was founded in 1903 by the Sisters of Charity. It had 489 girls, aged 5–18, and 7 boys in 1978.[39]

St. Benedict's school originated in a school opened in 1902 by Father Sebastian Cave, following the establishment of a temporary chapel in 1896 by Downside abbey.[40] As Ealing Catholic school, renamed Ealing Priory school in 1916, it occupied Orchard Dene in Montpelier Road from 1906 before moving to no. 56 Eaton Rise in 1924. Orchard Dene was retained for boarders, no. 54 Eaton Rise was acquired in 1929,[41] and new buildings were added in 1937.[42]

[1] Kelly's Dir. Ealing (1893–4); Mdx. County Times, 11 Nov. 1893, 29 Sept. 1894.
[2] M. E. R. Jones, 'Notes on Bygone Ealing' (TS. 1959, in Ealing libr.), 4–5.
[3] Mdx. Chron. 23 Jan. 1864.
[4] Ealing Post, 26 Mar., 2, 9, 16, 23, 30 Apr., 21 May 1864.
[5] Ibid. 27 Aug. 1864.
[6] Mdx. County Times, 27 Sept. 1879.
[7] M.R.O., D.R.O. 37/D1/2.
[8] Mdx. County Times, 3 Nov. 1866.
[9] Ibid. 22 Apr. 1876.   [10] Ibid. 10 Feb. 1883.
[11] Ibid. 6 Oct. 1883.
[12] Ibid. 7 Oct. 1908.
[13] Kelly's Dir. Ealing (1912, 1913).
[14] Ealing Illustrated (1893), 13; Mdx. County Times, 15 July 1882; Ealing As It Was, illus. 12.
[15] Mdx. County Times, 24 Dec. 1881.
[16] Ibid. 15 July 1882.   [17] Ibid. 21 Dec. 1889.
[18] Ibid. 25 May, 7 Dec. 1935.
[19] J. E. Sayers, Fountain Unsealed (1973), 11.
[20] Ibid. 148, 150–1, 161.
[21] Prospectus (1976); inf. from the headmistress and pupils.
[22] Kelly's Dir. Ealing (1916, 1917).
[23] Mdx. County Times, 23 Dec. 1893, 17 Oct. 1908.

[24] Sch. Roll for First 45 Years (1886–1930) (1931).
[25] Ealing libr., local colln. index.
[26] Prospectus (1921) in Ealing libr., local colln.
[27] Prospectus (1973) in Ealing libr., local colln.; Public and Prep. Schs. Year Bk. (1979).
[28] Inf. from the headmaster.
[29] Mdx. County Times, 17 Oct. 1908.
[30] Ibid. 24 July 1973.
[31] Inf. from the headmaster.
[32] Schools (1979), 298.
[33] Kelly's Dir. Ealing (1923).
[34] Pigot, Com. Dir. (1839); Faulkner, Brentford, Ealing and Chiswick, 248; Mdx. County Times, 2 June 1888; Kelly's Dir. Ealing (1903–4, 1904–5, 1911, 1922).
[35] Min. Educ. List 70 (1958); Mdx. County Times, 31 Dec. 1971.
[36] Production Engineer, Dec. 1974.
[37] Above, Rom. Catholicism; Mdx. County Times, 16 Apr. 1932.
[38] Catholic Educ. (1978).
[39] Inf. from the headmistress; Catholic Educ. (1978).
[40] 'Fifty Years: St. Benedict's Sch. 1902–52', Priorian, vi (9), 1–2.
[41] Ibid. 6, 8, 10; Kelly's Dir. Ealing (1908).
[42] Mdx. County Times, 13 Feb. 1937.

The school was called St. Benet's in 1938–9 and thereafter St. Benedict's. In 1948 the 445 boys included 200 juniors and in 1950 a separate middle school was formed. Elected to the Headmasters' Conference in 1951,[43] the school was still governed by Ealing abbey in 1979. There were then 220 boys in the junior school and 595 in the middle and upper schools, besides some girls in the sixth form.[44]

Ealing commercial college, a day and boarding school at nos. 1 and 2 Totnes Villas, Uxbridge Road, in 1888 replaced Eccleston collegiate school for boys.[45] Girls were taught at Ealing secretarial college, no. 51 the Mall, in 1912.[46] A branch of Clark's college was at no. 45 Uxbridge Road from 1910, then at no. 95 New Broadway, and finally, until 1965, at no. 83.[47] Pitman's college opened in 1914 at nos. 52–6 Uxbridge Road and leased part of Bilton House, built there in 1959, until c. 1968.[48] Gregg secretarial college started in 1926 at no. 3 Hamilton Road but by 1928 was at no. 36 Uxbridge Road and by 1954 at no. 8 Mattock Lane,[49] where it remained as the co-educational Gregg school in 1979.[50]

CHARITIES FOR THE POOR.[51] Early charities divide between those for Ealing parish and those for New Brentford. Some Ealing charities served the whole parish but others, through the donors' intentions or by custom, were limited to Upper Side or to Old Brentford, Lower Side, by 1822. A Scheme of 1904 created a group later called Ealing Charities for the Poor and excluded gifts used solely for Old Brentford, while allowing Old Brentford its share in the common charities. A second Scheme of 1918 created Brentford United Charities out of those for New Brentford, leaving Old Brentford's own charities to be administered separately.

EALING CHARITIES. *Almshouse charities*. There was a church house in 1492[52] which was said in 1547 to have been given for the relief of the poor[53] and later became the assistant curate's house.[54]

Almshouses were built in Uxbridge Road, later the Mall, in 1783 out of profits from inclosure of the waste.[55] Numbering seven by 1840,[56] they still lacked their own endowment in 1867, when they received the income from the poor's allotments, and were dilapidated in 1870. With the aid of subscriptions and sums from the reorganized Bowman's charity and the sale of Lammas land, the buildings were replaced by ten new houses between 1872 and 1876.[57] Pensions

were paid from £323 stock left by J. S. Prosser, by will dated 1874, and £134 given by John Goodchild in 1884, supplemented from a small endowment which existed by 1899. The almshouses were replaced by shops in 1902.[58]

New almshouses were built on land in Church Gardens bought in 1900 from Ealing Cottage Dwellings. The number of inmates was fixed at 12, a married couple to count as one, in 1907. From 1904 the almshouses could benefit from the income of other Ealing charities, although they continued to receive separate bequests, including £585 from James William Tidy by will proved 1911 and £650 stock from Francis Garner Gledstanes by gift of 1912. Those and later gifts were regulated by a Scheme of 1971 for St. Mary's church homes, as they were then called. A further endowment was provided by G. F. Browse, whose bequest produced over £1,000 a year for weekly allowances. The building, a two-storeyed range with half-timbering, survived in 1980.[59]

St. Stephen's Jubilee (later Victoria) homes, Castlebar Park, were opened in 1899 as flats for old couples, with the aid of a fund started in 1887. Near by six single flats, given by Miss M. Wheeler and known as the Wheeler homes, were opened in 1899. From 1958 both sets of flats were managed by Ealing Philanthropic Institution.[60]

Distributive charities. Edward Vaughan, by will dated 1612, left the rent from 4 a. equally between Upper Side and Lower Side for meat, coal, and bread at Christmas. In 1822 two-thirds of the income of £31 10s. was spent in Upper Side with money from Bowman's, Taylor's, and Payne's charities, on Christmas gifts to c. 150 families, the other third being reserved for Lower Side. By 1867 £30 was spent on fuel in Upper Side.

John Bowman of Ealing, canon of St. Paul's, by deed of 1630, endowed a lectureship with £40 and also gave rent charges totalling £22 a year for distribution at Christmas and other times. After increases in the rent and further purchases by the trustees, £30 was divided in 1822 between the vicar, for Upper Side, and Mrs. Trimmer, for Lower Side, and a further £11 12s. spent on apprenticing or casual relief. By 1867 £42 was spent on clothing or, occasionally, apprenticing in Upper Side. A Scheme of 1869 allotted ⁴⁄₇ of the total income from Bowman's property to ecclesiastical purposes and the remainder to general charitable purposes, which might include support of the almshouses.[61]

[43] *Priorian*, vi (9), 14, 30–2.
[44] *Public and Prep. Schs. Year Bk.* (1979).
[45] *Mdx. County Times*, 4 Aug. 1888; *Kelly's Dir. Ealing* (1888–9).
[46] *Ealing Boro. Official Guide* (1912).
[47] *Kelly's Dir. Ealing* (1911, 1938); *Kemp's Dir. Ealing* (1959).
[48] *Mdx. County Times*, 29 Aug. 1959; *Kemp's Dir. Ealing* (1969–70).
[49] *Mdx. County Times*, 6 Feb. 1926, 29 May 1954; *Kelly's Dir. Ealing* (1928).
[50] *Schools* (1979).
[51] Section based on *6th Rep. Com. Char.* H.C. 12, pp. 347–52, 370–7 (1822), ix; *Digest Endowed Chars. Mdx.* H.C. 433, pp. 12–13, 28–9 (1867–8), lii(1); *Endowed Chars.*

Mdx. H.C. 306, pp. 4–7, 10–11 (1899), lxx; Char. Com. files.
[52] P.R.O., SC 2/189/11, rot. 2.
[53] Ibid. E 301/34, no. 156. For furnishings, see *T.L.M.A.S.* xxiii. 299.   [54] Above.
[55] Lysons, *Environs*, ii. 238. Princess Amelia's gift of £500 to be distributed on her death may explain a statement that she founded the almshos.: Jackson, *Ealing*, 152.
[56] M.R.O., TA/EAL.
[57] Ibid. D.R.O. 37/A12/1–2, 5.
[58] Ealing town hall MS. 155; *Ealing As It Was*, illus. 26, 29.
[59] *Ealing As It Was*, illus. 5.
[60] *Kelly's Dir. Mdx.* (1908); *St. Stephen's, W. Ealing* (jubilee booklet 1976), 7.
[61] M.R.O., D.R.O. 37/F2/1.

Richard Taylor, by will dated 1715, left the rent from the later Lion brewhouse towards coal for 8 poor of Upper and 8 of Lower Side. The rent of £36 was divided equally in 1822, when in Upper Side it formed part of a distribution larger than that intended by the donor. By 1867 the rent was £50, spent on fuel in Upper Side.

Jonathan Gurnell, by will proved 1753, left stock to provide coal for householders in Upper Side. The income of £15 was spent on coal in 1822 and 1857.

Elizabeth Barne, by will proved 1758, left £400 for four widows. The income was £13 0s. 7d. in 1822, when paid quarterly to four widows of Upper Side, and 1867.

William Adair, by will proved 1783, left £100 for widows. The income was £3 in 1822, distributed to 24 recipients in Upper Side at Christmas, and 1867.

Henry York, by will proved 1793, left £250 stock in reversion for pensions. After a composition with his heirs,[62] the income was £4 1s. 8d. from £136 3s. 9d. stock in 1867.

Edward Payne, by will proved 1794, left £100 stock for coal. A further £100 was left by Sir Charles Morgan, raising the income to £9 6s. 8d. by 1822 and £12 8s. 10d. in 1867.

Hannah Harman, by will proved 1795, left £12 a year for coal, which was distributed in 1822 and 1867.

Thomas Denison Lewis, by deed of 1850, left £1,428 11s. stock in reversion to support poor women. No income had been received in 1867.

Ealing Dean common allotments. The £25 rent from allotments established on Ealing Dean common under the Poor Relief Act, 1832,[63] was spent on the almshouses in 1867. By 1904 c. 145 holders shared c. 20 a., which yielded £35 a year.

Ealing Charities for the Poor. All the above charities, including the almshouse ones, were regulated in 1904 as the charities of Bowman and others. The ecclesiastical share of Bowman's charity was continued, small sums from Bowman's and York's charities were assigned to educational purposes, and certain proportions from Taylor's, Vaughan's, and the residue of Bowman's were allotted to Old Brentford. The name was changed to Ealing Charities for the Poor in 1961 and the total income was c. £19,836 in 1974–5, after some of the allotment land had been sold.

BRENTFORD CHARITIES. *Apprenticing charities.* Dame Mary Spencer, by will proved 1659, left a rent of £6, charged from 1668 on the Butts closes, New Brentford, for apprenticing one boy a year. In 1822 apprenticing was effected at irregular intervals by the parish officers, in conjunction with the trustees of Lord Ossulston's charity.

John Bennet, Lord Ossulston (d. 1695), by deed dated 1692, gave £100 to apprentice

children whose parents were communicants at New Brentford chapel. The money was lent on interest until 1753, when £140 stock was bought. The amount had risen to £190 by 1822 and £200 by 1867, when the income, like that from Lady Spencer's, was £6.

Almshouse charities. There were almshouses in 1573,[64] presumably the queen's seven almshouses at Brentford which were to be repaired in 1576.[65] It is possible that they were the four old almshouses of 1811[66] later called the St. Paul's or Ferry Lane almshouses, at the corner of High Street and Ferry Lane, Old Brentford. Unendowed and of unknown origin in 1867, they numbered seven in 1870[67] and were demolished after closure in 1949.[68]

Four double almshouses, later called Salutation or St. George's, also stood on the south side of High Street, Old Brentford, near the Salutation inn.[69] They were built in 1794 by the churchwardens of Ealing, probably with the help of a gift from Henry Beaufoy of Castle Hill Lodge, were not endowed, and were demolished c. 1953.[70]

The almshouses' only income came from rent for land behind St. George's almshouses and from the use of a wall in Ferry Lane for advertisements. Stock was bought after the sites had been sold and a pension fund was established, yielding c. £174 in 1979, when it was distributed monthly among six widows.[71]

Distributive charities. Henry Redman, by will dated 1528, left the George and other property to support a minister at New Brentford. A rent charge of £6 was agreed in 1576 and divided equally between the minister and the inhabitants in 1714, although by 1822 the minister again received the whole of it. In 1867 £3 was spent on clothing, bread, and fuel, and in 1980 the entire £6 was distributed in small sums.[72]

John Middleton, by will dated 1624, left a rent charge of £5 for the poor of New Brentford. The income of £5 was distributed in bread and fuel, with Andrews's and Hubbold's charity and Townsend's and Williams's charity, in 1822 and 1867.

Richard and Mary Need, according to a list in Ealing church, in 1633 gave property in Old Brentford for the poor. In 1822 the income of £78 12s. was distributed in bread and coal near Christmas, together with John Taylor's charity and Old Brentford's £10 10s. share of Vaughan's charity. The Needs' charity was combined with John Taylor's in 1856, to provide £40 for bread and coal and the remaining money for schools.

Richard Andrews left £20 and Ann Hubbold, by will dated 1673, an additional £10 for coal in New Brentford. The income was £1 16s., spent on fuel and bread in 1822 and 1867.

John Taylor, according to a list in Ealing church, left land for the poor which was first let in

[62] Ibid. F1/1/1.
[63] Ibid. H7/1–2, 6.
[64] P.R.O., PROB. 11/62 (P.C.C. 29 Arundell).
[65] Cal. S.P. Dom. 1547–80, 526.
[66] Lysons, *Environs* (Suppl.), 132.
[67] M.R.O., D.R.O. 37/A12/5.

[68] C. Turner, 'Old Brentford Almshos.' (TS. in Chiswick libr.). [69] M.R.O., D.R.O. 37/A12/5.
[70] Lysons, *Environs* (Suppl.), 132; Turner, 'Almshos.'
[71] Turner, 'Almshos.'; inf. from chief executive's office, Hounslow L.B.
[72] Inf. from the vicar of Brentford.

1685. The rent came to be reserved for Lower Side and was £4 in 1822, when it was usually added to the Needs' charity.

Elizabeth, countess of Derby, by will proved 1717, left property for the poor of Kew and Old Brentford. The income of £15 from £500 stock, bought under a Chancery decree of 1719, provided pensions for 20 widows of Lower Side in 1822.

James Townsend, by will dated 1741, left £100 and Mary Williams, by will dated 1766, left an additional £5, together yielding £3 in 1822. It was then distributed with the charities of Middleton and of Andrews and Hubbold, as in 1867.

John Bennett gave £100 stock c. 1814, of which the income was distributed in cash at New Brentford in 1867.

Elizabeth Pitt, by will proved 1816, left £300 stock for New Brentford and the Half Acre district of Old Brentford. The income of £9 was distributed in fuel in 1867.

George Osborne, by will dated 1843, left £92 8s. 6d. stock, yielding £2 15s. 4d. for bread in New Brentford in 1867, and a like sum for Old Brentford.

Ann Northall, by will dated 1857, left £333 6s. 8d. stock, subject to the maintenance of a vault in New Brentford church. The income of £10 provided bread, fuel, and clothing in 1867.

Henry Chappell, by will dated 1860, left £100 stock, yielding £2 15s. for clothing 6 widows of Old Brentford in 1867.

Henry Meyers, by will proved 1873, left £100 stock, yielding £2 15s. for cash payments in New Brentford in 1899, and a like sum for the parishes of St. Paul and St. George, Old Brentford.

Thomas Layton, by will proved 1911, left the residue of his estate for the poor of St. George's, Old Brentford.[73] In 1980 the income was c. £620, distributed in monthly grants and at Christmas.[74]

Brentford United Charities. A Scheme of 1918, besides establishing a separate ecclesiastical charity with £40 out of Ann Northall's endowment, united the New Brentford charities of Townsend and Williams, Bennett, Pitt, Osborne, Northall, and Meyers. The total income in 1980 was £23, generally dispensed in gifts of at least £3 at Christmas.[75] The Old Brentford charities of Lady Derby, Osborne, and Chappell stayed separate under a Scheme of 1912, with an income of c. £45 in 1979, distributed at Christmas to 30 widows.[76] Those of Redman, in 1980 in the sole control of the vicar, Spencer, Middleton, and Layton also remained separate. The Needs' and John Taylor's eleemosynary charity, governed by a Scheme of 1966, in 1979 received £40 a year from the educational branch, which was distributed to local hospitals.

WEST TWYFORD

WEST TWYFORD, known in the 19th century as Twyford Abbey, was a separate parish[1] adjoining East Twyford (Willesden) and containing only 281 a. in 1901.[2] Although depopulated from the Middle Ages and subject in the 17th century to the parish officers of Willesden, West Twyford was later regarded as extra-parochial and acquired the status of a civil parish under the Extra-Parochial Places Act, 1857.[3] It was transferred to Willesden M.B. in 1934 but, after popular protest, was mostly returned to Ealing. The ancient boundaries were formed by the river Brent on the north and partly by Masons Green Lane on the west and Norwood Lane on the south.[4]

Except for some Taplow Gravel and alluvium along the Brent, West Twyford lay entirely on the London Clay which provided a gently undulating landscape rising from some 25 m. at the western end of the Brent to 44 m. at the southern border, where the ground rose towards Hanger Hill. A small stream ran northward from the southern boundary alongside the church to join

the Brent. The name Twyford or 'two fords' presumably referred to crossing points of the Brent, possibly those represented by Stonebridge in Willesden and Vicar's bridge a short way west of West Twyford in Alperton.[5] The Paddington branch of the Grand Junction canal was driven across the north-east quarter of West Twyford in 1801.[6]

Twyford Lane was described in the 13th century as a lane from the house and church of West Twyford to London,[7] by what route is uncertain. In the 18th century it ran south from the Brent and then west to Hanger Lane, which linked West Twyford with Ealing, Alperton, and Harrow. From Twyford Lane, Masons Green Lane ran south to Acton and Norwood Lane ran east from Masons Green Lane towards Harrow Road in Willesden.[8] Twyford Lane (later Twyford Abbey Road) was extended eastward from its bend south of the church to Twyford Abbey Farm and the canal towpath in the early 19th century. Norwood Lane had dwindled to a green lane by the 1820s and was obliterated by

[73] *Chiswick Times*, 10 Nov. 1911.
[74] Inf. from the vicar.   [75] Ibid.
[76] Inf. from chief executive's office, Hounslow L.B.
[1] Below, church.
[2] Para. based on *Census*, 1801–1931; C. Kearney, 'Hist. Twyford Abbey' (TS. in Grange Mus.); below, Willesden; above, Ealing.
[3] 20 Vic. c. 19.

[4] O.S. Map 6", Mdx. XVI. NW. (1864–7 edn.).
[5] Geol. Surv. Map 6", Mdx. XVI. NW. (1920 edn.); Milne, *Land Use Map of Lond.* (1800).
[6] *V.C.H. Mdx.* iv. 198.
[7] Bodl. MS. D.D. All Souls c 123/44.
[8] J. Rocque, *Map of Lond.* (1746), sheets 13–14; Milne, *Land Use Map of Lond.* (1800); O.S. Map 6", Mdx. XVI. NW. (1864–7 edn.).

the building of the G.W.R.'s Birmingham line in 1904; its course was nearly followed by Coronation Road, built to serve the Royal Agricultural Show at Park Royal.[9] The north end of Masons Green Lane had disappeared by 1894. The North Circular Road was built along the northern border of West Twyford in 1934–5 and suburban roads were built adjoining it shortly afterwards.[10]

West Twyford remained undeveloped until the opening of the Royal Agricultural Society's grounds at the beginning of the 20th century. The G.W.R. opened a station called Park Royal in Acton parish and in 1904 extended the line across the southern tip of West Twyford on its way to Greenford. The London Passenger Transport Board took over the line in 1947. In 1903 the Metropolitan District opened its line from North Ealing to South Harrow (and later to Uxbridge). The line passed very close to West Twyford's western boundary and a station called Park Royal and Twyford Abbey, in Hanwell detached, was opened in Twyford Abbey Road in 1903. In 1931 it was replaced by a station called Park Royal, from 1936 Park Royal (Hanger Hill), in Western Avenue in Ealing.[11]

West Twyford, like neighbouring settlements, probably originated as a clearing of the Middlesex forest in the late Saxon period. By 1086 there were six tenants there.[12] The small community, still comprising six holdings, was by 1181 served by a chapel[13] and had ten inhabited houses in the mid 13th century.[14] It was probably during the late 13th century that West Twyford became depopulated, later permitting the lords of the manor to inclose all the land into their demesne.[15] By 1593 the manor house was the only habitation in the parish and the church had become a private chapel.[16] A few people described as of West Twyford in the late 16th and early 17th centuries were servants at the manor house[17] and there was still only one house in 1801. When Thomas Willan rebuilt the manor house c. 1806, he built Twyford Abbey Farm for the principal tenant.[18] A third house, probably Canal Cottage, had been added by 1821, and a fourth by 1831. Nine houses were built between 1861 and 1881,[19] including Twyford House, a farmhouse south of Twyford Lane.

By 1907 there were buildings connected with mushroom farming west of Twyford Abbey Farm and a small mission hall south of the canal.[20] Mushrooms were grown at Twyford

Bridge farm by 1908[21] and at two other farms in 1925, but one was in the hands of building contractors by 1930 and the other was demolished c. 1935.[22] The first factory was built in Coronation Road in 1913 and more factories were opened during the First World War in the Park Royal area, part of which lay within West Twyford but which is treated as a whole under Acton. The construction of the North Circular Road in 1934–5 stimulated further building at Park Royal, both of factories and of housing estates. Guinness Brewery, which acquired property along the former boundary between West and East Twyford in 1933, built houses at Iveagh Avenue and Ramsford Road for its workers, besides its imposing factory buildings. Other housing included Brentmead Gardens in 1934–5 and the Waddington estate in 1937. In 1948 Guinness Brewery built another 46 houses at Moyne Place.[23]

The population was 8 in 1801, 43 in 1831, 87 in 1901, 311 in 1931, and 2,995 in 1951.[24]

MANORS. In 1086 Twyford was held by two canons of St. Paul's: Durand held 2 hides of the king, and Gueri held 2 hides described as a manor 'in the demesne of the canons'.[25] The estates are presumed to represent East and West Twyford respectively.[26] In 1102 the canons leased land at Twyford to Ulf and one heir after him.[27] Reiner held it before 1114 when the canons granted it to Walter of Cranford and his daughter Adelaide for their lives.[28] About 1183 Pain, son of Henry, and his wife Eileen, daughter of Adelaide's husband Morel, received the estate with warranty against the kin of Morel and Adelaide.[29] Grants were made at the end of the century to Robert and to Master Roger, sons of Morel.[30] Robert's widow Catherine quitclaimed her dower in 1200 in exchange for 10s. quitrent to Martin de Capella, who may have been Roger's son,[31] and in 1219 to Henry de Capella (d. c. 1248), to whom she surrendered the rent in 1225.[32] The estate descended to Henry's son Bartholomew (d. c. 1258) and Bartholomew's daughter Joan, still a minor in 1274, when rents were received by Sir Frank de Bohun, who had married Bartholomew's widow Nicole. For a time during the 1260s the estate had been seized by Sir Robert de Bruce and then by the servants of Lord Edward.[33] Sir Frank gave Joan in marriage to John (d. 1284), his son

[9] Below, Willesden, intro.; above, Acton, intro.; O.S. Map 6″, Mdx. XVI. NW. (1894–6 edn.).
[10] Kearney, 'Twyford Abbey'; O.S. Map 6″, Mdx. XVI. NW. (1938 edn.).
[11] A. E. Bennett and H. V. Borley, Lond. Transport Rlys. 21; J. E. Connor and B. L. Halford, Forgotten Stations of Gtr. Lond. 12, 35; above, Acton and Ealing.
[12] V.C.H. Mdx. i. 121.
[13] Below, church; P.R.O., CP 25(1)/146/2 no. 1; CP 25(1)/146/5, no. 7.
[14] 'Visitations of Churches belonging to St. Paul's', Camd. Misc. ix (Camd. Soc. N.S. liii), 5.
[15] Below, econ.; P.R.O., C 3/408/12.
[16] Norden, Spec. Brit. 41.
[17] e.g. John Cressy (d. 1585): Grange Mus., 4 I 3; Thos. Richardson and Geo. Collingwood in 1620: P.R.O., STAC 8/267/7.
[18] Census, 1801–11; Lysons, Environs (Suppl.), 323.
[19] Nos. hos. Census, 1801–1921.
[20] I. Holmes, W. Twyford (2nd edn. 1936), 8–9; O.S. Maps

6″, Mdx. XVI. NW. (1864–7, 1897, 1920 edns.).
[21] Kelly's Dir. Mdx. (1908).
[22] Kearney, 'Twyford Abbey'.
[23] Ibid.; J. C. Morris, Willesden Surv. (1949), pp. 20, 32, map 7, area 10B.
[24] Census, 1801–1951.
[25] V.C.H. Mdx. i. 121.
[26] Early Charters of St. Paul's (Camd. 3rd ser. lviii), p. xxiii; Le Neve, Fasti, 1066–1300, St. Paul's, London, 80. For East Twyford, see below, Willesden.
[27] Early Charters of St. Paul's, 137.
[28] Domesday of St. Paul's (Camd. Soc. [1st ser.], lxix), p. 127.   [29] St. Paul's MSS. A 39/1362–3.
[30] Early Charters of St. Paul's, 128, 132 (nos. 166, 171).
[31] P.R.O., CP 25(1)/146/2, no. 1; Rot. Cur. Reg. (Rec. Com.), i. 322–3. Master Roger may be identifiable with Master Roger 'capellanus', prebendary of Oxgate: Le Neve, Fasti, 1066–1300, St. Paul's, Lond. 68.
[32] P.R.O., CP 25(1)/146/5, no. 7; CP 25(1)/146/7, no. 55.
[33] 'Visitations of Churches', Camd. Misc. ix. 4–5; Cal. Inq. Misc. i. 246; P.R.O., SC 5/Mdx. (Tower Ser.), 1, m.2.

by his first wife. In 1281 the manor was sold by John Kirkby, later treasurer of England and bishop of Ely, to William Paynel, who was related by marriage to the de Bohuns[34] and may have been a trustee. In 1290 Kirkby died seised of the manor,[35] which descended to his brother William (d. 1302) and then to his sisters.[36] In 1304 Joan de Bohun and Mary, widow of Nutus of Florence, challenged the title of the Kirkby sisters, who claimed that John de Bohun had mortgaged the manor to Nutus and his brother Burgensus and that the brothers had sold it to John Kirkby after de Bohun's death.[37] Since de Bohun was still alive when Kirkby conveyed the manor in 1281, the manor may have been the subject of a trust similar to that which de Bohun made for his Sussex estates.[38] The manor appears to have been vested in 1313 in Joan de Bohun.[39]

By 1361 John Pecche, a London fishmonger, had been granted the manor to hold of St. Paul's for rent of a red rose at Midsummer, by Thomas Blondel, probably acting as trustee. Pecche granted a life estate to Sir Robert Aston, who held the manor at Pecche's death in 1380. Pecche's son and heir[40] Sir William, a London grocer, granted the rent from the manor to John Hadley, also a London grocer, who in 1403 had the wardship of Sir William's son John.[41] In 1433 Richard son of Adam Bamme, mayor of London, gave West Twyford in exchange to John Philpot (d. by 1439),[42] whose descendant John Philpot (d. 1485) was succeeded by his son John (d. 1510)[43] and that John's son Peter.[44]

Sir Peter Philpot sold the manor in 1540 to John Lyon, a London grocer and future mayor (d. 1564).[45] West Twyford then passed to John's nephew Richard (d. 1579), then probably to his sons Henry (d. 1591) and John (d. 1631), to John's nephew George (d. 1635), and his son George,[46] who in 1637 sold it to Robert Moyle.[47] Moyle (d. 1638) left the manor to his widow Margaret for life.[48] Margaret and her second husband, Sir Christopher Clapham, apparently occupied the house and estate until the marriage of Moyle's eldest son Walter in 1653.[49] Walter (d. 1660) similarly left a life interest to his widow Mary, who married Thomas Henslow in 1665.[50] Walter's son Walter, by will dated 1686, left the

manor to his sister Margaret, wife of Edward Bennett, for life, with remainder to his two half-sisters, Henslow's daughters.[51] The Bennetts sold their interest to Henslow in 1689 and he, as trustee for his daughters, sold the manor in 1692 to Sir Joseph Herne, M.P., a wealthy London merchant (d. 1699).[52] Sir Joseph was succeeded by his sons Frederick, a bachelor, and Joseph (d. 1723), also an M.P.[53]

The manor descended through Joseph's daughter Penelope, wife of John Cholmeley, to her grandchildren Sir Montague Cholmeley, Bt., and his sister Penelope, who jointly sold it in 1806 to Thomas Willan, a London stagecoach proprietor.[54] Willan was succeeded in 1828 by his daughter Isabella Maria (d. 1862) and her husband John Kearsley Douglas, later Douglas-Willan (d. 1833). In 1890 their son William Moffat Douglas-Willan sold the house, with 19 a. and the advowson, to William H. Allhusen, who in 1902 sold them to the Roman Catholic Alexian Brothers, the owners in 1981. Some other land was sold in 1897 to form part of the Willesden workhouse infirmary site and some in 1900 to the Royal Agricultural Society, becoming part of the Park Royal estate. Col. Douglas-Willan was still the chief landowner in 1908 but the remaining land was sold for building after the First World War, much of it in 1933 to Guinness Brewery.[55]

A manor house was mentioned in 1290,[56] and it may have been occupied by William Anderby, recorded as gentleman of West Twyford in 1430,[57] and by John Arundel, who had a lease of the estate for at least 20 years from c. 1531.[58] Sixteenth-century Flemish tiles have been found on the site.[59] The Lyons and the Moyles lived there, with several of their relations; in 1664 the house was assessed on 20 hearths.[60] From 1690 the house was leased,[61] and c. 1715 most of the 'fine old mansion house' was demolished and replaced with farm buildings, part of the great hall apparently surviving.[62] By 1800 the house, on a moated site, was plain and two-storeyed, a 'typical Georgian refronting of an earlier building'.[63] From that year the lessee was Thomas Willan,[64] who on buying the estate in 1806 filled in the moat and built a Gothic seat, which he called Twyford Abbey, to designs by William

[34] P.R.O., CP 25(1)/148/29, no. 105; *Early Charters of St. Paul's*, 134. For the de Bohuns, see *V.C.H. Suss.* iv. 77; *Genealogist*, N.S. xxviii. 1–16.
[35] P.R.O., C 133/57, no. 9.
[36] Ibid. C 133/105, no. 1; *Abbrev. Rot. Orig.* (Rec. Com.), i. 123.
[37] P.R.O., CP 40/151, m. 43d.; CP 40/153, m. 158d.; CP 40/159, m. 184d.; CP 40/161, m. 333.
[38] *V.C.H. Suss.* iv. 77.
[39] Lysons, *Environs*, iii. 606.
[40] *Cal. Inq. p.m.* xv, pp. 108–9; for Blondel, Newcourt, *Rep.* i. 539.
[41] P.R.O., E 40/14815.
[42] *D.N.B.* s.v. Sir John Philipot (d. 1384); Kearney, 'Twyford Abbey', quoting bp. of London's reg.
[43] P.R.O., C 141/6, no. 26.
[44] Ibid. E 40/12856.
[45] Ibid. C 54/418, no. 1.
[46] *Pedigrees* (Harl. Soc. lxv), 138; P.R.O. STAC 8/267/7; ibid. C 3/408/12; C 142/487/157; Kearney, 'Twyford Abbey.'
[47] P.R.O., CP 43/219, m. 33.
[48] M.R.O., Acc. 758/1.
[49] P.R.O., C 10/73/83; C 10/88/31.
[50] Ibid. C 10/161/51.

[51] Ibid. C 8/428/41.
[52] Ibid. CP 25(2)/852/1 Wm. & Mary, Trin.; 3 Wm. & Mary, Hil.; P.R.O., C 8/428/41.
[53] *Hist. Parl. Commons, 1715–54*, ii. 131, where Fred. is said to have d. 1723. Rawlinson in 1717 stated that Jos. had succeeded his brother: Bodl. MS. Rawl. B 389B, ff. 98–101.
[54] Burke, *Peerage* (1959), 457; Lysons, *Environs*, iii. 607; ibid. (Suppl.), 323.
[55] Holmes, *W. Twyford*, 35, 38–9; Kearney, 'Twyford Abbey'; M.R.O., BG/W 129/31; *Kelly's Dir. Mdx.* (1908).
[56] P.R.O., C 133/57, no. 9.
[57] *Cal. Fine R. 1422–30*, p. 323.
[58] P.R.O., C 54/418, no. 1; ibid. E 315/498, f. 40.
[59] Inf. from curator of Grange Mus.
[60] M.R.O., MR/TH/3 m.5. The rooms are mentioned in an inventory of 1666: P.R.O., C 10/161/51.
[61] P.R.O., C 8/428/41; C 8/607/37.
[62] Stukeley (MS. hist. of Mdx. 1755–62) quoted in Holmes, *W. Twyford*, 26–7.
[63] Plate facing p. 129, proof of evid. by G.L.C. Historic Bldgs. Div. in appeal by Alexian brothers, 1973 (TS. in Grange Mus.).
[64] Holmes, *W. Twyford*; Kearney, 'Twyford Abbey'; Grange Mus., 1 B 1 (poor rate bk. 1703–21).

Atkinson, a pupil of James Wyatt. The main part of the house is square in plan with a tower-like central block of three storeys, octagonal turrets, and embattled parapets. Built of brick faced with cement, the house was set in wooded grounds and was approached from the west. A service wing stood to the east and stables and coach-houses to the north. The Alexian brothers, who use the house as a rest home for the aged, enlarged it in 1905, 1914, and 1966 and much altered its appearance in 1935, when the parapets were removed, and in 1951 and 1959–62. In 1973 the brothers were refused permission to demolish the house.[65]

ECONOMIC HISTORY. On the 2 hides which apparently constituted West Twyford in 1086, there was one ploughteam in demesne and land for $\frac{1}{2}$ plough more.[66]. The demesne was described as a ploughland c. 1274[67] and as 100 a. of arable in 1290 and 1303.[68] In 1086 there were two villeins on a virgate, a bordar on 6 a., and three cottars.[69] There were six tenant estates c. 1200, mostly small and paying rents ranging from 7d. to 39d.,[70] and open arable fields called Perifield and Cotstedel in the 13th century.[71] By 1290 there were three free and seven customary tenants. The latter owed mowing and haymaking services, described in 1302 as 32 autumn works.[72] Although the Brent was near, no meadow was recorded in 1086; only 3 a. were recorded in 1290, but the haymaking services suggest that the acreage was higher.[73] In 1304 the manor was described as having 180 a. of meadow and no arable;[74] its depopulation may have been complete before the inclosing activities of the manorial lords, probably in the 15th or early 16th century.[75]

Woodland, sufficient for 50 pigs in 1086,[76] was described in 1290 as 5 a. and in 1304 as 4 a.[77] In 1635 George Lyon offered timber from Twyford for sale, some of it to the navy,[78] and by the mid 18th century West Twyford was wholly pasture.[79]

Grass was grown for hay by 1833[80] and was used for dairy cattle in the late 19th century. The Alexian brothers ran a home farm at Twyford Abbey until 1940, when they leased it to Guinness Brewery. The stock included 14 cows in 1940 and 25 in 1963, when the brewery changed to beef cattle, which remained in 1975.[81]

LOCAL GOVERNMENT. In 1290 the free tenants were said to owe suit of court every three weeks,[82] but in 1251 the tenants were said to be without a court and there is no evidence that courts were held.[83]

In 1650, in spite of Sir Christopher Clapham's protest that it was a parish in its own right, West Twyford was treated as a chapelry of Willesden,[84] with which it was assessed for the hearth tax[85] and to which it paid poor rates in the late 17th century.[86] In 1705, however, Edmund Life, tenant of the manor, brought a successful action against Willesden's parish officers, who had indicted him for failing in highway repairs.[87] During the 18th century the farmer of the manor acted as churchwarden and in 1795 avoided the burden of paupers by hiring servants for only 12 months at a time.[88] In 1801 West Twyford was described as extra parochial, as it remained until it became a civil parish under the Act of 1857.[89]

CHURCH. West Twyford church originated as a chapel and suffered many vicissitudes. In 1114 the tithes belonged to the canons of St. Paul's. By 1181 there was a chapel there paying to St. Paul's 12d. a year for tithes, independent of the neighbouring churches, and allowed by the chapter to baptize and bury. About 1183 Gilbert of Cranford, perhaps related to the Walter of Cranford who was granted the manor in 1114,[90] was instituted as rector, on the presentation of Pain, son of Henry, and Eileen, with tithes and the right to bury the dead of Twyford in neighbouring churchyards belonging to St. Paul's.[91] Henry de Capella (d. c. 1248), lord of the manor, was said in 1297 to have founded the chapel and to have given 12 marks rent to support two chantry chaplains, 1 mark for the maintenance of the church, and 1 mark to augment the rectory.[92] In 1251 Bartholomew de Capella was patron, presenting a chaplain, also called perpetual rector, to the dean and chapter, as ordinary. The rector had a house and 10 a. of arable, which was not enough to support him,[93] and by 1297 he had a house, 15 a., 4 marks a year from manors in Buckinghamshire where the Capellas had land,[94] and tithes; Gunnersbury manor in Ealing was also considered to belong to the chapelry, presumably paying tithes.[95]

The chapel was equipped much like a parish church in 1251, when there were three altars,[96]

[65] Brewer, *Beauties of Eng. and Wales*, x (5), 353 and plate facing p. 352; Kearney, 'Twyford Abbey'; proof of evid. by G.L.C. Historic Bldgs. Div.
[66] *V.C.H. Mdx.* i. 121.
[67] P.R.O., SC 5/Mdx. (Tower Ser.), 1, m.2.
[68] Ibid. C 133/57, no. 9; C 133/105, no. 1.
[69] *V.C.H. Mdx.* i. 121.
[70] P.R.O., CP 25(1)/146/2, no. 1; CP 25(1)/146/5, no. 11; CP 25(1)/146/6, no. 27.
[71] Bodl. MS. D.D. All Souls c 123/44.
[72] P.R.O., C 133/57, no. 9; C 133/105, no. 1.
[73] Ibid. C 133/57, no. 9.
[74] Ibid. CP 40/151, m. 43d.; CP 40/159, m. 184d.
[75] P.R.O., C 3/408/12.
[76] *V.C.H. Mdx.* i. 121.
[77] P.R.O., C 133/57, no. 9; ibid. CP 40/151, m. 43d.
[78] *Cal. S.P. Dom.* 1634–5, 450.
[79] Rocque, *Map of Lond.* (1746), sheets 13–14.
[80] *The Mirror*, 25 May 1833 (quoted in Kearney, 'Twyford Abbey').

[81] Kearney, 'Twyford Abbey'.
[82] P.R.O., C 133/57, no. 9.
[83] 'Visitations of Churches', *Camd. Misc.* ix. 4–5.
[84] Lysons, *Environs*, iii. 610.
[85] M.R.O., MR/TH/3, m.5; MR/TH/12, p. 33.
[86] e.g. Thos. Henslow (1678), Edm. Life (1706), Roger Life (1694, a national tax): Grange Mus. 1 B 27 (overseers' accts. 1678–1702); 1 B 1 (poor rate bk. 1703–21); M.R.O., F 34/281–6.
[87] P.R.O., C 8/607/37.
[88] Lysons, *Environs*, iii. 610.
[89] *Census*, 1801, 1861.
[90] *Domesday of St. Paul's*, 127, 152.
[91] Newcourt, *Rep.* i. 759.
[92] *Visitations of Churches belonging to St. Paul's* (Camd. Soc. n.s. lv), 64.
[93] 'Visitations of Churches', *Camd. Misc.* ix. 5.
[94] *V.C.H. Bucks.* iv. 223.
[95] *Visitations of Churches* (Camd. Soc. n.s. lv), 63–4.
[96] 'Visitations of Churches', *Camd. Misc.* ix. 4.

and 1297, when there was a churchyard although the chapel was said not to be consecrated.[97] The advowson was recorded as belonging to the lord of the manor in 1380[98] and rectors were recorded up to 1439,[99] but the payments from the Buckinghamshire manors and Gunnersbury lapsed and the chapel was worth only £2 a year in 1535.[1] Perhaps already the glebe and tithes had been merged in the manorial estate. The lord of the manor presented a rector in 1546, and in 1589 the rector of Perivale was presented to West Twyford in plurality. Another rector was presented in 1621,[2] and in 1635 the Crown presented after a vacancy of some years. The new rector, Thomas Lambe, brought an action to recover the rectory estate from the lord of the manor,[3] who as a result was ordered to pay the rector a stipend, which was £10 in 1650 and £6 in 1795.[4]

In 1650 the incumbent was a man who had been ejected from another living for scandal.[5] West Twyford may have been left vacant in the later 17th century; afterwards, until 1809, it was often held with Perivale rectory.[6] In the late 18th century services were performed by the rector or an assistant curate monthly or six times a year; in the early 19th century they were weekly,[7] as in 1872 when they were held by clergy from neighbouring parishes.[8] In 1885, however, the inhabitants went to church in Ealing. In 1862 the lessee of the manor had exercised the advowson but W. H. Allhusen, after acquiring the advowson with the manor house in 1890, failed to do so; services ceased and the church became dilapidated. When the Roman Catholic Alexian brothers attempted to use the church as their chapel the inhabitants protested, and when the brothers denied the rural dean access the bishop intervened. The church was reopened for Anglican worship in 1907, the curate of St. Stephen's, Ealing, being appointed to hold two services each Sunday and communion once a month, and the Crown presented an incumbent to what was thereafter called a vicarage, in the patronage of the bishop and later of the diocesan board of finance.[9] The benefice, augmented in 1912 by the Ecclesiastical Commissioners, was worth £150 a year in 1915,[10] and a Vicarage was built in Brentmead Gardens in 1934.[11]

The chapel of *ST. MARY*, so called *c.* 1300 and in 1535,[12] stood west of the manor house and was one of the smallest churches in Middlesex, seating *c.* 40 people.[13] It was rebuilt *c.* 1712 by Frederick Herne[14] and in 1800 was a plain gabled building of brick with round-headed windows, a western entrance, and a bellcot.[15] Thomas Willan and his architect William Atkinson removed the road between the church and the manor house, covering both buildings with cement to give the appearance of stone, and embellishing them with Gothic details.[16] To accommodate a growing population, a church hall was built in 1937 and used for worship until in 1958 a new church, incorporating the old one as a Lady Chapel, was built to the design of N. F. Cachemaille-Day.[17] Surviving monuments include alabaster and marble wall memorials to Robert Moyle (d. 1638) and Walter Moyle (d. 1660).[18]

The parish registers date from 1722.[19] The church owned a silver chalice in 1251 and in 1552, when it was kept at the manor house.[20] In 1666 the plate, described as two silver gilt flagons and a chalice, was included in the personal estate of Walter Moyle.[21] Plate stamped with the Moyle arms and dated 1697 was discovered in a London bank in 1918 and returned to the parish.[22]

ROMAN CATHOLICISM. The chapel of the Alexian brothers at Twyford Abbey, where mass was first celebrated in 1902, is a chapel of ease for St. John Fisher church, Perivale.[23]

PROTESTANT NONCONFORMITY. The Baptists of Ealing built a small iron mission hall in Abbey Road, south of the canal, *c.* 1905; it was replaced by factory buildings between 1938 and 1942.[24]

EDUCATION. West Twyford council school, opened in 1937 in temporary premises in St. Mary's church hall for 100 infants, was attended in 1938 by 46. It closed in 1939 and another school opened in 1942. The present primary school was built in 1967 and had a roll of 286 children in 1968.[25]

CHARITIES FOR THE POOR. None known.

[97] *Visitations of Churches* (Camd. Soc. N.S. lv), 63.
[98] *Cal. Inq. p.m.* xv, p. 109.
[99] Hennessy, *Novum Rep.* 432.
[1] *Valor Eccl.* (Rec. Com.), i. 434.
[2] Hennessy, *Novum Rep.* 176, 432.
[3] P.R.O., C 3/408/12.
[4] Holmes, *W. Twyford*, 21–2; Lysons, *Environs*, iii. 610.
[5] Lysons, *Environs*, iii. 610.
[6] Ibid.; Hennessy, *Novum Rep.* 432; *V.C.H. Mdx.* iv. 126.
[7] Holmes, *W. Twyford*, 29; Lysons, *Environs*, iii. 610; Brewer, *Beauties of Eng. & Wales*, x(5), 354.
[8] *N. & Q.* 4th ser. x. 273.
[9] Kearney, 'Twyford Abbey'; Holmes, *W. Twyford*, 40; *The Times*, 15 Apr. 1907; *Clergy List* (1915); *Lond. Dioc. Bk.* (1972).
[10] Crockford (1912); *Clergy List* (1915).
[11] Inf. from the vicar.

[12] Bodl. MS. D.D. All Souls c 123/44; *Valor Eccl.* (Rec. Com.), i. 434.
[13] Kearney, 'Twyford Abbey'.
[14] Bodl. Rawl. MS. B 389B, ff. 98–101.
[15] Plate facing p. 129.
[16] Proof of evid. by G.L.C. Historic Bldgs. Div. (TS. in Grange Mus.).
[17] Kearney, 'Twyford Abbey'.
[18] Hist. Mon. Com. *Mdx.* 121, plates 14, 133, 181.
[19] *T.L.M.A.S.* xviii (2), no. 40.
[20] *Camd. Misc.* ix. 4–5; P.R.O., E 315/498, f. 40.
[21] P.R.O., C 10/161/51.
[22] Kearney, 'Twyford Abbey'; M.R.O., Beavis Pkt. 41.
[23] Kearney, 'Twyford Abbey'.
[24] Holmes, *W. Twyford*; O.S. Map 6″, Mdx. XVI. NW. (1938 edn.); *Kelly's Dir. Lond.* (1942). It was not listed in 1903: Mudie-Smith, *Rel. Life.*
[25] Kearney, 'Twyford Abbey'; Mdx. C.C. *List of Educ. Svces.* (1957–64); Bd. of Educ., *List 21, 1938* (H.M.S.O.).

WILLESDEN

WILLESDEN parish, known until the Reformation for its cult of Our Lady, and more recently for the railway junction which in fact lies outside its boundaries, is roughly triangular in shape lying along the west side of Edgware Road between the second and fifth milestones from London. It contained 4,383 a. in the 1860s.[1] Willesden had a local board of health from 1874 and became an urban district in 1894 and a municipal borough in 1933. In 1934 Willesden M.B. gained 283 a. from Ealing M.B. and 37 a. from Wembley civil parish, but in 1937 some 72 a. were given back to Ealing. After minor changes in the boundaries Willesden M.B. covered 4,633 a. in 1965.[2] In that year it joined Wembley and Kingsbury in the London Borough of Brent.

Willesden was bounded on the north-east by the Roman Watling Street, later Edgware Road, on the north and west by the river Brent, and on the south-east by the Kilburn brook. An ancient track, some of it forming part of Harrow Road and Kilburn Lane, marked most of the southern boundary.[3] There were slight adjustments to the course of the Kilburn brook in 1840,[4] and in 1862 the boundary at that point between Willesden and Paddington, which had been obscured by building in the area, was redefined.[5] In 1875 there were complaints that boundary stones had been removed during building at Willesden Junction and the boundary between Willesden and Acton was disputed then and in 1892,[6] as a result of which a slight adjustment was made in 1895.[7] There were minor adjustments to the boundary with Wembley when the river Brent was straightened in 1938.[8]

The land rises from less than 30 m. along the Brent and the Kilburn brook to 73 m. at Dollis Hill and 75 m. at Mount Pleasant on the Brondesbury ridge. It lies on London Clay, with Taplow Gravel along the river Brent, glacial gravel at Dollis Hill, and Claygate Beds at Mount Pleasant.[9] The soil is mostly heavy and poorly drained clay, probably once covered by thick oak forest and well adapted to the grass farming that characterized the area from the 18th century.[10]

The river Brent, running from north-east to south-west, flooded frequently. It was dammed between 1835 and 1839 to form the Brent or Kingsbury reservoir (the Welsh Harp) along the northern boundary, but although the reservoir and feeders to the canal reduced the Brent it remained capable of serious flooding.[11] The principal tributary of the Brent in Willesden was the Mitchell brook which entered the Brent north of Stonebridge and was itself formed from two tributaries.[12] The northern branch, called the Sherrick or Slade brook, rose near Edgware Road at Cricklewood and flowed through Sherrick green where it was joined by a stream flowing northwards from Willesden Green.[13] The southern branch rose south of Willesden Green and flowed west and north through the open fields. South-east of the Brondesbury ridge the land drained into the Kilburn brook,[14] also known as West Bourne, Ranelagh Sewer, or Bayswater rivulet. The Paddington branch of the Grand Junction canal, which was opened in 1801, crossed East Twyford and was fed by a canal which ran through the common fields of Neasden and Stonebridge.[15]

COMMUNICATIONS.[16] The most important road in Willesden was Watling Street or Edgware Road, which is known, in stretches from south to north, as Kilburn High Road, Shoot-up Hill, and Cricklewood Broadway. In 1599 it was simply the London way. Local people were involved in attempts to improve the condition of the road, being named in a grant of pavage in 1389[17] and making gifts and bequests in the 16th and 17th centuries.[18] The largest were made by outsiders, John Lyon (1587) and Edward Harvist (1610), who founded charities for repairing the road from London to Edgware.[19] The charities were inadequate to cope with the constant traffic which made the road 'ruinous and dangerous' for six months of the year and in 1710 a turnpike trust was set up to repair the road between Kilburn bridge and Bushey (Herts.).[20] A turnpike gate

---

[1] O.S. Map 6″, Mdx. XI. SW., SE.; XVI. NW., NE. (1864–73 edn.).

[2] *Census*, 1931–61; Grange Mus., NM 9, 22, 184.

[3] M.R.O., EA/WIL; Bodl. MS. Gough Drawings a 3, f. 14.

[4] Grange Mus., O 6 (North colln.).

[5] Ibid. Wood F 23, pp. 211 sqq.

[6] Ibid. Wood F 10 (letter by overseers to local bd.); M.R.O., *Rep. Local Inqs.* 1889–97, 627–37 (Willesden and Acton boundary 1892).

[7] *Census*, 1901.

[8] Ibid. 1931–51; Grange Mus., NM 9, 22, 184.

[9] Geol. Surv. Map 6″, Mdx. XI. SW., SE.; XVI. NW., NE. (1920 edn.); relief map in A. Winterburn, 'Willesden: The Process of Urbanisation' (Univ. of Durham B.A. thesis, 1977) in Grange Mus., gen. files, topog.

[10] A. J. Garrett, 'Hist. Geog. of Upper Brent' (Lond. M.A. thesis, 1935), 13–18.

[11] *V.C.H. Mdx.* v. 2; S. Potter, *Story of Willesden* (1926), 4–6.

[12] M.R.O., EA/WIL (inclosure map); cf. Bodl. MS. D.D. All Souls c 123/45; All Souls Coll., Oxford, Hovenden maps II/18; W.A.M. 17039.

[13] P.R.O., E 40/11845; M. S. Briggs, *Mdx. Old and New* (1934), 162.

[14] G. F. Cruchley, *New Plan of Lond.* (1829); *Rep. on Bridges in Mdx.* 200; *P.N. Mdx.* 8, 112.

[15] *V.C.H. Mdx.* iv. 198; M.R.O., EA/WIL (inclosure map).

[16] Statements about roads dated 1599, 1746, 1749, and 1823 derive respectively from All Souls Coll., Hovenden maps II/20–1; J. Rocque, *Map of Lond.* (1746), sheets 11–14; Messeder Road Map (1749) in Grange Mus.; M.R.O., EA/WIL.

[17] *Cal. Pat.* 1388–92, 123.

[18] e.g. John (1596) and Ric. Franklin (1615); P.R.O., PROB 11/87 (P.C.C. 19 Drake); PROB 11/126 (P.C.C. 70 Rudd).

[19] Grange Mus., Wood F 23, pp. 313 sqq.; P.R.O., C 54/1059.

[20] 10 Anne, c. 3.

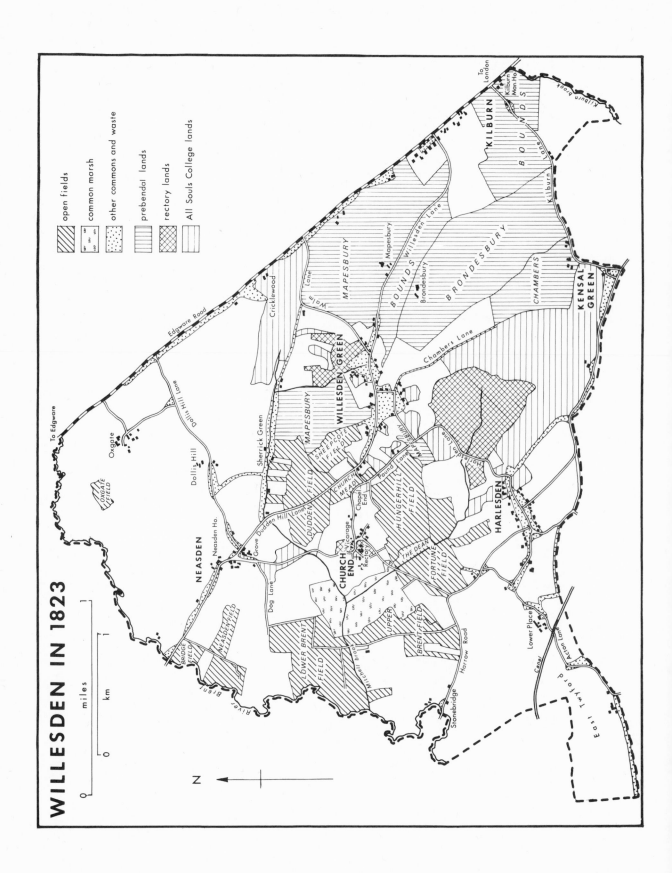

WILLESDEN IN 1823

open fields
common marsh
other commons and waste
prebendal lands
rectory lands
All Souls College lands

miles
km

N

To Edgware

To London
To London

KILBURN BOUNDS

MAPESBURY
Mapesbury
BOUNDS
Brondesbury
BRONDESBURY
CHAMBERS

KENSAL GREEN

Cricklewood
Walm Lane
Willesden Lane
Kilburn Lane

Edgware Road

Chambers Lane

WILLESDEN GREEN

MAPESBURY

Oxgate
OXGATE FIELD

Dollis Hill Lane

Dollis Hill

Sherrick Green

SHEEPCOTE FIELD

CHURCH MEAD
Chapel End

Pound Lane
Harlesden

HUNGERHILL FIELD

HARLESDEN

NEASDEN

Neasden Ho.

Grove Dudden Hill Lane

DUDDEN FIELD

Vicarage
CHURCH END
Rectory
THE DEAN

FORTUNE FIELD

Dog Lane

NEASDEN FIELD

UPPER

BRENT FIELD

BRIDGE FIELD

LOWER BRENT FIELD

Mitchell brook

River Brent

Stonebridge
Harrow Road

Lower Place

Canal

Acton Lane

East Twyford

Kilburn brook
Kilburn Man.Ho.

was erected just north of Kilburn bridge on the Willesden boundary.[21] It was moved in 1864 to the end of Willesden Lane and later to Shoot-up Hill where it stood when the road was disturnpiked in 1872.[22] Heavy waggons, shortage of gravel, dung-heaps alongside the road, encroachments, and highwaymen continued to make Edgware Road unpleasant for travellers and inhabitants alike throughout the 18th century. The commissioners of the metropolitan turnpike roads took responsibility for Edgware Road and the income of the Lyon and Harvist charities under the Metropolitan Roads Act of 1826. The commissioners made improvements, widening the road and lowering Shoot-up Hill. In 1872 they were replaced, under the Metropolis (Kilburn and Harrow) Roads Act by Edgware highway board and other local highway authorities.[23] In 1876 authority passed to Willesden local board which received its proportion of the Lyon and Harvist funds.[24]

Harrow Road, which left Edgware Road at Paddington, entered Willesden at Kensal Green, and formed the southern boundary until it turned northward to Harlesden green; thence it twisted through the open fields[25] and marsh to leave by Stonebridge for Wembley and Harrow.[26] John Lyon set up a charity for Harrow Road in 1582.[27] The road was turnpiked in 1801 after the Willesden vestry's request in 1800.[28] From 1826, when it was included in the Metropolitan Roads Act, its administration followed that of Edgware Road. The right-angle bend between Harlesden and Stonebridge was cut across in 1855,[29] to form the triangle of roads called Craven Park.[30] That name came to be used of Harrow Road as far as Harlesden, where the road is called High Street; west of Craven Park the road is called Hillside.[31]

Several roads ran west from Edgware Road to the hamlets in Willesden. The most northerly was the road to Neasden, Dollis Hill Lane, which was linked to the farms of Oxgate by Oxgate Lane. Walm Lane, recorded as Warne Lane in 1595,[32] ran west from Cricklewood, turning south to Willesden Green before it reached Sherrick green.[33] From Walm Lane a track westward across Sherrick green to Neasden was called Shirwykstrete in 1425,[34] and in 1746 it and the northern part of Walm Lane were called Sherrick Green Lane. Sherrick Green Lane had shrunk to a green lane by 1823 and a footpath by

the 1860s.[35] Willesden Lane, which by c. 1394[36] and until the 1860s[37] was called Mapes Lane, ran from Kilburn to Mapesbury manor house and Willesden Green, whence Churchend Lane in 1593,[38] or Churchend Road in 1823, later High Road, ran west. Kilburn Lane, so called in 1527[39] but Flowerhills Lane in 1649,[40] ran southwestward from just north of Kilburn bridge to Kensal Green. The inhabitants of Willesden were indicted for not repairing it in 1722.[41]

Apart from Harrow Road two roads ran westward out of the parish. A footway north from the parish church to Neasden in 1615[42] was called Neasden Lane in 1746; it then continued northwest as Brent Lane, and perhaps earlier under another name, across the Brent to Kingsbury. Later the north-west portion was called Neasden or Kingsbury Lane. It was widened as an access road to the Empire Exhibition at Wembley in 1924.[43] A second lane to Kingsbury in 1746 had disappeared by 1765.[44] Acton Lane followed a tortuous course from Harlesden green northwestward to Greenhill and then south-westward to Lower Place before turning southward to Acton. A road probably once ran the length of the southern boundary west from Kensal Green. Most of it remained in 1746. The most westerly section (Norwood Lane in 1823) had dwindled by 1823 to a green lane but it survived as a footpath until the development of Park Royal in the 20th century.[45] Another section, a green lane called Old Lane in 1823, ran from Harrow Road to Lower Place. Kims Lane Road (1823), called Old Oak Lane in 1599 and Old Oak Common Lane by 1894, ran south from Harlesden green across the boundary green lane to Old Oak common. With the development of Willesden Junction it became Station Road. A lane running south-east from the east end of Harlesden green to join Harrow Road was recorded as Prentice Lane in 1432[46] and Stub Lane in 1593;[47] it survived as a green lane in 1823 and was a tree-lined, rural grass track in 1873,[48] just before the estate was developed and it became Wrottesley Road. Sawyers Lane, in 1749 linking Harrow Road at Fortune Gate with Acton Lane at Greenhill, became Greenhill Park when the area was built up in the 1870s and 1880s.

Many lanes linked the hamlets of Willesden parish. Church Road, called le Chercheway in 1364[49] and Fortune Field Road in 1823, ran north

[21] Messeder Road Map (1749).

[22] J. C. Morris, *Willesden Surv.* (1949), 8; *Kilburn Times*, 6 July 1872.

[23] Grange Mus., Wood F 23, pp. 313 sqq.; Garrett, 'Hist. Geog. of Upper Brent', 89–92; Middleton, *View*, 305.

[24] 39 & 40 Vic. c. 76 (Local). For the later hist. of the funds see below, charities.

[25] As the highway to Harrow it formed an abutment to Fortune field in 1364: Bodl. MS. D.D. All Souls c 123/54.

[26] Part of the road is marked on All Souls Coll., Hovenden maps II/19, 20, 22.

[27] Grange Mus., Wood F 23, pp. 313 sqq.; P.R.O., C 54/1149. For other bequests see *V.C.H. Mdx.* iv. 172.

[28] Grange Mus., 1 D 29 (vestry order bk. 1722–1814); 41 Geo. III, c. 129 (Local and Personal).

[29] Grange Mus., Wood F 23, pp. 313 sqq.

[30] Ibid. O 6 (North colln.).

[31] O.S. Maps 6″, Mdx. XVI. NW. (1864–73, 1894–6, 1920, 1938 edns.).

[32] *Mdx. County Rec.* i. 229.

[33] All Souls Coll., Hovenden maps II/21 shows (1599) the

beginning of the southward turn but not the whole road to Willesden Green.

[34] P.R.O., E 40/10379.

[35] O.S. Map 6″, Mdx. XI. SW. (1864–73 edn.).

[36] *Public Works in Medieval Law*, ii (Selden Soc. xl), 75 sqq.

[37] O.S. Map 6″, Mdx. XVI. NE. (1864–73 edn.); P.R.O., HO 107/1700/135/3, f. 371. For a picture in the 18th cent. see Grange Mus., photo. files, Willesden Lane (NL 41).

[38] Bodl. MS. D.D. All Souls c 245/32.

[39] Ibid. c 124/85A.

[40] Guildhall MS. 11816B, pp. 115–17.

[41] Grange Mus., 1 D 29 (vestry order bk. 1722–1814).

[42] P.R.O., C 142/349, no. 155.

[43] Grange Mus., 2 B 24 ('Memories of Neasden').

[44] Grange Mus., Wood F 21 (map of 1765).

[45] Ibid. Map of Willesden U.D. 1901.

[46] Bodl. MS. D.D. All Souls c 123/64.

[47] Ibid. c 245/32; Messeder Road Map (1749).

[48] Grange Mus., photo. files, Wrottesley Rd. (NL 1587–8).

[49] Bodl. MS. D.D. All Souls c 123/54.

from Harrow Road at Fortune Gate to Church End. It was straightened at inclosure, the new course leaving Harrow Road farther north.[50] Harlesden Lane or Road followed a circuitous route from Harlesden green to Willesden Green. The northern section was called Golders Lane in 1424 and 1599[51] and Allsopps Lane in 1749. The section in the centre next to the rectory estate was called Yppelestrate c. 1280[52] and Nipley Lane in 1599, and that nearest Harlesden may be identifiable with Botis Lane of 1432.[53] Pound Lane, so called after 1851 and linking Harlesden Lane with Chapel End, was called Perrycroft or Petticoat Lane in 1593 and 1649[54] and Clarke's Lane in 1749.[55]

From Willesden Green south-eastward Chambers Lane, so called in 1593[56] and later called Chamberlayne Road, dwindled to a footpath before its junction with Kilburn Lane. Roughly parallel to the east Brand's Lane, recorded in 1649, and called Causeway in 1765, curved round Brondesbury manor house and reached almost to Kilburn Lane, but had been closed at either end by 1765.[57]

A short lane, later Glebe Road, ran west from Pound Lane to Hungerhill field in 1599. Dudden Hill Lane was recorded in 1593 as a warple way, i.e. a bridle way or green lane, called Dudding Lane between Willesden Green and Neasden. A track running west from Church End to the river probably existed in 1593[58] but had shrunk by 1749 to a short lane alongside the church. More lasting was Dog Lane, which as Stony Lane in 1420, Brent Field Lane in 1599, and Stones Lane in 1787, ran westward from Neasden Lane almost to the river.[59] By 1599 another lane ran southward from Dog Lane and by 1765 crossed the open fields to Harrow Road.[60] In 1823 it was a private road; by the 1860s the westward section of Dog Lane had disappeared, and the whole road from Neasden to Harrow Road was called Dog Lane.[61] It was greatly altered by the building of the North Circular Road, which left only the northern tip, as Dog Lane, and the southern half, renamed Brentfield Road.

Unlocated roads include Loverdes Lane and Crokes Lane in 1304.[62] The second was possibly the Crucestrate of 1322, which may be identifiable either with Neasden Lane because it was near Bury field, on which Dog Lane abutted, or with Willesden High Road, beside which lay

Cross close.[63] Old Street of 1383 was probably part of Edgware Road; no other record has been found of Marsh field and West field past which it ran. Lites Lane (1383) and Wolberd Lane (c. 1397) are unlocated.[64] Pulkyn or Halys Lane (1424) may have been at Neasden.[65]

Compared with the 17 miles of roads in the parish in 1749 and 18 miles in the care of the local authority in 1875 there were 90 miles for which the urban district was responsible in 1931. Roads which had been neglected during the First World War were asphalted in 1922, and during the 1920s and 1930s all the main roads were resurfaced and some were widened. The milage in 1931 did not include the North Circular Road, outside the local authority's control, which was begun in 1921 and completed in 1934, entering the parish at Stonebridge and running alongside the river Brent to Edgware Road.[66]

Kilburn bridge,[67] which was recorded in 1398 and thought to have been built in the mid 13th century by the prior of Kilburn,[68] carried Edgware Road across the Kilburn brook. In 1826 the original stone bridge with a Gothic arch survived, flanked by brick portions added at two different periods. By that date repair was shared between the trustees of Marylebone turnpike and of the Kilburn road. Edgware Road crossed the river Brent at Brent bridge, which was mentioned in 1383.[69] In 1774 Willesden vestry was doubtful of its obligation to repair the bridge.[70] Harrow Road crossed the Brent at Stonebridge which took its name from a bridge recorded in 1746 and replacing an earlier, wooden bridge or ford.[71] Neasden or Kingsbury Lane bridged the Brent at Kingsbury bridge, recorded in 1531 and the joint responsibility of the lords of Chalkhill (Kingsbury) and Neasden manors.[72] Sherrick bridge in 1425 bridged the Sherrick brook probably at the point where it was crossed by Dudden Hill Lane.[73] As Barley bridge it apparently still existed in 1805 but by 1826 the Sherrick brook, together with all the other tributaries of the Brent, had been culverted under roads.[74]

In 1768 a daily stage coach travelled from London along Edgware Road to Edgware and a coach went to Harrow twice a week over Harrow Road.[75] Two coaches making five return journeys a day operated between the City and Kilburn in 1825 and by 1834 a coach left the Six Bells, Willesden Green, for London every morning.[76]

[50] Grange Mus., NM 312.
[51] P.R.O., KB 29/57 Trin. m. 31; All Souls Coll., Hovenden map II/20.
[52] St. Paul's MS. A 29/384.
[53] Described as northern abutment of Prentice Croft: Bodl. MS. D.D. All Souls c 123/64.
[54] Ibid. c 245/32; St. Paul's MS. FB 3, ff. 70 sqq.
[55] P.R.O., HO 107/1700/135/3, f. 393v.
[56] Bodl. MS. D.D. All Souls c 245/32; All Souls Coll., Hovenden maps II/19.
[57] Guildhall MS. 11816B, pp. 61-3; Grange Mus., Wood F 21 (map of 1765).
[58] Bodl. MS. D.D. All Souls c 245/32.
[59] P.R.O., E 40/10366; All Souls Coll., Hovenden maps II/22; M.R.O., Chandos estate map 1787.
[60] All Souls Coll., Hovenden maps II/22; Grange Mus., Wood F 21 (map of 1765).
[61] O.S. Maps 6", Mdx. XI. SW.; XVI. NW. (1864-73 edn.).
[62] P.R.O., E 40/6800.
[63] Ibid. E 40/7871. For Cross close, M.R.O., EA/WIL.

[64] Public Works in Medieval Law, ii (Selden Soc. xl), 75 sqq.
[65] P.R.O., E 40/7644. It belonged to the Roberts estate. Hales croft was near Neasden House: Guildhall MS. CC. 169256.
[66] All Souls Coll., uncat. material, agents' reps. 1921; Winterburn, 'Willesden'.
[67] Para. based on Rep. on Bridges in Mdx. 152-3, 198-203, 210, 213.
[68] Cal. Pat. 1396-9, 386.
[69] Public Works in Medieval Law, ii (Selden Soc. xl), 75. For bridge see V.C.H. Mdx. v. 2; Brent Prints (publ. Brent L.B. libr. 1974).
[70] Grange Mus., 1 D 29 (vestry order bk. 1722-1814).
[71] Rocque, Map of Mdx. (1746); V.C.H. Mdx. iv. 172.
[72] V.C.H. Mdx. v. 51.   [73] P.R.O., E 40/10379.
[74] Bodl. MS. D.D. All Souls c 149/2.
[75] R. Baldwin, Guide to City of Lond. (1768), quoted in Garrett, 'Hist. Geog. of Upper Brent', 94.
[76] T. C. Barker and M. Robbins, Hist. Lond. Transport, i. 392; Pigot, Nat. Com. Dir. (1832-4).

Willesden 'contains an inordinate and bewildering jungle of railway lines'.[77] In spite of the opposition of the Grand Junction Canal Co. and landowners,[78] the London and Birmingham Railway, renamed in 1846 the London and North Western Railway (L. & N.W.R.), opened in 1837. It crossed the southern part of the parish, where a station at Acton Lane, called Willesden, was open for a short time after 1841 and again from 1844 to 1866, although it was not intended to provide a suburban service. Two stations just outside the parish had great influence on Willesden's development, Kilburn High Road from 1852 and Willesden Junction from 1866. Queen's Park station opened in 1879. In 1903 a branch line was opened to serve the Park Royal Exhibition site.

In 1860 the Hampstead Junction Railway (H.J.R.) was opened to form a link between the North London at Camden Town and the North and South West Junction (N. & S.W.J.) which had opened from Kew to Willesden Junction in 1853. Stations were opened in 1860 at Edgware Road (from 1873 called Brondesbury) and in 1861 at Kensal Green and Harlesden. Harlesden station, at the crossing with Green Lane (later Wrottesley Road), closed in 1873 and was replaced by one of the same name (from 1890 called Kensal Rise) at Chamberlayne Road. Brondesbury Park station opened in 1908. Although competition from trams and buses caused a sharp decline in the number of passengers using the line, the H.J.R. (then part of the North London Railway) was absorbed by the L. & N.W.R. and included in its electrification scheme of 1965.[79]

The Midland Railway's main line from Bedford to London, which ran east of and parallel to Edgware Road, opened in 1868 with a station in 1870 at Child's Hill (later Cricklewood). In 1868 a loop line, called the Midland and South West Junction (M. & S.W.J.) or Cricklewood and Acton branch, opened for freight between the main line at Cricklewood and the M. & S.W.J. line at Acton Wells. A passenger service operated on the line from 1875 to 1888 and 1893 to 1902 with stations at Dudding Hill and Harrow Road (called Stonebridge Park 1884 and Harlesden 1901).

The Metropolitan opened a line from Hampstead to Willesden Green in 1879, extending it to Harrow in 1880 and Aylesbury in 1892.[80] Stations were opened at Kilburn and Willesden Green in 1879, at Neasden (called Kingsbury and Neasden until 1932) in 1880, and at Dollis Hill in 1909. A connecting link was constructed for freight between the Great Central line and the M. & S.W.J. line at Neasden in 1899, and in 1906 the Great Central Railway (G.C.R.), which leased tracks on the line, built a link from Neasden to a line at Northolt.[81] The Metropolitan built a power station besides its sidings and workshops at Neasden in 1903 and electric trains, first used in 1905, gradually superseded steam.[82] New fast lines were introduced over the line from 1913, and in 1939 Bakerloo line trains were extended over it and new station buildings erected at Kilburn and Dollis Hill. In 1979 this section became part of the Jubilee line.

The L. & N.W.R., intending to open an electric service to Watford, built the New Line, tracks alongside the main line. In 1912 the New Line was opened for steam trains from Kensal Green tunnel to Harrow and stations were opened at Harlesden (near the earlier Willesden station) and just outside Willesden U.D. at Stonebridge Park. The electrified New Line was opened to Watford in 1917 and to Euston in 1922.

In 1915 the London Electric Railway (L.E.R.) brought its line to Kilburn Park, where it opened a new station, and thence to Queen's Park, where it joined the L. & N.W.R. line and the two companies ran jointly-owned trains over the New Line to Watford Junction. The last station in Willesden, Kensal Green, was opened on the line in 1916. Stonebridge power station was built in 1913 to supply electricity for trains on the Euston to Watford (L. & N.W.R.) and Broad Street to South Acton (H.J.R.) lines.[83] The original L. & N.W.R. main line was electrified in 1965.

In 1839 an omnibus ran between the Bank and Kilburn, and the Harrow to London coach stopped at Harlesden green each morning and evening.[84] By 1855 London omnibuses operated from Harlesden five times daily and from Kensal Green fourteen times daily.[85] In 1856 there were 22 omnibuses operating from Kilburn to London Bridge and Whitechapel, one from Harlesden green and two from Kensal Green to London Bridge.[86]

In 1876 a regular omnibus service was introduced between Edgware Road station and Kilburn, and a service operated between Neasden and Harlesden from 1880 to 1885.[87] By 1890 omnibuses ran to Charing Cross from Stonebridge Park every hour and from Harlesden every 12 minutes, and a service operated between Church End and Kilburn. The L. & N.W.R. ran a bus to meet trains at Willesden Junction from Stonebridge Park and Church End.[88]

Most bus routes radiated out from London, with a large number on Edgware Road. By 1896 there were 45 omnibuses an hour along the road to South Kilburn, 33 an hour to mid Kilburn, and 5 an hour to Cricklewood. Harrow Road carried 11 buses an hour to Kensal Green with 3 going on to Harlesden. Another route carried 16 buses an hour from Edgware Road to Queen's Park, while one route crossed north-east to south-west from Edgware Road at Kilburn to Harrow Road.[89]

[77] Briggs, *Mdx. Old and New*, 164. Following paras. based on M. Robbins, 'Railways and Willesden', *T.L.M.A.S.* xxvi. 309–18.
[78] All Souls Coll., uncat. material, agents' letters 1808–37, s.v. 1830.
[79] Barker and Robbins, *Lond. Transport*, ii. 162.
[80] Ibid. i. 210.
[81] Ibid. ii. 158.
[82] Ibid. ii. 106; plate 36.

[83] Datestone.
[84] Barker and Robbins, *Lond. Transport*, i. 399; Pigot, *Dir. Mdx.* (1839).
[85] *Kelly's Dir. Mdx.* (1855).
[86] Barker and Robbins, *Lond. Transport*, i. 404–12.
[87] Morris, *Willesden Surv.* pp. 76 sqq.
[88] *Kelly's Dir. Mdx.* (1890).
[89] Garrett, 'Hist. Geog. of Upper Brent', fig. 14 (1); Morris, *Willesden Surv.* map 26.

The London General Omnibus Co. (L.G.O.C.) opened stables at Cricklewood in 1899 and from 1901 to 1904 operated a horse-bus service from Cricklewood to Edgware.[90] In 1900 it bought land for stables at Willesden Green, to which seven buses an hour were running by 1903.[91] In 1902 the London Motor Omnibus Syndicate Ltd. opened a service along the Edgware Road to Cricklewood and in 1905 its successor, the London Power Omnibus Co., introduced a regular service from Brondesbury to the Law Courts. At the end of 1905 the L.G.O.C. decided to challenge its rivals directly, introducing motor buses on the route from Cricklewood to the Law Courts and converting its stables at Cricklewood into a garage which by 1951 held 181 buses.[92] The motor buses were not, initially, a complete success: local traders at Kilburn complained of the noise and smoke, mainly due to inexperienced drivers and frequent breakdowns.[93] In 1908 the L.G.O.C. absorbed its rivals and by 1911, following the introduction of more reliable buses, horse-bus services were withdrawn.[94] The system continued to expand. Buses along the Edgware Road to South Kilburn numbered 71 an hour by 1903 and 87 by 1914, while 15 an hour went to Cricklewood. Seven buses an hour went along Willesden Lane to Willesden Green by 1903 with a connecting service between the latter and Harlesden, which by 1914 was carrying 13 buses an hour. By then there were also services through Brondesbury and Cricklewood. Services had been extended to the north-western part of the area by 1925 when 44 buses an hour plied between Church End, Neasden, and Wembley, and 18 between Neasden and northern Cricklewood.[95] There were 17 bus routes by 1933.[96]

In 1888 the Harrow Road and Paddington Tramways Co. opened a horse-tram service with a tram every five minutes along Harrow Road from Paddington to Harlesden, with a branch line from Harrow Road to Malvern Road and Carlton Vale in Kilburn.[97] In 1902 the Middlesex County Council tramways schemes (electric) came into effect, transferring the Harrow Road trams to the Metropolitan Electric Tramways Co. (M.E.T.), which introduced electric cars and extended the service to Stonebridge in 1906 and on to Wembley in 1908. Under the same scheme electric trams were introduced in 1904 between Edgware and Cricklewood, extended in 1906 to Willesden Green and in 1907 to Harlesden.[98] In 1909 the M.E.T. opened services from Harlesden to Acton on London United Tramways' Uxbridge line.[99] In 1919 Willesden U.D. suc-cessfully opposed an L.C.C. scheme for a tramway along Edgware Road to Cricklewood;[1] in 1920 all tram and bus fares in Willesden were doubled and the 1d. fare was abolished, perhaps in an attempt to halt the expansion of the working-class population.[2]

There were four tramway routes in the borough in 1933,[3] just before the whole network was taken over by London Transport for trolleybuses in 1936. By 1948 most journeys to work were made by bus, mostly on the London Transport central bus system which operated 15 routes through Willesden, extending to Watford and Croydon. There were also six trolleybus routes.[4]

SETTLEMENT AND GROWTH. Apart from Roman Watling Street, evidence of man's activities in the Willesden area before the Saxon period is dubious. According to local tradition there were numerous Neolithic finds at Park Royal, Bronze Age vessels on the site of Brent reservoir, and Roman bricks at Neasden. There have also been suggestions of Iron Age tracks and hill-top forts.[5] From the late Anglo-Saxon period scattered, nucleated hamlets were established in clearings in woodland usually on elevated, well drained sites watered by streams and wells, at Willesden Green, Harlesden, and Neasden. Kilburn grew up where Watling Street crossed the Kilburn brook and Twyford at a bridging point of the Brent. Church End as a settlement probably followed the building of the church there, and Kensal Green evolved in the early modern period at the junction of Harrow Road and Kilburn Lane. The whole parish was in the hands of St. Paul's cathedral by 1000 and prebendal estates were carved out of it in the 11th and 12th centuries. There was a group of farms in the centre of Oxgate prebend by the 15th century and there may have been cottages on some of the other prebends. In general the settlement pattern remained unchanged from the early Middle Ages until well into the 19th century: in the centre and west hamlets lay around village greens, separated from each other by open fields, whereas the prebendal estates to the east comprised enclosed demesne lands with isolated farms.[6] Common meadow and pasture covered the badly drained lands bordering the Brent, and extensive woodland throughout the parish was steadily reduced until its final disappearance in the 19th century.

There were c. 240 communicants in the parish in 1547[7] and 158 males took the protestation oath

[90] Grange Mus., 1 A 2 (*Willesden Cit.* 16 Mar. 1951); A. A. Jackson, *Semi-Detached Lond.* (1973), 248.
[91] All Souls Coll., uncat. material, agents' reps. 1900; Garrett, 'Hist. Geog. of Upper Brent', fig. 14 (2).
[92] Barker and Robbins, *Lond. Transport*, ii. 123, 128, 130; *Willesden Cit.* 16 Mar. 1951.
[93] *The Times*, 24 July 1906.
[94] Jackson, *Semi-Detached Lond.* 29; Grange Mus., gen. files, topog. (M. Marks, 'Growth of Willesden').
[95] Garrett, 'Hist. Geog. of Upper Brent', figs. 14 (2–4).
[96] Willesden boro. *Local Community Svces. 1933*, in Grange Mus., gen. files, topog.
[97] Barker and Robbins, *Lond. Transport*, i. 268; *Kelly's Dir. Mdx.* (1890).

[98] Grange Mus., gen. files, topog. (Marks, 'Growth of Willesden'); J. R. Day, *Lond.'s Trams and Trolley Buses* (1977), 56.
[99] Jackson, *Semi-Detached Lond.* 27.
[1] *The Times*, 31 Oct. 1919.   [2] Ibid. 10 July 1920.
[3] Willesden boro. *Local Community Svces. 1933*.
[4] Morris, *Willesden Surv.* pp. 71, 76 sqq.
[5] Potter, *Story of Willesden*, 20, 28; Garrett, 'Hist. Geog. of Upper Brent', 26–8; none of the finds is listed in the archaeological gazetteers in *V.C.H. Mdx.* i.
[6] The lessee of Brondesbury in the late 16th cent. suffered from being 'far distant from any neighbours': P.R.O., REQ 2/293/28.
[7] Ibid. E 301/34, no. 181.

in 1642.[8] There were 102 houses in 1664, of which half were one-hearth cottages. The largest houses were Neasden House and East Twyford manor house, the rest being modest farmhouses.[9] Most inhabitants were farmers and Willesden was not an area attracting the nobility or London merchants in any number. Bridget, countess of Bedford, lived there in 1595,[10] and Willesden was sufficiently within the ambience of London to be affected by the plague of 1665. In the early 18th century the inhabitants included Tobias Eco, 'a black'.[11] By 1720 there were 77 ratepayers, divided between Harlesden (23), Kilburn (14), Church End (13), Willesden Green (10), Neasden (8), Sherrick green (4), Oxgate (3), and Dollis Hill (2).[12] Farmhouses had been built on the cleared woodland at Cricklewood and at Kensal Green by the mid 18th century,[13] and some 31 parcels of waste had been enclosed by 1792, some of them, for example at Dollis Hill, for new cottages.[14] By 1795 there were said to be c. 130 houses in the parish.[15] The census figure of 98 houses in 1801 is too low, and the number of houses grew steadily from 178 in 1811 to 254 in 1821 and 358 in 1831.[16] In 1834 it was said that a great many cottages, usually owned by tradesmen and occupied by the poor, had been built since inclosure in 1823.[17] Most building was on the former village greens, at Willesden, Harlesden, and especially Kensal Green. Until the mid 19th century, however, Willesden was celebrated as a place of rural tranquillity by artists like George Morland (d. 1804), Paul Sandby (d. 1809), and Julius Caesar Ibbetson (d. 1817) and by writers like John Dugdale in 1819.[18]

The outward expansion of the metropolis reached Willesden in the mid 19th century, when there were 578 houses in Willesden, engulfing south Kilburn in the 1850s and 1860s and north Kilburn in the 1870s and 1880s. Proceeding along Harrow Road, it affected Kensal Green and Harlesden, whose growth was also stimulated by the building of Willesden Junction station just outside the borders. The first entirely new developments, at Brondesbury and Stonebridge from the 1860s and 1870s respectively, took place in estates bordering main roads and served by railway.

The number of houses grew from 812 in 1861 to 2,233 in 1871, 8,162 in 1891, and 20,128 in 1905.[19] The earliest development, at Kilburn, Willesden Green, Brondesbury, and Stonebridge Park, was for upper-class housing for merchants and professional men working in the City. Although builders in the other areas would have liked to serve a similar market, the existence of railway workings at Willesden Junction, the proximity of working-class suburbs, and simple demand meant that most of the building in the 1880s and 1890s was for the lower middle and working classes. Willesden was just outside the metropolis with its strict building regulations, and land companies and small builders competed to buy up estates and to cram them with cheap houses. The United Land Co. began buying estates at Kilburn and Church End in 1869 and by 1881 had 17 estates in Willesden Green, Church End, and Harlesden.[20] In 1887 it owned 178 a. in Willesden, and four other building societies and land companies owned 62 a., mostly in Stonebridge.[21] The land companies usually leased to builders who often sub-leased to other, usually small, local builders with little or no capital working on a speculative basis.[22] There was considerable pressure from the lower classes for housing, many having been displaced from the metropolis by the railway works there. They included many Irish who came from areas like Paddington and moved from street to street, attracted by the new houses. They did not stay long enough to discover the defects in the houses or to agitate for better surroundings. There were many jerry-built houses and buildings stood isolated among mud and unmade roads.[23] The piecemeal development of different estates produced an often bizarre road-pattern.[24] At Stonebridge the parallel streets running north from Harrow Road reflected the narrow fields with their short frontages on the main road. That sort of layout was avoided on the prebendal estates to the east, where the whole area was owned by the Ecclesiastical Commissioners and there was no difficulty in building long access roads like Brondesbury Park and Salisbury Road. The commissioners did not, however, keep a tight control of the development, and it was on their property that some of the worst mistakes, such as building in unmade roads, were made at Kilburn. Some 5,700 houses had been built on the commissioners' estates by 1944, mostly before 1908.[25] The other large landowner, All Souls College, Oxford, began with a policy of selling land when it reached £800 an acre and sold land at Kensal Green to the United Land Company in 1882. After 1888, however, a more adventurous estates bursar (Henry O. Wakemen, 1888–99) followed the advice of the college agents and began to exploit the estates directly: the college built roads and assumed responsibility for the overall planning while individual plots were leased to builders.[26] The college also sought agreement

[8] H.L., Protestation Returns.
[9] M.R.O., MR/TH/3, mm. 5–6.
[10] Ibid. Acc. 565/45.   [11] Grange Mus., Wood F 33.
[12] Ibid. 1 B 1 (poor rate bk. 1703–21).
[13] Messeder Road Map (1749); Rocque, Map of Lond. (1746).
[14] Grange Mus., 1 D 29 (vestry order bk. 1722–1814).
[15] Lysons, Environs, iii. 621.
[16] Census, 1801–31.
[17] Rep. Com. Poor Law, H.C. 44, p. 185i (1834), xxxvi.
[18] For Morland and Ibbetson, below; Sandby painted Willesden Lane: Grange Mus., photo. files, Willesden Lane (NL 41); J. Dugdale, New Brit. Traveller (1819), 556.
[19] Census, 1861–1901; Morris, Willesden Surv. p. 9.
[20] Grange Mus., Wood F 19 (sales cat. 1/20).

[21] M.R.O., TA/WIL (tithe map and award).
[22] e.g. at Willesden Green: Wm. Martin of Victor Works, bankrupt in 1888: M.R.O., Acc. 549/76; Chas. Cowley and Wm. Drake, building in Balmoral Rd. in 1895: ibid.; Jas. Lambe and Rob. Wiggins at Villiers Rd. in 1892: ibid. Acc. 1329/1–2.
[23] Grange Mus., Wood F 9 (Bill to enable Willesden local bd. to appoint bldg. inspectors, 1887); F 23, pp. 281 sqq.; C. Booth, Life and Labour of People of Lond. 3rd ser. Religious Influences, 3 (1902), p. 145.
[24] Winterburn, 'Willesden'.
[25] Ch. Com., Clutton's rep. on Lond. estates, 1944, p. 63.
[26] All Souls Coll., uncat. material, docs. relating to estates 1887–95; G. Faber, Notes on Hist. of All Souls Bursarships (priv. print.), 38, 58–61, 78.

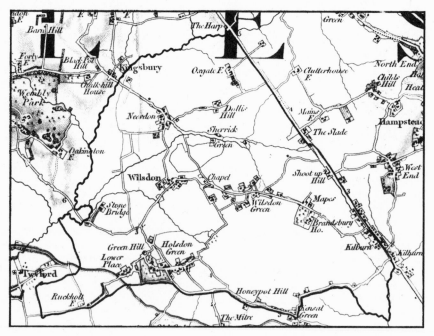

1822

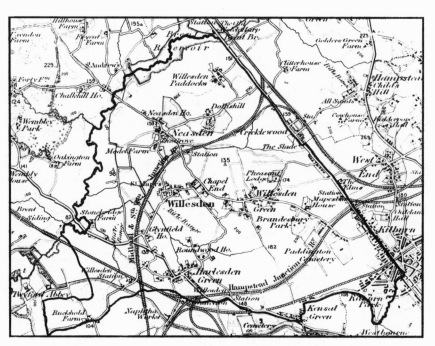

1877

WILLESDEN: EVOLUTION OF SETTLEMENT 1822–1914
(Scale 1 inch to 1 mile)

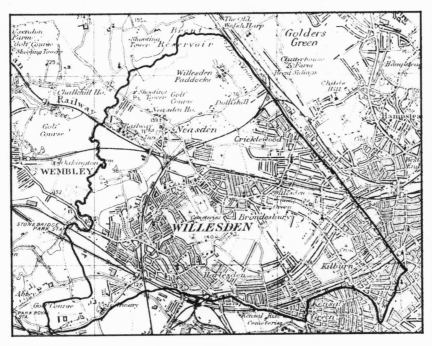

1914

with neighbouring landowners so that a more logical road pattern could be planned.[27]

Although the Willesden local board enforced building regulations after 1887, the tendency towards low-cost working-class housing continued. The pattern of growth was much influenced by the railway companies, which, beginning with the Metropolitan Railway in the late 1870s, bought land for railway sidings, workshops, and housing estates for their workers. Those developments attracted other industry, and it was usually the provision of transport, by rail as by buses and trams, that decided the success or failure of building schemes.

In the early years of the 20th century Willesden had an excellent transport system, flourishing shopping centres, and the beginnings of industry. It was primarily residential but it had already lost much of the middle-class character that predominated up to the 1880s. In 1901 the two largest categories of employed men worked in transport and building, with smaller numbers in the food, drink, and tobacco trades and working as clerks or in commerce. A third of the women worked, the largest group as domestic servants and many as dressmakers and laundresses.[28] There had long been areas of poverty, notably in Kilburn, and from c. 1906 to 1914 there was a slump. Some 45,000 meals were provided for underfed children by the Willesden Children's Aid Association during the winter of 1905–6, and the Willesden Distress Committee, financed partly by the Local Government Board,

found work for some of the unemployed in Willesden's parks in 1909.[29] Unemployment resulted partly from the decline in the building industry, which locally had outstripped demand. It was difficult to sell land in 1906[30] and by 1909 there were 1,113 houses and 1,129 tenements without occupants in Willesden. The First World War prevented the implementation of a scheme to provide council housing.[31]

The war also completed the transformation of Willesden from a largely middle-class residential suburb to a predominantly working-class part of the industrial belt of London. It stimulated the growth of industry, both in established centres like Church End and Kilburn and in newer areas like Cricklewood and Park Royal.

After the First World War industry continued to expand in the areas opened up by the munitions factories and linked by the North Circular Road. The council, anxious to avoid the unemployment and housing problems of the years before the war, encouraged building. The number of houses and flats increased to 24,919 in 1921, 31,000 in 1931, and 42,418 in 1939;[32] 7,368 dwellings, 226 factories and workshops, and 403 shops and offices were built between 1922 and 1934.[33] While the number of houses increased, the population initially increased even faster. There was a 4 per cent growth in the number of houses between 1911 and 1921 and a 7·4 per cent growth in population. In the late 1920s and the 1930s the rate of building was faster than the increase in population: the number of houses rose 28 per

[27] e.g. with the Eccl. Com. in 1883 and with Wright and Furness in 1900.   [28] *Census*, 1901.
[29] *The Times*, 22 Dec. 1906; 25 Nov. 1909.
[30] Faber, *All Souls Bursarships*, 57.

[31] *The Times*, 31 Aug. 1909; 18 Dec. 1913.
[32] *Census*, 1921–31; Willesden boro. *Year Bk.* (1958–9).
[33] Inst. of Mun. and County Engineers, *62nd Ann. Gen. Mtg.* (1935), in Grange Mus., gen. files, lectures.

cent 1921–31 and 36 per cent 1931–9 compared with population growth at 19 per cent and 13 per cent respectively.[34] Overcrowding persisted, as workers attracted by the new industry crowded into the houses built for City clerks. By 1934 a fifth of working-class families lived more than two persons to a room and 6 per cent of the population was classified as living in poverty. The newer houses tended to be occupied by the middle class and there was an increase in those employed in clerical and commercial occupations. In 1921 transport was still the largest employer of male workers while large numbers were employed in commerce and finance and as clerks, in metal work, in textiles and clothes, and in wood and furniture work. Domestic service was still the largest single category of women's work. There were smaller numbers of builders and bricklayers, electricians, and paper workers. Over half of Willesden's employed inhabitants worked outside its borders, while some 14,000 people travelled into Willesden to work.[35]

Willesden became a municipal borough in 1933 and Labour took control, drawing up a town planning scheme in the same year. The scheme designated three areas not yet covered by building: north Cricklewood, Neasden, and Dollis Hill; the western part of Stonebridge; and the area lying between Harlesden, Kensal Green, and Willesden Green. Industry was to be allowed in zones within each area, especially the first, and the rest was to be divided into housing zones of low density.[36] In its anxiety to avoid the housing densities of the old centres like Kilburn and Harlesden, the council neglected to leave sufficient open space for parks and recreation, and most of the land along the Brent was taken in the 1930s for factories and housing estates. The council concentrated its attention on the poorer, overcrowded areas in the south and east and produced its first slum clearance plan in 1937. By 1933 some 1,000 council houses had been built, mostly in the Brentwater estate, and in 1934 the council began building by direct labour. A large new council estate, Curzon Crescent, was built in the area between Harlesden and Church End in 1936.[37]

Some 1,300 homes were destroyed and 6,500 severely damaged during the Second World War. There was a considerable movement of population and by 1948 there were 11,750 families on the waiting list for council housing. The problem was alleviated by building prefabricated bungalows (some of which were still in use in 1965) and requisitioning empty houses, but a government survey in 1947 revealed the overcrowding, over-industrialization, and lack of planning which lay at the root of the problem. There was little sense of identity or community. Historically Willesden was a parish of separate hamlets and the building of canal, railways, and roads like the North Circular had served not to link but to divide them. The old parish church of St. Mary's had long ceased to be the focus of the area and no civic centre grew up to take its place. The population was unstable: people moved into Willesden from areas like Paddington and Marylebone and having achieved a certain level of prosperity moved farther out. In 1947, for example, more than half the inhabitants were said to have arrived since 1925. In 1971 the same proportion of Wembley's inhabitants had come from Willesden.[38]

Although most immigrants into Willesden came from other areas of London (42 per cent of the population in 1901 was born in London), from the 19th century there had been some immigrants from outside England. There had been Irish in Kilburn in 1841 and 1871 and in 1901 nearly 3 per cent of Willesden's population had been born in the British Empire (mostly in Ireland). By then Jewish immigration, particularly into Brondesbury and later into Cricklewood, had begun: 1·1 per cent of the population had been born in Europe, mostly in Germany.[39] American restrictions on immigrants in the 1920s and 1930s increased the flow of Irish to areas like Kilburn, which increased rapidly after the Second World War. The Irish had long been prominent in the building trade and they formed a high proportion of those crowding into the lodging houses.[40] In 1966 almost a fifth of Willesden's population had been born in Ireland.[41] Jewish residents came mostly as a result of the persecutions of the 1930s, as is reflected in the figures for 1951 when 3·5 per cent of the population was born in Germany, Poland, Russia, or Austria. From the 1950s most immigrants into Willesden were West Indians and, more recently, Asians. The few West Indians in 1951 were mainly students. By 1961 those born in the colonies and protectorates made up 5·5 per cent of the population, and most came from the Caribbean. By 1971 the proportion had risen to 13 per cent, nearly a third coming from Jamaica alone.[42]

The immigrants formed an increasing proportion of the population because as they moved in the older inhabitants, often skilled workers, moved out at a still faster rate. That was largely the result of the council's policy of encouraging Willesden's industry and workers to move to the new towns. In 1966 only a third of Willesden's male inhabitants were employed in middle-class occupations, compared with two fifths for Greater London, while of Willesden's West Indians nine tenths were manual workers.

Although extensive rebuilding in areas like Kilburn was undertaken by the council, the housing shortage, aggravated by the influx of working-class immigrants, remained. Willesden experienced all the problems of Rachmanism and squatting in the 1960s. The proportion of private rented accommodation in 1961 (45 per cent)

[34] Census, 1911–31; Willesden boro. Year Bk. (1958–9).
[35] Census, 1911–31; New Surv. of London Life and Labour (1934), vi, Social Survey, II. 459–62.
[36] V. Leff and G. H. Blunden, Willesden Story (1965), 30 sqq.; Grange Mus., NM 309.
[37] Inst. of Mun. and County Engineers, 62nd Ann. Gen. Mtg. (1935); Leff and Blunden, Willesden Story, 31 sqq.

[38] New Statesman, 22 Jan. 1971, in Grange Mus., gen. files, housing. [39] Census, 1901.
[40] J. A. Jackson, The Irish in Britain (1963), 13, 107.
[41] A. L. Weintraub, 'Race and local politics in Eng.: a case study of Willesden' (Columbia Univ. D.Phil. thesis, 1972, copy in Grange Mus.).
[42] Census, 1951–71.

was considerably larger than for Middlesex as a whole (27 per cent); twice as many dwellings lacked a bath, and three times as many people lived at a density of more than $1\frac{1}{2}$ persons per room. The council gradually increased its share of housing, from 4,274 dwellings in 1961 to 12,094 in 1970 and 18,729 in 1977. It also encouraged housing associations, financing six in 1964, to convert older property in areas like Kensal Green.[43]

The population of Willesden doubled from 751 in 1801 to 1,413 in 1821 and 2,957 (including 599 people in barns) in 1841. The development of Kilburn is reflected in the rise from 3,879 in 1861 to 15,869 in 1871. It was 61,265 by 1891 and 154,214 by 1911. It was 185,025 in 1931 but declined after the Second World War, to 179,697 in 1951 and 153,380 in 1971.[44]

WILLESDEN GREEN was the largest of the hamlets, a group of houses around the spacious green in the centre of the parish and its extension, East Green. The name Willesden, recorded in 939 as Wellesdune, has been interpreted as 'hill of the spring',[45] and the names 'Dune' and Willesden Dune were recorded c. 1280.[46] The hill referred to may have been Brondesbury ridge, which lay south and east of the settlement. One of the tributaries of the Sherrick brook rose in East Green.[47] There were several long-established farmhouses at Willesden Green, including one which probably dated back to the 14th century. At least three farmhouses with their barns and cottages were marked on the southern edge of the green in 1599 as was another in Pound Lane.[48] Eleven people were assessed for rates at Willesden Green in 1687.[49] By 1738 farmhouses and cottages were clustered all round the green.[50] There were at least 13 houses, mostly set in orchards and including the Spotted Dog inn, by the mid 18th century.[51]

In 1817 Willesden Green was a 'retired pleasant village, which appears as remote from London as at a distance of an hundred miles'.[52] At inclosure in 1823 it consisted of some 40 houses and cottages scattered around the large green.[53] They included the Spotted Dog, four farmhouses,[54] several houses of moderate size, and one 'of a rather superior description' built for Lord le Despenser and later part of William Weeden's estate. On a knoll commanding extensive views, the house can probably be identified with the

Grange at the entrance to Chambers Lane.[55] Willesden House, the property of the Waite family, stood in 6 a. of pleasure grounds on the north side of the green, near the Spotted Dog.[56]

There was some building of cottages in Willesden Green after inclosure. In 1828-9 there were a smith, a wheelwright, a coachmaster, and a brewer.[57] A grocer and a dame's school had been added by 1851 but the coachmaster and the brewer had gone. Most of the cottages were occupied by agricultural labourers and laundresses and there were some professional people, including George Waite, a surgeon dentist, at Willesden House, a surgeon, and several solicitors, including Richard Wright at Pheasant Lodge, built since inclosure.[58] Rose Villa, 'of Anglo-Italian style', set in pleasure grounds and 'park-like scenery', had been built by 1850 on the site of an earlier house at the junction of Walm and Willesden lanes.[59] Other middle-class villas built by 1855 included Willesden Lodge and the Villa.[60] Pound Lane contained a few cottages housing agricultural labourers and laundresses.[61]

Freehold building land fronting High Road, Willesden Green, was offered for sale in 1826[62] and there was an abortive attempt in 1856 to build on 13 a. at the eastern end of Sherrick green, where Melrose Avenue was laid out but still unbuilt on in 1894.[63] In 1876 the 'picturesque collection of old houses about the village green' had been replaced by rows of 'mean brick cottages',[64] probably cottages like those demolished in Grange Road in the 1930s and in Chapman Park in 1958[65] or the group clustered opposite the Spotted Dog.[66] The Grange estate was put up for sale in 1873 as suitable for 'a first-class building scheme'.[67] Although the estate was not built over for some time, it fell into the hands of the Furness family which opened its brickworks there.[68] In 1877 some 24 a. north-east of the green were put up for sale as potential building land, with views from high ground and the prospective construction of the Metropolitan line.[69]

The Metropolitan line with a station at Willesden Green opened in 1879 had a more immediate and masked effect upon development than earlier lines had done. Mrs. Catherine Nicol in 1877 sold Bramley's (Willesden) farm to the United Land Co. Within two years the company laid out streets south of the railway on each side of High Road,[70] selling plots to small builders who built

[43] Ibid. 1961–77; Weintraub, 'Race and local politics'; Grange Mus., gen. files, housing, housing assocs. and socs.; Brent L.B. *Year Bk.* (1970–1, 1977–8).

[44] *Census*, 1801–1971. The figs. for 1971 are of the 17 wards in Brent L.B. covering the area of Willesden.

[45] *P.N. Mdx.* (E.P.N.S.), 160–4. For the (spurious) charter of 939, below, manors.

[46] St. Paul's MSS. A 29/384; A 30/444.

[47] M.R.O., EA/WIL (inclosure map).

[48] All Souls Coll., Hovenden maps II/20–21.

[49] Grange Mus., 1 B 27 (overseers' accts. 1678–1702).

[50] M.R.O., Acc. 262/72/1, p. 32.

[51] Rocque, *Map of Lond.* (1746); Messeder Road Map (1749); Grange Mus., Wood F 21 (map of 1765).

[52] J. Hassell, *Picturesque Rides and Walks* (1817), i. 233.

[53] M.R.O., EA/WIL; Acc. 262/40, pt. 2 (inclosure claims 1816).

[54] Ibid. EA/WIL, nos. 647–50, 681, 741, 758; Cruchley, *New Plan of Lond.* (1829); O.S. Map 6″, Mdx. XVI. NW., NE. (1864–73 edn.).

[55] Brewer, *Beauties of Eng. and Wales*, x (5), 349.

[56] M.R.O., EA/WIL, nos. 666–7.

[57] Pigot, *Lond. and Provincial Dir.* (1828–9). For the brewery, south of High Road, Cruchley, *New Plan* (1829).

[58] P.R.O., HO 107/1700/135/3, ff. 380v.–388.

[59] W. Keane, *Beauties of Mdx.* (1850).

[60] *Kelly's Dir. Mdx.* (1855).

[61] P.R.O., HO 107/1700/135/3, ff. 388, 393v.

[62] M.R.O., Acc. 303/7.

[63] Grange Mus., Wood F 21, p. 296; O.S. Map 6″, Mdx. XI. SE. (1864–73, 1894–6 edns.).

[64] Thorne, *Environs*, 697–9.

[65] Grange Mus., photo files, Grange Rd. (NL 838–41); Chapman Park (NL 660–2); *Willesden Chron.* 23 May 1930; 3 Feb. 1939; 21 Nov. 1958.   [66] M.R.O., TA/WIL, no. 531.

[67] Grange Mus., Wood F 19 (sale cat. 1/4).

[68] M.R.O., TA/WIL, nos. 537–43.

[69] Grange Mus., Wood F 19 (sale cat. 1/28).

[70] i.e. Villiers, Chaplin, Belton, and Strode rds.: Grange Mus., NM 406–7.

crowded terraced houses which 'absolutely ruined all the centre of Willesden as a residential district'.[71]

The United Land Co. bought an estate at Pound Lane and the Willesden House estate by 1881.[72] By 1882 Willesden House had been demolished, semi-detached houses built along the north side of Willesden Lane, and roads and building plots laid out to the north.[73] Mount Pleasant and 9 a. belonging to it at Chambers Lane were offered in 1882 as building land.[74] Another of the small estates on the south-east side of the green was in the hands of builders by 1884.[75] The Pheasant Lodge estate to the north-east was sold to the Imperial Property Investments Co. and was being laid out for 'a superior class of house' in 1887; most building took place in the 1890s.[76] In 1891 the company bought Willesden Park estate, 17 a. surrounding the Willesden House estate, which by 1893 it had laid out in roads with names of royal association.[77] Chapter Road, parallel to the railway, was being built up between 1893 and 1900.[78] On adjoining land belonging to All Souls College, Oxford, building began in 1895,[79] and on the college's land south of High Road in 1899 on Willesden Green farm, of which the farmhouse had gone by 1904. In that year 125 houses were being built on the college estate at Willesden Green in addition to 55 already built.[80]

By 1896 building on both sides of the high street was well advanced, especially on each side of Willesden Green station. To the south-east building along Willesden Lane merged with the new district of Brondesbury, while houses reached on the west to Chapel End and on the south to Harlesden Lane and Chambers Lane.[81] North of the railway roads had been laid out, including Melrose Avenue, on the Buckingham estate, which had been sold in 1877, and by 1901 much building had been done.[82] By then the area between the high street and the railway was completely covered and north of the railway building was advancing westward from Walm Lane and eastward from Dudden Hill Lane. In the north-east Willesden Green merged with Cricklewood.[83]

A new parish, St. Andrew's, was formed in 1880 to serve the rapidly expanding district of Willesden Green. The numbers of houses in the parish increased from 145 in 1881 to 855 in 1891 and 1,764 in 1901. In 1898 a new parish, St. Gabriel's, was formed to serve the district on each side of Walm Lane north of the Metropolitan railway line and in 1901 it had 975 houses.

The population of St. Andrew's parish rose from 857 in 1881 to 5,570 in 1891 and 11,296 in 1901. St. Gabriel's then had 5,341 people and Willesden Green ward 18,948.[84] At the end of the 19th century Willesden Green's continually shifting inhabitants were described by the vicar of St. Andrew's as poor, 'utterly careless and irreligious', mostly unbaptized, rough, and accustomed to spending Sundays in bed.[85] As the older inhabitants moved out and the larger houses were pulled down, Willesden Green became wholly lower- and lower-middle class in character. In 1890 there were a few professional people, two farms, a jobmaster, and a nursery-man on the fringes of the district. There were three dairymen but they may have been retailers rather than agricultural workers. High Road had become a shopping centre with some 50 retail shops besides 19 craftsmen and 17 wholesalers. There were some 20 retail shops in other streets. Small-scale industry included 15 laundries, mostly in Villiers Road, printers, engravers, coachbuilders, 11 builders, and Furness's brick-works, which was probably the largest employer in the district.[86] Many travelled from Willesden Green station to work outside Willesden. The churches met some social needs: St. Andrew's, operating from temporary premises until a permanent church opened in 1886, provided a men's club, parish library, soup kitchen, and glee club besides schools and missions. Its services offered colour and drama, with incense, processions, and elaborate vestments in use during the 1880s and 1890s.[87] Baptist and Swedenborgian chapels were opened during the 1880s. There was less rivalry from public houses than in some parts of Willesden: only the Case is Altered in High Road and Rising Sun in Harlesden Lane had been added to the Spotted Dog by 1890.[88] High Road contained a concert hall and a working men's club by 1890 and a public library after 1894.

By 1911 the population of St. Andrew's parish was 16,718 and of St. Gabriel's 6,857. Willesden Green ward, reduced in area since 1901, had 15,187 inhabitants in 1911 and 16,565 in 1921. Growth after 1901 was most marked north of the Metropolitan line, in the new district of Dudden Hill, built by the Dudding Park Estate Co. and Ben Andrews, who in 1909 pressed the Metropolitan company to open Dollis Hill station as a stimulus to building.[89] There was some building in the central area, All Souls College for example completing some 36 houses between 1905 and 1914 and another 46, mostly in High Road, by

[71] Ibid. Wood F 23, pp. 286 sqq.; F 20 (sale cat. 2/6, 14); M.R.O., Acc. 549/76.
[72] Grange Mus., Wood F 19 (sale cat. 1/20); F 20 (sale cat. 2/31).
[73] i.e. Huddlestone and Lechmere rds.: ibid. NM 422-3.
[74] Ibid. Wood F 19 (sale cat. 1/49). Not built on for many years.   [75] M.R.O., Acc. 1353/31.
[76] Grange Mus., Wood F 23, pp. 288 sqq.; e.g. Blenheim, Stanley and Grosvenor gdns.: M.R.O., Acc. 1351/62; Grange Mus., 2 A 1 (H. Barnard, 'Memo. for hist. of Street Names'); All Souls Coll., uncat. material, docs. relating to estates, 1887-95.
[77] Grange Mus., Wood F 24, pp. 114 sqq.; NM 317-20.
[78] M.R.O., Acc. 584/2; Acc. 767; Acc. 891/2/9/59.
[79] i.e. Linacre and part of Balmoral and High rds.

[80] All Souls Coll., uncat. material, Bd. of Agric. orders (box of estate papers 1883-7): bursars' rentals 1896-8, 1904; agents' reps. 1899-1900.
[81] O.S. Map 6", Mdx. XVI. NW., NE. (1894-6 edn.).
[82] e.g. Riffel Rd., made up by council in 1902: M.R.O., Acc. 549/77.
[83] Grange Mus., Map of Willesden U.D. 1901.
[84] Census, 1881-1901.
[85] Grange Mus., gen. files, St. Andrew's church, Willesden Green (MS. notes by vicar).
[86] Kelly's Dir. Mdx. (1890).
[87] Grange Mus., gen. files, St. Andrew's church, Willesden Green (MS. notes by vicar).
[88] Kelly's Dir. Mdx. (1890).
[89] Jackson, Semi-Detached Lond. 229.

1924.[90] At Robson Avenue on the All Souls estate 30 houses were being built in 1934;[91] on the Furness estate south of the green the brickworks disappeared and the area was laid out in streets of large detached houses between 1925 and 1939; on the area next to it, south-east of the green, large semi-detached houses were built between 1920 and 1935; and north of the Metropolitan line, east of Dudden Hill, medium-sized semi-detached houses were built between 1927 and 1935. Most of the houses of the twenties and thirties, unlike earlier ones, were built for owner-occupiers.[92] The number of houses in Willesden Green ward rose from 2,762 in 1921 to 3,048 in 1931 while the population fell to 16,298.

In 1949 Willesden Green was defined as an area of 381 a., 4,260 houses, 1,196 flats, and 27,418 people. The average density of 72 persons to an acre covered a variation from 30 on the 1930s' Furness estate to 141 on the Imperial Land Co. estate of the 1890s. Except for the part next to Willesden Green station, the whole of the central district on either side of High Road was recommended for redevelopment, either because the houses were dilapidated or overcrowded or because industry was so mixed with housing.[93]

There was some small-scale demolition of early cottages in the 1950s[94] but plans for rebuilding in the early 1960s proved abortive[95] and the area continued to decline. In 1971 Willesden Green ward had a high proportion of inadequate houses.[96] The closure of a large co-operative store was taken in 1971 as symptomatic of the dying of Willesden Green as a shopping centre.[97] London Transport built houses for employees north of the Metropolitan railway line in 1977.[98] Like other areas in Willesden, Willesden Green received a considerable number of immigrants from the 1950s: 14 per cent of the people in Willesden Green ward in 1966 were Irish-born and 11 per cent were born in the West Indies.[99]

CHURCH END grew around the church, the site of which, at the edge of the marshes away from the main centres of settlement, may have been that of an earlier shrine associated with a well or grove[1] or may have been chosen because it was accessible from the three main settlements. The rectory and vicarage were built nearby. A few cottages joined them and by 1599 there were other houses grouped to the east, but there was never a village green.[2] By the mid 18th century Church End was a small village surrounded by open fields, the roads from Harlesden, Neasden,

and Willesden Green twisting round the church, vicarage, and rectory which formed its focus. It had two inns, the Five (later Six) Bells and the White Hart, and there was a group of wooden poorhouse cottages in the churchyard.[3] There were some 20 houses at inclosure, of which most were small cottages. A schoolroom and a round-house or lock-up had been added to the buildings of c. 1750.[4] The grouping around the church with its frame of elm trees, its extensive views and 'picturesque effect', attracted several painters in the late 18th and early 19th centuries, the work of George Cooke and John Varley being especially notable.[5]

William Harrison Ainsworth, who set his novel about the early 18th-century highwayman, Jack Sheppard, in Willesden, described it as he knew it in the 1830s as 'the most charming and secluded village in the neighbourhood of the metropolis', commenting on the 'grove of rook-haunted trees' and the old buildings of the church and rectory.[6] In 1828-9 the 'very retired little village' housed a bricklayer, a butcher, and a general dealer and by 1834 a coach left every morning for London from the Six Bells, which also served as a post office.[7]

At the eastern end of the village, midway between Church End and Willesden Green, a small settlement grew up called Chapel End, after the brick chapel built in 1820, or Queen's Town, to commemorate the visit of Queen Victoria in 1837.[8] Chapel Row had been built there by 1846[9] and in 1851 Queen's Town was a community of agricultural labourers, a bootmaker, and a carpenter. By that time a large farm, Dudden Hill Farm, had been built on the west side of the road leading from Chapel End to Neasden, and Mead House and another house, occupied by a wine merchant and the vicar respectively, had appeared on the north side of High Road. The rectory housed a tobacco manufacturer and most of the other houses, including the vicarage, were occupied by agricultural labourers; there were also a horsedealer, a schoolmaster, a builder, a bricklayer, and a fishmonger.[10] A large new vicarage was built in 1851, the White Horse in Church Road c. 1860, and the Elms opposite Mead House by the late 1860s.[11]

In 1868 the M. & S.W.J.'s (Acton branch) railway line was constructed west and north of Church End, and anticipation of the opening of a station (not achieved until 1875) stimulated the sale of land in Church End for building.[12] The

[90] All Souls Coll., uncat. material, bursars' rentals 1904, 1914, 1924.　　　[91] Ibid. 1934.
[92] Morris, *Willesden Surv.* p. 22, map 7.
[93] Ibid. pp. 18, 22, map 7, areas 1A-L.
[94] Grange Mus., photo. files, Chapmans Pk. (NL 660-2); Grange Rd. (NL 838-41).
[95] *Willesden Civic Review*, June 1960; *Rep. to Willesden, 1963-4* (Willesden boro. ann. review).
[96] *Profile of Brent* (1976), in Grange Mus., gen. files, race relations.　　　[97] *Willesden and Brent Chron.* 29 Jan. 1971.
[98] Winterburn, 'Willesden'.
[99] Weintraub, 'Race and local politics'.
[1] Below, churches.
[2] All Souls Coll., Hovenden maps II/21.
[3] Rocque, *Map of Lond.* (1746); Messeder Road Map (1749).

[4] M.R.O., Acc. 262/40, pt. 2 (inclosure claims 1816); ibid. EA/WIL; Guildhall MS. CC. 169193A.
[5] *Eng. Topog.* (Gent. Mag. Libr.), vii. 287-9; Grange Mus., photo. files, Neasden Lane, St. Mary's church (NL 26, 1235).
[6] W. H. Ainsworth, *Jack Sheppard* (1910 edn.), 144, 159-60, 173.
[7] Pigot, *Lond. and Provincial Dir.* (1828-9); Pigot, *Nat. Com. Dir.* (1832-4); *Eng. Topog.* (Gent. Mag. Libr.), vii. 287-9.
[8] Grange Mus., 1 A 2 (*Willesden Cit.* 23 July 1954).
[9] M.R.O., Acc. 549/78.
[10] P.R.O., HO 107/1700/135/3, ff. 388-98.
[11] O.S. Map 6", Mdx. XVI. NW. (1864-73 edn.); Grange Mus., photo. files, Church Rd. (NL 989).
[12] e.g. M.R.O., Acc. 1093/22.

church lost much of its picturesque appeal in the restorations of 1851 and 1872, and in 1866 the churchyard was extended by 4 a. and the old cottages there were pulled down.[13] The United Land Co. bought the Read estate at Chapel End in 1869,[14] which it had laid out by the late 1870s as the Meyrick Road estate.[15] In 1873 some 9 a. in the centre of Church End, then occupied by a house and Church End Paddocks, were put up for sale.[16] In 1875 Church Farm estate of 4 a. next to the White Horse, then containing the Timbers, an 'old-fashioned cottage residence,' and a small cottage and stables, was offered for residential or building property.[17] By 1875 there were 73 houses in Church End and Chapel End.[18]

Part of the Wright estate between Church Road and the railway was offered in 1879 as a good site for small villas.[19] The United Land Co. had acquired several estates upon which by 1880 it had laid out roads and building plots: at Chapel End (Beaconsfield Rd.), near the Church Farm estate (Cobbold Rd.), and on the east side of Neasden Lane, near the station opened in 1880 on the new Metropolitan line (Denzil Road).[20] In 1879 the vicar exchanged land with the rector, obtaining some $7\frac{1}{2}$ a. as protection around the Vicarage, and surrendering, *inter alia*, 4 a. between the railway and Church Road which were sold to the United Land Co. in 1881.[21] The company bought the field next to it and by 1882 roads had been laid out and building started.[22] On the west side of Neasden Lane, between the railway and the churchyard, was the last United Land Co. estate at Church End, bought by 1881.[23] In the late 1880s there were still a few old houses but 'one or two rows of mean houses' blocked the view from the church.[24] By the mid 1890s building was almost complete on all the land company's estates and by 1901 it had spread into the surrounding estates, on the rectory lands south of the church (Eric Road and Preston Gardens), on the Church Farm estate (Ilex Road), and on the north side of the High Road (Brenthurst Road). The opening of the Jewish cemetery at Pound Lane in 1873 and of Willesden cemetery next to it on the west in 1893 limited southward expansion from Chapel End.[25]

By 1890 Church End had a flourishing retail trade, especially in Church Road, but there was as yet no industry apart from the many laundries. There were seven retail shops in Queen's Town, where a new chapel had been built in 1878. Makers of blinds, picture frames, and cabinets had appeared in Church End by 1908,[26] and in

1907 the population of St. Mary's, then one of the poorest parishes in the diocese of London, was said to be almost entirely wage-earning.[27]

After the First World War the main development in Church End was in the growth of industry. By 1920 the cricket field north of the church had been replaced by several factories,[28] which by 1936 had spread eastward over Dudden Hill farm[29] and southward over Church End Paddocks. Willesden technical college was built north of Denzil Road in 1935 next to council housing built in 1933.[30]

In 1949 three areas of houses within Church End had population densities varying between 85 and 140 persons per acre and a total population of 2,535 in 464 houses. The area around Church Road housed 8,068 people in 1,116 houses and 314 flats at a density of 114 and 140 persons per acre. Almost all the housing was in closely-packed terraces and was thought fit for re-development.[31] The council started to purchase property in the 50 a. between Church Road, Craven Park, the railway, and Neasden Lane in 1963 and began rebuilding, starting from the southern end, in 1971. By 1980 the third stage was nearing completion.[32] Elsewhere Church End remained a mixture: the church, a few 19th-century cottages, the White Hart rebuilt in the late 19th century, the factory buildings of the 1920s and 1930s, and a school of the 1970s.

Of the 7,730 people in Church End ward in 1966, 6·9 per cent were born in the West Indies, 6·2 per cent in Ireland, 0·7 per cent in India and Pakistan, and a further 5·7 per cent elsewhere than in Great Britain.[33]

HARLESDEN, the name signifying Herewulf's farmstead,[34] was recorded in Domesday book and was one of the earliest and largest of the medieval settlements in the parish, with houses grouped together by 1319.[35] In the 16th century it was a linear village with houses along the edge of the green which bordered Harrow Road, separated from the other settlements to the north by the open fields. Its lands formed a prebendal manor and a manorial organization that survived relatively long, which probably helped to foster the sense of identity and separateness from the rest of Willesden which long characterized Harlesden. There were at least seven houses by 1599, including one of the main farmhouses of the All Souls estate.[36] Apart from farming there was some early industry in the form of tile-making.[37] There was an inn, the Crown, by the

[13] Thorne, *Environs*, 697–9.
[14] M.R.O., Acc. 1093/15–16, 22.
[15] Grange Mus., NM 424, 443; ibid. Wood F 19 (sale cat. 1/32A). [16] Ibid. Wood F 19 (sale cat. 1/5).
[17] Ibid. (sale cat. 1/14); photo. files, Church Rd.
[18] Willesden local bd. *San. Rep.* (1875).
[19] Grange Mus., Wood F 20 (sale cat. 2/24).
[20] Ibid. NM 420–1, 426–9, 440; ibid. Wood F 19 (sale cat. 1/20); F 20 (sale cat. 2/35); ibid. MS. 43.
[21] Ch. Com. file 59830.
[22] i.e. Mayo, Bourke, Carlton (later Garnet), Heron, and Talbot rds. and Church Lane: Grange Mus., NM 414–16, 418.
[23] Grange Mus., Wood F 19 (sale cat. 1/20).
[24] H. J. Foley, *Our Lanes and Meadow Paths* (1887), 56–7.
[25] O.S. Map 6", Mdx. XVI. NW. (1894–6 edn.); Grange Mus., Map of Willesden U.D. 1901.

[26] *Kelly's Dir. Mdx.* (1890, 1908).
[27] *The Times*, 23 Aug. 1907; 21 Dec. 1909.
[28] O.S. Map 6", Mdx. XI. SW., XVI. NW. (1920 edn.).
[29] Grange Mus., photo. files, Dudden Hill.
[30] O.S. Map 1/2500, Mdx. XI. 14 (1936 edn.); Inst. of Mun. and County Engineers, 62nd Ann. Gen. Mtg. (1935) in Grange Mus., gen. files, lectures.
[31] Morris, *Willesden Surv.* map 7, areas 8A, C, 11A–C, pp. 30, 32.
[32] Grange Mus., gen. files, housing estates; *Rep. to Willesden, 1963–4*; Brent L.B. *Year Bk.* (1977–8); hoardings on bldg. sites (1978); *Willesden and Brent Chron.* 4 Jan. 1980.
[33] Weintraub, 'Race and local politics'.
[34] *P.N. Mdx.* (E.P.N.S.), 162.
[35] Bodl. MS. D.D. All Souls c 123/43.
[36] All Souls Coll., Hovenden maps II/20.
[37] Below, industry.

late 17th century and another, the Green Man, by the mid 18th. At that time Harlesden contained a number of farmhouses set in orchards around the village green with scattered farms at Greenhill and Fortune Gate to the north-west. A network of roads led from Harrow Road to Acton, Old Oak common, Church End, and Willesden Green.[38] In 1816 Harlesden was described as a small village with several desirable houses.[39] There were some 30 houses by inclosure in 1823.[40]

The village grew slowly after inclosure. In 1828-9 there were two carpenters, a baker, and a wheelwright.[41] By 1839 the carpenters were replaced by a grocer, a shoemaker, a grocer and shoemaker, a tailor, a nurseryman, and a blacksmith, and another public house, the Royal Oak, had been opened. The coach from London to Harrow passed through Harlesden every day.[42] The London & Birmingham Railway (after 1846 the L. & N.W.R.) was built south of the village in 1837. A station called Willesden station was opened at Acton Lane in 1844 and six trains a day in each direction stopped there in 1849. It closed in 1866 when it was replaced by Willesden Junction station.[43] By 1851 the whole of the south-west corner of Willesden, including Harlesden, Twyford, and Stonebridge, had a population of 562 and 114 inhabited houses. Roundwood House, built 1834-8,[44] then occupied by Lord Ernest Brudenell Bruce, M.P., and Bramshill House, occupied by a stockbroker, had both been built since inclosure. There were four farms, including that at Lower Place, and most of the cottages were inhabited by labourers; there were also a few railway employees.[45] A Wesleyan chapel opened in High Street c. 1847. By 1855 Glynfield (Glenfield) House had been built on former open-field land. The tradesmen were much as they had been in 1839, with the addition of a beer-retailer and a butcher. The London coach still ran and an omnibus travelled daily to London from the Royal Oak.[46] In 1851 William Green, a builder from Paddington, erected Chapel Terrace next to the Wesleyan chapel on the north side of the High Street but went bankrupt in the process.[47] The Rectory estate was advertised for sale in 1858 as being 'admirably adapted to the erection of villas', mainly because of the ease of communications, being close to Willesden station on the L. & N.W.R. line and Harlesden Green station on the line from Kew to Fenchurch Street.[48] By

the late 1860s terraces and villas had been built on the east side of Harrow Road south of Harlesden green, a branch of Harlesden Lane had been extended northward (the later Longstone Avenue) to Knowles House and Roundwood Farm, and there was some building around Craven Park.[49] Anthony Trollope's description in 1869 of the setting of River's cottage as entirely rural, on a lane branching from Harrow Road at a 'country inn for hay-waggoners', presumably the Crown, was already out of date.[50] Houses were being built at the southern end of Church Road in 1870.[51] By 1875 there were 206 houses in the area between Harlesden green, Lower Place, and Stonebridge Park.[52] Although in 1876 Harlesden was said to have been 'a quiet rustic hamlet' that had been 'utterly spoiled' by the builder,[53] the building was still largely confined to High Street and existing roads.[54]

It was not until the later 1870s and the 1880s that farmland was sold and new streets laid out for building. Part of the Rectory estate, then called Willesden Manor, was sold in 1872 and a year later Uffington and Donnington roads had been laid out and the area divided into building plots for superior houses intended for commuters to London.[55] Michael Brown, a 'china man', began to issue 99-year building leases on the Greenhill estate to various builders in 1875 and sold the rest of the estate to the United Land Co. in 1880. By 1881 roads had been laid out and the area divided into plots, some of which were bought by Charles Penny, the Harlesden builder.[56]

Following the sale of the Taylors' estate in 1878 and 1879,[57] terraced houses were built, mainly by the United Land Co., at Station Road, Rucklidge Avenue, and Manor Park Road.[58] Nicoll Road had been built on the southern part of the Carr Glyn estate by 1879.[59] The United Land Co. bought the northern part, called Glynfield House estate, which it laid out in streets and building lots in 1881 and 1892.[60] An estate south of Acton Lane, near Willesden Junction, was developed by Col. R. J. Nightingale Tubbs as an area of terraced housing largely for railway employees. Charles Penny acquired building leases from Tubbs in 1884 and had laid out roads and plots for 100 houses by 1888.[61] Not all the building was by Penny, who often subleased to other builders.[62] The L. & N.W.R. built terraced housing for its employees in Harley Road.[63] In 1893 Penny was

---

[38] Messeder Road Map (1749); Rocque, *Map of Lond.* (1746).

[39] Brewer, *Beauties of Eng. and Wales*, x (5), 349-50.

[40] M.R.O., EA/WIL.

[41] Pigot, *Lond. and Provincial Dir.* (1828-9).

[42] Pigot, *Dir. Mdx.* (1839).

[43] *T.L.M.A.S.* xxvi. 310, 317-18.

[44] M.L.R. 1835/1/600; 1839/5/181.

[45] P.R.O., HO 107/1700/135/3, ff. 399 sqq.

[46] *Kelly's Dir. Mdx.* (1855).

[47] M.R.O., Acc. 1371/1-3.   [48] Ibid. Acc. 208/2.

[49] O.S. Map 6", Mdx. XVI. NW. (1864-73 edn.); above, communications.

[50] A. Trollope, *He Knew he was Right* (1869 edn.), ii. 135. The lane was a mile from [Kensal Green] cemetery on Harrow Road, which puts it in the centre of Harlesden green.

[51] M.R.O., Acc. 1284/1-4.

[52] Willesden local bd. *San. Rep.* (1875). Including Church

Road and St. Mary's Road.   [53] Thorne, *Environs*, 697-9.

[54] Morris, *Willesden Surv.* map 2.

[55] Grange Mus., Wood F 19 (sale cats. 1/7-8, 37); ibid. MS. 7.

[56] Ibid. NM. 436-7; ibid. Wood F 19 (sale cat. 1/57). Penny was still making leases to other builders on the estate in 1894: M.R.O., Acc. 538/2nd deposit/1204.

[57] Below, other est.

[58] Grange Mus., Wood F 20 (sale cat. 2/13, 18, 20); ibid. NM 439; ibid. photo. files, High St. Harlesden (NL 1039); M.R.O., TA/WIL.

[59] Ibid. Wood F 20 (sale cat. 2/18).

[60] Ibid. NM 273, 410-12; M.R.O., Acc. 1351/40.

[61] Grange Mus. NM 127; 2 A 1 ('Street Names'); M.R.O., Acc. 1351/30.

[62] e.g. M.R.O., Acc. 538/2nd deposit/1277.

[63] J. Ashdown and others, *Ind. Mon. of Gtr. Lond.* (1969), s.v. Brent.

building houses in Burns Road on land bought in 1891.[64] North of Harlesden green 20 a. of Roundwood Park, offered for sale as building land in 1886,[65] were sold in 1888 to the burial board for a cemetery and 26 a. in 1895 to the council for a park.[66] The area adjoining the cemetery to the west was being built up during the late 1890s.[67]

The number of houses in All Souls parish, Harlesden, increased from 399 (housing 2,390 people) in 1881 to 1,666 (housing 9,929 people) in 1891.[68] By 1894 almost the whole area between Burns Road and the railways had been built on. Building extended northward along Church Road to merge with Church End and west of the railway as Stonebridge Park.[69]

The rapid building brought problems, especially after the decision not to link Harlesden with the Metropolitan sewerage system.[70] On the Tubbs estate drainage was diverted to the Brent at Stonebridge but less scrupulous builders put in cesspools and in 1885 W. Tilbury, who was building in Church Road, was described as the 'worst builder in Willesden', putting up houses with 'every sanitary defect.'[71]

Harlesden was at the height of its prosperity at the turn of the century. Largely middle-class, it had a strong sense of identity compounded largely of civic pride and religious noncon-formity. Nine churches and chapels were built between 1876 and 1902 as were a court house, a library, a constitutional clubhouse, and a jubilee clock, the focus of High Street.[72] Willesden Hippodrome, a large music hall, opened in 1907. Much of High Street, a major shopping centre, was rebuilt in the Edwardian period.[73] To the east there were still several farms, Elmwood, Haycroft, Upper Roundwood, and Sellon's until the later 90s. In 1890 there were numerous jobmasters and dairy men, besides mansions occupied by men of business like George Furness, who had altered Roundwood House to create a stone-built Elizabethan-style mansion with barley-sugar chimneys, a tower, and pinnacles.[74] William Simpson (d. 1899), the artist and war correspondent, lived in Church Road from 1881.[75]

In 1900 All Souls College's agent, referring to the recent extraordinary growth in the neigh-bourhood and the splendid train service from Willesden Junction, advised the college to begin developing its Harlesden estate.[76] The estate lay south-east of the built-up area and the college began by building Wrottesley Road on the line of the old green lane to connect Harrow Road with Harlesden Lane and form the western boundary of the estate. Agreements were made with the neighbouring landowners for the joint develop-ment of the area. By 1904 Wrottesley Road had been laid out and c. 19 a. leased to various builders, of whom Langler and Pinkham were the most important, and some 77 middle-class houses were being built. In 1905 shops were under construction in Harlesden Lane, and Ridley Road was laid out and leased for building. By 1907, however, the builders asked to be released from their agreements as the effects of the building slump began to be felt. By 1910 building had virtually ceased and Furness pressed the college to allow cheaper houses to be built. Meanwhile on his own estate west of Wrottesley Road he was building small terraced houses in roads named after his father's foreign contracts.[77] By 1914 there were 392 houses on the All Souls estate east of All Souls Avenue and agreements had been made for another 128. By 1920 building was continuous between Harlesden and Kensal Green and was reaching towards Willesden Green in the north.[78]

Industry, already present in Harlesden before the First World War, was greatly stimulated by the war and in 1920 residential Harlesden north of the L. & N.W.R. line was flanked to the south and south-west by factories, power stations, and railway sheds.[79] The industry attracted workers who crowded into houses abandoned by the middle classes for whom they were built. Harlesden thus became a wholly working-class district.[80]

Building continued after the First World War on the unfinished portions of the All Souls and Furness estates.[81] The fringes of Roundwood formed part of an area planned by the council in 1933 to have a density of less than 15 houses to an acre.[82] It included land belonging to the college which the council purchased for its largest hous-ing estate, Curzon Crescent, built in 1936-7 for over 500 families.[83] By 1939 the last of the big old houses, Knowles Tower and Roundwood House, had been demolished and building had advanced eastward to Longstone Avenue. East of Harles-den Road (formerly Lane), the King Edward VII recreation ground was surrounded by residential streets as far as Willesden Green and Kensal Rise.[84]

In 1949 Harlesden could be identified as an area of 330 a. with a population of 28,789, living in 3,782 houses and 1,121 flats. In character it varied from Craven Park, with its large houses and gardens and a density of 43 persons per acre,

[64] M.R.O., Acc. 538/2nd deposit/2234-7.
[65] Grange Mus., Wood F 19 (sale cats. 1/6, 52).
[66] Below, pub. svces.
[67] Grange Mus., NM 272, 317-20.
[68] Census, 1881, 1891.
[69] O.S. Map 6", Mdx. XVI. NW. (1894-6 edn.).
[70] Below, pub. svces.
[71] Grange Mus., Wood F 23, pp. 281 sqq.; M.R.O., Rep. Local Inqs. 1889-97, 603-24 (Willesden local bd. 1889).
[72] Kelly's Dir. Mdx. (1890, 1908).
[73] e.g. Green Man site in 1901: M.R.O., Acc. 891/2/6/339; shops 1906: ibid. Acc. 1351/27.
[74] Kelly's Dir. Mdx. (1890); Grange Mus., photo. album 'Willesden'.
[75] Grange Mus., biog. files, Simpson.
[76] Para. based on All Souls Coll., uncat. material, agents'

reps. 1900-10; bursars' rentals 1904, 1914.
[77] Grange Mus., 2 A 1 ('Street Names'); M.R.O., Acc. 774; Acc. 1351/28. Geo. Furness was an engineering contractor.
[78] O.S. Map 6", Mdx. XVI. NW. (1920 edn.).
[79] Ibid. Mdx. XVI. NW. (1920 edn.); Grange Mus., gen. files, Aerofilms box 3, no. 175.
[80] Morris, Willesden Surv. p. 11. Observed in 1920 as a change 'of recent years': Nat. Soc. files, Harlesden, All Souls.
[81] All Souls Coll., uncat. material, bursars' rentals 1914, 1924, 1934; M.R.O., Acc. 1351/28.
[82] Grange Mus., NM 309 (town planning scheme, 1933).
[83] Leff and Blunden, Willesden Story, 32; Willesden Monthly Illus. 5 Oct. 1937.
[84] Morris, Willesden Surv. map 5; Brent planning and research dept., Age of Bldgs. Map; Grange Mus., photo. files, Roundwood Pk. (NL 897).

Stonebridge Park: proposed villas and church *c.* 1870

Neasden Green in 1818

WILLESDEN

EALING VILLAGE

WILLESDEN: CAMBRIDGE GARDENS, KILBURN

EALING: OFFICE BLOCKS IN UXBRIDGE ROAD

to Rucklidge Avenue, very small terraced houses in multiple occupation with a density of 160 persons per acre.[85] In 1952 Harlesden was 'crowded and unsightly' with 'no attractions to offer the visitor and few, perhaps, for the inhabitants'.[86]

Post-war demand for housing of any kind persuaded the council to abandon most of its plans to redevelop much of Harlesden. A temporary estate of prefabricated houses remained at Harlesden Road into the late 1960s.[87] By 1978 new flats had been built there and at Roundwood and there had been extensive rebuilding on the Church Road estate. Some landmarks, like the Willesden Hippodrome, which was replaced by an office block in 1961,[88] disappeared but generally High Street, with its parades of shops and congested traffic, remained much as it was in 1949, as did areas like Rucklidge Avenue.

The most striking change in Harlesden during the post-war period has been immigration, especially by West Indians. While the population in the three Harlesden wards fell from 39,527 in 1951 to 39,251 in 1961 and 26,970 in 1971, the proportion of immigrants increased. In 1966 the percentage of those born in the West Indies was 12 for Roundwood, 12 for Harlesden, and 11 for Manor ward. The percentages of those born in Ireland were, respectively, 10, 16, and 9. There were some problems associated with immigration, especially on the Curzon Crescent estate which during the 1960s was considered 'a dumping ground for the unfortunate and difficult'[89] and was in 1967 plagued by vandalism. In 1968 some 60 per cent of families housed on the estate were West Indians, increasing to 72 per cent in 1969–70, causing some resentment among the English population.[90] The West Indian influx has aggravated overcrowding[91] and unemployment but it has also brought a new vitality to Harlesden, reinforcing its sense of identity, bringing brightness to the drab 19th-century terraces and new life to its shops, social institutions, and chapels.

Before the Conquest NEASDEN may have been more important than Willesden. In a spurious charter dated 939 land was given at Neasden with Willesden, and in a list of c. 1000 Neasden, but not Willesden, was mentioned. The name indicates a hill and perhaps that it projected like a nose,[92] and the village had an elevated site. It lay around a green, surrounded by open fields and linked by lanes to Church End, Willesden Green,

and Kingsbury. In the Middle Ages there were several tenements with narrow frontages on an L-shaped lane called Bower Lane, which continued east and then south to Sherrick green.[93] Seven of the tenements, named after their medieval owners,[94] can be located. All of them passed into the hands of the Roberts family. Thomas Roberts (d. 1543) rebuilt or much enlarged one of them, Catewood's, bought by his ancestor in 1403. About 1656 Sir William Roberts pulled down the neighbouring medieval cottages and converted their sites and Bower Lane into gardens and orchards around his house, thereafter called Neasden House. A new route was created, on the line of the northern part of modern Dudden Hill Lane. One tenement, Bucklands, on the west side of Neasden Lane, north of Bower Lane, survived to become Neasden smithy.[95] By 1454 there was a house east of Neasden Lane, at its junction with Dog Lane, on Westminster abbey's estate.[96] Another house had been built on that estate west of Neasden Lane by 1566 and there were some cottages at the Neasden end of Sherrick green by 1599.[97] Turners and Wilsons or Brewers farmhouses were built north and south of Neasden House, probably for the tenants displaced c. 1656, and Neasden farm was built west of Neasden Lane probably about the same time. Thomas Wingfield (d. 1715), who bought the portion of the Roberts estate lying in the angle between Neasden Lane and Dudden Hill Lane, built the Grove, a two-storeyed brick and tiled building with attics and a central doorway fronting Neasden Lane, with a stable range facing the green. George, Lord Carpenter, added north and south wings after 1725 and there were formal gardens by 1746. By that date there was a building opposite, on the west side of Neasden Lane, north of its junction with Dog Lane, which by 1770 was licensed as the Spotted Dog. The Grove, which housed a boys' boarding school in the late 18th century, was sold in 1806 to a London solicitor, James Hall, who built new stables, converting the old ones into Rose Cottage, afterwards the Grange, which acquired its Gothic windows at that date.[98]

Neasden at inclosure in 1823 was a 'small village' or 'retired hamlet' of some six cottages, four larger houses or farms, a public house, and a smithy, grouped around the green.[99] There was a single cottage near the Kingsbury border. Most of the land surrounding Neasden had already been inclosed and was held mainly in consolidated blocks.[1]

[85] Morris, *Willesden Surv.* map 7, areas 8B, D–P, pp. 19, 30.

[86] Robbins, *Mdx.* 357–66.

[87] *Rep. to Willesden, 1963–4*; Grange Mus., gen. files, Harlesden Rd.

[88] Grange Mus., photo. files, High St. Harlesden (NL 1007).

[89] Ibid. gen. files, race relations ('Curzon Cres. Council Housing Survey, 1970').

[90] Ibid. gen. files, housing estates.

[91] An analysis of families on the Curzon Cres. estate in 1970 gave the average size of families by country of birth as U.K. 4·75; W. Indian 6·01; Irish 6·05; Grange Mus., gen. files, race relations ('Curzon Cres. Survey').

[92] *P.N. Mdx.* (E.P.N.S.), 162. For the charter and list, below, manors.

[93] Para. based on B.L. Stowe MS. 862, ff. 38 sqq.; Grange Mus., Wood F 24, pp. 285–6.

[94] For the Taylors, St. Paul's MS. A 29/383; for the Hales, P.R.O., E 40/6875; E 40/11588; E 40/11844; for the Bucklands, ibid. E 40/11648; E 40/12065; St. Paul's MS. A 39/1354.

[95] M.R.O., EA/WIL, no. 155.

[96] W.A.M. 17018.

[97] Ibid. 33187; All Souls Coll., Hovenden maps II/21–22.

[98] Grange Mus., gen. files, Neasden Lane, the Grange (G.L.C. dept. of archit. TS.); photo. files, Neasden Lane, the Grove, the Grange; Hist. Mon. Com. *Mdx.* 134. For the Spotted Dog, below, social; for the school, below, educ.

[99] Brewer, *Beauties of Eng. and Wales*, x (5), 349–50; *Eng. Topog.* (Gent. Mag. Libr.), vii. 287–9; above, plate facing p. 192.

[1] M.R.O., EA/WIL; ibid. Acc. 262/40, pt. 2 (inclosure claims, 1816).

In 1851 Neasden was still a rural community of farmers, farm labourers, grooms, gardeners, servants, a blacksmith, and publican. There was a solicitor at the Grove and a stockbroker at the Grange.[2] By the late 1860s Model Farm had been built on land belonging to All Souls College south of the junction of Dog Lane and Neasden Lane.[3] The M. & S.W.J. railway was built across the land to the south-east in 1868 and a station at Dudden Hill was opened in 1875; Londoners visited the Spotted Dog, which in 1876 was described as 'a sort of suburban tea-garden', and although Neasden was still the most rural part of Willesden it already had some 46 houses.[4]

In 1880 the Metropolitan line was extended from Willesden Green through Neasden to Harrow and a station was opened on Neasden Lane, south of the village. The railway company bought a considerable acreage between the Brent, the railway, and Neasden Lane. There it built an estate for its employees, naming streets (Quainton, Aylesbury, Chesham) after stations on the line.[5] In 1880 part of Model Farm was sold for building.[6] Some 112 houses had been built in Neasden by 1883 and the population increased rapidly.[7] In 1894 Model farmhouse remained but the triangle of Dog Lane, Neasden Lane, and Lansdowne Grove had been completely built up.[8] The railway estate faced Neasden Lane with a 'rather painful row of empty shops' in place of the 'pretty country lane' it had previously been. Although the old village remained, with its atmosphere of 'sleepy quietude', there were changes there too.[9] In 1891 the minister of St. Saviour's complained that in place of the gentlemen who contributed £20 a year each to the school horse dealers occupied two of the three large houses and that the population was almost entirely railway workers, horse dealers, and grooms.[10] The Grange was occupied by William Matthieu Williams (d. 1892), the scientific writer, and the Grove had since c. 1872 housed the Royal Canine Hospital.[11] In 1893 Neasden House, which the squire had long since left, was occupied by a golf club.[12]

Except for the building of Prout Grove and of an iron church, St. Catherine's, there was virtually no change in Neasden village between 1894 and 1901, but there was building to the south-east.[13] In 1823 the western part of the green lane called Sherrick green had some five scattered cottages.[14] The road fell out of use at inclosure, the M. & S.W.J. railway line was built through it, and by the late 1860s there were only two houses.[15] By 1901 a network of streets was laid out south of the railway near Dudden Hill station and within ten years had spread north of the line to form a continuous built-up area from Neasden village to Chapel End and Willesden Green.[16]

The second, and biggest, wave of building in Neasden followed the building of the North Circular Road (1921–34) and the widening of Neasden Lane in connexion with the Wembley Exhibition of 1924. Semi-detached houses of pre-cast concrete were added to the 19th-century cottages on the Metropolitan railway estate in 1925.[17] By 1930 semi-detached and terraced owner-occupied houses covered the district south-west of Neasden Lane and west of the North Circular; other houses, some built for the council, extended north-east of Neasden Lane on either side of the North Circular. In 1929 building was in progress on the golf course, which by 1937 was covered by semi-detached owner-occupied houses.[18] Neasden House survived a few years 'ignominiously behind a row of shops' but was replaced by flats, Neasden Court in Cairnfield Avenue, in 1933.[19] To the north 20 a. of Gravel Pit farm bordering the Brent were sold as building land in 1929 and in accordance with a scheme of 1933 the Coombe Road industrial area had been laid out there by 1938, bordered by Braemar Avenue, a high-density estate of flats in compact two-storeyed blocks built in 1937.[20] Industry had begun to spread northward from Church End on the eve of the First World War, reaching Neasden in the 1920s. The remaining open area south-west of the village was covered by a mixture of flats and houses during the 1930s.[21]

The centre of Neasden was transformed into that of a typical London suburb. A shopping parade and cinema (1932) were built along Neasden Lane and the Spotted Dog was rebuilt in Tudor style in 1932.[22] Model Farm, still a farmhouse in 1935, had gone by 1938 and the Grove was demolished in 1937. Even where old buildings remained, they were separated from their land and became dilapidated. Stud Farm (later Elmstead) had been leased to a cartage contractor by 1917 and became a depot.[23]

By 1949 Neasden had 2,325 houses, 1,508 flats, and 13,803 people. Density varied between 36 persons per acre in the area east of the village built in the 1930s and 84 per acre in the flats of Braemar Avenue. Though mainly residential, Neasden included railway works along the lines to the south-west and industry in the southern part of Neasden Lane and in the north at Coombe

[2] P.R.O., HO 107/1700/135/3, ff. 374v.–377v.; *Kelly's Dir. Mdx.* (1855).
[3] O.S. Map 6", Mdx. XI. SW. (1864–73 edn.).
[4] Thorne, *Environs*, 446, 697–9; Willesden local bd. *San. Rep.* (1875).
[5] Ashdown, *Ind. Mon. of Gtr. Lond.* s.v. Brent.
[6] Grange Mus., Wood F 20 (sale cats. 2/25, 37).
[7] The minister of St. Saviour's exaggerated in saying in 1883 that the pop. had risen from less than 60 a few months ago to over 1,500 and that it would be more than 4,000 in a few months: National Soc. files, Neasden.
[8] O.S. Map 6", Mdx. XI. SW. (1894–6 edn.).
[9] Foley, *Our Lanes and Meadow Paths*, 42, 55; Grange Mus., photo. files, Neasden Lane (NL 1612A); *Home Counties Mag.* iii. 121. [10] National Soc. files, Neasden, St. Saviour.
[11] *D.N.B.*; Grange Mus., biog. files, Glanfield.

[12] Below, social.
[13] Grange Mus., Map of Willesden U.D. 1901.
[14] M.R.O., EA/WIL.
[15] O.S. Map 6", Mdx. XI. SW. (1864–73 edn.).
[16] Grange Mus., Map of Willesden U.D. 1901; NM 350.
[17] Ashdown, *Ind. Mon. of Gtr. Lond.* s.v. Brent.
[18] Grange Mus., NM 9; Morris, *Willesden Surv.* p. 23; *Quarterly Rec. and Guide*, Oct. 1929.
[19] Grange Mus., gen. files, topog. (B.C. Dexter, press cuttings); *Estate Exchange Year Bk.* (1933).
[20] *Estate Exchange Year Bk.* (1929); Grange Mus., NM 309; Morris, *Willesden Surv.* p. 23; O.S. Map 6", Mdx. XI. SW. (1938 edn.).
[21] Morris, *Willesden Surv.* p. 23; below, industry.
[22] Briggs, *Mdx. Old and New*, 167; below, social.
[23] *Kilburn and Willesden Dir.* (1917–38).

Road. Neasden's main problem was traffic, especially at the intersection of Neasden Lane and the North Circular road, which formed the core of the shopping centre.[24] The Ministry of Transport drew up a scheme to bypass Neasden in 1963 but postponed it because of local opposition. In 1973, however, the North Circular was enlarged, slicing through Neasden Lane and the shopping quarter. Houses were demolished, Neasden Lane was diverted to an underpass, the shopping quarter declined, and north and south Neasden were divorced from each other. Stud Farm was demolished when a large roundabout was constructed on the site of Neasden green and the one remaining old house, the Grange, was saved only after a campaign led by Reg Freeson, M.P., and Councillor Ivor Davies. The house, purchased by the council in 1962, survived as the Grange Museum, a combined local museum, history library, and record repository.[25]

There was some building, mainly of flats, after the Second World War on small sites not already built on.[26] Office blocks included the 13-storeyed Radiation House built beside the North Circular Road in 1961, and factories were rebuilt in Neasden Lane in 1979.[27] Neasden High school was built on the site of London Transport's power station at Quainton Street in 1968 and from 1967 there was controversy, still unresolved in 1980, over the redevelopment of railway land mostly sited along the lines.[28] Neasden remained a distinct area, its name achieving widespread currency in the 1960s and 1970s when it was used by the satirical magazine *Private Eye* as 'the paradigm of faceless suburban nonentity and dreariness'.[29]

KILBURN, the settlement which grew up where Watling Street (later Edgware Road) crossed the Kilburn brook, straddled the boundaries of Willesden, Hampstead, and Paddington parishes. Within Willesden its hinterland was formed by the demesne lands of Bounds and Brondesbury manors and by the area later called Kilburn Park, which may have formed part of the lands of Kilburn abbey in the Middle Ages. A home farm for Bounds was built on Edgware Road in the late 16th century and there may have been an inn on the Willesden side before the Cock was built there in the 1760s. There were several houses along Edgware Road by c. 1677,[30] including by 1749 a terrace called Elm Row.[31]

In 1820 Kilburn had been 'rapidly increasing in extent and population for some years past',[32] but development had been mainly in the Hampstead and Paddington parts of the district. In 1829 building in the Willesden part of Kilburn was entirely confined to the strip along Edgware Road and even there large stretches of farmland remained. The densest concentration was around St. Paul's chapel (built 1825) and the Cock inn, behind which was a terrace of cottages.[33] In 1834 William Harrison Ainsworth was living at the Elms, the home of his father-in-law, the publisher John Ebers, which is probably identifiable with Elm Lodge on Edgware Road.[34] In 1851 there were only 254 houses and a population of 1,488 in the combined districts of Kilburn, Kensal Green, and Cricklewood. Manor farm, with its farmhouse on the Edgware Road, dominated the south-east and many of the inhabitants were still employed in agriculture. In Kilburn High Road there were some shopkeepers, but there were also larger houses, set in spacious grounds and occupied by men of the commercial and professional middle classes, including a leather merchant, wholesale perfumer, and a civil engineer at Elm Lodge.[35] Kilburn House was owned from 1840 to 1858 by the father of W. H. Smith, the bookseller and later M.P., and both father and son commuted to their Strand office from Kilburn.[36] Thomas Hardy lived in Clarence Place, Kilburn, in 1862–3 while he was studying architecture.[37]

Kilburn brewery and Kilburn mill represented early industry in the area. Kilburn was crossed by two railway lines, the London and Birmingham (later the L. & N.W.R.) in 1837 with a station at Kilburn (1852) and the Hampstead Junction railway with a station at Edgware Road (Brondesbury) in 1860.[38] The railways, however, played little part in the growth of Kilburn, serving less to connect the area with others than to divide it into sections.

Kilburn grew mainly with the outward spread of London along Edgware Road. Following the building in the 1830s and 1840s of villas and terraces in Maida Vale and the sale of Belsize manor to developers in 1841,[39] the Church Commissioners' agent in 1846 drew attention to the illegal building of a row of 'inferior' cottages on Edgware Road just within the Willesden boundary. He was fully aware of the potential as building land of the commissioners' Willesden manor estate with its long frontage on Edgware Road and Willesden Lane.[40]

Of the two other principal landowners[41] Lady Salusbury sold her interests to the commissioners in 1856[42] and the Revd. Edward Stuart in 1850 sold 47 a. of the southernmost part of Kilburn (Kilburn Park) to a consortium of five builders; in 1854 he also sold 25 a. south of

[24] Morris, *Willesden Surv.* map 7, areas 2A–J, pp. 18, 23; Grange Mus., gen. files, Aerofilms box 1, no. 93.

[25] *Willesden Civic Review*, Dec. 1963; *The Times*, 19 Feb. 1973; Grange Mus., gen. files, Neasden Lane, the Grange; inf. from Grange Mus.

[26] e.g. 24 flats in Press Rd. in 1956: *Willesden Civic Review*, June 1956.   [27] Grange Mus., gen. files, North Circular Rd.

[28] Grange Mus., gen. files, schools; Neasden; industries, Neasden sidings redevelopment; redevelopment; inf. from Brent L.B. development dept. (1979).

[29] *The Times*, 9 Feb. 1972.

[30] J. Ogilby, *Map of Mdx.* (1677).

[31] Messeder Road Map (1749).   [32] *Ambulator* (1820), 195.

[33] Cruchley, *New Plan of Lond.* (1829); M.R.O., Acc. 303/7.

[34] Elm Lodge was replaced by the State cinema in 1937: Grange Mus., biog. files, Ainsworth; *Willesden Green Libr. Rec.* Jan. 1904.

[35] P.R.O., HO 107/1700/135/3, ff. 329–366v.

[36] Grange Mus. red box, Kilburn; Sir H. Maxwell, *Life and Times of Wm. Hen. Smith* (1893), i. 43.

[37] Grange Mus., biog. files, Hardy. Clarence Place may have been near the later Clarence Rd., NE. of Willesden Lane near Paddington cemetery.

[38] Above, communications.

[39] Pevsner, *Lond.* ii. 295; Grange Mus., gen. files, industries and occupations (G. Hewlett, 'Development of Brent from the Ind. Revolution'.)

[40] Ch. Com., Surveys S 2, pp. 853–4, 857–70.

[41] M.R.O., EA/WIL.   [42] Below, manors.

Willesden Lane to Paddington burial board as a cemetery.[43] The builders laid out roads and sewers, divided the Kilburn Park estate among themselves, and sublet to small builders who put up a few houses on their individual plots, leaving them isolated among unmade and increasingly muddy roads as the money ran out. They began building in the ambitious style of St. John's Wood but potential customers were deterred by the surrounding desolation and even in 1887 most of the planned houses remained unbuilt.[44]

From 1857 the Church Commissioners made a series of agreements with James Bailey, a builder from Maida Vale who later moved to Brondesbury Terrace and then to Brondesbury Lodge. Bailey's first houses were on the Elm Lodge estate, between Edgware Road and Willesden Lane, where in 1859 he built Brondesbury Terrace.[45] In the same year he began building south of Kilburn Lane (Canterbury Road).[46] Building agreements for the surrounding blocks of land followed and were exchanged for 99-year leases when the houses were in carcase, capital being raised by mortgaging the almost completed buildings or selling the ground rents. Bailey used architectural pattern books and he had erected nearly 550 houses by 1867, when financial difficulties forced him to assign his leases to others.[47] In the course of the 1870s most of the leases were acquired by Real Property Trust Ltd.[48]

Other local builders began to build Brondesbury Road and Villas north of the L. & N.W.R. line in the 1860s.[49] Kilburn Square, part of which existed by 1851, lay immediately to the north; 14 a. stretching westward from it, occupied by the Victoria Rifle Volunteers from 1849, were sold for building in 1866. Semi-detached and terraced houses were built on the site, on roads named Victoria Road and Villas, during the 1870s and 1880s.[50] By 1871 there were 1,414 houses in the 400-a. parish of Holy Trinity, Kilburn.[51] They were overwhelmingly in the southern part of Kilburn, there being 1,310 houses in south Kilburn ward in 1875 compared with 330 houses in north Kilburn ward.[52] A few years earlier Charles Dickens had referred to Kilburn as 'a newly built district at the far end of the Edgware Road'.[53]

There was no building until the late 1880s on the area immediately south of the Hampstead Junction railway line although it had been leased by the Church Commissioners in 1858 to the Kilburn brewery, with permission to build houses.[54] The United Land Co. bought part of the Kilburn House estate in 1869 and the rest in 1882–3,[55] after it had been vacated by John Farmer, the largest employer in Kilburn, who had lived there from 1866 to 1882.[56] By 1884 three streets had been laid out and a dozen houses built and by 1890 they stretched westward to Paddington cemetery.[57] Between 1884 and 1893 the population of north Kilburn ward increased threefold, from 3,126 to 10,334.[58] The number of houses rose from 400 in 1881 to 512 in 1885 and 1,523 in 1891. In comparison those in south Kilburn increased from 1,605 in 1881 to 1,825 in 1885 and 2,095 in 1891.[59]

By 1887[60] Salusbury Road, running parallel to the Edgware Road, joined Kilburn to Brondesbury and Willesden Green. The whole of the Church Commissioners' estate east of Salusbury Road and south of the L. & N.W.R. had been built on and there were patches of building and a complete street layout on the Kilburn Park estate to the south. North of the L. & N.W.R. line the street plan was laid out as far as Victoria Road and building was complete on the former Tanners Mead (north of Kilburn Lane and west of Edgware Road)[61] and Elm Lodge estate. There was some building on both sides of the Hampstead Junction line. The rest of the area between the Hampstead Junction line and Willesden Lane was built up during the late 1880s.[62] South of Willesden Lane building stretched westward to Paddington cemetery and along Brondesbury Road as far as Salusbury Road by 1896. Most of the Kilburn Park estate was built up, and south of the L. & N.W.R. building stretched westward to merge with Kensal Green.[63]

A small part of Stafford Road, the only area south of the L. & N.W.R. line still empty in 1896, had been filled in by 1901. Queen's Park, opened in 1887 on land formerly used for the Royal Agricultural show, separated Kilburn from the new district of Kensal Rise to the west. The whole area of Kilburn between the two railway lines was by 1901 covered by streets of houses and some factories, save for Paddington cemetery, Queen's Park, and a small area north-east of the park, which was built on by 1920, probably following the opening of Brondesbury Park station in 1908.[64]

Kilburn reached its apogee during the Edwardian period. The town hall and a group of municipal buildings were built there during the

[43] Grange Mus., Wood F 22 (ii), pp. 66 sqq.; J. S. Curl, *Victorian Celebration of Death* (1972), 148.

[44] M.R.O., Acc. 1316/68; Acc. 1345/2–4; ibid. TA/WIL (tithe map); Grange Mus., Wood F 23, pp. 281 sqq.; ibid. 1 D 13 (vestry mins. 1871); O.S. Map 1/2,500, Mdx. XVI. 7, 8 (1865 edn.).

[45] Guildhall MSS. CC. 29222, 39516. Traces were still visible in 1978 behind shop fronts: G.L.C. Historic Bldgs. TS. (1978) in Grange Mus., gen. files, Kilburn.

[46] Guildhall MS. CC. 39518.

[47] Ibid. MSS. CC. 38338, 39501, 40963, 40987, 42129, 42133–4, 91987, 96157–8; Grange Mus., 3 H 7 (plans); G.L.C. Historic Bldgs. TS. (1978).

[48] M.R.O., Acc. 831.

[49] Guildhall MSS., CC. 40980, 40985–7, 41197.

[50] Grange Mus., Wood F 23, pp. 20 sqq.; ibid. 2 A 1 ('Street Names'); 3 H 7 (plans); see illus. in Brent L.B. *Official Guide* [1976], 22; M.R.O., Acc. 549/76; Acc. 1351/22.

[51] *Census*, 1871.

[52] Willesden local bd. *San. Rep.* (1875).

[53] Dickens, *Dictionary of Lond.* (1879).

[54] i.e. part of Mapesbury est.: Guildhall MS. CC. 40341.

[55] M.R.O., Acc. 1013/72; Acc. 1211; Grange Mus., NM 434, 441, 445.

[56] Grange Mus., S. W. Ball, 'Old Willesden' (TS.); ibid. Wood 24 (Willesden deeds xiv. 194); below, industry.

[57] *Kilburn and Willesden Dir.* (1883–90).

[58] M.R.O., *Rep. Local Inqs.* 1889–97, 639–62 (Willesden 1894).

[59] Grange Mus., Wood F 23, p. 171.

[60] M.R.O., TA/WIL (tithe map).

[61] Ibid. EA/WIL, no. 933.

[62] Grange Mus., Wood F 23, pp. 20 sqq.

[63] O.S. Map 6", Mdx. XVI. NE. (1894–6 edn.).

[64] Ibid. (1920 edn.); Grange Mus., Map of Willesden U.D. 1901.

1890s. The part of Edgware Road known as Kilburn High Road was an important shopping centre with more than 300 'handsome and imposing shops', including 40 drapers and 15 each of tailors, hosiers, jewellers, and bootmakers.[65] There were numerous public houses, several music halls[66] and (later) cinemas, and Edgware Road was crowded with competing buses and trams.

The population increased steadily. In 1871 Kilburn was socially mixed, not as high-class as the builders had hoped but still including a few large houses like Kilburn House and streets like Alexandra (later Princess) Road where more than half the houses employed servants. Commercial travellers, salesmen, and shopkeepers were among the inhabitants.[67] There was still a strong middle-class, mainly professional and commercial, element in the population, especially of north Kilburn, in the early 20th century. Among its inhabitants were the retired boxer Jem Smith in Torbay Road (1890–1914) and Salusbury Road (1914–31), the Zionist author Israel Zangwill in Oxford Road (1891–1900), and the popular illustrator of anthropomorphic cats, Louis Wain, in Brondesbury Road (c. 1900 to 1910).[68] From early on, however, the working classes predominated and contemporaries noted the horrifying conditions in which many of Kilburn's inhabitants lived. The overall density of 8 persons to a house in 1875 concealed streets like the newly built Pembroke (later Granville) Road in Kilburn Park where each house contained from four to six households.[69] It lay in the parish of St. John where 7,000 of the 9,000 residents in 1880 were said to be working-class, there were no wealthy people to give money for churches or schools, and in one group of streets 525 families lived in 81 houses.[70] Sickness was rife, and in 1875 Kilburn was castigated for its chronic pauperism, negligence, ignorance, and lack of cleanliness.[71] The people usually came from similar conditions in Paddington and Marylebone and included, already in 1871 but increasingly during the 20th century, recent Irish immigrants.[72] They included a shifting population of the temporarily employed, often bachelors working in the building industry and living in overcrowded lodging houses.[73] Social life centred around the public houses, said in 1949 to average one for every 424 people in south Kilburn compared with one to every 2,618 for the rest of

Willesden.[74] In the 19th century churches and chapels of all denominations offered an alternative social focus, especially at the colourful and theatrical Anglo-Catholic St. Augustine's where, a critic stated, 'free and easy' entertainments featuring coarse songs were allowed.[75]

The density of population in the whole of Kilburn remained at nearly 8 persons per house until well after the Second World War and in southern Kilburn was consistently over 10 people to a house. In 1881 in St. Luke's parish it was over 12 people to a house. In south Kilburn in 1921 there were 208 people to an acre.[76] In 1934 Pembroke Road was still notable for its poverty and overcrowding, and the poorest district in Willesden was the group of streets near Kilburn (Park) station.[77] A beginning was made of slum clearance in 1938 when houses were destroyed in Alpha Place, off Canterbury Road, but the Second World War intervened.[78] Surveys of the Church Commissioners' estates in 1944 and of the whole borough in 1948[79] showed that south Kilburn was grossly overcrowded and dilapidated.[80] Its large houses, often four-storeyed semi-detached or terraced, were divided into tenements, each occupied by several families described as very poor. The area between the two railway lines was more varied, in part subject to subletting and overcrowding but also having between Queen's Park and Paddington cemetery some late 19th-century houses which were occupied by 'a better standard of tenant,' characterized as employees of the London Passenger Transport Board, the borough council, or the post office. Light industry was scattered throughout the area, often in former commercial premises. Many houses were divided into single rooms for boarders, among whom in the 1950s was the writer V. S. Naipaul in St. Julians Road.

As part of a comprehensive plan for the redevelopment of south Kilburn the borough council bought 61 a. and began building in 1949 on bombed sites; in the 1950s and 1960s a further 59 a. were acquired.[81] The first stage of the projected redevelopment of Kilburn Square was complete by 1964, replacing the church and Victorian houses by a shopping precinct and 17-storeyed tower blocks.[82] As Kilburn was rebuilt and the total population fell the density declined from 133 persons per acre in 1949 to 87 in 1951, 78 in 1961, and 61 in 1971.[83]

Redevelopment relieved overcrowding but

[65] Grange Mus., gen. files, shops (Kilburn and Brondesbury Shops Exhib. Week, 1909). Not all the shops were in Willesden.
[66] Mostly not on the Willesden side: The Times, 2 Nov. 1907.
[67] Grange Mus., copy of census returns, 1871; G.L.C. Historic Bldgs. TS. (1978).
[68] Grange Mus., biog. files, Smith, Zangwill; red box, Kilburn.   [69] Willesden local bd. San. Rep. (1875).
[70] Nat. Soc. files, Kilburn St. John Evangelist.
[71] Willesden local bd. San. Rep. (1875).
[72] Grange Mus., census returns, 1871; Kilburn and Willesden Dir. (1883 and later edns.).
[73] Jackson, Irish in Britain, 18, 107.
[74] Morris, Willesden Surv. pp. 34 sqq. Some were exclusively Irish, e.g. Biddy Mulligan's in Edgware Rd.
[75] Nat. Soc. files, Kilburn St. John. St. Augustine's was outside Willesden but stood on the border in Kilburn Park Rd.

[76] Census, 1871–1921; Morris, Willesden Surv. p. 9.
[77] New Survey of Lond. Life and Labour (1934), vi, Social Survey, II. 459–62.
[78] The Times, 1 July 1931; 22 Oct. 1937; 26 Jan., 11 Feb. 1938.
[79] Ch. Com., Clutton's rep. on Lond. estates, 1944; Morris, Willesden Surv. map 7, areas 5A–F, 6A–B, pp. 26, 28.
[80] Grange Mus., photo. files, Albert Rd. (NL 478–9); Cambridge Rd. (NL 612); Canterbury Rd. (NL 619); Denmark Rd.
[81] Willesden boro. Year Bk. (1958–9); Willesden Civic Review, Oct. 1960; Dec. 1962; Oct. 1963; Grange Mus., photo. files, Albert Rd. (NL 480); Rep. to Willesden, 1963–4; Grange Mus., 1 A 2; The Times, 17, 26 Oct. 1967.
[82] Grange Mus., 1 A 2 (Willesden Cit. 24 Apr. 1964; Willesden Mercury, 14 Jan. 1966).
[83] Census, 1951–71; Morris, Willesden Surv. pp. 19, 26, 28.

brought new difficulties, associated particularly with high-rise flats described in 1972 as 'socially difficult'.[84] Immigration, still primarily of Irish, brought additional problems. In 1966 the percentages of those born in Ireland and in the U.K. were respectively 24·5 and 58 in Kilburn ward, 17·7 and 67·9 in Carlton ward, 9·8 and 66·8 in Queen's Park ward.[85] Objections to high-rise flats, the increasing costs of building, and a new appreciation for Victorian architecture led in the late 1970s to the preservation of the remaining mid-Victorian houses of south Kilburn and the return of middle-class residents.[86]

The first part of the name KENSAL GREEN was recorded as 'Kingisholt', the king's wood, in 1253, and the whole name in 1550.[87] The place was depicted in 1599 as a broad green at the junction of Harrow Road with Kilburn Lane, on the borders of the parishes of Willesden, Kensington, and the detached part of Chelsea.[88] The land north of the green lay in broad strips owned, from west to east, by All Souls College and the prebends of Chambers and Brondesbury. By the 1740s farmhouses of the prebendal estates had been built facing Kilburn Lane and the Plough inn at the road junction. South of Harrow Road a large house stood opposite the Plough and the Red House farther west.[89] A cottage had been built on the All Souls estate by 1800 and another next to the Plough by 1823.[90]

At inclosure in 1823 the green was divided into small plots which were sold as valuable sites at a junction on Harrow Road near the Paddington canal. Buildings, including a terrace of houses (Kensal Place), had gone up on all the plots by 1829 when Kensal Green was a village with a baker, a grocer, a milliner, a carpenter, a bookmaker, and two general dealers. There was also building south of Harrow Road,[91] where All Souls cemetery, opened in 1832, effectively blocked further building in Kensington parish. The London and Birmingham railway was driven through the Willesden portion of Kensal Green in 1837, cutting off the farmhouses in Kilburn Lane from much of their land.[92] Kensal New Town was built in the Chelsea portion south of Harrow Road with a church (St. John, 1844) and a school (1850) north of it, east of Kilburn Lane.[93] Between 1845 and 1855 building on the Willesden side of Kensal Green extended northward along Kilburn Lane and along the back of the existing houses in Harrow Road as All Souls College leased land to those who had already built on the former waste.[94] By 1851 Kensal

Green was a mixed community, including tradesmen, agricultural labourers, and farmers, two schoolteachers, the curate of St. John's, the author William Harrison Ainsworth at Kensal Manor House (built on the site of Red House, and demolished in 1939),[95] and people employed at the cemetery.[96]

The Hampstead Junction railway was built north of Kensal Green in 1860 with a station, Kensal Green and Harlesden (1861–73), at the junction of Harrow Road with Green Lane (later Wrottesley Road). The station was moved to Kensal Green (called Kensal Rise from 1890) in Chamberlayne Road in 1873.[97] The population of the Willesden part of the parish of St. John, Kensal Green, rose from 675, housed in 125 houses, in 1861 to 2,138, housed in 264 houses, in 1871.[98] By 1876 Kensal Green was 'most thickly covered'[99] and many of the houses were small, consisting of only two or four rooms, drained into open ditches and taking their water supply from butts. Many people kept pigs.[1]

The United Land Co. bought a 6-a. triangle of land between Harrow Road and the Hampstead Junction railway in 1879,[2] and an adjoining 21 a. from All Souls College in 1882.[3] The whole area was laid out as high-density terraced housing and shops as far east as College Road.[4] The college leased 13 a. south of the L. & N.W.R. line to Edward Vigers, who by 1888 had laid out roads and started building 134 small terraced houses. Rainham Road in the same area was let on building leases in 1895 and 30 houses had been built there by 1898. After 1888 the college began to exploit its lands more directly, laying out roads for the development of the whole estate. In 1893 it bought 5½ a. from the Ecclesiastical Commissioners to enable it to construct Chamberlayne Road, the eastern boundary of the estate and until then a country lane, as a link between Kensal Green and Willesden Green. Building north of the L. & N.W.R. line became possible after the surrender of a farming lease in 1888 and the college granted building leases, mainly to Charles Langler and Charles Pinkham who were building on what had become known as Kensal Rise, during the early 1890s. After a sewer had been constructed in 1895 the remaining 65 a. in the northern part of the estate were let on building leases. By 1898 400 houses had been built and another 243 were being built at Kensal Rise.[5] Among houses built at the time were those in Clifford Gardens whose gables depicted in stone scenes fashioned by an old Hampstead man employed by Langler and Pinkham.[6] By 1904

[84] *Kensington Post*, 18 Feb. 1972 (cutting in Nat. Soc. files, Kilburn, St. John).

[85] Weintraub, 'Race and local politics'.

[86] Grange Mus., gen. files, historic bldgs. (*Kilburn Times*, 8 July 1977); Dept. of Environment, list of bldgs., Brent L.B.

[87] *P.N. Mdx.* (E.P.N.S.), 162.

[88] All Souls Coll., Hovenden maps II/19.

[89] Rocque, *Map of Lond.* (1746); Messeder Road Map (1749).

[90] T. Milne, *Land Use Map of Lond.* (1800); M.R.O., EA/ WIL (inclosure map).

[91] M.R.O., EA/WIL; Cruchley, *New Plan of Lond.* (1829); Pigot, *Lond. and Provincial Dir.* (1828–9).

[92] Ch. Com., Surveys S2, pp. 411–20.

[93] Grange Mus., gen. files, Kensal Green.

[94] Bodl. MS. D.D. All Souls a 114, p. 21; a 124, p. 21. All

Souls Coll., uncatalogued material, plan of Mdx. estates 1861.

[95] Grange Mus., biog. files, Ainsworth; for illus. see ibid. photo. files, Harrow Rd. Ainsworth had lived in Kensal Green from 1835, at Kensal Lodge until 1841.

[96] P.R.O., HO 107/1700/135/3, ff. 332–52.

[97] *T.L.M.A.S.* xxvi. 313, 317–18.

[98] *Census*, 1861–71.   [99] Thorne, *Environs*, 697–9.

[1] Willesden local bd. *San. Rep.* (1876).

[2] Grange Mus., NM 432–3.

[3] Ibid. NM 430, 446–7; Bodl. MS. D.D. All Souls c 124/103.

[4] Morris, *Willesden Surv.* map 7, area 7H.

[5] All Souls Coll., uncat. material, docs. relating to estates 1887–95; bursars' rentals 1896–8; estate papers 1883–7 (Bd. of Agric. Orders); agents' reps. 1899.

[6] *Willesden Monthly Illus.* 5 Dec. 1937.

when building had spread north to Leighton Gardens and west to All Souls Avenue, there were 940 houses and another 181 houses being built. Building south of the L. & N.W.R. line at Kensal Green was complete, 311 houses having been built on the 13 a. leased in the 1880s.[7]

Building leases were being granted by the Ecclesiastical Commissioners at Kensal Green in 1884.[8] In 1894 the two prebendal farmhouses at Kilburn Lane remained but Allington Road had been built east of them, linking with building spreading west from Kilburn. North of the L. & N.W.R. line two roads, Harvist (in 1894 called Mortimer) and Chevening roads, had been laid out to link Chamberlayne Road with Kilburn.[9] Building leases on the commissioners' estate north of the L. & N.W.R. line were granted during the late 1890s and the 1900s.[10] By 1901 building was complete on both sides of Chamberlayne Lane south of the Hampstead Junction line, Queen's Park alone serving as a break between Kensal Rise and Kilburn. Roads had been laid out and some houses built north of the Hampstead line[11] and also on the Mount Pleasant estate, where houses were being built in 1904.[12]

Kensal Rise was affected by the building slump of the decade before the First World War. In 1910 Langler and Pinkham, who operated from Mortimer Works in Kensal Rise, said that they had not built a house for four years, being unable to let plots. In 1906 a building agreement for College Road was cancelled and land was let to sporting clubs and to the council for allotments. Between 1904 and 1914 only 19 new houses were built on the All Souls estate at Kensal Rise.[13] By 1920 building was continuous on the All Souls estate between Kensal Green and Harlesden. The extent of building had moved little farther north on the All Souls estate although it had advanced on the commissioners' and Mount Pleasant estates east of Chamberlayne Road. A church had opened at Kensal Rise in 1901 and there were several nonconformist chapels. Some light industry and shops had been established in Chamberlayne Road, but there was little sense of identity, either as a locality in its own right or as part of Willesden. Kensal Green and Rise were by 1920 part of the urban sprawl.[14]

Building resumed on the All Souls estate after the First World War, 156 houses being built by 1924 in Kensal Rise. By 1934 houses extended north of Leighton Gardens and agreements were current for some 130 houses on the 12 a. in the triangle formed by Chamberlayne Road, All Souls Avenue, and Hardinge Road.[15] Building there, mainly of semi-detached houses and

flats on rising ground next to the socially superior district of Brondesbury, was of a higher standard than earlier development to the south and described in 1949 as probably the most serious attempt at good housing layout in the borough. By 1939 building was continuous between Kensal Rise and Willesden Green and Brondesbury.[16]

The population of Kensal Rise ward declined steadily after the First World War, while the number of houses increased.[17] Kensal Rise and Green were defined in 1949 as an area of 329 a. containing 4,495 houses, 397 flats, and a population of 26,238. Densities varied from 20 persons per acre in the houses of the 1920s and 1930s on the north-east fringe to 176 persons per acre in those built between the L. & N.W.R. and Harrow Road in the 1880s. The second area, one of the most overcrowded in the borough, was in urgent need of redevelopment.[18]

The council bought up some property in Harvist Road for slum clearance in the 1950s[19] but very little was done and in 1973 a Kensal Green residents' association was formed to oppose the council's proposed redevelopment.[20] By 1978 many roads had been closed to traffic but the buildings remained and the whole area had a run-down and dilapidated appearance. In 1971 fewer than three quarters of dwellings in Kensal Rise ward had all amenities. Like most working-class districts in Willesden, Kensal Green attracted many immigrants in the post-war period, particularly during the 1960s and 1970s. The ward had the highest percentage (21·1) of West Indians in Willesden.[21]

The district of STONEBRIDGE, which may have included one of the three farmhouses recorded in the 16th century as at East Twyford,[22] took its name from the bridge, first recorded in 1746, carrying Harrow Road across the Brent. In 1746 there were apparently four buildings, all farms and cottages, clustered near the bridge.[23] An inn, the Coach and Horses, had been opened in the building south of Harrow Road by 1770, which was depicted by Julius Caesar Ibbetson in 1792 as the Angler's alehouse, and resorted to by another painter, George Morland.[24] Described as a very pretty spot in 1817, Stonebridge was in 1823 wholly rural, an area of low-lying meadow fringed on the north and east by open fields and crossed by a meandering feeder of the canal. It was linked to Harlesden by Harrow Road and to Neasden by Dog Lane.[25]

The London and Birmingham railway, built in 1837, and the Midland and S.W. Junction railway, in 1868, separated Sonebridge on the

[7] All Souls Coll., uncat. material, bursars' rentals 1904.
[8] Guildhall MSS. CC. 355996, 356001.
[9] OS. Map 6″, Mdx. XVI. NE. (1894–6 edn.).
[10] M.R.O., Acc. 1351/47.
[11] Grange Mus., Map of Willesden U.D. 1901.
[12] M.R.O., Acc. 969/152–4.
[13] All Souls Coll., uncat. material, agents' reps. 1906–10, 1920; bursars' rentals 1904, 1914.
[14] O.S. Map 6″, Mdx. XVI. NW., NE. (1920 edn.).
[15] All Souls Coll., uncat. material, bursars' rentals 1914, 1924, 1934.
[16] Morris, *Willesden Surv.* p. 29, map 5; M.R.O., Acc. 1351/29.

[17] *Census,* 1901–61.
[18] Morris, *Willesden Surv.* pp. 19, 29, map 7, areas 7A–N.
[19] Grange Mus., gen. files, housing.
[20] *The Times,* 1 Feb. 1973.
[21] Weintraub, 'Race and local politics'.
[22] Below, East Twyford.
[23] Rocque, *Map of Lond.* (1746); above, communications.
[24] Identified as Mrs. Reid's alehouse: Grange Mus., biog. files, Ibbetson. Mary Reed was the licensee of the Coach and Horses in 1790: M.R.O., MR/LV9/188. For Morland, J. Hassell, *Tour of Grand Junction Canal in 1819.*
[25] Hassell, *Picturesque Rides* (1817), i. 233; M.R.O., EA/WIL.

south and east respectively from the rest of Willesden. In 1851 Stonebridge Farm was occupied by a solicitor and being built on Harrow Road were a police station and 8 houses, probably St. Mary's Terrace and the cottages opposite.[26] There was a shopkeeper and beer retailer at Stonebridge by 1855, and by the late 60s Westend Farm stood on the site of a cottage on Harrow Road.[27]

Residential building in the area was stimulated by the presence of Harrow Road and the opening of Stonebridge Park station on the Midland line in 1875. A 35-acre site, running north from Harrow Road beside Dog Lane and originally called Harlesden Park, had by 1873 been laid out as Stonebridge Park and in 1876 contained 60 or 80 'smart new villas for City men', all detached or semi-detached.[28] A large hotel called Stonebridge Park was built on Harrow Road next to the new estate.[29] Subsequent development was not of such high quality. In 1879 land east of Stonebridge Park was laid out in streets (Bruce and Casselden roads) and building plots,[30] and the 55 a. west and north of Stonebridge Park was offered for sale.[31] In 1880 the United Land Co. had land south of Harrow Road laid out in 51 building plots in Shrewsbury, Stracey, and Knatchbull roads for 'small capitalists',[32] and building had started there a year later, when Melville Road north of Harrow Road was divided into building plots.[33] Houses were built there during the 1880s and 1890s, mostly small and in terraces, for the retail and other tradesmen such as launderers serving the middle-class district of Stonebridge Park.[34]

By 1901 building covered the area south of Harrow Road in the angle between the two railway lines as far west as Wesley Road, and north of Harrow Road reached Alric Avenue. Farther north, where Dog Lane turned east to Neasden, Willesden isolation hospital was built in 1894 and the Great Central Railway Co. built terraced houses between 1898 and 1900 in Woodheyes and Gresham roads for its workers.[35] A church, St. Michael's, was opened in 1892. Between 1901 and 1911 an increase in population without a corresponding amount of new building indicates that some of the larger houses were being divided.[36] Stonebridge Park retained its superior status into the 1930s, being the home of Willesden's historian, Frederick Augustus

Wood, and of many other members of the local board and council.[37] Like neighbouring Harlesden, however, Stonebridge was rapidly losing its middle-class character as industry moved into the area. By 1920 there were industrial premises, especially factory laundries, along the eastern and southern edges of the area by the railway lines and in Barry Road.[38] The population in 1921 was little more than in 1911.[39]

An attempt to develop the Brentfield estate in 1899 had failed,[40] and a broad stretch of land next to the river was leased to the council for sewage works and, after new sewage arrangements were made in 1911, for allotments.[41] The council's plan, under the Housing and Town Planning Act of 1919, to build 1,000 houses on the 63-a. Brentfield estate west of Dog Lane, the Stonebridge portion of which was renamed Brentfield Road, proved costly because of drainage difficulties, and in 1920, after some 260 houses had been built, the scheme was halted. In 1921 the North Circular Road was driven through the middle of the estate but in 1925 the council resumed the scheme, building another 420 houses.[42] In 1933 Brentfield was one of the areas included in Willesden's Town Planning Scheme.[43] Land adjoining the estate, conveniently close to the North Circular, was allocated to industry. Some council flats were built at Bridge Road near the railway estate in 1929.[44]

By 1949 there were several depots at Stonebridge, the trolleybus depot employing 886 and the railway goods depot 439.[45] Much land along the river remained unbuilt on and in use as allotments and recreation ground. In the Stonebridge area 17,641 people lived in 2,556 houses and 423 flats. Density ranged from 55 persons per acre in Stonebridge Park to 143 per acre south of Harrow Road (then called Hillside). An inadequate road system gave rise to traffic problems, there was residential overcrowding, and many buildings, including some of the large houses of Stonebridge Park where several had been converted to institutions or flats, were derelict.[46] In 1957 the council announced its plan to redevelop 100 a. bounded by the railways and the Brentfield estate, moving industry out of the area, redesigning the street plan,[47] and building 2,169 dwellings. The first blocks of flats were opened in 1967.[48] Building was well advanced by 1978 with blocks of flats and a shopping precinct

[26] P.R.O., HO 107/1700/135/3, ff. 403v.-404v.
[27] Kelly's Dir. Mdx. (1855); O.S. Map 6", Mdx. XVI. NW. (1864-73 edn.).
[28] Grange Mus., Wood F 19 (sale cats. 1/1-2); ibid. gen. files, Stonebridge Pk. (architect's impression of estate); Thorne, Environs, 697-9.
[29] Grange Mus., photo album 'Willesden'.
[30] Ibid. Wood F 20 (sale cat. 2/23).
[31] Ibid. (sale cat. 2/10).
[32] Ibid. (sale cat. 2/28); F 19 (sale cat. 1/47).
[33] Ibid. Wood F 20 (sale cat. 2/38).
[34] Ibid. Wood F 23, pp. 20 sqq.; Morris, Willesden Surv. p. 31; Kelly's Dir. Mdx. (1890); O.S. Map 6", Mdx. XVI. NW. (1894-6 edn.).
[35] Grange Mus., Map of Willesden U.D. 1901; Grange Mus. 2 A 1 ('Street Names'); Ashdown, Ind. Mon. of Gtr. Lond. s.v. Brent; Grange Mus., gen. files, railways (Forward: Jnl. of Gt. Central Rly. Soc. Dec. 1978).
[36] Census, 1901-11.
[37] Kelly's Dir. Mdx. (1890); Grange Mus., gen. files, Stonebridge Pk.
[38] O.S. Map 6", Mdx. XVI. NW. (1920 edn.); Grange Mus., gen. files, Gibbons Rd.
[39] Census, 1911-21 (Stonebridge ward).
[40] Grange Mus., NM 282.
[41] All Souls Coll., uncat. material, docs. relating to estates 1887-95; agents' reps. 1910.
[42] Grange Mus., gen. files, housing (Willesden U.D.C. Rep. 25 Feb. 1925); 1 A 5 (Willesden Chron. 16 July 1920; Willesden Cit. 23 July 1920); The Times, 8 Apr., 10 June, 30 Sept. 1919; All Souls Coll., uncat. material, agents' reps. 1921.
[43] Grange Mus., NM 309.
[44] Morris, Willesden Surv. p. 31.
[45] Ibid. pp. 63 sqq., map 6, map 7, areas 9A-H, 11D; Brent planning and research dept., Age of Bldgs. Map.
[46] Morris, Willesden Surv. map 7, p. 31.
[47] Willesden Civic Review, Feb. 1957.
[48] Grange Mus., gen. files, Stonebridge redevel.; 1 A 2 (Willesden Cit. 18 Dec. 1964; Willesden Mercury, 7, 14 Jan. 1966); Rep. to Willesden, 1963-4; O.S. Map 1/10,000, TQ 28 SW. (1975 edn.).

replacing the late 19th-century terraces. Some buildings, including St. Michael's church, Stonebridge Park hotel, and some of the large houses of Stonebridge Park remained.

North-west of the Brentfield estate the British Transport Commission sold a 17-a. depot site to the council in 1959 and 307 dwellings were built there in 1976.[49] During the 1960s and 1970s multi-storeyed office blocks were built along the North Circular Road. Among the most striking were the group at the crossing of the North Circular and Harrow Road, the 21-storeyed Station House on one side and two curved blocks on the other, opened in 1965 and 1975 respectively.[50]

In 1966 the population of Stonebridge included a proportion of immigrants higher than in neighbouring Church End but lower than in Harlesden, with 10 per cent born in Ireland and 7·3 per cent West Indian.[51]

BRONDESBURY. The land on either side of Willesden (formerly Mapes) Lane was, save for the section nearest its junction with Edgware Road, entirely prebendal, that to the north belonging to Mapesbury, that to the south to Bounds and Brondesbury.[52] In 1847 it was noted, with an eye to suburban development, that the Bounds and Brondesbury lands were inextricably mixed and that buildings on them included Brondesbury manor house which was leased with 27 a. to Charles Hambro. North of Willesden Lane, opposite Brondesbury manor house, stood Mapesbury House leased with 29 a. to William Anderson, a jobmaster. On Edgware Road there were two dilapidated cottages at the southern end and at Shoot-up Hill to the north a mill and a group of cottages and villas, some recently erected. The Mapesbury estate's long frontage on Edgware Road from just north of Willesden Lane to Walm Lane, the good access to all three estates from Willesden Lane, and at Brondesbury the elevated site were thought to make the land suitable for the better kind of villa.[53]

Building, begun in Willesden Lane by 1847, increased in pace after the Hampstead Junction line was driven through the middle of the area, with a station opened on Edgware Road in 1860. By the late 1860s there were a few houses at the western end of the prebendal estates at Willesden Green, two large villas, one called Brondesbury House, next to Brondesbury Park, and houses on both sides of the railway line south of Willesden Lane. The first new road, then called Cavendish Road, had been laid out south-west from Willesden Lane (along a stretch later called the Avenue) and some detached villas had been built.[54] Christ Church was built in 1866 to serve the new

district, named Brondesbury a year later.[55] In 1870 the Ecclesiastical Commissioners made an agreement with William White for building 16 detached or semi-detached houses of not less than £70 a year value on the north-east continuation of Cavendish Road.[56] Similar agreements were made during the 1870s.[57] By 1875 there were 106 houses in Cavendish Road and Willesden Lane,[58] described as a new district of genteel villas.[59]

Houses were being built in Christchurch Avenue in 1875[60] and in Winchester Road (later Avenue) in 1879.[61] In 1879 also 26 building plots along Willesden Lane, west of Christ Church, were offered for sale for 'first class residences' on 99-year leases.[62] Some had already been built, since William H. G. Kingston (d. 1880), the author of boys' adventure stories, lived in Stormont Lodge from c. 1877.[63] The Metropolitan railway built its line across the northern part of the district in 1879, with stations at Willesden Green and Edgware Road (called Kilburn and Brondesbury station). Building along Edgware Road, where the Ecclesiastical Commissioners had made building agreements for high-quality houses on some 17 a. in 1867 and 1868,[64] was continuous by 1887 to Walm Lane and beyond, and new roads and houses were advancing westward from Edgware Road on either side of the railway lines. On the south side of Willesden Lane detached houses were almost continuous from Willesden Green to the Hampstead Junction line, on the other side of which were the smaller terraced houses of Winchester Avenue and Kimberley Road. Salusbury Road, linking the area with Kilburn Lane, continued north as Brondesbury Park, which cut Brondesbury manor house off from its entrance on Willesden Lane.[65]

When Mapesbury farm was leased in 1893 it had been reduced to 120 a., large portions on the east and south having been lost to building.[66] By 1894 Mapesbury Road had been built and housing had almost engulfed Mapesbury House itself. There were houses along the northern side of Brondesbury Park and two, St. Monica's and Lady Adelaide homes, within the parklands of Brondesbury manor house, which had itself become a school.[67] By 1901 Brondesbury Park had been extended to Willesden Green and roads had been laid out on the northern and western boundaries with building from Kensal Rise advancing eastward across the Brondesbury demesne lands. On the Mapesbury estate the road pattern north of the Metropolitan line was complete by 1901 as was that south of the line as far west as Mapesbury Road, and housing in both areas was advancing westward.[68]

[49] Willesden Civic Review, Apr. 1957; Nov. 1959; Brent L.B. Year Bk. (1977-8); Grange Mus., gen. files, Neasden (Oct. 1977 map of housing redevel.).
[50] Grange Mus., 1 A 2 (Willesden Cit. 18 Dec. 1964; Willesden Mercury, 14 Jan. 1966); gen. files, Aerofilms box 3, no. 141; gen. files, Stonebridge Pk. (Willesden Observer 12 Sept. 1975).   [51] Weintraub, 'Race and local politics'.
[52] M.R.O., EA/WIL.
[53] Ch. Com., Surveys S1, pp. 592-603, 607-22, 857-70.
[54] O.S. Map 6", Mdx. XVI. NE. (1864-73 edn.).
[55] Lond. Gaz. 6 Aug. 1867, p. 4356.
[56] Guildhall MS. CC. 148864.

[57] e.g. ibid. MS. CC. 156578; M.R.O., Acc. 1351/12; Acc. 1351/58.   [58] Willesden local bd. San. Rep. (1875).
[59] Thorne, Environs, 697-9.
[60] M.R.O., Acc. 1351/51.
[61] Guildhall MS. CC. 199251.
[62] Grange Mus., Wood F 20 (sale cat. 2/17).
[63] Ibid. biog. files, Kingston.
[64] Guildhall MSS. CC. 126337, 126232.
[65] M.R.O., TA/WIL.
[66] Guildhall MS. CC. 255705.
[67] O.S. Map 6", Mdx. XVI. NE. (1894-6 edn.).
[68] Grange Mus., Map of Willesden U.D. 1901.

Brondesbury retained its intended character as a high-class residential district. In 1890 it housed four doctors, three artists, a solicitor, a professor of music, and three private schools. There was no industry and the nearest shops were at Willesden Green and Edgware Road.[69] In an area housing a high proportion of commuters there were three stations, and four from 1908 with the opening of Brondesbury Park on the Hampstead line, and in 1887 Metropolitan trains ran to Broad Street from Brondesbury every quarter hour.[70] In 1905 an omnibus ran from Brondesbury station to the Law Courts.[71]

A small area surrounding Mapesbury House was almost the only part of the estate which had not been built up by 1920. West of Brondesbury manor house Aylestone Avenue and Milverton Road had been laid out and some houses had been built.[72] Nearby 300 new dwellings were added by 1931.[73] In 1926 Brondesbury was still an area of City businessmen and professional men. There were six private schools, three nursing homes, bowling and tennis clubs, and a domestic servants' bureau. The only industry was a motor engineering works at Winchester Avenue.[74] In 1934 Brondesbury manor house and its remaining grounds were sold for building, the house was demolished and Manor House Drive built on the site.[75]

In 1949 Brondesbury was defined as an area of 318 a. containing 1,300 houses, 261 flats, and a population of 8,837, with a density on average of 27 persons per acre and at the most, in the Avenue, of 35. Although many of the large houses had been converted into flats, Brondesbury was still the most expensive residential area within the borough. Only at Shoot-up Hill was there dilapidated property,[76] which was cleared away in the 1950s and replaced by blocks of flats. The last remaining undeveloped land, Clement Road and Way, was built up in the 1960s.[77] Some 136 council houses were built in the area of Christchurch Avenue and Chatsworth Road and another 95 in Willesden Lane in 1975.[78]

Since the late 19th century Brondesbury had included a high proportion of Jewish residents, partly perhaps because it was an area of professional and City businessmen and partly because it contained flats. There was some immigration in the post-war period, though less than in other areas. Only a little over half of the population in 1966 was British-born: Jewish immigrants from Europe presumably formed a high proportion, perhaps as large as the 17·5 per cent born in Ireland. Brondesbury had the highest percentage of Indians and Pakistanis in Willesden.[79]

CRICKLEWOOD, OXGATE, AND DOLLIS HILL. The whole of the north-eastern corner of Willesden, north of Sherrick green and its continuation Walm Lane, belonged to the prebend of Oxgate. There was a settlement at Oxgate by the 13th century,[80] consisting of a group of farmhouses and cottages in the centre of the area, reached by lanes from Edgware Road and Dollis Hill Lane. There was also a group of buildings by the late 16th century at Dollis Hill.[81] Cricklewood, the remnants of the forest bordering Watling Street (later Edgware Road), was in 1599 an area of woodland extending westward on the north side of Walm Lane.[82] Clearings in it were extended until the whole area became farmland, centred certainly by the mid 18th and probably by the late 17th century on a farmhouse, called Cricklewood or the Slade, on Edgware Road. Another farmhouse (later Clock Farm) was built, probably about the same time, on Edgware Road farther north, but the hamlet of Cricklewood in the mid 18th century lay almost entirely on the Hendon side of Edgware Road.[83]

There had been little change before inclosure in 1823. The area, entirely made up of old inclosures, was divided into fairly compact estates centred on farmhouses. In 1815, to defray the expenses of inclosure, waste alongside Edgware Road was put up for sale as 'suitable for building',[84] and several houses had been built there by 1851, including Cricklewood Lodge and Oakland House. Besides farmers and labourers Cricklewood residents included a large-scale tailor, a frame manufacturer, the keeper of a boarding school, and several 'rustic chair-makers'.[85] The M. & S.W.J. railway was built across the centre of the area in 1868 by which time there were groups of houses along Edgware Road, especially on either side of the junction with Walm Lane and between the Slade and Clock Farm; the houses were more numerous on the Hendon side, near Child's Hill station, opened in 1870 on the Midland railway.[86] There were 36 houses in the Willesden portion of Cricklewood by 1875,[87] but Cricklewood was still a hamlet lying in a 'pretty rural tract' in 1876.[88] Dollis Hill Lane, described in the 1830s as 'more resembling the drive through a park than a public thoroughfare',[89] remained little changed for nearly a century, and Dollis Hill in 1876 was said to be elevated, well wooded, and picturesque.[90]

The transformation of Cricklewood began in the decade after 1876.[91] The Metropolitan railway line was built in 1879, and by 1887 George Furness was in possession of Clock farm, which

[69] Kelly's Dir. Mdx. (1890).
[70] Grange Mus., Wood F 9.
[71] Ibid. gen. files, topog. (M. Marks, 'Growth of Willesden').
[72] O.S. Map 6″, Mdx. XVI. NE. (1920 edn.).
[73] Census, 1931.
[74] Kelly's Dir. Mdx. (1926).
[75] Briggs, Mdx. Old and New, 166–7; Morris, Willesden Surv. p. 24.
[76] Morris, Willesden Surv. pp. 18, 24, map 7, areas 4A–D.
[77] Grange Mus., gen. files, housing; Willesden Civic Review, Aug. 1958, Nov. 1959; Rep. to Willesden, 1963–4; Brent planning and research dept., Age of Bldgs. Map.
[78] Brent L.B. Year Bk. (1977–8).
[79] Weintraub, 'Race and local politics'.

[80] P.N. Mdx. (E.P.N.S.), 163; P.R.O., E 40/7906.
[81] Below, other est.; Norden, Spec. Brit. map of Mdx.
[82] All Souls Coll., Hovenden maps II/21.
[83] Rocque, Map of Lond. (1746); below, manors.
[84] M.R.O., EA/WIL; ibid. Acc. 262/40, pt. 1 (sale cat. 1815).
[85] P.R.O., HO 107/1700/135/3, ff. 367–70, 378.
[86] O.S. Map 6″, Mdx. XI. SE. (1864–73 edn.); Grange Mus., Wood F 19 (sale cat. 1/15).
[87] Willesden local bd. San. Rep. (1875).
[88] Thorne, Environs, 697–9.
[89] W. H. Ainsworth, Jack Sheppard [1910 edn.], 173.
[90] Thorne, Environs, 697–9; Grange Mus., photo. files, Dollis Hill Lane (NL 766, 769, 1609).
[91] Grange Mus., Wood F 19 (sale cat. 1/28).

was described as building land.[92] Another building firm, Corsellis Son & Mossop, purchased a 12-a. site, probably the southern portion of the Clock farm estate, which it was proposing to develop in 1888.[93] In that year it applied to develop the Cricklewood estate of All Souls College, by that time the most southerly unoccupied space on the Willesden side of Edgware Road. The college agents, noting that trains ran every 10 minutes from Willesden Green station, that the local board was constructing main sewers, and that a railway depot and workshops had been built nearby, considered the whole area ripe for building.[94]

Building proceeded on the three estates during the 1890s and 1900s. On the Corsellis estate houses had been built in Rockhall Road by 1892[95] and streets and houses were well advanced by 1894.[96] Clock farmhouse was demolished c. 1892, and between 1893 and 1900 Furness laid out the estate which he called Cricklewood Park in roads named after trees and built terraced houses and the first factory, the Imperial Dry Plate works, in the area.[97] About half of Furness's 60-a. estate was built up by 1900 when the New River Co., which bought adjoining land for water works,[98] prevented Furness from building a road to link his estate to Parkside, then called Dudden Hill Park.[99] All Souls College built a group of roads named after fellows and leased building plots to, among others, Alexander McBain, Mackley Bros., Charles Cheshir, and Francis Buck.[1] By 1898 some 60 houses had been built on 8 a. of college land at Cricklewood and an agreement was current for another 60 on 13 a.[2]

In 1900 the college purchased 3 a. at the western end of the Cricklewood estate and began building west of Chichele Road, extending Anson Road to the end of the estate.[3] Further expansion westward was blocked by the Dollis Hill estate, which became a public park, Gladstone Park, in 1901. By 1904 there were 210 houses on 21 a. and 65 were being built on 12 a. at Cricklewood.[4] Slade farmhouse was demolished in 1906.[5] By that time, however, there was a recession in building. Applications were made to reduce the rent of leases at Cricklewood, it being 'almost impossible to sell houses'.[6] By 1914 there were 360 houses on 30 a. and leases were current for 33 more on 3½ a.[7] Residents in Chichele Road on the All Souls estate included

John E. Gunby Hadath, who wrote adventure stories from before the First World War into the 1950s.[8]

In 1897 Earl Temple planned to build on his land at Lower Oxgate north of Furness's estate,[9] and Temple Road had been built there by 1906; the farmhouse was not demolished until 1919.[10]

The identity of Cricklewood as a recognizable district was established in the two decades around 1900. A congregational church opened there in 1893, St. Gabriel's in 1898, a Baptist chapel in Anson Road in 1908, and St. Michael's in 1910. A shopping parade, in 'metropolitan electric' style was built in Edgware Road between 1900 and 1914,[11] and the stretch of road was named Cricklewood Broadway. A Cricklewood improvements association was formed in 1904, a horticultural association and a local newspaper in 1911.[12] The L.G.O.C. built stables in Cricklewood in 1897-8 and numerous motor bus and tram services were introduced during the same period.[13]

The First World War stimulated the growth of industry, especially near the junction of the M. & S.W.J. and Midland railway lines. By 1920 London Transport had opened a garage, and motor works had been built on the site of Lower Oxgate farm; terraced housing spread north of the M. & S.W.J. line in the area which became known as Dollis Hill.[14] St. Andrew's hospital was built in Dollis Hill Lane in 1913.

The north-east corner of the parish was, with Neasden, the main area involved in the expansion of the 1920s and 1930s. Building resumed on the All Souls estate, another 60 houses having been built between 1914 and 1924.[15] New building leases were sought in 1923[16] and building spread along avenues leading north and south from Anson Road, merging with Dudden Hill and Willesden Green. Only one road, Dicey Avenue, remained to be built after 1934.[17] Though Gladstone Park formed a barrier to westward expansion the tide of building spread northward from Dollis Hill Lane, engulfing the Oxgate farmlands. The farm cottages in Oxgate Lane were demolished c. 1937. Only Upper Oxgate farm was saved, being bought by an employee of the developers, Costain's, who preserved the 16th-century farmhouse in the midst of the new buildings.[18] The northern corner of Cricklewood

[92] M.R.O., TA/WIL, nos. 85-7, 89.
[93] In 1887 owned by Geo. Howard, furniture manufacturer: M.R.O., TA/WIL, nos. 90-3.
[94] All Souls Coll., uncat. material, docs. relating to estates, 1887-95.
[95] Grange Mus., NM 4.
[96] O.S. Map 6", Mdx. XI. SE. (1894-6 edn.).
[97] Grange Mus., Geo. Furness & Co. album of photos. and plans 1893-9; M.R.O., Acc. 549/76; Acc. 1351/28; Willesden Monthly Illus. 5 Mar. 1937.
[98] For the pumping station, built in 1905, Ashdown, Ind. Mon. of Gtr. Lond. s.v. Brent.
[99] Grange Mus., MSS. 34/12-13.
[1] All Souls Coll., uncat. material, docs. relating to estates 1887-95; ibid. Bd. of Agric. Orders 1891 for land at Cricklewood.
[2] Ibid. bursars' rentals 1896-8; M.R.O., Acc. 1351/21, 23, 31; Grange Mus., NM 4.
[3] All Souls Coll., uncat. material, agents' reps. 1900; M.R.O., Acc. 1351/23, 31.
[4] All Souls Coll., uncat. material, bursars' rentals 1904;

Grange Mus., NM 129.
[5] Grange Mus., S. W. Ball, scrapbk. ii, p. 0284 (newspaper cutting 5 Oct. 1906).
[6] All Souls Coll., uncat. material, agents' reps. 1906-10.
[7] Ibid. bursars' rentals 1914.
[8] Grange Mus., biog. files, Hadath.
[9] Ibid. MSS. 34/12-13.
[10] Ibid. NM 350; Kilburn and Willesden Dir. (1906, 1919).
[11] Robbins, Mdx. 82.
[12] Grange Mus., 1 E 7 (Cricklewood improvements assoc. min. bk. 1904-8); ibid. gen. files, Cricklewood.
[13] Ibid. gen. files, Cricklewood. For motor and horse buses at Cricklewood Broadway, Grange Mus., photo. files, Cricklewood Broadway (NL 761).
[14] e.g. at Dollis Hill Avenue in 1920: M.R.O., Acc. 1351/31, 42; O.S. Map 6", Mdx. XI. SE. (1920 edn.).
[15] All Souls Coll., uncat. material, bursars' rentals.
[16] Ibid. agents' reps. 1919-24.
[17] Ibid. bursars' rentals 1934, 1957; M.R.O., Acc. 1351/41.
[18] Grange Mus., 1 A 4 (Willesden Chron. 26 Nov. 1937).

was reserved in 1933 for industry, and factories[19] on each side of the North Circular Road as far south as Oxgate soon covered the area. Terraced housing for workers was built west of the industrial area in 1927–8, and intermingled semi-detached and terraced houses and blocks of flats were built in Oxgate and Dollis Hill between 1928 and 1935. In 1933 the Post Office research station was built on Dollis Hill farmland, which by 1939 was reduced to 3 a. around the farmhouse. The farmhouse was demolished shortly afterwards to make way for research buildings.[20]

Cricklewood was described in 1949 as an area with no clearly defined boundaries, possessing a good shopping centre which served a wide area outside Willesden borough; industry was intermixed with the residential parts and north Cricklewood was entirely industrial; 19,586 people lived in 3,600 houses and 842 flats, at densities varying from 28 persons per acre in Dollis Hill to 92 on the Furness estate.[21] There was some building, usually on small sites, after 1945[22] and plans were made for housing in Gladstone Park Gardens in 1969.[23] In 1966 Cricklewood had relatively high proportions of Irish and Jewish residents, who had arrived respectively from Kilburn and Brondesbury. Jewish enclaves were said to be a feature of Cricklewood and Dollis Hill in 1937.[24]

EAST TWYFORD AND PARK ROYAL. The south-west corner of the parish formed part of the district of Twyford which was already divided by 1086 into two estates. On the part which later came to be East Twyford in Willesden parish and the endowment of the prebend of East Twyford there were then three villeins.[25] There were three messuages in the 16th century although then or earlier one of them became the manor house. By the mid 18th century Lower Place (presumably the manor house site) consisted of two houses and barns. Farther south-west Ruckhold Farm, with cottages nearby, faced the green lane to Hanwell. The Coach and Horses at Stonebridge may represent the third of the 16th-century messuages.[26] A cottage had been built east of Lower Place green by 1800[27] and the Grand Junction canal was driven across the area, dividing Lower Place and Ruckhold farms, in 1801.[28] In 1837 the London and Birmingham railway was built north of the canal, effectively destroying the Lower Place cottages and running very close to the farm buildings. The Grand Junction Arms had been built where Acton Lane crossed the canal by the 1860s.[29]

Development in Twyford began at the end of the 19th century mainly as a result of the growth of Willesden Junction. In 1879 the United Land Co. bought land by the canal and within a year was offering 31 plots in Disraeli and Steele roads. Small terraced houses had been built there by 1885.[30] Some 4½ a. east of Acton Lane between the railway and the canal had been leased, presumably on building leases. By 1887 two roads of terraced houses, one called Wharf Road, had been built there.[31] They had gone by 1894, however, and by 1901 had been replaced by a power station. In 1897 the Willesden board of guardians bought 60 a. for a workhouse and infirmary next to Ruckhold Farm, which was demolished soon afterwards. By the end of the 19th century a farm in Acton opposite Ruckhold Farm was being called Lower Place and the original farm of that name was renamed Grange Farm. A large house called the Grange was built nearby. Waxlow Road led west from Acton Lane by 1901 and a biscuit factory and brick works had been built there by c. 1910.[32]

In 1901 the Royal Agricultural Society leased 117 a. west of the infirmary as a site for its annual agricultural shows. Although the Great Western Railway opened a station, called Park Royal after the site itself, in 1903, the shows were poorly attended and the site was abandoned after 1905. It was later used by Queen's Park Rangers football club and for other sporting events.[33] During the First World War the site housed an army horse compound and armaments factories, which were adapted after the war to civilian industrial use. By 1920, in addition to the factories west of the workhouse, industrial premises had been built at Lower Place, as had a school and children's homes.[34]

Following the building of the North Circular Road Park Royal became the major industrial area in Willesden,[35] spreading into Alperton, Acton, and West Twyford. Industry filled the remaining space at Lower Place, covering the area between the railway and the canal and reaching down Acton Lane to the infirmary. Grange farm was replaced by a sports ground in 1935, although the Grange survived in 1966.[36] In 1949 there were several sports grounds and allotments. At that date the 19th-century housing at Lower Place consisted of 136 dilapidated and overcrowded dwellings where 1,047 people lived.[37] In 1960 the council planned to remove the housing and make the area wholly industrial.[38]

[19] Grange Mus., NM 309.
[20] Ibid. NM 9; ibid. photo. files, Dollis Hill Lane (NL 605); Morris, *Willesden Surv.* p. 23; Robbins, *Mdx.* 357–60.
[21] Morris, *Willesden Surv.* map 7, areas 3A–C, 12, and 2K–Q, pp. 18, 23, 24, 32.
[22] Brent planning and research dept., Age of Bldgs. Map.
[23] Grange Mus., gen. files, Gladstone Pk. Gdns.
[24] Weintraub, 'Race and local politics'; *Willesden Monthly Illus.* 5 Oct. 1937.
[25] *V.C.H. Mdx.* i. 121.
[26] Grange Mus., Wood F 21 (map of 1765); M.R.O., EA/ WIL; below, manors.
[27] Milne, *Land Use Map of Lond.* (1800).
[28] M.R.O., EA/WIL.
[29] O.S. Map 6″, Mdx. XVI. NW. (1864–73 edn.).

[30] Grange Mus., Wood F 20 (sale cats. 2/9, 36); F 23, pp. 20 sqq.; ibid. NM 419, 449.
[31] M.R.O., TA/WIL, no. 267.
[32] O.S. Map 6″, Mdx. XVI. NW. (1894–6 edn.); Grange Mus., Map of Willesden U.D. 1901; ibid. NM 350; below, pub. svces.
[33] Grange Mus., photo. files, Park Royal; J. D. Allan Gray, *Central Mdx. Hosp.* (1963), 13.
[34] O.S. Map 6″, Mdx. XVI. NW. (1920 edn.).
[35] Grange Mus., NM 9, 184, 309.
[36] Brent planning and research dept., Age of Bldgs. Map. It had gone by 1975: O.S. Map 1/10,000, TQ 28 SW. (1975 edn.).
[37] Morris, *Willesden Surv.* map 7, pp. 20, 32.
[38] *Willesden Civic Review*, Feb. 1960.

SOCIAL AND CULTURAL ACTIVITIES.

In 1552 there were three alehouses[39] in Willesden and one in Kilburn.[40] William Huddle was jailed in 1615 for keeping an unlicensed alehouse.[41] The Anchor and Cable, which existed in 1670, may be identifiable with the Anchor at Harlesden (1688) and the Crown at Harlesden green, licensed from 1722.[42] There were eleven licensed houses, none of them named, in 1716 and fifteen in 1722. Among them were the Crown, two Lettice inns, one of which was the Dolphin in Harrow Road in 1726, the Parrot, the Great House at Neasden, and the Banqueting House on Edgware Road. One of two called the Green Man[43] was the inn south of Harlesden green[44] which in 1824 was the half-way house between London and Harrow. The Parrot is probably identifiable with the Five Bells, described as a newly erected cottage in 1724,[45] which stood north of High Road at Church End, near the Vicarage, and was used for vestry meetings.[46] By 1790 the name had changed to Six Bells. It ceased to be licensed some time before 1913 when the council decided to close it. The small square building survived into the later 20th century.[47]

The Plough, at the junction of Harrow Road and Kilburn Lane at Kensal Green, existed by 1749[48] and, though rebuilt, was still there in 1980. The White Hart (also called the Leather Bottle and the Gate) stood at the junction of Church Lane and High Road, Church End, by 1749 and was a brick and weatherboarded building with 19th-century pleasure gardens.[49] The Spotted Dog, High Road, north of Willesden Green, existed by 1762 and can probably be identified with the Dog at Willesden Green in 1751.[50] A dance hall had been added to the building by 1927.[51] There was a Cock in 1726 but it is not likely to have been the inn of that name on Edgware Road in Kilburn which was probably built in the 1760s. The inn was burned down and rebuilt c. 1794 and rebuilt again in 1900.[52] A second Spotted Dog was licensed in Neasden, at the junction of Neasden and Dog lanes, by 1770;[53] the small, square, brick and weatherboarded building, to which Londoners flocked as a 'suburban tea garden' in 1876, gave way to a building of c. 1900 which was demolished in 1932 and replaced by the large Tudor-style building sur-

viving in 1980.[54] A building on the site of the Coach and Horses on the south side of Harrow Road at Stonebridge in 1749 is unlikely then to have been an inn.[55] Called the Coach and Horses by 1790, it can probably be identified with the Stone Bridge, licensed in 1770. About 1900 it had a skittle alley and a gymnasium frequented by boxers. It was rebuilt in 1907.[56]

There were eight public houses in 1828, an average of one to every 177 persons, and in 1827 the vestry met to consider the number and to enforce the Sabbatarian legislation concerning them. The constables complained about only one, the Green Man, and the numbers were not reduced.[57] Other inns were opened: the Royal Oak, Harlesden green by 1839, the Case is Altered, Kensal Green by 1843, the Lion at Harlesden by 1851, the White Horse at Church End c. 1860, and the Victoria in Willesden Lane by 1865.[58] The spread of building brought new public houses, most developments reserving corner sites for them. By 1916 there were 35 licensed houses in Willesden and 42 by 1947, of which 10 were in Kilburn and only one in Neasden.[59] The numbers were much reduced when Kilburn was redeveloped. In the 1960s Kilburn High Street and Cricklewood Broadway were frequently disturbed by violence and noise, associated particularly with the Irish public houses and dance halls.[60]

In 1830 the duchess of Buckingham was paying an annual subscription of 2 guineas to a benevolent society which may have been set up by the vestry in 1811.[61] The Willesden union friendly society met at the Crown in 1816 and 1817; the Willesden provident society existed in 1830–1 and the Willesden association for the improvement of the condition of the working classes in 1856.[62]

The Cumberland sharpshooters, a volunteer unit founded in 1792, became in 1814 a civilian rifle club which, though based in Covent Garden, met for drill and practice at Wormwood Scrubbs and Kensal Green. It changed its name to the Royal Victoria rifle club in 1835, and in 1849, after a disagreement with the landlord of the Kensal Green ground, it leased 14 a. at Kilburn for a rifle range. In 1853 the group was reconstituted as a more military unit called the

[39] Inf. on public houses based on M.R.O., MR/LV3/4 (1716), 95 (1722); MR/LV4/30 (1726); MR/LV7/15 (1751); MR/LV8/65 (1770); MR/LV9/188 (1790); MR/LV11/133 (1810); MR/LV30 (1828–9).

[40] Mdx. County Rec. i. 11.

[41] M.R.O., Acc. 275/513; ibid. MJ/SBR 2/277.

[42] Ibid. EA/WIL, no. 422; Grange Mus., 1 B 27 (overseers' accts. 1678–1702); ibid. Ball, 'Old Willesden', 164.

[43] Guildhall MS. CC. 2199.

[44] M.R.O., EA/WIL, no. 373; ibid. Acc. 891/1/5/287.

[45] Ibid. EA/WIL, no. 522; M.L.R. 1724/4/315–16.

[46] Grange Mus., 1 D 29; ibid. Wood F 23, pp. 211 sqq.

[47] The Times, 19 June 1913; Grange Mus., gen. files, Neasden Lane, Six Bells; photo. files, Neasden Lane, Six Bells (NL 1254).

[48] M.R.O., EA/WIL, no. 831; Messeder Road Map (1749); Grange Mus., Ball, 'Old Willesden', 61.

[49] M.R.O., EA/WIL, no. 494; Messeder Road Map; M.R.O., Acc. 262/40, pt. 1 (1803); Grange Mus., photo. album.

[50] M.R.O., EA/WIL, no. 656; Grange Mus., gen. files, High Rd., Spotted Dog; photo. files, Church Rd., White Horse (NL 989 reverse).   [51] M.R.O., Acc. 1290/214, 221.

[52] M.R.O., EA/WIL, no. 951; ibid. Acc. 735/13–21; Grange Mus., 1 B 4 (poor rate bk. 1788–1804); not marked on Messeder Road Map (1749).

[53] M.R.O., EA/WIL, no. 141.

[54] Grange Mus., photo. files, Neasden Lane, Old Spotted Dog (NL 1252, 2024); Thorne, Environs, 446.

[55] Messeder Road Map (1749); M.R.O., EA/WIL, no. 254.

[56] Grange Mus., 1 A 2 (Willesden Cit. 6 June 1949).

[57] Ibid. 1 D 11 (vestry order bk. 1825–32).

[58] Pigot, Dir. Mdx. (1839); M.R.O., Acc. 735/1–5; Acc. 1290/177; P.R.O., HO 107/1700/135/3, f. 415; Grange Mus., Ball, 'Old Willesden', 158.

[59] Grange Mus., 2 A 1 ('Street Names'); Morris, Willesden Surv. p. 36, 89. In 1947 the average ratio of public houses to population in the London suburbs was 1 to 2,101, in Willesden 1 to 1,700, in Kilburn 1 to 424, in Neasden 1 to 14,000.

[60] Grange Mus., 1 A 2 (Willesden Cit. 14 Sept. 1962).

[61] Ibid. 1 D 29 (vestry order bk. 1722–1814); M.R.O., Acc. 262/65/3.

[62] P.R.O., FS 1/437/1602; FS 1/442/1790; FS 1/486A/3599.

Victoria Rifles, renamed the 1st Middlesex Rifle Volunteers in 1859, and it left Kilburn in 1867 when Victoria Road was built across the range.[63] Another rifle range on the Roundwood estate between Harlesden and Church End, described as newly erected in 1861 when the vestry complained of the danger to people in Harlesden Road, was still there in 1871.[64] The West Middlesex Rifle Volunteers had a drill hall at Regency Terrace, Willesden Green, in 1887 and a large drill hall opened in Pound Lane in 1911.[65] Willesden Green and District rifle club, which had previously met in an iron hall, opened a new rifle range at Cricklewood in 1909. It continued until the 1930s.[66] There was a miniature rifle association at Willesden Green in 1917, and there were shooting grounds at Kensal Green from c. 1861 to c. 1910 and at Neasden in 1920.[67]

Fishing rights on the Brent belonged in the 16th and 17th centuries to East Twyford manor.[68] Willesden was a favourite place for pigeon shooting c. 1790 and in the mid 19th century at Purdey's grounds.[69] In the 19th century packs of hounds, of which the Neasden Harriers were the best known, were kept both at Neasden House and at the Grove. The Grove hounds were sold in 1856 and those at Neasden House may not have survived the death in 1853 of Joseph Nicoll, who had his portrait painted as a huntsman.[70] Boxing matches and bull-baiting had taken place at Willesden Green for some years before 1810, when the vestry decided to stop them on the grounds that they attracted crowds from London and disrupted the hay harvest.[71] Cricket matches were being played in 1854 by the Black Lion Perseverance Club at its ground on the Willesden side of Kilburn.[72] Willesden cricket club existed by 1875 and had a ground at Church End until 1898; the lease then passed to the London Playing Field committee, which continued the use as a cricket pitch until the First World War.[73] There was another cricket ground at Neasden by 1894, and one south of Roundwood Park and one at Gladstone Park by c. 1910.[74] There were four cricket clubs by 1917 and 17 pitches by 1933.[75] There were two wholly West Indian cricket teams in 1964.[76]

Kilburn was one of the clubs present at the formation of the Football Association in 1863,[77] and Willesden football club existed by 1885.[78] Queen's Park Rangers was formed in 1886 by the amalgamation of two Paddington clubs, and used numerous grounds mostly within Willesden. The club became professional in 1898 and moved in 1907 to Park Royal, where its ground was taken over by the army during the First World War. In 1917 it moved out of Willesden to the Shepherd's Bush ground at Loftus Road where it has remained.[79] By 1933 Willesden had 26 football pitches.[80]

Willesden lawn tennis club existed by 1877,[81] Willesden Park c. 1904–34, Kensal Green from 1906, and Elmwood 1914–57.[82] There were 13 clubs by 1917, most of them serving small localities, and 36 courts by 1933.[83]

The National Athletic ground at Kensal Green was laid out in 1890 and steeplechases were last held on the site of the King Edward VII recreation ground in 1903.[84] It was used by the Aeroplane Building and Flying Society in 1911.[85] By 1914 the council was receiving so many applications for sports pitches that they had to be ballotted.[86] The number of applications revived after the war and by 1920 there were numerous athletic grounds, cricket pitches, and tennis courts.[87] Neasden golf club, founded in 1893, with its headquarters at Neasden House, survived until the area was engulfed by building in the 1930s.[88] A greyhound stadium was opened at Park Royal in 1931 and enlarged for use by Acton and Willesden rugby league club in 1935.[89] As building swallowed up all available land, sports grounds became concentrated in the public parks and recreation grounds. In 1965 Willesden stadium and sports centre was opened in the former King Edward VII recreation ground.[90]

Many of the earliest social clubs, including those for working men, were organized by the churches and chapels.[91] Regency working men's club existed at Regency Terrace, Willesden Green, by 1890[92] and still existed in 1980. Willesden working men's club had opened by 1917 at Villiers Road, where it remained in 1977.[93] Harlesden working men's club started in

[63] Grange Mus., gen. files, Victoria Rifle Ground; ibid. 2 A 1 ('Street Names'); *Brent Prints* (Brent L.B. libr.); Guildhall MS. CC. 22700.

[64] Grange Mus., Wood F 23, p. 275; 1 B 23 (sewer rate 1871).

[65] *Kelly's Dir. Mdx.* (1890); Grange Mus., photo. files, Pound Lane (NL 1300); gen. files, music; O.S. Map 6″, Mdx. XVI. NW. (1920 edn.); inf. from curator of Grange Mus.

[66] *The Times*, 20 Dec. 1909; All Souls Coll., uncat. material, agents' reps. 1909; bursars' rentals 1914, 1924, 1934.

[67] All Souls Coll., uncat. material, plan of estates 1861; *Kelly's Dir. Kilburn* (1917–18); O.S. Map 6″, Mdx. XI. SW. (1920 edn.); Grange Mus., NM 350.

[68] P.R.O., CP 25(2)/172/ 21 & 22 Eliz. Mic.; M.R.O., Acc. 276/480; Grange Mus., Wood F 30, ff. 292 sqq.

[69] Robbins, *Mdx.* 144; *V.C.H. Mdx.* ii. 266.

[70] Grange Mus., portrait; ibid. red box, Neasden; ibid. Ball, 'Old Willesden', 151.

[71] Ibid. 1 D 29 (vestry order bk. 1722–1814); ibid. gen. files, boxing (advert. for match, 1809).

[72] Ibid. poster.

[73] Ibid. Wood F 37/41; All Souls Coll., uncat. material, bursars' rentals 1883–7, 1896–8, 1904, 1914.

[74] O.S. Map 6″, Mdx. XI. SW. (1894–6 edn.); Grange Mus., NM 350.

[75] *Kelly's Dir. Kilburn* (1917–18); Grange Mus., 2 C 17 (souvenir of incorp. 1933).

[76] Grange Mus., gen. files, immigrants (*Immigrants in Lond.* 1964).   [77] *V.C.H. Mdx.* ii. 276.

[78] Grange Mus., Wood F 37/130.

[79] R. J. Hayter, *Queen's Park Rangers* (1948).

[80] Grange Mus., 2 C 17 (souvenir of incorp. 1933).

[81] Ibid. Wood F 37/41.

[82] All Souls Coll., uncat. material, bursars' rentals 1904, 1914, 1924, 1934, 1957; agents' reps. 1906.

[83] *Kelly's Dir. Kilburn* (1917–18); Grange Mus., 2 C 17 (souvenir of incorp. 1933).

[84] *Kelly's Dir. Mdx.* (1908); Grange Mus., gen. files, Kensal Green.

[85] *Aviation World Who's Who* (1911).

[86] *The Times*, 30 July 1915.

[87] O.S. Map 6″, Mdx. XI. SW., SE.; XVI. NW., NE. (1920 edn.).

[88] *V.C.H. Mdx.* ii. 278.

[89] Grange Mus., gen. files, Park Royal.

[90] Ibid. parks and gardens.

[91] e.g. St. Andrew's, founded in 1881: Grange Mus., gen. files, St. Andrew's ch.

[92] *Kelly's Dir. Mdx.* (1890).

[93] *Kelly's Dir. Kilburn* (1917–18); Brent L.B. *Social Clubs* (leaflet 1977).

Manor Park Road in 1909 and still flourished in 1950.[94]

Willesden choral association was founded in 1884 with a membership of 175 and a programme of two concerts a year.[95] Harlesden philharmonic orchestra was founded in 1912 and in 1956 the borough amenities committee proposed taking it over and expanding it.[96] There was a Willesden (later Brent) symphony orchestra by 1961.[97] Willesden operatic society, founded in 1921, still existed in 1971[98] and by 1933 there were eight operatic and choral societies.[99] Brass bands played in the parks in the early 20th century.[1] St. George's, Brondesbury, literary society existed by 1917 and Willgreen dramatic society by 1922.[2] Willesden People's Theatre Movement was founded in 1926 with plays performed at Harlesden Memorial hall by the Mansfield House and Willesden Players.[3] There were eleven dramatic societies by 1933.[4] A drama festival for local amateur groups was held annually in the Anson hall from 1945,[5] and by 1960 39 societies were taking part. Music, horticultural displays, and other activities were added.[6] The new London Borough of Brent formed an arts council which from 1965 organized the annual arts festival.[7]

There was a horticultural association by 1876, a parliamentary debating society in the 1880s, a Radical club and institute at Willesden Green by 1903,[8] and Cricklewood horticultural society, founded in 1911.[9] The Willesden Society, a general amenity society, was active by 1958 and Willesden Local History Society from 1974.[10] Numerous social and cultural groups associated with the various immigrant communities dated mostly from the 1960s and 1970s.[11]

Most early social activities took place in public houses or in buildings belonging to the churches and chapels. Willesden workmen's hall was built at the junction of High Road and Pound Lane at Chapel End in 1875 but the company owning it was bankrupt by 1877 and a Congregational chapel was built on the site in 1878.[12] Willesden library and institute, also for working men, had opened at Willesden Green by 1876 and survived in 1890.[13] The Regency drill hall at Willesden Green was being used for concerts and popular

entertainment in 1887 and 1890[14] but in 1891 Willesden Lyric Hall Ltd. was formed to provide a public hall and assembly rooms because there was no building suitable for meetings, dances, or similar activities.[15] The Willesden High school building at Craven Park, used from 1907 by Willesden club and institute, had by 1915 become a billiard club.[16]

In 1899 All Souls College planned to let land in Anson Road for a public hall to serve the tenants of their new estate at Cricklewood, but there was opposition to the 'proposed gambling hell'.[17] St. Gabriel's parish hall was founded in 1909 and took the name Anson hall in 1948 when it was leased to Willesden B.C.[18] There were c. 10 halls by 1917, several belonging to places of worship.[19] Demands in the 1920s for public halls and assembly rooms, to give the borough a social centre, were resisted on grounds of expense, and Willesden has remained a collection of local communities served by small, often short-lived, halls.[20] One of the more important was Harlesden Peace Memorial hall, opened in 1923 as a men's club and for other local activities. It was sold in 1965.[21] Local dramatic and music societies mostly used halls or schools for their plays and concerts.[22] In 1963 the former College Park Methodist church in Victor Road was leased to the Theatre Centre Co.[23]

Willesden Hippodrome opened in High Street, Harlesden, in 1907 as a music hall seating 3,000 people. It was later used for orchestral concerts and as a cinema. It was bombed in 1940 and demolished in 1957.[24] In 1909 several shops were giving cinema shows.[25] In 1917 Willesden Green Electric Palace opened in the former Willesden Congregational chapel at the junction of High Road with Dudden Hill Lane.[26] It was called the New Savoy by 1933 and the Savoy by 1947, and had closed by 1959.[27] There were seven other cinemas by 1917: the Rutland Park, opposite the Spotted Dog at Willesden Green,[28] and the Picture House Cinematograph Theatre, at no. 24 High Street, Harlesden, had closed by 1926, the Grand Electric Theatre, Salusbury Road, by 1947,[29] the Picardy, at no. 120 High Street, Harlesden, by 1959, the Coliseum in Manor Park

[94] Grange Mus., 1 A 2 (*Kilburn Times*, 23 June 1950).
[95] Ibid. gen. files, music; ibid. Wood F 37/1.
[96] *The Times*, 17 Mar. 1956.
[97] Grange Mus., 1 A 2 (*Municipal Jnl.* 23 June 1961); Brent L.B. *Music Societies* (leaflet 1976).
[98] Grange Mus., biog. files, groups.
[99] Willesden boro. *Local Community Svces. 1933*).
[1] Grange Mus., gen. files, parks and gdns.; *The Times*, 30 Mar. 1916.
[2] *Kelly's Dir. Kilburn* (1917–18); Grange Mus., gen. files, drama.
[3] Grange Mus., gen. files, *W. Willesden Cit.*
[4] Willesden boro. *Local Community Svces. 1933*.
[5] Grange Mus., gen. files, drama.
[6] Ibid. 1 A 2 (*Municipal Jnl.* 23 June 1961).
[7] Ibid. (*Willesden Mercury*, 29 Oct. 1965); ibid. gen. files, music.
[8] Thorne, *Environs*, 697–9; Grange Mus., Wood F 37/1; *The Times*, 18 May 1912. For political societies, below, local govt.
[9] Grange Mus., gen. files, Cricklewood.
[10] Ibid. Willesden Soc., Willesden Local History Soc.
[11] Ibid., immigrants (*Immigrants in London*, 1964); Brent L.B. *Social Clubs* (leaflet 1977).
[12] Grange Mus., Wood F 19 (sale cat. 1/32A); below, prot. nonconf.

[13] Thorne, *Environs*, 697–9; *Kelly's Dir. Mdx.* (1890).
[14] Grange Mus., gen. files, music; *Kelly's Dir. Mdx.* (1890).   [15] Grange Mus., Wood F 18.
[16] Ibid. gen. files, courts.
[17] All Souls Coll., uncat. material, agent's reps. 1899.
[18] Inf. from Grange Mus.
[19] *Kelly's Dir. Kilburn* (1917–18).
[20] Morris, *Willesden Surv.* 12.
[21] Grange Mus., gen. files, Harlesden Memorial hall; ibid. 1 A 2 (*Willesden Mercury*, 5 Nov. 1965); *The Times*, 8 Sept. 1923.
[22] e.g. Willesden choral assoc. at Willesden high school in 1884: Grange Mus., gen. files, music.
[23] *Willesden Civic Review*, Apr. 1963.
[24] Grange Mus., gen. files, theatres; photo. files, High St., Harlesden (NL 1007); ibid. 1 A 2 (*Willesden Chron.* 28 Sept. 1956).   [25] *The Times*, 15 Jan. 1909.
[26] Grange Mus., 2 A 1 ('Street Names').
[27] Inf. on cinemas based on *Kelly's Dir. Kilburn* (1917–18); *Kelly's Dir. Mdx.* (1926); *Kelly's Dir. Lond.* (1947, 1959, 1964, 1975); Morris, *Willesden Surv.* map 30; Willesden boro. *Local Community Svces. 1933*.
[28] Grange Mus., gen. files, *Willesden Chron.* (Suppl. 5 Mar. 1937). The building survived in 1980: inf. from curator of Grange Mus.
[29] Marked on O.S. Map 1/2,500, Mdx. XVI. 7 (1935 edn.).

Road, Harlesden, in 1972,[30] and the New Palace and the Pavilion, both in Chamberlayne Road, Kensal Rise, by 1975.

The Empire, later called the Granada, had opened at the north end of Church Road by 1926. It closed c. 1962 and by 1978 had become a bingo hall, used by Granada social club.[31] The Ritz opened in Neasden Lane in 1932 and closed in 1971.[32] The State cinema, opened at nos. 195-9 High Road, Kilburn, in 1937 with seating for 4,000, the largest cinema in the British Isles. It contained two cinemas in 1978.[33] The Odeon, Craven Park, Harlesden, opened in 1937, had closed by 1972, and reopened in 1977 as the Roxy theatre, a popular music centre seating 1,600.[34] The Envoy Repertory cinema at no. 399 Kilburn High Road had opened by 1947 and closed by 1959. The Classic cinema had opened by 1959 at no. 405 Kilburn High Road and remained in 1980.

The *Kilburn Times* was founded as an independent weekly newspaper in 1867 by Willesden Press Association Ltd. and taken over in 1892 by the North Western Printing and Publishing Association Ltd.[35] In 1877 the same owners produced the *Willesden Chronicle and Herald*, also an independent weekly, which changed its name in 1964 to the *Willesden and Brent Chronicle*.[36] Both papers were still published in 1980. The *Queen's Park Advertiser*, a progressive weekly printed in Harrow Road, flourished from 1881 to 1965. There were several short-lived newspapers in Kilburn in the 1880s: the *Kilburn and Queen's Park Post, Kilburn Free Press*, and *Kilburn News*, all published in 1882-3, and the *Kilburn Post*, published in 1886-7. Other papers were the *Willesden Advertiser* (1884) and the *Willesden Herald*, from 1893 the *Willesden Times* (1884-94). The Harrow Observer group, printing in Harrow, produced two versions for the Willesden area: the *Willesden Observer*, from 1897, and the *Cricklewood Observer* from 1900; both ceased between 1910 and 1920. The *Willesden Citizen*, a left-wing weekly printed at the Manor House, Kensal Green, was founded in 1901 and changed its name in 1965 to the *Willesden Mercury*, when it was published by Middlesex and West London Newspapers Ltd. It was absorbed into the *Willesden and Brent Chronicle* in 1975. The *Cricklewood and Willesden Advertiser*, one of the Hendon Advertiser series, was a left-wing weekly founded in 1910 and closed in the 1920s. The *Cricklewood News*, founded in 1911, had closed by 1920 and the *Willesden Call* flourished from 1913 to 1918. The *Comet and North West Startler*, from 1923 the *Comet and Bargain Seekers Guide*, circulated in south-east Willesden for almost a decade from

1922. The *Cricklewood Gazette*, an independent paper founded in 1923, had closed by 1940. The *Cricklewood Christmas Advertiser* existed from 1932 to 1936 and *Willesden Monthly Illustrated*, a monthly magazine, lasted only from January to December 1937.[37] There were several overtly political papers. The Conservative *West Willesden Advertiser* produced only four issues in 1929. Papers of the left included the Labour monthlies *West Willesden Citizen* or *Courier* (1930-9) and the *East Willesden Courier* (1934-9), the *Willesden Worker*, a Communist paper founded in 1949, and the *Willesden Clarion*, a London Co-operative Society quarterly first published in 1958 and flourishing in 1963. The borough council published the monthly *Willesden Civic Review* from 1956 until 1965, when it became *Brent Civic Review*.[38]

MANORS. A charter purporting to be a confirmation by King Athelstan c. 939 to St. Paul's monastery in London of estates including ten *mansae* at Neasden with Willesden is generally thought to be spurious.[39] Nevertheless St. Paul's certainly had estates there before the Conquest. A list attributed to c. 1000 of contributions of men for manning a ship includes, among other places belonging to the church of St. Paul, four men from Neasden and three from 'Forth tune', possibly to be identified with Fortune in Harlesden.[40] In 1086 the canons of St. Paul's held Willesden, assessed at 15 hides, the manor of Harlesden, assessed at 5 hides, a manor of 2 hides in Twyford held from them by a canon called Gueri, and 2 hides in Twyford said to be held of the king by a canon called Durand.[41]

The distinction between the lands of the bishop of London and those of the cathedral chapter of St. Paul's was established before the Conquest, and the beginnings of the prebendal system are apparent in the arrangements at Twyford. The system crystallized under bishop Maurice (1085-1107), the lists of prebendaries beginning mostly in the early 12th century.[42] Gueri's estate developed into the manor and parish of West Twyford.[43] Willesden parish, which included Durand's estate at Twyford and Harlesden manor, was divided between eight prebends: East Twyford in the south-west, Neasden in the north-west, Oxgate in the northeast, Harlesden in the centre and south, and Chambers, Brondesbury, Bounds, and Mapesbury in the east.

The manor or prebend of *BOUNDS* or *WILLESDEN* may have taken the former name from the position of its demesne lands, part in the south-east, on the boundary at Kilburn, and part

[30] Grange Mus., gen. files, cinemas.
[31] Ibid. photo. files, Church Rd. (NL 716).
[32] Ibid. Neasden (NL 2007).
[33] *Willesden Monthly Illus.* 5 June 1937.
[34] Ibid. 5 July, 5 Oct. 1937; Grange Mus., gen. files, cinemas.
[35] Inf. on newspapers based on *Willing's Press Guide* (1896, 1910, 1920, 1922 and subsequent edns.); B.L. Newspaper Cat.
[36] Grange Mus., gen. files, topog. (*Willesden and Brent Chron.* Suppl. 2 Feb. 1965).

[37] Bound copies in Grange Mus.
[38] Copies in Grange Mus.
[39] *Cart. Sax.* ed. Birch, ii, p. 451, no. 737; *A.-S. Charters*, ed. P. H. Sawyer, pp. 180-1, no. 453.
[40] *A.-S. Charters*, ed. A. J. Robertson, pp. 144-5, 389-90; inf. from English Place-Name Soc.
[41] *V.C.H. Mdx.* i, p. 121, nos. 20-3.
[42] *Domesday of St. Paul's* (Camd. Soc. [1st ser.], lxix), p. iv; *Early Charters of St. Paul's* (Camd. 3rd ser. lviii), pp. xviii-xxviii; C. N. L. Brooke and G. Keir, *Lond. 800-1216*, 340 sqq.   [43] Above, West Twyford.

Roundwood House *c.* 1890

Dollis Hill House *c.* 1917

WILLESDEN

St. Mary's Church in 1823

Kilburn National Schools *c.* 1860. The entrance to the Victoria Rifle Ground is on the right.

WILLESDEN

extending along Willesden Lane to Willesden Green.[44] The manor belonged to the prebendary of Bounds until it was vested in the Ecclesiastical Commissioners in 1848 under the Act of 1840.[45] It was sold in 1649 by the parliamentary commissioners to Ezechiel Tanner, a Willesden yeoman,[46] but reverted at the Restoration. In 1856 the commissioners purchased the leasehold interest in Bounds and Brondesbury, together with 42 a. of adjoining freehold land, from Lady Elizabeth Salusbury.[47] Apart from land sold to the railways and small sites given for churches and schools, the commissioners retained the freehold until after 1940 when it was sold piecemeal, mostly to the council and tenants of individual houses.[48]

In 1546 the prebendary leased Bounds for 21 years to Richard Fitzwilliams of Kilburn and his wife Elizabeth.[49] In 1563 Robert Weston, dean of Arches, obtained the reversion to Fitzwilliams's lease, which he sold to William Bovington of Kilburn, to whom a 50-year lease was made in 1567.[50] In 1612 the prebend was leased for three lives[51] to Richard Perrin (d. 1615) and held in 1623 by his widow Sarah and her second husband, Bevis Thewall, in spite of the claim of Perrin's daughter Lucy and her husband, John Anbourne.[52] Anbourne, to whom the prebend was leased in 1636, was still the lessee in 1649.[53]

By 1694 the lease was held by John Heath, a London distiller,[54] from whom it passed to Ann Heath (1711), Thomas Wood of Littleton (1720), John Miles of Hampstead (1721) and Sir John Lade, Bt., the Southwark brewer (1737).[55] On Lade's death in 1740 the lease, renewed in 1747 and 1778,[56] passed with his property in Finchley to John Inskip (d. 1759), who took the surname Lade and was created baronet. His son Sir John (d. 1838), a gambler,[57] sold the lease in 1784 to John Foster, coachmaker of Long Acre. Foster died in or soon after 1785.[58] In 1788 his trustees sold the lease to the widow of the judge Sir John Salusbury, Sarah (née Burroughs, d. 1804), who settled the estate in trust for her husband's nephew, the Revd. Lynch Salusbury (later Burroughs) for life. When Burroughs died in 1837 his daughter Elizabeth Mary, who had married her cousin Sir Thomas Robert Salusbury, Bt. (d. 1835), took possession of

Bounds together with neighbouring estates inherited under other settlements. In 1839 she bought out the interest of Charles Paulet, marquess of Winchester, who claimed as remainderman under Sarah's will.[59] In 1856 Lady (Elizabeth) Salusbury sold the leasehold interest to the Ecclesiastical Commissioners, who, increasingly from 1859, let the estate on 99-year building leases.[60]

In 1567 the lessee was given permission to build a dwelling house and by 1649 there was a six-room house.[61] It is to be identified with Kilburn Manor Farm or House in Edgware Road, which was marked on maps from the mid 18th century.[62] It survived as a brick farmhouse until engulfed by building in the 1860s.[63]

The manor or prebend of *BRONDESBURY*, *BRANDS*, or *BROOMSBURY* almost certainly derived its name from Brand (*c.* 1192–1215), listed as prebendary of Brownswood in Hornsey, evidently in confusion with Roger Brun (*c.* 1154), from whom Brownswood presumably took its name, listed as prebendary of Brondesbury.[64] The estate was held by the prebendaries until it was vested in the Ecclesiastical Commissioners in 1840 under the Act of that year.[65] In 1649 the parliamentary commissioners sold it to Ralph Marsh[66] but it reverted at the Restoration. The leasehold interest of Brondesbury was purchased with that of Bounds in 1856 and the Ecclesiastical Commissioners retained the freehold until the 1950s and 1960s.[67]

Forty-year leases were made of Brondesbury to William Peter, gentleman of London, in 1538 and to Thomas Young, a Willesden yeoman, in reversion in 1566.[68] In the first decade of the 17th century Young's widow Elizabeth and his daughter Christian lived at Brondesbury. In 1615 Christian's estranged husband, Henry Shugborow, brought an action for possession against the executors of the prebendary, who had re-entered because the rent had not been paid and had sublet to one Marsh, 'an ancient tenant'.[69] The estate was leased for lives in 1638 to Edward Roberts but Ralph Marsh, who in 1649 bought Brondesbury from the parliamentary commissioners, seems to have occupied the land.[70] Thomas and Ralph Marsh were described as of Brands in 1679 and 1694 respectively.[71] Ralph Marsh (d. 1709) was already in occupation

[44] In 1254 it was called Willesden Green: *Val. Norw.* ed. Lunt, 494–6.
[45] The Act vested estates in the Eccl. Commrs. on the vacancy of the prebend: 3 & 4 Vic. c. 113; *Lond. Gaz.* 18 Jan. 1859, p. 166. The names and dates of prebendaries, unless otherwise stated, are taken from Le Neve, *Fasti, 1066–1300, St. Paul's, Lond. 1300–1541; 1541–1857.*
[46] P.R.O., C 54/3479, no. 33.
[47] Guildhall MSS. CC. 30680–1.
[48] Ch. Com., Surveys S2, pp. 607, 862, 924–39.
[49] St. Paul's MS. C (Sampson), f. 176.
[50] Ibid. C (I Nowell), ff. 89, 212v.-214v.
[51] Leases for lives continued until 1856.
[52] P.R.O., C 2/Jas. I/A 7/14; C 3/330/22.
[53] Guildhall MS. 11816B; P.R.O., C 54/3479, no. 33.
[54] M.R.O., F 34/281–6; Guildhall MS. CC. 30609.
[55] Guildhall MSS. CC. 30607–8, 30610–7.
[56] St. Paul's MS. FB 3, prebendal leases 1721–96, ff. 121–5; Guildhall MS. CC. 30620.
[57] *V.C.H. Mdx.* vi. 61; G.E.C. *Baronetage*, v. 69–70; 109–10.
[58] Guildhall MSS. CC. 30621–3; M.R.O., Acc. 397/2.

[59] M.R.O., Acc. 397/2; Guildhall MSS. CC. 30624–5, 30657–9, 30674, 30697; Burke, *Land. Gent.* (1952), 2234; Grange Mus., Wood F 22, p. 35.
[60] Guildhall MSS. CC. 30680–1, 38338, 39501, 39518.
[61] St. Paul's MS. C (I Nowell), ff. 212v.-214v.; Guildhall MS. 11816B.
[62] e.g. Rocque, *Map of Lond.* (1746); Messeder Road Map (1749). Approx. on site of Cambridge Rd.
[63] Grange Mus., Wood F 26/11; Guildhall MS. CC. 39501; O.S. Map 1/2,500, Mdx. XVI. 8 (1865 edn.).
[64] For the catalogue, see C. N. L. Brooke, 'Composition of chapter of St. Paul's, 1086–1163', *Camb. Hist. Jnl.* x (1951), 111 sqq.
[65] *Lond. Gaz.* 18 Jan. 1859, pp. 164–5.
[66] P.R.O., C 54/3471, no. 2.
[67] Ch. Com., Surveys S2, pp. 596–9, 924–51.
[68] St. Paul's MS. C (Sampson), f. 48; Guildhall MS. 9531/13, f. 55.
[69] P.R.O., C 2/Jas. I/S 23/5. The Marsh fam. may have been undertenants for some time.
[70] Guildhall MS. CC. 11816B; P.R.O., C 54/3471, no. 2.
[71] P.R.O., C 6/231/34; M.R.O., F 34/281–6.

in 1708, when he received a lease for lives.[72] The estate was heavily mortgaged by the Marshes from 1725 and in 1749 Ralph Marsh sold the lease to John Stace, who obtained a new lease in 1757.[73] Stace sold the lease in 1765 to Joseph Gibson, the undertenant, who obtained a new lease in 1769[74] and whose widow Sarah and son Joseph tried to sell the estate in 1778.[75] In 1788 Lady (Sarah) Salusbury purchased the leasehold, and in 1799 she obtained a new lease for lives.[76] Brondesbury thereafter passed through the same ownership as Bounds, Lady Salusbury obtaining possession in 1842.[77]

A moated house existed by 1538.[78] It was described in 1649, probably with the remnants of the moat,[79] and was depicted in 1749 as a large, apparently L-shaped building with a central cupola.[80] It appears to have been rebuilt in the third quarter of the 18th century and by the time of Lady (Sarah) Salusbury was a three-storeyed villa with a central canted entrance bay rising the full height of the north front. A lower wing, presumably an addition, ran southward from the east end. In 1789 Humphry Repton landscaped the grounds of c. 10 a. and William Wilkins supplied drawings for a Gothic seat. In his 'Red Book' Repton commented favourably on the hilltop situation and enhanced the view towards London.[81] The house and some 23 a., increased by 1834 to 53 a., was occupied successively by Coutts (after 1821 Sir Coutts) Trotter, Bt. (1804–36), Lady Trotter (1836–40), Lady (Elizabeth) Salusbury (1840–3), and Charles Hambro (1843–9). The house was extended westward and a semicircular bay was added to the south front in the early 19th century.[82] By 1849 the surrounding estate had been reduced to 27 a. and the house, described in 1816 as being commodious although having 'no regularity of architectural character' and in 1822 as an 'elegant seat',[83] was three-storeyed.[84] It continued as a gentleman's residence under Mrs. Howard (1850–3), Henry Vallence (1853–6), Mrs. Geach (1856–61), John Coverdale (1862–7), and Thomas Brandon (1867–76),[85] and in 1877 was offered for sale with 52 a.[86] After remaining empty it was leased as a school, to Margaret Clark (1882–98) and Lucy Soulsby (1898–1915). In 1891 the school added a classroom and dormitory block on the east and subsequently a chapel

beyond that.[87] The house continued as a school until 1934 when, described as 'shabby-looking', it was bought by C. W. B. Simmonds, a builder, and was pulled down to make way for Manor Drive.[88]

The manor or prebend of *MAPESBURY* took its name from Walter Map, prebendary 1173–c. 1192. Except for the short period after 1649 when the parliamentary commissioners sold Mapesbury to George Perior, a London scrivener, it remained in the hands of the prebendaries until 1851, when it was vested in the Ecclesiastical Commissioners under the Act of 1840.[89] The freehold was sold in the 1950s, mostly to private tenants although the council bought up a block of land at Shoot-up Hill.[90]

Walter Map made leases in Willesden c. 1187,[91] and the estate was leased in the mid 15th century to John Dobue.[92] Sixty-year leases of Mapesbury were made in 1534 to Thomas Broke, merchant tailor of London, and in 1548 to Roger Gibbes, husbandman of Willesden.[93] Gibbes died in 1581, leaving the lease to trustees for his infant son Roger.[94]

In 1603 Nicholas Kempe of Finchley took a lease of Mapesbury for lives.[95] In 1628 the prebendary, John Bancroft, leased it to Richard Bancroft for lives.[96] A Richard Bancroft was outlawed in 1638 and in 1639 the lease passed to John Redwood, although James Noel, scrivener of London, who occupied the premises in 1649, claimed he did so by virtue of a sale made by Richard Bancroft in 1642.[97] After the Restoration the prebend was leased for lives to Thomas Willett of Fulham, whose widow Martha renewed the lease in 1675 and 1691.[98] Martha's daughter Martha, widow of Thomas Wightwick, renewed the lease in 1713 and her son Thomas was in possession by 1717. He had died by 1722 when the lease passed to his sister Martha and her husband, Charles White of the Middle Temple.[99] Charles renewed the lease in 1727; it was probably his son Charles, described as of Mapesbury, who renewed the lease in 1743.[1] By will proved 1752 he left the lease to his friend Henry Hyatt for life. Hyatt was described as of Mapesbury in 1754 but was dead by 1774 when the estate was leased to William White, a Lancashire merchant.[2] He renewed the lease in 1786 but he had already mortgaged it and in 1799 the lease was made to

[72] St. Paul's MS. FB 3, prebendal leases 1721–91, ff. 26–8.
[73] Guildhall MSS. CC. 1938, 30548–52, 30557–66.
[74] Ibid. CC. 30567–70, 30574.
[75] Ibid. CC. 30579, 30582–4. The descent in Lysons, *Environs*, iii. 614, is of the mortgage.
[76] Guildhall MSS. CC. 1941, 30585–7.
[77] Ibid. CC. 1943–4, 30653–6, 30680–1; Grange Mus., 4 I 10 (M.L.R. 1835/3/413).
[78] St. Paul's MS. C (Sampson), f. 48.
[79] Guildhall MS. 11816B; cf. B.L. Add. MS. 12546F.
[80] Messeder Road Map (1749).
[81] D. Stroud, *Humphry Repton* (1962), 39; pages from the Red Book are reproduced in Sotheby & Co.'s Sale Catalogue, 10 Apr. 1957, and J. Harris, *Cat. of Brit. Drawings for Archit. in American Collns.* (New Jersey, 1971).
[82] Grange Mus., photo. album 'Willesden'.
[83] Brewer, *Beauties of Eng. and Wales*, x (5), 349; *Eng. Topog.* (Gent. Mag. Libr.), vii. 287–9.
[84] Ch. Com., Surveys S1, pp. 592–603.
[85] Grange Mus., Wood F 31 (loose TS. listing occupiers).
[86] Ibid. Wood F 19 (sale cat. 1/22).
[87] Views and plans in L. H. M. Soulsby, *Brondesbury Ways*

(priv. print. 1916).
[88] Ibid. Wood F 31 (list); ibid. gen. files, Brondesbury Park; Briggs, *Mdx. Old and New*, 166–7.
[89] *Lond. Gaz.* 18 Jan. 1859, p. 166.
[90] Ch. Com., Surveys S2, pp. 604–6, 608–9, 623–30.
[91] B.L. Cott. Ch. xvi. 40.
[92] P.R.O., SC 6/1108/19.
[93] Ibid. E 40/1519; Guildhall MS. 9531/12, f. 123v.
[94] P.R.O., PROB 11/63 (P.C.C. 28 Darcy).
[95] St. Paul's MS. C (Overal), f. 121.
[96] Ibid. MS. C (Donne), ff. 140v.–141v.
[97] P.R.O., E 367/556; *Cal. S.P. Dom.* 1629–31, 353; 1635, 185; Guildhall MS. CC. 11816B. In 1649 it was not known whether Ric. Bancroft jr. was still alive.
[98] St. Paul's MSS. C (Sancroft 1670–7), f. 253 and v.; (Tillotson and Sherlock), ff. 66v.–67v.
[99] Ibid. MS. C (Godolphin 1700–15), f. 235 and v.; ibid. MS. FB 3, prebendal leases, ff. 68–69v., 72v.–74v.; M.L.R. 1717/1/5.
[1] St. Paul's MS. FB 3, prebendal leases, ff. 91v. sqq., 97v.–98v.; Guildhall MS. CC. 2196.
[2] Guildhall MSS. CC. 2197–8, 114541.

trustees for Charles, son of Thomas White, although William White still lived at Mapesbury.[3] William White died in 1805 and Charles and Peter White of Mapes House, presumably William's son and grandson, authorized the sale of the lease to Charles White of Manchester.[4] Charles renewed the lease in 1806 and by will proved 1811 left it to his grandson John White, who lived at Park Hall (Derb.) and renewed the lease in 1834 and 1842.[5] Capt. Thomas Linney White, described as John White's wife's son, inherited the lease in 1866, when he sold it to the Ecclesiastical Commissioners.[6] Building leases were granted from 1868.[7]

The mansion house was mentioned in 1534, and in 1548 the prebendary reserved part of it for his own use.[8] The house was neglected in the later 16th century, and in 1603 the lessee was instructed to rebuild at the prebendary's expense as much of the house as he thought necessary and to fill up the moat on three sides and make a new moat more distant from the house.[9] A detailed description was made of the house in 1649.[10] It was rebuilt in brick late in the 17th century and it had a two-storeyed main front of five bays, the central three surmounted by a wooden pediment which enclosed an oval attic window.[11] It was 'new and well built' in 1725 and 'substantial' in 1784.[12] There was a small formal garden on the south side in 1746.[13] Said in 1803 to be pleasantly situated on elevated land with a fine view of Hampstead,[14] the house became much dilapidated, and William Anderson, the Piccadilly jobmaster who subleased the estate from 1826, made improvements.[15] Edmund Yates, who lived there in 1863, described the house as a delightful place and made it the setting of his novel *Broken to Harness*.[16] Under William and John Anderson (1826–71) and Chester Foulsham (1872–1916) Mapesbury House was a horse-training centre, although the land surrounding it contracted with building; in 1925 the house was demolished.[17]

The manor or prebend of *CHAMBERS, CHAMBERLAYNE WOOD*, or *WILLESDEN GREEN* took its name from Richard de Camera, prebendary c. 1208–1215, and remained in the hands of the prebendaries until vested in the Ecclesiastical Commissioners in 1842 under the Act of 1840.[18] It was in lay hands for a short period from 1651 when the parliamentary com-

missioners sold it to Sir William Roberts.[19] The alternative name, Willesden Green, probably refers to the tenements held from the manor, many of which were at the green. The demesne, which was small, was concentrated in the south, at Kensal Green. The freehold was sold to private tenants mostly in 1958.[20]

In 1548 William Stacy, a London yeoman, took a lease of 48 a. of demesne for 50 years.[21] John Walbanck was the farmer in 1569, and in 1570 the whole prebend was leased to Robert Sandwith, another London yeoman, for 80 years.[22] In 1598, however, the court was held in the name of the prebendary and the demesne was divided between Henry Budder and John Wilde.[23] A lease for lives of the whole prebend was made in 1627 to Francis Roberts.[24] Another was made in 1694 and surrendered in 1717 when Thomas Steel, gentleman of Holborn, obtained a lease for lives. His wife Mary renewed the lease in 1731 and his nephew Robert sold his interest in 1753 to his son Thomas, who had sold it to William Godfrey the elder by 1755.[25] By will proved 1760 Godfrey left the lease to his son, William Godfrey of Paddington, who obtained a new lease in 1761 and died before 1801 when his son, William Godfrey of St. Marylebone, obtained a new lease, renewed in 1817.[26] Godfrey died c. 1823 and his interest passed to his friend John Harper. Trustees for the Harper family obtained a new lease in 1826, and in 1860 sold the leasehold to the Ecclesiastical Commissioners.[27]

A farmhouse had been built on Kilburn Lane by 1746[28] and it was probably the same house which was described in 1847 as of brick and tile and three storeys.[29] The London and Birmingham Railway, built in 1837, cut the farmhouse off from its lands, but the farm continued.[30] Building leases were being issued from 1884 but in 1920, when all the farmland had gone, the 18th-century farmhouse apparently remained.[31]

The manor or prebend of *HARLESDEN* was held by the prebendaries of Harlesden until it was vested in the Ecclesiastical Commissioners in 1840 and sold to the lessee in 1847.[32] It was in lay hands for a short period from 1651, when the parliamentary commissioners sold it to Sir William Roberts.[33] Before 1215 Gilbert de Plesseto, prebendary of Harlesden, granted all the houses on his prebend next the church and all

[3] Ibid. MSS. CC. 2200–1, 114537, 114541; Grange Mus., Wood F 21, p. 341.
[4] Guildhall MS. CC. 114541.
[5] Ibid. MSS. CC. 2205–6, 2212–14.
[6] Ibid. MSS. CC. 114549–53.
[7] Ibid. MSS. CC. 126232 sqq.
[8] P.R.O., E 40/1519; Guildhall MS. 9531/12, f. 123v.
[9] St. Paul's MS. C (Overal), f. 121.
[10] Ibid. MS. FB 3, prebendal leases, ff. 70 sqq.
[11] Grange Mus., photo. album 'Willesden'.
[12] St. Paul's MS. FB 3, prebendal bases, ff. 72v.–74v.; Guildhall MS. CC. 2199.
[13] Rocque, *Map of Lond.* (1746).
[14] Guildhall MS. CC. 2202.
[15] Ibid. CC. 2208, 114545; Grange Mus., photo. album 'Willesden'; Ch. Com., Surveys S2, pp. 607–22.
[16] Grange Mus., 1 A 2 (*The Star*, 8 Apr. 1915); ibid. Ball, 'Old Willesden', 76.
[17] Ibid. gen. files, Willesden Lane, Mapesbury Ho.; *Willesden Monthly Illus.* 5 Oct. 1937; Potter, *Story of Willesden*, 97; *Kilburn Dir.* (1871–2).
[18] *Lond. Gaz.* 18 Jan. 1859, p. 165.

[19] P.R.O., C 54/3583, no. 30.
[20] Ch. Com., Surveys S2, pp. 417, 940–7.
[21] Guildhall MS. 9531/12, f. 129v.
[22] Bodl. MS. D.D. All Souls c 124/82; St. Paul's MS. C (I Nowell), ff. 330v.–331v.
[23] St. Paul's MS. C (III Nowell), ff. 162v.–163.
[24] Guildhall MS. 11816B.
[25] St. Paul's MS. FB 3, prebendal leases 1721–96, ff. 28–30v.; Guildhall MS. CC. 1980; M.L.R. 1753/3/167; Grange Mus., Wood F 22, p. 72.
[26] Guildhall MS. CC. 1980–1; M.L.R. 1761/3/292; St. Paul's MS. FB 4, prebendal leases 1798–1834, ff. 71v.–77.
[27] Guildhall MSS. CC. 1985–6, 39214–17.
[28] Ibid. CC. 1978; Rocque, *Map of Lond.* (1746).
[29] Ch. Com., Surveys S2, pp. 411–20.
[30] Grange Mus., Wood F 22, f. 74; Guildhall MS. CC. 39214–16, 209236, 291245; P.R.O., HO 107/1700/135/3, f. 351v.; M.R.O., TA/WIL.
[31] Guildhall MSS. CC. 255561, 270143, 291245, 355996, 356001; O.S. Map 6", Mdx. XVI. NE. (1920 edn.).
[32] Ch. Com., Surveys S2, pp. 495, 500.
[33] P.R.O., C 54/3583, no. 30.

the land which his predecessor had possessed to Richard de Camera, prebendary of Chambers and rector.[34] As a result the demesne of Harlesden was reduced to Lords Croft (1a.) and 2 a. in the common fields and marsh. With a small allotment at inclosure in 1823, the total was 4 a.[35] The value of the manor lay in its lordship of the hamlet of Harlesden and when the manorial perquisites lapsed, as they seem to have done by Elizabeth I's reign, the small demesne was worth little.

The whole manor was leased for 21 years to Edmund Roberts in 1576.[36] In 1594 Francis Roberts took a lease for lives,[37] which in 1649 was held by his executor Sir William Roberts.[38] Sir William retained the lease after the Restoration, renewing it in 1661.[39] In 1674 Harlesden was leased to George Hill, probably as trustee, for Sir William Roberts, Bt.[40] The lease presumably formed part of the Harlesden estate which Roberts sold to Richard Taylor, a London vintner, to whom a new lease for lives was made in 1689.[41] Leases were renewed to Richard's son John in 1717, John's son John in 1729 and 1760, and the second John's son Richard in 1771.[42] Richard was still alive in 1824 but in 1835 the last of the three lives expired and a new lease for lives was made to John Belemore, gentleman of Harlesden green.[43] Belemore purchased the freehold at Harlesden green, which was still in the hands of his descendants in 1887, the open-field allotment then being held by the trustees of James Wright.[44]

A house was built on Lord's Croft at Harlesden green, in the junction between Harrow Road (Craven Park Road) and High Street, probably in the 17th century.[45] A two-roomed cottage in 1835, it was added to by John Belemore and in 1847 was a cottage of two storeys.[46] It was surrounded by building in 1887[47] and probably disappeared soon afterwards.

The manor or prebend of *OXGATE* belonged in theory to the prebendaries until it was vested in the Ecclesiastical Commissioners in 1843 under the Act of 1840.[48] In practice the prebendary's control may have been lost long before Oxgate was sold by the parliamentary commissioners to Sir William Roberts in 1651.[49] In 1691 the prebendary attempted to recover the manor, which he described as 300 a. in Willesden and Hendon, but Roberts successfully claimed that the Oxgate lands were small and impossible to distinguish from his own.[50] No prebendal leases

are recorded but the prebendary of Oxgate's lordship was acknowledged at inclosure in 1823, when 1 r. 27 p. at Edgware Road was allotted to him.[51] The Ecclesiastical Commissioners sold it to the Buckingham estate in 1860.[52]

The Willesden family had emerged as holders of Oxgate by 1425 and possibly earlier and although it is possible that they paid rent and acknowledged the overlordship of the prebendary, their title was treated as hereditary. Oxgate passed from Thomas Willesden (fl. 1389–1425)[53] to Bartholomew Willesden (fl. 1457–81)[54] and his son Thomas, who by will proved 1494 left his estate for his wife Joan for life and subsequent sale.[55] In 1495 Sir Thomas Frowyk sued the feoffees concerning Willesden's lands and in 1506 died seised of Oxgate manor.[56] Frowyk left the manor to his widow Elizabeth for life with remainder to his daughter Frideswide (d. 1528), wife of Sir Thomas Cheyney (d. 1559); through one of their three daughters, Anne (d. 1553) wife of Sir John Parrott, the manor seems to have been inherited by her son Thomas Parrott.[57] In 1587 he sold the manor to Francis Roberts, who in 1608 obtained from the prebendary a 21-year lease of the manorial perquisites and quitrents.[58] Oxgate thus became part of the extensive Roberts estates.[59]

The house of Bartholomew Willesden at Oxgate was recorded in 1472.[60] It was probably the easternmost of the three Oxgate farms in existence by 1587.[61]

The manor or prebend of *NEASDEN* belonged to the prebendaries until it was vested in the Ecclesiastical Commissioners in 1845 under the Act of 1840.[62] The prebendary was allotted ½ a. at inclosure in 1823, which was sold to the lessee Henry Hall in 1860.[63] A 30-year lease made in 1544 to Ursula, widow of Michael Roberts, referred to lands, rents, and courts,[64] and a 21-year lease to Francis Roberts in 1624 listed lands, tenements, and woods, but there is no evidence that there was any demesne. On inquiry in 1649 'the said lands were not yet discovered', and there was no claim for demesne when Sir William Roberts purchased the manor from the parliamentary commissioners in 1651.[65] Sir William Roberts, Bt., obtained a 15-year lease in 1690.[66] Manorial rights had probably lapsed by that date and there were no further leases.

The manor or prebend of *EAST TWYFORD* belonged in theory to the prebendaries from the time of the earliest, Durand, a canon who held 2

[34] St. Paul's MS. A 39/1369; below.
[35] M.R.O., EA/WIL, nos. 410–11, 204, 407.
[36] St. Paul's MS. C (I Nowell), f. 456v.
[37] Ibid. (III Nowell), f. 14.
[38] Guildhall MS. 11816B.
[39] St. Paul's MS. C (Nicholas), f. 40.
[40] Ibid. MS. C (Sancroft), ff. 226v.–227.
[41] Ibid. MS. C (Tillotson and Sherlock), f. 19; M.R.O., Acc. 621/Add. 7–8.
[42] St. Paul's MSS. C (Godolphin), f. 106; C (Hare), f. 143 and v.; Guildhall MSS. CC. 2038–9.
[43] M.R.O., Acc. 891/2/5/615; Guildhall MS. CC. 2042.
[44] M.R.O., TA/WIL, nos. 208, 395.
[45] Grange Mus., Wood F 26/35; Rocque, *Map of Lond.* (1746).
[46] Ch. Com., Surveys S2, pp. 495–501.
[47] M.R.O., TA/WIL.
[48] 3 & 4 Vic. c. 113; *Lond. Gaz.* 23 Aug. 1850, p. 2296.
[49] P.R.O., C 54/3583, no. 30.
[50] Ibid. C 6/271/54.

[51] M.R.O., EA/WIL.
[52] Ibid. Acc. 262/40, pt. 2 (1860).
[53] *Cal. Pat.* 1388–92, 123; P.R.O., E 40/10379.
[54] Bodl. MS. D.D. All Souls c 123/68, 123/70; Grange Mus., Wood F 30, f. 197.
[55] P.R.O., C 142/20/4; ibid. PROB 11/10 (P.C.C. 16 Vox).
[56] Ibid. C 1/201/72; C 142/20/4.
[57] Ibid. C 142/119, no. 114.
[58] Ibid. CP 25(2)/172/29 Eliz. I Hil.; Guildhall MS. 11816B.
[59] Below.
[60] Grange Mus., Wood F 30 f. 197.
[61] i.e. M.R.O., EA/WIL, no. 8. For the later history of the three estates, see below, other est.
[62] *Lond. Gaz.* 28 Aug. 1860, p. 3161.
[63] M.R.O., EA/WIL; Ch. Commrs. Surveys S2, pp. 631–3.
[64] St. Paul's MS. C (Sampson), f. 54.
[65] Guildhall MS. 11816B; P.R.O., C 54/3583, no. 30.
[66] St. Paul's MS. C (Tillotson and Sherlock), ff. 41v.–43.

hides there in 1086.[67] In 1523 the manor was said to be held in socage of the prebend of Twyford,[68] but in 1620 it was not known of whom it was held[69] and there was no further evidence of any connexion with the prebendary.

From an early date the manor seems to have been in the hands of powerful laymen who established a hereditary title and treated it as an independent lay estate. The Cornhills, of whom William was described in 1305 as of East Twyford, were dealing in land there in 1294.[70] Richard of Cornhill acquired a messuage, land, and rent in 1306 from William de Kele,[71] which he settled in 1325.[72] Richard was succeeded by his son John (fl. 1351–9) and granddaughter Alice, who married successively Henry Frowyk and Thomas Charlton.[73] In 1412 Alice, then a widow for the second time, was taxed at £5 in Willesden, the highest assessment in the parish.[74] By 1454 her son Henry Frowyk held property described as formerly Thomas Charlton's and previously William de Kele's.[75] If the estate was at least partly in East Twyford, it had passed by 1474 to Sir John Elrington who was then described as lord of the place of Twyford.[76] In 1479 he acquired a house and land from Richard Heyward and his wife Isabel, heir of John Twyford.[77] The manor descended in the direct male line from Sir John Elrington (d. 1488) to Simon (d. 1500), Thomas (d. 1523), Thomas (d. 1566), and Edward.[78] In 1579 Edward sold the manor to Richard Paramour, merchant tailor, and his wife Mary.[79] Paramour sold it in 1585 to Richard Payne (d. 1605) and his wife Margery, and in 1599 Payne sold it to Sir Robert Lee.[80] Hugh Lee died seised of the manor in 1620[81] and his son Robert granted it in 1640 to John Hooker,[82] apparently by way of mortgage.[83] John Hooker left the property by will dated 1659 to his daughter Ann (d. 1665) for life with remainder to his brother Sir William (d. 1697),[84] in whose family it remained until at least 1732.[85] By 1772 it was in the hands of Charles Brett, who had married the Hooker heiress. Charles (d. 1799) devised it to trustees for his nephew John (d. 1819) and John's son Charles.[86] At inclosure in 1823 the trustees were allotted ½ a. as lords of East Twyford manor and they exchanged c. 140 a. in the south-west corner of Willesden for

an estate in Acton with Thomas Willan of West Twyford.[87] In 1887 the trustees of George Arthur Brett possessed c. 178 a. The Willan estate followed the descent of West Twyford, c. 134 a. being held by Thomas Willan Douglas-Willan in 1887.[88]

In 1474 Sir John Elrington had a house at Twyford, he and his wife being granted indults for portable altars,[89] and it may have been at the house that they built the chapel where in 1525 Sir Thomas More's two daughters were married.[90] The house was described as decayed c. 1523[91] and Thomas Elrington was apparently in the middle of rebuilding it when he died in 1566.[92] Norden referred to the moated house built by the Elringtons but located it at Neasden.[93] The house was repaired in the 1640s and assessed for 18 hearths in 1664, when it was occupied by William Chute.[94] It is presumably identifiable with Lower Place Farm, depicted in 1765 beside Barretts green on Acton Lane as a group of buildings surrounded by drainage channels, presumably the remnants of the 16th-century moat,[95] and renamed Grange Farm in the late 19th century. In 1935 the site was used for a sports ground.

Willesden *RECTORY*, appropriated to the dean and chapter of St. Paul's, may have come to be regarded as the chief manor of the seven prebendal manors: in 1552 the dean and chapter were presented as chief lords of Willesden Green,[96] in 1847 the Willesden estate of St. Paul's was described as seven manors within the lordship and parsonage of Willesden,[97] and in the 19th century the main rectorial farm was called Willesden manor.[98] In 1181 the dean and chapter farmed the rectory to Germanus the clerk,[99] referred to as parson of Willesden.[1] Germanus may have been succeeded by William the clerk, possibly surnamed Pastorel.[2] Before 1215 Richard de Camera, prebendary of Chambers from 1200, was rector of Willesden,[3] and in 1217 the dean and chapter leased Willesden church and all its property to the prebendary of Harlesden for life.[4] In 1248 the bishop confirmed the income from the church to the use of the resident canons[5] but soon afterwards, c. 1250, the dean and chapter leased it, except for the vicarage, for life to the dean, Henry of Cornhill,[6] and c. 1275,

[67] *V.C.H. Mdx.* i, p. 121, no. 20.
[68] P.R.O., C 142/81, no. 229.
[69] Ibid. C 142/396, no. 154.
[70] Ibid. CP 25(1)/148/34, no. 237; *Cal. Close,* 1302–7, 327.
[71] P.R.O., CP 25(1)/148/38, no. 333.
[72] Ibid. CP 25(1)/149/52, no. 328.
[73] *Cal. Close,* 1349–54, 357, 361; Bodl. MS. D.D. All Souls c 123/48; Grange Mus., Wood F 24, p. 202.
[74] *Feudal Aids,* vi. 488.
[75] W.A.M. 17018.   [76] *Cal. Papal Reg.* xiii. 379.
[77] P.R.O., CP 25(1)/152/98, no. 69.
[78] Ibid. C 1/125/59–62; C 1/546/52; C 142/81, no. 229; ibid. PROB 11/48 (P.C.C. 25 Crymes, f. 420); T. Streatfield, *Excerpta Cantiana* (1836), pedigree of Elrington.
[79] P.R.O., CP 25(2)/172/21 & 22 Eliz. Mic.; CP 40/1367, rot. 436.
[80] Ibid. CP 25(2)/173/41 & 42 Eliz. Mic.
[81] Ibid. C 142/396, no. 154.
[82] Lysons, *Environs,* iii. 616; Grange Mus., Wood F 30, p. 292.
[83] P.R.O., C 10/65/88.
[84] Ibid. C 10/96/117; C 10/170/45.
[85] M.L.R. 1732/5/674.

[86] Lysons, *Environs,* iii. 616–17; Grange Mus., Wood F 30, pp. 292 sqq.
[87] M.R.O., EA/WIL.
[88] Ibid. TA/WIL.
[89] *Cal. Papal Reg.* xiii. 379.
[90] Inf. from Lady Norrington (Haddenham, Bucks.; writing biog. of More's 2nd wife). More was related to the Elringtons and was executor of the will of Thos. (d. 1523).
[91] P.R.O., C 1/546, no. 52.
[92] Ibid. PROB 11/48 (P.C.C. 25 Crymes, f. 420).
[93] B.L. Harl. MS. 570, f. 26.
[94] M.R.O., MR/TH/3, m. 5; P.R.O., C 10/96/117.
[95] Grange Mus., Wood F 21 (map of 1765).
[96] Hist. MSS. Com. 39, *15th Rep. II,* p. 257.
[97] Ch. Com., Surveys S2, p. 845.
[98] Grange Mus., Wood F 19 (sale cat. 1/7–8).
[99] *Domesday of St. Paul's,* 152.
[1] St. Paul's MS. A 29/335.
[2] Ibid. MSS. A 29/333–4.
[3] Ibid. MS. A 39/1369.
[4] Ibid. MS. A 29/331.
[5] Ibid. MS. A 35/943.
[6] St. Paul's MS. A 39/1364.

except for the advowson of the vicarage, during his canonry to Alan of Morton, a minor canon, who enlarged the glebe by purchase.[7] From before 1313 until 1502 the rectory was leased to members of the chapter, for life or during office.[8]

By 1504 the Paulet family, in which the lease of the rectory became hereditary, appears to have been in possession.[9] Thomas Paulet (fl. 1494) was described as rector and John Paulet was farmer in 1536.[10] In 1549 the dean and chapter made a lease directly to John Paulet, and from 1600 leases for 21 years were granted every seven years to his grandson John Paulet (d. 1630) and the latter's son John (d. 1657),[11] who bought the freehold from the parliamentary commissioners in 1650. His son John renewed the lease after the Restoration,[12] and that John or his son John, who died without issue, renewed it again in 1668 and 1677.[13] In 1685 the lease was renewed to Francis Brende, husband of Elizabeth, sister and heir of the last John Paulet.[14]

Brende had died by 1706, when the lease was renewed to Richard Lake in whom his estate was vested.[15] Lake's estate was purchased by Charles Eaton (d. 1735), whence it descended to his daughter Maria (d. 1765), who married General Charles Otway (d. 1764), and her daughters Caroline (wife of John Douglas John St. Leger) and Sophia (wife of William Wynyard).[16] Both moieties had passed by 1790 to Sophia's daughter, Maria Caroline Wynyard, who continued to renew the lease until 1811.[17] In 1812 William Coleman, in whom Maria's interest was vested, put the estate up for sale[18] and in 1818 a new lease was made to Cobbett Derby of the Inner Temple, who renewed it until 1868.[19] Probably long before then the main rectorial farm was being leased separately: Dr. Thomas Hughes (d. 1833) of Berkshire was in possession by 1814,[20] the estate passed to his son John, and before 1872 the trustees of Hughes's will purchased the reversion in fee simple.[21]

In 1181 the rectory included all tithes, great and small, except those from the demesnes of certain ecclesiastical lords, including the 40 a. of demesne of the nuns of Kilburn.[22] About 1195

the bishop of London assigned to the mastership of the schools the tithes of 68 a. in Wormholt and Harlesden.[23] The great tithes were leased separately from the rest of the rectory c. 1245,[24] but the lease of the rectory c. 1275 to Alan de Morton included the great tithes,[25] as did later leases of the rectory. A statement in 1694 that some lands in Willesden paid tithes to the rector of Chelsea probably resulted from the fact that the lands belonged to All Souls College, whose estate extended into Chelsea.[26] In 1805 an agreement was reached for the composition of tithes,[27] and in 1811 the dean and chapter leased the tithes in 11 separate parcels.[28] Under the Inclosure Act of 1815 corn rents totalling £1,293 were substituted for rectorial tithes and leases were made in 1825 and every 7 years thereafter of corn rents, on the same basis as the leases of 1811.[29] In 1887 the corn rents were converted into rent charges of £931.[30]

The rectory house stood beside the churchyard c. 1249.[31] About 1275 the lessee was responsible for the repair of the buildings.[32] The house was assessed for seven hearths in 1664.[33] With c. 11 a. at Church End it was leased separately from 1804.[34] The house had apparently been rebuilt by 1868,[35] and in 1887 was known as the Rookery.[36] It was demolished in the 1890s to make way for building.[37]

MALORIES was a sub-manor, paying quit-rent to the prebends of Oxgate, Chambers, Brondesbury, Bounds, and Harlesden and, for lands south of the Willesden border, to the lords of Wormholt and Chelsea.[38] The name presumably derived from Peter Malorre, who in 1310 sold a messuage, a carucate of arable, 3 a. of meadow, and 3s. 10d. rent in Willesden to John de Westcote.[39] In 1333 William of Colriche, Richard of Hameldon, Laurence of Papham, John of Fulguardeby, and their wives, respectively Alice, Sibyl, Alice, and Margery, who may have been coheirs, sold a messuage and carucate to Robert of Wodehouse.[40] In 1344 Wodehouse, who was archdeacon of Richmond and treasurer of the Exchequer, held a messuage, land, and rent in Willesden of the dean and chapter of St. Paul's,

[7] Ibid. MSS. A 29/336, 380-6, 397; A 30/444.
[8] St. Paul's MSS. A 39/1355-61.
[9] John Paulet's land in Hungerhill abutted that of All Souls Coll.: Bodl. MS. D.D. All Souls c 125/4. The college and parsonage had adjoining land there in 1621: W.A.M. 17039. For the descent of the Paulets, see Grange Mus., Wood F 24, p. 241.
[10] St. Paul's MS. A 56; P.R.O., PROB 11/10 (P.C.C. 16 Vox, will of Thos. Willesden; Bodl. MS., Rawl. B 389B, ff. 134-8.
[11] St. Paul's MSS. C (III Nowell), ff. 33, 199v.-200v.; (Overall), f. 132 and v.; (Carey), ff. 337v.-338v., 370, 465v.-466; (Donne), ff. 53v.-54v., 160; (Wynnyff), f. 377; (Nicholas), f. 106v.
[12] P.R.O., C 54/3474, no. 10; St. Paul's MS. C (Nicholas), f. 106v.
[13] St. Paul's MS. C (Sancroft), ff. 248, 312 and v.
[14] Ibid. MS. C (Stillingfleet), ff. 162-164v.
[15] Ibid. MS. C (Godolphin 1707-15), ff. 198, 223v.-225v.; (1715-20), ff. 302v.-303v.; (Hare 1727-33), ff. 39-40v.
[16] Lysons, *Environs*, iii. 620; Grange Mus., Wood F 24, p. 204; Grange Mus., MS. 22.
[17] M.L.R. 1790/8/55-6; Guildhall MSS. CC. 169269-73.
[18] Grange Mus., MS. 31.
[19] Guildhall MSS. CC. 169274-80.
[20] All Souls Coll., uncat. material, map of Willesden 1814; Guildhall MSS. CC. 169235, 169242.

[21] Guildhall MSS. CC. 169240; 169245; Grange Mus., Wood F 19 (sale cat. 1/7).
[22] *Domesday of St. Paul's*, 152.
[23] *Early Charters of St. Paul's*, 218.
[24] St. Paul's MS. A 39/1365.
[25] Ibid. MS. A 29/336.
[26] B.L. Add. MS. 15609, f. 12.
[27] Guildhall MSS. CC. 207219.
[28] M.R.O., Acc. 262/40 (inclosure claims 1816); Guildhall MSS. CC. 169241, 169249, 169253, 169256, 169281, 169284A.
[29] M.R.O., EA/WIL; Guildhall MSS. CC. 169231-61, 169284. [30] M.R.O., TA/WIL.
[31] 'Visitations of churches belonging to St. Paul's', *Camd. Misc.* ix (Camd. Soc. N.S. liii), 3.
[32] St. Paul's MS. A 29/336.
[33] M.R.O., MR/TH/3, m. 5.
[34] Grange Mus., 4 I 7 (M.L.R. 1804/3/667).
[35] Guildhall MS. CC. 169193A-169198; plan of 1868 with inclosure map.
[36] M.R.O., TA/WIL, nos. 290-2. For a photo. of the Rookery, Grange Mus., Wood F 26/41.
[37] O.S. Map 6", Mdx. XVI. NW. (1894-6 edn.); Grange Mus., Map of Willesden U.D 1901.
[38] Bodl. MS. D.D. All Souls c 124/81; c 268/213.
[39] P.R.O., CP 25(1)/149/41, no. 51.
[40] Ibid. CP 25(1)/150/56, no. 90.

a carucate at Kensal Green possibly of the lord of Chelsea, and 30 a. called Forstersland of the bishop of London as of Fulham manor.[41] Before 1354 William of Northwell, clerk, conveyed apparently the same estate, described as in Willesden, Harlesden, and Chelsea, to Sir Henry de Burghersh whose kinsman Sir Bartholomew de Burghersh conveyed it in 1354 to John Pecche, a Londoner.[42] Pecche died in 1380 seised of the reversion of Malories manor which he had granted for life to Sir Robert Aston. He was succeeded by his son Sir William,[43] whose son John leased the estate for life to William and Catherine Constantine in 1410.[44] In 1411 Pecche granted the reversion of Malories to Ellis Davy, a London mercer, to whom the Costantines conveyed their interest in 1413.[45] In 1432 Davy conveyed the manor to William Crowmere and other London citizens,[46] who in 1438 conveyed it to Thomas Chichele and other trustees of All Souls College.[47]

The demesne lands of Malories consisted of a block of land at Kensal Green, stretching northward in two prongs towards Willesden Green and Harlesden. Cricklewood probably formed part of the estate.[48]

The grant in 1438 included other estates. Robert Hubbard and others had granted unspecified lands to Thomas Fylkes and Thomas Daunt, London citizens who in 1422 granted them to Sir Thomas Charlton, Thomas and Henry Frowyk, and others, whence, in 1433, they were conveyed to William Crowmere and other trustees.[49] Other estates had been conveyed in 1432 to the trustees: Robert Algar granted a house and croft at Harlesden and strips in the open fields which had belonged to his father Edward before 1415;[50] Ellis Davy granted a house and croft at Willesden Green and scattered strips in the open fields and marsh, granted to him in 1415 by Robert Algar's brother John, husband of Agnes, heir of John and Alice Knight;[51] Laurence Hierde and others granted a house and crofts at Harlesden which they had acquired from John Noreys.[52]

The resulting estate, estimated at 453 a. in 1599 and 491 a. in 1823,[53] was normally leased except for the woods, which were kept in hand by the college. The estate, called Harlesden and Willesden, was initially leased to two people, probably reflecting its division into two farms.[54]

The farmers from 1471 apparently held both Harlesden and Willesden Green.[55] A lease was made in 1538 to William Walker, fellow of All Souls, and to successive members of the Shepherd family, possibly as beneficial lessees, from 1543 to 1568.[56] By 1572 the lease was held by John Franklin, in whose family it remained for almost a century.[57] John Franklin (d. 1596) of Little Stanmore left the lease of Harlesden to his son John.[58] The lease passed in a direct line from John (d. c. 1605) to Richard (d. 1615) of Dollis Hill, Sir John (d. 1647), and Sir Richard (d. 1685), who relinquished it c. 1668.[59] Dr. George Rogers was the lessee in 1669 and 1694; in 1716 his widow Elizabeth and son George sold the lease to a Mr. Peters and in 1747 William Peters conveyed it to William Godfrey.[60] A William Godfrey continued to lease the whole estate until 1826 and his executor until 1828.[61] After 1828 leases were made directly to the farmers. From the late 19th century the estates were developed, mainly for housing. The college retained the freehold until most of it was sold to the occupying lessees in the 1960s; some freeholds belonged to the college in 1980.[62]

The messuage conveyed by Peter Malorre in 1310[63] has not been located, and no manor house was mentioned in the conveyances of the following century.

MIDDLETONS sub-manor[64] was built up in the late 13th century by John of Middleton, a London draper, who made a number of purchases, mainly of land held from Neasden and Oxgate prebends. In 1295 he bought a messuage, a mill, 208 a., and 6s. rent in Willesden and Hendon from William of Breadstreet and John and Alice of Buneney (or Boveney), which they had acquired from Simon Goddard, a London citizen.[65] Middleton's other purchases between 1295 and 1322 were small, usually of open-field strips and quitrents, and were in the northern part of the parish, mostly in Neasden.[66] By 1335 he had died and at least some of his lands had passed to his son Thomas. There was another John of Middleton at the same time and from 1365 to 1388 the estate was held by William, son and heir of John Middleton.[67] William Middleton had apparently died by 1396 when the estate, described as a messuage, 500 a. of land, 10 a. of meadow, 30 a. of wood, and £1 6s. 8d. rent in Willesden and Hendon, was divided between

---

[41] *V.C.H. Mdx.* iv. 204; P.R.O., C 143/272, no. 14.
[42] Bodl. MSS. D.D. All Souls c 123/1–2.
[43] P.R.O., C 136/10, no. 8.
[44] Bodl. MS. D.D. All Souls c 123/4; S. Thrupp, *Merchant Class of Medieval Lond.* (1948), 359.
[45] Bodl. MS. D.D. All Souls c 123/5, 9–12.
[46] Ibid. c 123/13–19.
[47] Ibid. c 123/20, 38–9; c 76/89; *Cal. Pat.* 1441–6, 19–20; *Reg. Chichele* (Cant. & York Soc.), i, p. lvi.
[48] Bodl. MSS. D.D. All Souls c 123/74; c 124/81; c 268/213.
[49] Ibid. c 123/24–5. [50] Ibid. c 123/22–3.
[51] Ibid. c. 123/22–3, 45–54, 58–62.
[52] Ibid. c 123/64–6.
[53] All Souls Coll., Hovenden maps II/18; M.R.O., EA/WIL.
[54] Bodl. MSS. D.D. All Souls c 124/78, 80; c 125/1–2; c 268/213, 216; c 324.
[55] Ibid. c 125/3, 5; c 324–5.
[56] Ibid. c 125/8–11; c 326.

[57] Ibid. c 326.
[58] P.R.O., PROB 11/87 (P.C.C. 19 Drake).
[59] Bodl. MSS. D.D. All Souls c 329; c 125/17–18, 23–30; b 19/1–20; b 20/23–5; P.R.O., PROB 11/126 (P.C.C. 70 Rudd); Bodl. MS. Rawl. B 389B, ff. 134–8; for the Franklin fam. tree, Grange Mus., Wood F 24, pp. 212–13.
[60] Bodl. MSS. D.D. All Souls a 18/54–70; b 20/26–39; M.R.O., F 34/281–6; M.L.R. 1712/5/20; M.L.R. 1716/2/55–6; M.L.R. 1747/1/124.
[61] Bodl. MSS. D.D. All Souls a 20; a 30; a 81; a 94–7; c 245/34 h, p, s.
[62] Inf. from Daniel Smith, Briant & Done (college agents).
[63] P.R.O., CP 25(1)/149/41, no. 51.
[64] Descent given in B.L. Stowe MS. 862, ff. 49–50v.
[65] P.R.O., CP 25(1)/148/35, no. 258; ibid. E 40/7548.
[66] P.R.O., E 40/6655, 6800, 6806, 6809, 6874–5, 7871, 7890–4, 7906, 8008, 11585, 11588, 11623, 11648, 11844–5, 12065; E 42/83; ibid. CP 25(1)/149/47, no. 202; M.R.O., Acc. 262/42, pt. 1 (Chandos estate map 1787).
[67] P.R.O., E 40/7883, 10381; *Cal. Close*, 1364–8, 190.

Alice and Sarah, daughters and coheirs of William Willesden[68] and their husbands William Benyngton (or Bedyngton) and Robert Curson or Betele (d. 1409), respectively draper and mercer of London.[69] Curson purchased Benyngton's moiety.

Robert's son, Robert Curson, clerk, who was one of the largest landowners in Willesden, assessed in 1412 for £3 6s. 8d., continued to consolidate the estate by acquisition and exchange in Neasden.[70] The estate was probably held by trustees for Curson[71] and c. 1440 they granted it to John Gloucester or Jones, clerk of the Exchequer, and others, to whom all rights were relinquished in 1448.[72] Gloucester, who in 1442 was described as lord of many lands in Willesden, settled the estate in 1468 on himself for life with remainder to his daughter Joan and her husband John Staunton.[73] Staunton and his wife were in possession by 1471; in 1489 Joan and her second husband Thomas Barley had to pay the hitherto lapsed rents and services due to Neasden prebend. Thomas's son Robert was in 1510 in possession of the messuage called Middletons and 300 a. held in socage for which he paid rent to Neasden prebend.[74] In 1563 Richard Barley sold the estate, consisting of 5 houses, land, and rent in Willesden and Hendon, to Edmund Roberts.[75] It thereafter merged with the other Roberts estates but was described in 1632 as Middletons manor.[76]

Robert Curson, clerk, replaced the house bought by John of Middleton in 1295 with a new house, called Bedewell Hall c. 1420.[77] It was presumably there that in 1442 John Gloucester was granted an indult to have a portable altar.[78]

KINGSHOLT (Kensal) manor was a submanor of 240 a. held in the 1270s by Thomas de Basing (d. 1275), a minor, but seized by Sir Robert de Bruce. Its lands probably formed part of Malories.[79]

OTHER ESTATES. In 1468 John Careley granted to John Roberts and others a house and ·land in Neasden which he had acquired in 1454 and 1465. In 1480 Roberts and the others, at Careley's request, enfeoffed William Page of Harlesden, who in 1495 conveyed that and other property to trustees for Margaret, countess of Richmond; in 1506 she was licensed to alienate it to WESTMINSTER ABBEY.[80] In 1651 the parliamentary commissioners sold the property to Sir William Roberts but Westminster recovered it after the Restoration and retained it until 8 a. were sold in 1853[81] and the remaining 16 a. in 1864.[82]

Westminster abbey leased its estate to Thomas Roberts (c. 1516–1539),[83] John Roberts (c. 1553–1556),[84] Edmund Roberts (1566–9),[85] Sir William Roberts (temp. Chas. I, 1660–4),[86] and his son Sir William Roberts, who renewed the lease in 1676 and mortgaged it with other lands to William Hellier and Ann Carpenter, to whom a lease was made in 1685. His son repaid the mortgage and the lease assigned to him expired in 1706. It was purchased and renewed by William Hawkins, clerk.[87] Hawkins renewed the lease in 1721, 1728, and 1735, and in 1742 his brother and trustee George renewed the lease for William's son, a minor. The younger William renewed the lease in 1749 and 1762.[88] His widow and executrix Lydia renewed it in 1769 and 1776 and her executrix and devisee, Lydia Dawson (by 1784 wife of Thomas Moore) renewed it in 1778, 1784, and 1791.[89] In 1811 the estate was leased to James Hall and in 1818 it was divided, 8 a. south of the Grove being leased to Hall[90] (d. 1838) whose son Henry bought the freehold in 1853,[91] and 16 a. west of Neasden village to John Nicoll (d. 1819); Joseph Nicoll (d. 1853) devised the property to John William Prout, who bought the freehold in 1864.[92] The house conveyed in 1454 is to be identified with the one marked east of the junction of Dog Lane and Neasden Lane in 1599.[93] It was probably that with one hearth occupied in 1664 by Widow Moulder.[94] A second house had been built on the estate by 1566.[95] It was assessed for four hearths in 1670 and stood west of Neasden green.[96]

ST. BARTHOLOMEW'S HOSPITAL owned a house at Church End which in 1547 was granted to the City of London;[97] the City administered the estate on behalf of the hospital, which was still in possession in 1823. The house was still there in 1599 but had gone by 1816.[98]

By will dated 1692 Francis Millington of London devised £500 to buy land out of which CHRIST'S HOSPITAL was to pay pensions to disabled watermen of Wandsworth parish; 64 a. in north Neasden, bordering the Brent, were bought from the coheirs of the Roberts estate in

[68] Possibly an alias of Middleton.
[69] B.L. Stowe MS. 862, f. 49 and v.; P.R.O., CP 25(1)/151/80, no. 149; Cal. Plea and Mem. R. of City of Lond. 1381–1412, p. 241; Testamentary Rec. in Archdeaconry Ct. of Lond. (Index Libr. lxxxix).
[70] P.R.O., E 40/7644, 10366, 10379; Feud. Aids, vi. 489.
[71] e.g. P.R.O., E 40/6817.
[72] Ibid. E 40/5752, 5773.
[73] Cal. Papal Reg. ix. 315; P.R.O., E 40/12183.
[74] P.R.O., CP 25(1)/294/76, no. 77; B.L. Stowe MS. 862, ff. 33v., 50.
[75] P.R.O., CP 25(2)/171/5 Eliz. I Trin.
[76] P.R.O., C 142/482, no. 65; for the Roberts estates, below.
[77] B.L. Stowe MS. 862, f. 49v.; P.R.O., E 40/10366.
[78] Cal. Papal Reg. ix. 315.
[79] P.R.O., SC5/Mdx. (Tower ser.) 1, mm. 1–2; V.C.H. Mdx. vi. 56.
[80] W.A.M. 17018–26; Cal. Pat. 1494–1509, 517.
[81] P.R.O., C 54/3583, no. 30; Grange Mus., Wood F 21, p. 315; Wood 8 (Willesden deeds, v. 870).

[82] Ch. Com., D 142734, 145790; Grange Mus., Wood F 24 (Willesden deeds, xiv. 155).
[83] W.A.M. 4680, 4697, 4706; P.R.O., SC 6/Hen. VIII/2415, m. 16.
[84] W.A.M. 33185; Cal. Pat. 1555–7, 352.
[85] W.A.M. 33187.   [86] Ibid. 9644, 42167.
[87] B.L. Stowe MS. 862, ff. 38 sqq.; Ch. Com., D 142721.
[88] Ch. Com., D 142721–2.   [89] Ibid. 142723–7.
[90] Ibid. 142728–9; M.R.O., Acc. 262/40 (inclosure claims).
[91] Ch. Com., D 142735–8A; Grange Mus., Wood 8 (Willesden deeds, v. 870).
[92] Ch. Com., D 142730–4; Grange Mus., Wood 24 (Willesden deeds, xiv. 155).
[93] W.A.M. 17018; All Souls Coll., Hovenden maps II/22.
[94] M.R.O., MR/TH/3, m. 6; Ch. Com., D 142721; cf. Ch. Com., D 145789, 146075.
[95] W.A.M. 33187.
[96] M.R.O., MR/TH/12, p. 33; Ch. Comm., D 142721.
[97] L. & P. Hen. VIII, xxi (2), 415.
[98] All Souls Coll., Hovenden maps II/21; M.R.O., Acc. 262/40 (inclosure claims); ibid. EA/WIL.

1704. In 1835 and 1838 parts were sold for the Brent reservoir. W. Prout of Neasden purchased the remaining 47 a. in 1873.[99]

The large estate built up by the *ROBERTS* family[1] included land held at Sherrick and Sheeproad by William Roberts or Roberd (fl. 1295–1306) and in Neasden open fields by Thomas Roberts between *c.* 1307 and 1327.[2] Ralph Roberts (fl. 1365–94) held Taylors cottage in Neasden, was granted pavage on Edgware Road in 1389, and had a son Thomas (fl. 1406), whose son John alienated the Sherrick lands in 1449.[3] John was probably the same as the John Robert of Neasden who purchased John atte Wood's estate in 1403 and consolidated his lands at Sheeproad by exchange with Robert Curson in the 1420s.[4] It was presumably another John Roberts who had died by 1480[5] and whose son Thomas in 1510 held five houses in Neasden village and numerous crofts and open-field land from Neasden prebend.

Thomas Roberts, clerk of the peace and coroner of Middlesex, added to the estate, acquiring other property held from Neasden and Chambers prebends and holding leases of various estates.[6] He was succeeded in 1543 by his son Michael, who died young in 1544 leaving Fosters in Acton and some tenements in Harlesden to his brother John and the rest of his estate for life to his widow Ursula. She later married Benjamin Gonson.[7] Michael's brother Edmund Roberts (d. 1585) seems to have acquired all Michael's lands. In 1563 he greatly increased the Neasden estate by purchasing Middletons manor.[8] He held the lease of Harlesden prebend in 1576 and may have acquired other lands in Harlesden.[9] His son and heir Francis bought Oxgate manor in 1587 and the few remaining tenements in Neasden,[10] and held leases of the Westminster abbey estate and the prebends of Harlesden (1594), Oxgate (1608), Neasden (1624), and Chambers (1627).[11] When he died in 1632 he was said to be seised of 34 messuages and 1,654 a. in Willesden, a manor and land in Acton, a small estate in Kingsbury, and other estates in Lincolnshire.[12]

Francis was succeeded by his grandson William Roberts (d. 1662), knighted in 1624, who took the parliamentary side in the Civil War, in 1646 became one of the contractors to sell church lands, and in 1651 bought the prebends of Neasden, Oxgate, Harlesden, and Chambers and the estate of Westminster abbey. He was M.P. for Middlesex and a member of the committee to try Charles I although he did not sign the death warrant. He lost nothing at the Restoration, taking leases of the prebends when they reverted to the prebendaries.[13] He had also increased the estate by his marriage with Eleanor, daughter and heir of Robert Atye, with land in Hampstead and Kilburn.[14]

The Roberts estate began to contract after his death.[15] Eleanor sold *c.* 120 a. in Willesden and Hendon to Edward Nelthorpe in 1662.[16] Her right was apparently successfully challenged in the same year by her eldest son Sir William Roberts, Bt. (d. 1688)[17] who in 1664 was treating as his own land in Willesden, Kilburn, and Hampstead which Eleanor claimed should have gone to a younger son, Edward.[18] Sir William, described as a 'very careless man', inherited property already encumbered with mortgages and legacies, and fell deeper and deeper into debt.[19] He sold the Kilburn estate in 1664,[20] two estates in Harlesden, amounting to 248 a., in 1665–6 and 1671,[21] and smaller estates in the north in 1675[22] and in Kilburn in 1679.[23] His complicated mortgage transactions resulted in award in 1682 to the current mortgagee, Prisca Colborne, of temporary possession of Neasden manor and other property to the value of £627 a year.[24] Sir William was preparing to pay his debts by selling Oxgate when he died in 1688.[25]

His son Sir William died in 1698 and the estate passed to his cousin William Roberts (d. 1700).[26] William paid off remaining mortgages in 1698 and 1699, and in 1700 sold over 100 a. at Oxgate, Neasden, and Church End.[27] His widow Elizabeth, whose second husband was William Hutchenson, continued to live at Neasden and still had interests in the estate in 1725.[28] His brother and heir Thomas died in 1702, and in 1704 further sales were made.[29] Thomas was succeeded by his five sisters, Eleanor wife of Thomas Knight, Elizabeth or Edith wife of Thomas Launder, Margaret wife of Richard Lawton, Mary wife of William Hawkins, and Sarah wife of Hollis and later of George Paterson. Sarah (d. 1708) was abroad in 1702 and her share

[99] Grange Mus., Wood F 21, pp. 172 sqq.; ibid. 4 I 10 (M.L.R. 1838/4/266); M.R.O., EA/WIL.

[1] Account of the Roberts estate based on B.L. Stowe MS. 862, ff. 38 sqq.; Grange Mus., Wood F 24, pp. 254 sqq.

[2] P.R.O., E 40/6800, 6806, 6874, 7892–3, 11648, 11844–5.

[3] *Cal. Close*, 1364–8, 190; 1392–6, 199–200; 1405–9, 152; P.R.O., E 40/7253.

[4] P.R.O., E 40/7644, 10379.

[5] W.A.M. 17021–2.

[6] P.R.O., E 210/10147; Bodl. MS. D.D. All Souls c 124/ 85A. See also P.R.O., C 1/349/1; C 1/767/20.

[7] P.R.O., PROB 11/30 (P.C.C. 14 Pynnyng); ibid. C 1/1223/39.

[8] Above, manors.

[9] St. Paul's MS. C (I Nowell), f. 456v.

[10] B.L. Stowe MS. 862, ff. 48, 58 sqq.; above.

[11] Above, manors; see also P.R.O., C 142/349, no. 155; ibid. PROB 11/126 (P.C.C. 79 Rudd, f. 102).

[12] P.R.O., C 142/482, no. 65.

[13] Grange Mus., Wood F 24, pp. 254, 271 sqq.; Potter, *Story of Willesden*, 106; *Acts & Ords. of Interr.* ed. Firth & Rait, i. 889.

[14] *Genealogist*, v (1881), 300–7; P.R.O., WARD 5/30/432.

[15] For a map of the estate in 1662, Grange Mus., Wood F 24, p. 299.

[16] Ibid. p. 232.

[17] *Cal. S.P. Dom.* 1661–2, 98.

[18] P.R.O., C 6/168/99; C 8/320/171.

[19] Ibid. C 5/85/75; C 6/215/33; C 8/386/24.

[20] P.R.O., C 6/168/99; C 6/196/87; M.R.O., F 34/281–6.

[21] M.R.O., Acc. 621/Add. 7–8; P.R.O., C 8/386/24; Grange Mus., Wood F 24, p. 232; B.L. Add. Ch. 40602.

[22] B.L. Stowe MS. 862, f. 53v.; P.R.O., C 5/85/75; C 6/215/33; C 6/215/101.

[23] P.R.O., C 6/231/34.

[24] Ibid. C 8/386/24; C 5/167/142.

[25] Ibid. PROB 11/390 (P.C.C. 38 Exton).

[26] Ibid. PROB 11/445 (P.C.C. 130 Lort); G.E.C. *Baronetage*, iii. 233.

[27] Grange Mus., Wood F 24, pp. 232, 299; M.R.O., Acc. 262/37, pt. 1; Acc. 583/1–3.

[28] P.R.O., PROB 11/458 (P.C.C. 184 Noel); ibid. C 10/ 307/67; M.L.R. 1715/1/40; 1734/5/111; Grange Mus., Wood F 21, pp. 241 sqq.

[29] B.L. Stowe MS. 862, f. 47 and v.; P.R.O., C 10/307/ 67.

was divided among her sisters.[30] John Wilson bought Eleanor's share in 1710, Edith's in 1717, and part of Mary's in 1720, and conveyed them in 1733 to John Nicoll (d. 1747).[31] Eleanor Knight's children inherited part of Margaret Lawton's share, including her portion of Sarah's share in Neasden. They sold it in 1739 to Thomas Nicoll.[32] In 1752 Thomas Nicoll bought the rest of Margaret Lawton's share, sold in 1705 to Thomas Smartfoot, left in 1707 to his 10 grandchildren, and sold in 1728 and 1730 to Edward Sibley (d. 1730) and his daughter Elizabeth.[33]

John Nicoll (d. 1747) was said to be in possession of the whole of Neasden House and farm and three fifths of Oxgate and Dollis Hill.[34] He also brought a small estate at Church End in 1738 and a moiety of Fishes, 100 a. at Willesden Green and Sherrick green and in the open fields, from the Paynter family.[35] In 1753 his daughter and heir Margaret (d. 1768) married James Brydges, who later succeeded as duke of Chandos.[36] The Brydges estate was enlarged by the purchase of Margaret Lawton's share in 1754[37] and of part of Mary Hawkins's, from Lydia Hawkins, in 1771.[38] In 1787 the duke, who did not live in Willesden, had an estate there of c. 700 a.[39] On his death in 1789 it passed to his only child Anna Eliza, who in 1796 married Richard Temple-Nugent-Brydges-Chandos-Grenville (d. 1839), created duke of Buckingham and Chandos in 1822. Their son Richard Plantagenet (d. 1861) was succeeded by his son Richard Plantagenet Campbell (d. 1889) and by his nephew William Stephen Gore-Langton, Earl Temple (d. 1902) and his son Algernon W. S. Temple-Gore-Langton, Earl Temple (d. 1940).[40]

Parts of the estate were sold in 1803 to John Read, William M. Sellon, and Lady (Sarah) Salusbury,[41] and by 1816 the estate had shrunk to 550 a. In 1817 Buckingham sold the remaining one fifth of Dollis Hill to the tenant, Joseph Finch, who had bought the other four fifths from the Nicolls in 1784 and 1795, and in 1818 he sold his shares of Neasden House and two farms to John Nicoll, the tenant who owned the rest of them.[42] In 1823 Buckingham's lands amounted to c. 450 a.[43] The estate was offered for sale in lots in 1837,[44] and between 1838 and 1844 Edmund Tattersall bought 96 a. of Upper Oxgate, including the farmhouse, S. H. Bigg 39 a. at Sherrick green, and Joseph Nicoll the 153 a. of Neasden farm.[45] Lower Oxgate and the remaining eastern part of Upper Oxgate were put up for sale in lots in 1847 but not sold, and the duke of Buckingham still had 136 a. in 1887.[46] Building began on the estate in the late 1890s and was completed in the 1930s.[47]

The Nicoll family, lessees of Neasden lands from c. 1720,[48] owned the remaining fractions and after 1818 wholly owned Neasden House and the heart of the Roberts estates. John Nicoll (d. 1819), the owner in 1787 and 1816, was succeeded by his brother Joseph (d. 1823) and nephew Joseph (d. 1853) who devised the property to trustees for his cousin Catherine Nicoll Lewis Prout.[49] In 1873 Catherine married William Edward Nicol, a Scot not related to the Nicolls of Neasden.[50] Their descendants retained some of the estate in 1980.[51]

The Nicolls' estate, 149 a. in 1823, was increased by the purchases of Neasden farm from the duke of Buckingham, the Grove estate in 1856 from the Hall brothers, part of the Westminster abbey estate in 1864, and the Christ's Hospital estate (47 a.) in 1873,[52] to comprise c. 500 a.[53] In the late 1870s land at Willesden Green was sold for building and a large portion of the Neasden lands to the Metropolitan Railway Co.[54] By 1887 the estate had shrunk to 191 a.[55] All that land, including Neasden House, was used for building, mostly in the 1930s, although the Grange (part of the Grove estate) was not sold until 1962.

Thomas Roberts (d. 1543), whose predecessors had lived in a house on the east side of Neasden Lane, called Little's or Barnhaw, rebuilt or much enlarged another house, also on the east side of the lane, previously called Catewood's and afterwards Neasden House.[56] His son Michael (d. 1544) continued the building,[57] and Francis Roberts (d. 1632) and his grandson Sir William (d. 1662) added to the house and transformed its surroundings.[58] By 1664 Neasden House was assessed on 21 hearths, the largest house in Willesden.[59] It was depicted in 1749 as a large L-shaped building with a three-gabled front and a three-bay side wing.[60] It was occupied from 1735 by Thomas Nicoll, who rebuilt it c. 1755.[61]

[30] P.R.O., C 10/307/67; C 5/623/13; M.R.O., Acc. 262/37, pt. 1.

[31] M.L.R. 1710/3/51; 1717/2/86, 224; M.R.O., Acc. 262/37, pt. 1 (1734); 38 (1725).

[32] M.R.O., Acc. 262/37, pt. 1 (sale 1739).

[33] Ibid. 39 (abstract of settlement 1752); Acc. 262/47/68.

[34] Ibid. Acc. 262/40, pt. 2 (rental c. 1747); Acc. 262/54H.

[35] Ibid. Acc. 262/37, pt. 1 (bundle of docs. 1700–38); Acc. 262/38 (lease 1759).

[36] Complete Peerage, iii. 132.

[37] M.R.O., Acc. 262/39 (marriage settlement 1754).

[38] Ibid. (sale 1771); Grange Mus., gen. files, farms (abstract of title to Oxgate).

[39] M.R.O., Acc. 262/42 (Chandos estate map and survey 1787).

[40] Complete Peerage, ii. 408–10; Burke, Peerage (1959), 2204.

[41] M.R.O., Acc. 262/40, pt. 1 (1803); 40, pt. 2 (1803).

[42] Ibid. Acc. 262/40 (inclosure claims 1816); 40, pt. 1 (agreement 1817, sale draft 1818); 40 pt. 2 (draft release 1817).

[43] Ibid. EA/WIL.

[44] Ibid. Acc. 262/40, pt. 1 (sales cat. 1837); Acc. 262/61/1.

[45] Ibid. Acc. 262/40, pt. 1 (agreement for sale to Nicoll); Acc. 262/61/2; Grange Mus., Wood F 21, p. 296.

[46] F. M. L. Thompson, 'End of a Great Estate', Ec. H.R. 2nd ser. viii. 36 sqq.

[47] Above.

[48] Grange Mus., 1 B 1 (poor rate 1720).

[49] Ibid. gen. files, Neasden Lane, St. Mary's churchyard (Nicolls in churchyard); ibid. Wood F 21, p. 248.

[50] Ibid. biog. files, Miss Prout (Kilburn Times, 29 Nov. 1873).

[51] Inf. from Brent L.B.

[52] M.R.O., Hist. Notes 30/12/68.

[53] Grange Mus., Wood 24 (Willesden deeds xiv. 155); map in Grange Mus. c. 1870.

[54] Above.   [55] M.R.O., TA/WIL.

[56] B.L. Stowe MS. 862, ff. 38 sqq.; Grange Mus., Wood-F 24, pp. 285–6.

[57] P.R.O., PROB 11/30 (P.C.C. 14 Pynnyng).

[58] B.L. Stowe MS. 862, ff. 39v.–40.

[59] M.R.O., MR/TH/3, m. 5.

[60] Messeder Road Map (1749).

[61] Brewer, Beauties of Eng. and Wales, iv. 350; Grange Mus., Wood F 24, p. 282.

By the 19th century it was a three-storeyed stuccoed building with two large rounded bays.[62] After a period during the early 20th century as a golf clubhouse, it was demolished to make way for building in the early 1930s.[63]

The land at Kilburn which Sir William Roberts sold in 1664 was bought by William Morgan, who also seems to have acquired part of Roberts's land in Harlesden. Richard Morgan (fl. 1723) left his estate to Morgan Graves, whose son Walwyn sold the Kilburn estate in 1807 to Daniel Stuart and the Harlesden estate to James Denew.[64] Stuart sold Kilburn House, called the Great House in 1728, with 17 a. to Sir Samuel Auchmuty in 1815, and the Revd. Edward Stuart sold nearly 100 a. between 1850 and 1857.[65] Denew sold the Harlesden land between 1827 and 1843, including 3 a. in 1834 to the architect Charles Ayers who built Roundwood House there and sold it in 1838 to John Horsley-Beresford, Baron Decies.[66]

Another estate sold by Sir William Roberts was 128 a. mostly in Harlesden, which Richard Taylor bought in 1665 and 1671.[67] Until 1835 it descended with the leasehold of Harlesden prebend,[68] being owned in 1823 by Richard Taylor[69] whose daughter Emily sold part in 1878 and 1879 and retained 76 a. in 1887.[70] The last part of the estate was sold in 1925 by Capt. Frederick Gibbons, apparently a maternal relation of Emily.[71]

A third estate sold by Sir William Roberts was c. 120 a., which Richard Wingfield bought in 1666. In 1727 Wingfield sold 69 a. mostly in Harlesden to Robert Glynn, and in 1730 Thomas Wingfield sold 53 a. in Stonebridge to Edward Sibley.[72]

At UPPER OXGATE Sir William Roberts sold 53 a. in 1675 to Ezechiel Tanner, from whom it passed to John Tanner (d. 1744), John's wife Anne (d. 1748), and Anne's niece Sarah, wife of Thomas Howard. It was sold in 1759 to John Haley, who sold it in 1785 to Thomas Byron; Edmund Byron was in possession in 1887.[73] The house, called Old Oxgate or Oxgate Farm, was presumably one of the three recorded in 1587 and was assessed on five hearths in 1670.[74] It survived in 1980 as the oldest secular building in Willesden, timber-framed, of the 16th and 17th centuries. The northern range was thought to be part of a larger 16th-century building, a fact which, together with the moat still visible in 1823,

suggests that it was the principal house of Oxgate, possibly on the site of that owned by Bartholomew Willesden in 1472.[75]

A second holding at UPPER OXGATE was c. 100 a. sold from the Roberts estate in 1700 to Richard Hawe. Hawe's nieces sold it in 1734 to Jenkin Thomas Phillips, whose heir John Williams sold it in 1768 to John Saxon.[76] Saxon apparently divided the estate into moieties, of which one passed through the Heming family to Henry Richard Phillips, who owned 164 a. in 1887.[77] The third and largest holding at Oxgate, leased by the Robertses and their successors to the Franklins from 1669 to 1819, included the 96 a. of Upper Oxgate sold by the duke of Buckingham to Edmund Tattersall in 1838. Tattersall's devisees sold that land to H. R. and J. R. Phillips in 1852.[78] Tattersall carried out extensive building, converting both the house with four hearths occupied in 1670 by John Franklin and that with two hearths occupied in 1670 by Thomas Etheridge[79] into the model stud-farm known as Willesden Paddocks.[80]

The land of the Roberts family at DOLLIS HILL, previously leased as two farms, was leased as one holding in 1773 to Joseph Finch, who between 1784 and 1818 acquired the fragmented freehold.[81] The Finches sold the land south of Dollis Hill Lane for a public park in 1901, retaining the northern farm until 1939.[82] The principal house, perhaps that occupied by Richard Franklin (d. 1615)[83] and assessed on seven hearths in 1664,[84] lay north of the lane and was called Dollis Hill House in 1734 and Dollis Hill Farmhouse in 1787.[85] It was rebuilt in brick c. 1800 as a small farmhouse with a front of three bays and featured in Harrison Ainsworth's Jack Sheppard.[86] It became a veterinary hospital in the early 20th century and was demolished in the 1940s. A smaller house south of the lane was replaced in 1825 by the Finches, who lived at Dollis Hill until 1861.[87] The new house was afterwards occupied by Dudley Coutts Marjoribanks, later Lord Tweedmouth, until 1881, by his daughter and her husband, the earl of Aberdeen, until 1897, and by the newspaper proprietor Hugh Gilzean Reed until 1906, being used thereafter as a restaurant for Gladstone Park and later by Kilburn Polytechnic for students on catering courses.[88] George Eliot is said to have placed a scene in Daniel Deronda (1876) in the

[62] Grange Mus., photo. files, Neasden Ho. (NL 1186).
[63] Ibid. gen. files, Neasden Ho.
[64] P.R.O., C 6/168/99; C 6/196/87; M.R.O., F 34/281-6; Grange Mus., estate map of Ric. Morgan 1723; ibid. 4 I 7 (M.L.R. 1807/5/238; 1805/4/348); M.R.O., Acc. 262/40 (inclosure claims 1816).
[65] Grange Mus., Wood F 22, pp. 66 sqq.
[66] Ibid. F 22, pp. 177 sqq.; F 23, pp. 177 sqq.; ibid. 4 I 10 (M.L.R. 1835/1/600; 1839/5/181).
[67] M.R.O., Acc. 621/Add. 7-8; P.R.O., C 8/386/24; Grange Mus., Wood F 24, p. 232.
[68] Above, manors.
[69] M.R.O., EA/WIL.
[70] Ibid. TA/WIL; Grange Mus., Wood F 20 (sale cats. 2/7, 11, 13, 23).
[71] Grange Mus., gen. files, Gibbons Rd.; M.R.O., Acc. 621/7-9.
[72] B.L. Add. Ch. 40602; P.R.O., C 10/65/88; Grange Mus., Wood F 21, pp. 318 sqq.; F 22, pp. 145 sqq.
[73] Grange Mus., Wood F 21, pp. 160 sqq.; M.R.O., TA/WIL.

[74] P.R.O., CP 25(2)/172/29 Eliz. I Hil.; M.R.O., MR/TH/12, p. 33.
[75] Hist. Mon. Com. Mdx. 135; Grange Mus., Wood F 26/1; ibid. photo. files, Coles Green Rd. (NL 733, 2054); M.R.O., EA/WIL.
[76] Grange Mus., Wood F 21, pp. 167 sqq.; M.R.O., Acc. 583/1-12.   [77] M.R.O., TA/WIL.
[78] P.R.O., C 5/167/142; Grange Mus., Wood F 21, pp. 186 sqq.; M.R.O., Acc. 262/52/65-953 (rentals).
[79] M.R.O., MR/TH/12, p. 33.
[80] G. Tattersall, Sporting Archit. (1841), 10.
[81] M.R.O., Acc. 262/39 (abstract of title; settlement 1754), 42; M.L.R. 1710/3/51; 1718/4/50-2.
[82] Grange Mus., gen. files, Dollis Hill P.O. Research Sta.
[83] Above, manors (Malories).
[84] M.R.O., MR/TH/3, m. 5d.
[85] Ibid. Acc. 262/37, pt. 1 (sale 1734), 40 (Chandos estate map 1787).
[86] Grange Mus., photo. files, Dollis Hill Lane (NL 766-9).
[87] Ibid., gen. files, Dollis Hill P.O. Research Sta.
[88] Inf. from curator of Grange Mus.

drawing room, Lord Aberdeen received visits from Rosebery, Balfour, and especially Gladstone, whose name was used for the park,[89] Mark Twain lived there briefly in 1900, calling it 'divinely beautiful and peaceful'.[90] It was adapted for use as an emergency hospital in 1915 and the cabinet met in the 'Dollis Hill war room' in 1941.[91] The house is square, of two storeys, in yellow stock brick with a stuccoed porch and formerly had a verandah on the south side.[92]

ECONOMIC HISTORY. AGRARIAN HISTORY. In 1086 the three estates at Willesden contained enough land for a total of 20½ plough teams, 15 at the principal manor, 4 at Harlesden, and 1½ at East Twyford. The largest manor, which had no demesne, was held at farm by 25 villeins who had between them only 8 teams, and there were also 5 bordars. At Harlesden the demesne had 2 teams and the villeins ½ team though there were 12 villeins with 1 virgate each and 10 with ½ virgate each. No demesne was recorded at East Twyford, where 3 villeins had 2½ virgates. In the three estates together there was woodland for 700 pigs. Only East Twyford had increased in value since 1066, the main manor having decreased by nearly half and Harlesden by more than half.[93] By the early 12th century the three estates had evolved into the eight prebends and the rectory estate which provided the medieval framework of Willesden. It seems likely that the demesne estates of the prebends in the south-east, namely Bounds, Brondesbury, Mapesbury, and Chambers, existed in the Middle Ages. Leases exist for Mapesbury demesne in the 15th century and a prebendary was presented in 1383 for the state of the road bordering land traditionally part of the demesne. Early 16th-century leases of Mapesbury contained a clause reserving part of the manor house for the prebendary. The prebendary of Harlesden alienated most of his demesne c. 1200, leaving a demesne of only 3 a.; there is no evidence that the other prebends ever had lands in demesne.

Most of the landholders in Willesden in the Middle Ages were from local, often long-lived

families. Local place-names supplied surnames for the Willesden (1278–1494),[94] Twyford (1219–1902),[95] Harlesden (13th cent., 1327),[96] Oxgate (1298),[97] and Slade (1248–1306)[98] families. Other local names included Hacche (c. 1200–1441),[99] Cornhill (1274–1415),[1] Algar (c. 1280–1432),[2] Fayrsire or Veyser of Harlesden (1293–1510),[3] Stokke or Stokker (1295–1377),[4] Wood or Atwood (1307–1463),[5] Shepherd (1322–1675),[6] Erlich (1351–1510), Nelme (1359–1510),[7] Franklin (1454–1840),[8] Reding (1473–1630),[9] and, the most important, Roberts (1295–1702).[10]

Willesden was sufficiently near London to attract London merchants. Middletons manor originated in the sale by one London draper to another in 1295 and passed, a century later, to a draper and mercer.[11] A clothier died seised of Malories and West Twyford manor in 1380 and it was a group of London merchants, particularly the mercer Ellis Davy, who built up the estate which was acquired by All Souls College in the 15th century.[12] A sherman leased the rectory in 1462[13] and other London merchants who bought and sold land in Willesden, probably as investments rather than as country seats, included two goldsmiths[14] and a fishmonger[15] in the 14th century, two grocers,[16] a spicer,[17] a tailor,[18] a draper,[19] a carpenter,[20] and a sherman[21] in the 15th century. The looseness of the lords' control evidently facilitated the buying, selling, and exchanging of land by local families and Londoners, which resulted in the creation of estates like Middletons and Malories and the conversion of large areas of the open fields to closes.

The open fields of Willesden as recorded from the 17th century to the 19th,[22] stretching westward from the centre of the parish to the river Brent, were the residue of a more extensive layout. North-west of Willesden Green Sheepcote field (1351)[23] contained c. 21 a. in 1621 and 26 a. in 1722 and 1816. Dudden or Duddinghill field (1363)[24] to the north was c. 72 a. in 1621 and 1722 and 66 a. in 1816. At Chapel End Church mead seems to have been the rump of Church field (c. 1280),[25] which formerly ran eastward from the church. Hungerhill field (1415)[26] contained c. 72 a. Fortune field (1359)[27] was 64 a. in

[89] Ibid. gen. files, Dollis Hill Ho.; photo. files, Dollis Hill Ho. (NL 775).
[90] A. B. Paine, *Mark Twain*, ii. 1108–10.
[91] *Diaries of Sir Alex. Cadogan* (1971), 362.
[92] Plate facing p. 208.
[93] *V.C.H. Mdx.* i. 121.
[94] Grange Mus., Wood F 24, p. 252; above, manors (Oxgate).
[95] P.R.O., CP 25(1)/146/5, no. 11; Grange Mus., photo. files, Neasden Lane, Old Spotted Dog.
[96] St. Paul's MS. A 30/444; *Cal. Mem. R. 1326–7*, 160.
[97] P.R.O., E 40/7906.
[98] Grange Mus., Wood F 22, p. 216; P.R.O., E 40/11585.
[99] St. Paul's MS. A 39/1366; P.R.O., E 40/7591.
[1] P.R.O., SC 5/Mdx. (Tower ser.) 1, m. 2; Bodl. MS. D.D. All Souls c. 123/22.
[2] Connected with Harlesden and Twyford: St. Paul's MS. A 29/397; Bodl. MS. D.D. All Souls c 123/23.
[3] Grange Mus., Wood F 24, p. 209; B.L. Stowe MS. 862, f. 33.
[4] Mainly in Neasden: P.R.O., E 40/7892; B.L. Stowe MS. 862, f. 38.
[5] P.R.O., E 40/6806; *Cal. Pat. 1461–7*, 255.
[6] Mainly in Neasden: P.R.O., E 40/7871; ibid. C 6/215/33.
[7] Bodl. MS. D.D. All Souls c 123/46, 49; St. Paul's MS. C (I Nowell), f. 330v.

[8] Mainly concerned with Cricklewood and Oxgate: Bodl. MS. D.D. All Souls c 125/1; Guildhall MS. CC. 169260.
[9] Bodl. MS. D.D. All Souls c 324; P.R.O., C 142/715, no. 7.   [10] Above, other est.
[11] Above, manors (Middletons).
[12] Above, manors (Malories).
[13] St. Paul's MS. A 39/1359.
[14] P.R.O., CP 25(1)/149/47, no. 207; CP 25(1)/150/53, no. 19.   [15] Ibid. CP 25(1)/151/73, no. 516.
[16] Ibid. CP 25(1)/152/86, no. 16; ibid. E 40/10366.
[17] Ibid. CP 25(1)/152/86, no. 16.
[18] Ibid. C 1/33/162; ibid. CP 25(1)/152/93, no. 129; ibid. PROB 11/4 (P.C.C. 15 Stokton).
[19] Ibid. CP 25(1)/152/94, no. 163.
[20] Bodl. MS. D.D. All Souls c 123/58.
[21] P.R.O., CP 25(1)/152/94, no. 170; W.A.M. 17026.
[22] What follows is based on W.A.M. 17039 (survey of fields 1621); G.L.C. County Hall map colln. AT 602 (Senex, map of open fields 1722); M.R.O., Acc. 262/40 (inclosure claims 1816); M.R.O., EA/WIL (inclosure map 1823). Dates in brackets indicate the earliest mention of a name.
[23] Bodl. MS. D.D. All Souls c 123/46.
[24] Ibid. c 123/53.
[25] St. Paul's MS. A 29/385.
[26] Bodl. MS. D.D. All Souls c 123/22.
[27] Ibid. c 123/49.

1621 and 1722 and 76 a. in 1816. The common marsh, divided into Harlesden and Willesden marsh in 1364[28] and Great and Little marsh in 1599[29] and 1621, contained c. 53 a. in 1621, 73 a. in 1722, and 77 a. in 1816. Brent field (1415),[30] often divided into Lower and Upper Brent field, contained 115 a. in 1621, 151 a. in 1722 and 1816, its shape indicating that parts had been inclosed. Neasden field (1457)[31] apparently abutted Brent field in 1621 when it contained 53½ a. but by 1722 it had shrunk to 31 a., including what by 1823 was called Bridge field. Some other field names, like Willesden field (1298)[32] and Drayton field (1510),[33] were probably alternatives to those already mentioned, and some, like Deriches field (c. 1185),[34] are totally unlocated. Many more, however, were of open fields which by 1621 were wholly inclosed, particularly in the north, on the farmlands of Oxgate, Dollis Hill, and Neasden. Sherrick field (1307) and Nether Sherrick field (1432) or Nether field (1419), between Sherrick Lane and Cricklewood,[35] and Hakkers field (1420), also north of Sherrick Lane,[36] had been inclosed by 1449.[37] Bury field (1322) or le Bery (1420)[38] and Bedewell field (1305)[39] were in Neasden, probably in the west near Brent and Neasden fields,[40] and Sheeprode field (1306) was in Oxgate.[41] Numerous crofts remained divided into strips.[42]

The process of consolidating strips can be traced from the 13th century, when the rectory estate began to take shape as a few compact blocks of land through the activities of Alan of Morton.[43] The nucleus of Malories at Kensal Green and Harlesden was probably formed before 1310, further land being added in the 14th and 15th centuries. Middletons was built up by mostly small purchases between 1295 and 1322, and in the 1420s there was much buying, selling, and exchanging of land in the north as the Cursons, Robertses and Willesdens built up their Neasden and Oxgate estates.[44]

Such inclosure may have been partly to convert arable to pasture, but farming in Willesden in the Middle Ages seems to have been mixed, with arable predominant. Arable was more extensive than meadow, pasture, or woodland in conveyances except in Harlesden and Kilburn. There was much woodland in the south and east; meadow lay mostly along the streams. The farm

buildings of the rectory were equipped c. 1280 for mixed farming.[45] Willesden was one of the main producers of sheep near London in 1340,[46] and cattle destroyed the woods of Bounds prebend in 1422.[47] In the 15th century the All Souls estate produced large quantities of oats and sheep, sent oats and hay to the college's hospice in London, and also yielded wheat, cows, and oxen.[48]

In 1517 the prebendary of Brondesbury was indicted for inclosing his arable land for pasture, displacing half a ploughteam and making 12 people idle.[49] In 1552 Thomas Nicoll, described as a merchant of Willesden, was presented for paying rents that poor men could not afford.[50] Willesden lands were valued highly presumably because they were close to London. Mapesbury was leased to a London merchant tailor in 1534 and a scrivener in 1642, and a London alderman, possibly with local connexions, bought Twyford manor in 1599.[51] A London skinner bought c. 80 a. in 1525 and Richard Taylor, who purchased a Harlesden estate in 1676, was a London vintner.[52] Local families which appear during the period include those of Wingfield (1524–1738),[53] Newman (1527–1864),[54] Kempe (1538–1662),[55] Vincent (1544–1663),[56] Nicoll (1552–1853),[57] Marsh (1574–1770),[58] Haley (1613–1760),[59] Finch (1615–c. 1900),[60] and Weeden (1665–1820).[61]

From the early 18th century the boundaries of freehold estates tended to remain constant, the land being leased and frequently underleased, so that a farm was often made up of contiguous portions of land belonging to several landlords. In 1765 the largest holding, that of Thomas Nicoll at Neasden, comprised several farms amounting to 453 a., Isaac Messeder occupied most of the All Souls estate (288 a.), and there were eight farms of 100–200 a., twelve of 50–100 a., seven of 21–50 a., and eighteen of less than 20 a.[62] By 1801 the largest farm was that of the London butcher, Paul Giblett, who leased 402 a. from Lady Salusbury in the south-east. The next largest estate was that of Joseph Nicoll (258 a.) in Neasden. There were two other estates of over 200 a., 11 of 100 a.–200 a., 7 of 50 a.–100 a., and 4 of 21 a.–50 a.[63]

By the late 18th century the woodland had virtually all been cleared and much of the arable had been converted to grass. Hedgerows had

[28] Ibid. c 123/54.
[29] All Souls Coll., Hovenden maps II/18.
[30] Bodl. MS. D.D. All Souls c 123/22.
[31] Ibid. c 123/68.
[32] P.R.O., E 40/7906.
[33] B.L. Stowe MS. 862, f. 33.
[34] Ibid. Cott. Ch. xvi. 40.
[35] P.R.O., E 40/6874–5; Bodl. MSS. D.D. All Souls c 123/34, 67.
[36] P.R.O., E 40/10366, 10379.
[37] E 40/7253.
[38] E 40/7871, 10366.
[39] E 40/6806.
[40] E 40/7644, 10366.
[41] E 40/11585, 11648; M.R.O., Acc. 583/1.
[42] e.g. St. Paul's MS. A 29/384; P.R.O., E 40/11648.
[43] St. Paul's MSS. A 29/380–8, 397, 444; above, manors (Rectory).
[44] Above, manors; other est.
[45] St. Paul's MS. A 29/336.
[46] Inq. Non. (Rec. Com.), 196; Home Counties Mag. vi. 49.
[47] St. Paul's MS. A 39/1370.
[48] Bodl. MSS. D.D. All Souls c 124/78; c 125/2; c 324.

[49] P.R.O., C 47/7/2/2, m. 14.
[50] Hist. MSS. Com. 39, 15th Rep. II, Hodgkin, p. 257.
[51] Above, manors; for other 16th-cent. Lees in Willesden, P.R.O., CP 25(2)/61/475/5 Edw. VI Mich.; Grange Mus., Wood F 35.
[52] P.R.O., CP 25(2)/27/180/16 Hen. VIII Hil.; above.
[53] Grange Mus., Wood F 24, p. 254; M.L.R. 1738/5/159.
[54] P.R.O., CP 25(2)/27/180/18 Hen. VIII Hil.; Grange Mus., Wood 14.
[55] Grange Mus., 1 A 4; P.R.O., C 8/320/171.
[56] P.R.O., PROB 11/30 (P.C.C. 14 Pynnyng, will of Mic. Roberts); ibid. C 107/70.
[57] Hist. MSS. Com. 39, Hodgkin, p. 257; above, other est.
[58] P.R.O., C 2/Eliz. I/P 10/23; M.R.O., Acc. 262/52/65–953; Acc. 262/53.
[59] M.R.O., MJ/SR/521/60; ibid. Acc. 262/39 (1771).
[60] P.R.O., PROB 11/126 (P.C.C. 114 Rudd, will of Thos. Rotheram); above, other est.
[61] Mdx. County Rec. iii. 373.
[62] Grange Mus., Wood F 21 (copy of 1765 terrier).
[63] Ibid. Wood F 21, pp. 121 sqq.; ibid. gen. files, ratepayers (TS. list, 1801).

been grubbed up by Michael Roberts at Neasden in the 1540s.[64] On Mapesbury manor in the 16th century felling was limited at Mapes wood[65] and there were still 70 a. of woodland in 1649,[66] but Great Mapes wood had gone by 1716 and by 1725 woodland had been reduced to 12 a., woods at Baldwins north of Willesden Green besides Mapes wood having been converted to grass or tillage since 1666;[67] the woodland had all gone by 1784.[68] There were 18 a. of woodland at Bounds and 69 a. at Brondesbury in 1649, but 44 a. of the latter had been lost by 1708.[69] There were 7 a. of woodland on the Rectory estate in 1650,[70] but it had apparently all gone by 1692.[71] On the Oxgate estates woodland formed 15 a. of Tanner's estate in 1675 but had entirely disappeared by 1755,[72] 30 a. of the Franklin farm in 1686 when another 33 a. had been lately converted to arable,[73] and only 3½ a. on the Hawe estate in 1700.[74] There was no woodland left on any of the Brydges estates by c. 1790: Broadfield Grove (33 a.) had been cleared by 1705, Down Grove (30 a.) between 1705 and 1734, and Square Grove (20 a.) by 1733.[75]

Woodland on the All Souls estate included Cricklewood along Edgware Road, where some clearing had taken place by the 15th century, but nearly half the land was still woodland in 1599. The main estate in Kensal Green and south Harlesden had once been part of Wormholt woods, and in 1599 much woodland remained in thick bands around fields.[76] The woods were not leased with the rest of the estate. In the 15th century wood yielded more income than other produce,[77] and from the mid 15th century the college sold the right to take wood for periods of years, usually three, attempting to reserve young trees.[78] The woodland was nevertheless gradually cleared.[79] In 1662 there were 107 elms and 816 oaks on the All Souls estate, of which 79 oaks were at Cricklewood.[80] Another 20 a. had been grubbed up by 1665, and in 1685 the All Souls woodland in Willesden totalled 64 a., compared with 99 a. in 1599.[81] In 1752 less than a tenth of the estate was woodland, all at Kensal Green and Harlesden.[82] By 1787 there was barely enough wood for common repairs.[83]

Although the land cleared of trees was often initially used as arable, the general tendency was a movement from arable to grassland. The All Souls estate, with a relatively high proportion of

arable, had 43 per cent in 1599, reduced to 25 per cent by 1752 and 17 per cent by 1815.[84] Arable was 40 per cent of Franklin's farm at Oxgate in 1686 and 17 per cent c. 1790,[85] while at Tanner's farm, Oxgate, the arable increased from c. 40 per cent in 1675 to 52 per cent in 1755 because of conversion from woodland.[86] At Mapesbury the arable decreased from nearly a third in 1649 to less than a tenth in 1784.[87] Most of the south-eastern part of the parish, at Kilburn, was almost entirely pasture and meadow.[88]

In 1816 Willesden was said to consist mostly of meadow or pasture although because the open fields survived there was more land under the plough than was usual in a parish so near London.[89] Except for Neasden field the boundaries of the open fields altered hardly at all between 1599 and inclosure.[90] An Inclosure Act was passed in 1815 following a petition by the principal farmers, and in 1823 the award was completed, 560 a. of open-field arable, meadow, and waste being allotted.[91] The largest freehold estates were those of All Souls College (491 a.), the duke of Buckingham (452 a.), the prebend of Mapesbury (319 a.), Joseph Finch (301 a.), Charles Brett (252 a.), and the prebend of Brondesbury (248 a.).[92]

In 1827 All Souls College attempted to rationalize its estate further.[93] There were further exchanges of land from 1851 to 1887 under the Inclosure Acts,[94] and by c. 1870 the pattern of landowning was much more logical and direct leases had replaced complicated sub-leasing.[95] There were 60 people occupying land in 1870, 15 having holdings of over 100 a., 10 of 50–100 a., 17 of 20–50 a., 11 of 5–20 a., and 6 of less than 5 a. Another six had livestock but no land. The number of holdings had fallen to 27 by 1900 and 16 by 1910. Of the latter one owned and six rented farms of 50–300 a., three owned and four rented farms of 5–50 a., and two rented holdings of 1–5 a. By 1930 there were only four holdings, all less than 50 a.[96] There was little arable: in 1866 out of a total acreage of 3,203 a., 52 a. were under oats, 43 a. under wheat, and 34 a. under beans.[97]

The soil, described at Mapesbury in 1803 as a strong, wet clay, was naturally much better suited to grass, and a cart could fetch a load of dung from the metropolis twice a day.[98] One

[64] P.R.O., PROB 11/30 (P.C.C. 14 Pynnyng).
[65] Ibid. PROB 11/63 (P.C.C. 28 Darcy, will of Roger Gibbes); ibid. REQ 2/293/28.
[66] Guildhall MS. 11816B.
[67] M.L.R. 1717/1/5; St. Paul's MS. FB 3, prebendal leases, ff. 72v.–74v.
[68] Guildhall MS. CC. 2199.
[69] Guildhall MSS. 11816B; CC. 30588.
[70] P.R.O., C 54/3574, no. 10.
[71] St. Paul's MS. C (Tillotson and Sherlock), f. 93 and v.
[72] P.R.O., C 6/215/101; M.L.R. 1755/2/151.
[73] P.R.O., C 5/167/142.
[74] M.R.O., Acc. 583/1.
[75] Ibid. Acc. 262/37, pt. 1 (1734), 39 (1705), 42 (Chandos estate map 1787), 42, pt. 1, 50/49; M.L.R. 1734/5/190.
[76] All Souls Coll., Hovenden maps II/18–22.
[77] Bodl. MS. D.D. All Souls c 268/213.
[78] Ibid. c 123/68; c 242/6, 10, 27, 33, 47, 53–4, 61.
[79] Ibid. c 124/85A; c 243/25; c 245/F (box E).
[80] Ibid. c 30/56.   [81] Ibid. b 20/23; 39.
[82] Ibid. c 245/F (box E); erroneously called Stonebridge Wood in Rocque, Map of Lond. (1746).

[83] Bodl. MS. D.D. All Souls c 245/34H.
[84] All Souls Coll., Hovenden maps II/18; Bodl. MSS. D.D. All Souls c 245/F (box E); c 245/34P. In 1815 all the arable was in the open fields.
[85] P.R.O., C 5/167/142; M.R.O., Acc. 262/42, pt. 1 (Chandos estate map 1787), 50/49.
[86] P.R.O., C 6/215/101; M.L.R. 1755/2/151.
[87] Guildhall MSS. 11816B; CC. 2199; St. Paul's MS. FB 3, prebendal leases, ff. 72v.–74v.
[88] Milne, Land Use Map of Lond. (1800).
[89] Brewer, Beauties of Eng. and Wales, x (5), 347–8.
[90] All Souls Coll., Hovenden maps II/18–22.
[91] 55 Geo. III, c. 49; M.R.O., EA/WIL; Grange Mus., 2 A 2 (Willesden inclosure docs.).
[92] M.R.O., Acc. 262/40, pt. 2 (inclosure claims 1816).
[93] Bodl. MS. D.D. All Souls c 245/34S.
[94] P.R.O., MAF 11/106/1195; MAF 11/107/3925; MAF 11/109/184, 258, 307, 562, 4523, 5996.
[95] Grange Mus., map c. 1870.
[96] P.R.O., MAF 68/250, 2416, 3520.
[97] Ibid. MAF 68/43–4.
[98] Guildhall MS. CC. 2202.

author noted the number and size of the dunghills along the side of Edgware Road, which carried more dung than any other road in the county.[99] Leases required more than two cartloads of dung per acre and restricted the proportion of land that could be mowed twice a year.[1] By 1833 the Willesden Green farm which the All Souls agent had suggested selling in 1827 had been much improved by manuring.[2]

During the 16th and 17th centuries the main function of the grassland was to support animals as part of mixed farming. At Mapesbury in 1581 an equal acreage was sown with wheat and oats, and cattle and horses formed part of the stock.[3] The farm buildings in 1649 included corn-chambers, a cowhouse, a cheesechamber, and a henhouse. Brondesbury and Bounds at the same date contained no buildings for arable farming but milkhouses, a cheeseroom, a sheephouse, and a bolting room and a haybarn, a hayhouse, and a cowhouse respectively.[4] The parsonage in 1692 included a granary as well as a dairy, a cheese-room, a cowhouse, a henhouse, and an apple-house; there was a granary at Oxgate in 1760 although haymaking was the main activity.[5] There were cattle at Brondesbury in the late 16th century and on the main All Souls estate in 1662.[6] Some farms supported both sheep and cattle in the 17th century, especially at Oxgate and Neasden.[7] Field-names indicate sheep on the All Souls estate between Harlesden and Kensal Green[8] and at East Twyford.[9] There was still a sheephouse on the Franklin farm at Oxgate c. 1791[10] but by then grass was grown either for feeding cattle or for hay. At Mapesbury in 1784 there was a dairy, cowhouse, a haybarn, and a house for labourers in the hay harvest.[11] There were vast herds of cattle around Brondesbury in the late 18th century,[12] and Ralph Marsh (d. by 1758), lessee of Bounds and owner of a freehold at Kilburn, was a grazier.[13]

Londoners were often directly involved in farming. Leases were made of Brondesbury to a butcher of Hanover Square in 1799 and 1812,[14] of the All Souls Kensal farm to an Oxford Street butcher 1810-46,[15] of Chambers and part of the All Souls Kensal lands to cowkeepers of St.

Marylebone in 1845,[16] of Mapesbury to a Piccadilly horse dealer 1826-71,[17] of the All Souls Willesden Green farm to a St. Marylebone jobmaster in 1828-45,[18] of the All Souls Crickle-wood farm to the keeper of a Berkeley Square livery stable 1832-55,[19] and of Oxgate to blood-stock dealers from Hyde Park Corner 1837-52.[20]

Hay was the major crop on the Brydges-Temple estates, and Oxgate was leased to a hay salesman from Stanmore in 1819.[21] Robert Hodgson's farm at Willesden Green was also a hay farm, 1845-52.[22] There were several cow-keepers between 1827 and 1862.[23] Thomas Goddard at Harlesden Green (1839) and Edward and Henry Biggs on Edgware Road (1847-58) were cattle dealers.[24] A horse dealer and chapman had been a tenant of Bounds and Brondesbury in 1784[25] but it was during the earlier 19th century that horses became especially important in Willesden: keepers of livery stables and job-masters included William Bean at Church End (1828),[26] Thomas Kenrick (1833), William Vaughan at Stonebridge (1836-7),[27] and William Cripps at Willesden Green.[28] Among the most important was William Anderson who, soon after taking the lease of Mapesbury, began to drain the land and manure it and built stables for 58 hunters and carriage horses.[29] He had been succeeded by 1850 by John Anderson, who continued there as a horse dealer until 1871.[30] He was followed by Chester Foulsham (d. 1917) who continued the tradition, specializing in training steeplechasers and hunters, including those of the prince of Wales (later Edward VII).[31] The other important horse dealer was Edmund Tat-tersall who built a model stud farm at Willesden Paddocks.[32] There was still a horse dealer there in 1890 but on a reduced scale, most of the land having been given over to dairy farming.[33] There were stables at Neasden, Willesden Green,[34] and Church End[35] in the 1870s, and jobmasters and horse dealers in 1890 at Willesden Paddocks, Dudding Hill farm, Church farm, Withers farm at Willesden Green, and Neasden stud farm and on a smaller scale, mainly in mews, in Willesden Green, Neasden, Harlesden, and especially Kilburn.[36] Sidney Galvayne, an Australian

[99] Middleton, *View*, 305.
[1] M.R.O., Acc. 262/60/96, 65/13.
[2] All Souls Coll., uncat. material, agents' letters.
[3] P.R.O., PROB 11/63 (P.C.C. 28 Darcy, will of Roger Gibbes).
[4] Guildhall MS. 11816B.
[5] St. Paul's MS. C (Tillotson and Sherlock), f. 93v.; M.R.O., Acc. 262/52/122.
[6] P.R.O., REQ 2/293/28; Bodl. MS. D.D. All Souls c 30/56.
[7] P.R.O., PROB 11/12 (P.C.C. 17 Moone, will of Wm. Page); PROB 11/69 (P.C.C. 36 Windsor, will of John Baseley); ibid. REQ 2/16/37; M.R.O., MJ/SR/60, 175-6; M.R.O., Acc. 583/1.
[8] All Souls Coll., Hovenden maps II/20.
[9] P.R.O., C 142/396, no. 154.
[10] M.R.O., Acc. 262/50/49, no. 27.
[11] Guildhall MS. CC. 2199.
[12] Loudon, *Landscape Gardening of Humphry Repton*, 39.
[13] Guildhall MSS. CC. 30618-19.
[14] Ibid. 33099-100.
[15] Bodl. MS. D.D. All Souls c 126/45; Guildhall MS. CC. 39215.
[16] Guildhall MS. CC. 39214; Bodl. MS. D.D. All Souls c 124/100.
[17] Guildhall MS. CC. 2208.

[18] Bodl. MSS. D.D. All Souls c 127/54; a 114, p. 21; All Souls Coll., uncat. material, agents' letters.
[19] Bodl. MSS. D.D. All Souls c 127/57; a 114, p. 21; Grange Mus., Ball, scrapbk. ii. 0284.
[20] i.e. Edmund Tattersall: above, other est.
[21] M.R.O., Acc. 262/60/96; cf. ibid. Acc. 262/60/97, 101; Acc. 262/65/3, 20.
[22] Grange Mus., Wood F 31; P.R.O., HO 107/1700/135/3, f. 382v.
[23] Bodl. MSS. D.D. All Souls a 104, p. 21; a 124, p. 21; c 127/51, 57*; c 245/34s; M.R.O., Acc. 1370/8.
[24] Grange Mus., Wood F 33; Ch. Com., Surveys S2, p. 607; Guildhall MS. CC. 22142.
[25] Guildhall MSS. CC. 30584, 30597; M.R.O., Acc. 397/2.
[26] Bodl. MS. D.D. All Souls Coll. c 127/53.
[27] Grange Mus., Wood F 33.
[28] Bodl. MS. D.D. All Souls Coll. c 245/34s; uncat. material, agents' letters.   [29] Guildhall MS. CC. 2208.
[30] Grange Mus., Ball, 'Old Willesden', 76; ibid. 1 B 21-3 (lighting rate bk.); Keane, *Beauties of Mdx*. 223.
[31] *Willesden Monthly Illus*. 5 Oct. 1937; Grange Mus., gen. files, Willesden Lane, Mapesbury.
[32] Above, other est.   [33] *Kelly's Dir. Mdx*. (1890).
[34] Grange Mus., 1 B 23 (sewer rate 1871-3).
[35] Ibid. Wood F 19 (sale cat. 1/5).
[36] *Kelly's Dir. Mdx*. (1890).

described as a humane horse tamer, operated at Upper Oxgate in 1891 and was later at Model farm, Neasden and there was a riding school at the Slade in Cricklewood in 1892.[37] In 1870, after the peak for horse farming had been passed, there were 118 agricultural horses, 76 unbroken horses, and 8 breeding mares.[38]

The Act of 1864 making it illegal to keep cattle within the metropolis led to a rapid growth in dairy farming just outside the limits.[39] In Willesden the numbers of milk cows and other cattle (mainly calves) rose from 146 and 65 in 1866 to 806 and 170 by 1870. There were 815 milk cows and 156 other cattle in 1880. Numbers declined after 1880.[40] Joseph Bannister had sheds for 204 cows at the Rectory farm at Harlesden (Manor farm) in 1864, and after the estate was sold in the 1870s moved to Willesden Paddocks which he was still farming in 1897.[41] At Neasden there were sheds for 80 cows at Model Farm in 1878 and for 60 at Gravel Farm in 1880.[42] There were cattle at Dollis Hill in 1887,[43] and Upper Oxgate farm, which in 1851 had been a horse stud farm, was by 1871 occupied as a dairy farm.[44] Among the most important dairy farmers were Welford & Sons who had been farming since c. 1860 and who were appointed dairymen to the queen in 1876. By 1882 they had a large herd of pedigree cows and farmed over 300 a. in Willesden, much of it leased from All Souls College at Kensal Green where they had built a model dairy farm. The farm continued, though on a reduced scale, after building had swallowed up most of the farmland and the firm was absorbed into the United Dairies in the 1920s.[45] Another large dairy farm was Goddard's at Lower Place, which was closed in 1901 when the Royal Agricultural Society took over the land. At the time there were three dairy farms at Willesden Green, two at Kensal Green, and one each at south Kilburn and Harlesden.[46] There were seven cowsheds in 1910, when horse keeping was said to have been replaced by dairy farming because of the growth of motor traffic.[47]

By then, however, all farming was diminishing as farmland was sold for building. From 3,370 a. (3,035 a. grass) in 1870, the acreage had shrunk to 1,113 a. (1,037 a. grass) by 1900, 550 a. (494 a. grass) in 1920, and 52 a. (50 a. grass) in 1930. Farming persisted longest in the north, at Neasden, Dollis Hill, and Oxgate. There were sheep at Dollis Hill in the late 19th century and it was probably there that the flocks of 1,372 in 1866 and 462 in 1880 were kept. There were 464 pigs in 1866, 279 in 1900, and 77 in 1920.[48] Pigs were mainly kept by the poor in Kilburn and Kensal Green. There were some nurseries in the late 19th century, mainly in Kilburn and Brondesbury, but vegetables were probably grown on allotments or as fodder crops on farms. The highest acreages were of mangolds (29 a. in 1870, 32 a. in 1900, 4 a. in 1920). There were 8 a. of turnips and 7 a. of carrots in 1870 but the area of other crops was very small.[49]

The proportion of the population dependent on agriculture declined from 86 per cent in 1811 to 23 per cent in 1851. In 1841 the 599 people living in barns and tents at the time of the census were mainly itinerant haymakers but may also have included builders and navvies. The proportion employed in agriculture had dropped to 1 per cent in 1901.[50]

MILLS. A mill which formed part of a grant in 1325 by Richard of Cornhill to John, vicar of Willesden, was probably a watermill on the Brent.[51]

A windmill existed by 1295 on the estate conveyed by William of Breadstreet to John of Middleton.[52] It stood apparently north of the Sherrick brook[53] and was in ruins by 1365 when permission was given to Thomas Frowyk, the mortgagee, to take the timber from it.[54]

Soon after 1616 William Grey, a lessee of Francis Roberts, built a windmill in Dudden hill field at the point where Dudden Hill Lane entered it.[55] The mill was held by Robert Paltock in 1698 and sold by Henry Barnett to Edmund Frankland in 1727.[56] William Kilby had it in 1765[57] but it had gone by 1817 and probably by 1787.[58]

Isaac Ennos, a tenant of Mapesbury, built Kilburn windmill at Shoot-up Hill between 1784 and 1803.[59] He was succeeded c. 1832 by William Hale,[60] who in 1851 employed five men there[61] and was succeeded before 1867 by Charles Hale. The boarded mill was burnt down in 1863 and demolished c. 1900. A steam mill was built next to the damaged windmill in 1867.[62]

INDUSTRY. A tilekiln, first mentioned in 1438–9,[63] formed part of the All Souls estate at Harlesden, probably just south of the green, on

[37] Grange Mus., NM 4; inf. from Grange Mus. (1980).

[38] P.R.O., MAF 68/250.

[39] Grange Mus., gen. files, farms (*The Countryman*, Winter 1954, p. 259).

[40] P.R.O., MAF 68/250, 706, 1846, 2416, 2980.

[41] Grange Mus., gen. files, farms (*The Countryman*, Winter 1954, p. 259); ibid. Wood F 19 (sale cat. 1/52); Guildhall MS. CC. 291245.

[42] Grange Mus., Wood F 20 (sale cats. 2/25, 37).

[43] Foley, *Our Lanes and Meadow Paths*, 32.

[44] P.R.O., HO 107/1700/135/3, f. 378; Grange Mus., 1 B 23 (sewer rate 1871); *Cricklewood*, ed. B. W. Dexter (1905).

[45] Grange Mus., gen. files, industries (*Illus. Lond. News*, 16 Sept. 1882; *Daily Mirror*, 14 July 1977); All Souls Coll., uncat. material, docs. relating to estates 1887–95; bursar's rentals 1904.

[46] Willesden U.D.C. *Public Health Rep.* (1902).

[47] Ibid. (1910).

[48] P.R.O., MAF 68/43-4, 250, 706, 1846, 2980; Grange Mus., gen. files, parks and gdns.

[49] Grange Mus., 1 B 20 (rate 1862); 1 B 23 (sewage rate 1871); M.R.O., Acc. 1279/1; Guildhall MS. CC. 161227.

[50] *Census*, 1811–1901.

[51] P.R.O., CP 25(1)/149/52, no. 328.

[52] Ibid. CP 25(1)/148/35, no. 258.

[53] Ibid. E 40/11845, Milnefeld.

[54] *Cal. Close*, 1364-8, 190.

[55] P.R.O., C 3/439/8; W.A.M. 17039; G.L.C. County Hall map colln. AT 602 (Senex, map of open fields 1722).

[56] P.R.O., CP 25(2)/854/10 Wm. III Trin.; CP 25(2)/1037/13 Geo. I Hil.

[57] Grange Mus., Wood F 21 (map of 1765).

[58] M.R.O., Acc. 262/40, pt. 2 (1817); ibid. (Chandos estate map 1787); Bodl. MS. D.D. All Souls c 149/2.

[59] Guildhall MSS. CC. 2199, 2202.

[60] Grange Mus., 1 B 10 (rate 1830); Guildhall MS. CC. 2208. [61] P.R.O., HO 107/1700/135/3, f. 366v.

[62] Ch. Com., Surveys S2, pp. 607 sqq.; *Kelly's Dir. Mdx.* (1851); Grange Mus., exhibits 1979; ibid. 1 B 21 (rate 1867). For a photo, see Grange Mus., Wood F 26/9.

[63] Bodl. MS. D.D. All Souls c 124/78.

the site of the later Tyle or Tylers Close.[64] The kiln lasted throughout the 15th and early 16th centuries, producing tiles for London using imported wood and clay.[65] Tilekiln houses at Harlesden and Kilburn formed part of the Roberts estate at the beginning of the 16th century.[66] That at Kilburn can probably be identified with the Place, tilehouses and kilns on Edgware Road sold by Thomas Roberts to Thomas Marsh in 1679,[67] and with Tile Kiln farm or Kilburn Pits, owned by the Marsh family in the mid 18th century.[68] The kiln had probably long ceased to be worked by the late 18th century when the farm was merged in the Salusbury estate, although there were brickmakers in Kilburn in 1851 and 1867.[69]

Other tile and brick works are indicated by the reservation of 'daubing earth' by Bartholomew Willesden in 1465,[70] by a brickfield on the Nicoll estate in 1739,[71] a tilekiln field at Oxgate in 1787,[72] and kiln fields on the Brondesbury estate in 1834.[73] Tenants of All Souls were producing a million bricks a year at Kensal Green in 1825.[74] The Willesden Brick & Tile works in Chambers Lane, which were owned by the Furness family and established by 1882, provided many bricks for local building until they were demolished in 1937.[75] There was also a brick and lime works next to the railway at Stonebridge in 1914.[76]

There was some tanning in the 17th century, notably at Oxgate which contained tanyards and was leased to one tanner, John Plomer, in 1665 and offered for sale to another, Ezechiel Tanner, before 1675.[77] There was a tailor in Willesden in 1624[78] but few tradesmen or craftsmen other than the usual smiths, wheelwrights, and shoemakers before the 19th century. In 1811 only one family in ten in Willesden was dependent on trade, manufacture, or craft but by 1831 the proportion had risen to a quarter.[79] Craftsmen included a coachmaker in 1819, a glassblower at Harlesden in 1829, a piano maker at Harlesden in 1850,[80] and a wholesale perfumer with 22 employees on Edgware Road in 1851.[81] There was a brewery near Oxgate in 1819.[82] Kilburn brewery, established on the Mapesbury estate at Edgware Road by William and George Verey in 1832,[83] employed 22 men in 1851 and 66 in 1919, a year before it closed.[84]

As early as 1834 the 'contiguity' to London was adduced as the reason for the unusually large number of laundresses in Willesden, women who earned good wages to supplement the seasonal work of their husbands in agriculture and brickmaking.[85] As steam laundries developed in the later 19th century, 'factory' laundries predominated over the smaller 'domestic' laundries.[86] By 1902 there were 137 laundries employing 2,046 women. The numbers declined, to 60 factory and 28 domestic laundries in 1910, 53 and 23 in 1918, and 38 and 29 in 1934.[87] In 1919 there were 15 laundries each employing more than 40 women, the two largest, in Stonebridge and Craven Park, employing 180 and 364 respectively.[88]

From the mid 19th century the influence of London on industry became increasingly stronger, building spreading from the south to house labour for industries which often themselves moved from central London. Kilburn, the nearest area and the first to be developed, also provided early industry. A carriage manufacturer was located on Edgware Road in 1851,[89] and Elm Lodge on Edgware Road was a gelatine factory in 1858.[90] There were five coachbuilding and three cycle-manufacturing firms in Kilburn by 1890. By that date Kilburn also housed manufacturers of ladders, steel punches, perambulators, artificial limbs, and gold leaf and several masons in Willesden Lane near Paddington cemetery.[91] The largest Kilburn firm was the Patent Railway Signal Works, opened by John Saxby and John Farmer on a site between the railway line and Canterbury Road c. 1862. They provided employment for 700 men in 1872 and for 2,000 before the manufacture of signalling equipment moved to Chippenham in 1903. The premises were sold in 1906[92] and from 1911 to 1933 were occupied by Humber Ltd., motor manufacturers.[93]

Land in Acton Road next to the canal was advertised as suitable for a brickfield or factory in 1879[94] and industry multiplied in Harlesden and Kensal Green from the 1880s. Most firms there were small. Holland & Holland, makers of hand-made guns, opened a factory on Harrow Road in 1880 and employed 48 men in 1919; although it had relinquished its shooting range for building

[64] All Souls Coll., Hovenden maps II/20; Grange Mus., Wood F 21 (map of 1765).

[65] Bodl. MS. D.D. All Souls c 324; P.R.O., KB 29/138 Hil. m. 23; ibid. C 1/150/82.

[66] P.R.O., C 1/349/1.

[67] Ibid. C 6/231/34.

[68] M.L.R. 1745/3/451; Guildhall MSS. CC. 30636-7; M.R.O., EA/WIL, no. 948.

[69] P.R.O., HO 107/1700/135/3, ff. 353 sqq.; Grange Mus., 1 B 21 (lighting rate bk.).

[70] P.R.O., E 40/5767.

[71] M.R.O., Acc. 262/37, pt. 1.

[72] Ibid. Acc. 262/42 (Chandos estate map 1787).

[73] B.L. Add. MS. 12546F; M.R.O., EA/WIL, nos. 905-6.

[74] All Souls Coll., uncat. material, agents' letters 1808-37.

[75] Grange Mus., gen. files, Willesden Chron. (Suppl. 5 Mar. 1937); ibid. 1 A 4 (Willesden Chron. 18 Sept. 1936; 30 July 1937); ibid. Geo. Furness & Co., album of photos. and plans 1893-9; Kelly's Dir. Mdx. (1882).

[76] O.S. Map 1/2,500, Mdx. XVI. 1 (1914 edn.).

[77] P.R.O., C 6/215/101; ibid. PROB 11/132 (P.C.C. 127 Meade); PROB 11/236 (P.C.C. 1654 f. 28v., will of Thos. Marsh); PROB 11/347 (P.C.C. 46 Bunch, will of John Finch).

[78] Ibid. PROB 11/144 (P.C.C. 83 Byrde, will of Nic. Broche).

[79] Census, 1811, 1831.

[80] Grange Mus., Wood F 33.

[81] P.R.O., HO 107/1700/135/3, f. 366v.

[82] M.R.O., Acc. 262/65/12.

[83] Ibid. Acc. 947; Pigot, Nat. Com. Dir. (1832-4).

[84] P.R.O., HO 107/1700/135/3, f. 365; Willesden educ. cttee. Draft Rep. (1919); Kilburn and Willesden Dir. (1872-1921).

[85] Rep. Com. Poor Laws, H.C. 44, p. 185h (1834), xxxvi.

[86] e.g. Grange Mus., Wood F 20, pp. 20 sqq.

[87] Willesden U.D.C. Public Health Rep. (1902, 1910, 1918, 1934).

[88] Willesden educ. cttee. Draft Rep. (1919), pp. 24 sqq.

[89] P.R.O., HO 107/1700/135/3, f. 362.

[90] Guildhall MS. CC. 39516.

[91] Kelly's Dir. Mdx. (1890).

[92] Centenary of Signalling (copy in Grange Mus., gen. files, Kilburn); W. F. Harris, John Saxby (copy in Grange Mus., red box, Kilburn).

[93] Kilburn and Willesden Dir. (1906-34).

[94] Grange Mus., Wood F 20 (sale cat. 2/9).

by 1918, the factory survived in 1981.[95] By 1890 Harlesden had makers of washing machines and antiseptic fluids, an art metal company, monumental masons, and the Willesden Cycle Co.[96] In 1902 McVitie & Price opened a biscuit factory in Waxlow Road, Harlesden, and by 1919 was the largest employer in Willesden, with 1,150 workers.[97] Park Royal began to be developed during the First World War; the later industrial history of the area is treated elsewhere.[98]

Small-scale industry, masons, saw-mills, cycle-makers, printers, electrical engineering works, and makers of photographic apparatus and pencils, were established at Willesden Green and Church End in the three decades before the First World War.[99] The largest of the firms was British Thomson Houston Co. which opened its electrical engineering works north of the vicarage at Church End in 1913, employing 462 people in 1919 and 2,000 in 1949.[1] It had closed by 1964.[2] J. H. Dallmeyer, manufacturers of lenses and scientific instruments, moved to Denzil Road, Church End, from central London in 1907. They moved to High Road in the 1920s and built extensions in 1945 and 1952. By 1979 the firm employed c. 90 people on high-precision optical manufacture.[3] Industry spread northward from Church End along Neasden Lane. In 1913 the pencil works of B. S. Cohen were founded in the Britannia Works in the triangle between Neasden Lane and the two railway lines. Some 100 people were employed there in 1919. In 1926 the works passed to the Royal Sovereign Pencil Co. which established a second factory a little to the north in 1929 and by 1937 had 250 employees. By 1949 it had been replaced by Waterman's Pen Co., then employing 300 people.[4]

While Kilburn, Kensal Green, Harlesden, Willesden Green, and the northern part of Church End all used the railway lines along which they lay for transporting raw materials and finished goods, two areas were even more dependent on the railways. The low lying and poorly drained land along the river Brent was unattractive to speculative builders and in the 1880s the Metropolitan Railway Co. purchased 290 a. at Neasden, where it built a new depot and repair shops designed to employ 500 men and to replace its obsolete works in Marylebone. Houses were built for the workers employed in repairing and, from 1896, building engines and rolling stock.[5] A generating station, built in Quainton Street, Neasden, when the line was electrified in

1903–5, survived until 1967. The Great Central Railway established its depot south of the line at Neasden and c. 1900 erected housing for its workers.[6] In 1888 the Midland Railway Co. extended its workshops and sidings at Cricklewood,[7] which although in Hendon employed many people from Willesden. In 1921 the railways employed 3,277 Willesden men.[8] In 1949 London Transport's 50-a. depot at Neasden employed 500 people and British Railway's Eastern Region 109-a. works, also at Neasden, employed 650; London Midland Region's depot at Willesden Junction provided work for 820 residents of Harlesden and Stonebridge.[9]

Served by the railway and Edgware Road, industry began to establish itself at Cricklewood before the First World War. W. J. Fowler & Son, printers, was founded at Cricklewood Broadway in 1898.[10] On the All Souls estate factories were built for scene-painting (1906), motor repairs (1909), and firewood (1912),[11] but the largest works, that of the Imperial Dry Plate Co., manufacturers of photographic plates and paper, was built by George Furness & Co. c. 1893 a little farther north.[12] In 1919 it had 200 employees.[13]

The First World War was a strong stimulus to industry in Willesden, especially in the new districts of Cricklewood and Park Royal. Firms established at Cricklewood, near the airfields and factories of Hendon and Kingsbury, included Nieuport & General Aircraft Co. and British Caudron Co., manufacturers of aeroplanes, which employed 500 and 400 people respectively in 1919. Farther south, in High Road, Kilburn, the Central Aircraft Co. employed 350 workers and other aeroplane manufacturers in Willesden Lane had 200 and 70 employees respectively.[14] The largest factory in Cricklewood, S. Smith & Sons (later Smiths Industries Ltd.), opened on Edgware Road south of the railway in 1915 to manufacture fuses, instruments, and accessories.[15] By 1919 Smiths employed 1,000 munition workers.[16] In 1920 all manufacturing was transferred from the firm's headquarters in Great Portland St. to Cricklewood and the company survived the slump of the 1920s, acquiring before 1939 firms which made electrical motors and aircraft accessories and electric clocks, and forming a new subsidiary in 1944 to make industrial instruments. As the company grew it acquired other companies and sites overseas but Cricklewood remained the most important site, expanding from the original factory

[95] Ibid. 1 A 2 (*Willesden Cit.* 27 Jan. 1950); All Souls Coll., uncat. material, bursars' accts. 1896–8, 1904, 1914; ibid. agent's reps. 1918; Grange Mus., Willesden educ. cttee. *Draft Rep.* (1919), pp. 24 sqq.; *Kelly's Dir. Lond.* (1975); inf. from curator of Grange Mus.
[96] *Kelly's Dir. Mdx.* (1890).
[97] Willesden educ. cttee. *Draft Rep.* (1919), pp. 24 sqq.
[98] Above, Acton.
[99] *Kelly's Dir. Mdx.* (1890); All Souls Coll., uncat. material, bursars' accts. 1904, 1914; D. Jenkinson and C. Posthumous, *Vanwall*, 14; Grange Mus., 1 A 2 (*Willesden Cit.* 9 July, 11 Nov., 1949); O.S. Map 1/2,500, Mdx. XI. 14; XVI. 2 (1914 edn.).
[1] Grange Mus., gen. files, electricity; Grange Mus., 1 A 2 (*Willesden Cit.* 30 Dec. 1949); Willesden educ. cttee. *Draft Rep.* (1919).
[2] *Kelly's Dir. Lond.* (1959, 1964).
[3] Inf. from Dallmeyer Optics.

[4] All Souls Coll., uncat. material, agent's reps. 1924; Willesden educ. cttee. *Draft Rep.* (1919); *Willesden Monthly Illus.* 5 Jan. 1937; Grange Mus., 1 A 2 (*Willesden Cit.* 23 Dec. 1949).
[5] *T.L.M.A.S.* xxvi. 314; *Kelly's Dir. Mdx.* (1882).
[6] Ashdown, *Ind. Mon. of Gtr. Lond.* s.v. Brent.
[7] All Souls Coll., uncat. material, docs. relating to estates 1887–95.
[8] *Census,* 1921.   [9] Morris, *Willesden Surv.*
[10] Grange Mus., gen. files, printers.
[11] All Souls Coll., uncat. material, plan and photo. of Anson Rd. ind. bldgs.
[12] Grange Mus., Geo. Furness & Co., album of photos. and plans 1893–9; O.S. Map 6″, Lond. XXVI (1894–6 edn.).
[13] Willesden educ. cttee. *Draft Rep.* (1919).
[14] Ibid.
[15] Based on inf. from Smiths Inds. Ltd. (1978).
[16] Willesden educ. cttee. *Draft Rep.* (1919), pp. 24 sqq.

to house 8,000 employees in 1937[17] and 1978. Smiths, although the largest, was one of many firms involved in the motor industry, which received a great impetus from the First World War. Others included, by 1919, McCurd Lorry Manufacturing Co. and Lamplough Radiator & Engineering Co., each with 80 employees on Edgware Road at Cricklewood, the Grosvenor Carriage Co. and Humber Ltd. with 70 and 100 employees respectively in Kilburn, and the British Ensign Motor Co. with 130 at Willesden Green.[18] Park Ward opened as high-class coach builders in Willesden Green in 1919. It was purchased by Rolls Royce in 1939, and after 1971 as Rolls Royce Motors (Mulliner Park Ward Division) was one of two factories (together employing 600 workers in 1977) producing bodies for Rolls Royce cars.[19] The number of motor and cycle makers increased from 12 in 1918 to 32 in 1925 and 63 in 1934.[20]

Willesden changed from a dormitory exporting workers to a net recipient of incoming workers after the First World War. It remained a net recipient, even though many who had travelled from outside Willesden to work in the munitions and aircraft factories of Cricklewood and Park Royal moved into new housing within Willesden when munitions gave way to light industry. With the construction of the North Circular Road factories and council estates were built along the hitherto empty land of the Brent valley, linking the existing sites at Cricklewood and Park Royal.[21] The number of factories increased from 60 in 1910 to 166 in 1918 and 237 in 1925;[22] 226 factories and workshops were built during the period 1922–34[23] and by 1939 there were 461 firms, 57 of which had been established since 1929 at Staples Corner,[24] the area at Cricklewood named from Staples & Co., manufacturers of mattresses, who built their factory at the junction of the North Circular and Edgware Road in 1925.[25] Other firms at Cricklewood included Rolls Razor, which moved to Edgware Road from Battersea in 1926;[26] York Shipley (after 1956 York Division, Borg-Warner Ltd.), refrigerator manufacturers, which moved to the North Circular Road from Regent Street in 1927 and employed 150 people there in 1978;[27] Western Electric Co. (later Westrex), which opened in 1929 in Coles Green Road, where it employed c. 100 people in 1978;[28] and Shepherd Tobias & Co., which opened its glass works on the North Circular Road c. 1930, employing c. 150 workers in 1950.[29] By 1933 there were 32

factories employing 6,975 people in Cricklewood and along the North Circular.[30] The industries were light, depending upon road transport and showrooms in London, electrical or engineering skills, and often recent inventions. Motor cars and their accessories, wireless, and films featured among them.[31]

Industry in Neasden developed during the 1920s and 1930s, partly because of increased accessibility provided by the North Circular Road and the widening and straightening of Neasden Lane in connexion with the Wembley Exhibition of 1924. By 1933 three firms in the southern part of Neasden Lane, British Thomson Houston Co. (electrical engineers), the Royal Sovereign Pencil Co., and Neasden Waxed Paper Co., employed 2,500 people.[32] The last named had opened in 1926 and employed 230 workers, mostly women, by 1937.[33] Oxford University Press was established in Press Road off the northern part of Neasden Lane by 1932, primarily as a warehouse for the distribution of books; 356 people were employed there by 1979.[34] The Book Centre next to the North Circular opened in 1938 and by the 1970s contained warehouses with 11,000,000 books and employed 100 staff.[35] TI Gas Spares (formerly Ascot Gas Water Heaters) opened a factory on a 15-a. site on the North Circular at Neasden in 1934 and employed 400 people there in 1978.[36] Other factories on the North Circular at Neasden included the cosmetic firms Amami Silvikrin in 1945 and J. Grossmith & Son shortly afterwards.[37]

In 1928 Hall's Telephone Accessories (later Associated Automation Ltd.) opened a small factory in Dudden Hill Lane which expanded during the Second World War and in 1960, until by 1974 it employed some 920 people, reduced by 1978 to 600.[38] By 1939 Church End had become wholly industrial, with motor body, furniture, paint, sheet metal, and die-casting works.[39]

In the absence of town planning Willesden was saturated by the late 1930s. In 1937 it was described as the largest manufacturing borough in Britain.[40] A survey made after the Second World War to establish a plan to deal with over-industrialization and over-population found that there were 445 firms in 1948, compared with 462 in 1939. Over half had been established in the period 1919–39. Of the 37,000 people employed within Willesden borough, 30 per cent were employed at Park Royal, 19 per cent at Cricklewood, 14 per cent at Church End, and the rest in

[17] *Willesden Monthly Illus.* 5 Dec. 1937 (copy in Grange Mus.).
[18] Willesden educ. cttee. *Draft Rep.* (1919), pp. 24 sqq.
[19] Grange Mus., gen. files, industry (*Kilburn Times*, 16 Sept. 1977).
[20] Willesden U.D.C. *Public Health Rep.* (1918, 1925, 1934).
[21] Morris, *Willesden Surv.*
[22] Willesden U.D.C. *Public Health Rep.* (1910, 1918, 1925).
[23] Inst. of Mun. and County Engineers, *62nd Ann. Gen. Mtg.* (1935).
[24] Morris, *Willesden Surv.*
[25] Grange Mus., 1 A 2 (*Willesden Cit.* 13 Oct. 1950).
[26] Ibid. (24 Feb. 1950).
[27] Inf. from York Marketing Div. Borg-Warner Ltd.
[28] Inf. from Westrex.

[29] Grange Mus., 1 A 2 (*Willesden Cit.* 15 Sept. 1950).
[30] D. H. Smith, *Industries of Gtr. Lond.* 89.
[31] See list of firms in Grange Mus., petition of Willesden U.D.C. for incorp. (1932), Suppl. no. 1.
[32] Smith, *Ind. of Gtr. Lond.* 93.
[33] *Willesden Monthly Illus.* 5 Nov. 1937; *Kilburn and Willesden Dir.* (1926).
[34] Inf. from O.U.P. (1979); Grange Mus., petition for incorp. (1932), Suppl. no. 1.
[35] Grange Mus., gen. files, industry.
[36] Inf. from TI Gas Spares Ltd.
[37] Grange Mus., 1 A 2 (*Willesden Cit.* 14 Apr., 10 Nov. 1950).
[38] Inf. from Assoc. Automation Ltd.
[39] O.S. Map 1/2,500, Mdx. XVI. 2 (1935 edn.); Morris, *Willesden Surv.* map 6.
[40] *Willesden Monthly Illus.* 5 Jan. 1937.

the residential areas. Only one factory, Smiths of Cricklewood, employed more than 2,000 people. There were four others with more than 1,000 employees and twelve with 500–1,000.[41] In the older centres industry, commerce, and housing were mixed together and in those areas of small industry, like Kilburn and Willesden Green, three quarters of the workforce, mostly female, lived locally.[42] Industry often occupied obsolete buildings: a third of the premises in use in 1948 had been constructed before 1900, a quarter between 1919 and 1930. The policy of Willesden borough, in conjunction with the Greater London Plan, was to reduce the population and to move industry out to new towns, especially from the older, congested areas like Kilburn which were to become almost wholly residential. By c. 1960 there were 168 'conforming' firms employing 36,092 people in Willesden, of which 60 (with 10,861 workers) were at Staples Corner, 52 (with 14,464 workers) at Park Royal, and 26 (with 5,142 workers) in Church End. There were 345 non-conforming firms with 7,903 workers, mostly small concerns with a short history.[43]

Although the total number of factories increased, the number of jobs declined, dropping from 147,000 in 1967 to 88,000 in 1969 and contracting still further thereafter. The contraction was part of a national trend but also reflected local factors. Firms and skilled workers left the often obsolete and overcrowded Willesden sites for more spacious surroundings. When large firms moved out the smaller firms dependent on them had to close, and many of them were encouraged to move by the council's policy.[44]

As the skilled white workers left, immigrants, mostly unskilled from Ireland, the Caribbean, and the Indian subcontinent, moved in, creating unemployment at a time when firms were closing because of the lack of skilled labour.[45] The initial attractions of Willesden's proximity to London were offset by high cost of rents, rates, and wages.[46] In 1973 Willesden became a focus of national attention in the clash over union power in the film-processing firm of Grunwick at Church End. Grunwick's was typical of many firms in the area in reducing its work force, from nearly 500 in 1973 to c. 250 by 1977.[47] There was also a movement away from manufacturing towards offices and warehousing. Multi-storeyed office blocks were built along the North Circular for TI Gas Spares in 1961,[48] for the E. Alec Colman Group in 1963,[49] and for O.U.P. next to

their warehouse in Press Road in 1965.[50] During the 1970s vacated factory sites were often used for warehousing,[51] and several vacant sites along the North Circular Road and in Cricklewood were advertised for warehousing in 1978. As factories closed the sites were often given over to other uses.

LOCAL GOVERNMENT. Manorial government. In 1294 the dean and chapter of St. Paul's established their title to view of frankpledge, the assize of bread and of ale, and other liberties in Willesden as in their other estates in Middlesex.[52] No record of the exercise of that jurisdiction has been found. In 1552 they were indicted at the Middlesex sessions for failing to hold an annual court at Willesden, as had been the custom, and for not maintaining a pound.[53] Some of the dean and chapter's jurisdiction appears to have been exercised in the courts of the several prebendal manors, to which all the freehold tenants owed suit of court, but the records are very few. For Bounds manor courts leet and baron were in theory held every three years; the single court roll that survives, for 1422, records presentments for breaking the assize of ale.[54] No record of manorial jurisdiction in Brondesbury has been found beyond the mention in a sublease of 1799 of the manorial pound and of waifs and strays.[55] For Mapesbury 16th-century leases mentioned not only waifs and strays but courts and their perquisites.[56]

At Chambers manor, for which a court was held in 1510, the lessee in 1570 had the right to hold a court and take the profits,[57] and his successors in 1649 and 1717 were instructed to hold a court baron every seven years. A value of £1 was put on the manor's courts leet and baron in 1649, including waifs, strays, and felons' goods.[58] In 1598, for which a transcript of a court roll alone survives, the court was held in the prebendary's name by the steward of All Souls College and fined defaulters within the view of frankpledge.[59] In 1729 and 1847 it was recorded that in spite of the wording of the leases no court had been held.[60]

At Harlesden in the early 16th century the right to felons' goods was exercised on behalf of the prebendary.[61] The lease of the manor in 1576 conferred the right to hold courts,[62] and the view of frankpledge and court baron, with waifs and strays, were valued at £1 5s. in 1649.[63] For Oxgate a single court roll survives for 1330, recording only essoins, a distraint for non-

[41] Morris, *Willesden Surv.*
[42] Leff and Blunden, *Willesden Story*, 45.
[43] Brent planning and research dept. *Background to Brent* (1967).
[44] *Rep. to Willesden, 1963–4.*
[45] Weintraub, 'Race and local politics'; Grange Mus., gen. files, Park Royal (*Willesden and Brent Chron.* 15, 22 Apr. 1977); *Rep. to Willesden, 1963–4; Willesden Civic Review,* Feb. 1957.
[46] Grange Mus., gen. files, industry (*Kilburn Times,* 16 Sept. 1977); gen. files, topog. (*Willesden and Brent Chron.* 31 Mar. 1972).
[47] G. Ward, *Fort Grunwick* (1977), 3, 23, 25–6.
[48] Grange Mus., 1 A 2 (*Willesden Cit.* 12 May 1961).
[49] Ibid. (22 Mar. 1963).
[50] *Builder,* 29 Oct. 1965.

[51] Grange Mus., gen. files, race relations (*Profile of Brent,* 1976).
[52] *Plac. de Quo Warr.* (Rec. Com.), 475–6.
[53] Hist. MSS. Com. 39, *15th Rep. II, Hodgkin,* p. 257.
[54] Guildhall MS. 11816B; St. Paul's MS. A 39/1370.
[55] Guildhall MS. CC. 33099.
[56] P.R.O., E 40/1519.
[57] St. Paul's MS. C (I Nowell), ff. 330v.–331.
[58] Guildhall MS. 11816B; St. Paul's MS. FB 3, prebendal leases 1721–96, ff. 28–30v.
[59] St. Paul's MS. C (III Nowell), ff. 162v.–163.
[60] Ibid. MS. FB 4, prebendal leases 1798–1834, ff. 77–9; Guildhall MS. CC. 1988; Ch. Com., Surveys S2, p. 411.
[61] P.R.O., C 1/150/82.
[62] St. Paul's MS. C (I Nowell), f. 456v.
[63] Guildhall MS. 11816B.

attendance, and a rental;[64] in 1649 the profits of the court leet, including waifs and strays, were valued at 5s.[65] For Neasden a view of frankpledge and court were held in 1510,[66] and in 1649, with waifs and strays, they were valued at 6s. 8d.;[67] the right to hold a court was mentioned in the lease of the manor in 1544.[68] At East Twyford a court leet was mentioned in a conveyance of 1597.[69]

Manorial pounds were thought to belong to Brondesbury in 1799[70] and to Harlesden in 1847,[71] but the three pounds that existed at inclosure in 1823, near Neasden House, near the Crown inn in Harlesden, and in Petticoat (later Pound) Lane in Chapel End,[72] were presumably controlled by the vestry. The vestry in 1828 ordered a pound to be set up in Petticoat Lane, probably the brick building dismantled in 1895, and from 1828 regularly appointed a pound-keeper.[73]

PARISH GOVERNMENT.[74] Churchwardens were mentioned in 1510 when they held chantry property.[75] There were two from 1552.[76] A constable of Willesden was mentioned c. 1580 when he was ordered to put the lessee of Brondes-bury in the stocks.[77] From c. 1641 to 1853 there were two constables.[78] A collector for the poor was mentioned in 1608.[79] There were two overseers of the poor from 1678 and a salaried deputy or assistant overseer in 1794, 1798, 1826, and 1830. From 1678 there were usually two surveyors of highways although in 1706-7, 1711-14, and 1771 there were three. The parish clerk, mentioned in 1708, was paid in 1774 for doing the vestry clerk's work and in 1789-90 and 1802 the two offices were held by the same man.[80] William Twyford (d. 1826), dismissed for incompetence as vestry clerk in 1813, continued as parish clerk in 1818 and 1824 although unsatisfactory. Other officials included a beadle (1703), a dog-whipper (1778), an apothecary or surgeon,[81] appointed in 1809 and 1818 and dismissed for neglect in 1833, a sexton, whose office was combined 1806-26 with that of parish clerk, two examiners of weights and measures (1826), and a poundkeeper from 1828. Appointments were mostly annual, although one churchwarden served continuously from 1787 to 1793. From 1816 one churchwarden was appointed by the parish and one by the vicar. In 1826 there was a struggle between the vestry and the vicar over the appointment of the sexton.

From 1678 the assembled inhabitants were acting as a vestry although not by that name until 1693. Early vestries were held at irregular intervals, but by the early 19th century there were monthly meetings, usually attended by the vicar or curate, the churchwardens and overseers, and a few others. There were occasional larger attendances, 15 for example in 1798. During the 19th century attendances became larger and there were 64 present in 1847 when the church was threatened. A vestry house was mentioned in 1708 and 1735 but for most of the 18th and the early 19th century meetings were held at the Six Bells or in the church. In 1815 a vestry room was built on the north side of the church. By 1856 it had become too small and meetings were held in private houses until a vestry hall was built in 1857 in the churchyard.

Besides poor-law matters the vestry's deliberations included law and order in 1749, 1757, 1810, and 1820, straying cattle in 1821, and starting a parish school in 1809, a benefit society in 1811, and an association to prosecute offenders in 1820. Church rates, normally 3d. in the £ in the 18th century and 2d. in the early 19th, were used for a variety of purposes not necessarily connected with the church, particularly in the 18th century, including the repair of buildings, the purchase of two constables' staves in 1796, and payments to the sick poor, especially in times of smallpox. From c. 1840 payments were confined to church repairs and salaries.

A poor rate was levied, usually twice a year, from 1678. The annual total rose from £57 in 1678 to £90 in 1730, £140 in 1770, £303 in 1803, £564 in 1821, and £844 in 1831. The income was augmented by rent payable from enclosed waste land, of which there were 31 parcels in 1792. The overseers spent a small part of it on repairing bridges (1682) and constables' expenses (1688, 1779). Expenditure on the poor included weekly pay and sums for specific purposes like apprenticing, sickness, burial, clothing, brandy for a woman in labour in 1708, and port for a widow on the doctor's order in 1801. The poor were badged in 1706. Edgware Road brought in many poor from elsewhere including, in the 1730s, disabled soldiers, a sailor, and Turkish prisoners; the overseers were forbidden in 1736 to make casual payments to outsiders. In 1801 relief was given to 94 women and children travelling with passes. Gypsies and vagrants were causing trouble in 1820. In 1800 the overseers bought potatoes, herrings, split peas, and barley, and distributed coal and potatoes in 1801 and 1823.

Following the end of the Napoleonic wars, the series of bad summers, and agricultural depression,[82] the overseers were ordered in 1818 to employ all the men who wanted to work, and in 1824 to purchase flax or hemp to employ poor

[64] St. Paul's MS. A 39/1354.
[65] Guildhall MS. 11816B.
[66] B.L. Stowe MS. 862, f. 33.
[67] Guildhall MS. 11816B.
[68] St. Paul's MS. C (Sampson), f. 54.
[69] M.R.O., Acc. 276/480.
[70] Guildhall MS. CC. 33099.
[71] Ch. Com., Surveys S2, pp. 495-501.
[72] M.R.O., EA/WIL, nos. 93, 413, 503.
[73] Grange Mus., 1 D 11 (vestry bk. 1825-32); ibid. gen. files, High Rd. (Mdx. Courier, 21 June 1895).
[74] Based on Grange Mus., 1 D 10-13, 29 (vestry mins. 1722-1878); 1 B 1-5, 7-11 (poor rates 1703-35, 1770-1835); 1 B 6, 24-8 (overseers' accts. 1678-1710, 1775-1823, 1833-7); 1 B 12, 16-17, D 17 (church rate and churchwardens' accts.

1730-1869); 1 B 13-19 (highway rate and surveyors' accts. 1785-1832, 1842-52). See also ibid. Wood F 23, pp. 211 sqq.; Rep. Com. Poor Laws, H.C. 44, pp. 185f-185h (1834), xxxv-xxxvi.
[75] St. Paul's MSS. C (I Nowell), ff. 330v.-331v.; (III Nowell), ff. 162v.-163v.
[76] P.R.O., E 315/498, ff. 39-40.
[77] Ibid. REQ 2/293/28.
[78] B.L. Add. MS. 38856, f. 59.
[79] Bodl. MS. D.D. All Souls c 124/84.
[80] Grange Mus., Wood F 24, p. 82.
[81] Payments were made to a doctor in 1679 and apothecary in 1774 but they are unlikely to have been appointed by the parish.
[82] All Souls Coll., uncat. material, agents' letters 1808-37.

women. By 1834 some 49 able-bodied poor were receiving relief. Women and children were employed in spinning and the able-bodied men were set to work on the roads, without supervision. Money was given to induce men to seek work outside the parish. About half the poor were non-parishioners and probably many were Irish; the ease with which they obtained magistrates' orders for relief was resented.

Willesden had no workhouse but cottages in the churchyard were being used to house the old and widows by 1704. It may have been one of them that was referred to in 1781 as the church house. There were six in 1828,[83] one being used by the parish clerk, and seven in 1834.

Willesden became part of Hendon union under the Act of 1834 and the poor houses were converted in the 1840s into larger ones for the parish officers. They were replaced by the engine house and vestry hall in the 1850s and 1860s.[84] The parish continued in a much more limited way its care for the poor: in 1847 an association was set up to improve the condition of the labouring classes, and some 3 a. were leased for allotments; in 1857 a vestry committee reported on the state of the dwellings of the poor; in 1861 some ladies were organizing soup kitchens during the winter.

The vestry continued to appoint officers: in 1837, for example, overseer, constables, surveyors, assessors of land, sexton, and beadle. A keeper for the fire engine was appointed in 1840 and a poundkeeper in 1842; in 1857 a headborough was mentioned. One man often combined several offices, in 1857 for example as constable, poundkeeper, sexton, beadle, and engine-keeper. The Vestry Clerks Act was adopted in 1856.[85] In 1835, to avoid becoming part of the Metropolitan police district, the vestry adopted the Lighting and Watching Act, 1833, and in 1849 it adopted the lighting provisions for part of Kilburn.[86] Increasingly the work of the vestry was done by committees. By 1857 there were committees for allotments, parish charities, building a vestry hall, the state of the poor, and nuisances. In 1863 Willesden became part of Edgware highway district.[87] By 1871 a separate sewer rate was being levied,[88] to deal with problems that eventually led to the formation of Willesden local board.

LOCAL GOVERNMENT AFTER 1874. Under an Act of 1874[89] Willesden became an urban sanitary district, divided into four wards and governed by a local board of 15 members. South Kilburn had six members, North Kilburn, East Willesden and West Willesden three each. There was a constant struggle between the councillors for Kilburn, where development and its problems were most marked, and the minority led by George Furness for the more rural districts.[90] The board appointed a clerk, a surveyor, a medical officer of health, and a sanitary inspector. Their work increased as building, especially jerry-building, spread. In the decade after 1875 the expenditure of the engineer and surveyor's department increased fourfold but there was still only one building inspector in 1887. In that year an Act[91] empowered the board to appoint additional building inspectors at the expense of the builders themselves.[92] By 1890 there were three building inspectors, a road inspector, a treasurer, a rate collector, and assistants to the surveyor, sanitary inspector, and clerk.[93] Board meetings were held at White's Hotel in Shoot-up Hill, from 1882 at Hampton House (no. 297 High Road, Kilburn), and after 1891 at the new offices opened in Dyne Road and enlarged in 1900.[94] The board, sometimes in conflict with the Metropolitan Board of Works and Edgware highway board, made up streets, built a sewage farm, took control of the fire brigade, and opened free libraries and a public park.[95]

By 1894 the enmity between Kilburn and the rest of Willesden was lessening, and under the Local Government Act of that year Willesden became an urban district divided into seven wards, each represented by three councillors: North, Mid, and South Kilburn, Willesden Green (including Cricklewood), Kensal Green, Harlesden, and Church End (including Neasden and Stonebridge). In 1909 the wards were increased to eleven with the creation of Cricklewood and Brondesbury Park from Willesden Green, Stonebridge from Church End, and Roundwood from Harlesden. From 1925 each ward was represented by four councillors.[96] Voting in elections was apathetic. Between 12 and 22 per cent voted in 1919 and only 7 per cent at North Kilburn in 1920. The controversy over health policy in 1922 led to a particularly high vote, between 33 and 44 per cent. Voting was increasingly on party lines.[97] A Willesden ratepayers association was established in 1878 and one in Harlesden in or before 1901.[98] The local Conservative association was formed in 1879 with a branch at Kilburn by 1900 and at Stonebridge by 1910. There was a constitutional club and a Radical club in Harlesden by 1895, a Liberal club in Church End by 1895 and one in Kilburn by 1900, and a Radical club at Willesden Green by 1900. By 1910 there was a constitutional club at Kensal Rise, a progressive club in Church End, and a social democratic club at Willesden Green. An Independent Labour Party club was established in Harlesden by 1918.[99]

The U.D.C. was at first dominated by a few individuals like Charles Pinkham, a developer

[83] Pigot, *Lond. and Provincial Dir.* (1828-9).
[84] Grange Mus., Ball, 'Old Willesden', 117-34.
[85] *Lond. Gaz.* 6 June 1856, p. 2015.
[86] Below, pub. svces.
[87] *Lond. Gaz.* 13 Mar. 1863, p. 1480.
[88] Grange Mus., 1 B 23.   [89] 37 & 38 Vic. c. 152 (Local).
[90] Grange Mus., 1 A 4 (*Willesden Chron. Charter Suppl.* 8 Sept. 1933); ibid. Wood F 23, pp. 281 sqq.
[91] 50 & 51 Vic. c. 149 (Local).
[92] Grange Mus., Wood F 9 (Bill and mins. of evid. 1887).
[93] *Kelly's Dir. Mdx.* (1890).

[94] Grange Mus., gen. files, Dyne Rd.; photo. files (NL 785); ibid. Ball, 'Old Willesden', 89; *Kelly's Dir. Mdx.* (1882).
[95] Grange Mus., Wood F 23 pp. 281 sqq.; below, pub. svces.
[96] M.R.O., *Rep. Local Inqs.* 1889-97, 639-62 (Willesden 1894); Grange Mus., gen. files, ward boundaries.
[97] *The Times*, 5 Apr. 1922; Grange Mus., 1 A 5 (*Willesden Chron.* 3 Sept. 1920).
[98] Grange Mus., Wood F 37/15A; Wood 67.
[99] Ibid. Wood F 24, p. 258; *Kilburn and Willesden Dir.* (1895, 1900, 1910, 1918-19).

who was elected to the local board in 1888, became chairman of the U.D.C. for the fifth time in 1918, and was Unionist M.P. for West Willesden 1919–22.[1] Another Conservative, George Sexton, a member of the U.D.C. 1901–28 and five times chairman, was an architect.[2] From 1907 there were 14 Conservative, 6 Liberal, and 1 Independent councillor although they did not use those labels.[3] The first election to be held on party lines was in 1910, when 20 Municipal Reform (Conservative) and 13 Progressive and Labour members were returned.[4] Church End, Stonebridge, Kensal Rise, and Harlesden were represented by a new class of councillor, railwaymen and engineers. Percival Bond, elected as a Progressive in 1910, continued as a councillor for many years.[5] Labour had 15 council members in 1921 and although still in a minority was, by tactical voting, implementing its policy on a variety of issues, notably in public health.[6] An alliance between the ratepayers association and the British Medical Association in 1922 brought an increased poll and the reduction of the Labour members to 7, compared with 25 of the ratepayers association.[7] By 1930 the parties were more evenly balanced,[8] and in 1933 Labour took control. The first woman councillor was co-opted in 1917.[9]

Willesden U.D.C. assumed more powers than those of the local board, including police services.[10] Under the Housing Acts the U.D.C. had by 1931 built 744 houses and 262 flats on estates at Brentfield and Neasden. It was responsible for 90 miles of public roads, 3 fire stations, 5 public parks, 2 hospitals, 6 libraries, 26 council and 2 special schools, 112 a. of allotments, and 3 burial grounds.[11] It had encouraged the growth of industry and housing in the 1920s but had not attempted to curb building speculation or to buy land for public buildings and open spaces.[12] The increased work required staff,[13] and a separate finance department was formed in 1909.[14] The number of staff employed on maternity and child welfare was one cause of conflict in 1922.[15] In 1925 there were 979 council employees.[16]

In 1896 the U.D.C. was empowered to appoint overseers of the poor. For a time Willesden paupers continued to be sent to the workhouse at Hendon, and later lived in houses leased to the U.D.C. until a large building at Park Royal was opened as an infirmary in 1903 and a workhouse

was built next to it in 1908. In 1910 there were 1,000 people in the workhouse.[17]

When, after unsuccessful attempts in 1908, 1909, and 1919,[18] Willesden became a municipal borough in 1933 it was the most populous non-county borough in England.[19] Changes in the ward boundaries and representation during the 1930s yielded 13 wards and 39 councillors in 1937. The boundaries of all the wards were altered, Carlton and Kilburn corresponding roughly to the old South and Mid Kilburn wards. Two new wards were created, Manor out of Harlesden and Kensal Green, and Neasden out of Cricklewood.[20] In 1952 further adjustments were made, including renaming Neasden as Gladstone and the creation of Brentwater ward out of the northern part of Cricklewood.[21]

BOROUGH OF WILLESDEN. *Gules, a chevron or between in chief an orb or with a band sable, ensigned with a cross-crosslet or, and two swords saltirewise proper, pommelled and hilted or; and in the base three lilies in a pot or; all within a border or charged with eight roundels sable*
[Granted 1933]

The borough consistently had a Labour majority from 1933 except in 1947.[22] The Conservatives called themselves Moderates in the 1930s and lamented the intrusion of party politics into local government, but they adopted party labels after 1945. In 1937 antagonism between the parties erupted in brawling at council meetings but apathy was more characteristic and in the election of the same year there was no campaigning by candidates. Polling was consistently low. In 1937 a fifth of the electorate voted in municipal elections,[23] in 1956 and 1960 less than a third.[24]

Housing was the major problem facing the council, which adopted a town planning scheme for three areas in 1933 and tried to limit density of housing in the remaining unbuilt districts, especially in the north and at Stonebridge.[25] For the areas long built over, especially the south-east with its overcrowded houses, a slum clearance plan was formulated in 1937, and by 1939 some 500 families had been moved from Kilburn into a

[1] Grange Mus., biog. files, Chas. Pinkham; gen. files, elections, local; *The Times*, 26 Apr. 1918.
[2] Grange Mus., 1 A 2 (*Willesden Cit.* 28 Oct. 1949).
[3] *Willesden Cit.* 1, 8 Apr. 1910.
[4] *The Times*, 6 Apr. 1910.
[5] *Willesden Cit.* 1, 8 Apr. 1910; *Willesden Call*, 11 Apr. 1913; *Kelly's Dir. Mdx.* (1926).
[6] *The Times*, 4 Apr. 1922; below, pub. svces.
[7] *The Times*, 5 Apr. 1922; Grange Mus., 1 A 5 (*Willesden Cit.* 25 June 1920).
[8] Grange Mus., gen. files, *W. Willesden Cit./Courier* (July 1930).
[9] *The Times*, 29 June 1917.
[10] Leff and Blunden, *Willesden Story*, 18.
[11] Grange Mus., MF 352 (petition for incorp. 1931).
[12] Morris, *Willesden Surv.* pp. 10, 12.
[13] *Kelly's Dir. Mdx.* (1908).
[14] Grange Mus., 2 C 17 (souvenir of incorp. 1933).
[15] *The Times*, 18 Jan. 1922.

[16] Grange Mus., 1 D 23 (establishment bk. 1925).
[17] Ibid. 1 D 16 (overseers' min. bk. 1895–1904); ibid. gen. files, workhouses (*Municipal Jnl.* 20 Mar. 1903); ibid. MF 352 (petition for incorp. 1931); ibid. Wood F 23, p. 234; *The Times*, 14 Dec. 1908; 11 Jan. 1910; below, pub. svces. (Park Royal hosp.).
[18] *The Times*, 2 Nov., 2 Dec. 1908; 12 Feb. 1909; 15 Nov. 1910; 29 Oct. 1919. [19] Ibid. 2, 8 Sept. 1933.
[20] Grange Mus., NM 9 (map of ward boundaries); ibid. gen. files, ward boundaries; *Census*, 1921, 1931.
[21] Grange Mus., NM 22 (map of boundaries 1952); *Census*, 1961.
[22] Grange Mus., gen. files, elections, local.
[23] *Willesden Monthly Illus.* 5 Jan., 5 Oct., 5 Nov. 1937; Weintraub, 'Race and local politics'.
[24] *Willesden Civic Review*, June 1956; Grange Mus., gen. files, elections, local.
[25] Grange Mus., NM 309 (Willesden town planning scheme 1933).

new council estate at Roundwood.[26] War interrupted the scheme and added bomb damage to already dilapidated property; the pressure of population was intensified by problems associated with immigrants from Ireland and the new Commonwealth. Following a comprehensive survey of Willesden in 1947[27] the council in 1954 began to redevelop South Kilburn. Through the 1950s and 1960s the council also bought property elsewhere in the borough, built council houses, made improvement loans, and encouraged housing co-operatives.[28] While the council's 30-year record on housing was attacked by a Tory M.P. in 1963,[29] one of the leading policy makers was Reg Freeson, elected to the council in 1952, Labour leader 1958–65, M.P. for Willesden East and later for Brent East, and a junior minister for housing in 1974.[30]

The number employed by the council had grown to 1,550 by 1949.[31] The main council offices remained at Dyne Road in spite of complaints that they were too far from the centre of the borough and inadequate for the expanded services and staff.[32] In 1937 some departments used converted houses and stables. The council's proposal in 1960 to build a block of offices for three departments was vetoed by the government in 1963.[33]

LONDON BOROUGH OF BRENT.
Per chevron gules and vert, a chevron wavy argent between in dexter chief an orb and in sinister chief two swords crossed saltirewise or points upward and in base two seaxes crossed saltirewise passing through a Saxon crown or

[Granted 1965]

In 1965, against strong local opposition, Willesden was amalgamated under the London Government Act, 1963, with Wembley U.D. in the London Borough of Brent.[34] Of the 31 wards, each with two councillors, 17 represented the former Willesden borough.[35] Almost all departments were housed in the Wembley part of the borough, mainly in the town hall, and the Dyne Road offices were demolished in 1972.[36] In the new borough, where Conservative Wembley and Labour Willesden were evenly balanced,

party controversy intensified, particularly on housing and education.[37]

Willesden was a district in the Harrow parliamentary division of Middlesex[38] until 1918, when it became a parliamentary borough divided into two divisions each returning one member.[39] Conservatives sat for Willesden West until 1923 and 1931–5, and Labour members 1923–31 and 1935–74.[40] Except in 1923 when the seat was held by a Liberal and *The Times* referred to the 'traditional pastime' in Willesden of wrecking the meetings of opponents,[41] Willesden East was represented by Conservatives until 1945 and from 1959 to 1964, and by Labour members 1945–59 and 1964–74. In 1974 the parliamentary boundaries were revised, the former borough of Willesden being included in Brent East and Brent South; both returned Labour members.

PUBLIC SERVICES. A whipping post and stocks were erected in 1680. In 1749 there were complaints of 'idle and disordered' people destroying and stealing farmers' property. A parish cage was built following vestry resolutions of 1757 and 1791. The cage, called the Round House and repaired in 1798 and 1830, was in High Road near the church and was demolished in 1841, when its materials were used for the new National school building.[42] By 1828 the two parish constables were aided by a Bow Street horse patrol along 5½ miles of public road.[43] There were policemen at Stonebridge in 1839,[44] and in 1840 Willesden joined the Metropolitan police district.[45] By 1851 there were police stations at Stonebridge and in Kilburn Lane.[46] The Stonebridge station had by 1871 been replaced by a station at Fortune Gate in the junction between St. Mary's Road and Harrow Road.[47] In 1913 the Harlesden station moved to its present site at the junction of Craven Park and West Ella Road.[48] Kilburn was served by successive stations at Kempshall Terrace, Edgware Road (*c.* 1873–1885), nos. 11–13 High Road (1885–*c.* 1892), and Salusbury Road from *c.* 1892 until it closed in 1938.[49] The building was bombed during the Second World War and from 1965 a temporary station on the site[50] was used until a permanent station was opened in 1980.[51] Willesden Green station was opened at the junction of High Road and Huddlestone Road in 1896.[52]

[26] Leff and Blunden, *Willesden Story*, 30–33.
[27] Morris, *Willesden Surv.*
[28] Leff and Blunden, *Willesden Story*, 40 sqq.
[29] Grange Mus., 1 A 2 (*Willesden Cit.* 25 Oct. 1963).
[30] Weintraub, 'Race and local politics'; *Who's Who* (1977).
[31] Excluding 1,635 employed in educ.: Morris, *Willesden Surv.* p. 70.   [32] M.R.O., Hist. Notes 25/8/71.
[33] *Willesden Monthly Illus.* 5 Oct. 1937; *Willesden Civic Review*, Dec. 1957; Apr. 1960; June 1963.
[34] Grange Mus., 1 A 2 (*Willesden Cit.* 4 May 1962); *V.C.H. Mdx.* iv. 246; v. 82.
[35] *Brent Civic Review*, July 1965.
[36] Grange Mus., gen. files, health service.
[37] Weintraub, 'Race and local politics'.
[38] Based on *Whitaker's Almanack* (1918–75).
[39] Grange Mus., MF 352 (petition for incorp. 1931).
[40] *The Times*, 16 Nov. 1922; 28 Oct. 1931; Grange Mus., gen. files, Members of Parl.
[41] *The Times*, 28 Nov., 7, 8 Dec. 1923.

[42] Grange Mus., Wood F 23, p. 273; ibid. 1 D 29, 1 D 11 (vestry order bks. 1722–1814, 1825–32); cage described in W. H. Ainsworth, *Jack Sheppard* [1910 edn.], 159–60; located in M.R.O., EA/WIL (inclosure map).
[43] *Rep. Sel. Cttee. on Police of Metropolis*, H.C. 533, p. 406 (1828), vi.
[44] Grange Mus., Wood F 33 (par. reg.).
[45] *Lond. Gaz.* 13 Oct. 1840, p. 2250.
[46] P.R.O., HO 107/1700/135/3, pp. 332 sqq., 404.
[47] Grange Mus., 1 B 23 (sewer rate 1871); ibid. Wood F 20 (sale cat. 2/18); Wood F 23, pp. 281 sqq.
[48] Datestone.
[49] *Kilburn and Willesden Dir.* (1872–1940). Salusbury Rd. police sta. existed before the other public bldgs. were erected next to it in 1894: Guildhall MS. CC. 268029; *The Times*, 24 Feb. 1938.
[50] *Kilburn Times*, 2 Apr. 1965.
[51] Inf. from curator of Grange Mus.
[52] Datestone.

Willesden petty sessional court opened in St. Mary's Road, Harlesden, in 1887 and was rebuilt in 1889. Its jurisdiction includes Acton and Chiswick.[53] Willesden was subject to the jurisdiction of Marylebone county court until 1931 when a county court was opened at Craven Park, in the former high school. It was replaced in 1970 by a new county court in Acton Lane.[54]

A salaried fire-engine keeper was appointed in 1840[55] and the office, usually combined with those of constable and beadle, continued until 1884.[56] Following a disastrous fire at the windmill on Shoot-up Hill, which exposed the inadequacy of the fire service, the Kilburn, Willesden, and St. John's Wood volunteer fire brigade was established in 1863.[57] Equipped with a steam engine by 1872, it covered the eastern part of the parish from headquarters in Bridge Street, Kilburn, until control passed to the local board c. 1892. A new fire station in Salusbury Road, opened in 1894, served the Kilburn area until the Second World War.[58] Willesden volunteer fire brigade was founded in Church End in 1872 and was not officially disbanded until 1932, although it had ceased to function by 1910. Its main station was at the White Horse, Church End, until c. 1888 and then at the vestry hall in Neasden Lane. A small sub-station opened in Harlesden in 1883. The brigade bought a steam engine in 1888. The local authority had taken control by 1895. A temporary building in Harlesden Road in 1910 replaced the former Harlesden station and was replaced in turn by the central station in Pound Lane in 1934. A station opened at Stonebridge in 1932 and closed in 1960.[59]

In 1827, following a complaint that the sick poor in Willesden were left at the cage, a magistrate ordered the churchwardens to provide a more suitable place.[60] The local board's first sanitary report in 1875 revealed a death rate of over 24 per 1,000 (compared with the average 22) and the very high rate of 45 (compared with the average 32) for children under 5 years. Kilburn was the most unhealthy district, with diarrhoea, tuberculosis, and respiratory disease especially prevalent; in more rural districts there was much typhoid because of open drains.[61] In 1876 the board appointed a medical officer of health, arranged for smallpox patients to be sent to Highgate and fever patients, though not paupers, to be sent to the London Fever Hospital, and pleaded for a hospital in Willesden.[62] The Kilburn, Maida Vale, and St. John's Wood

general dispensary at no. 13 Kilburn Park Road (outside the boundary) was the only medical institution in the area in 1890.[63] The philanthropist Passmore Edwards paid for the cottage hospital named after him which opened in 1893 in Harlesden Road, with three wards accommodating 24 patients. It was extended in 1899, again after the First World War when it was renamed Willesden General hospital, and in 1926, by which time it had beds for 104 patients.[64] There were 127 beds for acute cases by 1950.[65]

In 1894 the local authority built an isolation hospital on a 10-a. site in Dog Lane, Neasden. After extension in 1904 the hospital provided beds for 150,[66] and changed its name to Willesden Municipal hospital during the First World War. In 1921 it was argued that it should be extended as a general hospital,[67] but it again became a fever hospital, with 138 beds, in 1922[68] and was extended in the 1930s, until by 1936 it had 200 beds. An eye block was added in 1958,[69] but the number of beds had been reduced by 1975 to 175 and in 1978 it was a geriatric hospital.[70] By 1901 St. Monica's Home for sick and incurable children, which had opened in the Hampstead part of Kilburn before 1890, had moved to Brondesbury Park.[71] It was closed as a children's home c. 1950 and reopened with 35 beds for chronic cases, becoming a geriatric hospital by 1975.[72] In 1901 the district council built a temporary smallpox hospital in Honeypot Lane, Kingsbury.[73] In 1929 Willesden joined the county council smallpox scheme and in 1931 opened the Kingsbury building as a maternity hospital, which it remained until it became a mental hospital in the 1970s.[74]

For a few years after it separated from Hendon union in 1896 the Willesden board of guardians used a former private house as an infirmary. In 1897 it acquired a 60-a. site in Acton Lane where a 'splendid new building' designed by Alfred Saxon Snell opened in 1903. It accommodated 400 people of whom 150 were sick; from 1907 it was used exclusively for the sick and was called Willesden Workhouse infirmary. When the boards of guardians were abolished in 1929 it became the Central Middlesex County hospital, also known as the Willesden Institution and the Park Royal hospital. Extensions were made in 1908, 1911, and 1914 and by 1930 it had 689 beds. There were further extensions and by 1939 there were 890 beds, but the buildings were badly damaged during the Second World War.[75] An extension housing 28 maternity beds was added

[53] Grange Mus., Wood F 23, pp. 281 sqq.; Kelly's Dir. Mdx. (1908).
[54] Grange Mus., gen. files, courts, Craven Pk.; The Times, 25 Oct. 1929; 21 Nov. 1930.
[55] Grange Mus., 1 D 12 (vestry order bk. 1832–62).
[56] Para. based on Grange Mus., gen. files, fire; Kilburn and Willesden Dir. (1872–1940); inf. from G.L.C. Fire Brigade (1979).
[57] Grange Mus., Wood 1/20 (church circular).
[58] Guildhall MS., CC. 268029.
[59] Inf. from curator of Grange Mus.
[60] Grange Mus., gen. files, Pound Lane (Morning Chron. 1 July 1827).
[61] Willesden local bd. San. Rep. (1875).
[62] Ibid. (1876); Grange Mus., 2 C 17 (souvenir of incorp. 1933).
[63] Kelly's Dir. Mdx. (1890); Grange Mus., Wood F 4.

[64] Kelly's Dir. Mdx. (1908, 1926); The Times, 26 Jan. 1898, 9 Feb. 1926; 29 June 1927.
[65] Hospitals Year Bk. (1950–1).
[66] Kelly's Dir. Mdx. (1908).
[67] The Times, 14 Jan., 26 Feb. 1921.
[68] Ibid. 5 Apr. 1922; Hospitals Year Bk. (1931).
[69] Willesden Cit. 4 Dec. 1964.
[70] Hospitals Year Bk. (1975, 1978).
[71] Census, 1901; Kelly's Dir. Mdx. (1890).
[72] Hospitals Year Bk. (1931, 1950–1, 1965, 1970, 1975).
[73] All Souls Coll., uncat. mat., agents' reps. 1906; V.C.H. Mdx. v. 83.
[74] Grange Mus., MF 352 (petition for incorp. 1931); Hospitals Year Bk. (1970, 1975); The Times, 31 Dec. 1934.
[75] Gray, Central Mdx. Hosp.; Hospitals Year Bk. (1939); Grange Mus., gen. files, workhos. (Municipal Jnl. 20 Mar. 1903).

in 1966[76] but the total number of beds was reduced to *c.* 736, mainly for acute cases.[77]

St. Andrew's Roman Catholic hospital in Dollis Hill Lane, financed by Marguerite Amice Piou and administered by the Sisters of the Little Company of Mary, opened in 1913 with 100 beds; enlargements in 1929, 1952, and 1963 raised the number of beds to 141, mostly for acute and chronic cases. Plastic surgery techniques were pioneered there in the 1930s but the hospital did not become part of the National Health Service and in 1972 was sold to Brent council which closed it a year later.[78] No. 14 Stonebridge Park, used as a military hospital during the First World War along with the Grove, Neasden, and Dollis Hill House,[79] became the Edgar Lee Home for boys with rheumatic hearts.[80]

The local authority appointed a health visitor in 1903 and began a policy of providing clinics and disease prevention[81] which developed with the appointment of G. F. Buchan as medical officer in 1912.[82] In that year the council published schemes for an ambulance service and for a sanatorium and dispensaries to treat tuberculosis.[83] In the event the county council took control of tuberculosis treatment, establishing clinics at Pound Lane and in Priory Park Road, Kilburn.[84] The death rate steadily declined from over 24 per 1,000 in 1875 to under 10 in 1910 and the infant mortality rate, 162 per 1,000 births in 1885, to 80.[85] An advice centre was opened for mothers at Lower Place and in 1913 a ringworm clinic was opened which later included eye treatment.[86] Maternity and child welfare centres were opened at Willesden Lane, Kilburn, in 1916 and at High Road, Willesden Green, in 1918. Midwives and home helps were provided for mothers in what was described as 'the most complete and comprehensive scheme of maternity and child welfare evolved by a municipal council'.[87] Dental clinics for mothers and children were also established and more health visitors appointed.[88] The cost was criticized by the ratepayers association, the medical profession, which attacked Willesden's 'municipal socialism', and the Minister of Health; health was the main issue in the local elections of 1922, and with Labour's defeat the scheme was curtailed, maternity cases being in future referred to Park Royal hospital.[89] The Conservative administration, in control until 1933, limited the expansion of the municipal hospital and restricted, but did not close, the

clinics; in 1930 it opened a third clinic at Stonebridge.[90] Immunization against diphtheria was introduced in 1927 and two cancer clinics were opened in 1929. A midwives scheme was introduced in 1937.[91] Many overseas visitors came to see Willesden's advanced medical administration under Buchan, who became one of the founders of the National Health Service.[92]

Under the National Health Act, 1946, the two municipal hospitals in Neasden and Kingsbury, the county hospital at Park Royal, and Willesden General hospital in Harlesden Road were grouped together under the North-West Metropolitan Regional Hospital Board. The health centres serving Willesden Green, Kilburn, and Stonebridge passed under the control of the county council.[93] A new maternity and school clinic opened in Pound Lane in 1957, another clinic in Neasden by 1960 and by 1969 there were eight clinics in the Willesden part of Brent.[94] In the 1950s overcrowding, atmospheric pollution, and Irish immigration made tuberculosis a special problem: in 1955 one third of the beds in the tubercular unit at Park Royal were occupied by Irish although they formed less than one twentieth of Willesden's population.[95] A health centre opened in Craven Park in 1972. The health authority was reorganized in 1974 as Brent health district.[96]

A burial board formed in 1866 opened Willesden cemetery and two mortuaries in 1868 on 5 a. next to St. Mary's churchyard.[97] The board bought 26 a. in 1888 to form Willesden New Cemetery, opened in 1893, with Anglican and nonconformist chapels and a central tower in an elaborate Gothic style.[98] In 1895 the powers of the burial board passed to Willesden U.D.C. which *c.* 1928 purchased 33½a. in southeast Kingsbury as an additional cemetery.[99] A mortuary formed part of the public buildings erected in Salusbury Road in 1894.[1] Willesden is divided into two natural drainage areas, the south-east corner (Kilburn, Kensal Green, and part of Harlesden) draining into the Kilburn brook and the rest of the parish into the Brent.[2] From 1807 the south-eastern area was under the control of the metropolitan commissioners. Landowners paid rates and made their own drains which connected to the metropolitan system by means of the Ranelagh sewer (the culverted Kilburn brook). An Act of 1855 replaced the commissioners by the Metropolitan Board of

[76] Grange Mus., 1 A 2 (*Willesden Mercury*, 19 Nov. 1965).
[77] *Hospitals Year Bk.* (1965, 1970).
[78] Ibid.; Grange Mus., gen. files, hosps.; photo. files, St. Andrew's hosp. (NL 1383); ibid. 1 A 2 (*Tablet*, 7 June 1952).
[79] Grange Mus., photo. files, Neasden Lane, the Grove; gen. files, Dollis Hill Ho.
[80] Grange Mus., 1 A 2 (*Lancet*, 15 June 1957).
[81] Leff and Blunden, *Willesden Story*.
[82] *Willesden Monthly Illus.*, 5 Aug. 1937.
[83] *The Times*, 20 Aug., 20 Dec. 1912.
[84] *Kelly's Dir. Mdx.* (1917); Gray, *Central Mdx. Hosp.* 105.
[85] Willesden local bd. *San. Rep.* (1875); Grange Mus., Willesden U.D.C. *Public Health Rep.* (1910).
[86] Leff and Blunden, *Willesden Story*, 20.
[87] *The Times*, 2 Aug. 1918; Leff and Blunden, *Willesden Story*, 24.
[88] Grange Mus., 1 A 5 (*Willesden Cit.* 27 Aug. 1920); *The Times*, 30 Sept. 1919.

[89] *The Times*, 1 Apr. 1919; 15, 19, 26 Nov., 8 Dec. 1921; 4, 18 Jan., 4, 5, 6, 7 Apr. 1922.
[90] Grange Mus., 2 C 17 (charter of incorp. 1933).
[91] Leff and Blunden, *Willesden Story*, 26, 33.
[92] Grange Mus., 1 A 2 (*Lancet*, 15 June 1957).
[93] Morris, *Willesden Surv.* p. 86, map 30; Leff and Blunden, *Willesden Story*, 46.
[94] Leff and Blunden, *Willesden Story*, 57, 61; Grange Mus., gen. files, health service; Brent L.B. *Council and Related Svces.* (1969).
[95] Gray, *Central Mdx. Hosp.* 105; Grange Mus., gen. files, topog. (S. Levitt, project on Willesden).
[96] Grange Mus., gen. files, health centre, hosps.
[97] Ibid. Wood F 23, p. 350.
[98] Ibid. 1 D 16 (overseers' min. bk. 1895–1904, containing loose copy of mins. 1888); ibid. photo. files, Roundwood Pk. (NL 639); *Kelly's Dir. Mdx.* (1908).
[99] *V.C.H. Mdx.* v. 83.
[1] Guildhall MS. CC. 268029.
[2] Winterburn, 'Willesden', fig. 2.

Works and redefined its area of jurisdiction, excluding suburban areas like Kilburn. Building in Kilburn accelerated from that time and the new houses continued to drain into the metropolitan system, overburdening the sewers, particularly at their junction at Kilburn bridge. In 1878 the board sued for an injunction prohibiting the drainage of any new building in Willesden parish into the Ranelagh sewer; in 1883 the injunction was refused in respect of Kilburn but granted in respect of Harlesden.[3]

The rest of the parish used open ditches, about which there were complaints in 1846.[4] In 1855 the vestry appointed a sewer committee which reported defective drainage but failed to take action and died in 1866. In 1871 the vestry, under pressure from Harlesden ratepayers, levied a sewer rate to build a sewer at Harlesden;[5] in 1875 the local board became the sanitary authority, and some drainage works had been constructed at Stonebridge Park and Nicoll Road, Harlesden, by 1877.[6] In 1880 the board acquired land for a sewage outfall near the Brent at Stonebridge, and in 1882 the watershed was accepted as the boundary between the two areas, named Metropolitan and Brent, each separately rated. The sewage farm at Stonebridge, completed in 1886,[7] had expanded by 1898,[8] and a new sewage farm was built in 1904.[9] It continued in use, draining into the Brent, until 1911 when, under an Act of 1908, a sewer connecting with the L.C.C. system was completed.[10]

There were only two or three wells from borings in the parish in the mid 19th century, one of them sunk at Willesden Green c. 1830. Most people relied on rainwater cisterns and ponds until companies began supplying water in the late 19th century.[11] The West Middlesex Water Co. supplied water until 1903 when it was superseded in Willesden by the Metropolitan Water Board, which had reservoirs at Harlesden Road and at St. Michael's Road, Cricklewood, where it also had a pumping station.[12] The latter survived in 1978 as the Cricklewood works of the Thames Water Authority.

Public meetings in 1883 resulted in a petition to the Corporation of the City of London to purchase the former agricultural show site as a park[13] for the densely populated Kilburn district.[14] The Church Commissioners, who owned the 30-a. site, presented it to the corporation, which opened Queen's Park there in 1887, naming it in honour of the queen's jubilee.

Willesden local board acquired 26 a. at Harlesden, part of the Roundwood House estate, which it opened as a park in 1895.[15] With aid from the county council, the urban district bought most of the Dollis Hill House estate in 1900: most of the 96-a. Gladstone Park was left as it was, the parkland and gardens of a country house, while 29 a. south of the railway became sports grounds. The council bought the house in 1908, opening it a year later as refreshment rooms.[16] Willesden U.D.C. in 1909 bought 31 a. at Harlesden, opened as the King Edward VII recreation ground and later called Willesden sports centre.[17] The council bought 14 a. near Gibbons Road in 1925 for playing fields,[18] and Neasden (20 a.) and Stonebridge (11 a.) recreation grounds had also been acquired by 1931, by which time there were 228 a. of public open space in Willesden. No new parks were acquired, and in 1949 public and private open space together totalled 564 a., compared with the 1,324 a. thought necessary for Willesden's population.[19] By 1966 the reduction in the population had relieved some of the pressure on the open spaces, but there had been no increase in the parks and playing fields accessible to the public.[20]

In 1849 the lighting provisions of the Lighting and Watching Act, 1833, were adopted for a small portion of Kilburn near Kilburn Bridge; five inspectors were appointed and rates levied. The lighted portion was extended along Edgware Road in 1861 and by 1867 it reached northward to Walm Lane and westward to Willesden Green.[21] The Gas Light & Coke Co., which supplied the gas, was still laying mains in 1895.[22] In 1898 the U.D.C. appointed an electrical engineer and was authorized to supply electricity. In 1903 it built a generating station in Taylors Lane, which it sold to the North Metropolitan Electric Power Supply Co. in 1904.[23] By 1908 the lighting of c. 4½ miles of principal roads had been converted from gas to electricity.[24] All the streets were electrically lit by the early 1920s, when electric dust-carts were also introduced.[25] Taylors Lane power station, with a staff of 200, closed in 1972.[26]

In 1891 the local board adopted the Free Libraries Act and opened three libraries in 1894: Kilburn, the largest, as part of the complex of public buildings in Salusbury Road,[27] Harlesden in Craven Park Road (then called High Road), and Willesden Green on the south side of High Road.[28] Willesden Green was extended in 1907.

[3] Grange Mus., Wood F 10 (Chancery case 1878); F 19 (Chancery case 1883); M.R.O., *Rep. Local Inqs.* 1889–97, 603–24 (Willesden local bd. 1889).

[4] Grange Mus., 1 D 12 (vestry order bk. 1832–62).

[5] Ibid. Wood F 23, p. 307; ibid. 1 B 23 (sewer rate 1871).

[6] Willesden local bd. *San. Rep.* (1877).

[7] M.R.O., *Rep. Local Inqs.* 1889–97, 603–24 (Willesden local bd. 1889); Grange Mus., Wood F 23, pp. 288 sqq.

[8] All Souls Coll., uncat. material, bursars' accts. 1883–7, 1896–8.

[9] Winterburn, 'Willesden'.

[10] *The Times*, 1 Nov. 1909; Grange Mus., gen. files, housing (Willesden U.D.C. Rep. 1925).

[11] Grange Mus., gen. files, geol.; ibid. Wood F 23, pp. 281 sqq.

[12] *Willesden Civic Review*, Oct. 1957.

[13] Para. based on Grange Mus., gen. files, parks and gdns.

[14] *The Times*, 11 May 1885.   [15] Ibid. 13 May 1895.

[16] Ibid. 4 Nov. 1908; Grange Mus., gen. files, Dollis Hill Ho.; above, other est.

[17] *The Times*, 28 July 1910; All Souls Coll., uncat. material, agents' reps. 1909.

[18] Grange Mus., gen. files, Gibbons Rd.

[19] Morris, *Willesden Surv.* p. 81, map 6.

[20] Brent planning and research dept. *Background to Brent* (1967), 91, 94–5.

[21] Grange Mus., Wood F 23, p. 279; ibid. 1 B 20–2 (lighting rate bks. 1862–7).

[22] All Souls Coll., uncat. material, docs. relating to estates 1887–95.

[23] Grange Mus., gen. files, electricity.

[24] *Kelly's Dir. Mdx.* (1908).

[25] Grange Mus., 2 C 17 (souvenir of incorp. 1933).

[26] Grange Mus., gen. files, electricity.

[27] *The Times*, 4 Jan. 1894; Guildhall MS. CC. 268029.

[28] Grange Mus., Wood F 23, p. 281.

Mark Twain performed the opening of a fourth library, at Bathurst Gardens in Kensal Rise, in 1900. It was extended in 1904 and 1926. Other libraries were opened at Olive Road, Cricklewood, in 1929 and on the North Circular Road at Neasden in 1931.[29]

A public open-air swimming pool, the first in the country, was opened in Gladstone Park in 1903. Others were opened in the King Edward VII recreation ground in 1911 and at Craven Park in 1936.[30] In 1937 an indoor swimming bath, slipper baths, and a public laundry were built in Granville Road.[31] Slipper baths opened at Park Royal about the same time.[32] The Willesden sports centre, opened in 1965, included a swimming pool and baths.[33]

From 1933 to 1957 Willesden's rubbish was dumped on open ground at Twyford tip by the North Circular Road; thereafter it was sent to Yiewsley.[34]

Nurseries were introduced for the children of women working in munitions factories in the First World War.[35] At the end of the Second World War there were 12 nurseries. They had been reduced to nine by 1964 when two were opened in South Kilburn, and others were added shortly afterwards at Harlesden and Cricklewood.[36] By 1976 there were five day nurseries, two nursery schools and in addition schools with nursery departments.[37]

Willesden old people's welfare committee was established in 1958, provided with money and staff by the council.[38] In 1969 the council maintained 10 homes for the elderly.[39] The local council of social service was reorganized in 1960 with a grant from the borough council.[40]

The Willesden International Friendship committee was formed in 1958 to deal with the problems of immigration. The council appointed a liaison officer in 1960 and opened a community relations centre at Dollis Hill in 1972.[41]

CHURCHES. Willesden church, mentioned in 1181,[42] was the parish church for the whole of Willesden until 1867. The rectory belonged to the dean and chapter of St. Paul's, London.[43] A vicarage was first mentioned in 1249–50 as having all the altar dues, a house and garden next the church, and some land.[44] The advowson of the vicarage always belonged to the dean and chapter of St. Paul's and was reserved from leases of the rectory in the 13th century but was leased with the rectory during the later Middle Ages, when the lessees were canons.[45]

In 1297 the vicarage was taxed at £2;[46] in 1474 the vicar was allowed to be non-resident because of the small value of the vicarage,[47] but in 1535 its annual value was £14.[48] It was £40 in 1650[49] and £160 in 1847.[50] The vicar's property in 1297 consisted of a house and garden, 9 a. of arable, and 4 marks a year from the chamber of St. Paul's.[51] In 1652 £50 a year was voted as augmentation for the vicar[52] but from 1668 lessees of the rectory were required to pay £20 a year to the vicar.[53] In 1823 the vicar's glebe consisted of some 15 a. at Church End and his tithes were commuted to a corn rent then worth £129.[54] In 1887 the corn rent was converted into a rent charge of £84. By that time the vicarial glebe had shrunk to 5 a.[55] The vicar had conveyed a small piece of the glebe for the parish school in 1840[56] and in 1881 he exchanged his lands southwest of the church for rectorial glebe surrounding the vicarage.[57] The vicarage received grants from the Common Fund of £10 a year in 1849, £30 a year in 1863, £120 a year for a curate in 1867, and £560 for a parsonage in 1881;[58] the gross income increased from £169 a year in 1851[59] to £507 a year by 1896.[60]

The vicarage house was assessed on six hearths in 1664.[61] Rebuilt as a plain brick house in the 18th century,[62] it was in a very bad condition by 1851 when, aided by a grant from Queen Anne's Bounty, it was replaced by a solid building designed by Thomas Tinkler on a site further north.[63] In 1904 that was in turn replaced by a large building designed by W. D. Caroë on the same site. In 1939 N. F. Cachemaille-Day designed a new vicarage, sited to the south, and the old vicarage was turned into flats in 1975.[64]

A gift of property by Ralph Fairsire of Harlesden by will proved 1349 for a chantry before the altar of St. Catherine in Willesden church[65] had no mortmain licence; the king confiscated it and granted it to a layman in 1392.[66] Thomas Willesden, by will proved 1494, gave the residue of his money for a chantry chaplain and an obit, but there is no evidence of any such chantry or obit.[67] Obits were founded by William Barber (fl. mid

[29] *The Times*, 27 July 1926; opening programmes in Grange Mus.
[30] Morris, *Willesden Surv.* p. 88.
[31] *Willesden Monthly Illus.* 5 Jan. 1937.
[32] Morris, *Willesden Surv.* p. 88, map 30.
[33] Leff and Blunden, *Willesden Story*, 63.
[34] *Willesden Civic Review*, Aug. 1957.
[35] Leff and Blunden, *Willesden Story*, 23.
[36] Ibid. 59; Grange Mus. 1 A 2 (*Willesden Cit.* 28 Aug. 1964).
[37] Brent L.B. *Official Guide* [1976].
[38] Leff and Blunden, *Willesden Story*, 60.
[39] Brent L.B. *Council and Related Svces.* (1969).
[40] Leff and Blunden, *Willesden Story*, 66.
[41] Grange Mus., gen. files, health service.
[42] *Domesday of St. Paul's*, 152.
[43] Above, manors.
[44] 'Visitations of Churches', *Camd. Misc.* ix. 3.
[45] Above, manors.
[46] *Visitations of Churches belonging to St. Paul's* (Camd. Soc. N.S. lv), 61.
[47] *Cal. Papal Reg.* xiii. 383.

[48] *Valor Eccl.* (Rec. Com.), i. 434.
[49] Lysons, *Environs*, iii. 620.
[50] Ch. Com., Surveys S2, p. 845.
[51] *Visitations of Churches* (Camd. Soc. N.S. lv), 61.
[52] Lysons, *Environs*, iii. 620.
[53] St. Paul's MS. C (Sancroft), f. 248.
[54] M.R.O., EA/WIL, nos. 182, 187, 479, 487, 518, 524.
[55] Ibid. TA/WIL.   [56] P.R.O., C 54/12284, no. 3.
[57] Ch. Com., file 59830.
[58] *Lond. Gaz.* 10 Aug. 1849, p. 2486; 28 July 1863, p. 3736; 22 Nov. 1867, p. 6229; 5 Aug. 1881, p. 4088.
[59] M.R.O., Acc. 1083/11.
[60] *Crockford* (1896).   [61] M.R.O., MR/TH/3, m. 5d.
[62] Messeder Road Map (1749).
[63] M.R.O., Acc. 1083/11; Grange Mus., photo. album 'Willesden'; C. Hodgson, *Queen Anne's Bounty*, Suppl. (1864), pp. xxvi, lxix.
[64] Inf. from G. Hewlett (Brent planning dept.) and curator of Grange Mus., 1980.
[65] *Cal. Wills in Ct. of Husting*, ed. R. R. Sharpe, i. 553.
[66] *Cal. Pat.* 1391–6, 111; *Cal. Close*, 1392–6, 199–200.
[67] P.R.O., PROB 11/10 (P.C.C. 16 Vox, f. 125).

14th century),[68] William Page (1500),[69] and Thomas Paulet (fl. 1494),[70] the endowments being confiscated and sold in 1548-9.[71] In 1297 the church contained a great cross with images of the Virgin and St. John the Evangelist on the beam next the chancel besides images of St. John the Baptist, St. Nicholas, and St. Catherine.[72] Of the Virgin there were two large sculptured images and a red banner with a gold image in 1249-50[73] and two images with tabernacles in 1297.[74]

The cult of St. Mary at Willesden,[75] for which the evidence belongs mostly to the later Middle Ages, attracted pilgrims from London and generous offerings, although even before the Reformation it was regarded with some suspicion. It may have originated either with the 'distant tradition' that the Virgin appeared in the church-yard and caused a spring to flow or with the veneration of an ancient image of the Virgin. The tradition suggests that the church was built on the site of a holy well, perhaps that which gave Willesden its name.[76] The image was described by a woman who in 1509 was ordered to do penance for her blasphemy as 'a brunt-tailed elf on a brunt-tailed stock',[77] and c. 1535 was found to be of wood 'in colour like ebony, of ancient workmanship', covered with silk and jewels; it was taken away and burnt at Chelsea in 1538.[78]

The medieval church had been rich in ornaments, plate, vestments, and books.[79] Some vestments, altar cloths, and a chalice were stolen in 1550 although a considerable quantity still remained.[80] By the Civil War period puritanical influence was strong; the parish was dominated by the parliamentarian William Roberts who conducted marriages at his house and took charge of the registers during the Interregnum.[81] Roberts may have had a hand in the appointment of Edward Perkins, vicar from 1645 until ejected in 1662, described in 1649 as a 'learned and able minister'.[82]

Many of the vicars of Willesden, especially from the late 17th to the mid 19th century, were also canons of St. Paul's, prebendaries, and pluralists.[83] One prebendary, Francis Hawkins, vicar 1670-99, was followed by another, William Hawkins, vicar 1699-1736, presumably his kinsman and perhaps his son, who married one of the coheirs of the Roberts estate. William

Hawkins, whose brother George acted as his curate in 1714,[84] was also minister of Kingsbury as were several other vicars in the 18th century and the early 19th. One such was Moses Wright (1764-94), a canon and a fashionable London preacher, who seems to have been reasonably conscientious in the cure of Willesden and Kingsbury: in 1777 services were held at Willesden at 8 and 10 a.m. on most Sundays. Kingsbury people were expected to attend usually at Willesden.[85]

There had been chaplains to assist the vicar in the 13th century,[86] 1381,[87] 1547,[88] 1559, and 1562.[89] Curates were common from the 1680s.[90] In 1807 the vestry requested the vicar to pay the parish occasional visits and to appoint a resident curate, and when the vicar replied that he could not afford to, the parish made an annual collection and a salaried curate was appointed.[91] In 1820 on the vicar's death the vestry petitioned the dean and chapter of St. Paul's for a regular afternoon service, as especially needed by servants and the poor; its lack was allegedly a cause of the recent foundation of a dissenting meeting house.[92] In 1871 a winter evening service was introduced to supplement the summer one, and prayers and the litany were said twice on weekdays. In 1873 there was a morning, afternoon, and evening service on Sundays with communion on alternate Sundays and at the chief festivals. In 1875 women were removed from the choir and surplices were worn. Joseph Crane Wharton, vicar 1864-88, was the first for a long time who was not a pluralist; his curates evangelized the rapidly increasing population, running missions in various parts of the parish, especially during the vicar's absence through illness in the 1880s.[93] A parish magazine, edited by a curate, was started in 1872.[94] By 1886 there was a young men's institute, a temperance society, and a choral association.[95]

By 1903 St. Mary's was attended on one Sunday by 123 in the morning and 304 in the evening, only slightly above the average for Willesden's 17 Anglican churches.[96] One of the poorest parishes in the diocese of London, St. Mary's in 1907 ran two missions and needed funds for three assistant clergy, a trained nurse, and a parish sister.[97] Proposals were made in 1897 for a mission room in Taylor's Lane for 200 people. The room, in use by 1900, was attended by 68 people on the evening of one Sunday in

[68] Cal. Close, 1346-9, 145; Inq. Non. (Rec. Com.), 196.
[69] P.R.O., PROB 11/12 (P.C.C. 17 Moone, f. 130); ibid. E 318/Box 26/1461.
[70] Mentioned in Thos. Willesden's will: above; P.R.O., E 301/34 no. 181.
[71] P.R.O., E 315/68, f. 366; ibid. E 36/258, f. 65v.; Cal. Pat. 1549-51, 145; 1547-8, 286-8.
[72] Visitations of Churches (Camd. Soc. N.S. lv), 59.
[73] 'Visitations of Churches', Camd. Misc. ix. 1-3.
[74] Visitations of Churches (Camd. Soc. N.S. lv), 60.
[75] Para. based on H. M. Gillett, Shrines of Our Lady in Eng. and Wales, 371; T.L.M.A.S. iv (1874), 173-87; see also L. & P. Hen. VIII, x. 189; Potter, Story of Willesden, 73-4.
[76] P.N. Mdx. (E.P.N.S.), 160.
[77] Black Virgin of Willesden (pamphlet in Grange Mus.).
[78] Holinshed's Chronicles (1808 edn.), iii. 806.
[79] 'Visitations of Churches', Camd. Misc. ix. 1-3; Visitations of Churches (Camd. Soc. N.S. lv), 59-60; P.R.O., PROB 11/12 (P.C.C. 17 Moone, f. 130); PROB 11/19 (P.C.C. 4 Ayloffe, f. 30).
[80] P.R.O., E 315/498, ff. 39-40.

[81] Grange Mus., Wood F 24, p. 271.
[82] Calamy Revised, ed. Matthews, 386; Grange Mus., Wood F 24, pp. 50 sqq.
[83] Hennessy, Novum Rep. 459.
[84] Grange Mus., Wood F 33, p. 9.
[85] Ibid. 1 B 12 (ch. rate and accts. 1773-1827, s.v. 1777); ibid. Wood F 24, pp. 50 sqq.; F 33, p. 13.
[86] St. Paul's MSS. A 29/384, 388; P.R.O., E 40/7906.
[87] Church in Lond. 1375-92 (Lond. Rec. Soc. xiii), pp. 20-1.
[88] P.R.O., E 301/34, no. 181.
[89] Grange Mus., Wood F 24, p. 48.
[90] Ibid. Wood F 23, pp. 211 sqq.
[91] Ibid. 1 D 29 (vestry order bk. 1722-1814).
[92] Ibid. 1 D 10 (vestry order bk. 1814-25).
[93] Ibid. Wood F 3 (vicar's ann. reps.); F 24, pp. 24v., 72 sqq.
[94] Ibid. F 24, pp. 70 sqq.   [95] Ibid. F 3 (ann. reps.).
[96] Average 414 total attendances: Mudie-Smith, Rel. Life, 414.
[97] The Times, 23 Aug. 1907; 21 Dec. 1909.

1903. It still existed in 1937. In 1899 St. Mary's opened an iron mission in Dog Lane for railway employees. It was attended on a Sunday in 1903 by 26 in the morning and 31 in the evening. It was used as a church hall for St. Raphael's, Garden Way (q.v.), which replaced it, from 1910 until 1924.[98]

The suffragan bishopric of Willesden was founded in 1911.[99]

The church of *ST. MARY*,[1] so called by *c.* 1280,[2] is built of ragstone rubble and flint with freestone dressings and consists of a chancel with north and south chapels, aisled nave, south-west tower and south porch. The oldest surviving part of the church is the mid 12th-century font, one of six Norman fonts in Middlesex.[3] A narrow 12th-century window, found in the north wall, was destroyed in 1872. Two mid 13th-century cylindrical columns survive in the south and one in the north arcade of the nave, suggesting that the church then had north and south aisles. In 1297 the chancel roof was adequate while those of the bell-tower and nave needed improvement;[4] at the end of the 14th century the church was described as being in a disgraceful state.[5] The complaint by parishioners may have prompted the indulgence offered in 1395 to all who contributed to the upkeep of Willesden church. As a result the chancel and south-west tower were rebuilt *c.* 1400. In the early 16th century a south chapel was added and the outer wall of the south aisle rebuilt; the chancel was renovated and the chancel arch rebuilt, and possibly at that time the north aisle was removed and the arcade filled.[6] A south porch was added perhaps in the 17th century. In 1750 a small square turret with a pyramidal roof surmounted the tower;[7] in 1785 it was falling in and was repaired, but it was removed soon afterwards, probably in 1793 when a peal of bells was given.[8] New pews were added *c.* 1805, and a vestry was built north of the chancel in 1813. A gallery, in existence by 1810, was altered to accommodate pews in 1821, when an organ gallery was built and the windows were modernized. In 1824 more seats were needed.[9] Roof bosses were removed from the chancel *c.* 1848[10] and the church was 'grievously dilapidated' in 1849.[11] An unusually large vestry meeting defeated a proposal to pull down the church and build a new one, deciding instead to

preserve the exterior and repair the interior to give 120 more sittings.[12] In 1852 the chancel was repaired and the nave extended westwards under the architect W. Little.[13] The church was restored in 1872 under E. J. Tarver: the western gallery was removed, the north aisle and chapel and an entrance porch were built, adding 227 seats to the 520 already there, the cement and whitewash were removed from the exterior, and the tower was opened to the interior.[14] Other restorations were made to the nave roof in 1895, the south-east chapel in 1917, and the whole church in 1960–4.

There is a fine 14th-century door in the south porch, a piscina in the chancel, an Easter sepulchre in the south-east chapel, and an Elizabethan communion table.[15] Brasses, rescued after they had been thrown onto a rubbish heap in the course of restoration, include these of Bartholomew Willesden and his wife (1494), the vicar William Lichfield (1517), Margaret wife of Thomas Roberts (1505), Edmund Roberts with his two wives and nine children (1585), Jane Barne and her daughters (1609), and a mid-16th century unidentified woman with six children. There is a sculptured monument to Richard Paine and his wife (1606) and monuments, mostly in black marble, to John Barne (1615), Richard Franklin (1615), John Franklin (1647), Francis Roberts (1631), his wife Mary (1623), Sir William Roberts, Bt. (1688), his wife Sarah (1682), Sir William Roberts (1698), William Roberts (1700), and Elizabeth wife of Francis Brende (1667).[16] The author Charles Reade (d. 1884) is buried in the churchyard,[17] which contains many striking 19th-century monuments.

Willesden had two bells in 1297 and four in 1552.[18] All had been replaced or recast by 1717 when there were five bells, including three dated 1661, 1694, and 1704.[19] Thomas Mears was paid for a peal of bells in 1793,[20] of which five survived in the 20th century, together with two given in 1913 from the church of St. Peter-le-Poer, one of 1859, and a sanctus of 1696.[21]

Plate included a silver chalice in 1249–50[22] and 1297,[23] a chalice given by Thomas Willesden (d. 1494),[24] and a gilt chalice by the vicar William Lichfield (d. 1517).[25] In 1552 after the theft of a chalice there remained a silver and gilt chalice and paten and two masers used for bride-ales.[26]

[98] Mudie-Smith, *Rel. Life*, 414; Grange Mus., Wood F 24, pp. 80, 98; ibid. gen. files, *Willesden Chron.* (Suppl. 5 March 1937); ibid. 1 A 2 (*Willesden Chron.* 3 Dec. 1954).
[99] *V.C.H. Mdx.* i. 141.
[1] Based on Hist. Mon. Com. *Mdx.* 132–4; L. R. Dowse and H. Egan, *Brent Parish Churches* (pamphlet 1970); Pevsner, *Mdx.* 172–4; *T.L.M.A.S.* xviii (2).
[2] St. Paul's MS. A 29/384.
[3] See drawings made in 1839: Grange Mus., MS. 1; above, plate facing p. 209.
[4] *Visitations of Churches* (Camd. Soc. n.s. lv), 59.
[5] St. Paul's MS. A 39/1368.
[6] *T.L.M.A.S.* xxii. 37–40; Bodl. MS., Rawl. B 389B, ff. 134–8.
[7] Grange Mus., photo. files, Neasden Lane, St. Mary's par. ch. (print 1750).   [8] Ibid. MS. 1.
[9] Ibid. 1 B 12 (ch. rate and accts. 1773–1827); 1 D 10, 29 (vestry order bks. 1722–1814, 1814–25); *Eng. Topog.* (Gent. Mag. Libr.), vii. 287–9.
[10] Grange Mus., Wood F 27/8–13, 20–3. One survives in Grange Mus.
[11] J. H. Sperling, *Church Walks in Mdx.* (1849), 96–9.

[12] Grange Mus., Wood F 24, pp. 9 sqq.
[13] Potter, *Story of Willesden*, 158; Grange Mus., 1 B 16 (church rates 1828–69).
[14] Thorne, *Environs*, 697–9; Grange Mus., Wood F 3 (bldg. cttee. ann. rep.).
[15] A communion table was bought in London in 1777: Grange Mus., 1 B 12 (chwdns.' accts. 1773–1827).
[16] Bodl. MS. Rawl. B 389B, ff. 134–8; B.L. Add. MSS. 32490, Z 23, CC 31, HH 5, AAA10.
[17] Reade was the executor of Laura Seymour, who founded a Willesden charity but had no other connexion with Willesden: Robbins, *Mdx.* 357–60; Char. com. files.
[18] *Visitations of Churches* (Camd. Soc. n.s. lv), 59; P.R.O., E 315/498, ff. 39–40.
[19] Bodl. MS. Rawl. B 389B, ff. 134–8.
[20] Grange Mus., 1 B 12 (chwdns.' accts. 1773–1827).
[21] *T.L.M.A.S.* xix. 112; *The Times*, 14 June 1913.
[22] 'Visitations of Churches', *Camd. Misc.* ix. 1–3.
[23] *Visitations of Churches* (Camd. Soc. n.s. lv), 59.
[24] P.R.O., PROB 11/10 (P.C.C. 16 Vox, f. 125).
[25] Ibid. PROB 11/19 (P.C.C. 4 Ayloffe, f. 30).
[26] Ibid. E 315/498, ff. 39–40.

In the late 19th century the oldest plate was a cup dated 1606.[27] The registers begin in 1569.[28]

Other C. of E. churches were:[29]

ALL SOULS, Station Rd., Harlesden. Mission services held by curate of St. Mary's at Harlesden institute 1858. Dist. formed 1875 from Willesden, Acton, St. John's, Kensal Green, and Hammersmith.[30] Patron Crown and bp. of London alternately. One asst. curate by 1881, two by 1896, three by 1907. Attendance 1903: 360 a.m.; 477 p.m. High Church tradition broken 1906 but restored in 1970s.[31] Iron church 1869.[32] Brick bldg. in plain Gothic style 1879 by E. J. Tarver, extended 1890: chancel, nave, N. and S. aisles, central octagon, shallow polygonal apse. Extensive repairs 1967. Worship restricted to octagon 1970. Octagon restored and nave demol. 1979. Missions: St. Mark (q.v.); Old Oak Lane, Willesden Junction, Acton, c. 1902–c. 1926; 10A Rucklidge Ave. c. 1902.

CHRIST CHURCH, Willesden Lane, Brondesbury.[33] Dist. formed 1867 from St. Mary's under Dr. Charles W. Williams (d. 1889) and financed by his sisters.[34] Declared a rectory with tithe-charges transferred from St. Mary's 1868.[35] Williams, patron and first rector, succeeded by son, Charles D. Williams 1889–1913. Patronage sold to parish c. 1930 and transferred to Lord Chancellor c. 1957. United with St. Lawrence's (q.v.) 1971. One asst. curate by 1896, two by 1926. High Church. Attendance 1903: 300 a.m.; 447 p.m. Limestone bldg. in 13th-century style by C. R. B. King: chancel, north tower and spire, nave, N. aisle, N. transept, and NW. porch 1866, S. aisle and S. transept 1899, choir vestry 1909. Damaged by land mine 1940, restored 1948. Missions: St. Lawrence (q.v.); Poplars Ave. c. 1918; Avenue Close 1903–39.

GOOD SHEPHERD, Acton Lane, Lower Place. Mission services held by curate of St. Michael's, Stonebridge, c. 1883. New mission bldg. 1890.[36] Attendance 1903: 40 a.m., 20 p.m. Closed after 1908.

HOLY TRINITY, Brondesbury Rd., Kilburn. Founded by min. of St. Paul's, Kilburn (q.v.). Dist. formed 1867 from St. Mary's.[37] Patron trustees, by 1955 Church Patronage Soc. United with St. Paul's, Kilburn, 1936 and from 1953 held with St. Anne's (q.v.). Low Church. Attendance 1903: 116 a.m.; 108 p.m. Buff brick bldg. 1867 with stone facings by F. and F. J. Francis, seating 1,100. Destroyed by fire 1950

except tower and spire which were demol. by 1970. Mission in Canterbury Rd. 1903–48.[38]

ST. ANDREW, High Rd., Willesden Green. Dist. formed 1880 from St. Mary's.[39] Patron bp. of London and Crown alternately. Benefice suspended under Pastoral Measures Act 1976 and held with St. Francis of Assisi (q.v.).[40] Four asst. curates by 1896, three by 1926, two by 1947, one by 1970; employed two members of Sisters of Community of Church 1882–3. High Church. Attendance 1903: 235 a.m.; 263 p.m. Iron churches at junction of Villiers and Chaplin Rds. 1880–2, on High Rd. site 1882–7.[41] Brick bldg. with stone facings in 13th-century style 1887 by J. Brooks, extended 1897, seating 1,000: chancel with N. and S. chapels, aisled and clerestoreyed nave, shallow transepts.[42] Flemish reredos and 16th-century processional cross from Seville cathedral. Missions: infant sch. in Chaplin Rd. c. 1887–c. 1908;[43] St. John the Baptist (q.v.).

ST. ANNE, Salusbury Rd., Brondesbury. Originated as mission of London Diocesan Home Mission 1899.[44] Parish formed 1905 from Christ Church, Holy Trinity, and St. John's, Kensal Green. Patron bp. of London, from 1953 alternately with Church Patronage Society. Held with Holy Trinity (q.v.) from 1953. Two asst. curates by 1907, one by 1926, none after 1947. Attendance 1903: 62 a.m.; 97 p.m. Iron church 1900. Brick bldg. with stone dressings in 14th-century style 1905 by J. E. K. and J. P. Cutts, seating 750: chancel with two S. chapels, N. vestry, aisled and clerestoreyed nave.

ST. CATHERINE,[45] Dudden Hill Lane, Neasden. Chapel of ease to St. Andrew's, Kingsbury, 1901; parish formed 1934. Patron dean and chapter of St. Paul's. Held with St. Paul's, Oxgate, 1980. Attendance 1903: 41 a.m.; 110 p.m. Iron chapel at corner of Neasden Lane and Prout Grove, enlarged 1903. Brick bldg. with stone dressings on new site in 14th-century style 1916 by J. S. Alder:[46] chancel, S. chapel, aisled nave; W. extension in 13th-century style by E. B. Glanfield, 1954.

ST. CECILIA, Acton Lane, Harlesden. Mission of St. Michael's, Stonebridge, 1895. Attendance 1903: 51 a.m.; 66 p.m. Closed 1956.[47]

ST. FRANCIS OF ASSISI, Fleetwood Rd., Gladstone Park. London Diocesan Mission church 1911; parish formed 1934. Patron bp. of London. Held from 1976 with St. Andrew's (q.v.). High Church. Temp. church seating 350 blt. 1911. Buff brick bldg. in style of lower

[27] Freshfield, *Communion Plate*, 55.
[28] *T.L.M.A.S.* xiv. 106; Grange Mus., Wood F 33.
[29] Inf. about patronage based on Hennessy, *Novum Rep.*; *Clergy List* (1881 and later edns.); *Crockford* (1896 and later edns.); about architecture on *T.L.M.A.S.* xviii (2); Dowse and Egan, *Brent Parish Churches*; inf. for 1979 from the curator, Grange Mus.; about missions on *Kelly's Dir. Mdx.* (1855 and later edns.); attendance figs. for 1903 from Mudie-Smith, *Rel. Life*, 414. For abbreviations used see above, p. 37 n. 68.　　[30] *Lond. Gaz.* 14 May 1875, p. 2580.
[31] Inf. from the curator, Grange Mus. (1979).
[32] Grange Mus., Wood F 24, pp. 70, 99.
[33] Based on *Par. Ch. of Brondesbury* (*Christ Church*) *Centenary Booklet, 1866–1966*.
[34] *Lond. Gaz.* 6 Aug. 1867, p. 4356.
[35] Ibid. 15 May 1868, p. 2807.
[36] Grange Mus., Wood F 3 (ann. reps.); F 24, p. 134.

[37] *Lond. Gaz.* 6 Aug. 1867, p. 4356.
[38] Morris, *Willesden Surv.* pp. 34 sqq.
[39] *Lond. Gaz.* 17 Sept. 1880, p. 4948.
[40] Inf. from clergy.
[41] Grange Mus., gen. files, St. Andrew's ch. (diary); *St. Andrew's Kalendar*, Nov. 1881.
[42] Grange Mus., Wood F 28/4; ibid. photo. files, St. Andrew's ch.
[43] Nat. Soc. files, St. Andrew, Willesden Green.
[44] Grange Mus., gen. files, Brondesbury Park (*Willesden Chron.* 8 July 1904).
[45] G. H. Ayerst, *Short Acct. of Par. of Neasden-cum-Kingsbury* (pamphlet c. 1907); O.S. Map 1/2,500, Mdx. XI. 14 (1914 edn.).
[46] Grange Mus., photo. files, Neasden (44.1977d).
[47] Ibid. NM 350; *Willesden Chron.* 29 Nov. 1895; 17 Aug. 1956.

basilica at Assisi 1933 by J. H. Gibbons, seating 446: chancel with vestries, short central tower with transepts, aisled nave.[48]

ST. GABRIEL,[49] Walm Lane, Cricklewood. Dist. formed from St. Andrew's (q.v.) under auspices of London Diocesan Home Mission 1890 with additions from Christ Church (q.v.) 1896. Patron bp. of London. Attendance 1903: 296 a.m.; 444 p.m. Iron church in Chichele Rd. 1891, enlarged 1892 and 1894 to seat 400. Stone bldg. in early 14th-century style 1897 by W. Bassett Smith and R. P. Day: chancel, N. chapel, S. vestry, aisled and clerestoreyed nave with N. transept, W. saddleback tower. Damaged by lightning 1900, restored 1903, seating 940.

ST. JOHN THE BAPTIST, Dudden Hill Lane. Mission founded from St. Andrew's (q.v.) with aid from bp. of London's fund. Attendance 1903: 53 a.m.; 60 p.m. Bldg. 1901, seating 350. Closed after 1937.[50]

ST. JOHN THE EVANGELIST, Cambridge Gdns., Kilburn. Perpetual curacy founded 1860. Dist. formed from Holy Trinity (q.v.) 1872.[51] Patron trustees, by 1907 Church Patronage Soc. One asst. curate by 1877, two by 1882,[52] one by 1926, none after 1935. United with St. Augustine's, Kilburn, 1971.[53] Attendance 1903: 134 a.m.; 262 p.m. Founded as Low Church mission from St. Paul's, Kilburn Square (q.v.), in rivalry with High Church St. Mary's, Kilburn. Min. forced to resign when introduced surplices and services 1875.[54] V. complained of 'Romish tendencies' of St. Augustine's, Kilburn, 1880.[55] Iron church, seating 2,000, opened at junction of Carlton and Kilburn Park roads and destroyed by fire 1860. Rebuilt 1862.[56] Buff brick bldg. with red brick dressings 1871 by F. and F. J. Francis, seating 1,100: apsidal chancel, nave, N. and S. aisles, NE. chapel, SE. crypt chapel, SW. tower with octagonal bell-turret and spirelet. Closed 1971 and burnt down 1975.

ST. LAWRENCE, Chevening Rd., Brondesbury.[57] Mission founded from Christ Church, Brondesbury, c. 1903. Parish formed from Christ Church 1905. Patron bp. of London. United with Christ Church (q.v.) 1971. High Church. Attendance 1903: 79 a.m.; 105 p.m. Iron church c. 1903. Red brick bldg. with stone dressings 1906 by J. E. K. and J. P. Cutts, seating 537: nave, N. and S. aisles, W. baptistery;[58] never completed. Closed 1971 and subsequently demol.

ST. MARK, Bathurst Gdns., Harlesden.[59] Founded as mission from All Souls (q.v.) 1903. Parish formed, with endowment transferred from St. Olave's, Mile End, 1915. Patron trustees of St. Olave's, Hart Street. Iron church 1903, seating 500. Brick bldg. with stone facings in 14th-century style 1914 by J. S. Alder, seating 500: chancel with chapels, aisled and clerestoreyed nave; W. front completed 1968 by Riley and Glanfield.

ST. MARTIN, Mortimer Rd., Kensal Rise. Founded 1899 as memorial church to Charles J. Vaughan (d. 1897), headmaster of Harrow and dean of Llandaff. Parish formed from St. Mary's, St. John's, Kensal Green, Hammersmith, and Kensington 1900. Patron bp. of London. Attendance 1903: 200 a.m.; 480 p.m. Red brick bldg. with stone dressings in 13th-century style 1899 by J. E. K. and J. P. Cutts, seating 750: chancel with S. chapel, aisled and clerestoreyed nave, base for SW. tower, narthex. Mission in Harrow Rd. by 1899, closed by 1908,[60] attendance 1903: 89 a.m.; 121 p.m.

ST. MATTHEW, St. Mary's Rd., Willesden.[61] Founded by London Diocesan Home Mission 1894. Parish formed from St. Mary's and All Souls (q.v.) 1902. Patron bp. of London. One asst. curate by 1899, three by 1905, two by 1912, one from 1928. Attendance 1903: 228 a.m.; 241 p.m. High Church. Musical tradition established c. 1918. Iron church 1895, seating 300.[62] Brick bldg. with stone facings in mixed style 1901 by W. D. Caroë, seating 878: chancel, SE chapel, nave, passage aisles, N. and S. transepts, narthex. Medieval oak statue of St. Matthew possibly from Glastonbury rood screen. Missions: St. Thomas Rd. 1908; Roundwood Rd. 1926.

ST. MICHAEL, St. Michael's Rd., Cricklewood.[63] Founded by London Diocesan Home Mission 1907. Parish formed from St. Gabriel's (q.v.) 1910. Patron bp. of London. Benefice sequestrated, in charge of V. of St. Gabriel's 1941–5. Benefice suspended because of friction between V. and parishioners 1949–51. Mission church 1907, later parish hall. Ashlar bldg. in 14th-century style 1909 by J. S. Alder, seating 754: chancel with N. chapel, aisled and clerestoreyed nave, base for NW. tower.

ST. MICHAEL AND ALL ANGELS, Hillside, Stonebridge. Mission meetings in rented rooms 1876. Mission room in Melville Rd. 1879. London Diocesan Home Mission provided new mission 1885.[64] Parish formed from St. Mary's and All Souls (q.v.) 1892. Patron bp. of London. One asst. curate by 1926. Attendance 1903: 179 a.m.; 263 p.m. Red brick bldg. with stone dressings in late 13th-century style 1891 by Goldie and Child, enlarged 1904, seating 750: chancel with N. and S. chapels (1904), aisled and clerestoreyed nave. Missions: Good Shepherd (q.v.); St. Cecilia (q.v.); St. Peter (q.v.).

---

[48] Grange Mus., gen. files, Gladstone Park (*New Churches Illus.* 1936).

[49] G. M. Clibborn and C. F. G. Turner, *St. Gabriel's Ch. Willesden Green* (pamphlet c. 1903 in Grange Mus.).

[50] Grange Mus., gen. files, St. Andrew's ch. (diary); gen. files, *Willesden Chron.* (Suppl. 5 Mar. 1937).

[51] *Lond. Gaz.* 23 Feb. 1872, p. 693.

[52] Ibid. 23 Mar. 1877, p. 2206; 30 June 1882, p. 3032.

[53] *Kilburn Times,* 3 Jan. 1975.

[54] Grange Mus., Wood F 24, pp. 118, 258.

[55] Nat. Soc. files, Kilburn.

[56] Grange Mus., Ball, scrapbk. i, p. 0194 (*S. Lond. Chron.* 1 Dec. 1860); O.S. Map 6″, Mdx. XVI. NE. (1864–73 edn.).

[57] Inf. from John G. F. Miller (1978).

[58] Grange Mus., photo. files, Chevening Rd. (NL 696, 699).

[59] *St. Mark's Ch. Harlesden, 1914–74* (diamond jubilee booklet).

[60] P.R.O., C 54/19314, m. 20.

[61] *St. Matthew at Willesden 1901–51* (golden jubilee handbk.).

[62] Grange Mus., Wood F 24, pp. 72 sqq.

[63] *St. Michael, Cricklewood, 1910–60* (golden jubilee booklet).

[64] Grange Mus., Wood F 3 (ann. reps.); F 24, pp. 70 sqq., 134.

ST. PAUL, Kilburn Sq., Edgware Rd. Proprietary chapel founded by Francis Nalder and John M. Close 1825. Proprietor and min. *c.* 1840–1847 John Heming.[65] Patron Charles Bradley 1863–7, Elizabeth Heming 1868–97. Parish formed 1897. Patron Church Patronage Soc. Attendance 1851: 461 a.m.; 218 p.m.;[66] 1903: 203 a.m.; 458 p.m. Low Church under evangelical James J. Bolton 1852–63[67] and George Despard 1863–7. Congregation split and min. left to found Holy Trinity (q.v.) 1867. Musical reputation established by Henry G. Bonavia Hunt 1887–1905. Bldg. of 1826 enlarged 1887–94, seating 600. Chancel rebuilt by 1908. Church demol. and parish united with Holy Trinity 1936.[68]

ST. PAUL, Dollis Hill Lane, Oxgate.[69] Opened in iron church *c.* 1934 and moved to bldg. (later church hall) in Oxgate Gdns. *c.* 1936. Patron bp. of London. Brick and concrete bldg. 1939 by N. F. Cachemaille-Day, seating 360: shallow chancel, aisled nave; 18th-century seating from City church. Closed 1980 and united with St. Catherine, Neasden.

ST. PETER, Harrow Rd., Stonebridge. Mission founded from St. Michael's, Stonebridge (q.v.), by 1902. Attendance 1903: 119 a.m.; 68 p.m. Closed after 1937.[70]

ST. RAPHAEL, Garden Way, Neasden. London Diocesan Home Mission chapel for Great Central Railway estate 1910. Iron church at apex of Gresham and Woodheyes roads 1910, seating 200. Bldg. at Garden Way 1924.[71]

ST. SAVIOUR, Quainton St., Neasden.[72] London Diocesan Home Mission chapel for Metropolitan Railway estate 1883. Dist. of St. Saviour and St. Andrew, Kingsbury, formed 1885. Replaced by old St. Andrew's, Kingsbury, 1885.[73] Brick bldg. 1883, seating 220, used for sch. 1884 and closed 1945.

ROMAN CATHOLICISM. There were no papists in Willesden *c.* 1641 or *c.* 1714,[74] and in spite of the early Irish immigration Roman Catholic churches and convents were not established until the late 19th century. That may have been because there were particularly active centres just over the border, for example at Quex Road. A church and convent were established at Harlesden in the 1880s, and the introduction of annual processions to the shrine of Our Lady of Willesden in 1903 provoked attacks by Protestants.[75] A church and two convents were opened at Willesden Green in the 1900s and a church and hospital (St. Andrew's) at Dollis Hill at the time

of the First World War. There was a mission at Brondesbury by 1920 and there were churches at Stonebridge in 1926 and Kilburn in 1948; another convent opened at Willesden Green in 1928. Most convents have been small ones, opened in the 1960s and 1970s in newer areas like Cricklewood, although a convent and church opened in Kensal Rise in 1977. The movement to Cricklewood reflects the general movement of the Irish north from Kilburn. The drop in the attendance figures of the Immaculate Heart of Mary at Kilburn from 1961 to 1978 is explained by the replacement of Irish by West Indian and Indian immigrants.[76] Individual churches and convents are described below.[77]

Our Lady of Willesden originated in services held in private house in Tubbs Rd., Harlesden, 1885. Iron chapel in Manor Park Rd. 1886. Attendance 1903: 354 a.m.; 106 p.m. Replaced by church of Italian terracotta in Romanesque style in Crownhill Rd. 1907, seating 200. Became part of Jesus and Mary convent on building of red brick church with companile in modern Romanesque style at junction of Acton Lane and Nicoll Rd. 1930 by Wilfred C. Mangan. Wooden statue of Our Lady given by Cardinal Vaughan, object of attempt to revive pre-Reformation cult of Our Lady of Willesden.[78]

St. Catherine's chapel of ease, no. 59 Chaplin Rd., Willesden Green, registered 1902. Replaced 1905 by chapel at no. 28 Park Ave., 1908 by Our Lady of Compassion, Linacre Rd., and 1939 by St. Mary Magdalen, brick church in Harlesden Rd. Close connexions with Polish Jesuits of House of Our Lady (q.v.). Masses in Polish.[79]

St. Mary and St. Andrew built 1915 in Dollis Hill Lane and replaced 1933 by brown brick church.[80]

Church of the Five Precious Wounds, Knatchbull Rd., Stonebridge, registered 1926. Replaced 1957 by church in Woodheyes Rd. and 1967 by brick church seating 400 in Brentfield Rd.[81]

Oblates of St. Mary Immaculate opened church of Immaculate Heart of Mary as chapel of ease to Sacred Heart of Jesus, Quex Rd. (Hampstead), 1948 in former Methodist chapel in Stafford Rd. (Percy Rd.), Kilburn. Average attendance at mass 1961: 3,900; 1978: *c.* 1,200.[82]

Church of the Transfiguration opened in former Methodist chapel 1977 in Chamberlayne Rd., Kensal Rise. Red-brick building altered to seat 1,100.[83]

The Catholic Missionary Society ran a mission ho. *c.* 1920–*c.* 1940 at Restormel, Brondesbury Park.

[65] Ibid. F 33, pp. 13 sqq.; Guildhall MS. CC. 30688.
[66] P.R.O., HO 129/135/3/1/2.   [67] *D.N.B.*
[68] Grange Mus., gen. files, Kilburn Sq. (*Mdx. Courier*, 23 July, 6 Aug. 1897; *Willesden Chron.* 18 Oct. 1895; 22 May 1936).   [69] Inf. from vicar (1978).
[70] Grange Mus., gen. files, *Willesden Chron.* (Suppl. 5 Mar. 1937).
[71] Ibid. 2 B 24 ('Memories of Neasden'); ibid. gen. files, railways (*Forward, Jnl. of Gt. Central Rly. Soc.* Dec. 1978).
[72] Ayerst, *Neasden-cum-Kingsbury*; Grange Mus., Wood F 24, p. 141; Nat. Soc. files, Neasden.
[73] Grange Mus., Wood F 4 (ann. reps.); *V.C.H. Mdx.* v. 85.
[74] B.L. Add. MS. 38856, f. 59; M.R.O., MR/RR 19/4.
[75] Gillett, *Shrines of Our Lady*, 379.

[76] Inf. from the par. priest (1978).
[77] Based on *Cath. Dir.*; *Westminster Year Bk.*
[78] *Story of Our Lady of Willesden* (pamphlet 1928 in Grange Mus.); Gillett, *Shrines of Our Lady*, 379; inf. from the par. priest (1978); G.R.O., Worship Reg. 31369, 42910, 52989; Mudie-Smith, *Rel. Life*, 416; Dept. of Environment, list of bldgs., Brent L.B. (*c.* 1978).
[79] G.R.O. Worship Reg. 39368, 41354, 42920, 59198; datestone 1938; inf. from superior of Our Lady of Mercy (1978).   [80] G.R.O. Worship Reg. 46505, 54493.
[81] Ibid. 50468, 66279, 70951; inf. from the par. priest (1978).
[82] G.R.O. Worship Reg. 64474; inf. from the par. priest (1978).
[83] *Kilburn Times*, 28 Oct. 1977; below, prot. nonconf.

The Congregation of Jesus and Mary opened convents 1886 in Crownhill Rd., Harlesden, c. 1908 in Park Ave., Willesden Green,[84] and 1977 at 58 Wrentham Ave., Kensal Rise.[85]

The Religious Society of Marie Réparatrice flourished c. 1900 at Sharstead, Donnington Rd., Willesden Green, but had gone by 1920.

The Little Company of Mary or Sisters of Mercy ran St. Andrew's hospital 1913–73 in Dollis Hill Lane.[86]

A small community of the Daughters of Charity of St. Vincent de Paul was established 1928 in St. Paul's Ave., Willesden Green. Moved to no. 247 Willesden Lane where hostel opened for working girls 1932. Bombed 1940 and closed until 1942. Ran probation hostel for girls 1942–69. Premises converted into 10 flatlets for unmarried mothers 1970. Contains chapel for public worship.[87] Another community of Daughters of Charity of St. Vincent de Paul 1978 at nos. 72 and 74 Anson Rd. Cricklewood.

The Canossian Sisters established the Holy Family convent by 1970 at no. 9 Hillcrest Gardens, Dollis Hill.

A small convent of the Sisters of the Holy Family of Bordeaux moved 1974 from Kilburn (Hampstead) to no. 83 St. Gabriel's Rd., Cricklewood. Private chapel.[88]

The Sisters of Charity of Jesus and Mary, a nursing order, was established 1975 at no. 13 Station Rd. Harlesden. Private chapel.[89]

The Divine Word Missionaries moved 1975 from Totteridge common to no. 8 Teignmouth Rd., Cricklewood. Hostel for students training as overseas missionaries.[90]

Polish Jesuits opened the House of Our Lady 1959 at no. 182 Walm Lane, Cricklewood, as centre for pastoral work among Poles in NW. London. Chapel registered 1962.[91]

The Hungarian Roman Catholic Chaplaincy of Our Lady, the administrative office of the chaplaincy in the United Kingdom, moved from Kensington 1964 to no. 56 Randall Ave., Neasden.[92]

PROTESTANT NONCONFORMITY.[93]

During the second decade of the 19th century Protestant dissenters began meeting in private houses in Willesden Green.[94] One of the houses belonged to the mother of Oliver Nodes who visited her each Sunday and read from the sermons of the Evangelist George Burder. They were joined by neighbours, forming the congregation which in 1820 founded Willesden Green Independent (Congregational) chapel.[95] Houses were registered for worship by dissenters in the

1830s at Fortune Gate, Harlesden, Willesden Green, and Kensal Green.[96] A Wesleyan chapel opened in Harlesden c. 1847, a Baptist chapel in West Kilburn in 1865, and a Presbyterian church at Fortune Gate in 1875.

The great expansion of nonconformity from the late 1870s until the First World War mirrored the growth of building in Willesden, chapels and mission halls opening in the rapidly developing districts of Kilburn, Harlesden, and Willesden, especially during the 1880s and 1890s. The parish, increasingly working-class with poor church attendance, was compared in 1903 with Stepney or St. Pancras. Most of those attending places of worship were Protestant nonconformists.[97] In areas like Kilburn the division was less between Church and Dissent than between High and Low Church. The Irish Roman Catholics and ritualist High Anglicans were vehemently opposed by the Low Church Anglicans and nonconformists; people moved frequently from one nonconformist sect to another.[98]

By 1903 there were 45 Protestant nonconformist places of worship, attended on one Sunday by 4,111 people in the morning and 7,512 in the evening, nearly three fifths of those worshipping in Willesden on that day. The Methodists, with 2,982 attendances at 10 chapels, formed the largest denomination, followed by the Presbyterians (1,748 attendances at 6 chapels), Baptists (1,738 at 5 chapels), and Congregationalists (1,411 at 4 chapels). Of the 45 chapels and halls, Kilburn and Willesden Green each had 10, Harlesden 8, Kensal Green and the area stretching from Stonebridge to Church End 5 each, Neasden 4, Brondesbury 2, and Cricklewood 1.[99]

Between 1903 and 1914 the Baptists opened five chapels or halls and built a larger chapel at Willesden Green, and there was limited expansion by the other established sects. Several mission halls closed, and after the First World War closures were more frequent than openings in spite of the spread of building to Neasden and Cricklewood in the 1930s. There were 41 chapels and halls by 1933 and 27 by 1963.[1] Since then 13 have closed and 8 opened. As the established sects have contracted, newer sects, often Pentecostalist, have expanded, often using old chapels, especially in areas like Harlesden where membership is largely West Indian.[2]

CONGREGATIONALISTS. Congregation of 'Protestant Dissenters' met in house of Kelita Kilby at Willesden Green 1815. Independents met at house of Oliver Nodes 1817.[3] Small, plain

[84] Chapel reg. 1960: G.R.O. Worship Reg. 67772.
[85] Inf. from the sister superior (1978).
[86] Above, pub. svces.
[87] Inf. from Sister Eileen (1978).
[88] Inf. from Sister Veronica Tracy (1978).
[89] Inf. from Sister Kathleen O'Connor.
[90] Inf. from the rector (1978).
[91] G.R.O. Worship Reg. 68611; inf. from the superior (1978).
[92] Inf. from R.C. Hungarian chaplain in the U.K. (1978).
[93] For abbreviations used see above, p. 40 n. 51. Attendance figures for 1903 from Mudie-Smith, Rel. Life, 414 sqq.

[94] Guildhall MS. 9580/4.
[95] Potter, Story of Willesden, 162.
[96] P.R.O., RG 31/3, no. 1754; RG 31/6, nos. 2, 3, 11.
[97] Mudie-Smith, Rel. Life, 339, 342, 443.
[98] C. Booth, Life and Labour of the people in Lond. 3rd ser. Religious Influences, 3 (1902), p. 208.
[99] i.e. within Willesden: there were other chapels in the Hendon portion of Cricklewood.
[1] Willesden boro. Local Community Svces. 1933; Willesden Inf. Handbk. [1963].
[2] e.g. Willesden Mercury, 20 Jan. 1967.
[3] Guildhall MS. 9580/4. Kilby conveyed the site for the chapel in 1820.

chapel with pedimented front and round-headed windows built 1820 at junction of High Rd. and Dudden Hill Lane.[4] Attendance 1851: 20 a.m.; 30 p.m.[5] Larger chapel built 1878 to west, at junction of High Rd. and Pound Lane.[6] Attendance 1903: 108 a.m.; 131 p.m. Original bldg. used for Sunday sch. until closed 1907.[7]

St. James's iron Cong. chapel opened in Cambridge Rd., Kilburn, by 1872 and closed by 1903.[8]

Independent mission chapel opened in Carlton Rd. (later Vale) by 1890 and closed 1913.[9] Attendance 1903: 49 a.m.; 98 p.m.

Iron mission chapel in Cricklewood Lane (Hendon) opened by Lyndhurst Rd. (Hampstead) church 1885.[10] Congregation moved to brick bldg., Lown memorial hall in Howard Rd., Cricklewood 1893. New chapel in Gothic style with tower opened 1902 in Chichele Rd.[11] Attendance 1903: 187 a.m.; 402 p.m. Had 21 members 1978.[12] Closed and reopened as mosque by 1980.[13]

Congregation met in constitutional hall in St. Mary's Rd., Harlesden before foundation stone of chapel laid at corner of Church and West Ella roads 1899.[14] Red brick bldg. with stone dressings in Gothic style with asymmetrical SW. tower, designed by Spalding and Spalding for 800. Chapel and adjoining lecture hall reg. 1901.[15] Attendance 1903: 153 a.m.; 283 p.m. Declining numbers led to leasing of chapel to film company c. 1962, congregation thereafter using hall. Membership 1963-4: 71; 1978: 30.[16]

Chapel opened at Craven Hill (Bayswater) 1846. Congregation moved 1912 to new chapel in Wrentham Ave., Brondesbury Park. Had 79 members 1963-6. Closed by 1972 and bldg. used for youth and community service 1978.[17]

Hamilton hall, 375-7 High Rd., Willesden Green, licensed for worship by Cong. 1914-25.[18]

METHODISTS. Wes. chapel built c. 1847 on north side of Harrow Rd. (High St., Harlesden) and closed c. 1856.[19] Replaced by Willesden (Junction) Wes. chapel, accommodating 300, on eastern side of Harrow Rd., opposite Crown inn 1869-81.[20] Bldg. used as Sunday sch., then shop after new chapel accommodating 1,030, of red brick with stone dressings in early Gothic style

with tower and spire by Charles Bell, opened 1882 on adjacent site (25 High St.).[21] Attendance 1903: 240 a.m.; 435 p.m. Opened Tavistock hall, seating 500, 1906. Chapel damaged 1940 and demol. 1941. New brick chapel, seating 250, built 1956 in plain, modern style by A. MacDonald. Hall used as youth and community centre 1978.[22]

Chapel of stock bricks with slate roof built 1878 at junction of Cambridge and Malvern Rds., Kilburn Park for Free (later United) Meths. Attendance 1903: 35 a.m.; 104 p.m. Closed 1934.[23]

Peel Rd. chapel in Percy Rd. Kilburn Park reg. for Bible Christians 1880. Attendance 1903: 81 a.m.; 166 p.m. Recertificated for Bible Christian United Meths. 1907 and closed 1948. Used as Roman Catholic church of Immaculate Heart of Mary (q.v.).[24]

Wes. Meths. met 1886 in ho. in College Rd., Kensal Rise. Tin chapel opened 1887 in Hiley Rd. Brick chapel with stone dressings in Gothic style with tower and spire opened 1900 at corner of Chamberlayne Wood Rd. and Ladysmith Rd. (later Wrentham Ave.). Attendance 1903: 330 a.m.; 568 p.m. Chapel sold to Roman Catholics (q.v.) 1977 and Meths. met in adjacent hall.[25]

Wes. services held in cottage in Quainton St., Neasden 1880s and shop in Kingsbury Rd. leased rent-free from Metropolitan Rly. Co. 1896. Attendance 1903: 37 a.m.; 13 p.m. Iron chapel accommodating 300 built 1905 at corner of Neasden Lane and Verney St. on railway land and supported by Rly. Mission Co. Iron chapel moved 1928 to new site at junction of Neasden Lane and North Circular. Replaced 1937 by brown-brick chapel accommodating 400 on new site in Neasden Lane, north of North Circular Road. Damaged 1945 and reopened after repairs 1947.[26] Closed 1980 and services held in hall.

Free (later United) Meth. chapel seating 250 built 1888 in Tubbs Rd., Harlesden. New chapel for 450 built 1901. Attendance 1903: 96 a.m.; 134 p.m. Closed 1963.[27]

Hamilton hall, High Rd. Willesden Green reg. for Wes. Meths. 1889-1902.[28]

Primitive Meth. chapel opened in High Rd., Willesden Green by 1897. Attendance 1903: 96 a.m.; 144 p.m. Rebuilt 1904. Closed 1963.[29]

[4] M.R.O., Acc. 958/5; Grange Mus., 1 D 10 (vestry bk. 1814-25); OS. Map 1/2,500, Mdx. XVI. 2 (1865 edn.).
[5] P.R.O., HO 129/135/3/1/5.
[6] Grange Mus., photo. files, High Rd., Willesden Green (NL 972); ibid. NM 421.
[7] M.R.O., Acc. 958/6; G.R.O. Worship Reg. 24616; Grange Mus., Ball, scrapbk. ii. 0673.
[8] Kilburn Dir. (1872-81); Kelly's Dir. Mdx. (1890).
[9] G.R.O. Worship Reg. 33392; Kelly's Dir. Mdx. (1890).
[10] Based on Hist. Cricklewood Cong. Ch. (1927, pamphlet in Grange Mus.) and inf. from sec. (1978).
[11] G.R.O. Worship Reg. 34104, 39300; Grange Mus., photo. files, Chichele Rd. (NL 700).
[12] United Reformed Ch. Year Bk. (1978).
[13] Below, Islam.
[14] Based on inf. from sec. (1978).
[15] G.R.O. Worship Reg. 38230; Pevsner, Mdx. 172-4.
[16] Cong. Year Bk. (1963-4); United Reformed Ch. Year Bk. (1978).
[17] Brondesbury Park Cong. Ch. 1913-63 (pamphlet in Grange Mus.); G.R.O. Worship Reg. 15196, 45494; Cong. Year Bk. (1963-4); Free Ch. Dir. (1968-9); Kelly's Dir. Lond. (1972).
[18] G.R.O. Worship Reg. 46035; below, Methodists, Brethren.
[19] M.R.O., Acc. 1371/1; P.R.O., RG 31/3, no. 2335; Kelly's Dir. Mdx. (1855); Nat. Soc. files, Harlesden All Souls.
[20] Based on Harlesden Meth. Ch. 1869-1969 (pamphlet in Grange Mus.).
[21] G.R.O. Worship Reg. 26504; Grange Mus., Wood F 20 (sale cat. 2/18); Wood F 37/14; ibid. 1 A 4 (Willesden Chron. 21 Jan. 1938); ibid. photo. files, High St. Harlesden (NL 1014, 1468).
[22] Inf. from the minister (1978); The Builder, 21 Dec. 1956.
[23] M.R.O., Acc. 1351/18; G.R.O. Worship Reg. 28256.
[24] G.R.O. Worship Reg. 25118, 42548.
[25] Kensal Rise Meth. Ch. 1900-60 (pamphlet in Grange Mus.).
[26] Neasden Meth. Ch. Souvenir Handbk. 1958 (pamphlet in Grange Mus.); inf. from sec. (1978); The Times, 3 Apr. 1928.
[27] G.R.O. Worship Reg. 31168, 39167; Kelly's Dir. Mdx. (1890, 1926); Grange Mus., 1 A 2 (Willesden Cit. 6 Sept. 1963); below, Church of the God of Prophecy.
[28] G.R.O. Worship Reg. 31897; Grange Mus., 1 A 2 (Willesden Chron. n.d.); above and below, Congregationalists, Brethren.
[29] P.R.O., C 54/19812, m. 32; G.R.O. Worship Reg. 36276, 40460; below, New Testament Church of God.

Primitive Meth. chapel built 1897 at corner of Harrow Rd. and Victor Rd., College Pk. Attendance 1903: 80 a.m.; 130 p.m. Closed 1958.[30]

Trinity Wes. chapel built 1899 at corner of Walm Lane and Dartmouth Rd., Cricklewood. Large brick and stone bldg. by W. D. Church & Son with tower and steeple. Attendance 1903: 125 a.m.; 256 p.m. Closed 1948.[31]

Metropolitan Rly. Mission hall opened in Neasden Lane by Wes. by 1890. Attendance 1903: 40 a.m.; 73 p.m. Closed by 1933.

Primitive Meth. Metropolitan Rly. Mission hall opened in Dog Lane, Neasden by 1903 when attendance 25 a.m.; 31 p.m. Closed by 1933.[32]

United Meths. reg. rooms at 7 Stafford Rd., Kilburn, 1929–35.[33]

For Welsh Calvinistic Meth. chapel in Willesden Lane, see below, Presbyterians.

BAPTISTS.[34] Stock brick chapel with stone dressings in classical style with pedimented front and round-headed windows built 1865 for 550 in Canterbury Rd., West Kilburn. Attendance 1903: 47 a.m.; 140 p.m. Had 68 members 1977–8.[35]

Congregation, formed at Willesden Green after open-air mission by Spurgeon's students 1881, met in cottage, stable, and shop until chapel built 1884 at corner of High Rd. and Huddlestone Rd. Membership 1889: 120. Chapel enlarged 1892 to seat 300. Attendance 1903: 235 a.m.; 223 p.m. Old chapel, named Huddlestone hall, used for Sunday sch. after new red-brick chapel with stone dressings in Gothic style with spire, built 1907 by Messrs. J. Wills & Sons to seat 800. Membership 1924: 450. Doctrinal controversy led to split and formation of Willesden Christian Fellowship (see below). Membership 1977–8: 151.[36]

Particular Bapt. chapel in red brick and stone, consisting of baptistery, nave, aisles, short transept, tower, and spire, built 1890 for 860 in Acton Lane, Harlesden.[37] Attendance 1903: 133 a.m.; 321 p.m. Membership 1977–8: 81.

Kensal Rise tabernacle opened for 900 in Chamberlayne Wood Rd. by 1894.[38] Attendance 1903: 184 a.m.; 422 p.m. Membership 1977–8: 74.

Bapt. mission room opened 1899 in Chaplin Rd., Willesden Green. Attendance 1903: 15 a.m.; 18 p.m. Closed by 1926.[39]

Old Bapt. Union opened hall 1899 at the Green, Willesden. Closed and members transferred to other chapels 1901.[40]

Harlesden Evangelical mission hall seating 300 opened 1905 in Leghorn Rd. by Acton Lane chapel. Recertificated as Bapt. chapel 1933. Membership 1977–8: 31.[41]

Strict Bapts. met at 18 Manor Terrace, Harrow Rd., Kensal Green by 1908.[42]

Bapt. mission room in Disraeli Rd., Lower Place opened by 1908. Closed after 1933.[43]

Red-brick and stone chapel with tower accommodating 450 built 1908 by Arthur Keen to seat 450 in Anson Rd., Cricklewood. Dalsey hall built next to it 1930.[44] Membership 1977–8: 57.

Bapts. from Marylebone opened Streatley hall 1908 in Streatley Rd., Brondesbury. United with Kilburn Vale, Hampstead chapel after 1925.[45]

Steele Rd., Lower Place mission room used by Bapt. by 1917–18.[46] Closed c. 1971.[47]

PRESBYTERIANS. Willesden Presb. church opened 1875 in hall seating 150 at Fortune Gate, Harlesden. St. Margaret's, a cruciform chapel in Gothic style built 1876 at junction of Nicoll Rd. and Craven Park Rd. and enlarged 1884 to seat 645. Galleries added 1894. Attendance 1903: 294 a.m.; 378 p.m. Name changed to St. Margaret United Reformed church 1959 and St. Margaret and St. George United Reformed and Moravian church 1974. Membership 1963–4: 90.[48]

St. George's church, consisting of chancel, nave, aisles, and transepts built 1888 in Early English style to seat 550 in Willesden Lane, Brondesbury. Attendance 1903: 140 a.m.; 190 p.m. Closed 1973 and congregation united with that of St. Margaret's (above).[49] Bldg. used for Hindu temple.

St. John's Wood Presb. church opened Pembroke mission hall c. 1880 in Granville (formerly Pembroke) Rd., Kilburn. Attendance 1903: 33 a.m.; 170 p.m. Closed by 1959.[50]

St. Margaret's built mission hall 1888 in Oak Rd., Harlesden. Enlarged 1894. Attendance 1903: 84 a.m.; 150 p.m. Closed by 1954.[51]

St. Andrew's church, Salusbury Rd., West Kilburn, built 1896 to seat 300. Attendance 1903:

[30] P.R.O., C 54/20128, m. 13; datestone; G.R.O. Worship Reg. 36759; above, social.

[31] Trinity Wes. Ch. Cricklewood Official Handbk. (1903, in Grange Mus.); Grange Mus., photo. files, Walm Lane (NL 2001); G.R.O. Worship Reg. 37182.

[32] Kelly's Dir. Mdx. (1890, 1926); Grange Mus., NM 350; Willesden boro. Local Community Svces. 1933.

[33] G.R.O. Worship Reg. 52086.

[34] Membership figs. for 1977–8 from Bapt. Union Dir. (1977–8).

[35] Inf. from the minister (1978); Whitley, Bapts. of Lond. 199; Grange Mus., photo. files, Carlton Vale (NL 2234–7).

[36] Willesden Green Bapt. Ch. 1882–1932 (booklet in Grange Mus.); Kelly's Dir. Mdx. (1908, 1926).

[37] Whitley, Bapts. of Lond. 302; G.R.O. Worship Reg. 32210; Kelly's Dir. Mdx. (1926).

[38] G.R.O. Worship Reg. 34226. Re-reg. 1900: ibid. 37539.

[39] Whitley, Bapts. of Lond. 302; Kelly's Dir. Lond. (1908, 1926).

[40] Whitley, Bapts. of Lond. 249.

[41] Ibid. 302; datestone (1904); G.R.O. Worship Reg. 41023, 54874.

[42] Kelly's Dir. Mdx. (1908). For Manor Terrace: Grange Mus., Wood F 23, pp. 20 sqq. (s.v. Harrow Rd.).

[43] Kelly's Dir. Mdx. (1908); Willesden boro. Local Community Svces. 1933.

[44] Inf. from the minister (1978); Whitley, Bapts. of Lond. 254.

[45] Whitley, Bapts. of Lond. 249; Kelly's Dir. Kilburn (1917–18).

[46] Kelly's Dir. Kilburn (1917–18). Whitley, Bapts. of Lond. 257, is therefore wrong in giving 1925 as the foundation date.

[47] G.R.O. Worship Reg. 43938. For the mission's existence before 1917, below, Evangelical.

[48] Story of Willesden Presb. Ch. 1874–1925 (booklet in Grange Mus.); Kelly's Dir. Mdx. (1890, 1908); G.R.O. Worship Reg. 23621; Presb. Ch. of Eng. Official Handbk. (1963–4).

[49] Foundation stone; G.R.O. Worship Reg. 30897; Kelly's Dir. Mdx. (1890).

[50] P.R.O., C 54/19598, m. 5; Kelly's Dir. Mdx. (1890, 1908); Kelly's Lond. Suburban Dir. (1880); Kelly's Dir. Lond. (1952, 1959).

[51] Willesden Presb. Ch. 1874–1925; G.R.O. Worship Reg. 34539; Kelly's Dir. Lond. (1947).

59 a.m.; 128 p.m. Used as hall when new red-brick and stone chapel built in Gothic style next to it 1911.[52] Membership 1963-4: 142.[53]

Chapel at no. 265 Willesden Lane, called Welsh Meth. or Presb. Church of Wales, reg. 1900 for worship to Welsh Calvinistic Meths.[54] Attendance 1903: 32 a.m.; 71 p.m.

St. George's opened mission hall by 1902 at no. 247 High Rd., Willesden Green.[55] Attendance 1903: 9 a.m.; 111 p.m. Closed by 1947.[56]

Mission room opened by 1894 in Strode Rd., Willesden Green. Closed by 1933.[57]

SALVATION ARMY. Barracks opened in Percy Rd., Kilburn 1889. Attendance 1903: 81 a.m.; 283 p.m. Closed by 1971.[58]

Wendover hall in Wendover Rd., Harlesden reg. 1893. Attendance 1903: 57 a.m.; 184 p.m. Closed 1903 and citadel opened 1904 in Manor Park Rd.[59]

Barracks reg. 1901 at Hiley Rd., Kensal Rise. Attendance 1903: 35 a.m.; 62 p.m. Moved 1908 to Alexandra hall, Doyle Gdns. Closed 1913.[60]

Citadel opened in High Rd., Willesden Green, by 1902.[61] Attendance 1903: 93 a.m.; 239 p.m.

Goodwill Centre reg. 1971 in Chichester Rd., Kilburn.[62]

EVANGELICAL. Kilburn hall opened for Evangelical Mission by 1880 in High Rd., Kilburn, near Willesden border. Closed 1913.[63]

Evangelical Mission opened Willesden hall 1893 for 500 at junction of Aldershot Rd. and Willesden Lane, Kilburn. Attendance 1903: 50 a.m.; 186 p.m. Bombed 1944 and prefabricated bldg. seating 150 erected 1947. Name changed to Kilburn Evangelical Free church 1954. New bldg. seating 200 opened 1962.[64]

Willesden Evangelical church opened 1896 in iron bldg. in Church Rd. Attendance 1903: 133 a.m.; 177 p.m. Closed by 1978.[65]

Kilburn Protestant and Evangelical sch. and mission opened by 1885 and reg. at nos. 78-86 Kilburn Park Rd. 1900. Attendance 1903: 45 p.m. Closed 1913.[66] City Mission hall opened in Kilburn Park Rd. by 1890.[67]

Mission hall at Lower Place by 1899.[68] Reg. 1909 as mission hall for Evangelical Christians at Steele Rd., Lower Place.[69] Bapt. mission by 1918 (q.v.).

London City Mission in Stonebridge Park by

1903 when attendance 5 a.m.; 27 p.m. Evangelical mission hall at no. 9 Melville Rd. by 1908. Mission hall built at junction of Melville and Harrow roads 1913. Replaced 1972 by new chapel seating 120 in Hillside.[70]

BRETHREN. Plymouth Brethren ran a small sch. in Kilburn 1881.[71] Opened Cambridge hall in Cambridge Ave. by 1896. Attendance 1903: 135 a.m.; 203 p.m. Closed by 1954.[72]

Shrewsbury gospel hall opened in Shrewsbury Rd., Stonebridge by 1901. Attendance 1903: 112 a.m.; 142 p.m. Replaced 1971 by hall in Winchelsea Rd., Harlesden.[73]

Hamilton hall, Willesden Green, attendance 1903: 26 a.m.; 53 p.m.[74]

Open Brethren reg. Kings hall, Harlesden Rd., 1907-54.[75]

Mission room opened at no. 10A Rucklidge Ave., Harlesden by 1915. Closed and new meeting room opened 1937 at no. 28A Fortune Gate Rd., Craven Park. Closed 1977.[76]

Plymouth Brethren reg. Belton hall, Willesden Green, 1925-32.[77]

OTHER DENOMINATIONS AND UNSPECIFIED MISSIONS. The Reformed Episcopal Church erected Christ Church 1884, an iron bldg. seating 200, in St. Albans Rd., Harlesden. Used as Sunday sch. and hall when red-brick church seating 650 built beside it 1893-4.[78] Attendance 1903: 152 a.m.; 221 p.m.

The Swedenborgian Church of the New Jerusalem built 1889 to seat 120 in High Rd., Willesden Green. Attendance 1903: 43 a.m.; 43 p.m. Replaced by small brick chapel 1910.[79]

A Friends meeting ho. opened 1900 in Harlesden Rd. Attendance 1903: 43 a.m.; 45 p.m. Enlarged 1910. Closed 1953.[80]

Seventh Day Adventists opened mission room by 1909 in no. 38A Harley Rd., Harlesden. Closed and replaced 1917 by hall in Wendover Rd. Closed 1925.[81]

Willesden Christian Fellowship, house in Donnington hall, Donnington Rd., founded as breakaway from Willesden Green Bapt. chapel (q.v.) before 1932.

The People's Own Mission opened by 1933 in iron tabernacle in Church Path, Harlesden. Reg. by Brotherhood Movement 1953.[82]

Christian Spiritualists met by 1934 in room in

[52] Inf. from the minister (1978); Kelly's Dir. Mdx. (1908).
[53] Presb. Ch. of Eng. Official Handbk. (1963-4).
[54] G.R.O. Worship Reg. 37632; Kelly's Dir. Mdx. (1908, 1926); Kelly's Dir. Kilburn (1917-18).
[55] Kelly's Lond. Suburban Dir. (1902).
[56] Kelly's Dir. Lond. (1942, 1947).
[57] O.S. Map 1/2,500, Mdx. XVI. 2 (1894 edn.); Kelly's Dir. Mdx. (1926); Willesden boro. Local Community Svces. 1933.
[58] G.R.O. Worship Reg. 31343; Kelly's Dir. Lond. (1964, 1971).   [59] G.R.O. Worship Reg. 33978, 40398.
[60] Ibid. 38193, 43307.   [61] Ibid. 38866.
[62] Ibid. 72610, 73106.
[63] Ibid. 32819; Kelly's Lond. Suburban Dir. (1880); Grange Mus., NM 350.
[64] Kilburn Evangelical Free Ch. (leaflet); Willesden Hall, 1893-1946 (booklet); Fellowship (Mag. of Fellowship of Indep. Evangelical Churches) Oct.-Dec. 1962, all supplied by pastor (1978).
[65] P.R.O., C 54/20055, m. 30; G.R.O. Worship Reg. 37236.

[66] G.R.O. Worship Reg. 37915.
[67] Kelly's Dir. Mdx. (1890).
[68] Willesden sch. bd. Rep. of Cttee. (1899, in Grange Mus.).   [69] G.R.O. Worship Reg. 43938.
[70] Inf. from the pastor (1978); Kelly's Dir. Mdx. (1908).
[71] Nat. Soc. files, St. John Evang. Kilburn.
[72] G.R.O. Worship Reg. 35482.
[73] Ibid. 38221, 72655.
[74] Above, Congregationalists, Methodists.
[75] G.R.O. Worship Reg. 42591. Taken over by King's Hall Community Assoc. by 1959: Kelly's Dir. Lond. (1959).
[76] G.R.O. Worship Reg. 46640, 57798.
[77] Ibid. 49619; All Souls Coll., uncat. material, agents' reps. 1924.   [78] Kelly's Dir. Mdx. (1890, 1908).
[79] G.R.O. Worship Reg. 31469, 44407; Kelly's Dir. Mdx. (1890).
[80] List of Friends' Mtg.-hos. in Friends' Ho., Euston Rd.; All Souls Coll., uncat. material, agents' reps. 1910.
[81] G.R.O. Worship Reg. 43996, 47158.
[82] Ibid. 63812; Willesden boro. Local Community Svces. 1933.

Hassop Rd., Cricklewood. Housed by 1963 in Ashford hall, Ashford Rd.[83]

Christian Scientists met 1936–54 in rooms at no. 92 Walm Lane, Cricklewood.[84]

'Free Christians' reg. the Fifth church of the Good Shepherd 1951 at no. 5, Bramshill Rd., Harlesden. Recertificated 1954 as church of St. John the Divine for the New Catholic and Free Church. Closed by 1964.[85]

The New Testament Church of God opened 1964 in former Meth. chapel at no. 179 High Rd., Willesden Green.[86]

The Apostolic Church of God opened Beulah church by 1964 in Denton Rd., Stonebridge Pk. Closed 1978.[87]

The Jehovah's Witnesses opened a Kingdom hall by 1967 at nos. 192–212 High Rd., Willesden.[88]

The Church of the God of Prophecy opened in former Meth. (q.v.) chapel 1967 in Tubbs Rd., Harlesden.[89]

The Associated Gospel Assembly opened 1971 in former Roundwood mission in Longstone Ave., Harlesden.[90]

The Medical mission hall opened for undenominational worship by 1897 in Heron Rd., Church End. Attendance 1903: 82 a.m.; 68 p.m. Closed by 1926.[91]

Oxford mission hall, Oxford Rd., Kilburn, opened for undenominational worship by 1903 when attendance 2 a.m.; 100 p.m. Closed by 1917.[92]

The United Christian Society opened by 1916 Providence hall, Hampton Rd., Kilburn Park. Closed by 1942.[93]

Willesden Revival centre opened 1964 in no. 334 High Rd., Willesden. Changed name to Willesden Deeper Life Christian centre 1973.[94]

Railway mission by 1902 at no. 152 High St., Harlesden. Attendance 1903: 64 a.m.; 83 p.m. Closed by 1908.[95]

Willesden Junction Railway mission opened by 1903 in Harrow Rd., next to Scrubbs Lane, when attendance 51 a.m.; 39 p.m. Closed by 1926.[96]

Other undenominational missions were St. James, Manor Park Rd., Harlesden, open by 1890 and closed by 1903;[97] Croft at the Croft, Harlesden, open by 1908, closed by 1933; Claremont Rd. hall at Midland Brent Terrace, Queen's Park, flourished 1917–18;[98] Harley Rd., Harlesden, flourished in former Seventh Day Adventist hall (q.v.) 1926 and reg. 1943;[99] Roundwood at Longstone Ave., Harlesden, 1930–71.[1]

RUSSIAN ORTHODOX CHURCH IN EXILE. The Convent of the Annunciation opened in Brondesbury Park in 1960. The community had originated in Palestine and moved to England in 1954. The convent contains a chapel open to the laity and the nuns run a Sunday school for the children of parishioners.[2]

JUDAISM.[3] There was considerable Jewish immigration at the end of the 19th century into Brondesbury and Willesden Green. In 1902 an iron building was erected for services and religious classes on a site in Salusbury Road and in 1905 a permanent synagogue, affiliated to the United Synagogue, was opened at the junction of Chevening and Carlisle roads. Called Brondesbury synagogue, it was a red-brick building in an oriental style with Moorish domes and arches. There was a fire there in 1965 and the synagogue closed in 1974.[4]

A second wave of immigration took place in the 1920s and 1930s leading to the establishment of several synagogues. In 1928 a house at no. 137 Walm Lane, Cricklewood, was registered for worship, and in 1931 the second United synagogue, Cricklewood synagogue, was built next door at nos. 131–5 Walm Lane. A two-storeyed brick building with rounded doors and windows was in use in 1978.[5]

In 1929 Jews in the developing districts of Neasden, Dollis Hill, and Gladstone Park met to consider opening a synagogue. Services were held at the L.M.S. institute in Edgware Road and in 1930 at Neasden mission hall in Dog Lane.[6] In 1931 the foundation stone was laid of a synagogue in Clifford Way, Neasden. A Federation synagogue, it was called Gladstone Park and Neasden synagogue or Abravath Shalom. The foundation stone of a new synagogue was laid at the same site in 1967.[7]

A synagogue, which in 1937 became a district member of the United Synagogue, opened in 1933 in Parkside, Dollis Hill. A larger, concrete synagogue by Walter Landauer seating 524 men and 392 women opened in 1938, the original building becoming the Joseph Freedman hall.[8]

[83] G.R.O. Worship Reg. 55478; *Willesden Inf. Handbk.* [1963].

[84] G.R.O. Worship Reg. 56630.

[85] Ibid. 62908, 64600.

[86] Ibid. 69808.

[87] Ibid. 69455.

[88] Ibid. 70886.

[89] Ibid. 71639; *Willesden Mercury*, 20 Jan. 1967.

[90] G.R.O. Worship Reg. 72501; below.

[91] G.R.O. Worship Reg. 36358; *Kelly's Dir. Kilburn* (1917–18); *Kelly's Dir. Mdx.* (1926).

[92] G.R.O. Worship Reg. 42503; *Kelly's Dir. Mdx.* (1908); *Kelly's Dir. Kilburn* (1917–18).

[93] G.R.O. Worship Reg. 46833; Willesden boro. *Local Community Svces. 1933*; *Kelly's Dir. Lond.* (1942).

[94] G.R.O. Worship Reg. 69460.

[95] *Kelly's Dir. Mdx.* (1908); *Kelly's Lond. Suburban Dir.* (1902).

[96] *Kelly's Dir. Mdx.* (1926); *Kelly's Dir. Kilburn* (1917–18).

[97] *Kelly's Dir. Mdx.* (1890, 1908). Possibly later used by Salvation Army (q.v.).

[98] *Kelly's Lond. Suburban Dir.* (1902); *Kelly's Dir. Mdx.* (1908, 1926); *Kelly's Dir. Kilburn* (1917–18); Willesden boro. *Local Community Svces. 1933*.

[99] G.R.O. Worship Reg. 60660.

[1] Ibid. 52761.

[2] Inf. from the mother superior (1978); *What's on in Lond.* 6 Jan. 1961 (cutting in Grange Mus.).

[3] Based on *Jewish Year Bks.*

[4] *Brondesbury Synagogue, Semi-Jubilee Celebration Rec.* (pamphlet in Grange Mus.); G.R.O. Worship Reg. 41012; *The Times*, 15 Mar. 1965.

[5] G.R.O. Worship Reg. 51327, 53118.

[6] *Dollis Hill Synagogue Re-dedication* (pamphlet 1956 in Grange Mus.).

[7] Dated foundation stones; G.R.O. Worship Reg. 53680, 58135.

[8] *Dollis Hill Synagogue Re-dedication*; G.R.O. Worship Reg. 54678, 57901, 61542; *Arch. Rev.* lxxxiii (1938).

Willesden synagogue was established in Brondesbury Park in 1934. As Willesden Hebrew Congregation it was registered at no. 17 Heathfield Road in 1935 and re-registered as Willesden Green Federation synagogue in 1936. In 1939, when presumably a synagogue was built, it was registered as Willesden (later Willesden and Brondesbury) synagogue and became a member of the United Synagogue. The building was desecrated in 1967 but still in use in 1978.[9]

Khal Yisroel synagogue was registered at no. 185 Willesden Lane 1935–1947.[10]

Ohel Shem Beth Hamedrash, a member of the Federation of Synagogues, was established in 1945 at no. 263 Chamberlayne Rd., Kensal Rise.[11]

Cricklewood Beth Hamedrash or Keser Torah had opened at no. 62 St. Gabriel's Road by 1949 when it was a member of the Union of Orthodox Hebrew Congregations. From 1950 it was a Federation affiliated synagogue.

Dollis Hill Beth Hamedrash, also a member of the Union of Orthodox Hebrew Congregations, existed at no. 152 Fleetwood Road from before 1950 until after 1960.

An independent congregation, Kilburn and Brondesbury Chevra Torah, existed at no. 9 Brondesbury Rd. from 1953 until after 1963.[12]

By 1978 the emigration of Jews from Willesden and the general decline in religious observance led the United Synagogue to 'streamline' its Willesden synagogues and a single rabbi served the congregations of Cricklewood, Willesden, and Dollis Hill.[13]

A Jewish cemetery opened in 1873 on 12 a. near Pound Lane. It contained three buildings in stone designed by N. S. Joseph, and the graves of Baron Mayer de Rothschild (1874) and Sir Anthony de Rothschild (1876).[14]

HINDUISM. The Shree Swaminarayan temple in the former St. George's Presbyterian church in Willesden Lane was registered by Hindus in 1975.[15]

In 1980 a site in Meadow Garth, Neasden, was consecrated for the largest Hindu temple outside India.[16]

ISLAM. A mosque and Islamic centre had opened in the former Congregational chapel in Chichele Rd., Cricklewood, by 1980.[17]

BUDDHISM. In 1975 a Tibetan Buddhist centre, called Orgyen Chö Ling, opened in Chatsworth Rd., Kilburn. It moved out of Willesden in 1976 but returned in 1977 to no. 76 Princess Rd., Kilburn. The building contains a shrine but is primarily a centre for meditation and study used mainly by Europeans.[18]

EDUCATION. A schoolhouse near the church was mentioned in 1686, and although Willesden did not feature in the list of charity schools in Middlesex in 1724 the schoolhouse was mentioned again in 1735.[19] It had presumably disappeared, however, before Richard Freelove, by will dated 1776, gave £200 to erect and endow a charity school and a special vestry in 1777 passed a resolution to build a school. Nothing was done, however, until 1809 when a parish school was opened in Willesden, Freelove's gift being used to build a schoolroom and voluntary contributions to finance it.[20] The farmers feared that it would 'render the children of the poor unfit for useful and contented labour.'[21] It opened as a Sunday school, attended in 1819 by 90 children, and by 1818 a National day school for 80 children was also held there.[22] The poor were then said to possess sufficient means of education, although the parish could scarcely support the school.[23] The Independents opened a Sunday school at Chapel End in 1820,[24] described in 1833 as an infants' school where 40 boys and 30 girls were instructed at their parents' expense. The National school was by then wholly a day school, attended by 43 boys and 37 girls and financed by endowment and school pence. The Independents also had a day school for 16 boys and girls and there were two day schools at which 36 boys were educated, all three financed by school pence.[25] Willesden National school was still considered adequate to meet the educational needs of all the district in 1846,[26] although the vestry had in 1843 taken a decision to build a school in Kilburn for the poor. During the later 19th century the different hamlets and districts within Willesden began to acquire their own National schools. Kilburn was the first with St. Paul's, opened in 1847 and replaced in 1867 by Holy Trinity. The early nonconformist schools closed but a Wesleyan school was opened in Harlesden in 1871 and a Roman Catholic school in Kilburn in 1872.

In 1870 there was accommodation for 726 children in three public schools. All were said to be connected with the Church or the National Society.[27] By 1875 the three National schools provided accommodation for 1,078 children, the

[9] G.R.O. Worship Reg. 55948, 57092, 58959; *Willesden Mercury*, 1 Sept. 1967. The synagogue, between Brondesbury Pk. and Heathfield Rd., could be given either address: *Willesden Inf. Handbk.* [1963] refers to it as Willesden Green synagogue, Heathfield Rd.
[10] G.R.O. Worship Reg. 55771.   [11] Ibid. 61698.
[12] *Willesden Inf. Handbk.* [1963].
[13] Grange Mus., gen. files, Jewish Community (*Kilburn Times*, 12 May 1978). There were said to be 20,000 Jews in Brent in 1976: ibid. (*Jewish Chron.* 1 Oct. 1976).
[14] Thorne, *Environs*, 697–9; *Kelly's Dir. Mdx.* (1908).
[15] G.R.O. Worship Reg. 74114.
[16] *Daily Telegraph*, 21 July 1980.
[17] *Kelly's Dir. Lond.* (1980); Char. Com. reg. 272500.
[18] Inf. from Patrick Gaffney (Orgyen Chö Ling, 1978).

[19] P.R.O., C 78/925, no. 5; [T. Cox], *Magna Britannia* (1724), iii. 51; Grange Mus., 1 D 17 (chwdns.' accts. 1730–70).
[20] *14th Rep. Com. Char.* H.C. 382, pp. 809–12 (1826), xii; Grange Mus., 1 B 3 (poor rate bk. 1770–87); 1 D 29 (vestry order bk. 1722–1814).
[21] Brewer, *Beauties of Eng. and Wales*, iv. 352.
[22] Grange Mus., 1 D 10 (vestry order bk. 1814–25).
[23] *Digest of Returns to Sel. Cttee. on Educ. of Poor*, H.C. 224, p. 536 (1819), ix (1).
[24] Potter, *Story of Willesden*, 178.
[25] *Educ. Enq. Abstract*, H.C. 62, p. 554 (1835), xliii (2).
[26] *Church Schools Inquiry, 1846–7*, *Mdx.* 12; Grange Mus., 1 D 12 (vestry order bk. 1832–62).
[27] *Returns relating to Elem. Educ.* H.C. 201, pp. 242–3 (1871), lv.

Wesleyan and Roman Catholic schools for 382, and other National schools on the borders of the parish (St. Augustine's, Kilburn, and St. John's, Kensal Green) for 589, a total in all of 2,049 places. The Education Department served notice on Willesden parish that 350 more places were needed.[28] Within a year the accommodation had risen to 3,319 but the increase was mainly due to the schools outside Willesden, especially the Kilburn schools of St. Augustine's and St. Luke's (opened for 620 children in 1876). By 1882 there were 4,577 places and another 432 were being built. The Education Department refused in 1877 to consider St. Luke's or St. John's, Kensal Green, as Willesden schools, arguing that there was a deficiency of accommodation and that a school board was necessary. It made an order for the compulsory formation of a school board in Willesden in 1882.[29]

The churches, which had formed an association to fight against the imposition of a school board, continued their opposition with some success for another decade. They dominated the board and prevented the opening of a board school.[30] Instead a number of new Church schools were established in the rapidly growing but poor districts of Willesden: Brondesbury in 1878, Willesden Green and St. John's, Kilburn, in 1882, Stonebridge in 1883, and Neasden in 1884. The Church Extension Association, working through the Anglican community of the Sisters of the Church, which was based in Kilburn Park Road, opened four schools: Gordon Memorial in Kilburn in 1887, Keble Memorial and the People's College in Harlesden, and Princess Frederica in Kensal Rise in 1889. A Roman Catholic school opened in Harlesden in 1887 and a Protestant school in Kilburn in 1891. Generally, however, the nonconformists became the driving force behind the movement for board schools.

The Anglicans had the patronage of the largest landowners in the area, the Ecclesiastical Commissioners and All Souls College, who often donated sites and subscriptions for new schools, but they lacked a wealthy middle class to which they could appeal for donations. They complained of the enmity of the Education Department and of the Metropolitan Railway Co. which leased land at Neasden on advantageous terms to nonconformists while demanding the full rent from Anglicans.[31]

The Education Department refused grants to Church schools, and although it failed in its attempt to close All Souls school it compelled Willesden to open a temporary board school in the Wesleyan lecture hall in Harlesden in 1885 and to build its first board school there in 1891. Before it was superseded in 1904 Willesden school board opened another 12, mainly large,

schools and several special schools. The 15 voluntary schools provided 10,217 places and the board schools another 10,876.[32]

In 1904 Willesden U.D. became an autonomous part III authority under the 1902 Education Act and a council education committee replaced the school board.[33] Under pressure from the Board of Education,[34] the council had opened another 13 schools by 1916 and although those and the 13 former board schools included some which were temporary, there were still 20 council schools in existence by 1919, providing accommodation for 19,396 children, compared with 7,094 places in the 12 non-provided schools. Another 1,177 Willesden children were educated in London public elementary schools, just outside the borders. Willesden also maintained special schools for physically handicapped and mentally defective children. Only in secondary education was the provision inadequate.[35]

There was a higher grade department for boys at St. Andrew, Willesden Green, after 1892. Willesden U.D.C. agreed in 1909 to contribute to the enlargement of Brondesbury and Kilburn high school for girls (opened 1892)[36] and made grants for scholarships there and to Kilburn grammar school for boys and, after 1922, to the Roman Catholic Convent of Jesus and Mary for girls.[37] In 1926 a Central school was established at Pound Lane. Secondary education was, however, primarily the responsibility of the county, which took over Kilburn grammar school in 1908, aided (and in 1938 took over) Brondesbury and Kilburn high, and in 1924 opened Willesden county grammar school.

Four council schools and one Roman Catholic school were opened between 1927 and 1930 but no new schools were opened thereafter until the 1950s. Following the Hadow report, eight council and two Church schools were organized into senior and junior departments between 1927 and 1932, and another seven and two respectively between 1932 and 1938.

In 1946 Willesden education committee drew up a development plan for 13 secondary modern,[38] 5 grammar, and 2 secondary technical schools but the committee, even at that early stage, adopted the principle of comprehensive education and set out a plan for converting the existing schools in two stages into six fully comprehensive schools.[39] The first stage was implemented in 1967 when some senior schools became fully comprehensive, others were reorganized as junior and senior high schools, others were closed or amalgamated, and one new comprehensive, Willesden high, was opened. The second phase took place 1971–3 when the junior and senior high schools were amalgamated, more schools were closed, especially those in board and early council school buildings, and

[28] Following paras. based on Grange Mus., Wood F 23, pp. 336 sqq.

[29] Lond. Gaz. 23 May 1882, p. 2409; see also Grange Mus., Wood F 10 (correspondence with Educ. Dept.); Wood F 3 (ann. reps. on parochial schs.).

[30] Grange Mus., gen. files, Willesden Chron. (Suppl. 5 Mar. 1937). [31] Nat. Soc. files, passim and esp. Neasden.

[32] Grange Mus., gen. files, schs. (Willesden sch. bd. dinner 9 Feb. 1903).

[33] Mdx. C.C. Primary and Secondary Educ. in Mdx. 1900–65, 31. [34] The Times, 22 May 1909; 10 July 1912.

[35] Willesden educ. cttee. Draft Rep. (1919, in Grange Mus.).

[36] Mdx. C.C. 6th Ann. Rep. of Mdx. Educ. Cttee. (1909).

[37] Willesden educ. cttee. Mins. (1921–2).

[38] Counting Dudden Hill boys and girls as separate schools.

[39] Willesden educ. cttee. Mins. (1946), 15 July 1946.

three new large comprehensives were opened. By 1978 there were ten comprehensives.[40]

There were 34 primary schools in 1978, mostly successors to board and council schools founded before 1930. They included six of the eleven Church of England schools which had existed in 1900, seven Roman Catholic, and one Jewish school. Eight new primary schools had been opened since 1950 and many of the older schools were accommodated in new buildings.

Public schools. The general sources are those indicated above, p. 44, with the addition of Grange Mus., gen. files, schools (*Origin of Schs. in Willesden*, 1953), and the same abbreviations are used.

ALL SOULS C.E., Harlesden. Abortive attempt to found sch. 1856. Nat. sch. for 150 G and I opened 1867 in iron bldg. adjoining temp. church of All Souls. 1874 a.a. 60 G and I. Sch. pence 1874 (1*d.* and 2*d.*). Iron classroom opened 1882 for 138 I. By agreement B attended Harlesden Wesleyan sch. until 1882. New sch. built 1883 in Station Rd. for 589 BGI. 1890 a.a. 466. Financed by parl. grant and vol. contributions. Reorg. from 1927 into JM and I; closed 1932.

ANSON PRIMARY, Anson Rd., Cricklewood. Opened 1952 for JM and I. Huts added. Roll 1978: 326.

AYLESTONE HIGH, Aylestone Ave., Brondesbury. Opened 1956 as sec. mod. for 500 SM. Reorg. 1967 as S high sch. and extended 1971 as comprehensive for 1,650 SM. Roll 1978: 1500.

BRAINTCROFT PRIMARY, Warren Rd., Brentwater Estate. Opened 1928 as council sch. for 494 JM and I. Reorg. and extended 1932 for 414 JM, 504 I. 1936 a.a. 400 JM, 424 I. Roll 1978: 475 JM, 246 I, 60 nursery.

BRENTFIELD PRIMARY, see Gibbons Rd.

BRIDGE RD. PRIMARY, Neasden. Opened 1913 as temp. council sch. for 400 M and I. Replaced 1915 by permanent council sch. for 1200 BGI. 1919 a.a. 228 B, 232 G, 258 I. Reorg. by 1932 into JB, JG, I, and 1942 into JM, I. Nursery unit added 1978. Roll 1978: 327 JM, 138 I, 28 nursery.

BRONDESBURY C.E., see Christ Church.

BRONDESBURY AND KILBURN HIGH, Salusbury Rd., Kilburn. Formed 1967 as comprehensive for SM by amalg. of Brondesbury and Kilburn high for G and Kilburn grammar for B. Reorg. 1973 as comprehensive. Acquired former Brondesbury synagogue for extra accn. 1975. Roll 1978: 850 SM.

BRONDESBURY AND KILBURN HIGH FOR G, Salusbury Rd., Kilburn. Opened 1892 as G demonstration sch. for ladies' training college (later called Maria Grey). Aided by Willesden U.D.C. and Mdx. C.C. from 1909.[41] Taken over 1938 by Mdx. C.C. as grammar sch. for G. In 1940 Maria Grey moved to Twickenham and part of sch. bldg. destroyed in war. Rebuilt 1951.

Amalg. with Kilburn grammar for B 1967 as Brondesbury and Kilburn high.

BULLER RD. TEMP., Kensal Green. Opened 1901 as bd. sch. for 172 B in hall belonging to Baptist chapel. Closed 1908.[42]

CAMBRIDGE RD. TEMP., Kilburn. Opened 1905 as council sch. for 150 B in Methodist Free Church Sunday sch. Superseded 1912 by Percy Rd.[43]

CARDINAL HINSLEY R.C. HIGH, Harlesden Rd., Harlesden. Opened 1958 as vol. aided R.C. sec. mod. for B. Reorg. 1967 as comprehensive and extended. Roll 1978: 900 B.

CARLTON VALE I, Kilburn. Opened 1913 as council sch. for 400 G, 416 I. 1927 a.a. 363 G, 371 I. 1938 a.a. 217 G, 296 I. Reorg. 1939 into sec. mod. for G, I. Sec. mod. 1967 became J high and amalg. 1972 with Percy Rd. as South Kilburn high when bldgs. became Carlton community centre. I sch. moved to new bldgs. 1970. Roll 1978: 151 I, 23 nursery.

CHAMBERLAYNE WOOD PRIMARY, Chamberlayne Rd., Kensal Rise. Opened 1904 as council sch. for 400 B, 400 G, 420 I. 1919 a.a. 359 B, 358 G, 269 I. Reorg. by 1932 for 320 SB, 320 SG, 400 I, and between 1936 and 1938 into SM, I. 1938 a.a. 274 SM, 218 I. S sch. became sec. mod. under 1944 Act, J high 1967 and closed 1970. I sch. reorg. 1977 as JM and I. Roll 1978: 270 JM and I, 30 nursery.

CHRIST CHURCH C.E., Willesden Lane, Brondesbury. Sch. for 60 G and I opened 1878 by vicar in hired premises. School pence 1878 (2*d.* to 4*d.*). Joined Nat. Soc. 1887. Permanent sch. opened 1889 for 120 I. 1890 a.a. 58 I. Financed by parl. grant and vol. contributions. Sch. for 62 B, 62 G built next to it 1893.[44] 1908 a.a. 68 B, 63 G, 128 I. By 1919 accn. 152 B, 152 G, 110 I. 1927 a.a. 144 B, 144 G, 105 I. Reorg. between 1932 and 1936 into JB, JG, I and by 1948 into JM and I.[45] Roll 1978: 196 JM and I.

COLLEGE RD. TEMP., Kensal Rise. Opened 1913[46] as council sch. for 400 M. 1919 a.a. 400 M. 1927 a.a. 282 M. Closed 1929.

CONVENT OF JESUS AND MARY R.C. HIGH, Crown Hill Rd., Harlesden. Opened 1888 as private R.C. day and boarding sch. for G. Bldgs. erected 1887–96. Became day sch. for G 1939. Reorg. under 1944 Act as grammar sch. for SG. Vol. aided status from 1952. Reorg. 1956 as bilateral grammar and sec. mod. for G.[47] Extended 1959.[48] Reorg. 1966 as comprehensive. Additions 1972, 1978. Roll 1978: 1,000.

CONVENT OF JESUS AND MARY R.C. I, Park Ave., Willesden Green. Opened 1908 as private R.C. sch. (below, private schs.). Reorg. 1967 as state-aided I sch. Roll 1978: 280 I.

DISRAELI RD. TEMP., Acton Lane, Harlesden. Opened 1900 as bd. sch. for 180 M. Reorg. 1902 for 190 I. Closed 1916.[49]

DOLLIS HILL TEMP. Opened 1929 as council sch. Closed 1930.

DONNINGTON PRIMARY, Uffington Rd. Opened

[40] i.e. within the Willesden part of Brent L.B.: inf. from Brent L.B. educ. dept. (1978).
[41] Mdx. C.C. *6th Ann. Rep. of Mdx. Educ. Cttee.* (1909).
[42] Willesden bd. of educ. *Mins.* (1901); Willesden educ. cttee. *Mins.* (1908–9).
[43] Willesden educ. cttee. *Mins.* (1904–5, 1912–13).
[44] Datestones and notices on bldgs. (1978).
[45] *Schs. of Willesden and Dist.* [1948] (in Grange Mus.).
[46] Willesden educ. cttee. *Draft Rep.* (1919).
[47] Willesden educ. cttee. *Mins.* (1956–7).
[48] *Willesden Chron.* 24 July 1959.
[49] Willesden educ. cttee. *Mins.* (1915–16, 1916–17).

1972 for JM and I. Roll 1978: 218 JM and I, 18 nursery.

DUDDEN [DUDDING] HILL LANE. Opened 1897 as bd. sch. for 1,250 BGI. 1906 a.a. 399 B, 386 G, 437 I. Reorg. by 1938 into 1,100 SB, SG, I. 1938 a.a. 323 SB, 301 SG, 265 I. Under 1944 Act SB, SG became sec. mod. which closed 1964. I closed 1960, replaced by Northview. Bldgs. taken over by Willesden College of Technology.

FURNESS PRIMARY, Furness Rd., Harlesden. Opened 1908 as council sch. for 1,256 SM, JM, I. 1919 a.a. 351 SM, 329 JM, 344 I. Reorg. 1925 as BGI. 1938 a.a. 262 B, 242 G, 268 I. Part bombed and rebuilt after war. Reorg. 1949 into JM, I. Roll 1978: 378 JM, 244 I.

GIBBONS RD., Stonebridge. Opened 1902 as bd. sch. for 800 M, 418 I. 1927 a.a. 549 M, 312 I. Reorg. by 1932 for 480 SM, 350 I. 1938 a.a. 397 SM, 228 I. Under 1944 Act SM became sec. mod.; I moved 1949 to temp. accn. in Conduit Way. Hall built 1959 and name changed 1960 to Brentfield I. Sec. mod. merged 1969 into Slade-brook high which continued to use old bldgs. I sch. rebuilt in Meadow Garth and reorg. 1975 as JM and I. Roll 1978: 213 JM and I.

GLADSTONE PARK PRIMARY, Sherrick Green Rd., Dollis Hill. Opened 1914 as temp. council sch. Reopened 1915 as permanent council sch. for 400 M. 1919 a.a. 352 M. New bldg. and reorg. 1937 for 300 JM, 280 I. 1938 a.a. 242 JM, 174 I. Extension built 1976. Roll 1978: 330 JM, 256 I.

GORDON COMMERCIAL. Recorded 1890 for 233 G and I, a.a. 98.

GORDON MEMORIAL C.E., Cambridge Rd., Kilburn. Opened 1885 by Sisters of the Church for I in bldg. belonging to Methodist chapel. New bldg. 1887 for 1,240 BGI. 1890 a.a. 277 B, 274 G, 432 I. Financed by parl. grant and vol. contributions. 1938 a.a. 136 B, 109 G, 99 I. Closed 1953 and bldgs. acquired by St. Mary's R.C. sch.[50]

HARLESDEN C.E., see All Souls.

HARLESDEN PRIMARY, Acton Lane, Harlesden. Opened 1891 as first bd. sch. for 350 M, I. Financed by parl. grants and vol. contributions. Expanded 1900 to 472 M, I. 1908 a.a. 298 M, 178 I. Reorg. by 1932 for 380 JM and I. 1932 a.a. 332 JM and I. Roll 1978: 280 JM and I.

HARLESDEN R.C., see St. Joseph, Harlesden, R.C.

HARLESDEN WESLEYAN (Willesden Junction), Craven Park Rd., Harlesden. Opened 1871 for 129 BG next to Wesleyan chapel. Financed by subscriptions and sch. pence (3d. and 4d.). Agreement with All Souls to take B only. 1880 a.a. 83 B. Parl. grant but closed 1882 for lack of funds.[51]

HARLESDEN GREEN, see People's College.

HOLY TRINITY C.E., Kilburn. Opened 1867 as Nat. sch. for 220 B in bldgs. of St. Paul's, Kilburn, Nat. sch. in Edgware Rd. Nat. sch. for 440 G and I opened 1868 in Canterbury Rd. 1890 a.a. 148 B, 96 G, 129 I. Financed by parl. grants, vol. contributions, and sch. pence (1s. 5d.). B closed 1925. 1927 a.a. 99 G, 122 I. Reorg. by 1932 for 340 B. Council acquired site 1937 in exchange

for one in Alpha Place. Closed 1939 and demol. early 1950s.

JOHN KELLY HIGH, Crest Rd., Neasden. Opened 1958 as sec. mod. for B, G. Reorg. 1967 as comprehensives for SB, SG. Additions made 1970 and 1974. Roll 1978: 660 B, 1,000 G.

KEBLE MEMORIAL C.E., Crown Hill Rd., Harlesden. Opened 1889 by Sisters of the Church for 150 B, 180 G, 250 I. 1890 a.a. 90 B, 95 G, 100 I. Financed by parl. grant, vol. contributions, and sch. pence (7s.). 1919 a.a. 173 B, 230 G, 129 I. Reorg. 1955 as JM, I. Control passed 1965 to London Diocesan Bd. of Educ. Vol. aided. Modernized and extended 1973. Roll 1978: 250 JM, 180 I.

KENSAL GREEN TEMP. Opened 1896 for B, 1897 for G, in bldgs. belonging to St. John's parish. Closed 1898.

KENSAL RISE PRIMARY, Harvist Rd. Opened 1898 as bd. sch. for 1,270 BGI. 1908 a.a. 396 B, 399 G, 440 I. Reorg. 1930 into 400 JB, 400 I, and by 1936 into 1,200 JB, JG, I. 1938 a.a. 248 JB, 219 JG, 325 I. Reorg. 1977 into JM, I. Roll 1978: 251 JM, 162 I, 16 nursery.

KILBURN GRAMMAR, Salusbury Rd. Opened 1898 in Willesden Lane as choir sch. by vicar of St. Paul's, Kilburn. Moved 1900 to Salusbury Rd.,[52] opposite Brondesbury and Kilburn high for G, and became grammar sch. for B. Roll 1900: 120. Acquired by Mdx. C.C. 1908 and enlarged 1927.[53] Damaged in war and rebuilt 1951–2. Amalg. with Brondesbury and Kilburn high for G 1967 as Brondesbury and Kilburn high.

KILBURN ORPHANAGE, see Percy Rd. Orphanage.

KILBURN PARK, Kilburn Park Rd. Opened 1907 by council for 150 G, 174 I in premises of Kilburn Protestant sch. 1927 a.a. 318 GI; 1938 a.a. 190 GI. Moved to new site in Malvern Rd. 1972. Roll 1978: 217 JM.

KILBURN PARK, Percy Rd. BGI sch. opened 1879 in rooms under chapel of Bible Christians. Financed by sch. pence (3d.). Roll 1880: 90 BGI.

KILBURN PROTESTANT, Kilburn Park Rd. Opened for BGI in bldgs. of Kilburn Protestant and Evangelical church 1900.[54] Financed by vol. contributions and sch. pence (1d.). Taken over by council 1907 as Kilburn Park sch.

KILBURN R.C., see St. Mary R.C.

KILBURN ST. PAUL, see St. Paul, Kilburn.

KILBURN TRINITY, see Holy Trinity.

KING ALBERT BELGIAN, Wrentham Ave., Kensal Rise. Opened 1916 by council for M children of Belgian refugees. Closed 1919.

LEOPOLD PRIMARY, Leopold Rd. Opened 1897 as bd. sch. for 1,250 BGI. 1908 a.a. 438 B, 445 G, 460 I; 1932 a.a. 270 B, 231 G, 270 I. Reorg. by 1936 into 550 SM, 400 I. 1938 a.a. 365 SM, 247 I. After 1944 Act SM became sec. mod. and closed 1966 when pupils transferred to Willesden county and bldg. used as annexe for St. Joseph's, Harlesden, R.C. I reorg. 1976 into JM and I. Roll 1978: 115 JM and I.

LOWER PLACE, Barretts Green Rd., Harlesden. Opened 1915 as council sch. for 800 M, I on site

[50] Willesden educ. cttee. Mins. (1952–3); Grange Mus., photo. files, Cambridge Rd. (NL 609).
[51] Grange Mus., Wood F 23, pp. 336 sqq.; Harlesden Meth. Ch. 1869–1969 (booklet).
[52] Opening Programme (1900, in Grange Mus.).
[53] The Times, 8 Dec. 1908; date on rainwater head; Grange Mus., gen. files, Kilburn grammar sch.
[54] P.R.O., C 54/20662, mm. 1–7.

next to temp. sch.[55] (see below). 1919 a.a. 351 M, 241 I; 1936 a.a. 197 M, 112 I. Reorg. by 1938 for 556 JM and I. 1938 a.a. 189 JM and I. Closed 1977.[56]

LOWER PLACE TEMP., Barretts Green Rd., Harlesden. Opened 1902 as bd. sch. for 680 BGI and closed 1915.

MALOREES PRIMARY, Christchurch Ave., Brondesbury. Opened 1953 as council sch. for JM and I. Reorg. 1958 into JM, I. Extensions 1969. Roll 1978: 310 JM, 185 I.

MORA PRIMARY, Mora Rd., Cricklewood.[57] Opened 1907 as council sch. for 400 B, 400 G, 400 I. 1919 a.a. 315 B, 306 G, 188 I; 1936 a.a. 350 B, 316 G, 331 I. Reorg. 1937 for 400 SM, 380 JM, 400 I. After 1944 Act SM became sec. mod. which closed 1958 when John Kelly schs. opened. New block added 1950s and nursery unit 1978. Roll 1978: 240 JM, 142 I, 31 nursery.

NEASDEN C.E. Opened 1884 as Nat. sch. for 168 M in St. Saviour's mission church at junction of Neasden Lane with Quainton St. Iron room for I added 1889. 1890 a.a. 109 M. Permanent sch. for 106 I added 1893. Financed by parl. grant and vol. contributions. 1908 a.a. 127 M, 58 I. Reorg. by 1932 for 224 JM and I. 1932 a.a. 164 JM and I; 1938: 99 JM and I. Closed 1945.

NEASDEN HIGH, Quainton St. Opened 1973 as SM comprehensive in new bldgs. Roll 1978: 785 SM.

NEASDEN TEMP. Opened 1927 as council sch. for 40 I. 1932 a.a. 64 I. Closed 1937.

NORTH-WEST LONDON JEWISH, 180 Willesden Lane, Brondesbury. Opened 1945 as vol. aided Jewish sch. for JM and I in Minster Rd. (Hampstead) and moved to Willesden Lane 1958.[58] Roll 1978: 253 JM and I, 26 nursery.

NORTHVIEW PRIMARY, Northview Cres., Neasden. Opened 1960 as council sch. for I to replace Dudden Hill Lane. Extended and reorg. for JM and I 1973. Roll 1978: 215 JM and I, 38 nursery.

OLDFIELD PRIMARY, Oldfield Rd. Opened 1907 as council sch. for 1,200 BGI.[59] 1919 a.a. 355 B, 355 G, 335 I; 1927 a.a. 237 B, 277 G, 268 I. Reorg. by 1932 for 346 SM, 354 JM. Reorg. by 1936 for 380 JM, 380 I. 1938 a.a. 336 JM, 290 I. Reorg. after 1964 into JM and I. Roll 1978: 349 JM and I.

OUR LADY OF GRACE R.C. PRIMARY, Dollis Hill. Opened 1967 as vol. aided R.C. sch. for JM and I in Dollis Hill Lane. Bldgs. extended 1972 and sch. reorg. for JM. Separate sch. for I opened at junction of Dollis Hill Ave. and Edgware Rd. 1972. Roll 1978: 300 JM, 238 I.

OUR LADY OF LOURDES R.C. PRIMARY, Wesley Rd., Stonebridge. Opened 1973 as vol. aided R.C. sch. for JM and I in part of bldgs. formerly occupied by Wesley Rd. sch. Roll 1978: 330 JM and I, 38 nursery.

PEEL RD. R.C., Kilburn. Opened 1868 in Hampstead part of Kilburn by church of Sacred Heart, Quex Rd. As St. Joseph's, reopened 1872

for 150 G, 120 I in Peel Rd. 1890 a.a. 120 G, 84 I. Closed c. 1892 when St. Mary R.C. opened.[60]

PEOPLE'S COLLEGE, Manor Park Rd., Harlesden Green. Opened 1889 as higher grade and elementary sch. for 200 G, 50 I by Church Extension Assoc. in temp. iron bldg. 1890 a.a. 84 GI. Reorg. by 1894 for 341 M. Financed by parl. grant, vol. contributions, and sch. pence (30s.). Closed c. 1895.[61]

PERCY RD., Kilburn. Opened 1912 as council sch. for 400 B. 1927 a.a. 372 B; 1938 a.a. 256 B. Extended 1939. Became sec. mod. under 1944 Act. Became J high 1967 and amalg. 1972 with Carlton Vale sec. mod. as South Kilburn high.

PERCY RD. ORPHANAGE, Kilburn. Opened 1865 by C.E. New bldg. 1872. Financed by parl. grant, vol. contributions, and sch. pence (2d.). 1882 a.a. 30 G, 20 I; 1894 a.a. 87 M. By 1906 an R.C. orphanage. 1906 a.a. 40 M.

POUND LANE, Willesden Green. Opened 1903 as bd. sch. for 860 M, 418 I. 1908 a.a. 790 M, 390 I; 1938 a.a. 411 M, 164 I. Reorg. 1927 as selective central sch. for 480.[62] Reorg. after 1944 Act as sec. mod. Amalg. 1967 with Willesden county as Willesden high.

PRINCESS FREDERICA C.E., College Rd., Kensal Rise. Opened 1889 as Nat. sch. for 1,805 BGI by Sisters of the Church. 1894 a.a. 762 BGI. Financed by parl. grant, vol. contributions, and sch. pence (2s.). Accn. reduced 1906 to 1,320 BGI. 1908 a.a. 388 B, 376 G, 303 I; 1938 a.a. 163 B, 164 G, 191 I. Reorg. by 1948 into JM, I. Control passed 1965 to London Diocesan Bd. of Educ. Extended and modernized 1975. Reorg. 1978 into JM and I. Roll 1978: 300 JM and I.

ST. ANDREW C.E., Willesden Green. Opened 1882 as Nat. sch. for 170 I in mission bldg. in Chaplin Rd.; high sch. for B opened in same bldg. 1884. Nat. sch. for BGI opened 1885 at corner of High Rd. and St. Andrew's Rd. New B sch. opened 1887. Dept. for 172 G added 1889. 1890 a.a. 91 B, 107 G, 170 I. Financed by parl. grants, vol. contributions, and sch. pence (5s. 6d.). Enlarged 1892 for 270 I; 334 G, and upper grade dept. for 188 B opened 1893.[63] 1908 a.a. 400 B, 330 G, 230 I; 1927 a.a. 223 B, 214 G, 130 I. Additions to I sch. 1956 and 1977. Reorg. 1964 of B, G into JM. New sch. blt. 1974 for 320 JM in Belton Rd. Roll 1978: 160 JM, 121 I, 42 nursery.

ST. GEORGE'S HALL TEMP., High Rd., Willesden Green. Opened 1901 as bd. sch. for B in hall of Presbyterian church.

ST. JOHN C.E., Granville Rd., Kilburn. Opened 1871 for G and I in bldgs. belonging to St. John's church. Opened 1882 as Nat. sch. in new bldg. for 314 upper M, 221 lower M, 249 I. Enlarged 1895 for 81 more children. Financed by parl. grant, vol. contributions, small endowment, and sch. pence (1d.). 1908 a.a. 280 B, 206 G, 210 I; 1927 a.a. 231 B, 153 G, 198 I. Reorg. by 1932 for 160 G, 272 I. 1938 a.a. 141 G, 131 I. Reorg. 1947 into JM and I.[64] New sch. blt. 1972 for 245 JM and I. Roll 1978: 117 JM and I, 27 nursery.

---

[55] Willesden educ. cttee. *Draft Rep.* (1919).
[56] Note on card index in Grange Mus.
[57] A. Walker, *Mora, 1907, 1977* (pamphlet).
[58] *Jewish Year Bk.* (1950, 1960); *Willesden Chron.* 14 Nov. 1958.
[59] Willesden educ. cttee. *Draft Rep.* (1919).
[60] Inf. from par. priest of Immaculate Heart of Mary R.C. ch., Kilburn (1978). [61] M.R.O., Acc. 549/76.
[62] Grange Mus., 2 C 17 (souvenir of incorp. 1933).
[63] Ibid. photo. files, Chaplin Rd. (NL 659); gen. files, St. Andrew's ch.
[64] Willesden educ. cttee. *Mins.* (1946-7).

ST. JOSEPH R.C., Harlesden. Opened 1887 for 170 M in iron bldg. beside R.C. chapel in Manor Park Rd.[65] Run by nuns of convent of Jesus and Mary, Crown Hill Rd.; 1890 a.a. 95 M. Financed by parl. grant and vol. contributions. Iron bldg. condemned and sch. moved to another bldg. 1897. Dept. for 86 I opened 1908 in Park Parade.[66] New premises opened on Park Parade site 1934 and reorg. for 240 M and I. 1938 a.a. 262 M and I. SB transferred 1958 to Cardinal Hinsley R.C.; SG transferred 1959 to Convent of Jesus and Mary R.C. and sch. reorg. as JM and I. Extended 1965. JM moved to Leopold annexe in Goodson Rd. 1966. Roll 1978: 760 JM and I.

ST. JOSEPH R.C., KILBURN, see Peel Rd. R.C.

ST. MARGARET CLITHEROW R.C. PRIMARY, Quainton St., Neasden. Opened 1973 for I. Reorg. 1977 for JM and I. Roll 1978: 230 JM and I.

ST. MARY C.E., Willesden. Opened 1809 as Nat. Sunday sch. for 80 poor children in High Rd., Church End, next to vicarage. Became day sch. 1818. 1821 a.a. 65 B, 51 G.[67] New sch. built on site 1853 for 195 BG.[68] Sch. for 119 I built 1858 on site in Pound Lane given by All Souls College.[69] Sch. pence 1858 (2d.). 1880 a.a. 113 BG, 71 I. Extended 1876, 1886, 1892 for 380 B, 264 G, 280 I. Financed by parl. grant, vol. contributions, small endowment, and sch. pence (2s. 6d.). 1908 a.a. 300 B, 250 G, 190 I; 1922 a.a. 160 B, 169 G, 89 I. Reorg. 1934 for 400 JM and I. New sch. blt. 1972 in Garnet Rd. next to church. Nursery added 1978. Roll 1978: 240 JM and I.

ST. MARY R.C., Kilburn. Opened 1892 for 125 M, 160 I in Granville Rd. Financed by parl. grant and vol. contributions. 1908 a.a. 135 M, 140 I; 1938 a.a. 206 M, 125 I. Acquired former Gordon Memorial sch. premises 1953 in Cambridge Rd. Reorg. 1964 into JM at Cambridge Rd. and I in new bldg. in Granville Rd.[70] New sch. built 1974 in Canterbury Rd. Roll 1978: 471 JM, 362 I.

ST. MARY MAGDALEN R.C., Linacre Rd., Willesden Green. Opened 1928 for 300 M and I.[71] 1932 a.a. 162 M and I; 1938 a.a. 263 M and I. Reorg. by 1960 for JM and I and by 1966 for JM. Roll 1978: 360 JM.

ST. MICHAEL AND ALL ANGELS C.E., Melville Rd., Stonebridge. Opened 1883 for 77 I. Sch. pence (2d.). 1890 a.a. 69 I. Financed by parl. grants and vol. contributions. Closed c. 1900.

ST. PAUL NAT., Edgware Rd., Kilburn. Opened 1847 as Nat. sch. for 100 B, 80 G.[72] 1866 a.a. 252 BG. Parl. grant 1866. Became part of Holy Trinity schs. 1867.

ST. SAVIOUR, see Neasden C.E.

SALUSBURY PRIMARY, Salusbury Rd., Kilburn. Opened 1899 as temp. bd. sch. for 744 M, 420 I in iron bldg.[73] Permanent bd. sch. opened 1902 for 860 M, 400 I. 1908 a.a. 860 M, 433 I; 1932 a.a. 597 M, 337 I. Reorg. 1936 for 400 SM, 300 JM,

460 I. 1938 a.a. 275 SM, 224 JM, 248 I. After 1944 Act SM became sec. mod. dept. which closed 1970 when children transferred to Aylestone high. Bldgs. modernized 1971–2. Roll 1978: 230 JM, 150 I (including nursery).

SLADEBROOK HIGH, Brentfield Rd., Stonebridge. Opened 1969 as SM comprehensive formed by amalg. of Willesden Sch. of Building (Kilburn Polytechnic),[74] Gibbons Rd. sec. mod., and Wesley Rd. sec. mod. Opened in new bldgs. using Gibbons Rd. sec. mod. bldgs. as annexe. Roll 1978: 1,107 SM.

SOUTH KILBURN HIGH, Stafford Rd., Kilburn. Opened 1972 as SM comprehensive, formed by amalg. of Carlton Vale and Percy Rd. J high schs. Opened for 1,200 in new bldgs. incorporating Percy Rd. premises. Roll 1978: 900 SM.

STONEBRIDGE C.E., see St. Michael and All Angels C.E.

STONEBRIDGE PRIMARY, Shakespeare Ave. Opened 1900 as bd. sch. for 460 B, 460 G, 440 I. 1908 a.a. 433 B, 398 G, 411 I; 1927 a.a. 275 B, 267 G, 279 I. Reorg. by 1932 for 350 JB, 350 JG, 350 I. 1938 a.a. 255 B, 243 G, 315 I. Reorg. 1955 for JM, I. Bldgs. modernized and extended 1975–8. Roll 1978: 337 JM, 205 I.

TUBBS RD. TEMP., Harlesden. Opened 1899 as bd. sch. for 51 B in Methodist chapel bldg. Accn. increased to 190 B by 1908. 1908 a.a. 140 B. Closed 1908.[75]

WESLEY RD., Stonebridge. Opened 1910 as council sch. for 520 JM, 400 I. 1922 a.a. 433 JM, 308 I. Reorg. by 1932 for 400 SB, 400 SG. 1938 a.a. 247 SB, 211 SG. After 1944 Act became sec. mod. New bldgs. 1956. Closed 1969. Pupils transferred to Sladebrook high and part of bldgs. used by Our Lady of Lourdes R.C.

WILLESDEN COUNTY, Doyle Gdns. Opened 1924 as SM county grammar sch. for 336 SM. Extended 1932 and 1965.[76] Amalg. 1966 with sec. mod. dept. of Leopold as Willesden county grammar-technical sch. Merged 1967 into Willesden high.

WILLESDEN HIGH, Doyle Gdns. Opened 1967 as SM comprehensive formed by amalg. of Willesden county with sec. mod. dept. of Pound Lane. Housed in county sch. bldgs., which were extended using Pound Lane sch. as annexe. Roll 1978: 1,600 SM.

WILLESDEN NAT., see St. Mary C.E.

WILLESDEN GREEN R.C., see St. Mary Magdalen R.C.

WILLESDEN JUNCTION, see Harlesden Wesleyan.

WILLIAM GLADSTONE HIGH, Park Side, Dollis Hill. Opened 1974 as SM comprehensive. Roll 1978: 867 SM.

WYKEHAM PRIMARY, Aboyne Rd., Neasden. Opened 1930 as council sch. for 600 SM, 672 JM and I. Reorg. by 1936 for 640 SM, 624 JM and I.

[65] Inf. from par. priest of Our Lady of Willesden R.C. ch. (1978).

[66] Bldg. dated 1900; 1908 inf. from headmistress; O.S. Map 1/2,500, Mdx. XVI. 6 (1935 edn.) shows Park Parade site as I sch.

[67] Grange Mus., 1 D 10 (vestry order bk. 1814–25); M.R.O., EA/WIL, no. 517; Digest of Returns to Sel. Cttee. on Educ. of Poor, H.C. 224, p. 536 (1819), ix(1).

[68] Brent Prints (publ. Brent L.B. libr.).

[69] Grange Mus., Wood F 27/38.

[70] Ibid. 1 A 2 (Kilburn Times, 17 Sept. 1965).

[71] The Times, 26 Mar. 1928.

[72] Guildhall MSS. CC. 22700, 30688.

[73] Willesden sch. bd. Rep. of Cttee. (1899).

[74] Below, technical educ.

[75] Willesden sch. bd. Rep. of Cttee. (1899); Willesden educ. cttee. Mins. (1908–9).

[76] Grange Mus., gen. files, housing; Opening of Extension (1932).

1936 a.a. 496 SM, 464 JM and I. After 1944 Act SM became sec. mod. Bldgs. damaged in war and rebuilt. Sec. mod. dept. closed 1973 when Neasden high opened. Roll 1978: 452 JM and I (including nursery).

Special schools.

BARRETTS GREEN, Harlesden. Opened 1968 as sec. sch. for maladjusted in bldgs. vacated by Lower Place special sch. Roll 1978: 30 SM.

FURNESS RD., Harlesden. Opened by 1910 for 60 physically handicapped children.[77] Closed between 1928 and 1933.

GRANVILLE RD., Kilburn. Opened 1899 for mentally deficient and physically handicapped in Presbyterian mission hall. Superseded 1912 by Leinster Rd.[78]

LEINSTER RD., Kilburn. Opened 1912 for 80 mentally deficient children. Moved by 1948 to College Rd., Kensal Rise.[79] Closed after 1954.[80]

LEOPOLD RD. Opened 1902 for 40 physically handicapped children. Closed 1928.[81]

LOWER PLACE, Barretts Green, Harlesden. Opened c. 1947 for 160 physically handicapped on ground floor of Lower Place council sch. Moved 1968 to Grove Park, Kingsbury.[82]

MANOR PRIMARY, the Avenue, Brondesbury Park. Opened 1959 as Woodfield sch. for educationally sub-normal children in Kingsbury.[83] Reorg. 1969 and primary sch. moved 1970 to Brondesbury Park. Extended 1971 and 1977. Roll 1978: 101 JM.

OLDFIELD RD. Opened 1928 for mentally deficient children. Closed by 1948.[84]

VERNON HOUSE, Willesden Lane, Brondesbury. Opened 1968 for maladjusted children. Roll 1978: 50 JM.

Technical education. In 1893 Willesden local committee for technical education organized classes in Willesden town hall and in 1896 Middlesex C. C. bought the St. Lawrence institute in Priory Park Road, Kilburn, and placed it at the disposal of the local committee which opened it as Willesden Polytechnic.[85] By 1898 there was an enrolment of 1,571,[86] and a new building was opened in Glengall Road, Kilburn, in 1904. A needle-trades school for girls was established there from 1910 until it moved to an annexe at the Hyde, Edgware Road, in 1952; it closed in 1962. An art school had been established as part of the polytechnic by 1919 and a school of building opened in 1925.[87] In 1934, in

anticipation of the opening of Willesden College of Technology, Willesden Polytechnic was reorganized as Kilburn Polytechnic and the old St. Lawrence hall was replaced by a four-storeyed block. In 1978 there were 1,400 full-time and 4,500 part-time enrolments.

In 1934 Middlesex C. C. opened Willesden College of Technology in Denzil Road to provide the technical courses originally provided by the polytechnic, including the schools of art and building.[88] There were extensions in 1952[89] and 1972, and in 1964 the college took over the buildings of Dudden Hill Lane school. The art school closed in 1959,[90] and in 1969 the school of building amalgamated with other schools to form Sladebrook high school. There were 8,000 enrolments in 1978.

Private schools.[91] Mr. and Mrs. Raikes ran a boarding school at the Grove, Neasden, for the sons of gentlemen in the early 1780s.[92] There were schoolmasters at Kilburn in 1822 and 1828 and at Kensal Green in 1831.[93] In 1845 there was a preparatory school at Willesden Green, an academy and ladies' school in Kilburn, and a boys' boarding school, which still existed in 1855, at Cricklewood.[94] Kensal academy existed in 1848 at the northern edge of Kensal Green.[95] In 1851, besides the master and mistress of St. Mary's parochial school, there were two schoolmistresses in Kensal Green, a schoolmaster and schoolmistress in Kilburn, the boarding school in Cricklewood, and a dame school in Willesden Green.[96] The last was probably taught by the 'woman in the village' who provided some education in Willesden in 1857.[97] There was a temporary private school for 120 children, supported by school pence of 6d., in Kilburn in 1867.[98] In 1870 two private schools were attended by 37 boys and 51 girls.[99]

The number of schools began to multiply with the spread of building in Willesden and, especially, in Kilburn from the 1870s. There were 14 by 1872, including Claremont House in Cambridge Road, Kilburn, which still existed in 1890. There were 19 by 1880, 37 by 1890, and 40 by 1908. Most schools, in spite of their often pretentious names, were short-lived, probably small schools in private houses. Among the longer-lived were Brondesbury College, a boys' secondary school which opened in 1864 in Quex Road east of Edgware Road and had moved by 1890 to Willesden Lane, just west of Edgware

---

[77] Willesden educ. cttee. *Mins.* (1909–10, 1928, 1933).

[78] Willesden sch. bd. *Rep. of Cttee.* (1899); Willesden educ. cttee. *Mins.* (1912–13).

[79] Willesden educ. cttee. *Mins.* (1912–13, 1933); *Schs. of Willesden and Dist.* [1948].

[80] Willesden boro. *Ann. Health Rep.* (1954).

[81] Willesden educ. cttee. *Mins.* (1928–9).

[82] *V.C.H. Mdx.* v. 88; Willesden boro. *Ann. Health Rep.* (1954).

[83] *V.C.H. Mdx.* v. 88.

[84] Willesden educ. cttee. *Mins.* (1928, 1933); *Schs. of Willesden and Dist.* [1948].

[85] Based on *Short Hist. of Kilburn Polytechnic* (pamphlet, 1968); inf. from the principal (1978).

[86] *The Times*, 4 Jan. 1898.

[87] Willesden educ. cttee. *Draft Rep.* (1919); *The Times*, 26 May 1925; M.R.O., Acc. 965/2.

[88] Based on inf. from the principal (1978); *Official Opening* (1934, in Grange Mus.).

[89] *The Builder*, 9 Jan. 1953.

[90] *The Times*, 11 Mar. 1957; Willesden educ. cttee. *Mins.* (1959).

[91] Subsection based on: *Kilburn Dir.* (1872); *Kelly's Dir. Mdx.* (1890, 1908, 1926); *Kelly's Lond. Suburban Dir.* (1880, 1902); *Kelly's Dir. London* (1934, 1942, 1947, 1952, 1964, 1975, 1978); *Kelly's Dir. Kilburn* (1917–18); Willesden boro. *Local Community Svces. 1933.*

[92] Hist. MSS. Com. 42, *15th Rep. VI, Carlisle*, pp. 450, 476, 566, 569.

[93] Grange Mus., Wood F 33.

[94] *Home Counties Dir.* (1845); *Kelly's Dir. Mdx.* (1855); P.R.O., HO 107/1700/135/3, f. 367v.

[95] *Environs of Lond.* (1848, map printed by Jas. Wyld).

[96] P.R.O., HO 107/1700/135/3, ff. 332 sqq., 354, 364, 367v., 386v., 394v.

[97] Nat. Soc. files, St. Mary I.   [98] Ibid. Holy Trinity.

[99] *Returns relating to Elem. Educ.* H.C. 201, pp. 242–3 (1871), lv.

Road.[1] It closed between 1919 and 1926.[2] Willesden high school in Craven Park existed from 1880 to 1906. Brondesbury Manor housed a girls' boarding school from 1882 to 1934.[3] Brondesbury and Kilburn high school for girls functioned as a private school from its foundation in 1892 until the county council took it over in 1938, as did Kilburn grammar school, founded in 1898 and taken over in 1908.[4]

Eight schools (Vernon House,[5] Bestreben high, Miss Watkins's school, Lady Margaret, and Sunbury House, respectively at nos. 163, 197, 275, 292, and 294 Willesden Lane, Roundwood College in Harlesden Park Road, Miss A. Edmonds's school in Dyne Rd., Kilburn, and A. Ferreira's school in Victoria Rd. Kilburn) flourished from c. 1902 to c. 1933. Geneva House (also called Brondesbury high) in Shoot-up Hill, Edgware Road, a girls' secondary school and kindergarten, existed from 1891 to c. 1964.[6] A private Roman Catholic preparatory school was opened by the convent of Mary and Jesus in Willesden Green in 1908. Initially a boarding and day school, it had become a day school by 1950 and entered the state system in 1967.[7]

The numbers of schools began to decline after 1910. There were 29 in 1917 and 1926, including Clark's College (c. 1917–1964) and Gladstone House (c. 1917–c. 1934) both in Shoot-up Hill, Cricklewood; in 1933 there were 15 and by 1950 only 9, including Blenheim House in Oxgate Gardens (c. 1942–1964) and St. Helen's preparatory school in Blenheim Gardens (c. 1942–1964). Hillel House, a mixed school for juniors and infants, was opened by the Zionist Federation educational trust in Chamberlayne Road in 1947 and had approximately 130 children on the books in 1978.[8] Other Jewish schools were shorter-lived. By 1978 there were only two private schools in the area, Hillel House and the London Welsh school, a mixed pre-preparatory school for 30 children which was owned by the Welsh Presbyterian church and had moved to Willesden Lane from Paddington in 1962.[9]

CHARITIES FOR THE POOR. William Barber (fl. 1319–46) gave a rent charge from which 12d. a year was for bread and ale for the poor, and Thomas Paulet (fl. 1494) directed that bread and drink were to be distributed on the anniversary of his obit. Neither charity survived the Reformation.[10] In 1624 Francis Roberts granted £2 a year for distribution to the poor at Eastern and Whitsun.[11] In 1686 the churchwardens successfully sued William Roberts for the restitution of the £2 and for £180 given in trust to buy a rent charge of £8 a year to be distributed in coal.[12] In the 18th century payments called the coal money were from 2s. to 5s., to people whose names were listed by the churchwardens and overseers and approved by the occupier of Neasden House.[13] After 1823 the money was applied with other charities in coal and bread[14] until 1882. During the 19th century the rent charges were replaced by £334 stock. In 1977 the income of £9 a year was distributed in cash.[15]

An unknown donor, perhaps Thomas Young, gave an annual rent charge of £1 for the poor of Willesden.[16] Other charities listed in 1826 were the parish close (3 a. at Fortune Gate which was leased by the overseers) and the poor's land, ⅛ a. next to the churchyard, divided between the poor houses[17] and a garden which was let.[18] Their origins were unknown, and the poor's land probably derived from the Middle Ages. The income was applied in bread and coal each Christmas until 1882,[19] but in the 1850s the trustees failed to present accounts and much of the land was sold and the proceeds were invested in stock. In 1874 a Scheme consolidated all the charities except the Roberts charity but including Freelove's gift for the school; the trustees, who were to make payments to the school and apply the rest in clothes, fuel, or medical aid,[20] were largely representative of the established church and were opposed by a faction led by W. James Wright (d. 1887), a low churchman in constant conflict with the vicar.[21] By 1903 the income was spent on the poor and scholarships;[22] in 1978 it was £1,942.[23]

Laura Seymour by will dated 1863 gave a sum represented by £333 stock, the income, £10 in 1880 and £8 in the 1960s, to be used for widows and orphans.[24]

Edward Harvist's charity, founded by will in 1610 for the maintenance of the Edgware and Harrow roads, was in 1975 applied by statutory instrument to the relief of sickness and distress and to educational and recreational facilities in the five boroughs through which the roads passed. Brent L.B.'s share of the income was £34,000 in 1976.[25]

[1] Sch. Bd. Map of London [c. 1904].
[2] Willesden educ. cttee. Draft Rep. (1919).
[3] Grange Mus., gen. files, Brondesbury Manor.
[4] Above, public schs.
[5] Above, special schs.
[6] Schs. of Willesden and Dist. [1948].
[7] Cath. Dir. (1920 and later edns.); above, public schs.
[8] Inf. from the sec. (1978).
[9] Inf. from the headmaster (1978); The Guardian, 31 Mar. 1976.
[10] Bodl. MS. D.D. All Souls c 123/43; Cal. Close, 1337–47, 476; P.R.O., E 301/34, no. 181.
[11] The land concerned once supported Wm. Page's obit: Grange Mus., Wood F 24, p. 145; above, churches.
[12] P.R.O., C 78/925, no. 5; 14th Rep. Com. Char. H.C. 382, pp. 209–12 (1826), xii.
[13] M.R.O., Acc. 262/40, pt. 2 (Chandos estate map 1787); Grange Mus., 1 B 3.
[14] 14th Rep. Com. Char.; Grange Mus., Wood F 24, pp. 145 sqq.   [15] Char. Com. reg. 211130.
[16] 14th Rep. Com. Char.; Willesden Par. Year Bk. (1902–3), where Young was mentioned. A Thos. Young was lessee of Brondesbury in the 16th cent.
[17] Above, local govt.
[18] M.R.O., Acc. 262/40, pt. 1 (inclosure claims 1816); M.R.O., EA/WIL, nos. 183, 200–1; Grange Mus., MS. 66/5.
[19] Grange Mus., 1 B 29 (bread and coal accts. 1800–82).
[20] Ibid. MS. 66/8.
[21] Ibid. Wood F 24, pp. 156 sqq.
[22] Willesden Par. Year Bk. (1902–3).
[23] Char. Com. reg. 211132.   [24] Ibid. 207587.
[25] Ibid. 211970; Grange Mus., gen. files, charities.

INDEX

INDEX

INDEX

CORRIGENDA TO VOLUMES IV, V, AND VI

Earlier lists of corrigenda will be found in Volumes I, III, IV, V, and VI

Vol. IV, page 169*a*, line 28 from end, *for* 'eastern' *read* 'western'
        177*b*, line 15 from end, *for* 'north-eastern' *read* 'north-western'
        197*b*, line 23 from end, *for* 'south-westward' *read* 'south-eastward'
        243*a*, line 7, *for* 'vicar' *read* 'headmaster of Harrow School'
        262*a*, line 10, *for* 'The chapel' *read* 'A new chapel'

Vol. V, page 12*a*, line 5 from end, *for* '1868' *read* '1870'
        22*a*, line 12 from end, *for* 'Susanna' *read* 'Catherine'
        229*b*, note 98, *for* 'pas.rts' *read* 'parts'
        263*a*, line 26, *for* '1852' *read* '1850'
        408*a*, s.v. Nicholl, *insert* 'Cath., 22' *and delete* 'Mrs. Susanna (fl. 1828), 22'

Vol. VI, page x, line 9, *for* '1900' *read* '1905'
        9*a*, lines 12–13 from end, *for* 'c. 1931 by the London Passenger Transport Board, later London Transport'
          read 'in 1925 by the London General Omnibus Co. and extended in 1929–32'
        9*b*, lines 24–5, *for* '1904, along the Great Northern and City Railway to Moorgate.' *read* '1875, over the
          North London Railway to Broad Street.'
        9, note 64, *for* '222' *read* '223'
        9, note 67, *for* '222' *read* '223'
        9, note 79, *for* 'G. R. Grinling' *read* 'C. H. Grinling'
        9, note 85, *delete whole footnote and substitute* 'M. Robbins, *North Lond. Rly.* (1946), 7.'
        27, note 96, *for* '203' *read* '223'
        32 (facing), line 1, *for* '1900' *read* '1905'
        40, map, *for* 'Lang Lane' *read* 'Long Lane'
        40, map, *for* 'Bull Lane' *read* 'Bulls Lane'
        42*a*, line 6, *for* 'Pymmes' *read* 'Pymme's'
        46*a*, line 4, *for* 'Bull' *read* 'Bulls'
        73, note 9, *for* 'B.H.L.H.' *read* 'B.L.H.L.'
        91*b*, line 27, *for* 'North Way' *read* 'Northway'
        106*b*, line 17 from end, *delete* 'to Fenchurch Street station'
        106, note 28, *for* 'G. H. Grinling' *read* 'C. H. Grinling'
        107*a*, line 22 from end, *after* 'type' *insert* 'in Europe'
        111*b*, line 16 from end, *for* '1872' *read* '1863'
        116, note 17, *for* 'wh reeotherwise' *read* 'where otherwise'
        118*a*, line 25, *for* 'End,' *read* 'End.'
        120*a*, line 2 from end, *for* 'a seven-storeyed tower' *read* 'linked seven-storeyed blocks'
        121*b*, line 17 from end, *after* 'Muswell' *insert* 'Hill'
        133*a*, lines 14–15 from end, *for* 'c. 1947' *read* 'in 1939'
        136*b*, line 2 from end, *for* 'Pennithorne' *read* 'Pennethorne'
        141, note 48, *for* 'of' *read* 'in'
        156*a*, line 7 from end, *after* 'Schneytler' *insert* 'or Snetzler'
        221*a*, s.v. Pennithorne, *for* 'Pennithorne' *read* 'Pennethorne'